DEUTERONOMY

THE NIV APPLICATION COMMENTARY

From biblical text . . . to contemporary life

DEUTERONOMY

THE NIV APPLICATION COMMENTARY

From biblical text . . . to contemporary life

DANIEL I. BLOCK

ZONDERVAN®

ZONDERVAN.com/
AUTHORTRACKER
follow your favorite authors

We want to hear from you. Please send your comments about this book to us in care of zreview@zondervan.com. Thank you.

ZONDERVAN

The NIV Application Commentary: Deuteronomy
Copyright © 2012 by Daniel I. Block

This title is also available as a Zondervan ebook.
Visit www.zondervan.com/ebooks.

Requests for information should be addressed to:
Zondervan, *Grand Rapids, Michigan 49530*

Library of Congress Cataloging-in-Publication Data

Block, Daniel Issac.
    Deuteronomy / Daniel I. Block.
        pages. cm. — (The NIV application commentary)
    Includes bibliographical references and indexes.
    ISBN: 978-0-310-21048-1
    1. Bible. O.T. Deuteronomy — Commentaries. I. Title.
  BS1275.53.B56 2012
  222'.15077 — dc23   2011049625

Printed in the United States of America

13 14 15 16 17 18 /DCI/ 24 23 22 21 20 19 18 17 16 15 14 13 12 11 10 9 8 7 6 5 4 3

To my grandchildren,
Calvin, Brennig, Kate, Megan, Ella, and Eric
The LORD your God is a merciful God;
he will not abandon or destroy you
or forget the covenant with your forefathers.
(Deuteronomy 4:31)

The NIV Application Commentary Series

When complete, the NIV Application Commentary
will include the following volumes:

Old Testament Volumes

Genesis, John H. Walton
Exodus, Peter Enns
Leviticus/Numbers, Roy Gane
Deuteronomy, Daniel I. Block
Joshua, Robert L. Hubbard Jr.
Judges/Ruth, K. Lawson Younger Jr.
1-2 Samuel, Bill T. Arnold
1-2 Kings, August H. Konkel
1-2 Chronicles, Andrew E. Hill
Ezra/Nehemiah, Thomas and Donna Petter
Esther, Karen H. Jobes
Job, John H. Walton
Psalms Volume 1, Gerald H. Wilson
Psalms Volume 2, Jamie A. Grant
Proverbs, Paul Koptak
Ecclesiastes/Song of Songs, Iain Provan
Isaiah, John N. Oswalt
Jeremiah/Lamentations, J. Andrew Dearman
Ezekiel, Iain M. Duguid
Daniel, Tremper Longman III
Hosea/Amos/Micah, Gary V. Smith
Jonah/Nahum/Habakkuk/Zephaniah,
    James Bruckner
Joel/Obadiah/Malachi, David W. Baker
Haggai/Zechariah, Mark J. Boda

New Testament Volumes

Matthew, Michael J. Wilkins
Mark, David E. Garland
Luke, Darrell L. Bock
John, Gary M. Burge
Acts, Ajith Fernando
Romans, Douglas J. Moo
1 Corinthians, Craig Blomberg
2 Corinthians, Scott Hafemann
Galatians, Scot McKnight
Ephesians, Klyne Snodgrass
Philippians, Frank Thielman
Colossians/Philemon, David E. Garland
1-2 Thessalonians, Michael W. Holmes
1-2 Timothy/Titus, Walter L. Liefeld
Hebrews, George H. Guthrie
James, David P. Nystrom
1 Peter, Scot McKnight
2 Peter/Jude, Douglas J. Moo
Letters of John, Gary M. Burge
Revelation, Craig S. Keener

To see which titles are available,
visit our web site at www.zondervan.com

Contents

NIV Application Commentary
Series Introduction

THE NIV APPLICATION COMMENTARY Series is unique. Most commentaries help us make the journey from our world back to the world of the Bible. They enable us to cross the barriers of time, culture, language, and geography that separate us from the biblical world. Yet they only offer a one-way ticket to the past and assume that we can somehow make the return journey on our own. Once they have explained the *original meaning* of a book or passage, these commentaries give us little or no help in exploring its *contemporary significance.* The information they offer is valuable, but the job is only half done.

Recently, a few commentaries have included some contemporary application as *one* of their goals. Yet that application is often sketchy or moralistic, and some volumes sound more like printed sermons than commentaries.

The primary goal of the NIV Application Commentary Series is to help you with the difficult but vital task of bringing an ancient message into a modern context. The series not only focuses on application as a finished product but also helps you think through the *process* of moving from the original meaning of a passage to its contemporary significance. These are commentaries, not popular expositions. They are works of reference, not devotional literature.

The format of the series is designed to achieve the goals of the series. Each passage is treated in three sections: *Original Meaning, Bridging Contexts,* and *Contemporary Significance.*

 THIS SECTION HELPS YOU understand the meaning of the biblical text in its original context. All of the elements of traditional exegesis—in concise form—are discussed here. These include the historical, literary, and cultural context of the passage. The authors discuss matters related to grammar and syntax and the meaning of biblical words. They also seek to explore the main ideas of the passage and how the biblical author develops those ideas.

After reading this section, you will understand the problems, questions, and concerns of the *original audience* and how the biblical author addressed those issues. This understanding is foundational to any legitimate application of the text today.

THIS SECTION BUILDS A bridge between the world of the Bible and the world of today, between the original context and the contemporary context, by focusing on both the timely and timeless aspects of the text.

God's Word is *timely*. The authors of Scripture spoke to specific situations, problems, and questions. The author of Joshua encouraged the faith of his original readers by narrating the destruction of Jericho, a seemingly impregnable city, at the hands of an angry warrior God (Josh. 6). Paul warned the Galatians about the consequences of circumcision and the dangers of trying to be justified by law (Gal. 5:2–5). The author of Hebrews tried to convince his readers that Christ is superior to Moses, the Aaronic priests, and the Old Testament sacrifices. John urged his readers to "test the spirits" of those who taught a form of incipient Gnosticism (1 John 4:1–6). In each of these cases, the timely nature of Scripture enables us to hear God's Word in situations that were *concrete* rather than abstract.

Yet the timely nature of Scripture also creates problems. Our situations, difficulties, and questions are not always directly related to those faced by the people in the Bible. Therefore, God's word to them does not always seem relevant to us. For example, when was the last time someone urged you to be circumcised, claiming that it was a necessary part of justification? How many people today care whether Christ is superior to the Aaronic priests? And how can a "test" designed to expose incipient Gnosticism be of any value in a modern culture?

Fortunately, Scripture is not only timely but *timeless*. Just as God spoke to the original audience, so he still speaks to us through the pages of Scripture. Because we share a common humanity with the people of the Bible, we discover a *universal dimension* in the problems they faced and the solutions God gave them. The timeless nature of Scripture enables it to speak with power in every time and in every culture.

Those who fail to recognize that Scripture is both timely and timeless run into a host of problems. For example, those who are intimidated by timely books such as Hebrews, Galatians, or Deuteronomy might avoid reading them because they seem meaningless today. At the other extreme, those who are convinced of the timeless nature of Scripture, but who fail to discern its timely element, may "wax eloquent" about the Melchizedekian priesthood to a sleeping congregation, or worse still, try to apply the holy wars of the Old Testament in a physical way to God's enemies today.

The purpose of this section, therefore, is to help you discern what is timeless in the timely pages of the Bible—and what is not. For example, how do the holy wars of the Old Testament relate to the spiritual warfare of the New? If Paul's primary concern is not circumcision (as he tells us in Gal. 5:6), what *is* he concerned about? If discussions about the Aaronic priesthood or Melchizedek seem irrelevant today, what is of abiding value in these passages? If people try to "test the spirits" today with a test designed for a specific first-century heresy, what other biblical test might be more appropriate?

Yet this section does not merely uncover that which is timeless in a passage but also helps you to see *how* it is uncovered. The authors of the commentaries seek to take what is implicit in the text and make it explicit, to take a process that normally is intuitive and explain it in a logical, orderly fashion. How do we know that circumcision is not Paul's primary concern? What clues in the text or its context help us realize that Paul's real concern is at a deeper level?

Of course, those passages in which the historical distance between us and the original readers is greatest require a longer treatment. Conversely, those passages in which the historical distance is smaller or seemingly non-existent require less attention.

One final clarification. Because this section prepares the way for discussing the contemporary significance of the passage, there is not always a sharp distinction or a clear break between this section and the one that follows. Yet when both sections are read together, you should have a strong sense of moving from the world of the Bible to the world of today.

THIS SECTION ALLOWS THE biblical message to speak with as much power today as it did when it was first written. How can you apply what you learned about Jerusalem, Ephesus, or Corinth to our present-day needs in Chicago, Los Angeles, or London? How can you take a message originally spoken in Greek, Hebrew, and Aramaic and communicate it clearly in our own language? How can you take the eternal truths originally spoken in a different time and culture and apply them to the similar-yet-different needs of our culture?

In order to achieve these goals, this section gives you help in several key areas.

(1) It helps you identify contemporary situations, problems, or questions that are truly comparable to those faced by the original audience. Because contemporary situations are seldom identical to those faced by the original audience, you must seek situations that are analogous if your applications are to be relevant.

(2) This section explores a variety of contexts in which the passage might be applied today. You will look at personal applications, but you will also be encouraged to think beyond private concerns to the society and culture at large.

(3) This section will alert you to any problems or difficulties you might encounter in seeking to apply the passage. And if there are several legitimate ways to apply a passage (areas in which Christians disagree), the author will bring these to your attention and help you think through the issues involved.

In seeking to achieve these goals, the contributors to this series attempt to avoid two extremes. They avoid making such specific applications that the commentary might quickly become dated. They also avoid discussing the significance of the passage in such a general way that it fails to engage contemporary life and culture.

Above all, contributors to this series have made a diligent effort not to sound moralistic or preachy. The NIV Application Commentary Series does not seek to provide ready-made sermon materials but rather tools, ideas, and insights that will help you communicate God's Word with power. If we help you to achieve that goal, then we have fulfilled the purpose for this series.

The Editors

General Editor's Preface

SOME SCHOLARS CALL THE book of Deuteronomy "The Gospel According to Moses." Others, instead of comparing Moses to a gospel writer, compare him to Paul, the great New Testament theoretician. Daniel Block, in this wonderfully written commentary on Deuteronomy, uses both these ascriptions and more to describe the incredible theological value of this Old Testament book. At one point he claims it is "the most systematic presentation of theological truth" in the entire Bible, rivaled perhaps only by Paul's Romans.

Deuteronomy? you may be wondering. Isn't it just an Old Testament book? How can it be "gospel" without Jesus? Doesn't it predate Jesus by at least a millennium? Isn't this kind of reliance on Old Testament law just what Paul warns us against?

Listen! If you have even an ounce of such nomo-phobia, start reading this commentary. You will find your prejudices quickly taking flight. As Professor Block shows us, what Moses did *was* gospel. It was good news to the Israelites who heard it on the Plains of Moab. And in the hands of this excellent biblical exegete, it becomes gospel for us today.

This may sound surprising to you, and it is true that there are surprises awaiting you when you study this book. First, you will be surprised at who Moses is. Second, you will probably be surprised with what Moses asks Israel to do in his speeches, not because of what he says, but with how much sense it makes to you as a non-Israelite some three thousand-plus years after the fact.

Moses can be summed up in this statement: Moses is more of a pastor than a lawgiver. Admittedly this goes against the grain of what we think we know about him. One of our most enduring images of Moses is his Olympian moment of anger, smashing two stone tablets of law on the rocks when he saw the golden calf. At first glance this seems to be all about law. God has given the law, Moses is bringing the law, the children of God are breaking the law. Can't be much more law-filled than that, right? And wasn't that really who Moses was?

But consider the occasion presented to us in Deuteronomy. The Israelites are poised to enter the Promised Land. It is a moment of hope. But hope, by its very nature, always has an element of uncertainty, and thus anxiety always accompanies hope. Things could go wrong. What if . . . ? Or what if . . . ? They need the reassurance of a pastor's hand, not the remonstrances of an authority figure. Moses supplies that.

The second surprise is that what Moses tells the Israelites makes so much sense to us today. He tells them they need to be in a covenant relationship with God, that God wants them to be his people. Moses challenges the Israelites to respond by declaring that Yahweh alone is their God, and then by doing what God asks them to do.

Several years ago my wife and I taught abroad for a year and offered our home to a Jewish couple from Israel who were teaching in the United States. They asked if they could affix a mezuzah to our doorpost, a metal tube with the Shema in it, a passage from Deuteronomy 6 in Hebrew on a piece of paper (it also includes a similar passage from Deuteronomy 11). The Shema in just a few short verses captures so much of what Moses taught and counseled, beginning with the well-known phrase, "Hear, O Israel, the LORD our God, the LORD is one." After the briefest of considerations, we couldn't think of anything more appropriate to be on our doorpost. That is what we want to be constantly reminded of—the one Lord and our allegiance to him. And that is what we want to say to the world about who we are, and whose we are. The mezuzah is still on our doorpost.

Since then, the verses from Deuteronomy 6:4–9 have become one of my favorite biblical passages:

> Hear, O Israel: The LORD our God, the LORD is one. You shall love the LORD your God with all your heart, with all your soul, and with all your strength. And these words which I command you today shall be in your heart. You shall teach them diligently to your children, and shall talk of them when you sit in your house, when you walk by the way, when you lie down, and when you rise up. You shall bind them as a sign on your hand and they shall be a frontlet between your eyes. You shall write them on the doorposts of your house and on your gates.

One does not have to be an Old Testament Israelite to fully embrace the identity that this passage describes and to live it to the full. Jesus in his teaching ministry realized the spiritual goldmine of this passage and others like it that Deuteronomy represents. In his teaching he quotes more often from Deuteronomy than from any other biblical book. And this rich resource is as available to us—perhaps even more so—as it was to Jesus.

Terry C. Muck

Author's Preface

THE ADVENTURE REPRESENTED BY this volume began more than a quarter century ago when I taught a Hebrew exegesis course on Deuteronomy for the first time, and it intensified after Zondervan graciously invited me to write this commentary for the NIVAC series. Whereas in an earlier phase of my life I had spent fifteen years with Ezekiel, for the past decade I have been engaged in a lively conversation with Moses. When I read Deuteronomy, I hear the voice of Moses. But sometimes I don't understand what I am hearing, so I ask for clarification. Sometimes what I hear him saying sounds so different from what my ears have been trained to hear and my mind has been taught to accept. This leaves me puzzled and confused. Sometimes I hear the message clearly, but I don't like what I hear, and I protest. He challenges my theology and my understanding of piety. Sometimes I hear him pleading with me to abandon my idols and to follow the Lord more fully, and I resist his plea. Then the voice of Moses exposes my self-centeredness and my hypocrisy. I do not love the Lord with all my heart and mind, with all my being, and with all my resources (cf. Deut. 6:4–5), and I certainly do not love my neighbor as myself. But thank you, Moses, for revealing to me the way of freedom and forgiveness and for reminding me of God's relentless pursuit of his people and his lavish grace.

The present volume is a distillation of a much larger work. Unfortunately the limitations of the series has forced me to eliminate much of my exegetical homework and more detailed consideration of many subjects. We have tried to let the theological cream rise to the top and present that in a coherent and helpful form. As I see it, a commentary like this must serve three purposes: (1) It must help readers actually understand the text. (2) It must integrate the theological message of the text with teachings found in the rest of Scripture. (3) It must provide preliminary guidance for readers of Scripture — particularly pastors and teachers — on the relevance of the message of biblical texts for today. How successful we have been only readers and time will tell.

I agreed to write this commentary more than a decade ago, when my life was rather simple. However, shortly thereafter administrative duties (as president for the Institute for Biblical Research and as Associate Dean for Scripture and Interpretation at the Southern Baptist Theological Seminary in Louisville, Kentucky) complicated my life and ate up a lot of time and energy that might have gone into this project. This pilgrimage was put on virtual standstill for more than a year when we moved to Wheaton College in 2005. Finally, by the grace of God and the patience of the editors of this series, this stage of the project is finished. It is still far from perfect, and, while the Word of God is authoritative and reliable, our comments on the Scriptures are always in soft lead pencil, subject to correction, modification, and even erasure. We present this work to the church with the prayer that despite its imperfections, it will help to make the Scriptures, particularly the gospel according to Moses, come alive for a new generation of readers.

The people who have assisted me in the pilgrimage are too many to count. While Moses has been speaking to me, there have been many who have aided him by supporting me in my study of this remarkable book. Whether in classroom situations or in seminars and sermon series offered in churches—many have walked with me as I have walked with Moses, offering welcome insights into both the broader themes of Deuteronomy and the details of particular passages, and many have helped me refine the ways in which I communicate my discoveries. I must acknowledge in particular a series of graduate students who have lent me invaluable aid in research, in proofreading drafts, and in being sounding boards for some of my discoveries: Greg Mathias [deceased], Jason DeRouchie, Greg Smith, Kenneth Turner, Bryan Cribb, Rebekah Josberger, Nathan Elliott, Chris Ansberry, Jerry Hwang, Charlie Trimm, Jason Gile, Rahel Schafer, Matt Newkirk, Matthew Patton, and Daniel Owens. This work could never have been accomplished without their friendship and their assistance. I must also express my gratitude to Carmen Imes and my wife, Ellen, who assisted me in the tedious task of indexing this work.

However, I owe a special debt of gratitude to Chris Ansberry, who spent countless hours at the end of this process trying to reduce a 1,250 page manuscript to approximately 800 pages as required by the editors of this series without losing my voice or the spirit of the larger work. Having worked so closely with Chris for six years, he knows the pulse of my heart. This final stage was funded by monies that came with the Leland Ryken Award for Teaching Excellence graciously granted me in the fall of 2010.

I would be remiss if I did not also express my thanks to the institutions that invested in this project through their library resources and funding provided for attending professional conferences where my ideas could be presented and tested: Bethel Theological Seminary, Southern Seminary, Wheaton College, and the Tyndale Library in Cambridge, where I was generously hosted during two sabbaticals (2002, 2010). Special thanks to Danny Akin, the dean of Southern Seminary, who graciously granted me a sabbatical leave in 2001–2002, and to Jeff Greenman, Jill Baumgartner, and Stan Jones, who granted me a generous leave in 2010. I am also grateful for the invitation by Zondervan and the NIVAC editorial board to make this contribution to the series. I am especially appreciative of the support I have received from Katya Covrett along the way. I must also express my deep gratitude to Bud and Betty Knoedler, who have given so generously to underwrite my professorial chair. It is a special grace to know them not only as supporters of Wheaton College, but also as personal friends. Ellen and I are grateful for their daily prayers on our behalf.

I eagerly also acknowledge Ellen, the delight of my life, who has stood by me as a gracious friend and counselor for more than four decades. Without her love and wisdom, the work represented here would either never have been finished, or it would have taken a dramatically different turn. Ellen has walked with me on this pilgrimage, not only listening to my private expressions of frustration and joy throughout this process, and patiently hearing many of my sermons and lectures on this book, but also providing me with a tranquil and peaceful world in which to do my work. I am also thankful for my family, who has taught me so much about celebrating the grace of God in everyday experiences of life. This book is dedicated to my grandchildren with deep love and affection.

Ultimately, all praise for this and any other accomplishment must go to God, who has lavished his grace on us in Christ Jesus and in his Torah.

May the favor of the Lord our God rest upon us;
   establish the work of our hands for us—
   yes, establish the work of our hands. (Ps. 90:17)

Daniel I. Block
May 2011

Abbreviations

AB	Anchor Bible
ABD	*Anchor Bible Dictionary*. Ed. David N. Freedman. 6 vols. New York, 1992.
ACEBT	*Amsterdamse Cahiers voor Exegese en bijbelse Theologie*
AfO	*Archiv für Orientforschung*
AJSL	*American Journal of Semitic Languages and Literature*
AnBib	Analecta biblica
ANEP	*Ancient Near Eastern Texts in Pictures*. Ed. J. Pritchard. Princeton, 1954
ANET	*Ancient Near Eastern Texts Relating to the Old Testament*. 3rd ed. Ed. J. Pritchard. Princeton, 1969.
AOAT	Alter Orient und Altes Testament
ARAB	*Ancient Records of Assyria and Babylonia*. Ed. D. D. Luckenbill. 2 vols. Chicago, 1926–1927.
ARM	Archives royales de Mari
AUSS	*Andrews University Seminary Studies*
BASOR	*Bulletin of the American Schools of Oriental Research*
BBB	Bonner biblische Beiträge
BBR	*Bulletin of Biblical Research*
BECNT	Baker Exegetical Commentary on the New Testament
BETL	Bibliotheca ephemeridum theologicarum lovaniensium
BHQ	*Biblia Hebraica Quinta*
BHRG	*Biblical Hebrew Reference Grammar*. Ed. C. H. J. Van der Merwe. Sheffield, 1999.
BHS	*Biblia Hebraica Stuttgartensia*
Bib	*Biblica*
BibOr	Biblica et orientalia
BIS	Biblical Interpretation Series
BJS	Brown Judaic Studies
BN	*Biblische Notizen*
BRev	*Bible Review*
BSac	*Bibliotheca sacra*
BST	Bible Speaks Today
BTB	*Biblical Theology Bulletin*
BWANT	Beiträge zur Wissenschaft vom Alten und Neuen Testament
BZ	*Biblische Zeitschrift*

BZAW	Beihefte zur Zeitschrift für die alttestamentliche Wissenschaft
CahRB	Cahiers de la Revue biblique
CAD	*The Assyrian Dictionary of the Oriental Institute of the University of Chicago.* 1956.
CANE	Civilizations of the Ancient Near East
CAT	*Cuneiform Alphabetic Texts from Ugarit, Ras Ibn Hani, and Other Places* [=CTU]. Ed. M. Dietrich, O. Loretz, J. Sanmartin. Münster, 1995.
CBC	Cambridge Bible Commentary
CBQ	*Catholic Biblical Quarterly*
CH	Code of Hammurabi. Ed. M. T. Roth. *Law Collections from Mesopotamia and Asia.* Atlanta, 1997.
chap(s).	chapter(s)
ConBOT	Coniectanea biblica: Old Testament Series
COS	*Context of Scripture.* Ed. W. W. Hallo. Leiden, 1997–.
CurBR	*Currents in Biblical Research*
DBAT	*Dielheimer Blätter zum Alten Testament*
DCH	*Dictionary of Classical Hebrew.* Ed. D. J. A. Clines. Sheffield, 1993–.
DDD	*Dictionary of Deities and Demons in the Bible.* Ed. K. van der Toorn et al. Leiden, 1995, rev. ed. 1998.
DDS	*Deuteronomy and the Deuteronomic School.* By M. Weinfeld. Winona Lake, 1992
DJD	*Discoveries in the Judaean Desert.* Oxford University Press. 44 vols. 1955–.
DOTP	*Dictionary of the Old Testament: Pentateuch.* Ed. T. D. Alexander and D. W. Baker. Downers Grove, 2003.
EGL	*Eastern Great Lakes*
EncJud	*Encyclopaedia Judaica.* Jerusalem, 1972.
ErIsr	*Eretz-Israel*
ESV	English Standard Version
ETL	*Ephemerides Theologicae Lovanienses*
EvQ	*Evangelical Quarterly*
ExAud	*Ex auditu*
ExpTim	*Expository Times*
FAT	Forschungen zum Alten Testament
FRLANT	Forschungen zur Religion und Literatur des Alten und Neuen Testaments
HALOT	*Hebrew and Aramaic Lexicon of the Old Testament.* Ed. L. Koehler, W. Baumgartner, and J. J. Stamm. 2 vols. Leiden, 1994–2000.

Abbreviations

HAR	*Hebrew Annual Review*
HAT	Handbuch zum Alten Testament
HBS	*Herder biblische Studien*
HBT	*Horizons in Biblical Theology*
HDT	*Hittite Diplomatic Texts*. Ed. G. Beckman. 2nd ed. Atlanta, 1999.
HKAT	Handkommentar zum Alten Testament
HL	Hittite Laws Ed. M. T. Roth. *Law Collections from Mesopotamia and Asia*. Atlanta, 1997.
HS	*Hebrew Studies*
HSM	Harvard Semitic Monographs
HSS	Harvard Semitic Studies
HTR	*Harvard Theological Review*
HUCA	*Hebrew Union College Annual*
IBD	*Illustrated Bible Dictionary*
ICC	International Critical Commentary
IDB	*Interpreter's Dictionary of the Bible*
IEJ	*Israel Exploration Journal*
Int	*Interpretation*
JANES	*Journal of the Ancient Near Eastern Society*
JAOS	*Journal of the American Oriental Society*
JATS	*Journal of the Adventist Theological Society*
JBL	*Journal of Biblical Literature*
JBQ	*Jewish Bible Quarterly*
JEA	*Journal of Egyptian Archaeology*
JETS	*Journal of the Evangelical Theological Society*
JHS	*Journal of Hebrew Scriptures*
JJS	*Journal of Jewish Studies*
JNES	*Journal of Near Eastern Studies*
JNWSL	*Journal of Northwest Semitic Languages*
JPA	Jewish Publication Society
JQR	*Jewish Quarterly Review*
JSJ	*Journal for the Study of Judaism in the Persian, Hellenistic and Roman Periods*
JSNTSup	Journal for the Study of the New Testament: Supplement Series
JSOT	*Journal for the Study of the Old Testament*
JSOTSup	Journal for the Study of the Old Testament: Supplement Series
JSS	*Journal of Semitic Studies*
JTI	*Journal of Theological Interpretation*

JTS	*Journal of Theological Studies*
KTU	*Die Keilalphabetischen Texte au Ugarit* [=CTU]
LCC	Library of Christian Classics
LE	Laws of Eshnunna. Ed. M. T. Roth. *Law Collections from Mesopotamia and Asia.* Atlanta, 1997.
LH	Laws of Hammurabi. Ed. M. T. Roth. *Law Collections from Mesopotamia and Asia.* Atlanta, 1997.
LL	Laws of Lipit-Ishtar. Ed. M. T. Roth. *Law Collections from Mesopotamia and Asia.* Atlanta, 1997.
LNTS	Library of New Testament Studies
LX	Laws of X (an unknown ruler). See M. T. Roth, *Law Collections from Mesopotamia and Asia.* Atlanta, 1997.
LXX	Septuagint
m.	*Mishnah*
MAL	Middle Assyrian Laws. Ed. M. T. Roth. *Law Collections from Mesopotamia and Asia.* Atlanta, 1997.
MT	Masoretic Text
MWBS	Midwest Biblical Societies
NAC	New American Commentary
NCB	New Century Bible
NIB	*New Interpreter's Bible*
NIBC	New International Biblical Commentary
NICNT	New International Commentary on the New Testament
NICOT	New International Commentary on the Old Testament
NIDB	New International Dictionary of the Bible. Ed. J. D. Douglas and Merrill C. Tenney. Grand Rapids, 1987.
NIDOTTE	*New International Dictionary of Old Testament Theology and Exegesis.* Ed. W. VanGemeren. 5 vols. Grand Rapids, 1997.
NIV	New International Version
NIVAC	NIV Application Commentary
NJPS	New Jewish Publication Society
NKJV	New King James Version
NLT	New Living Translation
NovT	*Novum Testamentum*
NovTSup	Novum Testamentum Supplements
NRSV	New Revised Standard Version
NTS	*New Testament Studies*
OBO	Orbis biblicus et orientalis
OBT	Overtures to Biblical Theology
OTL	Old Testament Library
OTS	Old Testament Studies

Abbreviations

OtSt	Oudtestamentische Studiën
PEQ	*Palestine Exploration Quarterly*
RB	*Revue biblique*
RevExp	*Review and Expositor*
RevQ	*Revue de Qumran*
RIME	The Royal Inscriptions of Mesopotamia: Early Periods
SAA	State Archives of Assyria
SANE	Sources from the Ancient Near East
SBA	Studies in Biblical Archaeology
SBJT	*Southern Baptist Journal of Theology*
SBLABS	Society of Biblical Literature Archaeology and Biblical Studies
SBLDS	Society of Biblical Literature Dissertation Series
SBLMS	Society of Biblical Literature Monograph Series
SBLSP	*Society of Biblical Literature Seminar Papers*
SBLWAW	Society of Biblical Literature Writings from the Ancient World
SBT	Studies in Biblical Theology
SHANE	Studies in the History of the Ancient Near East
SSI	*Textbook of Syrian Semitic Inscriptions.* Ed. J. C. L. Gibson. 3 vols. Oxford, 1971–82.
STDJ	Studies in the Texts of the Desert of Judea
StEv	*Studia evangelica*
TA	*Tel Aviv*
TCS	Texts from Cuneiform Sources
TDOT	*Theological Dictionary of the Old Testament.* Ed. G. J. Botterweck and H. Ringgren. 15 vols. Grand Rapids, 1974–.
TJ	*Trinity Journal*
TLOT	*Theological Lexicon of the Old Testament.* Ed. E. Jenni and C. Westermann. 3 vols. Peabody, MA, 1997.
TWOT	*A Theological Wordbook of the Old Testament.* Ed. R. L. Harris, G. L. Archer, and B. K. Waltke. 2 vols. Chicago, 1980.
TynBul	*Tyndale Bulletin*
UF	*Ugarit-Forschungen*
UNP	Ugaritic Narrative Poetry. S. B. Parker. SBLWAW 9. Atlanta, 1997.
v(v).	verse(s)
VF	Verkündigung und Forschung
VT	*Vetus Testamentum*
VTE	Vassal Treaties of Esardhaddon. Ed. M. T. Roth. *Law Collections from Mesopotamia and Asia.* Atlanta, 1997.

VTSup	Vetus Testamentum Supplements
WBC	Word Biblical Commentary
WMANT	Wissenschaftliche Monographien zum Alten und Neuen Testament
WTJ	*Westminster Journal of Theology*
ZAW	*Zeitschrift für die alttestamentliche Wissenschaft*

Introduction to Deuteronomy

THE THEOLOGICAL SIGNIFICANCE OF Deuteronomy can scarcely be overestimated. Inasmuch as this book offers the most systematic presentation of theological truth in the entire Old Testament, we may compare its place to that of Romans in the New Testament. Moreover, since Deuteronomy reviews so much of Israel's historical experience of God's grace as recounted in Genesis through Numbers, a comparison with the gospel of John may be even more appropriate. Just as John wrote his gospel after several decades of reflection on the death and resurrection of Jesus, so Moses preached the sermons in Deuteronomy after almost four decades of reflection on the significance of the Exodus and God's covenant with Israel. Thus, like the gospel of John, the book of Deuteronomy functions as a theological manifesto, calling on Israel to respond to God's grace with unreserved loyalty and love.

History of Interpretation

DEUTERONOMY IS THE FIFTH and final book of what Jewish tradition knows as the *Torah*, and Christians refer to as the Pentateuch. In popular Hebrew tradition the book is *sēfer dᵉbārîm* ("book of words"), which is an adaptation of the official Hebrew name *ᵓēlleh haddᵉbārîm* ("These are the words"), taken from the first two words of the book. In the third to second centuries BC the translators of the LXX set the course for the history of interpretation of Deuteronomy when, instead of translating the Hebrew title *to biblion tôn logôn* ("the book of words") or more simply *logoi* (words"), they designated the book *deuteronomium* ("second law").[1] This Greek heading probably became determinative because the book does indeed reiterate many of the laws found in Exodus through Numbers, and in chapter 5 it cites the Decalogue of Exodus 20 almost verbatim. But the name "Deuteronomy" overlooks the true nature of the book: It presents itself as a series of

---

1. Cf. Deut. 17:18, where LXX misinterprets *mišnēh hattôrâ* ("a copy of the Torah") as *to deuteronomiom*. Since the LXX was translated by Jews for Jews, not surprisingly, in Jewish tradition rabbis often referred to Deuteronomy as *Mishneh Torah* ("The Repetition of the Torah"). See J. H. Tigay, *Deuteronomy* (JPS Torah Commentary; Philadelphia: JPS, 1996), xi; M. Weinfeld, "Deuteronomy, Book of," *ABD*, 2:168.

sermons that review events described in the narratives of earlier books and challenges the people to faithful living in the future. Where laws are dealt with (e.g., the central sanctuary regulation in Deut. 12), the presentation is often in the form of exposition rather than a recital of the laws themselves.

Prior to the rise of the source-critical method, both Jewish and Christian readers assumed Mosaic authorship of the book, a fact reflected in the common designation of the Pentateuchal books outside the English world as the Five Books of Moses. During the time in which Jesus ministered and spoke, some looked on him as the eschatological prophet like Moses whom Yahweh promised to raise up (Deut. 18:15; cf. Matt. 11:9; John 1:21, 25; 6:14; 7:40). While Jesus himself rejected this interpretation (John 1:21), judging by the number of quotations from Deuteronomy, this was Jesus' favorite book. This impression is reinforced by his distillation of the entire law into the simple command to love Yahweh with one's whole being and to love one's neighbor as oneself (Matt. 22:37; Mark 12:30; Luke 10:27). This form of the command is thoroughly deuteronomic. While appeals for love for one's neighbor and the stranger occur earlier in the Pentateuch (Lev. 19:18, 34), the command to love God occurs only in Deuteronomy (Deut. 6:5; 11:1, 13; 13:3[4]; 30:6).

Paul repeatedly cites texts from Deuteronomy to buttress his positions (Rom. 10:19; 11:8; 12:19; 1 Cor. 5:13; 9:9; Eph. 6:2–3; etc.). However, it is clear that Paul interpreted not only the entire history of God's revelation, but also Deuteronomy in particular in the light of Christ and the cross (Rom. 10:6–8; 1 Cor. 8:6; Gal. 3:13). In so doing, Paul functioned as a second Moses, not only in providing a profoundly theological interpretation of God's saving actions in Christ, but also in reminding his readers that salvation comes by grace alone. In Romans and Galatians Paul's argumentation is addressed to those who would pervert the "law" (a narrow legalistic interpretation of Hebrew *Torah*) into a means of salvation, rather than treating it as a response to salvation as Moses perceived it. In his own disposition toward the "law" Paul was in perfect step with Moses: obedience to the law was not a means for gaining salvation but a willing and grateful response to salvation already received. There is nothing revolutionary in Paul's definition of a true Jew as one who receives the praise of God because he is circumcised in the heart (Rom. 2:28–29; cf. Deut. 10:16–21; 30:6), nor in his praise of the law as holy, righteous, and good (Rom. 7:12; cf. Deut. 6:20–25), nor in his distillation of the whole law into the law of love (Rom. 13:8–10; cf. Deut. 10:12–21).

The early church fathers tended to follow Paul's lead in interpreting Deuteronomy christologically, but in their application of the laws they often resorted to spiritualizing the details. For example, by marshaling the

Shema (Deut. 6:4–5) to defend the doctrine of the Trinity, they obscured the original contextual meaning of the statement.[2] Of the Reformers Luther tended to read Deuteronomy through the lenses of Paul's rhetorical seemingly antinomian statements (Rom. 7:4–9; 2 Cor. 3:6; Gal. 3:10–25). His own debilitating experience of works-righteousness within the Roman Catholic Church contributed significantly to his view of a radical contrast between the law (which kills) and the gospel (which gives life). His emphasis on the dual function of the law (civic—to maintain external order on earth; theological—to convict people of sin and drive them to Christ)[3] completely missed the point of Deuteronomy, which presents the law as a gift of grace to the redeemed to guide them in the way of righteousness and lead to life (cf. Deut. 4:6–8; 6:20–25). Like Luther, Calvin insisted that no one can be justified by keeping the law, but he also emphasized that through the gift of the law, Israel was instructed on how to express their gratitude for their redemption and bring glory and delight to God.[4]

These approaches tended to dominate the disposition of interpreters of Deuteronomy until the Enlightenment, when the attention of critical scholars shifted from the theological value of Deuteronomy to hypotheses concerning the origin of the book. By the second half of the nineteenth century the documentary approach to Pentateuchal studies was firmly entrenched, and Deuteronomy had been isolated as a source separate from J (Yahwist), E (Elohist), and P (Priestly). Critical scholars generally agree that on the one hand, Deuteronomy either provides the occasion or is the result of the Josianic reform, and on the other hand that the speeches in Deuteronomy are pseudepigraphic, being fictionally attributed to Moses to lend weight to the voice of the parties whose interests are represented in the book.[5] Whether they attribute the bulk of Deuteronomy to country Levites writing shortly before 701 BC,[6] prophetic circles of northern Israel,[7] or sages in the Jerusalem court,[8] many interpret the book as a sort of manifesto, written in support

---

2. Cf. D. I. Block, "How Many Is God? An Investigation into the Meaning of Deuteronomy 6:4–5," *JETS* 47 (2004): 193–212; reprinted in D. I. Block, *How I Love Your Torah, O LORD: Studies in the Book of Deuteronomy* (Eugene, OR: Cascade, 2011), 73–97.

3. Cf. B. Lohse, *Martin Luther's Theology* (Minneapolis: Fortress, 1999), 270–74.

4. J. Calvin, *The Four Last Books of Moses* (Grand Rapids: Eerdmans, 1950), 363.

5. At the end of a thorough study on how Deuteronomy presents itself as a written document, J.-P. Sonnet (*The Book within the Book: Writing within Deuteronomy* [BIS 14; Leiden: Brill, 1997], 262–67) dismisses all the attributions to Moses that he has explored as pseudepigraphic.

6. G. von Rad, *Deuteronomy* (trans. D. Barton; OTL; Philadelphia: Westminster, 1966), 23–27.

7. E. W. Nicholson, *Deuteronomy and Tradition* (Philadelphia: Fortress, 1967), 58–82.

8. Weinfeld, "Deuteronomy, Book of," 2:181–82; idem, *Deuteronomy 1–11* (AB 5; New York: Doubleday, 1991), 62–65; idem, *Deuteronomy and the Deuteronomic School* (Winona Lake, IN: Eisenbrauns, 1992), 244–307 (hereafter referred to as *DDS*).

of Josiah's efforts to centralize the religion of Israel in Jerusalem. Weinfeld views Deuteronomy not only as a remarkable literary achievement, but also as a profound monument to the theological revolution advocated by the Josianic circles. This revolution attempted to eliminate other shrines and to centralize all worship of Yahweh in Jerusalem, as well as to "secularize," "demythologize," and "spiritualize" the religion.[9]

These interpretations go back to Julius Wellhausen, who proposed that Deuteronomy 12–26 represents the original core of the book, which was written by a prophet (some suggest Jeremiah) ca. 622 BC (cf. 2 Kings 22–23) to promote the reform of Israel's religious practices (2 Chron. 34–35) and centralize the cult in Jerusalem. Whereas previously all had recognized Deuteronomy as the last book of the Pentateuch, Martin Noth argued that the book serves as a theological prologue to the Deuteronomistic history (Joshua–Kings), whose purpose was to demonstrate that the demises of Israel and Judah in 722 BC and 586 BC respectively were the direct result of Israel's worship of strange gods and her failure to obey Yahweh's demands.[10]

More recently some have proposed that Deuteronomy was originally produced by a coalition of dissidents (scribes, priests, sages, and aristocrats). According to Richard D. Nelson, the book has its roots in a time of crisis (seventh century), when loyalty to Yahweh was being undermined by the veneration of other gods, the well-being of many was being jeopardized by exploitative royal policies, and the prophetic institution was out of control.[11] The inconsistencies and ambiguities in the Deuteronomic legislation reflect the varying interests of the dissident groups.[12]

While many scholars admit that some of the ideas in the book may derive from earlier times, in their minds the Moses we hear in Deuteronomy is a legendary figure and the speeches in the book are pseudepigraphic. Like

---

9. See further Weinfeld, "Deuteronomy, Book of," 2:175–78; idem, *Deuteronomy 1–11*, 53–57; idem, *DDS*, 158–79.

10. See M. Noth, *The Deuteronomistic History* (JSOTSup 15; Sheffield: Univ. of Sheffield Press, 1981).

11. R. D. Nelson, *Deuteronomy* (OTL; Louisville: Westminster John Knox, 2002), 4–9; cf. R. Albertz, *A History of Israelite Religion in the OT Period*, 2 vols. (OTL: Louisville: Westminster John Knox, 1994), 1:194–231. P. D. Miller (*Deuteronomy* [Interpretation; Louisville: Westminster John Knox, 1990], 5–8) recognizes that the book contains prophetic, priestly, and scribal (wisdom) features, but he refuses to choose among these, let alone recognize that Moses was one of the few persons in the history of ancient Israel whose life and ministry bore the stamp of all three interest groups.

12. See also K. van der Toorn's complex reconstruction of the composition of Deuteronomy in *Scribal Culture and the Making of the Hebrew Bible* (Cambridge, MA: Harvard Univ. Press, 2007), 143–72.

many ancient writers, the author of the book expresses his ideology by putting programmatic speeches into the mouth of this figure, who towers above all others in Israelite history as the epitome of wisdom and spirituality.[13]

But this reconstruction of the origins and provenance of Deuteronomy is diametrically opposed to the internal evidence of the book. Nothing about the book of Deuteronomy or the speeches embedded therein points to a pseudepigraphic work. On the contrary, the image of Moses reflected in the addresses, particularly in the first speech, is hardly the stuff of idealized legend. Moses is keenly aware of his honorific role as the mediator of divine revelation (cf. 5:4–5) and the mouthpiece for God (1:42; 2:2, 31; 3:2; 6:1), but his transparently sour disposition toward the people, and even toward God because he cannot enter the land of Canaan, is anything but laudatory. The first speech in particular creates the impression of a tired and bitter old man, disillusioned with his people, frustrated with God, and discouraged with his task (1:37; 3:26; 4:21). This is not the normal stuff of pseudepigraphy and argues strongly for the integrity of the speeches as authentic records of Mosaic speeches.

Not all are willing to date Deuteronomy late. Some argue that the religious and political vision of the book does not fit the Josianic period as described in 2 Kings. On the contrary, according to McConville, "Deuteronomy, or at least a form of it, is the document of a real political and religious constitution of Israel from the pre-monarchical period."[14] As such it challenges prevailing ancient Near Eastern royal-cultic ideology, replacing this with a prophetic vision of Yahweh in direct covenant relationship with his people and a people governed by Torah. Through the Torah the prophetic authority of Moses, the spokesperson for Yahweh, extends to the community. The "Book of the Torah," deposited next to the ark and formally read before the assembly, provides a constant reminder of the will of the covenant Lord and a guide for expressing its loyalty to him.[15]

13. For discussion see Weinfeld, *Deuteronomy 1–11*, 4–6. B. T. Arnold ("Deuteronomy as the *Ipsissima Vox* of Moses," *Journal of Theological Interpretation* 4 [2010]: 53–74) argues that Deuteronomy preserves the voice (*vox*) of Moses, but not his words (*verba*). The book represented the culmination of the Mosaic legal tradition and is the result of a complex scribal history.

14. J. G. McConville, *Deuteronomy* (Apollos; Downers Grove, IL: InterVarsity Press, 2002), 34. Juha Pakkala ("The Date of the Oldest Edition of Deuteronomy," *ZAW* 121 [2009]: 388–401) offers ten arguments for dating Deuteronomy in the Persian period. Most of his arguments fit more naturally in the premonarchic period than in the time he suggests.

15. For additional critiques of these critical views, see I. Wilson, *Out of the Midst of the Fire: Divine Presence in Deuteronomy* (SBLDS 151; Atlanta: Scholars Press, 1995); S. L. Richter, *The Deuteronomistic History and the Name Theology: lᵉšakkēn šᵉmô šām in the Bible and the Ancient Near East* (BZAW 318; Berlin/New York: de Gruyter, 2002); P. Vogt, *Deuteronomic Theology and the Significance of Torah: A Reappraisal* (Winona Lake, IN: Eisenbrauns, 2006).

Taken at face value, Deuteronomy tells us more about its composition than any other book in the Old Testament. Inside the book we find many references to the written Torah (6:6−9; 11:18−21; 17:18−20; 27:1−8; 28:58−61; 29:14−29[13−28]; 30:8−11), which point to an early transcription of the Torah that Moses delivered in oral form. Deuteronomy 31:9−13 specifically declares that Moses wrote down this Torah and placed it in the custody of the priests who carried the ark of the covenant. We may infer that this applied to all the addresses recorded in the book: the first address (1:6−4:40), the second address (5:1b−26:19; 28:1−29:1[28:69]), and the third address (29:2[1]−30:20). Deuteronomy 31:22 also indicates that Moses wrote down the song that Yahweh dictated to him and Joshua that same day (32:1−43), and there is every reason to believe that he did the same with the fragments that now constitute the blessing of the tribes (33:2−29).

It seems likely that when Joshua and the Israelites crossed the Jordan River after Moses' death, they had in their possession a written copy of all this material. The book identifies the individual addresses as *Torah.* Eventually, the scope of this term was expanded to include the added narrative sections (1:1−5; 27:1−10; 34:1−12; etc)—and finally, when the book of Deuteronomy was combined with the preceding books (Genesis−Numbers), to the Pentateuch as a whole.

The book of Deuteronomy presents itself as the record of a series of addresses delivered orally by Moses to his countrymen on the verge of crossing over into the Promised Land, and immediately committed to writing (31:9).[16] However, in accordance with ancient Near Eastern literary conventions, strictly speaking the book as we have it is anonymous. We may speculate when the individual speeches of Moses were combined, arranged, and linked with their present narrative stitching. Within the book we observe a series of features that suggest Moses was not responsible for the final form of the book: (1) references to Moses in third person in the narrative stitching at the boundaries of the respective speeches,[17] and in the formulaic introductions to the blessing fragments in chapter 33;[18] (2) details that reflect a context later than the speeches themselves (*post-Mosaica*);[19] (3) the language of Deuteronomy.[20] Nevertheless, several fea-

---

16. D. I. Block, "Recovering the Voice of Moses: The Genesis of Deuteronomy," *JETS* 44 (2001): 385−408; reprinted in D. I. Block, *The Gospel According to Moses: Theological and Ethical Reflection on the Book of Deuteronomy* (Eugene, OR: Cascade, 2011), 21−51.

17. See 1:1−5; 4:41−5:1a; 27:1−11; 29:1−2[28:69−29:1]; 31:1, 30; 32:44−52; 34:1−12.

18. See 33:1, 7, 8, 12, 13, 18, 20, 22, 23, 24.

19. (a) Expressions like (lit.) "across the Jordan in the wilderness in the Arabah opposite Suph" (1:1), and "to this day" (2:22; 3:14; 10:8); (b) parenthetical historical notes (2:10−12;

tures within the book point to much earlier context: (1) archaic or at least archaizing features in the language,[21] which occur both in Moses' speeches (as might be expected: 4:6; 10:10; 20:20; 24:4; 30:11,12,13) and in the narrative comments (3:11); (2) the literary style of Deuteronomy;[22] (3) the names used to identify the original inhabitants of the Transjordanian territories of Moab and Ammon in Moses' first address;[23] (4) the anecdotal reference to Og's huge bed of iron in 3:11, which invites ancient readers to check the narrator's veracity and confirm the magnitude of Israel's victory; and (5) the structure of Deuteronomy, which bears a closer resemblance to late second millennium Hittite treaties than to neo-Assyrian structures.[24]

Taking these features into account, it seems that although the speeches of Deuteronomy derive from Moses himself, the book as we have it was produced later. A reasonable *terminus a quo* (earliest possible date) would be during the tenure of Joshua after the Israelites had crossed the Jordan; a *terminus ad quem* (latest possible date) would be the ninth century, prior to the ministries of Elijah and Elisha, after which the style of prophetic preaching seems to have changed dramatically. The Torah referred to in texts like Joshua 1:8; 8:31–34; and 23:6 may have consisted minimally of the written versions of Moses' second address (including the covenant curses and the

---

2:20–23; 3:9, 11, 13b–14); (c) the use of the past tense in 2:12, "just as Israel did in the land the LORD gave them as their possession"; (d) the obituary of Moses (32:48–52; 34:1–12); (e) the reference to Dan as a northern extremity (34:1); (f) the use of Israelite tribal names for geographic regions of Canaan (34:1–3); (g) the observation that since the death of Moses no prophet like him has risen in Israel, that is, no one whom Yahweh knew face to face (34:10), which makes sense only if the narrator was aware of the historical significance of Moses' own prediction concerning the prophetic institution in 18:15–22 and knew at least a few prophetic figures with whom Moses could be compared.

20. While the poems at the end (chs. 32 and 33) appear ancient, the speeches seem to be cast in classical Jerusalem dialect of Hebrew as represented by Jeremiah. On the evolution of the language, see G. J. Wenham, "The Date of Deuteronomy — The Linch-pin of OT Criticism," *Themelios* 10/2 (1985): 18–19.

21. E.g., the use of the masculine third person singular pronoun *hû*' ("he") for the feminine, on which see G. A. Rendsburg, "A New Look at Pentateuchal *HW*'," *Bib* 63 (1982): 351–69.

22. Some argue the sermonic form of Deuteronomy antedates the poetic form of prophets like Amos and Hosea and has more in common with the utterances of Samuel and Elijah. See C. Rabin, "Discourse Analysis and the Dating of Deuteronomy," in *Interpreting the Hebrew Bible: Essays in Honour of E. I. J. Rosenthal* (ed. J. A. Emerton and S. C. Reif; Cambridge: Cambridge Univ. Press, 1982), 171–77.

23. On these names see the commentary below.

24. See K. A. Kitchen, *On the Reliability of the Old Testament* (Grand Rapids: Eerdmans, 2003), 283–94; Markus Zehnder, "Building on Stone? Deuteronomy and Esarhaddon's Loyalty Oaths (Part 1): Some Preliminary Observations," *BBR* 19 (2009): 341–74; "(Part 2): Some Additional Observations," *BBR* 19 (2009): 511–35.

Song of Yahweh), and maximally of Moses' three major speeches and the songs now preserved in Deuteronomy. However, it is reasonable to suppose that by David's time Deuteronomy more or less as we have it existed as the last scroll of the Pentateuch.

While critical scholars tend to assume that the Pentateuch arose in response to the crisis of the exile,[25] it remains equally possible that Israel's canonical Scriptures were produced in the context of peace and heightened religious fervor. In an earlier time, God's self-revelation and his entry into covenant relation with Israel at Sinai represented a climactic spiritual experience whose significance is documented in writing in the Decalogue and the statutes, ordinances, and laws preserved in the books of Exodus, Leviticus, and Numbers. One can imagine that David's transfer of the ark to Jerusalem, the choice of Zion as the permanent residence of Yahweh, the receipt of the blueprint for the temple, the organization of the cult personnel, and the gathering of the materials for the construction of the temple sparked a new enthusiasm for the worship of Yahweh throughout the land (1 Chron. 22–29).

One may also imagine that David's religious reforms called for a canonical Scripture to be used in worship and to serve as a guide for daily living as Israel looked forward to a new social and religious order under monarchic rule. David's organization of the temple worship provides a logical context for the production of a canonical Scripture.[26] Exercising their role as gatekeepers of Israel's theological ideas,[27] the priests and Levites would use these Scriptures in worship and in instructing the citizenry in the life of covenantal fidelity. The conjunction of this energized religious climate with the peace and security that David had won for the nation set the stage for the high point of Israel's cultural achievements, which could reasonably have included the literary masterpiece we know as the Pentateuch as a whole and the book of Deuteronomy in particular.

Whether Deuteronomy, more or less as we have it, was produced by Samuel or under the auspices of David, this was probably the document

---

25. See Nelson, as cited in n. 11 above.

26. David's charge to Solomon at the end of his life in 1 Chron. 22:12–13 assumes a canonical Torah, and the description of his organization of the cultic personnel in chs. 23–26 seems to reflect some canonical awareness (cf. 23:31; 24:19; 28:1, 8), though clearly (see 28:9–19) the instructions for some of this was communicated by means of a new written document.

27. On this role of the relation of religious specialists and written religious literature, see J. Goody, *The Logic of Writing and the Organization of Society* (Studies in Literacy, Family, Culture, and the State; Cambridge: Cambridge Univ. Press, 1986), 16–18. Goody observes, "Once the Holy Word has been written down in book form and institutionalized in a church, it becomes a profoundly conserving force, or better a force for continuity—its own continuity, not necessarily the state's, despite changes in the polity or economy" (20).

according to which David charged Solomon to rule in 1 Kings 2:2–4. Unfortunately, as already anticipated by Moses, the periods when Israel as a whole and her kings in particular would live by the Torah were few and far between. During the reign of Manasseh in the seventh century, the book was suppressed altogether, and thoroughly pagan forms replaced its injunctions (2 Kings 21; 2 Chron. 33), which accounts for the response of Josiah when he heard the Torah read by Shaphan (2 Kings 22). The narrative suggests that the Torah had long been recognized as canonical; it was not some recent literary composition.

Later expressions like "Book of Moses" and "Torah of Moses" do not demand that Moses' own hand produced the book in its final form. We do not doubt the historicity of Moses, nor the authenticity of his speeches, nor the fundamentally Mosaic authority behind the entire Pentateuch, any more than we question the authenticity of the speeches of Jesus in the Gospels. The editor of Moses' final speeches and the biographer who preserved for us the account of Moses' final days was himself a prophet in the Mosaic tradition. The book he produced is the Torah, which the priests were to teach and model,[28] which psalmists praised,[29] to which the prophets appealed,[30] and by which faithful kings ruled[31] and righteous citizens lived (Ps. 1). In short, the book of Deuteronomy provides the theological base for virtually the entire Old (and New) Testament and the paradigm for much of its literary style.

Deuteronomy and the Canon

THE WRITTEN COPIES OF Moses' last addresses to Israel were to be recognized as authoritative and canonical from the beginning. Not only did Moses prohibit adding to or deleting from his words (4:2; 12:32), but he also commanded the Levites to place the written copy of the Torah beside the ark of the covenant (31:9–13). That this written Torah was placed *beside* the ark rather than *in* it does not suggest a lesser authority than the Decalogue *inside the ark* but a different significance and use. Whereas the tablets with the Decalogue symbolized the covenant (4:13; 10:1–4) and were placed in the ark as a reminder to God of his covenant with Israel, the Torah was Moses' inspired commentary on the covenant for the people (1:3).

The theological stamp of Deuteronomy is evident throughout the Old Testament and into the New Testament. If in Deuteronomy the term *Torah*

---

28. Deut. 33:10; 2 Chron. 15:3; 19:8; Mal. 2:6, 9; cf. Jer. 18:18; Ezek. 7:26; Ezra 7:10.
29. Pss. 19:7–14[8–15]; 119; etc.
30. Isa. 1:10; 5:24; 8:20; 30:9; 51:7.
31. 1 Kings 2:2–4; 2 Kings 14:6; 22:11; 23:25.

applies expressly to the speeches of Moses, eventually it was applied to the entire Pentateuch, for which Deuteronomy represents the conclusion. The stamp of Deuteronomy on the so-called "Deuteronomistic History" (Joshua–Kings) is evident not only in the style of these books,[32] but especially in its theology.[33] Specifically Solomon's emphasis on the temple as a place for the "name" of Yahweh to dwell in 1 Kings 8 harks back to Deuteronomy 12 et passim. More generally, when the nation of Israel was destroyed and the Davidic monarchy dismantled, it was because they failed in their covenant relationship with Yahweh as outlined in Deuteronomy.

The influence of Deuteronomy is less obvious on Chronicles and Ezra-Nehemiah, but in the Latter Prophets one hears echoes of Moses' orations throughout. Particularly in Hosea and Jeremiah, the links are so direct that scholars often debate which came first, Deuteronomy or the prophet. Prophetic pronouncements of judgment and restoration appear often to be based on the covenant curses of Deuteronomy 28 and promises of renewal in chapter 30. Indeed, the canonical collection of prophets as a whole and the book of Malachi specifically end with a call to return to the "law of my servant Moses" (Mal. 4:4–6[Heb. 3:22–24]), which, while having its base in the revelation at Sinai, refers fundamentally to Moses' exposition of that law. In the Psalms Deuteronomic influence is most evident in the so-called "Torah" Psalms (1; 19; 119), which highlight the life-giving purpose of the law, but also in the "wisdom" psalms, with their emphasis on the fear of Yahweh (111:10; cf. 34:8–12[9–13]). The Psalms are so rooted in Deuteronomy that unless Christians accept this book as authoritative, they have no right to find inspiration in the Psalms.[34]

New Testament texts like Luke 24:44 suggest that by the time of Christ, the expression "Law of Moses" served as the standard designation of the first part of the Jewish canon (alongside "the Prophets" and "the Psalms"). As noted earlier, the Pentateuchal location of Deuteronomy, which provides theological exposition of the events narrated in the previous books, may have influenced the canonical location of John, the most overtly theological of the Gospels. While many Christian interpreters see in Jesus a second Moses, this actually reflects a low Christology, for the New Testament presents Jesus as Yahweh incarnate. If there is a second Moses in the

---

32. Many of the embedded speeches sound like Deuteronomy. E.g., Josh. 23; 24; 1 Sam. 12; etc.

33. Cf. J. G. McConville, *Grace in the End: A Study in Deuteronomic Theology* (Grand Rapids: Zondervan, 1993).

34. Patrick Miller has rightly argued that when the Psalter refers to the Torah, it has in mind primarily Deuteronomy. See "Deuteronomy and the Psalms: Evoking a Conversation," *JBL* 119 (1999): 3–18.

New Testament, that person is Paul. Like Moses, this apostle of liberty was specially called not only to lead the community of faith in the mission to which God had called it, but especially to draw out the theological and soteriological significance of God's saving actions and to instruct God's people in the life of covenant faith. In so doing Paul responded sharply to those who insisted that adherence to the law of Moses was a prerequisite to salvation, and he called his hearers to salvation by faith in the redeeming work of Christ. Like the book of Deuteronomy, Paul's letters (such as Romans) often divide into two parts, the first being devoted to theological exposition (e.g., Rom. 1–11; cf. Deut. 1–11), and the second to drawing out the practical and communal implications of the theology (e.g., Rom. 12:16; cf. Deut. 12–26).

Hearing the Message of Deuteronomy

BECAUSE OF A PERVASIVE if latent Marcionism and adherence to theological systems that are fundamentally dismissive of the Old Testament in general and the book of Deuteronomy in particular, its message has been largely lost to the church. This is a tragedy because few books in the Old or New Testament proclaim such a relevant word of grace and gospel to the church today. But how can readers today rediscover the message of the book? The following hermeneutical steps should help.

(1) It is important to "hear" the word of Deuteronomy. At significant junctures Moses appeals to his people to "hear" the word he is proclaiming (5:1; 6:3–4; 9:1; 20:3). In 31:9–13 he charges the Levitical priests to read the Torah that he has just transcribed (i.e., his speeches) before the people every seven years at the Feast of Booths. This statement highlights the critical connection between hearing the Torah in the future and the life of God's people. This link may be represented schematically as follows:

Reading ▸ Hearing ▸ Learning ▸ Fear ▸ Obedience ▸ Life

A similar relationship between reading/hearing the words of "this Torah" and one's future well-being is expressed in 17:19, where Moses charges future kings to read the Torah for themselves so they may embody the covenant fidelity he has espoused in his addresses to the people.

(2) To hear the message of Deuteronomy we must recognize its genre and form. At one level, Deuteronomy represents the final major segment of the biography of Moses that began in the first chapter of Exodus.[35] Accordingly,

---

35. Cf. R. P. Knierim. *The Task of Old Testament Theology: Substance, Method and Cases* (Grand Rapids: Eerdmans, 1995), 355–59, 372–79.

Deuteronomy may be interpreted as narrative with a series of lengthy embedded speeches. At another level, the manner in which the first two speeches have been arranged is strikingly reminiscent of ancient Near Eastern treaty forms, especially second millennium Hittite suzerainty treaties. Recognition of the fundamentally covenantal character of Deuteronomy has significant implications for the message we hear in the book. Yahweh is the divine suzerain, who graciously chose the patriarchs and their descendants as his covenant partner (4:37; 7:6–8), and he demonstrated his covenant commitment (ʾāhab, "love") by rescuing them from Egypt (4:32–40), entering into an eternal covenant relationship with them at Sinai (4:9–31), revealing to them his will (4:1–8), and providentially caring for them in the desert (1:9–3:29), and he is now about to deliver the Promised Land into their hands (1:6–8; 7:1–26).

As a true prophet of Yahweh, Moses challenges the Israelites to respond by declaring that Yahweh alone is their God (6:4) and by demonstrating unwavering loyalty and total love for him through acts of obedience to him (6:5–19; 10:12–11:1; etc.). Although Moses realistically anticipates Israel's future rebellion against her suzerain, leading ultimately to her banishment from the land promised on oath to Abraham, Yahweh's compassion toward his people and the irrevocable nature of his covenant mean that exile from the land and dispersion among the nations cannot be the last word; Yahweh will bring them back to himself and the land (4:26–31; 30:1–10; 32:26–43). Moses perceives the covenant being renewed with Yahweh as an extension of the covenant made with Israel at Sinai (29:1[28:69]), and ultimately this is an extension of the covenant made with their ancestors (29:10–13[9–12]).

(3) At a third level the book of Deuteronomy presents itself as a series of addresses by Moses to Israel immediately prior to their entrance into the land of Canaan and prior to his own decease. The narrative preamble to the book (1:1–5) should be determinative for how we hear the message of the book. The preamble identifies Moses' words as *hattôrâ hazzōʾt* ("this Torah"). The Hebrew term *tôrâ* means "instruction," being derived from the verb *hôrâ* ("to teach"), and the *sēper hattôrâ* (e.g., Deut. 29:21[20]; Josh. 1:8; etc.) means "the book of the instruction" rather than "the book of the law." Although *tôrâ* was applied to specific instructions earlier (e.g., Ex. 12:49; 24:12; Lev. 7:1; Num. 19:14; etc.), here the word identifies Moses' sermons in Deuteronomy.[36] Both the book and the word itself are represented much

---

36. Although Deuteronomy incorporates much prescriptive material deriving from the Sinai revelation, legal lists analogous to the forms of other ancient Near Eastern law codes tend to be concentrated in only seven chapters (chs. 19–25), but even these are punctuated by strong rhetorical appeals and a fundamental concern for righteousness rather than mere legal conformity.

---

more accurately by the Greek *didaskalia* and *didachē* as used in the New Testament[37] than by the word *nomos*.

Moses' role in Deuteronomy is not that of a lawgiver[38] but a pastor (Num. 27:17; Isa. 63:11).[39] Knowing that his death is imminent, like Jacob in Genesis 49, Joshua in Joshua 24, and Jesus in John 13–16, Moses gathers his congregation and delivers his final homily, pleading with the Israelites to remain faithful to Yahweh. The texts he has left us are not to be read primarily as law, but as discourses on the implications of the Israelite covenant for a people about to enter the land promised under the Abrahamic covenant (cf. Gen. 15:7–21; 26:3; Ex. 6:2–8).

How, then, are Christians to interpret and apply the book today? The following represent a few guiding principles.[40] (1) Rather than beginning with what the New Testament has to say about Deuteronomy, we should read the book as an ancient Near Eastern document that addresses issues current well over a thousand years before Christ in idioms derived from that cultural world. Although the New Testament church accepted this book, along with the rest of the Old Testament, as its authoritative Scripture, the book seeks primarily to govern the faith and life of the nation of Israel composed largely of ethnic descendants of the patriarchs.

(2) We should recognize the book as a written deposit of eternal truth. Some of these verities are cast in explicit declarative form (4:35, 39), while others are couched in distinctive Israelite cultural dress, for which we need to identify the underlying theological principle (22:8). Unless the New Testament explicitly declares a Deuteronomic ordinance to be passé, we should assume minimally that the principle underlying each command remains valid.

---

37. Greek *didachē* is used to designate "teaching" in general (Mark 1:27; Acts 17:19; 1 Cor. 14:6; 2 Tim. 4:2; Titus 1:9; Heb. 6:2); Jesus' teaching (Matt. 7:28; 22:33; Mark 1:22; 4:2; 11:18; 12:38; Luke 4:32; John 7:16–17; 18:19; Rev. 2:24); the apostles' teaching (Acts 2:42; 5:28; 13:12; Rom. 16:17; 1 Cor. 14:26; 2 John 9–10); the teaching of the Pharisees and Sadducees (Matt. 16:12); and false teaching (Rev. 2:14–15). The Greek word *didaskalia* in the sense of "instruction, doctrine" is used of human teaching (Matt. 15:9; Mark 7:7; Col. 2:22); of teaching in general or the apostles' teaching (Rom. 12:7; Eph. 4:14; 1 Tim. 1:10; 4:6; 5:17; 6:1, 3; 2 Tim. 3:10; 4:3; Titus 1:9; 2:1, 7); of teaching about God (Titus 2:10); of the teaching of demons (1 Tim. 4:1); of the Old Testament Scriptures (Rom. 15:4; 2 Tim. 3:16); and of Timothy's teaching (1 Tim. 4:13, 16).

38. Isa. 33:22 attributes this role (*mᵉḥôqēq*) to Yahweh.

39. For full discussion, see D. I. Block, "Will the Real Moses Please Rise? An Exploration into the Role and Ministry of Moses in the Book of Deuteronomy," in D. I. Block, *The Gospel According to Moses*, 68–103.

40. For a discussion of these issues see D. I. Block, "Preaching OT Law to NT Christians," in D. I. Block, *The Gospel According to Moses*, 104–36; idem, "The Grace of Torah: The Mosaic Prescription for Life (Deut. 4:1–8; 6:20–25)," *BSac* 162 (2005): 3–22; reprinted in D. I. Block, *How I Love Your Torah, O LORD*, 1–20.

(3) Having established the meaning of a specific Deuteronomic passage in its original context, we must reflect on the significance of the passage in the light of the later revelation, the incarnation, the cross, and the resurrection of Christ. Christ has indeed fulfilled the law (and the prophets, Matt. 5:17), which means not only that he is the perfect embodiment of all that the law demands and the perfect interpreter of its meaning, but also that he represents the climax of the narrative that includes Yahweh's gracious self-disclosure at Sinai and his mediated self-disclosure through Moses on the plains of Moab. We need to abandon the low Christology that sees Moses as a type of Christ, or Christ as a second Moses in the Gospels, particularly in Matthew 5–7. The message of the New Testament is that Yahweh, the One who spoke directly at Sinai and indirectly through Moses, is none other than Jesus Christ, Yahweh incarnate in human form, and that Moses was his prophet.

Deuteronomy and Theology

THE FUNCTION OF THE book of Deuteronomy is to call every generation of Israelites to faithful covenant love for Yahweh in response to his gracious salvation and his revelation of himself (cf. 6:20–25) and in acceptance of the missional role to which he has called them (26:19). In developing this theme Moses presents a theology that is remarkable, both for its profundity and its scope.

(1) Israel's history begins and ends with God. Deuteronomy instructs Israel and all subsequent readers on Yahweh's absolute uniqueness (4:32–39; 6:4; 10:17; 32:39; 33:26), eternality (33:27), transcendence (7:21; 10:17; 32:3), holiness (32:51), justice and righteousness (32:4; cf. 10:18), passion (jealousy) for his covenant and his relationship with his people (4:24; 5:9; 6:15; 9:3; 32:21), faithfulness (7:9), presence (1:41; 4:7; 6:15; 7:21; 31:17), compassion (4:31), and especially his covenant love (4:37; 7:7, 8, 13; 10:15, 18; 23:5[6]). But in this book none of these is a mere abstraction. Yahweh lives in relationship with human beings, which explains why Moses never tired of speaking of God's grace. This grace was expressed in many different concrete actions toward Israel: his election of Abraham and his descendants (4:37; 7:6), his rescue of Israel from the bondage of Egypt (4:32–36), his establishment of Israel as his covenant people (4:9–31; 5:1–22; 26:16–19), his providential care (1:30–33; 8:15–16), his provision of a homeland (6:10–15; 8:7–14), his provision of leadership (16:18–18:22), and his provision of victory over their enemies (7:17–24).

(2) Deuteronomy offers a comprehensive picture of the community of faith, the chosen people of Yahweh. In this book the doctrine of divine

election plays a prominent role. The book speaks of the divine election (*bâḥar*) of the place for Yahweh's name (12:5, 11; 14:23–24; 16:6–7; etc.), of Israel's king (17:15), and of the Levitical priests (18:5; 21:5). However, Yahweh's election of Israel to be his covenant people receives special attention. Deuteronomy 4:32–40 places Yahweh's rescue of the nation of Israel within the framework of cosmic history, declaring this event to be unprecedented and unparalleled in human experience. Elsewhere Moses emphasizes that Yahweh's election of Israel had nothing to do with physical or spiritual superiority (7:6–8; 9:1–23), but was an act of sheer grace, grounded in his love for the ancestors (4:32–38) and their descendants (7:6–8). In so doing the book of Deuteronomy presents the nation of Israel as an incredibly privileged people. As the objects of Yahweh's gracious redemption and covenantal love, they are a holy people belonging to him (7:6; 14:2; 26:19; 28:9), his adopted children (14:1) and his treasured possession (*sᵉgullâ*, 7:6; 14:2; 26:18).

Although Yahweh had called the nation as a whole to covenant relationship with himself, the true community of faith consists of persons who love their God with their entire being and who demonstrate that love through ethical conduct characterized by righteousness (*ṣᵉdâqâ*, 6:25; *ṣedeq*, 16:20), which includes the repudiation of all other gods and the compassionate pursuit of justice and righteousness toward others (10:16–20). The frequent alternation of singular and plural forms of direct address in the book suggest the existence of two Israels. Physical Israel consisted of the descendants of Abraham, while spiritual Israel only included those persons who, like Caleb and Joshua, demonstrated unqualified devotion to Yahweh by walking in his ways.

(3) No other book in the Old Testament presents as thorough a treatment of covenant relationship as Deuteronomy. The covenant Yahweh made with Israel at Sinai/Horeb represents the fulfillment of the covenant he had made with Abraham and an extension of his commitment to his descendants (cf. Gen. 17:7). And the covenant ceremonies that underlie the book of Deuteronomy represent the present generation's own commitment to that covenant (26:16–19). It is within this covenantal context that we may understand the nature and role of the law in ancient Israel. According to Deuteronomy, within that relationship obedience to the law is:

- not a burden but a response to the supreme and unique privilege of knowing God's will (Deut. 4:6–8)
- not a precondition to salvation but the grateful response of those who had already been saved (6:20–25)
- not primarily a duty imposed by one party on another but an expression of covenant love (26:16–19)

- not merely an external act but evidence of the circumcision of one's heart and the internal disposition of fear of and love for God (10:12–11:1; 30:6–9)
- not a pressured response to a tyrant but a willing subordination of one's entire being to the gracious divine suzerain (6:4–9; 10:12–13)

In short, obedience to the law offers visible proof of righteousness, which is a precondition to Israel's fulfillment of the mission to which she had been called and to her own blessing (4:24–25; chs. 11; 28). This obedience is both reasonable and achievable (30:11–20).

(4) Deuteronomy presents a highly developed theology of land. Moses' cosmic awareness is expressed by his appeal to heaven and earth to witness Israel's renewal of the covenant (4:26; 30:19; 31:28). But in 11:12 Moses declares that the land set aside for Israel is the special object of his perpetual care (*dāraš*). He is delivering this land into the hands of the Israelites as their special grant (*naḥºlâ*, 4:21, et passim), as an act of grace and in fulfillment of his oath to the ancestors (1:8, et passim). The Deuteronomic vision of the nation's relationship to the land within the context of the tripartite association of deity–land–people may be illustrated diagrammatically as follows:

At Sinai Yahweh had formalized his covenant relationship with Israel. On the Plains of Moab Moses led this generation of Israelites in a covenant renewal ceremony by which their relationship with Yahweh was cemented prior to their entrance into the land. Once the Israelites had crossed the Jordan, their first order of business would be to bring the land into this relationship by means of a special ceremony at Mounts Gerizim and Ebal (27:1–26).

The relationships involving Yahweh, the people, and the land were perceived as dynamic relationships, which meant that the response of the land to Israel's occupation would depend entirely on the people's fidelity to Yahweh. If they will be faithful to him, the land will yield bountiful produce (7:11–16; 11:8–15; 28:1–14); but if they prove unfaithful and go after other gods, the land will stop yielding its bounty, and Yahweh will sever his ties with it (4:25–28; 8:17–20; 11:16–17; 28:15–26). However, although the nation's infidelity seems inevitable, in the distant future, when the population would be removed from the land because of their sin, this would not represent a cancellation or repudiation of the covenant but the application of its fine print (cf. Dan. 9:4–16). Because of Yahweh's immutable covenant commitment to Abraham and his descendants (4:31), he must and would bring Israel back to the land and to himself (30:1–10). Accordingly, the "new covenant" of which Jeremiah speaks in Jeremiah 31:31–34 and the eternal covenant of which Ezekiel writes in Ezekiel 16:60 (cf. Ezek. 34:25–31) anticipate the full realization of God's original covenant made with Abraham, ratified and fleshed out at Horeb and renewed on the Plains of Moab, when the boundaries of physical and spiritual Israel would finally be coterminous.

(5) The book of Deuteronomy presents a remarkable approach to administration of the covenant community. From beginning to end, it is clear that Israel is a theocracy, with Yahweh as her divine suzerain (though the kingship of Yahweh receives scant explicit attention; cf. 33:5). The Torah provides for judicial officials appointed by the people (1:9–15; 16:18), and kings, priests, and prophets appointed and/or raised up by Yahweh (17:14–18:22). However, in seating responsibility for the administration of justice with the people, it envisions a covenant community under the authority of Torah and governed by "righteousness" (*ṣᵉdāqâ/ṣedeq*).

Conclusion

FOR MODERN READERS PLAGUED by a negative view of the Old Testament in general and Old Testament law in particular, the book of Deuteronomy offers a healthy antidote. Through the work of Christ not only is Israel's relationship made possible, but also the church, the new Israel of God, is grafted into God's covenant promises. As with Israel, access to these promises remains by grace alone, through faith alone. However, having been chosen, redeemed, and granted covenant relationship, Yahweh's people will gladly and without reservation demonstrate their allegiance to him wholeheartedly and with full-bodied obedience (Rom. 12:1–12).

For Christians today Deuteronomy remains an invaluable resource for a biblical understanding (1) of God, especially his grace in redeeming those bound in sin; (2) of the appropriate response to God, entailing love for God and for our fellow human beings; and (3) of the sure destiny of the redeemed. More than any other book in the Old Testament (if not the Bible as a whole), Deuteronomy concretizes the life of faith in real life. In the New Testament Jesus Christ, the incarnate God of Israel's redemption, summarizes the spiritual, moral, and ethical pronouncements of Deuteronomy with the Supreme Command: to demonstrate covenant commitment to God with one's entire being (love) and covenant commitment to one's fellow human beings (Matt. 22:34–40). Christians who live by this "law of Christ" (Gal. 6:2) will have their feet firmly on the ground and will resist the temptation to retreat into interior and subjective understandings of the life of faith so common in Western Christianity.

Structure and Design

AS NOTED ABOVE, THE book of Deuteronomy is dominated by the speeches of Moses—speeches he delivered to his congregation on the Plains of Moab and then committed to writing. Some time later these addresses were assembled, and narrative frameworks were composed for each speech. The pattern of addresses and narrative frames may be illustrated generally as follows (the proportions are not exact).

Hearing the Words of Moses

Moses' First Adress	Moses' Second Adress	Moses' Third Adress	The Song of Yahweh / Moses	Moses' Benediction
1:1–5	4:44–5:1a	29:2a [29:1a]	31:14–30	32:48–33:2a
1:6–4:40		29:2b–30:20 [29:1b–30:20]	32:1–43	33:2b–29
			32:44–47	34:1–12
4:41–43	5:1b–26:19	31:1–13		
27:1–26 →	28:1–68			
	29:1 [28:69]			

The Gospel According to Moses

I. Moses' First Address: Remembering the Grace of Yahweh
(1:1–4:43)
  A. The Preamble to Moses' First Address (1:1–5)
  B. The Essence of Moses' First Address: The Grace of Calling
(1:6–4:40)
    1. Recollections of Yahweh's Grace to the Exodus
Generation (1:6–2:1)
      a. Recollections of Mount Horeb (1:6–18)
      b. Recollections of the Journey from Horeb to Kadesh
Barnea (1:19)
      c. Recollections of Kadesh Barnea (1:20–46)
      d. Recollections of the Desert (2:1)
    2. Recollections of Yahweh's Grace to the New Generation
(2:2–3:29)
      a. Recollections of Israel's Encounters with their
Transjordanian Relatives (2:2–23)
      b. Recollections of Israel's Encounters with the Amorite
Kings (2:24–3:11)
      c. Moses' Personal Recollections (3:12–29)
    3. Recollections of Yahweh's Grace with the Future in Mind
(4:1–40)
      a. Recollections of the Grace of Torah (4:1–8)
      b. Recollections of the Grace of Covenant (4:9–31)
      c. Recollections of the Grace of Salvation (4:32–40)
  C. The Epilogue to Moses' First Address (4:41–43)
II. Moses' Second Address: Explaining the Grace of Yahweh
(4:44–29:1[28:69])
  A. The Preamble to Moses' Second Address (4:44–5:1a)
  B. The Essence of Moses' Second Address: The Grace of
Covenant (5:1b–26:19)
    1. The Revelation of the Principles of Covenant
Relationship (5:6–6:3)
      a. The Context of the Revelation (5:1b–5)
      b. The Content of the Revelation (5:6–22)
      c. The Response to the Revelation (5:23–6:3)

2. Proclaiming the Privilege of Covenant Relationship
(6:4–11:32)
  a. The Essence of Covenant Relationship: A Call to
  Covenant Love (6:4–8:20)
    (1) The Call to Exclusive Covenant Commitment
    (6:4–9)
    (2) The Tests of Covenant Commitment
    (6:10–8:20)
      (a) The Trial of Faith, Part I: The Internal and
      External Tests of Covenant Commitment
      (6:10–25)
        • The Nature of the Tests (6:10–19)
        • The Response to the Tests (6:20–25)
      (b) The Trial of Faith, Part II: The External
      Test of Covenant Commitment (7:1–26)
        • The Nature of the Test (7:1–16)
        • The Response to the Test (7:17–26)
      (c) The Trial of Faith, Part III: The Internal
      Test of Covenant Commitment (8:1–20)
        • The Nature of the Test (8:1–10)
        • The Response to the Test (8:11–20)
  b. The Sheer Grace of Covenant Relationship
  (9:1–10:11)
    (1) Disputing False Claims to Divine Favor
    (9:1–24)
      (a) The Nature of the Claim (9:1–6)
      (b) The Refutation of the Claim (9:7–24)
    (2) Pleading for Renewal of Divine Favor (9:25–29)
      (a) The Nature of Moses' Plea (9:25–29)
      (b) Yahweh's Response to the Plea (10:1–11)
  c. The Fundamental Demands of Covenant
  Relationship (10:12–11:1)
  d. The Importance of Covenant Relationship
  (11:2–28)
    (1) A Lesson from History: Reviewing the Mighty
    Acts of Yahweh (11:2–7)
    (2) A Lesson from Economic Geography:
    Recognizing the Provision of Yahweh
    (11:8–28)
  e. Anticipating the Completion of the Covenantal
  Triangle: Yahweh–Israel–Land (11:29–32)

3. Proclaiming the Dimensions of Covenant Relationship
   (12:1–26:19)
   a. Celebrating Covenant Relationship with Yahweh:
      Part I (12:2–14:21)
      (1) Responding to Yahweh's Invitation to Worship
          in His Presence (12:2–14)
      (2) Responding to Yahweh's Generosity at Home
          (12:15–28)
      (3) Responding to Yahweh's Call for Exclusive
          Relationship (12:29–13:18[19]
      (4) Responding to Yahweh's Invitation to Feast at
          His Table (14:1–21)
   b. Demonstrating Covenant Relationship with Yahweh
      (14:22–15:18)
      (1) Soft Hearts and Open Hands, Part I: Generosity
          in Worship (14:22–29)
      (2) Soft Hearts and Open Hands, Part II:
          Generosity at Home (15:1–18)
          (a) Showing Kindness to the Poor (15:1–11)
          (b) Showing Kindness to Debt–Slaves
              (15:12–18)
   c. Celebrating Covenant Relationship with Yahweh:
      Part II (15:19–16:17)
      (1) Unscheduled Feasting in the Presence of
          Yahweh and at Home (15:19–23)
      (2) Scheduled Feasting in the Presence of Yahweh
          (16:1–17)
          (a) The Festival of Passover (16:1–8)
          (b) The Festival of Weeks (16:9–12)
          (c) The Festival of Booths (16:13–15)
          (d) The Summary Statement (16:16–17)
   d. Covenant Relationship and the Pursuit of
      Righteousness (16:18–18:22)
      (1) The Judiciary as the Executors of Covenant
          Righteousness (16:18–17:13)
      (2) The King as the Embodiment of Covenant
          Righteousness (17:14–20)
      (3) The Levites as Community Barometers of
          Covenant Righteousness (18:1–8)
      (4) The Prophets as Agents of Covenant
          Righteousness (18:9–22)

e. Pursuing Covenant Righteousness in Matters of Life
and Death (19:1–21:9)
   (1) Righteousness in Cases of Manslaughter (and
     Greed) (19:1–13)
   (2) Righteousness in Courts of Law (19:15–21)
   (3) Righteousness in Military Engagement (20:1–20)
   (4) Righteousness in the Face of Unsolved Crime
     (21:1–9)
f. Pursuing Covenant Righteousness in Marriage and
Family: Part I (21:10–23)
   (1) Righteousness in the Treatment of War Brides
     (21:10–14)
   (2) Righteousness in the Treatment of the Firstborn
     (21:15–17)
   (3) Righteousness in the Treatment of a Rebellious
     Son (21:18–21)
   (4) Righteousness in the Treatment of a Criminal's
     Remains (21:22–23)
g. Pursuing Covenant Righteousness in Marriage and
Family: Part II (22:1–30[23:1])
   (1) Righteousness in the Treatment of Animals and
     Other Domestic Issues (22:1–12)
   (2) Righteousness in the Face of Marital Infidelity
     (22:13–21)
   (3) Righteousness in the Face of Sexual Promiscuity
     (22:22–30[23:1])
h. Pursuing Covenant Righteousness as the Holy
People of Yahweh (23:1–14[2–15])
   (1) Righteousness in the Assembly of Yahweh
     (23:1–8[2–9])
   (2) Righteousness in the Camp of Israel
     (23:9–14[10–15])
i. Pursuing Covenant Righteousness in Social and
Economic Relationships: Part I: (23:15–25[16–26])
j. Pursuing Covenant Righteousness in Marriage and
Family: Part III:
   (1) Righteousness in the Face of Divorce (24:1–4)
   (2) Righteousness in the Face of a Call to Arms (24:5)
k. Pursuing Covenant Righteousness in Social and
Economic Relationships: Part II (24:6–25:16)
l. Interlude: Taking Care of Unfinished Business: The
Amalekite Question (25:17–19)

Select Bibliography
on Deuteronomy

Readers who wish to pursue the study of Deuteronomy in greater depth may find these works helpful. Fuller bibliographic information is provided by Christensen (below).

Bergey, R. "The Song of Moses (Deuteronomy 32.1 – 43) and Isaianic Prophecies: A Case of Early Intertextuality?" *Journal for the Study of the Old Testament* 28 (2003): 33 – 54.

Biddle, Mark E. *Deuteronomy*. Smyth & Helwys Bible Commentary. Macon, GA: Smyth & Helwys, 2003.

Block, Daniel I. *The Gospel According to Moses: Theological and Ethical Reflection on the Book of Deuteronomy*. Eugene, OR: Cascade, 2012.

———. *How I Love Your Torah, O LORD! Studies in the Book of Deuteronomy*. Eugene, OR: Cascade, 2011.

———. *The Gods of the Nations: Studies in Ancient Near Eastern National Theology*. Revised edition. Evangelical Theological Society Monographs. Grand Rapids: Baker, 2000.

———. *Judges and Ruth*. New American Commentary 6. Nashville, TN: Broadman & Holman, 1999.

———. "Marriage and Family in Ancient Israel." Pages 33 – 102 in *Marriage and Family in the Biblical World*. Edited by K. Campbell. Downers Grove, IL: InterVarsity Press, 2003.

———. "My Servant David: Ancient Israel's Vision of the Messiah." Pages 17 – 56 in *Israel's Messiah in the Bible and the Dead Sea Scrolls*. Edited by Richard. S. Hess and M. Daniel Carroll R. Grand Rapids: Baker, 2003.

Braulik, Georg. *The Theology of Deuteronomy: Collected Essays of Georg Braulik, O.S.B*. Translated by U. Lindblad. Bibal Collected Essays 2. N. Richmond Hills, TX: Bibal, 1994.

———. "Law as Gospel: Justification and Pardon according to the Deuteronomic Torah." *Interpretation* 38 (1984): 5 – 14.

Brown, Raymond. *The Message of Deuteronomy*. The Bible Speaks Today. Downers Grove, IL: InterVarsity Press, 1993.

Brueggemann, Walter. *Deuteronomy*. Abingdon Old Testament Commentaries. Nashville: Abingdon, 2001.

Calvin, John. *Commentaries on the Four Last Books of Moses*. Translated by Charles William Bingham. Grand Rapids: Eerdmans, 1950.

Christensen, Duane L. *Deuteronomy 1:1 – 21:9*. Revised edition. Word Biblical Commentary 6A. Nashville, TN: Nelson, 2001.

———. *Deuteronomy 21:10 – 34:12*. Word Biblical Commentary 6B. Nashville, TN: Nelson, 2002.

———, ed. *A Song of Power and the Power of Song: Essays on the Book of Deuteronomy*. Studies in Biblical Theology 3. Winona Lake, IN: Eisenbrauns, 1993.

Clarke, Ernest G. *Targum Pseudo-Jonathan: Deuteronomy*. Aramaic Bible 5B. Collegeville, MN: Liturgical, 1998.

Craigie, Peter C. *The Book of Deuteronomy*. New International Commentary on the Old Testament. Grand Rapids: Eerdmans, 1976.

Crüsemann, F. *The Torah: Theology and Social History of Old Testament Law*. Translated by A. W. Mahnke. Minneapolis: Fortress, 1996.

DeRouchie, Jason S. *A Call to Covenant Love: Text Grammar and Literary Structure in Deuteronomy 5 – 11*. Gorgias Dissertations 30. Piscataway, NJ: Gorgias, 2007.

Driver, S. R. *A Critical and Exegetical Commentary on Deuteronomy*. International Critical Commentary. Edinburgh: T&T Clark, 1902.

Falk, Ze'ev W. *Hebrew Law in Biblical Times*. 2nd edition. Provo, UT: Brigham Young University Press, 2001.

Firmage, E. B., et al., eds. *Religion and Law: Biblical-Judaic and Islamic Perspectives*. Winona Lake, IN: Eisenbrauns, 1990.

Fishbane, M. *Biblical Interpretation in Ancient Israel*. Oxford: Clarendon, 1985.

Harrelson, W. *The Ten Commandments and Human Rights*. Revised edition. Macon, GA: Mercer Univ. Press, 1997.

Hugenberger, Gordon. *Marriage as a Covenant: Biblical Law and Ethics as Developed from Malachi*. Biblical Studies Library. Winona Lake, Indiana: Eisenbrauns, 1998.

Hwang, Jerry. "The Rhetoric of Remembrance: An Exegetical and Theological Investigation into the 'Fathers' in Deuteronomy." Ph.D. Dissertation, Wheaton College, 2009.

Kaufman, Stephen. "The Structure of the Deuteronomic Law." *Maarav* 1 (1979): 105 – 58.

King, P. J., and L. E. Stager. *Life in Biblical Israel*. Library of Ancient Israel. Louisville, KY: Westminster John Knox, 2001.

Kitchen, Kenneth A. *On the Reliability of the Old Testament*. Grand Rapids: Eerdmans, 2003.

Knoppers, Gary. "Rethinking the Relationship between Deuteronomy and the Deuteronomistic History." *Catholic Biblical Quarterly* 63 (2002): 393 – 415.

———. "The Deuteronomist and the Deuteronomic Law of the King: A Re-examination of a Relationship." *Zeitschrift für die alttestamentliche Wissenschaft* 108 (1996): 329 – 46.

Levinson, Bernard M. *Deuteronomy and the Hermeneutics of Legal Innovation.* Oxford: Oxford University Press, 1998.

—. *"The Right Chorale": Studies in Biblical Law and Interpretation.* Winona Lake, IN: Eisenbrauns, 2011.

Lienhard, S. J. *Exodus, Leviticus, Numbers, Deuteronomy.* Ancient Christian Commentary on Scripture. Old Testament 3. Downers Grove, IL: InterVarsity Press, 2001.

MacDonald, Nathan. *Deuteronomy and the Meaning of "Monotheism."* Forschung zum Alten Testament 2/1. Tübingen: Mohr (Siebeck), 2003.

Mayes, A. D. H. *Deuteronomy.* New Century Bible. Grand Rapids: Eerdmans, 1981.

McBride, S. Dean, Jr. "Polity of the People of God: The Book of Deuteronomy." *Interpretation* 41 (1987): 229–44.

McCarthy, Carmel, ed. *Deuteronomy.* Biblia Hebraica Quinta 5. Stuttgart: Deutsche Bibelgesellschaft, 2007.

McConville, J. G. *Deuteronomy.* Apollos Old Testament Commentary. Downers Grove, IL: InterVarsity Press, 2002.

—. *Grace in the End: A Study in Deuteronomic Theology.* Grand Rapids: Zondervan, 1993.

—. *Law and Theology in Deuteronomy.* Sheffield: JSOT Press, 1984.

McConville, J. Gordon, and J. G. Millar. *Time and Place in Deuteronomy.* Journal for the Study of the Old Testament Supplement Series 179. Sheffield: Sheffield Academic, 1984.

Merrill, Eugene H. *Deuteronomy.* New American Commentary. Nashville, TN: Broadman & Holman, 1994.

Millar, J. G. *Now Choose Life.* Grand Rapids: Eerdmans, 1998.

Miller, P. D. *Deuteronomy.* Interpretation. Louisville, KY: John Knox, 1990.

—. "Deuteronomy and the Psalms: Evoking a Biblical Conversation." *Journal of Biblical Literature* 118 (1999): 3–18.

—. "'Moses My Servant': The Deuteronomic Portrait of Moses." *Interpretation* 41 (1987): 245–55.

—. *The Ten Commandments.* Interpretation. Louisville, KY: Westminster John Knox, 2009.

Nelson, R. *Deuteronomy.* Old Testament Library. Louisville, KY: Westminster John Knox, 2002.

Nicholson, E. W. *Deuteronomy and Tradition: Literary and Historical Problems in the Book of Deuteronomy.* Philadelphia: Fortress, 1967.

Olsen, Dennis T. *Deuteronomy and the Death of Moses: A Theological Reading.* Overtures to Biblical Theology. Minneapolis: Fortress, 1994.

Otto, Eckart. *Das Deuteronomium.* Beihefte zur Zeitschrift für die alttestamentliche Wissenschaft 284. Berlin: de Gruyter, 1999.

Patrick, Dale. *Old Testament Law.* Atlanta: John Knox, 1985.

Phillips, Anthony. *Ancient Israel's Criminal Law: A New Approach to the Decalogue.* Oxford: Blackwood; New York: Schocken, 1970.

Polzin, R. *Moses and the Deuteronomist: A Literary Study of the Deuteronomistic History.* New York: Seabury, 1980.

Pressler, Carolyn. *The View of Women Found in the Deuteronomic Family Laws.* Beihefte zur Zeitschrift für die alttestamentliche Wissenschaft 216. Berlin/ New York: de Gruyter, 1993.

Rad, G. von. *Deuteronomy: A Commentary.* Old Testament Library. Philadelphia: Westminster, 1966.

————. *The Problem of the Hexateuch and Other Studies.* London: SCM, 1966.

————. *Studies in Deuteronomy.* Studies in Biblical Theology 9. London: SCM, 1953.

Richter, Sandra. *The Deuteronomistic History and the Name Theology:* lešakkēn šemô šâm *in the Bible and the Ancient Near East.* Beihefte zur Zeitschrift für die alttestamentliche Wissenschaft 318. Berlin: de Gruyter, 2002.

Roth, Martha. T. *Law Collections from Mesopotamia and Asia Minor.* 2nd ed. Society of Biblical Literature Writings from the Ancient World 6. Atlanta: Scholars, 1997.

Sohn, Seock-Tae. *The Divine Election of Israel.* Grand Rapids: Eerdmans, 1991.

Sonnet, Jean-Pierre. *The Book within the Book: Writing in Deuteronomy.* Leiden: Brill, 1997.

Thompson, J. A. *Deuteronomy: An Introduction and Commentary.* Tyndale Old Testament Commentaries. Downers Grove, IL: InterVarsity Press, 1974.

Tigay, J. *Deuteronomy.* Jewish Publication Society Torah Commentary. Philadelphia: Jewish Publication Society, 1996.

————. *You Shall Have No Other Gods: Israelite Religion in the Light of Hebrew Inscriptions.* Harvard Semitic Monographs 31. Atlanta: Scholars, 1986.

Toorn, K. van der, B. Becking, and P. W. van der Horst, eds. *Dictionary of Deities and Demons in the Bible.* Revised edition. Leiden: Brill, 1999.

Turner, Kenneth J. *The Death of Deaths in the Death of Israel: Deuteronomomy's Theology of Exile.* Eugene, OR: Wipf & Stock, 2011.

Vogt, Peter. *Deuteronomic Theology and the Significance of Torah: A Reappraisal.* Winona Lake, IN: Eisenbrauns, 2006.

Watts, James W. *Reading Law: The Rhetorical Shaping of the Pentateuch.* Biblical Seminar 59. Sheffield: Sheffield Academic, 1999.

Weinfeld, M. "Deuteronomy." In *Anchor Bible Dictionary.* Edited by D. N. Freedman, 2:168–83. Garden City, NY: Doubleday, 1992.

————. *Deuteronomy 1 – 11: A New Translation with Introduction and Commentary.* Anchor Bible 5. New York: Doubleday, 1991.

————. *Deuteronomy and the Deuteronomic School.* 1972; reprint Winona Lake, IN: Eisenbrauns, 1992.

Wenham, Gordon. J. "Deuteronomy and the Central Sanctuary." *Tyndale Bulletin* 22 (1971): 103 – 18.

Wevers, John W. *Notes on the Greek Text of Deuteronomy.* Septuagint and Cognate Studies 39. Atlanta: Scholars, 1995.

Wilson, Ian. *Out of the Midst of the Fire.* Society of Biblical Literature Dissertation Series 151. Atlanta: Scholars, 1995.

Wright, Christopher J. H. *Deuteronomy.* New International Biblical Commentary. Peabody, MA: Hendrickson, 1996.

————. *The Mission of God: Unlocking the Bible's Grand Narrative.* Downers Grove, IL: InterVarsity Press, 2006.

————. *The Mission of God's People: A Biblical Theology of the Church's Mission.* Grand Rapids: Zondervan, 2010.

————. *Old Testament Ethics for the People of God.* Downers Grove, IL: InterVarsity Press, 2004.

Zehnder, Markus. "Building on Stone? Deuteronomy and Esarhaddon's Loyalty Oaths (Part 1): Some Preliminary Observations." *Bulletin for Biblical Research* 19 (2009): 341 – 74.

————. "Building on Stone? Deuteronomy and Esarhaddon's Loyalty Oaths (Part 2): Some Additional Observations." *Bulletin for Biblical Research* 19 (2009): 511 – 35.

Deuteronomy 1:1–5

T hese are the words Moses spoke to all Israel in the desert east of the Jordan—that is, in the Arabah—opposite Suph, between Paran and Tophel, Laban, Hazeroth and Dizahab. ²(It takes eleven days to go from Horeb to Kadesh Barnea by the Mount Seir road.)

³In the fortieth year, on the first day of the eleventh month, Moses proclaimed to the Israelites all that the LORD had commanded him concerning them. ⁴This was after he had defeated Sihon king of the Amorites, who reigned in Heshbon, and at Edrei had defeated Og king of Bashan, who reigned in Ashtaroth.

⁵East of the Jordan in the territory of Moab, Moses began to expound this law, saying:

DEUTERONOMY OPENS WITH A formal editorial introduction, which describes the nature and content of the book and provides a series of details that readers must take into account.

The authorities behind the book. Although Deuteronomy consists largely of proclaimed divine truth, the voice of God is heard directly only five times: 31:14b, 16b–21, 23b; 32:49–52; and 34:4b. This introduction alerts the reader to the voice of Moses, which we will hear throughout. But his voice is not an independent voice; he speaks only what Yahweh "had commanded him" (1:3). This man, who served as mediator of Yahweh's covenant with Israel and as the human conduit of divine revelation at Sinai, speaks as the authoritative spokesman for God.

The addressees in the book. The addressees are identified as "all Israel" in verse 1 and "the descendants of Israel" in verse 3 (NIV "Israelites"), two expressions that are scattered throughout the book. The former suggests that Moses speaks to the community of faith; the latter highlights the nation's ethnic cohesion (they are the descendants of Jacob/Israel).

The location of the events described in the book. The introduction locates the addresses of Moses geographically as "east of the Jordan" in general and "in the territory of Moab" in particular. Based on 32:49 and 34:1, these events happen at the northern edge of Moab.

The syntax of verse 1b creates the impression that Moses delivered these addresses in the desert, somewhere in the Arabah. The following list of place names supposedly clarifies the location: "opposite Suph, between Paran and Tophel, Laban, Hazeroth and Dizahab." Since those places that can be identified are located south of the Dead Sea, this list seems to refer to a series of way stations along the route the Israelites took from Sinai/ Horeb to Kadesh Barnea. Verse 2 notes that under normal circumstances the journey could be completed in eleven days. However, because the people had rebelled at Kadesh Barnea—the point of entering the Promised Land (Num. 13–14)—their entrance into Canaan had been delayed almost forty years.

The time of the events described in the book. The narrator fixes the time of Moses' address "in the fortieth year, on the first day of the eleventh month." According to Exodus 12:2, the people's departure from Egypt marks the beginning of Israel's history (Gen. 15:7–21; Ex. 3:6–8; 6:2–8).[1] Now forty years later, a new generation of Jacob's descendants stands at the Jordan, ready to enter Canaan. Verse 4 adds a second chronological marker: Moses delivers these addresses after the defeat of the two Amorite kings east of the Jordan. The victories over Sihon and Og provide concrete proof that when Israel is faithful to Yahweh, he will fight for them.

The genre of the book. The book opens with "These are the words Moses spoke." Verse 3 reiterates that Moses "proclaimed" (*dibber*) to the Israelites all that Yahweh commanded him. This suggests that in this book Moses does not function primarily as a lawgiver but as a prophet (18:15; 34:10) and as the people's pastor (cf. Num. 27:17; Isa. 63:11), delivering his final sermons before he passes from the scene. The narrator's description of his activity as *hôʾîl . . . bēʾēr* (NIV "he began to expound") speaks of more than mere verbal exposition. Through the proclamation and the performance of the covenant renewal rituals implied in the book, the Israelite covenant ratified at Horeb[2] is put in force with this generation.[3]

The expression "this Torah" (*hattôrâ hazzōʾt*) characterizes what follows as instruction rather than legislation.[4] This interpretation is confirmed by

---

1. The narrator's chronological marker is synchronized with the rest of the Pentateuch (cf. Ex. 16:1; 19:1; 40:17; Num. 1:1; 9:1; 12:11; 33:38).

2. Consistent with the common designations of the other biblical covenants (Abrahamic/ patriarchal covenant, Noachian/cosmic covenant, Davidic covenant), throughout I will refer to this covenant as "the Israelite covenant." The covenant made at Sinai was not made *with* Moses, but *through* him; Moses was not the covenant partner.

3. Hebrew *bēʾēr* is cognate to Akkadian *burru*, "to confirm," that is, "to put a legal document in force". Cf. *CAD* 2 (1965),127.

4. The noun *tôrâ* derives from the verb *hôrâ* ("to teach") (*HALOT*, 436–37). The word occurs twenty-two times in Deuteronomy: Deut. 1:5; 4:8, 44; 17:11, 18, 19; 27:3, 8, 26; 28:58, 61; 29:21[20]. , 29[28]. ; 30:10; 31:9, 11, 12, 24, 26; 32:46; 33:4, 10.

the way the book depicts Moses. He "teaches" (*limmēd*) the people (4:5, 14; 5:31; 6:1; 31:19) and they "learn" the Torah (4:10; 5:1; 17:19; 31:12 – 13). The bulk of the book consists of pastoral instruction and exhortation, and even when earlier laws are cited, they are surrounded with hortatory appeals.

Deuteronomy involves two kinds of Torah: oral and written. Deuteronomy 1:5 and 4:8 obviously classify Moses' first address as the former. However, within the reports of Moses' second (6:6 – 9; 11:18 – 21; 17:18 – 20; 27:1 – 8; 28:58 – 61) and third (29:14 – 29[13 – 28]; 30:8 – 11) addresses, we find numerous references to a written Torah, which refers to the transcribed version of his oral speeches. As if to dispel any doubt about the genre of the book, the introduction concludes with a verb of speech ("saying," *lē᾿mōr*) rather than legislation. Moses stands before the people as pastor, delivering his final sermons at the command of Yahweh and pleading with the Israelites to remain faithful to their God once they cross the Jordan and settle down in the land promised to the ancestors.

 MOST READERS OF SCRIPTURE recognize the significance of Moses in the history of Israel. Raised in the courts of Pharaoh but exiled for forty years in the Midianite wasteland, Moses reluctantly answered God's call to lead his people out of Egypt. The prologue to the gospel of John captures his role in the history of revelation perfectly:

> From the fullness of his grace we have all received one blessing [read "grace"] after another. For the law [read "Torah"] was given through Moses; grace and truth came through [read "happened in"] Jesus Christ. (John 1:16 – 17)

Here the contrast is not between law and grace, but between mediated grace ("through Moses") and embodied grace ("in Jesus Christ"). John understood the revelation of the Torah through Moses as a climactic moment of grace, superseded only by the incarnation. As the interpreter of the covenant and the Horeb revelation, Moses served Israel as a mediator of divine grace.

But Moses' authority derives from God himself. According to verse 3, Moses speaks to the Israelites according to all that Yahweh has commanded him. This is the Old Testament's way of describing the process of inspiration. Since Moses functions as Yahweh's mouthpiece, whatever he declares to the Israelites is as binding on them as the Sinai revelation, which Exodus – Leviticus consistently presented as direct divine speech. But the process of inspiration does not stop with the oral delivery, or even with Moses' own transcription of his speeches (cf. 31:9). The same Holy Spirit who guided Moses as he proclaimed the Torah also guided the person who collated and edited the speeches and stitched them together with the narrative seams, including this narrative introduction. The inspiration of the Scriptures renders them authoritative for believers and guarantees their transformational effectiveness. In Deuteronomy we encounter the heart of the Scriptures that Paul characterized as an effective resource for instructing, rebuking, correcting, and training God's people in righteousness, so that they may be competent and equipped for every good work (2 Tim. 3:16–17).

Indeed, the book of Deuteronomy offers a full-bodied portrayal of the meaning of the word Torah. As "authoritative instruction," it may indeed involve laws and commands (4:44–45),[5] but the addresses that follow demonstrate that it is much more. It includes divine speeches (1:6–8); autobiographical reminiscences (1:9–18; 3:23–28); reviews of historical events (1:19–3:17); promises of blessing as a reward for fidelity to Yahweh (7:12–16; 11:18–27; 28:1–14); paraenetic exhortation (4:9–24); warnings against defection (7:25–26; 8:11–20; 12:29–13:18[19]), including the threat of curse for infidelity (11:28; 27:14–26; 28:15–68); recitation of the Decalogue (5:6–21); catechetical instruction (6:4–9, 20–25; 10:12–22; 26:1–15); invitations to regular fellowship in the presence of Yahweh (2:1–19); the granting of specific requests (12:20–28; 17:14–20); specific instructions on diet (14:1–21) and cultic worship (14:22–29; 16:1–17); administrative instructions (16:18–18:22); instructions on military policy (7:1–11; 20:1–20; 23:9–14[10–15]); specific instructions concerning the administration of justice (16:18–19; 17:2–13; 19:15–21); ecological, economic, and agricultural practices (19:14; 20:19–20; 22:1–11; 24:19–22; 25:13–16); sexual morality (22:13–30) and marriage (21:10–14; 24:1–5; 25:5–12); appeals for compassion toward those economically and socially marginalized (10:18–19; 15:1–18; 24:17–22); the national anthem (32:1–43); and Moses' final benedictions of the tribes (33:1–29).

All these fall under the rubric of "Torah." The semantic breadth of the term also explains how the designation Torah could so easily be extended to the entire Pentateuch, which is actually dominated by narrative rather than law. Surely when the Psalter opens with reference to delighting in the Torah (Ps. 1:2) the psalmist is not thinking primarily of "law," for without the gospel narrative in which the laws are embedded, the laws are a burden rather than a delight.

---

5. Cf. 4:1; 5:1; 6:1; 11:1; 12:1; 26:17; 30:11. Note the sole application of the term to the Decalogue in Ex. 24:12.

FOR MANY CHRISTIANS THE Old Testament in general and Deuteronomy in particular is a dead book. Consequently, the favorite book of Jesus is ignored, the source of much Johannine and Pauline theology is discarded, and the life-giving power of the Word of God is cut off. Unless we rediscover this book, we will not treasure the Old Testament as a whole. As we will see in the commentary, this book presents the gospel according to Moses. This is a gospel of divine grace lavished on undeserving human beings. Moses' vision for his own people serves as a microcosm for the divine vision of humanity as a whole. The book points the reader to the Lord God, who has redeemed his people and assigned them the mission of radiating his grace to the world.

At the same time, in the book we catch a glimpse of pastoral ministry at its finest. The speeches represent the farewell address of a man who had pastored this congregation for forty years, guiding them in exciting times and caring for them when circumstances were difficult. We will hear reminiscences of Moses' frustrations with his own people (1:37; 3:26; 4:21), of Yahweh's rebuke for his own sins (32:48–52), and of his refusal to grant a personal request (3:24–26), but in many respects Moses functions as a model pastor. He knows his audience well; they have been rebellious from the day he first knew them (9:24), and as soon as he has exited from the stage they will apostasize (31:27–29).

Unlike many pastors today, Moses also knows his role as their teacher (Deut. 4:1, 5, 10, 14). He challenges them to keep alive the memory of Yahweh's gracious acts and instructs them in the dimensions of covenant life. He also pleads with them to guard their very beings against spiritual lethargy and defection. But most important, Moses introduces them to God. Fulfilling the ideals of Malachi, the last in the train of prophets that he heads, Moses worked tirelessly as pastor to bring about his parishioners' life and peace; he stood in awe of the name of Yahweh; he taught truth; he walked with Yahweh in *shalom* and uprightness; and he turned many from iniquity (Mal. 2:5–6).

But Moses also knew his role in relation to Yahweh. He was a voice, crying in the desert, "Prepare the way of the LORD" (Isa. 40:3; John 1:23). But he was also a righteous intercessor through whose prayers much was accomplished (9:19–20; cf. James 5:16). And as he faced his own death, he was not preoccupied with personal legacy; his energies were focused on his flock. Here was a man who pastored "according to God" (*kata theon*), that is, as God would have done were he physically present (1 Peter 5:2).

Deuteronomy 1:6–18

🕊

Introduction to Moses' First Address (Deuteronomy 1:6–4:40)

BEFORE WE COMMENT ON specific segments of Moses' first address, we must examine the nature and rhetorical strategy of chapters 1–4. Structurally this speech divides into two parts, 1:6–3:29 and 4:1–40 respectively. The transition to the second is signaled formally by "Hear now, O Israel" (4:1) and by a marked shift in style and tone. Whereas 1:6–3:29 consists largely of historical recollections, 4:1–40 bears a distinctly sermonic stamp as Moses calls on his people to guard themselves lest they forsake Yahweh and go after other gods. Even so, chapters 1–3 and 4 are linked by at least four theological themes: Yahweh's presence,[1] Yahweh's election of Israel,[2] obedience as the appropriate response to divine grace,[3] and the land of Canaan as Yahweh's gracious grant to his chosen people.[4]

In developing these themes Moses tells Israel's story backwards in four stages: (1) Yahweh's care and guidance of Israel from Horeb to the plains of Moab (1:6–3:29); (2) Yahweh's revelation of his will (4:1–8); (3) Yahweh's covenant relationship with Israel (4:9–31); (4) Yahweh's salvation of Israel from the slavery of Egypt (4:32–38). In 4:37 Moses actually identifies a fifth and even earlier stage: Yahweh's love and election of their ancestors. By recounting significant events in Israel's recent past and concluding with an impassioned appeal, Moses calls his people to not be rebellious like their ancestors (1:6–3:29), but to respond to Yahweh's amazing grace with wholehearted devotion. Only then will their future be secure (4:39–40).

We noted earlier that the overall structure of Deuteronomy is patterned after the order of ancient Near Eastern suzerain-vassal treaties. Following

---

1. Compare 1:30–33, 42; 2:7 and 4:9–14, 36–39.

2. Although chap. 2 casts a broader vision, declaring that Yahweh has allotted their respective lands to the Edomites, Moabites, and Ammonites (2:5, 9, 19), Israel's title to the land is based on the election of the ancestors and the divine promise of land to them (1:8, 21, 35). The rescue of Israel from Egypt is the decisive proof of Israel's elect status (1:27, 30; 3:24; 4:32–33).

3. In 1:19, 26–46 obedience means heading for and entering the land of Canaan; in chapter 4, obedience involves adherence to Yahweh's will revealed at Horeb, especially the prohibition of idolatry (vv. 1–8, 15–24, 40).

4. Compare 1:7–8, 20, 36; 2:29; 3:20, 24–28; and 4:1–5, 21–26, 38–40. To these features we should add Moses' expressed disposition toward his people (1:37; 3:26; 4:21).

---

the introduction of the suzerain, second millennium BC Hittite treaties in particular tended to begin with a historical prologue summarizing the history of the relationship between suzerain and vassal. In this first address Moses highlights Yahweh's faithfulness in fulfilling his promise to the fathers (1:6–8), providentially caring for Israel in the desert (1:31; 2:7), and providing victory over Israel's enemies (2:24–3:11; note esp. 2:30; cf. 1:28). But he also highlights the people's faithlessness, particularly in refusing to enter the land from Kadesh Barnea (1:19–46). By noting Yahweh's anger in the face of the people's infidelity (1:34, 42; 4:24, 25), Moses reminds them that they are not to take their covenant relationship with Yahweh for granted.

As we read this first address, we should note Moses' attitude toward God, toward himself, and toward the people. In keeping with the style of ancient Near Eastern historiography, Moses recognizes God as the prime mover in all events. With reference to himself, Moses exhibits a high view of his own office with frequent references to his own initiative,[5] to Yahweh's speaking to him (1:42; 2:2, 31; 3:2; but cf. 1:6, "us"), and to his role as mediator between Yahweh and Israel (1:22, 29, 41; 2:4; 3:18–22). Perhaps Moses' disposition toward the people is the most surprising feature of this speech. Three times he blames the people for Yahweh's anger toward himself (1:37; 3:26; 4:21–22). Combined with the way he belabors the people's rebellion and his sharp words in 1:26–46,[6] we get the impression of a bitter old man, who is disillusioned with his people, frustrated with/by God, and discouraged with his task.

Eleven occurrences of the expression "at that time" highlight the chronological dimensions of the first address.[7] The relationship between narrated time and narrative time in 1:6–3:29 may be plotted geographically as follows:[8]

---

5. Note the prevalence of verbs with Moses as the subject: "I commanded," "I said," "I charged," "I acted," etc.: 1:15, 16, 18, 20, 23, 29, 43; 2:26; 3:18, 21, 23.

6. They were unwilling to go up (v. 26); they rebelled against the command of Yahweh (v. 26); they grumbled in their tents (v. 27); they accused Yahweh of hatred toward them and deliberately plotting to kill them (v. 27); they admitted their loss of heart (v. 28); they feared the Canaanites (v. 29); they did not trust Yahweh (v. 32); they were an evil generation (v. 35); they refused to listen (v. 43); they rebelled against Yahweh's command (v. 43); and they acted presumptuously (v. 43).

7. Deut. 1:9, 16, 18; 2:34; 3:4, 8, 12, 18, 21, 23; 4:14. The expression occurs elsewhere in 5:5; 9:20; 10:1, 8.

8. Cf. N. Lohfink, "Narrative Analyse von Dtn 1,6–3,29," in *Mincha: Festgabe für Rolf Rendtorff zum 75. Geburtstag* (ed. E. Blum; Neukirchen–Vluyn: Neukirchener, 2000), 133.

Text	Location	Estimated Narrated Time	%	Narrative Time (number of verses devoted to subject)	%
1:6—18	At Horeb	2 months[9]	.4%	13	12%
1:19	From Horeb to Kadesh Barnea	42 weeks[10]	2.2%	1	1%
1:20—46	At Kadesh Barnea	2 weeks[11]	.1%	27	25%
2:1	In the desert south of Kadesh Barnea	38 years	97%	1	1%
2:2—23	Encounters with the Transjordanian relatives	1 month	.2%	22	21%
2:24—3:11	Encounters with the Transjordanian Amorites	1 month	.2%	25	23%
3:12—29	Preparing for the conquest of Canaan	1 month[12]	.2%	18	17%

Remarkably the thirty-eight years of circling in the desert (97 percent of narrated time) are dispensed with in a single verse (1 percent of narrative time), while the two tragic weeks at Kadesh Barnea receive one-fourth of the attention.

The LORD our God said to us at Horeb, "You have stayed long enough at this mountain. [7]Break camp and advance into the hill country of the Amorites; go to all the neighboring peoples in the Arabah, in the mountains, in the western foothills, in the Negev and along the coast, to the land of the Canaanites and to Lebanon, as far as the great river, the Euphrates. [8]See, I have given you this

---

9. The time needed to organize the camp, after Yahweh's command to set out, which may have been given on the one-year anniversary of Israel's departure from Egypt (cf. Ex. 12:2 and Num. 10:11).

10. Based on a two-week stopover at each of the twenty-one camps sites listed in Num. 33:16—37.

11. This number yields a total of one year from the command to leave Sinai to the fiasco at Kadesh Barnea. Adding this year to the year from the Exodus from Egypt to the command to leave Sinai and the thirty-eight years in the desert (2:14) yields a total of forty years (cf. 2:7).

12. Prior to the delivery of the addresses and the covenant renewal rituals implied in the book of Deuteronomy.

---

land. Go in and take possession of the land that the LORD swore he would give to your fathers—to Abraham, Isaac and Jacob—and to their descendants after them."

⁹At that time I said to you, "You are too heavy a burden for me to carry alone. ¹⁰The LORD your God has increased your numbers so that today you are as many as the stars in the sky. ¹¹May the LORD, the God of your fathers, increase you a thousand times and bless you as he has promised! ¹²But how can I bear your problems and your burdens and your disputes all by myself? ¹³Choose some wise, understanding and respected men from each of your tribes, and I will set them over you."

¹⁴You answered me, "What you propose to do is good."

¹⁵So I took the leading men of your tribes, wise and respected men, and appointed them to have authority over you—as commanders of thousands, of hundreds, of fifties and of tens and as tribal officials. ¹⁶And I charged your judges at that time: Hear the disputes between your brothers and judge fairly, whether the case is between brother Israelites or between one of them and an alien. ¹⁷Do not show partiality in judging; hear both small and great alike. Do not be afraid of any man, for judgment belongs to God. Bring me any case too hard for you, and I will hear it. ¹⁸And at that time I told you everything you were to do.

THE COMMAND TO LEAVE Horeb (1:6−8)
MOSES BEGINS WITH A verbatim quotation of Yahweh's speech to the Israelites thirty-eight years ago, instructing the Israelites to leave Horeb and head for Canaan (1:6−8; cf. Num. 10:11−13). The order consists of three parts. (1) Moses recalls Yahweh's telling the people that they had camped at the mountain long enough; his goals at Horeb had been achieved. (2) Moses describes the destination, the hill country of the Amorites, the Arabah of their neighbors, and the seacoast and lowland of the Canaanites. (3) Moses reiterates Yahweh's promise to the ancestors (v. 8). Adapting an ancient grant formula, with deliberately legal language Yahweh announces he has given the land into the hands of his vassal Israel. Alluding to Genesis 15:7−17, he adds that it is the land he had sworn to give their ancestors and their descendants.

Administrative Details (1:9–18)

AFTER VERSE 8 WE expect Moses to report that the Israelites immediately set out from Horeb. Instead he speaks of some administrative homework dealt with prior to their departure—reoganizing Israel's military structures. Exodus 18 provides background to this report, but Moses' recollection differs in some details from the earlier account. However, the differences are not fundamentally contradictory, and neither text claims to be exhaustive; condensation and expansion are possible in each account. After almost four decades of hassling by these people, it is understandable that Moses' reminiscences would exhibit distinctive properties.

Verses 9–18 divide into three sections: (1) Moses' explanation of the need to reorganize Israel's administrative structures (vv. 9–12); (2) his explanation of how the assistants were appointed (vv. 13–15); and (3) his report of the charge given to those who had been appointed (vv. 16–18).

(1) In the first part (vv. 9–12), Moses acknowledges that the burden of the Israelites had become heavier than he could bear (v. 9). Remarkably, the underlying cause was Yahweh's faithfulness: he had fulfilled his promise to the ancestors and transformed Israel from a small clan into this innumerable host (v. 10). The statement is hyperbolic, since the troops had in fact been counted (Num. 1:46; 2:32). Moses' plea to God to multiply them a thousandfold suggests that numbers was not the real problem (v. 11). The problem lay with the character and conduct of the people; to Moses they were a pain and a burden, and their bickering was intolerable (v. 12).

(2) To take the pressure off himself, Moses proposed that the people pick men of wisdom, understanding, and experience from each of the tribes as leaders over them (vv. 13–15). With this stereotypical triad of qualities (cf. Eccl. 9:11) Moses emphasizes the leaders' maturity and intellectual qualifications, in contrast to Jethro's focus on their spiritual and moral qualities in Exodus 18:21. Continuing his pattern of triads, Moses identifies the officials who were chosen with three expressions (vv. 13, 15): (a) "Leading men" (*rā'šîm*) refers to those who bear responsibility for the well-being of a social group; (b) "commanders" (*śārîm*) refers to military leaders within specific spheres of jurisdiction; (c) "tribal officials" (*šōṭᵉrîm lᵉšibṭêkem*) refers to a literate group called upon to record decisions or to muster the troops.[13] The vocabulary and pattern of organization suggest that Israel was structured socially as a military camp; they were "the LORD's divisions" (Ex. 12:41; lit., "the hosts of Yahweh").

---

13. *Šōṭᵉrîm* seems to be an archaic word, later replaced by *sōpᵉrîm* ("scribe"). In 16:18 the word is paired with *šōpᵉṭîm* ("judges") to create a hendiadys, "scribal judges." The word appears in explicitly military contexts in Deut. 20:5; 1 Chron. 27:1; and 2 Chron. 26:11. Cf. *HALOT*, 1441.

(3) Moses reports his charge to the officials whom he had installed as leaders of the Israelites (vv. 16—18), now identified as "judges" (*šōpᵉṭîm*). In the charge Moses makes four basic points. (a) These men were instructed to hear the people's disputes and judge "fairly" (*ṣedeq*) (v. 16b). This called for decisions based on the divine standard of righteousness and in the interest of *šālôm* between disputing parties.[14] This principle was to govern all disputes, whether between two Israelites ("your brothers") or between Israelite and aliens attached to them. By extending the commitment of righteousness to the "alien," Moses hints at the humanitarian emphasis we find throughout Deuteronomy. In Israel the economically and socially vulnerable are to be as secure as native Israelites.

(b) The men were not to "show partiality" in their judging (v. 17a); they were expected to hear the cases of the small and the great alike (cf. Lev 19:15).

(c) The officials were to judge boldly ("do not be afraid"); they must not fear the accused, a member of the accused's family, or a superior, because the "judgment belongs to God." The last clause seems intentionally vague. It could mean: (i) God's judgment will support the official's verdict; (ii) the official judges by divine authority; (iii) the official receives wisdom for rendering a just decision from God; (iv) the law by which the official renders judgment is administered on behalf of God, from whom it derives; or (v) the judge will ultimately answer to God for how he has administered justice.

(d) The officials had to recognize their limitations (v. 17b). In keeping with Jethro's advice in Exodus 18:22, Moses invited the officials to bring cases they found too difficult to handle to him. Judges were not expected to be omniscient (cf. Prov. 16:33).

THE THEOLOGICAL SIGNIFICANCE OF Moses' word to Israel at Horeb is obvious. (1) Yahweh is faithful to his covenant promises. To the fathers he had promised descendants as numerous as the stars of the sky, a special privileged covenant relationship, and a land where they would fulfill his intentions and from which they would be a blessing to the world.[15] The first promise was fulfilled in Egypt (cf. Ex.

---

14. W. Brueggemann (*Theology of the Old Testament: Testimony, Dispute, Advocacy* [Minneapolis: Fortress, 1997], 130) defines righteousness as "Yahweh's ready capacity to be present in situations of trouble and to intervene powerfully and decisively in the interest of rehabilitation, restoration, and well-being."

15. Cf. D. J. A. Clines, *The Theme of the Pentateuch* (JSOTSup 10; Sheffield: JSOT, 1978), esp. 31—37.

1:1–7), and the second at Horeb. Standing east of the Jordan, the Israelites are about to witness the fulfillment of the third.

That Israel should have camped at the foot of Horeb for more than a year was neither a sign of divine indecision nor loss of focus, for here Yahweh had formally brought the nation into the covenant he had made with Abraham centuries earlier (Gen. 17:7–8), and here they became his vassals.[16] However, as Yahweh had promised in Exodus 6:6–8, the confirmation of the covenant would not be the end of the journey; Yahweh brought them out of Egypt to deliver into their hands the land he had promised to the ancestors. Despite the weight of the Israelites on Moses' shoulders, their presence before Yahweh was testimony to his faithfulness in fulfilling the ancestral promise to make their descendants as numerous as the stars of the sky (cf. Gen. 15:5; 22:17; 26:4; Ex. 32:13).

(2) While the administration of the community of faith involves economic and judicial decisions, it must be rooted in a robust theology. God defines and demands righteousness; God embodies perfect fairness (Deut. 10:17); God calls and authorizes human leaders to administer the community on his behalf; God remains the ultimate arbiter before whom all will stand; and as Abraham had learned, the Judge of all the earth does indeed judge rightly (Gen. 18:25). With this statement we recognize the transcendent dimension of Israelite constitutional law. While God delegates to humans the responsibility of administering justice, behind Israel's law stands the God to whom justice belongs.[17]

THE MISSION OF GOD for Israel. Yahweh's speech in verses 6–8 describes the mission of God for Israel. When he rescued his people from slavery in Egypt, he had promised them the land of Canaan, which would provide the context from which they would fulfill their mission as a light to the nations (cf. 26:19). However, this generation would perish in the desert, which would prove that they were not true children of the promise, nor had they been born of the Spirit (cf. Gal. 4:29). Physically they had come out of Egypt, and at Sinai they declared their allegiance to Yahweh, but they remained captive to sin.

This perspective underlies Paul's argument with the Judaizers in Galatians 4:21–31. His detractors seem to have forgotten that the law was

---

16. In the exodus narratives (e.g., Ex. 3:12; 4:23) the verb ʿābad means generally "to serve [Yahweh] as his vassals." At Sinai those who had formerly been slaves (ʿᵃbādîm) of the Egyptians became Yahweh's privileged servants.

17. Cf. C. J. H. Wright, *Deuteronomy* (NIBC; Peabody, MA: Hendrickson, 1996), 27.

not the end goal, nor did it represent the essence of God's call. While the covenant and the revelation of God's will were to be received as incredible graces, the promise looked beyond Sinai, and the mission lay far beyond. This is not to minimize the significance of the law; it is simply to emphasize that possession of it is not the end goal. The Lord calls us that we might delight in the fulfillment of his promise, and that in that fulfillment the world may see what he can do for them.

Paradigm for the church. Several features of Moses' reorganization of the administration of Israel are paradigmatic for the church. (1) Moses' appointment of and charge to the leaders assumes that God provides the community of faith with the gifts and the personnel needed to govern that community. As Paul would declare so eloquently in 1 Corinthians 12, God has placed within the body of Christ the members needed for its health and effective functioning (v. 18), and he has appointed those who should exercise leadership in the body (v. 28).

(2) While ministers are prone to forget that the mission in which they are engaged is God's mission, and they are often tempted to act as if both the burden of the mission and the credit for its successes are their own (cf. v. 9–10), the success of the mission depends on casting the burden on God's strong shoulders and letting him energize his people.

(3) The stresses of service in God's kingdom may be relieved through the sanctified engagement of common sense and the distribution of responsibilities. Moses' and God's answer to his personal fatigue was to delegate administrative duties to wise and experienced leaders of the community.

(4) Those who lead God's people must be committed fundamentally to the promotion of righteousness. Righteous (*ṣedeq*) administration demands uncompromising fairness for all, without respect to the social standing of the persons involved. As Leviticus 19:15 recognizes, the righteous administration of justice may easily be derailed by showing either deference to the rich and powerful or sentimentality toward the poor (cf. Deut. 10:17; 16:19; 24:17). Moses' inclusion of aliens reminds us that those who adjudicate on covenantal matters must be blind to status, race, and citizenship. It may be too much to expect that the world will operate this way, but the current climate of hatred toward specific people groups offers the church a glorious opportunity to display the compassion of God himself (10:17).

(5) In their exercise of authority, leaders must recognize that they do so on God's behalf and for the achievement of his goals. In cases that exceed the competence of human minds, he provides wisdom, and in cases involving unfair outcomes, he holds those who abuse the office accountable.

Deuteronomy 1:19–2:1

Then, as the LORD our God commanded us, we set out from Horeb and went toward the hill country of the Amorites through all that vast and dreadful desert that you have seen, and so we reached Kadesh Barnea. ²⁰Then I said to you, "You have reached the hill country of the Amorites, which the LORD our God is giving us. ²¹See, the LORD your God has given you the land. Go up and take possession of it as the LORD, the God of your fathers, told you. Do not be afraid; do not be discouraged."

²²Then all of you came to me and said, "Let us send men ahead to spy out the land for us and bring back a report about the route we are to take and the towns we will come to."

²³The idea seemed good to me; so I selected twelve of you, one man from each tribe. ²⁴They left and went up into the hill country, and came to the Valley of Eshcol and explored it. ²⁵Taking with them some of the fruit of the land, they brought it down to us and reported, "It is a good land that the LORD our God is giving us."

²⁶But you were unwilling to go up; you rebelled against the command of the LORD your God. ²⁷You grumbled in your tents and said, "The LORD hates us; so he brought us out of Egypt to deliver us into the hands of the Amorites to destroy us. ²⁸Where can we go? Our brothers have made us lose heart. They say, 'The people are stronger and taller than we are; the cities are large, with walls up to the sky. We even saw the Anakites there.'"

²⁹Then I said to you, "Do not be terrified; do not be afraid of them. ³⁰The LORD your God, who is going before you, will fight for you, as he did for you in Egypt, before your very eyes, ³¹and in the desert. There you saw how the LORD your God carried you, as a father carries his son, all the way you went until you reached this place."

³²In spite of this, you did not trust in the LORD your God, ³³who went ahead of you on your journey, in fire by night and in a cloud by day, to search out places for you to camp and to show you the way you should go.

³⁴When the LORD heard what you said, he was angry and solemnly swore: ³⁵"Not a man of this evil generation shall

see the good land I swore to give your forefathers, [36]except Caleb son of Jephunneh. He will see it, and I will give him and his descendants the land he set his feet on, because he followed the LORD wholeheartedly."

[37]Because of you the LORD became angry with me also and said, "You shall not enter it, either. [38]But your assistant, Joshua son of Nun, will enter it. Encourage him, because he will lead Israel to inherit it. [39]And the little ones that you said would be taken captive, your children who do not yet know good from bad—they will enter the land. I will give it to them and they will take possession of it. [40]But as for you, turn around and set out toward the desert along the route to the Red Sea."

[41]Then you replied, "We have sinned against the LORD. We will go up and fight, as the LORD our God commanded us." So every one of you put on his weapons, thinking it easy to go up into the hill country.

[42]But the LORD said to me, "Tell them, 'Do not go up and fight, because I will not be with you. You will be defeated by your enemies.'"

[43]So I told you, but you would not listen. You rebelled against the LORD's command and in your arrogance you marched up into the hill country. [44]The Amorites who lived in those hills came out against you; they chased you like a swarm of bees and beat you down from Seir all the way to Hormah. [45]You came back and wept before the LORD, but he paid no attention to your weeping and turned a deaf ear to you. [46]And so you stayed in Kadesh many days—all the time you spent there.

[2:1]Then we turned back and set out toward the desert along the route to the Red Sea, as the LORD had directed me. For a long time we made our way around the hill country of Seir.

IN THE REST OF chapter 1, Moses recounts the critical events that transpired at Kadesh Barnea. Verse 19 summarizes the Israelite response to Yahweh's command in verse 7 given at Mount Sinai and telescopes in one verse a month or two of Israel's history. Moses limits his report to a few basic facts. The route from Sinai took them through an inhospitable desert (cf. 8:15), described as "vast and dreadful." He highlights his audience's own experience of Yahweh's providential care through this life-threatening wasteland by adding "that you have seen." While the goal of the journey was the hill country of the Amorites (cf. v. 7), they headed for Kadesh Barnea. Throughout, the standard of operation was "as the LORD our God commanded us." Yahweh had acted as Commander-in-Chief of this vast Israelite army on the march.

It is clear from verses 20–46 that Kadesh Barnea represented a turning point in Israel's history. The nation had finally arrived on the bank of destiny, with the Promised Land lying before them. How would the people respond? Moses answers this question in remarkable detail. His recollections of Kadesh Barnea divide into five parts: (1) his charge to take the land (vv. 20–21); (2) the people's faithless response (vv. 22–33); (3) Yahweh's reaction (vv. 34–40); (4) the people's presumptuous response (vv. 41–45); and (5) an epilogue (v. 46).

Moses' Charge to Take the Land (vv. 20–21)

THE OPENING TO MOSES' reminiscences of Kadesh Barnea contains three promising observations: the Israelites had arrived at their destination (vv. 7, 19); Yahweh had placed his grant of land before them (cf. v. 8); and Yahweh, the God of their ancestors, had kept his word. Moses' alternation of "the LORD your God" and "the LORD, the God of your fathers" reflected his conviction that this nation stood in covenantal solidarity with the patriarchs. Based on these observations, Moses challenged the people with three verbs: "take possession of [the land]," "do not be afraid," and "do not be discouraged."[1] Exhortations by deities not to fear in the face of threatening situations are common in ancient Near Eastern accounts and were often accompanied by divine promises of victory and/or protection.

The People's Faithless Act of Rebellion (1:22–33)

THE ISRAELITES RESPONDED TO Moses' charge by proposing to send a party of men to scout out the territory. This account differs dramatically from Numbers 13:1–2, but neither report claims to tell the whole story. In this rendition Moses agreed to the people's request, selected a man from each tribe, and sent them out (v. 23; cf. Num. 13:4–16.). The detail with which he now recounts the people's infidelity in verses 26–45 suggests Moses may have acted on his own, and after thirty-eight years of reflection he seems to have recognized this was a wrong move. Under normal circumstances such a reconnaissance mission might have made good sense (Josh. 2:1; 7:2; Judg. 18:2), but coming immediately after God's command, the

---

1. The verb *ḥātat* means literally "to be shattered, broken to pieces" (cf. Isa. 7:8; Mal. 2:5), and in a derived sense (as here), "to be emotionally distraught."

proposal itself seemed to betray a lack of faith (cf. 9:23). The outcome of the mission reinforced this conclusion.

Verses 24–25 describe the scouts' mission and report. Moses notes that they went up into the hill country and scouted out the land as far as the Valley of Eshcol, near the city of Hebron (cf. Num. 13:21–24). His recollection illuminates the ironies of the situation. (1) They went out to gain information to be used to determine military strategy, but their report focused on fruit, concrete evidence of the fertility of the land. (2) They reported that the land was good, but promptly demonstrated they did not think it worth the risk of an invasion. (3) They referred to the land as "a good land that the LORD our God is giving us," but they refused to accept it from his hand. God's promises concerning the land were true, but the obstacles loomed too large in their minds.

In verses 26–33 Moses recalls the people's reaction to the scouting report. Omitting many details found in Numbers 13–14, he concentrates on their shameful attitude (vv. 26–27a) and reprehensible actions (vv. 27b–28). He describes the former with three expressions: they were unwilling to go up; they rebelled against the command of Yahweh; and they muttered/grumbled in their tents. The people expressed their rebellion and sullenness with a troubling speech, accusing Yahweh of deliberately trying to destroy them (v. 27b) and fixating on the enemy (v. 28).[2] They complained that Yahweh's actions were directed *against* them and motivated by hostility, rather than being performed *on their behalf* and driven by his covenant commitment, that is, his love (cf. 7:8, 13; 10:15–19; 23:5[6]). They also despaired of finding any strategy that would work against the occupants of the land.[3]

Moses cites three reasons for the Israelites' demoralization: the inhabitants of the land were larger and taller than they; their cities were huge and impregnable, with sky-high walls (cf. Num 13:28); and the inhabitants included descendants of the Anakites (cf. 9:2).[4] On the surface, everything

---

2. The expression "our brothers have made us lose heart [lit., 'made our hearts melt']" expresses the same effect that rumors of what Yahweh had done for the Israelites would have on the Canaanites (Josh. 2:11; 5:1).

3. The rhetorical question, "Where can we go?" (v. 28)—which expects a negative answer, "Nowhere"—answers to "the route we are to take" in v. 22.

4. According to Josh. 15:13 and 21:11, Anak was the son of Arba, who had founded Kiriath-Arba, that is, Hebron. Num. 13:33 suggests the Anakites were a subgroup of the Nephilim, the legendary giants whose name derives from the antediluvian offspring of the "sons of God" and earthly women (cf. Gen. 6:1–4). Num. 13:22 identifies by name three Anakites whom the scouts encountered in Hebron: Ahiman, Sheshai, and Talmai. Deut. 2:10–11 and 20–21 associates the Anakites with the Rephaites, referred to as the Emites and Zamzummites by the Moabites and Ammonites respectively.

about the scouts' report was true. The land was indeed fertile and productive, and the inhabitants seemed invincible. But they forgot that their divine Commander-in-Chief had already disposed of a much more powerful enemy in the Egyptians, and they blamed their demoralization on the scouts (cf. Num. 13:30–33; 14:36–38).

Trying to correct the people's flawed perspective, Moses' response focused entirely on Yahweh. After an opening call for calm and confidence (v. 29), he tried to encourage them with three arguments (vv. 30–31): (1) Yahweh was present with them and going before them; (2) Yahweh, the divine Warrior and Captain of his hosts (cf. Josh. 5:13–15), would fight for them; (3) Yahweh had taken care of them in the past by defeating the Egyptians before their very eyes[5] and sustaining them through the great and terrifying desert (v. 19). With sensitive pastoral touch, Moses compared Yahweh's care to that of a father who carries his son through danger to safety.

It is obvious from verses 32–33 that Moses' exhortation had no effect. Reiterating how foolish and faithless the people had been, he reminded the present generation that their security and success rested neither with human generals nor in human wisdom; Yahweh always marched ahead of them. However, instead of speaking of his fighting for them (cf. v. 30), Moses says that Yahweh went before, scouting out[6] places for them to set up their (military) camps and directing their actions, that is, to attack the enemy. The sight of the pillar of fire by night and cloud by day rendered the original rebellion even more tragic (cf. Ex. 13:21; Num. 14:14). But the people ignored both the evidence of their own experience and the visible proof of Yahweh's commitment to them. The real challenge was neither physical nor military, but spiritual. Would they trust God? Verse 32 declares that they would not!

Yahweh's Reaction to the People's Faithlessness (1:34–40)

MOSES' RECOLLECTION OF YAHWEH'S response abbreviates Numbers 14 drastically. He simply announces Yahweh's anger at the sound of the people's words and moves immediately to his final decision, expressed with an oath. The terms of the oath may be summarized in three statements.

---

5. This fact was recognized by the Egyptians themselves in Ex. 14:25 (cf. Moses' promise in v. 14). The motif of Yahweh's fighting for Israel is common in Deuteronomy and the literature influenced by this book. See Deut. 3:22; Josh. 10:14, 42; 23:3, 10.

6. In Num. 10:33–36 the ark is said to have gone before the people to seek out (*tûr*) a resting place for the people. Deuteronomy never portrays the ark as a symbol of Yahweh's presence.

(1) Because of their faithlessness not one man among "this evil generation," would experience the good land he had sworn to their ancestors (v. 35). (2) There would be two notable exceptions: Caleb and Joshua (vv. 36, 38).[7] In view of their efforts to encourage the people to trust in Yahweh (Num. 13:30; 14:5 − 10), Moses declares Yahweh's favor toward these two men in unequivocal terms.[8] (3) Yahweh swore that he would give the land to the little children of that faithless generation. Innocent children who could not distinguish good from bad (i.e., were not yet morally responsible)[9] would replace "this evil generation" (v. 35) of adults who had signed on to the covenant at Horeb and had been charged to go in and take the land. The children would not be judged for the sins of their parents.

Within the context of Yahweh's oath, Moses' personal gripe in verse 37 is intrusive. He blames the Israelites that he is unable to enter the Promised Land with Caleb and Joshua. The statement is remarkable on several counts. (1) Far from associating Moses with the rebellion of the people, in the narratives of Numbers 13 − 14 Yahweh offered to start over with Moses and to have his descendants replace Israel as his covenant people (Num. 14:12). (2) The reasons given for God's refusing Moses entrance into the Promised Land in the earlier narratives relate to an entirely different incident — his failure to treat Yahweh as holy by striking the rock rather than speaking to it at Meribah (Num. 20:2 − 13; cf. Deut. 32:48 − 52). With this act of faithlessness, Moses personally disqualified himself from achieving the prize. How then could he blame the Israelites for his failure to enter the land? The answer is actually simple. If the Israelites had trusted Yahweh at Kadesh Barnea and entered the land at his command, the event recorded in Numbers 20 would never have

---

7. In verse 38 we encounter the root *nḥl* for the first time. Although elsewhere in the Old Testament the land of Israel and Zion are referred to as Yahweh's *naḥᵃlâ*, in Deuteronomy Moses calls Israel Yahweh's *naḥᵃlâ* and the land of Canaan Israel's *naḥᵃlâ*. While NIV follows longstanding tradition in translating the word with inheritance terminology, it is preferable to associate it with landed property, reflecting "the practice of giving loyal servants the utilization of land as a reward for past service — fundamentally military service is involved — and in expectation of future service" (H. O. Forshey, "The Hebrew Root *NHL* and Its Semitic Cognates" [Th.D. diss., Harvard University, 1973], 233).

8. Of the two exceptions, Caleb presents the more interesting case. Identified elsewhere as "Caleb son of Jephunneh the Kenizzite" (Num. 32:12; Josh. 14:6, 14) and as a descendant of Kenaz a grandson of Esau (Gen. 36:11, 15, 42; cf. 1 Chron. 1:36, 53), apparently Caleb's family were proselytes of Edomite descent. But Caleb was so thoroughly integrated into the faith and life of Israel that he represented the tribe of Judah and was one of only two who demonstrated total covenant loyalty to Yahweh (Num. 14:24; 32:11 − 12; Josh. 14:8 − 9, 14).

9. Cf. Jonah 4:11, where Yahweh characterizes the innocent of Nineveh as "those who cannnot tell their right hand from their left."

occurred. However, since the people's faithlessness precipitated a series of unfortunate events, including Meribah, in a sense Moses was right. However, as we will learn from Deuteronomy 3:23 – 26, Yahweh will not listen to such arguments.

In verse 40 Yahweh called for a literal and figurative turning point in Israel's history. He commanded the people to retrace their steps back to the desert and set their sights on the Red Sea. In one stroke the exodus was annulled and the nation's history reversed. Those whom Yahweh had brought out of Egypt were rejected as heirs of the promise to the fathers.

The People's Presumptuous Act of Rebellion (1:41 – 2:1)

THE KEY EXPRESSIONS IN this paragraph are "rebelled against the LORD's command" and "arrogance" (v. 43).[10] (1) The people expressed their defiance by glibly confessing their sin against Yahweh. On the surface, their confession looked like a serious response to Yahweh's sworn decree. But they failed to recognize that with the intervening events, everything had changed. What had previously been called for as an act of faith now became an act of rebellion.

(2) They armed themselves for battle and casually marched up to the hill country. Lest they be destroyed at the hands of the Canaanites, Yahweh sent Moses to warn them not to proceed.

(3) They refused to listen to Moses. Defying their divine Commander (cf. Num. 14:44) and without any assurance of divine protection, they attacked those whom they had feared only a short time ago. Adding the sin of presumption to rebellion, they forgot that God is not obligated to those who do not take him seriously.

From a military standpoint this misadventure was a fiasco (vv. 44–45). The Amorites of the hill country[11] responded like wild bees in a disturbed hive. The Israelites discovered that the land "flowing with milk and honey" also produced stinging bees, which swarmed around them, chased them off, and struck them down at Hormah in Seir. The spiritual consequences of this event were more tragic than the physical. Having swung emotionally from despair to self-confidence, the people returned to the base camp and wept before Yahweh. But Yahweh's ears were stopped; he refused to listen. God demanded obedience, not tears.

---

10. The Hebrew *zûd* refers to "a presumptuous, premeditated offense against God and his religious and moral order" (S. Scharbert, "זוד," *TDOT*, 4:48.

11. The ethnic term *Amorites* is used indiscriminately for the inhabitants of Canaan. Num. 14:45 identifies them more precisely as Amalekites and Canaanites.

Verse 46 brings formal closure to the Kadesh Barnea chapter. The statement declares that the Israelites "stayed in Kadesh many days," though it is unclear how long "many days" was. But in obedience to Yahweh's command, they turned around and headed southeastward into the desert in the direction of the Red Sea (2:1). Moses' observation that they milled around in circles for many days in the vicinity of Seir represents a classic understatement, for those days turned out to be 13,880 days. During these thirty-eight years (cf. v. 14) the Israelites made no progress whatsoever toward the fulfillment of the mission on which they had embarked when they came out of Egypt.

Yahweh had one primary goal for their desert wanderings—to get rid of that rebellious generation (vv. 14–16). For almost four decades Israel was a death camp, a walking mortuary, in which the dominant sound was the death wail. The irony is inescapable. So long as they were slaves in Egypt, Israel's population mushroomed; as soon as they were free, it shrank.

SOME OF THE PERMANENT theological lessons deriving from Moses' recollections at Kadesh Barnea are obvious; others are subtle. It may be helpful to categorize these by asking two questions: What does this text teach us about God? About God's people?

Teachings about God. The first question is answered with three powerful metaphors: God is a divine Warrior, a divine Guide, and a divine Father. (1) *God as divine Warrior.* If judgment in Israel's internal affairs belongs to God (v. 17), the same is true of the battles this nation would fight against foreign foes (2 Chron. 20:15). Whether Egyptian or Amorite, anyone who stands in the way of Israel stands in the way of God.

(2) *God as divine Guide.* Throughout Israel's travels, Yahweh had gone before them in the cloud and the fire, seeking places for Israel to camp and showing them which way to go (v. 33). The God who had brought Israel to himself at Horeb had faithfully brought Israel to the boundary of the Promised Land. We hear allusions to this notion in Zechariah's celebration of God's mercy in guiding "our feet into the path of peace" (Luke 1:78–79), and Revelation 7:15–17, which speaks of the Lamb leading his sheep to springs of living water.

(3) *God as divine Father.* Verse 31 presents a tender image of God as a loving father who firmly carries his child through the vast and dreadful desert (8:15). However, the Israelites learned that the fatherhood of

God has two sides. He who lavishes grace on his son also gets angry when his son defies him and refuses to trust him (v. 34). Yahweh disciplines his son (cf. 8:5; Prov. 3:12), but when discipline fails, the heavenly Father turns a deaf ear to the wailing of a rebellious son (v. 45). In the New Testament Jesus invites his followers to address God as Father when they pray and to call on him to lead them (though not into the wilderness of temptation), to fight their battles ("deliver us from the evil one"), and to give them the daily bread they need (Matt. 6:9–13). But Hebrews 12:6 reminds us that the fatherhood of God still has another side: "The Lord disciplines those he loves, and he punishes everyone he accepts as a son."

Teachings about God's people. Few passages in Scripture provide a fuller study in human faithlessness. (1) Faithlessness results from and is expressed in faulty vision. Here Moses highlights the motif of "seeing" (vv. 19, 22–23, 25, 28, 30, 31, 33), but faithless "eyes" are selective in what they allow to register in the heart. These people were blind to God's gracious providences, and they saw only the obstacles in their road. Because of their blindness to the greater One among them (1 John 4:4), they would not "see" the prize (vv. 35–36).

(2) This passage teaches us the many faces of faithlessness. According to verses 19–33 faithlessness suppresses the truth (v. 32) and is expressed in stubbornness and rebellion against the command of God (v. 26), grumbling behind the leader's and God's back, bitterness, misreading the heart of God, accusations against other members of the community (v. 28), fear and loss of nerve (v. 29), and perhaps most tragic of all, a loss of memory (vv. 30–33). Within this book, Moses will return repeatedly to this "theology of remembrance," emphasizing that many of Israel's cultic and constitutional institutions were purposefully designed to keep alive the memory of God's many interventions on their behalf (6:20–25; 26:5–11).

(3) Faithlessness assumes that the mere mouthing of penitential words will win the favor of God (v. 41), and it forgets that the proof of fidelity is obedience to God's will. Faithlessness assumes a fickle God (vv. 26–40) and presumes upon his presence. Faithlessness yields alienation so acute that God refuses to respond to the prayers of faithless supplicants, regardless of the passion with which they plead with him.

Nevertheless, despite the pervasive unbelief of Israel, every age knows a faithful remnant. We may contrast Caleb and the rest of the Israelites by juxtaposing his response as described in Numbers 13–14 with the characteristics of Israel as illustrated in Moses' recollections:

Characteristics of the Israelites as a Whole	Characteristics of Caleb
- unwilling to go up (v. 26)	- eager to go up (cf. Num. 13:30)
- rebellious against Yahweh's command (v. 26)	- encouraging people not to rebel against Yahweh (cf. Num. 13:30)
- sulking in their tents (v. 27; Ps. 106:25)	- calming the people (cf. Num. 13:30)
- accusing Yahweh of hatred and betrayal (v. 27)	- assuring the people of Yahweh's favor and presence (Num. 14:9)
- melting hearts (v. 28)	
- terrified and fearful (v. 29)	- challenging the people not to fear (cf. Num. 14:9)
- refusing to trust Yahweh their God (v. 32)	- fully confident in Yahweh (cf. Num. 13:30; 14:8–9)

The case of Caleb demonstrates that from the beginning of the nation's history there have been two Israels: (a) ethnic Israelites who participated in the exodus from Egypt, claimed descent from the patriarchs, and viewed themselves as the automatic heirs of the promises; (b) true Israelites who may or may not have been physical descendants of the ancestors, but who possessed the Spirit of God like the ancestors and were therefore their true spiritual heirs. In Numbers 14:24 Yahweh recognizes a different spirit with Caleb, demonstrated in following Yahweh fully. While this could mean simply that Caleb's disposition differed from that of the rest the population, it is more likely that "to be accompanied by a different Spirit" is equivalent to being circumcised of heart (Deut. 30:6), to having experienced a divine heart transplant, or to having had Yahweh put his "spirit" within a person (Ezek. 36:26–27). The indwelling Spirit yielded a life of total obedience to Yahweh. Caleb, the Gentile proselyte, illustrates the Pauline adage:

> A man is not a Jew if he is only one outwardly, nor is circumcision merely outward and physical. No, a man is a Jew if he is one inwardly; and circumcision is circumcision of the heart, by the Spirit, not by the written code. Such a man's praise is not from men, but from God. (Rom. 2:28–29)

Few have received more enthusiastic approval by God himself than Caleb.

Contemporary Significance

AFTER THE ISRAELITES LEFT Egypt, they faced a series of tests of their fidelity and faith in Yahweh. He had proved himself faithful to them at every turn; at Kadesh Barnea they were challenged to rely on him to complete his mission and to deliver the vastly superior Canaanites into their hand. Christians in every age have encountered representatives of the kingdom of darkness who stand in the way, obstacles to the fulfillment of the mission to which God has called us. Admittedly our enemies are not specific ethnic or racial groups, and the prize of our struggle is not physical territory, but the challenge is no less real. Paul paints the picture of our struggle in graphic strokes in Ephesians 6:10 – 13:

> Finally, be strong in the Lord and in his mighty power. Put on the full armor of God so that you can take your stand against the devil's schemes. For our struggle is not against flesh and blood, but against the rulers, against the authorities, against the powers of this dark world and against the spiritual forces of evil in the heavenly realms. Therefore put on the full armor of God, so that when the day of evil comes, you may be able to stand your ground, and after you have done everything, to stand.

Sadly, like Israel, the church as a collective and Christians as individuals have often proved faithless, being more impressed by the power of the enemy than the power of God and the resources he makes available to his people. But the example of Caleb inspires us in our pursuit of God and provides the key to passing the tests we face: possession of a different Spirit, that is, the Holy Spirit of God, and unqualified commitment to God and his mission. To those who persevere the Lord promises not a plot of land but the eternal reward of an inheritance with him (Eph. 1:3 – 14).

Deuteronomy 2:2–23

❦

Then the LORD said to me, [3]"You have made your way around this hill country long enough; now turn north. [4]Give the people these orders: 'You are about to pass through the territory of your brothers the descendants of Esau, who live in Seir. They will be afraid of you, but be very careful. [5]Do not provoke them to war, for I will not give you any of their land, not even enough to put your foot on. I have given Esau the hill country of Seir as his own. [6]You are to pay them in silver for the food you eat and the water you drink.'"

[7]The LORD your God has blessed you in all the work of your hands. He has watched over your journey through this vast desert. These forty years the LORD your God has been with you, and you have not lacked anything.

[8]So we went on past our brothers the descendants of Esau, who live in Seir. We turned from the Arabah road, which comes up from Elath and Ezion Geber, and traveled along the desert road of Moab.

[9]Then the LORD said to me, "Do not harass the Moabites or provoke them to war, for I will not give you any part of their land. I have given Ar to the descendants of Lot as a possession."

[10](The Emites used to live there—a people strong and numerous, and as tall as the Anakites. [11]Like the Anakites, they too were considered Rephaites, but the Moabites called them Emites. [12]Horites used to live in Seir, but the descendants of Esau drove them out. They destroyed the Horites from before them and settled in their place, just as Israel did in the land the LORD gave them as their possession.)

[13]And the LORD said, "Now get up and cross the Zered Valley." So we crossed the valley.

[14]Thirty-eight years passed from the time we left Kadesh Barnea until we crossed the Zered Valley. By then, that entire generation of fighting men had perished from the camp, as the LORD had sworn to them. [15]The LORD's hand was against them until he had completely eliminated them from the camp.

[16]Now when the last of these fighting men among the people had died, [17]the LORD said to me, [18]"Today you are to

pass by the region of Moab at Ar. ¹⁹When you come to the Ammonites, do not harass them or provoke them to war, for I will not give you possession of any land belonging to the Ammonites. I have given it as a possession to the descendants of Lot."

²⁰(That too was considered a land of the Rephaites, who used to live there; but the Ammonites called them Zamzum-mites. ²¹They were a people strong and numerous, and as tall as the Anakites. The LORD destroyed them from before the Ammonites, who drove them out and settled in their place. ²²The LORD had done the same for the descendants of Esau, who lived in Seir, when he destroyed the Horites from before them. They drove them out and have lived in their place to this day. ²³And as for the Avvites who lived in villages as far as Gaza, the Caphtorites coming out from Caphtor destroyed them and settled in their place.)

IN DEUTERONOMY 2 – 3 Moses deals with a new generation: before him stand the children of the faithless exodus generation. Here he recounts six episodes in which the divine Commander-in-Chief directed his Israelite army from somewhere in the vicinity of Seir to a position east of the Jordan from which they would enter the Promised Land (2:2 – 3:29). Verses 1, 8, and 13b – 15 represent the narrative skeleton of 2:2 – 23. The remainder consists largely of speeches by Yahweh to Moses (vv. 2 – 7, 9, 13a, 17 – 19) and inserted footnotes identifying the original inhabitants of the lands of Moab, Ammon, and Edom (vv. 10 – 12, 20 – 23).

Beyond this narrative skeleton, we observe again Moses' penchant for tripling elements, as he deals successively with the Israelites' interaction with the Edomites (vv. 2 – 8a), Moabites (vv. 8b – 15), and Ammonites (vv. 16 – 24a). The keywords of this text are obviously "to cross over, pass through" (ʿābar, 8x; vv. 4, 8, 13, 14, 18, 24) and "to possess, dispossess"/"possession" (yāraš/yᵉruššâ, 9x; vv. 5, 9, 12, 19, 21, 22). After thirty – eight years of aimlessly circling the desert, Israel was on the march, passing successively through the territorial possessions of Edom, Moab, and Ammon.

Moses does not explain why Yahweh had the Israelites enter Canaan from the east across the Jordan rather than relaunching the campaign from Kadesh Barnea in the south. But to get to the eastern shore of the Jordan, the Israelites needed to negotiate their way carefully through a series of states, all of which were related to the Israelites by blood and were themselves just coming into their own. The Edomites living in Seir were the closest relatives, being descendants of Esau, the brother of Jacob (cf. Gen. 36). The Moabites and Ammonites were descendants of Abraham's nephew Lot by his two daughters (Gen. 19:30–38; cf. Deut. 2:9, 19).

Moses' Recollections of Seir/Edom (2:2–8a)

IN THIS OPENING EPISODE, Moses remembers Israel's encounter with the Edomites. After circling Mount Seir for many days, Yahweh broke his silence,[1] telling Moses that they had milled around long enough and that the time had come to head north. But first they had to seek permission to pass through territory occupied by the descendants of Esau. Moses does not recount how the Israelites conducted their negotiations with the Edomites (cf. Num 20:14–21). In verses 2–7 he simply recalls verbatim the divinely prescribed policy for dealing with Edom: the Israelites were simply to pass through, treating the Edomites with respect and not provoking them in any way.

This policy appears to have been based on five considerations. (1) The Edomites were the Israelites' relatives (Heb. ʾaḥîm, "brothers," v. 4a).

(2) The Edomites were fearful of the Israelites (v. 4); apparently the story of their escape from Egypt and defeat of the Amalekites (Ex. 17:8–16) forty years ago had reached them (cf. Num. 22:3–4).

(3) Just as Yahweh had allocated the land of Canaan to Israel, so he allocated Seir as the rightful possession of Esau and his descendants. Whereas ancient Near Easterners tended to perceive patron deities as having jurisdiction only over their own territories, Yahweh, the God of Israel, exercises supranational authority and providential care over other nations.[2] As Yahweh's vassal, Israel was not to claim territory given by him to another.

(4) Yahweh prohibited the Israelites from looting or stealing from the Edomites; instead, they were to pay for any food or water that they would need with silver.

(5) Israel was to continue relying entirely on the direct provision of Yahweh (v. 7). In typical Mosaic style, he grounds this point in three facts. (a) Yahweh had blessed every activity to which the people had put their

---

1. The narratives of Numbers suggest Yahweh had spoken to Moses on numerous occasions, issuing more constitutional directives, advising Moses on administrative matters, and responding to the people's faithfulness.

2. For discussion of the ancient Near Eastern perceptions of the relationship between patron deities and national territory, see Daniel I. Block, *The Gods of the Nations* (Grand Rapids: Baker, 2000), 75–111.

hands. (b) Yahweh had watched over[3] the Israelites during their travels through the vast and dreadful desert (cf. 8:3−5). (c) Yahweh had been with his people for the past forty years,[4] providing everything they needed. In verse 8a Moses notes that rather than risking a violation of the policy, the Israelites traveled around Edomite territory to the east, apparently avoiding the King's Highway that ran through the Edomite heartland.[5] Because verse 8a is vague, the route is not clear.[6] But Yahweh's speech represented a test of faith for the new generation. From what follows they obviously passed this test.

Since verses 12 and 22 also concern the Edomites we may consider them here. Verses 10−12 and 20−23, which review how the Transjordanian nations came to occupy the lands in which they lived, provide context for Israel's conquest of Canaan. The pre-Edomite/Esauite occupants of Seir are identified as Horites (cf. Gen. 36:20−30). The comment in verse 22, "The LORD had done the same for the descendants of Esau," suggests we should view Edom's displacement of the Horites as paradigmatic. Just as Yahweh had destroyed the Horites and delivered their land into the Edomites' hands, so he had done for the Ammonites, and so he would do for Israel. While verse 12 has the Edomites destroying the Horites, verse 22 attributes the action to God.

Moses' Recollections of Moab (2:8b−15)

MOSES' RECOLLECTIONS OF THE second phase of the journey open like the first, but the account is shorter. The report of this encounter involves only verses 8b−9 and 13, most of which is taken up with a verbatim recollection of Yahweh's speech to Moses at the time. The parallels between verse 9 and verse 5 suggest Moses' comments concerning the descendants of Esau also applied to the sons of Lot, that is, the Moabites (v. 9) and the Ammonites (v. 18).

When the Israelites arrived at the edge of Moab (v. 8b), Yahweh commanded that the policy that governed their treatment of Edom was also to apply to Moab. They were not to harass them or pick a fight with them (cf.

---

3. The verb *yādaʿ* ("to know") often bears the sense, "to care for, to protect." Cf. Gen. 39:6, 8; Job 9:21; 35:15; Pss. 1:6; 31:8[9]; Prov. 27:3.

4. "Forty" is a round number that includes the time spent traveling from Egypt to Sinai, the time at Horeb, and the wandering in the desert. Numbers 14:27−35 notes that the forty years represented one year of wandering for every day the scouts had been surveying the land of Canaan; this is how much time it would take to replace the faithless generation with a new one.

5. So also Barry J. Beitzel, *Moody Atlas of Bible Lands* (Chicago: Moody Press, 2009), 33.

6. Literally, "Then we crossed over away from our brothers, the sons of Esau who lived in Seir, away from the way of the Arabah, away from Eilat, and away from Ezion-Geber."

v. 5). Just as Yahweh had given Seir to Edom, so he gave Ar to the Moabites as their possession. Remarkably, Yahweh posed as Moab's patron deity, claiming a role normally ascribed to Chemosh, the god of Moab.[7] The reference to Moab as one of the sons of Lot alludes to Genesis 19:30 – 38. While the location of Ar is unknown, the name probably identifies the capital city located somewhere in the Moabite heartland rather than a larger region (Num. 22:36; Isa 15:1). Numbers 21:28 reports that Sihon of Og burned Ar of Moab, following a policy regarding conquered cities that was common in the ancient Near East. After a parenthetical insertion (vv. 10 – 12), in verse 13 Yahweh commanded Israel to arise and cross the brook Zered, the natural boundary between Edomite and Moabite territory. Since the Israelites did not actually pass through Moabite territory, the crossing must have occurred some twenty or thirty miles upstream to the east.[8]

Verses 10 – 12 function as a footnote (cf. vv. 20 – 22; 3:9, 11, 13), clarifying ethnographic and geographic issues raised in Moses' speech. As noted earlier, the relatives of the Israelites in the Transjordan (Edom, Moab, Bene Ammon) were not indigenous to the region. While the circumstances of the displacement of populations is unknown, in verse 21 Moses credits Yahweh with destroying them and delivering the territories into the hands of the newcomers, even as he would do for Israel in Canaan. Verse 10 suggests that the earlier inhabitants of Moab, the Emites, were as fearsome as the Anakites, their counterparts west of the Dead Sea, for they too were great, numerous, and tall. Whereas the Moabites identified these gigantic races of people as Emites, the Israelites called them Rephaites (cf. vv. 20 – 21).[9]

Syntactically verses 14 – 15 also function as a parenthetical footnote. It seems that for Moses, crossing the Wadi Zered was a significant milestone. The recollection of Yahweh's charge to cross the Zered (v. 13) triggered a reflective glance backward. The generation that had been lost in the desert perished not for lack of water or food, but because Yahweh had become their enemy and had taken action against them, just as he had sworn. The book of Numbers records several specific events that precipitated the unleashing of Yahweh's wrath, but these account for only a small fraction of the casualties of divine fury. Yahweh's hand that had fought so

---

7. On Chemosh as the god of Moab, see 1 Kings 11:33 and 2 Kings 23:13; on the Moabites as "the people of Chemosh," see Num. 21:29.

8. The brook Zered is generally identified with modern Wadi Ḥasa, which in the rainy season flows into the Arabah Valley at the south end of the Dead Sea.

9. See Job 26:5; Ps. 88:10[11]; Prov. 2:18; Isa. 14:9; 26:14, 19. On the Rephaites, see H. Rouillard, "Rephaim," *DDD*, 692 – 700.

triumphantly against the Egyptians[10] was now turned against the Israelites and would not cease its devastating work until every member of that generation had been rooted out.

Moses' Recollection of Bene Ammon (2:16–23)

BECAUSE MOSES IS FOCUSED on getting the Israelites to the Promised Land rather than reporting encounters with the Moabites, he moves immediately to the next phase of the nation's adventures.[11] Like the previous episode, this one consists of a narrative introduction (vv. 16–17), a quotation of a speech by Yahweh (vv. 18–19), and a parenthetical historical note (vv. 20–23).

Once the last warriors of the faithless generation had died, Yahweh ordered the Israelites to move into the homestretch of their long journey, past the territory of the Ammonites. Like the Moabites, the Ammonites were descendants of Lot through his (younger) daughter. The conventional national name *benê ʿammôn* memorializes the incestuous sexual affair in the cave outside Sodom more explicitly than "Moab." Yahweh's instructions concerning Bene Ammon in verse 19 were virtually identical to his comments concerning Moab in verse 9. He prohibited the Israelites from harassing the Ammonites or from trying to take any of their territory, for he had given their land as their own possession. Here he claims authority normally attributed the Milkom, the acknowledged patron deity of Bene Ammon.[12]

The remainder of the report concerning Bene Ammon is taken up with a parenthetical note concerning the persons they displaced as occupants of the land (vv. 20–23). Their territory encompassed an amorphous region northwest of Moab around Rabbath-Ammon (modern Amman, Jordan) under the rule of Sihon king of Heshbon. But like the Moabites, the Ammonites had their own name for the fearsome indigenous population they displaced; they called them Zamzummites (Gen. 14:5). All these names reflect the terrorizing effect these gigantic people had on outsiders: Rephaites ("ghosts"), Emites ("terror"), Anakites ("giants"), and Zamzummites ("confused/threatening sound"). Just as Yahweh had enabled the descendants of Esau to dispossess and destroy the Horites in Seir and to occupy their land

---

10. Cf. Ex. 3:20; 7:4–5; 9:3, 15; 13:3, 9, 14, 16; 15:6, 9, 12; 18:10; 32:11. Ironically, this was precisely the fate the Israelites had requested in Ex. 16:3.

11. Num. 21:13 summarizes the trek around Moab with one simple sentence. The Israelites had several critical encounters with the Moabites, but these all transpired after the defeat of the Amorite kings while they were camped at Shittim on the plains of Moab opposite Jericho (Num. 22–25).

12. On Milkom, the patron deity of Bene Ammon, see E. Puech, "Milcom," *DDD*, 575–76.

(v. 22), so he had destroyed the Zamzummites and allowed the Ammonites to dispossess them and occupy their land (v. 21).

Verse 23 adds a puzzling reference to historical events far away in the region of Philistia on the southwest coast of Palestine, where the Avvites were destroyed and dispossessed by the Caphtorites or Philistines (cf. Josh 13:3−4). While scholars debate how the Philistines might have traveled to Palestine, their original goal seems to have been to settle in Egypt. However, Rameses III defeated them in about 1190 BC and settled the vanquished forces in the coastal towns of southern Canaan. In the mid-twelfth century, the Philistines drove out their Egyptian overlords, forming the Philistine Pentapolis, a federation of five major city-states: Ashdod, Ashkelon, Ekron, Gath, and Gaza. In the providence of God, the Philistines arrived in Palestine (which is named after them) from the west, at the same time as the Israelites were moving in from the east and trying to establish their authority over the land. Conflict was inevitable.[13]

THE PERMANENT THEOLOGICAL LESSONS deriving from this part of Moses' first address relate especially to God's providential activity, both with respect to his own people and with broader humanity.

Faithful to his promises. Centuries earlier Yahweh had promised to Abraham, Isaac, and Jacob that their descendants would one day claim this land. While this plan may appear to have been forgotten for thirty-eight years, the progress of the Israelites from Kadesh Barnea to the Gulf of Aqaba, around Seir to the Wadi Zered, and on past the land of Moab demonstrates that Yahweh had not forgotten his oath. He was setting the stage for their triumphant entry into the Promised Land from across the Jordan opposite Jericho.

Faithful to his threats. This part of Moses' speech also demonstrates that God is faithful to his threats. Because the faithless Israelites had refused to enter the Promised Land from Kadesh Barnea, Yahweh swore to destroy that generation in the desert and start over with a new people. The image of two million Israelite corpses (if one takes the registrations of Numbers 2 and 26 at face value) buried in the desert is not only tragic, but also seems shamefully wasteful to the modern reader. Could God not have relented just a little from his harsh response to their infidelity? And were not many of the Israelites victims of the system and particularly faithless leadership?

But Yahweh's actions are not governed by sentimentality; he acts according to principle. For a people who were ungrateful for divine grace

---

13. See Judg. 13−16; 1 Sam. 4−6; etc.

experienced over and over again and who repeatedly clamored to return to Egypt, the penalty did indeed suit the crime. God is not obligated to people who do not take seriously the privileges of divine election, salvation, covenant, and care.

God's involvement in human affairs. This text also teaches a profound lesson on God's involvement in all human affairs. In later times the Israelites would take pride in their unique election for covenant relationship with God. However, as Amos will remind his hearers in Amos 9:7, apart from faith and covenant loyalty, the migration of Israel from Egypt was a migration like that of any other nation. And as Paul would declare to the Athenians more than a millennium later, "From one man he made every nation of men, that they should inhabit the whole earth; and he determined the times set for them and the exact places where they should live" (Acts 17:26).

God has been involved in the migration of peoples from the beginning. Even though they made no claim of allegiance to the God of Israel, behind the displacement of the Horites by the descendants of Esau, the Emites by Moabites, the Zamzummites by the Bene Ammon, and the Avvites by the Philistines, Moses recognizes the hidden hand of God. Yahweh, the God of Israel, exercises sovereignty over all nations in all times. Like pieces on a chessboard, he moves them around; he removes some and replaces them with others, and he determines their places.

As the story of Israel in the land unfolded, we observe that Yahweh's response to persistent rebellion would be to hand them the same fate as the Horites, Emites, Zamzummites, and Avvites. A series of invasions punctuated Israel's history in the first millennium BC, but each came in God's time and in God's order. In the end Yahweh used the Assyrians to discipline the northern kingdom, deporting their population and replacing them with foreigners.

But this could not be God's final strategy, for he had made an eternal promise to Abraham that his descendants would be his people in his land forever. So to punish Judah and Jerusalem he brought in the Babylonians, who settled the Judaeans in advantageous circumstances by the Kebar River, where they could maintain their communal institutions and be preserved for future renewal. When the time for restoration came, God brought in a new player, the Persians, who assumed that happy gods would look on them with favor. So the Persian emperors authorized the return of subject peoples to their homelands, encouraging them to reconstruct their sacred temples and reinstitute indigenous religions.[14] As benefactors of this

---

14. See the inscription on the renowned Cyrus cylinder in *ANET*, 315−16; *COS*, 2:314−316.

---

general imperial policy, the Judaeans returned to Jerusalem in 538 BC to rebuild the community of faith in their homeland.

ON THE SURFACE THIS text seems removed from the world in which we live. Exotic names like Horites, Zamzummites, Emites, Avvites, and Anakites are the stuff of myths and legends. However, this passage reminds us that human history is a history of migrations, conflicts, and claims to land. But behind the movements of peoples we see the hand of God—the same hand that guided Moabites and Edomites and Israelites also guided the aboriginal North Americans in their migration across the Bering Strait and in the past four or five centuries European migrations to North America. Nor are the movements of Asians and Latinos to formerly largely Anglo North America beyond the divine control. This does not mean migrating peoples are justified in abusing indigenous populations, but nothing happens by chance. The observation that Edomites dispossessed the Horites (v. 12) and then that Yahweh destroyed the Horites before them (v. 22) point to the synergy between free human and sovereign divine actions.

This text has special significance for the present crisis in the Middle East, reminding us that God's eyes are not only on his chosen people. They are also on the Transjordanian lands, now taken up by the Hashemite kingdom of Jordan, and the Sinai peninsula, which is part of Egypt. The same God who preserved this land for Moabites and Ammonites has given it to the Jordanians and Egyptians. The church would do well to encourage modern Israel to treat their neighbors with the respect that Yahweh had demanded from the ancestors of this people more than three thousand years ago. Israelite title to the land is not unconditional. Apart from faith the migration of the Israelites is merely one migration among many (Amos 9:7). There is no automatic title to God's promises for those who refuse to trust him and serve him. This is true for the physical descendants of Jacob as well as for those who claim to be his spiritual heirs.

Finally, from a terrestrial perspective, this text teaches Israel and all who read it that land is a gift delivered by Yahweh himself. The references to these fearful peoples highlight the truth that when God begins to do his work of grace, no one can stand in his way. The enemies may appear huge, numerous, and strong, but the church must remember that Yahweh, the God of Israel, is mightier than all. Greater is he who is in you than he who is in the world (1 John 4:4).

‎۱۷

"Set out now and cross the Arnon Gorge. See, I have given into your hand Sihon the Amorite, king of Heshbon, and his country. Begin to take possession of it and engage him in battle. ²⁵This very day I will begin to put the terror and fear of you on all the nations under heaven. They will hear reports of you and will tremble and be in anguish because of you."

²⁶From the desert of Kedemoth I sent messengers to Sihon king of Heshbon offering peace and saying, ²⁷"Let us pass through your country. We will stay on the main road; we will not turn aside to the right or to the left. ²⁸Sell us food to eat and water to drink for their price in silver. Only let us pass through on foot—²⁹as the descendants of Esau, who live in Seir, and the Moabites, who live in Ar, did for us—until we cross the Jordan into the land the LORD our God is giving us." ³⁰But Sihon king of Heshbon refused to let us pass through. For the LORD your God had made his spirit stubborn and his heart obstinate in order to give him into your hands, as he has now done.

³¹The LORD said to me, "See, I have begun to deliver Sihon and his country over to you. Now begin to conquer and possess his land."

³²When Sihon and all his army came out to meet us in battle at Jahaz, ³³the LORD our God delivered him over to us and we struck him down, together with his sons and his whole army. ³⁴At that time we took all his towns and completely destroyed them—men, women and children. We left no survivors. ³⁵But the livestock and the plunder from the towns we had captured we carried off for ourselves. ³⁶From Aroer on the rim of the Arnon Gorge, and from the town in the gorge, even as far as Gilead, not one town was too strong for us. The LORD our God gave us all of them. ³⁷But in accordance with the command of the LORD our God, you did not encroach on any of the land of the Ammonites, neither the land along the course of the Jabbok nor that around the towns in the hills.

³:¹Next we turned and went up along the road toward Bashan, and Og king of Bashan with his whole army marched out to meet us in battle at Edrei. ²The LORD said to me,

"Do not be afraid of him, for I have handed him over to you with his whole army and his land. Do to him what you did to Sihon king of the Amorites, who reigned in Heshbon."

³So the LORD our God also gave into our hands Og king of Bashan and all his army. We struck them down, leaving no survivors. ⁴At that time we took all his cities. There was not one of the sixty cities that we did not take from them—the whole region of Argob, Og's kingdom in Bashan. ⁵All these cities were fortified with high walls and with gates and bars, and there were also a great many unwalled villages. ⁶We completely destroyed them, as we had done with Sihon king of Heshbon, destroying every city—men, women and children. ⁷But all the livestock and the plunder from their cities we carried off for ourselves.

⁸So at that time we took from these two kings of the Amorites the territory east of the Jordan, from the Arnon Gorge as far as Mount Hermon. ⁹(Hermon is called Sirion by the Sidonians; the Amorites call it Senir.) ¹⁰We took all the towns on the plateau, and all Gilead, and all Bashan as far as Salecah and Edrei, towns of Og's kingdom in Bashan. ¹¹(Only Og king of Bashan was left of the remnant of the Rephaites. His bed was made of iron and was more than thirteen feet long and six feet wide. It is still in Rabbah of the Ammonites.)

AS MOSES PROCEEDS IN his historical review, his recollections become more detailed. This section consists of three parts: two battle reports, the first describing Israel's defeat of Sihon king of Heshbon (2:24–37), and the second recounting the victory over Og king of Bashan (3:1–7), followed by a summary statement and footnote (3:8–11).

The Conquest of Sihon of Heshbon (2:24–37)

IF WE DISREGARD FOR a moment verses 20–23, which are parenthetical, we notice that verse 19 flows smoothly into verse 24. The absence of any reference to Yahweh as speaker and the use of second person imperatives in verse 24 confirm that verses 24–25 continue his speech in verses 18–19. This episode begins with a directive from the divine Commander to cross the Wadi Arnon (modern Wadi el-Mujib), which served as the boundary between the Moabites and the Amorites of the Transjordan (Num. 21:13). After the instructions on how to deal with the Ammonites in verses 18–19, we expect an encounter with these people, but this does not happen. Instead, Yahweh's eyes are fixed on another challenge. Once Israel had crossed the Arnon the Amorites represented the only obstacle separating them from the Promised Land.

Sihon ruled the southern Amorites from his capital Heshbon, modern Tell Hesban.[1] His territory extended from the Jordan in the west to the land of Bene Ammon and the desert on the east, and from Wadi Jabbok in the north to Wadi Arnon in the south. God's promises of land to the patriarchs never included the territory east of the Jordan. The narratives in Numbers suggest that Israel's claim to this region was an afterthought, in response to the vacuum created when the Israelites eliminated the Amorites. In Moses' reminiscences both the defeat of the Amorites and the Israelite claim to this land seem to have been foregone conclusions.[2]

Yahweh's command to the Israelites consists of six imperatives (the first is not represented in the NIV): "Arise! Set out! Cross the Wadi Arnon! Begin! Take possession! Engage him in battle!"[3] This charge is accompanied by two significant promises: Yahweh had already given Sihon into the Israelites' hands,[4] and from this day on, he would send shockwaves throughout the earth, causing people to tremble in fright when they heard of Israel's triumphs. Remarkably the statement highlights Israel's actions and places Yahweh in the background. The peoples throughout the world (lit., "the peoples under the whole heaven") would tremble and writhe (in anguish) *before them* when they heard reports *of them* because they were in dread *of them* and in awe *of them*.[5] Rahab's testimony in Joshua 2:9–11 and the narrator's comment in Numbers 22:3 indicate that this actually happened among the Canaanites and Moabites.

Moses reports that from Kedemoth[6] he dispatched an emissary[7] to Sihon ostensibly with an offer of peace and a request for permission for safe

---

1. On Heshbon, see L. T. Geraty, "Heshbon," *ABD*, 3:181–84.

2. Moses' overtly theological interpretation of these events contrasts sharply with the Numbers account (Num. 21:21–32), which does not even mention the name of Yahweh.

3. Israel is commanded to do to Sihon what they were prohibited from doing to the Edomites, Moabites, and Ammonites. Note the use of the same verb, *hitgārâ* ("to provoke," "engage in battle") as in vv. 5, 9, 19.

4. The promise reverses Israel's accusation in 1:27 that Yahweh had given them into the hands of the Amorites.

5. Cf. Ex. 23:27, which has Yahweh sending out "my terror" as if it were a concrete object going ahead of Israel.

6. Josh. 13:18 locates Kedemoth in the territory of Reuben, suggesting that Moses had crossed the Arnon before he sent the envoys.

7. A *malʾāk*, whether human or angelic, is an officially authorized messenger commissioned by a superior to conduct business on his behalf.

passage through Sihon's territory. While the text does not say that Moses did so in response to Yahweh's command, since the action was in line with policies concerning conflicts with foreign peoples outlined later in Deut. 20:10–15, these Amorites were not by definition targets of Israelite conquest. Moses' request for safe passage through Sihon's territory echoes Yahweh's earlier instructions on dealing with the Edomites (vv. 4–6) and the actual account of his overtures to Edom as reported in Numbers 20:14–17. Moses promised to stay on the highway; his forces would not leave the road to pillage the countryside as invading armies customarily did. But they would need resources, so he requested that Sihon provide them with food and water, for which the Israelites would gladly pay; they were just passing through (cf. Num. 20:19).

Given the negative picture of the Edomite response in Numbers 20:14–21 and the Moabite hostility in Numbers 22–24, Moses' positive portrayal of these nations in verse 29 is surprising. Has he forgotten so quickly? Obviously not, for later he will single out Ammonites and Moabites for *not* having offered them bread or water. These comments sound like diplomatic rhetoric, stretching the truth for the sake of argument, a common feature in political negotiations (cf. Jephthah's speech in Judg. 11).

The description of Sihon's response to Moses' overture recalls the hardening of Pharaoh's heart in Exodus 5–11. Although like Pharaoh, Sihon was inexcusable for his disposition, Moses attributes his response directly to Yahweh, who "made his spirit stubborn" and "his heart obstinate." He also declares explicitly the divine purpose in hardening Sihon: "in order to give him into your hands." With the concluding phrase, (lit.) "as [it is] this day," he draws attention to a present reality whose roots lay in past actions.

In verses 31–37 Moses describes the battle against Sihon. The narrative provides few details, but in its general structure it provides a model for how the Israelites would engage the Canaanites in their battles for the Promised Land. As Commander-in-Chief Yahweh ordered the attack, offering words of encouragement and promises of victory, to which Israel responded by defeating the enemy forces, utterly destroying the population, and claiming the territory promised. The sevenfold repletion of "all" in verses 32–37 emphasizes the completeness of Israel's obedience and the totality of victory. This pattern continues in the sequel (3:3–10).[8]

Verse 32 describes Sihon's response as if he imagined himself to be a free moral agent. Apparently thinking this Israelite rabble would be easy

---

8. Moses hereby contrasts the faithfulness of the people in this event with the infidelity and faithlessness of the previous generation at Kadesh Barnea. So also Tigay, *Deuteronomy*, 32.

picking, the Amorite king brought his troops out of their fortifications and committed them all to battle at Jahaz.[9] In verses 33 – 34 Moses summarizes the outcome of the battle. His description reflects two key principles involved in the biblical perspective on historical events. (1) As Sovereign over all nations and over all historical events, Yahweh delivered Sihon into Israel's hands. It is assumed that Sihon's gods could not defend him. (2) The victory was achieved by concentrated human effort. Moses notes three specific actions: they captured every one of Sihon's fortifications,[10] they completely annihilated the populations of every town,[11] but they excluded the animals and the property from the law of *ḥērem* and claimed them as booty.[12]

Verses 36 – 37 describe the scope of Israel's victory. From Aroer[13] on the edge of the Wadi Arnon in the south to the Gilead highlands in the north, no Amorite fortification could hold back the Israelites. While the description assumes the Jordan River marked the western extremity of the territory conquered by Israel, Moses defines the amorphous eastern fringe of Sihon's territory ethnically. In keeping with Yahweh's instructions (vv. 18 – 19), the Israelites did not encroach on the territory of Bene Ammon, who occupied the land to the east, on the other side of the Jabbok (modern Wadi Zerqa).[14]

The Conquest of Og of Bashan (3:1 – 11)

STANDING ON THE THRESHOLD of the Promised Land, the Israelites had one more battle to fight — against Og king of Bashan. The name Bashan

---

9. Like Kedemoth this site was included in Reuben's tribal allotment (Josh. 13:18) and later designated a Levitical city (Josh. 21:36), though later prophets (Isa. 15:4; Jer. 48:21, 34) agree with the indigenous Mesha inscription in locating Jahaz within Moabite territory. The location of Jahaz is unknown, but of the sites that have been proposed, Khirbet Medeiniyeh on the Wadi al Themed seems the most likely. See J. A. Dearman, "Jahaz," *ABD*, 3:612.

10. The NIV reads "towns." See the comment on 1:22 above.

11. The verb *beḥʿrîm* (the verb occurs only in the causative Hiphil and Hophal stems), rendered "completely destroyed" in the NIV (see NIV text note), involves a sacred act of irrevocable consecration to God and absolute proscription from human use. For further discussion of the concept of *ḥērem* and its ethical implications, see below on 7:2.

12. The addition of "we left no survivor" occurs especially in accounts of wars with the Canaanites. Cf. Deut. 3:3; Josh. 8:22; 10:28 – 40; 11:8; but see also 2 Kings 10:11.

13. Aroer is identified with Khirbet Araʿir, a strategic fortress a mile up the hill from the stream that guarded the King's Highway at the southern checkpoint on the territorial border. "The town in the gorge" probably refers to a secondary fortress in the valley, perhaps guarding Aroer's water supply. Technically the name Gilead derives from the range of hills running parallel to the Jordan from the Wadi Hesban to the Wadi Yarmuk.

14. Although for most of its course the Jabbok flows from east to west, the wadi begins northeast of Rabbath Ammon and arcs from south to north for a considerable distance near its source in the eastern highlands.

---

refers to the mountain range north of the Jabbok River, east of the Sea of Galilee, as far as Mount Hermon southwest of Damascus (Deut. 32:14; Ps. 22:12[13]; Amos 4:1). Verse 10 suggests Og's kingdom extended south to Salecah and Edrei (cf. 1:4). Situated strategically on a tributary of the Yarmuk, the southern border of Og's territory, and on the King's Highway, Edrei was to this king what Aroer was to Sihon (cf. above on v. 36).[15] Ashtaroth (modern Tell Ashterah) was located approximately ten miles up the King's Highway, twenty miles east of the Sea of Galilee.

Omitting a command from Yahweh to continue the campaign northward (cf. v. 24), Moses recalls rather matter-of-factly that the Israelites "turned and went up along the road toward Bashan," as if this were merely one more stage in Israel's itinerary of "turning" (2:1), "passing by" (2:8), "crossing" (2:13), and "setting out and passing through" (2:24) one land after another. Og interpreted the Israelites' movements as a hostile military maneuver. Like Sihon (2:32), he mobilized his troops and challenged Israel to battle at Edrei.

Then the voice of Yahweh broke through to Moses with a word of encouragement and a challenge (v. 2). Yahweh encouraged him and his people not to fear, because he had already delivered Og, all his people, and his land into their hands. But as elsewhere in the Scripture, for every divine promise there is a call for human response. Yahweh challenged Moses to deal with Og exactly as he had with Sihon in Heshbon.

In verses 3 – 7 Moses describes the course of the battle. With stereotypical language, he begins with a summary statement reporting the divine involvement ("the LORD our God also gave into our hands Og king of Bashan and all his army") and the human response ("we struck them down"). In the recollection that follows, Moses highlights the scope of the Israelites' victory: (1) Yahweh delivered Og and *all* his people over to Israel; (2) they captured *all* his towns; (3) they took the *entire* Argob region; (4) *all* these towns were heavily fortified; (5) they imposed the law of ḥērem on *all* these towns; and (6) they took *all* the animals and spoils as booty. Furthermore, they struck them until not a single person survived (v. 3).

Clarifying the meaning of "too strong/high" in 2:36, verse 5 adds that the towns were fortified with high walls and gates. Since the fortified towns were not able to withstand Israel's onslaught, it is not surprising that they also captured all the unwalled villages. Entering the towns, the Israelites annihilated the population according to the law of ḥērem and claimed all the livestock and property as booty (vv. 6–7).

---

15. Archaeologists identify the site with modern Darᶜa in southern Syria near the Jordanian border.

Moses concludes his recollections of the battles against Sihon and Og with a summary statement of the Israelites' conquests (v. 8). They took the Amorite region east of the Jordan from the Wadi Arnon in the south to Mount Hermon in the north (cf. Josh 12:5; 13:11).[16] Verse 9 interrupts the review with another parenthetical comment, this time clarifying the reference to Mount Hermon. Apparently Mount Hermon was the Israelite name for a mountain that the Sidonians (representing the Phoenicians) called Hermon Sirion, and one that the Amorites (who previously controlled it) called Senir.[17] In verse 10 Moses reiterates the scope of the Israelites' conquests, focusing on the highlands. Moving from south to north, he lists the conquered regions.[18]

A final footnote at the end of Moses' recollection of the defeat of Sihon and Og notes that as a Rephaite, Og was one of the last survivors of the gigantic pre-Amorite aboriginal peoples in this region.[19] As concrete evidence of his size Moses refers to Og's bed, which apparently was on display in Rabbah of Bene Ammon (the Ammonite capital) at the time this note was written. Og's bed was impressive. It was huge: nine cubits long by four cubits wide (13.5 feet by 6 feet). And it was made of iron. Since iron was a precious metal in the Late Bronze Age, this was probably a bed made of wood and adorned with iron, similar to Solomon's great throne, which 1 Kings 10:18 describes as (lit.) "a throne of ivory."[20] This note invites the

---

16. Modern Jebel al-Sheikh, "mountain of the chieftain," which rises to a height of 9,323 feet at the south end of the Anti-Lebanon range. The name Hermon (*ḥermôn*) derives from the same root as *ḥērem*, probably because it was considered a "consecrated place." See further R. Arav, "Hermon, Mount," *ABD*, 3:158–60.

17. Both names recur in the Old Testament (1 Chron. 5:23; Ps. 29:6; Song 4:8; Ezek. 27:5–6) and are attested in extrabiblical writings.

18. "All the towns on the plateau" refers to the fortifications in the highlands between the Arnon and the Wadi Heshbon and the Jabbok (cf. 4:43; Josh. 13:9, 16, 17, 21; etc.); "all Gilead" refers to the uplands between the Wadi Heshbon and the Yarmuk River, divided in half by the Wadi Jabbok; and "all Bashan," refers to the hill country north and east of the Yarmuk, the southern border being marked by Salecah and Edrei. On Edrei, see above on v. 1. Salecah is usually identified with modern Salkhad, a town on the southwest base of Mount Hauron.

19. On the Rephaites, see above on 2:10–11.

20. Similarly the "iron chariots" in Josh. 17:16 and Judg. 1:19; 4:3, 13. For discussion, see A. R. Millard, "King Og's Bed and Other Ancient Ironmongery," in *Ascribe to the Lord: Biblical and Other Studies in Memory of Peter C. Craigie* (ed. L. Eslinger and G. Taylor; JSOTSup 67; Sheffield: Sheffield Academic, 1988), 481–92. This interpretation is preferable to the older view that what is described as an iron bed was actually a sarcophagus made of basalt, whose color and metallic appearance remind an observer of iron. See A. D. H. Mayes, *Deuteronomy* (NCB; Grand Rapids: Eerdmans, 1981), 144.

ancient reader to check the narrator's veracity and to confirm the magnitude of Israel's victory.[21]

WHAT PEOPLE OF FAITH can achieve. Moses' recollections of the conquests of the Transjordanian Amorite kingdoms teach us what people of faith can achieve. In contrast to the previous generation, which through rebellion and unbelief had disqualified itself from entry into the Promised Land from Kadesh Barnea, this account shows there is no limit to what God is able to do for and through his people if they trust him. Sihon and Og, the giants of the Transjordan, symbolize all that was opposed to Yahweh. Whereas earlier in Hebron the scouts had incidentally observed the presence of gigantic figures (1:28), here the giants were in charge. By sending his people into the Rephaite heartland, Yahweh sent an early signal that when his people entered the conflict with faith and courage, no one could stand in their way. This provided the Israelites with an important precedent as they entered the Promised Land.

Principles of a theology of war. This narrative account illustrates several principles that underlie the Mosaic theology of war.[22] Israel's military engagements with outsiders were always deemed theological affairs. Although economic factors (e.g., the need for *Lebensraum*, "space to live") and political ambition (kings' desire for greater power) often contributed to the initiation and the conduct of war, like their ancient Near Eastern neighbors, the Israelites believed that ultimately God determined the outcome of all their military engagements. The Israelites' wars of conquest, particularly their seizure of the land of Canaan, have often been referred to as "holy wars."[23] Although the expression rightly acknowledges the sacral nature of war in the Old Testament, because the expression never occurs in the

---

21. How the bed found its way to Rabbah of Bene Ammon (modern Amman) we may only speculate. Perhaps the Ammonites claimed it as booty taken from the Israelites during the time of Jephthah (Judg. 10–12).

22. More will be said on the subject in the commentary on Deut. 7 and 20.

23. G. von Rad, in particular, has popularized the notion of "holy war." He writes, "These wars were then holy wars, in which Jahweh himself fought in defence of his own people; they were sacral operations, before which men sanctified themselves—submitted, that is, to abstention from sexual intercourse—and whose termination was the ban (*ḥrm*), the assignment of the spoil to Yahweh." G. von Rad, *Old Testament Theology*, vol. 1, *The Theology of Israel's Historical Traditions* (trans. D. M. G. Stalker; New York: Harper & Row, 1962), 17. Cf. idem, *Studies in Deuteronomy* (trans. David Stalker; SBT 9; London: SCM, 1953), 45–59; idem, *Holy War in Ancient Israel* (trans. M. J. Dawn; Grand Rapids: Eerdmans, 1991), 115–27.

Bible and because of its negative connotations today, the expression is best avoided and replaced with an expression like "Yahweh wars."[24]

Although the theology of warfare reflected in Deuteronomy shares many features with perceptions of war among the surrounding nations,[25] it also offers a distinctly Israelite perspective.

1. As the divine Commander-in-Chief, Yahweh identifies the military target. He excludes Edomites, Moabites, and Ammonites, and he zeroes in on the Amorite kings and their people in the Transjordan, presumably because they stood in the way of his people's manifest destiny.

2. Yahweh initiates the war, telling the Israelites when to engage the enemy.

3. Yahweh determines the strategy for the war—in this instance, telling Israel to cross the Jordan, possess the land, and contend with him in battle (2:24), capturing the cities, annihilating the population, and claiming the property as booty (2:34–37).

4. Yahweh accompanies Israel into battle. Although there is no explicit reference here to Yahweh's presence within the Israelite military camp, with an eye on 1:42, we may conclude that this is the case here as well.

5. Yahweh engages in psychological warfare, controlling the disposition of the enemy toward himself and toward Israel, so that ultimately his objectives are achieved. Specifically, Yahweh hardened the heart of the enemy king so he would reject overtures of peace (2:30), and he put the fear and dread of Israel on the peoples everywhere, demoralizing them totally (2:25).

6. Yahweh delivered the enemies and their lands into Israel's hand (2:30–31, 33, 36; 3:3).

In this picture Israel functions as the army of Yahweh. But Moses says nothing about specific military actions taken by the Israelites. He states simply that they took the cities, imposed *ḥērem* on the population, and claimed the animals and property as booty, but he seems uninterested in the logistics of the campaign—how this unwieldy band of citizen soldiers marched from city to city, the weapons they used, how the battles were

---

24. So also T. Longman III, "Warfare," *New Dictionary of Biblical Theology* (ed. T. D. Alexander et al.; Downers Grove, IL: InterVarsity Press, 2000), 836.

25. For discussion, see M. Weinfeld, "Divine Intervention in War in Ancient Israel and in the Ancient Near East," in *History, Historiography and Interpretation: Studies in Biblical and Cuneiform Literature* (eds. H. Tadmor and M. Weinfeld; Jerusalem: Magnes and Hebrew Univ. Press, 1983), 124–31.

actually conducted, what methods they employed to capture the superbly fortified cities with walls and towers reaching to the sky and elaborate gate systems, or how they actually captured Sihon and Og. Moses' silence on these matters throws into sharp relief his contention that the primary resources needed by the people for the battles ahead were courage and faith in Yahweh, who would fight for them.

In portraying Israel's battles this way, especially his treatment of Sihon, Moses' address forces the reader to contemplate the relationship between divine sovereignty and human freedom. Just as Yahweh had done to Pharaoh forty years earlier, he hardened the heart of Sihon in order that Yahweh's goals might be achieved. But this did not rob Sihon of personal freedom to act, nor did it absolve him of responsibility for his actions. The divine action does not reduce him to a puppet on a string, nor does it make God into a divine puppeteer. Deuteronomy and the rest of the Scriptures affirm with equal vigor divine sovereignty over earthly affairs and human freedom and responsibility for one's own conduct. How these two factors can both be true at the same time defies human logic. People of faith can only stand back in awe and wonder.

SOME YEARS AGO MY son and his wife were involved in a Bible study going through the book of Joshua. The entire group was troubled by the Israelites' treatment of the Canaanites. In fact, few issues in Old Testament interpretation are as difficult as the Lord's command to the Israelites to dispossess the Canaanites and take over their land, along with his command to wipe out the Amorites east of the Jordan. How could a good God command the elimination of a whole race, including men, women, and children? Is this not genocide of the worst sort? And what is to stop us from carrying out similar actions in the name of God against entire peoples in our own time?

These texts are so troubling that many reject the Old Testament and its God because of this single issue, and many refuse the gospel of the New Testament because of its guilt by association, for the Old Testament is part of the Christian Bible. How should we answer these questions? While none of the following responses below is satisfying in and of itself, all represent factors to be considered in coming to grips with the issue.[26]

---

26. See also C. J. H. Wright, *Old Testament Ethics for the People of God* (Downers Grove: InterVarsity, 2004), 472–80; idem, *The God I Don't Understand: Reflections on Tough Questions of Faith* (Grand Rapids: Zondervan, 2008), 76–108.

1. As Creator of all things and all human beings and as sovereign over all, God can do anything he wants with anyone and be right in doing so. He was Israel's Commander-in-Chief. He accounts to no one for his actions or his commands, and by definition he does what is right. If he decides to command the Israelites to eliminate the Canaanites, he is perfectly within his rights. Obviously this answer will satisfy few but hardcore Calvinists.

2. The ways of God are a mystery. Since we will never completely understand him, we might as well relax with the questions in our minds. Isaiah 55:8–9 offers some consolation.

3. According to the biblical picture of the Canaanites, these peoples were extremely wicked, and their annihilation represented God's judgment for their sin. The destruction of the Canaanites was neither the first nor the last time God would do this. The differences between the Canaanites' fate and the fate of humanity (except for Noah's family) as described in Genesis 6–9 involve scale and agency. With the Canaanites, as with many others in history, Yahweh used human beings rather than natural disasters or plagues and sickness (Lev. 26; Deut. 28).

4. God never intended for the Israelites to make the policy of *ḥērem* as a general policy toward outsiders. Deuteronomy 7:1 expressly identifies and thereby delimits the target peoples. The Israelites were not to follow these policies against Aramaeans or Edomites or Egyptians, or anyone else (cf. Deut. 20:10–18). Contrary to the way Christians have often used these texts in past history, this policy provides no justification at all for Christian atrocities committed against Jews and Muslims in the context of the Crusades or for Europeans' claim to some sort of "manifest destiny" in their dispossession and slaughter of native North Americans.

5. The Canaanites suffered a fate that ultimately all sinners will face: the judgment of God. The difference between them and other lost peoples is that they (especially the children) met their doom earlier than most. But in the last analysis, apart from the grace of God we are all Canaanites, and it is only by divine grace that modern nations are not cut off as they were.

6. During biblical times people assumed a sense of corporate identity that is difficult for modern Westerners to understand. According to the ancient Near Eastern ideal, one found one's significance and identity in relation to the community. When one member hurt, they all hurt; when one prospered, they all prospered (1 Cor. 12–14). Accordingly, few ancients would have objected to the fact that the

general population shared the fate of kings and children shared the fate of their parents.

7. God's elimination of the Canaanites was a necessary step in the history of salvation. In order for Israel to achieve the goals that God had established for them — that they might declare to the world his glory and grace — they needed a clean slate and a holy land. Because they resisted Israel's migration through their territory, the war of extermination against Canaanites was extended to Sihon and Og.

8. Although the Canaanites as a whole were targets of God's judgment, they had at least forty years of advance warning (see Rahab's confession in Josh. 2:8–11). The conquest of Canaan caught few by surprise. Rahab illustrates the gracious fact that any individual who declared faith in Yahweh would be spared. Rahab's incorporation into the community of faith was so complete that she became the ancestor of Jesus! (Matt. 1).

9. God really does not play favorites. Yes, he chose Abraham and his descendants to be his covenant people, but Deuteronomy warns the Israelites repeatedly that if they ever forget God and behave like Canaanites, they will experience the same fate as the Canaanites (4:25–28; 7:25–26; 8:19–20; 28:15–68).

None of these answers will satisfy everyone, and none of them should be taken in isolation. But when we consider this complex of considerations, we may relax, knowing that God is good and God is always right. The challenge for us is that we treasure his grace in our own lives and pray for him to extend that grace to others. Perhaps when they see what God has done for us, like Rahab non-Christians will confess faith in our God.

Deuteronomy 3:12-29

Of the land that we took over at that time, I gave the Reubenites and the Gadites the territory north of Aroer by the Arnon Gorge, including half the hill country of Gilead, together with its towns. ¹³The rest of Gilead and also all of Bashan, the kingdom of Og, I gave to the half tribe of Manasseh. (The whole region of Argob in Bashan used to be known as a land of the Rephaites. ¹⁴Jair, a descendant of Manasseh, took the whole region of Argob as far as the border of the Geshurites and the Maacathites; it was named after him, so that to this day Bashan is called Havvoth Jair.) ¹⁵And I gave Gilead to Makir. ¹⁶But to the Reubenites and the Gadites I gave the territory extending from Gilead down to the Arnon Gorge (the middle of the gorge being the border) and out to the Jabbok River, which is the border of the Ammonites. ¹⁷Its western border was the Jordan in the Arabah, from Kinnereth to the Sea of the Arabah (the Salt Sea), below the slopes of Pisgah.

¹⁸I commanded you at that time: "The LORD your God has given you this land to take possession of it. But all your able-bodied men, armed for battle, must cross over ahead of your brother Israelites. ¹⁹However, your wives, your children and your livestock (I know you have much livestock) may stay in the towns I have given you, ²⁰until the LORD gives rest to your brothers as he has to you, and they too have taken over the land that the LORD your God is giving them, across the Jordan. After that, each of you may go back to the possession I have given you."

²¹At that time I commanded Joshua: "You have seen with your own eyes all that the LORD your God has done to these two kings. The LORD will do the same to all the kingdoms over there where you are going. ²²Do not be afraid of them; the LORD your God himself will fight for you."

²³At that time I pleaded with the LORD: ²⁴"O Sovereign LORD, you have begun to show to your servant your greatness and your strong hand. For what god is there in heaven or on earth who can do the deeds and mighty works you do? ²⁵Let me go over and see the good land beyond the Jordan—that fine hill country and Lebanon."

²⁶But because of you the LORD was angry with me and would not listen to me. "That is enough," the LORD said. "Do not speak to me anymore about this matter. ²⁷Go up to the top of Pisgah and look west and north and south and east. Look at the land with your own eyes, since you are not going to cross this Jordan. ²⁸But commission Joshua, and encourage and strengthen him, for he will lead this people across and will cause them to inherit the land that you will see." ²⁹So we stayed in the valley near Beth Peor.

ALTHOUGH VERSES 12–17 follow logically after the accounts of the victories over Sihon and Og, the construction of the opening line, "Of the land," signals a turn in the plot, shifting attention from actions involving the nation to Moses' own actions. Moses' recollections here divide into four parts, each of which is signaled by the chronological marker "at that time"[1] and is controlled by a specific verb cast in the first person.[2] In these episodes Moses' focus shifts from the conquered land (vv. 12–17), to the two and one-half tribes of Israel (vv. 18–22), to Joshua (vv. 21–22), and to himself (vv. 23–28). Verse 29 provides an epilogic conclusion.

Moses' Assignment of the Transjordanian Lands (3:12–17)

MOSES' RECOLLECTION OF THE distribution of the Amorites' lands to the tribes of Reuben, Gad, and the half-tribe of Manasseh differs from the procedure Yahweh prescribed for the apportionment of the land west of the Jordan (Num. 26:52–56), and the process actually followed in the event (Josh. 14–19). Moses does not mention Yahweh, so one might conclude he was acting on his own. However, since the memory of the event was still vivid in the people's minds, there was no need to give all the details.

Numbers 32 tells the full story. Observing that the hills of Gilead and Bashan were ideal for raising livestock, the tribes of Reuben and Gad approached Moses for permission to claim this land as their possession (32:5). At first Moses interpreted the request as an act of rebellion against Yahweh (32:14–15), but when they assured him they would cross the

---

1. The reference being to the time of the allocation of the land to the two and a half tribes.

2. Verses 12–17, "I gave" (vv. 12, 13, 15, 16); verses 18–20, "I commanded" (v. 18); verses 21–22, "I commanded" (v. 21); verses 23–28, "I pleaded" (v. 23).

Jordan with the rest of the tribes and assist them in the conquest of Canaan, he granted their request.[3]

Moses' description of the allocations of the Transjordanian lands seems disjointed and repetitive, but the account exhibits a chiastic A B C B′ A′ structure:

A The allotments to Reuben and Gad (v. 12)
B The allotments to the half-tribe of Manasseh (v. 13a)
C The parenthetical historical/geographic note (vv. 13b–14)
B′ The allotment to the half-tribe of Manasseh: Makir (v. 15)
A′ The allotments to Reuben and Gad (vv. 16–17)

Moses treats the tribes of Reuben and Gad as a unit, perhaps because they had requested permission to claim this land together (Num. 32:1–5). The territory he assigned them extended from Kinnereth (Sea of Tiberias/Galilee; cf. Josh. 12:3; 13:27) to the slopes of Pisgah[4] and the Salt Sea (the Dead Sea); it corresponded roughly to the territory of Sihon.[5] The Jabbok served as a boundary between Manasseh and Reuben-Gad in the highlands of Gilead, though the eastern part of the Jordan Valley (here referred to as the Arabah), including the valley north of the Jabbok, was actually assigned to the latter. The territory assigned to the half-tribe of Manasseh included the rest of Gilead, that is, the hill country north of the Jabbok as far as the Yarmuk River, and all of Bashan (vv. 13a, 15). Gilead in particular Moses assigned to Makir, the descendants of the grandson of Joseph (cf. Num. 32:39).

Another parenthetical geographical/historical note interrupts Moses' report of the Manassite assignment (vv. 13b–14).[6] After reminding the reader that Bashan has traditionally been known as the land of the Rephaites, the note observes that the clan descended from Jair, the great-great-grandson of Manasseh (1 Chron. 2:21–22), took the region of Argob (i.e., Bashan), adjacent to the Geshurites and Maacathites, and renamed it Havvoth Jair ("settlements/villages of Jair") after himself.[7]

---

3. Even though Numbers 32 does not mention Moses consulting with Yahweh, the Reubenites and Gadites interpreted his permission to be the words of Yahweh (v. 32).

4. Since Pisgah always occurs with the article, this may actually be a common noun, meaning something like "the ridge," perhaps the mountain ridge of which Nebo is the peak. Some argue that Pisgah is the lower of the two peaks of Jebel Shayhan, modern Ras es-Siyagha (G. Mattingly, "Pisgah," *ABD*, 5:373–74).

5. The NIV glosses over the awkwardness of the Hebrew. We expect "from Aroer along the Wadi Arnon to the Jabbok" (cf. v. 16), but instead the Hebrew reads literally, "from Aroer along the Wadi Arnon and half the hill country of Gilead and its cities."

6. Cf. 2:10–12, 20–23.

7. Geshur was a small Aramaean kingdom, located east of the Sea of Galilee on the western slopes of the southern Golan Heights. It seems to have resisted the power of Og of

Moses' Charge to the Transjordanian Tribes (3:18–20)

HAVING AUTHORIZED THE TWO and one-half tribes to settle east of the Jordan, Moses charged them to aid the rest of Israel in the conquest of the actual Promised Land (cf. Josh. 1:12–15). The charge consists of four parts. (1) Moses credits Yahweh with granting the land to the two and one-half tribes. This is striking because Yahweh is never mentioned in verses 12–17 and especially because he plays no active role in the fuller account of Numbers 32. But Moses acknowledges God's role in Israel's affairs; his decisions are by definition divine decisions.

(2) Moses issues the specific command: the two and one-half tribes must commit all their "able-bodied men" to the campaign so that their "brothers," the "Israelites," can wage war on the other side of the Jordan. Crossing the river ahead of their brothers fully armed, they are to function as the vanguard of the Israelite army.

(3) Moses authorizes the women, children, and livestock belonging to the two and one-half tribes to remain east of the Jordan in the towns he granted them.[8]

(4) Moses defines the time the two and one-half tribes are to commit themselves to the greater national interest—until "the LORD gives rest to your brothers," just as he had given rest to those across the Jordan. Here Moses introduces the notion of "rest, resting place" for the first time. In this book, "rest" results from eliminating all outside threats, possessing the grant of land (*naḥᵃlâ*) as their "the resting place" (*hammᵉnûḥâ*), and living in security (*beṭaḥ*, 12:9–10). This "rest" is always portrayed as a gift from Yahweh (3:20; 12:10; 25:19; cf. Josh. 1:13; 11:23), and is a prerequisite to Yahweh's choosing a permanent place for his name to dwell (12:10).

Moses' Public Charge to Joshua (3:21–22)

HAVING REMINDED THE TWO and one-half tribes of their obligations to their kinsmen, Moses recalls his earlier charge to Joshua as well. Since he uses the same verb "to command" (*ṣiwwâ*) and adds "at that time," these two charges

---

Bashan (Josh. 12:5) and retained its independence from the newly arrived Israelites (Josh. 13:13). Later David would marry Maacah, the daughter of Talmai, king of Geshur, from which union Absalom was born (2 Sam. 3:3). On the Geshurites, see Z. Ma'oz, "Geshur," *ABD*, 2:996. Maacah was another Aramaean kingdom located north of Geshur between the Sea of Galilee and Mount Hermon. Later the Maacathites would join the Ammonites and the petty Aramaean territories of Beth Rehob, Zobah, and Tob in resisting David's Transjordanian expansion (2 Sam. 10:6–8).

8. The parenthetical note suggests that by now these tribes have distinguished themselves by their wealth in livestock.

seem to have been issued in close succession after the defeat of Sihon and Og. While Numbers 27−32 includes a variety of additional details and situates the commissioning of Joshua (27:18−23) before Moses authorized the two and one-half tribes to settle in the Transjordan (chap. 32), here Moses seems unconcerned about the chronological order of events. Nevertheless, the commissioning accounts are linked by the verb "command/charge" (*ṣiwwâ*, cf. Num. 27:19, 23), which suggests that Moses recalled the actual words he had used in the original context.

Moses' charge to Joshua consisted of three elements. (1) He reminded Joshua of his own past experience of Yahweh's intervention on Israel's behalf, which Joshua had seen with his own eyes. (2) Moses declared that Yahweh's triumph over Sihon and Og was paradigmatic for what he would do against the kingdoms on the other side of the Jordan. (3) Moses promised the continued presence of Yahweh, for Yahweh is the divine Warrior fighting for them.

The shift from singular ("You have seen with your own eyes") to plural ("all that the LORD your [pl.] God has done to these two kings") suggests that while Moses issued the charge to Joshua, he also intended his message for the wider audience. This conclusion is reinforced by the plural verb in the injunction, "[You (pl.)] do not be afraid," and by grounding confidence in the presence of Yahweh, who fights for *them*. A personal charge has become a public challenge and is now recalled in order to renew the courage and faith of this congregation.

Moses' Private Prayer (3:23−29)

THIS PARAGRAPH CATCHES THE reader by surprise on several counts. First, Moses' prayer seems embarrassingly self-serving. From other texts we learn that he would pray for others, even to the point of sacrificing his own life for them (Ex. 32:30−34; cf. Deut 9:19−20, 25−26). But not since his call in Exodus 3−5 have we observed him so preoccupied with his personal fate.[9] Although Numbers 20:1−12 provides the background to this prayer and Numbers 27:12−14 probably describes the context, the only clue Moses provides here to the occasion for this prayer is the phrase "at that time" (v. 23), that is, after the defeat of the Amorite kings. Israel's overwhelming triumph over the enemy must have excited this 120-year-old man, and we should understand his intense desire to see his dream of entering the Promised Land fulfilled. From where he stands he can see the land just across the Jordan. In the prayer Moses pleads with Yahweh to be gracious and let

---

9. Along with his blaming the people for not being allowed to enter the Promised Land (1:37; 3:26; 4:21), the negative image of Moses argues for the authenticity of this passage.

him cross. The prayer itself takes up only verses 24 and 25, but it contains several typical features of biblical prose prayers.[10]

1. The invocative address: "**O Sovereign LORD.**" The double invocation establishes contact with God (cf. 9:26). By opening with *ʾadônāy* ("lord, master, suzerain"), Moses expresses his subordination before God, a disposition that he reinforces by referring to himself as "your servant."[11] But Moses also addresses God by name, which is possible only because God in his grace has revealed it to him (cf. Ex. 3:13 – 15; 34:6 – 7). Indeed Moses has the courage to address Yahweh because of his personal relationship with Israel's gracious Suzerain.

2. The description. "You have begun to show to your servant your greatness and your strong hand. For what god is there in heaven or on earth who can do the deeds and mighty works you do?" In prayers imbedded in Old Testament narratives, the opening invocation is often followed by a description of the divine addressee, proclaiming his power and uniqueness.[12] This particular declaration consists of a statement followed by a rhetorical question. The former alludes to Yahweh's mighty acts; this is the beginning of demonstrations of Yahweh's greatness and "strong hand."[13] In effect Moses laments that he has been able to witness only the beginning of Yahweh's great project. The rhetorical question asks whether there is any other god in heaven or earth who can match what Yahweh has done for Israel. The question obviously anticipates an emphatic negative response: "There is no god like Yahweh!" Moses will elaborate fully on this notion in the next chapter (4:32 – 40).

3. The petition. Next comes Moses' petition: "Let me go over and see the good land beyond the Jordan — that fine hill country and Lebanon." Moses expresses his desire forthrightly and passionately. The intensity of his pain at the prospect of missing this opportunity is reflected by his heaping of adjectives to describe the goal: "the good [i.e., fertile] land," "that fine [i.e., fertile] hill country," "and Lebanon," which serves as a metaphor for any lush landscape.

It is difficult for visitors to the land of Palestine today to conceive of the region as the fabulously good land described here. In trying to understand

---

10. For a helpful study of prayers in biblical narratives, see M. Greenberg, *Biblical Prose Prayer as a Window to the Popular Religion of Ancient Israel* (Berkeley: University of California Press, 1983).

11. In prayers, "your servant" functions as more than a courtesy; it expresses humility and subjugation even as it reflects the hope that the "servant" will receive a measure of goodwill from his "master, lord." See further H. Ringgren, "עבד," *TDOT*, 10:392.

12. While these statements sound like flattery, intended to gain a favorable hearing, to modern readers, we should interpret them as expressions of respect.

13. This expression "strong hand" (*yād ḥªzāqâ*) occurs also in 4:34; 5:15; 6:21; 7:8, 19; 9:26; 11:2; 26:8; 34:12.

Moses, we should keep in mind three factors. (1) Archaeologists and climatologists agree that in the Late Bronze Age and Early Iron Age the landscape of Palestine differed markedly from what we find there today. The invention and manufacture of more efficient agricultural implements in the Early Iron Age (1200—900 BC) enabled the clearing of large tracts of land to make way for human settlement and agriculture, which over time denuded the landscape and precipitated erosion of the soil to bedrock.[14]

(2) This description may be passionately hyperbolic. To anyone who had been wandering around in the desert of Sinai for forty years, the landscape across the Jordan would have seemed Edenic.

(3) For Moses, the land of Canaan was much more than a geographic place; it was a theological idea. Seen with spiritual eyes, the land was good, not because it was fertile, but because it was the land that Yahweh had reserved for his people; this was the destination that Yahweh had set for Moses when he called him to lead the people out of Egypt (Ex. 3:8).

With intense pain, in verses 26—28 Moses describes Yahweh's response to his prayer. (1) Angry with Moses because he had not accepted as final his earlier pronouncement (Num. 20:9—11), Yahweh refused to grant his request with an emphatic order for Moses to stop making this request;[15] he would hear no more about the matter. As he had done in 1:37, Moses had blamed the people for Yahweh's anger with him, obviously overlooking his own culpability in the event at Meribah (Num. 20:1—13). Technically he was correct. If Israel had trusted Yahweh at Kadesh Barnea and entered the land, the events at Meribah would never have happened. But the image of this great leader passing off responsibility is disappointing.

(2) Yahweh offered him a consolation prize: he could climb Mount Pisgah and take in the sight of the Promised Land, gazing in all directions across the Dead Sea and the Jordan River.[16]

(3) Adding insult to injury, Yahweh charged Moses to prepare Joshua his lieutenant to take his place, to lead the people across the Jordan, and to deliver the grant of land into the people's hands.[17] Since the Canaanites were as formidable as ever (cf. 1:28), Moses must "encourage" and "strengthen" Joshua.[18]

---

14. For discussion, see Beitzel, *Moody Atlas of Bible Lands*, 53—54.

15. Here the expression is strong, in effect, "Shut up!"

16. If Pisgah is modern Ras es-Siyagha, which rises 2,329 feet above sea level and projects westward from the tableland, it affords magnificent views of the country, from the Negeb in the south to Hermon in the north.

17. On the significance of the root *nḥl*, "to receive/deliver as a grant," see on 1:38.

18. In 2:30 this same word had been used of Yahweh's hardening Sihon's heart, and in 15:7 it is used of people hardening their own hearts.

Moses concludes his recollections of this painful episode abruptly by noting simply that he and the people remained in the valley opposite Beth Peor on the plains of Moab (34:1), the place where he delivered this address. The valley in question was probably Wadi ʿAyn Musa, "The Valley of Moses' Well," at the foot of Pisgah. Beth Peor is probably an abbreviation for the fuller name, Beth Baal Peor, "the house of Baal of Peor," which suggests the location of a shrine to Baal (cf. 4:3).[19] The Israelites are still at the place where they had recently engaged in spiritual prostitution and physical harlotry (Num. 25:1−9).

THE TRANSJORDANIAN TRIBES. EACH of the four sections of this text has its own enduring theological significance. In the short run, the request of the two and one-half tribes to retain this land seems both logical and reasonable. This was a fertile region, especially suitable for grazing herds and flocks, as the two tribes recognized. Moreover, the Israelites' elimination of the Amorites had created a power vacuum in the region. Nevertheless, this land had previously never been envisaged as part of the Promised Land, and one may assume that if the Israelites had entered from the south thirty-eight years earlier, it would never have become part of the land of Israel. Although Moses declared that these lands were Yahweh's gift to the two and one-half tribes (3:18), the accounts here and in Numbers are strangely silent on the involvement of God in the process. Assuming Moses' had access to God's will on this matter, we are still surprised that God would allow the expansion of the territory of Israel in response to the people's desires.

Nevertheless, in long-range terms, granting the people's request yielded disastrous consequences. Whereas God's original plan envisaged the Jordan as a barrier between Israel and the Transjordanian nations, in a matter of months it would divide the nation itself. The theological implications of their request dawned on the two and one-half tribes immediately after the backbone of Canaanite resistance had been broken (Josh. 22). Fearing the western Israelites would treat their descendants as second-class citizens, excluded from the people of Yahweh, they built an altar on the west bank of the Jordan to memorialize their membership in the people of

---

19. The place is named variously as "Baal Peor" (Num. 25:3, 5; Deut. 4:3; Ps. 106:28; Hos. 9:10), "Beth Peor" (Deut. 3:29; 4:46; 34:6; Josh. 13:20), or simply "Peor" (Num. 25:18; 31:16; Josh. 22:17). Peor was a mountain near Mount Nebo to which Balak took Balaam to have him curse Israel (Num. 23:28).

Yahweh (vv. 24−25). Had cool heads not prevailed, this decision would have resulted in a civil war within Joshua's own lifetime.

With the increasing Canaanization of Israelite society in the post-conquest period, on several occasions east and west came to blows with disastrous consequences.[20] In the centuries that followed, these tribes would be the first to feel the ravages of foreign armies. Remarkably, in the sixth century BC, Ezekiel's vision of the restored nation leaves the heartland of these Transjordanian territories between the Wadi Arnon and the Yarmuk River out of the picture of the Promised Land (Ezek. 47:15−20). The fact that the boundaries of the land apportioned to the other tribes corresponds closely to the territory promised to Abraham (Gen. 15)[21] raises questions of what Yahweh really thought about the matter.

Moses' charge to the two and one-half tribes (3:18−20) highlights the unity and solidarity of the people of Yahweh. Not only was the Promised Land Yahweh's gift to all Israel, but the conquest of Canaan was also a national agenda; no tribe could be excused until the goal had been achieved and God had given rest to all. Unfortunately, in subsequent history this principle would be honored more in the breach than in the observance. The narratives of Judges demonstrate how quickly this unity would dissolve. The narrator of Judges laments the fact that instead of keeping alive the memory of Yahweh's gracious saving acts on behalf of the entire nation, the Israelites forgot Yahweh and behaved more and more like Canaanites (Judg. 2:10−23). The inter-city rivalries of the peoples they displaced[22] gave way to intertribal parochialism and jealousies.

Moses' charge to Joshua. Moses' charge to Joshua (vv. 21−22, 28) demonstrates that if courage and faith are prerequisites for serving in the infantry of Yahweh's army, they are even more so for those who lead in kingdom work. Joshua's confidence could not be based on his personal experience, qualifications, or training, but had to be based on God, and on God alone. This faith would be buttressed by keeping alive the memory of God's past actions, by being reminded of God's firm promises of future action, and by celebrating his presence in the conflict.

Moses' request to enter Canaan. This is the first and last time we hear of Moses' frank conversation with God about his request for permission to enter the Promised Land. However, having included this episode, the death of Moses outside the land hangs like a pall over the entire book. In fact, the

---

20. See Judg. 8 and 12.

21. It includes the highlands of Bashan and runs far north of Damascus, but excludes the southern Transjordan. For discussion see Block, *Ezekiel Chapters 25−48* (NICOT; Grand Rapids: Eerdmans, 1998), 703−24.

22. As witnessed by the Amarna correspondence. See *ANET*, 483−90.

addresses that follow take on the function of a last will and testament or a prefunerary oration. In 31:2 Moses acknowledges that his end has come, and he takes further steps to get his house in order before his demise. Yahweh will remind him again in 32:48−52 of the reason for his refusal, and in 34:1−4 Moses receives the consolation prize—sight of the Promised Land from one end to the other. However, not another word is said in the book or the rest of the Old Testament of Moses' prayer and God's rebuff. With time the image of Moses was increasingly idealized. In Jewish tradition the rabbis would debate whether or not Moses even died or was transported directly to heaven.[23]

ON THINGS ABOVE. THE apportionment of the land east of the Jordan to the two and one-half tribes (3:12−17) illustrates the ambiguities that often characterize the life of faith. Like Lot in Genesis 13, these tribes desired the good land east of the Jordan, and God gave them what they desired. Although their request seemed reasonable, in the long term it proved a disaster. The episode reminds readers today to set their affections on things above, not on things below (Col. 3:2). It is not that what seems attractive to us is fundamentally wrong; it may even be logically defensible and economically wise. But when earthly considerations eclipse the divine agenda, we are in danger of losing our place in both.

Moses' charge to the two and one-half tribes reminds readers today that a biblical ethic is not only driven by heavenly rather than earthly values; it also seeks the well-being of the next person ahead of our own. Flush from the victories over the Canaanites, in Joshua 22 these tribes declared their identity with their kinsfolk to the west. But within a generation the nation would begin to unravel. When people lose sight of their common spiritual heritage and their common mission, their sense of community also vanishes.

The nature and purpose of prayer. Verses 23−29 are extremely instructive on the nature and purpose of prayer. Some of the lessons to be learned from Moses' conversation with God are obvious; others are not so clear. (1) *Prayer is an act of worship.* True worship involves reverential acts of submission and homage to the divine superior in response to his gracious revelation of himself and in accordance with his will. When Moses addressed

---

23. For bibliography and discussion see A. J. Heschel, *Heavenly Torah: As Refracted through the Generations* (ed. and trans. G. Tucker; New York: Continuum, 2007), 353−54.

God as "Sovereign LORD" and referred to himself as "your servant," he illustrated the psychological and spiritual posture that is prerequisite to receiving a hearing with God.

(2) *Prayer must be grounded in correct theology*, which in biblical prayers is often expressed through exuberant adoration of the great and glorious God and doxologies of praise for his gracious but concrete acts on people's behalf (4:32−40). David takes Moses doxology to a new level in 1 Chronicles 29:10−13:

> Praise be to you, O LORD,
> > God of our father Israel,
> > from everlasting to everlasting.
> Yours, O LORD, is the greatness and the power
> > and the glory and the majesty and the splendor,
> > for everything in heaven and earth is yours.
> Yours, O LORD, is the kingdom;
> > you are exalted as head over all.
> Wealth and honor come from you;
> > you are the ruler of all things.
> In your hands are strength and power
> > to exalt and give strength to all.
> Now, our God, we give you thanks,
> > and praise your glorious name.

But this is a prayer of praise. Although it is longer and more detailed, the prayer of petition by Peter and John in Acts 4:24−30 follows the pattern of Moses' plea:

> Invocation: "Sovereign Lord,"
> Description: "you made the heaven and the earth and the sea, and everything in them. You spoke by the Holy Spirit through the mouth of your servant, our father David...."
> Petition: "Now, Lord, consider their threats and enable your servants to speak your word with great boldness. Stretch out your hand to heal and perform miraculous signs and wonders through the name of your holy servant Jesus."

Like the prayer Jesus taught his disciples (Matt. 6:9−13), this is a helpful pattern for us, reminding us who we are in relation to God and who he is in relation to the universe. Confident prayer is based on the relationship that God has graciously established with his people.

(3) *Prayer is an incredible privilege.* As Moses will assert in the next chapter (4:8), of all the nations only Israel has a God so near that he hears them

whenever they call on him. But even in prayer, God remains the Sovereign, and he retains the right to say "yes" or "no" to a human supplicant's requests. Taking into account the overall biblical perspective, the effects of prayer may vary. As Moses had experienced in Exodus 32 and Numbers 14, through the effectual fervent prayer of a righteous person, God's disposition may be changed, and he may withdraw threats he had previously pronounced on people (cf. also Jonah 3−4). In other contexts, God may answer prayer affirmatively by effecting a change in one's external circumstances, as we witness in the case of Peter in Acts 12:5−17.

(4) Finally, *through prayer the persons praying may themselves be changed.* Rather than being a means by which supplicants get God to do what they desire, sometimes prayer becomes the process whereby God brings the wills of those who pray into conformity with his own. As was the case with Moses, our faith may not necessarily be measured by the extent to which we can move God. Strong faith also may demand that we accept God's "no" and get on with the tasks to which he has called us. Sometimes his "no" is final.

Some decades ago now, for nine months I served as the interim preacher of a wonderful church. The week I arrived we learned that a thirty-two-year-old woman, the mother of two lovely children, was diagnosed with terminal cancer. Her friends rallied around her, organizing round-the-clock prayer vigils. Sadly, eight months later, as one of my last duties as interim pastor, I conducted her funeral. By then most of her best friends had left the church, disillusioned and angry with the congregation for not praying seriously and for not having faith strong enough to heal this person. God could have granted Moses' request. God can and does heal miraculously. But painful though it was, this family and congregation had to come to terms with God's "no." The measure of faith is not necessarily established by what we can get God to do for us; sometimes strong faith means simply casting ourselves into his loving and gracious arms, trusting him to be with us even in grief.

Responsible pastoral leadership. Finally, through Moses' actions in these episodes, we learn a series of lessons on the nature and style of responsible pastoral leadership. (1) As the leader of this massive congregation, Moses was sensitive to the desires *and* needs of his people. He heard the two and one-half tribes' request for land, and he granted the request. But this was not merely a sentimental acquiescence to their appetites; Moses also recognized the implications of the decision for the congregation as a whole. Accordingly, even as he granted the privilege of possessing the land east of the Jordan, he also highlighted their obligations toward the community of faith as a whole.

(2) Responsible pastoral leaders have the well-being of all the members of the congregation in mind (v. 19). Even as Moses impresses the men of

the eastern tribes with their obligations to the larger community, he provides for the well-being of the vulnerable—their wives and children, not to mention their livestock. In so doing he both guarantees their security and spares them the horrors and violence of the wars to come.

(3) Responsible leaders recognize the symbiotic relationship that exists between divine and human activity (v. 20). Moses knows that the men must cross the Jordan to engage the enemy with the rest of the nation, but they will go confident in God's promise to give rest to the warriors in particular and to the nation in general. Then they may return home and celebrate the rest he has provided.

(4) Responsible pastoral leaders hold up before the people a high view of God (vv. 22–24). Moses knows that the God of Israel is like no other, and he realizes the importance of keeping alive the memory of God's saving action on behalf of his people. With this lofty theology, the people may charge onto the battlefield with confidence, realizing that the gods of the enemies they face are but foolish figments of a depraved human imagination.

(5) Responsible pastoral leaders place the well-being of the congregation over their own fortune. Moses had led the people for almost four decades through horrible physical circumstances and many bitter experiences, knowing full well that in the end he would be denied the trophy. But through all those years, he did not cease to represent the people before God and God to the people.

(6) Even responsible pastoral leaders are subject to the pressures of the office, which often drive them to bitter venting of personal feelings before God. On several occasions in this first address, Moses becomes embarrassingly transparent, openly expressing his disappointments and frustrations toward the people. Many leaders can identify with him in this critical moment and find some consolation in knowing that even the greatest leaders have feet of clay.

(7) Responsible leaders maintain open lines of communication with God. Not only was Moses open to the instruction and guidance of Yahweh at every turn, but he had also learned to cast his cares on Yahweh, knowing that God cared for him. Exodus 33 characterizes Moses' relationship with God as a relationship of friendship—Yahweh used to speak to him face-to-face (i.e., directly) as a man speaks to a friend. In his plea to enter the land, Moses does indeed recognize his inferior position in this relationship, but the form of his request and the form of Yahweh's answer are precisely how friends converse—directly, forthrightly, and without equivocation, ambiguity, or evasion. Moses walks away from this conversation with God bitterly disappointed, but he remains the friend of God.

(8) Responsible pastoral leadership knows when it is time to relinquish authority to a successor and to do so with grace and dignity. Although Moses is transparently bitter for having been refused entrance to the land and cynical toward the people because of it, with respect to Joshua he extends unwavering support. Despite the disappointment of unfulfilled dreams, he passes the mantle to his lieutenant and faithfully prepares him to take the reins of leadership.

Deuteronomy 4:1–8

❦

Introductory Comments on Deuteronomy 4:1–40

IN CHAPTER 4 MOSES' first address reaches its climax. Although the chapter exhibits numerous links with the preceding,[1] it is obviously a literary subsection in its own right. (1) Verse 1 opens with (lit.) "and now" (w$^{e\varsigma}$attâ), which signals a turning point in the address.[2] (2) For the first time Moses appeals to his specific audience to "hear."[3] (3) This chapter displays a significant change in style—from basically historical reminiscences to explicitly hortatory proclamation. (4) At the same time in this chapter Moses recalls several additional events—Yahweh's judgment at Baal Peor, the revelation of the Torah and the establishment of the covenant at Horeb, and the exodus from Egypt—with each place symbolizing greater spiritual realities. (5) The chapter is characterized by a perplexing alternation between singular and plural second person forms.[4] This alternation serves a rhetorical/sermonic goal. When Moses views Israel as a collective, he uses the singular; when he uses the plural, he recognizes that ethics and faith must be applied individually.[5] By shifting to a more obviously sermonic style, Moses seeks to recapture in his audience the effect that the original theophany at Horeb should have had on the previous generation—wholehearted devotion to Yahweh.

Although Moses continues his backward look in chapter 4, he actually has his sights set on the future, preparing the Israelites for life in the land.

---

1. See above, pp. 60–62.

2. On w$^{e\varsigma}$attâ, "and now," signaling a turning point, see also 10:12 and 1 Sam. 12:13.

3. Elsewhere in the book the imperative "Hear" (š^{e}ma$^\varsigma$) always opens new sections (5:1; 6:4; 9:1; 20:3; 27:9), though the phrase w$^{e\varsigma}$attâ š^{e}ma$^\varsigma$, (lit.) "And now, hear," never appears at the absolute beginning of a speech.

4. This issue is obscured in translation because English uses a common expression, "you," for both singular and plural: vv. 1–8, plural, except for "Hear" (v. 1), the end of v. 3, the beginning of v. 5; vv. 9–10, singular; vv. 11–16, plural; v. 19, singular; vv. 20–28, plural, with exceptions in vv. 21, 23, 24, and 25; vv. 29–40, singular, with exceptions in the opening of v. 29, and two in v. 34.

5. On this issue, see esp. J. G. McConville, "Singular Address in the Deuteronomic Law and the Politics of Legal Administration," *JSOT* 97 (2002): 19–36. Based on the alternation of singular and plural forms, many scholars argue that 4:1–40 is a patchwork of smaller pieces combined and inserted here during the exile to give hope to a spiritually despondent community. The reference to exile from the land in 4:27–30 is critical for the postexilic dating of this chapter. See, e.g., Jon D. Levenson, "Who Inserted the Book of the Torah," *HTR* 68 (1975): 222. However, removing 4:1–40 creates an intolerably harsh transition from 3:29 to 4:41 and fails to recognize the rhetorical climactic function of this chapter.

Yahweh has indeed given Israel eternal title to the land (v. 40), but actual possession of it and experiencing well-being in it are contingent on the people's compliance with the revealed will of God (vv. 1, 5, 14, 40). Moses heightens the urgency of a correct response now by repeatedly inserting "today" (*yôm*, e.g., v. 4, 8, 26, 38), which turns out to be a perpetual "today." Every time one hears or reads this passage, one must respond.[6] The Israelites' physical journey may end when they cross the Jordan, but their spiritual pilgrimage never ends.

But chapter 4 also looks forward in that here Moses introduces many theological issues that will drive his preaching in the addresses that follow.[7] In so doing this chapter sets the sermonic (rather than the legal) tone for the rest of the book and declares Moses' central concern in the book: to call his people to covenant love demonstrated in actions that please their Redeemer.

The chapter is made up of three main parts, with a large prescriptive core (vv. 9−31), framed by a reflective prologue (vv. 1−8) and a challenging epilogue (vv. 32−40). Continuing the motif that pervades chapters 1−3, each section focuses on a specific demonstration of divine grace: the grace of Torah (vv. 1−8), the grace of covenant (vv. 9−31), and the grace of salvation (vv. 32−40). But with impressive rhetorical effect, Moses reverses the historical order of the graces. He has begun with the most recent past (chaps. 1−3), and now works backward to Horeb (4:1−31), ending with the dramatic moment of the nation's birth (4:32−40), and beyond to Yahweh's covenant love for the ancestors (v. 37). In so doing, Moses reminds his people that they must constantly retrace their steps back to their spectacular rescue from Egypt, which was the determinative moment in their history (vv. 32−40).

---

6. Cf. J. Gordon McConville and J. G. Millar, *Time and Place in Deuteronomy* (JSOTSup 179; Sheffield: Sheffield Academic, 1984), 42−43; J. G. Millar, *Now Choose Life: Theology and Ethics in Deuteronomy* (Grand Rapids: Eerdmans, 1998), 77−78. For a discussion of the gnomic use of *yôm*, see S. J. de Vries, *Yesterday, Today and Tomorrow: Time and History in the Old Testament* (Grand Rapids: Eerdmans, 1975), 45.

7. (1) Yahweh's love for the ancestors/Israel (v. 37; cf. 7:7, 8, 13; 10:15, 18; 23:5[6]); (2) Yahweh's gracious election of the ancestors/Israel (v. 20; cf. 7:6, 7; 10:15; 14:2; 26:18); (3) Yahweh's establishment of Israel as his own people (v. 20; cf. 7:6; 14:2; 26:18; 27:9; 28:9; 29:13[12]); (4) Yahweh's covenant relationship with Israel (vv. 13, 23, 31; cf., e.g., 5:2, 3; 7:2, 9, 12; 8:18); (5) Yahweh's rescue of Israel from the clutches of another nation (vv. 20, 32−39; cf., e.g., 5:6, 15; 6:21−23; 7:8, 19; 8:14; 24:18; 26:6−8; 33:29); (6) Yahweh's gracious presence (vv. 7, 10, 36; cf. 5:22−27; 7:21; 18:16; 23:14[15]; 31:6, 8, 23; 33:2−3, 5; contra 31:16−18); (7) Yahweh's demand that Israel recognize him as the only God and love/fear him alone (vv. 15−24, 35, 39; cf., e.g., 5:7−8; 6:4−5; 10:12, 20; 11:1, 22; 13:2−5[3−6]); and (8) Yahweh's demand that Israel demonstrate covenant fidelity through obedience to his revealed will (vv. 1, 5, 8, 14, 40; cf., e.g., v. 45; 5:1, 31; 6:1, 20, 25; 7:11; 10:12−13; 11:1; 31−32; 12:1; 26:16−18; 27:1, 10; 28:1, 15).

Hear now, O Israel, the decrees and laws I am about to teach you. Follow them so that you may live and may go in and take possession of the land that the LORD, the God of your fathers, is giving you. ²Do not add to what I command you and do not subtract from it, but keep the commands of the LORD your God that I give you.

³You saw with your own eyes what the LORD did at Baal Peor. The LORD your God destroyed from among you everyone who followed the Baal of Peor, ⁴but all of you who held fast to the LORD your God are still alive today.

⁵See, I have taught you decrees and laws as the LORD my God commanded me, so that you may follow them in the land you are entering to take possession of it. ⁶Observe them carefully, for this will show your wisdom and understanding to the nations, who will hear about all these decrees and say, "Surely this great nation is a wise and understanding people." ⁷What other nation is so great as to have their gods near them the way the LORD our God is near us whenever we pray to him? ⁸And what other nation is so great as to have such righteous decrees and laws as this body of laws I am setting before you today?

HERE NOW, O ISRAEL (4:1)

IN A SENSE, THESE eight verses summarize the entire chapter, highlighting the importance of obedience as the proper response to Yahweh's grace expressed by the revelation of his will. Moses begins by calling for the people's attention: "Hear now, O Israel, the decrees and laws that I am about to teach you."[8] The Hebrew word for "decrees" (*ḥōq*) refers to laws prescribed by a superior and "inscribed" with a sharp object on some writing material (clay, stone, etc.). The word for "laws" (*mišpāt*), literally "judgments," may suggest laws based on precedent, that is, decisions by a judge, though it seems more likely that in this context it means "divine decisions concerning the way of covenant righteousness." In Deuteronomy the word

---

8. The pair of expressions "decrees and laws" (*ḥuqqîm* and *mišpātîm*) occurs repeatedly in this chapter (vv. 1, 5, 8, 14, 45) and nine times hereafter—especially at critical structural junctures (5:1; 11:32; 12:1; 26:16). They also appear in association with other expressions: "command[s]" (*miṣwâ/miṣwôt*, 5:31; 6:1; 7:11) and "stipulations" (*ʿēdôt*, 4:45; 6:20).

pair "decrees and laws" is shorthand for the entire revelation received earlier at Horeb and along the way from Egypt to Kadesh Barnea.[9]

By "teaching" (*limmēd*) the "decrees and laws," Moses functions as a pastor-teacher (Eph. 4:11), reiterating earlier revelation, applying that revelation specifically to life in the land, declaring the essence of covenant relationship, and highlighting the importance of a correct response to the revealed will of God. Moses does not view himself as a lawgiver; the only office he and the person who edited the book claim for him is that of prophet (18:15; cf. 34:10). Moses was the communicator and interpreter of divine revelation, not its source. Even so, as the authorized spokesman for God, everything he said about the "decrees and laws" was as binding as the original laws themselves, as he will declare in verse 2.

Moses declares his pedagogical goals in verse 1b (cf. 30:11–14). His immediate objective is to inspire Israel to "follow," that is "do" (*ʿāśâ*) the decrees and laws. What he offers is not theoretical speculation but practical instruction for life demonstrated through obedient action. Moses expresses his long-range hope in terms of Israel's high calling: life, entry into, and possession of the land that Yahweh is giving them. The life spoken of here is not so much eternal life but the full enjoyment of Yahweh's blessings in the land promised to the ancestors.[10]

Why Obedience to the Torah Is Crucial (4:2–8)

IN VERSES 2–8 Moses explains why obedience to the Torah is crucial. (1) The Torah itself is normative by definition (4:2). By warning his hearers not to add anything to his word, Moses declares that *only* that which he (on Yahweh's behalf) prescribes is normative, and by warning them not to delete anything from his word, he declares that *all* that he (on Yahweh's behalf) prescribes is normative.[11]

(2) Obedience to the Torah is the key to life (4:3–4); in fact, as Moses will reiterate at the end of his final address (30:15–20), obedience to Yahweh is a matter of life and death. This was demonstrated recently in the

---

9. Some understand the pair to refer to the entire promulgation at Moab, including Moses' paraenetic exhortations. See J. G. Millar, "Living at the Place of Decision," in *Time and Place in Deuteronomy* (ed. J. G. McConville and J. G. Millar; JSOTSup 179; Sheffield: Sheffield Academic, 1984), 35–42; idem, *Now Choose Life*, 75–80.

10. For eloquent discussions of these issues, see Millar, *Now Choose Life*, 55–66; C. J. H. Wright, *Knowing Jesus through the Old Testament* (Downers Grove, IL: InterVarsity Press, 1992), 64–102.

11. These warnings follow a widespread ancient Near Eastern tradition of warnings (often curses) against altering documents. Rev. 22:18–19 echoes the wording of Deut. 4:2 (cf. 1 Macc. 8:30). See further, Weinfeld, *DDS*, 262.

treacherous worship of Baal at Peor,[12] which Moses takes to be paradigmatic. Whereas Yahweh destroyed all who "followed" after Baal of Peor, the people standing before Moses are alive today because they "held fast" to Yahweh.[13] They are living testimony to the importance of obedience to the divine will. The emphatic "See" in verse 5 suggests the challenge will be heightened rather than reduced once the Israelites have crossed the Jordan. Having referred to Baal Peor, Moses reminds the people that he is not looking back as much as he is looking forward to the people's occupation of the land. As at Kadesh Barnea thirty-eight years earlier, and more recently at Baal of Peor, the people's fidelity will be tested every day once they have entered the Promised Land.

(3) Obedience to the Torah is the highest privilege imaginable (4:6−8). In light of verses 2−5, the first two verbs in verse 6 are almost predictable: "Observe them [the decrees and laws] carefully," that is, "keep them by doing them." However, the following declaration emphasizes that compliance with the law is not a burden imposed on the people; it is a special privilege that will make them the envy of the nations. Moses highlights his point by introducing hypothetical respondents who, having watched Israel and learned of the ordinances that govern their lives, express their amazement and envy. The incredulity of outside observers to Israel's privilege is reflected in the opening particle *raq* ("surely"), whose sense may be captured colloquially by "Wow!"[14] Observing Israel's "wisdom" and "understanding," they will ascribe "great nation" status to them, thereby fulfilling God's promise to Abraham[15]

(4) Israel is indeed great. But what is it that makes Israel so great, wise, and understanding in the eyes of the nations? In verses 7−8 Moses declares that the nation's greatness does not derive from her own qualities, but from Yahweh their God. The question is asked twice, "What other nation is there [like Israel?]" The implied answer is "None!" for two reasons. (a) The Israelites are uniquely privileged because their God is near to them and he answers their prayers. When other peoples pray to their gods, they remain both aloof and silent. Craftsmen may design them with big ears, but they do not hear (cf. 4:28; Ps. 115:4−8). Ironically, although the Israelites' God

---

12. See Num. 25:1−9. "Baal of Peor" identifies the local manifestation of Baal as worshiped by the Moabites at the place called Peor. Cf. comment on 3:29 above.

13. The verb *dbq* denotes decisive and irreversible commitment (cf. Gen. 2:24; Ruth 1:14). It recurs in 10:20; 11:22; 13:4[5]; and 30:20. This is the strongest biblical expression for "sticking together" (cf. Job 29:10) and answers to the action of the idolaters who had "yoked themselves" to Baal of Peor (Num. 25:3).

14. Cf. Deut. 33:26−29, where outsiders' response to Israel's privileged status is expressed with *ʾašrêykā*, usually translated "Blessed are you," but better rendered, "O how privileged are you!" or even "Congratulations to you!"

15. Gen. 12:2; 18:18; 46:3.

was not represented by images they could set up in their homes or anywhere else, he was near; and although he had no ears, he heard their cries
whenever they called on him.[16]

(b) The Israelites are uniquely privileged because they know what their
God expects of them, and what he expects is absolutely righteous. The
Israelites were not the first nation to possess a set body of laws,[17] nor were
only their laws deemed by someone to be just. However, whereas elsewhere, tainted by self-interest, the people who promulgated the laws were
the ones who deemed them to be just, it is outsiders who look at Israel
and conclude that their entire Torah (which includes the laws and Moses'
interpretation of them) is "righteous."[18]

For Moses "righteousness" is not an abstraction but adherence to an
objective norm, demonstrated in concrete ethical acts that seek the interests of others and results in perfect harmony between them and their Ruler.
In 16:20 Moses will declare the watchword of the Torah: "righteousness,
only righteousness" (ṣedeq, 16:20, pers. trans.). Israel's laws are righteous
because they derive from God, who is absolutely righteous and upright
(32:4), and because adherence to them always achieves righteous results.
Israel may be the least significant people on earth with respect to size and
numbers (7:7), but with regard to status Yahweh has elevated them high
above the nation for his "praise, fame and honor" (26:19; 28:1, 9−10). His
intent is that they might be a blessing (Gen. 12:2−3; 18:18; 22:18; 26:4;
28:14) and light (Isa. 42:6; 49:6; 51:4) to the nations.

THE POSITIVE VIEW OF Israel's law and the Torah
of Moses reflected here is celebrated with unrestrained delight in Psalms 19:7−11[8−12] and
119, which is composed as a glorious "Ode to
Torah." These texts provide a welcome and necessary corrective to the
common perception of the law in the Old Testament as a burden, a noose
around the Israelites' neck to drag them to their deaths. Moses' reference to
foreign observers reminds us that we must evaluate Israel's law first and
foremost within the context of the world in which it was given.

Having rescued his people from Egypt, Yahweh could have left them
to figure out on their own what an appropriate response to his gracious

---

16. Cf. also Pss. 22:11, 19−20[12, 20−22]; 34:15−18[16−19]; 145:18.

17. The ancient laws are conveniently gathered by M. Roth (*Law Collections from Mesopotamia and Asia Minor* (SBLWAW; Atlanta: Scholars, 1997), and *COS*, 2:332−68, 408−14.

18. This is the only place in the OT where the form ṣaddîq/ṣaddîqîm describes anything
other than a person (as in 16:19).

redemption might be. This is the plight of all who lack access to the mind and will of God. Whereas the Israelites knew the will of their God because he had revealed it to them, the way other peoples related to their gods was always experimental. The best they could do was guess what should please their gods, but even then they would never know whether their assessment was right, whether their conclusions measured up to the standard of "righteousness," and whether adherence won the goodwill of the gods. Their plight is illustrated by an ancient Sumerian prayer preserved in the library of Ashurbanipal (seventh century BC) in Nineveh:

Prayer to Any God[19]

May (my) lord's angry heart be reconciled,
May the god I do not know be reconciled,
May the goddess I do not know be reconciled,
May the god, whoever he is, be reconciled,
May the goddess, whoever she is, be reconciled,
May my (personal) god's heart be reconciled,
May my (personal) goddess's heart be reconciled,
May (my) god and (my) goddess be reconciled (with me)!
May the god who [has turned away] from me [in anger be re]
    conciled,
May the goddess [who has turned away from me in anger be
    reconciled],
[I do not know] what wrong [I have done],
[   ] the wrong [ ]....
I could not eat for myself the bread I found,[20]
I could not drink for myself the water I found.
I have perpetrated un[wittingly] an abomination to my god,
I have unwittingly violated a taboo of my goddess.
O (my) lord, many are my wrongs, great my sins,
O my god, many are my wrongs, great my sins,
O my goddess, many are my wrongs, great my sins,
O god, whoever you are, many are my wrongs, great my sins,
O goddess, whoever you are, many are my wrongs, great my sins!
I do not know what wrong I have done,

---

19. As translated by B. R. Foster, *From Distant Days: Myths, Tales, and Poetry of Ancient Mesopotamia* (Bethesda, MD: CDL Press, 1995), 269–71. While this "prayer, confession, lament, and concluding supplication, could be used for any deity" (p. 269), it also exposes the fundamental problem with any religion not grounded on revelation.

20. That is, he offered it all to his gods in vain.

I do not know what sin I have committed,
I do not know what abomination I have perpetrated,
I do not know what taboo I have violated!
A lord has glowered at me in the anger of his heart,
A god has made me face the fury of his heart,
A goddess has become enraged at me and turned me into a sick
    man,
A god, whoever he is, has excoriated me,
A goddess, whoever she is, has laid misery upon me!...
When I wept, they would not draw near.
When I would make a complaint, no one would listen.
I am miserable, blindfolded, I cannot see!
Turn towards me, merciful god, as I implore you.
I do homage to you, my goddess, as I keep groveling before you,
O god, whoever you are, [turn towards me, I implore you],
O goddess, [whoever you are, turn towards me, I implore you],
O lord, tur[n towards me, I implore you],
O goddess, lo[ok upon me, I implore you],
O god, [whoever you are, turn towards me, I implore you],
O goddess, whoever [you are, turn towards me, I implore you]!...
How long, O god whosoever you are, until y[our angry heart is
    calmed]?
How long, O goddess, whosoever you are, until your estranged
    heart is reconciled?
Men are slow-witted and know nothing,
No matter how many names they go by, what do they know?
They do not know at all if they are doing good or evil!...
O my god, though my wrongs be seven times seven, absolve my
    wrongs,
O my goddess, though my wrongs be seven times seven, absolve
    my wrongs....
Absolve my wrongs, let me sound your praises!
As if you were my real mother, let your heart be reconciled,
As if you were my real mother, my real father.

This pathetic piece provides a remarkable window into the psyche of
the ancients. This person is sure of three things: the gods are angry with
him; his sin has caused this anger; and he must do something about the sin
to placate the gods' wrath. But his ignorance is also threefold: he does not
know which god is angry; he does not know what the crime is that provoked the divine fury; and he does not know what it will take to placate
the wrath of the gods.

Into this dark world the Torah of Moses shines its beacon of glory and grace. Israel's God has revealed himself; Israel's God has declared the boundaries of acceptable and unacceptable conduct; and Israel's God has provided a way of forgiveness that actually solves the human problem of sin. No wonder psalmists celebrated with such joy the life to be found in the Torah (Ps. 119). Even as Moses recognizes Israel's extraordinary privilege as bearer of the revealed will of God, he also declares the nation's missionary function. In the plan of God through the obedience of his people, they would demonstrate their greatness to the nations and so fulfill the promise to the ancestors and serve as agents of worldwide blessing. To borrow the language of Paul in 2 Corinthians 3:3, Israel was to be a letter from God to the world, written not with ink but with the Spirit of the living God, not on tablets of stone but on tablets of human hearts.

Sadly, the nation as a whole failed in this mission, and the individuals within the nation who fulfilled this calling were rarely more than a remnant. But Israel's failure negates neither the grace nor the power of the Torah to yield life when treasured with proper perspective. Israel's failure testifies simply to the hardness of the human heart.

KNOWING GOD AND HIS will as Israel's supreme privilege. This paragraph highlights two commonly forgotten or intentionally dismissed realities for Christians. It reminds us that along with the experience of salvation itself, the presence of God and the knowledge of his will represent the supreme privileges of his people. Moses will conclude his final speech by declaring that the word, that is, the revealed will of God, is near to Israel, presenting them with the opportunity to choose life or death (30:11 – 20, esp. v. 14).

In a strange hermeneutical move, Paul will explicitly quote that statement in Deuteronomy 30:12 – 14 and apply it to Christ, who is the climactic demonstration both of God's nearness and his revelation (Rom. 10:7 – 11). However, the christological significance of our present passage finds expression more naturally and more fully in the prologue to the gospel of John, which reaches a climax in 1:14: "The Word became flesh and made his dwelling among us. We have seen his glory, the glory of the One and Only, who came from the Father, full of grace and truth." And then John exclaims, "From the fullness of his grace we have all received one blessing after another. For the Torah was given through Moses; grace and truth happened through Jesus Christ" (John 1:16 – 17). The contrast here is not between law and grace, but two ways of expressing grace: mediated and embodied. John is referring to the two climactic gracious revelatory moments in history. For the Israelites, possession of the Torah was a supreme grace (Rom. 9:4), a grace exceeded and superseded only by Christ, for he is Immanuel, "God with us."

The significance of God's revealed will in a believer. At the same time, this paragraph reminds us of the significance of God's revealed will in the life of a believer. The Torah and the rest of the Scriptures have not been given to us to display in beautifully decorated family Bibles on the coffee table, or to be the subjects of high-sounding creedal statements on the inerrancy and infallibility of the Scriptures. A high view of God's revealed will is demonstrated in lives that conform to God's will as revealed. Moses spends much more time calling his people to orthopraxy than to orthodoxy. The missional goal of God's people is not fulfilled with precise theological formulas, but through the life-giving and transforming power of the divine Word.

In our Western cultural context Christians as individuals and as the church are increasingly dismissed by outsiders as irrelevant, hypocritical, and self-serving. But in his own farewell address to his disciples Jesus reminded his followers of the relationship between spiritual claims and life:

- If you love me you will obey my commands (pers. trans., John 14:15).
- If you obey my commands, you will remain in my love, just as I have obeyed my Father's commands and remain in his love (John 15:10).

Here "keep/obey my commands" does not mean simply, "Do as I tell you from now on." The expression "my commands" alludes to specific commands revealed long ago as God's will. When the disciples hear these words from Jesus' lips, they are hearing the voice of the One who revealed his "decrees and laws" long ago at Horeb. This Jesus who speaks in the upper room is the same One who spoke directly to the people at Sinai and through his prophet Moses. Through obedience to Jesus Christ we demonstrate our covenantal commitment ("love") to him, but we also display to the world the privilege of salvation, divine presence, knowledge of his will, and blessing. Delighting in obedience to the revealed will of God represents the key to fulfilling the divine mission of reaching the world with his grace.

Deuteronomy 4:9-31

O nly be careful, and watch yourselves closely so that you do not forget the things your eyes have seen or let them slip from your heart as long as you live. Teach them to your children and to their children after them. [10]Remember the day you stood before the LORD your God at Horeb, when he said to me, "Assemble the people before me to hear my words so that they may learn to revere me as long as they live in the land and may teach them to their children." [11]You came near and stood at the foot of the mountain while it blazed with fire to the very heavens, with black clouds and deep darkness. [12]Then the LORD spoke to you out of the fire. You heard the sound of words but saw no form; there was only a voice. [13]He declared to you his covenant, the Ten Commandments, which he commanded you to follow and then wrote them on two stone tablets. [14]And the LORD directed me at that time to teach you the decrees and laws you are to follow in the land that you are crossing the Jordan to possess.

[15]You saw no form of any kind the day the LORD spoke to you at Horeb out of the fire. Therefore watch yourselves very carefully, [16]so that you do not become corrupt and make for yourselves an idol, an image of any shape, whether formed like a man or a woman, [17]or like any animal on earth or any bird that flies in the air, [18]or like any creature that moves along the ground or any fish in the waters below. [19]And when you look up to the sky and see the sun, the moon and the stars—all the heavenly array—do not be enticed into bowing down to them and worshiping things the LORD your God has apportioned to all the nations under heaven. [20]But as for you, the LORD took you and brought you out of the iron-smelting furnace, out of Egypt, to be the people of his inheritance, as you now are.

[21]The LORD was angry with me because of you, and he solemnly swore that I would not cross the Jordan and enter the good land the LORD your God is giving you as your inheritance. [22]I will die in this land; I will not cross the Jordan; but you are about to cross over and take possession

of that good land. [23]Be careful not to forget the covenant of the LORD your God that he made with you; do not make for yourselves an idol in the form of anything the LORD your God has forbidden. [24]For the LORD your God is a consuming fire, a jealous God.

[25]After you have had children and grandchildren and have lived in the land a long time — if you then become corrupt and make any kind of idol, doing evil in the eyes of the LORD your God and provoking him to anger, [26]I call heaven and earth as witnesses against you this day that you will quickly perish from the land that you are crossing the Jordan to possess. You will not live there long but will certainly be destroyed. [27]The LORD will scatter you among the peoples, and only a few of you will survive among the nations to which the LORD will drive you. [28]There you will worship man-made gods of wood and stone, which cannot see or hear or eat or smell. [29]But if from there you seek the LORD your God, you will find him if you look for him with all your heart and with all your soul. [30]When you are in distress and all these things have happened to you, then in later days you will return to the LORD your God and obey him. [31]For the LORD your God is a merciful God; he will not abandon or destroy you or forget the covenant with your forefathers, which he confirmed to them by oath.

IN THESE RECOLLECTIONS MOSES leapfrogs over thirty-eight years of desert wandering from Baal Peor back to Horeb. As pastor he interjects his recollections with repeated appeals to "guard" (NIV "watch") against forgetting past events (vv. 9, 15, 23) and against corrupt behavior (vv. 16, 19, 23).[1] The term "covenant" (*bᵉrît*), which occurs three times in this section (vv. 13, 23, 31), provides the key to both the main idea and the literary structure of these verses. Each occurrence relates to a particular moment in the covenantal story: (1) the grace of covenant past: the origins of the covenant (vv. 9 – 14); (2) the grace of covenant present: the essence of the covenant (vv. 15 – 24); (3) the grace of covenant future: the permanence of the covenant (vv. 25 – 31).

---

1. In each case the call for self-watch is followed by motive clauses, both negative (introduced with "so that ... not," *pen*, vv. 9b, 16, 19, 23) and positive (introduced with "for," *kî*, vv. 15, 24, 25[?]).

The Grace of Covenant Past:
The Origins of Yahweh's Covenant with Israel (4:9−14)

VERSES 9−14 involve one long sentence governed by the twofold appeal to absolute vigilance in verse 9a,[2] and a twofold warning (lit.), "lest you forget," and (lit.) "lest they leave your minds."[3] The verb "forget" does not mean simply a loss of memory, but failure to take into account what the memory recalls—the special relationship Yahweh had established with his people. Throughout his addresses Moses refers to details not to be forgotten,[4] reinforcing the impression created here that Israel's memory is not simply to involve abstract notions about God, but his specific acts in history on their behalf. With the charge, "Teach them to your children and to their children after them" (v. 9b), Moses highlights both the importance of Yahweh's revelation and the antidote to Israel's bad memory (cf. v. 25). The Israelites' greatest enemy will not be the Canaanites out there, but their own mind and heart within them (Judg. 2:10; Hos. 4:6).

As is often the case with modern preachers, Moses' passion is reflected in the awkward style of verses 9−14.[5] The object of "do not forget" in verse 9 is clear: "the things [events]" that the people's own eyes had witnessed. Verses 10−14 are best interpreted as commentary on "the things," highlighting especially one of the most significant "days" (v. 10) in Israel's history. Moses recaptures the aura of past events with the last three words of verse 11, which echo Exodus 19:16 and 20:21: that was a day of "darkness, cloud, and deep gloom" (NIV "black clouds and deep darkness").

Moses' recollections of Horeb focus on actions, first by the Israelites (vv. 10−11) and then by Yahweh (vv. 12−14). On that day the people stood before Yahweh their God; they came near and stood at the foot of the blazing mountain. This is formal court language. For a brief moment Horeb was transformed into a sacred place, the throne room of Yahweh,

---

2. The double appeal is framed by two strong particles, *raq*, "only, above all," and *mᵊʾôd*, "closely, diligently."

3. In Hebrew the word *lēb* represents both the heart and the mind.

4. Yahweh, their God (8:11, 19); Yahweh, who gave birth to Israel (32:18); how Yahweh rescued Israel from the slavery of Egypt (5:15; 6:12; 7:18; 8:14; 15:15; 16:3, 12; 24:18, 22); the revelation of Yahweh at Horeb (4:9); the covenant at Horeb (4:23); Yahweh's provision in the desert (8:2); what Amalek did to Israel (25:17) and Yahweh's victory over Amalek (25:19); the commands (26:13); what Yahweh did to Miriam (24:9); that Yahweh is the source of Israel's power and wealth (8:18); the nation's national anthem (31:21); Israel's own sin in the desert (9:7); and the past in general (32:7). In 24:19 Moses refers to the mundane matter of remembering a sheaf left out in the field.

5. The NIV solves the problem by inserting "Remember" in v. 10, which is lacking in the Hebrew.

and his subjects were invited to an audience with their divine Sovereign (cf. 18:7). Sometimes the Old Testament associates the divine fire with Yahweh as a warrior,[6] but in Deuteronomy fire is usually linked with the theophany at Horeb.[7] The combination of fire and light on one hand with cloud and darkness on the other introduced the Israelites both to the radiance of divine glory and to its lethal force.

The human actions provide the syntactical skeleton for verses 10—11, but these actions were possible only because of the divine Sovereign's gracious invitation. While the charge "Assemble the people before me" (v. 10) recalls Yahweh's own summary of the events in Exodus 19:4 (cf. Ex. 3:12), here Yahweh summarizes the agenda for the encounter: He will let them hear his voice so they might learn to "revere" him and never stop "revering" him. The Hebrew word for "to revere" (*yârēʾ*) bears a wide range of meanings in the Old Testament. Depending on the relationship between subject (the fearer) and object (the one feared), it could denote either fright (Ex. 20:18) or reverence and awe in the presence of a superior.[8] The latter is obviously the case here. For Israel this sort of "fear" will be a precondition to unqualified obedience, which in turn will be a precondition to life and prosperity in the land. The generation that came out of Egypt learned this fear through the physical sight of Yahweh's glory. Throughout his addresses Moses assumes that present and future generations must be taught this fear (Deut. 4:10; 14:23; 17:19; 31:12—13) through hearing the words of Yahweh (4:10), participating in formal worship (14:23), and hearing the Torah (17:19; 31:12—13).

Accepting the invitation, the people stood at the foot of the mountain eagerly anticipating the address of the divine king (v. 11).[9] When Yahweh spoke, he introduced them to his "covenant" (*bᵉrît*). The covenantal nature of Deuteronomy is evident in both the structure and the tone of the book, but this is the first occurrence of this word. In the Old Testament the word *bᵉrît* generally speaks of established or confirmed relationships and usually carries with it nuances of obligation.[10] The word is used of agreements, pacts, and treaties of all kinds, ranging from marriage contracts to legal declarations of promise and obligation.

---

6. Deut. 9:3, but see esp. 2 Sam. 22:8—16.

7. Deut. 4:11—12, 15, 33, 36; 5:4—5, 22—26; 9:10, 15, 21; 10:4; 18:16.

8. Deut. 4:10; 5:29; 6:2, 13, 24; 8:6; 10:12—13, 20; 13:4[5]; 14:23; 17:19; 28:58; 31:12—13.

9. Against the views of some, Moses' view of Israel's appearance and response before Yahweh is entirely positive.

10. Cf. W. J. Dumbrell, *Creation and Covenant: A Theology of Old Testament Covenants* (Nashville: Nelson, 1984), 16.

Moses notes two significant details about this covenant. (1) He identifies the covenant as Yahweh's covenant. Like all covenants involving Yahweh in the Old Testament, this covenant is monergistic: that is, Yahweh initiates it, identifies the covenant partner, defines the terms, and determines the consequences for compliance or noncompliance. However, unlike Hittite and Assyrian suzerainty treaties, this covenant was not imposed by an overlord upon a defeated vassal. The background is found in Yahweh's miraculous and undeserving rescue of the Israelites from the clutches of an oppressive overlord, that he might establish a relationship with them — a relationship that, from start to finish, serves their interests and well-being.

(2) Moses associates the covenant with (lit.) "the Ten Words"[11] (v. 13). Contrary to most translations and to pervasive popular usage, the Old Testament never refers to this document as the "Ten Commandments"; these are "ten words" (cf. 10:4; Ex. 34:28). Given the semantic range of the term *dᵉbārîm*, we should follow the early Greek translation and refer to this document as the *Decalogue*, that is, "the ten words/declarations," or even "the ten principles of covenant relationship." While the Old Testament never explains why there were ten words or explicitly numbers them,[12] the number ten seems to have been selected to correspond to the fingers on our hands and to facilitate memorization.

Having declared the foundational principles of the covenant,[13] Yahweh produced two written copies of the document on tablets of stone (cf. Ex. 24:12; 31:18; 32:15–16). The provision of two identical copies follows the ancient Near Eastern custom of giving each party to a covenant a copy of the agreement.[14] Whereas second millennium BC Hittite sources suggest

---

11. Here LXX translates *ta deka rhēmata*; in 10:4 and Ex. 34:28 LXX translates *tous deka logous*. For further discussion, see D. I. Block, "Reading the Decalogue Right to Left: The Ten Principles of Covenant Relationship in the Hebrew Bible," in *How I Love Your Torah, O LORD*, 24–25.

12. Based on discourse and syntactical features of the Decalogue I follow the Catholic and Lutheran, rather than the Reformed, numbering. For discussion, see Block, ibid., 56–60.

13. NIV treats "the Ten Commandments" as appositional to "covenant," but verse 13 consists of two clauses. The first declares the principal idea and the second clarifies it: "Then he declared to you his covenant, that is, he commanded you to do the Ten Words." Grammatically "the Ten Words" is the object of the infinitive "to do." For discussion, see most recently J. Hwang, "The Rhetoric of Remembrance: An Exegetical and Theological Investigation into the 'Fathers' in Deuteronomy" (Ph.D. Dissertation, Wheaton College, 2009), 292–98. The expression "to declare [*higgîd*] a covenant" occurs nowhere else in the Old Testament.

14. A longstanding Jewish tradition assumes the ten words were distributed five on each tablet (Josephus, *Ant.* 3.5.8) but this means that the first tablet has 146 words and the second only 26. In Christian tradition the first tablet is associated with the vertical commands (##1–4 in Calvin's numbering), and the second with the horizontal (##5–10). However, this approach has no contextual merit. See further, Block, "Reading the Decalogue Right to Left," 35–36.

the subordinate's copy was kept in the temple of his chief deity,[15] Deuteronomy 10:5 notes that both Yahweh's and Israel's copies of the Decalogue were stored in the ark of the covenant.

Moses concludes his report of the events at Horeb by adding that Yahweh commanded him to teach the Israelites "decrees and laws," which they were to put into practice in the land that they were to enter and possess (v. 14). The statement reinforces his role as authorized interpreter of the covenant. The book of Deuteronomy testifies to his fidelity to this charge.

The Grace of Covenant Present:
The Essence of Yahweh's Covenant with Israel (4:15–24)

THIS SECTION SUBDIVIDES INTO three main parts. Moses begins the first (vv. 15–19) and last (vv. 23–24) with strong appeals to the Israelites to "watch [guard]" themselves against abhorrent behavior, while the center (v. 20) functions as the rhetorical fulcrum. In verses 21–22 Moses inserts a parenthetical personal note, dividing this section into two almost identical halves and linking this chapter with the preceding recollections (cf. 1:37–38; 3:26).[16] While this section (as well as the rest of vv. 9–31) obviously serves as a warning against idolatry, the inverted word order in verse 20 places this warning within the broader context of Yahweh's grace in rescuing Israel from Egypt and taking them as his covenant people. Moses reinforces this conclusion with a climactic appeal not to forget the covenant (vv. 23–24), reminding the people of Yahweh's passion/jealousy and drawing expressions from the preamble and the first command of the Decalogue: Yahweh will not tolerate rivals.

Moses elaborates on the general prohibition of idolatry by listing four classes of forbidden creaturely representations of divinity: large land creatures, flying creatures, crawling dirt creatures, and creatures of the sea, categories borrowed directly from Genesis 1. By worshiping them humans violate Yahweh's formlessness (v. 15) and displace him with creatures, but they also challenge his rule by submitting as vassals to the creatures they were to govern.[17] Whereas idolaters worship forms that have mouths but

---

15. Thus Gary M. Beckman, *Hittite Diplomatic Texts* (Atlanta: Scholars, 1996), 3. He cites specific examples on pp. 46–47 and 91.

16. Not counting ʾet, the marker of a definite direct object, vv. 15–19 contain 75 words, vv. 20–24 contain 74.

17. This warning highlights the fundamental difference between the aniconism of Israelite religion and the forms of worship that prevailed among Israel's neighbors. On the nature and history of aniconism in Israel against its ancient Near Eastern cultural background, see T. Mettinger, *No Graven Image? Israelite Aniconism in Its Ancient Near Eastern Context* (ConBOT 42; Stockholm: Almqvist & Wiksell, 1995).

do not speak, the Israelites worshiped the One who has no form but who speaks and calls on the Israelites to serve as his representatives.

Moses then turns to a second form of religious perversion: the worship of the sun and moon and stars (v. 19; cf. 2 Kings 21:3; 23:5). Ancient Near Easterners generally perceived these as representations of divine beings who governed earthly existence. Moses uses five expressions to describe worshipers' relationship to them: they raise their eyes heavenward; they gaze devotedly at "all the heavenly array"; they are seduced by them; they prostrate themselves before them; and they submit to the gods as vassals.

Theologically the last clause of verse 19 may be the most difficult in the entire book of Deuteronomy. Many take the verse to mean that Yahweh allotted these heavenly objects to the other nations as objects of worship, while reserving himself for Israel's worship. However, this interpretation flies in the face of the Old Testament's consistent antipathy toward idols of any kind[18] and reads too much into this verse. The text is silent on the allotment, and the assumed purpose, "as objects of worship," must be supplied from outside. Furthermore, this explanation excludes Israel from "all the nations under heaven" and assumes this nation has no relationship to the heavenly bodies.

Finally, this interpretation of verse 19 misses the links between this passage and Genesis 1. Having borrowed the categories of creatures from Genesis 1:20–23, Moses moves back to day four of creation, when God created these heavenly bodies. His comment that they were apportioned "to all the nations under heaven" represents a legitimate interpretation of Genesis 1:14–19. These objects were not created as objects to be worshiped but as instruments of divine providence, governing the world, and guaranteeing the annual rhythm of life for all its inhabitants. Even if the objects function as ciphers for heavenly beings, this passage does not identify them as legitimate objects of worship by anyone.[19] If Israel is sidetracked and worships them, they will deny divine election and their special covenant standing with Yahweh.

Verse 20 represents the focal point of this passage, highlighting the utter treachery and perversion of idolatry. Moses highlights Israel's special rela-

---

18. See further D. I. Block, "Other Religions in Old Testament Theology," in *Biblical Faith and Other Religions: An Evangelical Assessment* (ed. D. W. Baker; Grand Rapids: Baker, 2004), 60–74; reprinted in *The Gospel According to Moses*, 200–236.

19. Cf. 32:8. The verb used here is used of apportioning the land of Canaan among the tribes of Israel (Josh. 14:1; 18:2) or distributing the spoils of battle (Josh. 22:8). See further, M. Heiser, "Deuteronomy 32:8 and the Sons of God," *BSac* 158 (2001): 71; idem, "Monotheism, Polytheism, Monolatry, or Henotheism? Toward an Assessment of Divine Plurality in the Hebrew Bible," *BBR* 18/1 (2008): 4–13.

tionship with Yahweh with three statements: (1) they are the product of Yahweh's gracious saving actions;[20] (2) they were rescued from the furnace specifically to be Yahweh's covenant partner;[21] (3) they have been claimed by Yahweh as his own "special possession." By referring to Israel as his *naḥ^alâ*, Moses highlights Yahweh's loving and caring relationship with this nation.

In verses 21–22 Moses digresses momentarily to express his frustration over Yahweh's refusal to let him enter the land. As in 1:37 and 3:26 he recognizes that this prohibition arises from Yahweh's anger toward him, but he blames the people for that anger. His bitterness is reflected in complaining that he will die outside the Promised Land, characterized as a "good" land that Yahweh has given to the Israelites as their special "possession" (*naḥ^alâ*).[22]

If verse 20 is the fulcrum of this passage, then verses 23–24 represent the climax. Once more Moses charges his people to guard themselves against forgetting "the covenant of the LORD your God" that he made with them, and against manufacturing any images that would supplant Yahweh in this relationship. He grounds this warning with two clauses, each of which contributes significantly to Deuteronomy's vision of God: "Yahweh is Consuming Fire; he is Impassioned El" (pers. trans.).[23] On the surface, the first expression extends the visual metaphor of Horeb (Exod 3:2–3; 24:17), except that there, remarkably, the fire did not consume. Here the fire represents not merely the personal presence of Yahweh, but his burning fury in the face of covenantal infidelity, expressed specifically in idolatry.[24]

---

20. By frontloading the object and choosing verbs for their assonantal effect, Moses contrasts Yahweh's indirect management of the rest of the world with his direct involvement with Israel. Note the word play: the verb *lāqaḥ*, "he took," here, and *ḥālaq*, "he apportioned," at the end of verse 19, contain the same consonants and vowels.

21. The purpose clause at the end of verse 20 adapts the covenant formula, "I will be your God, and you shall be my people." See Deut. 29:10–13[9–12]. Also Ex. 6:7; Lev. 26:12; Jer. 7:23; 11:4; 30:22; Ezek. 36:28.

22. The exclusion of Moses is a dark theme running through Deuteronomy (cf. Millar, *Now Choose Life*, 97). D. T. Olson's interpretation of Moses as "a paradigm for the vocation of sacrificial giving" (*Deuteronomy and the Death of Moses: A Theological Reading* [OBT; Minneapolis: Fortress, 1994], 17–22) is unnecessarily idealistic.

23. Like most translations, the NIV treats both predicates as adjectives. However the pattern of verbless clauses in the Pentateuch suggests the second element in both functions as a proper noun. See F. I. Andersen, *The Hebrew Verbless Clause in the Pentateuch* (SBLMS 14; Nashville/New York, Abingdon, 1970). Elsewhere *ʾēl qannāʾ* may mean "a jealous/passionate God" (Ex. 34:14b; Deut. 6:15; Josh. 24:19; Nah. 1:2), but Ex. 34:14a explicitly identifies Qanna' as a proper title for God. So also J. Hoftijzer, "The Nominal Clause Reconsidered," *VT* 23 (1973): 494.

24. See P. A. Kruger, "A Cognitive Interpretation of the Emotion of Anger in the Hebrew Bible," *JNWSL* 26 (2000): 181–93, esp. 189.

Moses' characterization of Yahweh as El Qanna' (Impassioned El) is equally dramatic. The usual interpretation of *qn'* as "jealous" is misleading because we commonly view jealousy as an illegitimate disposition akin to envy or covetousness.[25] However, in the Old Testament, this term usually speaks of the legitimate passion that is aroused when interference from a third party threatens a proper relationship, particularly a marriage relationship when another "lover" enters the picture. Yahweh is an impassioned God, who treasures Israel as his covenant people. This love is fueled, not by an exploitative need to dominate, but by ardor for the well-being of the object.

The Grace of Covenant Future: The Permanence of the Covenant (4:25−31)

NOW MOSES SHIFTS HIS gaze to the role of the covenant in the distant future. While the first part of this section is dominated by a tone of doom (vv. 25−28), the second opens windows of hope (vv. 29−31). Here Moses the pastor describes the consequences of abandoning Yahweh and the covenant relationship: the tripartite covenant relationship involving Yahweh, Israel, and the land will disintegrate. Although the mood is pessimistic, Moses ends on a positive note.

Moses envisions Israel's descent into idolatry when they are well-established in the land. He restates his own warning in verse 15a almost verbatim: they will act corruptly, making images and all kinds of shapes, and committing the "evil in the eyes of the LORD your God." That this idiom commonly occurs with the article ("the evil") suggests a particular kind of evil; violating the Supreme Command ("You shall have no other gods before me," 5:7) by manufacturing competing images of worship,[26] which "provoke" Yahweh's ire. Before Moses elaborates on the divine anger, he appeals to the heavens and the earth to testify *against* Israel (cf. 31:28).[27] Then he lists five consequences of infidelity that await the Israelites: (1) they will certainly and quickly be removed from the land ; (2) they will be utterly destroyed, ending their dream of long life in the land; (3) Yahweh

---

25. Though the Hebrew word may be used of envy (Gen. 26:14; Ezek. 31:9).

26. "The evil" is picked up in the sevenfold refrain of the book of Judges: 3:7, 12 [2x]; 4:1; 6:1; 10:6; 13:1.

27. The act of calling witnesses is drawn from ancient Near Eastern custom, which often included long lists of divine witnesses in treaty documents. See, e.g., Esarhaddon's succession treaty, *ANET*, 534−41. For discussion, see S. Parpola and K. Watanabe, *Neo-Assyrian Treaties and Loyalty Oaths* (Helsinki: Helsinki Univ. Press, 1988), xxxvii. Given Moses' strict monotheism and the nature of his warnings, "heaven and earth" is a merismic expression for "all creation" (Gen. 1:1; Deut. 32:1; Isa. 1:2; cf. Jer. 6:19; Mic. 1:2) substituting for the gods.

will scatter them among the peoples, driving them to another place like a shepherd drives his flock; (4) a few will survive in the lands where Yahweh has driven them; (5) in the lands where the worship of senseless gods is the norm, they will have their fill of idolatry (v. 28).

Moses' last threat drips with irony and poetic justice as he promises the people exactly what their insatiable lust demanded. Exposing the folly of idolatry, Moses observes sarcastically how roles have reversed. (1) Instead of the creature worshiping the Creator, the creator worships creature: idols are the work of human hands. (2) Idolatry directly contradicts Yahweh's self-revelation (vv. 12, 15): lifeless and physical material replaces what is formless but living and spiritual. (3) These images have organs of perception and communication, but they are blind, deaf, and dumb. In effect, Yahweh says through Moses, "If idolatry is what you want, fine — but not in my land!" For their sin, the Israelites face a total disintegration of the deity – nation – land relationship that Yahweh had established for the sake of his mission to the world, and in Israel's interest.

But suddenly the tone changes (v. 29). Beyond the judgment Moses sees a change in the people's disposition. From the land of the Israelites' exile and from the land where they worship their worthless idols, they will again seek Yahweh, and amazingly he will let himself be found by them. Unlike the gods of the peoples, he is not primarily a territorial deity; rather, he is the personal God of Israel. The opening clause of verse 30 specifies the context of the reversal: when people are "in distress," when all these threats have been fulfilled,[28] and "in later days."[29]

Moses begins verse 29 by spelling out the human preconditions of hope, and then he declares the divine basis for that hope. He describes the response required of Israel with four verbs arranged in logical order. (1) From the land of exile the Israelites will seek Yahweh their God.[30] (2) They will find him if they abandon all other searches and seek Yahweh alone (with their whole being). (3) They will turn around (*šûb*) and walk toward Yahweh rather than toward the other gods. (4) They will listen to Yahweh's voice. Here "the voice" refers to the covenantal words Yahweh delivered at Sinai and the words being preached presently by his spokesman Moses.

---

28. As in v. 9, *haddᵉbārîm* may refer to events or Moses' words. NIV's "things" obscures the emphasis on Moses' utterance and the certain fulfillment of his predictions.

29. This phrase does not mean the eschatological end of time (as in Isa. 2:2) but a point in the distant future, i.e., "ultimately." So also Tigay, *Deuteronomy*, 54; Peter C. Craigie, *Deuteronomy* (NICOT; Grand Rapids: Eerdmans, 1976), 141.

30. "To seek" (*bqš*) Yahweh does not mean to look for him as if he were lost, but to seek him out, to approach him humbly with renewed devotion, and plead for return of his favor.

Although Deuteronomy's version of the covenant curses ends with judgment,[31] perhaps inspired by Yahweh's own words in Leviticus 26, here Moses declares that Israel's story cannot end in judgment. In the end, Yahweh's disposition and character guarantee their hope: "the LORD your God is a merciful God (v. 31). The word *raḥûm* speaks of warm and tender affection, like the love of a mother toward a child (Ex. 34:6–7).[32] Yahweh's passion does indeed burn with vexation and rage at infidelity, but it also burns with compassion for Israel, his child (cf. Hos. 11:8–9).

Moses then cites three evidences of Yahweh's compassion (v. 31): Yahweh will not "drop" or abandon Israel, he will not destroy Israel, and he will not forget his covenant with Israel's ancestors. Although the emphatic verbs framing verse 26 seemed to suggest that Yahweh would respond to Israel's apostasy by completely annihilating them, the reference to a remnant in verse 27 had opened the door ever so slightly to divine grace. Now Yahweh declares in unequivocal terms that because he is gracious, he will neither destroy Israel nor allow Israel to destroy herself. Israel may forget the covenant of Yahweh (v. 23), but Yahweh will never forget the covenant of the "forefathers." Israel's future is as secure as the eternal covenant and the unchangeably gracious character of God.

Bridging Contexts

WHAT SHALL WE MAKE of "the covenant with your forefathers, which he confirmed to them by oath"? Does this refer to the covenant with the patriarchs as described in Genesis, the covenant made with the exodus generation at Sinai (as in v. 23), or the covenant renewed here on the Plains of Moab? While some argue in favor of the first,[33] the weight of the evidence is elsewhere.

1. The distinction many make between the Abrahamic covenant as unconditional and the Israelite covenant as conditional is false. All

---

31. Chapter 28 provides exposition and expansion of Deut. 4:26–28.

32. It derives from the same root as *reḥem*, the word for "womb" (Isa. 49:15; Jer. 20:17). Cf. *HALOT*, 1216–18.

33. (1) In previous occurrences of the expression, "which he swore to X," in Deuteronomy, the clause has referred to Yahweh's covenant promise of land to the patriarchs (1:8, 35). This contrasts with the narratives dealing with the covenant ratification ceremony at Sinai, which never speak of Yahweh's "swearing" to Israel to keep the covenant. (2) Biblical narratives often refer to the covenant with the patriarchs as God's covenant with Abraham, Isaac, and Jacob (Ex. 2:24; cf. 6:4; Lev. 26:42; 2 Kings 13:23; 1 Chron. 16:15–18 = Ps. 105:8–11). (3) The covenant curses in Leviticus 26 base Israel's hope for renewal on God's covenant with the patriarchs. See further Eugene Merrill, *Deuteronomy* (NAC; Nashville: Broadman & Holman, 1994), 129.

covenants involve relationships, the health of which depends on the actions of each party vis-à-vis the other. As anticipated in Genesis 17:7, the Israelite covenant ratified at Sinai was the means by which the promise made within the Abrahamic covenant was fulfilled.

2. Although we read of God's covenant with Abraham, Isaac, and Jacob, this covenant is never referred to elsewhere as "the covenant of your forefathers."

3. Leviticus 26:45 explicitly associates the "covenant of the ancestors" (*berît riʾšōnîm*), used here, with those "whom I brought out of Egypt in the sight of the nations to be their God."

4. In this chapter (esp. vv. 9−31), the central issue has been the covenant that Yahweh made with Israel at Horeb and that is embodied in the Decalogue.

5. Moses' reference to Yahweh's remembering his covenant with the forefathers deliberately contrasts his fixed memory with the Israelite lapse of memory (cf. v. 23).

6. Since Moses is speaking of the distant future (v. 30) and specifically refers to when "you have had children and grandchildren" (v. 25), "your forefathers" could refer to the exodus generation or even to the present generation.

7. While some cite the absence of an oath at Horeb as evidence for the Abrahamic covenant, we should note first that in the ancient Near East covenants would rarely have been made without an oath.[34] Moreover, later prophetic tradition actually speaks of Yahweh's commitment on oath to this covenant.[35]

8. Finally, borrowing heavily from Deuteronomy, Jeremiah explicitly identifies the exodus generation as the forefathers with whom Yahweh made a covenant (34:13).

In the end, there is no need to choose between the patriarchal covenant and the Israelite covenant. Rather than focusing on the land—as promised to the patriarchs—in verse 31 Moses' attention is on Yahweh's relationship with his people: "He will neither fail *you* nor destroy *you*" [pers. trans.]. Furthermore, the "return" spoken of in verses 29−31 is not to the land but to Yahweh.[36] The issue in this chapter is much greater than land. Unlike

---

34. Weinfeld notes (*TDOT*, 2:256) that oaths were essential to give covenants their binding validity.

35. See Ezek. 16:8 and 20:5. Cf. Daniel I. Block, *Ezekiel Chapters 1−24* (NICOT; Grand Rapids: Eerdmans, 1997), 625−26.

36. Cf. the references to the "land" as that which he swore to the ancestors in 1:8, 35; 6:10; 7:13; 10:11; 11:9, 21; 26:3; 28:11; 30:20; 31:20.

the gods of the nations, who were primarily interested in territory and only secondarily concerned about people, Yahweh's primary concern lies with his people and his relationship to them (cf. Gen. 17:7).[37] The covenant he remembers is the one made with Abraham, extended to his descendants at Horeb, and about to be confirmed with this generation on the Plains of Moab.[38]

In Deuteronomy the covenant with the fathers is one.[39] In the future Yahweh may suspend the benefits of the covenant (4:25–28; cf. Lev. 26:14–39; Deut. 28:15–68), but this will not affect the covenant itself.[40] On the contrary, the judgments are written into the covenant, but so is the restoration; the judgment cannot be the last word. In the end, when God circumcises the Israelites' hearts and they repent of their rebellion (Lev. 26:41; Deut. 4:30; 30:6–10), he will renew his covenant relationship with them and bring them back to the land he promised the ancestors.

In this paragraph Moses continues his attack on idolatry, portraying Israel's worship of other gods not only as rebellion against Yahweh, but as foolish and futile. Finally Yahweh gives them up to the folly of their own minds. If the Israelites want to worship objects of wood and stone made with human hands, with eyes that do not see, ears that do not hear, and mouths that do not eat, let alone speak, then let them—but not in Yahweh's land! Echoes of this polemic are heard not only in Isaiah's spoofs of idolatry in Isaiah 44:9–20, but especially in Psalm 115:3–11:

> Our God is in heaven;
> > he does whatever pleases him.
> But their idols are silver and gold,
> > made by the hands of men.
> They have mouths, but cannot speak,
> > eyes, but they cannot see;
> they have ears, but cannot hear,
> > noses, but they cannot smell;
> they have hands, but cannot feel,
> > feet, but they cannot walk;
> > nor can they utter a sound with their throats.

---

37. In 4:37a Moses notes that Yahweh chose the ancestors' descendants "after them." This phrase occurs five times in Gen. 17:7–10.

38. References to the covenant "that Yahweh swore with the forefathers" (pers. trans.) recur in Deut. 7:12 and 8:18. The identity of the ancestors in each case must be determined according to the evidence of each context.

39. As argued convincingly by Hwang, "Rhetoric of Remembrance," 302–8.

40. On the eternality of God's covenant with Israel, see Ex. 31:16–17; Lev. 24:8; Judg. 2:1; Ps. 111:2–9; Isa. 54:4–10.

Those who make them will be like them,
  and so will all who trust in them.
O house of Israel, trust in the LORD—
  he is their help and shield.
O house of Aaron, trust in the LORD—
  he is their help and shield.
You who fear him, trust in the LORD—
  he is their help and shield.

THE COVENANT AT SINAI represented a remarkable expression of God's grace. Deuteronomy
4:9–31 makes a profound contribution both to
Deuteronomy's vision of the grace and the glory
of God. First, the covenant made at Sinai represented a remarkable expression of God's grace. Within God's gracious redemptive-historical plan, his
covenant with Israel plays an important role. It demonstrates what is true
of all divine covenants: the privilege of relationship with God is available
only to those whom he in his gracious sovereignty chooses and must be
answered with grateful obedience to his will as revealed in the context of
the covenant.

Even so, all covenants are grounded in and made possible by the finished work of Christ (1 Peter 1:13–21). When Jesus instituted what we call
"the Lord's Supper," he declared to the disciples, "This is my blood of the
covenant, which is poured out for many for the forgiveness of sins" (Matt.
26:28).[41] This statement echoes Moses' words of institution in the context
of the covenant ratification at Sinai: "See the blood of the covenant, which
the LORD has made with you" (Ex. 24:8 [pers. trans.]). Through Christ the
vast gulf between the gracious but holy God and sinful human beings is
spanned. Based on his work, the benefits summarized in the new Israelite
covenant were granted to believers in Israel and have also become ours: (1)
the Torah written on our hearts; (2) covenant relationship with God; (3)
the knowledge of God; (4) forgiveness of sins.[42]

The covenant made at Sinai represented a remarkable expression of
God's glory. God does indeed condescend to speak with mortals, but he
does so without sacrificing any of his glory. In fact, only the cloud and the
deep darkness spared the Israelites from God's lethal radiance. And to this
day, those who have been drawn to God in covenant relationship will give

---

41. Cf. Heb. 13:20–21.
42. Jer. 31:33–34; cf. Heb. 8:8–13; 9:15.

expression to their gratitude, meager as that expression may be. In 1867 W. Chalmers Smith attempted to capture the glorious enigma of God as revealed at Sinai in his famous hymn:

> Immortal, invisible, God only wise,
> In light inaccessible hid from our eyes,
> Most blessed, most glorious, the Ancient of Days,
> Almighty, victorious, the great name we praise.

> Great Father of glory, pure Father of light,
> Thine angels adore Thee, all veiling their sight;
> All laud we would render: O help us to see —
> 'Tis only the splendour of light hideth Thee.[43]

More recently, with powerful rhetorical flourish, a sermon easily accessible on the Internet has captured a measure of the indescribable glory and grace of God:[44]

> He is the First and Last, the Beginning and the End!
> He is the keeper of Creation and the Creator of all!
> He is the Architect of the universe and the Manager of all times.
> He always was, He always is, and He always will be....
> Unmoved, Unchanged, Undefeated, and never Undone!
> He was bruised and brought healing! He was pierced and eased pain!
> He was persecuted and brought freedom! He was dead and brought life!
> He is risen and brings power! He reigns and brings Peace!
> The world can't understand Him, the armies can't defeat Him,
> The schools can't explain Him, and the leaders can't ignore Him.
> Herod couldn't kill Him, the Pharisees couldn't confuse Him,
> and the people couldn't hold Him!
> Nero couldn't crush Him, Hitler couldn't silence Him,
> The New Age can't replace Him, and Donahue can't explain Him away!
> He is light, love, longevity, and Lord.
> He is goodness, Kindness, Gentleness, and God.
> He is Holy, Righteous, mighty, powerful, and pure.

---

43. The lyrics are widely available on the Internet; e.g., www.worshipmap.com/lyrics/immortal.html.

44. Some attribute the sermon to the great African American preacher S. M. Lockeridge. See http://blessingsforlife.com/favforwards/everydayisablessing.htm (accessed February 4, 2009).

His ways are right, His word is eternal,
His will is unchanging, and His mind is on me. . . .

He is everything for everybody, everywhere, every time, and every
    way.
He is God, He is faithful. I am His, and He is mine!
My Father in heaven can whip the father of this world.
So, if you're wondering why I feel so secure, understand this. . . .
He said it and that settles it.
God is in control, I am on His side, and that means all is well with
    my soul.
Everyday is a blessing, for GOD Is!

**The covenant made at Sinai testifies to God's right to our exclu-
sive devotion.** Calvin asserted that human nature is "a perpetual factory of
idols."[45] The urgency of Moses' warning testifies to the truth of this assertion. While we who read this text today may be shocked at how quickly
the Israelites would abandon Yahweh in favor of other gods, this problem
is common to all humanity. Paul may have had Deuteronomy 4:15 – 24
in mind when he wrote Romans 1:18 – 23. When people forget the grace
of God in redemption, revelation, and covenant, they become ungrateful,
have no fear of God (*asebeia*, rendered "ungodliness" by the NIV), and act
corruptly (*adikia*, rendered "unrighteousness" by the NIV).

In our text idolatry involves reverential acts of homage and submission
to objects other than God—objects made either by human hands or by
God's own hands. While modern Westerners tend not to create concrete
objects to be worshiped, we are constantly crafting new substitutes for
God. Indeed an idol may be defined as anything (whether concrete or
abstract) that rivals God—anything to which we submit and which we
serve in place of God himself. The stuff of idols is not necessarily bad. The
sun, moon, and stars are good; they govern the universe. Wood and stones
are good and useful for limitless projects and tasks. But when we pervert
their function and treat them as ultimate things on which our well-being
and destiny depend, they rival God—and that makes them an idol.

Ask Job. He had a clear idea of the forms and the seductive power of
idols (Job 31:24 – 26). Idols are not necessarily physical. Many have identified money, sex, and power as pervasive idols in our day.[46] However, the
same may be true of our spouses, our children, our hobbies, our books. If

---

45. John Calvin, *Institutes of the Christian Religion* (ed. J. T. McNeill and trans. F. L. Battles
(LCC 20; London: SCM, 1960), 1:108.

46. For an eloquent discussion of this issue, see Tim Keller, *Counterfeit Gods: The Empty
Promises of Money, Sex, and Power, and the Only Hope That Matters* (New York: Penguin, 2009).

we are unwilling to give them up for the sake of the kingdom, they have become idols and God is robbed of the exclusive worship he deserves.

The covenant made at Sinai served as a call to worship. The privilege of covenant relationship with God calls for humble submission and homage to the divine Suzerain, demonstrated in grateful and unreserved obedience, as acts of reverent worship. God's invitation to Israel to the mountain was an invitation to worship—with fear and trembling. We may live on this side of the incarnation, but echoing the sights and sounds of Horeb, the author of Hebrews reminds us that God still seeks worshipers who will worship him in fear (Heb. 12:18–29).

Deuteronomy 4:32–40

A sk now about the former days, long before your time, from the day God created man on the earth; ask from one end of the heavens to the other. Has anything so great as this ever happened, or has anything like it ever been heard of? ³³Has any other people heard the voice of God speaking out of fire, as you have, and lived? ³⁴Has any god ever tried to take for himself one nation out of another nation, by testings, by miraculous signs and wonders, by war, by a mighty hand and an outstretched arm, or by great and awesome deeds, like all the things the LORD your God did for you in Egypt before your very eyes?

³⁵You were shown these things so that you might know that the LORD is God; besides him there is no other. ³⁶From heaven he made you hear his voice to discipline you. On earth he showed you his great fire, and you heard his words from out of the fire. ³⁷Because he loved your forefathers and chose their descendants after them, he brought you out of Egypt by his Presence and his great strength, ³⁸to drive out before you nations greater and stronger than you and to bring you into their land to give it to you for your inheritance, as it is today.

³⁹Acknowledge and take to heart this day that the LORD is God in heaven above and on the earth below. There is no other. ⁴⁰Keep his decrees and commands, which I am giving you today, so that it may go well with you and your children after you and that you may live long in the land the LORD your God gives you for all time.

MOSES' FIRST ADDRESS REACHES a glorious climax in 4:32–40.[1] The God whom he has declared to be incomparably gracious in the revelation of his will (vv. 1–8) and in his invitation to covenant relationship (vv. 9–31) is also incomparable in the gracious salvation he accomplishes for his people. In this short section Moses demonstrates

---

1. On the discourse significance of *kî* (first word in v. 32) see C. M. Follingstad, *Deictic Viewpoint in Biblical Hebrew Text: A Syntagmatic and Paradigmatic Analysis of the Particle kî* (Dallas: SIL International, 2001).

that of all the graces reviewed in this first address, this grace surpasses them all.

On the basis of style and content this paragraph divides into five parts:

A The History Lesson Part I (vv. 32–34)
  B The Theology Lesson Part I (v. 35)
A´ The History Lesson Part II (vv. 36–38)
  B´ The Theology Lesson Part II (v. 39)
    C The Practical Lesson (v. 40)

Three dominant imperatives trace the logic of the passage: "ask" (v. 32); "acknowledge [know]" (v. 39); "keep" (v. 40). With keen homiletical sense, Moses challenges his hearers to reflect on the historical facts (vv. 32–34), to draw the right theological conclusions from those facts (vv. 35–39), and to order their lives according to the theology that derives from those facts (v. 40).

The History Lesson, Part I (4:32–34)

A CENTRAL HISTORICAL FACT drives the first paragraph: Israel's experience of salvation is without parallel or analogy in all of human history. With the opening imperative, "Ask," Moses invites his audience to engage in exhaustive historical research[2] in pursuit of the answers to four questions. The first two questions are general; the third and fourth are more specific. (1) Has any great event like this ever happened before?[3] (2) Has anybody ever heard about anything like this? (3) Has any people ever heard the voice of God? And having heard it have they lived to tell about it?[4] (4) Has any god dared to do what Israel's God has done in taking for himself one nation from the midst of another nation?"

The last question, of course, is purely hypothetical, since there are no other gods (v. 35). Even if there were, this is not how ancient Near Eastern gods typically behaved. In self-interest they would indeed battle other nations and their gods, but not to rescue people; their goal was expanding their own territory. In an unprecedented act Yahweh had invaded Egypt, snatched Israel from the clutches of Pharaoh and Egypt's gods, and brought them to himself (Ex. 19:4). The verb *nissâ* ("to test") captures

---

2. "From the day God created man on the earth" specifies the chronological scope; "from one end of the heavens to the other" specifies the geographic scope.

3. Contra NIV, the question is not whether an event as great as this has happened, but whether a great event *like this* has happened before. So also Wright, *Deuteronomy*, 55.

4. Underlying this question is the biblical notion that no one can see God and live; the radiation of divine glory is lethal. Cf. Ex. 3:6; 24:10–11; 33:20–23; Judg. 6:22–23; 13:22; Isa. 6:5.

the nature and significance of Yahweh's actions (v. 34):[5] They challenged both human powers and the gods of the land where the people were enslaved.

Moses describes Yahweh's valorous acts with seven expressions: "daring acts" (NIV "testings"), "miraculous signs and wonders," "war," "a strong hand and an outstretched arm," and "great and awesome deeds." With these four questions and this catalogue of divine actions Moses declares that Yahweh's rescue of Israel from Egypt is unparalleled either in historical records or in fictional portrayals; the notion is unheard of, the experience is intolerable, and the divine power displayed is awesome.

The Theology Lesson, Part I (4:35)

A CENTRAL THEOLOGICAL FACT drives this paragraph: The God of Israel is *sui generis* — in a class all his own. Having ended verse 34 with a reminder that these acts were all performed for Israel's sake, he reiterates this point in verse 35: "You were shown ... so that you might know."[6] The purpose of Yahweh's awesome acts was revelatory: these events demonstrated that he alone deserves the title God (*ʾelōhîm*) and that there is no other in his class. He is indeed "God of gods" (10:17).

The History Lesson, Part II (4:36 – 38)

MOSES BEGINS TO ADDRESS the second pair of rhetorical questions from verses 33 and 34 by affirming that Yahweh is *both* in heaven, his true residence, *and* on earth in the very midst of the fire (cf. vv. 11 – 15). Indeed, the fire serves as the visible symbol of his presence.[7] Although unstated here (cf. 8:5), based on verses 10 and 35, his goal was obviously to promote fear of Yahweh and demonstrate that Yahweh alone is God.

In verses 37b – 38 Moses addresses the fourth question, summarizing again Yahweh's great past and anticipated future acts on Israel's behalf: (1) He chose Israel; (2) he personally and with his own great strength brought his people out of Egypt; (3) he will drive out greater and stronger nations than Israel; (4) he will deliver their land over to the Israelites as their "special grant" (*naḥᵃlâ*, NIV "inheritance"). This is the first reference

---

5. NIV's "tried" (v. 34) misconstrues this merely as an attempt. Cf. the reference to "great trials" in 7:19 and 29:3[2], which in context signify acts of "daring-do."

6. The wording of "you were shown" is both emphatic (note the addition of an explicit subject with a passive verb) and enigmatic (shown what?).

7. For full discussion of the real presence of Yahweh in Deuteronomy, see I. Wilson, *Out of the Midst of the Fire: Divine Presence in Deuteronomy* (SBLDS 151; Atlanta: Scholars, 1995), esp. 66 – 73.

to Yahweh's prior election of Israel in the book. The objects of his election are the "descendants" of the ancestors, that is, the Israelites as a people (cf. Gen. 17:7).

Moses' declaration that Yahweh has chosen Israel and is acting on the nation's behalf "because he loved your forefathers" introduces us for the first time to a key theological motif in Deuteronomy. Although in the Old Testament the term ²āhab ("to love") may bear a wide range of meanings,[8] in Deuteronomy "love" denotes "covenant commitment demonstrated in actions that serve the interests of the other person."[9] This statement is revolutionary, since the notion of love is virtually absent from the vocabulary of divine-human relationships in the ancient orient.

The Theology Lesson, Part II (4:39)

REITERATING THE STATEMENT OF verse 35, Moses heightens the urgency and relevance of acknowledging Yahweh for the Israelites poised to cross the Jordan by adding "this day" (*hayyôm*). What the people had witnessed at Sinai has enduring significance. The people may cross the Jordan confidently, knowing that though Yahweh is supreme in heaven, he is present with them on earth.

The Practical Lesson (4:40)

A SINGLE PRACTICAL FACT drives the final verse: awareness of the history of Yahweh's actions on Israel's behalf and knowledge of his status as supreme over all must inspire behavior in line with the will of this gracious God. Moses appeals to his people to obey the will of Yahweh for their own good and for the good of their descendants. If they will keep alive the memory of Yahweh's gracious actions, if their theology remains pure, and if their response is right, God's mission for them will be fulfilled. The land has indeed been promised them as an eternal possession, but enjoyment of the promise is conditional.[10] Each generation must commit itself anew to being the people of God in God's land for God's glory.

---

8. See P. J. J. S. Els, "אהב," *NIDOTTE*, 1:277–99.

9. For discussion of the notion of "love" as the basis of ancient Near Eastern treaty relationships, see William L. Moran, "Ancient Near Eastern Background of the Love of God in Deuteronomy," *CBQ* 25 (1965): 77–87. The Amarna letters speak of allied princes "loving" each other, of vassals loving the pharaoh, and the pharaoh loving the vassal. Cf. A. O. Haldar, "אהב," *TDOT*, 1:101.

10. Cf. Deut. 5:29; 6:24; 11:1; 14:23; 18:5; 19:9; 28:29–33.

Bridging
Contexts

FEW TEXTS IN SCRIPTURE are more profound or exhilarating than verses 32–40. We hear echoes of Moses' reminiscences of Yahweh's mighty acts repeatedly in Deuteronomy[11] and throughout the Scriptures. While later poets pick up the motif of "signs and wonders" and flesh it out with recollections of the fate of Pharaoh and his forces,[12] Jeremiah 32:20–22 provides the clearest echo of the present passage:

> You performed miraculous signs and wonders in Egypt and have continued them to this day, both in Israel and among all mankind, and have gained the renown that is still yours. You brought your people Israel out of Egypt with signs and wonders, by a mighty hand and an outstretched arm and with great terror. You gave them this land you had sworn to give their forefathers, a land flowing with milk and honey.

In context Jeremiah observes that Israel has wasted these memories of Yahweh's mighty acts by failing to draw the theological conclusions and practical implications spelled out in Deuteronomy 4:40 and refusing to live according to God's will. Yahweh's past signs and wonders provide the backdrop for answering the question, "Is anything too hard for [Yahweh]?" (Jer. 32:27). For Jeremiah the specific issue is Israel's ultimate restoration to the land, a hope symbolized by the prophet's purchase of the plot of land in Anathoth. In a manner similar to the later rabbinic method of arguing from the greater to the lesser, he declares that if Yahweh could rescue the Israelites from Egypt and deliver Canaan into their hands in the first place, surely he is able to rescue his people from exile and restore their fortunes in the land promised to their ancestors.

But allusions to the motifs of Deuteronomy 4:32–40 are common elsewhere in the Old Testament as well. The linkage of the notion of exodus with a polemic against idolatry are especially striking in Isaiah 40. Moreover, the motif of divine signs and wonders carries over into the New Testament. Increasingly scholars are recognizing that one of the fundamental agendas of the Gospels is to present Jesus as Yahweh, who ushers in the kingdom of God with signs and wonders that climax in his resurrection.[13]

---

11. Deut. 6:22; 7:19; 11:3; 13:2[3]; 26:8; 29:3[2]; 34:11.

12. See Neh. 9:9–11; Pss. 78:43–53; 105:26–45; 135:8–9; 136:10–15.

13. Drawing esp. on Isaiah. See R. Watts, *Isaiah's New Exodus and Mark* (WUNT 2/88; Tübingen: Mohr-Siebeck, 1997); idem, *Isaiah's New Exodus in Mark* (Grand Rapids: Baker, 2000); D. W. Pao, *Acts and the Isaianic New Exodus*, (WUNT 2/130; Tübingen: Mohr-Siebeck, 2000); idem, *Acts and the Isaianic New Exodus* (Grand Rapids: Baker, 2002).

References to signs and wonders occur repeatedly in the book of Acts as signs of the dawning of the new eschatological age,[14] validating the work of the apostles as a continuation of the work of Jesus. While Isaiah's and other prophets' use of exodus language to describe the return of Israel from captivity in Babylon and her restoration to the Promised Land obviously inspired New Testament authors, ultimately these notions derive from the exodus narratives themselves and from Moses' reflections on those narratives, as in our passage.

TEXTS LIKE DEUTERONOMY 4:32 – 40 should be as inspiring to Christian readers today as they were to Moses' original hearers, not only because of their vibrant style, but especially because of the eternal lessons they teach.

(1) **God's salvation is achieved at great expenditure of divine energy and power.** For Israel, God's saving actions involved the plagues of Egypt, through which he not only declared Israel to be his chosen people but also revealed to the watching world his glory and grace. But what he did for this nation of slaves is paradigmatic for what God has done for sinners, enslaved not to an evil earthly empire but to sin. In fact, in the death and resurrection of Christ, we witness a surpassing demonstration of power and glory by which he proves that he is indeed supreme over all. In 2 Peter 1:16 – 17, Peter gathers the motifs of story and power, divine majesty, honor, glory, and the voice of revelation from heaven on the sacred mountain. But in Christ, God's glory and grace are revealed even more dramatically. Paul adds his insight concerning the surpassing power demonstrated in the gospel of Christ in Romans 1:16 – 17:

> I am not ashamed of the gospel, because it is *the power of God for the salvation* of everyone who believes: first for the Jew, then for the Gentile. For in the gospel a righteousness from God is revealed, a righteousness that is by faith from first to last, just as it is written: "The righteous will live by faith." [italics mine]

If the exodus represented the supreme moment of divine revelation and founding event of Israel's history, this is what the cross is for New Testament believers.

(2) **In this brief sermon on "the grace of salvation," Moses demonstrates how saving grace always works.** Of his own free choice and by his

---

14. Acts 2:19, 22, 43; 4:30; 5:12; 6:8; 7:36; 14:3; 15:12.

own power, God delivers captives from their bondage and ushers them into a new life of freedom and celebration. However, while the call to salvation is without preconditions, the fulfillment of God's calling for his people is contingent on grateful obedience to his will. Unlike the ancient Egyptians and Mesopotamians, the response demanded by the Savior is not defined primarily in liturgical and cultic obligations (like the "care and feeding of the gods"), but through moral obedience. This is how his people render to God sacrifices of praise and proclaim his grace to the watching world.

(3) **This passage offers pastors a paradigm for preaching, not only in its content, but also in its proportion.** In a text consisting of 163 words, Moses uses 109 to tell the story of Israel's historical experience of grace; he uses 26 to reflect theologically on those events; and then he concludes with 26 words of application. This paradigm contrasts with much contemporary evangelical preaching, which, in its drive to be practical, fails to develop the story of God's gracious redemption (or tells it in hurried and passion-less tones) and consequently also fails to show the theological implications of that story. Instead we spend our time on pointed but trite and facile application.

This text reminds us that our ethic must derive from our theology, which in turn derives from the memory of God's gracious intervention in human history. Tragically, the evangelical church is not only losing its theology; it is losing the story. For this reason we must continue boldly proclaiming God's amazing acts of redemption. This is why we preach Christ and him crucified. In the cross alone is there any hope of salvation for anyone.

But the crucifixion of Christ was not simply an interesting and unprec-edented historical event. It was also a profoundly theological event, for through the death and resurrection of Jesus his supreme divinity is pro-claimed (Rom. 1:2 – 6). Concerning Christ Jesus Paul writes in Philippians 2:7 – 11:

[He] made himself nothing,
   taking the very nature of a servant,
   being made in human likeness.
And being found in appearance as a man,
   he humbled himself
   and became obedient to death—even death on a cross!
Therefore God has exalted him to the highest place
   and gave him the name that is above every name,
that at the name of Jesus every knee should bow,
   in heaven and on earth and under the earth,
and every tongue confess that Jesus Christ is Lord [Yahweh],
   to the glory of God the Father.

Through his death and resurrection Jesus proves his identity with Yahweh, the Redeemer of Israel. If Yahweh's rescue of the Israelites from their bondage to Pharaoh and his kingdom demanded a tremendous act of divine power, how much more our rescue from sin and the dominion of darkness. But this is what Jesus has accomplished for us, and in so doing he has demonstrated that he alone is God; there is no other.

The implications of God's gracious acts of deliverance for Israel and for us are the same. Having been redeemed, why would we not commit ourselves to joyful obedience? This was and remains the key to the Lord's blessing on our lives. Jesus himself instructs us, "If you love me (that is, if you are covenantally committed to me), you will keep my commands" (John 14:15 [pers. trans.]). To paraphrase Jesus' words in John 14:21, "Those who have my commands and keep them are those is who are covenantally committed to me. And those who are covenantally committed to me will be the object of my Father's covenantal commitment, and I will be covenantally committed to him and manifest myself to him." And again, "If any are covenantally committed to me, they will keep my word, and my Father will demonstrate his covenantal commitment to them, and we will come to them and make our home with them. Whoever is not covenantally committed to me does not keep my words" (John 14:23−24; cf. 15:10−11). It is all part of this same wonderful picture. Indeed we may bring out the relevance of Deuteronomy 4:32−40 for us who have experienced the grace of God in Christ by recasting this entire section from Deuteronomy in Christian vocabulary:

> Ask now of the days that are past, which were before you, since the day that God created humankind on the earth, and ask from one end of heaven to the other, whether such a great thing as this has ever happened or was ever heard of. Did any people ever encounter their gods directly, as you have encountered him, and still live? Or has any god ever dared to invade the kingdom of darkness and take for himself a people from the midst of that kingdom by trials, by signs, by wonders, and by war, by a mighty hand and an outstretched arm, and by great deeds of terror, all of which Jesus Christ your God has done for you on the cross before your eyes?
>
> To you it was shown, that you might know that Jesus Christ is Yahweh, God; there is no other besides him. Out of heaven he came as the divine Word, that he might reveal the Father to you, and on earth he revealed his glory, the glory as of the only begotten of the Father, full of grace and truth (John 1:14).
>
> And he loved the ancestors and chose their spiritual offspring after them and brought you out of the kingdom of darkness by his great power, disarming the rulers and authorities and putting them

to open shame, by triumphing over them in him (Col. 2:15), in order to grant us an inheritance, since we have been predestined according to the purpose of him who works all things according to the counsel of his will (Eph. 1:11).

Know therefore today, and lay it to your heart, that Jesus Christ is Yahweh; he is God in heaven above and on the earth beneath; there is no other.

Therefore walk in a manner worthy of Jesus Christ the LORD, fully pleasing to him, bearing fruit in every good work and increasing in the knowledge of God, being strengthened with all power, according to his glorious might, for all endurance and patience with joy, and giving thanks to the Father, who has qualified you to share in the inheritance of the saints in light (Col. 1:10–12).

Deuteronomy 4:41–43

🔥

T hen Moses set aside three cities east of the Jordan, [42]to which anyone who had killed a person could flee if he had unintentionally killed his neighbor without malice aforethought. He could flee into one of these cities and save his life. [43]The cities were these: Bezer in the desert plateau, for the Reubenites; Ramoth in Gilead, for the Gadites; and Golan in Bashan, for the Manassites.

FROM A LITERARY PERSPECTIVE, this short paragraph is a narrative epilogue to Moses' first address. By setting aside three towns[1] of refuge east of the Jordan, Moses fulfilled part of Yahweh's instruction in Numbers 35:9–34 (cf. Josh. 20). The narrator is content to record his actions and to offer a summary statement of the function of these towns (cf. 19:1–13).

The principles underlying the towns of refuge accord with the humanitarian interests of the book of Deuteronomy as a whole. While Numbers 35:6–34 incorporates this law fully into the Israelite system of justice, any system that invests relatives of the victims of a crime with responsibility for administering justice is vulnerable to abuse. To protect a potential secondary victim, Yahweh required the Israelites to designate six towns as refuges to which a person who had accidentally caused another person's death could flee for asylum. This would give communities affected by the tragedy time to investigate the circumstances of the death. The towns so identified by Moses were distributed so all who lived east of the Jordan would have ready access: Bezer in Reuben's tribal land, Ramoth in Gilead of the Gadites, and Golan in Bashan for the eastern half of the Manassites.[2]

---

1. It is preferable to render Hebrew ʿîr as "town" rather than NIV's "city." In English "city" is misleadingly associated with large population centers. In the OT an ʿîr was by definition a settlement with defensive walls and gate structures—irrespective of size. These were necessary features for a site to function as a place of refuge.

2. On the nature and function of cities of refuge, see J. R. Spencer, "Refuge, Cities of," *ABD*, 5:657–58.

WHY THE EDITOR OF Moses' speeches closed his first address with this account is unclear. However, in its present location this episode reminds readers that as the Israelites approached the time for crossing the Jordan, the tribes who remained east of the river were subject to the same ethical standards as those who would cross over into the actual Promised Land. Furthermore, these cities of refuge served as memorials to the faithfulness of Yahweh. If the Israelites will conduct their campaign west of the Jordan the way they had fought Sihon and Og in the east, they will soon have their own cities of refuge to memorialize God's faithfulness.

WE WILL REFLECT ON the theological implications of this policy more intensely when we return to the subject of cities of refuge in 19:1 – 3. For now we note that except for the archival notes in 1 Chronicles 6, after Joshua's allocation of the cities of refuge west of the Jordan in Joshua 20, the topic never reappears in the Old Testament. But what are modern Christians supposed to do with a literary and judicial fossil like this? While it is difficult to domesticate the picture of justice here and square it with the needs of twenty-first century life, the passage yields a couple of insights of special relevance for our time.

(1) Whereas this provision presupposes that the Israelites will execute murderers, it recognizes the danger of potentially escalating cycles of revenge. It also recognizes that whenever one person accidentally or inadvertently causes another's death, there are actually two victims: the one whose physical life was taken and the one deprived of social life. This policy illustrates the need for all judicial systems to take into account the lives of potential secondary victims. Even as it grieves over accidental loss of life, a just society will guard against unwarranted violent responses to innocent acts.

(2) As Moses will keep reminding us, God's people need memorials to keep alive the memory of God's actions on their behalf and to remind us to be open to his continued action on our behalf. When Israel trusted in Yahweh and engaged the enemy on his terms, the victory was certain. So it is for the church that engages the kingdom of darkness on his terms.

Deuteronomy 4:44 – 5:5

※

This is the law Moses set before the Israelites. ⁴⁵These are the stipulations, decrees and laws Moses gave them when they came out of Egypt ⁴⁶and were in the valley near Beth Peor east of the Jordan, in the land of Sihon king of the Amorites, who reigned in Heshbon and was defeated by Moses and the Israelites as they came out of Egypt. ⁴⁷They took possession of his land and the land of Og king of Bashan, the two Amorite kings east of the Jordan. ⁴⁸This land extended from Aroer on the rim of the Arnon Gorge to Mount Siyon (that is, Hermon), ⁴⁹and included all the Arabah east of the Jordan, as far as the Sea of the Arabah, below the slopes of Pisgah.

^{5:1}Moses summoned all Israel and said:

Hear, O Israel, the decrees and laws I declare in your hearing today. Learn them and be sure to follow them. ²The LORD our God made a covenant with us at Horeb. ³It was not with our fathers that the LORD made this covenant, but with us, with all of us who are alive here today. ⁴The LORD spoke to you face to face out of the fire on the mountain. ⁵(At that time I stood between the LORD and you to declare to you the word of the LORD, because you were afraid of the fire and did not go up the mountain.) And he said:

Original Meaning

THE PROLOGUE TO THE SECOND ADDRESS (4:44 – 5:1A)

THE BOUNDARIES OF MOSES' long second address (4:44 – 26:19; 28:1 – 29:1[28:69]) are fixed by the narrative prologue (4:44 – 5:1a) and the narrative colophon in 29:1[28:69].[1] The prologue (4:44 – 5:1a) begins with a double heading, consisting of vv. 44 and 45 respectively. The NIV rendering of *tôrâ* as "law" in the first heading misconstrues both the word and the content of the second address, since little of chapters 5 – 11 and 12 – 18 actually fits the literary category of "law." As Moses had declared in 4:1 and will reiterate in 5:1 and 6:1, he

---

1. I interpret 29:1[28:69] as the conclusion to this address, not the introduction to the third. See further below. Chapter 27 interrupts the smooth flow from 26:19 to 28:1.

stands before the people as a pastor-teacher, seeking to inspire his audience with a particular vision of God and to convince them to order their lives accordingly. On first sight, verse 45 seems to provide a more natural introduction to the second address (cf. 4:1, 5, 8, 14) than verse 44, since the expression "decrees and laws" occurs at critical junctures in the speech.[2] But here this pair is preceded by a third expression, "stipulations." The article on all these expressions point to the covenant stipulations given at Sinai and other regulations delivered prior to the present addresses (cf. Num. 36:13).

Like the introduction to the first address, the prologue to the second describes the historical context of the speech. By itself, verse 45 seems to suggest that Moses delivered this address when the Israelites left Egypt. However, in verse 46 he clarifies the situation, linking the speech to the defeat of the Amorite kings and describing the geographical scope of those campaigns. In so doing he collapses the first forty years of Israel's history as a nation into one short statement.[3] The prologue concludes in 5:1a with the notice of Moses' summons to the people to hear him. The use of the word "he said" reminds the reader to interpret what follows as the address of a pastor rather than laws promulgated by a legislator.

The Context of the Revelation of Covenant Relationship (5:1b–5)

THE SECOND ADDRESS DIVIDES into two parts. The first (5:1b–11:32) is largely sermonic, while parts of the second (12:1–29:1[28:69]) are more formal, making more direct use of previously revealed prescriptions and concluding with covenant blessings and curses. However, throughout we hear the voice of Moses the pastor.[4] In the first we hear a pastoral exhortation to covenant faith, and in the second more detailed pastoral application of covenant faith to life.

Chapters 5–11 subdivide into three parts, each of which begins with "Hear, O Israel" (5:1b; 6:4; 9:1).[5] Homiletically, these three parts represent

---

2. Deut. 5:1, 31; 6:1, 20; 7:11; 11:32; 12:1; 26:16, 17.

3. Verses 46–49 contain little new information. The parenthetical note identifying Mount Siyon with Hermon recalls the note in 3:9, which reminds readers that Sidonians and Amorites refer to Mount Hermon as Mount Siryon and Mount Senir, respectively. Siyon may refer to a particular peak or section of Siryon. Thus Y. Ikeda, "Hermon, Sirion, and Senir," *AJSL* 4 (1978): 44, n. 58.

4. Critical scholars tend to isolate the paraenetic materials as later deuteronomistic insertions. However, these are vital in determining the genre of the book and are much more extensive in chaps. 12–28 than is generally recognized.

5. By word count these sections increase progressively in length: Deut. 5:1b–6:3 consists of approximately 570 words; 6:4–8:20, approximately 830 words; and 9:1–11:32, approximately 1,150 words.

three constituents of authoritative preaching: (1) the Scripture lesson (5:1b – 6:3), highlighting the foundations of covenant relationship; (2) the theology arising from the Scripture (6:4 – 8:20), focusing on the essence of covenant relationship; (3) the appropriate response arising from that theology (9:1 – 11:32), demonstrating love for Yahweh as evidence of covenant relationship.[6]

It is fitting that Moses should begin this discourse on Yahweh's relationship with Israel by reciting the original covenant document, the Decalogue (cf. 4:13). This was the official testament to the covenant.[7] Since most in this generation had grown up after the original revelation at Sinai, it was especially important for them to hear these words from Moses himself.

Moses' purpose in 5:1b – 5 is twofold: to challenge the present generation to seize hold of what their parents had rejected at Sinai, and to highlight the importance of his teaching. His message is the same as that revealed at Sinai, and he delivers it as the very message of God.

With the opening summons, "Hear, O Israel," Moses both challenges his hearers to listen and calls for obedience to the will of the Suzerain. But this summons also introduces the content of Moses' message: "the decrees and laws," that is, the revelation given by Yahweh through Moses at Sinai. Given this introduction, Moses' hearers may have expected him to launch immediately into instructions regarding specific laws. However, the preacher digresses in verses 2 – 5, which in turn leads to a lengthy digression covering chapters 5 – 11. Not until 11:32 does he pick up the train of thought begun here. As in 4:1, with this summons Moses also declares the goal of his address: the laws are to be "learned" and rigorously applied.[8]

However, before Moses gets to the "decrees and laws," he declares shockingly that Yahweh did not make a covenant with "our fathers" at Horeb, but "with us," that is, the people standing before him (vv. 2 – 3). He reiterates this point in verse 3 with seven expressions: "with us," "we,"

---

6. Cf. the structure based on text-linguistic considerations identified by J. DeRouchie, *A Call to Covenant Love: Text Grammar and Literary Structure in Deuteronomy 5 – 11* (Piscataway, NJ: Gorgias, 2007), 229.

7. The second-millennium BC vassal treaty that Muwattalli III of Hatti imposed on Alaksandu of Wilusa includes this clause: "Furthermore, this tablet which I have made for you, Alaksandu, shall be read out before you three times yearly, and you, Alaksandu, shall know it. These words are by no means reciprocal. They issue from Hatti." As translated by Beckman, *Hittite Diplomatic Texts*, 91.

8. The construction, *šāmar laᶜ ᵃśôt* ("keep by doing"), contrasts with 4:6, which used finite verbs for both, "keep and do." This form occurs often in the book (5:29; 6:3, 25; etc.), and is reminiscent of Gen. 18:19, where Yahweh calls on Abraham's descendants to "keep [*šāmar*] the way of Yahweh by doing [*laᶜ ᵃśôt*] justice and righteousness." On this gerundive use of the infinitive construct, see WO §36.2.3e; Joüon §124o.

"these," "here," "today," "all of us," "[who are] living." But this declaration raises a problem: How could Yahweh make a covenant with this generation at Horeb, when most of them had not yet been born? Equally problematic is the reference to "your fathers" in verse 3. If Moses had in mind the former generation, his statement contradicts Exodus 19–24, according to which God had in fact made the covenant with the fathers.

Some account for the problem by treating 5:2–5 as a late insertion;[9] others suggest that in Deuteronomy "fathers" always refers to the patriarchs,[10] in which case the contrast here is between the Horeb covenant and the covenant God made with Abraham. But Deuteronomy blurs the distinctions between these covenants, interpreting the covenant rituals at Horeb and in Moab as the means whereby the patriarchs' descendants were incorporated in the covenant made originally with them (cf. Gen. 17:7). It is most natural to treat "your fathers" as the exodus generation. The association of "the stipulations, decrees and laws" with the descendants of Israel "when they came out of Egypt" in 4:45 suggests this was how the editor understood the matter.

Moses' comment should not be interpreted literally but as a rhetorical statement, acknowledging the ineffectiveness of the covenant to which the exodus generation had signed on (cf. 1:19–40; 9:7–21). But Yahweh's offer remains on the table, presently to be received by those gathered on the plains of Moab.[11] This is their chance to sign on to the covenant ratified at Horeb whose terms are embodied in the Decalogue, as well as the "decrees and laws."[12]

Verses 4–5 summarize the roles played by the respective parties when Yahweh made his covenant with Israel at Horeb. On the one hand, Yahweh spoke directly with the people from the midst of the fire (v. 4). But on the other hand, Moses stood between Yahweh and the people to declare the divine word to them (v. 5). Moses' parenthetical comment is an interruptive reminder that the revelation at Sinai involved two dimensions: direct divine speech and mediated divine speech. As he will iterate in verse 22, the people heard only the Ten Words directly from Yahweh; the rest was communicated from God to his people via Moses. His momentary recollection of the people's fearful response to the revelation from the fire, which precipitated his assuming the role of mediator thereafter, will be fleshed out in verses 22–33.

---

9. See Weinfeld, *Deuteronomy 1–11*, 237–39.

10. Tigay, *Deuteronomy*, 61.

11. Interpreting *lōʾ ... kî*, which is usually rendered "not ... but," as "correlative," rather than "absolute" negation: "not only ... but also." Cf. Wright, *Deuteronomy*, 62.

12. Similarly, Millar, *Now Choose Life*, 82; idem, "Time and Place," 57–58.

MOSES' INTRODUCTION TO THE second address reiterates that Yahweh is a communicating deity. What separates him from other gods is not only that he speaks, but also that he speaks in a language humans can understand. This notion is picked up frequently in the prophets. In the books of Jeremiah and Ezekiel we often read something like this, "The word of the LORD came to me, saying."[13] But Ezekiel highlights Yahweh as a communicating God more specifically with the repeated expanded version of the divine self-introduction formula: "I am Yahweh; I have spoken, and I will do [what I have said]" (pers. trans.).[14] As the opening to the book of Hebrews declares, Yahweh has spoken in the past in many contexts and in many different ways. Sometimes he has spoken directly, sometimes through a mediator, but always his revelation of himself has been a gracious act of self-disclosure. At Horeb Yahweh spoke through Moses his mediator, but he also spoke directly from the midst of the fire.

These two forms of communication are recognized in John 1:17: "For the law was given through Moses; grace and truth came through Jesus Christ." The directness of God's speech climaxes in the incarnation, for in the Son, Jesus Christ, Yahweh has personally entered our world and spoken with a clarity never seen before. The prologue to the gospel of John recognizes this not only by declaring that in the beginning the Word was God, but also that the Word became flesh and dwelt among us, and in him we behold the glory of Yahweh, full of grace and truth (John 1:14).

IT IS POSSIBLE FOR us today to hear the voice of God and still not to hear the voice of God. The exodus generation heard Yahweh's voice clearly, but because of the hardness of their hearts, they rejected what they heard. Consequently, like the branches of a vine that refuses to bear fruit (John 15:6), they were cut off by the vinedresser and thrown into the fire. Those who abide in the vine bear the fruit of belief and covenant commitment (love) shown in obedience to the revealed will of God. This passage declares that if we reject the revelation of God, we reject God himself.

But what does it mean to receive the revelation of God? It is surely more than decorating the document with a nice cover and putting it on

---

13. Both first and third person forms of the "word event formula" occur in Jeremiah: 1:2; 28:12; etc. In Ezekiel the formula is always in first person (3:16; etc.).
14. Ezek. 17:24; 22:14; 24:14; 36:36; 37:14.

the coffee table as ornamentation. Yahweh's goal in revealing his will to his people is to affect life. They are to hear the decrees and laws that they might learn them and do them. This does not mean signing high-sounding creedal statements about one's high view of Scripture, but actually doing what God expects of those whom he has redeemed. In Jesus' words, those who love him (i.e., are covenantally committed to him) will keep his commands (John 14:15, 21, 23; 15:10).

But how will God's people walk in the ways of the Lord if they have not learned his ways, and how will they learn those ways if they have not heard his revelation? This brief text highlights the indispensable role of the ministry of the Word in the corporate worship of God's people. Pastors today would do well to follow the model of Moses, in teaching the Word of God clearly, systematically, and with practical intent.

Deuteronomy 5:6–22

I am the LORD your God, who brought you out of Egypt, out of the land of slavery.

[7]"You shall have no other gods before me.

[8]"You shall not make for yourself an idol in the form of anything in heaven above or on the earth beneath or in the waters below. [9]You shall not bow down to them or worship them; for I, the LORD your God, am a jealous God, punishing the children for the sin of the fathers to the third and fourth generation of those who hate me, [10]but showing love to a thousand generations of those who love me and keep my commandments.

[11]"You shall not misuse the name of the LORD your God, for the LORD will not hold anyone guiltless who misuses his name.

[12]"Observe the Sabbath day by keeping it holy, as the LORD your God has commanded you. [13]Six days you shall labor and do all your work, [14]but the seventh day is a Sabbath to the LORD your God. On it you shall not do any work, neither you, nor your son or daughter, nor your manservant or maidservant, nor your ox, your donkey or any of your animals, nor the alien within your gates, so that your manservant and maidservant may rest, as you do. [15]Remember that you were slaves in Egypt and that the LORD your God brought you out of there with a mighty hand and an outstretched arm. Therefore the LORD your God has commanded you to observe the Sabbath day.

[16]"Honor your father and your mother, as the LORD your God has commanded you, so that you may live long and that it may go well with you in the land the LORD your God is giving you.

[17]"You shall not murder.

[18]"You shall not commit adultery.

[19]"You shall not steal.

[20]"You shall not give false testimony against your neighbor.

[21]"You shall not covet your neighbor's wife. You shall not set your desire on your neighbor's house or land, his manservant or maidservant, his ox or donkey, or anything that belongs to your neighbor."

²²These are the commandments the LORD proclaimed in a loud voice to your whole assembly there on the mountain from out of the fire, the cloud and the deep darkness; and he added nothing more. Then he wrote them on two stone tablets and gave them to me.

THE DECALOGUE IS FOUND twice in the Pentateuch: Exodus 20:1−17 and Deuteronomy 5:6−21.[1] When we compare these two texts, the Deuteronomic version appears expansionistic, stylistically less formal, and more humanitarian in outlook. The variations may suggest that at the time of this address Moses recited the principles of covenant relationship from memory. This was necessary because he would not have had access to the actual tablets, which were deposited in the ark of the covenant (10:5).

Moses' comment in verse 22 that "he [Yahweh] added nothing more" (cf. 10:2, 4) suggests the communication of a fixed version of a document familiar to his audience. But as we will see, despite his caution against adding to or subtracting from the decrees and laws that he is teaching in 4:2, Moses introduces several significant changes to the wording of the document. These changes are not corrections intended to supersede the original in the ark. Rather, they reflect the pastoral context and the paraenetic aims of this recitation.[2] Moses hereby highlights the importance of the original document, while affirming that its authority extends to life as people actually live it. His fresh recitation of the text assumes that the process of inspiration extends beyond Yahweh's original proclamation to Moses' interpretation.

Although some scholars view the Decalogue as a late distillation of Yahweh's will for his people,[3] the narratives of Exodus and the present context paint the opposite picture. This document was the fountainhead from which later revelation springs and on which it will expound. The Decalogue itself is cast as a complete entity. Resembling ancient Near Eastern treaties, the document includes its own formal introduction (v. 6), its own discrete number of terms (vv. 7−21), and a transcriptional epilogue (v. 22).

---

1. Before the discovery of the Qumran scrolls, the Nash papyrus, a liturgical fragment from the Maccabean period containing the Decalogue and the Shema (Deut. 6:4−5), was the oldest witness to the Hebrew text of the Old Testament. Cf. E. Tov, *Textual Criticism of the Hebrew Bible* (Minneapolis: Fortress, 1992), 118.

2. Note his addition of "as the LORD your God has commanded you" in vv. 12 and 16.

3. R. Albertz, *A History of Israelite Religion in the Old Testament Period* (trans. John Bowden; Louisville: Westminster John Knox, 1994), 214−16.

The Historical Prologue (5:6)

AS IN ANCIENT TREATIES, the prologue is a fundamental part of the document, introducing the Suzerain and summarizing the history of the relationship between the two parties to the covenant. However, unlike many vassal treaties, this covenant did not reflect a superior's conquest of a people. Rather, behind this document lie the gracious actions of the divine Superior, who rescued this people from those who held them in bondage. The law is preceded by gospel; obedience to God's will as outlined in the commands that follow represents a supreme act of worship, involving reverential human acts of submission and homage before the divine Sovereign in response to his gracious revelation of himself.

The Covenant Stipulations (5:7−21)

THE TERMS OF THE covenant are cast as second person commands, for the most part without preconditions or declaration of consequences. Except for the Sabbath ordinance and the command to honor parents, the stipulations are negative in form, and motive clauses are the exception rather than the rule. The commands are cast in terms that are absolute, universal, and permanent. Since they are so general as to be virtually unenforceable, we should not interpret this document as a law code. Rather, this document seeks to create a worldview intended to govern the relationship between the redeemed and their Redeemer on the one hand, and among members of the community on the other.[4]

As noted above on 4:13, the Old Testament consistently identifies this unit as "the Ten Words" (Ex. 34:28; Deut. 10:4). Apparently the principles of the covenant have been reduced to ten to facilitate memorization—one command for each of our ten fingers. However, there is some question how the words should be numbered. The Reformed tradition counts verses 8−10 as the second command, distinct from verse 7, and treats verse 21 as a single command. However, based on discourse linguistic grounds, it is preferable to follow the Lutheran and Roman Catholic numbering, with verses 7−10 representing the first command and splitting verse 22 into two commands.[5]

By this system the first two commands (vv. 7−11) govern the Israelites' vertical relationship with Yahweh, and the last seven governing horizontal relationships between members of the covenant community (vv. 16−21).

---

4. Comparing the Decalogue to the American Constitution, P. D. Miller rightly observes that it provides the basis for later specification of the laws in the Book of the Covenant, the Holiness Code and the so-called Deuteronomic Code. See "The Place of the Decalogue in the Old Testament and Its Law," in *The Way of the Lord: Essays on Old Testament Theology* (Grand Rapids: Eerdmans, 2004), 3−16.

5. For discussion, see Block, "Reading the Decalogue Right to Left," 56−60.

The Sabbath principle (#3; vv. 12–15) is transitional. By basing it on the divine pattern of creation, the Exodus version (Ex. 20:8–11) highlights the theological dimension of the Sabbath; by emphatically extending the Sabbath rest to the entire household and basing it on Israel's experience of deliverance from slave labor, the Deuteronomic version transforms it into a humanitarian/horizontal command.

Although the principles of the Decalogue apply ultimately to every member of the covenant community, strictly speaking, the commands are addressed to *every man*, specifically adult males who are heads of households with wives and children and who possess property. If we assume patricentric social structures, the document views strong domestic leadership as the key to a healthy community. Whereas some argue that the Decalogue seeks to protect the power and privileges of wealthy male Israelites,[6] it actually does the opposite, intentionally reining in potential abuse of power by male heads of households.[7] In so doing this document functions as an Israelite version of a bill of rights.[8] However, unlike modern bills of rights, the document does not protect one's own rights but the rights of the next person. Each of the terms may be recast as a statement of another person's rights and the adult males' responsibility to guard the rights first of the covenant Lord, and second of fellow Israelites:

The Divine Rights
1. The Supreme Command: Yahweh has the right to exclusive allegiance (vv. 7–10).
2. Yahweh has the right to proper representation (v. 11).

The Human Rights
3. All in the household have the right to humane treatment by the head (vv. 12–15).[9]
4. One's parents have the right to respect (v. 16).
5. One's neighbor has the right to life (v. 17).
6. One's neighbor has the right to purity and fidelity in marriage (v. 18).
7. One's neighbor has the right to his property (v. 19).

---

6. D. J. A. Clines, "The Ten Commandments, Reading from Left to Right," in *Interested Parties: The Ideology of Writers and Readers of the Hebrew Bible* (JSOTSup 205; Sheffield: Sheffield Academic Press, 1995), 26–45; C. S. Rodd, *Glimpses of a Strange Land: Studies in Old Testament Ethics* (OTS; Edinburgh: T&T Clark, 2001), 87–89.

7. See further D. I. Block, "Reading the Decalogue from Right to Left," 36–42; idem, "'You shall not covet your neighbor's wife,'" in *The Gospel According to Moses*, 137–68.

8. Though we agree in general with W. Harrelson, *The Ten Commandments and Human Rights* (Philadelphia: Fortress, 1980), 186–93, who treats this document as a "charter of human freedom."

9. According to the Exodus version the Sabbath command expresses a divine right; Yahweh has the right to the Israelites' time and trust (Ex. 20:8–11).

8. One's neighbor has the right to honest and truthful testimony in court (v. 20).
9. One's neighbor has the right to security in marriage (v. 21a).
10. One's neighbor has the right to his own household property (v. 21b).

The first principle of covenant relationship: Yahweh's right to exclusive allegiance (5:7 – 10). Israel is to have no other gods[10] besides Yahweh. This command prohibits the worship of any other deity alongside Yahweh, as if he were one member or even the head of a larger pantheon. While the command does not explicitly deny the existence of other gods, it denies any a share of his authority, power, or jurisdiction.[11]

Verses 8 – 10, which serve as commentary on verse 7, break down into three verbal statements: "you shall not make"; "you shall not bow down [before what you make]"; and "[you shall not] worship [what you make]" (cf. 4:15 – 19). The prohibition is exhaustive in scope, banning the manufacture of any image of deity after the models of God's own creation in Genesis 1. The prohibitions are followed by a motive clause (v. 9): because Yahweh is El Qanna', "Impassioned God" (NIV "a jealous God").[12] Whereas other gods tolerated their devotees' simultaneous worship of other deities, as El Qanna' Yahweh will brook no rivals. The key expressions are obviously "those who reject me" (NIV, "who hate me") and "those who love me" or are covenantally committed to me. The final clause (v. 10) declares that like divine love, human love is not merely an emotion; it is commitment demonstrated in action, in this instance by keeping Yahweh's commands.

Yahweh warns those who reject him that he will "visit their iniquity" (NASB) on the children to the third and fourth generation.[13] While the idiom "to the third and fourth generation" is commonly interpreted vertically, the phrase should be understood horizontally.[14] In the ancient world a domestic unit could consist of up to four generations, all under the leadership of the "father." This warning is based on a notion of corporate solidarity according to which the actions of one member of the household, particularly the father, implicate all the members. If the opposite of "reject" is "love,"

---

10. This is a recurrent theme in Deuteronomy: 5:17; 6:14; 7:4; 8:19; 11:16, 28; 13:2[3], 6[7], 13[14]; 17:3; 18:20; 28:14, 36, 64; 29:26[25]; 30:17; 31:18, 20.

11. See further, J. H. Walton, "Interpreting the Bible as an Ancient Near Eastern Document," in *Israel — Ancient Kingdom or Late Invention* (ed. D. I. Block; Nashville: Broadman & Holman, 2008), 305 – 9.

12. For the significance of this expression, see comments on 4:24.

13. The divine intervention is expressed by *pqd*, which may be either positive (Ruth 1:6) or negative. "To visit the guilt of fathers on children" occurs elsewhere in Ex. 20:5; 34:7; Num. 14:18.

14. This principle is illustrated by the execution of Achan and his entire household in Josh. 7:16 – 26.

then the opposite of "visit the guilt upon" is to demonstrate *ḥesed* (NIV, "show love") toward them (v. 10). Like the Hebrew word for "love" (*ʾāhab*), *ḥesed* belongs to the covenantal semantic field, encompassing those qualities that move a person to act for the benefit of another irrespective of self-interest: love, mercy, grace, kindness, goodness, benevolence, loyalty, fidelity, and covenant faithfulness.[15] Yahweh does so "to a thousand generations," which highlights his long-term commitment to his people and his delight in covenant grace in contrast to his short-lived expression of wrath (v. 9).[16]

This first principle of covenant relationship (vv. 7 – 10) represents "the Supreme Command," which Moses has in mind whenever he uses the singular expression "the command" in connection with the plural forms "the decrees and laws" (5:31; 6:1; 7:11). This principle will find its obverse in the Shema (6:4 – 5). The following nine commands represent specific ways of demonstrating one's exclusive devotion to Yahweh.

The second principle of covenant relationship: Yahweh's right to proper representation (5:11). Whereas Jewish tradition tends to see here a ban on the flippant use of the divine name in oaths,[17] Christians often view it simply as a taboo on verbal profanities. Some treat it as a prohibition on the magical use of Yahweh's name to exercise power over another person.[18] Literally the Hebrew translates, "You shall not bear/carry the name of Yahweh your God emptily." The idiom derives from the ancient practice of branding slaves with the name of their owner.[19] To bear the name of Yahweh means to claim him as one's owner and to accept the role of representing him (cf. Isa 44:5). At issue is Israel's status and function as the people of Yahweh. They may not claim Yahweh as their covenant Lord and then live as if they belonged to Baal.[20] The consequences of misrepresenting Yahweh are declared only in the vaguest of terms: these Yahweh will not acquit (NIV "hold guiltless").

The third principle of covenant commitment: the right of all members of the household to humane treatment (5:12 – 15). Whereas the Exodus version of the Decalogue grounds the Sabbath in creation (Ex. 20:8 – 11; cf. Gen. 1:1 – 2:4a), Moses transforms this institution into a symbol of the right of all to humane treatment from the head of the household. He does not hereby negate the original meaning of the Sabbath, but ensures that the

---

15. On the word see D. A. Baer and R. P. Gordon, *NIDOTTE*, 2:211 – 18.

16. Cf. the use of this expression in Ex. 34:6 – 7; also Jer. 9:23.

17. See Tigay, *Deuteronomy*, 67.

18. See Walton, "Interpreting the Bible as an Ancient Near Eastern Document," 313 – 18.

19. See further D. I. Block, "Bearing the Name of the LORD with Honor," in *How I Love Your Torah, O LORD!* 61 – 72.

20. Compare the New Testament application of this principle in 2 Tim. 2:14 – 26 and 1 Peter 4:12 – 19.

gift of Sabbath rest extends to the entire household, while the amount of space devoted to the Sabbath reflects the importance of this ordinance.[21] Structurally, this command consists of three parts: (1) a summary command (v. 12); (2) an exposition of the command (vv. 13 − 14); and (3) a declaration of the grounds for the command (v. 15).

Like the command to respect parents, this one is cast as an affirmative statement.[22] The Sabbath is kept "by keeping it holy," that is, by sanctifying it, separating it from the other six days as a day of rest and recognizing that it belongs to Yahweh (v. 13; cf. Gen 2:3). As suggested by verses 13 − 14, the word *šabbat* derives from a root meaning "to cease, stop," indicating that the Sabbath was not primarily a day of assembly but of quiet, when all work associated with everyday life was to cease.[23]

In ancient Israel it would have been tempting for the head of the household and his immediate family to observe the Sabbath while the rest of the household carried on as usual. To prevent this, the command specifically lists others in the economic unit to be included in the privilege: children (male and female), servants (male and female), draft animals (ox and donkey),[24] and all outsiders temporarily residing in the town. The added motive clause insists that in their right to Sabbath rest these were all on a par with the householder; the Sabbath was a gift for all. In grounding the "holiday" on Israel's memory of their own experience in Egypt (v. 15), Moses calls for a sympathetic disposition toward those under one's authority. In their treatment of children, servants, animals, and outsiders, the heads of households were to embody the superior righteousness of the revealed laws of Yahweh (Deut. 4:8).

Although the weekly Sabbath rest was designed to serve several functions,[25] the Old Testament offers remarkably little information on how the

---

21. The 60+ words compares with 50 devoted to the first command.

22. The verb "observe" ("keep") replaces "remember" in Ex. 20:8.

23. Preparing food (Ex. 16:23 − 30), working the fields (Ex. 34:21; Neh. 13:15−21), lighting fires (Ex. 35:3), gathering wood (Num. 15:32 − 36), hauling goods (Jer. 17:21 − 22), and engaging in commerce (Amos 8:5). The ban did not include emergency situations. Note Jesus' response to the Pharisees in Matthew 12:9 − 14 and Luke 14:1 − 6.

24. For other laws calling for humane treatment of animals, see Ex. 22:30[29]; Lev. 22:27 − 28; Deut. 22:6 − 7, 10; 25:4.

25. (1) It addressed the utilitarian need of all for regular rest from the stress of everyday work. (2) By patterning the rhythm of life after the creative work of God himself, the weekly Sabbath offered an opportunity for Israelites to declare their fundamentally theological perspective on life. (3) Like the rainbow in relationship to the covenant God made with Noah and the cosmos (Gen. 9:12, 13, 17), the Sabbath served as a "sign" of Yahweh's eternal covenant with Israel (Ex. 31:16−17). The construction is emphatic: to ignore the Sabbath is to renounce one's membership in the covenant community and cut oneself off from the grace of God—hence the treatment of Sabbath violation as a capital crime (see Ex. 31:14− 15; 35:2; Num. 15:32 − 36). (4) It offered Israelites a means of regularly

Israelites were to keep and sanctify it (cf. Lev. 24:8; Num. 28:9−10). The first reference to Israelites keeping the seventh-day Sabbath is found in Exodus 16:22−30. This demonstrates that the pattern was in place before the Israelites got to Sinai,[26] and this was not part of the ritual system associated with tabernacle or temple worship, but a fundamentally ethical ordinance. The seventh-day Sabbath was to be celebrated as a blessed day (Gen. 2:3), set apart for all to "rest" and "to catch their breath."[27]

The fourth principle of covenant relationship: parental right to respect (5:16). Although using a different verb, like Leviticus 19:3, the fourth command calls on Israelites to honor (*kabbēd*) both mother and father.[28] The terms "father" and "mother" should not be restricted to biological parents, let alone living parents; nor is the principle valid only when one is young. Since the Decalogue is directed primarily to adult males, the scope of this ordinance extends even to deceased parents. The added motive clause links people's well-being with their disposition toward their parents. This is not ancestor worship; one's fate or fortune does not depend on the deceased's continued power; well-being is a blessing granted by Yahweh in response to proper respect for one's parents.

The fifth principle of covenant relationship: the right to life (5:17). The verb *rāṣaḥ* is used elsewhere of accidental manslaughter (4:42; 19:2,

---

commemorating Yahweh's mighty acts of liberation and celebrating their privilege of being the vassals of Yahweh rather than the slaves of Pharaoh. (5) It provided a context for free Israelites to declare their identification with the marginalized and economically vulnerable, reflecting Deuteronomy's general concern for the alien (cf. 10:18−19; 16:11; 26:11). (6) It provided a means whereby Israelites could declare that all of life is sacred (cf. Lev. 19:1). As Yahweh had set Israel apart as his holy people (Ex. 19:5; Deut. 10:14−15), so he had sanctified the seventh day, for every day in which Yahweh is involved is a holy day. By "guarding" (*šāmar*) the Sabbath as the holiest day of all, Israelites reminded themselves and the world that all of life is holy.

26. The revelation of the seventh-day Sabbath ordinance is separated from and antedates the revelation of all other cultic observances. Later texts associate a Sabbath with visits to the prophets (2 Kings 4:23), special assemblies (Isa. 1:13), prostration before Yahweh (Isa. 66:23), enthusiastic thanksgiving (Ps. 92), and celebration (Isa. 58:13; Hos. 2:11[13]; Lam. 2:6), but these probably involved monthly or annual festivals rather than the weekly Sabbath. Cf. the link of Sabbaths (plural) with New Moon festivals in Isa. 1:13; 66:23; Hos. 2:11[13].

27. Although Gen. 2:1−4a does not use the word *nûaḥ* ("to rest") of God, this verb occurs in Ex. 20:11 with God as the subject. Exodus 31:17 uses an even stronger anthropomorphic expression: *yinnāpaš* ("to catch one's breath").

28. The piel verb means "to ascribe weight to"; it is usually used in the sense of "to treat with respect," the way one treats a master (Mal. 1:6), an envoy of Yahweh (Judg. 13:7), or God himself (1 Sam. 2:30; Ps. 50:15). Its opposite is represented by the verb *qallēl* ("to treat with contempt, to denigrate" (Ex. 21:17; Lev. 20:9), often translated as "to curse." Echoes of this command are heard in 2 Sam. 10:3 (=1 Chron. 19:3) and Mal. 1:6.

4, 6), but here it refers to intentional, premeditated homicide.[29] But this is not merely a prohibition against murder. It also calls for proactive prevention of accidental deaths. The command is rooted in the unique sanctity of human life that derives from our status as the image of God (Gen. 9:6). To take the life of another person is to rob God of a representative and deputy, which is the highest form of treason. Unlike Babylonian laws, this command draws no distinctions in value of life based on status, race, or gender. The life of all human beings is equally sacred.

The sixth principle of covenant relationship: the right to fidelity in marriage (5:18). Strictly speaking, "adultery" involves voluntary sexual relations between a married person and someone other than his or her spouse.[30] Adultery was considered a capital crime because it undermined the integrity and covenant of marriage, violated the sanctity of sexual union, defiled a human being as the image of God, and threatened the stability of the community.[31] Like murder, adultery pollutes the land and ultimately causes it to spew out its inhabitants (Lev. 18:20, 24–25). And like murder, adultery is not only a crime against one's spouse or children or parents; it is a crime against God (cf. Gen. 39:9). Whereas elsewhere instructions on adultery focus on the female adulteress, this regulation focuses on male adultery.

The seventh principle of covenant relationship: the right to own property (5:19). Since the verb *gānab* is sometimes used of stealing persons (Ex. 21:15; Deut. 24:7), in Jewish tradition some have interpreted this command as a prohibition on kidnapping. However, it should not be restricted to stealing people.[32] This is a categorical prohibition of all theft, particularly of items one is tempted to covet, as listed in the last principle (v. 21b).

The eighth principle of covenant relationship: the right to an honest and fair hearing in court (5:20). This ordinance may apply to all conversations, but it envisages particularly a legal setting where a person is called to testify in a case involving his neighbor. While Exodus 20:16 and Deuteronomy 19:18 characterize the forbidden form of testimony as a "falsehood, lie," the NIV's reading misses the present point, which prohibits "empty" testimony. The concern is testimony that does not move the case forward, that hedges the truth, or that detracts from the pursuit of justice

---

29. Num. 35:16–34; Hos. 4:2; Jer. 7:9; 1 Kings 21:19. The common rendering, "You shall not kill," is too broad, suggesting a prohibition on slaughtering animals, capital punishment, engagement in war, or cutting down trees.

30. Extramarital relations of a married man were only considered adulterous if the woman involved was married. See Tigay, *Deuteronomy*, 71. This ordinance does not condone extramarital sexual relations, though the present concern is to protect the integrity of marriage.

31. On adultery in the OT, see E. A. Goodfriend, "Adultery," *ABD*, 1:82–86. On this "great sin/crime" in Ugaritic and Egyptian texts (*ANET*, 24), see W. L. Moran, "The Scandal of the 'Great Sin' at Ugarit," *JNES* 18 (1956): 280–81.

32. See Weinfeld, *Deuteronomy 1–11*, 314–15.

with misleading and trivial responses.[33] The seriousness of false testimony is reflected by the call for the death penalty in 19:15–21.

The ninth principle of covenant relationship: the right to marital security (5:21a). That verse 21 concerns a disposition of the heart or a mental state reinforces the conviction that the Decalogue is not a legal code to which judges could appeal to enforce proper conduct, but a body of principles by which to live. The syntactical division of this verse into two distinct clauses follows the version in Exodus 20:17, but now Moses modifies the command in three significant respects. (1) He changes the word for covet in the second from *ḥāmad* to *hit'awwâ*.[34] (2) He reverses the order of "house" and "your neighbor's wife" and isolates this prohibition as a separate command. (3) He creates a natural pair in the second by adding "his field" to "his house."

The significance of these shifts is monumental.[35] The ambiguity of the word "house," as well as the location of "your neighbor's wife" in the Exodus version, opens the door to irresponsible males justifying treating their wives merely as household property. Here Moses removes the ambiguity and elevates the marital relationship above all other domestic relationships. Whereas the sixth command sought to ensure the purity of marriage, this ordinance seeks to ensure the security of the relationship. Men do not covet their neighbor's wives only with lustful and adulterous sexual intentions. In an exploitative environment, women are also coveted for the contribution they make to the domestic economy, to enhance the status of a man, and to provide more children for the household. Moses' modifications to the ninth principle of covenant relationship establish a trajectory in domestic relations that will be pursued throughout Deuteronomy, intentionally reining in potential abuse of power by the heads of household.

The tenth principle of covenant relationship: the right to secure ownership of household property (5:21b). Having separated the wife from the rest of the household, Moses forbids Israelites from lusting after their neighbor's economic assets. These assets include the entire domestic compound: house and field, male and female servants, ox and donkey, as well as "anything [else] that belongs to your neighbor."

The aim of these last two commands is to create a climate of trust and security within the covenant community. By concluding the Decalogue

---

33. In the modern American context it could involve pleading the Fifth Amendment to protect oneself, when one knows this will not promote the cause of justice, or trivial preoccupation with semantics, as in President Clinton's comment, "It depends on what the meaning of the word 'is' is."

34. Since *ḥāmad* ("to covet") may be used of healthy desires (*DCH*, 3:247–48), the word is not intrinsically negative.

35. For detailed study see Block, "'You shall not covet your neighbor's wife,'" in *The Gospel According to Moses*, 137–68.

on this note Yahweh recognizes that actions arise from within,[36] and that neither proper behavior by the individual nor the security of the community can be legislated. These are achieved only as all the members purpose within their hearts to place the interests of others ahead of themselves.

The Transcriptional Epilogue (5:22)

WHILE MANY CONSIDER THIS verse to be the introduction to the next literary section that extends from 5:22 to 6:3, on form-critical grounds and based on comparison with ancient treaties, this verse is best understood as the conclusion to Moses' recitation of the Decalogue (cf. Ex. 24:12 – 18; 31:18). Moses recalls that Yahweh's revelation at Sinai was visual, oral, and textual.[37] Indeed he highlights the identification of the oral with the textual revelation: what Yahweh said, that he wrote, and no more. Having produced the written document himself, Yahweh handed it to his authorized representative and interpreter. By reciting the Decalogue, Moses has laid the foundations for the rest of the second address.

The transcription of the Decalogue on a pair of durable tablets of stone rather than perishable materials like parchment or papyrus reflects both its official nature and its permanent validity. Longstanding tradition has it that one tablet[38] contained the commands that dealt with Israel's relationship to God, and the second those that governed horizontal relationships.[39] This interpretation is groundless exegetically and contextually. Ancient Near Eastern custom required duplicate copies of treaties be produced, one for each party to the agreement.[40] Exodus 33:15 observed that the words of the Decalogue covered the stone slabs front and back, reinforcing the conclusion that Yahweh gave Moses two identical copies: one for the people and one for himself.

---

36. Cf. Isa. 32:6; 59:13; Matt. 5:27 – 28; 12:34; 15:18; Eph. 6:6. In Eph. 5:5 and Col. 3:5, Paul links this last principle with the first two claiming that in essence covetousness and greed are idolatry.

37. Elsewhere we read that at the top of the mountain, Yahweh handed Moses the two stone covenant tablets "inscribed by the finger of God" (Ex. 31:18; cf. 32:15 – 16; Deut. 5:22).

38. References to "two" tablets occur often in the Old Testament: Ex. 31:18; 32:15; 34:1, 4a, 4b, 29; Deut. 4:13; 5:22; 9:10, 11, 15, 17; 10:1, 3; 1 Kings 8:9; 2 Chron. 5:10; cf. additional plural references without specifying "two": Ex. 24:12; 32:1, 19, 28, 29; Deut. 9:9; 10:2, 4, 5.

39. Calvin, *Institutes of the Christian Religion*, 2.8.11 (pp. 376, 377). The tradition dates as far back as Philo, who wrote, "We find that He divided the ten into two sets of five which he engraved on two tables, and the first five obtained the first place, while the other was awarded the second" (*Decalogue*, 12.50). Similarly Josephus, *Ant.* 3.5.8; 3.6.5.

40. See further, M. G. Kline, "The Two Tables of the Covenant," *WTJ* 22 [1960]: 138 – 46. According to Hittite custom, each party deposited his copy of the treaty in the temple of the deity, where they would be overseen by the respective gods, but from where they could be retrieved and read aloud at prescribed intervals. For an example, see the treaty between Suppiluliuma I of Hatti and Shattiwaza of Mittani in *Hittite Diplomatic Texts*, 6A §13, pp. 46 – 47.

IN CHRISTIAN TRADITION THE Decalogue has been elevated above all the rest of the Torah as the essence of God's moral law, permanently and universally valid as the basis of ethics, in stark contrast to the rest of the laws, which have little or no relevance for us. The Decalogue is indeed a special document. Produced by the finger of God, it was the official covenant document. It reduced the divine will to ten statements that could be easily memorized and recited in a liturgical setting. Nevertheless, there is no evidence within the Old Testament or the New Testament that the Decalogue was ever treated as more authoritative or weighty than any other parts of the Sinai revelation.[41] Rather, we should perceive its relationship to the other constitutional documents as organic, like that of a seed that sprouts and grows and eventually yields its full beautiful flowers.[42] The relationships among these documents may be illustrated as follows:

The Evolution of Israel's Constitutional Tradition

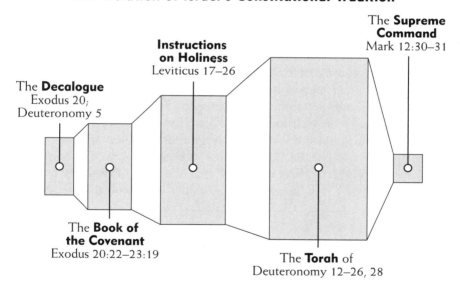

It is difficult to determine what role the Decalogue played in Israel's worship. In the present context on the Plains of Moab, Moses recites it as

---

41. So also F. Crüsemann, *The Torah* (Minneapolis: Fortress, 1996), 356–57.

42. The notion that the Decalogue is the source of all laws dates back as far as Philo, who wrote, "Never forget this, that the ten words are the sources of the laws which are recorded in appearance before the entire legislation in the sacred books" (Philo, *Decalogue*, 29.154).

the Scripture on which he will base his second address (Deut. 4:44 — 26:19 and 28:1 — 29:1[28:68]). In 6:1 — 11:32 he provides a detailed exposition of the first ["Supreme"] Command, while in 12:1 — 26:19 (misleadingly identified by many as the Deuteronomic Code) he expounds on the worldview presented by the rest of the Decalogue.[43] Few texts in the Old Testament have been inspired directly by the Decalogue. Leviticus 19 may be one such text, but changes in language and forms of expression cast doubts on viewing the Decalogue as the primary inspiration.

The spiritual commitment and social ethic called for by the Decalogue are reflected in the preaching of the prophets (Jer. 7:9; Hos. 4:2), but no unequivocal echoes of the document itself are found either in the Prophets or the Psalms. Ezekiel's lists of righteous actions in Ezekiel 18 display few formal or stylistic links with the Decalogue. If Psalms 15 and 24 did indeed originate in "entrance liturgies,"[44] it is remarkable that these texts reveal no influence of the Decalogue. Psalm 50:16 — 21 quotes God as questioning the right of the wicked to "recite my laws" and to "take my covenant on your lips," since they refuse to live by it. This may refer to the glib memorization and recitation of the Decalogue as a religious exercise, without any sense of personal spiritual obligation to the God who speaks in the document. However, the language suggests it may also be inspired by other constitutional texts. Psalm 81:9 — 10[10 — 11] obviously remembers the revelation at Sinai and seems to allude specifically to the preamble and the first principle of the Decalogue, but any theory of how the Decalogue might have been used in Israel's cult is speculative.[45]

The citation of the Decalogue in the Nash papyrus (second century BC) and the Tefillin (phylacteries) found at Qumran[46] shows that the Decalogue played an important liturgical role in early Judaism. The Mishnah (*m. Tamid* 5:1) suggests it was originally recited as part of the daily temple service. Whereas Christian tradition has tended to exploit the Decalogue

---

43. S. Kaufmann's attempt ("The Structure of the Deuteronomic Law," *Maarav* 1/2 [1978]: 105 — 58) to see the structure of the Decalogue reflected in the structure of this "Code" is forced.

44. Thus S. Mowinckel, *Le décalogue* (Paris: Félix Alcan, 1927), 141ff.

45. M. Weinfeld (*Deuteronomy 1 — 11*, 262, 267 — 75; idem, "The Decalogue in Israel's Tradition," in *Religion and Law: Biblical and Judaic-Islamic Perspectives* (ed. E. B. Firmage [Winona Lake, IN: Eisenbrauns, 1990], 38 — 39) proposes that the Decalogue was read at the Feast of Weeks (Shebuot), on the fifteenth of Sivan, three months after the exodus (Ex. 18:1). The day the Decalogue was heard is known as "the day of the assembly" (Deut. 9:10; 10:4; 18:16; cf. 4:10 — 14). Weinfeld suggests that the original event was regularly dramatized in a ritual by which the people took the Decalogue upon themselves by covenant and oath.

46. See G. Vermes, "Pre-Mishnaic Jewish Worship and the Phylacteries from the Dead Sea," *VT* 9 (1959): 65 — 72.

independently of its biblical context, Judaism refused to isolate it from the larger corpus of biblical law.[47]

While the New Testament never formally cites the Decalogue as a cultic or liturgical document, it obviously provides the basis for both Jesus' and Paul's ethical teaching. The antitheses in Jesus' Sermon on the Mount feature the Decalogue (Matt. 5:21 – 37), but elsewhere he reduces the principles of covenant relationship to two commands: "You shall love the Lord your God with all your heart ... and ... your neighbor as yourself" (Matt. 19:16 – 30; Mark 10:17 – 31; Luke 18:18 – 30), which capture precisely the two dimensions of covenant relationship spelled out in the Decalogue. Both James (Jas. 2:8 – 13) and Paul (Rom. 8:7 – 13; 13:8 – 10; Eph. 6:1 – 4) explicitly cite the Decalogue.[48] In 2 Corinthians 3 Paul contrasts the law engraved on stone letter by letter, which dispenses only death, with the law written on the heart by the Spirit, which dispenses life. This externalism often associated with the first covenant finally gives way in the new covenant.[49] Paul's ready use of the document reflects longstanding Jewish catechetical tradition and the importance of the Decalogue in early Christian preaching. Even so, there is no evidence in the New Testament that it had unique authority for Christians.

WHAT IS THE CHRISTIAN today to make of the Decalogue? Should Christians support the posting of the "Ten Commandments" in our courthouses and schools? Or does our freedom in Christ absolve us of obligation to all Old Testament laws, including the Decalogue? In seeking to answer these questions, we need to keep in mind several considerations.

Addressed to the redeemed. First, the Decalogue is addressed to those who have been redeemed. The ten principles of covenant relationship were not revealed to the Egyptians or Canaanites, but to the people of God, chosen to represent him and proclaim his grace and glory among the nations. The past tense of the verb ("who brought you out," v. 6) is neither

---

47. On the use of the Decalogue in early Judaism, see F. E. Vokes, "The Ten Commandments in the New Testament and in First Century Judaism," *StEv 5* (ed. F. L. Cross; Berlin: Akademie Verlag, 1968): 146 – 54.

48. Vokes (p. 153) observes that for Paul, "The Law as law passes away, but as an ethical norm it still remains."

49. In this he agrees with Jer. 31:31 – 34. But this internal aspect of the new covenant is not new absolutely. Every element of the new covenant cited by Jeremiah was operative in the hearts of true believers under the prior covenant.

coincidental nor irrelevant; it reminds all who hear this document of the proper relationship between obedience to the divine will and Yahweh's saving actions. The law (including the Decalogue) was neither a way of salvation nor a burdensome obligation; it was a gracious gift, a guide for God's people so they might knowingly respond to his grace according to his will.[50]

This means that impulses to post the Decalogue in public schools and courthouses are fundamentally misplaced. The problem with American society is not that people do not keep the "Ten Commandments"; it is that most have never left Egypt. It is unrealistic and unbiblical to expect those who have not been redeemed to live according to the principles and commitments of the redeemed. They have neither the motivation nor the indwelling Spirit to empower them do so.

Covenant relationship. Second, the terms of the Decalogue are revealed within the context of the establishment of a covenant relationship. Yahweh brought Israel to himself before he brought the laws to them (Ex. 19:4–6). Accordingly, the Israelites were not called primarily to follow a code of conduct but to enter a relationship with God ("I am the LORD your God"). Commitment to the revealed will of God is secondary to acceptance of the privilege of covenant relationship with him. Apart from the experience of salvation and covenant relationship, insistence on obedience to the "Ten Commands" is sheer moralism.

Complete acceptance. Third, if one accepts some terms of the Decalogue as normative for Christians, one must accept all. This document must be received as a package, beginning with the preamble and ending with the command against coveting. The principles are cast as absolute and unconditional commands, without qualification, and for the most part without declared motivation.

This includes the seventh-day Sabbath. Some argue for the normativeness of the "Ten Commands" as a guide for Christian behavior, but then remove the Sabbath ordinance as an exception, claiming this to be part of the ceremonial law that ended in Christ. However, this approach is indefensible. (1) The seventh-day Sabbath ordinance is embedded in the Decalogue as a fundamental principle of covenant relationship, along with the prohibition of any other gods, of murder, and so on. One may not treat it differently from the rest.

---

50. Note the similar evaluation of J. J. Stamm (*The Ten Commandments in Recent Research* [trans. M. E. Andrew; SBT 2nd series; London: SCM, 1967], 114): "The Decalogue was the charter of freedom which Yahweh had presented to his people delivered from Egypt. The people received it not as a burden, but as a gift, which was seen as a privilege and as an occasion for thanks."

(2) According to the Exodus version of the Decalogue, the six-plus-one weekly rhythm is fundamental to the cosmic order. Exodus 20:11 grounds the human practice in the pattern of divine creative work.

(3) In its origin the Sabbath is separated from Israel's ceremonial laws. In fact, Israelites were observing it as a matter of course before they got to Sinai (Ex. 16).

(4) The Sabbath command is not primarily a cultic ordinance. In intent and character it was both humanitarian (a gift offering people rest and refreshment from life-sustaining labor) and theological—offering Israelites an opportunity to declare their fundamentally theological perspective on life (God is Creator of all), their confidence in him to provide for the seventh day, their acceptance of covenant relationship, their gratitude for salvation from slavery, and their compassion for the poor.

(5) Nowhere does the New Testament declare the seventh-day Sabbath passé in Christ. On the contrary, Jesus (e.g., Luke 3:16) and the early disciples observed it (Acts 13:14, 27, 42, 44; 15:21; 16:13; 17:2; 18:4). Where Paul appears to minimize the Sabbaths (plural), he speaks of those annual or monthly festivals actually associated with the Israelite ceremonial calendar (Rom. 14:5–6; Gal. 4:10; Col. 2:16).[51]

It seems that by the first half of the second century AD Christians increasingly gathered for worship on Sunday, though many continued to observe the Sabbath on Saturday.[52] Along with circumcision, the rite of initiation into the covenant (which was replaced by baptism), and the Passover (which was transformed into the Lord's Supper), early Christians transformed the seventh day of rest into the first day of celebration of resurrection and new life.[53] They did not abolish the Sabbath; as the seventh-day Sabbath was the sign of the covenant for Israel (cf. Ex. 31:17), so the first-day Sabbath became the sign of the new covenant for Christians.[54] If Sunday is to Christians what the Sabbath was to Israel, then by observing this day we too declare our fundamentally theological perspective on life (God is creator of all), our confidence in him to provide for the sanctified

51. To cite Hebrews 4:9 as evidence of the end of the Sabbath rest in Christ is to misunderstand metaphors; the use of the seventh-day Sabbath as a picture of rest we enjoy in Christ does not affect the reality on which it is based.

52. Though Sunday was not the official day of rest until it was decreed so on March 7, AD 321, by Constantine I.

53. In Russian, the word for "Sunday," *Voskresenie*, means "Resurrection day."

54. It seems that behind the expression "on the Lord's day" in Rev. 1:10 lies the Hebrew phrase, "a day belonging to Yahweh," perhaps an abbreviation of "the seventh day is a Sabbath to the LORD your God" (Ex. 20:10). In that case John applies the old covenant expression to a new covenant reality. Elsewhere we read of the first day as the day for corporate worship and receiving donations for the poor (Acts 20:7; 1 Cor. 16:2).

day, our acceptance of covenant relationship, our gratitude for salvation from slavery to sin, and our compassion for the poor.

Jesus and the Decalogue. Finally, Jesus shows us how we are to understand the Decalogue. In reducing the revealed will of God to the simple command, "You shall love the Lord your God with all your heart ... and ... your neighbor as yourself" (Matt. 22:34 – 40; Mark 12:28 – 34), Jesus captured both the essence and the heart of all the law. Patrick Miller observes, "The Commandments are ... the starting point of a rich trajectory of meaning and effects, principles and actions, that tell the community of faith how to live its life in relation to God and neighbor."[55]

True godliness is demonstrated by acts of covenant commitment that seek the pleasure of God and the well-being of others. Assuming the Decalogue to be normative for his followers, Jesus quoted it explicitly (Matt. 19:18 – 19) and rebuked the Pharisees for hypocritically substituting their own laws for weightier matters of Torah (Matt. 15:4 – 20; 23:1 – 12). Even so, as Yahweh incarnate, the One who had spoken to Israel at Horeb, Jesus personally retained complete freedom toward this ordinance and declared himself to be the Lord of the Sabbath (Mark 2:27 – 28). When he commended the young inquirer for keeping the commands and called on him to follow *him* (Matt. 19:16 – 22; Mark 10:17 – 22; Luke 18:18 – 30), Jesus spoke as Yahweh in the Decalogue. Eternal life is gained through relationship with him, the covenant Lord.

---

55. P. D. Miller, *The Ten Commandments* (Interpretation; Louisville: Westminster John Knox, 2009), 6.

Deuteronomy 5:23–6:3

W hen you heard the voice out of the darkness, while the mountain was ablaze with fire, all the leading men of your tribes and your elders came to me. ²⁴And you said, "The LORD our God has shown us his glory and his majesty, and we have heard his voice from the fire. Today we have seen that a man can live even if God speaks with him. ²⁵But now, why should we die? This great fire will consume us, and we will die if we hear the voice of the LORD our God any longer. ²⁶For what mortal man has ever heard the voice of the living God speaking out of fire, as we have, and survived? ²⁷Go near and listen to all that the LORD our God says. Then tell us whatever the LORD our God tells you. We will listen and obey."

²⁸The LORD heard you when you spoke to me and the LORD said to me, "I have heard what this people said to you. Everything they said was good. ²⁹Oh, that their hearts would be inclined to fear me and keep all my commands always, so that it might go well with them and their children forever!

³⁰"Go, tell them to return to their tents. ³¹But you stay here with me so that I may give you all the commands, decrees and laws you are to teach them to follow in the land I am giving them to possess."

³²So be careful to do what the LORD your God has commanded you; do not turn aside to the right or to the left. ³³Walk in all the way that the LORD your God has commanded you, so that you may live and prosper and prolong your days in the land that you will possess.

⁶:¹These are the commands, decrees and laws the LORD your God directed me to teach you to observe in the land that you are crossing the Jordan to possess, ²so that you, your children and their children after them may fear the LORD your God as long as you live by keeping all his decrees and commands that I give you, and so that you may enjoy long life. ³Hear, O Israel, and be careful to obey so that it may go well with you and that you may increase greatly in a land flowing with milk and honey, just as the LORD, the God of your fathers, promised you.

MOSES' RECOLLECTIONS OF THE sequel to the revelation of the Decalogue divide into three roughly equal parts, in each of which we hear a different voice: the voice of the people (vv. 23–27), the voice of Yahweh (vv. 28–32), and the voice of Moses (5:32–6:3).

The People's Response to the Theophany at Horeb (5:23–27)

UPON HEARING THE THUNDER of Yahweh's voice, a delegation consisting of all the leaders of the tribes and elders approached Moses. The way they approached Moses reflects their excitement. They acknowledged that Yahweh had revealed his glory and majesty and that they had heard his voice from the midst of the fire. They expressed amazement that they survived the experience (v. 24), but then they were not so sure they had actually escaped (vv. 25–26). They expressed their fear with two rhetorical questions: "Why should we die?" and "What mortal man[1] has ever heard the voice of the living God speaking out of fire, as we have, and survived?" Yahweh's fiery presence has convinced them that he is indeed the living God, but they fear that the One who lives will take their life. To ward off the danger, the people request that Moses serve as mediator (v. 27), and they promise from now on to listen to him and to treat the voice of Moses as if it were the voice of God.

Yahweh's Response to the People's Proposal (5:28–31)

YAHWEH ACKNOWLEDGED THAT HE overheard the people's request to Moses (cf. 4:28) and affirmed their response. He also expressed his wish that the Israelites would never lose their present reverential disposition toward him.[2] If they would demonstrate it by obedience to all his commands forever, then their well-being would be assured forever. The remainder of Yahweh's comments were directed to Moses. He was to send the people home to their tents while he remained in Yahweh's presence to receive further revelation, identified as "the whole command" (NIV, "all the commands"), and the "decrees and laws."

The singular form of the first expression is striking. As elsewhere,[3] it refers to the first command of the Decalogue (the Supreme Command) and

---

1. Hebrew *bāśār* (NIV "mortals") may be used of living creatures (Gen. 6:17, 19; Num. 18:15) but usually refers to humankind (Gen. 6:12, 13; Isa. 40:5, 6; etc.).

2. This idiom recurs in 28:67; variations appear in Ex. 16:3; Num. 11:29; Job 6:8; 11:5; 13:5; 14:3; 19:23; 23:3.

3. Deut. 6:1, 25; 7:11; 8:1; 11:8, 22; 30:11.

its obverse, as expressed in the Shema (6:4–5),[4] which underlies all, while the "decrees and laws" refer to the specific stipulations of the covenant. Moses is to teach these to the Israelites that they might live by them in the Promised Land.

The verb "teach" (*limmēd*) offers the hermeneutical key to the second address. In chapters 6–11 Moses will instruct the people on the nature and dimensions of the Supreme Command, and in chapters 12–26 he will teach them the decrees and laws. This will not mean simply reciting them as they have been previously given, but explaining the principles that underlie them and applying them to new situations.

The Mediator's Exhortation (5:32–6:3)

ASSUMING HIS ROLE AS official spokesman, Moses seizes the opportunity to exhort the people to a life of obedience. His exhortation divides into three parts, each with its own charge, goal, and declaration of place: 5:32–33; 6:1–2; 6:3 (cf. 4:40). The first highlights Yahweh as the source of the commands; the second, Moses as the teacher of the commands; and the third, the people as learners and doers of the commands.

Moses' first charge (vv. 32–33) moves from a simple call to covenant commitment to a metaphorical exhortation (cf. 4:40).[5] He speaks of Yahweh's commands as a road down which he has commanded his people to travel, and he warns them not to get sidetracked by turning off "to the right or to the left." If they stay on course, they will reach the threefold goal of life, well-being, and length of days in the land they are to possess (cf. 28:1–14).

Moses' second charge (6:1–2) focuses on what Yahweh has commanded him to teach the people. His goal was not mere memorization but a permanent fear of God that will inspire them and their descendants to obedience and yield the desired result of long life.

As pastor-teacher, he opens his third charge (v. 3) with an appeal to listen,[6] followed by a call to "be careful to obey/keep by doing." His declared goal, defined in terms of well-being for the people and extreme multiplication of the population, links this statement to the narratives of Genesis (e.g., Gen. 13:16; 22:17; 28:14). Cryptically he described the geographic context

---

4. So also Weinfeld, *Deuteronomy 1–11*, 326; Lohfink, *Das Hauptgebot; eine Unterschung literarischer Einleitungstragen zu Dtn 5–11* (Rome: Pontifical Biblical Institute, 1963), 55–56.

5. On the construction "keep by doing," see above on 5:1. While the concern here is to keep alive the memory of God's revelation at Sinai, the emphasis on "guarding oneself" recalls 4:9, 15, 23.

6. Appeals to hear occur esp. in teaching contexts (Prov. 1:8; 4:1, 10; 8:32; cf. 4:20; 5:1; 7:24. See further Weinfeld, *DDS*, 305–6.

in which both the charge and the promise will be fulfilled as in "a land oozing [NIV 'flowing'] with milk and honey."[7] Milk and honey represent products the land produces spontaneously, in contrast to the artificial and irrigational nature of agricultural production in Egypt.[8] Oozing with milk and honey, the Promised Land also represented the antithesis to the desert, where for nearly forty years these people had had nothing to eat but manna.

ALTHOUGH MOSES HAS ACKNOWLEDGED earlier that the present generation is not faithless like their parents (4:4:3–4), for the first time he hints that all is not what it appears to be. Verses 28–29 suggest that Yahweh lacks confidence in his people and that their present enthusiasm will be short-lived.

This motif will return in chapter 31, where Yahweh declares explicitly that as soon as Moses is gone, the people will go after other gods, abandon him, and break his covenant (31:16). But Yahweh goes further. When he has brought the people into the land "oozing with milk and honey" and they prosper, they will serve other gods, spurn Yahweh, and break his covenant (31:20). Moses concurs. He knows how rebellious and stubborn the people are, even while he is alive; as soon as he has died, they will give full vent to their rebellion (31:27). The history of Israel proves how warranted Yahweh's present reservations are here. Within a generation or two of Moses' death (Judg. 2:1–23) they have turned from the way of Yahweh to a course that persisted until finally in 586 BC, the fire of divine fury engulfed the nation.

YAHWEH AS A CONSUMING **fire.** This portion of Moses' speech contains little that we have not heard before. However, in its recapitulative nature, it reminds modern readers of several fundamental spiritual lessons. First, Yahweh is a consuming fire before whom mortals rightfully recoil. Although the "Word becoming flesh" in Christ highlights God's continued determination to communicate with human

---

7. This idiom, describing the richness of the land of Palestine, will recur in Deuteronomy (11:9; 26:9, 15; 27:3; 31:20) and elsewhere in the Old Testament (Ex. 3:8, 17; 13:5; 33:3; Lev. 20:24; Num. 13:27; 14:8; 16:13, 14; Josh. 5:6; Jer. 11:5; 32:22; Ezek. 20:6, 15). On this expression and the nature of the Palestinian landscape in ancient times, see S. D. Waterhouse, "A Land Flowing with Milk and Honey," *AUSS* 1 (1963): 152–66.

8. For a comparable early second-millennium BC Egyptian's description of northern Palestine, see *COS*, 1:38 (p. 79).

beings, he does so in ways that sacrifice nothing of his glory (John 1:14). As he was before ancient Israel, so God remains before all who have been grafted in and made heirs of the promises. He is a consuming fire, before whom acceptable service will always arise out of deep reverence and awe (Heb. 12:28–29).

The disposition of fear. The proper human disposition before the glorious and gracious God remains fear, the deep sense of awe in his presence, which alone will produce acceptable liturgical response and the worship of daily obedience. Where there is no fear, there is no sense of obligation and no sense of gratitude that we have stood in the presence of God and lived to tell about it. Without fear, the privileged life of obedience is reduced to a burdensome duty.

Yahweh's longing for devotion. Third, Yahweh's longing for constancy of devotion (5:29) reminds us of the fundamental depravity of the human heart. Moses knows only too well how short-lived will be the Israelites' fearful disposition. While in 10:16 he will call on the Israelites to circumcise their hearts, ultimately he will declare (30:6) that this too involves a divine act of grace. People with hearts of stone rebel against God and insist on their own ways; those with circumcised hearts fear God and walk in his ways.

Deuteronomy 6:4–9

❧

Introduction to Deuteronomy 6:4–8:20

LIKE A PREACHER TODAY, after reciting Scripture in the form of the Decalogue, Moses launches into a theological exposition of that text. His primary goal in the first major part of the second address (6:4–11:32) is to impress on the people the privilege and sheer grace of the special relationship they enjoy with Yahweh. However, this grace may not be received casually; it must be embraced with grateful and unreserved devotion to their Redeemer and covenant Lord.

But this section subdivides into several segments. As in 5:1, the beginnings of the first two are signaled by Moses' summons, "Hear, O Israel," in 6:4 and 9:1. Between these two markers (6:4–8:20) Moses expounds on the essence of covenant relationship with Yahweh. He announces this grand theme with the Shema in 6:4 and then develops it from several different angles. The flow and structure of 6:4–8:20 may be illustrated diagrammatically as follows:

Thesis Statement	Deuteronomy 6:4–9: A Call to Covenant Love[1]		
Rhetorical presentation of the test	6:10–25	7:1–26	8:1–20
	The internal and external tests (6:10–19)	The external test (7:1–16)	The internal test (8:1–16)
Audience response	Question from child: What is the meaning of these commands? (6:20)	Question from audience: How can I dispossess these nations? (7:17)	Conclusion by audience: I have achieved this myself. (8:17)
Rhetorical answer	Moses' catechetical answer (6:21–25)	Moses' promise and warning (7:18–26)	Moses' reminder and warning (8:18–20)

While 6:4–5 embodies the central idea, in the rest of chapters 6–8 Moses' concretizes his understanding of unreserved love for Yahweh with a series of tests of devotion that life in the Promised Land will present.

---

1. This theme is captured in the title of J. DeRouchie's work, *A Call to Covenant Love: Text Grammar and Literary Structure in Deuteronomy 5–11* (Piscataway, NJ: Gorgias, 2007).

Hear, O Israel: The LORD our God, the LORD is one. ⁵Love the LORD your God with all your heart and with all your soul and with all your strength. ⁶These commandments that I give you today are to be upon your hearts. ⁷Impress them on your children. Talk about them when you sit at home and when you walk along the road, when you lie down and when you get up. ⁸Tie them as symbols on your hands and bind them on your foreheads. ⁹Write them on the doorframes of your houses and on your gates.

THIS FIRST SUBSECTION OF 6:4 – 8:20 may be the shortest, but it may also be the most profound. Readers tend to fix their attention on the opening, "Hear, O Israel," but this šᵉmaᶜ is just the first of a series of imperatives that dominate the paragraph: "hear," "love," "impress," "talk," "tie," and "write."

The Focus of Covenant Commitment (6:4)

THE SHEMA IS ONE of the most important symbols of Judaism.[2] To this day, orthodox Jews recite verses 4 – 5 twice daily as part of their prayers (cf. v. 7).[3] Despite its importance in Jewish and Christian tradition, the Shema is enigmatic. The sense of the first two words is clear. But the construction of the remainder is unparalleled in the entire Old Testament, so any interpretation, including our own, should be deemed provisional. On the surface the four words appear to be arranged in an ABAB parallelistic order, translated literally:

Hebrew transliteration	Literal translation	NIV
yhwh ʾᵉlōhênû	"Yahweh our God"	"The LORD our God"
yhwh ʾeḥād	"Yahweh one"	"The LORD is one"

---

2. Its significance in ancient Judaism is reflected by its inclusion after the Decalogue in the Nash papyrus, a second century BC liturgical text (Emmanuel Tov, *Textual Criticism of the Hebrew Bible* [Minneapolis: Fortress, 1992], 118); and in a first century AD phylactery text from Cave 8 at Qumran, in which the Shema is written in a rectangle and surrounded by other texts (published by M. Baillet, *Discoveries in the Judaean Desert* 3 [1962]: 149 – 51).

3. Thereby taking "the yoke of the kingdom," that is, placing themselves under kingship of Yahweh. For discussions of the Shema in early Judaism, see L. Jacobs. "Shema, Reading of," in *Encyclopaedia Judaica* (rev. ed.; New York: Macmillan, 2007), 18:453 – 56; S. D. McBride, "The Yoke of the Kingdom: An Exposition of Deut. 6:4 – 5," *Int* 27 (1973): 273 – 306, esp. 275 – 79.

The first line could be interpreted either as a sentence, "Yahweh is our God," or appositionally, "Yahweh our God," though the latter creates problems for interpreting the second line. The critical word in the second part is obviously *ʾeḥād*, which in the overwhelming number of occurrences represents the cardinal number "one."[4] However, in a half dozen instances, the word functions as an equivalent to *lᵉbaddô*, "unique, only, alone."[5] Within the immediate and the broader contexts the purpose of this statement is not to answer the question, "How many is God?" but "Who is the God of Israel?" To this question the Israelites were to respond in unison and without compromise or equivocation, "Our God is Yahweh, Yahweh alone!"[6]

Moses' concern here is whether God's people would remain devoted exclusively to Yahweh or be seduced by the gods of Canaan. His exposition of the Shema in the remainder of 6:5–19 confirms this interpretation. Answering to the Supreme Command, by uttering the Shema the Israelites were declaring their complete, undivided, and unqualified devotion to Yahweh. This is not strictly a monotheistic confession (cf. 4:35, 39) but a cry of allegiance, an affirmation of covenant commitment that defines the boundaries of the covenant community. It consists of those who claim this utterance as a verbal badge of identity and who demonstrate this identity with uncompromising covenant commitment, a subject to which Moses now turns.

The Locus of Covenant Commitment (6:5)

VERSE 5 EXPLAINS WHAT Moses means by exclusive allegiance to Yahweh. As noted earlier (4:37), Hebrew *ʾāhab* ("love") refers to covenant commitment demonstrated in actions that seek the well-being and pleasure of one's covenant partner. Here Moses calls on the people to back up the verbal commitment expressed in verse 4 with wholehearted and full-bodied love.

---

4. This is clearly how LXX understood it: *akoue Israēl kyrios ho theos hēmôn kyrios heis estin*. For discussion, see J. W. Wevers, *Notes on the Greek Text of Deuteronomy* (Atlanta: Scholars, 1995), 114. So also the Nash papyrus, which adds a pleonastic *hûʾ* at the end of v. 4.

5. Josh. 22:20; 2 Sam. 7:23 (// 1 Chron. 17:21); 1 Chron. 29:1; Job 23:13; 31:15; Song 6:9; Zech. 14:9. Cf. the similar use of *lᵉbaddô* in 2 Kings 19:19; Isa. 2:11, 17. The ambiguity of the Hebrew text of the Shema is resolved in this direction also in a fourth-century AD Samaritan inscription, which adds an appositional *ldbw*, "he alone," to the Shema. See G. Davies, "A Samaritan Inscription with an Expanded Text of the Shema," *PEQ* 131 (1999): 3–19.

6. For a detailed discussion of the Shema and a defense of the interpretation represented here, see D. I. Block, "How Many Is God? An Investigation into the Meaning of Deuteronomy 6:4–5," in *How I Love Your Torah, O LORD!* 73–97. Cf. Nathan MacDonald, *Deuteronomy and the Meaning of 'Monotheism'* (FAT 2/1; Tübingen: Mohr Siebeck, 2003).

Moses highlights the intensity of this commitment with a triad of qualifiers, which the NIV renders as "with all your heart and with all your soul and with all your strength." The rendering is traditional, but it is somewhat misleading and obscures the profundity of this statement. Although some have interpreted verse 5 as a Greek psychological statement reflecting a tripartite anthropology, this is intended as an emphatic reinforcement of the absolute and singular devotion to Yahweh called for by verse 4.[7] Proceeding from the inside out, the three Hebrew expressions, *lēb, nepeš, mᵉʾōd*, represent three concentric circles, each of which represents a sphere of human existence (see figure).

The Dimensions of Covenant Commitment
An Interpretation of Deuteronomy 6:5

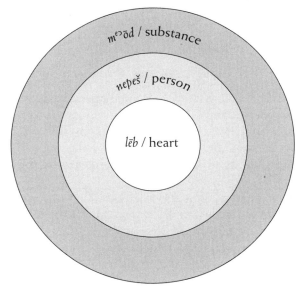

The Hebrew word *lēb* ("heart") often functions metaphorically for the seat of the emotions and will, but equally often it refers to the "mind" or the seat of thought. Here the word serves comprehensively for one's inner being, including the "heart" and "mind."[8] Concretely *nepeš* means "throat, gullet," but the word is used in a variety of derived metaphorical senses: "appetite/desire" (Prov. 23:2; Eccl. 6:7); "life" (Gen. 9:5; 2 Sam. 23:17;

---

7. McBride, "The Yoke of the Kingdom," 273–306.

8. Which explains why, in Mark's citation of Jesus' quotation of this verse, he uses four Greek words for Deuteronomy's three: *kardia* (= Heb. *lēb*), *psychē* (= Heb. *nepeš*), *dianoia* (= Heb. *lēb*), and *ischys* (= Heb. *mᵉʾōd*).

Jonah 2:5[6]); a person as a "living being" (Ezek. 4:14; etc.); the whole self (Lev. 26:11); even a corpse, that is, a body without life/breath (Lev. 21:11). Here the word refers to one's entire person. The NIV's rendering of *mᵉʾôd* as "strength" follows the LXX, which reads *dynamis*, "power" (cf. *ischys* in Mark 12:30), but this flattens the sense required by the Hebrew. Except for this text and 2 Kings 23:25, which echoes this statement, elsewhere *mᵉʾôd* always functions adverbially, meaning "greatly, exceedingly."[9] Here its meaning is best captured by a word like "resources," which includes physical strength, but also economic or social strength, and it may extend to the physical things an Israelite owned: tools, livestock, a house, and the like.

The progression and concentricity in Moses' vocabulary now become apparent. Calling all Israelites to love God without reservation or qualification, Moses begins with the inner being, then moves to the whole person, and ends with all that one claims as one's own.[10] This is the "yoke of the kingdom" — covenant commitment rooted in the heart, but extending to every level of one's being.

The Dimensions of Covenant Commitment (6:6 – 9)

CONTINUING THIS CENTRIFUGAL PATTERN, in the remainder of this paragraph Moses emphasizes that this unreserved commitment is to permeate all of life. (1) The commitment expressed in the Shema and the call for unreserved love for Yahweh must be indelibly written on one's own inner being (v. 6). Israelite faith is not to be defined by ritual acts but by deep internal commitment to Yahweh.[11]

(2) This covenant commitment is to be a family matter, demonstrated by the indoctrination of children and the spontaneous discussion of the issue with the members of one's household (v. 7). This is to be accomplished by "impressing" these words on children (vv. 4 – 5). This means repeating them constantly,[12] when God's people sit in their homes and walk on the

---

9. Cognate adjectival expressions occur in both Ugaritic (*mad/mid*, "great, strong, much"; *Kirta* 1.ii.35 [Parker, *Ugaritic Narrative Poetry*, 15]; *Baal Cycle* 10.v.15 [*Ugaritic Narrative Poetry*, 130]), and Akkadian *mâdum*, "many, numerous," and *maʾdu*, "quantity, fullness," from the verb *mâdum*, "to become numerous," *AHw*, 573. Cf. *HALOT*, 2:538.

10. Just as "iniquity, rebellion, and sin" in Ex. 34:7 refer to "every conceivable sin," so here "inner being, person, and resources" function superlatively for every part of a person.

11. On the actual internalization of the will of God in the hearts of believers, see Pss. 37:31; 40:8[9]; 119:11; Isa. 51:7.

12. The verb *šinnēn*, "to repeat, to inculcate by repetition," occurs only here in the Old Testament. It has traditionally been thought of as deriving from a root *šānan*, "to whet, sharpen" (BDB, 1042; Weinfeld, *Deuteronomy 1 – 11*, 332 – 33). However, in the light of Ugaritic texts, which use the cognate *tnn*, "to repeat, to do twice," the word is better interpreted as a denominative of the numeral *šēnî/šᵉnayim*, "two." Cf. Craigie, *Deuteronomy*, 170, n. 17.

road; when they lie down and when they rise up.[13] In this case, every adult Israelite is to be a teacher, seizing every opportunity for instruction.

(3) This commitment is to be a public matter. Moses continues his pattern of triadic expression by charging his people to bind these words on their hands, apply them as phylacteries on their foreheads (lit., "between their eyes"), and inscribe them on the doorposts of their buildings (cf. Ex. 13:9, 16). That which is bound is apparently the Shema and the call for wholehearted covenant love (vv. 4 – 5).[14] What kind of object Moses intends to be bound on the hands we cannot know — nor even if he intends this injunction to be taken literally.[15] If we associate this act with the inscription of the divine name on one's hand (cf. Deut 5:11; Isa. 44:5), this action signifies more than a tattoo or brand on the hand.[16] The binding concretizes the declaration of allegiance and ownership by Yahweh as declared orally in the Shema.

The second act is even more enigmatic: These words are to serve as *ṭôṭāpōt* between the eyes, that is, the forehead (cf. 14:1; Dan. 8:5, 21). The etymology of *ṭôṭāpōt* is uncertain, making any interpretation tentative. Some interpret the command metaphorically, but several factors speak for a literal application. (a) This seems to be the case with the actions called for in verse 9. (b) The medallion worn by the high priest (Ex. 28:36 – 39) and extrabiblical evidence for ornaments worn on the forehead in Egypt and Mesopotamia support a literal intention here.[17] (c) Two silver plaques inscribed with biblical texts from the seventh century BC attest to an analogous custom

---

13. Contra the NIV, *dibbēr . . . bᵉ* does not mean "to speak about," but to recite the text itself. See E. Talstra, "Texts for Recitation, Deuteronomy 6:7; 11:19," *Unless Someone Guide Me . . . Festschrift for Karel A. Deurloo* (ed. J. W. Dyk et al.; ACEBTSup 2; Maastricht: Shaker, 2001), 67 – 76.

14. Whether left or right hand is intended is unclear. Since most people are right-handed, it would be more convenient to bind them on the left hand, in which case the sign is intended primarily for the person wearing it. Thus B. Jacob, *The Second Book of the Bible: Exodus* (trans. W. Jacob; Hoboken, NJ: Ktav, 1992), 369. But since the right hand was generally recognized to be more important than the left (cf. Rev. 13:16) and was used in greeting and oaths, this would fit better in this context.

15. For a literal interpretation also of Ex. 13:9 and 16, see Ibn Ezra, *Commentary on the Pentateuch: Exodus (Shemot)* (trans. H. N. Strickman and A. M. Silver; New York: Menorah, 1996), 262.

16. So also C. Houtman, *Exodus*, 3 vols; vol. 2, *Chapters 7:14 – 19:25* (Historical Commentary on the Old Testament; Kampen: Kok, 1996), 218 – 20. For further discussion, see O. Keel, "Zeichen der Verbundenheit: Zur Vorgeschichte und Bedeuting der Forderungen von Deuteronomium 6:8f. und Par," in *Mélanges Dominique Barthélemy* (OBO 38; Freiburg/Göttingen: Vandenhoeck & Ruprecht, 1981), 212 – 15.

17. For documentation, see J. Gamberoni, *TDOT*, 5:319 – 21; Jeffrey H. Tigay, "On the Meaning of *ṭ(w)ṭpt*," *JBL* 101 (1983): 328 – 30; Keel, "Zeichen der Verbundenheit," 212 – 15.

in the First Temple Period.[18] (d) Finally, this text provided the basis for the practice of wearing phylacteries (Aramaic *t*fillîn*) in the late Second Temple Period.[19] In any case, the purpose of all three elements was to mark Israelites as those who claimed Yahweh as their covenant Lord and committed themselves to loving him wholeheartedly.[20]

(4) Moses concludes this call for public declarations of covenant commitment with a command to write these words on the doorposts of their houses and on their gates (v. 9).[21] In so doing Israelites will remind themselves that their primary allegiance is to Yahweh whenever they leave from or return to their homes, and that love for Yahweh must govern all activities inside and outside the house. Furthermore, it will declare to guests and all who pass by that in this household Yahweh is not only the unseen guest but also the supreme head. The inscription on the gates extends this commitment to the entire community, reminding citizens and visitors alike of Yahweh's rule over the town and the nation as a whole. Since city gates also functioned as courthouses, these inscriptions will also remind those participating in legal or administrative proceedings that all must be done in honor and on behalf of the divine ruler.

FEW TEXTS IN THE Old Testament are as pregnant with significance as this passage. (1) The Shema functioned as Israel's pledge of allegiance. Whenever Israelites recited this pledge, they acknowledged that the God who redeemed them was not some amorphous and unknowable deity. He is Yahweh, who intervenes in history on behalf of his chosen people and calls them to covenant relationship with himself. No other god, ancient or modern, has done this.

---

18. For discussion, see G. Barkay, *Ketef Hinnom: A Treasure Facing Jerusalem's Walls* (Jerusalem: The Israel Museum, 1986), 29 – 31; idem, "The Priestly Benediction on the Ketef Hinnom Plaques," *Cathedra* 52 (1989): 37 – 76 [Hebrew]. Cf. Tov, *Textual Criticism*, 118 and plate 1. These plaques have holes for the string that was used to attach them to the body.

19. These *t*fillîn* were small cubical boxes of leather attached to the wrist or the forehead with leather strips. Inside the boxes were small pieces of parchment inscribed with biblical texts from the Decalogue, Ex. 13:1 – 16, and Deut. 6:4 – 9; 11:13 – 21. Cf. Matt. 23:5. For discussion and documentation of the Qumran phylacteries, see L. H. Schiffman, "Phylacteries and Mezuzot," in *Encyclopedia of the Dead Sea Scrolls* (Oxford: Oxford Univ. Press, 2000), 2:675 – 77.

20. Similarly, Houtman, *Exodus Chapters 7:14 – 19:25*, 2:219. It seems likely that these ornaments would have been worn on special occasions, perhaps the Sabbath, or during Passover and Unleavened Bread (Ex. 13:9, 16).

21. On sacred inscriptions on doorposts of houses in ancient Egypt, see Keel, "Zeichen der Verbundenheit," 183 – 92.

Given the theological and confessional weight of the Shema, it is remarkable how faint are its echoes in the Old Testament. Indeed we hear the only certain echo at the very end, in Zechariah 14:9, where the enigmatic verbless clause is transformed into a clear verbal declaration: "The Lord [Yahweh] will be king over the whole earth. On that day there will be one Lord [Yahweh], and his name the only name."[22] As in the original Shema, the issue here is not the unification of God in one deity, but expanding the boundaries of those who claim only Yahweh as their God to the ends of the earth.

References and allusions to the Shema in the New Testament are both fascinating and exciting. While Jesus cites it as a sort of creedal statement in connection with the Supreme Command (Mark 12:30), it falls to Paul to draw out its christological significance. He does so most pointedly in 1 Corinthians 8:1 – 6, where he roots his polemic against idolatry in Deuteronomy 6:4 – 5 and beyond.[23] Like Moses, Paul declares the uniqueness and exclusive existence of Yahweh in contrast to the nothingness of idols. Reflecting a thorough understanding of the Shema in its original context, in 1 Corinthians 8:5 – 6, Paul declares hypothetically that even if one concedes the existence of other gods (which, in the light of v. 4, he will not do), "for us there is but one God, the Father, from whom all things came and for whom we live; and there is but one Lord [i.e., Yahweh], Jesus Christ, through whom all things came and through whom we live." The christological effect of inserting the name "Jesus Christ" after "Lord" is extraordinary,[24] in that Paul identifies Jesus unequivocally with Yahweh, the one and only God to whom true Israelites declared allegiance (cf. Rom. 3:29 – 30; 10:13). What the Old Testament has said about Yahweh may now be said about the Christ.[25]

(2) Whereas elsewhere the Old Testament in general and Deuteronomy in particular spoke of commitment to Yahweh in terms of "fear" and "clinging to Yahweh," here for the first time in the Pentateuch, Moses picks up

---

22. Cf. the NJPS, footnote, "i.e., the Lord alone shall be worshiped and shall be invoked by his true name."

23. On Paul's reformulation of the Shema in 1 Corinthians 8, see N. T. Wright, "Monotheism, Christology and Ethics: 1 Corinthians 8," in *The Climax of the Covenant: Christ and the Law in Pauline Theology* (Edinburgh: T&T Clark, 1991), 120 – 36; L. Hurtado, *One God, One Lord: Early Christian Devotion and Ancient Jewish Monotheism* (London: SCM, 1988), 97 – 100.

24. N. T. Wright, "Monotheism, Christology and Ethics: 1 Corinthians 8," 129. This compares with the application of the title, "God of gods and Lord of lords," taken from Deut. 10:17, to the Lamb in Rev. 17:14.

25. So also R. W. L. Moberly, "Toward an Interpretation of the Shema," in *Theological Exegesis: Essays in Honor of Brevard A. Childs* (ed. C. Seitz and K. Greene-McCreight; Grand Rapids: Eerdmans, 1999), 142.

on a notion expressed in the Decalogue and speaks of the proper response to God as "love" (*ʾāhab*). In the Decalogue Yahweh promised covenant faithfulness (*ḥesed*) to those who demonstrate love for him by keeping his commands (5:10; Ex. 20:6; cf. Deut. 7:9), but from this point in Deuteronomy, this word will become increasingly important as an expression of the human disposition toward God. However, this kind of love is not merely an emotion, nor may it be taken for granted — Moses commanded it.[26] In the face of temptation to withhold love or to give it to other gods, the Shema provided Israelites with a necessary and constant reminder to commit themselves to Yahweh alone.[27]

Given the emphasis on loving God here and throughout Deuteronomy, and given the general assumption that the pious do "love" Yahweh/God (Ps. 97:10), it is remarkable that only once in the Old Testament is anyone said to have "loved" (*ʾāhab*) God.[28] When it speaks of individuals who appear to have measured up to the standard of Deuteronomy 6:5 the verb is changed.[29] Even more striking, especially in light of current habits in worship, the verb *ʾāhab* never occurs with a first person subject when it has Yahweh/God as the object. No one (not even the psalmists) ever declares that he or she loves Yahweh.[30] This probably explains why Peter will say he loves Jesus in the sense of *phileô*, but he will not claim *agapaô*

---

26. Moses reiterates the command in various forms in 10:12; 11:1, 13; 13:3[4], and speaks of obedience to them "by loving" Yahweh (11:22; 19:9; 30:16, 20). Cf. similar injunctions to "love" in Josh. 22:5; 23:11; Ps 31:23[24].

27. References and appeals for "wholehearted" devotion to Yahweh are common in the Old Testament: with "all one's heart": 1 Kings 8:23 = 2 Chron. 6:14; etc.; with "a wholesome heart": 2 Kings 20:3 = Isa. 38:3; 1 Chron. 28:9; 29:9; with, "one/a single heart": Jer. 32:39; Ezek. 11:19.

28. Solomon may be the exception that proves the rule: "Solomon showed his love (*ʾâhab*) for the LORD, walking according to the statutes of his father David, except that he offered sacrifices and burned incense on the high places" (1 Kings 3:3). Does the narrator anticipate his latter-day apostasy (1 Kings 11)? Cf. J. D. Hays, "Has the Narrator Come to Praise Solomon or to Bury Him? Narrative Subtlety in 1 Kings 1 – 11," *JSOT* 28 (2003): 149 – 74.

29. See esp. 2 Kings 23:25, where we hear a clear echo of Deut. 6:5: Josiah "turned [*sûb*] to the Lord ... with all his heart [*lēb*] and with all his soul [*nepeš*] and with all his strength [*mᵉʾôd*], in accordance with the Law of Moses." Hezekiah claims to have walked before Yahweh with a whole heart (2 Kings 20:3 = Isa. 38:3).

30. Ps. 18:12[13] deliberately avoids *ʾāhab*, reading *rāḥam*, "to feel compassion," which is odd, since typically the greater feels compassion toward a needed lesser person. The psalmist's discomfort with the notion may be reflected in his use of the Qal; elsewhere the verb always appears in the Piel or Pual stem. Ps. 116:1 translates literally, "I love because Yahweh has heard my voice and my supplications." This compares with 1 John 4:19, "We love, because he first loved us."

(John 21:15–19).[31] And how could he? He just demonstrated a total lack of "covenant commitment" by denying Jesus three times—the opposite of the love called for by Deuteronomy 6:6–9.

TRUE SPIRITUALITY. MOSES TAUGHT his people and he teaches us and Christians everywhere that true spirituality arises from the heart and extends to all of life. Those who claim to be religious tend to be subject to two temptations: either to treat spirituality as primarily interior and private, or to treat it as a matter of external performance. True love for God is rooted in the heart, but it is demonstrated in life, specifically a passion to speak of one's faith in the context of the family and to declare one's allegiance publicly to the world. This passage suggests that the very decoration of our homes should bear testimony to our faith, declaring to all guests and passers-by the fundamentally theological outlook of those who live within, and serving as reminders to residents to live in dependence on God and to realize that blessing is contingent on obedience.

My wife and I witnessed a striking illustration of this in 1968 when, for two months we lived in Soest, Germany. In the older part of town many of the half-timbered houses were decorated on the exterior by inscriptions, often religious. Into the black doorframe of one memorable house was carved and painted in gold the declaration, "An Gottes Segen ist alles gelegen," which translates loosely as, "Everything depends on the blessing of God." While we cannot make any judgments about the present residents, for the person originally responsible for the inscription, the text served two noble purposes, declaring to passers-by the theological outlook of those who lived within and reminding residents to live in dependence on God.

The meaning of love. Our text also reminds us today of the biblical understanding of love and its expression. Speaking biblically "love" is not merely an emotion, a pleasant disposition toward another person, but covenant commitment demonstrated in actions that seek the interest of the next person. Christians must indeed praise God for the love he has demonstrated in Christ Jesus and in his many providences. However, from biblical patterns we might learn to be more modest about professions of love for God in both prayer and song; the self-laudatory confessions so ubiquitous

---

31. For recent defense of this interpretation, see D. Shepherd, "'Do You Love Me?' A Narrative-Critical Reappraisal of ἀγαπάω and φιλέω in John 21:15–17," *JBL* 129 (2010): 777–92. Whether or not there is any etymological relationship between Hebrew ʾāhab, "to love," and Greek *agapaō*, "to love," the assonantal links are striking, facilitating the translation of the former with the latter in the LXX.

in contemporary worship find no precedent or warrant in Scripture. Words come easily. Just as in marriage true love is demonstrated not merely or even primarily by roses and verbal utterances of "I love you," but in actions that seek the well-being and delight of one's spouse, so true love for God is demonstrated primarily in active obedience to God. After all, did not Jesus himself say, "If you love me, you will obey what I command" (John 14:15)? Such obedience is the fruit of union with Christ (John 15:1 – 11).

True religion in the Old Testament. Finally, this passage should correct a common misunderstanding of true religion in the Old Testament. We often hear it said that whereas in ancient Israel, God demanded the sacrifices of animals and produce of the fields, in the New Testament he calls for sacrifice of our very bodies. However, not only does this view drive an unfortunate wedge between the Testaments; it is also patently false. Deuteronomy 6:4 – 5 is the Old Testament equivalent of Romans 12:1 – 2. As is true for us, in ancient Israel the truly godly were covenantly committed to him in their inner beings, with their entire bodies, and with all their resources. Paul and Moses are on the same page.

Deuteronomy 6:10–25

When the LORD your God brings you into the land he swore to your fathers, to Abraham, Isaac and Jacob, to give you—a land with large, flourishing cities you did not build, ¹¹houses filled with all kinds of good things you did not provide, wells you did not dig, and vineyards and olive groves you did not plant—then when you eat and are satisfied, ¹²be careful that you do not forget the LORD, who brought you out of Egypt, out of the land of slavery.

¹³Fear the LORD your God, serve him only and take your oaths in his name. ¹⁴Do not follow other gods, the gods of the peoples around you; ¹⁵for the LORD your God, who is among you, is a jealous God and his anger will burn against you, and he will destroy you from the face of the land. ¹⁶Do not test the LORD your God as you did at Massah. ¹⁷Be sure to keep the commands of the LORD your God and the stipulations and decrees he has given you. ¹⁸Do what is right and good in the LORD's sight, so that it may go well with you and you may go in and take over the good land that the LORD promised on oath to your forefathers, ¹⁹thrusting out all your enemies before you, as the LORD said.

²⁰In the future, when your son asks you, "What is the meaning of the stipulations, decrees and laws the LORD our God has commanded you?" ²¹tell him: "We were slaves of Pharaoh in Egypt, but the LORD brought us out of Egypt with a mighty hand. ²²Before our eyes the LORD sent miraculous signs and wonders—great and terrible—upon Egypt and Pharaoh and his whole household. ²³But he brought us out from there to bring us in and give us the land that he promised on oath to our forefathers. ²⁴The LORD commanded us to obey all these decrees and to fear the LORD our God, so that we might always prosper and be kept alive, as is the case today. ²⁵And if we are careful to obey all this law before the LORD our God, as he has commanded us, that will be our righteousness."

 IF THE SHEMA INTRODUCES the theme of covenant commitment, the rest of this chapter and chapters 7−8 answer the question, "What does it mean to be totally committed to Yahweh?" Moses answers the question by challenging his audience to be prepared for three tests of that commitment. These tests are arranged in an ABA order, with the first (6:10−25) and last (8:1−20) involving internal tests—Israel's response to prosperity in the land—and the center test (7:1−26) involving an external challenge—Israel's response to enemies who stand in their way. Deuteronomy 6:10−25 divides into two major parts: future challenges to Israel's commitment (vv. 10−19), and the importance of that commitment (vv. 20−25).

The Nature of the Test (6:10−19)

VERSES 10−12 are cast as one long sentence with the principal clause being delayed to the very end: "Be careful that you do not forget the LORD, who brought you out of Egypt." Previously Moses had warned against forgetting the events at Horeb (4:9) or the covenant of Yahweh (4:23), but now he goes back one stage further, highlighting the importance of remembering Yahweh as the one who had brought Israel out of Egypt, the slave house (cf. 5:6).

Moses sets the stage for the warning in verse 12 by describing the context in which the temptation to forget Yahweh will arise: when Yahweh has brought them to the land that he swore to their ancestors (v. 10a), when they have eaten, and when they are full (end of v. 11).[1] However, in verses 10−11 he devotes most of his attention to describing the place where the danger will lurk. To be sure it is the land that Yahweh had promised the ancestors,[2] but it is occupied by a settled agrarian population, and symbols of human cultural achievements—fortified towns (NIV "cities"), houses, cisterns, vineyards, and olive groves—dominate its landscape.[3] Yahweh will indeed deliver into the Israelites' hands the fruits of Canaanite efforts, ready made for their enjoyment. However, Moses warns the people that instead of evoking praise to their divine Benefactor, prosperity may yield a lapse of memory, especially concerning the source of the gifts.

---

1. Deuteronomy uses the expression "to eat and be satisfied" in both positive (8:10; 14:29; 26:12) and negative senses; in the latter it leads to self-sufficiency or idolatry (6:11; 8:12; 11:15; 31:20).

2. The statement echoes 1:8, as well as Yahweh's promise to Moses in Ex. 6:2−8 and Ex. 13:11. As in 9:5; 29:13[12]; and 30:20, he lists the ancestors by name: Abraham, Isaac, and Jacob (cf. also 9:27).

3. For a comparable description see Josh. 24:13. For a poetic exposition of this description, see Neh. 9:24−25.

In verses 13–19 Moses describes how the Israelites should respond to prosperity. Expounding on the Shema, he begins with three emphatic positive statements: "Fear the LORD your God, serve him only and take your oaths in his name." These statements cover most of life.[4] Fear (*yārē*) denotes the fundamental disposition of holy reverence and submission before Yahweh demonstrated by obedience.[5] Serving Yahweh involves accepting one's role as his vassal, not only by performing religious duties but especially by walking in his ways. Swearing by his name alone involves invoking only his name to guarantee the truthfulness of one's word. No other gods are to be invoked, even in oaths.[6]

The negative command of verse 14 presents the flip side of verse 13: Israel is not to walk after other gods. The idiom "to walk after a god" may derive from religious festivals in which devotees of a deity would follow in procession behind the image of the god. In Deuteronomy it is always used in a metaphorical sense of loyal devotion to Yahweh demonstrated by living in accordance with his revealed will and/or behaving as God himself does (10:18–19).

Verse 15 presents the basis for this prohibition in the form of three motive clauses. The positive motivation we have heard before: Yahweh is an impassionate God (*ʾēl qannāʾ*; NIV, "jealous God"), zealous for his honor and jealous toward his covenant partner.[7] Thus, Moses adds, should Israel betray him by going after other gods, he will destroy them off the face of the earth (Num. 11:1–3, 33; cf. also 25:3–4; Deut. 9:22).[8] In short, if Yahweh's people behave like Canaanites, they may expect the fate of the Canaanites. The God in their midst prefers to act for their good, but by the terms of the covenant he is not obligated to those whose devotion is compromised.

The reference to Yahweh's presence "among you" in verse 15 seems to have triggered in Moses' mind an illustration from Israel's own experience. In verse 16 he adds an unexpected imperative with a cross reference to Massah (Ex. 17:7), "place of testing." Massah became notorious as the place where Israel challenged God to prove himself, to keep his word,[9] even though in suzerain-vassal relationships it is inappropriate for the inferior

---

4. Cf. 10:20; 13:4[5].

5. Deut. 5:29; 6:2, 24; 10:12; 13:4[5]; 17:19; 31:12–13.

6. Cf. Ps. 63:11[12]; Isa. 48:1; 65:16; Jer. 4:2; 5:2; 12:16–17.

7. In contrast to 4:24, this clause clearly uses the description attributively rather than as a title.

8. On this combination of divine anger and destruction of the people, see 7:4; 11:17; 29:20, 23, 27[19, 22, 26]; 31:17; 32:22.

9. Cf. Deut. 9:22 and 33:8. The name recurs also in Ps. 95:8–9.

to challenge the superior (cf. Num. 14:22). Ironically, at Massah Yahweh was in fact testing the spiritual mettle of the Israelites (cf. Deut. 8:2−3; Ps. 81:7[8]). However, they had twisted his test of them into their own test of Yahweh,[10] demanding he prove his presence by indulging them with their physical desires and making his response a condition of following him.

But there is another irony in Moses' addition of "as you did at Massah." Whereas in the past Israel's loyalty to Yahweh had been tested by deprivation, in the future they will be tested by being "satisifed" (v. 11). Crises of need tempt people to demand a response from Yahweh, but crises of prosperity tempt them to forget him and to become self-sufficient. For this reason, Moses charges his people to guard their conduct (v. 17). Faith and fidelity are not merely matters of the heart, religious service, and/or verbal declarations of allegiance (v. 13); they must be demonstrated in life, specifically in obedience to the revealed will of God.[11]

In verses 18−19 Moses pleads for loyalty to Yahweh one more time, though now he expresses the demand in most general terms: "Do what is right and good in the LORD's sight."[12] The Hebrew article on both "right" and "good" suggests specific content is attached to "the right" and "the good," namely, unqualified allegiance to Yahweh alone and loving him with one's entire being as summarized in the Supreme Command and the Shema.[13] This is a precondition to enjoying the benefits of covenant relationship. The last clause in verse 19 shifts attention momentarily to the external test of Israel's commitment. As they do what is right in Yahweh's sight, he will do what is right, namely, to drive out the Canaanites (Ex. 23:27−28; cf. Deut. 11:23−25).

The Response to the Test (6:20−25)

HERE WE WITNESS MOSES at his pastoral best, instructing his congregation on the importance of passing the faith on to succeeding generations.[14]

---

10. Cf. Ps. 78, esp. vv. 18, 41, 56; Ps. 106, esp. v. 14. Mal. 3:10−12 is the exception that proves the rule.

11. On the meaning "commands," "stipulations," and "decrees," see comments on 4:1−2, 45.

12. The root twb/ytb is a key word in this chapter. Cf. "good" cities and houses full of "good" things in v. 10; the "good" land, doing "good," and experiencing "good" in v. 18. Deuteronomy 28:1−14 fleshes out what "good" means in terms of the covenant blessings.

13. The expression, recurs in Deut. 12:25; 13:18[19]; and 21:9. The opposite idiom is "doing what is [the] evil in the eyes of the LORD" (4:25; 9:18; 17:2; 31:29), or "do what is [the] right in one's own eyes" (cf. 12:8).

14. For fuller discussion of 6:20−25, see D. I. Block, "The Grace of Torah: The Mosaic Prescription for Life (Deut. 4:1−8; 6:20−25)," in *How I Love Your Torah, O LORD!* 11−17.

This short paragraph consists of a child's question (v. 20) and the adult's prescribed response (vv. 21–25). Moses assumes that when faced with the challenge of competing cultures, children will ask their parents for an explanation of their way of life.[15] The question the child asks concerns the stipulations, decrees, and laws that Yahweh commanded Israel (cf. 4:45). Whether the question arises out of ignorance, curiosity, or cynicism, the child is in effect asking, "Why are we governed by this set of regulations?"

The answer Moses prescribes for this question has been interpreted as a "family catechism."[16] Instead of getting straight to the point and talking about the laws, Moses offers a four-sentence exposition of the prologue to the Decalogue (vv. 21–23). In so doing he declares that Israelites' lives were to be driven not primarily by a system of rules but by a knowledge of Yahweh, particularly his saving acts on their behalf and their special relationship with him. By highlighting four critical moments in the nation's history, the confession declares in a nutshell the essential elements of Old Testament theology.

1. The history of Israel as a nation began with the people's need of salvation: They were slaves of Pharaoh in the land of Egypt (v. 21a).
2. Yahweh rescued the Israelites from their desperate situation with a mighty hand (v. 21b; cf. 4:32–34).
3. Yahweh performed great and devastating signs and wonders in Egypt in the sight of the Israelites (v. 22; cf. 4:34).
4. Yahweh had brought Israel out of that land, in order to bring them into the land he had promised on oath to the ancestors (v. 23).

Taken as a whole, Yahweh's rescue of the Israelites was a judicial act whereby he freed them from slavery to Egypt and claimed them as his own vassals—a status symbolized by the stipulations, decrees, and laws he had revealed to them.

In verses 24–25 Moses finally addresses the question raised in verse 20. In his mind Yahweh had revealed the stipulations, decrees, and laws for four purposes: (1) to govern Israel's conduct ("to obey all these decrees"); (2) to instill in them reverent awe for their God ("to fear the LORD"); (3) to ensure Israel's well-being in perpetuity ("so that we might always prosper"; cf. 28:1–14); (4) to maintain/sustain Israel's life. The emphatic construction of verse 25 signals the climax of this semicreedal statement: "And righteousness it will be for us if ..." [pers. trans.].

---

15. The forms of the question and the answer are also found in Ex. 12:26–27; Josh. 4:6–7, and 21–23.

16. G. Braulik, "Gesetz als Evangelium: Rechtfertigung und Begnadigung nach der deuteronomischen Tora," in *Studien zur Theologie des Deuteronomiums* (SBA 2; Stuttgart: Katholisches Bibelwerk, 1988), 135.

As noted earlier, in Deuteronomy "righteousness" (ṣᵉdāqâ) denotes behavior that conforms to norms established in the stipulations of Yahweh's covenant (cf. 33:21).[17] The Hebrew word order suggests righteousness will be credited to faithful Israelites when Yahweh observes their scrupulous obedience to the Supreme Command (*hammiṣwâ*, "this law").[18] To those who do so, Yahweh will announce, "You are righteous" (cf. 24:13).[19] Herein lies the significance of the statutes and ordinances: In his mercy Yahweh rescued Israel from Egypt and revealed to his people the appropriate response to grace that they might fear and obey him. If they do, they will not only live and prosper, but they will also hear his approval, "Well done, good and faithful servant [vassal].... Enter into the joy of your master [suzerain]."

TESTING BY YAHWEH. MERIBAH and Massah became proverbial for Israel's testing Yahweh and blatantly violating the rules governing suzerain-vassal relationships. The taboo on a vassal testing a superior forces us to reevaluate biblical characters like Gideon, who tested Yahweh repeatedly.[20] But Gideon seems not to have realized that in testing Yahweh he was actually proving his own faithlessness.

The notion of Yahweh's testing his people occurs frequently in the Old Testament.[21] The purpose of his tests generally is either to prove people's faith (cf. Gen. 22:1) or to refine their faith (Deut. 8).[22] The former is illustrated by Jeremiah 17:10: "I the LORD search the heart and examine the mind, to reward a man according to his conduct, according to what his deeds deserve." The latter principle is described by Zechariah: "This third I will bring into the fire; I will refine them like silver, and test them like gold. They will call on my name and I will answer them; I will say, 'They are my people,' and they will say, 'Yahweh is our God'" (Zech. 13:9; pers. trans.).[23]

Both dimensions of testing carry over into the New Testament. In Acts 5:9 Peter accuses Ananias and Sapphira of testing the Spirit of the Lord,

---

17. See comments on 4:8.

18. Thus Braulik, "Gesetz als Evangelium," 140.

19. Similarly Weinfeld, *Deuteronomy 1−11*, 337.

20. Note the explicit reference in Judg. 6:39.

21. See Gen. 22:1; Ex. 15:25; 20:20; Pss. 17:3; 66:10; 81:7[8]; 105:19; Prov. 27:21 (implied); Zech. 13:9.

22. See further, G. S. Smith, "The Testing of Our Faith: A Pentateuchal Theology of Testing" (Ph.D. dissertation, The Southern Baptist Theological Seminary, Louisville, KY, 2005), esp. 56−95.

23. Cf. 1 Cor. 3:13; 1 Pet. 4:12.

and in Acts 15:10 he charges Christians with Pharisaic backgrounds with putting God to a test by imposing on Gentile converts the yoke of the Torah of Moses. The New Testament seems to transfer the taboo on testing Yahweh in the Old Testament to a taboo on testing Christ. The Gospels are replete with stories of people who test Jesus, oblivious to his status as Yahweh incarnate.[24] Paul's appeal to the Corinthians not to test Christ as the Israelites did in the desert is especially striking (1 Cor. 10:9).[25] First Thessalonians 2:4 speaks expressly of God as testing the hearts of his own.[26]

Deuteronomy 6:20–25 is significant because it highlights the importance of deliberate strategies for transmitting the faith and the memory of the gospel of Yahweh's saving actions from generation to generation. As Judges 2 testifies, with the loss of the memory of his saving grace, apostasy and the Canaanization of culture followed closely behind. When we move to the New Testament, we discover repeated exhortations for passing on the faith (2 Tim. 2:2). Jesus deliberately transformed the Passover as prescribed in Exodus 12–13 into the Lord's Supper to keep alive the memory of his saving actions (Luke 22:19; 1 Cor. 11:24).

Law and grace. Even more significant theologically, this passage teaches clearly the relationship between law and grace within the divine plan of salvation and sanctification. Moses hereby declares that when members of the covenant community conscientiously obey the whole command,[27] Yahweh accepts their actions as evidence of righteousness.

In trying to understand this statement and the relationship between human works and righteousness, we must avoid two extremes. (1) We must reject the notion that Moses viewed obedience to the commands as the *basis* of covenantal relationship. He had just declared (vv. 21–23) that the Israelites' position as the people of Yahweh rested entirely on his past saving actions, independently of any Israelite merit (cf. 9:1–24).[28] (2) We must reject the notion that one may enjoy a relationship with God without obedience to his commands, as if status can exist without concrete evidence

---

24. Matt. 16:1; 22:18, 35; Mark 8:11; 10:2; 12:15; Luke 10:25; 11:16; John 8:6.

25. Most manuscripts read *kyrios*, but for the textual evidence for *Christos* as the preferred reading see B. Metzger, *A Textual Commentary on the Greek New Testament* (London: United Bible Society, 1971), 560.

26. See also 1 Chron. 29:17; 2 Chron. 32:31; Ps. 26:2; Jer. 12:3.

27. It is not clear whether the singular "all this law" (v. 25) refers to all the stipulations, decrees, and laws of v. 20 as a collective, or the Supreme Command particularly. See comments on 5:28.

28. This is even clearer in Ex. 19:4–5; Yahweh took care of the Egyptians and brought Israel to himself before he revealed to them his commands. Braulik ("Gesetz als Evangelium," 148) speaks of a repudiation of a "works piety" (*Werkfrömmigkeit*), that is, a legal claim before God based on one's own righteousness

of the status. Genesis 15:6, which provides a close analogue to the present text, does not contradict this interpretation. Abraham's faith was indeed accounted to him as righteousness, but even before this event the patriarch had demonstrated his faith and his righteousness with obvious acts of obedience. Moses' point here is that when acts of obedience arise out of genuine faith and fear, Yahweh accepts them as proof of righteousness and responds with blessing and life. Conversely, it may be assumed that in the absence of obedience, faith is lacking and the covenant relationship rejected, to which Yahweh responds with the curse and death.[29]

The Scriptures are consistent in asserting that no one may perform works of righteousness sufficient to merit the saving favor of God.[30] In the New Testament words of Paul, "all have sinned and fall short of the glory of God" (Rom. 3:23). However, within the gospel of salvation by grace alone through faith alone, Yahweh graciously reveals the standard of righteousness by which his people may live and be confident of his approval. There is no conflict here between law and grace. The Torah is a gracious gift through which Yahweh provided his people with an ever-present reminder of his deliverance, power, covenant faithfulness, and the way of life and prosperity.

But how is this perspective to be reconciled with Paul's outspoken statements regarding the death-dealing effect of the law in contrast to the life that comes by the Spirit?[31] However we answer the question, we must keep in mind several important considerations. (1) Moses' statement concerning the life-giving/sustaining effects of the law is consistent with his teaching in 30:15−20, and with the teaching of the Old Testament elsewhere (cf. Lev. 18:5; Ezek. 20:11, 13; Neh. 9:29). The Psalter begins with an ode to the life-giving nature of the Torah (NIV "law," Ps. 1), and Psalm 119, by far the longest piece in this collection, is devoted entirely to the positive nature and function of the law. The psalmist does not hesitate at all to declare the relationship between keeping the law and life (vv. 17, 40, 77, 93, 116, 144, 156, 159, 175). Ezekiel offers an extended exposition of this notion in Ezekiel 18:1−23,[32] presenting three cases in which the conduct of a person leads directly to pronouncements of life or the sentence of death. The prophet assumes that outward actions reflect a person's inner spirit,[33] on the basis of which a judgment concerning the spiritual state of the person may be made and the sentence of life or death rendered.

---

29. See further Ps. 24:1−5; Ezek. 18:1−23; Hab. 2:4.

30. Pss. 14:1, 4; 51:4−5[6−7]; 53:1, 3 [2, 4]; Isa. 64:6[5].

31. Rom. 2:12−13; 4:13−15; 7:8−9; 8:2−4; 10:4−5; 2 Cor. 3:6; Gal. 3:12−13, 21−24; 5:18.

32. For detailed discussion of this chapter, see Block, *Ezekiel Chapters 1−24*, 554−90.

33. This principle is operative also in Jesus' teaching (Matt. 7:15−23).

(2) In trying to reconcile Paul and Moses we need to recognize also that from a hermeneutical and theological perspective, later revelation cannot correct earlier revelation, as if there were some defect in it. Later revelation may be more precise and more nuanced, but it cannot be more true. Accordingly, Paul cannot be interpreted as correcting Moses, as if Moses' teaching were erroneous. If Moses attributed a life-giving/sustaining function to the law (cf. Lev. 18:5), and Paul appears to have declared the opposite as a dogmatic assertion, then he would have failed the traditional and primary test of a true prophet: agreement with Moses (cf. Deut. 18:15–22). Paul's statements must be interpreted not only in the light of Moses, but also as rhetorical assertions made in the context of particular arguments.

In both Romans and Galatians, Paul is responding to those who insist that salvation comes by the works of the law, as represented by circumcision. To those who represent this view, he replies that if one looks to the law as a way of salvation, it will lead to death, but if one looks to the law as a guide for those already saved, it yields life (cf. Gal. 5:13–25). Indeed, Paul himself recognizes that although believers enjoy the status of righteous persons through the work of Christ, he still anticipates a future time when, based on faith demonstrated in acts of love (covenant commitment), believers will stand before God and hear his words of approval: "You are righteous" (cf. Gal. 5:5–6). On this matter Moses and Paul agree. In fact, Paul himself says, "It is not those who hear the law who are righteous in God's sight, but those who obey the law who will be declared righteous" (Rom. 2:13). The notion of "the obedience of faith" (Rom. 1:5 NASB)— that is, a faith demonstrated through acts of obedience—is common to Old and New Testaments.[34] The same paradigm applies:

> Yahweh's gracious (i.e., unmerited) saving actions yield the fruit of a redeemed people.
> A redeemed people produces the fruit of righteous deeds.
> Righteous deeds yield the fruit of divine approval and blessing.

MOSES WILL HAVE MORE to say on the subject of this short passage in chapter 8, but for the moment we may summarize several dimensions of the enduring relevance of its message. In our twisted thinking, we often turn moments of deprivation into daring

---

34. For a helpful discussion of these and related issues from the New Testament perspective, see S. J. Hafemann, *Paul, Moses, and the History of Israel: The Letter/Spirit Contrast and the Argument from Scripture in 2 Corinthians 3* (WUNT 81; Tübingen: Mohr Siebeck, 1995).

challenges for God rather than into opportunities simply to cast ourselves on him in faith. However, if need can serve as a test of faith and loyalty, the same is true of excess. As Paul will eloquently declare in Romans 1:18−23, the wrath of God in the face of ungodliness and unrighteousness did not die with the turning of the ages. In Paul's thinking, thanklessness is the essence of idolatry.

Dangers of wealth and excess. With the wealth and excess we in the Western world enjoy, it is easy to forget that everything we have is a gracious gift of God. Sadly, too many of us fail the test of fidelity and faith that prosperity represents. We become like the rich farmer of Jesus' parable (Luke 12:14−21)—smug and self-sufficient in our excess but paupers toward God. But the principle extends beyond personal, material, or physical well-being to the health of the church as well. Difficult days for a congregation test the faith of God's people, but so do times of growth and apparent effectiveness. When our buildings are large and our congregations huge, then more than ever we must guard ourselves so that our commitment extends beyond glib confessions of love for God, or regurgitation of creedal affirmations, or emotional passion in cultic worship, to the daily obedience of faith. Jesus said, "If you love me, you will obey my commands" (John 14:15).

The significance of God's commands. If we ask the question today, "What is the significance of the stipulations, the ordinances, and laws that God commanded the Israelites to observe?" the responses we receive vary greatly. Some shake their heads in bewilderment and wonder seriously whether there is any point to many of these laws, such as the food laws in Deuteronomy 14. Some feel sorry for the Israelites because they were saddled with a burden that no one can bear, for no one can keep the laws perfectly. Some, with cultural and antiquarian interests, find in these laws a helpful window into the society of ancient Israel, especially when compared with other ancient Near Eastern legal traditions, like those found in the Law Code of Hammurabi, king of Babylon in the nineteenth century BC.

However, at the popular level, especially in contemporary Western evangelicalism, some view the law as the way of salvation for ancient Israel. That is, whereas in the New Testament people are saved by grace, under the old covenant people were saved by keeping the law.[35] Others have the opposite disposition to the law. For Israel, the law was not a way of salvation, but the way of death (Rom. 4:15; 7:6; Gal. 3:10−13, 23−24;

---

35. Despite Paul's arguments to the contrary, particularly his reference to Abraham as an illustration of salvation by faith alone (Rom. 4; Gal. 3:1−12).

4:21–31). The significance of the law lies in its power to bind those who are under the law, to subject them to the curse and the wrath of God, and to demonstrate their desperate need of a Savior. While on the surface this seems to be the way the New Testament perceives the law, it raises serious questions concerning both the justice and mercy of God. How and why would God rescue the Israelites from the burdensome and death-dealing slavery of Egypt (cf. Ex. 20:2) only to impose on them an even heavier burden of the law, which they in any case were unable to keep, and which would sentence them to an even more horrible fate—damnation under his own wrath? When you look at the exodus this way, it turns out not to be such a good deal after all.

The Reformers spoke of three functions of the moral law: (1) to exhibit the righteousness of God and convict and finally condemn humans; (2) to guide civil authorities in curbing unrighteousness and lawlessness; and (3) to offer believers a guide for life in conformity with the will of God.[36] While Luther paid little attention to the last, in truth, this is the only function of the law that Deuteronomy knows. In fact Deuteronomy 6:20–25 emphasizes that the law is a gracious gift for the redeemed, that they might have a clear view of the Lord's expectations. Unlike other nations, the Israelites did not need to resort to guesswork or experimentation to learn the will of God. He revealed it to them directly in order that, motivated by gratitude and reverent awe, they might obey, as a result of which Yahweh would bless them with well-being, life, and his declaration of righteousness.

Some years ago, when our children were still home, at the supper table we were having a rather warm conversation over ethical issues and how we as Christians respond to them. In frustration my teenage son blurted out, "Why do we have to be such a prehistoric family?" While the tone of his voice left something to be desired, his question was profound. How do we respond when our children ask these questions? Do we say simply, "This is how we have always done it," or "This is what the church teaches," or "This is how we are obligated as Christians to live"? Such responses border on legalism at worst and moralism at best. Or do we take these as glorious opportunities to declare the gospel—how God has lavished on us his

---

36. This is the order we find in John Calvin's *Institutes of the Christian Religion* 2.7.6–12. This compares with the Lutheran view, as expressed in the The Formula of Concord, Article VI: (1) that "thereby outward discipline might be maintained against wild, disobedient men [and that wild and intractable men might be restrained, as though by certain bars]"; (2) that "men thereby may be led to the knowledge of their sins"; and (3) that "after they are regenerate ... they might ... have a fixed rule according to which they are to regulate and direct their whole life" See *Triglot Concordia: The Symbolical Books of the Evangelical Lutheran Church* (ed. and trans. F. Bente and W. H. T. Dau; St. Louis: Concordia, 1921), Epitome VI.1.

grace in our salvation from the power of sin, our hope of eternal life, and the privilege of knowing his will and gratefully living to please him. The Eucharist certainly offers Christians both an opportunity to keep awareness of Christ's sacrifice fresh in their own minds and an occasion for curious questions by outsiders and children. Perhaps when such questions arise, we might respond with a recast version of this semicreedal statement of Deuteronomy 6:20—25:

When our children ask us in days to come, what is the meaning of the ordinances and customs that we observe, then we will say: "We were slaves to sin, but the Lord rescued us from the kingdom of darkness and ushered us into his glorious kingdom of light, with a strong hand, and great signs and wonders. He has brought us out in fulfillment of his promises and in accordance with his glorious plan of salvation, conceived before the foundation of the world. So the Lord commanded us to demonstrate our fear and love for him by keeping his commands for our good always and as expressions of our covenant relationship with him, as it is this day. And it will be righteousness for us before him if we are careful to show that we love God with all our hearts by doing all that he commanded us. Then we too will hear him say, "Well done, good and faithful servant. Enter into the joy of your Lord."

Deuteronomy 7:1–26

When the LORD your God brings you into the land you are entering to possess and drives out before you many nations—the Hittites, Girgashites, Amorites, Canaanites, Perizzites, Hivites and Jebusites, seven nations larger and stronger than you—²and when the LORD your God has delivered them over to you and you have defeated them, then you must destroy them totally. Make no treaty with them, and show them no mercy. ³Do not intermarry with them. Do not give your daughters to their sons or take their daughters for your sons, ⁴for they will turn your sons away from following me to serve other gods, and the LORD's anger will burn against you and will quickly destroy you. ⁵This is what you are to do to them: Break down their altars, smash their sacred stones, cut down their Asherah poles and burn their idols in the fire. ⁶For you are a people holy to the LORD your God. The LORD your God has chosen you out of all the peoples on the face of the earth to be his people, his treasured possession.

⁷The LORD did not set his affection on you and choose you because you were more numerous than other peoples, for you were the fewest of all peoples. ⁸But it was because the LORD loved you and kept the oath he swore to your forefathers that he brought you out with a mighty hand and redeemed you from the land of slavery, from the power of Pharaoh king of Egypt. ⁹Know therefore that the LORD your God is God; he is the faithful God, keeping his covenant of love to a thousand generations of those who love him and keep his commands. ¹⁰But

> those who hate him he will repay to their face by destruction;
> he will not be slow to repay to their face those who hate
> him.

¹¹Therefore, take care to follow the commands, decrees and laws I give you today.

¹²If you pay attention to these laws and are careful to follow them, then the LORD your God will keep his covenant of love with you, as he swore to your forefathers. ¹³He will love

you and bless you and increase your numbers. He will bless the fruit of your womb, the crops of your land—your grain, new wine and oil—the calves of your herds and the lambs of your flocks in the land that he swore to your forefathers to give you. ¹⁴You will be blessed more than any other people; none of your men or women will be childless, nor any of your livestock without young. ¹⁵The LORD will keep you free from every disease. He will not inflict on you the horrible diseases you knew in Egypt, but he will inflict them on all who hate you. ¹⁶You must destroy all the peoples the LORD your God gives over to you. Do not look on them with pity and do not serve their gods, for that will be a snare to you.

¹⁷You may say to yourselves, "These nations are stronger than we are. How can we drive them out?" ¹⁸But do not be afraid of them; remember well what the LORD your God did to Pharaoh and to all Egypt. ¹⁹You saw with your own eyes the great trials, the miraculous signs and wonders, the mighty hand and outstretched arm, with which the LORD your God brought you out. The LORD your God will do the same to all the peoples you now fear. ²⁰Moreover, the LORD your God will send the hornet among them until even the survivors who hide from you have perished. ²¹Do not be terrified by them, for the LORD your God, who is among you, is a great and awesome God. ²²The LORD your God will drive out those nations before you, little by little. You will not be allowed to eliminate them all at once, or the wild animals will multiply around you. ²³But the LORD your God will deliver them over to you, throwing them into great confusion until they are destroyed. ²⁴He will give their kings into your hand, and you will wipe out their names from under heaven. No one will be able to stand up against you; you will destroy them. ²⁵The images of their gods you are to burn in the fire. Do not covet the silver and gold on them, and do not take it for yourselves, or you will be ensnared by it, for it is detestable to the LORD your God. ²⁶Do not bring a detestable thing into your house or you, like it, will be set apart for destruction. Utterly abhor and detest it, for it is set apart for destruction.

DEUTERONOMY 7 PRESENTS ONE of the most problematic, if not offensive, texts in all of Scripture. While early church fathers tended to interpret Yahweh's charge to eliminate the Canaanites allegorically, today many treat the policies prescribed here and in chapter 20 as textual fossils from a primitive time, when ethical and religious ideals had not risen to the level of later prophets and were certainly inferior to the ethic espoused in the New Testament by Jesus (Matt. 5:44; Luke 6:27, 35). However, since the policy presented here is remarkably similar to that attested elsewhere in the ancient Near East,[1] others appeal to progress in revelation: God apparently adapts prevailing practices to his own sacred agenda, though never with the intention of this becoming permanent or universal policy nor of this being the ultimate ideal.[2] But this solution raises questions about the consistency of God, unless of course the early heretic Marcion was right, that the God of Israel and the God of the New Testament were two different gods.

Since the prohibition on covenants and intermarriage with Canaanites in verses 3–4 follows immediately after the demand to exterminate the population, some have argued the *ḥērem* ordinance was never intended to be applied literally, but rather functions as a metaphor for absolute religious fidelity.[3] Had Moses intended a literal understanding, the destruction of the Israelites for failing to carry out the policy as commanded in verses 4 and 26 should also be interpreted literally. But within Deuteronomy, even Moses foresees an Israelite remnant surviving the judgment of exile (4:29–31; 30:1–10). The conquest narratives may also cast doubt on a literal interpretation of the *ḥērem* ordinance. Although the Gibeonites feared the Israelites would execute the policies of Deuteronomy 20:15–18 (Josh. 9), the accounts in Joshua and Judges suggest the policy was carried out in only four places: Jericho (Josh. 6:24), Ai (8:28), Hazor (11:13–14), and Laish (Judg. 18:27; cf. Josh. 19:47). This accords with the archaeological record, which does not see evidence for widespread destruction of Canaanite cities,[4] and with texts in Deuteronomy that authorize the Israelites to take intact fortified cities (Deut. 6:10–11).

---

1. Like the Mesha Inscription from Moab. *ANET*, 320–21; *COS*, 2:23. For discussion of this text, see P. D. Stern, *The Biblical Herem: A Window on Israel's Religious Experience* (BJS 211; Atlanta: Scholars, 1991), 19–56. Stern also discusses additional ancient Near Eastern texts that potentially involve similar institutions (see pp. 57–87).

2. J. Bright, *The Authority of the Old Testament* (Grand Rapids: Baker, 1975 [reprint of 1967 edition]), 246–51; L. E. Toombs, "War, Holy," *IDB*, 4:796–801.

3. Moberly, "Toward an Interpretation of the Shema," 136.

4. For discussion of the evidence see V. P. Long, *A Biblical History of Israel* (Louisville: Westminster John Knox, 2003), 173–83.

Perhaps the problem is solved by paying closer attention to the genre of Deuteronomy 7. Instead of interpreting this book as legislation, we should treat it as rhetoric.[5] It is observed that chapter 7 is not concerned primarily with the practice of *ḥērem;* rather, it focuses on Israel's status as the people of Yahweh (7:6, 9 – 10).[6] That the instructions regarding *ḥērem* demonstrate Israel's status is reinforced by the concentric pattern of motifs:[7]

A The *ḥērem* principle, grounded in Israel's status as a holy people (vv. 1 – 6)
 B Past victory (exodus), grounded in Yahweh's love for Israel and oath to the ancestors (vv. 7 – 8)
  C The character of Yahweh, the ground of Israel's present conduct (vv. 9 – 10)
   D Obedience, the response to Yahweh's command (v. 11)
  C´ The character of Yahweh, the ground of Israel's future hope (vv. 12 – 16)
 B´ Future victory (in Canaan), grounded in Yahweh's presence with Israel (vv. 17 – 24)
A´ The *ḥērem* principle, grounded in Israel's holiness (vv. 25 – 26)

Although Exodus 23:20 – 33 obviously underlies this chapter, a comparison of the two texts reveals the differences between law and legislation.[8] The stamp of rhetorical oration is most evident in the elements not found in Exodus 23:20 – 33. In other words, Exodus 23:20 – 33 is to Deuteronomy 7 what a text of Scripture is to a sermon: the latter draws out the significance of the former.

Despite these considerations, Deuteronomy 20:15 – 18 makes it difficult to interpret the *ḥērem* law simply as metaphor. Nevertheless, in 7:2 – 5 and 20:18 Moses' primary concern is not ethnic elimination, but ethical scrupulosity.[9] Based on the structural features recognized above, chapter 7 divides into two main segments, the first describing the nature of the test of Israel's fidelity (vv. 1 – 16), and the second presenting possible responses to the test (vv. 17 – 26).

---

5. W. Crump ("Deuteronomy 7: A Covenant Sermon," *ResQ* 17 [1974]: 224) observes that its contents include "encouragement, warning, promise, remembrance, and admonition."
6. Moberly, "Toward an Interpretation of the Shema," 135 – 37.
7. Cf. the scheme of Wright, *Deuteronomy,* 108 – 09.
8. Ex. 23:20 – 33 comprises approximately 150 words in Hebrew, Deut. 7 has 350.
9. The narratives of Joshua prove the issue to be devotion to Yahweh rather than ethnicity. Cf. L. D. Hawk, "Conquest Reconfigured: Recasting Warfare in the Redaction of Joshua," in *Writing and Reading War: Rhetoric, Gender, and Ethics in Biblical and Modern Contexts* (ed. B. E. Kelle and F. R. Ames; SBL Symposium Series 42; Atlanta: Society of Biblical Literature, 2008), 145 – 60.

The Nature of the Test (7:1–16)

THE CONTEXT OF THE test (7:1–2a). Deuteronomy 7 opens with series of temporal clauses that set the stage for the presentation of the test of Israel's love for Yahweh (v. 2b). The policy of *ḥērem* is to be implemented when (1) Yahweh has brought the Israelites into the Promised Land, (2) he has cleared away the opposition, (3) he has delivered the Canaanites into the hands of the Israelites, and (4) the Israelites have defeated them. As in 6:10, the test of Israel's love for Yahweh will come when God's promises have been fulfilled.

Moses describes the anticipated hostilities from the perspectives of both divine and human protagonists. Yahweh's role will be to "drive out"[10] the inhabitants of the land and "deliver" them into the hands of the Israelites. As for the Israelites, they must defeat (*nākâ*, lit., "strike") and utterly destroy (*beḥᵉrîm*)[11] the Canaanites. These four statements represent the pillars on which Israelite war policy regarding the Canaanites rested. While acknowledging that this is Yahweh's war,[12] Moses also insists that the Israelites must enter the fray and attack the enemy themselves.

Moses' introduction of the antagonists makes it clear that the challenges a previous generation of Israelites faced have not diminished in the intervening thirty-eight years (1:28). He highlights the strength of the enemy with five expressions: (1) the nations are many; (2) they are the same nations that had faced their ancestors;[13] (3) they are seven nations (a literary figure representing the totality of the population); (4) they are more numerous; (5) and they are stronger than Israel. This is a frank assessment of the challenge facing his people (cf. v. 17).

The elements of the test (7:2b–5). The emphatic construction *baḥārēm taḥᵃrîm*, rendered "you must destroy them totally," signals the principal element of the test and reinforces the sacred nature of the agenda. The noun *ḥērem* and its cognate verb *beḥᵉrîm* ("to commit to *ḥērem*") combine military (3:6) and sacred nuances (13:15–17[16–18]). The root itself belongs to the same semantic field as *qdš*, which means "to consecrate" for divine service. While

---

10. The relatively rare verb *nāšal* occurs again in verse 22. As in 2 Kings 16:6, it is a military term, referring to clearing a conquered territory or city of its population.

11. For the meaning of this term, see below.

12. The expression "holy war" rightly recognizes the sacral character of the campaign for the land of Canaan, but the phrase is too closely associated with Islamic *jihad* and other radical movements, and it should be abandoned. See B. C. Ollenburger, "Gerhard von Rad's Theory of Holy War," in his introduction to the English edition of von Rad's work, *Holy War in Ancient Israel*, 22–33.

13. For discussion of the identities of these peoples, see Merrill, *Deuteronomy*, 177–79; Tigay, *Deuteronomy*, 84–85.

many argue that *ḥrm* means "to reserve" for divine service,[14] the nuance of consecration was also involved. Based on a recently published Hittite text describing the ritual, the emphatic verbal expression *haḥᵃrēm taḥᵃrîm* ("to destroy totally") seems to serve as shorthand for a complex series of actions: (1) defeating the military forces of a city; (2) slaughtering the population; (3) burning the town; (4) sowing it with salt (Judg. 9:45); (5) pronouncing a curse on it (Josh. 6:26); (6) consecrating it to Yahweh.[15] Most of these elements are featured in Deuteronomy 13:15 – 16[16 – 17], which provides the fullest description of the policy.

In the remainder of verses 2b – 5 Moses' explains how this policy should work. (1) The Israelites may not under any circumstances enter into agreements or treaties with the peoples of the land. (2) They may not show any mercy toward the Canaanites; sentimentality must not interfere with the pursuit of the divine agenda. (3) The Israelites may not intermarry with Canaanites. Moses' concern here is obviously not to safeguard Israel's ethnic purity (cf. Gen 34:16), but the danger intermarriage poses for fidelity to Yahweh. Foreign spouses will turn the people's hearts away from Yahweh to serve other gods, thereby violating the Supreme Command and annulling commitments as declared in the Shema (cf. 6:10 – 14).[16] The consequences of compromise on the issue of *ḥērem* described in the last clause of verse 4 reflects the seriousness of this policy: to adopt the lifestyle and the religious commitments of a Canaanite is to render oneself a Canaanite and thus provoke the ire of Yahweh.

Having specified prohibited actions and dispositions within Israel's *ḥērem* policy, in verse 5 Moses outlines the actions the policy demands. He lists four, all directed against the Canaanites' cultic installations:[17] (1) Tear down

---

14. Josh. 6:17 – 25 presents a case study of this policy. Everything in the city was subject to *ḥērem*, which should have meant that everything would be destroyed. However, the silver and gold were reserved for Yahweh and placed in the tabernacle treasury. The root *ḥrm* was fairly widespread among Semitic languages, but the biblical usage involving "consecration to destruction" is attested only in Moabite and possibly Ugaritic. See Stern, *Biblical Herem*, 16.

15. For the Hittite practice, see the autobiographical reports of Muršili II (ca. 1321 – 1295 B.C.), in H. Roszkowska-Mutschler, "'… and on its site I sowed cress …': Some Remarks on the Execration of Defeated Enemy Cities by the Hittite Kings," *Journal of Ancient Civilizations* 7 (1992): 6; G. F. Del Monte, "The Hittite *Ḥērem*," in *Babel und Bibel 2: Memoriae Igor M. Diakonof, Annual of Ancient Near Eastern, Old Testament, and Semitic Studies* (ed. L. Kogan; Orientalia et Classica 8; Winona Lake, IN: Eisenbrauns, 2006), 25. Compare the reconstruction of events by Roszkowska-Mutschler, "Some Remarks," 11 – 12. For the ritual text, which includes offerings to the gods of the targeted town to ensure the god's favor toward the conqueror, see Del Monte, "The Hittite *Ḥērem*," 40 – 43.

16. So also Mal. 2:10 – 11, which speaks of intermarriage as marrying "the daughters of a foreign god," and views this as an act of treason/treachery against the covenant community.

17. By opening each clause with the object, Moses focuses on the symbols themselves. The verse echoes Ex. 34:13.

their altars, (2) smash their pillars, (3) chop down their Asherim, and (4) burn the images of their divinities in fire. Altars were viewed as the tables of the gods,[18] on which worshipers presented offerings of food and beverage.[19] In pagan cultic contexts, "pillars" (*maṣṣēbôt*) were upright stones often engraved with religious symbols, symbolic of the male deity. Asherah poles were wooden symbols representing the female principle in the Canaanite fertility religion.[20] They were probably carved in the form of a woman with exaggerated sexual features. *Pᵉsîlîm* is a generic term for carved images, though sacred images were often plated with gold or silver.

At one level the demolition of sacred objects was intended to eradicate evidence of the pagan practices of the Canaanites within the land. However, at a deeper level, it represented a polemic against idolatry. The lesson for Israel should have been obvious: If idols cannot defend themselves, of what use are they to their worshipers (cf. Judg 6:31−32)?[21]

The basis of the test (7:6−8). Moses' discussion of Israel's version of the *ḥērem* policy reaches a climax in verses 6−8, where he specifies its grounds. If the Shema and the Supreme Command had addressed the first element of the covenant formula ("I will be your God"), then this statement addresses the second part ("You will be my people"), for here Moses reflects on Israel's awesome privilege as Yahweh's covenant partner. In the Hebrew text, Moses' assertion of Israel's privileged position consists of six sentences (two per verse) arranged in three pairs. The first pair declares Israel's special status before Yahweh (v. 6), and the last two declare the divine actions by which that status was achieved/demonstrated (vv. 7, 8).

In the first couplet (v. 6), Moses refers to the Israelites' status with two special expressions: they are "a people holy to the LORD" and "his treasured possession" (cf. 14:2; 26:18−19). Although obviously inspired by Yahweh's own words in Exodus 19:4−5, Moses substitutes the cold political term *gôy*

---

18. Cf. Ezek. 39:17−20; 41:22; 44:16; Mal. 1:7, 12.

19. The verb is associated with the demolition of altars in Ex. 34:13; Judg. 2:2; 6:30−32 (Gideon); 2 Kings 23:12, 15 (Josiah); of high places in 2 Kings 23:8; and of the sacred pillar and temple of Baal in 2 Kings 10:27.

20. The Authorized Version rendered this word as "groves." However, in the light of abundant extrabiblical evidence that surfaced in the last century, Asherah is now known to have been a prominent goddess in Canaanite mythology, the wife of the high god El and mother of seventy gods. The seductive power of the Asherah cult is attested by several Hebrew inscriptions from the period of the monarchy that speak of "Yahweh and his Asherah." See further, J. M. Hadley, *The Cult of Asherah in Ancient Israel and Judah: Evidence for a Hebrew Goddess* (Cambridge: Cambridge Univ. Press, 2000); N. Wyatt, "Asherah," *DDD*, 99−105; J. Day, "Asherah," *ABD*, 1:483−87.

21. On biblical polemics against idolatry, see Block, "Other Religions in Old Testament Theology," in *The Gospel According to Moses*, 200−236.

("nation") with the warm relational term ʿam ("people")[22] and views Israel's status as his "holy people" to be the grounds of their actions against the Canaanites and their pagan installations, rather than the result of covenant obedience. In effect, he contrasts persons and objects "devoted to destruction" (ḥrm) with those devoted to God for a sacred relationship.[23] The reference to Israel as Yahweh's sᵉgullâ ("treasured possession") involves a rare word that occurs only eight times in the Old Testament. While six of these use it metaphorically of Israel,[24] the key to understanding the concept is found 1 Chronicles 29:3 and Ecclesiastes 2:8, where the word denotes valued possessions, specifically the treasure of kings.[25]

But how did Israel become "a people holy to the LORD" and "his treasured possession"? In verses 7–8 Moses highlights four divine actions behind Israel's holy status. (1) Israel is the beneficiary of Yahweh's affectionate grace (v. 7a).

(2) Israel is the beneficiary of Yahweh's electing grace. Out of all people groups, he has chosen her that she might be his treasured possession.[26] In verse 7a Moses insists that Yahweh's election of Israel for covenant relationship with himself had nothing to do with their personal qualifications, for they are the least significant of the peoples.

(3) Israel is the beneficiary of Yahweh's saving grace (v. 8a). Lest the Israelites claim merit as a basis for their privileged position, Moses declares that Yahweh was the one who brought them out of Egypt.

(4) Israel was the beneficiary of Yahweh's redemptive grace (v. 8b). For the first time in the book Moses employs the word pādâ ("to redeem").[27] This word seems more formal than the kinship term gāʾal.[28] Whereas the latter speaks of the intervention of a close relative when persons are in distress and helpless to save themselves,[29] pâdâ is associated with rescuing a slave through

---

22. See D. I. Block, "Nation, Nationality," *ISBE* (rev. ed.), 3:492–96; idem, "Nations/Nationality," *NIDOTTE*, 4:966–72.

23. On the meaning of the root qdš, see W. Kornfeld, *TDOT*, 12:521–30.

24. Ex. 19:5; Deut. 7:6; 14:2; 26:18; Ps. 135:4; Mal. 3:17.

25. The Authorized Version's "peculiar people" is based on the sense of the underlying Latin, *peculium*, "personal/private property," and has nothing to do with "odd, weird." The Septuagint reads *periousion* (a people "of his possession"), which undertranslates the word. See also Titus 2:14; Eph. 1:14; and 1 Peter 2:9.

26. On the verb bāḥar, see comments on 4:37; cf. also 10:15; 14:2.

27. On pādâ as a metaphor for Yahweh's salvation of Israel from the bondage of Egypt, see Deut. 9:26; 13:5[6]; 15:15; 21:8; 24:18; 2 Sam. 7:23 = 1 Chron. 17:21; Neh. 1:10; Ps. 78:42; Mic. 6:4.

28. Gāʾal is used metaphorically of Yahweh's act of salvation outside Deuteronomy in Ex. 6:6; 15:13; Pss. 74:2; 77:15[16]; 78:35; 106:10.

29. For a discussion of the functions of a gōʾēl and further literature, see Block, *Judges, Ruth*, 674–75; R. Hubbard, "פדה," *NIDOTTE*, 3:578–82.

the payment of a ransom. Used metaphorically in Deuteronomy, the word speaks of Yahweh's ransoming Israel from the slave house of Egypt and from the strong hand of Pharaoh. Although these statements all focus on God, Israel's redemption was not simply an act of divine *machismo*; it was driven by his love (*ʾâhab*) for this people and his fidelity to his oath to their ancestors.

In verses 6–8 Moses contemplates the question, "Why does God love Israel?" He does not actually answer the question, except to suggest that God loves Israel because God loves Israel. Driven by fidelity to his promise to the forefathers and his covenant commitment to their descendants, through a miraculous act of grace, Yahweh secured Israel's freedom and called this nation from the kingdom of darkness into the kingdom of his marvelous light (cf. 1 Peter 2:9).

The importance of the test (7:9–15). Thematically, verses 11–12 function as the fulcrum of this passage: Moses renews his charge to the people to keep the Supreme Command (cf. 5:31; 6:1) and the detailed stipulations of the covenant ("decrees and laws") that he is issuing this day "to follow them." According to the logic of this paragraph, knowledge of the character of Yahweh and his fidelity to the covenant, whose terms include both blessings and curses (vv. 9–10), is the precondition to scrupulous conformity to his will (v. 11). At the same time, scrupulous conformity to Yahweh's will (v. 12a) is the precondition to experiencing the blessings rather than the curses (vv. 12b–13a). Moses' thinking flows as follows:

Knowledge ▸ Obedience ▸ Blessing

Because Moses' rhetorical goal here is to secure the first element, he begins with the pseudo-imperative, "Know therefore," as if one can be commanded to know something. The body of knowledge is cast in semicatechetical form (cf. 4:35, 39). To the affirmation that Yahweh is *"the* [one and only] God," he adds, "He is the faithful El" (pers. trans.). The adjective "faithful" (from the same root as our "Amen") means "to be true, trustworthy, reliable." In the patriarchal narratives of Genesis, God frequently introduces himself as El.[30] As El Shadday he made the covenant with Abram/Abraham (Gen. 17:1–8), but as Yahweh he proved to be faithful, fulfilling these promises and confirming the covenant (Ex. 6:2–8).[31]

---

30. Often in combination with other words: El El Olam (Gen. 21:33), El Roi (16:13), El Elyon (14:18–22), and El Shadday (17:1; 28:3; 35:11).

31. On the relationship between the names El Shadday and Yahweh, see G. J. Wenham, *Genesis 16–50* (WBC; Dallas: Word, 1994); xxx–xxxv; idem, "The Religion of the Patriarchs," in *Essays on the Patriarchal Narratives* (eds. A. R. Millard and D. J. Wiseman; Leicester: Inter-Varsity Press, 1980), 157–88; R. W. L. Moberly, *The Old Testament of the Old Testament: Patriarchal Narratives and Mosiac Yahwism* (Minneapolis: Fortress, 1992), 85–87.

The remainder of verses 9–10 spells the meaning of this confessional statement for Israel. As "the faithful El," Yahweh keeps his "covenant of love" (lit., "his covenant and his *ḥesed*"). The last word speaks of that quality that moves a person to act for the benefit of another without respect to the advantage it might bring to the one who expresses it.[32] However, here and in verse 12, together "the covenant" and "the *ḥesed*" mean "the gracious covenant."[33] Borrowing language directly from the first principle of the Decalogue (5:10), Moses identifies the objects of Yahweh's faithful covenant love as those who "keep his covenant of love to a thousand generations of those who love him and keep his commands." But verse 10 departs significantly from the Decalogic statement. In place of the vague God as one who "punishes" sin (6:9), Moses declares him as one who "repays . . . by destruction"; in place of the corporate application of the punishment to "the children," Moses declares the judgment to be direct and personal, "to their face" (twice); and in place of "to the third and fourth generation," Moses declares that Yahweh will not hesitate to repay the guilty person. Memory of God's grace and knowledge of his character should motivate his people to do anything he asks (vv. 11–12a).

In verses 12b–16 Moses elaborates on the blessings promised to those who respond to grace with obedience. He begins with a statement of principle: Yahweh, the God of Israel, keeps the gracious covenant (cf. on v. 9) that he made on oath to the fathers. While many assume he is speaking of the covenant with the patriarchs, the blessings listed in verses 13–15 actually summarize the blessings of the covenant made at Horeb (cf. Ex. 23:25–26; Lev. 26:1–13), a conclusion reinforced by Moses' references to "a covenant . . . with an oath" in his last address (29:12, 14, 21[11, 13, 20]). Moses tries to motivate fidelity by following up with three promises, each expressed with a single word. If the Israelites will be faithful, Yahweh will demonstrate his covenant commitment (NIV "love") to them, bless them, and multiply them.[34] Whereas the size of Israel's population had nothing to do with their election (v. 7), in the future an increase in their numbers will be their reward for obedience.

In verses 13b–15 Moses elaborates on the promises made in verse 13a. The blessing involves positive promises of fertility (vv. 13b–14a) on the one hand, and the removal of threats to multiplication (vv. 14b–15) on the other. He begins by cataloguing those areas of life on which people are most dependent for their security. Whereas "the fruit of your womb" and

---

32. For the meaning of this word see comments on 5:10. In 2 Sam. 7:15, the word functions as a virtual substitute for *bᵉrît*, that is, "the covenant promises."

33. A hendiadys. So also Weinfeld, *Deuteronomy 1–11*, 370.

34. Cf. Gen. 17:2; 22:17; 26:4, 24; 28:3; 32:12[13]; 35:11; 48:4; Ex. 32:13; Lev 26:9.

"the crops [lit., 'fruit'] of your land" are shorthand expressions for all areas of life and agricultural activities on which humans are reliant, the remaining terms seem deliberately chosen to challenge the claims of the idolatrous system that governed the lives of Canaanites.

All the expressions in verse 13b are linked with the Canaanite pantheon. *Dāgān* ("grain") recalls Dagon, later the primary god of the Philistines (Judg. 16:23; 1 Sam. 5:2–7), though worship of this deity was widespread among the Canaanites.[35] For "wine," Moses substitutes the common word *yayin* (cf. 14:26) with *tîrôš*, which is cognate to the name of the god Tirshu/Tirash, attested in the El-Amarna letters and in Ugaritic texts.[36] For olive "oil," Moses substitutes the common word *šemen* (cf. 8:8) with *yiṣhār*, from a root meaning "shiny." Some speculate that Yishar is the name of the god of olive oil.[37] The rare expression for "calves of your herds" (lit., "the increase of your cattle") occurs elsewhere only in 28:4, 18, 51, and in Ex. 13:12. Replacing the more common *ʿēgel* (cf. 9:16, 21), *šgr* seems to be linked to the name of the deity Shaggar/Sheger, whose veneration has been attested in Ugaritic, Emar, Deir ʿAlla, and Punic texts.[38]

However, the mythological connection is most transparent in the designation for "lambs of your flocks" (*ʿašterōt ṣōʾnekā*), which substitutes for the more common *kebeś* (cf. Ex. 29:39) or *keśeb* (Deut. 14:4). The veneration of Ishtar/Astarte, the goddess of fertility, was among the most widespread of any divinity in the ancient Near East.[39] Moses' preference for these rare expressions seems a deliberate stab at the jugular of Canaanite religion. In the land that Yahweh promised on oath to the ancestors, he alone guarantees the fertility of crops and herds.[40] The pastor of Israel ends this promise of blessing in verse 14a with a final comprehensive promise: Israel will be blessed more than all the peoples.[41]

---

35. Reflected in the place name, "Beth-Dagon" ("house of Dagon"), attested in Judah (Josh. 15:41) and Asher in the north (Josh. 19:27). On this deity, see L. Feliu, *The God Dagan in Bronze Age Syria*, trans. W. G. E. Watson (Culture and History of the Ancient Near East 19; Leiden: Brill, 2003), 278–88.

36. See further J. F. Healey, "Tirash," *DDD*, 871–72.

37. Cf. N. Wyatt, "Oil," *DDD*, 640.

38. Sheger apparently refers to the deity of the full moon, which was commonly thought to influence conception and birth. For further information on Sheger/Shaggar, see K. van der Toorn, "Sheger," *DDD*, 760–62.

39. On Ishtar in the Near Eastern religion, see T. Abusch, "Ishtar," *DDD*, 452–56; on Astarte, see N. Wyatt, "Astarte," *DDD*, 109–14. See *ANEP* ##464, 465.

40. The sequence of grain, wine, cattle, and sheep is found in the blessings in the Phoenician inscription by Azatiwada (early seventh century BC). For the text, see *COS*, 2:31, iii.2–11 (p. 150). Cf. Weinfeld, *Deuteronomy 1–11*, 373.

41. On Israel's supreme economic standing among the nations as a reward for scrupulous obedience to the covenant, see 15:5–6; 26:16–19; 28:12–14.

The remainder of verses 14 and 15 clarify what Moses had meant by "he will . . . increase your numbers" at the beginning of verse 13. In ancient times people recognized two primary inhibitors to well-being: the curse of barrenness (cf. Gen. 30:1) and the curse of premature death. Now Moses promises that if Israel will be faithful to Yahweh, neither will be a problem either for the human population or the livestock. At the other end of the life cycle, Yahweh will remove all sickness and hold off all the "horrible diseases" they knew from their time in Egypt.[42] This statement seems to be based on Exodus 15:26, which uses similar vocabulary for the covenant requirements to link obedience and health.

The concluding call for obedience (7:16). Verse 16 is transitional, bringing the preceding conversation to a conclusion with a plea for decisive action against the Canaanites and setting the stage for the response expressed in verse 17. Employing vocabulary different from verses 1–5, Moses calls on his people to destroy (ʾākal, lit., "to consume, eat") all the peoples whom Yahweh delivers into their hands. Again he warns against letting sentimentality interfere with the grim resolve to execute the divine mandate: "your eyes shall not pity them" (pers. trans.).[43] The concluding command, "do not serve their gods," recognizes the seductive pull of the entire system of fertility worship, which promises life but will deliver death (cf. 12:30).[44]

The Response to the External Test of Covenant Commitment (7:17–26)

As in 6:10–25, Moses follows up his exhortation to covenantal fidelity by imagining a hypothetical though realistic reaction to the charge, to which he then gives a response. This text divides into two parts: the question (v. 17) and the answer (vv. 18–26).

The question (7:17). The question posed reflects the original rhetorical situation. Whereas in 6:20 the imaginary respondent is a descendant of a person in his audience, here the hypothetical person is someone in the gathering before Moses. We may readily imagine that as Moses lays the challenge of verses 1–16 before the people, he picks up nonverbal

---

42. The expression, which also occurs in 28:60, derives from a root meaning "to be faint, ill." The diseases would include malaria, dysentery, elephantiasis, etc. On diseases in ancient Egypt, see Pliny, *Natural History* 26.1.5.

43. This idiom is especially prominent in Ezekiel, where it is used of God or his agent: 5:11; 7:4, 9; 8:18; 9:5, 10; 20:17; 24:14. For discussion of the idiom, see S. Wagner, "חוס," *TDOT*, 4:271–77.

44. Whereas Ex. 23:33 looks forward to the future, the present verbless clause treats the issue as a real and present danger. The word translated "snare" denotes a fowler's net used to catch birds. For illustrations, see O. Keel, *The Symbolism of the Biblical World: Ancient Near Eastern Iconography and the Book of Psalms* (trans. T. J. Hallett; New York: Seabury, 1978), 89–94.

signals of incredulity or despair from some in the crowd. Perhaps with the response of the previous generation at Kadesh Barnea still in mind (cf. 1:26–28), he expresses out loud what the people are thinking ("you say in your heart/mind" [pers. trans.]) but apparently do not have the nerve to ask. Picking up on a word he used to describe the seven nations (v. 2), his hypothetical interlocutor raises a problem: the obvious numerical superiority of the nations the Israelites are about to face. Speaking for all Israel in first person, he asks (lit.), "How can I dispossess them?"

Moses' answer (7:18–26). Moses' response divides into a promise (vv. 18–24) and a warning (vv. 25–26). His pastoral heart and rhetorical skill are both evident in the former as he appeals to the power of positive thinking in carefully crafting the response. His word of promise divides into two parts, in Hebrew each being introduced by a three-word admonition: "Do not be afraid of them" (v. 18a); and "Do not be terrified by them" (v. 21). Exhibiting remarkable proportion, the words of encouragement that follow these exhortations are virtually identical in length: the first consists of forty-five words, the second of forty-seven.

In verses 18b–20 Moses encourages his audience with two principal points: remember what Yahweh has done for you in the past (vv. 18b–19), and recognize that Yahweh is with you in the present (v. 20). In reminding the Israelites of Yahweh's past actions, Moses echoes what we have heard before in 4:34 and 6:22.[45] Now, adopting a method of argument that would be widely used in later Judaism, *qal waḥomer* ("from the heavy to the light"), Moses does not minimize the power of the seven Canaanite nations, who do indeed pose a formidable foe. His point is that if Yahweh was able to rescue them from the Egyptians, then these petty kingdoms, which have for some time been subject states to the pharaohs, are nothing at all to him.

And for those in his audience who might think the weapons Yahweh had used against the Egyptians (as listed in v. 19) might be insufficient or ineffective, in verse 20 Moses adds one more. Literally the word *ṣirʿâ* denotes a species of wasp/hornet whose sting may be fatal, especially if one is attacked by an entire swarm. Moses has precisely this image in mind when he changes the identity of the hornets' targets from the Canaanite tribes in Exodus 23:28 to "the survivors who hide from you." When Yahweh commissions the swarm of insects to attack the Canaanites, they will pursue them relentlessly into every cave and bush to which they flee, and will sustain that attack until all perish, as had been the case with peoples of Sihon and Og.[46]

---

45. For a discussion of these terms, see comments on 4:34.

46. Hornets are not mentioned either in Num. 21 or Deut. 2:26–3:11, but, quoting Yahweh, in Josh. 24:12 Joshua attributes the defeat of Sihon and Og to the hornet (singular) that God had sent against them.

In the second half of this word of promise (vv. 21–24), Moses' attention shifts from the invincible power of Yahweh to his awesome presence. Like the statement concerning the presence of Yahweh in 6:15, the declaration in verse 21 is semicatechetical: the Israelites shall not dread the enemy, "for the LORD your God, who is among you, is a great and awesome God [El]." In the face of threats from rival deities, it is Yahweh's passion/jealousy that is aroused; when other nations threaten his people, it is his transcendent and awesome strength. As in verse 9, Moses equates Yahweh, the God of Israel, with El. But unlike the senile and otiose El of Canaanite mythology, Yahweh is supremely great and terrifying to all who stand in his way.[47]

In verses 22–24 Moses explains how this awesome God will pursue his campaign of conquest. As the supreme Commander of Israel's forces and the divine Warrior who fights for them, his strategy is clear: He will clear away the nations of Canaan before the Israelites (v. 22); he will hand them over to the Israelites (v. 23); he will throw them into great confusion[48] until they are destroyed (v. 23; cf. v. 2); and he will deliver the kings of Canaan into the Israelites' hands (v. 24). With these promises, Moses challenges his people to trust in Yahweh. This is his war, not theirs. His awesome presence will create pandemonium among the enemies' forces, and he will deliver their leaders into Israel's hands.

However, to prevent his hearers from imagining that all they need to do is stand passively by and watch (Ex. 14–15), Moses adds a series of caveats to his promises of divine involvement. (1) Although Yahweh will clear away the Canaanites, he will not do so in a single moment, but "little by little" (v. 22). He recognizes that the Israelites presently lack both the resources to eliminate them quickly and the population to occupy all the land that has been promised (cf. Ex. 23:30). The elimination of the population all at once would create a vacuum leading to a dangerous increase in the number of wild animals—presumably involving both scavenging creatures like jackals and more aggressive wolves and lions that actually threaten the Israelites (cf. 2 Kings 17:24–26).

(2) In verse 24b Moses declares that Yahweh will deliver the kings into the Israelites' hands so they may obliterate their names from under the heavens (cf. 4:32). Since the ancients thought that people lived on in their children, the worst fate one could experience was to have his seed cut off

---

47. See comment on 10:17.

48. The verb *bûm* means, "to make noise, create a din." Combined with its cognate noun, *mᵉhûmâ*, "din, noise," and the adjective *gᵉdōlâ*, the image recalls the pandemonium involved in Gideon's attack on the Midianites (Judg.7:19–22).

and his name destroyed from his father's household.[49] The battle reports in the book of Joshua name several kings who opposed the Israelites, but the absence of royal names in the catalogue of defeated kings in Joshua 12:7–24 seems intentional.

(3) The concluding clause in verse 24, "you will destroy them," summarizes the Israelites' obligation in the conquest. Moses' use of the same verb for "destroy" in verses 23 and 24 (*hišmîd*) reflects the synergy of divine and human involvement.

Shifting from promise to warning in verses 25–26, Moses' mood changes significantly. He now returns to the issues with which he had begun the chapter, especially verse 5. The NIV correctly captures the emphatic structure of the first sentence with its inversion of the normal word order—object, subject, verb. The directive to burn the images of the Canaanites' gods summarizes the four commands concerning pagan cult installations in verse 5. But now the significance of the images has changed. Instead of focusing on the images as problematic theological symbols that seduce the Israelites and deflect their allegiance away from Yahweh, Moses' interest is in the material of which the images were made.

Borrowing a verb from the ninth command, he warns against "coveting" the silver and gold used in the manufacture of images.[50] He hereby forecloses the temptation to rationalize salvaging and recycling the precious metals when carrying out the policy of *ḥērem* against enemy establishments. The fact that images have been demolished does not mean the metals used to decorate them have lost their spiritual significance. No, the materials take on the character of the images themselves. Because idols are abominable to Yahweh, the God of Israel, the materials of which they are made pose exactly the same threat to the Israelites as the gods represented by those images: they will ensnare the people of Yahweh.[51]

The word *tôʿēbâ* ("abomination"; NIV "detestable") occurs in verses 25 and 26 for the first time in the book[52] and serves as Moses' favorite expression for the abhorrent nature of idolatry (cf. 12:31; 13:14[15]; 17:4; 32:16). In verse 26 he identifies the root of the problem. Idolatry is not only seductive ("a snare") and an abomination to Yahweh; the "abomination"

---

49. See 1 Sam. 24:21[22]; 2 Sam. 14:7. To prevent this, Absalom set up a memorial for himself because he had no children to proclaim his name after his death (2 Sam. 18:18). See also Ps. 37:28; Isa. 14:20–21.

50. The same verb is used of Achan's sin in Josh. 7:21.

51. In v. 16 Moses had warned that the service of the gods would be a "snare" to the Israelites; now he says they will be "ensnared" (same root, *yqš*) by silver and gold with which they were plated.

52. The word derives from a root *tʿb* ("to abhor, to reject as utterly disgusting").

is contagious. Contact with abominable objects neutralizes the Israelites' status as a holy people and reduces them to being simply one among the nations, but it also renders the Israelites absolutely defiled and fundamentally degraded. There is only one solution for anything or anyone declared to be *tôʿēbâ*: the rigorous application of the policy of *ḥērem*.

THEOLOGY OF WARFARE. ALONG with chapter 20, Deuteronomy 7 is critical for understanding the theology of warfare in the Old Testament. As we noted in our comments on the battles against Sihon and Og,[53] the policy of *ḥērem* was intended to secure for the Israelites a clean land, where they could develop and grow as a nation, not for their own sakes, but for the glory of God and to testify to his grace to the nations.[54] Yahweh was handing the land over to them as a gift, to complete the covenantal deity – nation – land triangle.

In Israel the policy of *ḥērem* was not driven by fundamental antipathy to outsiders, but by the need to eliminate all rivals to God, who is at the top apex of this triangle. Deuteronomy 7:4 – 11 excludes any room for compromise in respect to the Supreme Command and the Shema.

It is remarkable how the accounts of the battles of conquest mute this factor. The only references to alien gods in Joshua occur in the leader's speeches at the end. While it is clear that Achan's sin involved a violation of this ordinance (esp. vv. 25 – 26), a link with Canaanite religion depends on familiarity with Deuteronomy 7. Achan's crime is characterized as being unfaithful (Josh. 7:1), sinning (7:11, 20), violating Yahweh's covenant (7:11, 15), stealing (7:11), lying (7:11), a disgraceful thing (7:15), coveting (7:21; cf. Deut. 7:25), and especially a violation of the *ḥērem* ordinance.[55] However, the account contains no explicit reference to idolatry or idolatrous

---

53. See above pp. 95 – 97.
54. See below on Deut. 26:19.
55. Forms of the root *ḥrm* occur eight times in Josh. 7:1 – 15 (vv. 1, 11, 12, 13, 15).

objects or installations. Although the clause "they have been made liable for destruction" is true insofar as certain objects subject to the *ḥērem* law were not destroyed (Josh. 7:12) and thus clearly echoes "it is to set apart for destruction" (Deut. 7:26), the narrator presents Achan's crime as an act of personal covetousness without overt reference to its religious significance.

While the narratives of Joshua are relatively silent on Joshua's disposition toward pagan cult objects, they are explicit in highlighting Yahweh's fulfillment of the promise to deliver the land into the Israelites' hands (Deut. 7:1). After the initial conquests of Jericho and Ai, the focus seems to be particularly on the kings of the land,[56] in fulfillment of Deuteronomy 7:24. Even so, the center of gravity in the book of Joshua as a whole is on the distribution of the territorial spoils of the war among the tribes (Josh. 13:1–21:45). Not until Joshua's speeches at the end do we hear clear allusions to the religious ideology of the war as laid out in Deuteronomy 7.

Intermarriage. In his farewell address Joshua expressly warns the Israelites not to intermarry[57] with the Canaanites, because Yahweh will use them as a "snare" (Josh. 23:13; cf. Deut. 7:16), and they will perish from the good land Yahweh is giving them. Beginning with the accounts in the book of Judges, the history of Israel is a story of compromise with pagan ideologies, and in the end the nation is destroyed because of the seductive power of idolatry. Later royal sponsorship of idolatry makes matters worse. Among the kings of Israel, the principal exception is Josiah, who is said to have turned to Yahweh "with all his heart/mind, being, and resources" (pers. trans. of 2 Kings 23:25), and who literally fulfills Moses' instructions regarding pagan cult installations by demolishing the altars, sacred pillars, Asherim, and high places throughout the land (2 Kings 23:12–15).

Behind the firm boundaries that Moses draws between the kingdom of God and the kingdoms of this world is the conviction of the special status of the people of God. As noted above, that blessed status is reflected in five expressions in verses 7–8: Israel is a holy people belonging to Yahweh, the object of his gracious election, his treasured people, the object of his affection, and the beneficiary of his covenant love. This privileged status is awarded Israel as a free gift of God—unmerited, undeserved, and unsought. While the rest of the Old Testament tends to highlight the holiness of God, in Deuteronomy this notion surfaces only in 32:51. Furthermore, whereas the holiness of the people of God is rarely mentioned

56. Josh. 5:1; 9:1; 10:1–12:24.
57. The verb *hithattēn* ("to intermarry") occurs especially in contexts involving intermarriage with Canaanites: Gen. 34:9; Deut. 7:3; Josh. 23:12; cf. also Ezra 9:14.

elsewhere,[58] this notion is fundamental to the theology of Deuteronomy (7:6; 14:2, 21; 26:19; 28:9).[59]

The degenerating effect of intermarriage with pagans is a common theme in the Old Testament. The link between intermarriage and spiritual recidivism is explicitly declared in Judges 3:5—8a:

> The Israelites lived among the Canaanites, Hittites, Amorites, Perizzites, Hivites and Jebusites. They took their daughters in marriage and gave their own daughters to their sons, and served their gods.
>
> The Israelites did [the] evil in the eyes of the LORD; they forgot the LORD their God and served the Baals and the Asherahs. The anger of the LORD burned against Israel.

For all his wisdom, Solomon turns out to be the ultimate fool. He loved many foreign women, who turned his heart away from Yahweh to go after other gods. Departing from the commitment of his father David, his heart was not fully devoted to Yahweh, he went after foreign gods, and he did evil in the sight of Yahweh (1 Kings 11:1—8). Whereas in the days of the judges the problem seems to have involved the general population, with Solomon for the first time idolatry was sponsored by the court. Just as Moses had predicted, loving foreign women led to loving foreign gods. Because of Israel's persistent spiritual rebellion, eventually first the northern kingdom (2 Kings 17:1—18) and then the kingdom of Judah (2 Kings 24—25) were declared abominable in the sight of Yahweh and suffered the fate of the Canaanites.

Although the exile seems to have weaned the nation as a whole of idolatry, at the personal level the problem persisted until the closing days of Israel's recorded history. Malachi notes the symptoms of the absence of fear of Yahweh among the postexilic community of the fourth century BC, including intermarriage with pagans. They profaned the covenant of their fathers with treacherous actions against each other and against God, behaving abominably, and desecrating the sanctuary "by marrying the daughter of a foreign god" (Mal. 2:10—11). In accordance with Deuteronomy 7:24—25, on these the prophet invokes a curse: "As for the man who does this, whoever he may be, may the LORD cut him off from the tents of Jacob—even though he brings offerings to the LORD Almighty" (Mal. 2:12).

---

58. Isa. 63:18 (lit., "people of your holiness") and Dan. 12:7 ("holy people") are exceptions.

59. This notion has its roots in Ex. 19:6.

Echoes of this passage reverberate through the New Testament. Paul undoubtedly had this text in mind when he opens his letter to the Ephesian Christians by celebrating their privileged status in Christ (Eph. 1:1 – 14). Like Israel of old, those who are faithful in Christ Jesus are chosen so that they should be holy. In love God has adopted as his children to the praise of the glory of his grace, the objects of his redemption and the recipients of his inheritance, "in order that we, who were the first to hope in Christ, might be for the praise of his glory" (1:12; cf. Col. 3:12). While the opening of 1 Peter 2:9 – 12 has its roots in Exodus 19:6, the commentary that follows is Deuteronomic:

> But you are a chosen people, a royal priesthood, a holy nation, a people belonging to God, that you may declare the praises of him who called you out of darkness into his wonderful light. Once you were not a people, but now you are the people of God; once you had not received mercy, but now you have received mercy.
>
> Dear friends, I urge you, as aliens and strangers in the world, to abstain from sinful desires, which war against your soul. Live such good lives among the pagans that, though they accuse you of doing wrong, they may see your good deeds and glorify God on the day he visits us.

DIVINE WAR POLICY. FOR many readers today Deuteronomy 7 raises serious ethical questions. How could a God who claims to be gracious and merciful command the extermination of whole populations? And how could human beings accept these instructions as part of their official war policy? We have dealt with some of the ethical implications of this text earlier in the context of our discussion of the extermination of the Amorites east of the Jordan.[60] Unfortunately, the history of the church is severely tarnished by unwarranted extension of these policies "in the name of Christ" to any who oppose Christians. It has been too easy to assume innocence, to declare one's own agenda to be the agenda of the kingdom of God, and to brand those who stand in our way as infidels deserving of the sentence called for here — whether the enemy be Muslims, Jews, Franks and Goths, "pagan" aboriginal peoples, communists, and even other Christians. We forget the distinctive circumstances addressed in Deuteronomy 7 and displace love and compassion as the primary marks of God's people with aggressiveness and violence.

---

60. See above, pp. 95 – 97.

This is not to say that the boundaries between the kingdom of God and the kingdoms of this world should be blurred. The relevance of this text for contemporary Christians is obvious. Like Israel, we are called to fight against the kingdom of darkness. Admittedly "our struggle is not against flesh and blood, but against the rulers, against the authorities, against the powers of this dark world and against the spiritual forces of evil in the heavenly realms" (Eph. 6:12); but this demands the same vigilance and the same reliance on divine resources as were required of the Israelites. In this battle, alliances with the kingdom of darkness remain a particular problem. In our culture the intermarriage of believers with unbelievers is widespread. Paul's response to such alliances in 2 Corinthians 6:14—16, particularly his rooting of his instructions in our status as the holy covenant people of God, sounds remarkably Mosaic:

> Do not be yoked together with unbelievers. For what do righteousness and wickedness have in common? Or what fellowship can light have with darkness? What harmony is there between Christ and Belial? What does a believer have in common with an unbeliever? What agreement is there between the temple of God and idols? For we are the temple of the living God. As God has said: "I will live with them and walk among them, and I will be their God, and they will be my people."

The problem represented by intermarriage begins much earlier in the dating patterns of young people. Even if 97 percent of young people say that the religious preferences of the other person plays no role in whom they date, for Christians this is intolerable. Until and unless Christians recover a sense of the incredible privilege of being a holy people belonging to God, the objects of his gracious election, his treasured people, and targets of his affection, and until they recover the missional significance of this calling, the Western church will remain pathetic and powerless in the face of the challenges of our age.

The last verse of Deuteronomy 7 serves as a stern reminder to us not to limit the recognition of Yahweh as our God to creedal affirmations and luxuriating in one's sense of privilege. Spiritual commitment must be expressed in actions that accord with the will of God, who has so graciously revealed himself to his people. To be governed by that which is right in one's own eyes rather than what is right in the sight of Yahweh is to prove oneself in effect a Canaanite and to bring on oneself the judgment to which the Canaanites were sentenced.

Struggling with sin. For the everyday struggles with sin and the pressures posed by the kingdom of darkness, Deuteronomy 7:17—24 is particularly relevant. This paragraph presents three indispensable keys to a victorious Christian life. (1) Recognize God's past grace in salvation. Just as Moses could argue from greater to lesser, so we may encourage each other by observing that if God could deliver us from death to life in the first place (Eph. 2:1—5), he is surely able to defeat the enemy in everyday skirmishes.

(2) Recognize his power in the present. In 1 John 4:4 the beloved apostle declares, "The one who is in you is greater than the one who is in the world."

(3) Recognize our own responsibility to engage the enemy by keeping ourselves unspotted from the world. The trappings of pagan cultures may be attractive to those who claim to be God's holy people, but they are seductive and drag people down, so that in the end they are condemned along with those responsible for devising these ungodly notions.

Deuteronomy 8:1–20

B
e careful to follow every command I am giving you
today, so that you may live and increase and may
enter and possess the land that the LORD promised
on oath to your forefathers. ²Remember how the LORD your
God led you all the way in the desert these forty years, to
humble you and to test you in order to know what was in
your heart, whether or not you would keep his commands.
³He humbled you, causing you to hunger and then feeding
you with manna, which neither you nor your fathers had
known, to teach you that man does not live on bread alone
but on every word that comes from the mouth of the LORD.
⁴Your clothes did not wear out and your feet did not swell
during these forty years. ⁵Know then in your heart that as
a man disciplines his son, so the LORD your God disciplines
you.

⁶Observe the commands of the LORD your God, walking in his ways and revering him. ⁷For the LORD your God
is bringing you into a good land—a land with streams and
pools of water, with springs flowing in the valleys and hills;
⁸a land with wheat and barley, vines and fig trees, pomegranates, olive oil and honey; ⁹a land where bread will not
be scarce and you will lack nothing; a land where the rocks
are iron and you can dig copper out of the hills.

¹⁰When you have eaten and are satisfied, praise the
LORD your God for the good land he has given you. ¹¹Be
careful that you do not forget the LORD your God, failing to observe his commands, his laws and his decrees that
I am giving you this day. ¹²Otherwise, when you eat and
are satisfied, when you build fine houses and settle down,
¹³and when your herds and flocks grow large and your silver
and gold increase and all you have is multiplied, ¹⁴then
your heart will become proud and you will forget the LORD
your God, who brought you out of Egypt, out of the land
of slavery. ¹⁵He led you through the vast and dreadful
desert, that thirsty and waterless land, with its venomous
snakes and scorpions. He brought you water out of hard

rock. [16]He gave you manna to eat in the desert, something your fathers had never known, to humble and to test you so that in the end it might go well with you. [17]You may say to yourself, "My power and the strength of my hands have produced this wealth for me." [18]But remember the LORD your God, for it is he who gives you the ability to produce wealth, and so confirms his covenant, which he swore to your forefathers, as it is today.

[19]If you ever forget the LORD your God and follow other gods and worship and bow down to them, I testify against you today that you will surely be destroyed. [20]Like the nations the LORD destroyed before you, so you will be destroyed for not obeying the LORD your God.

MOSES CONTINUES TO ADDRESS the challenges to faith that the Israelites will encounter in the Promised Land. In this chapter that threat emerges because Yahweh is faithful to his promises. Moses' fivefold appeal to keep alive the memory of Yahweh's actions on Israel's behalf (vv. 2, 11, 14, 18, 19) suggests that the notion of remembering/forgetting is a key motif in the chapter.[1] In addition, Moses' charge to keep the commands of Yahweh by walking in his ways and fearing him (v. 6; cf. v. 11) points to the heart of the matter: Will Israel serve Yahweh in the land, or will they not? This is the same question Moses had raised in chapter 7, though now the nature of the test has changed dramatically.

While some question the place of verses 19–20 in this chapter, the parallels between the structure of this unit and the preceding units argue for its integrity.[2] This interpretation is buttressed by the structural and thematic links between 6:10–15 and chapter 8, as illustrated by the following synopsis of the principal elements of each:

---

1. Note (1) Moses' positive charges to "remember" (vv. 2, 18); (2) his appeals for scrupulous guarding of oneself with a negative purpose clause, "lest you forget" (vv. 11, 14); (3) his warning against spiritual amnesia, "if you ever forget" (v. 19).

2. Compare the views of the structure of this text in Wright, *Deuteronomy*, 121; R. O'Connell, "Deuteronomy VIII 1–20: Asymmetrical Concentricity and the Rhetoric of Providence," *VT* 40 (1990): 437–52.

Heading	Clarification	6:10−15	8:1−20
The context of the test	In the land Yahweh had promised the ancestors	6:10a	8:1
The nature of the test	Limitless opportunity and prosperity	6:10b−11	8:7−10[3]
The wrong response to the test	Forgetting Yahweh	6:12	8:11−17
The correct response to the test	Fearing/remembering Yahweh	6:13−14	8:18
The final warning	Elimination from the land	6:15	8:19−20

While chapter 8 resumes and expands on the subject of chapter 6, verse 17 plays a critical role in the chapter's overall scheme. Grammatically and syntactically, the verb, "you may say" is the last of a series of clauses governed by "lest" (*pen*) back in verse 12 and triggers Moses' answer to the response in verses 18−20.

The Nature of the Internal Test (8:1−10)

THE VERB ŠĀMAR ("TO guard, keep"; NIV "be careful, observe") occurs three times in this chapter (vv. 1, 6, 11), but the shift from "keeping" the commands of Yahweh in the first two to "keeping" oneself in verse 11 signals a transition from the first to the second part. The first ten verses describe the nature of the test of Israel's faith in four parts: (1) an introduction, which sets the context for the test (v. 1); (2) a retrospective look at Israel's desert experience as a paradigm for the future tests (vv. 2−5); (3) a prospective view of the future, when Israel's faith will again be tested (vv. 6−9); (4) a concluding prescription on what is required to pass the test (v. 10).

The context of the test (v. 1). Moses begins by reminding his audience of Yahweh's ancient goal for Israel: life and prosperity in the land that he had sworn to give to their descendants. The emphatic construction of the main clause, coupled with the use of the singular "the whole command" (NIV, "every command"), suggests Moses has in mind the Supreme Command (6:5). By adding the word "follow" (lit., "do"), he reiterates that the divine will is kept by putting it into action. Allegiance to Yahweh is not merely a matter of verbal utterances of the Shema or any other creed; it is demonstrated in behavior, the nature of which will be fleshed out generally in 30:16. If Israel will be faithful to Yahweh, they will achieve life, increase (of population), entrance into the land, and possession of it.

---

3. Deut. 8:2−5 lacks a counterpart in 6:10−15.

The desert experience as a paradigm for the future test (vv. 2–5).
This paragraph forms a self-contained unit framed by the appeal to remember in verse 2 and the appeal to draw the right theological conclusions in verse 5.[4] The opening appeal, "Remember how the LORD your God led you all the way," functions as a thesis-type statement, which the rest of verses 2 and 3 will develop. Here "way" (*derek*) refers metaphorically to the course of conduct that Yahweh prescribes for the Israelites (v. 6),[5] and to Yahweh's manner of dealing with people and the underlying motivation for his actions (cf. Ex. 33:13). Moses clarifies the expression by citing four actions that any outside observer could have recognized: Yahweh led Israel for forty years in the desert, he humbled them, he caused them to hunger, and he fed them manna.

But Moses' concern here is with the divine motivation: Why did Yahweh treat Israel the way he did? To this question he provides three answers. (1) Yahweh was intentionally depriving Israel of normal food to humble them. (2) Yahweh was testing his people to assess the quality of the vassal's fidelity (8:2) and to enhance Israel's covenant commitment through discipline (8:5). Just as the metallurgical process of refining precious metals involves extraction of impurities from ore through intense heat, so metaphorical refinement involves a demanding and painful process.[6] (3) Yahweh was exposing the shallowness of the people's commitment to him. This aim is expressed explicitly by the clause "to know what was in your heart," and the method involved observing whether or not the Israelites would keep his commands. Moses' present statement echoes Yahweh's words in Exodus 16:4 and assumes that people's actions express what is inside their hearts/minds.[7]

Although some argue that God needs "to test" Israel because he lacks knowledge of the people's level of commitment,[8] this interpretation flies in the face of other texts that declare generally that God knows everything about us. It also contradicts fundamental assumptions in Deuteronomy that Yahweh knows what is in the Israelites' hearts and where this will lead them long range (4:25–31; cf. 5:29). The verb "to know" (*yādaᶜ*), which occurs

---

4. For a similar pedagogical pattern see comments on 4:32–40 (esp. vv. 35, 39) and 7:8–10.

5. So also 5:33; 9:12, 16; 10:12; 11:22, 28; 13:5[6]; 19:9; 26:17; 28:9; 30:16; 31:29.

6. Cf. Ezekiel's use of the metaphor as a description of judgment, rather than refinement in 22:17–22.

7. Jesus' allusion to the Decalogue in Matt. 15:18–19 suggests that such behavior proves the words of the covenant have not been written on the heart.

8. J. Crenshaw, *A Whirlpool of Torment* (OBT; Philadelphia: Fortress, 1984), 2; Brueggemann, *Theology of the Old Testament*, 202; Tigay, *Deuteronomy*, 92.

three times in verses 2−3, should be interpreted something like "to prove" or "bring to light," so that observers (including the Israelites themselves) would know the level of commitment (cf. v. 3b).

As metallurgical metaphors, these tests were intended to refine Israel by burning off the dross and purifying that which is of value — specifically, to enhance Israel's relationship with Yahweh. The fact that God tests/ refines Israel demonstrates that he cares about them and that he acts to deepen that relationship.[9] This "refining" interpretation gives new meaning to verse 4, which reads like a casual aside. But the statement is patently ironic. Everyone in Moses' present audience knows that their parents were the ones tested and that they had failed the test. It was not the length of the journey that killed them (their feet did not swell); they all died in the desert because they were dross.[10] What survived the test was the divine provision — their clothing and the manna that was there on the ground every morning to greet the survivors.

The commentary Moses gives on God's novel provision of the manna in verse 3b (cf. Ex. 16:15) reinforces this interpretation. Neither this generation nor their fathers had ever experienced anything like this white flakelike substance that resembled coriander seed and bdellium. All sorts of natural explanations have been given for manna, but all are speculative and miss the point. Manna was a supernatural provision to keep the stomachs of the Israelites full during their thirty-eight years in the desert, but also to teach them that full stomachs do not ensure life. The key to life is not found in the food one eats, but in the nourishment that comes from the mouth of God. Moses' statement is literarily poetic and proverbial, but the metaphor borders on the grotesque, casting God in the image of a bird, which, upon returning from the hunt to its young, regurgitates its food for them.

Understood spiritually, Moses declares that it is more important to feed one's inner self with the word of God than to feed the body with physical food.[11] This interpretation fits the Deuteronomic emphasis on reading the Torah (cf. 17:18−20; 31:9−11), as well as texts that suggest that a person's life depends on "the word addressed to him by God."[12] However, the issue in this context is in fact real physical life — first the life of the previous

---

9. Cf. Moberly, *Abraham and God in Genesis 22*, 106−8. Commenting on Gen. 22:12, Wenham (*Genesis 16−50*, 110) speaks of "confirming his [God's] knowledge."

10. The Baal Peor incident reported in 4:1−5 is never called a test, but it had the same effect. The dross was destroyed, but those who held fast to Yahweh survived.

11. Cf. S. R. Driver, *A Critical and Exegetical Commentary on Deuteronomy* (ICC; Edinburgh: T&T Clark, 1896), 107−8.

12. Thus von Rad, *Deuteronomy*, 72. See 30:15 and 32:47.

generation in the desert, and second the life that awaits this people across the Jordan in the land.[13]

Some interpret that which comes from the mouth of God to be "every provision decreed by YHWH," in contrast to that which one gains by one's own efforts.[14] Since the first line speaks of ordinary food produced by human effort but which by itself cannot sustain life, and the second line speaks of manna, the daily miraculous provision of food, the test supposedly was intended to engender a lasting disposition of dependence on God. However, this understanding forces an unwarranted wedge between bread and manna and overlooks the problem the Israelites actually faced in the desert: they had no bread at all. According to the first part of verse 3, Yahweh himself had deprived them of food, necessitating the manna, which was their bread. The stark reality was that even though the people had this daily supply of food, none of that generation survived. They had plenty to eat and their stomachs were full, but they died.

Therefore, it seems best to understand that "which comes from the mouth of God" to be his revealed will, represented by the Supreme Command and all the stipulations, decrees, and laws. The chapter opens with the challenge to obey the commands of Yahweh "so that you may live" (v. 1); it ends with a sentence of death on all who think they can live by feasting on physical food but neglect the will of God (v. 20). To live one must also ingest (take to heart, 6:6) the life-giving commands that come from the mouth of Yahweh, and let them energize one to do his will (cf. 17:19 – 20; 31:11 – 13).

In verse 5 Moses drives home the significance of the illustration of the testing in the desert. He challenges the people to draw the right conclusions about the "way" of Yahweh (cf. v. 2a) and to fix the lesson indelibly in their minds: "know then in [with] your heart [mind]." Reaching back to a notion he had introduced in 1:31, Moses declares that Yahweh's relationship to Israel is like that of a father to a son. But here the issue is not primarily food or Yahweh's providential care for his children; it is how he trains them. The purpose of the deprivation in the desert was to refine his people through "discipline." Whether punitive or educational, Yahweh's fatherly disciplinary action is always administered in love for the good of his people. This is the lesson the present generation must take with them as they cross the Jordan into the Promised Land.

---

13. For a different perspective, see J. T. Willis, "Man Does Not Live by Bread Alone (Deut. 9:3 and Mt. 4:4)," *Restoration Quarterly* 16 (1973): 145 – 47.

14. Thus O'Connell, "Deuteronomy VIII 1 – 20," 450, following Willis, with some modification. Cf. Tigay's comment (*Deuteronomy*, 92), "Man does not live on natural foods alone but on whatever God decrees to be nourishing."

The nature of the future test (vv. 6—9). This illustration of Israel's deprivation in the desert serves as a foil for the future test: How will the Israelites respond to prosperity and excess? By casting the first clause of verse 10 as a temporal clause, the NIV obscures the rhetorical strategy of this section, which is driven by four verbs in verses 6—10 (lit.): "you will keep [observe] the commands ... you will eat ... you will be satisfied ... you will bless [praise]." The first three summarize the nature of the test, and the last expresses how they should have responded to it.

Moses opens this paragraph on a familiar note with a renewed call to obedience to the commands of Yahweh, the divine suzerain (v. 6). The pair of infinitive expressions that follow explain how the commands are to be kept: *by* walking in his ways and *by* fearing him.[15] The particle *kî* (NIV, "For") in verse 7 signals a momentary shift in focus to establish the grounds of the Israelites' future obedience: Yahweh's act of escorting the Israelites into the good land. If the key motif of this paragraph concerns the Israelites' response to this grace, the key word is undoubtedly "land" (*ʾereṣ*), which occurs seven times.[16] The final clause of verse 10, "on the good land he [Yahweh] has given you," creates an effective inclusio with the opening statement in verse 7. The general reference to the land as "a good land" functions as an introductory thesis statement, whose meaning will be clarified in the following verses, and it contrasts the land ahead with the desert the Israelites have left behind.

Whatever Moses' personal feelings about not being permitted to enter the land (3:23—26), his literary style rises to a new semipoetic register as he describes the Edenic world that awaits his people beyond the Jordan. This "Ode to the Promised Land" breaks down into five stanzas, each introduced by the word "land" (*ʾereṣ*, which stands in apposition to "a good land" at the beginning) and each lauding the land for a particular contribution it will make to Israel's well-being. This is a land with a limitless supply of fresh water (v. 7b), food rich in variety (v. 8a), agricultural staples and luxuries (v. 8b), limitless supply of all that one needs (v. 9a), and minerals easily mined (v. 9b). This image of a land spontaneously yielding its bounty elaborates on the previous description of the land as "flowing with milk and honey" (6:3) and presents a dramatic contrast to the description in 6:10b—11.

Each stanza deserves brief comment. The fact that Moses begins (v. 7) by praising the land for its water resources reflects Israel's unceasing need for this precious commodity. Rather than focusing on rainfall, Moses speaks

---

15. On this construction, see the comments on 5:1.
16. The NIV omits translating one of the occurrences of *ʾereṣ* at the end of v. 8 ("[a land] of olive oil and honey").

of ground resources: brooks ever flowing with water, and springs and foun-tains[17] bursting forth in every valley and on every hill. This description takes the focus off the heavens and fixes it on the earth.

In the second and third stanzas (v. 8), Moses catalogues the most impor-tant horticultural products of the land. Wheat and barley were the main grains of the region, used especially in the baking of bread and other pas-tries, but also in the production of beer.[18] Vines provided a valuable source for both food (grapes and raisins) and drink (wine).[19] Figs and pomegran-ates were the staple fruits, both of which could be eaten fresh or dried.[20] Olives for oil provided one of the most valuable commodities in ancient households. The oil was used for cooking, lighting, ointments, perfumes, cosmetics, lubrication, anointing the sick, and sacred services.[21] If the term for "honey" is understood as the product of bees, it seems out of place. Most therefore interpret the word to denote the nectar of fruit, particularly "date honey," used as a sweetener.[22]

In verse 9a Moses interrupts his discussion of food with a general evalu-ation of the fertility and bounty of the land. But this sentence is transitional; the first half summarizes the preceding, and the second half prepares for the last stanza. Nowhere is Moses' description more idealized than in verse 9b: The rocks of the Promised Land are iron, and its hills wait for miners to come and extract the copper ore. This description is strangely utopian, since only tiny amounts of iron ore and copper have actually been found in Palestine.

---

17. The Hebrew word denotes the subterranean waters, but as used here it refers to the fountains from which the subterranean waters gush forth. See further, D. T. Tsumura, *Creation and Destruction: A Reappraisal of the* Chaoskampf *Theory in the Old Testament* (rev. ed.; Winona Lake, IN: Eisenbrauns, 2005), 50.

18. On these grains, see Oded Borowski, *Agriculture in Iron Age Israel* (Winona Lake, IN: Eisenbrauns, 1987), 87–92; Michael Zohary, *Plants of the Bible: A Complete Handbook* (Cam-bridge: Cambridge Univ. Press, 1982), 74–76.

19. On viticulture in Palestine, see Borowski, *Agriculture in Iron Age Israel*, 102–14; Zohary, *Plants of the Bible*, 54–56. For a fuller study, see C. E. Walsh, *The Fruit of the Vine: Viticulture in Ancient Israel* (HSM 60; Winona Lake, IN: Eisenbrauns, 2000).

20. Pomegranates were also valued as symbols of fertility (Song 4:13; 6:11; 7:12) and as motifs in religious art. For tabernacle (Ex. 28:33–34; 39:24–26) and temple decoration (1 Kings 7:18, 42) and for the head of the priest's mace, see A. Lemaire, "Probable Head of Priestly Scepter from Solomon's Temple Surfaces in Jerusalem, *BAR* 10/1 (1984): 24–29. On the importance of pomegranates in the ancient economy, Borowski, *Agriculture in Iron Age Israel*, 116–17; Zohary, *Plants of the Bible*, 62.

21. Cf. Borowski, *Agriculture in Iron Age Israel*, 117–26; Zohary, *Plants of the Bible*, 56–57.

22. Borowski, *Agriculture in Iron Age Israel*, 126–28; Zohary, *Plants of the Bible*, 60–61; Tigay, *Deuteronomy*, 435–36.

The correct response to the future test (v. 10). Moses continues the grammatical sequence begun in verse 6. If the people are true to the covenant, they will eat and be satisfied. But the third verb declares the proper response to the bounty the land provides: "Then you shall bless Yahweh your God on the good land that he has given you" (pers. trans.). Here "to bless" (*brk*) functions as a virtual synonym for "to give thanks" (cf. Pss. 105:1; 106:1; 107:1) and represents the antithesis to "forgetting the LORD your God" in 6:12. It was one thing for the previous generation to lean on Yahweh in the desert when they were directly dependent on God for food, but for this and future generations the test will be the opposite. In response to the gift of the land and the food it produces, the people were to acknowledge Yahweh (cf. 26:3—11).

The Response to the Internal Test (8:11–20)

THE WRONG RESPONSE TO the test (vv. 11–17). Having described the nature of the internal test and the correct response, Moses goes on to describe the wrong response (vv. 11–17). He begins with a charge, involving the same verbal root as he had used in verses 1 and 6 (*šāmar*), but he calls on Israel to "be careful." If keeping the commands of Yahweh is fulfilled *by* "walking in his ways and revering him" (v. 6), then forgetting Yahweh is expressed *by* "failing to observe his commands, his laws and his decrees" that Moses is commanding them (v. 11). The threat envisioned is not the Canaanite nations but the Israelites themselves. If, in the midst of prosperity, they forget Yahweh, they become their own worst enemy.

Verses 12–17 elaborate on the charge. These verses consist of a single, complex statement opening with "lest" (*pen*), which governs a series of eight verbs: "lest you eat, and are satisfied, and build good houses, and live [in the land],[23] and everything you own multiplies, and your heart is lifted up, and you forget Yahweh . . . and you say in your heart" [pers. trans.]. The potential problem emerges in verse 14: instead of blessing Yahweh, the Israelites' hearts will be tempted to "rise" with pride.[24] Moses clarifies what he means by "a lifted heart" in verse 17: this is a disposition that causes people to take credit for all their successes and to think that their wealth is the result of their own efforts. Moses highlights the perversion of this kind of thinking by treating "my power" and "the strength of my hands" as

---

23. The NIV translates "and you settle down," but this should probably be interpreted as an abbreviated variant of "to live in/on the land" (cf. 11:31; 12:10, 19, 29; 17:14; 26:1; 30:20).

24. The idiom *rûm lēb*, "the heart is lifted up" (NIV "become proud"), recurs in 17:20 (cf. Ezek. 31:10; Dan. 5:20; Hos. 13:4—6).

the subject of "produce," whereas they should say, "the LORD [our] God" has done all this.

Verses 14b – 16 highlight the tragedy of this response to the test by reviewing the kindnesses Yahweh has lavished on Israel: he is Yahweh "your God, who brought you out of Egypt" (v. 14b), "led you through the vast and dreadful desert" (v. 15a), "brought you water out of hard rock" (v. 15b), and "gave you manna to eat in the desert" (v. 16). The first provision reiterates the historical prologue of the Decalogue (cf. 5:6), while the second focuses on the constant dangers associated with the great and terrifying desert—a place infested with dangerous serpents and scorpions, and totally lacking in water.

The third benefaction answers the problem alluded to in the previous sentence. Miraculously Yahweh had provided water from a most unlikely source—impervious rock.[25] Yahweh's fourth provision involved food in the desert—manna. As in verse 3, Moses observes that this was food of which their ancestors had never heard. However, he interprets the manna shockingly as the means of Israel's deprivation and testing/refinement. Every day Yahweh tested the Israelites to see whether or not they would be a grateful people.[26] From the declared purpose in verse 16 (lit., "so that in the end it might go well with you"), we learn that the manna was not given merely to satisfy the Israelites' immediate hunger but to purify and refine commitment.

Moses' review of the divine benefactions in the desert and their refining/testing function provides a context for the verbal response of the hypothetical interlocutor in verse 17. The claims of the Israelites to have achieved the prosperity described in verses 12 – 13 through their own efforts provide clear evidence of hearts that have been lifted up and that have forgotten Yahweh (v. 14a), from whom all blessings flow. Not only have those who think this way failed the test; the trial has also proved the people themselves to be dross (cf. vv. 19 – 20).

The correct response to the future test (v. 18). In contrast to the wrong response to the test (vv. 11 – 17), Moses now provides three elements of the correct response. (1) When the Israelites prosper in the land, they must "remember the LORD." As elsewhere the verb *zâkar* involves more than simply acknowledging his existence; it means to take seriously his presence and actions. (2) Even if the Israelites prosper through hard work, they must recognize that the skill and energy needed to do that

---

25. Cf. Ex. 17:6; Num. 20:7 – 11. The word recurs in Deut. 32:13; Ps. 114:8; Isa. 50:7.

26. For a narrated illustration of the failed test at Taberah, see Num. 11:1 – 9, to which Moses will allude in 9:22.

work is a gift from Yahweh. (3) They must remember that Yahweh gives strength not primarily for their prosperity, but to confirm his covenant with the ancestors. Moses' use of the expression "to confirm his covenant" proves he is not speaking of a new covenant, but the fulfillment of a previous covenant, here identified as the covenant he made with the ancestors of his audience.

The NIV renders ᵃᵇōṭēḳā as "your forefathers," following a longstanding tradition of identifying this as the covenant Yahweh made with the patriarchs.[27] However, in light of verses 3 and 16, it seems more likely that Moses has the exodus generation in mind.[28] This interpretation is reinforced by the fact that although Yahweh promised to bless Abraham and his descendants in general (Gen. 12:2; cf. 17:20), this is not a prominent theme in the references to the Abrahamic covenant.[29] The profusion of material blessings lavished on Israel in verses 7−9 (cf. 7:12−16) represent the fulfillment of the blessings promised within the covenant made with Israel at Horeb/Sinai (Lev. 26:1−13; Deut. 28:1−14).[30]

The final warning (vv. 19−20). Moses ends this topic with a final frightful warning, declaring the dire consequences of the wrong response to the test/refinement presented by prosperity in the Promised Land. Employing expressions encountered earlier, Moses reviews the conditions that are absolutely unacceptable to Yahweh: forgetting Yahweh (cf. vv. 2, 11, 14, 18), going after other gods (cf. 5:7; 6:14; 7:4), serving them (4:19, 28; 5:9; 6:13; 7:4, 16), and prostrating themselves in homage and submission to them (cf. 4:19; 5:9). All these responses represent betrayals of allegiance to Yahweh and a violation of the Supreme Command (6:4−5).

Moses opens his announcement of judgment with a call for witnesses. As in 4:26, the invocation is a response to anticipated future apostasy.[31] In effect, if the Israelites go after other gods, they will surely perish like the nations whom Yahweh destroyed before them. To forget Yahweh in the midst of prosperity is to reduce oneself to the status of the Canaanite nations whom the Israelites were to displace and to become the object of divine fury.

---

27. This interpretation goes back as far as the Samaritan Pentateuch and the LXX[L379], which insert the names of Abraham, Isaac, and Jacob at this point. Cf. *BHQ*, 75*, and 49*−50* on 1:8.

28. So also Hwang, *Rhetoric of Remembrance*, 328−29.

29. The narratives speak of Yahweh's blessing Abraham (24:1["in every way"], 35) and Isaac (25:11; 26:12−14, 29).

30. The addition of "as it is today" strengthens this interpretation.

31. Apparently based on 4:26, several manuscripts of LXX add "the heavens and the earth." See *BHQ*, s.v.

The final clause reminds Moses' hearers of the reason for their horrible fate: they refused to listen to the voice of God. The reference to "hearing the voice of Yahweh" (NIV "obeying the LORD") brings to a conclusion not only this chapter, but also the long section that began in 6:4 with "Hear O Israel." But it also concludes a chapter that has highlighted the "mouth" and communication of Yahweh. "That [which] comes from the mouth of the LORD" (v. 3) is the gracious revelation of his will in the form of stipulations, commands, decrees, and instructions. The formulas for life that have been operative in the past and that will operate in the future may be represented as follows:

Past ▸ miraculous provision (manna) + gratitude and obedience ▸ life

Future ▸ the bounty of the land (plenty) + gratitude and obedience ▸ life

Whereas in the past Yahweh had tested and refined his people with deprivation and manna, in the future he will do so with prosperity. His aim in both is to produce a nation that brings praise and glory to him in the sight of the nations (26:19). If they fail the test and refuse to be refined, he will discard them again like dross and consign them to the slag heap (cf. Ezek. 22:17 – 22).

MANNA. REFERENCES TO MANNA are remarkably rare in the Old Testament. Outside the narratives involving the provision (Ex. 16:15, 31, 33, 35; Num. 11:6, 7, 9) and Moses' present reflections on this provision (Deut. 8:3, 16), this miraculous food is mentioned only five times. Joshua 5:12 notes that Yahweh ceased providing manna the day after the Israelites ate the produce of the land for the first time (cf. Ex. 16:35). The present text is remembered in the prayer of the Levites in Nehemiah 9:19 – 20, which notes that among Yahweh's many gracious provisions during the forty-year sojourn in the desert, Yahweh provided manna and water, and then adds that "their clothes did not wear out nor did their feet become swollen," an obvious allusion to Deuteronomy 8:4. Later poets spoke of the manna as "bread of heaven" (Ps. 105:40), "grain of heaven" (Ps. 78:24), and even more colorfully, "bread of angels" (Ps. 78:25).

Indeed the manna was deemed such a special gift that Moses had Aaron placed an omer of it before the ark of the covenant as a permanent reminder of Yahweh's provision during the forty years of their journey through the desert (Ex. 16:31 – 35). Moses' association of manna with the revealed will of God in Deuteronomy 8:3 may have been inspired by the fact that the tablets that symbolized Yahweh's verbal revelation shared this most sacred space with the manna.[32]

In John 6:31–51 Jesus makes a claim that the Jewish leaders viewed outrageous; he is "the bread of heaven" that gives life, in contrast to the manna, which the people ate in the desert but which failed to produce life (6:31). According to Moses, in the desert people lived by eating that which came from the mouth of God, that is, his revealed word, rather than through physical food taken into one's own mouth. Now Jesus identifies himself as the very bread of God that has come down from heaven and gives life to the world (John 6:33; cf. 1:1–4). He invites people to come and eat of him, for he is the bread of life, and those who eat of him will live forever.

Paul alludes to our text in 1 Corinthians 10:3–5. While his statement is enigmatic, he observes that the ancestors all ate the same spiritual food and drank the same spiritual drink, from a spiritual rock; but most of them died, because they did not receive the approval of God. While most commentators assume the spiritual food was the manna,[33] which was in fact very physical,[34] Paul has in mind "every word that comes out of the mouth of the LORD" (Deut. 8:3), that is, his verbal revelation embodied in the commands and ordinances of the covenant. When he says that the people ate but God was not pleased with them, he recognizes that the ancestors all had access to the revelation, but they refused to keep the commands of Yahweh their God, to walk in his ways, and to fear him (Deut. 8:6).

The best-known allusions to Moses' discourse on the manna are found in the gospel narratives of Jesus' temptation in the desert (Matt. 4:1–4; Luke 4:1–4). Seeing Jesus' famished condition after a forty-day fast, the devil challenged him: If he was the Son of God, turn the stones into bread. By quoting Moses in Deuteronomy 8:3, Jesus acknowledges that even if stones were turned to bread, this would not guarantee life. In John 4:31–34 Jesus expresses his own disposition toward physical and spiritual food. In his response to his disciples urging him to eat, "My food . . . is to do the will of him who sent me and finish his work," Jesus claims to embody the ideal of Deuteronomy 8:3.

---

32. While Heb. 9:4 suggests the manna and Aaron's rod were kept in the ark along with the tablets of the covenant, 1 Kings 8:9 (= 2 Chron. 5:10), as well as Philo (*Moses* 9.97) and Josephus (*Ant* 3.6.5; 8.4.1), suggest otherwise. The note in Hebrews must either be based on some other tradition (Cf. C. R. Koester, *Hebrews: A New Translation with Introduction and Commentary* [AB 36; New York: Doubleday, 2001], 395) or reflect a later reality when the objects were transferred from *before* the ark *into* the ark.

33. In which case *pneumatikon brōma* is equivalent to *leḥem šāmayim*, "bread of heaven."

34. According to Ex. 16:31 it resembled white coriander seed, and its taste was like wafers with honey. Num. 11:7 adds that it sparkled like bdellium.

Even as this text highlights God's character as a graciously providing and disciplining father, it also provides a dramatic contrast between the God of Israel and other so-called gods, particularly with respect to their responses to humans. Whereas the pagans portray their images of gods with prominent eyes and ears and mouths (cf. 4:28), Yahweh has none of these. Nevertheless, he sees and hears and perhaps most remarkably, he talks. Contrary to the view of many today, the words that come from his mouth are life-giving; to receive them, to take them to heart, and to live by them is evidence of righteousness that yields life, well-being, and the affirmation of God (6:24–25). No wonder the psalmist could declare with such enthusiasm, "Oh, how I love your law [read: Torah]! I meditate on it all day long" (Ps. 119:97).

OBEDIENCE TO THE WILL of God. The significance of this chapter for contemporary Christians may be recognized at many levels. First, and most obviously, like Israel of old, Christians do not live by bread alone but by obedience to the will of God. If we are preoccupied with physical well-being to the neglect of our spiritual life, we too will perish. This is a particular problem in the Western church, where with our prosperity we have forgotten that all good things come from God, including the ability to make wealth. Not only have we forgotten to give thanks to God; we have also become increasingly resistant to letting his revealed will govern our lives.

Testing. Second, the image of God as a father testing and disciplining his children offers valuable perspective on the tests and trials we face. The wise man of Israel teaches us the proper disposition toward the discipline of God in Proverbs 3:11–12:

> My son, do not despise the LORD's discipline
>   and do not resent his rebuke,
> because the LORD disciplines those he loves,
>   as a father the son he delights in.

Peter seems to have understood the purpose of such testing when he wrote in 1 Peter 1:6–7 that trials have come so that "faith—of greater worth than gold, which perishes even though refined by fire—may be proved genuine and may result in praise, glory and honor when Jesus Christ is revealed." Like the Israelites' disposition toward Yahweh, though Peter's readers have not seen Jesus Christ, they love him; and though they do not see him now, they still believe in him and are filled with inexpressible and glorious joy, knowing that it is for their good in the end and the goal of their faith, the salvation of their souls. The echoes from our text are evident throughout this passage (see also the connections in 1 Peter 4:12–18)

The road to idolatry. Third, this passage declares that the first stage on the road to idolatry is ingratitude. Deuteronomy 8:10 has had a profound impact on Judaism, providing the basis for the threefold blessing after meals[35] and should provide inspiration for Christians today to acknowledge the gracious and generous work of God on their behalf, particularly in sustaining our daily life. Moses reminds his audience and us that the only appropriate response to eating of the bounty that God provides is to bless Yahweh. But this chapter exhibits a downward spiral, in which forgetting Yahweh (vv. 2, 11) leads to ingratitude (vv. 12–16), which leads to self-sufficiency (v. 17), which leads to idolatry (v. 19). Paul plots a similar course in Romans 1:21–23.

The danger of success. Fourth, the second half of this chapter reminds us of the potential danger that lurks with success. Indeed success may be more tragic than failure, especially if it causes us to forget God and results in pride, smugness, and self-sufficiency. This applies not only to economic ventures, but especially to those who serve as ministers of the gospel. When we look over our accomplishments, whether they are the megachurches we have built, the books we have written, or the busy schedules people impose on us, we too are tempted to say to ourselves, if not publicly, "My power and the strength of my hands have produced this church for me." And we are tempted to forget that every service we render has its roots in the gracious and unmerited call of God, and that every achievement is possible only because the Lord God has graciously endowed us with the abilities to preach a fine sermon, to lead a large church, or to write an impressive tome.

In our day, God's tests come in many additional forms. When all our needs are met, God is testing us: when we win a scholarship to a prestigious university, receive accolades for a beautiful painting or poem, are promoted in business, or gain a windfall fortune on the stock market. But this is also true of the more mundane accomplishments: when we learn to read or ride a bicycle, master a new computer program, or strike a hole-in-one on the golf course, God is testing us. Will we give him praise for giving us the wits and the skills for these accomplishments? Our faith and faithfulness are not tested only when the Lord drives us to the end of ourselves; they are also tested when everything is going our way. Indeed, the more successful we are, the stiffer the test and the greater the reason to praise God, and at the same time, the greater the danger of self-sufficiency.

---

35. See the discussion in Weinfeld, *Deuteronomy 1–11*, 392–94.

A sober warning. Finally, the last verse in this passage provides a sober warning to those seduced by the idolatry of success: If our lives are governed by the values of the world, we incur the wrath of God and will share its fate. This may be particularly true for people who come from humble beginnings and rise to the top professionally or economically. Many live under the illusion that having crossed the Red Sea figuratively (having said the sinner's prayer or been baptized), they are forever well and God is obligated to grant them prosperity. When they prosper, they take this as evidence of God's favor. In the meantime, they forget the God who redeemed them and the God who gave them the gifts and opportunities to succeed. But success may not be proof of either personal well-being or divine favor. Failure to acknowledge God in success proves that we are at root Canaanites, and that our faith is just a modern version of ancient fertility religion. Nothing provokes the ire of God like ingratitude for his grace.

From my childhood I remember a farmer who provided a striking illustration of the problem. He was a leader in the church, who regularly taught Sunday school and served on the church council; occasionally he preached. When I first met him, he operated a modest farm, working 960 acres of land. That year his whole family was relaxed; they took off several days to fish in the beautiful lakes of northern Saskatchewan and to participate in community activities. The next year he worked over 1,900 acres. The fishing trip was canceled. The third year he worked 3,360 acres, and by the fourth year it had grown to more than 5,100 acres. I had never seen an operation like this. Everything he touched seemed to turn to gold.

The neighbors clamored to have him work their land, because the way he farmed they would make a greater profit if they received one-third of the crop as rent than if they farmed it themselves. In the meantime I watched him shrivel up spiritually. His success went to his head. When a machine broke down, he had illusions of conspiracies by jealous neighbors. When he was runner up for "Farmer of the Year" award, he went into a fit of rage. As the pressures mounted, the turmoil in his family increased, he had less time for the community and especially for the community of faith, he became abusive to his hired hands, and he resorted to a dangerous and unhealthy lifestyle. He died in his late fifties, a totally broken and bankrupt man. While only God can judge the state of his soul, by all appearances, he had failed the test.

The disposition called for by Moses is reflected in a song we learned in the late 1970s while worshiping with a blessed Brethren Assembly in Liverpool, England:[36]

---

36. Composer unknown.

The wise may bring their learning,
The rich may bring their wealth;
And some may bring their greatness,
And some their strength and health.
We too would bring our treasures
To offer to the King;
We have no wealth or learning
What gifts then shall we bring?

We'll bring the many duties
We have to do each day;
We'll try our best to please him,
At home, at school, at play.
And better are these treasures
To offer to the King
Than richest gifts without them,
Yet these we all may bring.

We'll bring him hearts that love him;
We'll bring him thankful praise,
And souls forever striving
To follow in his ways.
And these shall be the treasures
We offer to the King;
And these are gifts that ever
Our grateful hearts may bring.

Deuteronomy 9:1-24

🔥

Introduction to Deuteronomy 9:1-11:32

WITH THE OPENING "HEAR, O ISRAEL!" (v. 1), Moses signals the beginning of the third major section (9:1–11:32) of his second address (4:45–26:19). This large section subdivides according to its temporal vision, shifting successively from Israel's future (9:1–6), to the past (9:7–10:11), to the present (10:12–11:1), to the past (11:2–7), to the future (11:8–25), to the present (11:26–32).

Despite the shift between 9:6 and 7, Deuteronomy 9:1–10:11 is a self-contained literary subunit whose boundaries are marked by Moses' anticipation of crossing the Jordan and claiming the land in 9:1, and by Yahweh's command to Moses to lead the people away from Sinai/Horeb to go and possess the land he had sworn to their ancestors (10:11). The intervening material is held together by the motif of Israel's rebellion, the tone of tension between Israel and Yahweh, and the temporal phrase "forty days and forty nights."[1]

Hear, O Israel. You are now about to cross the Jordan to go in and dispossess nations greater and stronger than you, with large cities that have walls up to the sky. ²The people are strong and tall—Anakites! You know about them and have heard it said: "Who can stand up against the Anakites?" ³But be assured today that the LORD your God is the one who goes across ahead of you like a devouring fire. He will destroy them; he will subdue them before you. And you will drive them out and annihilate them quickly, as the LORD has promised you.

⁴After the LORD your God has driven them out before you, do not say to yourself, "The LORD has brought me here to take possession of this land because of my righteousness." No, it is on account of the wickedness of these nations that

---

1. Five of the nine occurrences of this phrase in the Old Testament occur here. It took forty days and nights (1) for Yahweh to deliver the Decalogue to Moses (9:9–10); (2) for the Israelites to prove the shallowness of their covenant commitment (9:11–17); (3) for Moses to deal with the sin of the people, including his confession before Yahweh and his destruction of "the sin" (9:18–21); (4) for Moses to convince Yahweh to withdraw his threat to annihilate his people (9:25–10:5); (5) to complete the work of atonement and to hear Yahweh's marching orders to renew the trek to the Promised Land (10:10–11).

the LORD is going to drive them out before you. [5]It is not because of your righteousness or your integrity that you are going in to take possession of their land; but on account of the wickedness of these nations, the LORD your God will drive them out before you, to accomplish what he swore to your fathers, to Abraham, Isaac and Jacob. [6]Understand, then, that it is not because of your righteousness that the LORD your God is giving you this good land to possess, for you are a stiff-necked people.

[7]Remember this and never forget how you provoked the LORD your God to anger in the desert. From the day you left Egypt until you arrived here, you have been rebellious against the LORD. [8]At Horeb you aroused the LORD's wrath so that he was angry enough to destroy you. [9]When I went up on the mountain to receive the tablets of stone, the tablets of the covenant that the LORD had made with you, I stayed on the mountain forty days and forty nights; I ate no bread and drank no water. [10]The LORD gave me two stone tablets inscribed by the finger of God. On them were all the commandments the LORD proclaimed to you on the mountain out of the fire, on the day of the assembly.

[11]At the end of the forty days and forty nights, the LORD gave me the two stone tablets, the tablets of the covenant. [12]Then the LORD told me, "Go down from here at once, because your people whom you brought out of Egypt have become corrupt. They have turned away quickly from what I commanded them and have made a cast idol for themselves."

[13]And the LORD said to me, "I have seen this people, and they are a stiff-necked people indeed! [14]Let me alone, so that I may destroy them and blot out their name from under heaven. And I will make you into a nation stronger and more numerous than they."

[15]So I turned and went down from the mountain while it was ablaze with fire. And the two tablets of the covenant were in my hands. [16]When I looked, I saw that you had sinned against the LORD your God; you had made for yourselves an idol cast in the shape of a calf. You had turned aside quickly from the way that the LORD had commanded you. [17]So I took the two tablets and threw them out of my hands, breaking them to pieces before your eyes.

[18]Then once again I fell prostrate before the LORD for forty days and forty nights; I ate no bread and drank no

water, because of all the sin you had committed, doing what was evil in the LORD's sight and so provoking him to anger. [19]I feared the anger and wrath of the LORD, for he was angry enough with you to destroy you. But again the LORD listened to me. [20]And the LORD was angry enough with Aaron to destroy him, but at that time I prayed for Aaron too. [21]Also I took that sinful thing of yours, the calf you had made, and burned it in the fire. Then I crushed it and ground it to powder as fine as dust and threw the dust into a stream that flowed down the mountain.

[22]You also made the LORD angry at Taberah, at Massah and at Kibroth Hattaavah.

[23]And when the LORD sent you out from Kadesh Barnea, he said, "Go up and take possession of the land I have given you." But you rebelled against the command of the LORD your God. You did not trust him or obey him. [24]You have been rebellious against the LORD ever since I have known you.

MOSES CONTINUES HIS RECOLLECTIONS of events at Horeb. These reminiscences are cast as a modified disputation speech, a form commonly used by later prophets to refute faulty thinking. Typical disputation speeches consist of an introduction, quotation of a popular saying presented as a thesis/hypothesis concerning a fact, a dispute negating the hypothesis, and a counter-thesis offering an alternative interpretation. Several of these elements are evident here:[2]

Introduction: A call to attention and announcement of fact (vv. 1–3)
Thesis: An explanation of the fact, expressed by means of a direct quotation (v. 4a)
Counter-thesis: An alternative explanation of the fact (vv. 4b–6)
Refutation: A denial of the thesis and the reasons for its rejection (verses 9–24).

Although the rhetorical signals marking the transitions from one part to the other differ from later prophetic oracles and the last two features are reversed, the similarities are striking.

---

2. On disputation speeches in the prophetic books, see A. Graffy, *A Prophet Confronts His People: The Disputation Speech in the Prophets* (AnBib 104; Rome: Biblical Institute Press, 1984); Block, *Ezekiel Chapters 1–24*, 329–40.

The Nature of the False Claim (9:1 – 6)

WITH THE PROMISE OF Yahweh's confirmation of the covenant to the fathers in the background (8:18), Moses speaks of Yahweh's dispossessing the Canaanites and handing over their land to Israel.[3] This raises the question: Why should Yahweh be interested in the Israelites at all? Moses answers this question first by refuting any claim to merit as the basis for the divine favor, and then by highlighting the mercy of Yahweh in getting them to the Promised Land. Loosely following the form of a disputation speech, this section divides into two major paragraphs (vv. 1 – 3 and vv. 4b – 6), separated by a hypothesis explaining Yahweh's interest in Israel, cast as direct speech in the mouth of a hypothetical interlocutor (v. 4a).

Introduction (vv. 1 – 3). Following the opening call to attention, Moses announces the fulfillment of the divine agenda presented in Exodus 3:8 (cf. Ex. 6:1 – 8): rescuing Israel from the bondage of Egypt (v. 6), establishing them as Yahweh's covenant people at Sinai (v. 7), and taking them to the Promised Land (v. 8) — elements familiar from previous utterances (cf. 1:28; 4:38; 7:1). Obviously the challenge facing this generation is no different than it had been thirty-eight years earlier. The quotation in verse 3, "Who can stand up to the sons of Anak?" [pers. trans.], has a proverbial ring.[4] Assuming a negative answer, in effect the Canaanites were saying, "You may have dispossessed Sihon and Og, but no one can dislodge us from our land."

This reminder of the enemies' apparent invincibility sets the stage for Moses' confident declaration in verse 3, namely, that the key to the Israelite's future is not to be found in their own strength but in the strength of their divine Commander-in-Chief. The description of the one who is crossing over ahead of the Israelites reinforces this notion. This one is identified by name — "Yahweh"; by his relationship to Israel — "your God"; by epithet — ʾEsh ʾOkelah; and by his actions on Israel's behalf: (1) "He is the one crossing over before you"; (2) "He will destroy them"; and (3) "And he will subdue them before you" [all pers. trans.].

Here, ʾEsh ʾOkelah ("Devouring Fire") functions as a quasi-titular designation. Whereas in 4:24 the reference to the fiery passion of Yahweh was intended to motivate Israelite fidelity and warn against worshiping other

---

3. The sevenfold repetition of the root *yrš* ("to possess, dispossess") in this short paragraph is obscured in the NIV, which renders the term variously: "dispossess" (v. 1), "drive them out" (vv. 3, 4, and 5), "take possession" (vv. 4 and 5), and "possess" (v. 6). This verb involves the conquest of another people or nation, thereby gaining the right to rule its territory. Cf. N. Lohfink, "ירש," *TDOT*, 6:371.

4. The elliptical nature of the statement buttresses this impression: "You have heard [people say] . . ." On the renowned strength of the Anakites, see 1:28; 2:10 – 11.

gods, here Moses promises that the same fury will be turned against the enemy. This is what the Israelites should "know" as they dispossess and destroy the enemy. As we have seen elsewhere (e.g., 7:1), the credit for the conquest will go to Yahweh, but his people are to engage the enemy, who will capitulate, just as Yahweh promised them.

The hypothesis (v. 4a). In verse 4a Moses again introduces a hypothetical interlocutor to speak for the people. As in 7:17 and 8:17, the response is cast as internal ("in your heart"; NIV "to yourself") rather than external speech, as if one would think this but never dare actually to say it. As a judicial term, "righteousness" speaks of virtuous character, reflecting an upright heart (lit., "straightness of heart," v. 5) and demonstrated in conduct aligned with covenantal standards (6:20). In this context its opposite is represented by "wickedness" (vv. 4, 5).[5] The hypothetical speaker imagines himself to be virtuous, but the word speaks of smug self-righteousness and inflated self-esteem. According to this hypothesis, Yahweh's transfer of the land from the Canaanites to Israel is a reward for the latter's moral superiority.

Moses' counter-thesis (vv. 4b–6). If this were a pure disputation speech, Moses would have begun his response to the mistaken hypothesis by explicitly disputing the claim. He does indeed do so twice in this short paragraph—in verse 5a and then in verse 6. However, around these repudiations of the hypothesis, he weaves his counter-thesis, which consists of three arguments, each relating to a different party in this equation.

(1) *The Canaanites.* Yahweh's act of driving out the Canaanites is not grounded in Israel's righteousness but is a response to the wickedness of the Canaanites.[6]

(2) *Yahweh.* Yahweh is driving out the Canaanites to fulfill the promise that he made to the patriarchs, listed here by name as Abraham, Isaac, and Jacob (v. 5; cf. 1:8; 8:18).

(3) *Israel.* Saving the most devastating argument for last, Moses declares that far from claiming "righteousness" as their characteristic attribute, the Israelites are fundamentally "a stiff-necked people." This idiom is based on the image of draft animals, especially yoked oxen, whose locus of power is perceived to be in the neck, but who often refuse to work as their master directs.[7]

---

5. Ezekiel 18 provides classic presentations of the contrast between "righteousness" and "wickedness." For detailed discussion see Block, *Ezekiel 1–24*, 554–90.

6. Moses' negative evaluation of the Canaanites accords with the perspective of the rest of the Pentateuch. See Gen. 15:16; Lev. 18:24–30; 20:23; Deut. 18:12.

7. See G. Abramson, "Colloquialisms in the Old Testament," *Semitics* 2 (1972): 12–13. In v. 13 Moses recalls Yahweh's own use of the expression in the aftermath of the golden calf affair (Ex. 32:9; 33:3, 5).

With his verdict of "stiff-necked" Moses pricks Israel's balloon of inflated self-esteem and sets the stage for his portrayal of the Israelite's fundamentally flawed character. They have nothing to commend themselves to God: no physical greatness (7:7), or power (8:17), or moral character. Their election, occupation of the land, and prosperity within it are all gifts of divine grace, granted to them in spite of their lack of merit.

The Refutation of the Claim (9:7–24)

THE OPENING DOUBLE IMPERATIVE, "remember this and never forget how you provoked the LORD your God to anger in the desert," signals a new movement in this speech. Having declared that rather than commending her to Yahweh, Israel's character is actually repelling him, Moses gathers evidence for this counter-thesis, urging his people to see themselves as God sees them.

Verse 7b begins the exposition of the thesis announced in verse 7a. In fact, it functions as a front bookend for this subsection, whose final counterpart occurs in verse 24. These two statements mirror each other both with respect to content and structure:

A From the day you left Egypt until you arrived,
B you have been rebellious against the LORD. (9:7)
B′ You have been rebellious against the LORD
A′ ever since I have known you. (9:24)

Moses will spend the rest of this speech reminiscing on Israel's past troublesome relationship with Yahweh. In verses 7b–21 he concentrates on the most dramatic event as evidence of his thesis. However, in case this is insufficiently convincing, he adds three more illustrations in verses 22: Taberah, Massah, and Kibroth Hattaavah. And for good measure, in verse 23 he brings back the events of Kadesh Barnea, which he had already recounted in chapter 1. His opening statement (v. 7) describes the Israelites from God's perspective with two new expressions: they have a habit of "provoking the LORD your God to anger," and they have been in constant rebellion against him.[8] The recollections of the golden calf incident at Horeb (vv. 8–21) display strong links with the narratives of Exodus 32–33.

Continuing the emphatic word order used in verses 4–6, Moses identifies Horeb as a symbol of Israel's true character (vv. 8–10). This was the mountain where the Israelites were formally received as Yahweh's covenant partners, where they had committed themselves to total and unreserved obedience to Yahweh (cf. Ex. 19:8; 24:3, 7), and where their representatives had eaten the covenant meal in the presence of God (Ex. 24:9–11).

---

8. Cf. 1:26, 43; 9:23, 24.

This was also the place where they had demonstrated their true colors. So intense was Yahweh's provocation at their rebellion that within forty days of sealing the covenant, he threatened to destroy them (v. 8). So much for moral superiority! Instead of the Israelites' righteous character commending them to Yahweh, these people have earned divine fury.

As background to the rebellion at Horeb, Moses briefly describes what he was doing at the time (vv. 9–11). In his recollections we again hear clear echoes of the narrative in Exodus, with additional details found earlier in the first address.[9] According to verse 9, Moses seems to have fasted whenever he went up the mountain to meet with Yahweh. His asceticism stands in sharp contrast to the activity of the Israelites below. The process of making the calf probably required time, in which case the people's rebellion must have surfaced shortly after they had sworn fidelity to the covenant.[10]

To understand the significance of Moses' climb to the top of Horeb we are dependent on Exodus 24:12–18. The basic terms of the covenant had been revealed, the people had committed themselves to the covenant, the ratification ritual had been completed, and the covenant meal celebrating the new relationship had been eaten in the presence of God. All that remained was documentation of the event in written text, which was the purpose of Moses' ascent up the mountain.[11] But while Moses was on the mountain on official business on behalf of the people, they searched for a replacement for him (Ex. 32:1).[12] In his recollection Moses highlights the transformation in the symbolism of Horeb from a place of grace and glory, of revelation and response, of covenant and promise, to a place of human rebellion and divine fury.

After announcing Israel's rebellion and providing background information, Moses shifts attention to Yahweh's response (vv. 12–14). As in the Exodus account, Moses casts Yahweh's response in the form of two direct speeches, verse 12 (cf. Ex. 32:7–8) and verses 13b–14 (cf. Ex. 32:9–10). Although the present text exhibits many links with Exodus 32:7–10, Moses' language here is more intense, reflecting his own heightened emotion. This is seen most

---

9. His focus here is on the covenant as the basis for the relationship between Yahweh and Israel, not on the stipulations of the covenant themselves. "Out of [the midst of] the fire" (v. 10) recalls 4:12, 15, 36, and 5:22; "on the day of the assembly" echoes 4:10 and 5:22. The expression "tablets of the covenant" (*luḥôt habbᵉrît*) that Yahweh made with them occurs only here and in verses 9, 11, and 15 (though it recalls 4:13; cf. 1 Kings 8:9), and replaces "tablets of the stipulations" (*luḥôt hāʿēdut*) in Ex. 31:18 (cf. 32:15; 34:29).

10. The Exodus account does not indicate how quickly the idolatrous behavior surfaced, but Yahweh uses the word "quick" in Ex. 32:8.

11. Cf. Ex. 31:18; Deut 5:22.

12. Verse 11 suggests it took forty days and nights to produce the written copy of the covenant.

dramatically in the fate with which Yahweh threatened Israel. The choice of *hišmîd* ("to destroy," Deut. 9:14a) in place of *killâ* (lit., "to put an end to," Ex. 32:10) links Yahweh's disposition here with the fate of the Canaanites in Deuteronomy 7:24. Yahweh's determination to "blot out their name from under heaven" (9:14) is shocking. If Moses' presentation of Yahweh's fury is stronger than in the earlier narrative, the same is true of the honor Yahweh promised him (9:14b). Whereas Exodus 32:10 had simply echoed God's general promise to make Abraham a great nation, Moses remembers it as a promise to make of him into a nation stronger and more numerous than the Canaanites.

Upon closer examination of Yahweh's speech, several features stand out. (1) Yahweh distances himself from the Israelites by referring to them as "your people whom you brought out of Egypt" (v. 12). The people gathered at the foot of the mountain are not the product of God's redeeming work, nor a people in covenant relationship with himself, but just another group of people on the move (cf. Amos 9:7). Reinforcing this disposition in verse 13, Yahweh refers to the Israelites contemptuously as "this people"[13] and "a stiff-necked people." The phrase "stiff of neck," which literally speaks of an ox resisting the yoke of his master, may have been prompted by the sight of the golden calf; with classic irony the people have become like the image they worshiped.

(2) Yahweh seems reticent to talk about the people's specific actions. This contrasts with the earlier narrative, where he had noted a series of specific concrete offenses (Ex. 32:8). Although Moses will identify the image as a "calf" (*ʿēgel*) in verse 21, here Yahweh refers to the image generically as a "an idol cast [*massēkâ*] in the shape of a calf" (v. 16). Suppressing interest in the form of the image and the ritual involved in its worship, the primary significance of the event lies in its implications for the covenant.

(3) In "begging" Moses to leave him alone that he might give full vent to his fury (Ex. 32:10) and destroy Israel, paradoxically Yahweh opens the door for his intervention.[14] As an idiom meaning "Let me alone" (v. 14),[15] Yahweh's request reflects the extraordinary relationship between him and Moses.

---

13. Cf. Num. 14:11; Deut. 31:16; Isa 6:9–10; 8:6, 11–12; 9:16; 29:13–14; etc.

14. Cf. R. W. L. Moberly, *At the Mountain of God: Story and Theology in Exodus 32–34* (JSOTSup 22; Sheffield: JSOT, 1983), 50. According to S. Balentine (*Prayer in the Hebrew Bible: The Drama of Divine-Human Dialogue* [OBT; Minneapolis: Augsburg, 1993], 136), this is "a form of invitation by prohibition."

15. C. Houtman (*Exodus Chapters 20–40* [Historical Commentary on the Old Testament; Leuven: Peeters, 2000), 3:645] translates the idiom, "Do not stop me." Targums Pseudo-Jonathan and Onqelos read, "Desist from your prayer to me" (thus trans. by E. G. Clarke, *Targum Pseudo-Jonathan: Deuteronomy* [Aramaic Bible 5B; Edinburgh: T&T Clark, 1998], 32). Targum Neofiti is even more explicit and expansive: "Refrain yourself before me from begging mercy for them" (trans. by M. McNamara, *Targum Neofiti 1: Deuteronomy* [Aramaic Bible 5A; Edinburgh: T&T Clark, 1997], 61).

In effect, Yahweh said he would not act against Israel without Moses' release. He removed all incentive for intercession by promising Moses that he would make of him a nation stronger and more populous than the Canaanites. Had Moses accepted this offer, he would have replaced Abraham, Isaac, and Jacob as the ancestor of the nation and the history of God's people would have been written as the history of the "Mushites" rather than "Israelites."

Moses' reaction to Israel's rebellion (vv. 15—21). As Moses recalls the events at Horeb, he leaves his hearers momentarily wondering how he would respond to Yahweh's challenge (vv. 15—21). Unlike the narrative of Exodus 32, Moses skips over the details associated with his descent from the mountain (Ex. 32:15—20) as well as his verbal response. Instead, he concentrates entirely on his nonverbal reaction—he will report his prayer later (vv. 25—29). Moses' report of his own actions consists of four summary parts: (1) He smashed the tablets (vv. 15—17); (2) he interceded before Yahweh (vv. 18—19); (3) he interceded for his brother Aaron (v. 20); and (4) he disposed of the calf (v. 21).

Moses' smashing of the tablets (vv. 15—17). When Yahweh finished his speech of verses 13—14, Moses turned around and headed back down the fiery mountain, carrying the symbols of the covenant in his hands. The reference to the fire links this event with the day that Moses had declared the words of the covenant "out of the fire, on the day of the assembly" (v. 10),[16] but it also links this scene with the divine epithet ʾEsh ʾOkelah ("Consuming Fire") in verse 3. Exodus 24:16—18 suggests the people's request for Aaron to make the image arose from a conviction that Moses himself had been consumed by the fire that shrouded the mountain. However, the people should have realized that the blazing fire symbolized not only Yahweh's theophanic presence, but also his consuming fury, particularly in the face of idolatry (4:23—24; cf. 29:20[19]).

Later Moses will state that as he came down the mountain, he feared that Yahweh's wrath would blaze against the people (v. 19). The added note that Moses descended the mountain with the two tablets of stone seems like an incidental detail, except that these are "the tablets of the covenant," concrete symbols of the relationship that had been established. The opening words of verse 16 highlight Moses' shock at what he saw: "And I looked, and behold!" [pers. trans.].[17] Ironically, in the fifteen words

---

16. Cf. the references to the fire on the mountain in 4:11—12, 15, 24, 33, 36; 5:4—5, 22—26.

17. The NIV's "When I looked, I saw" flattens the rhetorical significance of the redundancy, especially the use of the particle *hinnēh* ("Behold"). The particle often follows verbs of perception and focuses attention on what follows. Cf. C. H. J. van der Merwe, et al., *Biblical Hebrew Reference Grammar* (Sheffield: Sheffield, 1999), 329—30.

that follow, only two involve a visible object: "a cast/molten calf." The rest represent interpretive comments on that object.

The precise significance of the calf is not clear. If it was intended as an image of Yahweh, it was a blasphemous act reducing the formless deity to physical form, directly contravening Yahweh's warning in 4:15. But if the calf was intended as an image of another deity,[18] it represented a blatant violation of the first commandment of the Decalogue and flagrant denial of the Shema. Whatever the people's perception of the image, Yahweh interpreted its manufacture and worship as "corrupt" acts and a "turning away" from his way (v. 12), and Moses characterized it as "sin" and "turning aside ... from the way that the LORD had commanded" (v. 16). This was rebellion of the first order.

Moses describes his reaction to the people's rebellion in three dramatic acts: he seized the two tablets, threw them to the ground, and smashed them in full view of all the people. These actions were both legal and symbolic, analogous to the Mesopotamian custom of breaking tablets on which contracts were written when the agreement had been violated. As the representative of Yahweh, by smashing the tablets Moses declared the covenant null and void even before the people had a chance to see the divinely produced written documentation.

Moses' intercession for the people (vv. 18–19). Although he delays reporting the contents of his prayer until verses 25–29, in these verses Moses the statesman becomes Moses the prophetic intercessor par excellence. Here the focus is entirely on his physical gestures and on the urgency of his intercession, when he "fell prostrate before the LORD," begging for mercy and fasting for forty days.[19] Whereas previously Moses had given up food and drink to concentrate on his official role as recipient of communication *from* Yahweh to the people (v. 9), here his fast arises from his intercessory role *to* Yahweh on behalf of the people.

Verses 18b–19 clarify the nature of Moses' intercession. (1) Moses characterizes Israel's crime as "all the sin the people had sinned by doing the evil in Yahweh's eyes" (pers. trans.; cf. 4:25). The definite article on the word for "evil" suggests a specific crime, in this case and generally elsewhere, the violation of the first commandment. (2) Moses reveals the inner emotion

---

18. Perhaps the Egyptian bull Apis, sacred to and emblematic of the god Ptah; or El, the chief Canaanite deity, who is called "Bull El" in the Ugaritic literature; or Baal, the fertility deity, who sired an ox in one of the Ugaritic myths; or merely a precursor to the metal figurines of bulls and calves that have been discovered at several Palestinian sites. For further discussion of these options, see Tigay, "Excursus 12: The Golden Calf," *Deuteronomy*, 445–46.

19. Cf. Gen. 43:18; Ezra 10:1. On the symbolic significance of the act, see M. Gruber, *Aspects of Nonverbal Communication in the Ancient Near East* (Studia Pohl 12/1; Rome: Biblical Institute Press, 1980), 131–33.

behind his actions: he was frightened at the prospect of Yahweh's anger, whose superlative intensity is expressed by heaping up a triad of Hebrew expressions for anger. Moses feared that Yahweh would destroy his people.

Although Moses' report of Yahweh's response here lacks the drama of Exodus 32:14, the relief in his voice is still evident thirty-eight years later when he adds, "But again the LORD listened to me." The addition of the particle *gam* ("also, as well") alludes to some other crises during the desert wanderings when the people were spared because of his intercession.[20] It also reflects the extraordinary relationship between Yahweh and his representative. The prayer of this righteous man was indeed powerful and effective (James 5:16).

Moses' intercession for Aaron (v. 20). Moses interrupts his report of the national crisis with a surprising reference to his brother Aaron.[21] Because Aaron had participated in the rebellion, Yahweh's fury burned against him as well, and he threatened to destroy him. However, through Moses' intercession, Yahweh's threat on Aaron's life was also lifted. Nonetheless, for his involvement in this event, Aaron was barred from entrance into the Promised Land.[22]

Moses' disposal of the golden calf (v. 21). Moses concludes this phase of his report of the rebellion at Horeb by describing how he disposed of the calf itself. Referring to the "calf" as "that sinful thing of yours" (lit., "your sin"), he describes his actions against it with a rapid-fire sequence of verbs: He "took" it, "burned it," "ground it to power as fine as dust," and "threw the dust" into the stream flowing down the mountain, flushing it away as excrement.[23] Josiah's similar treatment of idolatrous objects in 2 Kings 23:12—16 suggest these were stereotypical procedures for dealing with offensive pagan objects (cf. 7:5).[24]

---

20. Cf. Ex. 14:15; 15:25; Num. 11:2; 12:13—14; 14:13—20; 21:7—9.

21. While the exodus narratives (MT) omit the reference to Moses' intercession for Aaron, the Samaritan Pentateuch and *4QpaleoEx*[m] [4Q22] from Qumran include it, apparently under the influence of this verse.

22. Even though Num. 20:22—29 links Aaron's premature death with his conduct at Meribah, Moses' reference to his death in 10:6 suggests a link also with the calf incident. See further below on 10:6.

23. Ex. 32:20 adds that he made the people drink the water into which he had dumped the remains.

24. For other texts involving obliteration of idolatrous cult places and objects, see Ex. 23:24; 34:13; Lev. 26:30; Num. 33:52; Deut. 7:5, 25; 1 Kings 15:13 (cf. 2 Chron. 15:16); 2 Kings 10:26—27. On extrabiblical analogues, see C. T. Begg, "The Destruction of the Calf (Exod 32,20/Deut 9,21)," in *Das Deuteronomium: Entstehung, Gestalt und Botschaft* (ed. N. Lohfink; BETL 68; Leuven: Leuven Univ. Press, 1985), 208—51. But for a cautionary note, see Houtman, *Exodus Chapters 20—40*, 3:660. The resemblance between Moses' actions and Anath's disposal of Mot's body in a late second millennium Ugaritic document is especially striking. See *CTA*, 6: ii.30ff., as translated by D. Pardee in *COS*, 1:270.

The postscript (vv. 22−24). As if the golden calf incident were insufficient evidence for Israel's fundamentally rebellious disposition vis-à-vis Yahweh, Moses offers four additional illustrations of their unrighteousness. For the first three he simply lists place names that serve as code words for different dimensions of their rebellious character. Taberah ("Burning") symbolizes Yahweh's response to Israel's sour disposition; it illustrates both Yahweh's destructive power as "a consuming fire" and the constant need for Moses' intervention (Num. 11:1−3). Massah ("Place of Testing") is a code word for Israel's contentious disposition toward Moses (the place was also called Meribah, "Place of Contention") and testiness toward Yahweh (Ex. 17:1−7). At Kibroth Hattaavah ("Graves of Craving"), the people had expressed their boredom with Yahweh's provision by complaining about the manna (Num. 11:4−34), to which Yahweh responded by providing quail and punishing by plague. Regarding Kadesh Barnea, in verse 23 Moses summarizes in a sentence what he had described in great detail in 1:26−43. Here the Israelites' refusal to enter the land from Kadesh Barnea was paradigmatic of their rebellion, unbelief, and disobedience (cf. 1:26, 32).

Moses concludes his recitation of the Israelites' fundamentally unrighteous character with one final sweeping generalization: They have been in revolt against Yahweh from the day he was first introduced to them. Although this is obviously rhetorical hyperbole, the history of sour relations between the people, on the one hand, and Yahweh and Moses, on the other, can be traced as far back as Exodus 5:20−23.

ISRAELITE IDOLATRY. THE MEMORY of Israel's rebellion at Sinai/Horeb would not die out with Moses and his generation. We hear echoes of the account of the golden calf in Exodus 32 most clearly in Jeroboam's speech dedicating the two calves at Bethel and Dan as symbols of the northern kingdom's religious unity: "Here are your gods, O Israel, who brought you up out of Egypt" (1 Kings 12:28).[25] The use of the name Horeb (rather than Sinai) in Psalm 106:19 suggests the psalmist has been inspired by Moses' recollections of the event when he remembered the utter folly of this sort of idolatry (Ps. 106:19−22).

Centuries later Stephen remembered this event not only as an act of folly but also of willful disobedience and rebellion, repudiating Yahweh and

---

25. Except for the first word, this speech echoes Aaron's in Ex. 32:4. Hosea deals with these calves in Hos. 8:5; 10:5.

turning to other gods (Acts 7:39−41). But Stephen went even further. In a shocking turn, with obvious echoes of Deuteronomy 10, Stephen accused the members of the Sanhedrin of being stiff-necked and "uncircumcised of heart" (Acts 7:51), resisting the Holy Spirit just like their ancestors.[26] The use of a bovine metaphor like stiff-neckedness is especially apt in contexts involving the worship of the calf.

However, in Israel's subsequent history the rebellion tended not to take the form represented here, involving an image of a calf. This was clearly a case of syncretism, combining a pagan form with orthodox theology. Within a generation Israel's apostasy would take on less subtle forms. From the time of the judges (Judg. 2:11−23) to the days of Manasseh and beyond (2 Kings 21:1−9), doing "the evil in the eyes of the LORD" involved the overt worship of pagan gods: the Baals, the Ashtaroth, and the Asherim. It is no wonder, then, that in the end Yahweh's fury should rage against his people. They had rejected the one who had so graciously redeemed them, invited them to covenant relationship, revealed to them his will, and cared for them in the desert, in favor of lifeless idols.

However favorably the Israelites might have told their own story, Ezekiel told it the way God saw it. Despite Yahweh's grace in calling her to life and elevating her to the status of queen (Ezek. 16:1−14) and despite her claims to nobility, by going after other "lovers" (vv. 15−34) she proved her true parentage; her father was an Amorite and her mother a Hittite (vv. 3, 44−50).

BY GRACE, NOT BY **merit**. Earlier Moses had denied that the call to salvation and mission for the kingdom of God might be based either on the greatness (Deut. 7:7) or the special giftedness (8:17−18) of those called. This episode opens with a truth that pervades all of Scripture, namely, that the call to relationship with God is never based on merit. In response to Israelites, who might be tempted to attribute their status in the divine scheme to their superior righteousness (in contrast to the Canaanites), Moses demonstrates that the Israelites had been undeserving of the mission to which God had called them; from the beginning they had demonstrated that they were fundamentally depraved and that if they had been rescued from Egypt and would be handed the Promised Land as their grant, these were privileges granted by grace alone. And so it is with us. As Paul reminds Titus:

---

26. References to circumcision of the heart and stiff-neckedness appear together only here and in Deut 10:16.

> At one time we too were foolish, disobedient, deceived and enslaved by all kinds of passions and pleasures. We lived in malice and envy, being hated and hating one another. But when the kindness and love of God our Savior appeared, he saved us, not because of righteous things we had done, but because of his mercy. He saved us through the washing of rebirth and renewal by the Holy Spirit, whom he poured out on us generously through Jesus Christ our Savior, so that, having been justified by his grace, we might become heirs having the hope of eternal life. (Titus 3:3 – 7)

Paul goes on to challenge those who have trusted in God to be careful to devote themselves to doing what is good, for these things are excellent and profitable for everyone (Titus 3:8). With respect to the call to salvation, human righteousness counts for nothing with God. Indeed, apart from God's grace we are all Canaanites.

The nature of idolatry. Israel's rebellion at Sinai/Horeb is typical of the human race in general and, sadly, of the church in particular. Like Israel, humankind was created as the image of God and charged to reflect the glory and grace of God in their government of the world. But however privileged this role was, the status of vassals was not good enough. By eating of the forbidden fruit we thrust God from the throne and defined reality on our own terms (Gen. 3). We were not satisfied to let God be God on his terms and our role in the universe to be defined on his terms. Such is the nature of idolatry. It dethrones the one and only God and substitutes him with pathetic and grotesque images. It robs the living God of the credit for creation and redemption and ascribes sovereignty to lifeless substitutes. In the words of John Calvin, the heart is an "idol factory."

What is particularly shocking about Israel's act at Horeb is that it flies in the face of all that they had just witnessed of the living God and in the face of their threefold declaration, "We will do everything the LORD has said" (Ex. 19:8; 24:3, 7), and with the "blood of the covenant" by which they had been bound to Yahweh in an exclusive relationship (24:8). Yahweh had not even produced the covenant document before they broke their vows. In this respect Israel is not only typical of humanity in general, but those who call themselves the redeemed people of God in particular. Like the church at Ephesus, we too are so prone to forsake our "first love" (Rev. 2:4), which is the one and only Savior to whom we have committed ourselves by covenant. Scarcely have we declared our conversion and been baptized upon our confession of faith, when we forget the Lord and return to the gods of this world.

But the rebellion at Horeb represents a particularly sinister form of idolatry. This is syncretism at its cleverest. In his dedication speech Aaron had declared, "These are your gods, O Israel, who brought you up out of Egypt"

(Ex. 32:4), constructed an altar before it, and then announced the following day as a holiday, "a festival to the LORD" (v. 5). The words and actions appear orthodox, but the form is entirely pagan and in direct violation of Yahweh's explicit command.

This is a serious and pervasive problem in Western worship—even the worship of evangelicals, with their high claims to regeneration and new birth and authentic Christianity. We are quick to declare our love for God, but we hate his "law." We are passionate in our expressions of worship, but we refuse to ask him what kind of worship pleases him. Instead we take our idioms from the pagans around us. We claim new life in Christ, but then we reduce Christianity to a fertility religion, perverting slogans like "God has a wonderful plan for your life" into a health and wealth gospel. We take God's good gifts and corrupt ourselves by making idols out of them. The Israelites took their precious metals and made them into a divine image; we take our families, the books we write, our toys, and our money, and we make them the focus of our devotion and homage.[27] We have forgotten that *true worship involves reverential acts of homage and submission before the divine Sovereign in response to his gracious revelation of himself and in accordance with his will.*[28]

---

27. For an excellent discussion of the problem see Timothy Keller, *Counterfeit Gods: The Empty Promises of Money, Sex, and Power, and the Only Hope That Matters* (New York: Dutton, 2009). Keller defines idolatry as "anything more important to you than God, anything that absorbs your heart and imagination more than God, anything you seek to give you what only God can give," xvii.

28. For development of this theme, see Daniel I. Block, *For the Glory of God: Recovering a Biblical Theology of Worship* (Grand Rapids: Baker, forthcoming).

I lay prostrate before the LORD those forty days and forty nights because the LORD had said he would destroy you. ²⁶I prayed to the LORD and said, "O Sovereign LORD, do not destroy your people, your own inheritance that you redeemed by your great power and brought out of Egypt with a mighty hand. ²⁷Remember your servants Abraham, Isaac and Jacob. Overlook the stubbornness of this people, their wickedness and their sin. ²⁸Otherwise, the country from which you brought us will say, 'Because the LORD was not able to take them into the land he had promised them, and because he hated them, he brought them out to put them to death in the desert.' ²⁹But they are your people, your inheritance that you brought out by your great power and your outstretched arm."

¹⁰:¹At that time the LORD said to me, "Chisel out two stone tablets like the first ones and come up to me on the mountain. Also make a wooden chest. ²I will write on the tablets the words that were on the first tablets, which you broke. Then you are to put them in the chest."

³So I made the ark out of acacia wood and chiseled out two stone tablets like the first ones, and I went up on the mountain with the two tablets in my hands. ⁴The LORD wrote on these tablets what he had written before, the Ten Commandments he had proclaimed to you on the mountain, out of the fire, on the day of the assembly. And the LORD gave them to me. ⁵Then I came back down the mountain and put the tablets in the ark I had made, as the LORD commanded me, and they are there now.

⁶(The Israelites traveled from the wells of the Jaakanites to Moserah. There Aaron died and was buried, and Eleazar his son succeeded him as priest. ⁷From there they traveled to Gudgodah and on to Jotbathah, a land with streams of water. ⁸At that time the LORD set apart the tribe of Levi to carry the ark of the covenant of the LORD, to stand before the LORD to minister and to pronounce blessings in his name, as they still do today. ⁹That is why the Levites have no share or inheritance among their brothers; the LORD is their inheritance, as the LORD your God told them.)

¹⁰Now I had stayed on the mountain forty days and nights, as I did the first time, and the LORD listened to me at this time also. It was not his will to destroy you. ¹¹"Go," the LORD said to me, "and lead the people on their way, so that they may enter and possess the land that I swore to their fathers to give them."

THE CHAPTER DIVISION BETWEEN chapters 9 and 10 creates a false impression, inviting readers to separate these two chapters from each other. However, these parts belong together as cause and effect, or action and response.

The Nature of Moses' Plea (9:25–29)

ALTHOUGH MOSES' REPORT OF his intercessory prayer fits more logically after verses 18–19, its inclusion there would have been rhetorically disruptive, because in the prayer his attention shifts from the sinful disposition of the people to God himself. Moses' intercession exhibits a masterful combination of pathos and argumentation. As we have seen throughout this chapter, Moses' recollections of his words are linked to the version of this prayer found in Exodus 32:11–14. However, Moses' concern about what the nations will say if Israel is destroyed (Deut. 9:28) bears a closer resemblance to a statement in his other great intercessory prayer for Israel in Numbers 14:13–19 (esp. v. 16).

Despite these similarities, the present recollections conform fully to the literary style of Deuteronomy. The distinctive argumentation of the prayer may be highlighted by comparing it with the versions of Moses' prayers elsewhere:

Exodus 32:11–14	Numbers 14:13–19	Deuteronomy 9:26–29
Israel is Yahweh's people, not his (v. 11a).		Israel is Yahweh's people, not his (v. 26a).
Yahweh has invested great effort in saving the Israelites from the bondage of Egypt; by implication, to destroy them would mean this effort was wasted (v. 11b).	Yahweh has invested great effort in saving the Israelites from the bondage of Egypt; by implication, to destroy them would mean this effort was wasted (v. 13).	Yahweh has invested great effort in saving the Israelites from the bondage of Egypt; by implication, to destroy them would mean this effort was wasted (v. 26b).

Yahweh's reputation among the nations will be damaged if he destroys Israel; they will think his intent was malicious from the beginning—to destroy Israel in the desert (v. 12).	Yahweh has been uniquely close to his people; he is in their midst and has been personally leading them; by implication, it makes no sense to destroy them (v. 14).	Hold back for the sake of the patriarchs; overlook the sin of their descendants (v. 27).
Hold back for the sake of the patriarchs; to them he promised to multiply their seed and give them the land of Canaan as their possession forever (v. 13).	Yahweh's reputation among the nations will be damaged if he destroys Israel; they will think that he slaughtered them in the desert because he was unable to carry through on his promise to give them the land (vv. 15—16).	Yahweh's reputation among the nations will be damaged if he destroys Israel; they will think that he brought them out to destroy them in the desert because he was unable to carry through on his promise to give them the land, and because he hated them (v. 28).
	Yahweh's gracious character is in question; he has proved himself merciful in the past—may he be gracious again and forgive his people (vv. 17—19).	Israel is Yahweh's people, not his (v. 29a).
		Yahweh has invested great effort in saving the Israelites from the bondage of Egypt; by implication, to destroy them would mean this effort was wasted (v. 29b).

Structurally, Deuteronomy 9:25—29 consists of a prose preamble (vv. 25—26a) and an extended quotation of Moses' prayer (vv. 26—29). Unlike both Exodus 32:11—14 and Numbers 14:13—19,[1] here Moses fails

---

1. In the former, Yahweh "relented" and withheld the disaster (v. 14); in the latter Yahweh "forgave."

to report the divine response to the prayer or his intercessory effectiveness (cf. 9:19). Instead, he moves directly to the problem of reproducing the tablets of the covenant that he had destroyed (10:1–5). The preamble to the prayer (9:25–26a) consists almost entirely of expressions we heard in verses 18b–19. However, Moses introduces a new generic designation for his verbal response to God: *hitpallēl*. The word usually means "to make intercession for," which suits the present context perfectly.[2]

With the vocative opening to the prayer, (lit.) "O Adonay Yahweh," Moses uses the personal name of God and acknowledges his own vassal status. Unlike many other biblical prayers that include descriptions of the divine addressee,[3] Moses immediately launches into his demands: (1) "Do not destroy your people" (9:26); (2) "remember your servants, Abraham, Isaac and Jacob" (v. 27a); and (3) "overlook the stubbornness of this people, their wickedness and sin" (v. 27b). His boldness in making these demands contrasts with his stubbornness at the time of his call (Ex. 3–5). In that encounter Yahweh would not take "no" for an answer; here it is Moses who refuses to accept a divine "no."

Moses' first demand, that Yahweh not annihilate his people, is striking. He had used the same verb "to destroy, exterminate" (*hišḥît*) in 4:31, where he reassured his people that Yahweh is a compassionate God; he will not fail his people or "destroy" them, nor will he forget his covenant with the ancestors. Tossing the ball back into Yahweh's court, Moses declared that for Yahweh to destroy Israel would be for him to eliminate his partner in covenant. Whereas Yahweh had distanced himself from the Israelites in verse 12, Moses turned the tables, reminding Yahweh that Israel is "your people" and "your special possession" (*naḥalâ*; NIV "inheritance"), and that Israel is the product of his own extraordinary saving efforts (see Ex. 6:2–7; Lev. 25:55). He had "redeemed"[4] them himself "with his greatness" and brought them out of Egypt "with a strong hand." Moses would take neither the credit (cf. the people's statement in Ex. 32:1) nor the blame (cf. Yahweh's statement in v. 12) for the people who had gathered at Mount Sinai.

Moses' second demand is expressed cryptically. Without specifying the purpose, he pleaded for Yahweh to remember his servants Abraham, Isaac, and Jacob. Based on Exodus 32:13, he must be thinking of Yahweh's covenant promises to multiply their descendants like the stars of the sky, and to

---

2. While *hitpallēl* is often used of intercession for someone else (Gen. 20:7; Num. 21:7; 1 Sam. 7:5; Job 42:8), this is not always the case. See 1 Sam. 1:10; 2 Sam. 7:27; 1 Kings 8:30, 35, 42, 44, 48; 2 Chron. 7:14; Dan. 9:4.

3. See Gen. 32:9–12[10–13]; 2 Kings 19:15b–19; 1 Chron. 29:10–29; Dan. 9:1–27.

4. On Moses' use of the verb *pādâ* ("to redeem")," see comment on 7:8.

give them the land as their eternal possession. By referring to the ancestors as "your servants," Moses recognized them as Yahweh's vassals.[5]

Moses' third demand was the most dramatic, as he pleaded with Yahweh to overlook the "stubbornness" (lit., "stiff-neckedness"), "wickedness," and "sin" of "this people" (v. 27). Neither excusing his people nor minimizing their crime, Moses daringly warned Yahweh that if he destroyed the Israelites, the nations would conclude that either he was unable to carry through on his mission of bringing them to the land, or that he had intentionally brought them in the desert to slaughter them. Assuming the Egyptians would not distinguish between immediate divine causation and the Israelites' ultimate responsibility for their own fate, what was supposed to be a gracious scheme of salvation would look like a diabolical plot. Moses therefore argued that Yahweh's own reputation was at stake; he could not afford to destroy his people.

Moses concluded his prayer with a positive foundation for this appeal. Repeating his opening statements, he declared that Israel was Yahweh's people; they were his personal possession, and saving them was to his advantage. Therefore he had to overlook their rebellion and simply carry on. Although Moses had noted in verse 19 that Yahweh listened to his prayer, now he is silent on Yahweh's response (cf. Ex. 32:12).

Modern readers may wonder if Yahweh accepted Moses' argumentation, but his audience knew they were living proof of the effectiveness of Moses' intercession. Moses' own reticence on this matter probably relates to his immediate concern, which is to demonstrate to his audience that if Israel ever made it to the Promised Land, it was by sheer grace. This story is not about him or his power as intercessor; it is about God and his people. Yahweh is not delivering the Promised Land into their hands as a reward for their superior righteousness. Nor is it because of their leader, however fearless he may have been in his intercession. Ultimately the credit for the success of the present mission will go entirely to Yahweh, their covenant God.

The Lord's Response to the Plea
for Renewal of Favor (10:1 – 11)

AS NOTED ABOVE, THE chapter division obscures the relationship between this section and the ending to chapter 9. Located immediately after his plea to spare Israel, Moses recalls the production of the new set of tablets and suggests that Yahweh's renewal of the covenant was the answer to

---

5. Although Yahweh had spoken of Abraham as "my servant" in Gen. 26:24, in Ex. 32:13 Moses was the first to apply the epithet to all three ancestors.

his prayer. As in chapter 9, Moses has telescoped a series of events into a straight line from prayer to tablets (cf. Ex. 34:1–4, 28). Structurally this text is complex. The primary action involves Yahweh's reaffirmation of the covenant made with Israel at Horeb (vv. 1–5, 10a). Verses 6–9 are parenthetical, presenting the Levites as custodians of the covenant document, and verses 10b–11 provide a narrative conclusion to the unit that began in 9:1.

Yahweh's reaffirmation of the Israelite covenant (10:1–5). The opening expression, "at that time," links Yahweh's speech (vv. 1–2) with Moses' prayer. Yahweh's commands were simple. (1) Moses was to cut out two tablets of stone to replace the ones he broke and bring them up to Yahweh on the mountain (cf. Ex. 34). Moses' recollection leaves no doubt that these new tablets were to function like the original tablets ("like the first ones," v. 1), and they were inscribed with "the words that were on the first tablets" (v. 2), "what he had written before" (v. 4a), that is, "the Ten Words" (v. 4b), that Yahweh had proclaimed "on the mountain, out of the fire, on the day of the assembly" (v. 4c). Furthermore, Moses recalls that he remained on the mountain for forty days and nights like "the first time" (v. 10).

(2) Moses was to make an ark and put these new tablets into it. He does not describe the ark here, except to say it was made of acacia wood (v. 3). This was not the permanent "ark of the covenant" later placed in the Most Holy Place of the tabernacle. That ark had not yet been made, and in any case it was crafted by the divinely endowed craftsman Bezalel (Ex. 35:30–36:1). Whereas this ark served as a temporary receptacle for the tablets (cf. Deut. 31:9, 26), that one would also function as a throne for the invisible deity, which figured in the Day of Atonement ritual (Lev. 16:11–14). This one played no part in the cult, but that one served as a visible symbol of Yahweh's presence and was a central feature in Israelite's worship. This distinction is reinforced by the rare reference to the receptacle as "an ark" (v. 1; NIV "a wooden chest") as opposed to "the ark" (v. 3).[6] Although the ark served more than one function,[7] given Deuteronomy's concern with covenantal issues, it is not surprising that in this book this chest functions primarily as the official depository of the covenant documents.[8]

---

6. Of almost 200 references to the official ark of the covenant, the indefinite form occurs only in Ex. 25:10, where Yahweh first introduces the subject. Thereafter, it is always called "the ark" and never "an ark."

7. So also I. Wilson, "Merely a Container? The Ark in Deuteronomy," in *Temple and Worship in Biblical Israel* (ed. J. Day; London: T&T Clark, 2007), 212–49; idem, personal communication on ʿāmad lipnê, "to stand before."

8. See the discussion above on 5:22.

Moses reports the outcome of Yahweh's instructions in verses 3–5. By reversing the order of Yahweh's instructions in verse 1, he focuses on the divine action (v. 4), particularly Yahweh's inscription of the terms of the covenant. The report concludes with a summary notice of Moses' descent and his depositing the tablets in the ark he had made. He ends with a final note: they are still there, just as Yahweh had commanded him. In introducing the ark as the repository of the covenant document, Moses has struck on its primary covenantal significance in Israel's tradition. In keeping with ancient Near Eastern custom, by placing the tablets of the covenant in the ark and later depositing it before Yahweh in the Most Holy Place, Yahweh was invoked as a witness to and guarantor of the covenant.[9] Later Moses will instruct the Levites to place his Torah document beside the ark rather than inside it.[10]

Introduction of the custodians of the covenant (vv. 6–9). Moses' report on the reaffirmation of the covenant is interrupted briefly by a parenthetical note, consisting of a geographical comment concerning several stages in the Israelites' trek through the desert (vv. 6–7) and an explanation for the Levites' current role in relationship to the covenant.[11] The geographic fragment apparently derives from a tradition of Israel's journeys that existed alongside the official itinerary in Numbers 33. The reference to Aaron's death between two geographic notes referring to water is striking. Moses does not explain why Yahweh refused to let Aaron enter the land or describe how the priestly garments were transferred from Aaron to his son Eleazar. Moses' recollection reduces this event to the barest facts (Deut. 10:6b).

In verses 8–9 the narrator returns to the subject that interests him most—the ark of the covenant and its relationship to the Levitical priests. "At that time" (v. 8) seems to associate the elevation of the Levites with the death of Aaron and his replacement by Eleazar (v. 6). However, the phrase should probably be linked with verse 1, where the identical form ties the reaffirmation of the covenant with the rebellion of Israel at Horeb. The narrative of that event juxtaposes Aaron's lame excuse for his involvement in the affair (Ex. 32:21–24) with the gallant reaction of the Levites (32:25–29). This forms the basis for the narrator's comment in Deuteronomy 10:8–9: The Levites are a privileged group, set apart for divine service.

---

9. For a fourteenth century BC Hittite analogue to the Israelite storage of the Decalogue, see Beckman, *Hittite Diplomatic Texts*, 46; M. Haran, *Temples and Temple Service in Ancient Israel: An Inquiry into Biblical Cult Phenomena and the Historical Setting of the Priestly School* (Winona Lake, IN: Eisenbrauns, 1985), 255.

10. On the ark and manna and Aaron's rod, see the Bridging Contexts section of 8:1–20.

The narrator summarizes the professional privileges/duties of the Levitical priests with four infinitive purpose clauses: (1) "to carry the ark of the covenant of the LORD,"[12] which means to serve as custodians of the tablets inside, and by implication of the covenant itself; (2) "to stand before the LORD," which elsewhere represents official court language authorizing entrance into the presence of the king (cf. Dan. 1:4);[13] (3) "to minister" to Yahweh, a reference to the cultic service they would render by presenting offerings and sacrifices on the altar,[14] maintaining the tabernacle/temple as Yahweh's residence (Num. 18:1–6; Ezek. 44:11), and resolving disputes on God's behalf (Deut. 21:5); and (4) "to pronounce blessings" before the people in the name of Yahweh, which probably involved pronouncing the "Aaronic benediction" of Numbers 6:24–26 (cf. Lev. 9:22; 1 Chr. 23:13).[15]

Since the note makes no reference to the tabernacle, all these roles are covenantal. The Levitical priests were responsible for maintaining the relationship between the two parties to the covenant.[16] The note ends with a reference to their spiritual privilege. Whereas the rest of the tribes of Israel would receive their apportioned allotment in the form of real estate, the Levitical priests' portion is defined in spiritual and theological terms; Yahweh promised himself as their grant. Aaronic status and privilege was extended to the Levites as a whole.

Moses' narrative epilogue (vv. 10–11). When Moses' own voice returns in verses 10–11, he resumes the main subject at hand: Yahweh's reaffirmation of his covenant with Israel. Recapitulating information provided in 9:18 and 9:25 (because of the intervening material), he recounts his intercession and Yahweh's response. Like a courtier before a king, Moses stood before Yahweh pleading on behalf of the people. Yahweh responded as he had done previously (cf. 9:9) and withdrew his threat to destroy

---

11. Moses' own speech flows smoothly from v. 5 to vv. 10–11. The note was probably added by the final editor of the book (see also 2:10–12, 20–23; 3:9, 11, 13b–14).

12. Deuteronomy is not overly concerned about the distinctions between priests and Levites, hence the references to "the Levitical priests": 17:9, 18; 18:1; 24:8; 27:9 (and elsewhere, Josh. 3:3; 8:33; Jer. 33:18, 21), "the priests, the sons of Levi" (31:9), or simply "the Levites" (18:7; 27:14; 31:25). See chap. 18 below. But the book is not unaware of priestly-Levitical distinctions. Verse 6 explicitly recognizes the hereditary nature of the Aaronic priesthood. See further McConville, *Law and Theology in Deuteronomy*, 138–39.

13. The expression is also used of the heavenly host standing at Yahweh's right and left hand (2 Chron. 18:18), prophets (1 Kings 17:1; 18:15; Jer. 15:1; 18:20; 23:18), and Levitical priests (10:8; 18:5, 7; cf. 2 Chron. 29:11; Zech. 3:1).

14. Which, however, was restricted to the priests; cf. Num. 18:7; Ezek. 44:15–16.

15. The importance of this blessing is reflected in two silver amulets from the seventh century BC found in Jerusalem, inscribed with this blessing. See Barkay, *Ketef Hinnom*, 29–31.

16. This is reinforced by four later texts in Deuteronomy: 17:18; 31:9–10, 24–26; 33:10.

his people. Yahweh's words in verse 11 reaffirm his acceptance of Moses' intercession and the full restoration of the covenant. The double command, "Arise, go" (NIV reads only "Go") — that is, "Hurry up and go" — reflects Yahweh's eagerness to get on with the mission. The reminder of the promise of land to the ancestors provides concrete proof that the covenant relationship was fully restored.

THE POWER OF PRAYER. Although in Nehemiah 9:18–19 the Levites remember both the contemptuous actions of the Israelites in making the golden calf and Yahweh's compassion in sparing them, that text is silent on Moses' role in bringing about this response. This is not the case with Psalm 106:19–23, which credits Moses, Yahweh's "chosen one," with standing "in the breach" and turning away divine fury that would otherwise have destroyed them. Like our text, this recollection highlights the power of prayer. James's declaration that "the prayer of a righteous man is powerful and effective" (James 5:16) may also allude to this text.

However, since neither of these passages explicitly characterizes Moses as righteous, this must be inferred from our text and the antecedent narrative in Exodus 32. Moses' righteousness is seen in several aspects of his response: (1) his wrestling for mercy from God on behalf of his people despite their blatant rebellion; (2) his rejection of Yahweh's heady offer to start his program over with him; (3) the argument of his prayer, which focused on preserving Yahweh's reputation in the eyes of the nations. Moses' self-portrayal in Deuteronomy 9 is also remarkably modest in that he says nothing of his offer to give up his life if Yahweh will only spare his people (Ex. 32:32).

Apart from Moses' role as intercessor, his petition exhibits a profound theology of prayer. From beginning to end it reflects the same perspective as we find in the prayer Jesus taught his disciples (Matt. 6:8–13). (1) It is addressed to Yahweh, whom he had earlier compared with a father concerned for the well-being of his children (Deut. 8:5). (2) It is concerned above all with the reputation of God (cf. "Hallowed be your name"). If Yahweh destroys his people, the nations will draw the wrong conclusions, which will bring shame to his name. (3) He prays for forgiveness for his people.

But there is more. Moses appeals to Yahweh's integrity, reminding him of the patriarchs to whom he had committed himself. Perhaps what is most remarkable is his utter selflessness at this point. In rejecting Yahweh's offer to make a great nation out of him, Moses served as a model for all who lead in the kingdom of God. The biblical paradigm of leadership always manifests the interests of the people ahead of oneself.

Understanding the covenant. Moses' recollections of the episode involving the golden calf have important bearing on our understanding of the covenant. On the surface, his symbolic gesture of smashing the tablets suggests that the covenant Yahweh had made with Israel was off, and when Yahweh offered to start over with Moses, the covenant with the patriarchs seems also to have been suspended. However, the emphasis on the new tablets as duplicates of the originals and the inscription thereon being "like the first ones" (10:1 – 4) highlight the continuity between the covenant that the Israelites ratified in Exodus 34 and the covenant in force when they left Mount Horeb.

Moreover, since Moses began his second address by reciting the Decalogue, this is also the covenant that the people renewed on the Plains of Moab (cf. 29:10 – 13[9 – 12]). This is the covenant that ensures Israel's future, even after judgment (4:32; cf. 30:1 – 10), a notion that is developed more fully centuries later in the context of the exile by Ezekiel (Ezek. 16:60 – 63; cf. 34:25 – 31; 37:25 – 28). Indeed, in Isaiah 54:7 – 10 the prophet compares the irrevocability of this covenant (which he calls "my covenant of peace," 54:10) with the cosmic covenant made in the days of Noah (cf. Gen. 9).[17]

LESSONS ON PRAYER. THIS passage demonstrates the depths of the mercy of God. Immediately after having mouthed their unqualified allegiance to Yahweh, the Israelites proved their true colors with blatant idolatry. However, on account of Moses' intercession, Yahweh took his people back and renewed the covenant with them. This response highlights the importance of prayer in linking human needs with the divine store of mercy.

In so doing, this text offers some profound lessons on prayer. Those who pray with firm trust in God will be prepared for three possible outcomes of their prayer. (1) Sometimes prayer is the process whereby external circumstances are changed. I will never forget the motto my parents hung above the dining room table in the farmhouse in which I grew up: "Prayer changes things." It certainly did for Peter in Acts 12:1 – 17. In answer to the people's prayer Peter walked out of prison a free man. (2) Sometimes

---

17. On the irrevocability of Yahweh's covenant with Israel ratified at Sinai see Ex. 31:16 – 17; Lev. 24:8; Judg. 2:1; Ps. 111:2 – 9; Isa. 24:4 – 5; Jer. 31:35 – 37.

prayer is the process whereby the will of the person praying is changed and brought into conformity with God's will. God does not always answer prayer the way we want him to. Moses had recounted his own earlier bitter experience of this fact (Deut. 3:23–29).[18] (3) But sometimes prayer may be the process whereby the will of God is brought into conformity with the will of the person praying. The narrative of Exodus 32 reports that in response to Moses' intercession on behalf of his people, Yahweh "relented" and withdrew his threat to destroy them (32:14).

But lest we be seduced into thinking that prayer is simply a formula by which we manipulate God to get anything we want (like the genii in Aladdin's lamp), it is important to emphasize that in this case, Moses actually sacrificed his own self-interest in the interests of his people. Furthermore, in his forty-day wrestling bout with God, his single interest was the will and reputation of God, which he was convinced would be best served by sparing the people who had rebelled against him rather than starting over with Moses. When wicked people turn from their sin in full repentance (Jonah 3) or when a righteous intercessor pleads with God on behalf of sinners, God's fury is turned back and his grace is extended to undeserving people. This is one more exhilarating dimension of the gospel according to Moses.

Lessons on leadership. This text also offers contemporary readers several important lessons on leadership. We have already noted Moses' self-sacrificing performance and his close relationship with God. However, in observing the job description of the Levitical priests, leaders of God's people recognize important roles that they should play. But these roles should not be restricted to the professionals but extended to the entire community of faith. What the Levitical priests were to the congregation of Israel, the people of God are to the world. Peter's reference to the priesthood of all believers in 1 Peter 2:9 has less to do with laypersons having "the same right as ordained ministers to communicate with God, interpret Scripture, and minister in Christ's name,"[19] than with the community of faith as a whole representing the gracious God to a needy world. Like the Levites, Israel as a whole, and now as those who have been grafted into the olive tree (Rom. 11:17–23) and adopted as children of God (Rom. 8:15, 23), Christians are custodians of the new covenant (Rom. 9:4). To us has been granted the new "temple" service (Rom. 9:4), and we have been called to be agents of blessing to a world under the curse of sin (Gal. 3:14).

---

18. See also Amos 7:1–9.

19. The official statement of the Southern Baptist Convention, accessible at www.sbc.net/aboutus/pspriesthood.asp.

At the same time, this statement of the duties and privileges of the Levitical priests anticipates the ministry of our Savior Jesus Christ. Endowed with a priesthood superior even to that of Aaron the high priest, he is not only the custodian of the covenant, but the one who makes covenant relationship possible in the first place. When he instituted the Eucharist and blessed the wine he said, "This is my blood of the covenant, which is poured out for many for the forgiveness of sins" (Matt. 26:28). Apart from his sacrificial work, there is no forgiveness of sin. The central message of the book of Hebrews is that Jesus Christ is a perfect Intercessor, a perfect Priest, and a perfect Sacrifice. He stands before God the Father, performing the service of sacrifice on our behalf and pronouncing blessing in his name (Deut. 10:8; cf. Heb. 4:14–5:10).

Deuteronomy 10:12–11:1

And now, O Israel, what does the LORD your God ask of you but to fear the LORD your God, to walk in all his ways, to love him, to serve the LORD your God with all your heart and with all your soul, ¹³and to observe the LORD's commands and decrees that I am giving you today for your own good?

¹⁴To the LORD your God belong the heavens, even the highest heavens, the earth and everything in it. ¹⁵Yet the LORD set his affection on your forefathers and loved them, and he chose you, their descendants, above all the nations, as it is today. ¹⁶Circumcise your hearts, therefore, and do not be stiff-necked any longer. ¹⁷For the LORD your God is God of gods and Lord of lords, the great God, mighty and awesome, who shows no partiality and accepts no bribes. ¹⁸He defends the cause of the fatherless and the widow, and loves the alien, giving him food and clothing. ¹⁹And you are to love those who are aliens, for you yourselves were aliens in Egypt. ²⁰Fear the LORD your God and serve him. Hold fast to him and take your oaths in his name. ²¹He is your praise; he is your God, who performed for you those great and awesome wonders you saw with your own eyes. ²²Your forefathers who went down into Egypt were seventy in all, and now the LORD your God has made you as numerous as the stars in the sky.

^{11:1}Love the LORD your God and keep his requirements, his decrees, his laws and his commands always.

Original Meaning

THE ELEVATED STYLE OF Deuteronomy 10:12–11:1 suggests that Moses' second address is nearing a climax.[1] As in chapter 4, Moses signals the climactic moment with "and now" (*wᵉᶜattâ*). He is about to declare the moral and spiritual implications of the

---

1. The significance of this text in ancient Judaism is evident from its utilization in the phylacteries and mezuzot found at Qumran. For detailed analysis of these phylacteries, see Y. Yadin, *Tefillin from Qumran* (Jerusalem: Israel Exploration Society and the Shrine of the Book, 1969), 11–36.

privilege of covenant relationship that he has been preaching to this point of the second address.[2] Apart from this rhetorical marker, the boundaries of this unit are demarked by an opening question (10:12a) and the summary answer in 11:1. On the surface, the unit appears repetitious. However, Moses is a preacher, not an essayist. Based on the syntax, we observe that he addresses a single issue from three different but complementary angles. The relationships of the parts may be highlighted by juxtaposing more or less literal translations of each, as in the synopsis below:

The Issue	So what does Yahweh your God ask of you? (10:12a)		
	I (10:12b–15)	II (10:16–19)	III (10:20–22)
The Requirement	You shall fear Yahweh your God, walk in all his ways, love him, and serve Yahweh your God with all your heart and with all your soul, and keep the commands and statutes of Yahweh, which I am commanding you today for your good. (10:12b–13)	Circumcise therefore the foreskin of your heart, and be no longer stubborn. (10:16)	You shall fear Yahweh your God. You shall serve him and hold fast to him, and by his name you shall swear. (10:20)
The Basis of the Requirement — The Doxology	Behold, to Yahweh your God belong heaven and the heaven of heavens, the earth with all that is in it. (10:14)	For Yahweh your God is God of gods and Lord of lords, the great, the mighty, and the awesome God, who is not partial and takes no bribe. (10:17)	He is your praise. He is your God, who has done for you these great and terrifying things that your eyes have seen. (10:21)
The Basis of the Requirement — The Application	Yet Yahweh set his heart in love on your fathers and chose their offspring after them, you above all peoples, as you are this day. (10:15)	He executes justice for the fatherless and the widow, and loves the sojourner, giving him food and clothing. Love the sojourner, therefore, for you were sojourners in the land of Egypt. (10:18–19)	Your fathers went down to Egypt seventy persons, and now Yahweh your God has made you as numerous as the stars of heaven. (10:22)
The Conclusion	You shall therefore love Yahweh your God and keep his charge, his statutes, his rules, and his commands always. (11:1)		

2. Cf. E. Talstra, "Deuteronomy 9 and 10: Synchronic and Diachronic Observations," *Oudtestamentsche Studien* 34 (1995): 196–200.

The issue raised (v. 12a). Moses begins his reflection on the practical implications of the covenant with a question: In view of the grace that Yahweh has lavished on his people, what does he require of Israel? And with this question we realize that we are about to encounter the heart of the covenant — in Jesus' words, "the more important matters of the law" (Matt. 23:23). Moses answers his own question from three different angles. These statements consist of doxologies of praise to Yahweh, followed by reflection on the implications of the doxological statement for Israel. The result is a glorious theology of covenant relationship built on three pillars of cosmic theology and grounded on three marvelous acts of grace.

Moses' first answer (vv. 12b–15). Moses' first response consists of five infinitive phrases, all of which been heard before and will be heard repeatedly hereafter: (1) fear Yahweh your God; (2) walk in all his ways; (3) love Yahweh your God; (4) serve Yahweh your God with your whole being; (5) keep the commands and decrees of Yahweh. This combination captures in a nutshell the message of this book, especially as it relates to the human response to divine grace. The common denominator is the importance of allegiance to Yahweh as the God of the covenant.[3] The list consists of responses that involve fundamental dispositions (fear, love) and active expressions (walk, serve, keep). Attitude and action are interrelated. Fear is primary and love (covenant commitment) is at the core. Without these, the actions are legalistic efforts to gain the favor of God. Without the actions, fear and love are useless and dead.[4]

Moses signals the shift to the grounds for these demands in verse 14 with the focus particle "look" (*bēn*, not represented in NIV), which introduces us to Yahweh's sovereignty over the universe as the ground for fidelity. Moses highlights the comprehensiveness of Yahweh's rule by means of *merismus* (referring to polar opposites — heavens and earth) and superlative expressions.[5] With "the highest heavens" Moses declares that whatever cosmic entity one may imagine to exist out there or however far one may travel in space, it all belongs to Yahweh, the God of

---

3. So also Craigie, *Deuteronomy*, 204; Weinfeld, *DDS*, 83–84.

4. "Faith and love" express covenant commitment. Together they represent the Mosaic counterpart to the New Testament *pistis*. James has caught the spirit of this text precisely in James 2:14–26; on which, see R. Stein, "'Saved by Faith [Alone]' in Paul Versus 'Not Saved by Faith Alone' in James," *SBJT* 4/3 (2000): 4–19.

5. On the "heaven of heavens" to express the highest heaven superlative degree, cf. 1 Kings 8:27 = 2 Chron. 6:18; 2 Chron. 2:6[5]; Neh. 9:6; Pss. 68:33[34]; 148:4. Compare expressions like "holy of holies," "song of songs," and "king of kings," as well as "God of gods" and "Lord of lords" in verse 17.

Israel.[6] But Yahweh is also sovereign over the earth and all it contains. Under this expression, Moses includes the earth's occupants, human beings, as well as animals large and small. Yahweh owns all.

While Yahweh's ownership of the universe might have inspired worship in and of itself in another context, verse 15 suggests that Moses has presented this doxology to set the stage for something even more dramatic and relevant to Israel's situation: Yahweh's election of this people. Moses hereby emphasizes that although Yahweh owns everything in the universe, out of all the peoples he chose Israel's ancestors to be the object of his affection and love and to be his covenant people (cf. 7:6–8). In light of this gracious election, the call for total devotion in verses 12b–13 is utterly reasonable.

Moses' second answer to the question (vv. 16–19). While Moses' first answer called for external acts of covenant commitment, his second focuses on the internal disposition, employing a strange metaphor, the circumcision of the heart/mind. This figure of speech may have been prompted by the reference to Yahweh's election of the ancestors, since physical circumcision represented the seal by which Israelite men declared their acceptance of covenant relationship with God (Gen. 17). Since outsiders would not see the sign, the only evidence of membership within the covenant community they would see would be the life the person lived.[7] It seems odd that Moses would have introduced this metaphor here, since apparently none of the men standing before Moses had been circumcised (Josh. 5:4–7). The picture is ironic: their fathers, who came out of Egypt, apparently had all been circumcised externally (Ex. 12:43–51), but by their faithlessness they proved it was merely an external act. The people standing before Moses now were physically uncircumcised, yet by clinging to Yahweh in the face of the apostasy at Baal Peor (Deut. 4:4), they apparently proved themselves to be circumcised of heart.

Moses' charge in verse 16 consists of two commands: circumcise the foreskin of your hearts (*lēb*, which also means "mind"), and stop stiffening your necks. He does not explain at this point what he means

---

6. Jewish tradition speaks of as many as seven heavens, and even in the New Testament we read of multiple heavens generally (Eph. 4:10; Heb. 4:14) and the third heaven specifically (2 Cor. 12:2). On these traditions, see J. E. Wright, *The Early History of Heaven* (New York/Oxford: Oxford Univ. Press, 2000), 145–50.

7. Unlike the Shema, which was to be written on one's hands, worn on the forehead, and inscribed on houses and gates. On circumcision in Israel, see J. S. DeRouchie, "Circumcision in the Hebrew Bible and Targums: Theology, Rhetoric, and the Handling of Metaphor," *BBR* 14 (2004): 161–74; J. Goldingay, "The Significance of Circumcision," *JSOT* 88 (2000): 3–18.

by "circumcising the heart," except to contrast it with "stiffening the neck" in the second command. The latter expression links this statement to 9:6 and 13, where Moses had denounced his people as persistently "stiff-necked." Mixing metaphors involving two body parts, Moses suggests that a circumcised heart/mind represents a disposition that is soft and sensitive toward Yahweh and has ceased resisting his will (cf. 30:6 – 8). The earliest reference to this metaphor occurs in Leviticus 26:41. Looking beyond Israel's judgment for persistent infidelity, there Yahweh spoke of the people's uncircumcised heart being humbled so they would make amends for their iniquity, treachery, and hostility toward Yahweh.

In verses 17 – 18 Moses grounds the demand for spiritual circumcision on Yahweh's supremacy over all powers. He highlights the scope of Yahweh's authority by ascribing to him superlative epithets, "God of gods" and "Lord of lords." The first expression uses "gods" either as pagan deities that do not actually exist but are alive in people's imagination, or lesser ranked supernatural beings that actually exist and are either at home in the heavens, like the "sons of God" in Job 1:6 (see NIV text note), or are opposed to Yahweh, like the "sons of God" in Genesis 6:1 – 4. Whether it refers to pagan deities or supernatural beings, Moses does not hereby recognize other gods alongside or equal in status to Yahweh (cf. 4:35, 39); his statement is rhetorical. If "God of gods" declares Yahweh's supremacy over all heavenly powers, then "Lord of lords" speaks to his supremacy over earthly rulers.[8]

Moses also highlights the supremacy of Yahweh with the title "the great, mighty, and awesome El."[9] As we noted on 7:9, in Canaanite mythology El was the head of the pantheon — the husband of Asherah and father of seventy gods. By attaching the article to El Moses declares Yahweh to be *the* only El worthy of the name. He reinforces the notion of Yahweh's supremacy with a triad of descriptors: he is "great," "mighty," and "awesome."[10] These expressions seem intended as a deliberate polemic against the Canaanite El, whom the thirteenth-century BC texts from Ugarit depict as an otiose and senile old deity.

---

8. "Lord of lords" appears elsewhere in the Old Testament only in Ps. 136:3, but occurs in the New Testament in 1 Tim. 6:15; Rev. 17:14; 19:16. Elsewhere supreme earthly rulers are referred to as "king of kings" (Ezra 7:12; Ezek. 26:7; Dan. 2:37; cf. 1 Tim. 6:15; Rev. 17:14; 19:16).

9. NIV translates "the great God, mighty and awesome."

10. On this term, see comments on 7:21.

Moses combines these transcendent attributes of Yahweh with four verbal declarations of his immanence (cf. Ex. 33:18−34:8). He begins with a double-barreled, thesis-type statement: Yahweh "shows no partiality and accepts no bribes" (Deut. 10:17). The first involves the idiom "to lift the face," which is court language derived from the common though unjust practice of lifting the plaintiff's face so the king or judge may identify him before he declares his judgment. Thus the adjudicator perverts justice by letting the identity and status of the person—whether poor or the rich (cf. Lev. 19:15)—affect the decision.

But Yahweh, who is supreme in his power, is also supreme in his justice.[11] As if all who come before him have bags over their heads, he judges not by what he sees nor hears but by the objective merits of the case. The second statement reinforces this interpretation: Yahweh cannot be corrupted by bribes. The frequency with which the Old Testament speaks about bribery attests to its prevalence in ancient Near Eastern life.[12] However, Yahweh's favor cannot be bought.

Having declared in principle Yahweh's absolute justice, in verse 18 Moses explains how this is implemented to the advantage of the vulnerable in society: the fatherless, the widow, and the alien. All three classes of people are easily preyed upon and subject to abuse because they lack a father or husband or older brother to protect and care for them.[13] The picture is remarkable. The God of gods and Lord of rulers executes justice on behalf of the little people.

The term *gēr* ("alien") refers to an outsider who has chosen to leave the security of family and homeland to try to make a living in a foreign context. Remarkably Yahweh, the God of Israel, is not so ethnocentric as to be blinded to the plight of the non-Israelites in their midst. Going beyond the privileges granted to resident aliens in Exodus 12:48, Moses declares that Yahweh extends to the alien the same covenant commitment ("love") he had demonstrated toward their ancestors (4:37; 10:15). He does so not with mere words but in action, providing them with "food and clothing."

---

11. He embodies perfectly what he demands of human judges (cf. 1:16−17; 16:19; Isa. 11:3).

12. Ex. 23:8; Deut. 10:17; 16:19; 27:25; 1 Sam. 8:3; 1 Kings 15:19; 2 Kings 16:8; Job 6:22; Pss. 15:5; 26:10; Prov. 6:35; 17:8, 23; 21:14; Isa. 1:23; 5:23; 33:15; 45:13; 47:11; Ezek. 16:33; 22:12; Mic. 3:11; 7:3.

13. For a discussion of these and other terms for the underprivileged in the Old Testament, see M. R. Jacobs, "Toward an Old Testament Theology of Concern for the Underprivileged," in *Reading the Hebrew Bible for a New Millennium: Form, Concept, and Theological Perspective,* vol. 1, *Theological and Hermeneutical Studies* (ed. D. H. Ellens et al.; Studies in Antiquity & Christianity; Harrisburg, PA: Trinity International, 2000), 211−14.

Moses had used these same words in 8:3−4 in reference to Israel, suggesting that he also thinks of this people as an alien nation.

Moses' reference to the alien in verse 18 triggers a practical exhortation in verse 19. Because the Israelites know what it is like to be an alien, they should be especially sensitive to the plight of aliens in their midst (cf. Lev 19:33−34). As in his modification of the Sabbath command of the Decalogue (Deut. 5:14−15), Moses' appeal for compassion by the Israelites is based on a memory of their own experience as aliens (cf. Ex. 22:21[20]; 23:9).[14]

Moses' third answer to the question (vv. 20−22). Moses' third answer to the demand in verse 12 consists of four statements. In each case the syntax highlights the call for unqualified devotion to Yahweh:

> [Only] Yahweh your God you shall fear.
> [Only] him you shall serve.
> [Only] to him you shall hold fast.
> [Only] by his name you shall swear (pers. trans.; cf. 6:13).

The elements in the first pair are borrowed from verses 12b−13, while the last pair involves expressions used elsewhere in Deuteronomy.[15] If verses 12b−13 expand on the Supreme Command (6:5), then verse 20 clarifies the Shema proper (6:4).

Moses begins his presentation of the grounds for this demand with a third doxology: "He is your praise; he is your God" (v. 21). With the second clause he declares in second person what the Shema confesses in first person. The first clause, "He is your praise,"[16] could mean either that Yahweh is the object of Israel's praise or that when other nations look at Israel, they will praise Yahweh (cf. 33:26−29). As in 26:19, Moses' ambiguity here is probably intentional, adding depth and perspective to his picture of divine grace.

In verse 21b Moses explains how Yahweh has manifested himself in Israel through "great and awesome" demonstrations of power. Although elsewhere such expressions refer to the events of the exodus (4:32−40) or the theophany at Horeb (4:9−14; 5:22−27), here Moses recalls Yahweh's multiplication of Israel's population in Egypt: Israel went down to Egypt a small clan consisting of seventy persons,[17] but Jacob's descendants stand

---

14. See also Deut. 1:16; 14:29; 16:11−14; 24:14−15, 17−18, 19−22; 26:11−13; 27:19.

15. On holding fast to Yahweh see 4:4; 11:22; 13:4[5]; 30:20.

16. "He is your praise" is paralleled elsewhere only in Ps. 109:1 and Jer. 17:14.

17. The number derives from Gen. 46:26 and Ex. 1:5. In Acts 7:14 Stephen follows the LXX in reading seventy-five rather than seventy.

before Moses now as a nation innumerable "as the stars in the sky." This simile (cf. 1:10) is drawn from the patriarchal promises. Since the registration of Israel's troops in Numbers 1–2 and 26 demonstrates that the population could still be counted, this statement is obviously hyperbolic. Nevertheless, what has happened to Jacob's descendants can only be attributed to a marvelous work of Yahweh.

The issue concluded (11:1). Moses concludes this section by synthesizing the three answers he has given to the question raised in 10:12. He reduces the divine requirement to two simple statements, the first of which obviously abbreviates the Supreme Command (6:5), and the second reiterates the call for obedience to the revealed will of God in its entirety. However, Moses prefaces the traditional triad of familiar expressions ("his decrees, his laws and his commands") with a new word: *mišmartô* ("his requirements"). Although in contexts involving tabernacle and temple personnel, the phrase *šāmar mišmeret* denotes "to perform guard duty,"[18] here *mišmeret* refers to obligations and injunctions in a general sense.[19] Since Moses tends to work with triplets and triads, the addition of the fourth term here completes the points of a compass. What does Yahweh require of his covenant people: obedience, no matter from which direction one approaches the issue.

MORAL OBEDIENCE. WITH THE opening question Moses raises a subject that surfaces frequently in the Old Testament. His answers should put to rest a common misperception that under the old covenant religion was an external matter focused on sacrifices and other forms of external cultic service. Moses' call to fear and love Yahweh, to walk in his ways and serve him, and to keep all his commands places the center of gravity on faith and covenant commitment to Yahweh. Remarkably, he omits any reference to sacrifices or other forms of worship. In placing greater stock in moral obedience than in cultic performance, Moses prepared the way for the prophets.

---

18. Lev. 8:35; 22:9; Num. 1:53; 3:7, 28, 32, 38; 8:26; 9:19, 23; 18:4; 31:30, 47; Ezek. 40:45–46; 44:8, 14, 15, 16. Cf. Jacob Milgrom, *Leviticus*, 3 vols. (AB; New York: Doubleday, 1999–2001), 1:7; idem, "The Levites: Guards of the Tabernacle," in *Numbers* (JPS Torah Commentary; Philadelphia: JPS, 1990), 341–42; Block, *Ezekiel Chapters 25–48*, 537–38; John R. Spencer, "The Tasks of the Levites: *Smr* and *Ṣbʾ*," *ZAW* 96 (1984): 267–71.

19. As in Gen. 26:5; Josh. 22:3; 1 Kings 2:3; Mal. 3:14. In Lev. 18:30 and 22:9 the expression involves specific sexual and purity/impurity commands.

- Like Moses, Samuel declared, "To obey is better than sacrifice, and to heed is better than the fat of rams" (1 Sam. 15:22).
- Like Moses, Amos taught that the practice of "justice" and "righteousness" took precedence over the noise of festivals and offerings (Amos 5:21 – 25).
- Like Moses, Hosea affirmed that Yahweh found greater delight in "mercy" and personal relationship with him than in sacrifices of every sort (Hos. 6:6).
- Like Moses, in Micah's mind true piety is demonstrated not in extravagant sacrifices but in doing justice, loving kindness, and walking humbly with God (Mic. 6:6 – 8).[20]
- Like Moses, Isaiah announced that if ethical righteousness, demonstrated especially on behalf of the marginalized, was lacking, no liturgical celebrations would impress Yahweh (Isa. 1:10 – 17).
- Like Moses, Jeremiah believed that acceptance with God was dependent on ethical behavior rather than attendance at the house of God (Jer. 7:1 – 15).

This perspective is also found in the Psalms, which emphasize that acceptable worship is preconditioned by lives that demonstrate covenant commitment to Yahweh and to one's neighbor (Pss. 15; 24).

This paradigm carries through to the New Testament. Jesus castigates Jewish religious leaders for tithing mint and dill and cummin but neglecting weightier matters of Torah (i.e., love for God and one's neighbor; Matt. 23:23; Luke 11:42). Sounding like Moses, James declares that "religion that God our Father accepts as pure and faultless is this: to look after orphans and widows in their distress and to keep oneself from being polluted by the world" (Jas. 1:27). The same is true of Paul, who calls believers to offer themselves as "living sacrifices" (Rom. 12:1) and then explains what this means (12:2 – 15:13).

Imitation of God. In Deuteronomy 10:12 – 11:1 Moses not only points to the essence of grace-filled religion, but he also provides the basis for the same: knowledge of the absolute sovereignty of God over all and of his particular favor to Israel, which should inspire their own compassion toward the marginalized. Moses' association of the notion of the supremacy of Yahweh over all with his defense of the weak and downtrodden is picked up and celebrated with great enthusiasm in Psalm 146:5 – 10:

---

20. See esp. Micah's question "And what does the Lord require of you?" (Mic. 6:8).

Blessed is he whose help is the God of Jacob,
   whose hope is in the LORD his God,
the Maker of heaven and earth,
   the sea, and everything in them —
   the LORD, who remains faithful forever.
He upholds the cause of the oppressed
   and gives food to the hungry.
The LORD sets prisoners free,
   the LORD gives sight to the blind,
the LORD lifts up those who are bowed down,
   the LORD loves the righteous.
The LORD watches over the alien
   and sustains the fatherless and the widow,
   but he frustrates the ways of the wicked.
The LORD reigns forever,
   your God, O Zion, for all generations.
Praise the LORD.

The principle of *imitatio dei*, the imitation of God, represents one of the fundamental pillars of biblical ethics — Old and New Testaments. If elsewhere Yahweh calls on people to be holy as he, Yahweh their God, is holy (Lev. 11:44; 19:2; 20:7; 1 Pet. 1:16), here Moses calls on Israel to imitate Yahweh's compassion. Just as he is distinguished for his compassion to the widow, the fatherless, and the alien, so should his people be. Jesus applied this principle to his disciples when he called on them to be covenantally committed to love one another, just as he is covenantally committed to them (John 13:34; 15:12). And the apostle builds on this notion when he challenges his readers to love one another, not only because Christ has commanded us to do so (1 John 3:23), but because God is covenantally committed to us (1 John 4:11), and the love believers demonstrate is the proof that God indwells them (1 John 4:7, 12).

"WHAT DOES THE LORD ask of us?" In contemporary wars over worship style and worship idioms, leaders in our churches are often driven by questions like this: "What do the unchurched or marginal church members ask for?" Thus, in our efforts to fill our sanctuaries and appear successful, worship is planned to satisfy the tastes and demands of the greatest number of potential clients. A text like this reminds us how misplaced such issues may be. The principal question God's people should always be asking is: "What does the Lord ask of us?" Like Israel, we often forget that unless we are walking in the ways of the Lord during the rest of the week, nothing we do in corporate liturgical worship on Sunday or any other day will impress God. This text reminds us again that walking in the ways of the Lord, accepting our vassal status before him, and obeying his commands are the fruit he seeks as evidence of reverent awe and covenant commitment (love) to him. Mouthing words of devotion ring hollow without the life of devotion.

Furthermore, it is tempting for evangelicals to think that creedal statements of faith provide sure tests of devotion to Christ. However, this text reminds us again that true faith is not demonstrated so much in the defense of truth as in the life of truth. God's people refuse to bear his name in vain, which is to say, to claim they belong to him but to act as if they belong to some other god or gods. As Paul tells the Galatians, true faith will be demonstrated by a transformed life, refusing to live according to fleshly "Canaanite" values and instead yielding the fruit of the Spirit in abundance (Gal. 5:13–26).

Sadly, recent studies have shown that attitudes of professing Christians and non-Christians toward critical ethical issues like divorce, materialism, the poor, sexual immorality, and racism are scarcely distinguishable.[21] The ethics of many who call themselves "Christian" look more like the ethics of the world than the ethics of Christ. The recently drafted "Evangelical Manifesto" represents a step in the right direction.[22]

Specifically, Moses reminds believers of every age that true faith is demonstrated especially in compassion for the socially and economically marginalized. Sadly, in North American politics evangelical Christians are associated with heartless right wing politics, which runs roughshod over the backs of the marginalized. To cite just one example, the disposition of evangelicals toward undocumented aliens in this country differs little from that of non-Christians, and in some instances the rhetoric is less compassionate. Our memories are short. Many of us are only two or three generations removed from immigrant forebears who sought refuge in North America.

More fundamentally, apart from God's grace we are all aliens, slaves of sin and citizens of the kingdom of darkness. However, in his mercy

---

21. For discussion of the evidence see R. J. Sider, *The Scandal of the Evangelical Conscience* (Grand Rapids: Baker, 2004), and an excerpted chapter, "The Scandal of the Evangelical Conscience: Why Don't Christians Live What They Preach?" in *Books and Culture: A Christian Review* 11/1 (January/February, 2005): 8.

22. The document is available at www.anevangelicalmanifesto.com.

the Lord has rescued us and made us his children and citizens of heaven. If Christians would demonstrate toward undocumented aliens and other immigrants in our communities the compassion they have freely received in Christ, outside observers would be drawn to him and glorify our Father in heaven (Matt. 5:16). For us the ethic of compassion and commitment to the well-being of the marginalized must take precedence over legality. If we heed this call, immigrants will know when they encounter us that they have crossed the border into a community of distinctively gracious people.[23]

---

23. For two perspectives on the issue see M. D. Carroll R., *Christians at the Border: Immigrations, the Church, and the Bible* (Grand Rapids: Baker, 2008), and J. K. Hoffmeier, *The Immigration Crisis: Immigrants, Aliens, and the Bible* (Wheaton, IL: Crossway, 2009).

Deuteronomy 11:2–28

Remember today that your children were not the ones who saw and experienced the discipline of the LORD your God: his majesty, his mighty hand, his outstretched arm; ³the signs he performed and the things he did in the heart of Egypt, both to Pharaoh king of Egypt and to his whole country; ⁴what he did to the Egyptian army, to its horses and chariots, how he overwhelmed them with the waters of the Red Sea as they were pursuing you, and how the LORD brought lasting ruin on them. ⁵It was not your children who saw what he did for you in the desert until you arrived at this place, ⁶and what he did to Dathan and Abiram, sons of Eliab the Reubenite, when the earth opened its mouth right in the middle of all Israel and swallowed them up with their households, their tents and every living thing that belonged to them. ⁷But it was your own eyes that saw all these great things the LORD has done.

⁸Observe therefore all the commands I am giving you today, so that you may have the strength to go in and take over the land that you are crossing the Jordan to possess, ⁹and so that you may live long in the land that the LORD swore to your forefathers to give to them and their descendants, a land flowing with milk and honey. ¹⁰The land you are entering to take over is not like the land of Egypt, from which you have come, where you planted your seed and irrigated it by foot as in a vegetable garden. ¹¹But the land you are crossing the Jordan to take possession of is a land of mountains and valleys that drinks rain from heaven. ¹²It is a land the LORD your God cares for; the eyes of the LORD your God are continually on it from the beginning of the year to its end.

¹³So if you faithfully obey the commands I am giving you today—to love the LORD your God and to serve him with all your heart and with all your soul—¹⁴then I will send rain on your land in its season, both autumn and spring rains, so that you may gather in your grain, new wine and oil. ¹⁵I will provide grass in the fields for your cattle, and you will eat and be satisfied.

¹⁶Be careful, or you will be enticed to turn away and worship other gods and bow down to them. ¹⁷Then the LORD's

anger will burn against you, and he will shut the heavens so that it will not rain and the ground will yield no produce, and you will soon perish from the good land the LORD is giving you. ¹⁸Fix these words of mine in your hearts and minds; tie them as symbols on your hands and bind them on your foreheads. ¹⁹Teach them to your children, talking about them when you sit at home and when you walk along the road, when you lie down and when you get up. ²⁰Write them on the doorframes of your houses and on your gates, ²¹so that your days and the days of your children may be many in the land that the LORD swore to give your forefathers, as many as the days that the heavens are above the earth.

²²If you carefully observe all these commands I am giving you to follow—to love the LORD your God, to walk in all his ways and to hold fast to him—²³then the LORD will drive out all these nations before you, and you will dispossess nations larger and stronger than you. ²⁴Every place where you set your foot will be yours: Your territory will extend from the desert to Lebanon, and from the Euphrates River to the western sea. ²⁵No man will be able to stand against you. The LORD your God, as he promised you, will put the terror and fear of you on the whole land, wherever you go.

²⁶See, I am setting before you today a blessing and a curse—²⁷the blessing if you obey the commands of the LORD your God that I am giving you today; ²⁸the curse if you disobey the commands of the LORD your God and turn from the way that I command you today by following other gods, which you have not known.

Original Meaning

DEUTERONOMY 11:2−28 is a complex package, characterized by frequent repetitions, interruptive appositions, and parenthetical comments. This is not the stuff of legislation but the style of a preacher, who uses any means possible to burn his message deep into the hearts of his congregation. A structural break occurs between verses 7 and 8 as Moses moves from recollection to exhortation. Thus this part of the second address ends like the first (4:32−40). Moses moves from history to theology to a call for obedience. He ends this lesson with an exhortation in 11:8a; this challenge is expounded in much greater detail in verses 8b−28.

A Lesson from History:
Reviewing the Mighty Acts of God (11: 2–7)

VERSES 2–7 comprise one complex sentence in Hebrew.[1] Referring twice in verses 3 and 7 to the deeds Yahweh has performed, Moses' primary concern is to review again his mighty acts on Israel's behalf. Moses frames this recitation with awkward references to his audience (vv. 2a, 7), keenly aware that the addressees are not equally familiar with what he will describe. This review of past events provides vital background for verses 8–28, especially verses 26–28, in which Moses calls for decision by the people standing before him.

Apart from the interruption in verse 2, Moses' presentation is deliberate. He opens with a thesis statement: "Know today the lesson of Yahweh your God" (pers. trans.). Although NIV translates the key word *mûsâr* as "discipline,"[2] we should follow the lead of the Septuagint and render the term "lesson, education." The "lesson of Yahweh your God" refers either to the lesson that Yahweh taught them (as in 8:5) or the lesson about Yahweh. The subject of study is Yahweh's actions, but through those mighty acts the Israelites learn about him.

The actual lesson divides into two parts: three simple pointers to Yahweh's person (v. 2b), and a series of manifestations of Yahweh's power (vv. 3–6). The former are all familiar from Moses' previous preaching: Yahweh's "majesty,"[3] his "mighty hand,"[4] and his "outstretched arm."[5] Moses frames the latter with "his [attesting] signs" and "the things he did" in verse 3a, and "these great things the LORD has done" in verse 7. The key phrase within these frames is obviously "what he did to X" (vv. 3b, 4, 5, 6), which signals four dimensions of Yahweh's great deeds. Each represents an emphatic declaration that Yahweh is not only a God who acts in history, but also a God who acts on behalf of his people and against those who stand in the way of his agenda.

In the crosshairs of Yahweh's awesome power were, first, Pharaoh and all his land (cf. 6:22),[6] and second, his military forces,[7] including his horses

---

1. The problems posed by this text are reflected in the variations in the renderings in translations. For the major possibilities see Nelson, *Deuteronomy*, 131–32.

2. The word is often used this way, but since we generally associate discipline with punishment for misbehavior (this could apply to the case of Dathan and Abiram, v. 6), this translation is misleading.

3. See also 3:24; 5:21; 9:26; 32:3.

4. Cf. 3:24; 4:34; 5:15; 6:21; 7:8, 19; 9:26; 26:8.

5. Cf. 4:34; 5:15; 7:19; 9:29; 26:8.

6. For additional references to "signs" performed in Egypt against Pharaoh and his land, see 4:34; 7:19; 29:3[2]. As in our text, in each case Moses highlights the fact that Israelites were eyewitnesses to these signs.

7. The use of *ḥayil* for "army" links this comment to Ex. 15:4. The Song of the Sea (Ex. 15:1–12) celebrates Yahweh's triumph over the Egyptians in most exuberant terms.

and chariots (see Ex. 14). Moses casts Yahweh in the role of a puppeteer, who "rolled back the waters of the Red Sea over their faces" (pers. trans.). With the final note, "how the LORD brought lasting ruin on them," (NJPS "once for all"), Moses acknowledges the results of a momentous event: Israel is standing on the threshold of the Promised Land.

Yahweh's third target catches the reader by surprise. Contra NIV, the syntax of verse 5 demands this statement be rendered, "what he did to you in the desert until you came to this place" (cf. ESV). Moses has in mind Yahweh's punitive acts against the Israelites themselves for their faithlessness and rebellion (cf. Ex. 32; Num. 25; Deut. 1:22 – 45).

Moses concludes with a fourth target, Dathan and Abiram (v. 6). He recalls how the earth swallowed them up as ringleaders in a rebellion, along with their entire households, including their tents (cf. Num. 16:32).[8]

Moses' ends his recitation of Yahweh's powerful acts with a reminder that the people in his audience were eyewitnesses to the events he has just described (v. 7).[9] The positive experiences of Yahweh's salvation at the exodus, his provision of manna in the desert, and his speech from the midst of the fire on Mount Horeb represent only one side of the Israelites' experience of Yahweh's power; his power to destroy is equally awesome. Awareness of how fearful it is to fall into the hands of the living God (Heb. 10:31) should provide lasting motivation for uncompromising covenant fidelity and a constant reminder that the benefits of covenant relationship with Yahweh should never be taken for granted (vv. 8 – 25).

A Lesson from Economic Geography: Recognizing the Gracious Provision of God (11:8 – 28)

THIS LARGE SECTION BREAKS down into four segments. The first three begin with a challenge to covenantal obedience and are arranged thematically in an ABA order (vv. 8 – 12, 13 – 21, 22 – 25); the last segment (vv. 26 – 28) is Moses' concluding appeal. The clear echoes of 4:40 in verse 8 suggest that 11:8 – 25 presents another case of "resumptive exposition," as Moses picks up the notions of the earlier text and develops them more fully in this new context. In so doing Moses now offers the most comprehensive statement on his theology of land. But he does not treat the land in isolation; it represents the third member of the triad involved in Yahweh's covenant relationship with Israel: deity — people — land.

---

8. The phrase "every living thing" occurs elsewhere only in Gen. 7:4, 23, where it refers to human beings and animals that perished in the great flood. See also Josh. 7:15, 25 – 26.

9. This is a recurring motif in the book. Cf. 1:30; 3:21; 4:3, 9, 34; 7:19; 9:17; 10:21; 29:2[1].

Part I: The land as gift (vv. 8 – 12). The land represents the climactic element in a series of gifts Yahweh promised to the ancestors.[10] Moses opens his discussion of the place of the land in Israel's relationship with Yahweh with a charge to keep the Supreme Command in all its dimensions.[11] By following this command with two purpose clauses, he presents it as a virtual condition for the fulfillment of the promise that follows (vv. 8b – 9).[12] The first clause lists three objectives: "that you may be strong, that you may enter, and that you may possess the land" (pers. trans.). While the second and third are formulaic, the first is new.[13] The second clause introduces a fourth objective, which we have also seen repeatedly, "that you may live long in the land." Each purpose statement ends with a comment on the land. The first (v. 8b) looks forward to Israel's crossing of the Jordan, while the second (v. 9a) looks back to Yahweh's ancient covenantal promise to the ancestors (Gen. 17:8; Ex. 3:6 – 8; 6:8). In this moment past and future meet.

Moses' excitement at Israel's prospect of entering the land (vv. 9b – 12) is evident in his excursus extolling its virtues even more effusively than in 6:10 – 11 and 8:7 – 9. Unlike Egypt, this land yields its bounty spontaneously. Moses develops this point with three basic statements. (1) This land flows naturally with milk and honey (v. 9b).[14] (2) This land contrasts sharply with Egypt, from where the Israelites have come (v. 10) and where food production depended entirely on human effort.[15] (3) This is a land of hills and valleys that drink water from the rains of heaven (v. 11). Clarifying his comment in 8:7, Moses invites his hearers to imagine ever-flowing streams of fresh water coursing down the hills and watering the landscape, in contrast to the stagnant and brackish waters of the Nile Delta.

---

10. On Deuteronomy's vision of the land as gift, focusing on this text, see W. Brueggemann, *The Land* (OBT; London: SPCK, 1978), 47 – 53.

11. NIV's rendering "all the commands" obscures the regular use of the singular *kol hammiṣwâ* as shorthand for the Supreme Command. See 5:31; 6:25; 8:1; 11:8, 22; 15:5; 19:9; 26:13; 27:1; 31:5. Cf. 6:1; 7:11; 17:20; 30:11.

12. Equivalent to the conditional clauses in vv. 13 and 22.

13. Cf. the reuse of this combination of expressions in 31:6 and 7 (also Josh. 1:6).

14. For discussion of this idiom, see comments on 6:3 (also cf. 26:9, 15; 27:3).

15. Some interpret watering plants "by foot" as carrying water in buckets to where it is needed, or using the feet to operate water wheel devices (Arabic *shaduf*) to pump water from the Nile or ditches into canals and holding areas from which it could be distributed to the plants (Merrill, *Deuteronomy*, 208; Weinfeld, *Deuteronomy 1 – 11*, 445). However, since water wheels were generally operated by hand rather than by foot, this phrase probably alludes to some aspect of the work involved in operating Egypt's elaborate irrigation system. So also Tigay, *Deuteronomy*, 112; Craigie, *Deuteronomy*, 210; L. Eslinger, "Watering Egypt (Deuteronomy XI 10 – 11)," *VT* 37 (1987): 85 – 90.

As in 6:10−11 and 8:7−9, Moses' comments are utopian. Although Egypt receives virtually no rainfall, because of the annual inundation of the Nile Delta with silt and the constant flow of the river, any farmer would have preferred the gardens of Egypt to the rocky and hilly terrain of Palestine. This is obviously not the objective report of a government surveyor, but the dream of a man who can only see the land from a distance but cannot enter it. With this speech Moses tries to excite his people about the prospects awaiting them on the other side of the Jordan. Moses envisions the Promised Land through the eyes of faith. The land is good, not only because it represents the fulfillment of the promises to the ancestors, but also because it drives its inhabitants to depend on God. To the eyes of faith this is paradise indeed.

In verse 12 Moses adds a fourth reason why the land is special: it is the object of Yahweh's special attention and care (v. 12). He "cares for" (*dāraš*) it continuously, and his eyes are fixed on it from one year to the next. This statement expresses Yahweh's disposition toward the land more dramatically and tenderly than any other in Scripture. Here the verb *dāraš* does not bear its common meaning, "to seek" something that is lost (22:2), but a nuance of election (cf. Lev. 25:23). Just as Yahweh has chosen Israel out of all the peoples of the earth, so he has chosen the land of Canaan (Palestine) from all the territories of the earth.

But there is more. Since the participle of *dāraš* (lit., "seeking") and the adverb "continually" imply continuity, "to seek the land" is an elliptical expression for "to seek the peace and well-being of the land" (cf. 23:6[7]).[16] The added reference to "the eyes of the LORD" on the land year round speaks of focused attention and constant providential care (cf. vv. 13−15).

In the added phrase "from the beginning of the year to its end," we recognize a subtle polemic against the fertility cults of the ancient Near East. The mythologies of Mesopotamia and Ugarit perceived the seasonal rhythm of rain and drought as reflections of the fertility deity's (Tammuz in Mesopotamia, Baal in Canaan) descent to the netherworld at the beginning of the dry season and his return at the beginning of the rainy season. Fertility gods were unable to attend to their land or their devotees while they were away, leaving the peoples' fate in the hands of gods of drought and death (Nergal in Mesopotamia, Mot in Canaan). Unlike Baal (cf. 1 Kings 18:27), Yahweh is never distracted; he never leaves, and he never sleeps (cf. Ps. 121). Through summer and winter, seedtime and harvest, his eyes are on the land (Lev. 26:3−6, 9).

---

16. For similar use of the verb, see Job 3:4; Ps. 142:4[5]; Isa. 62:12; Jer. 30:14, 17.

Part II: The land as test (vv. 13−21). Following an approach that is common in wisdom literature[17] and anticipating what he will declare explicitly in verses 26−28 (cf. 30:1, 19), Moses presents life in the land as a test, with significant consequences (cf. 6:10−15; 8:6−20). The land symbolizes a choice between two ways: the way of blessing, prosperity, and life, or the way of the curse, adversity, and death. Moses presents the options before the people in two frames almost identical in length[18] and remarkably parallel in content and form, as the following synopsis of relatively literal translations shows:

The Test of Faith

	The Passing Grade Deuteronomy 11:13−15	The Failing Grade Deuteronomy 11:16−17
The human response to the test	So if you faithfully obey the commands I am giving you today—to love the LORD your God and to serve him with all your heart and with all your soul,	Be careful, or you will be enticed to turn away and worship other gods and bow down to them.
The divine evaluation of the test	then I will send rain on your land in its season, both autumn and spring rains,	Then the LORD's anger will burn against you, and he will shut the heavens so that it will not rain
The interim result	so that you may gather in your grain, new wine and oil.	and the ground will yield no produce,
The end result	I will provide grass in your fields for your cattle, and you will eat and be satisfied.	and you will soon perish from the good land the LORD is giving you.

Moses begins by defining the passing grade, the correct response to the test (vv. 13−15). His exhortation involves themes we have heard before. The Israelites are to listen carefully to the commands and demonstrate their covenant commitment ("love") as well as their unreserved vassaldom to Yahweh ("serve"). As elsewhere, by adding "today" Moses creates a sense of urgency. His injunctions are not for the distant future but are to be applied immediately. The Israelites must commit themselves today, even before they cross the Jordan, and in the perpetual present once they have crossed.

By speaking with Yahweh's voice in verses 14−15, Moses draws attention to the following statements as both *divine* promise and *divine* evaluation

17. E.g., Ps. 1; Prov. 9.
18. Verses 13−15 consists of thirty-five words; verses 16−17 of thirty-three words.

286

of their response to the test.[19] Extending the picture of the utopian land (vv. 8–12), Yahweh makes two promises, each introduced by (lit.) "I will give." Each promise subdivides further into two parts, the first emphasizing the divine response to the human performance, and the second the human benefit. In both we recognize a polemical critique of the fertility religion of Canaan, as Yahweh claims for himself the functions Canaanites attributed to Baal, their storm god.

In verse 14 Yahweh promises to provide rain in abundance. He begins with a general statement, promising "rain on your land in its season." This expression is defined with "early rain"[20] and "latter rain"[21] (NIV, "autumn and spring rains").[22] Here Yahweh declares that because of his gift of rain, the land will yield its produce and the people will bring home grain, wine, and olive oil. As in 7:13, these expressions both speak of the literal bounty of the land and subtly challenge the prevailing fertility deities of the region. If Yahweh's first gift (rain) is of immediate benefit to the land, the second gift (grass) benefits animals, which naturally results in the people eating well and being satisfied (v. 15).

Earlier Moses had recognized that affluence and satisfaction may lead either to forgetting Yahweh (6:10–12) or to taking prideful credit for what one has achieved (8:17). While he does not hesitate to declare that the people's well-being and satisfaction with life are divinely intended goals, he does not promise them unconditionally. Instead he draws a direct line from the people's response to the demands of relationship to their enjoyment of the full blessings of the Promised Land.

In verses 16–17 Moses describes the failing grade and in so doing addresses head-on a problem from the past and what he fears is a danger in the future—defection from Yahweh and his covenant. Returning to a motif he had dealt with at length in chapters 6 and 8—the test represented by prosperity—Moses begins with a call for self-watch, which he follows up with a series of potential dangers introduced with the particle "lest." The four verbs in verse 16 identify four kinds of actions against which the

---

19. The switch to first person in vv. 14–15 reflects Moses' role as mouthpiece for Yahweh.

20. The early rain falls intermittently October–November and is needed to soften the ground so it can be prepared for seeding. In Palestine 70 percent of the annual rainfall falls in December–February.

21. The late rain falls between late March and early May and is crucial for an abundant and high quality harvest.

22. To this day the agricultural economy of Israel stands or falls on the timely arrival of the early and late rains. On the importance of timely rains see Lev. 26:4; Deut. 28:12; Jer. 5:24; Ezek. 34:26. For discussions of the climate of Palestine, see D. Ashbel, "Israel, Land of Climate," *EncJud* (2nd ed.), 10:132–33.

Israelites must guard themselves: being open-minded about other gods, turning to them, accepting vassaldom to them, and prostrating themselves in submission and homage before them. Only the first requires comment. "To have an open mind/heart" (NIV "be enticed") is an elliptical version of an idiom that speaks of being easily seduced by the attractions of pagan religion.[23]

In verse 17 Moses declares that open-mindedness toward the worship of gods other than Yahweh is fatal. If the people fix their devotion elsewhere, instead of being the objects of Yahweh's favor, he will unleash his fury against them,[24] "turning off the taps" in the sky,[25] thereby stopping the rain and preventing the ground from yielding its produce. Consequently the Israelites will perish quickly from the good land that they had received as a gift. Yahweh's design was for himself, the Israelites, and the land to exist in harmonious symbiotic relationship to one another, each contributing to the other's delight and each finding delight in the other. The curse represents the complete opposite of the blessing: instead of divine favor, Israel incurs his wrath; instead of abundant rain in its season, drought; instead of fruit, infertility; instead of life abundant, death — and ultimately divorce from the land.

In verses 18 – 21 Moses takes a surprising turn. After his warning of the consequences of covenant betrayal, he repeats the sequel to the Shema (6:6 – 9) almost verbatim. Most of the changes from the earlier text reflect Moses' renewed passion, especially in the wake of his rehearsal of Israel's history of apostasy in chapter 9 and his brief consideration of the unthinkable in verses 16 – 17.[26] Whereas in the original context "these words" to be put on the people's hearts would probably have been Deuteronomy 6:4 – 5, here the antecedent of "these" is Moses' utopian description of the land and his presentation of two ways of responding to the gift of land in verses 8 – 16. While everything Moses has said since 6:4 – 5 is in effect com-

---

23. Moses does not identify the influences to which the Israelites' minds might be open. Clues to the riddle may be found in Job 31:26 – 28 and Deuteronomy 4:15 – 19.

24. See also 6:15; 7:4; 29:27[26]; 31:17.

25. The idiom (lit.) "to shut/restrain the heavens" occurs also in 1 Kings 8:35=2 Chron. 6:26; 7:13. Later in the covenant curse section Moses will speak more graphically of the heavens above being like bronze and the earth like iron (Deut. 28:23).

26. The following adjustments are the most significant: (1) shifting pronouns from singular to plural; (2) a more direct introduction, "Fix these words," instead of "These words shall be," on your heart; (3) "these *my* words," instead of "these words that I am commanding you"; (4) adding "and minds" after "in your hearts" (cf. 6:5); (5) advancing the injunctions to bind these words as signs on one's hands and wear them on one's forehead; (6) replacing the rare word "to inculcate" in 6:7 with the more common "to teach"; and (7) adding a lengthy conclusion (v. 21), in keeping with the new context in which this text has been inserted.

mentary on these verses, he repeats what he had said earlier to imprint the message indelibly on their minds and on their hearts.

Verses 18–21 hold the key to the future relationship of deity, people, and land. In order to ensure that God's design for Israel will be realized, the people must commit themselves wholeheartedly to him and his covenant. Yahweh's desire is to see their population explode as the lifespan of each generation increases on the land that he had promised the ancestors. The final temporal reference, "as many as the days that the heavens are above the earth" (v. 21), alludes to the eternality of Yahweh's covenant commitment to his people.[27] Although Yahweh has previously characterized his covenant with Israel as eternal,[28] this is first time the cosmic symbols are applied to it (cf. Gen. 8:22).

But how can Moses say in one breath that Israel will be destroyed, and in the next appeal to the cosmos as a symbol of the eternality of God's covenant with the nation? The answer is found in the fact that every generation and all individual Israelites must accept the covenant by faith and demonstrate fidelity to Yahweh through obedience. Moses seems to think that Israel's exile is inevitable, but he knows it will not be the last word (4:31; 30:1–10). Yahweh's promise to Israel is firm, like the cosmos itself.

Part III: The land as promise (vv. 22–25). Moses concludes this part of the address by presenting the second issue raised by the land: Yahweh's promise to dispossess the Canaanites (v. 8). Having offered the land as a test in verses 18–21 and concluded with a glorious word of promise, in verse 22 Moses yanks his audience back to reality with a third expression of conditionality. Yahweh is under no obligation to the Israelites unless they keep the Supreme Command in its entirety,[29] by "putting it into practice," by "loving Yahweh your God," by "walking in all his ways," and by "holding fast to him" (pers. trans.). As in 10:12 the alternation of expressions for actions and dispositions reinforces the comprehensive nature of covenant commitment. There is really only one command, to love Yahweh with one's whole heart, but love without obedience is not love at all.[30]

Using strong military language, verses 23–25 spell out the rewards for having met these conditions:[31] Yahweh will dispossess all the Canaanite

---

27. On this and similar formulas, see S. Paul, "Psalm 72:5—A Traditional Blessing for the Long Life of the King," *JNES* 31 (1972): 351–55. Similar formulas are attested in Sumerian, Akkadian, Aramaic, Ugaritic, Phoenician, and Punic texts.

28. See Ex. 31:16–17; Lev. 24:8. Cf. Judg. 2:1; Ps. 111:2–9; Isa. 24:4–5; 54:4–10.

29. Returning to the singular word for "command" of v. 8 (see comment), after having used the plural in v. 13.

30. Cf. Jesus' words in John 14:15, 23–24; 15:10.

31. This leads Weinfeld (*Deuteronomy 1–11*, 449) to classify vv. 22–25 as a military oration.

nations in advance of the Israelites (v. 23a),[32] and Israel will "possess" nations stronger and mightier than they are. By juxtaposing these statements, Moses declares that human history involves both divine and human activity, with the divine actions being determinative. In verse 24 he concretizes the promise in geographic terms: in fulfillment of Genesis 13:17, the Israelites will stake their claim to every inch of ground on which the soles of their feet tread.[33]

Moses' specification of the boundaries authorizes them to claim the territory from "the desert" (Negev) in the south to "Lebanon" in the north; from the "Euphrates River" in the far northeast to the "western sea" (the Mediterranean). As in 1:7, he defines the Promised Land in terms of Yahweh's promise to Abraham in Genesis 15:18 and later reaffirmed to Moses in Exodus 23:31. Apparently in deference to the tribes of Reuben, Gad, and one-half of Manasseh, he avoided any reference to the Jordan River as the eastern boundary (Num. 34).[34]

Echoing 7:24, Moses concludes this paragraph with a promise that after the Israelites have crossed the Jordan, no enemy will be able to withstand them. Verse 25 explains why this will be so: Yahweh will impose the "terror and fear" of the Israelites on all the land they claim as they tread up and down the land.[35] Moses concludes with a reminder that this will occur in fulfillment of Yahweh's earlier word (Ex. 23:27−31; Deut. 7:19−24). While Rahab will soon testify to the fulfillment of this promise (Josh. 2:8−11), the present audience must remember that these promises are all contingent on Israel's fidelity to the covenant Lord.

Part IV: The land as opportunity (vv. 26−28). As pastor, Moses concludes this part of the sermon with a climactic appeal for decision. He calls his people to attention with "See," and follows this with a statement of principle: "I am setting before you today a blessing and a curse." Elsewhere Moses describes his verbal actions as "setting before" the people specific instructions (4:8; 11:32); here he is handing them the options of "blessing" and "curse."[36] Moses summarizes the conditions determining which of these the Israelites

---

32. Cf. 4:38; 9:4−5, and later in 18:12. Cf. also Ex. 34:24 and Num. 14:12. The element of "elimination" is confirmed by the combinations of "dispossess" and "destroy" in 2:12; 2:21, and similarly 2:22; 12:29; 19:1.

33. This verse is echoed almost verbatim in Yahweh's encouragement to Joshua in Josh. 1:3.

34. The significance of the Jordan as a boundary between these tribes and the rest of Israel is illustrated dramatically in Josh. 22. Ezekiel's later idealized vision also views the Jordan as the eastern border (Ezek. 47:18).

35. Here "the land," which cannot express emotion, functions metonymically for the people who live on the land.

36. This is the first occurrence of both of these expressions in the book.

will experience in verses 27 and 28. For the content of the blessing and the curse we may look back to verses 14−17, with the first half (vv. 14−15) describing the blessing, and the second half (vv. 16−17) describing the curse. Moses will spell them out in greater detail in chapter 28.

The symmetry of the introductory clauses setting the conditions for the blessing and the curse reflects the formality of the present circumstance. In verse 27 "the commands of the LORD your God" are equated with "that I am giving you today." In verse 28 "disobeying the commands of the LORD your God" is explained as to "turn from the way that I command you today by following other gods, which you have not known."[37] This is shorthand for what Moses had said in verse 16. The formality of the situation is reinforced by the repetition of "today" in the presentation of the blessing and the curse. While the nature of the occasion is unclear, it seems that the covenant renewal ceremony reflected in 26:16−19 underlies this text. By choosing the blessing the people formally accept their status as Yahweh's covenant people and him as their covenant Lord.

If this view of the context is correct, then the structure of the second address recapitulates the structure of the original covenant event on Mount Horeb (Ex. 19−24). Like Exodus 19, the burden of Deuteronomy 5:1−11:32 has been to challenge, inspire, and convince the Israelites to commit themselves to Yahweh. This section expounds in detail what Yahweh had declared to the people in Exodus 19:3b−6. The principles underlying Exodus 19:3b−6 are precisely those Moses has been presenting in Deuteronomy 5−11. (1) Israel's relationship with Yahweh is rooted in his gracious act of deliverance from the bondage of Egypt. (2) The covenant primarily involves a relationship with the covenant Lord rather than a commitment to a code of conduct. (3) Yahweh's call to covenant relationship is purposeful: that Israel might be his special treasure, that the people might be holy, and that they might serve as an agent of grace to the nations from which they were called. (4) Israel's enjoyment of the blessings of the covenant and the nation's fulfillment of the divine mission are contingent on a positive response to Yahweh's voice.

In the original context, once Moses presented these fundamental issues to the people and they responded (Ex. 19:8), Yahweh commenced the revelation of his will, which included first the Decalogue (Ex. 20:1−17), and then the "Book of the Covenant" (20:22−23:19). In this context Moses began the second address by reciting the Decalogue and then expounding

---

37. Here and elsewhere in the book (13:2, 6, 13[3, 7, 14]; 28:64; 29:26[25]), "gods that you have not known" are gods with whom the Israelites have had no experience. Cf. Tigay, *Deuteronomy*, 116.

on the implications of claiming Yahweh as covenant Lord. Deuteronomy 5–11 functions as the equivalent to his report of Yahweh's speech to the people in Exodus 19:7.[38] The present appeal for decision on the plains of Moab corresponds to Moses' call for decision in Exodus 19:8. This reinforces the image of the ceremonies on the Plains of Moab as a second Horeb experience. Like Sinai/Horeb, the Plains of Moab was a place of both revelation and decision. With his call to decision in 11:26–32, Moses challenges the new generation to respond with greater fidelity than their parents had done. Their future in the land depends on it.[39]

VISION OF THE LAND. As noted above, this chapter offers the fullest picture of Deuteronomy's vision of the land. As we move into the more detailed presentation of life in the Promised Land in chapters 12–26, we must keep in mind the essential elements of that vision.

1. Israel's land is a gift from Yahweh in fulfillment of his covenant promises to the ancestors (v. 9).
2. Israel's land offers the covenant people a paradise-like context in which to fulfill their destiny (vv. 9–11).
3. Israel's land is the special object of Yahweh's election and his perpetual care (v. 12).
4. Israel's land offers the people a geographic context for an ethical response to the covenant (vv. 8, 13, 22).
5. Israel's land fulfills its intended role within the triangular covenant relationship only as Yahweh providentially enables it to do so (vv. 14–17).
6. Israel's possession of the land is contingent on Yahweh's giving it to the people, and their retention of it is contingent on their fidelity to the covenant (vv. 22–25).

The challenge and promise of this passage will become urgent for the Israelites within a matter of days or weeks, the moment they cross the Jordan and take their first steps in the Promised Land (Josh. 1:3–9). The nation's history will prove how deaf to Moses' voice the people's ears will be. Within a generation spiritual recidivism will set in, and the allure of the gods of Canaan will prove too strong (Judg. 2:11–23). But Yahweh

---

38. The narrator of Exodus and Moses in Deuteronomy use different verbs, but both mean "He set X before them."

39. See Millar, *Now Choose Life*, 80–88; idem., "Living at the Place of Decision," 52–69.

will build his church; despite their propensity to apostatize and commit "the evil," the nation will survive and the historian will report that several centuries later, during the reigns of David and Solomon the ideals of this passage are fulfilled (1 Kings 4:20–28).

But this ideal does not last. With his own sponsorship of idolatry, Solomon adds the weight of the crown to the apostasy that eventually brings the nation to ruin at the hands successively of Assyrians (eighth century BC) and Babylonians (sixth century BC). But even as Nebuchadnezzar's armies are in sight of Jerusalem, the people cling to the promises of this passage, demanding that Yahweh rescue them. They assume that since his covenant commitment to them is eternal, their enjoyment of his favor is unconditional. They fail to read the fine print of the covenant, which declares that God's promises are contingent. Each generation and each individual must claim the promises by faith and demonstrate its allegiance to the divine Suzerain by conformity to his will—particularly the Supreme Command. Yahweh is not obligated to bless those who forget him and his gracious acts and go after other gods. The land is a gracious gift, and to forget the Giver and give credit to other gods is the height of ingratitude and rebellion.

But Israel's relationship to the land of Palestine serves as a microcosm of the relationship between the human population of the earth and the globe. Yahweh delights in the productivity of the soil and in those made in his image enjoying its bounty. The covenantal triangle involving Yahweh, Israel, and the Promised Land applies to the cosmos as a whole.

At creation, God established a trialogical arrangement linking the well-being of humankind directly to their devotion to him. In response to faithful service to Yahweh, the earth yields its produce for the benefit of all living creatures and for the glory of the Creator.

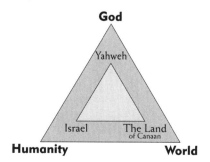

Blessing and curse. Human awareness of the alternatives of blessing and curse, dependent on the people's response to God, is as old as the human race. Although Genesis 2–3 avoids the terms "covenant," "blessing," and "curse," this is what the trees in the garden of Eden represented. The Tree of Life symbolized the reward for obedience to the divine Suzerain, while the Tree of the Knowledge of Good and Evil, whose fruit would yield death, symbolized the consequences of disobedience (Gen. 2:9, 16–17). The promises to the patriarchs held out the blessing and the curse for all the families of the earth, depending on their disposition to the ancestors as agents of blessing (Gen. 12:3).[40] Admittedly the blessing and curse are never formally presented to the patriarchs as consequences of their response to Yahweh,[41] but they are implicit in the narratives. The test of Abraham in Genesis 22 assumes that blessing is contingent on obedience, though elsewhere material blessing seems disconnected from moral response (Ishmael, 17:20; Abraham, 24:1, 35; Isaac, 25:11; 26:12–14).

Indeed, the accounts seem to emphasize the transfer of blessing from one generation to the next through performative speech acts by the ancestors.[42] However, in Genesis 26:3–5 Yahweh expressly transfers the promise to Isaac *because of* Abraham's complete obedience to his revealed will.[43] In any case, the characters in the narratives are keenly aware of the alternatives of blessing and curse (cf. 27:12). Although the terms "blessing" and "curse" do not occur in Leviticus 26, the recitation of benefactions in 26:3–13 and disasters in 26:14–39 demonstrates that these two options represented integral elements of Yahweh's covenant with Israel. Later, in Deuteronomy 28 Moses expands on these blessings and curses in great detail.

For the narrators of Israel's history, especially the deuteronomistic historian (Joshua–2 Kings), the blessings and curses provide the determinative grid for assessing interim events,[44] but especially for the final fate of the nation, which went into exile for their covenantal infidelity precisely as predicted.[45] And later prophets, raised in the tradition of Moses (cf. Deut. 18:15), repeatedly challenged the people to choose life and blessing instead of death and the curse.[46] In effect, Joshua's final challenge to his

---

40. The promise is fulfilled in 30:27, 30 (to Laban the Aramaean) and 39:5 (the Egyptians).

41. In Gen. 12:2 Yahweh simply promises to bless Abraham, but this promise is missional in character—that he may be a blessing to the nations.

42. See esp. Gen. 27 and 48. While ostensibly presented as a blessing, in contrast to the blessing of Jacob (27:27–29), the pronouncement concerning Esau (27:39–40) sounds more like a curse than a blessing.

43. Remarkably, in Gen. 26:5 Abraham is credited with complying fully with the will of God as revealed at Sinai and expounded by Moses in Deuteronomy. The expressions for the divine regulations sound Deuteronomic: Abraham listened to Yahweh's voice and kept his charge (cf. Deut. 11:1), his commands, his decrees, and his instructions.

44. See, e.g., Judg. 2:1–5; 6:7–10; 10:10–16; 1 Sam. 12:8–15.

45. See 2 Kings 17:7–23; 21:10–15; 22:15–17.

46. Cf. Daniel's reflection in Dan. 9:4–16.

people to "choose for yourselves this day whom you will serve" was a challenge to choose life by fearing Yahweh and serving him in sincerity and truth rather than going after other gods (Josh. 24:14–26).

THE PRESENT STATE OF **Israel**. This passage is critical for contemporary discussions of the relationship of the state of Israel to God's ancient covenantal promises. Prophetic visions of the restoration of Israel following the judgment were grounded in Yahweh's eternal and irrevocable promises (Ezek. 34:1–31; 36:16–38; 37:1–28). However, the vision of Israel's restoration that Moses paints in Deuteronomy 30:1–10 and that is presented by the prophets who follow assume a regenerate people, with circumcised hearts, wholly devoted to Yahweh, walking in his ways and keeping the commands (30:6–9). In Judaism it has long been assumed that what God requires of his people is primarily to keep Torah—particularly but not limited to the dietary laws of *kashrut* and the proper celebration of the ancient festivals. This view is reflected in Jesus' pronouncement of woe on the scribes and Pharisees, who were scrupulous in tithing mint, dill, and cumin, but neglected the weightier matters of Torah: justice, mercy, and faithfulness (Matt. 23:23). It is also reflected in some of the early rabbinic conversations, like the following:

A. R. Hunah, R. Jeremiah, in the name of R. Hiyya bar Abba: "It is written, 'Me they have abandoned' (Jer. 6:11).
B. "Is it possible that they have kept my Torah? Would that they would abandon Me but keep my Torah.
C. "For if they had abandoned Me but kept My Torah, then in the course of their study of the Torah, the yeast that is in it would have brought them back to Me."[47]

However, this is precisely the opposite of the perspective advocated by Moses in Deuteronomy. Israel's first allegiance was to be to Yahweh, not to the law. Obedience to the will of God should be an expression of one's prior love for God. Otherwise it degenerates to moralism and legalism. Those who have been redeemed will consider their relationship with God the supreme privilege and respond with fear and love, demonstrated in acts that please him and serve the well-being of others. Rooted in love for God, from Zion and the Promised Land as a whole, the causes of justice and peace are to flow out to the nations.

---

47. As cited by Jacob Neusner, in *Theological Dictionary of Rabbinic Judaism* (Lanham, MD: University Press of America, 2005), 1:219.

While the existence of the state of Israel today testifies to Yahweh's permanent commitment to the physical descendants of Abraham, given their abusive policies and actions against the Palestinians, both Muslim and Christian, the present state cannot be the fulfillment of the ancient promises. Furthermore, since the New Testament equates Jesus Christ with Yahweh, the Redeemer of Israel, allegiance to the God of Israel must be expressed by devotion to Christ, for salvation from sin and from the wrath of God is to be found in Christ, and in Christ alone (Acts 4:9—12; Rom. 10:1—15; Phil. 2:4—11).[48]

In reinforcing the messages of Deuteronomy 6—8, this passage reminds Israel that occupation of the land provides the context and motivation for decision, as well as the reward for obedience.[49] But it also reminds Gentile Christians, who have been grafted into the promises to Israel (Rom. 11:11—24), who have been blessed with every blessing in Christ, and who have obtained a spiritual inheritance as God's own possession, to the praise of his glory (Eph. 1:3—14), that the proof of covenant commitment is undivided devotion to Christ, our Redeemer, demonstrated in a life of obedience to him. On the one hand, this means repudiating all other gods and serving Christ alone, and on the other hand, this serves as a solemn warning that there is no eternal security for those who live in sin. Paul may well have had texts like this one in mind when he presents the options in Romans 2:4—13.

Each day a day of decision. Finally, as was the case for the Israelites, for those who claim to be God's people, every day is a day of decision. Our commitment to Yahweh must not only be renewed at significant junctures in our lives, but daily. The blessings associated with the covenant are not to be taken for granted or viewed as automatic rights. The covenant established by Christ involves a special relationship, which demands constant investment of energy and devotion. The options open to the Israelites— blessing and curse—are open to us, but how we experience them depends on our covenant commitment to Christ, demonstrated by active obedience.

Our Savior illustrated the two ways graphically with his metaphor of the vine in John 15. Branches that do not abide in Christ experience the curse. Because they do not bear fruit (i.e., keep his commands, v. 10), they are cut off, discarded, and thrown into the fire (v. 6). Contrariwise, those who abide in him experience his blessing. Because they abide in him, they

---

48. See further, Daniel I. Block, "Who Do Commentators Say "the Lord" Is? The Scandalous Rock of Romans 10:13," in *On the Writing of New Testament Commentaries: Festschrift for Grant Osborne* (ed. S. Porter and E. Schnabel; Leiden: Brill, 2012), forthcoming.

49. Cf. Millar, *Now Choose Life*, 55—66.

bear abundant fruit; that is, they demonstrate their covenant commitment with righteous acts of obedience and are rewarded by having the Father do for them whatever they wish (v. 7). Just as Israel's obedience and blessing brought great glory to Yahweh (Deut. 26:19), so our obedience and blessing bring great glory to God (John 15:8).

Deuteronomy 11:29–32

🔥

When the LORD your God has brought you into the land you are entering to possess, you are to proclaim on Mount Gerizim the blessings, and on Mount Ebal the curses. ³⁰As you know, these mountains are across the Jordan, west of the road, toward the setting sun, near the great trees of Moreh, in the territory of those Canaanites living in the Arabah in the vicinity of Gilgal. ³¹You are about to cross the Jordan to enter and take possession of the land the LORD your God is giving you. When you have taken it over and are living there, ³²be sure that you obey all the decrees and laws I am setting before you today.

THE GRAMMATICAL CONSTRUCTION OF the beginning of verse 29 signals the beginning of a new, albeit short, section.[1] Now Moses' attention shifts from the present covenant renewal ceremony to an anticipated event on the other side of the Jordan. The opening clause sets the temporal context: when the Israelites have arrived at their destination. As always, Moses is careful to credit Yahweh for their arrival in the land to which they have been headed (v. 29).

Moses' description of the ceremony is sketchy in the extreme, consisting of only nine words in the Hebrew (v. 29b). Interpreted literally, Moses seems to envisage "the blessing" and "the curse" as tangible if not concrete objects to be carried across the Jordan and deposited on Mounts Gerizim and Ebal. From the Plains of Moab he could undoubtedly see these twin peaks, some forty miles to the northwest. This enigmatic text leaves unanswered many questions concerning the nature of the event. These questions will not be answered until chapter 27, which the editor of Moses' addresses has inserted near the end of this second address.

Geography is the key to the significance of these verses. Having identified Mounts Gerizim and Ebal as the place for the ceremony, by means of a complex rhetorical question (not apparent in most Eng. translations, but see KJV) Moses offers a convoluted description of the location. It is

---

1. The phrase *wᵉhāyâ kî* (lit.., "and it will be that") signals new literary [sub]units in 6:10; 26:1; 30:1; 31:21. Cf. *BHRG*, 331.

across the Jordan,[2] beyond the road that leads west from the Jordan River to Shechem, between Gerizim and Ebal, in the land of the Canaanites, who live in the Arabah opposite Gilgal north of Jericho, next to the great trees of Moreh. Although the Arabah obviously refers to the Jordan Valley gorge that runs from the Sea of Galilee in the north to the Red Sea in the south, the remainder of the verse is obscure.[3]

The phrase "trees of Moreh" may provide a key to the meaning of the ceremony anticipated here. The expression occurs elsewhere only in Genesis 12:6, marking the spot near Shechem where Abraham first camped when he entered the land. At that time Yahweh had appeared to him and confirmed "this land" as the gift that he would give to his descendants. Earlier we noted that Yahweh's establishment of his covenant with Israel at Sinai, as well as the renewal of that covenant with this generation on the Plains of Moab, represented the fulfillment of Yahweh's covenant promise to Abraham and his descendants to be their God and to claim them as his covenant people (Gen. 17:7). But these were bilateral ceremonies involving only Yahweh and his people. Since both the ratification of the covenant at Horeb and the renewal ceremonies on the Plains of Moab had transpired on alien soil, the land had yet to be brought into the relationship. Apparently the purpose of this ceremony was to complete the covenantal triangle, though confirmation of this interpretation must await the commentary on chapter 27.

In verse 31 Moses confidently announces the end of the journey for his people. They are about to cross the Jordan to receive their gift of land from Yahweh. His comment that they will possess that land and establish permanent residence there seems redundant, but this should not surprise us if we remember that Moses is speaking pastorally and personally. As a pastoral note, it reminds the people of the significance of the event that lies immediately before them: they will claim what Yahweh in his grace is giving them.

But on the personal level, Moses' fixation on the crossing betrays his own bitter disappointment at being refused entrance to the land (3:23–26). With this note Moses also reiterates the role of the Jordan as the boundary between alien soil and the Promised Land to be received as a gift. One can only imagine what the two and one-half tribes who had requested the Transjordanian territory as their land might have thought about this.

---

2. As in 3:20, 25, Moses' perspective in vv. 30 and 31 differs from that of the narrator, for whom "beyond the Jordan" is east of the river (see 1:1, 5; 4:41, 46–47).

3. Assuming that Gilgal is the well-known site north of Jericho (cf. Josh. 4:19–5:12), and the "oaks of Moreh" is a prominent grove in the vicinity (cf. Gen. 12:6), Moses seems to be referring to a route running parallel to the Jordan, until it meets up with "Sunset Boulevard" (Tigay, *Deuteronomy*, 116), which heads west to Gerizim and Ebal.

Moses concludes the first section of his second address (5:1b–11:32) with another appeal for the Israelites "today." There is no point in dreaming about the future if they do not commit themselves *now* to full obedience to the decrees and laws that he is giving them.

THESE VERSES ARE CONCERNED with a future one-time ritual on Mounts Gerizim and Ebal. While Moses will expand on this summary charge in chapter 27, it will fall to Joshua to carry out these instructions. According to Joshua 8:30–35, after the Israelites had conquered Jericho and Ai, they gathered at these mountains, where Joshua led them in a ritual observance precisely as Moses had prescribed. When the Israelites headed for this sacred spot, they retraced the steps of their ancestor Abraham (Gen. 12:6–7). At the great trees of Moreh, at the very spot where Yahweh had appeared to Abraham for the first time in the Promised Land, where he had declared, "To your offspring I will give *this land,*" and where Abraham had built his first altar, there Joshua also built an altar to Yahweh.

With this altar and the accompanying ritual, the Israelites celebrated Yahweh's faithfulness in fulfilling his promise given centuries earlier, and formally the Promised Land was incorporated into the tripartite covenant relationship involving Yahweh, Israel, and the land. In so doing Joshua laid the foundation not only for Israel's longstanding claim to the land, which they had received as a grant from their divine Suzerain, but also for the prophetic hope that after the ultimate judgment of exile from the land and the departure of the divine presence, these three parties to the covenant would be reunited.[4]

THIS PASSAGE HAS PROFOUND significance for contemporary Christians in two particular respects. First, it reminds us that God is faithful; he always keeps his promises. Just as he had held the land of the Canaanites in reserve for his people as their special grant and inheritance, so he holds in reserve for those who believe in Jesus the Christ an eternal heavenly grant (Eph. 1:3–14). Our possession is not an earthly allotment but a spiritual reality; we have been redeemed and have been given the Holy Spirit as a pledge of our inheritance to the praise of his glory. Like every other benefit, this is an unmerited and undeserved gift from God.

---

4. See esp. the restoration oracles in Jer. 30–33 and Ezek. 34; 36–37; and 40–48.

Deuteronomy 12:1–14

🔥

Introduction to Deuteronomy 12:1–26:19

DEUTERONOMY 12:1 INTRODUCES A new section, leading readers to expect a formal series of laws comparable to those found in the Book of the Covenant (Ex. 20:22–23:19). However, in tone and style much of this material bears a closer resemblance to Moses' preaching in chapters 6–11 than to the Covenant Code, the Holiness Code (Lev. 17–25), or Mesopotamian laws. Consequently, to refer to Deuteronomy 12–26 as "the Deuteronomic Law Code" misrepresents the genre of the material as a whole. Moses does indeed draw on specific laws and regulations received at Sinai, but his aim is pastoral rather than legislative.

The literary boundaries of this section are set by Deuteronomy 12:1, which functions as a formal heading, and 26:16–19, which represents a formal conclusion. Together these texts create an effective frame around 12:2–26:15, similar to that found bookending the Book of the Covenant:

Exodus 20:22–23:19		Deuteronomy 12:2–26:15	
A	Principles of worship (20:23–26), highlighting Israel's cultic expression of devotion to Yahweh	A	Principles of worship (12:2–16:17), highlighting Israel's cultic expression of devotion to Yahweh
B	Casuistic and apodictic laws (21:1–23:9), highlighting Israel's ethical expression of devotion to Yahweh	B	Casuistic and apodictic instruction (16:18–25:19), highlighting Israel's ethical and civil expression of devotion to Yahweh
A´	Principles of worship (23:10–19), highlighting Israel's cultic expression of devotion to Yahweh	A´	Principles of worship (26:1–15), highlighting Israel's cultic expression of devotion to Yahweh

Some argue that Moses' presentation of the covenant obligations in Deuteronomy 12–26 is structured after the Decalogue.[1] However, this approach seems forced.[2] The flow of thought is best grasped by outlining the material on the basis of content. The logic of the overall structure is clear. Viewing Israel as a theocracy, Moses begins with the nation's direct

---

1. See S. Kaufman, "The Structure of Deuteronomic Law," *Maarav* 1/2 (1978/1979): 105–58.

2. This approach is also rejected by Tigay, *Deuteronomy*, 534, n. 19.

obligations to Yahweh (12:2–16:17), then moves successively to the offices through which Yahweh will exercise his kingship once the people have settled in the Promised Land (16:18–21:9), family law (21:10–22:30), a reminder of the boundaries of the covenant community (23:1–8[2–9]), regulations regarding many different aspects of Israelite life (23:9[10]–25:19), and ending with further instructions for worship (26:1–15).

Apparently taking cues from both the Decalogue and the Book of the Covenant, Moses begins his exposition with the vertical dimensions of covenant relationship. The dominant motif in 12:2–14:21 is worship of Yahweh in liturgical settings. This motif spills over into 14:22–27 and returns in 15:19–16:17, deliberately framing horizontal concerns. By adopting this structure Moses the pastor teaches his congregation that worship and life are intricately intertwined; acceptable vertical expressions of covenant are preconditioned by fidelity in horizontal relationships, which offer opportunities for corporate celebration of the vertical.

These are the decrees and laws you must be careful to follow in the land that the LORD, the God of your fathers, has given you to possess—as long as you live in the land. ²Destroy completely all the places on the high mountains and on the hills and under every spreading tree where the nations you are dispossessing worship their gods. ³Break down their altars, smash their sacred stones and burn their Asherah poles in the fire; cut down the idols of their gods and wipe out their names from those places.

⁴You must not worship the LORD your God in their way. ⁵But you are to seek the place the LORD your God will choose from among all your tribes to put his Name there for his dwelling. To that place you must go; ⁶there bring your burnt offerings and sacrifices, your tithes and special gifts, what you have vowed to give and your freewill offerings, and the firstborn of your herds and flocks. ⁷There, in the presence of the LORD your God, you and your families shall eat and shall rejoice in everything you have put your hand to, because the LORD your God has blessed you.

⁸You are not to do as we do here today, everyone as he sees fit, ⁹since you have not yet reached the resting place and the inheritance the LORD your God is giving you. ¹⁰But you will cross the Jordan and settle in the land the LORD your God is giving you as an inheritance, and he will give you rest from all your enemies around you so that you will live in safety. ¹¹Then to the place the LORD your God will choose as

a dwelling for his Name—there you are to bring everything I command you: your burnt offerings and sacrifices, your tithes and special gifts, and all the choice possessions you have vowed to the LORD. ¹²And there rejoice before the LORD your God, you, your sons and daughters, your menservants and maidservants, and the Levites from your towns, who have no allotment or inheritance of their own. ¹³Be careful not to sacrifice your burnt offerings anywhere you please. ¹⁴Offer them only at the place the LORD will choose in one of your tribes, and there observe everything I command you.

AS ALREADY NOTED, DEUTERONOMY 12:1 marks the transition from the exposition of the Supreme Command (chaps. 5–11), to the exposition of the stipulations of the covenant in chapters 12–26. As elsewhere (4:45; 5:1; 26:16–17), "the decrees and laws" represent the covenantal obligations that Yahweh revealed at Sinai. Continuing the second address begun back in 5:1, this opening statement echoes many of the expressions found in 11:32, the conclusion to the previous section. Using familiar phrases this opening makes four points.

1. Moses specifies the genre of the material to follow. Although they will be presented in a profoundly hortatory way, these are "decrees and laws."
2. He declares his goal—to govern conduct: "Keep them by doing them" (pers. trans.).³
3. He links his instructions with the gift of land: They are to be obeyed in the land that "the LORD, the God of your fathers, has given you to possess."⁴
4. He identifies the context to which they apply: They are to be obeyed "as long as they live in the land."

Deuteronomy 12:1 actually performs a dual purpose, introducing readers to the chapters 12–26 as a whole, but also to the following literary subunit (12:2–27). This interpretation is buttressed by verse 28, which,

---

3. On this expression, see comments on 5:1.

4. This is the last time keeping the covenant stipulations is linked to occupation of the land. Cf. 4:1, 5, 14; 5:31; 6:1. Similar to 11:8–28, Moses summarizes the tripartite relationship that existed among deity, population, and territory to reinforce the contingency of the promise to the ancestors: Israel needs to accept the privilege of covenant relationship and the gift of land, and demonstrate her gratitude through scrupulous observance of the divine Suzerain's will.

together with verse 1 creates an effective frame around these verses. Structurally 12:2–27 divides into two parts, virtually identical in size.[5] The first involves sacrificial slaughter (vv. 2–14), while the second authorizes profane slaughter throughout the land. Functioning as two sides of a coin, these texts are held together by the word "place," the tenfold repetition of "there,"[6] and the sixfold repetition of the "place formula," by which Yahweh calls for worship at a single shrine, the place that he will choose. These six are evenly distributed: three in the first panel (vv. 5, 11, 14), and three in the second (vv. 18, 21, 26).

Deuteronomy 12:1–14 subdivides further into three parts: two invitations to celebration in the presence of Yahweh (vv. 2–7 and 8–12) and a concluding exhortation (vv. 13–14). The invitations are remarkably symmetrical in length[7] and structure, consisting respectively of negative charges (vv. 2–4; vv. 8–9) and positive invitations (vv. 5–7; vv. 10–12). Like most translations, the NIV treats this unit as a series of legal prescriptions, despite the sermonic injunctions that punctuate it (vv. 4, 8–9, 13–14).

The First Invitation to Celebrate in the Presence of Yahweh (vv. 2–7)

LIKE THE DECALOGUE AND the Book of the Covenant, Moses' discourse on the decrees and laws begins with instructions on Israel's vertical relationship with Yahweh. This first version of the invitation anticipates two phases of application: purging the land of any vestiges of Canaanite idolatry (vv. 2–3) and replacing these pagan practices with those approved by Yahweh (vv. 5–7). Verse 4 is transitional.

Moses' charge to clear the land of Canaanite worship consists of three parts: an emphatic general command to destroy all pagan cult centers (v. 2), a specific command to destroy all cult paraphernalia (v. 3a–d), and a sweeping command to eliminate all the claims that Canaanite deities might have to the land (v. 3e). He refers to Canaanite places of worship as "places ... where the nations ... worship their gods," in contrast to "the place" (singular) that Yahweh will choose to place his name. The triad of expressions—"all the places" where the nations worship their gods, "on the high mountains and on the hills," and "under every green tree"—highlights the pervasiveness, intensity, and futility of pagan worship in the land (cf. 4:28).

---

5. Vv. 2–14 consist of 199 words; vv. 15–27 of 200 words (counting the sign of the direct object with the noun).

6. "Place": vv. 3, 5, 11, 13, 14, 18, 21, 26; "there": vv. 2, 5a, 5b, 6, 7, 11a, 11b, 14a, 14b, 21. These are apparent in the Hebrew text, not necessarily in the NIV.

7. Vv. 2–7 consist of 85 words; vv. 8–12 of 89 words.

Because verse 3a echoes 7:2 – 5, we need only to reiterate our earlier comment that ancient approaches to religion were concretized in specific places and acts rather than in abstract systems of belief. Moses assumes that obliterating the physical symbols of paganism will reduce the temptation of idolatry. Thus, he commands the Israelites to obliterate the name of their gods from every place where they are worshiped. This action will remove all reminders of their existence, delegitimize the sites as centers of worship, neutralize the respective divinities' claim to the sites and the surrounding regions, and set the stage for Yahweh's election of a place for himself, and with this his exclusive claim to the land.

Moses concludes with a simple but direct command not to behave like the people whom the Israelites will displace (v. 4). The warning not to treat Yahweh like this means that they are not to serve Yahweh the way Canaanites served their gods — multiplying shrines and constructing all kinds of cultic accoutrements for their worship.[8] Moses follows this general proscription with a positive alternative in verses 5 – 7, a remarkably gracious invitation to a more personal relationship with Yahweh their God. This invitation is dominated by five verbs: "you may make a pilgrimage to the place" (*dāraš*),[9] "there you may come/enter" (v. 5), "there you may bring your offerings" (v. 6), "there you may eat" (v. 7a), and "there you may rejoice in all activities" (v. 7b; all pers. trans.).

Verse 5 contains the first of twenty-one occurrences of "the place formula" in Deuteronomy: "the place the LORD will choose to put his Name."[10] The formula occurs in a variety of forms, ranging from the most elemental (16:16; 31:11) to the most complex (12:5).[11] The present form of a formula makes four fundamental statements concerning "the place." (1) It is a place that Yahweh will *choose*.[12] The verb *bāhar* ("to choose") represents the most explicit term for "election" in Deuteronomy. Moses does not say how that choice will be revealed, but this eventually happens to David through Gad the prophet (2 Sam. 24:18 – 25; 1 Chron. 21:18).

---

8. These verses look like commentary on Ex. 23:24.

9. The verb *dāraš* ("to seek") may mean to look for something that is lost, or to "to inquire," or even "to care for, to seek the welfare of" (11:12). However, the expression used here functions idiomatically for "to make a pilgrimage to the place," "to visit the place with spiritual intent." Cf. Tigay, *Deuteronomy*, 120. See also Amos 5:5; Isa. 11:10.

10. See 12:5, 11, 14, 18, 21, 26; 14:23, 24, 25; 15:20; 16:2, 6, 7, 11, 15, 16; 17:8, 10; 18:6; 26:2; 31:11. For variations/echoes of the formula in later writings, see Josh. 9:27; 2 Kings 21:7; 23:27; Ezra 6:12; Neh. 1:9; Jer. 7:12.

11. Scholars agree that Moses' intent with this statement and with verses 5 – 28 as a whole is to clarify the version of the altar law found in Ex. 20:24 – 26.

12. On the initiative of deities in ancient Near Eastern accounts of temple construction see V. (A.) Hurowitz, *"I Have Built You an Exalted House": Temple Building in the Light of Mesopotamia and Northwest Semitic Writings* (JSOTSup 115; Sheffield: Sheffield Academic, 1992), 135 – 67.

(2) The place will be chosen "from among all your [pl.] tribes," a comment rendered only slightly more concrete by "in one of your [sing.] tribes" in verse 14. "Your tribes" refers to the territorial tribal allotments predicted in Numbers 34 and fulfilled by Joshua in Joshua 14 – 19. Although Exodus 20:24 seems to allow for the simultaneous worship of Yahweh in more than one sanctuary, it does not demand this interpretation. It may simply envision the adaptation of Israelite worship to changing circumstances.[13] In verses 4 – 14 Moses clarifies the ambiguity of the earlier statement, ensuring that in the future the people will have regular access to Yahweh.

(3) The place will have Yahweh's name on it. As in 12:21 and 14:24, the phrase "to put his Name there"[14] indicates divine ownership. Just as a person who bears the name of Yahweh is recognized as belonging to Yahweh,[15] so the place bearing the imprint of his name is recognized as his possession.[16] The expression alludes to the practice of inscribing the name on the foundation stone by the founder of a building, in this case validating the location and declaring it to be a locale where he could be worshiped and invoked.[17]

(4) The place will be the goal of Israel's pilgrimages. Translating the verbs at the end of verse 5 modally, "you may make a pilgrimage and you may come there" (pers. trans.), this statement represents a gracious invitation by Yahweh to come to the place where he has set his name. The choice of the verb "to come" (*bô'*) rather than "to go" (*hālak*) reinforces this interpretation, suggesting these instructions are given from Yahweh's point

---

13. The successive interpretation of "the place that the LORD will choose" has been well argued by G. J. Wenham, "Deuteronomy and the Central Sanctuary," *TynB* 22 (1971): 103 – 18; J. G. McConville, "Time, Place, and the Deuteronomic Altar-Law," in J. G. McConville and J. G. Millar, *Time and Place in Deuteronomy* (JSOTSup 179; Sheffield: Sheffield Academic, 1994), 89 – 139.

14. Cf. 1 Kings 9:3; 11:36; 14:21; 2 Kings 21:4, 7; 2 Chron. 6:20; 12:13; and "for his name to be there" in 1 Kings 8:16, 29; 2 Kings 23:27.

15. See comments on 5:11. Cf. Isa. 44:5. Isa. 18:7 speaks of the temple as the place of Yahweh's name. Note also the references to building a house "for the name of the LORD" (2 Sam. 7:13; 1 Kings 3:2; 5:3 – 5[17 – 19]; 8:17 – 20, 44, 48).

16. For equivalent expressions in Akkadian texts, see EA 287:60 – 63 (*ANET,* 488; cf. EA 288:5, *ANET,* 488); in an Egyptian text, Rameses III refers to building a temple for Amon "as the vested property of your name" (*ANET,* 261). Here the expression serves as the equivalent of "the place where Yahweh causes [people] to remember his name" in Ex. 20:24 (pers. trans.), or "the place on which my name is called/read," which later always refers to the city of Jerusalem (Jer. 25:29) or the temple/house of Yahweh (1 Kings 8:43; Jer. 7:10, 11, 14, 30; Jer. 32:34; 34:15). The same expression is used of Israel as the elect people of Yahweh in Deut. 28:10 and 2 Chron. 7:14, and is applied to a prophet in Jer. 15:16.

17. See S. D. McBride, Jr., *The Deuteronomic Name Theology* (PhD diss., Harvard University, 1969), 93 – 94, 204 – 10; S. L. Richter, *The Deuteronomistic History and the Name Theology: lᵉšakkēn šᵉmô šām in the Bible and the Ancient Near East* (BZAW 318; Berlin/New York: de Gruyter, 2002); idem, "The Place of the Name in Deuteronomy," *VT* 57 (2007): 342 – 66.

of view. Moses hereby offers his people regular access to Yahweh, just as the previous generation had enjoyed at Sinai.[18]

Verses 6—7 declare the purpose of Yahweh's invitation by explaining what is to happen at the place Yahweh establishes for his name. Again the choice of verbs and the nature of the activities suggest that this paragraph should be interpreted as an invitation rather than a law. Not only are the Israelites invited to "come" to the place (v. 5), but they are also invited to "bring" rather than "take" their offerings. Both verbs view the movement of the Israelites from the perspective of the person at the destination rather than the person beginning the journey.

Although verses 6—7 provide the fullest statement of the purpose of the place to which Yahweh invites his people in the book, occurrences of the place formula elsewhere suggest the Israelites are invited to the place for a variety of reasons. (1) Moses invites the Israelites to bring all their sacrificial gifts to the place. Here he lists seven types of offerings: (a) "[whole] burnt offerings," animal sacrifices in which the entire carcass was consumed by fire on the altar (Lev. 1:1—17; 6:8—13[1—6]); (b) "sacrifices," a general expression for animal sacrifices in which the blood and fat were burned on the altar and the meat eaten by the worshiper and the priests in the presence of Yahweh (Lev. 7:11—18); (c) "tithes," the tenth part of the crops and livestock (cf. 14:23); (d) "sacred donation of your hand" (NIV "special gifts"), contributions dedicated to Yahweh; (e) "votive offerings" (NIV "what you have vowed") presented in fulfillment of a vow;[19] (f) "free-will offerings," spontaneous expressions of happiness;[20] (g) "the firstborn of your herds and flocks," defined elsewhere as "what breaches the womb" (Ex. 13:2, 12—15; 34:19—20; cf. Deut. 15:19—23). The list is obviously not exhaustive,[21] because Moses is not presenting a comprehensive manual for worship. Rather, he offers his people a theology of worship.[22] To have the

---

18. Compare not only the emphasis in the Exodus narratives on Sinai as a place where Israel would "serve" Yahweh (Ex. 3:12; 4:23; 7:16, 26[8:1]; 8:16[12]; 9:1,13; 10:3, 7—8, 11, 24, 26; 12:31), offer sacrifices to him (Ex. 3:18; 5:3, 8, 17; 8:4[7:29]; 8:21—25[17—21]; 10:25), and celebrate a festival in his honor (Ex. 5:1; cf. 10:9), but also Yahweh's words to Israel in Ex. 19:4: "You yourselves have seen what I did to the Egyptians, and how I carried you on eagles' wings *and brought you to myself*" (italics added).

19. For more detailed instruction involving vows see Deut. 23:21—23[22—24]; also Lev. 27:1—34; Num. 30:1—16[2—17].

20. Thus Milgrom, *Leviticus 1—16*, 419—20.

21. Missing are offerings such as "peace offerings," "thanksgiving offerings," "Passover sacrifices," "sin/purification offerings," "cereal offering," and "liquid libations."

22. Although these offerings were distinctly Israelite in their form and significance, most of Israel's rituals resembled the practices of peoples outside Israel. See M. Weinfeld, "Social and Cultic Institutions in the Priestly Source against Their Ancient Near Eastern Background," *World Congress of Jewish Studies* (Jerusalem: Magnes, 1981): 95—129, esp. 105—11.

chosen people offering specially chosen gifts in the place chosen by Yahweh—this is the key to maintaining the covenant relationship established at Sinai in the land.

(2) Moses invites the Israelites to eat in the presence of Yahweh their God. In the ancient world, eating together was an act of fellowship and communion, often the culmination of a covenant-making ritual (Gen. 31:54; Ex. 24:5–11). In this instance, the food would be taken from offerings that were not wholly consumed on the altar (v. 6). The location of the meal "there, in the presence of the LORD your God" (v. 7), is crucial for grasping the significance of this act. As Yahweh's vassal, Israel eats in his presence, but not with him.[23] The place that Yahweh chooses for his name ensures a means of communion with all Israel in perpetuity, analogous to his communion with them at Horeb, except that here Moses democratizes the experience. At Horeb only a privileged few ate in Yahweh's presence; here Moses opens fellowship with him to everyone (vv. 12, 18; 31:10–12).

(3) Moses invites the Israelites to celebrate the blessing of Yahweh on their work. Linking human efforts with the blessing of God, he coins a new phrase: "that to which one extends one's hand" (pers. trans.). The expression refers either to one's labor or to the products of one's labor[24] and heightens the contrast with pagan idols in verses 2–3, described elsewhere as man-made (4:28; 27:15). Moses views worship as the joyful and celebrative response of everyone in the community to Yahweh's invitation to his presence.[25] He seems to have seized on Leviticus 23:40, which contains the only occurrence of a verb for joy or celebration in the Sinai legislation and made it normative for any worship that transpires before Yahweh.

The Second Invitation to Celebrate in the Presence of Yahweh (vv. 8–12)

THIS PARAGRAPH CLARIFIES THE key issue raised in verses 2–7: the centralizing of national worship, beginning with an appeal to stop current problematic practices (vv. 8–9). Although the first part of the exhortation

---

23. In Ex. 18:12 Moses, Aaron, and the elders of Israel ate with Jethro "in the presence of God." Compare Uriah's eating before David (2 Sam. 11:13), Adonijah's supporters eating before him (1 Kings 1:25), Jehoiachin's eating before his overlord, the king of Babylon (2 Kings 25:29//Jer. 52:33), and the prince eating "in the presence of the LORD" (Ezek 44:3).

24. The expression occurs elsewhere in 12:18; 15:10; 28:8, 20.

25. The verb "to rejoice, celebrate" (*śāmaḥ*) occurs seven times in connection with appearing before Yahweh (12:7, 12, 18; 14:26; 16:11, 14, cf. v. 15; 26:11; cf. also 27:7). The root also occurs in 24:5 and 33:18 of rejoicing in other circumstances. For further discussion see D. I. Block, "The Joy of Worship: The Mosaic Invitation to the Presence of God (Deut. 12:1–14)," in *How I Love Your Torah, O LORD!* 98–117.

answers to verse 4, in substance it corresponds to verses 2–3. Apparently the people were worshiping how and where they pleased—doing as everyone saw fit; despite the permanent ordinance restricting sacrifice to the "Tent of Meeting" (Lev. 17:1–9), unacceptable forms of worship persisted in the camp. Centralizing worship is presented as the answer to Canaanite evils and current Israelite malpractices.[26]

The motive clause in verse 9 recognizes that Israel is still in a transitional historical stage. Only when they have come to their "resting place" and the "inheritance" of land Yahweh has reserved for them will the ideal of exclusive devotion to Yahweh (6:4–5) be matched by exclusive worship at a central shrine. Speaking of security, that is, freedom from fear of enemies outside and tranquility and prosperity inside (Isa. 32:16–18), Moses envisions a time when the covenantal triangle (Yahweh—Israel—the land) will exist in perfectly harmonious relationship.

In verses 10–12 Moses returns to positive instructions regarding Israel's future worship in the land. Echoing verses 5–7, he reiterates that Yahweh will choose the place for his name to reside (v. 11a). In verse 10 he establishes the context for Yahweh's revelation of the place he has chosen for his name, specifying four preconditions: the Israelites have crossed the Jordan, they occupy the land that Yahweh has apportioned to them as their inheritance, Yahweh has given them rest, and they live safely in the land.[27] As Moses celebrates in his final benediction (33:27b–28a), that security is achieved by Yahweh, who has taken care of the enemies.

In verses 11b–12 Moses describes the nature of worship at Yahweh's chosen place. Building on verses 6–7, he reiterates that it will involve sacrifices to Yahweh and rejoicing in his presence. The new catalogue of sacrifices includes most of those found earlier, but by prefacing the list with "everything I command you," he reminds his audience that the list is not necessarily complete. At the end of verse 11, he expands on the votive offerings: they are "choice possessions" that the worshiper has vowed to Yahweh.

Moses ends this second invitation by specifying those whom Yahweh invites to "rejoice" in his presence. The persons listed are those who normally make up "the families" or households in verse 7 (sons, daughters, male and female servants), but he expands the invitation to Levites who live within towns but have no tribal allotment or land grant (*naḥᵃlâ*, NIV "inheritance"; cf. 18:6–8).[28] Given the association of Levites with aliens,

26. Cf. Weinfeld, *DDS*, 170.

27. The strange locution involving rest from enemies all around occurs also in 25:19; Josh. 23:1; 2 Sam. 7:1, 11; 1 Chron. 22:9.

28. The Levites' lack of a territorial allotment is a repeated concern of Moses (cf. 14:27, 29; 18:1, 8).

orphans, and widows elsewhere,[29] "the Levite who is in your gates" (pers. trans.) represents all whom established Israelites might marginalize.[30]

A Concluding Exhortation (vv. 13–14)

MOSES CONCLUDES THE PRESENT instructions on worship with a warning not to make decisions regarding worship practices on the basis of personal preferences, and a specific charge to offer their sacrifices only at the place that Yahweh chooses. The former begins like many exhortations in the book, (lit.) "guard yourselves lest,"[31] which reinforces the sermonic tone of this entire chapter. Anticipating future temptations for them to perform sacrificial rituals "anywhere you please," Moses warns his people not to pervert or forget the divine choice in the place formula that follows. Responding to the indiscriminate and ubiquitous worship of their gods by the Canaanites in verse 2, he reiterates that Israelites are to worship Yahweh only at the place he will choose within one of the tribal allotments. "There" (šā'm occurs twice) they shall present their sacrifices and perform all the other rituals as Moses has commanded them.

Bridging Contexts

THE PLACE FORMULA. MANY scholars associate the centralization of worship called for here with the religious reforms of Josiah (2 Kings 23), and many view this ordinance as a revolutionary theological notion. Whereas people previously believed that Yahweh actually resided within the sanctuary—as symbolized by the Shekinah Glory—in Josiah's day Yahweh was seen to reside only in heaven. The temple was not the actual residence of deity, but a place where worshipers could deliver their prayers to God, who lives in heaven. Supposedly this revolution aimed to eradicate the notion that Yahweh sits enthroned above the cherubim and to eliminate the inherent corporality of this imagery. Furthermore, sacrifice was transformed from an institutional to a personal practice, functioning as a humanitarian occasion for sharing with the poor and as an expression of gratitude to God for his blessing.[32] The "place" that Yahweh would choose

---

29. Cf. Deut. 12:18–19; 14:27, 29; 16:11, 14; 18:6; 26:11–13. When Moses refers to the Levites as an economically vulnerable group, he uses the singular (*hallēwî*, "the Levite"); when he refers to them carrying out official duties, he tends to use the plural (17:9, 18; 18:1, 7; 24:8; 27:9, 14; 31:25).

30. "Gates" functions metonymically for "towns" (see NIV), which by definition refer to settlements with defensive walls and gate structures.

31. Deut. 4:9; 6:12; 8:11; 12:13, 19, 30; 15:9.

32. For a convenient summary of this position see Weinfeld, "Deuteronomy, Book of," *ABD*, 2:175–78.

obviously refers to Jerusalem, which Josiah made the center of all worship by eliminating all competing shrines outside this city.

However, this interpretation reflects a fundamental misunderstanding of the place formula.[33] (1) The expression "to put the Name there" does not express an abstraction of God, but declares his claim to ownership and authorization of the place as a cult center.

(2) Rather than abstracting the presence of Yahweh and focusing on divine transcendence, the expression "in the presence of the LORD" (*lipnē yhwh*) actually heightens the sense of his real presence.[34]

(3) The emphasis here and elsewhere in Deuteronomy is not on the place itself, but on Yahweh's right to determine the place of worship and his freedom regarding his own worship.

(4) The deuteronomistic historians acknowledged the fulfillment of the place formula in a succession of locations: Shechem, Shiloh, Bethel, and ultimately Jerusalem.[35]

(5) Even if Deuteronomy 12 had emphasized Yahweh's transcendence, the notion of Yahweh dwelling *in the temple* need not conflict with the notion that Yahweh actually dwells *in heaven*. The theology of the tabernacle reflects the same tension, even in the designations for the structure: "Holy Place" (*miqdāš*) highlights his transcendence, while "dwelling place" (*miškān*) highlights his immanence.

(6) The theory interprets the text anachronistically. Since Jerusalem and the temple were at the heart of Josiah's reforms, it is odd that neither should ever be mentioned in Deuteronomy. And the reference to Yahweh choosing the place "from among all the tribes" (12:5, 14) makes no sense in later times.[36]

While all scholars assume that Deuteronomy 12 played a crucial role in Josiah's reforms, the earliest allusion to this passage does not occur in 2 Kings 22—23.[37] It would be a mistake to read later highly developed Zion theology into Moses' vague reference to the place that Yahweh would choose, but the one who inspired him in this address ultimately had Jerusalem in mind,

---

33. For fuller discussion see J. Gordon McConville, "Time, Place and the Deuteronomic Altar-Law," in *Time and Place in Deuteronomy*, 88–141.

34. See Wilson, *Out of the Midst of the Fire*.

35. Deuteronomy never implies that the choice is permanent or irrevocable. Cf. Wenham, "Deuteronomy and the Central Sanctuary," 103–18.

36. S. Bakon ("Centralization of Worship," *Jewish Bible Quarterly* 26 [1998]: 31) observes that by Josiah's time "the tribal division had ceased for almost 400 years, since the time when Solomon had instituted a division of the United Kingdom into 12 districts. The term 'tribe' does not appear even once in the Books of Kings."

37. For discussion see T. N. D. Mettinger, *The Dethronement of Sabaoth: Studies in the Shem and Kabod Theologies* (ConBOT 18; Lund: CWK Gleerup, 1982).

even as he would have David in mind in 17:15.[38] After David had brought to Jerusalem "the ark of God, which is called by the Name, the name of the LORD Almighty [Yahweh Sabaoth]" (2 Sam. 6:2) and after "the LORD had given him rest from all his enemies around him" (7:1), David thought the time had come to build a temple for Yahweh. The use of "to give rest" suggests the narrator viewed the construction of the temple as a fulfillment of Deuteronomy 12.[39] Moreover, 2 Samuel 7:13 links Yahweh's covenant with David with the construction of a house for Yahweh's name and associates Yahweh's residence with the kingship and residence of David.

Solomon's prayer consecrating the temple in 1 Kings 8 repeatedly alludes to the place formula in Deuteronomy. In verse 16 Solomon recognizes that along with choosing a "city" from all the tribes of Israel to build a house for his name, Yahweh has chosen a man, David, to be over his people Israel. In verses 17−21 he acknowledges that from David he has inherited the privilege of building a house for the name of Yahweh and preparing a place for the ark, which contained the "covenant of the LORD."[40] But Solomon recognizes that, although he has built a house for the name of Yahweh, Yahweh's true residence is in heaven—for no earthly construction can actually house Yahweh.[41] In 1 Kings 9:3 Yahweh responds to the prayer, declaring that he has consecrated the temple that Solomon built by putting his name there forever. First Kings 11:36 expressly applies the place formula to Jerusalem (cf. 14:21; also 2 Chron. 6:20; 12:13).

Jeremiah frequently alludes to the place formula. Speaking of Jerusalem, in 3:17 he predicts a time when all nations will be gathered to the city "to honor the name of the LORD" (NIV). In chapter 7, after identifying Shiloh as the place where Yahweh made his name dwell at first (7:12), Jeremiah deals in considerable length with the temple in Jerusalem (7:9−14, 30).

No text demonstrates the significance of the place where Yahweh's name dwells more dramatically than Daniel 6:10[11]. Even though the city of Jerusalem and the temple lay in ruins, Daniel prayed toward this place three times a day. His passion for the city is evident in 9:17−19, where he pleads with Yahweh to take note of the desolation of the city that is called

---

38. Ps. 78:69−71 links the election of Judah/Zion (as opposed to Joseph/Ephraim) as Yahweh's eternal dwelling place with the election of David as king.

39. Psalm 132 links Yahweh's election of and covenant with David with the election of Zion as his dwelling place.

40. Note the function of the ark—not as the throne of Yahweh, but as the repository of the covenant of Yahweh (cf. Deut. 10:1−5). On this matter see Wilson, "Merely a Container? The Ark in Deuteronomy," 212−49.

41. Cf. 1 Kings 8:27, 30, 39, 43, 49. The notion is also reflected in Deut. 26:15; Ps. 33:13−14; Isa. 63:15.

by his name and to act for his own sake because his people and his city are called by his name.

Yahweh's initiative in inviting Israel to worship in his presence contrasts sharply with worship in pagan religions, where images represent human responses to the need for divine presence. Whereas iconographic religions offer symbols of presence, the gods are absent. Yahweh requires no physical representations of presence — indeed he forbids them — yet he offers his real presence. This notion seems to underlie Jesus' response to the Samaritan woman in John 4. Whereas Samaritans associated the "place" with Mount Gerizim, they acknowledged that for the Jews, the "place" was Jerusalem (John 4:20). However, Jesus announces the time when all these debates about place will be irrelevant. A day is coming when those who worship God will do so in spirit and truth. Apparently commenting on the current state of affairs in Gerizim and Jerusalem — where worship apparently was not driven by the Spirit and lacked integrity — he anticipates a time when it will have both.

This does not mean that Israel's worship was never true worship or that it was never driven by the Spirit; rather, it means that the vision of spiritual and true worship envisioned by Moses will be recovered because once again worshipers will focus on the object of worship — Yahweh incarnate in Christ — rather than the place itself.[42]

THEOLOGY OF WORSHIP. FOR contemporary readers, Deuteronomy 12:1 – 14 offers a profound theology of worship. (1) This text declares that Yahweh, the creator of heaven and earth, the God of Israel, and Redeemer of humankind, who appeared among us as the divine incarnate Son, Jesus Christ, is the only legitimate object of worship. Whether they be the man-made forms like those created by ancient Canaanites or the cleverly devised idols of moderns, all other objects of worship are not only illegitimate; they are abominable. As envisioned here, true worship perceives God alone as the divine host, with redeemed human beings as his guests.

(2) Worship must be designed to please the object of worship, not the worshipers. If Moses had to call a stop to the Israelites of his day worshiping in any way they pleased (v. 8), the same is true today. In the end, the divine verdict on our worship is the only verdict that matters. True worship

---

42. See also Jesus' references to destroying "this temple" and rebuilding it in three days (Mark 14:58; John 2:19). For fuller discussion see Daniel I. Block, "'In Spirit and in Truth': The Mosaic Vision of Worship," *The Gospel According to Moses*, 272 – 98.

involves an audience with the divine King and transpires in God's place by God's invitation on God's terms. Contrary to some, ultimately acceptable forms and styles of worship are not determined by worshipers, let alone the unregenerate or marginally spiritual. The invitation to enter the presence of God is extended to those who worship him with their lives (Deut. 10:1; Pss. 15; 24; Isa. 1:2 – 17; Mic. 6:6 – 8) and is to be accepted with humility and awe.

(3) In true worship the location has always been less important than the presence of the divine host. Deuteronomy suggests that Jesus' words on the location to the Samaritan woman in John 4:21 – 24 may not have been as radical or revolutionary as we tend to imagine. Whatever else "in spirit and in truth" means, worship "in spirit" involves worship driven by the regenerating and animating work of the Spirit of God. Worship "in truth" is worship with integrity — participation in actions that please God and arise out of lives that please him as well. As Stephen declared in Acts 7:47 – 50, Israel's spiritual pilgrimage took a wrong turn when they lost sight of the divine Resident and became preoccupied with his earthly residence.

(4) The redeemed anticipate worship with both delight and sobriety. On the one hand, those who worship God in spirit and in truth realize the incredible grace that God has lavished on them, first in his redemption, and second in his invitation to enter his presence (cf. Ps. 95:1 – 5). On the other hand, those who worship God in spirit and in truth are awed by the responsibility. True worship is never flippant or casual.

(5) True worship is communal rather than private. While we recognize that for believers all of life should be worship and that private basking in the presence of God is a great privilege and delight, when God's people gather for corporate worship, they gather to bring collective praise or petition to God. This text also emphasizes the inclusion of the marginalized. Those who are genuinely grateful will share their gifts with the less fortunate and marginalized believers and invite them to walk with them into the presence of God.

This issue has become especially acute in our day. Reflecting on the ethnic make-up of congregations, authorities on worship have often said that the worship hour on Sunday morning is the most segregated hour of the week. Whereas in the past the comment lamented the division of God's people on ethnic and racial grounds, to these fractures in recent times we have added segregation based on age and maturity. When churches split their services on the basis of race or age or musical tastes, the enemy has achieved his goal — a house divided. Worshipers who are overwhelmed by their own unworthiness on the one hand and the grace of God on the other will be more concerned about worship that pleases him than about pleasing themselves. If God's people are united about anything, it should be about the joy and privilege of worshiping him — together!

Deuteronomy 12:15–28

Nevertheless, you may slaughter your animals in any of your towns and eat as much of the meat as you want, as if it were gazelle or deer, according to the blessing the LORD your God gives you. Both the ceremonially unclean and the clean may eat it. ¹⁶But you must not eat the blood; pour it out on the ground like water. ¹⁷You must not eat in your own towns the tithe of your grain and new wine and oil, or the firstborn of your herds and flocks, or whatever you have vowed to give, or your freewill offerings or special gifts. ¹⁸Instead, you are to eat them in the presence of the LORD your God at the place the LORD your God will choose—you, your sons and daughters, your menservants and maidservants, and the Levites from your towns—and you are to rejoice before the LORD your God in everything you put your hand to. ¹⁹Be careful not to neglect the Levites as long as you live in your land.

²⁰When the LORD your God has enlarged your territory as he promised you, and you crave meat and say, "I would like some meat," then you may eat as much of it as you want. ²¹If the place where the LORD your God chooses to put his Name is too far away from you, you may slaughter animals from the herds and flocks the LORD has given you, as I have commanded you, and in your own towns you may eat as much of them as you want. ²²Eat them as you would gazelle or deer. Both the ceremonially unclean and the clean may eat. ²³But be sure you do not eat the blood, because the blood is the life, and you must not eat the life with the meat. ²⁴You must not eat the blood; pour it out on the ground like water. ²⁵Do not eat it, so that it may go well with you and your children after you, because you will be doing what is right in the eyes of the LORD.

²⁶But take your consecrated things and whatever you have vowed to give, and go to the place the LORD will choose. ²⁷Present your burnt offerings on the altar of the LORD your God, both the meat and the blood. The blood of your sacrifices must be poured beside the altar of the LORD your God, but you may eat the meat. ²⁸Be careful to obey all

these regulations I am giving you, so that it may always go well with you and your children after you, because you will be doing what is good and right in the eyes of the LORD your God.

THE INVITATION TO PRESENT sacrifices to Yahweh at the place he chooses raises questions about the slaughter of domesticated animals as food for the population. The Sinai revelation required that all domestic animals used for food be slaughtered in front of the sanctuary and involve the priests (Lev. 17:1–16). This arrangement was workable as long as the people were in transit and lived around the tabernacle, positioned in the middle of the camp. However, once they settled in the land, such restrictions would be problematic. Without modifications to the Sinai legislation, everyday diet would be restricted to wild game and vegetarian foods, and the people would have to be satisfied with eating the meat of domesticated animals only at celebrations at the central sanctuary. In this passage Moses modifies the previous regulations, removing a legal constriction of Israelite life in the land and inviting the people to enjoy the products of their labor and the blessing of Yahweh (cf. v. 7).

Like the previous section (12:2–14), this passage divides into two panels (A: vv. 15–19 B: vv. 20–27), and ends with a general charge (v. 28). Both panels subdivide further into two segments: the first part of each opens the door to nonsacrificial (profane) slaughter of domestic animals (vv. 15–16; vv. 20–25), while the second closes the door on eating animals intended for sacrifice away from the central sanctuary (vv. 17–19; vv. 26–27). Whereas the first segments deal largely with the same issues, the second ones emphasize different aspects of worship at the central sanctuary. Indeed, the purpose of verses 26–27 seems to be to clarify verses 17–19. This commentary will treat the first segments together and then proceed to the second.

Moses' Instructions on Profane Slaughter (12:15–16, 20–25)

IN THESE PASSAGES MOSES expresses his positive disposition toward profane slaughter through the principal verbs. First he declares, "You may slaughter," and "eat as much of the meat as you want"; then he adds: "Both the ceremonially unclean and the clean may eat it" (v. 15). In the second part he is even more emphatic: "You may eat meat" (v. 20); "you may slaughter" (v. 21a); "you may eat" (v. 21b); "eat them" (v. 22a); "both the ceremonially unclean and the clean may eat it" (v. 22b).

The need for this instruction is created by the fact that an individual will crave meat but will be far from the central sanctuary. Verse 15 specifies the context as (lit.) "in your gates," a figure of speech for "your towns" (NIV) within the allotted tribal territories where the Israelites reside (cf. v. 12). Moses' own clarification in verses 20–21 confirms this interpretation: when Yahweh has fulfilled his promise and enlarged the individual's territory (Ex. 34:23–24), and the person lives far from the place "where the LORD your God chooses to put his Name."

Moses highlights the craving for meat with the threefold repetition of "in all the desire of your soul/person" (pers. trans. of vv. 15, 20b, 21b), and casting it in direct speech, "I would like some meat" (v. 20a).[1] Moses responds to this craving by opening wide the door to "profane" consumption with four significant comments. (1) The people may slaughter and eat meat proportionate to the blessing that Yahweh lavishes on them (v. 15; cf. 16:17). This comment suggests that butchering an animal for meat may be a profane act (i.e., not directly associated with the cult), but it is never secular.[2] The demand to drain the blood (vv. 16, 23), and the addition of "as I have commanded you" (v. 21) reinforce this conclusion.[3]

(2) Israelites may slaughter and eat meat "in your gates/towns to your hearts' content" (pers. trans.), as well as in proportion to the blessing of Yahweh (vv. 15, 20–21).

(3) Anyone, whether clean or unclean, may eat the meat (vv. 15b, 22b).[4] To restrict consumption of the meat to those who were ceremonially pure would prove unworkable, since at any given time a large portion of the population would be in a state of ceremonial impurity. Indeed, the act of slaughtering an animal would render one unclean.

(4) The people may eat meat of domestic animals ("from the herds and flocks") like the meat of wild game. The pair "gazelle or deer" in verses 15b and 22 is a shorthand expression for all wild game authorized for human consumption (14:5–6; 15:22).

---

1. The expression that the NIV translates "as much as you want" may also be interpreted,"whatever you desire" (NKJV; Christensen, *Deuteronomy 1:1–21:9*, 250), temporally, "whenever you desire" (NJPS; NRSV; McConville, *Deuteronomy*, 210–211), or locatively, "wherever you desire" (NLT; Tigay, *Deuteronomy*, 124; cf. 2 Sam. 3:21; 1 Kings 11:37).

2. Normally *zābaḥ* ("to slaughter") refers to a sacrificial act, but occasionally it serves as a synonym for *ṭābaḥ* ("to butcher") or *šāḥaṭ* ("to slaughter"). So also 1 Sam. 28:24; 1 Kings 19:21; 2 Chron. 18:2; Ezek. 34:3.

3. According to Milgrom (*Leviticus 1–16*, 714–18) this clause "signifies that common slaughter must follow the same method practiced in sacrificial slaughter."

4. "The ceremonially unclean and the clean" involves a *merism* meaning "all Israelites." Ceremonial impurity could result from touching a corpse or a carcass, from certain diseases, or from bodily discharges (cf. Lev. 11–15; Num. 19).

Having opened the door to the consumption of meat of domestic animals away from the central sanctuary does not mean that Israelites can treat these animals callously, or that this slaughter could be considered amoral or secular. Verses 16 and 23 specify that when they kill an animal, the blood must not be consumed but poured out on the ground like water. In verse 23 Moses elaborates on the terse prohibition of verse 16 by specifying the grounds: Because the blood is the life, the blood is not to be eaten with the meat.[5] This identification of the blood with life derives from observing the life of an animal or person ebbing away as blood is lost. Because life is sacred and the blood is identified with the life, consuming blood is viewed as an attack on life itself, which explains Moses' explicit comment in verse 23, "You must not eat the life with the meat."

Although the blood of an animal slaughtered for its meat did not require satisfaction, in a sense all slaughter is sacrificial and substitutionary: a life for a life.[6] Whereas Leviticus 17:10–14 stressed the taboo on the blood of slaughtered animals by threatening to cut violators off from their people, in verse 25 Moses takes a more positive and pastoral approach. Compliance is the precondition to well-being for them and their children, and it guarantees the approval of Yahweh. After all, they "will be doing what is right in the eyes of the LORD."[7]

Moses' Instructions on Sacred Offerings (12:17–19, 26–27)

AS NOTED EARLIER, WHEREAS the first part of these two segments deal with the same issues, the concerns of the second parts diverge. While they exhibit some common features,[8] in the details they go their own ways and are best dealt with separately.

Following his summary authorization of profane slaughter (vv. 15–16), in verses 17–19 Moses reminds his people of the other side of this coin. Permission to slaughter domestic animals in all their towns whenever they crave meat does not mean that all livestock are candidates for profane con-

---

5. These prescriptions regarding blood are more general than Lev. 3:17; 7:26–27; 17:10–14, which required the blood of game animals and birds be poured out and covered with earth. See Milgrom, *Leviticus 17–22*, 1481–84.

6. Contra Weinfeld (*DDS*, 214), who suggests that "pouring the blood out like water" means "the blood has no more a sacral value than water has." This comparison relates to its liquid state rather than its religious significance.

7. "Doing what is right in the eyes of the LORD" answers directly to verse 8, where Moses had called on the people to stop doing (lit.) "what was right in their own eyes."

8. Both subdivide further into two parts (vv. 17 and 18–19; vv. 26 and 27); both segments have the first part deal with offerings at the sanctuary (v. 17; vv. 26–27a); and both segments refer to "the place the LORD your God will choose" (vv. 18, 26).

sumption. In fact, this restriction extends to horticultural products as well (cf. 7:13; 12:6). Animals and produce of the field that have been set apart as sacred offerings may not be eaten at home; this food may be consumed only in the presence of Yahweh at the place he chooses. The juxtaposition of "before the LORD your God" and "in your towns" does not mean Yahweh is not present with the Israelites in the towns where they will live. Rather, for purposes of cultic worship his presence is localized in the place he will choose.

Moses follows up the command to eat these products as sacrificial meals at the central sanctuary by specifying who may participate in these events (v. 18a). This list is identical with verse 12, except that he now refers to the addressee in the second person singular instead of the plural. Verse 18 concludes with another invitation to celebrate before Yahweh with all the products of the Israelites' labor. Almost as an afterthought, Moses ends the first panel with a stern warning not to neglect the Levite as long as the Israelites live in the land (v. 19).

Verses 26–27 follow Moses' more detailed instructions on profane slaughter (vv. 20–25). Once again (cf. v. 17) he restricts the meals authorized for consumption in the towns by excluding sacred offerings. But rather than listing the kinds of forbidden offerings, he speaks generally of "your consecrated things and whatever you have vowed to give." The former represent contributions required by the cultic rituals; the latter are gifts voluntarily promised to Yahweh. For these offerings the Israelites should go to the place Yahweh chooses.

The panel concludes with summary instructions on what worshipers are to do when they arrive at the sanctuary: perform (ʿāśâ; lit. "do"; NIV "present") the rituals of the whole burnt offerings and the other sacrifices. With burnt offerings the flesh and blood are consumed entirely by fire on the altar; with the rest the meat is eaten by worshipers and the blood is poured out on the altar.

Conclusion (12:28)

FOREVER THE PASTOR, MOSES concludes his instructions regarding the central sanctuary and profane slaughter with a final exhortation to pay careful attention to all that he has said. Characterizing his instructions as "words" (NIV "regulations") rather than as commands or ordinances does not suggest this has been a casual conversation. On the contrary, heeding his instructions is the precondition for the well-being of the present generation and their descendants in perpetuity. Furthermore, when they bring their sacrifices to the sanctuary and butcher animals for food according to the instructions given, they not only obey him; they also do "what is good and right in the eyes of the LORD your God."

A GRACIOUS DISPOSITION. THIS passage reflects the fundamentally gracious disposition of Moses and Yahweh toward the people. They recognize the logistical problems created by the call for worship at the central sanctuary and are sensitive to the personal appetites of the people. Rather than hemming in Israelite behavior, with remarkable generosity Moses affirms the people's desire to enjoy the meat of animals in their own towns. A similar disposition toward the people's desires is reflected in 17:14–20. Anticipating the people's future request for a king Moses authorizes them to set a king over themselves. However, as in this case, the permission is qualified by specifying who may or may not be candidates for the office and then prescribing the boundaries of the king's performance.

Slaughtering animals. The notion of clean and unclean animals is as old as the human race. According to Genesis 7:2, in addition to pairs of all the other species of animals, Noah took into the ark seven clean animals. The narrative assumes Noah knew the boundaries between clean and unclean. Presumably God had revealed this information to Adam and Eve as they left Eden. The subject will return in chapter 14, where Moses spells out in considerable detail which animals are clean (i.e., fit for Israelite consumption) and which are not (cf. Lev. 11). For now we note only that this passage is concerned more with how slaughtered animals are handled than which animals are authorized as food for Israelite consumption.

The taboo on eating the blood reflected in this passage also goes back to the fountainhead of humanity (Gen. 9:4), in which God forbids the consumption of blood by any of Noah's descendants. The original ordinance reinforces the notion that respect for the sanctity of animal life was never perceived as a uniquely Israelite concern; it applies to all humanity. In Acts 15:20 the council of Jerusalem recognized the permanence and supra-Israelite validity of the ban on blood, binding Gentile Christians to this ordinance.[9] The principle of the sanctity of all life transcends the Torah of Deuteronomy and ethnic Israel.

---

9. For discussion of the relationship of these apostolic injunctions to, and their grounding in, Lev. 17–18, see R. Davidson, "Which Torah Laws Should Gentile Christians Obey? The Relationship between Leviticus 17–18 and Acts 15," paper presented to the Evangelical Theological Society, November 15, 2007, in San Diego.

Contemporary Significance

ETHICAL TREATMENT OF ANIMALS. The picture of God painted here surprises many readers. Perceiving the God of the Old Testament to be dour and angry, if not violent and bloodthirsty, more intent on punishing than in showing mercy, some will be surprised by the ease with which Moses (and Yahweh, who inspires him) accedes to the people's desire to eat meat wherever they live. Yes, meals eaten in the presence of God are special, and when Yahweh the divine host turns around and serves his guests the food they have brought to him as offerings, this is a great privilege and honor. But how welcome to hear him say, "Go ahead. Do not wait until you are at the sanctuary to celebrate the goodness of God. Rejoice in his blessing and eat freely of the food—including the meat—that he has provided." Incidentally, Scripture does not assume a vegetarian diet.

However, even as this passage encourages us to enjoy the provision of God, it does so with a profound ethical sensitivity. The slaughter of animals for meat could easily degenerate into savagery and a ruthless disregard for the life of the animal. However, the ritual of draining the blood reminds the persons who slaughtered the animal and those who eat its meat that even the life of the creature is sacred. If the meat is eaten with its blood, the blood will cry out to God and the offender will become the target of divine fury. While the flesh is sanctioned for human consumption, life itself is inviolable, and God remains the guarantor of the sanctity of the life of the animal.[10]

However, there is another aspect of the ordinance that is seldom noted. It is easy to imagine a hunter being calloused toward the life of his victim, especially when the animal is killed from a distance with a projectile (arrow, spear) or in a trap. This ordinance forces those who kill animals for their meat to identify with the creature by touching it and personally bearing responsibility for its death. This identification with a nonhuman animal in its death enhances humans' appreciation for all life and forces them to grieve over the loss, even as they take advantage of the benefit the animal offers them. Since all slaughter is sacrificial and substitutionary—a life for life—the slaughter of animals may be profane (dissociated from the cult), but it is never secular. So whether the occasion is a festive Thanksgiving dinner or a common meal, when we sit down to feast on the turkey or mutton set before us, we need to give thanks to God who has blessed us by providing food, but we also need to thank him for the animal that has given its life for us.

---

10. For detailed discussion of these passages in Leviticus, see Milgrom, *Leviticus 1–16*, 704–13; idem, *Leviticus 17–22*, 1469–84.

After studying this passage I understand better my father's emotional stress every fall when it was time to fill the larder with meat for his large family. He was uncomfortable selecting one of the animals and then having to kill it that we might have food. But cutting the jugular and watching the blood drain onto the ground was for him a religious experience. We youngsters should be grateful to God and his creation for this provision. This text speaks to the ethical problems posed by some practices in slaughterhouses across the country. If factory farms have depersonalized and dehumanized animal husbandry, gigantic slaughterhouses have desecrated the life of these animals. While the Scriptures offer no warrant for vegetarianism, and we obviously cannot go back to the small family farm where hogs were recognized by personality and temperament and every cow had a name, Christians need to be in the forefront of efforts to ensure the ethical treatment of animals from birth to death.[11]

---

11. For further study and bibliography, see Daniel I. Block, "All Creatures Great and Small: Recovering a Deuteronomic Theology of Animals," in *The Old Testament in the Life of God's People: Essays in Honor of Elmer A. Martens* (ed. J. Isaak; Winona Lake, IN: Eisenbrauns, 2009), 283–305; reprinted in *The Gospel According to Moses*, 174–99.

Deuteronomy 12:29–13:18[1]

The LORD your God will cut off before you the nations you are about to invade and dispossess. But when you have driven them out and settled in their land, [30]and after they have been destroyed before you, be careful not to be ensnared by inquiring about their gods, saying, "How do these nations serve their gods? We will do the same." [31]You must not worship the LORD your God in their way, because in worshiping their gods, they do all kinds of detestable things the LORD hates. They even burn their sons and daughters in the fire as sacrifices to their gods.

[32]See that you do all I command you; do not add to it or take away from it.

[13:1]If a prophet, or one who foretells by dreams, appears among you and announces to you a miraculous sign or wonder, [2]and if the sign or wonder of which he has spoken takes place, and he says, "Let us follow other gods" (gods you have not known) "and let us worship them," [3]you must not listen to the words of that prophet or dreamer. The LORD your God is testing you to find out whether you love him with all your heart and with all your soul. [4]It is the LORD your God you must follow, and him you must revere. Keep his commands and obey him; serve him and hold fast to him. [5]That prophet or dreamer must be put to death, because he preached rebellion against the LORD your God, who brought you out of Egypt and redeemed you from the land of slavery; he has tried to turn you from the way the LORD your God commanded you to follow. You must purge the evil from among you.

[6]If your very own brother, or your son or daughter, or the wife you love, or your closest friend secretly entices you, saying, "Let us go and worship other gods" (gods that neither you nor your fathers have known, [7]gods of the peoples around you, whether near or far, from one end of the land to the other), [8]do not yield to him or listen to him. Show him

1. For the sake of convenience, in the commentary on chap. 13 all references are to the English verse numbers. Because the Hebrew begins chap. 13 at 12:29, all verse numbers are higher by one.

323

no pity. Do not spare him or shield him. ⁹You must certainly put him to death. Your hand must be the first in putting him to death, and then the hands of all the people. ¹⁰Stone him to death, because he tried to turn you away from the LORD your God, who brought you out of Egypt, out of the land of slavery. ¹¹Then all Israel will hear and be afraid, and no one among you will do such an evil thing again.

¹²If you hear it said about one of the towns the LORD your God is giving you to live in ¹³that wicked men have arisen among you and have led the people of their town astray, saying, "Let us go and worship other gods" (gods you have not known), ¹⁴then you must inquire, probe and investigate it thoroughly. And if it is true and it has been proved that this detestable thing has been done among you, ¹⁵you must certainly put to the sword all who live in that town. Destroy it completely, both its people and its livestock. ¹⁶Gather all the plunder of the town into the middle of the public square and completely burn the town and all its plunder as a whole burnt offering to the LORD your God. It is to remain a ruin forever, never to be rebuilt. ¹⁷None of those condemned things shall be found in your hands, so that the LORD will turn from his fierce anger; he will show you mercy, have compassion on you, and increase your numbers, as he promised on oath to your forefathers, ¹⁸because you obey the LORD your God, keeping all his commands that I am giving you today and doing what is right in his eyes.

ALTHOUGH MOST COMMENTATORS DIVIDE the text according to the chapter divisions, on grounds of form and substance 12:29 begins a new unit that extends to the end of chapter 13.[2] Whereas the principal concern of 12:1–28 is the *place* of legitimate worship, in 12:29–13:18 the concern shifts to the *object* of legitimate worship—no gods but Yahweh. The style and tone of a preacher continue as Moses calls his people to abandon all other gods and cling to Yahweh alone. This rhetorical agenda is evident throughout.

Deuteronomy 12:29–32 functions as a thesis statement, warning the people against the seduction of Canaanite gods, while 13:1–18 presents

---

2. The conclusion in 13:18 answers to 12:28, which signals the end of the preceding subsection.

three hypothetical circumstances under which such seduction might occur (13:1–5; 13:6–11; 13:12–18). Each of the four parts begins with a temporal/conditional clause introduced by "when/if" (*kî* in 12:29; 13:1, 6, 12). The required response is cast in the form of general exhortations to "guard yourself" (12:30, NIV "be careful") not to act a certain way (12:31), not to listen to those who would lead you astray (13:3, 8), not to yield to them (13:8), and not to pity, spare, or conceal them (13:8). Positively Moses exhorts his hearers to follow Yahweh their God, fear him, keep his commandments, listen to his voice, and cling to him (13:4). The most emphatic charges occur at the end of the preamble (12:32), in 13:4, and in the concluding clause (13:18). The entire section is laced with motive clauses, positive statements being introduced with "for, because" (12:31; 13:3, 5, 10, 18) and negative motivations with "lest" (12:30; cf. 13:11).

Moses makes his case for exclusive devotion to Yahweh by putting the critical statements in the mouths of hypothetical interlocutors.[3] In the preamble (12:30) the general warning is cast as a question; the other three cast the interlocution as cohortative statements by third persons who try to incite the Israelites to abandon Yahweh in favor of other gods (13:2b, 6b, 13). As in chapter 4, singular and the plural forms of pronouns alternate. The collective singular predominates, but occasional shifts to the plural[4] indicate that corporate character depends on individual compliance.

Throughout Moses appeals to the loyalty of the people by reminding them of their special relationship with Yahweh; twelve times in twenty-two verses he identifies Yahweh as "your God"[5] and contrasts him with the gods of the Canaanites, "gods you have not known"[6] (13:2, 6, 13). This is not the style of legislation but the language of a pastor, passionate about the spiritual well-being of his flock after he is gone.

The General Warning against Spiritual Defection (12:29–32)

MOSES BEGINS BY DESCRIBING the circumstances in which the danger identified in verse 30 will lurk:[7] when Yahweh cuts off the seven nations of the land (7:1) and the Israelites settle in the land, dispossess them, and occupy their territory. Once again the test of Israel's faith will come when

---

3. Cf. the discussion on 6:20–8:20 above.

4. The second person plural occurs in 12:32a, 2c, 3b–5a, 7, 13b.

5. See 12:29, 31; 13:3a, 3b, 4, 5a, 5b, 10, 12, 16, 18a, 18b. Moses refers to Yahweh without the qualifier only in 12:31b.

6. Verse 6 has an expanded version: "gods that neither you nor your fathers have known."

7. The NIV's translation of v. 29 obscures the "When ... then ..." construction of the Hebrew. In casuistic laws the protasis introduced by *kî* prepares the reader for the specific situation that a command addresses.

they are enjoying the fulfillment of the promise to Abraham and the deity–nation–land relationship is fully operative.

Moses casts the warning not to behave like the people they dispossess with an exhortation, "Guard yourself" (NIV "be careful"), followed by two lurking dangers.[8] (1) They are to be careful not to get caught in the trap that has destroyed the nations that preceded them in the land, the trap being a metaphor for destruction at Yahweh's hands. (2) This warning (v. 30b) is more specific, cautioning the people against fascination with the gods of the nations in Canaan. He concretizes their potential curiosity by introducing an interlocutor who asks, "How do these nations serve their gods?" and then declares his determination: "I will do the same."[9] Moses' rejection of such impulses echoes his earlier statement in verse 4: "You shall not treat Yahweh this way" (v. 31a, pers. trans.). Whereas the earlier reference to "this way" had involved multiplying shrines all over the land, this prohibition on serving Yahweh as the Canaanites worship their gods is more general.

Moses grounds the prohibition in two considerations. He first declares that everything that Yahweh abhors and hates the Canaanites do for their gods.[10] Then Moses identifies the most despicable offense; they even offer their children as burnt offerings to their gods (cf. 18:10). Although direct archaeological evidence for this practice among the Canaanites is missing, classical sources speak of it in Phoenicia and her colonies.[11] Whereas to Canaanites such actions represented supreme acts of piety (cf. Mic. 6:6–7), to Yahweh this was the ultimate in depravity.

In verse 32 Moses challenges his hearers once more to keep every word that he is commanding them (cf. 5:1). He also warns them not to supplement his instructions with their own cultic improvisations or borrowing practices from their neighbors. Moses sets the stage for the three hypothetical scenarios in chapter 13, then, with the charge neither to add to nor to subtract from what he is commanding them (cf. 4:2).

---

8. Introduced by "lest" (Heb. *pen*). Cf. 4:9, 16, 23; 6:12; 8:11–12, 17; 11:16; 12:13, 19, 30; 15:9.

9. The NIV uses the plural, but the construction literally translates: "And I will do thus, I too."

10. Contra NIV, it is not merely that all they do is repugnant to Yahweh, but all that is repugnant to Yahweh they do.

11. For an illustrated popular discussion, see L. E. Stager and S. R. Wolff, "Child Sacrifice at Carthage—Religious Rite or Population Control," *BAR* 10/1 (1984): 30–51. On child sacrifice, often associated with the cult of Molech, see J. Day, *Molech: A God of Human Sacrifice in the Old Testament* (Cambridge: Cambridge Univ. Press, 1989); Tigay, "Excursus 15: Child Sacrifice and Passing Children through Fire," in *Deuteronomy*, 464–65.

The Specific Warnings against Spiritual Defection (13:1–18)

CHAPTER 13 REPRESENTS ONE of the most logically constructed literary units in the book. Critical scholars tend to interpret this chapter as an adaptation of late neo-Assyrian loyalty oaths.[12] However, the style and wording of neo-Assyrian (and Sefire) oaths were conventional and rooted in a centuries-old literary treaty and loyalty oath tradition.[13] Furthermore, the conceptual links of Deuteronomy 13 with second millennium BC Hittite loyalty oaths are as strong as, if not stronger than, the eighth–seventh century neo-Assyrian connections.[14] Indeed, counterparts to virtually every feature of the present passage may be adduced from second millennium BC Hittite diplomatic correspondence. The parallels do not prove that Deuteronomy is dependent on Hittite loyalty treaties for its phraseology and its basic ideas, but they demonstrate that conceptually this chapter is at least as at home in the second millennium as in the first.

The unity of Deuteronomy 13 is evident in the form with which Moses presents the three seditious scenarios. Each is divided into three major parts: the protasis, introduced by an "if/when" clause in the third person; an apodosis in the second person, prescribing the appropriate response to the conspirators; and a complex motive clause.

It has been claimed that Deuteronomy 13 is "the only biblical law aimed at those who might *proselytize* for other deities."[15] While the classification of this chapter as law is questionable, the theological point is correct. In

---

12. As represented, e.g., in the Vassal Treaties of Esarhaddon (hereafter VTE). For transliteration, translation, and discussion of VTE, see S. Parpola and K. Watanabe, *Neo-Assyrian Treaties and Loyalty Oaths* (SAA 2; Helsinki: Helsinki Univ. Press, 1988), 28–58. For defenses of this view, P.-E. Dion, "Deuteronomy 13: The Suppression of Alien Religious Propaganda in Israel during the Late Monarchical Era," in *Law and Ideology in Monarchic Israel* (ed. B. Halpern and D. W. Hobson; JSOTSup 124; Sheffield: Sheffield Academic, 1991), 197–98; B. M. Levinson, "Textual Criticism, Assyriology, and the History of Interpretation: Deuteronomy 13:7a as a Test Case in Method," *JBL* 120 (2001): 236–41.

13. For discussion of the persistence of conventional language through centuries of Assyrian records, see J. J. Niehaus, *The Deuteronomic Style: An Examination of the Deuteronomic Style in the Light of Ancient Near Eastern Literature* (unpublished manuscript, 1985).

14. For critique of the view that this chapter is inspired by VTE, see M. Zehnder, "Building on Stone? Deuteronomy and Esarhaddon's Loyalty Oaths (Part 1): Some Preliminary Observations," *BBR* 19/3 (2009): 348–51; idem, "Building on Stone? Deuteronomy and Esarhaddon's Loyalty Oaths (Part 2): Some Additional Observations" (*BBR* 19/4 [2009]: 511–30, esp. 511–16). See also Joshua Berman, "CTH 133 and the Hittite Provenance of Deuteronomy 13," paper presented to the Society of Biblical Literature in Atlanta, GA, November, 2010. For the Hittite texts, see Gary Beckman, *Hittite Diplomatic Texts* (2nd ed.; SBLWAW 7; Atlanta: Scholars, 1999), 11–124, but especially the Treaty between Arnuwanda I of Hatti and the Men of Ismerika, 13–17.

15. Dion, "Deuteronomy 13," 147; italics his.

chapter 13 Moses moves from the soil in which the seeds of apostasy sprout (12:29−31) to three ways the seeds may be planted. In so doing he declares the dire consequences of spiritual sedition and prescribes a preventative strategy: undivided and unreserved love for Yahweh, demonstrated in obedience to his voice (vv. 3−4, 18) and in remembrance of his saving grace (vv. 5b, 10b).

Scenario 1: apostasy instigated by a prophet or an oneiromantic (vv. 1−5). False prophets represent the first potential source of spiritual sedition. This is the first occurrence in Deuteronomy of the word "prophet" (*nābîʾ*). The Old Testament has a rich vocabulary of prophecy,[16] but *nābîʾ* is the most common expression. The word refers to "one summoned by God."[17] The primary role of prophets was to proclaim to divinely determined audiences messages they received from the deity (cf. Ex. 7:1−2; Jer. 23:16−22). Since the institution of prophecy was common throughout the ancient Near East,[18] that a prophet might appear proclaiming a message antithetical to the will of Yahweh is not surprising. Indeed, the conflict between true and false prophets is a prominent motif in Israel's later history.[19]

The second potential source of spiritual sedition is identified as a "dreamer of dreams," that is, a professional who has access to the mind of deity through dreams. Oneiromancy (divination through dreams) was widespread in the ancient world.[20] These dreams tended to be of two types: symbolic dreams that required interpretation by a gifted interpreter (Gen. 37:5−11; 40:9−19; 41:1−7; Dan. 2:1−49), and message dreams involving straightforward communication (Gen. 15; 28:10−22; 1 Kings 3:5−15 = 2 Chron. 1:6−12). Unlike Deuteronomy 18:15−19, the present context does not disapprove of dreams or prophecy in principle.[21]

---

16. Prophets are referred to variously as "seer" (1 Sam. 9:9), "man of God" (2 Kings 4:7), "servant [of the LORD]" (2 Kings 17:13), "messenger [of the LORD]" (2 Chron. 36:15, 16; Isa. 44:26).

17. This is an I-class passive from a hypothetical root, *nābâʾ*, "to call,." See further J. Huehnergard, "On the Etymology and Meaning of Hebrew *nābîʾ*," *ErIsr* 26 (1999): 88*−93*.

18. See H. B. Huffmon, "Prophecy," *ABD*, 5:477−82.

19. 1 Kings 22:1−23; Jer. 23:16−40; Ezek. 13:1−19.

20. For surveys of the phenomenon in Egypt see J. Bergman et al., *TDOT*, 4:421−27. For analysis of dreams in Mesopotamia, see A. L. Oppenheim, *The Interpretation of Dreams in the Ancient Near East: With a Translation of an Assyrian Dream Book* (Philadelphia: American Philosophical Society, 1956).

21. On dreams as a means of revelation in ancient Israel see R. Gnuse, *The Dream Theophany of Samuel: Its Structure in Relation to Ancient Near Eastern Dreams and Its Theological Significance* (Lanham, MD: Univ. Press of America, 1984); F. H. Cryer, *Divination in Ancient Israel and Its Near Eastern Environment: A Socio−Historical Investigation* (JSOTSup 142; Sheffield: Sheffield Academic, 1994), 263−72.

In this context the dreamer makes a formal pronouncement (v. 3b) and then announces an authenticating sign. Moses casts the prophetic utterance in the form of direct speech,[22] as the dreamer invites Israelites to join him in worshiping "other gods," defined more closely as "gods you have not known" (cf. vv. 6, 13).[23] Verse 7 specifies these as the gods of the Canaanites referred to in 12:29–30.

As in 8:2–3 and 16, that which is unknown functions as a test of Israel's commitment to Yahweh (cf. v. 4). However, here the roles are reversed. Whereas with the manna the Israelites were challenged to cease relying on the familiar and trust in the unknown, here Moses challenges the Israelites not to abandon the known in favor of that which is foreign and new. The glorious truth for the Israelites was that Yahweh their God had actually revealed himself through word and deed (1:5–3:29; 4:1–40). By contrast, the gods of the nations were merely man-made images with mouths that could not speak, eyes that could not see, and ears that could not hear (4:28). To exchange the God of Israel for these figments of depraved imaginations (cf. 4:35, 39) is the height of treason (Moses' principal point here) and folly. As new objects of devotion, they are rivals to Yahweh, in violation of the first principle of covenant relationship (5:7) and the people's commitment expressed in the Shema (6:4–5).

Moses anticipates that prophets and dreamers who call for defection to other gods will try to prove their authenticity with an attesting "sign or wonder" (v. 2a; cf. 4:34). These expressions do not speak merely of an accompanying miraculous act (Ex. 4:1–9) but of a verbal wonder, a prediction of a specific natural or extraordinary event that would supposedly prove the person was a genuine divine messenger.[24] For the sign to authenticate the medium's call to worship other gods, the predicted event had to transpire within a short period of time. If an event would happen just as the prophet predicted, people whose faith was weak would be convinced that both the person and the message were genuine — even if it contradicted what they had been taught about Yahweh and the other gods. Perhaps recalling his own encounters with the magicians of Egypt (Ex. 7:11, 22; 8:7[3]), Moses recognizes that false prophets are sometimes able to work wonders.

---

22. On the significance of "to walk after/follow other gods," see comments on 6:14. On the significance of "to serve other gods," see comments on 7:4. See also 11:16; 13:6, 13[7, 14]; 17:3; 28:36, 64; 29:26[25]; cf. also 4:19; 8:19; 30:17.

23. On this expression, see 11:28.

24. For analogous authenticating "signs," see 1 Sam. 10:1–13, cf. v. 7 (the choice of Saul as king), 1 Kings 13:1–5 (the utterance of an unnamed prophet at Bethel), and 2 Kings 20:8–11 (the message of Isaiah to Hezekiah).

In 13:3–5 Moses prescribes how the Israelites are to respond to prophets or dreamers who encourage defection from Yahweh. Focusing on the Israelites' disposition toward the invitation, Moses explicitly charges the Israelites to refuse to give prophets or dreamers who incite spiritual sedition an ear (vv. 3–4). But then he offers a surprising theological explanation for the overture to defection. Like the manna in 8:2–3, 16, Moses interprets the occasion as a "test" from Yahweh of Israel's loyalty to him (13:3a). While some interpret this as divine disingenuity, as with the magicians in Egypt, we should interpret this either as Yahweh's permission of the instigator to have access to the Israelites, or as his permission of the signs accompanying the invitation to be fulfilled.[25] Whatever the origin or source of a temptation to abandon Yahweh, such occasions always constitute a test of love for him.

The anticipated form of the test is at home in the context of ancient Near Eastern treaties[26] and within the book of Deuteronomy: Do the Israelites love Yahweh with their entire beings?[27] With emphatic syntax, Moses summarizes the evidence of unreserved love, using six familiar verbs: "after Yahweh their God they shall walk";[28] "him they shall fear"; "his commandments they shall keep"; "to his voice they shall listen"; "him they shall serve"; and "to him they shall cling" (all pers. trans.).[29]

Moses instructs the people on how to treat a prophet or dreamer who incites sedition with one simple statement: He "must be put to death" (v. 5a). If in political contexts encouraging subjects of one king to change allegiance to another king is considered worthy of the death penalty, how much more would the appeal to the Israelites to abandon Yahweh in favor of other gods call for capital punishment.[30]

Moses then provides the rationale for such harsh treatment of the conspirators (vv. 5b–c): The prophet or dreamer has falsely claimed to have received a message from God and has tried to turn the Israelites away from the way prescribed by Yahweh. Because the first expression suggests that,

---

25. Similarly Tigay, *Deuteronomy*, 130.

26. See W. L. Moran, "The Ancient Near Eastern Background of the Love of God in Deuteronomy," *CBQ* 25 (1965): 77–97.

27. Cf. 5:10; 6:5; 7:9; 10:12; 11:1, 13, 22; 19:9; 30:6.

28. As opposed to "other gods." "Walking after Yahweh" occurs only here in Deuteronomy, undoubtedly to answer to temptation to "walk after other gods," expressed three times in vv. 2b, 6b, and 13b. Elsewhere Moses speaks of "walking in [Yahweh's] way/ways [*derek*]": 8:6; 19:9; 26:17; 28:9; 30:16.

29. This expression occurs elsewhere in 4:4; 10:20; 11:22; 30:20.

30. The absolute use of the passive "he must be put to death" occurs elsewhere in Deuteronomy only in 21:22 and functions as a technical term for capital punishment (cf. Ex. 21:29; 35:2; Lev. 19:20; 24:16, 21; Num. 1:51; 3:10, 38; 18:7). Deuteronomy tends to prefer the active mood *wāmēt/ûmēt*, "And he shall die" (see v. 10; 17:12; 18:20; 19:12; 21:21; 22:21, 22, 24, 25; 24:7, though the NIV usually translates these as passives too).

through the sign, Yahweh has authorized the worship of other gods,[31] the issue involves an Israelite who creates the impression that he speaks in the name of Yahweh and suggests that, like other gods in the ancient world, Yahweh tolerates the worship of other deities.[32] With the second expression, Moses describes the potential effect of such seditious prophecy: it is seductive and entices the people from Yahweh's prescribed course. This statement summarizes the six verbs used in the previous verse.

As their pastor, Moses heightens the significance of such treacherous counsel by reminding the Israelites that Yahweh, the one who brought them out of Egypt and redeemed them from the house of slavery (cf. 7:8), is their God. His call for the death penalty for one who encourages spiritual defection from Yahweh may seem harsh, but the final clause declares Moses' fundamental concern: to "purge the evil from among you."[33] Whereas in verse 5a Moses had used the passive, "and be put to death," without specifying the agent, here he places responsibility for the purging the evil on the people themselves. He recognizes that the sin of sedition is like a virus whose influence in Israel can only be stopped by exterminating those infected with it. Yahweh requires a community united in its devotion to him and rigorous in its preservation of its own character as a holy people (cf. 7:1–6).

Apostasy instigated by a member of the family (vv. 6–11). Whereas the first seditious scenario had involved treachery inspired by persons posing as professional spokespersons for Yahweh, the second involves treachery at home. To highlight the potential problem Moses lists five close acquaintances who might incite defection away from Yahweh: a full brother, a son, a daughter, a wife, or a friend. The expressions highlight the intimacy of relationships between potential ringleader and follower. Presupposing a social environment in which polygamy was common, by qualifying "your brother" with (lit.) "son of your mother,"[34] Moses stresses full blood relationship as opposed to one's half brother.[35]

---

31. Cf. Tigay, *Deuteronomy*, 130–31.

32. Note also the clear identification of the instigators of sedition as Israelites in vv. 6 and 11. On divine tolerance of the worship of other gods in the ancient Near East generally, see Block, *The Gods of the Nations*, 62–71.

33. The formula "to purge [exterminate] the evil from" recurs in 17:7, 12; 19:19; 21:21; 22:21, 22, 24; 24:7. Cf. Judg. 20:13; 2 Sam. 4:11; 1 Kings 4:10. Except for Deut. 19:19, in Deuteronomy all these occurrences involve the death penalty.

34. NIV "your very own brother" obscures the emphasis. The LXX and Samaritan Pentateuch read "the son of your father or of your mother." Cf. also 11QTemple [11Q19] 54:19.

35. For the pairing of "brother" and "son of mother," see Gen. 27:29; 43:29; Judg. 8:19; Pss. 50:20; 69:8[9], and second millennium Ugaritic texts (Kirta, *CAT* 1.14.I.7–9 [cf. Parker, *UNP*, p. 12]; *KTU* 1.6.VI.10–11, 14–16 [*UNP*, p. 162]) and a first century Akkadian treaty text (VTE ll. 94, 270, 341–43). See Levinson, "Textual Criticism," 224–27.

By adding "daughter," Moses personalizes the issue even more. In a patricentric world sons were expected to take responsibility, but to imagine one's daughter leading the charge in defection from Yahweh is striking. While "wife of your bosom" (NIV "wife you love") speaks of the most intimate and affectionate relationship (Mic. 7:5),[36] the final expression, "your neighbor who is like yourself" (NIV "your closest friend") refers to someone close outside the family, one's "bosom buddy." Viewed as a whole, this list imagines those who are closest and dearest as potential conspirators intent on leading the family and the community away from the worship of Yahweh.[37] Like most seditious plots, this action is urged "secretly," presumably within the walls of one's home — as if Yahweh or his spies are unable to see what goes on inside. To "entice" people to follow a different god is treason of the highest order.[38]

The appeal that the local instigator of rebellion presents (v. 6b) is essentially the same as that of the prophetic dreamers in verse 2b, though the characterization of alien gods is more elaborate. They are strange not only to the present generation, but have also been unknown to their ancestors, presumably a reference to the ancestors of the generation envisioned here rather than the patriarchs. In contrast to Yahweh, these are new gods, who have played no role in Israel's history. By inciting family members to abandon Yahweh, the leaders of sedition violate both the Supreme Command and Israel's longstanding religious tradition. The specification of the alien gods as the gods of the Canaanites, whether local or elsewhere in the land,[39] deliberately eliminates any and every god as potential rivals to Yahweh.

In verses 8 – 10a Moses prescribes the proper Israelite response to close relatives and friends who attempt to lead them astray. The instructions are detailed, beginning with five negative commands, followed by three positive orders. By heaping up the former (v. 8) Moses addresses the tendency to let sentimentality interfere with the proper administration of justice. Whereas earlier Moses had simply urged his people not to listen to prophets or dreamers (v. 3), in verse 8 he intensifies the command with a direct appeal to the will of the hearer: "Do not yield to him or listen to him," and

---

36. The expression recurs in 28:54, and in 28:56, referring to a man as "husband of her bosom."

37. This list is reminiscent of a list of conspirators in VTE 10.

38. Similarly 2 Kings 18:32; 2 Chron. 32:11, 15; Isa. 36:18; Jer. 43:3. Job 36:18 speaks of being "enticed" by riches. In some instances God himself is the subject of the verb, inciting humans to action: 1 Sam. 26:19; 2 Sam. 24:1 (cf. 1 Chron. 21:1; 2 Chron. 18:31); Job 36:16.

39. "Around you, whether near or far" and "from one end of the land to the other" are merisms involving polar opposites to express totality.

follows this up with a twofold charge not to let natural human emotions deflect from what needs to be done. The first, "Show him no pity," discourages persons charged with carrying out punishment from being lenient toward the offender.[40] The second, "Do not spare him," prohibits feeling sorry for or showing compassion toward the person.[41] The last command, "Do not ... shield him," demands that relatives and close friends expose the perpetrator of the crime — they are not to give him asylum.[42]

To modern readers the demand to execute the conspirator in verses 9 – 10a seems ruthless and heartless. But Moses' tone is emphatic: "You must certainly put him to death." The singular verb suggests that the family member who hears a relative or neighbor propose sedition must take immediate action. This impression is reinforced by the added comment: "Your hand must be the first in putting him to death" (cf. 17:5 – 6). Nevertheless, the following clause reins in the temptation to individual vigilantism; this is in fact a community concern. Reinforcing the charge in verse 8, verse 9 insists that allegiance to Yahweh must take precedence over family ties. Because Israel's identity was bound up with her covenant relationship with him, defection was a capital offense, the prescribed form of punishment being execution by stoning (v. 10a). The Old Testament requires this form of punishment for actions considered "high treason" against Yahweh.[43] By stoning the criminal the executioners avoided direct contact with objects contaminated by holiness/unholiness (e.g. Ex. 19:13).

As Israel's pastor, in verse 10b Moses returns to his principle concern: guarding the relationship between Yahweh and his people. The close relative or neighbor is to be executed because he tried to lure a person away from Yahweh his God. By identifying Yahweh as the God "who had brought you [sing.] out of Egypt, out of the land of slavery," Moses reminds the people that all Israelites owe their existence and freedom to Yahweh's redemptive grace. To go after other gods is to repudiate this grace and to renounce one's status as his people. All Israelites have a vested interest in

---

40. Cf. Weinfeld, *DDS*, 209. Elsewhere the idiom (lit.) "the eye shall not pity" is associated with exterminating Canaanites (7:16), executing murderers (19:13), dealing with false witnesses (19:21), and responding to a woman guilty of immodesty (25:12).

41. On this expression, see M. Tsevat, *TDOT*, 4:470–72.

42. Thus McConville, *Deuteronomy*, 233. Compare a similar charge to expose conspirators in VTE 10.

43. The worship of other gods (13:10; 17:5; Lev. 20:2; cf. Ex. 8:26[22]); defiance against Yahweh by stepping on territory he has declared to be holy (Ex. 19:13), or taking items subject to the law of *ḥerem* (Josh. 7:25); killing a human being [as an image of God] (Ex. 21:28–32[an ox]); blasphemy (Lev. 24:14, 16, 23; 1 Kings 21:10, 13–14; cf. Acts 7:54–60); sorcery (Lev. 20:27); violating the Sabbath (Num. 15:35–36); a son's insubordination (Deut. 21:21); sexual/adulterous crimes (Deut. 22:21, 24; cf. Ezek. 16:40; 23:47).

taking drastic measures, even against close relatives or neighbors. Fear of a similar fate should deter anyone else who might be tempted to promote spiritual sedition.

Apostasy instigated by anyone else in Israel (vv. 12 – 18). The third scenario is the most serious of all — the defection of an entire town. This time Moses' instructions are not addressed to potential defectors but to witnesses to defection. Verse 12 sets the context: one of the towns that Yahweh has given to the Israelites. The issue involves a rumor that has reached the ears of the addressee (singular): Certain worthless fellows from one of Israel's own towns have gone out and lured their fellow citizens to desert Yahweh in favor of other gods that are unfamiliar to them (v. 14).[44] The text characterizes those responsible for this mass defection as "men, sons of Belial" (NIV "wicked men"). The last phrase translates literally as "sons of worthlessness," that is, men without honor.[45] The moral sense of the idiom is reflected by the kinds of people so characterized: murderers, rapists, false witnesses, corrupt priests, drunks, boors, ungrateful and selfish folk, rebels, and those who do not know Yahweh.

Because this scenario envisages rumors of spiritual sedition rather than direct contact with those who lead in the defection from Yahweh, instead of immediately calling for the death penalty Moses demands careful investigation to determine whether the rumors of "this detestable thing"[46] are true or false (v. 14a). The seriousness of the inquiry is reflected in the verbs describing the process: "to inquire, seek," "to probe, search out," and "to investigate [thoroughly]."

Once it is established that the rumors are true,[47] the punishment of the town is to be decisive and comprehensive. (1) Moses calls for the

---

44. As in vv. 2b and 6b, Moses quotes the seductive speech: "Let us go and worship other gods."

45. Cf. *HALOT,* 420. For other possibilities, see S. D. Sperling, "Belial," *DDD,* 322 – 27; T. J. Lewis, "Belial," *ABD,* 1:654 – 56. For variations of expression, see Judg. 19:22; 20:13; 1 Sam. 1:16; 2:12; 10:27; 25:7, 25; 2 Sam. 16:7; 20:1; 1 Kings 21:10, 13; 2 Chron. 13:7; Prov. 16:27.

46. The expression *tôʿēbâ* ("abominable act") links this chapter with the preamble in 12:31.

47. The clause in v. 14b ("and look, if the matter is established as true," pers. trans.) recurs in 17:4. The particle *wᵉhinnēh* (lit., "and look") focuses attention on the results of the investigation.

48. Moses' duplication of (lit.) "by the mouth [blade] of a sword" is emphatic. His command resembles the prescription for a treasonous town in the eighth-century BC Sefire Treaty between the Aramaean kings of KTK and Arpad. For the text, translation, and discussion see John C. L. Gibson, *Textbook of Syrian Semitic Inscriptions,* vol. 2, *Aramaic Inscriptions including Inscriptions on the Dialect of Zenjirli* (Oxford: Clarendon, 1975), 2:48 – 49, 54; Weinfeld, *DDS,* 99.

indiscriminate slaughter with the sword of all living things in the town (v. 15).[48] By adding "Destroy it completely, both its people and its livestock," Moses declares that if Israelites go after the gods of the peoples they were to dispossess, they were themselves to be utterly devoted to destruction.[49]

(2) Moses prescribes how the Israelites are to treat the inanimate material found in the renegade town (v. 16). Referring to the "stuff" as "plunder" captured in war, it is to be collected and piled up in the square of the condemned town. Then the pile and the city itself are to be torched and totally burned up as a sacrifice to Yahweh.[50] The ash heap that remains is to be preserved as a permanent memorial, reminding all who see it of the fate of those who defect from Yahweh and serve other gods. The city is never to be rebuilt. For good measure, Moses adds that none of the objects reserved for destruction is to be allowed to stick to the hands of those who carry out the punitive/sacrificial action (v. 17a; cf. Josh. 7:21–26).

Following the pattern of the previous cases, Moses concludes his prescription for the response to incited apostasy by explaining why the guilty persons are to be treated so mercilessly (v. 17b). The sternness of his tone reflects the seriousness with which Yahweh looks on spiritual defection. The only way to placate his burning wrath and to renew his compassion is to offer up an entire town to Yahweh as a whole burnt offering. His renewed favor will then be demonstrated concretely in the multiplication ("increase") of the population in accordance with his oath to their ancestors (cf. Gen. 15:5; 22:17; etc.).

Moses ends this chapter with a general pastoral reminder of the conditionality of Yahweh's renewed favor (v. 18). Employing familiar language, he sets out three conditions: Israel must obey the voice of Yahweh in whatever he says, keep all his commandments that Moses is giving them this day, and do what is right in his eyes. This is an efficient summary of the essence of Israel's vassaldom. As the trophy of divine grace, her devotion must be directed to Yahweh alone, and her love for him demonstrated in unreserved and unqualified obedience.

THE SERIOUSNESS OF IDOLATRY. The drastic response against idolaters demanded by this passage has been illustrated in two prior events: the Levites' zeal for Yahweh in their confronta-

---

49. On *ḥeḥʾrîm*, "to devote to destruction," see comments on 3:6 and 7:2. Cf. 7:26.

50. The expression *kālîl* (lit., "totality") is used occasionally of offerings that are totally consumed by fire (Lev. 6:15–16[8–9]; Deut. 33:10).

tion with the worshipers of the golden calf (Ex. 32:25–29), and more recently, Phinehas's stand against the worshipers of Baal Peor (Num. 25). Although later historiographic texts never appeal explicitly to this passage, the spirit, values, and procedures presented here undoubtedly underlay the ruthless actions taken in later times in defense of an uncompromising Yahwism: Elijah versus the prophets of Baal at Mount Carmel (1 Kings 18); Jehu versus the worshipers of Baal (2 Kings 10:18–28); the Judahites versus the priest of Baal (11:18); Josiah versus the Manassite installations in Jerusalem and Judah (23:4–14), and Josiah's extension of the crusade to the northern kingdom (23:15–20).

The actions of Josiah, the only person in the entire Old Testament said to have turned to Yahweh "with all his heart/mind and with all his being and with all his resources, in accordance with all the Torah of Moses" (pers. trans. 2 Kings 23:25; cf. comments on Deut. 6:5), come closest to the fulfillment of Deuteronomy 13. Indeed Deuteronomy 13 offers the clearest statement of what critical scholars have come to describe as the Yahweh-alone policy, whose aim was to stamp out all ideological competition. Moses' passion for the exclusive claims of Yahweh on Israel also underlies later prophetic preaching, denouncing all idolatrous forms and calling for exclusive devotion to him.[51]

The case of the Benjamite town of Gibeah in Judges 19–20 represents the nearest example of judgment inflicted on a town that had apostasized.[52] Although the crime for which Gibeah was attacked is not overtly identified as idolatry, given the repeated refrain referring to Israel's degeneration into idolatry that punctuates the book of Judges[53] and the arrangement of the narratives in the book,[54] the Gibeahites represent a community of Israelites that had been thoroughly Canaanized. The links with our text are both lexical and thematic: The perpetrators of the moral offense are identified as (lit.) "men, sons of Belial" (Judg 19:22; 20:13); the aim of the Israelite army with respect to Gibeah was to purge the evil from Israel; the town was first

---

51. For a recent study of the exclusivism of Yahwistic faith in ancient Israel see Block, "Other Religions in Old Testament Theology," in *The Gospel According to Moses*, 200–236.

52. Rightly suggested by McConville, *Deuteronomy*, 240–41.

53. "And the Israelites did [the] evil in the eyes of the LORD" occurs in 2:11 and six times thereafter (3:7, 12; 4:1; 6:1; 10:6; 13:1). In three of these the clause is followed immediately by references to defection from Yahweh and/or the worship of other gods (2:11–13; 3:7; 10:6–16).

54. The narratives are arranged to create the impression of deeper and deeper apostasy, climaxing in chapter 19, where the people of Gibeah are portrayed as later versions of Sodom and Gomorrah in Gen. 19. On the structure of the book and the significance of the Gibeahite narrative, see Block, *Judges, Ruth*, 50–67, 532–40.

struck with the edge of the sword (Judg. 20:37), and then it was burned up as one huge pyre, presumably as a "burnt offering."

The Old Testament provides several cases that seem to invert the intentions of Deuteronomy 13. Based on Deuteronomy 13, Gideon, the son of Joash, should probably have executed his own father for promoting the worship of Baal and Asherah in his backyard. When he tore down the altar of Baal and the image of Asherah, in defense of the idolatrous cult the townspeople perversely demanded the death of the one who had demolished the installation. Jeremiah 11:18 – 23 reports Jeremiah's townspeople of Anathoth taking action against the prophet of Yahweh for denouncing the nation's treacherous going after Baal. According to Jeremiah 37:11 – 16, his enemies arrested and imprisoned the true prophet for preaching sedition because he had encouraged them to submit to the Babylonians.

In Galatians 1:8 – 9 Paul picks up the tone and vocabulary of Deuteronomy 13: "But even if we or an angel from heaven should preach a gospel other than the one we preached to you, let him be eternally condemned! As we have already said, so now I say again: If anybody is preaching to you a gospel other than what you accepted, let him be eternally condemned!" The Greek expression *anathema* (NIV, "eternally condemned") is borrowed from LXX, which uses this word to translate the Hebrew *hāyîtâ herem* ("to be devoted to destruction") in Deuteronomy 7:26. Perhaps with Deuteronomy 13 in his mind, in responding to those who were preaching another gospel in Galatians 1:6 – 12, Paul sounds like a second Moses.

How so? (1) Paul demands compliance with the message he has proclaimed (cf. Deut. 12:32; 13:18). (2) He introduces a hypothetical preacher of good news who disturbs the people (Gal. 1:7).[55] (3) He identifies the "seducer" as either himself or "an angel [messenger] from heaven." While the latter alludes to the prophet or dreamer of Deuteronomy 13:1, by including himself Paul shockingly places himself in the role of the relative (13:6) or "son of Belial" (13:13). (4) He pronounces the curse on the seducer (cf. 13:17). (5) Later in Galatians 3:1 Paul refers to the impact of the seducer as "bewitching," the sinister effect of hostile words, which seems to allude to the seductive ("to turn you away," Deut. 13:5, 10, 13; cf. "to entice" in 13:6) influence of those who preach a false gospel. For Paul, preaching a gospel contrary to the "gospel of Christ" (Gal. 1:7), which secured our deliverance from the present evil age (1:4), is equivalent to leading the Israelites away from Yahweh, who brought them out of Egypt and redeemed them from the slave house (13:5) to follow other gods.

---

55. Though without putting the seductive words in his mouth. Cf. Deut. 13:2, 6, 13.

 PRESERVING THE FREEDOM YAHWEH has pro-
vided. While modern readers might dismiss this
chapter as totalitarian and link its call for the
members of one's family and the community to
act violently against their own relatives and neighbors when they observe
them "secretly" worshiping other gods, with Stalinist-style "secret police,"
Moses' message here is not about repressing personal freedoms and imposing thought control. It is about preserving the freedom that Yahweh by
grace has wrought on Israel's behalf. If they abandon Yahweh, they will not
only cut themselves off from his grace, but will also cease to be his people,
Israel. Yahweh had called Israel to a position of praise and fame and honor
above all the nations (Deut. 26:18 – 19), but if they follow the gods of the
nations, they will lose their identity in the mass of humankind and attract
the fury of their own God. However, this chapter reminds Christians today
that commitment to Yahweh is not only a national affair; it must also be
rigorously pursued at the personal, family, and community level.

This agenda carries over into the New Testament with Jesus' own claim
to be the only way of salvation and his assertion that no one comes to the
Father but through him (John 14:6). In Acts 4:12 Peter also declares that
"salvation is found in no one else, for there is no other name under heaven
given to men by which we must be saved."

But such statements do not reach the tone and severity of Deuteronomy
13. For that we turn to two Pauline texts: Galatians 1:8 – 9 (discussed above)
and 1 Corinthians 16:22, with which he closes this long letter: "If anyone
does not love the Lord — a curse be on him. Come, O Lord!" Paul does not
charge Christians to engage in pogroms against those who would incite
them to abandon the Lord Jesus Christ, but his invocation of the curse
on an apostate is no less sharp than the words of Moses here. This is also
true of Peter's warning in 2 Peter 2:1, "But there were also false prophets
among the people, just as there will be false teachers among you. They
will secretly introduce destructive heresies, even denying the sovereign
Lord who bought them — bringing swift destruction on themselves." As
Yahweh had graciously rescued Israel from bondage and called the nation
to freedom from the slavery of Egypt, so Jesus Christ has graciously called
us to freedom from the bondage of sin. In the wake of this incredible grace,
total and uncompromising devotion to Jesus Christ is a most reasonable
and spiritual service (Rom. 12:1 – 2).

At the same time, this passage is not that far removed from Jesus' own
statement in Luke 14:26: "If anyone comes to me and does not hate his
father and mother, his wife and children, his brothers and sisters — yes,

even his own life—he cannot be my disciple." For those who have been redeemed from sin through the gracious work of Christ, devotion to the Savior must still take precedence over the closest family ties. This text offers a stern warning to anyone who seeks to deflect another's devotion away from Jesus Christ (who is Yahweh incarnate) to any other god. Of course, apostasy is not restricted to the worship of physical idols, made of wood or stone or precious metal. Job grasped this truth in his climactic declaration of personal integrity and fidelity to God:

> If I have put my trust in gold
> or said to pure gold, "You are my security,"
> if I have rejoiced over my great wealth,
> the fortune my hands had gained,
> if I have regarded the sun in its radiance
> or the moon moving in splendor,
> so that my heart was secretly enticed,
> and my hand offered them a kiss of homage,
> then these also would be sins to be judged,
> for I would have been unfaithful to God on high. (Job
> 31:24 – 28)

Since we do not worship images of wood and stone, idolatry in our context may actually be more subtle. An idol is anything that deflects our devotion to Jesus Christ. It could be our career, our family, our hobbies, or our home. Preachers of a health and wealth gospel in our day push personal happiness and material success as if they were the ends for which we live and on the basis of which we make all our decisions. But this too is idolatry, twisting the gospel of divine grace and its call to take the name of Christ as a badge of honor and his cross as a privileged burden into a modern version of the fertility religions of the ancient Near East.

Deuteronomy 14:1–21

You are the children of the LORD your God. Do not cut yourselves or shave the front of your heads for the dead, ²for you are a people holy to the LORD your God. Out of all the peoples on the face of the earth, the LORD has chosen you to be his treasured possession.

³Do not eat any detestable thing. ⁴These are the animals you may eat: the ox, the sheep, the goat, ⁵the deer, the gazelle, the roe deer, the wild goat, the ibex, the antelope and the mountain sheep. ⁶You may eat any animal that has a split hoof divided in two and that chews the cud. ⁷However, of those that chew the cud or that have a split hoof completely divided you may not eat the camel, the rabbit or the coney. Although they chew the cud, they do not have a split hoof; they are ceremonially unclean for you. ⁸The pig is also unclean; although it has a split hoof, it does not chew the cud. You are not to eat their meat or touch their carcasses.

⁹Of all the creatures living in the water, you may eat any that has fins and scales. ¹⁰But anything that does not have fins and scales you may not eat; for you it is unclean.

¹¹You may eat any clean bird. ¹²But these you may not eat: the eagle, the vulture, the black vulture, ¹³the red kite, the black kite, any kind of falcon, ¹⁴any kind of raven, ¹⁵the horned owl, the screech owl, the gull, any kind of hawk, ¹⁶the little owl, the great owl, the white owl, ¹⁷the desert owl, the osprey, the cormorant, ¹⁸the stork, any kind of heron, the hoopoe and the bat.

¹⁹All flying insects that swarm are unclean to you; do not eat them. ²⁰But any winged creature that is clean you may eat.

²¹Do not eat anything you find already dead. You may give it to an alien living in any of your towns, and he may eat it, or you may sell it to a foreigner. But you are a people holy to the LORD your God.

Do not cook a young goat in its mother's milk.

IN CHAPTER 14 MOSES' attention shifts from the specific rejection of Canaanite gods to the general rejection of Canaanite ways. This chapter divides into two parts, both concerned with eating. Yahweh's people are to be distinguished by what they do and do not eat in everyday life (vv. 1−21) and by where and how they eat in the very presence of God (vv. 22−29). In so doing, this chapter exhibits a chiastic relationship with the key motifs of chapter 12:

A Eating in the Presence of Yahweh (12:5−14)
B Eating in your Towns (12:15−28)
C Remaining True to Yahweh (13:1−18[2−19])
B′ Eating in your Towns (14:1−21)
A′ Eating in the Presence of Yahweh (14:22−29)

In both sections of chapter 14 Moses picks up topics he had dealt with in chapter 12: he expands on 12:5−7 and 11−12 in 14:22−29, and he elaborates on and concretizes 12:15−27 in 14:1−21.[1]

Speaking of eating, Deuteronomy 14:1−21 is constructed like a sandwich, with verses 1−3 at the beginning and verse 21 at the end serving as the "theological bread," and the large center section (vv. 4−20) representing the "meat." Actually, verses 4−20 function as commentary on verse 3, fleshing out what Moses means by the prohibited "detestable" food. These verses are a self-contained literary unit, stylistically distinct from the surrounding frame, not only by its lists of various kinds of animals but also by its relative secularity.[2] This does not mean this material is lacking in theological significance; the fourfold reference to uncleanness (vv. 7, 8, 10, 19) confirms that the concern here goes far beyond the mere listing of clean and unclean foods.

The linkage between verses 4−20 and Leviticus 11 is intriguing. Although these texts share a concern for dietary distinctions,[3] the tone of the text in Deuteronomy seems more positive. Twice it authorizes the Israelites to eat kosher flying creatures (Deut. 14:11 and 20). More significantly, Leviticus 11:2−23 (cf. vv. 41−43) expresses the repugnancy of unclean food much more sharply with its eightfold use of the root *šqṣ* ("to detest").[4] This word is missing in Deuteronomy 14:1−21, though

---

1. This "resumptive exposition" of notions raised in chap. 12 continues in chaps. 15 and 16.

2. Verses 4−20 represent the second longest continuous text in Deuteronomy without any reference to the name of Yahweh. Only 21:11−22 is longer by word count.

3. Note the frequent occurrences of the root *ṭm*ʾ ("to be unclean") in both.

4. The noun *šeqeṣ* ("detestable thing"; Lev. 11:10, 11, 12, 13, 20, 23) and the verb *šiqqēs* ("to detest," vv. 11, 13).

the prohibition on eating any "detestable thing" in the preamble (v. 3) compensates for this lack.[5] Nevertheless, occasionally our text replaces "it is/they are a detestable thing for you" in Leviticus 11 with milder expressions: "You may not eat [it]" (14:10; cf. Lev. 11:10), and "[it is] unclean for you" (Deut. 14:19; cf. Lev. 11:20).[6] Leviticus 11 seems more concerned to define precise boundaries between clean and unclean animals, as evidenced by the explicit distinctions drawn for aquatic animals (11:10—11), the principles by which objects/persons that have been contaminated by contact with cadavers should be treated (11:24—40), and instructions on low carriage land animals (11:41—44).[7]

With these modifications Moses transforms the legal dietary document (Lev. 11) into a moral document (Deut. 14), declaring how Israel's status as Yahweh's "holy people" is to be reflected in actions as fundamental as eating. Here the focus of Israel's pastor is on affirming what the Israelites may do rather than on prohibiting what they may not do. That Moses seems more concerned to open doors rather than to close them is reinforced by the opening declaration ("You are the children of the LORD your God," v. 1a) and his framing verses 4—20 with statements that are profoundly ethical (vv. 1b—3 and v. 21). The positive introductions to the categories of food are equally striking (vv. 4, 9, 11, 20), suggesting these statements are better understood as grants of permission and invitation than as legal proscriptions. Being the covenant people of Yahweh implicates all aspects of life—even as mundane a matter as eating.

As already noted, the concern with kosher food and the expression "detestable thing/act" (v. 3) link 14:1—21 with chapters 12—13.[8] Whereas 12:15—28 referred in passing to cattle and sheep (as representative of domestic animals; cf. v. 17) and gazelles and deer (as representative of wild game [cf. v. 22]), in 14:4—5 Moses lists ten species of animal approved for food. The verb "to eat"[9] occurs fourteen times, also tying 14:1—21 to the following verses (vv. 23, 26, 29; cf. 15:20, 22—23; 16:3, 7—8). This link is strengthened by the social concern reflected in references to the resident alien and the stranger in verse 21 (cf. 14:29; 15:3).

---

5. The word *tôʿēbâ* links this text with 12:31 and 13:14[15]; In Leviticus this word is used only of incestuous crimes (18:22—30; 20:13). Deuteronomy reserves the root *šqṣ* for detestable idolatry (7:26; 29:17[16]).

6. Milgrom (*Leviticus 1—16,* 657) argues that "detestable" animals refers to creatures that contaminate by touch, while "unclean" animals contaminate by touch and ingestion.

7. On zoological classifications in the Old Testament see R. Whitekettle, "Where the Wild Things Are: Primary Level Taxa in Israelite Zoological Thought," *JSOT* 93 (2001): 17—37.

8. The word *tôʿēbâ* also occurs in 12:31 and 13:14[15].

9. See vv. 3, 4, 6, 7, 8, 9a, 9b, 10, 11, 12, 19, 20, 21a, 21b.

The Guests at Yahweh's Table (14:1 – 3)

WHEREAS LEVITICUS SPEAKS OF Israel's holiness as a quality to be practiced through imitation of Yahweh her holy God (11:44 – 45; 19:2; 20:7,26), here Moses speaks of holiness as a quality that Israel possesses. Whereas in chapters 12 and 13 Moses had challenged Israel to demonstrate her status as the covenant people of Yahweh by rejecting Canaanite gods and Canaanite ways of worshiping, now he calls her to prove her holy status in her diet. Commenting primarily on the dietary laws in Leviticus 11, E. Firmage observes:

> The dietary law originates ... in a self-conscious attempt ... to put a singular tenet of Israelite theology into practice — that Israel be holy, not simply pure (in the technical meaning of "free from impurity"). Thus, unlike the laws of personal impurity which applied even to non-Israelites, the dietary law was to be kept by Israelites alone.[10]

If this was true of the priestly legislation in Leviticus, it is even more so in the present text.

Without verses 1 – 3 the dietary regulations in verses 4 – 20 are external laws imposed by a suzerain upon a vassal (cf. 5:6). The introduction changes everything, for here Moses declares that Israelite life was not to be governed so much by external laws as by the relationship they enjoyed with Yahweh, a privilege they celebrate by eating at Yahweh's table. He highlights their unique status with four expressions. They are: (1) the children of Yahweh; (2) a holy people, belonging to Yahweh their God; (3) the elect people of Yahweh, chosen from all the peoples on the face of the earth, to be (4) Yahweh's own treasured possession. Since verse 2 reiterates 7:6, here we need to comment only on the first: Israel's status as "the sons [*bānîm*] of the LORD."

This is not the first time Moses has compared Yahweh's relationship to Israel to that of a father and son (cf. 1:31; 8:5). However, now he strengthens the image by using a metaphor rather than a simile: Yahweh not only *treats* Israel like a father treats a son, he *is* Israel's father. The metaphor derives from ancient Near Eastern political relationships (cf. 2 Kings 16:7). Within this relationship the suzerain's status was referred to as "fathership" and the status of the vassal was referred to as "sonship."[11]

---

10. E. Firmage, "The Biblical Dietary Laws and the Concept of Holiness," in *Studies in the Pentateuch* (ed. J. A. Emerton; Leiden: Brill, 1990), 184.

11. *ARM*, 2:119r.8. Cf. *CAD*, 10/1:321. See, e.g., the fourteenth-century BC treaty between Shattiwaza of Mittanni and Suppilulima I of Hatti, in Beckman, *HDT* 6B §3 (p. 45). For additional references and discussion, see Weinfeld, "The Covenant of Grant," *JAOS* 90/2 (1970): 191 – 94.

While Deuteronomy never speaks explicitly of Yahweh's entrance into covenant relationship with Israel with adoptive language, this is how Jeremiah 3:19—20 interprets it. By opening this unit with "Sons you are to Yahweh your God" (pers. trans.), Moses announces that whatever follows reflects Israel's acceptance of this privileged status. In chapter 13 Moses dealt with the prospect of defection from covenantal allegiance to Yahweh by going after other gods and serving them. Now we learn that for Israelites to go after these gods would mean to deny their status as the children of Yahweh. This status as the elect vassal of Yahweh provides the basis for their participation in table fellowship with him.[12]

Earlier Moses had grounded the prohibition on intermarriage with the Canaanites and the total destruction of every vestige of Canaanite religion on Israel's standing as Yahweh's elect and holy covenant people (7:6). According to 14:1—3, Yahweh's election provides the grounds for two additional regulations. (1) The Israelites were not to gash their bodies or cut their hair in certain ways. On the surface, both seem to be associated with the cult of the dead, since such actions were connected with mourning rites for the dead. Non-Israelites believed the deceased continued to exercise both beneficent and malevolent power over the living, and that the favorable influence of departed ancestors could be secured through mortuary rites. However, the present prohibition seems not to allude to the ancestor cult but simply to rites of mourning. Moses hereby insists that the taboos extended beyond contact with corpses to contact with the "vital forces" of the deceased.[13]

The exact style of haircut cannot be determined,[14] but the Hebrew allows for a variety of ways of producing baldness: cutting, shaving, plucking, pulling. Although the expressions used are different, similar practice is reflected in Leviticus 19:27—28. Whereas that text grounds Israel's ethic in the principle of *imitatio dei*—they are to be holy as Yahweh their God is holy (v. 2)—here Israel's ethic is grounded on their status before Yahweh. The meaning of these prohibitions against pagan practices in the present context seems to be bound up with the dietary laws themselves. Viewing this text as an invitation to eat at Yahweh's table, it is important that the participants be ritually clean (cf. 26:14).[15] If physical contact with a corpse

---

12. The present portrayal of Israel as the privileged vassal eating at Yahweh's table is reflected in Ps. 23:5.

13. First Kings 18:28 and Hos. 7:14 suggest some pagan rituals involved lacerating oneself. Jer. 16:5—7; 41:5; 47:5; and Mic. 4:14 associate these with lamentation and shaving the head, mourning rites for the dead.

14. The Hebrew translates literally, "And you shall not make baldness between your eyes."

15. Ps. 106:28 links the worship of Baal Peor with eating sacrifices offered to the dead.

was deemed defiling (cf. Lev. 11:24–40), how much more objectionable for the holy people of Yahweh to attempt spiritual contact with the dead.[16]

(2) The second demand arising from Israel's status as children of Yahweh involves food, specifically prohibiting any food that Yahweh deems "detestable." Earlier Moses had applied this expression to the religious practices of the pagans (12:31; 13:13[14]). In chapter 7, with which 14:1–2 displays direct lexical and conceptual links, the expression applied both to the abhorrent practices of the nations and the silver and gold of which their idols were made (7:25–26).[17] Moses does not explain why certain foods are classified as "detestable" (*tôʿēbâ*), nor the consequences of so doing. Perhaps if the contagion could be contracted by touching abominable artifacts, how much more by ingesting food that Yahweh had declared "detestable."

Against this backdrop, the regulations regarding edible and inedible food that follows should be regarded as a gracious gift, seeking to protect Israel's status as Yahweh's holy people. Eating foods forbidden by Yahweh involves more than the ingesting of "unclean food" (vv. 7, 8, 10, 11); its association with false religion also represents a breach of covenant relationship.

The Fare at Yahweh's Table (14:4–20)

MOSES' ADDITION OF "FOR you" (*lākem*) in verses 7, 8, and 10 ties the dietary rules to the covenant people. Because Israelites are the holy people of Yahweh, the meat in their diet must be like the food that God "eats" in the sacrifices offered to him. Through everyday observance of the dietary boundaries, Israelites declared to one another and to outsiders their unique proximity to Yahweh. By eating at his table they declared their sanctified status as his covenant people "in every encounter with the animal kingdom and at every meal."[18]

After appealing to Israel to avoid abominable food, Moses reminds them of the established boundaries between kosher[19] and prohibited food. Many cultures have their own rules defining boundaries between the clean and unclean. The rationale for the boundaries described here is not clearly

---

16. Hence the taboo on consulting the dead in 18:11–12.

17. Elsewhere Deuteronomy links the expression to the worship of astral deities (17:2–4), the manufacture of idols (27:15), the sacrifice of blemished animals to Yahweh (17:1), divination, sorcery, and necromancy (18:9, 12), cross-dressing (22:5), offering the fees of prostitutes or "dogs" to Yahweh (23:18[19]), a man returning to a woman he has divorced (24:4), and dishonesty in commercial dealings (25:16).

18. M. Douglas, *Purity and Danger: An Analysis of Concepts of Pollution and Taboo* (London: Routledge & Kegan Paul, 1966), 57.

19. The Yiddish term *kosher* derives from an apparently common West Semitic root *kāšar* ("to be appropriate, deemed fit"). For the Hebrew, see *HALOT*, 503.

understood,[20] Scholars have proposed a variety of theories for taboos on unclean food: cultic (they were associated with Canaanite religious practices), aesthetic (they are loathsome or repulsive), hygienic (they cause illness), sociological (they have ambiguous form and lack physical integrity), and didactic (they illustrate/teach wrongful behavior).[21]

Our text links the lists of clean and unclean animals with Israel's holiness, but it does not spell out why clean animals cohere with the biblical notion of holiness or why unclean animals violate those notions. It seems most likely that the forbidden animals are rejected because of their association with death. (1) Leviticus 11:24−40 emphasizes the defiling effect of contact with animal carcasses. (2) The dietary instructions in Deuteronomy 14 are introduced with reference to rituals related to the cult of the dead (v. 1). (3) The account concludes with regulations concerning animals that have died a natural death (v. 21).[22] In addition, we note that most of the animals designated unclean are carnivores, or scavengers that feed on carrion, or ground creatures in constant contact with unclean matter.

In the end we admit that the Old Testament never spells out the reasons for the boundaries. They may seem arbitrary to modern readers, but Yahweh's covenant with Israel is a suzerainty covenant—the terms are not negotiated and need not even make sense to the vassal. They are simply to be accepted because they represent the will of the divine Lord. This does not mean that they are burdensome impositions. On the contrary, the mere fact of knowing the boundaries is an enviable grace (cf. 4:8). Furthermore, both Leviticus 11 and Deuteronomy 14 provide ample incentive to accept willingly these dietary boundaries; because the Israelites are the objects of Yahweh's gracious redemption, election, and exceptional favor, obedience to all he required should be a delight.

The list of edible and inedible animals follows the traditional taxonomy recognizing four broad categories of animals: high carriage land animals (vv. 4−8), sea creatures (vv. 9−10), birds (vv. 11−18), and insects (vv. 19−20). (See Figure 1 on p. 347). Moses' attention to these categories is uneven. He provides long lists of creatures in the land animal and bird categories, but he disposes of sea creatures and insects with one or two general sentences. The lists of land animals and birds present a study in contrasts: the former consists primarily of edible creatures; the latter, exclusively of forbidden birds. Moses' fourfold taxonomy involving land animals, aquatic

20. Lev. 11:43−47 explicitly links Israel's dietary laws with her status as a holy people.
21. See W. Houston, *Purity and Monotheism* (Library of Hebrew Bible/Old Testament Studies; Sheffield: Sheffield Academic, 2009), 68−123.
22. Isa. 65:2−7 associates nocturnal and necromantic activity with eating swine's flesh (cf. also 66:17).

Clean and Unclean Animals According to Leviticus 11 and Deuteronomy 14

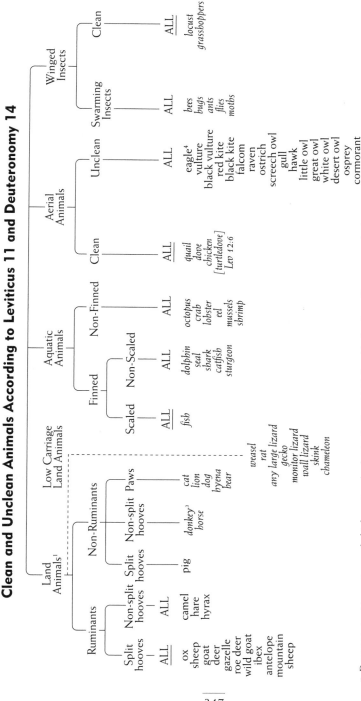

1. Deuteronomy 14 mentions only high carriage land animals. Lev 11:29-31 adds the class of low carriage land animals that "swarm on the ground." Lev. 11:10-11 refers to corresponding aquatic "swarmers."
2. Underlined: permitted as food.
3. Italic font: examples, not named in Leviticus 11 or Deuteronomy 14.
4. The identity of some of these birds is uncertain.

animals, two-legged aerial animals, and six-legged aerial animals represents one version of several attested in the Old Testament.[23] These categories agree precisely with the colophonic ending to Leviticus 11:46–47.

We might have expected the opening statement in verse 4 to be followed by principles by which kosher animals could be identified. Instead Moses lists ten animals permitted as food (vv. 4b–5). Three are domesticated species (ox, sheep, and goats), whose blood Yahweh will accept as sacrifices (cf. 12:23–27). Seven are wild (deer, gazelle, roebuck, wild goat, addax,[24] antelope, mountain sheep) and may be considered undomesticated equivalents of the domesticated species. All are not only ruminants and split-hoofed, but also horned, at least the males of the species, though Moses makes nothing of this.[25] The list expands the four basic categories of cattle, flock, gazelle, and deer referred to in 12:21–22.

Having listed clean animals, Moses explains that permissible meat may come only from animals with split hooves that chew the cud (v. 6). To illustrate this point he identifies four creatures that possess one feature but lack the other (vv. 7–8).[26] The first three (v. 7) apparently chew the cud but they do not have split hooves.[27] The pig is also mentioned, because it reverses the features of the previous three. Nothing is said of its disgusting habits,[28] its association with trichinosis, or its role in pagan sacrificial rites or rites performed in graveyards (Isa. 65:4; 66:3, 17). The pig is rejected simply because it does not chew the cud.[29] Moses' demand that people not

---

23. Gen. 1:26 provides a basic fourfold division: fish of the sea, birds of the sky, high carriage land animals, and "crawlies," which crawl on the ground. On biblical taxonomies, see Whitekettle, "Where the Wild Things Are," 17–37.

24. NIV reads "ibex," but see E. Firmage, "Zoology," *ABD*, 6:1153, 1157.

25. The identification of some is uncertain (e.g., the fourth, which some read as "fallow deer," and the eighth, which some read as [old world] "bison" or "aurochs").

26. Firmage ("Biblical Dietary Laws," 188) observes that these four species are the only ones in Israel's immediate environment that met one but not both criteria.

27. Rabbits and coneys are included with those that chew the cud because the way they chew resembles the chewing of ruminants. Hebrew definitions of species are based on observable habits or features rather than scientific criteria as we understand science. On biblical understanding of biodiversity and species, see Daniel I. Block, "To Serve and to Keep: Toward a Biblical Understanding of Humanity's Responsibility in the Face of the Biodiversity Crisis," in *Keeping God's Earth: The Global Environment in Biblical Perspective* (ed. N. J. Toly and D. I. Block; Downers Grove, IL: InterVarsity Press, 2010), 116–21.

28. Even Babylonians and Assyrians, who otherwise had no aversion to pork, recognized the disgusting habits of pigs: "The pig is unholy [...] bespattering his backside, Making the streets smell, polluting the houses"—as translated by W. G. Lambert, "Morals in Ancient Mesopotamia," *Ex Oriente Lux* 15 (1957–58): 189.

29. For a discussion of the pig in the ancient Near East and in Israel see E. Firmage, "Zoology," *ABD*, 6:1130–35.

even touch the carcasses (cf. v. 21) reflects the strength of Israelite revulsion toward hogs.[30]

In verses 9—10 Moses distinguishes between clean and unclean aquatic animals. He continues the positive tone of verses 4—6 by first describing those that may be eaten—they have fins and scales—and then prohibiting those that lack these features. Not only has Moses drastically abbreviated the treatment of edible and inedible marine animals in Leviticus 11:9—12, but he has also softened the taboo, characterizing them as "unclean" for Israel rather than "detestable" and dropping any reference to their carcasses.

The most detailed listing of animals involves aerial creatures. As in the previous categories, Moses begins with a permissive declaration. However, unlike the previous two cases, he offers no criteria for classifying birds as clean or unclean. Also in contrast to the first list, after the opening line he pays no attention to edible birds but follows up the previous statement with the negative counterpart, listing birds that the Israelites may not eat.

The list of birds prohibited consists of twenty-one entries. With minor exceptions, the species named are identical to those found in Leviticus 11:12—19, suggesting that Moses is recalling that list from memory. The identities of most of the birds named are uncertain.[31] They tend to be either carnivorous or scavengers. The fourfold addition of "any kind of" intentionally broadens the scope of prohibitions to species closely related to those listed. Bats are obviously mammals, but they are included with birds because Israel's definition of "bird" was an animal with wings or that flies.

Moses concludes with a brief reference to "insects" (lit., "swarmers [*šereṣ*] of the wing [*ḥā‘ôp*]," vv. 19—20). By itself *šereṣ* refers to creatures that swarm or crawl and could include rodents and snakes, except that *ḥā‘ôp* ("of the wing") limits it here to insects. Abbreviating Leviticus 11:20—23, Moses declares simply that all swarming insects are unclean and may not be eaten. But then, in keeping with the generally positive tone of this text, he adds, "All clean winged [insects] you may eat." These include leaping insects like locusts and crickets, which are not associated with carrion or filth.

A Final Reminder for Those Who Eat at Yahweh's Table (14:21)

IN THE EPILOGUE (V. 21) Moses returns to the fundamental issue that has occupied his mind since the beginning of this chapter: Israel's status as

---

30. Lev. 11:24—40 extends the prohibition to all carcasses, cataloguing advertent and inadvertent circumstances where such contacts occur and the means whereby one who has been ritually defiled through contact may be purified.

31. Rather than create a false impression of certitude, Houston (*Purity and Monotheism,* 29—30) leaves most of the designations for birds untranslated. For a helpful survey of these birds see Firmage, *ABD,* 6:1155, 1157—58.

Yahweh's holy people. Having explained in detail what he had meant by his prohibition of "detestable things" (v. 3), he recognizes two further culinary implications of Israel's privileged place in the divine agenda. (1) Yahweh's covenant people must avoid meat from animals that have died a natural death.[32] The prohibition is probably connected with the need to drain the blood of animals before eating it (cf. 12:16, 23, 27; 15:23). Arising from his conviction that the entire nation of Israel is holy, Moses hereby extends to all the people a principle that Leviticus 22:8 applied only to priests. Since resident aliens and foreigners are not part of the "holy people," these taboos do not apply. So the food may be given to the former as an act of charity or sold to the latter as a business transaction.

(2) Those who eat at Yahweh's table must avoid certain ways of preparing the food. The proscription on boiling a kid in its mother's milk remains a riddle.[33] Scholars have proposed a variety of explanations for this regulation, but three commend themselves above all others. (a) The ordinance may arise out of a humanitarian concern, similar to that underlying the prohibition on killing a mother bird and taking its young or its eggs at the same time (Deut. 22:6−7; cf. Ex. 22:30[29]; Lev 22:27−28). (b) Boiling a kid in its mother's milk may represent a fundamental and perverse violation of natural law — that which is intended for nourishment is used as an instrument of death. (c) Given the prohibition of eating animals from which the blood has not been drained, this proscription may be concerned with avoiding all appearance of the consumption of blood. Linking this taboo with others that forbid the slaughter of an animal less than eight days old, we note that in the first few days after giving birth, a mother animal's milk is rich in colostrum, often giving it a reddish color. Eating the meat of a kid cooked in its mother's milk may be considered eating meat with blood.[34]

It is difficult to decide which of these three possibilities is best. While this strange prohibition occurs in identical form in Exodus 23:19 and 34:26, its association with the annual pilgrimage festivals suggests it may allude to fertility rites performed in honor of a Canaanite deity.

---

32. On this matter, see K. Sparks, "A Comparative Study of the Biblical *blh* Laws," *ZAW* 110 (1998), 594−600.

33. See R. Ratner and B. Zuckerman, "A Kid in Milk?" *HUCA* 57 (1986): 15−60; M. Haran, "Seething a Kid in Its Mother's Milk," *JJS* 30 (1979): 23−35; C. J. Labuschagne, "'You Shall Not Boil a Kid in Its Mother's Milk': A New Proposal for the Origin of the Prohibition," in *The Scriptures and the Scrolls* (ed. F. G. Martínez, et al.; VTSup 49; Leiden: Brill, 1992), 6−17.

34. Thus Labuschagne, "A New Proposal," 14−15.

FOOD LAWS IN THE rest of the Bible. Allusions to these food laws in the Old Testament are rare. Isaiah 65:4 and 66:17 include eating swine's flesh with other provocative actions that incite Yahweh's fury. Hosea 9:3 mentions eating unclean food in exile as a consequence of Israel's rebellion. In Ezekiel 4:14 the exilic prophet protests that (as one in line for priestly service) he has never defiled himself by eating the flesh of an animal that has died by itself or been torn by wild animals; no contaminated meat has ever entered his mouth. However, here the defilement would derive from cooking pastry over human dung.[35] In Ezekiel 44:31 the prophet reiterates the prohibition of Deuteronomy 14:21 for priests in the new spiritual order envisaged after the exile. According to Daniel 1:8, after Daniel was brought into Nebuchadnezzar's court, he requested permission to abstain from the rich fare offered by the king that he might not defile himself. Although in exile in Babylon, he obviously viewed the dietary regulations of Deuteronomy 14 still to be in force.

Several New Testament texts suggest Jesus' coming signaled the end of Israel's food laws. According to Mark 7:19, all foods are clean—though in context the point is that defilement is caused primarily by actions arising out of the heart rather than ingesting food. In Acts 10:10—16 God reveals to Peter that in the post-resurrection community of faith, the dietary boundaries of the Old Testament community of faith are erased (as are the walls between Israelites and Gentiles). Paul declares in Romans 14:14, the old objective criteria for clean and unclean have been replaced by subjective perceptions. In Acts the apostles (including Paul, 21:26) continued to observe Israel's ceremonial regulations when they were in Jerusalem, but they invited non-Jews to the messianic community without forcing them to become cultural Jews.[36]

Israel's dietary regulations served as boundary markers and symbolized God's election of this ethnic group as his holy people. The successive expansion of the boundaries of the covenant community in the postresurrection period from converted Christian Jews (Acts 2:5—21), to converted Samaritans (half-Jews physically and spiritually, 8:14—17), to Gentile "God-fearers" in the land of Israel (10:44—48), to people in foreign lands (19:1—7) rendered the old dietary boundaries between Israel and the nations obsolete. With the resurrection of the Messiah, on the one hand,

---

35. See further, Block, *Ezekiel 1—24*, 186.

36. For a helpful discussion of the erasure/redrawing of the old boundaries in the Christian community, see Houston, *Purity and Monotheism*, 258—82.

and the opening of the door of salvation and the privilege of being God's holy people to all humankind, on the other, those laws lost their symbolic significance.

A THEOLOGY OF PRIVILEGE and holiness. Christians today do not generally follow these regulations concerning haircuts and tattoos and diet and dietary boundaries. But this does not mean that Moses' pastoral counsel to Israel has no bearing for us. Underlying Deuteronomy 14 is a profound theology of privilege and holiness whose relevance transcends the old covenantal order. Like the Israelites, we, the people of God, should treasure his grace in election and his claims upon us as his holy people. Expression of our holy status should not be reserved for worship services but should be demonstrated in all areas of life. Those who bear the brand of Christ's name represent him wherever they go.

But Christians today are conflicted over the degree to which the regulations of Deuteronomy 14:1−21 apply.[37] While the significance of tattoos and certain hairstyles changes from culture to culture and generation to generation, it could be argued that whenever specific forms of these practices are linked with pagan or ungodly notions, they are to be avoided. After all, as sons and daughters of the living God, chosen in Christ before the foundation of the world "to be holy and blameless in his sight," and predestined "to be adopted as his sons through Jesus Christ ... to the praise of his glorious grace" (Eph. 1:4−6), and chosen to be his special treasure, that we should "declare the praises of him who called you out of darkness into his wonderful light" (1 Pet. 2:11−20), we are to avoid every appearance of evil.

But what about the dietary regulations, which on the surface appear morally neutral? On a recent visit to Hong Kong, I preached on Deuteronomy 14:1−21 to a Chinese congregation, well aware that much of what these people eat, especially the food brought in from offshore—violates Israel's food laws: octopus, squid, shrimp, and the like have neither scales nor fins. When the people saw the sermon title, "Banqueting at the Table of the Lord: The Grace of Israel's Food Laws," some were visibly nervous. But they were relieved when I focused on the privileges that are ours in Christ—we are adopted as children of God, we are the elect, his special treasure, his holy people—and when I explained that in Christ these dietary regulations are removed.

---

37. For a broader study of the dietary prescriptions of chap. 14 within the context of Deuteronomy's overall theology of animals, see D. I. Block, "All Creatures Great and Small," 283−305.

While these dietary restrictions no longer apply to Christians, according to Acts 15:20 at the council of Jerusalem, the first generation of disciples reaffirmed the prohibition on consuming blood and the meat of animals that had not been properly slaughtered,[38] along with prohibitions on idolatry and sexual immorality. The taboo on eating blood is not rooted in Israelite covenantal stipulations but goes back to the fountainhead of humanity; in Genesis 9:4 God forbids the consumption of blood by any of Noah's descendants. In binding Gentile Christians to this ordinance, the council of Jerusalem recognized that all life is sacred.

According to the Babylonian Talmud, "A man's table is like an altar."[39] In a sense every meal, especially those involving the meat of animals, is a sacrifice — an animal gives its life for our sakes. Rather than calling for a vegetarian diet, both Old and New Testaments authorize the consumption of animals, provided the consumer continues to respect the sanctity of the life of the animal. Moskala rightly declares that "both sacrifice and food should be taken with or as an expression of gratitude and thankfulness."[40] But this thankfulness is not only expressed in verbal declarations to God for his gracious provision, but is also felt toward the animal world that has provided both pleasure and nourishment to God's vice-regent.

Apart from this concern for the life of the creature, in the end, the significance of the dietary regulations for Christians is probably best understood as a corollary of Israel's sacrificial system. If indeed Deuteronomy 14 involves Yahweh's invitation to eat of the food in which he himself takes delight in the form of sacrifices (12:5−14), then with the termination of all sacrifices in Christ, these food regulations also become passé. Since we no longer present these offerings to God but celebrate the sacrificial work of Jesus Christ, whenever we partake of the bread and the wine of communion, we participate in the feast to which the Lord has graciously invited us.

Indeed, when Jesus transforms the annual Israelite Passover into the regular communion meal and institutes the Lord's Supper, he acts not only as the divine host who invites us to eat in his presence, but as God in the flesh, inviting redeemed sinners, children of God, his holy people, his chosen ones, his special treasure, to eat of him. For he who said to his disciples, "Take and eat; this is my body," also took the cup, gave thanks, and offered

---

38. Davidson ("Which Torah Laws Should Gentile Christians Obey?") rightly observes that the prohibitions are the same as those applied to native Israelites and aliens who by faith had attached themselves to Israel as the holy community of faith.

39. *Hagigah* 27a.

40. J. Moskala, *The Laws of Clean and Uunclean Animals in Leviticus 11: Their Nature, Theology, and Rationale (An Intertextual Study)* (Adventist Theological Society Dissertation Series; Berrien Springs: Adventist Theological Society, 2000), 106.

it to them, saying, "Drink from it, all of you. This is my blood of the covenant, which is poured out for many for the forgiveness of sins. I tell you,
I will not drink of this fruit of the vine from now on until that day when I
drink it anew with you in my Father's kingdom" (Matt 26:26–29). What
an amazing declaration! The Lord invites us to his table and then offers
himself as the sacrifice. Through him our admission to the family of God
is secured. Hallelujah, what a Savior!

Deuteronomy 14:22–29

❧

Introduction to Deuteronomy 14:22–15:18

DEUTERONOMY 14:22–29 is transitional, bringing to a conclusion a chapter on eating in the presence of Yahweh and introducing a series of instructions on charity that extends through chapter 15. With the latter it shares a common concern to loosen the Israelites' hold on their material possessions. Indeed, the term "hand/hands" serves as a key motif in chapter 15, being represented by two clauses that appear at the precise midpoint of the passage: "You shall not harden your heart nor close your hand" (15:7, pers. trans.).[1] The first clause, which speaks to interior motivation, is reinforced by three wrongful dispositions: (1) a hardened heart (15:7); (2) a heart/mind that harbors perverse thoughts (15:9); (3) an evil heart (15:10). The second clause, which speaks of external action, is likewise reinforced by seven additional occurrences of the word *yâd* ("hand"),[2] two of which occur within the same central paragraph. Indeed 15:7–11 presents the heart of the matter. Although the words "hand" and "heart" are missing from 15:19–23, the concern in this subunit is also readiness to relinquish one's hold on material possessions.

Taken together 14:22–15:18 pleads for a soft heart and open hands, demonstrated in giving up the tithe (14:23–29), pledges (15:1–11), indentured members of the family (15:12–18), and the firstborn (15:19–23). These motifs exhibit an ABBA structure, with the outside segments dealing with hands and hearts that are open toward God, and the middle sections with hands and hearts that are open toward the marginalized in the community. However, these distinctions are not absolute. The first concludes with an appeal to include the Levites in one's generosity toward God, and the middle two discuss compassion for the poor in the context of Yahweh's open hands toward Israel[3]—even speaking of debts in 15:2 as Yahweh's remission.

In this larger section these appeals for charity toward the poor are sandwiched between two texts dealing with worship before Yahweh at the place he chooses (14:22–26; 16:1–17). Furthermore, Moses reinforces the humanitarian concern within the lengthy latter unit with another reminder

---

1. The Hebrew text has 244 words before these clauses and 242 thereafter.
2. See 14:25, 29; 15:2, 3, 7, 8, 10, 11.
3. Note the references to his blessing (15:4, 6, 10, 14, 18; cf. 14:24, 29), his gift of land (v. 7), and his redemption (v. 15).

---

to heads of households to include the needy in their worship (16:11). In so doing he reminds his hearers of the relationship between life as worship and formal cultic service. True worship is not limited to the latter; in fact, if the former is lacking, the latter is of no positive consequence for the worshiper.[4]

> Be sure to set aside a tenth of all that your fields produce each year. [23]Eat the tithe of your grain, new wine and oil, and the firstborn of your herds and flocks in the presence of the LORD your God at the place he will choose as a dwelling for his Name, so that you may learn to revere the LORD your God always. [24]But if that place is too distant and you have been blessed by the LORD your God and cannot carry your tithe (because the place where the LORD will choose to put his Name is so far away), [25]then exchange your tithe for silver, and take the silver with you and go to the place the LORD your God will choose. [26]Use the silver to buy whatever you like: cattle, sheep, wine or other fermented drink, or anything you wish. Then you and your household shall eat there in the presence of the LORD your God and rejoice. [27]And do not neglect the Levites living in your towns, for they have no allotment or inheritance of their own.
>
> [28]At the end of every three years, bring all the tithes of that year's produce and store it in your towns, [29]so that the Levites (who have no allotment or inheritance of their own) and the aliens, the fatherless and the widows who live in your towns may come and eat and be satisfied, and so that the LORD your God may bless you in all the work of your hands.

ON FIRST SIGHT, 14:22–29 continues the series of instructions begun in chapter 12, inviting Israelites to celebrate their vertical covenant relationship with Yahweh. Indeed, not until verse 27 do we learn that the primary concern is actually elsewhere: the well-being of those who are economically vulner-

---

4. Links between 14:22–29 and chapter 12 reinforce the connection between formal and informal worship: (1) both consist of two parts, involving feasting at the central sanctuary (14:22–26; cf. 12:1–14) and meals eaten at home (14:27–29; cf. 12:15–27); (2) both involve offerings at the place Yahweh chooses to establish his name; (3) both involve the tithe; (4) both integrate religious and social issues by singling out Levites as needy (14:27–29; cf. 12:18–19); (5) in both the emphasis is more on the privilege of feasting on food authorized by Yahweh than on commands.

able. Like the Decalogue, all these instructions are addressed to economically independent households, particularly their heads. Moses assumes that covenant relationship with Yahweh is demonstrated fundamentally by active commitment to the poor. For those with means, that commitment begins by identifying with the poor and inviting them to join them when they celebrate in the presence of Yahweh.

The Annual Tithe Festival (14:22–26)

ALTHOUGH THIS PARAGRAPH BEGINS with an emphatic command annually to set aside one tenth of all that the fields produce (v. 22), the remainder reads more like an invitation to a celebration than a cultic ordinance. (1) Moses introduces the place where the banquet will be held: at the place that Yahweh "chooses as a dwelling for his Name"(v. 23). This is not merely a geographical location. In specifying "in the presence of the LORD your God," he identifies Yahweh as the divine host.[5] (2) Moses introduces the banquet fare: the tithe of their crops and their livestock (cf. 7:13, 11:14). As in 7:13, he completes the picture with "the firstborn of your herds and flocks." Whatever the Israelites bring to Yahweh they may eat. (3) Moses declares the purpose of the banquet: that the Israelites may learn to revere Yahweh their God "always." It is not the eating that teaches people to fear Yahweh, but eating in the presence of Yahweh. Thus the presentation of the tithe provided a means by which the settled people could participate annually in the kind of event that the elders of Israel had experienced on Horeb (4:10; Ex. 24:9–11).[6] Reverent awe and gratitude were to characterize the people of Yahweh.

Moses' sympathetic disposition toward the people is evident in verses 24–25, where he recognizes the logistical difficulties that the requirement might pose for those who live far from the central sanctuary. When the Israelites experience the fulfillment of Yahweh's blessing (7:13; 11:13–15), how will they carry the tithe, whether horticultural or animal, to the place of worship?[7] Moses' solution is both liberal and practical. Instead of packing up these goods and transporting them, the people may convert their value into silver.[8] The worshipers were to wrap the silver in a cloth or bind

---

5. On the phrase "in the presence of the LORD," in Deuteronomy, see Wilson, *Out of the Midst of the Fire*, 131–97. In Leviticus instructions for eating at the sanctuary speak of eating "in a holy place" (Lev. 6:16, 26[9, 19]; 7:6; 24:9) or "in a ceremonially clean place" (10:14). For the image of Yahweh preparing a banquet for his devotee see Ps. 23:5–6.

6. Tigay (*Deuteronomy*, 142) suggests the reverence will be learned from the priests, who will teach Torah piety in the chosen city.

7. Similar concerns lie behind 12:20–21 and 19:8–10.

8. NIV rightly resists translating *kesep* as "money," since inscribed coins were not minted in Palestine until the fifth century BC.

it in a bag and carry it by hand to the place that Yahweh would choose to establish his name. Upon arrival at the sanctuary, the silver could be exchanged for beef or veal from the herd, mutton or lamb from the flock, and wine[9] or other alcoholic drink.[10]

To Moses the tithal meal was obviously not intended as a burdensome legal or ceremonial requirement. It was to be welcomed as an occasion for eating and celebrating in the presence of Yahweh their God.[11] For this reason, he makes it easy for all citizens to participate and redundantly invites not only the heads of families but entire households to eat anything that their hearts desire at the festival. Remarkably, the text omits any reference to the most common foods (cf. v. 23). Apparently meat was always desirable fare for a banquet.

The Triennial Tithe Festival (14:27–29)

PICKING UP WHERE 12:12 and 12:17b–18 had left off, this paragraph encourages the landed citizenry to take advantage of tithal festivals to demonstrate generosity toward those less fortunate than themselves. Since the blessings of Yahweh come most directly to those who own agricultural land, they could easily treat worship events self-indulgently, shutting out those who had no access to land as a means of livelihood. The Torah does not envision a welfare system administered by a political bureaucracy and based on a centralized system of taxation. The well-being of the potentially marginalized depends on the charity of all citizens.

Coming immediately after the instructions regarding the tithal festival, 14:27 suggests that the landed citizenry are expected to invite Levites to accompany them on their pilgrimages to the place that Yahweh will choose (cf. 12:12, 17b–18) and to join them in celebrating in the presence of Yahweh. In good years this would not create a hardship for the households, since in the few days of the festivals they could not possibly have consumed the tenth of their produce. So the appeal to invite Levites living in their towns is both reasonable and charitable.

However, concerned about the Levites' general economic well-being throughout the year, in verses 28–29 Moses calls for a third-year tithe,

---

9. This is the first occurrence of *yayin*, the common word for "wine." Cf. *tîrôš* ("new wine") in 7:13; 11:14; 12:17; 14:23; 18:4; 28:51; 33:28.

10. Whereas *yayin* is derived from grapes, *šēkār* ("fermented drink") refers to any kind of intoxicating drink, whether made from dates or figs or pomegranates or grain (beer). For discussion of the word, see P. P. Jenson, "שכר," *NIDOTTE*, 4:113–14.

11. On formal worship in the presence of Yahweh as an occasion for joy and celebration, see comments on 12:7.

an institution found nowhere else in the Old Testament.[12] Rather than bringing their tithes to the central sanctuary, in the third and sixth years the farmers must deposit their tithes in their towns. It is unclear whether everyone must do this in the same third and sixth years of the seven-year cycle,[13] or whether they are to be staggered, which would ensure a continuous supply of food for the Levites. Although in verse 27 "your gates" functions metaphorically for "your towns" (NIV), verse 28 uses the expression in its literal sense. Here they can be stored and distributed to the Levites.

But Levites are not alone in lacking direct access to the blessing of Yahweh through the crops of the fields and the herds and flocks. In keeping with his humanitarian concern for all who are economically marginalized, Moses expands the economic safety net to the alien, the fatherless, and the widow.[14] These should all be invited to the gates to receive food they can take home and eat until they are satisfied. Moses anticipates some stratification of Israelite society, but he envisions communities whose landed citizenry are compassionate and whose economically marginalized are cared for (cf. chap. 15). With the last clause of verse 29 he suggests that demonstrated compassion to the poor is precondition for continued blessing.[15]

THE THEOLOGICAL AND SOCIAL **significance of the tithe.** Although we first hear of the tithe in Genesis 14:20 and 28:22, the antecedents to Moses' current discussion are found in Leviticus 27:30—33 and Numbers 18:21—32. The former presents the tithe as Yahweh's holy possession reserved for priests and Levites (cf. Lev. 27:21) and calls for the tithing of both horticultural products and livestock. However, people are given the option of paying the tithe in silver instead of in kind, though in such instances one-fifth of its monetary value must be added.

---

12. Moses will return to the subject of the third-year tithe in 26:12—15. The most likely candidate for a link with this tithe occurs in Amos 4:4—5, which may represent an intentional caricature of the third-year tithe.

13. Thus Tigay, *Deuteronomy*, 144.

14. On this triad see comments on 10:18. These marginalized classes had been referred to earlier in 1:16; 5:14; 10:18.

15. "In all the work of your hands that you do" (pers. trans.) expands a phrase that occurs frequently in Deuteronomy: 2:7; 4:28; 16:15; 24:19; 27:15; 28:12; 30:9; 31:29; 33:11.

The laws of purity that applied to sacrificial offerings do not apply to tithes. Animals presented to Yahweh are to be selected randomly, which meant that whether the lot falls on a desirable or defective specimen, it must not be substituted. In Numbers 18:21 – 32 Yahweh declared that the tithe be given to the Levites as their remuneration for the spiritual service they render to the nation and as compensation for not receiving any grants of land. Levites in turn must offer a tithe of the tithe they receive from the people, giving the best part of what they had received to the high priest.

As the Levites' source of food, the tithe can be consumed wherever they live. However, because the people have dedicated the gifts to Yahweh, the Levites are to treat what is brought to them as sacred. Standing on the shores of the Jordan before a people about to enter the land, here Moses highlights both the theological and social significance of the tithe, with minimal attention to administrative logistics.

Like the rest of the cultic festivals prescribed by the Torah, it is difficult to determine the extent to which the Israelites' performance measured up to the ideals laid out so clearly. Malachi is well aware of the link between the people's stinginess with respect to the tithes that should have been brought to the storehouses (presumably of the temple) and their irreverence toward Yahweh. Going against the stream of divine injunctions elsewhere, in Malachi 3:7 – 12 he challenges his postexilic contemporaries to bring in their tithes faithfully and thus to test Yahweh to see if he would not pour out his blessing on them. While this invitation to test Yahweh is extraordinary, the prophet recognizes the link between fidelity in these offerings and the divine blessing of the land, as laid out in Deuteronomy 14:22 – 29.

In reading the Old Testament prophets, one surmises that the people's participation in religious festivals was often little more than external performance (cf. Isa. 1:10 – 17; Hos. 6:6; Amos 5:21 – 24; Mic. 6:6 – 8), devoid of the joy in the privilege of feasting in the presence of Yahweh envisioned here. Furthermore, landed citizens' participation in these festivals seems to have been disconnected from life in general and compassion for the poor in particular. In a similar vein, in the New Testament Jesus accuses the Jewish leaders of being scrupulous in adhering to the tithing ordinance while disregarding the weightier matters of Torah: justice, mercy, and faithfulness.

This will happen when access to divine favor is considered a right, especially by those who conform externally to the ceremonial requirements of the law but forget that worship in the presence of the Lord is a supreme privilege to be greeted with awe and a sense of unworthiness. As Moses had pleaded in 10:12 – 22, those who worship God rightly are grateful for

God's blessing and commit themselves to an ethic of *imitatio dei* ("imitation of God"), particularly in showing compassion to the poor.

A BAROMETER OF AUTHENTIC **spirituality.** We leave a fuller discussion of the contemporary significance of the tithe until we have examined the festivals in chapter 16. For now we note that the disposition of the church toward the marginalized continues to be a primary barometer of authentic spirituality. Christians should not wait for the state to take care of the poor in their communities. On the contrary, through charity and compassion the church functions as the "wings" of Yahweh (Ruth 2:12) and the hands and feet of Christ (cf. Matt. 25:34—46).

Some today draw sharp contrasts between the external and ritualistic worship of the Old Testament and the internal spiritual worship in the New Testament.[16] But this interpretation fails to distinguish between flawed Israelite practice and the ideals of the Old Testament itself and completely misreads the book of Deuteronomy. If the previous text grounded the dietary regulations in Israel's spiritual relationship with Yahweh (14:1—2, 21), the present text highlights the institution of the tithe as a means and opportunity to celebrate the generosity and the blessing of Yahweh in his presence, to learn to fear him, and to show compassion to the marginalized. Little is said about the nature of the rituals.

In his call for worship "in spirit and in truth" (John 4:23—24), Jesus has recaptured the vision of Deuteronomy, which is a far cry from the way in which the Israelites tended to perform their liturgical acts of worship. But the problem of reducing worship to externals and rituals was not unique to the ancient Israelites. It characterized the Pharisees of Jesus' day (Matt. 23:23; Luke 11:42), quickly contaminated the worship of the early church (Acts 5:1—5), and plagues the church to this day. The defense against such ritualism is a heart that is soft toward God and toward those in need, and hands that gladly give up what they hold.

Christians today often debate whether they are obligated to tithe. The question itself is curious and somewhat hypocritical, because these same people spend little time discussing whether or not other aspects of the Old Testament law continue in force. It seems that when we ask, "Do Christians need to tithe?" we have asked the wrong question. At issue is not the institution but the heart and mind of God, which are to be reflected in the hearts

---

16. See e.g., John Piper, in a sermon, "Worship God!" (www.desiringgod.org/Resource-Library/Sermons/Worship-God--2/; accessed October 6, 2011).

and minds of his people. This passage is not concerned so much about the tithe as about providing another occasion to celebrate in the presence of God and to encourage generosity among God's people. Consequently we should rephrase the question this way: How might Christians demonstrate the compassion for the economically marginalized that the institution of the tithe tries to foster? This gets us off the externals and focuses on the primary issue: soft hearts and open hands.

Deuteronomy 15:1–18

A t the end of every seven years you must cancel debts. ²This is how it is to be done: Every creditor shall cancel the loan he has made to his fellow Israelite. He shall not require payment from his fellow Israelite or brother, because the LORD's time for canceling debts has been proclaimed. ³You may require payment from a foreigner, but you must cancel any debt your brother owes you. ⁴However, there should be no poor among you, for in the land the LORD your God is giving you to possess as your inheritance, he will richly bless you, ⁵if only you fully obey the LORD your God and are careful to follow all these commands I am giving you today. ⁶For the LORD your God will bless you as he has promised, and you will lend to many nations but will borrow from none. You will rule over many nations but none will rule over you.

⁷If there is a poor man among your brothers in any of the towns of the land that the LORD your God is giving you, do not be hardhearted or tightfisted toward your poor brother. ⁸Rather be openhanded and freely lend him whatever he needs. ⁹Be careful not to harbor this wicked thought: "The seventh year, the year for canceling debts, is near," so that you do not show ill will toward your needy brother and give him nothing. He may then appeal to the LORD against you, and you will be found guilty of sin. ¹⁰Give generously to him and do so without a grudging heart; then because of this the LORD your God will bless you in all your work and in everything you put your hand to. ¹¹There will always be poor people in the land. Therefore I command you to be openhanded toward your brothers and toward the poor and needy in your land.

¹²If a fellow Hebrew, a man or a woman, sells himself to you and serves you six years, in the seventh year you must let him go free. ¹³And when you release him, do not send him away empty-handed. ¹⁴Supply him liberally from your flock, your threshing floor and your winepress. Give to him as the LORD your God has blessed you. ¹⁵Remember that you were slaves in Egypt and the LORD your God redeemed you. That is why I give you this command today.

¹⁶But if your servant says to you, "I do not want to leave you," because he loves you and your family and is well off

with you, ¹⁷then take an awl and push it through his ear lobe into the door, and he will become your servant for life. Do the same for your maidservant.

¹⁸Do not consider it a hardship to set your servant free, because his service to you these six years has been worth twice as much as that of a hired hand. And the LORD your God will bless you in everything you do.

THIS CHAPTER CONTINUES THE appeal for soft hearts and open hands begun in 14:22 by appealing for generosity toward the poor in one's own family (vv. 1 – 11) and toward those enslaved (vv. 12 – 18). Although on first sight, verses 1 – 3 seem to have a legal flavor, Moses the pastor spends more than 80 percent of his time trying to motivate the people to adopt the policy.[1] These are practical instructions for the congregation on the life of godliness.

Showing Kindness to the Poor (15:1 – 11)

THE YEAR FOR CANCELING debts (vv. 1 – 5). The section opens formally with an announcement: "At the end of every seven years you must cancel debts." Whether "the end of seven years" means at the beginning,[2] sometime within, or at the end[3] of the seventh year of the seven-year cycle, Deuteronomy 31:10 associates "the time of the year of the release" with the Festival of Booths (cf. 16:13 – 16).[4] The present passage does not link the release with this festival, though the reference to a formal proclamation at the end of verse 2 makes most sense in this festival context. The required action is specified literally as "to practice/enact release" (NIV "cancel debts"). Whereas earlier regulations on the sabbatical year focused on rest for the land,[5] with characteristic humanitarian concern this text focuses on the institution's implications for the people, particularly the poor. Here

---

1. On the rhetorical style of vv. 4 – 6 see William S. Morrow, *Scribing the Center: Organization and Redaction in Deuteronomy 14:1 – 17:13* (Atlanta: Scholars, 1995), 101 – 2.

2. Verse 12 speaks of an indentured servant serving his master for six years (cf. Driver, *Deuteronomy*, 174).

3. Jewish tradition places it on the last days of the seventh year. See Tigay, *Deuteronomy*, 145.

4. The initial temporal phrase, "at the end of seven years," occurs elsewhere only in 31:10, where Moses adds the clarifying comment, "in the year for canceling debts, during the Feast of Tabernacles."

5. On Ex. 23:10 – 12 and Lev. 25:1 – 7, 18 – 22, see D. L. Baker, *Tight Fists or Open Hands: Wealth and Poverty in Old Testament Law* (Grand Rapids: Eerdmans, 2009), 223 – 32.

Moses highlights the spirit of the ordinance, recognizing that merely allowing the poor access to privately held lands during the sabbatical year will not solve the long-term danger of economic stratification.

Beginning with a formal heading, verses 2 – 3 clarify what Moses means by "enacting release" (v. 1). (1) In general terms Moses calls on creditors to release their claims on debtors.[6] The Hebrew expression *maśśēh yād* (lit., "the [secured/guaranteed] loan of the hand" reflects the ancient custom of leaving property with a creditor as collateral and a guarantee that one intends to repay the loan. The property could be some valuable possession or in extreme cases the debtor himself (cf. vv. 12 – 18). By this understanding the present statement means something like, "Every creditor who holds a loan-pledge shall release what has been pledged to him by his neighbor who is indebted to him."[7] If so, this does not mean the absolute cancellation of all debts, nor even the suspension of payments during the sabbatical year, but the return of all properties that a creditor is holding against loans by those indebted to him, enabling the original owner once more to enjoy the economic benefit of those properties.

(2) Moses calls on all creditors to refrain from pressuring neighbors or "fellow Israelites" to pay off the loan (v. 2). Debtors would naturally feel the release of pressure if the creditor renounced all claims to the property given as pledge, and even more so if he suspended the payment for the loan that was due in the seventh year. Just as allowing land a year to lie fallow (Ex. 23:10 – 11) provided it with an opportunity to rejuvenate itself, so by suspending his rights to the loan and the pledge for one year, the creditor would offer the debtor an opportunity to catch his breath and hopefully get back on his feet economically.

Moses grounds the call for release in the fact that "the LORD's time has been proclaimed for canceling debts." The verb "proclaim" (*qārā᾽*, "to call out") suggests a formal proclamation, but the meaning of *layhwh* (lit., "to Yahweh") can be interpreted several ways.[8] If it means "belonging to

---

6. The meaning of the Hebrew behind "every creditor shall cancel the loan" is debated. For a discussion of the options see C. J. H. Wright, *God's People in God's Land: Family, Land, and Property in the Old Testament* (Grand Rapids: Eerdmans, 1990), 169 – 73; cf. Nelson, *Deuteronomy,* 189; McConville, *Deuteronomy,* 255.

7. Similarly Robin Wakely, "נשׂא," *NIDOTTE,* 3:176, following C. J. H. Wright, "Sabbatical Year," *ABD,* 5:858; idem, *God's People in God's Land,* 170 – 72.

8. The closest analogue in Deuteronomy concerns the Sabbath command in the Decalogue, which grounds the six-day rhythm of work in the fact that the seventh day is Sabbath *layhwh* ("of/to Yahweh your God," cf. Lev. 23:3). The language of issuing a proclamation "for/to Yahweh" is borrowed from Lev. 25:2 – 7, which refers to the sabbatical institution of the release of land in the seventh year as a Sabbath *layhwh* ("Yahweh's Sabbath"). By echoing the language of the sabbatical year in effect Moses declares, "Observe the release of debts *in addition to* the release of the land, because both have been proclaimed as Yahweh's." Thus Milgrom, *Leviticus 23 – 27,* 2245.

Yahweh," then Yahweh claims it as his own and retains the right to deter-mine the boundaries of appropriate human activity on that day (cf. 5:14). If it means "by Yahweh," the emphasis falls on the divine origin of the ordinance. If *layhwh* means "in honor of Yahweh" (NIV "the LORD's time"), this ordinance calls for a theological perspective on all of life. By showing compassion for the poor before the watching world, Israelites will imitate the compassionate character of their God (cf. 10:17–19).

Remarkably Moses permits Israelites to keep the pressure on the for-eigner (v. 3a). At the moment Moses is not concerned about foreigners' well-being or about Israelites who make business loans.[9] The focus is on Israelites, who for whatever reason have fallen into debt (e.g., perhaps because of crop failure, accident).

In verses 4–11, with keen pastoral insight Moses recognizes that it is not enough simply to announce the policy regarding the indebted poor; his people must be motivated to adopt this policy. After opening with "How-ever" or "On the other hand," Moses seeks to do so by describing the eco-nomic ideal (vv. 4–6) and then pleading for compassion and generosity toward the poor (vv. 7–11).

Moses' picture of Israel's ideal economic future sounds utopian. He opens with an announcement: "There should be no poor among you." The book of Deuteronomy expresses great concern for widows, the fatherless, and aliens,[10] but references to the "poor" as *ᵓebyôn* occur only here (vv. 7, 9, 11, 15) and in 24:14. This expression involves individuals who through landlessness or lack of resources are economically deprived and dependent on others for relief from their poverty. The emphatic construction[11] sug-gests that despite (or because of obedience to) the charge in verses 1–3, the Israelites may anticipate a future when this ordinance will no longer be needed. But this future is not inevitable.

In verses 4b–5 Moses identifies two preconditions to the realization of the ideal. (1) Yahweh must show favor toward his people by delivering the land of Canaan into the hands of the Israelites as their grant (NIV "inheri-tance")[12] and possession, and then by blessing his people in the land.[13] (2) Israel must adhere scrupulously to the will of Yahweh (v. 5). Moses'

---

9. So also Tigay, *Deuteronomy*, 145, following early Jewish tradition reflected in *m. Šeb.* 10.

10. Cf. the references to the orphan, the widow, and the alien in 10:18; 24:17; 27:19.

11. The infinitive absolute + imperfect of the root *brk* (NIV "richly bless") occurs only here in Deuteronomy.

12. For echoes of the divine land grant formula, see 4:21, 38; 15:4; 19:10; 20:16; 21:23; 24:4; 25:19, 20.

13. The specific nature of the blessing is described in 7:13–16; 11:14–15 (cf. v. 26); and 28:1–14.

demand for total obedience is as emphatic as his declaration of Yahweh's blessing,[14] yielding the following logic:

> If you obey Yahweh scrupulously, he will bless you richly.
> If he blesses you richly, there will be no poor among you.

In verse 6 Moses' attention shifts from personal economics to corporate implications of Yahweh's blessing. For rhetorical effect he repeats the divine blessing formula, adding "as he has promised," a reference to a previous ordinance outside the book.[15] Moses summarizes the evidence of Yahweh's blessing for Israel as a nation with four statements declaring Israel's economic and political hegemony over the rest of the world, cast in symmetrical and chiastic parallelism (vv 6b, 6c):

> You will lend to many nations, but you will borrow from none.
> You will rule over many nations, but none will rule over you.

Instructions on how to treat the poor (vv. 7–8). In verses 7–11 Moses moves from describing the ideal future to the reality that awaits the people once they cross the Jordan. Here we witness Moses' pastoral and rhetorical strategy as clearly as anywhere in the book.[16] (1) Having presented the ideal in verses 4–6, he begins where the people are in the real historical context. (2) Moses appeals to Israel's sense of family. Four of the seven occurrences of "brother" in this chapter occur in these verses (vv. 7a, 7b, 9, 11). (3) Moses addresses the fundamental sinfulness of the people. But here he is not interested in the personal sin that might underlie the poor person's indebtedness, but the propensity of the rich to sin against their poor brothers (v. 9). (4) Moses addresses both the interior and the exterior dimension of ethics. When he speaks of the "heart"/"mind" of the rich, his concern is their disposition toward the poor; when he speaks of the "hand," his concern is their action. (5) Moses punctuates his comments with direct speech — first a hypothetical comment by the addressee (v. 9), and then a quotation of divine speech (v. 11). Based on the syntax and the flow of ideas, this paragraph divides into three parts arranged in an ABA pattern as follows: instructions on how to treat the poor (vv. 7–8); a warning,

---

14. The earlier construction for *brk* of infinitive absolute + imperfect is matched in v. 5 for the verb *šmᶜ*, with the nuance "you must indeed listen/obey."

15. Cf. Ex. 23:22–26 and Lev. 26:3–13. See J. Milgrom, "Profane Slaughter and a Formulaic Key to the Composition of Deuteronomy," *HUCA* 47 (1976): 1–17.

16. For a helpful general discussion of the "pastoral strategy" of Deuteronomy, see John Goldingay, *Theological Diversity and the Authority of the Old Testament* (Grand Rapids: Eerdmans, 1987), 153–66.

signaled by "be careful" (v. 9); more instructions on how to treat the poor (vv. 10–11).

On the surface the opening clause of verse 7 appears to contradict verse 4. However, the contradiction evaporates when we recognize that the earlier statement represents an ideal, whereas this statement recognizes the realities of life. Moses clarifies what he means by the poor "among you" with three expressions reflecting an expanding scope. "Your brothers" refers fundamentally to the members of a household, but as we have seen, in Deuteronomy it applies to all Israel, which is perceived as an extended kinship group. As elsewhere in this book, "your towns" is strictly speaking "your gates" (cf. 3:5), while "the land" refers to the entire territory that Yahweh had delivered to the Israelites. With this statement Moses reiterates that Israelites are responsible for each other's well-being.

Verse 7b specifies the required disposition toward the poor: Israelites are to be softhearted and openhanded. This demand is expressed with two negative statements. The first ("do not be hardhearted") uses a word that in 2:30 had been used of Sihon's hardened disposition toward Israel. The second ("do not be ... tightfisted") speaks of clenching what one holds in the hand—in particular, the article the debtor has deposited as security for his debt. This interpretation is confirmed by verse 8, which appeals for a compassionate disposition, freely opening one's hands to those in need and generously lending to one another.

Warnings against hardheartedness and tightfistedness (v. 9). The imperative in verse 9, "Be careful not ...," signals the climax of this paragraph.[17] The text identifies three pathological dispositions that plague those who are economically well-off. (1) The first malady is a twisted mind. The characterization of tightfistedness as a "wicked thought" in one's heart places a lack of compassion toward the poor in the same category as plots to lead people into apostasy (cf. 13:13[14]). Moses concretizes the "mean-spirited" notion with a hypothetical quotation by this Scrooge: "The seventh year, the year for canceling debts, is near." The thinking is, the closer the year of release, the less the creditor has to gain from the debtor's indebtedness. The antidote to such twisted thinking is a generous heart concerned about the well-being of the poor rather than one's own advantage. Loans were to be granted freely for the benefit of the poor, not the creditor, who has no need to capitalize on the plight of his brother.

(2) The second malady is an evil eye (NIV "ill will"). Deuteronomy recognizes that there is a time and a place for the eye to express no pity

---

17. For variations, see 4:9; 6:12; 8:11; 12:13, 19, 30. This is the only imperatival form in the chapter.

but hostility,[18] but when faced by a countryman in poverty, the eye is to be compassionate.[19]

(3) The third pathology is tightfisted hands. Admittedly, "hand" does not appear until verse 10, but the statement "so that you ... give him nothing," the association of the hard heart with closed hands in verse 7, and the plea for open hands in verse 8 all suggest that here Moses is thinking of open hands that give liberally to the poor what they need. The verb "to give" contrasts the stinginess of potential Scrooges with the generosity of Yahweh, who has given the land as an undeserved grant to the Israelites (v. 7).

The ending of verse 9 describes the consequences of such stinginess; it will force the impoverished to take their appeal directly to Yahweh and rouse him to declare a verdict on mean-spirited and tightfisted creditors (cf. Ps. 69:33[34]). As Moses declared in 10:18—19, Yahweh executes justice on behalf of the fatherless, the widow, and the alien (10:18—19), and in so doing he provides a model for human conduct. The verdict, "you will be found guilty of sin," contrasts with 6:25, where Moses announces the effect of wholehearted obedience: "That will be our righteousness" (cf. 24:10—15).

Further instructions on how to treat the poor (vv. 10—11). Verses 10 and 11 go on the offensive, describing the disposition and actions that should characterize the rich and adding the consequences of such conduct. Reversing the subjects dealt with in verse 9, Moses again calls on the rich to be generous toward the poor and to give without regret. Whereas in verse 9 Moses had spoken of eyes as "evil" (*rā'â*), here he applies the corresponding verb (*r'h*) to the "heart." Since elsewhere a heart that is evil is "sad," Moses is speaking of giving "generously" and "without a grudging heart" (1 Sam. 1:8; Neh. 2:2).[20] In so doing he attempts to get his audience beyond the letter of the law to its spirit: concern for the well-being of a brother alone should motivate generous and free-spirited giving.

In verse 10b Moses declares the consequences of cheerful generosity toward the poor. The promise that Yahweh will bless the creditor "in all

18. Toward the Canaanites (7:16); a member of the family who attempts to lead Israelites into idolatry (13:8[9]); a person guilty of willful murder (19:13); a malicious witness (19:21); a woman who seizes the genitals of one who is not her husband (25:12). For discussion of the "no-pity formula," see Block, *Ezekiel Chapters 1—24*, 209—10.

19. In 28:54—57, the only other reference to an evil eye, Moses describes a community besieged by the enemy where otherwise tender and delicate parents heartlessly devour their children.

20. As elsewhere, *ṭôb* ("good") and *rā'* ("evil") represent polar opposites; a "sad heart" is the opposite of a "good heart," that is, a "merry/delighted heart." Cf. Judg. 18:20; 19:6; Ruth 3:7; 1 Kings 21:7.

your work" and "in everything you put your hand to" takes the wind out of the sails of those who regret the nearness of the year of release, who seek to capitalize on the articles the poor have deposited as security, or who demand quick return on their loans. Yahweh will reward those who are kind and generous to the needy.

In verse 11 Moses ends this paragraph with another realistic reminder that the poor will always be around. Although the utopia he described in verses 4–6 may never be achieved, it is an ideal for which to strive. He ends this paragraph strengthening his earlier appeal (v. 8) by reminding those with means to care for "your brothers ... the poor and needy in your land."

Showing Kindness to Debt-Slaves (15:12 – 18)

MOSES CONTINUES HIS DISCUSSION of obligations of Israelites who are self-sufficient toward those who are economically dependent with instructions of debt-servitude.[21] These instructions build on Exodus 21:2–11 and Leviticus 25:39–46, but as pastor, Moses adapts the discussion in anticipation of the people's imminent entrance into the Promised Land. The focus shifts from the debt-servant's rights to the master's responsibilities, and the text is more paraenetic in tone.

Verses 12–18 must be interpreted not only in the light of antecedent biblical documents but also in the light of related customs as attested in writings from the ancient Near East.[22] The institution of slavery was widespread in the ancient world. Although Israelites would gain possession of non-Israelite slaves who were captives of war (Num. 31:7–12; Deut. 21:10–14) or through purchase in the slave trade, Israelite indentured servants usually landed in this state through indebtedness or destitution.[23] Having sold their property to pay off a debt or having given it as security for a loan, they became a part of a creditor's household, as a debt-servant or hireling.[24] Even if creditors were within their legal rights to take on

---

21. Since this text assumes the Israelite voluntarily submitted to this role (vv. 16–17), the expression "debt-servant" is preferable to "debt-slave."

22. The law code of Hammurabi (§117–119) provides the nearest analogue, on which see G. C. Chirichigno, *Debt-Slavery in Israel and the Ancient Near East* (JSOTSup 141; Sheffield: Sheffield Academic, 1993), 67–72, 144.

23. See I. Mendelsohn, "Slavery in the OT," *IDB*, 5:384–85. On slavery in Israel, see Z. W. Falk, *Hebrew Law in Biblical Times: An Introduction* (2nd ed.; Provo, UT: Brigham Young Univ. Press, 2001), 114–18.

24. See Lev. 25:25–34, 35–38, 39–55, on which see Milgrom, *Leviticus 23–27*, 2191–241. The third stage is illustrated in 2 Kings 4:1–7, which describes the plight of the widow of one of the sons of the prophets who was about to lose her two sons because the creditor was coming to take them as "slaves."

debt-servants, both Leviticus 25:39–46 and Deuteronomy 15:12–18 deny them the moral right to do so.[25] By placing boundaries around the conduct of creditors, Moses seeks to prevent future abuses of indentured Israelites' rights. His instructions divide into three major parts, with a parenthetical interlude in verse 17b: principles governing the treatment of indentured Israelites (vv. 12–15); principles governing exceptional cases (vv. 16–17a); a concluding appeal (v. 18).

Principles governing the treatment of indentured Israelites (vv. 12–15). The situation addressed here involves one Israelite falling into hands of another through an economic transaction. Normally the verb *mâkar* (to sell") involves handing something over in exchange for payment, but in a derived sense here it means simply to deliver something/someone into the power of another.[26] In contrast to Exodus 21:2, here the poor person apparently sells himself/herself.[27]

As in verses 1–11, Moses identifies the impoverished person as "your brother," treating creditor and indentured servant as kin. He highlights the ethnic factor by referring to the indebted person as "a fellow Hebrew, a man or a woman." In the Old Testament Israelites generally use "Hebrews" as a self-designation, in contrast to outsiders.[28] Here Moses is obviously dealing with inner-Israelite social and economic relations, not the disposition of Israelites toward foreigners within or outside their community. That he should mention both male and female servants highlights the need for identical compassion toward both genders.

Moses here instructs the Israelites on how those with means were to treat indentured countrymen. He permits them to use the services of indentured Israelites for six years. The six-year period envisioned here differs from the release ordinance of verses 1–11, which had linked the time of release to the national sabbatical year (cf. v. 9). The present ordinance seems to base the timing of the indentured servant's release on the date when he was pressed into service: "in the seventh year."[29] This guarantees independent Israelites seven years' service by anyone who indentures

---

25. As in the Decalogue, the second person addresses the owner as a potential violator of the debt-servant's rights.

26. See Judg. 2:14; 3:8; 4:2; 10:7.

27. Since Ex. 21:7–8 seeks to regulate the case of a father selling his daughter as a debt-servant, it is possible *yimmākēr* in our text should be interpreted passively, "is sold." NIV's reflexive highlights the debtor's initiative.

28. The words for "Hebrew man" (*ʿibrî*) and "Hebrew woman" (*ʿibriyyâ*) occur only here in Deuteronomy, reinforcing the link with Ex. 21:2–11, which deals with the plight of the indentured "Hebrew slave" (v. 2). See J. W. Marshall, *Israel and the Book of the Covenant: An Anthropological Approach to Biblical Law* (SBLDS 140; Atlanta: Scholars, 1993), 113–16.

29. Lev. 25:40 speaks only of a release in the year of Jubilee.

himself/herself—but the creditors may not demand more time. Indeed, here Moses transforms an impoverished person's legal right (Ex. 21:2) into a creditor's moral obligation—he must release the debt-servant, granting him independence as a fully free citizen of Israel.[30] Verses 13–14 charge those whom the impoverished person has served to help "jumpstart" their economic independence by liberally loading them with meat, grain, and wine in proportion to the blessing of Yahweh.

According to verse 15 the memory of Israel's slavery in Egypt and Yahweh's undeserved redemption should keep the creditor's heart soft toward his impoverished brother or sister (cf. 10:17–19).[31] Since the verb "redeem" (*pâdâ*) is naturally at home in contexts of slavery (cf. Ex. 21:8),[32] here the word strengthens the analogy between the liberation of Israel from Egyptian bondage and the liberation of the debt-servant. This link is reinforced by verse 13, which recalls Yahweh's own provision for the Israelites as they left Egypt. Just as the Israelites had left with the Egyptians' goods in their possession (cf. Ex. 3:21–22),[33] so creditors must ensure that when debt-servants leave, they have been lavishly provided for.

Principles governing an exceptional case (vv. 16–17a). In verses 16–17 Moses contemplates the possibility of an Israelite preferring permanent servitude to economic independence. He personalizes the situation by casting the resolve as a direct quotation from the debt-servant.[34] The text does not specify circumstances that might motivate him to reject freedom, but it focuses on the relationship that had developed between creditor and servant. Because the servant fared so well in the household of his creditor, he developed a genuine love (*ʾāhēb*) for those whom he served. Therefore he rejects the offer of freedom, preferring to cast his lot with the creditor and his family for the rest of his life.

Verse 17 summarizes the juridical procedure by which a debt-servant's decision to remain would be legally established: the master is to pierce his ear with an awl and pin his lobe to the door. Although Exodus 21:6 does

---

30. Whereas Ex. 21:3–4 suggests that the state of "freedom" involved less than total independence, Deut. 15:13–14 and Lev. 25:41 treat the manumission as the restoration of complete freedom. Cf. N. Lohfink, "חָפְשִׁי," *TDOT*, 5:114–18.

31. Moses inspires compassion toward fellow Israelites by reminding them of their experience of slavery in Egypt elsewhere in 5:15; 16:12; 24:18; 24:22.

32. See also 7:8 and 13:5[6], which also speak of Yahweh redeeming Israel "from the land of slavery," though often the verb "bring out" (*hôṣîʾ*) is used; see 5:6; 6:12; 8:14; 13:11.

33. Cf. Ex. 11:2–3; 12:35–36; Ps 105:37.

34. Though his rhetorical strategy may have been determined by Ex. 21:5, which does the same thing.

35. See J. I. Durham, *Exodus* (WBC 2; Waco: Word, 1987), 321. Extrabiblical support for this interpretation is often drawn from the Laws of Eshnunna §37 (cf. Roth, *Law Collections*, 65).

not prescribe pinning the ear to the door, based on the reference to God in that text, some argue this ceremony was to be performed at the sanctuary.[35] This would have been difficult logistically, unless the sanctuary was a local shrine. Therefore, it seems preferable to interpret "to God" in the earlier text as a reference to a divinely legitimated legal authority, perhaps with particular jurisdiction in cases involving families.[36] Perhaps the ritual officials so designated would come to the home of the creditor, representing God, who was a divine witness to the proceeding. The pierced ear served as a badge declaring the slave's commitment to his master and presumably the master's commitment to him;[37] he was his slave for life.[38] Whether the master could or would ever have negotiated a separation is unknown, but hereafter neither party could legally break this contract without the consent of the other.[39]

The concluding appeal (v. 18). Following a reminder that the policies for treating servants were to be the same for men and women (v. 17b), Moses concludes the discussion on debt servitude by returning to normal cases, in which indentured servants would accept their freedom. In verses 7 and 10 Moses had warned creditors not to be hardhearted or tightfisted in their treatment of their debtors. Now he admonishes them not to "consider it a hardship" or to feel cheated for needing to grant manumission to debt-servants when the sixth year comes to an end. Instead, they should be grateful for the contribution the debt-servants had made to the domestic economy.

The NIV's reading "worth twice [*mišneh*] as much as that of a hired hand" suggests landowners could get twice as much out of slaves as out of a hired person, presumably because they can force them to work harder or because they are available around the clock. However, here *mišneh* means "equivalent to,"[40] in which case the master should gladly release the indentured servant,

---

36. Thus Marshall, *Israel and the Book of the Covenant*, 134–38. This usage also occurs in Ex. 22:8[9].

37. After the ear was pierced, the creditor may have inserted a ring or cord with a metal or clay tag bearing his name, analogous to Egyptian and Mesopotamian customs of branding or stamping slaves with their owner's names or forcing them to wear other symbols of their status. See I. Mendelsohn, "Slavery in the OT," *IDB*, 5:385; M. Dandamaev, *Slavery in Babylonia: From Nabopolassar to Alexander the Great (626–331 BC)* (ed. M. A. Powell and D. B. Weisberg; trans. V. A. Powell; rev. ed.; DeKalb, IL: Northern Illinois Univ. Press, 1984), 229–35.

38. The expression "servant for life" occurs in 1 Sam. 27:12 and Job 41:4[40:28]. See further Craigie, *Deuteronomy*, 239.

39. The last law in the Code of Hammurabi (§282) involves a slave who repudiates his status by declaring, "You are not my master."

40. As in Jer. 16:18 (and Deut. 17:18, where *mišneh* refers to a "copy" of a document). *HALOT*, 650. A second millennium BC text from Alalakh uses the cognate expression *mištannu* for compensation given the owner of a slave when his human chattel is returned to him. Cf. M. Tsevat, "Alalakhiana," *HUCA* 29 (1958): 125–26.

knowing he has had the benefit of his work without cost for six years. As in verses 4, 6, and 10, Moses ends with a motive clause: the reward for this gracious disposition toward persons who are granted their freedom will be the blessing of Yahweh on all that the creditor sets his hands to do.

HISTORY OF GOD'S PEOPLE **on these commands.** In Deuteronomy 15:1 – 11 Moses has caught the spirit of life within the covenant community. Israel's ethic is not grounded in a system of laws written on tablets of stone, but on living relationships that exist between them and Yahweh their God on the one hand, and between individuals within the covenant community on the other. Pleading pastorally for a willing application of the first and foremost commandment, Moses calls the people to demonstrate their love for Yahweh by loving their neighbors. The sage of Israel would put it another way:

> He who oppresses the poor shows contempt for their Maker,
> but whoever is kind to the needy honors God. (Prov. 14:31)

> He who mocks the poor shows contempt for their Maker;
> whoever gloats over disaster will not go unpunished.
> (Prov. 17:5)

It is difficult to assess the extent to which Moses' instructions regarding debtors and slaves in verses 12 – 18 were fulfilled in the history of Israel. The Elijah-Elisha narratives are set within the broader context of a general polemic against the worship of Baal. In the heart of these narratives, the case of the prophetic apprentice's widow and her sons illustrates how the abandonment of Yahweh in favor of other gods resulted in the breakdown of the social values espoused here in Deuteronomy (2 Kings 4:1 – 7). Whether or not the creditor was within his legal rights, this episode demonstrates that Israel's spiritual recidivism was accompanied by loss of moral integrity; because the community had failed to take care of this widow and her fatherless children, the creditor was coming to claim the boys as debt-servants.[41]

Later prophets repeatedly railed against those with economic and political power for their exploitation of the poor.[42] In the eighth century Amos

---

41. Cf. the repeated injunctions in Deuteronomy to care for widows and orphans (lit., "fatherless").

42. Isa. 3:14 – 15; 10:1 – 2; 58:6 – 7; Ezek. 18:11 – 12; 22:29; Amos 2:6 – 8; 8:4 – 6; Zech. 7:8 – 12.

cites tightfistedness and hardheartedness as the supreme evil in the northern kingdom of Israel:

> This is what the LORD says:
> "For three sins of Israel,
>   even for four, I will not turn back ⌞my wrath⌟.
> They sell the righteous for silver,
>   and the needy for a pair of sandals.
> They trample on the heads of the poor
>   as upon the dust of the ground
>   and deny justice to the oppressed.
> Father and son use the same girl
>   and so profane my holy name.
> They lie down beside every altar
>   on garments taken in pledge.
> In the house of their god
>   they drink wine taken as fines." (Amos 2:6 – 8)

A century later Jeremiah denounces the people of Judah for violating the policies outlined by Moses in this text (Jer. 34:12 – 22). The oracle acknowledges that after a history of failure to observe the year of release for debt-servants, the prophet's generation had implemented the actions called for here. However, "your fathers ... did not listen to me or pay attention to me," because they changed their minds and reclaimed the freed persons as their debt-servants. Consequently, instead of the blessing that Moses promised to those who are generous, openhanded, and softhearted, Jeremiah pronounces on them the full weight of the curses of Deuteronomy 28.

Responding to those who would condemn the woman for pouring out her ointment on Jesus' head, in Mark 14:7 the Savior expresses his own realism regarding the community, reminding his own disciples that "the poor you will always have with you, and you can help them any time you want." At the same time, Moses' declaration of the ideal in Deuteronomy 15:4 points to a future when all wrongs will be righted. The NIV renders the verse, "There should be no poor among you," but it could just as well be rendered indicatively as a promise: "There will be no poor among you" (ESV, NRSV), for when Yahweh lavishes his blessing on his people in the ultimate grant that he gives them, the utopian ideal will be reality.

John envisions the fulfillment of this covenantal ideal in the holy city, the new Jerusalem:

> And I heard a loud voice from the throne saying, "Now the dwelling of God is with men, and he will live with them. They will be his people, and God himself will be with them and be their God. He

will wipe every tear from their eyes. There will be no more death or mourning or crying or pain, for the old order of things has passed away." (Rev 21:3 – 4; cf. 7:14 – 21)

THE SPIRIT OF CHARITY. In Deuteronomy 15:1 – 11 Moses presents his people with a vision of the community of faith and the spirit of charity that should characterize God's people in every age. The softheartedness and openhandedness called for here are clearly reflected in 1 John 3:17 – 18: "But if anyone has material possession and sees his brother in need yet has no pity on him, how can the love God be in him? Dear children, let us not love with words or tongue but with actions and in truth." This spirit of compassion must begin in the household of faith (Gal. 6:10), but then extend to all economically marginalized, including those trapped in the ghettoes of our cities and the "hollers" of Appalachia, legal immigrants and undocumented aliens fleeing desperate situations for a better life,[43] and the elderly who are often abandoned by their families. There is no better opportunity for Christians to distinguish themselves from the self-indulgent Canaanites of this land than through their generosity and charity toward the poor. To paraphrase 1 John 4:19, "We are covenantally committed to others and seek their well-being through concrete acts of 'love,' because the Lord was first covenantally committed to us and sought our well-being through concrete acts of 'love.'"

Although Christians for the most part do not live in the land of Palestine and are not "brothers" in an ethnic sense, the relevance of the principles arising from Deuteronomy 15:1 – 11 and 12 – 18 are obvious to all who have eyes that see the reality of a world fractured by alienation and ears that hear the divine response to this pervasive dysfunction.[44] On the one hand, this passage proves that the institution of servitude need not be oppressive by definition. All owners of servants should treat their subjects as brothers or sisters, by virtue of their common humanity as descendants of Adam and their common nobility as images of God (Gen. 5; Job 31:15; Ps. 8; Prov. 14:31; 17:5). On the other hand, members of the household of faith and children of God have special motivation for compassion toward

---

43. Combining prophetic zeal with a tender pastoral tone, Carroll R. (*Christians at the Border: Immigration, the Church, and the Bible*) appeals to Christians to adopt a distinctively Christian disposition to the issue of undocumented immigrants.

44. See the excellent discussion of the contemporary significance of this chapter by Jeffries M. Hamilton, *Social Justice and Deuteronomy: The Case of Deuteronomy 15* (Atlanta: Scholars, 1992), 144 – 58.

the poor and needy. We the redeemed remember that God in his grace has rescued us from the bondage of sin and adopted us as his sons, lavishing on us his provision in accordance with our needs. Knowing not only the pain of deprivation and slavery but also the grace of redemption, we look at the world through the eyes of our heavenly Father and are inspired to treat others as he has treated us.

The implications of this fact are profound and varied. (1) The poor and marginalized should not need to defend their rights or beg for charity from the well-to-do and the powerful. Concern for social justice is a barometer of the health of the church.

(2) God's people will be gracious toward those who are indebted to them, being more concerned about the satisfaction of the needs of the poor than the defense of their own rights to private property. Openhanded generosity and softhearted compassion toward the poor and needy are the duty especially of those with the means to help.

(3) Godly persons in economical and social positions of power will treat those for whom they are responsible with compassion, so that even those who are formally inferior recognize that their lot in life is "good" (*tôb*).

(4) Although we recognize the social and economic problems of the world outside the church to be symptomatic of a deeper spiritual problem that can be resolved only through the miraculous and gracious redemption wrought through Christ, God's people will support all efforts to break down walls of alienation and oppression. In so doing, they will not only be obeying the commands of the Lord, but they will also be declaring to the world how exceptionally righteous are his ways (Deut. 4:7–8).

(5) The rich and powerful should never pride themselves in their accomplishments but rejoice in God's favor, knowing that the blessing of the Lord is not a right but an expression of his generosity and his fidelity to his promise to bless those who represent him well.

(6) Worship provides a context in which economic and social barriers may and should be torn down. The powerful must guarantee equal rights for all for access to the presence of God and need to take the initiative to invite the poor and needy to the Lord's table.

For these and many other reasons, Christians should be at the forefront of movements that seek both the common good and the well-being of the underprivileged and socially defenseless, like Sir William Wilberforce (1759–1833), who led the charge against slavery in Britain. In a post-slavery world they will do the same by generously providing the poor with economic resources, safeguarding their justice, and protecting them from exploitation and abuse. In short, like Boaz, as the "wings" of the Lord they offer security to the vulnerable (cf. Ruth 2:12).

Deuteronomy 15:19–23

et apart for the LORD your God every firstborn male of
your herds and flocks. Do not put the firstborn of your
oxen to work, and do not shear the firstborn of your
sheep. [20]Each year you and your family are to eat them in the
presence of the LORD your God at the place he will choose.
[21]If an animal has a defect, is lame or blind, or has any serious flaw, you must not sacrifice it to the LORD your God.
[22]You are to eat it in your own towns. Both the ceremonially
unclean and the clean may eat it, as if it were gazelle or deer.
[23]But you must not eat the blood; pour it out on the ground
like water.

Original Meaning

IN 15:19–16:17 Moses returns to his instructions on the vertical dimensions of covenant
relationship that were interrupted by instructions regarding the poor (14:22–15:18). The
first section (15:19–23) is transitional, dealing with eating in the presence
of Yahweh at the central sanctuary and at home; the second (16:1–17)
invites the people regularly to celebrate before him.

Whereas chapter 16 will deal with scheduled celebrations in the presence of Yahweh, 15:19–23 invites Israelites to be ready to celebrate any
time. Regulations concerning the offering of the firstborn are found elsewhere in the Pentateuch (Ex. 13:2, 11–16; 22:29b–30[28b–29]; Num.
18:15–18). While critical scholars tend to highlight the inconsistencies
in these texts,[1] conservative scholars often try to harmonize them.[2] Both
approaches tend to overlook the distinctive emphases of each text, especially the role they play in the broader contexts in which they are embedded.[3] Given the appeal for open hearts and open hands in 15:1–18, this
treatment of offerings at the place Yahweh will choose (v. 20) creates an
effective inclusio with 14:22–29 and brings this larger unit on open hands
and a soft heart to an effective conclusion.

---

1. E.g., Weinfeld, *DDS*, 215–16.
2. E.g., C. F. Keil, *Biblical Commentary on the Old Testament* (with F. Delitzsch), vol. 1, *The Pentateuch* (Grand Rapid: Eerdmans, 1953), 357–58.
3. So also McConville, *Law and Theology in Deuteronomy*, 88–90.

Earlier Moses had instructed the people to present the firstborn of herd and flock to Yahweh along with a series of other gifts (12:5–6, 17–18; 14:23). Now he focuses on this offering in greater detail. According to Exodus 13:1–2, because every firstborn of every creature belongs to God, it must be consecrated to him and thereby removed from profane, everyday use. Although usually translated "firstborn,"[4] *bᵉkôr* connotes sociological rank rather than chronological priority,[5] which probably explains why Exodus 13:12 adds "the first offspring of every womb." This phrase confirms that those claimed by Yahweh are the firstborn of a mother rather than of a father.[6]

Deuteronomy 15:19 restricts the law, first by specifying firstborn males, and second by requiring perfect specimens. Taking into account Exodus 13:13, which eliminates donkeys, and Numbers 18:15–16, which eliminates unclean animals, the successive narrowing of the field of candidates may be illustrated diagrammatically as follows:

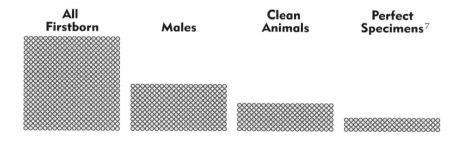

All Firstborn	**Males**	**Clean Animals**	**Perfect Specimens**[7]

Since no more than about 15 percent of firstborn animals will have been sacrificed, the economic consequences of the law of the firstborn was minimal. Furthermore, the animals were not to be simply disposed of or sacrificed as whole burnt offerings; rather, their meat was eaten in celebration at the central sanctuary (v. 20).

---

4. Thus *HALOT*, 131; *DCH*, 1:170; M. Tsevat, "בכור, *bᵉkôr*," *TDOT*, 2:121–27.

5. See Block, "Marriage and Family in Ancient Israel," 82–85; F. E. Greenspahn, *When Brothers Dwell Together: The Preeminence of Younger Siblings in the Hebrew Bible* (New York/Oxford: Oxford Univ. Press, 1994), 19, 27, 59–62.

6. A father's eldest child is referred to as "the first sign [beginning] of his father's [procreative] strength" (Deut. 21:17; cf. Gen. 49:3; Pss. 78:51; 105:36).

7. Compared to mortality rates today, the number of firstborns that survived the eight days required by Ex. 22:30[29] may have been fewer than 60 percent. Of these a significant number will have had one blemish or another.

The paragraph opens with a forthright command, calling Israelites to consecrate the firstborn in their herds and flocks to Yahweh their God. Whereas Numbers 3:13 establishes the basis for this demand, the supplementary commands in our text prohibit the use of these animals for normal domestic purposes. Firstborn male cattle were not to be used as draft animals, pulling wagons or plowing the fields, and the sheep and goats were not to be shorn. Since yearling cattle are strong enough for some tasks and since the finest wool comes from lambs six to twelve months old, Israelites might be tempted to compromise the integrity of these animals by using them for domestic purposes prior to consecrating them.[8] Although the text does not specify the time of year to consecrate the firstborn, the expression "each year" (lit., "year by year") suggests they were to be presented at the central sanctuary at one of the annual festivals.[9] This means that some firstborn may have been as young as a few days, others could have been almost a year old.

But how shall we reconcile these instructions with Yahweh's direct command in Exodus 22:30[29] to consecrate the firstborn on the eighth day? Apparently it depends on the location and timing of the consecration ritual. Since Numbers 18:16 sets the redemption price according to the "sanctuary shekel," this might have transpired at the tabernacle. However, once the tribes had scattered to their allotted territories, it would have been logistically impossible for the men to trek to the central sanctuary on the eighth day after the birth of every firstborn. Perhaps the functions of Levites living in Levitical cities (Num. 35:1−8) included receiving these offerings and the money that was paid to redeem other animals. In any case, once Moses called for the presentation of the firstborn at the central sanctuary, earlier regulations were suspended in favor of new guidelines in keeping with the new situation.

Verse 20 invites the head and the entire household to a banquet in the presence of Yahweh when the firstborn are consecrated.[10] Although Yahweh himself does not eat the meat, as divine host he invites his family to partake of food that has been dedicated to him. Lest they become careless about their offerings, Moses reminds the Israelites that the only meat worthy of Yahweh's table is that which comes from flawless animals (v. 21). Although he specifies defective as lame and blind, the addition

---

8. So also Tigay, *Deuteronomy*, 151.

9. On which see Deut. 16:1−17. This timing might explain Ezekiel's simile in Ezek. 36:37−38.

10. This statement abbreviates Num. 18:17−18, which requires that the blood of the firstborn be sprinkled on the altar and that the fat be burned up as an offering to Yahweh prior to the consumption of the meal.

of "any serious flaw" suggests these expressions function as shorthand for any conceivable defect.[11] They may be physically flawed, but they represented ceremonially clean species of animals. Therefore, like wild game, they could be eaten by anyone, whether in a state of cleanness or uncleanness in the towns where the people lived, provided the blood was properly drained during slaughtering.[12]

IN CONTRAST TO EXODUS 12–13 and Numbers 18, this paragraph offers a minimalist description of the consecration and sacrifice of the firstborn animals.[13] Building on Deuteronomy 12:6, it focuses on the firstborn as God's provision of table fare for his people who are invited to come regularly and eat in his presence. Yahweh delights in their presence before him. Every birth of a firstborn male among cattle, sheep, or goats signaled a call from Yahweh to the household to come to his sanctuary to declare their gratitude and to fellowship with him. The fertility of the herds and flocks was not to be taken for granted. The ability of a ewe or cow to conceive and give birth was a gift and a mark of divine blessing.

Thus the consecration of the firstborn should not have been viewed merely as an external ritual requirement; these young animals symbolized Yahweh's delight in his people. At the same time, this passage reflects Yahweh's concern for economy. Defective animals were not to be wasted or treated as trash; they too reflected his delight in the people, for he authorizes them to eat their meat in their homes—provided they respect the sanctity of the life of the animals. In a sense, even these meals are sacrifices, for an animal gives its life for the people in the family of God.

The book of Malachi describes a society in which divine grace and blessing were taken for granted. The loss of reverence for Yahweh, the loss of sight of his covenant love, and the loss of the privilege of sonship (Mal. 1:1–6; cf. Deut. 14:1) were reflected in the people's trivialization of worship. Instead of rejoicing at the prospect of worship in the presence of Yahweh, the people of Malachi's day responded to his invitation to fellowship with cynicism and ingratitude (Mal. 1:7–14). They were bored with

---

11. Lev. 21:18–20 speaks of defects that disqualify a male descendant of Aaron from priestly service, and Lev. 22:22–24 lists defects that render animals unacceptable.

12. A comparison of vv. 22–23 with 12:21b–24 suggests this is an abbreviation of the earlier text.

13. For discussion of the significance of the consecration of the firstborn in connection with the Passover, see P. Enns, *Exodus* (NIVAC; Grand Rapids: Zondervan, 2000), 253–59.

the ritual, and they profaned Yahweh's table by presenting to him lame and sickly animals.

THIS IS A PROBLEM in our own day. We often view the Lord's blessing as a right rather than a privilege. But God's people cannot afford to lose sight of the grace of covenant relationship with him, concretized in his blessing on our work and his invitation to worship in his presence. Success in every venture, whether agricultural, industrial, academic, or domestic, depends on God's favor (Ps. 90:16−17). And every meal is still a sacrifice, but it is also a gracious provision of God.

If this is true of the meals we eat in our homes, how much more of the meals he invites us to eat in his presence. Every time we gather to partake of the bread and the wine of communion, Jesus, who is Yahweh incarnate, serves us at his table. However, he does not merely take the offerings we bring and then invite us to eat of it; the firstborn Son of God offers himself, saying, "Take and eat, this is my body, given for you" (Matt. 26:26−27; Mark 14:22−23; with Luke 22:19−20; 1 Cor. 11:24−25). God's people should never treat eating at the Lord's table as a wearisome ritual, a waste of time and resources. On the contrary, this is a precious ritual, for the invitation to eat at this meal sets us apart from all others and provides us with a constant reminder of his immeasurable grace. In the words of the angel of Revelation 19:9, "Blessed are those who are invited to the wedding supper of the Lamb!"

Deuteronomy 16:1–17

O bserve the month of Abib and celebrate the Passover of the LORD your God, because in the month
of Abib he brought you out of Egypt by night.
²Sacrifice as the Passover to the LORD your God an animal
from your flock or herd at the place the LORD will choose as
a dwelling for his Name. ³Do not eat it with bread made with
yeast, but for seven days eat unleavened bread, the bread of
affliction, because you left Egypt in haste—so that all the
days of your life you may remember the time of your departure from Egypt. ⁴Let no yeast be found in your possession in
all your land for seven days. Do not let any of the meat you
sacrifice on the evening of the first day remain until morning.

⁵You must not sacrifice the Passover in any town the LORD
your God gives you ⁶except in the place he will choose as a
dwelling for his Name. There you must sacrifice the Passover
in the evening, when the sun goes down, on the anniversary
of your departure from Egypt. ⁷Roast it and eat it at the
place the LORD your God will choose. Then in the morning
return to your tents. ⁸For six days eat unleavened bread and
on the seventh day hold an assembly to the LORD your God
and do no work.

⁹Count off seven weeks from the time you begin to put
the sickle to the standing grain. ¹⁰Then celebrate the Feast
of Weeks to the LORD your God by giving a freewill offering
in proportion to the blessings the LORD your God has given
you. ¹¹And rejoice before the LORD your God at the place he
will choose as a dwelling for his Name—you, your sons and
daughters, your menservants and maidservants, the Levites in
your towns, and the aliens, the fatherless and the widows living among you. ¹²Remember that you were slaves in Egypt,
and follow carefully these decrees.

¹³Celebrate the Feast of Tabernacles for seven days after
you have gathered the produce of your threshing floor and
your winepress. ¹⁴Be joyful at your Feast—you, your sons
and daughters, your menservants and maidservants, and the
Levites, the aliens, the fatherless and the widows who live in
your towns. ¹⁵For seven days celebrate the Feast to the LORD

your God at the place the LORD will choose. For the LORD your God will bless you in all your harvest and in all the work of your hands, and your joy will be complete.

¹⁶Three times a year all your men must appear before the LORD your God at the place he will choose: at the Feast of Unleavened Bread, the Feast of Weeks and the Feast of Tabernacles. No man should appear before the LORD empty-handed: ¹⁷Each of you must bring a gift in proportion to the way the LORD your God has blessed you.

AS THE COUNTERPART TO 14:22–29, Deuteronomy 16:1–17 completes the theological framework surrounding the ethical injunctions in chapter 15. Here Moses instructs God's people on the three annual religious festivals, which have been introduced in three earlier contexts: Exodus 23:14–17; 34:18–25; Leviticus 23:1–44. The present text shares with the first two the formal announcement of the requirement to appear before Yahweh three times a year, though here this declaration comes at the end (vv. 16–17) rather than at the beginning. The present chapter exhibits a well-defined structure based on the three pilgrimage festivals: Passover and Unleavened Bread (vv. 1–8), Weeks (vv. 9–12), and Booths (vv. 13–15).

The Festival of Passover (16:1–8)

THE ORIGINS OF THE Festival of Passover and the Festival of Unleavened Bread are described in detail in Exodus 12 and elsewhere. The present version of this festival differs from earlier treatments in several significant respects.[1] Since some scholars exploit these differences as insurmountable contradictions, a brief response may be helpful. If we read the Pentateuchal books as a continuous narrative, these tensions all find ready answers.

The location of the festival. Exodus 12 presents the Passover as a domestic observance in contrast to a centralized festival. However, tech-

---

1. Scholars often exploit these differences to defend the Josianic date of the book and argue for the theologically revolutionary nature of Deuteronomy's vision of Israel's worship. See B. M. Levinson in *Deuteronomy and the Hermeneutics of Legal Innovation* (Oxford: Oxford Univ. Press, 1998), 53–97; idem, "The Hermeneutics of Tradition in Deuteronomy: A Reply to J. G. McConville," *JBL* 119 (2000): 269–86. For a response, see J. G. McConville, *Law and Theology in Deuteronomy* (JSOTSup 33; Sheffield: JSOT, 1984), 99–123; idem, "Deuteronomy's Unification of Passover and *Maṣṣôt*: A Response to Bernard M. Levinson," *JBL* 119 (2000): 47–58.

nically, the rituals prescribed in verses 1 – 14 do not pertain to the annual festival commemorating the exodus from Egypt; these are instructions for the one-time historical event involving Yahweh's envoy of death passing over the Israelites' houses in the final plague that swept through Egypt. Since the Israelites in Egypt lacked a central place of worship, a reference to such a place in Exodus 12 would have been anachronistic. Furthermore, whereas Leviticus 23:4 – 8 classifies the memorial festival of Passover as a *miqrā' qôdeš*, which may mean "sacred proclamation"[2] or "sacred assembly" (NIV), Exodus 12:6 opens the way for a centralized observance with the expression, "the people of the community of Israel."

Our text uses the expression ʿ *ʿṣeret* (NIV "assembly"), which suggests a mandatory celebration for Yahweh (Deut. 16:8), with the people gathering at a particular place. The designation of the Passover elsewhere as a "pilgrimage festival" reinforces this understanding. Since the exodus involved freeing a "people," a national—rather than family— commemoration of that event is appropriate. Thus while the original Passover was observed in Israelites' homes, a national celebration was anticipated from the beginning.

The sacrificial victim. While Deuteronomy's inclusion of animals from the "herd" (16:2) differs from Exodus 12:3 – 5, this is not a contradiction. "Sheep" and "goats" were natural victims in the original context, because the event required an animal that could be easily butchered and consumed in one evening. Although cattle were sacrificed at Sinai, their number in the Israelite camp may have been limited until the slaughter of the Midianites.[3] Furthermore, since cattle were acceptable for other sacrifices, to sacrifice bovines at the Passover is not extraordinary.[4]

Boiling the meat of the sacrificial animal. The verb *bâšal* may indeed mean "to boil" (Ex. 12:9; Deut. 14:21), but this is not required when fire is the specified agent (2 Chron. 35:13). This Hebrew verb means "to cook" generally, which may involve boiling in liquid, but could also mean roasting over a fire (cf. NIV) or frying in a pan.[5] While Exodus 12:9 prohibits boiling the Passover meat in water, Deuteronomy is silent on how the food may or may not be prepared.

Merging the Festivals of Passover and Unleavened Bread. Many scholars maintain that the festivals of Passover and Unleavened Bread have

---

2. See Milgrom, *Leviticus* 23 – 27, 1957.

3. According to Num. 31:33, the booty from this battle included 72,000 cattle.

4. According to 2 Chron. 35:7 one-tenth (3,000) of the Passover offerings sacrificed by Josiah were bulls.

5. According to Ex. 16:23, manna may be baked or cooked another way. "Boil" is possible, but no more likely than preparing it like a flapjack on a griddle or in a pan.

separate origins[6] and that Deuteronomy's conjunction of the two is innovative.[7] However, Exodus 34:18–25 links these festivals, and the account of the original Passover integrates unleavened bread firmly into the narrative (Ex. 12:8, 15–20, 34, 39). Furthermore, although Deuteronomy 16:1–8 treats the Passover as a pilgrimage festival, the notion that Deuteronomy robs the Festival of Unleavened Bread of this character is contradicted by verses 16–17.[8] The tensions between Deuteronomy 16:1–8 and 16 do not rise to the level of contradictions.

With respect to style and structure, Deuteronomy 16:1–17 appears more legislative than any previous text. Although this text lacks formal imperatives, verb forms with imperatival force anchor every independent clause. Nevertheless, motive and modifying clauses continue as Moses seeks to inspire the Israelites with the joy of feasting in the presence of Yahweh. Structurally, this passage divides into three parts: (1) the charge to keep the Passover (v. 1); (2) instructions for keeping the Passover (vv. 2–7); (3) the charge to keep the Festival of Unleavened Bread (v. 8). The outer elements echo the Sabbath command of the Decalogue, creating an effective "sabbatical envelope" around the entire unit.

The charge to keep the Passover (v. 1). Following the instructions on feasting in the presence of Yahweh in 14:22–15:23, Moses announces, "Observe the month of Abib." Because everyone was aware that Passover was to be celebrated on Abib/Nisan 14, there was no need to specify the date here.[9] Abib was the first month of the year,[10] which may suggest that this celebration also functioned as a New Year Festival.[11] The command

---

6. Exodus 12 clearly distinguishes between the Festivals of Passover and Unleavened Bread, and Ex. 23:15 names only the latter as one of the required three annual festivals.

7. See, e.g., Levinson (*Deuteronomy and the Hermeneutics of Legal Innovation*, 72–81), who argues that Deuteronomy transforms the Passover from a domestic festival to a pilgrimage festival, secularizes the Festival of Unleavened Bread, and deprives it of its pilgrimage character.

8. Levinson ("Reply to J. G. McConville," 282–83) interprets verse 16 as a cynical chiastic redeployment of the colophon from the Covenant Code to provide continuity "with tradition that the new festival calendar lacks."

9. See Ex. 12:6, 18; Lev. 23:5; Num. 9:3, 5; 28:16; Josh. 5:10; 2 Chron. 35:1; Ezra 6:19; Ezek. 45:21.

10. Cf. Exodus 12:1–6. The name Abib, meaning "the new ears of grain," reflects the time of year (March–April) when barley heads begin to emerge from the stalks. Later the month was known by the Babylonian name Nisan. Cf. J. C. VanderKam, "Calendars, Ancient Israelite and Jewish," *ABD*, 1:815.

11. Several significant events in Israel's history occurred on the first day of the year: the erection of the tabernacle (Ex. 40:2, 17); the beginning of the consecration of the temple (2 Chron. 29:17); the departure from Babylon of the returnees under Ezra's leadership (Ezra 7:9); the completion of marital reforms (Ezra 10:17). However, unequivocal evidence for a New Year Festival in ancient Israel is lacking. See further D. I. Block, "New Year," *ISBE* (rev. ed.), 3:529–32.

to observe a month seems odd and probably refers to all the ceremonies scheduled for that month (cf. Ex. 12:3; Lev. 23:9 – 14).

Passover was the most important festival of the month and probably the entire liturgical year. While the English rendering "to pass over" has a long history linked to the word's association with ʿābar ("to pass by," Ex. 12:23), the verb pāsaḥ should probably be understood as "to offer protection for." To translate pesaḥ simply as a synonym for ʿābar obscures the primary significance of the celebration: to commemorate Yahweh's protection of the houses of Israel from the envoy of death the night of their departure from Egypt. This interpretation is reinforced by the explanatory clause at the end of verse 1, which focuses on Yahweh's rescue of Israel from Egypt. The qualification "at night" reminds readers that Yahweh's acts of protection preceded their exodus (cf. Num. 33:3).

Instructions for keeping the Passover (vv. 2 – 7). Like the other Pentateuchal accounts of the Passover, Deuteronomy 16:1 – 8 offers only a bare outline of the rituals involved in the festival. (1) Israelites were to celebrate the Passover at the place Yahweh would choose to establish his name (vv. 2, 6, 7b).[12] Moses categorically prohibits observing the Passover in Israelite towns.

(2) The Passover involved eating.[13] The verb "sacrifice" (zābaḥ, v. 2) refers to the ritual slaughter of an animal, which for Israel usually meant a meal eaten by worshipers in the presence of Yahweh. Moses' expansion of the fare to include cattle anticipates Israel's transition from a nomadic people dependent on sheep and goats to a settled agricultural economy, in which cattle play an important role (cf. Deut. 32:13 – 14).

The text only hints at how the people are to prepare the sacrificial victim, and the clues are not presented in chronological order. We may rearrange the four significant stages as follows. (1) The Passover animal[14] is slaughtered in the evening as the sun sets (v. 6), to coincide with the timing of Israel's exodus from Egypt.[15]

(2) The meat of the animal is cooked (v. 7). Since Exodus 12:9 prohibits boiling the meat in water, this probably involved roasting it directly over a fire or indirectly in a pan.

---

12. For discussion of the formula, which appears three more times in this chapter (vv. 11, 15, 16), see above on 12:5.

13. In keeping with repeated references to eating in Yahweh's presence: 12:7, 27; 14:23, 26; 15:20; 16:7 – 8; 27:7.

14. In vv. 2 and 5, the word "the Passover" applies to the sacrificial victim rather than the holy day itself.

15. Ex. 12:6 has the victim slaughtered "at twilight." If the instructions for the original event (Ex. 12:1 – 13) applied to later memorial celebrations, the animal would be selected four days earlier, on the tenth of the month (v. 3).

(3) The people eat the Passover. Occurring three times in verses 3–7, the verb "to eat" functions as the key word of this passage. In keeping with Exodus 12:10, verse 4b specifies that none of the meat from the evening slaughter may be left over until the next morning. The reference to the Passover as "the first day" (v. 4) assumes the conjunction of Passover with the Festival of Unleavened Bread.

(4) Having eaten, in the morning the worshipers return to their tents (v. 7b)—temporary dwellings that the people have pitched in the vicinity of the central sanctuary. The reference to "tents" rather than "houses" echoes Moses' earlier report concerning the events at Sinai (5:30) and reinforces the notion that the purpose of "the place [Yahweh would] choose as a dwelling for his Name" was to enable the Israelites to fellowship with him in the land in perpetuity.

In summarizing the Passover ritual, we have jumped ahead of the text, for the reference to "the first day" (v. 4) links this event with the Festival of Unleavened Bread (*maṣṣôt*, vv. 3–4).[16] The prohibition on eating leavened bread at the Passover (v. 3a) opens the door naturally for an aside on the Festival of Unleavened Bread.[17] Except for the repeated phrase "with it," which binds the festivals together, the opening command, "for seven days eat unleavened bread," echoes Exodus 13:6a, which marks the transition from the Passover to instructions regarding the Festival of Unleavened Bread. Although Moses alludes to the need for haste in the journey out of Egypt as necessitating unleavened bread (v. 3c), by referring to the *maṣṣôt* as "bread of affliction," he links the Festival of Unleavened Bread with the Israelites' experience of slavery in Egypt.

The last clause of verse 3 provides the rationale for the Festival of Unleavened Bread. It serves as an annual reminder of the day the Israelites left Egypt. In verse 4a Moses strengthens the prior prohibition by banning all leaven from Israel's borders throughout the seven-day observance (cf. Ex 13:7). However, the meaning of "your borders" (*gᵉbûl*; NIV "your land") is uncertain. If this term applies to the boundaries of the temporary village set up around the central sanctuary, then the injunction involves those gathered for worship at the central shrine. However, if the term refers to the boundaries of individuals' personal allotments or the national territory of Israel (cf. 19:3, 8, 14), the prohibition applies to all Israelites, whether or not they attend the Festival of Unleavened Bread at the central location.

16. For critique of scholarly views of the relationship between the *maṣṣôt* and Passover elements in vv. 1–18 and defense of the literary unity of vv. 1–18, see Morrow, *Scribing the Center*, 138–47.

17. References to the festival occur elsewhere in Ex. 12:15–20; 13:3–10; 23:15; 34:18; Lev. 23:4–8.

Since only males are required to participate in the festival (v. 16), presumably women and children who remained at home would also be subject to the prohibition.

The charge to keep the Festival of Unleavened Bread (v. 8). The instructions on Passover conclude with a final summary, highlighting three primary features of the Festival of Unleavened Bread (v. 8). (1) Whatever else the Israelites eat during the festival, for six days their bread must be unleavened. (2) On the seventh day the community is to gather in holy convocation before Yahweh—a mandatory assembly of worshipers on the eighth day of the festival (Lev. 23:36; Num. 29:35).[18] Referring to the last day of the Festival of Unleavened Bread as the seventh day (rather than the eighth day) prevents blurring the boundary between the Festivals of Passover and the Unleavened Bread and links the pattern of this week more closely to the seven-day weekly rhythm of life.[19]

The Festival of Weeks (16:9–12)

AMONG ANCIENT ISRAEL'S MAJOR religious festivals, the Festival of Weeks exhibits several distinctive features. (1) It is never assigned a precise date on the religious calendar (v. 9; cf. Lev. 23:15–16). (2) Though our text links the festival with Israel's experience in Egypt (v. 12), the festival is never associated with specific events in their history. Instead, it has the appearance of an agricultural festival. (3) References to the festival are rare in the Old Testament. In keeping with its harvest associations, it is referred variously as "the Festival of the Harvest" (Ex. 23:16), or "the Day of Firstfruits" (Num. 28:26a).[20] Being celebrated fifty days after Passover (Lev. 23:16), later Greek texts refer to this festival as Pentecost.[21]

Whereas Leviticus 23:15–21 and Numbers 28:26–31 deal with technical aspects of the offerings on the Festival of Weeks, the treatment here is anything but clinical. The prescriptive style of the previous verses continues, but the tone is more pastoral. Here Moses seeks to motivate Israelites to keep the Festival of Weeks from an understanding of the profound

---

18. These links suggest the seven-day Festival of Unleavened Bread in the first month represented the spring counterpart to the eight-day Festival of Booths in the autumn. Echoes of Num. 29:35 in Deut. 16:8 reinforce this interpretation. Lev. 23:36 links the expression with "sacred assembly."

19. Milgrom (*Leviticus 23–27*, 2030–31) speculates the purpose of the assembly was to pray for a successful harvest.

20. As Ex. 34:22 suggests, this does not mean any firstfruits, but "the firstfruits of the wheat harvest."

21. Tob. 2:1; 2 Macc. 12:31–32; Josephus (*Ant* 3.10.6; etc.; *J.W.* 1.13.3; etc.); Philo (*Decal.* 160; *Spec. Laws* 2.176); Acts 2:1; 20:16; 1 Cor. 16:8.

theology that underlies it. Our headings below reflect the threefold structure of the text.

The timing of the Festival of Weeks (v. 9). Although the name of the festival does not appear until verse 10, the word from which it derives its name, *šᵉbuʿôt* ("weeks"), occurs in verse 9. Instead of specifying a date for its celebration, twice the opening statement calls on the people to "count off seven weeks." The point of reference is "the time you begin to put the first sickle[22] to the standing grain." In the context of Leviticus 23:11–16, this "time" would probably be the last day of the Festival of Unleavened Bread, which is identified as "a sacred assembly."[23] Here the festival would have fallen in the month of Sivan (May-June), so that the Festivals of Unleavened Bread and Weeks respectively served as bookends on either side of the grain harvest.

The essence of the Festival of Weeks (vv. 10–12a). The description of the Festival of Weeks provides three important details. (1) It is a pilgrimage festival (v. 10). Although Leviticus 23 and Numbers 28 do not refer to it as a "pilgrimage festival," the use of the word *ḥag* ("Feast") here and in Exodus 34:22 places the festival alongside Passover and the Festival of Booths. In contrast to the detailed list of offerings prescribed in Leviticus 23:15–21 and Numbers 28:26–31, our text simply invites Israelites to present a generous freewill offering to Yahweh "in proportion to" the harvest. The expression for offering refers to a gift offered spontaneously and joyfully, without regard to cause. The standard for the offering, as "the LORD your God has given you," links it with the treatment of debt-servants (15:12–18). Moses hereby declares that those who are genuinely grateful for the grace of God in the harvest will be liberal in their offerings.

(2) The Festival of Weeks is to be a joyful celebration (v. 11). Although pilgrimages to the place of worship would require considerable effort, the Festival of Weeks is cast as an opportunity to celebrate before Yahweh. And with greater enthusiasm than earlier invitations (12:12, 18), the catalogue of participants includes every imaginable member of the community. Combating natural tendencies toward marginalization of outsiders, the list draws all of them, beginning with members of the household, but including outsiders to the community and the economically vulnerable.

(3) The Festival of Weeks is a memorial celebration (v. 12a). Breaking rank with other accounts, Moses links the observance of this festival

---

22. On sickles, see D. M. Howard, "Sickle," *ISBE* (rev. ed.), 4:499. Given variations in climate and regional topography, the timing of the first sickle would vary from year to year and from place to place.
23. Cf. Mark J. Olson, "Pentecost," *ABD*, 5:222–23; J. C. VanderKam, "Weeks, Festival of," *ABD*, 6:895–97.

with Israel's experience in Egypt. By associating what was otherwise an agricultural festival with Egypt, he highlights the conviction that everything Israel has is to be received as a gift. Like his provision of salvation, Yahweh's provision of harvest calls for free and spontaneous expressions of gratitude.

The concluding charge to observe the Festival of Weeks (v. 12b–c). The instructions on the Festival of Weeks conclude more formally than any witnessed previously with a double call to observe these ordinances. The combination of verbs "and you shall keep and do"[24] (NIV translates "follow carefully") and the phrase "these decrees" link this text with 26:16.[25] The vocabulary places this interpretation of the Festival of Weeks on par with the earlier announcement and explanations of the festival.

The Festival of Booths (16:13–15)

OF THE THREE ANNUAL pilgrimages, the Festival of Booths (NIV "Tabernacles") receives the least attention. While Exodus 23:16b and 34:22b identify it as "the Festival of Ingathering," the present designation, "Festival of Booths" (*hassukkôt*), derives from Leviticus 23:34.[26] Although Exodus 23:16 ties this festival to the end of the agricultural cycle, technically it is not a harvest festival. The term "ingathering" does not refer to the harvest of agricultural products, but to the collection of processed grain and unfermented grape juice and their storage for winter in granaries and vats. Rejoicing over the blessing of harvest and the safe processing of the foodstuffs, the Festival of Booths is the happiest of all the festivals.[27]

Interpreted together, Leviticus 23:33–44 and Numbers 29:12–39 provide a manual for the observance of the Festival of Booths, identifying the specific features of the festival and the prescriptions for its celebration. The style and tone of Deuteronomy 16:13–15 are different. Assuming familiarity with the rituals, as in the treatment of the Festival of Weeks above, this text focuses entirely on the theological and communal significance of the festival.

The timing of the Festival of Booths (v. 13). The paragraph opens with a call to "celebrate" the Festival of Booths. The term "booths" (*sukkôt*) derives from the character of the temporary dwellings the Israelites

---

24. Cf. 5:1 and 23:24.

25. The expression occurs elsewhere only in 4:6; 6:24; 17:19.

26. Num. 29:12–39 offers a detailed presentation, but instead of referring to the festival by name, it speaks generally of "a sacred assembly" (v. 12), an "assembly . . . [with] no regular work" (v. 35), and includes it in the sacred appointments (v. 39).

27. See further Tigay, *Deuteronomy*, 157–58.

were to live in during the seven-day festival (cf. Lev. 23:40). According to Exodus 23:16 and 34:22 the festival was to be observed "at the end of the year" and "at the turn of the year," respectively. These expressions seem to relate to the agricultural year, defined unofficially as the time between two "ingatherings."[28] Leviticus 23:34 and Numbers 29:12 fix the date on the fifteenth day of the seventh month (Tishri 15 = September-October). This results in a remarkably symmetrical calendar, with important observances in the first and seventh months at opposite ends of the cycle anchoring life.[29] The present text sets the time of the Festival of Booths more generally: "after you have gathered the produce of your threshing floor and your winepress." This phrase confirms that the festival occurs not when crops are harvested but when the agricultural products have been processed and stored.

The essence of the Festival of Booths (vv. 14–15). These verses suggest the Festival of Booths serves two purposes. (1) It affords Israelites an occasion to celebrate their sense of community in a weeklong festival of joy. If we translate the opening statement of verse 14 modally, then this may be interpreted as an invitation to celebrate rather than as a command. Like the Festival of Weeks in the spring, this invitation is extended to the entire community: "you, your sons and daughters, your menservants and maidservants, and the Levites, the aliens, the fatherless and the widows who live in your towns" (cf. v.11).

(2) Coming at the end of the agricultural cycle, the Festival of Booths affords the Israelites an opportunity for corporate thanksgiving in the presence of Yahweh at the place he would choose as his residence. Verse 15 leaves no doubt concerning its purpose: to praise Yahweh for his blessing, for he has rewarded the efforts of human hands by granting an abundance of crops from the field. Unlike 4:28; 27:15; and 31:29, the expression "work of [one's] hands" refers to legitimate work engaged in to make a living.[30] Like 14:29 and 15:10, 18 the statement recognizes that Israel's well-being depends on Yahweh's favor, and that Yahweh fulfills his promise to bless those who love and serve him wholeheartedly.

The concluding charge to rejoice (v. 15b). This short paragraph reaches a crescendo with the final charge to participate wholeheartedly in the celebration. Above all else and above all other feasts, when the

---

28. See also the Gezer Calendar, which begins with "months of ingathering."

29. However, the symmetry is not exact. Whereas the Festival of Unleavened Bread follows immediately after the Passover, five days separate the the Festival of Booths from the Day of Atonement (cf. Lev. 23:27), which Deuteronomy never mentions.

30. Cf. 2:7; 14:29; 16:15; 24:19; 28:12; 30:9. Except for 28:12, where Yahweh blesses the work of the hands, the work of their hands provides the occasion for Yahweh to bless *Israel*.

Israelites come to worship Yahweh at the Festival of Booths, they are to be overflowing with joy and prepared to express that joy for an entire week.

The Summary Statement (16:16–17)

THE SUMMARY STATEMENT IN verses 16–17 recalls Yahweh's words in Exodus 23:14–17. However, here Moses opens (rather than closes) by declaring that all Israelite males are to appear before Yahweh three times a year. In keeping with the androcentrism of the earlier text,[31] this statement requires all males to attend the three festivals—though earlier Moses had encouraged the men to bring along their daughters, female slaves, and widows (vv. 11, 14). Participation in the annual pilgrimage festivals was *mandatory* for all males, but the *invitation* to appear before Yahweh is extended to all who identified with the covenant people, apparently without respect to ethnic identity or gender.

By referring to deity as "the LORD your God," instead of "the Sovereign LORD" (i.e., *hāʾādôn yhwh*) as in both Exodus 23:17 and 34:24, Moses subtly adjusts the tone of the observances. Whereas "the Sovereign LORD" highlights Yahweh's sovereignty over Israel, "the LORD your God" emphasizes the covenant relationship between deity and people.[32] The idiom "to appear in the presence of Yahweh" (pers. trans.) is royal court language, denoting entering his court and paying homage before him. Whereas Exodus 23:14–17 and 34:23–24 identified the location of the festival generally as "before the LORD," for the sixth time this chapter specifies the destination as "the place [the LORD your God] will choose." Following 12:5, Yahweh graciously allows himself to be sought and encountered at the place he chooses. While noting with Exodus 23:15 that worshipers are not to appear before Yahweh empty-handed, here too Moses notes this, and (cf. v. 10) adds that these gifts are to be proportional to the blessing that Yahweh has lavished on the worshiper. The divine host delights in the generosity of his people.

---

31. The society as a whole was androcentric, but households were patricentric. See Block, "Marriage and Family in Ancient Israel," 38–44.

32. J. W. Watts (*Reading Law: The Rhetorical Shaping of the Pentateuch* [Biblical Seminar 59; Sheffield: Sheffield Academic, 1999], 108) argues that fidelity and obedience are demanded and enforced because Yahweh rules in Israel. However, T. Fretheim ("Law in the Service of Life: A Dynamic Understanding of Law in Deuteronomy," in *A God So Near: Essays on Old Testament Theology in Honor of Patrick D. Miller* [ed. B. A. Strawn and N. R. Bowen; Winona Lake, IN: Eisenbrauns, 2003], 194) rightly counters that God gives the law and commands obedience for the sake of the life and well-being of the creatures, not out of the self-serving notion that the people *must* obey because God is, after all, their Ruler.

SUBSEQUENT HISTORY OF THE **festivals**. Moses, the authoritative interpreter of Israel's legal tradition and pastor of the people of Yahweh, demonstrates great respect here for the nation's spiritual heritage. However, he is also mindful of the new circumstances that await God's people. Assessing the influence that Moses' instructions on these festivals had on Israel's history is difficult. The memory of Moses' injunction to keep the Passover seems to have been short-lived. According to Joshua 5:10–11, Joshua timed the crossing of the Jordan so that as soon as they entered the Promised Land, the Israelites could celebrate this feast and the Festival of Unleavened Bread. On the fourteenth day of the month (which month is not specified), before they launched their campaigns against the Canaanites, they paused for worship. Whether or not the Passover was celebrated at Sinai or during the desert journeys, the two accounts in Exodus 12–13 and Joshua 5:10–11 stand as bookends on either side of Yahweh's great acts of salvation, provision in the desert, covenant ratification, and guidance to the Promised Land.

The narrator of these events caught their significance by noting that the day after the Passover celebration, the Israelites feasted on the produce of the land. More than any other festival, the Passover defined Israelite identity; and more than any other festival, it declared who Yahweh was. Joshua and his generation recognized that they were the products of Yahweh's grace and that he had kept all his promises.

Subsequent records indicate that hereafter the Festival of Passover was more honored in the breach than in the observance. The Chronicler observes that in the wake of Solomon's construction of the temple, he led the people in the celebration of all the holy days in Israel's religious calendar, including the three mandatory pilgrimage festivals: Unleavened Bread, Weeks, and Booths (2 Chron. 8:13). In light of the close association of Passover and the Festival of Unleavened Bread in Deuteronomy 16:1–8, we may assume the observance of the Festival of Unleavened Bread began with the Passover celebrations. Except for a late retrospective reference to Samuel (2 Chron. 35:18), the narratives are silent on the Passover until the time of Hezekiah, who led Judah in the celebration and even attempted to engage Israelites in what was by then the Assyrian province of Samaria (2 Chron. 30). However, the Chronicler adds that the Passover and the Festival of Unleavened Bread were celebrated one month late because the priests had not been adequately prepared (30:2–3, 13). This observance seems to have stirred the conscience of the people, precipitating a nationwide campaign against pagan and syncretistic forms of worship (31:1). But this revival was short-lived. Under Manasseh, the festivals devoted to Yahweh were suppressed and displaced by pagan rituals.

Finally, toward the end of the seventh century BC, as part of the reforms of Josiah, Manasseh's grandson, the Passover was celebrated one more time. Both the deuteronomistic historian (2 Kings 23:22) and the Chronicler (2 Chron. 35:17–19) observe that the Passover had not been celebrated like this since before the founding of the monarchy. This event provides a terminal bookend to match Joshua's in Joshua 5:10–11, but it was too little, too late. Because of their infidelity to Yahweh as prescribed by Moses in the book of the Torah, the doom of Judah had already been sealed (2 Kings 22:15–20). The nation was destroyed and its population dragged off into exile. Not until they had experienced a new exodus and the temple, the symbol of Yahweh's presence in Jerusalem, had been rebuilt, would they celebrate these most fundamental festivals again (Ezra 6:19–22). At that time, in accordance with Deuteronomy 12:5, they sought Yahweh in the place he had chosen to establish his name, and in accordance with 16:1–8 they celebrated the Passover in his presence.[33]

The Festival of Weeks seems to have suffered from even more serious neglect. Except for the Chronicler's reference to this festival as one of the three annual mandatory pilgrimages that Solomon observed in conjunction with the building of the temple (2 Chron. 8:13), the Old Testament is completely silent on this observance.

The Festival of Booths seems to have fared slightly better. Indeed, some suggest that this festival was the most important festival in preexilic Israel.[34] Although the festival is mentioned by name only five times,[35] on several occasions it is referred to as "the festival of the LORD" (Judg. 21:19; Hos. 9:5; cf. Lev. 23:39), or simply "the festival."[36] Later in Deuteronomy Moses will highlight the significance of the Festival of Booths by calling for the reading of the Torah every seven years at this festival (31:9–13), which is what the Israelites did in Nehemiah 8:13–18.

Of these three festivals the Passover (together with the Festival of Unleavened Bread) is by far the most prominent in the New Testament. The Festival of Unleavened Bread is mentioned six times, but only once apart from the Passover connection.[37] The Passover, on the other hand,

---

33. The celebration of the Passover is anticipated in Ezekiel's vision of the future (Ezek. 45:21–25).

34. Thus Marvin Tate, *Psalms 51–100* (WBC 20; Dallas: Word, 1990), 318.

35. 2 Chron. 8:13; Ezra 3:4; Zech. 14:16, 18–19.

36. The date identifies it as the Festival of Booths in 1 Kings 8:2 (cf. also v. 65); 12:32; 2 Chron. 7:8; cf. Isa. 30:29 (without the date); the mention of the shophar ("horn") in Ps. 81:3[4] suggests this festival (cf. Num. 10:10).

37. Acts 20:6; cf. Mark 14:1, 12; Luke 22:1, 7; Acts 12:3.

is mentioned dozens of times. However, only Hebrews 11:28 recalls the original Passover event. According to Luke 2:41, Jesus' parents demonstrated their piety every year by attending the Passover. John 6:4 highlights its centrality in the Jewish religious calendar by calling it "the Passover, the feast of the Jews." Remarkably, all the remaining references to the feast in the Gospels are associated with the passion of the Messiah.[38]

While the New Testament never mentions the Festival of Weeks by this name, "Pentecost" is mentioned three times (Acts 2:1; 20:16; 1 Cor. 16:8). If this festival involved covenant ceremonies (including the reading of the Decalogue), as some suggest,[39] then the significance of the events of Pentecost described in Acts 2 is heightened dramatically. Believers in Jesus specifically have become the heirs of the covenant. Indeed, the book of Acts traces the expansion of the boundaries of the covenant community with the recurrence of these "Pentecostal" phenomena to include Samaritans (Acts 8:14 – 17), Gentile proselytes in Judea (10:44 – 48; cf. 9:17), and people of Asia Minor, including Gentiles (19:1 – 6).

John 7:2 contains the only reference to the Festival of Booths in the New Testament, but this is sufficient to demonstrate that this festival was still observed in the days of Jesus.

CHRISTIANS AND THESE FESTIVALS. Although the book of Hebrews declares that the ceremonial and festival calendar of ancient Israel is rendered obsolete through the sacrifice of Christ, remarkably the Passover is not actually abrogated. Instead, it is radically transformed.[40] At his Last Supper, which was itself the Passover meal, Jesus declares himself the Passover Lamb, through whose death the judgment of God is averted and the redemption of his people is bought. Jesus is the Lamb without blemish who gives his life — though without a

---

38. Matt. 26:2, 17–19; Mark 14:1,12, 14, 16; Luke 22:1, 7–8, 11, 13, 15; John 12:1; 13:1; 18:28, 39; 19:14.

39. See *b. Meg.* 31a; *t. Meg.* 4:5. Thus M. Greenberg, "Decalogue (The Ten Commandments)," *EncJud* (2nd ed.), 5:525; M. Weinfeld, "The Decalogue: Its Significance, Uniqueness, and Place in Israel's Tradition," in *Religion and Law: Biblical-Judaic and Islamic Perspectives* (ed. E. B. Firmage, B. G. Weiss, and J. W. Welch; Winona Lake, IN: Eisenbrauns, 1990), 28–32, 34; idem, "The Uniqueness of the Decalogue and Its Place in Jewish Tradition," in *The Ten Commandments in History and Tradition* (ed. B.-Z. Segal and G. Levi; Jerusalem: Magnes, 1990), 21–27.

40. Since the festivals of Passover and Unleavened Bread were instituted in Egypt, technically they stand apart from the rituals and festivals associated with the tabernacle ritual as revealed at Sinai.

bone of his body being broken—so that all who partake of him might be free.[41]

With Paul the identification is complete, for in 1 Corinthians 5:7 he declares, "Get rid of the old yeast that you may be a new batch without yeast. For Christ, our Passover lamb, has been sacrificed." Decades after the death of Christ, John explicitly speaks of the Passover as "the Passover of the Jews" (John 2:13; 6:4; 11:55), suggesting perhaps that by then it was distinguished from "the Passover of Christians."

Admittedly, apart from the Lord's Supper, the New Testament never prescribes specific festivals and celebrations for God's new covenant people. However, this should not be interpreted to suggest we need not bother with commemorative rituals and events. On the contrary, the church as a whole and individual congregations in particular would do well to establish memorial festivals that bind us to believers everywhere (Easter, Pentecost, Christmas, etc.) and to keep alive in our minds the reality of God's work on our behalf. But even as we celebrate the ecumenical festivals of the church year and the commemorative festivals of our local congregations, like the ancient Israelites we must beware of the danger of mere externalism. In Deuteronomy 16 Moses the pastor reminds us that acceptable worship must be conducted in spirit and in truth—that is, driven and energized by the Spirit of God, enacted according to the revealed will of God, and practiced by those who faithfully embody covenant righteousness.

Christmas and ascension. Although the Festival of Passover has been transformed by the gospel and the festivals of Weeks and Booths are no longer mandatory for Christians, the North American church would do well to observe festivals marking the events associated with the birth of the church and its foundation as the new Israel of God. Judging by the attention it receives, the most important event on the church calendar is Christmas, which supposedly celebrates the birth of Christ. We should not be surprised if the world tries to remove "Christ" from "Christmas" and to secularize this holiday as a winter festival. However, even in Christian circles this observance has been cluttered by so many distractions—Santa Claus, Christmas trees, holly and ivy, overindulgent exchange of gifts, and raw commercialism—that its roots and meaning are scarcely recognizable. From a biblical perspective, the birth of Jesus was indeed an occasion for cosmic celebration (Luke 2:14), but we need to remember the dismal

---

41. Matthew's version of the institution of the Lord's Supper (Matt. 26:28) conflates motifs derived from the Festival of Passover (substitutionary death), the covenant ratification ritual at Sinai ("blood of the covenant"; cf. Ex. 24:1–11), and the sin offering ("for the forgiveness of sins"). While the oppressive sin of the Egyptians may have been a factor in the original Passover event, the sin of those being redeemed was never mentioned.

backdrop to this event: that Jesus was born to die. He is Immanuel ("God with us") indeed, but he is also "Jesus," who saves his people from their sins. This event should commemorate both God's grace to us and our depraved and rebellious undeservedness.

When I was a child, I can recall services commemorating the ascension of Jesus forty days after Easter, and Pentecost (in our Mennonite circles Pfingsten) ten days later on the seventh Sunday after Easter. But outside Anglican and Lutheran circles among evangelicals in North America, these observances have been largely forgotten. Tragically, the loss of the observance has been accompanied by a loss of consciousness of the original events and of an appreciation for their momentous theological significance. Aware of Jesus' ascension, we anticipate his immanent return (Acts 1:11), and mindful of the outpouring of the Spirit on the disciples at Pentecost, we celebrate the inclusion of all who believe in Jesus in the reconstituted covenant community.

A biblical theology of worship. Whatever our disposition toward these memorial events, Deuteronomy 16:1 – 17 presents Christians with an extraordinarily rich resource for developing a biblical theology of worship. Among the lessons we might apply to contemporary worship, the following deserve consideration. (1) True worship involves an engagement with God and is focused on him. According to Jesus himself, true worship focuses not on the place but on the person of Christ, who is Yahweh incarnate (John 4:21 – 24).

(2) True worship occurs at the invitation of the Lord and must be conducted on his terms.

(3) True worship is communal. In worship the redeemed gather to celebrate the kindness that God has lavished on us collectively, without merit and without prejudice. Furthermore, true worship tears down the barriers of gender, class, and race. As Paul writes in Galatians 3:28, in the presence of God "there is neither Jew nor Greek, slave nor free, male nor female, for you are all one in Christ Jesus."

(4) True worship is driven by a deep sense of gratitude to God, first for his redemption, and second for his lavish daily provision. In true worship our focus is not on what we are doing for him but on what he has done for us. For this reason true worship should be a joyful event, not a burden to be legalistically borne.

(5) Finally, true worship involves the lavish offering of one's resources and even oneself (Rom. 12:1) in sacrifice to and for the service of Christ.

Deuteronomy 16:18–17:13

❧

Introduction to Deuteronomy 16:18–18:22

HAVING APPEALED FOR SOFT hearts toward those in need and for joy in the worship of Yahweh, Moses resumes a theme he had left earlier in chapter 13, the maintenance of religious fidelity in Israel. This text is part of a larger subsection of Moses' second address (16:18–18:22), whose significance for the Deuteronomic disposition toward Israel's civil and religious administrators is widely recognized.[1] Indeed many interpret this material as a utopian constitution for Israel,[2] drafted after the exile.[3] However, this approach assumes Deuteronomy was composed to bolster the centralizing reforms of Josiah[4] and overloads these sections with undue political freight, at the expense of the central issues, which are spiritual and religious.

The declaration in 16:20 ("Righteousness [ṣedeq], only righteousness you shall pursue,"[5] pers. trans.) highlights the central issue in this section — covenant righteousness — and identifies the primary audience — "you." What follows is not a manual for judges, kings, priests, and prophets, but an appeal to the people to be involved in the maintenance of righteousness. Although NIV's rendering of ṣedeq as "justice" coheres with most translations, the issues addressed range far beyond social justice, from personal morality to idolatry. Furthermore, no officials are addressed directly, and the subunits exhibit a lack of concern with the formal duties of these leaders. In every case, the ultimate concern is righteousness (ṣedeq), demonstrated in the people's fidelity to Yahweh.[6] As agents of the people and

---

1. Note the headings ascribed to this section: Nelson, "Constitutional Proposals" (*Deuteronomy*, 210, 226); Tigay, "Civil and Religious Authorities" (*Deuteronomy*, 159); N. Lohfink ("Distribution of the Functions of Power: The Laws concerning Public Offices in Deuteronomy 16:18–18:22," in *Great Themes from the Old Testament* [trans. R. Walls; Chicago: Franciscan Herald, 1981], 68; reprinted in *A Song of Power and the Power of Song* [ed. D. L. Christensen; Winona Lake, IN: Eisenbrauns, 1993], 346).

2. Thus B. Halpern, *The Constitution of the Monarchy in Israel* (HSM 25; Chico, CA: Scholars Press, 1981), 226–33; S. D. McBride, "The Polity of the Covenant People: The Book of Deuteronomy," *Int* 41 (1987): 229–44; Nelson, *Deuteronomy*, 212.

3. Thus Lohfink, "Distribution of the Functions of Power," in *Song of Power and the Power of Song*, 346.

4. For critique of this approach, see Peter Vogt, *Deuteronomic Theology and the Significance of Torah: A Reappraisal* (Winona Lake, IN: Eisenbrauns, 2006), 32–93.

5. Throughout this section I will be translating ṣedeq ṣedeq as "righteousness, only righteousness" (NIV "justice and justice alone").

6. Cf. Vogt, *Theology and the Significance of Torah*, 209–26.

Yahweh, the officials to be appointed are to support the people in their maintenance of righteousness.

Appoint judges and officials for each of your tribes in every town the LORD your God is giving you, and they shall judge the people fairly. ¹⁹Do not pervert justice or show partiality. Do not accept a bribe, for a bribe blinds the eyes of the wise and twists the words of the righteous. ²⁰Follow justice and justice alone, so that you may live and possess the land the LORD your God is giving you.

²¹Do not set up any wooden Asherah pole beside the altar you build to the LORD your God, ²²and do not erect a sacred stone, for these the LORD your God hates.

¹⁷:¹Do not sacrifice to the LORD your God an ox or a sheep that has any defect or flaw in it, for that would be detestable to him.

²If a man or woman living among you in one of the towns the LORD gives you is found doing evil in the eyes of the LORD your God in violation of his covenant, ³and contrary to my command has worshiped other gods, bowing down to them or to the sun or the moon or the stars of the sky, ⁴and this has been brought to your attention, then you must investigate it thoroughly. If it is true and it has been proved that this detestable thing has been done in Israel, ⁵take the man or woman who has done this evil deed to your city gate and stone that person to death. ⁶On the testimony of two or three witnesses a man shall be put to death, but no one shall be put to death on the testimony of only one witness. ⁷The hands of the witnesses must be the first in putting him to death, and then the hands of all the people. You must purge the evil from among you.

⁸If cases come before your courts that are too difficult for you to judge—whether bloodshed, lawsuits or assaults—take them to the place the LORD your God will choose. ⁹Go to the priests, who are Levites, and to the judge who is in office at that time. Inquire of them and they will give you the verdict. ¹⁰You must act according to the decisions they give you at the place the LORD will choose. Be careful to do everything they direct you to do. ¹¹Act according to the law they teach you and the decisions they give you. Do not turn aside from what they tell you, to the right or to the left. ¹²The man who shows

contempt for the judge or for the priest who stands ministering there to the LORD your God must be put to death. You
must purge the evil from Israel. ¹³All the people will hear and
be afraid, and will not be contemptuous again.

ALTHOUGH THE FLOW OF thought in this passage
is rough,[7] this section displays more evidences
of coherence than is often recognized. Stylistically from beginning to end the main clauses are
dominated by the second person singular of direct address (16:18, 20–22;
17:1–5b, 7c–9b, 10–11, 12c).[8] As signaled by 16:20, this text exhibits a
pervasive concern for "righteousness" (NIV "justice"). The threefold occurrence of *ṣedeq* in verses 18–20 sets the tone for this literary unit, and the
variation in expressions for culpable behavior keeps the focus on the key
issue (16:22; 17:1, 2, 3, 4, 5, 7, 12, 13). Deuteronomy 17:11 establishes the
Torah as the basis of all judgments,[9] while 16:21–17:1 and 17:2–13 illustrate the kind of infidelity that Yahweh abhors.

The central concern of 16:18–17:13 is, therefore, not the administration of social justice or the promotion of a secular judicial institution in
support of the centralization of Israelite polity and religion, but the engagement of the entire community in the promotion of righteousness as defined
by the Torah.[10] Consequently, this unit divides into three parts: (1) a call
for communal commitment to righteousness (16:18–20); (2) three examples of righteousness violated (16:21–17:1); (3) the prescription for righteousness violated (17:2–13).

A Call for Communal Commitment to Righteousness (16:18–20)

THE OBJECT-VERB STRUCTURE OF the opening line signals the beginning of
a new section.[11] A second heading in verse 20, whose grammar imitates

---

7. Levinson (*Deuteronomy and the Hermeneutics of Legal Innovation*, 98) finds 16:18–17:13 as
"one of the most problematic 'case studies'" with respect to "topic selection, sequencing,
and ostensible redundancy."

8. The text switches to the third person five times: 16:18b; 17:5c–7b; 17:9c; 17:12a;
17:13.

9. N. Lohfink, "Distribution of the Functions of Power," 344; idem, *Great Themes from the
Old Testament*, 65.

10. Cf. P. T. Vogt, *Religious Concepts in the Theology of Deuteronomy* (Gloucester, UK: Univ.
of Gloucestershire Press, 2003), 224–26.

11. The Hebrew reads, "Judges and officials you shall appoint" (cf. 12:32[13:1]; 14:1,
9, 11; 16:9, 13).

verse 18a, signals the primary concern. These two statements provide a framework around an important theme in Deuteronomic theology: justice in the service of righteousness. Verse 18 also echoes an earlier statement in 1:15, which associates the "officials" with other leaders in Israel: heads, staff-holders, elders.[12] While some view "judges" and "officials" as different classes of officials, "judges and officials" is probably intended as a hendiadys, that is, "scribal judges."[13]

Many interpret verse 18 as provision for a judiciary composed of professional judges and officials appointed by the monarch to replace the elder-based judiciary of a by-gone era[14] and to support centralizing authority in the crown.[15] However, this view rests on speculative arguments from silence.[16] The absence of elders here does not mean they have been pushed aside; their involvement is assumed (cf. 25:1 – 3). Furthermore, it flies in the face of sociological analyses of judicial structures in kinship-based societies, in which "the existence of dual but complementary judicial institutions" is common.[17] Who hears which case depends on the socio-political implications of the dispute.[18]

As in Deuteronomy 1:15, the verb "to appoint" is represented by *nātan* ("to give"), which in contexts like this means "to provide for by installing."[19] Whereas in the earlier text Moses had installed leaders whom the people presented to him, here he assigns responsibility to the people. Presumably elders, acting on behalf of the people, will make the appointments, selecting persons from their own ranks for the office of "scribal judge" in accordance with the qualifications specified by Moses in 1:13 – 15.[20] The charge to appoint judges "in all your gates" (NIV "in every town") ensures distribu-

---

12. Cf. Deut 29:10[9]. Deut. 31:28 pairs the expression with "the elders of your tribes." This association with elders also occurs in Num. 11:16; Josh. 8:33; 23:2; 24:1.

13. Thus A. Rofé, "The Organization of the Judiciary in Deuteronomy [Deut 16.18–20; 17,8–13; 19.15; 21.22–23; 24.16; 25.1–3]," in *The World of the Aramaeans I: Biblical Studies in Honor of Paul-Eugène Dion* [ed. P. M. M. Daviau, J. W. Wevers, and M. Weigl; JSOTSup 324; Sheffield: Sheffield Academic, 2001]), 99. On the titles here, see comments on 1:15–18.

14. See Levinson, *Hermeneutics*, 126, 138; A. Rofé, "Organization of the Judiciary," 95.

15. According to Rofé (ibid.) the appointment originated "in the capital city, the seat of the king and the administrative center."

16. So also Timothy M. Willis, *The Elders of the City: A Study of the Elders-Laws in Deuteronomy* (SBLMS 55; Atlanta: Scholars, 2001), 86.

17. Ibid., 88.

18. Ibid., 50–67. This complementarity of two or more judicial institutions common among modern kinship-based peoples also existed among many of the peoples surrounding Israel (ibid., 67–82).

19. Cf. Ex. 31:6; Num. 14:4; Deut. 17:15; Josh. 20:2, 8; 1 Sam. 2:28; 12:12; 2 Sam. 11:16; 2 Kings 23:5; 2 Chron. 32:6; Ezra 8:20; Neh. 9:17.

20. Thus Willis, *Elders of the City*, 66–67.

tion of responsibility for the maintenance of righteousness throughout the land. While elsewhere "gates" functions metonymically for "towns," here the word specifies the location of judicial proceedings (cf. Ruth 4:1 – 12). Moses qualifies "towns" as those that "the LORD your God is giving you," assuming that kinship-based tribal structures and a settled agrarian life will coexist in Israel.[21]

Moses' call for judges to "judge the people fairly" (v. 18) adapts a statement in Leviticus 19:15 addressed to all the people. This is the only comment in this entire unit concerned with the conduct of judges, calling them to render righteous judgments. Though *mišpāṭ* ("judgment") and *ṣedeq* ("righteousness") form a standardized pair in biblical Hebrew, the phrase "righteous judgment" (*mišpaṭ ṣedeq*) occurs only here (cf. Isa 58:2). Moses hereby appeals for judgment that accords with covenantal standards as outlined in the Torah.

In verse 19 Moses refocuses on the Israelites as a community. Broadening the scope and reducing the judicial flavor of earlier injunctions, Moses calls on the people to imitate Yahweh in not perverting justice[22] through partiality[23] or bribery. The latter clouds the vision of those who must make judgments[24] and subverts the pronouncements of the righteous (cf. Prov 22:12).[25]

In the emphatic word order and the repetition of verse 20 we hear not the measured tone of a legislator but the passionate voice of a preacher, who pleads with his congregation to put first things first. Moses hereby announces the issue that will concern him throughout the rest of the second address — fidelity to Yahweh, demonstrated in righteous behavior. He ends this statement by stressing the importance of pursuing "righteousness,

---

21. For later evidence of tribal self–consciousness, see 2 Chron. 34:6; Ezek. 48; Matt. 4:13, 15; Rev. 7:4 – 8; 21:12.

22. On "perverting justice," see Piotro Bovati, *Re-Establishing Justice: Legal Terms, Concepts and Procedures in the Hebrew Bible* (trans. M. J. Smith; JSOTSup 105; Sheffield: JSOT, 1994), 191 – 92.

23. Impartiality is also emphasized in 1:17 and 10:17. This statement condenses Lev. 19:15: "You shall not lift the face of the poor nor honor the face of the great" (pers. trans.).

24. Cf. 1:13 and 15, where the people installed as *šōṭ^rîm* are characterized as "wise." For the association of clear-sightedness with wisdom, see Eccl. 2:14; for pointed description of the effects of bribery, see Eccl. 7:7.

25. NIV's rendering, "twists the words of the righteous," preserves the ambiguity of the Hebrew, but it leaves unclear what is perverted: the cause of the accused, or the judgment of the adjudicator? However, the parallelism suggests "the righteous" in the second statement corresponds to "the wise" in the first. The plural "words of the righteous" renders a singular translation like "cause of the righteous" unlikely.

only righteousness." It is a prerequisite to the achievement of Yahweh's goal for his people: life and possession of the land that Yahweh is giving to them.[26]

Three Examples of Righteousness Violated (16:21 – 17:1)

MOSES FOLLOWS UP THE declaration of principle in verse 20 with warnings of three specific dangers that violate the principle of "righteousness, only righteousness." The first command warns against spiritual syncretism (v. 21). The perversity in question involves compromising one legitimate act (building an altar for Yahweh their God) with an illegitimate act (setting up an Asherah pole beside the altar of Yahweh). In Canaanite religion Asherah was a female goddess, the consort of El, who represented the female principle in the fertility religion. However, to Moses an Asherah pole is merely a piece of wood made from "any tree" and "planted" by human hands."[27] Whether Israelite worshipers understood such a pole as a symbol of the fertility they expected of Yahweh (cf. 7:12 – 14), or as a consort of Yahweh, by erecting it next to Yahweh's altar, they were violating the Supreme Command (cf. 5:7).[28]

The meaning of the second prohibition is less certain (v. 22). The association of pillars with Asherim in 7:5 and 12:3 suggests this is a stone erected to symbolize Baal, who represents the male principle in the fertility religion. However, the singular form may suggest a symbol of Yahweh himself, who claimed responsibility for the productivity of the soil and the livestock (7:12 – 14). While in an earlier time stone pillars were tolerated as religious symbols (Gen. 28:18 – 22), by the time the Israelites entered Canaan these representations of deity were so identified with the Baal cult that they were strictly forbidden (cf. 7:5; 12:3). The concluding clause, "these the LORD your God hates," expresses Yahweh's fundamental disposition toward idolatry.[29]

The third prohibition shifts the focus from forbidden cult objects to prohibited sacrifices — from overtly apostate actions that Yahweh hates to apostate dispositions that he finds detestable. To an observer any cultic action might appear pious, but when the sacrificial animal is defective,

---

26. These are familiar Deuteronomic expressions. For the former, see 4:1; 5:33; 6:24; 8:1; for the latter, see 3:20; 6:18; 10:11.

27. See comments on 7:7 and 12:3.

28. This problem is illustrated in several ninth–eighth century pithoi inscriptions from Kuntillet ʿAjrud. See Block, *Gods of the Nations*, 67 – 68; M. S. Smith, *The Early History of God: Yahweh and the Other Deities in Ancient Israel* (2nd ed.; Grand Rapids: Eerdmans, 2002), 108 – 47. The cited texts are discussed on pp. 118 – 25.

29. Later writings use "sacred stones and Ashera" as shorthand for all kinds of idolatrous cult objects: 1 Kings 14:23; 2 Kings 17:10; 23:14; 2 Chron. 14:3; 31:1.

seemingly correct worship is rejected by Yahweh. This warning represents the obverse of 15:19–21. It is not merely a matter of giving the best; perfect specimens speak of wholeness.[30] The characterization of blemished sacrifice as a "detestable [thing]" (*tôʿēbâ*) of Yahweh places such worship in the same category as overtly pagan actions (cf. 7:26; 12:31; 18:9; 20:18).

The Prescription for Righteousness Violated (17:2–13)

IN VERSES 2–3 Moses prescribes the response to violations of the principle of "righteousness, only righteousness" as stated in 16:20. This section divides into two panels of identical length (vv. 2–7 and vv. 8–12),[31] followed by a summary conclusion (v. 13). Each panel opens with a complex clause setting the context (vv. 2–4a; v. 8a), is followed by a lengthy prescribed response (vv. 4b–7a; vv. 8b–12a), and concludes with a declaration of the goal (v. 7b; v. 12b). The symmetry of structure and the verbal links suggest that verses 2–7 and 8–12 have been intentionally composed to develop a common point—how to deal with unrighteous behavior. The first involves relatively clean cases; the second involves the procedure for cases insoluble by ordinary means of investigation.

Panel A: How to deal with idolaters (vv. 2–7). Harking back to 12:29–13:18[19], almost every phrase and clause echoes corresponding elements in chapter 13.[32] Because the borrowed items derive from all three panels of chapter 13, Moses presents a comprehensive policy for idolatrous crimes, to be applied regardless of the instigator.[33] The instructions for dealing with idolaters divide into three sections: the problem (vv. 2–4b); (2) the prescription (vv. 4c–7b); and the goal (v. 7c). Since Moses' role is that of a pastor rather than legislator, it is not surprising that the flow is not necessarily logical by our standards, but neither is it pedantic. The instructions are precise, but added clauses concerning the violation of the covenant and the purgation of evil afford this text extraordinary *gravitas*. The goal is obviously not merely legal exactitude but the preservation of Israel in the land Yahweh has given them.

The problem (vv. 2–4a). Moses introduces the first case with a complex conditional clause that ends with "and this has been brought to your attention" (v. 4a). In this instance there is no reference to how the discovery

---

30. Cf. McConville, *Deuteronomy*, 289.

31. Both vv. 2–7 and vv. 8–12 consists of 103 words.

32. Levinson, *Deuteronomy and the Hermeneutics of Innovation*, 102–10; Morrow, *Scribing the Center*, 182–86.

33. The Temple Scroll from Qumran places 17:2–13 immediately after chapter 13. See F. G. Martínez and E. J. C. Tigchelaar, *The Dead Sea Scrolls: Study Edition* (Grand Rapids: Eerdmans, 1997/1998), 2:1274–77.

was made, which may explain why this phase ends with "and it is reported to you," and "and you hear" (pers. trans.). These expressions represent part of the discovery phase: A report of the crime to the community[34] is to trigger the response that follows.

Like 13:1[2], the text notes the context of the crime. Here the term "gates" (NIV "towns," v. 2) sets the hearer up for the judicial proceedings in the city gate (v. 8) and implies that the offense has been flagrantly committed in public. Characterizing the "gates" as those that "the LORD gives you" links this text with the appointment of judges in 16:18. Where Israel appoints judges, there the danger lurks. The statement also implies that since the towns themselves are gifts from Yahweh,[35] they are not to be polluted by worship of other gods.

Before specifying the crime, Moses comments on its spiritual significance: it represents "doing [the] evil in the eyes of the LORD your God" and "a violation of his covenant" (v. 2). The article on "the evil" points to a specific evil, violating the first command of the Decalogue. The second expression highlights what is at stake: honoring Yahweh's right to exclusive allegiance.[36] In verse 3 Moses finally announces the offense: "walking [after]," "serving," and "prostrating before" other gods (pers. trans.). While the first two expressions derive from the appeal in 13:2, 6, 13[3, 7, 14], this text exhibits a subtle shift of emphasis. Whereas chapter 13 sought to root out apostasy by eliminating those who led others away from Yahweh, here the concern is with those who have been seduced. The inclusion of women (v. 2) recognizes that if they have full access to the privileges of covenant relationship and the worship of Yahweh (cf. 12:12, 18; 16:14), they are equally susceptible to the temptation of idolatry and equally accountable to Yahweh.

The forbidden objects of worship are identified as "other gods" in general (v. 3; cf. 13:2, 6, 13[3, 7, 14]), and astral deities (sun, moon, and stars) in particular (4:15–19). The list ends awkwardly with "contrary to my command" (note that the NIV places this phrase forward; the Hebrew places at the end of v. 3). This has often been interpreted as litotic understatement, "which I have commanded you not to do." However, it should probably be read in light of 4:19 and understood as "which I did not authorize" as legitimate objects of worship.

The prescription (vv. 4b–7b). Based on the amount of space given to the matter, the response Moses prescribes is obviously the center of gravity of

---

34. The second person singular bears a collective sense throughout.

35. Cf. 6:10, which speaks of Yahweh giving Israel great and splendid towns that they did not build.

36. While specific references to the covenant are missing in chapter 13, the word "covenant" answers to the summary conditions of obedience in 13:18[19].

this paragraph. He begins by outlining the investigative procedure (v. 4b), warning his people not to base judicial decisions on hearsay and rumors, especially in capital cases. If someone reports that a man or woman is worshiping other gods, the charges must be investigated thoroughly in order to establish guilt beyond a shadow of a doubt (cf. v. 6). The rest of verse 4 assumes the inquiry proves positive. The declaration of the outcome adapts a similar statement in 13:14[15]. Moses' reference to "this detestable thing" (*hattô‘ēbâ*) rather than a concrete expression for idolatry reflects his pastoral concern; the charges strike at the heart of Israel's relationship with Yahweh.

The prescription for confirmed spiritual defection is execution by stoning (v. 5). Whereas Leviticus 24:14 and Numbers 15:35 call for the execution of criminals "outside the camp,"[37] here the sentence is to be administered in the city gates. The former treatment was reasonable, as long as the Israelites camped together with the tabernacle in the center. However, once they scattered to their tribal territories and towns, maintaining sanctity throughout the land would need to be localized. Executing criminals in the gate would make a spectacle of them and demonstrate the heinousness of their "evil deed" (v. 5b).

As in 13:10[11], stoning is specified as the form of execution, presumably to prevent the executioners from being ritually contaminated by direct contact with the accused. Having demanded at least two witnesses (v. 6), in verse 7 Moses calls on these witnesses to cast the first stones, after which all the people must join in.[38] Placing primary responsibility for executing the sentence in the hands of the witnesses safeguards against frivolous accusations by a neighbor (cf. 19:15−21). However, Moses places responsibility for maintaining righteousness in the hands of the people rather than with political leaders.

The goal (v. 7c). Although the judicial process ends with execution, the purpose of the procedure is not merely to give criminals their due. The concluding declaration summarizes the goal: to "purge the evil" from the midst of Israel.[39] Moses' concern for communal health leaves no room for sentimentality or prejudice. Yahweh's agenda requires a people united in its devotion to him and rigorous in its preservation of its own character as a holy people (cf. 7:1−6). Eliminating those guilty of capital crimes eradicates the evil from the land and the people.

---

37. Cf. Milgrom, *Leviticus 23−27*, 2113.

38. Cf. Jesus' challenge in John 8:7, "If any one of you is without sin, let him be the first to throw a stone at her."

39. The clause is borrowed verbatim from 13:5[6]. On this and related expressions (which recur in v. 12; 19:13, 19; 21:9, 21; 22:21, 22, 24; 24:7), see Bovati, *Re-Establishing Justice*, 385−86.

Panel B: How to deal with difficult cases (vv. 8 – 12). The judicial structures established in Exodus 18, with difficult cases coming to Moses, were practicable as long as Moses led the people. The purpose of this text is to provide a means of resolving insoluble cases after he is gone. While the reference to cases of dispute that come "before your gates" (NIV "courts") links this text with the preceding, the focus shifts from cases the people can solve to those that cannot be adjudicated by normal and local means, and from issues involving Israel's vertical relationship with Yahweh to horizontal relationships among Israelites. Remarkably, in this arrangement those submitted to communal courts are religious in nature (vv. 2 – 7), while cases involving civil and criminal offences are submitted to the central "theocratic" tribunal (vv. 8 – 12).[40] As noted above, the literary structure of this panel is identical to verses 2 – 7.

The problem (v. 8a). Contrary to prevailing opinion,[41] the primary concern in this paragraph is neither to establish the makeup of Israel's supreme court nor to describe its principal functions. As in verses 2 – 4, with a conditional clause Moses announces the issue: cases for judgment that are too difficult for the local court to settle in the gates. The verb *niplā³* denotes "beyond one's power to unravel or adjudicate" (cf. 1:17; Ex. 18:26).[42] The present instructions concern only the last stage of the process: how the people should proceed when they cannot reach a decision in a disputed case. Moses identifies three kinds of cases that might lead to an impasse:[43] murder/unintentional manslaughter, civil or criminal disputes, and physical assaults. Such cases are to be sent on to the higher tribunal.

The prescription (vv. 8b – 12b). Although Moses introduces Levitical priests and a judge as final adjudicators (v. 9), his primary addressee continues to be ordinary citizens, and his concern is still the involvement of the people in maintaining righteousness in judicial matters.[44] While the actions of the priest/judge are presented in one short statement (v. 9c), those required of the people

---

40. On these two panels, see Levinson, *Deuteronomy and the Hermeneutics of Legal Innovations*, 130 – 37.

41. Note the titles to this section in commentaries: "The High Court of Referral" (Tigay, *Deuteronomy*, 163), "The Supreme Court" (Mayes, *Deuteronomy*, 266), "The Jurisdiction of the Central Tribunal" (Craigie, *Deuteronomy*, 251), "Law of the Central Tribunal — A Court of Referral" (Christensen, *Deuteronomy*, 371).

42. The word also denotes "to be unusual, wonderful." See *HALOT*, 927. Throughout this literary unit (16:18 – 17:13), *mišpāṭ* refers to a concrete judicial decision, rather than "justice."

43. For these scenarios, see Bovati, *Re – Establishing Justice*, 32. Each case involves an identical binary form translated formally. For discussion of the idioms, see Levinson, *Deuteronomy and the Hermeneutics of Legal Innovations*, 128 – 29.

44. Note the preponderance of second person verbs. Though cast in the third person, even the last sentence (v. 12a – b) impresses on the people the importance of carrying out the sentence exactly as determined at the central sanctuary.

are presented in two stages: their duty to present the case to the central tribunal (vv. 8b–9), and their responsibility to execute its decision (vv. 10–12b).

When confronted with an insoluble case, the people are to "arise and go up" (pers. trans. of v. 8b)[45] to the place that Yahweh will choose and present the case to the Levitical priests and the judge in office at the time. Moses suggests that the central sanctuary will not only be a place of worship but also a court of last resort; he thus implies the role of God in the pursuit of righteousness. The court of appeal does not provide the accused with another opportunity to have the case reviewed but serves as a resource for local adjudicators.[46]

Moses identifies the adjudicators as "the priests, who are Levites, and . . . the judge." This refers to a subgroup of the Levites, who performed priestly duties before Yahweh at the central sanctuary.[47] Although the priestly writings (esp. Leviticus) never ascribe a judicial role to priests, Numbers 5:11–31 alludes to this function. The cryptic nature of Moses' statement here suggests this judicial role was widely recognized.

But what are we to make of "the judge who is in office at that time"? Most view him as a layperson who joins a group of priests (note the plural) to hear the case (cf. 19:15–21).[48] However, the twofold reference to the central sanctuary in this context (vv. 8, 10), plus the fact that he is to officiate "in the presence of the LORD" (19:17),[49] render a lay interpretation unlikely. It is preferable to treat "the judge" as loosely appositional to "the priests, who are Levites," specifying an individual selected from among them to head the tribunal and/or announce the decision. The explanatory clause, "who is in office at that time," leaves open whether these persons served for life like high priests or rotated off when their term expired.

How would this tribunal operate? Versions that read the verb "inquire" as a third person plural[50] suggest the central tribunal would repeat the lower

---

45. The verb ʿālâ (v. 8) not only reflects the common practice of erecting sanctuaries on hilltops, but also anticipates Mount Zion, the place that Yahweh will eventually choose to establish his name.

46. So also Nelson, *Deuteronomy*, 221.

47. The expression "Levitical priests" appears here for the first time, but it recurs in v. 18; 18:1–2; 24:8; 27:9. Sometimes this group is identified simply as "the priests," without qualifying them as "Levites" (19:17; 21:5) or "the priests, the sons of Levi" (21:5; 31:9). On their duties, see 10:7–8; 18:1, 3; 26:4; 27:9–10; 31:9–11, 24–26). See further McConville, *Law and Theology in Deuteronomy*, 124–53; M. D. Rehm, "Levites and Priests," *ABD*, 4:303–5.

48. Weinfeld (*Deuteronomy and the Deuteronomic School*, 235) goes farther, arguing that two judicial traditions that were originally independent have been combined.

49. Exodus 21:6 and 22:8–9[7–8] also speak of judicial cases being resolved "before God."

50. LXX and the Samaritan Pentateuch read wᵉdārᵉsû, "and they shall inquire," rather than wᵉdārastâ ("and you shall inquire").

court's investigative procedure (cf. 13:14[15]; 17:4). However, if we interpret *dâraš* as "to make inquiry"[51] rather than "to investigate," the verb refers to seeking guidance from Yahweh. The last clause of verse 9 reinforces this interpretation. The noun *mišpāṭ* is sometimes used of a divine pronouncement in response either to inquiry (Judg. 13:12; 1 Sam. 2:12–13; 8:10–11) or to a cry for rescue (Judg. 4:5).[52] As priestly "judge," the designated official is heir to Moses, who at first heard all the disputes of the people and then inquired of God (Ex. 18:15–16). However, unlike Moses, the priestly judge could probably use the Urim and Thummim to determine the mind of God.[53]

If we abandon the political interpretation of the broader context (16:18–18:22), this interpretation explains several features in the text: (1) the characterization of difficult cases with the verb *niplā'*, a root used elsewhere of miraculous or "wonderful" divine actions rather than the mundane variants (1:17; Ex. 18:26); (2) the emphasis on the location of the inquiry at the sanctuary rather than in the city gates (vv. 8, 10); (3) the absence of any reference to an investigation by priests or judge (the tribunal simply declares the outcome); (4) the phrase used for the decision, which suits an oracular context perfectly (cf. v. 11); (5) the twofold use of the idiom "according to the decisions [*dābar*]" (vv. 10, 11), which the adjudicators apparently do not establish but only declare (vv. 9, 10, 11); (6) the later reference to "the priest who stands ministering there to the LORD your God" (v. 12). These elements all fit an oracular context perfectly, but they are difficult to square with a judicial inquiry conducted by a lay official. As prescribed, the procedure emphasizes that Yahweh is the highest court of appeal, and his verdicts are declared through his priestly representative at the central sanctuary.

Moses' charge to execute the verdict of the tribunal is the center of gravity in this panel (vv. 10–12b). Since verse 10 demands action, "the word of judgment" (NIV "verdict") apparently would include both a declaration of guilt or innocence and the actions to take against a person declared guilty. While the second reference to the place of decision as "the place the LORD will choose" (v. 10) reinforces the divine authority of the verdict, the importance of executing the judgment is emphasized by the threefold use of the verb "to do" (vv. 10a, 10b, 11a), and by the emphatic construction, "and you shall keep by doing" (NIV "be careful to do ..."). Four times

---

51. Thus *DCH*, 2:474.

52. On the oracular use of *mišpāṭ* and extrabiblical parallels, see D. I. Block, "Deborah among the Judges: The Perspective of the Hebrew Historian," in *Faith, Tradition, and History: Old Testament Historiography in Its Near Eastern Context* (ed. A. R. Millard et al.; Winona Lake, IN: Eisenbrauns, 1994), 247.

53. On the oracular use of the Urim and Thummim carried in the priest's breastpiece, see Ex. 28:30; Lev. 8:8.

Moses declares that the sentence is to be carried out precisely as instructed: "according to the word they declare to you" (v. 10a); "according to all they teach you" (v. 10b); "according to the instruction they teach you" (v. 11a); "according to the pronouncement they say to you" (v. 11b; all pers. trans.). While some treat these repetitive features as secondary insertions,[54] they reflect the text's rhetorical and sermonic genre.

If the "word" the adjudicators declare and the verdict they communicate represent the divine judgment on the case that normal procedures have failed to resolve, what is to be made of the *tôrâ* that the tribunal teaches (v. 11a)? While the immediate context might suggest specific instructions related to the case at hand,[55] the usage of *tôrâ* elsewhere in the book, as well as the priests' role as custodians and instructors of Torah (17:18; 31:9–13; 33:10), argues in favor of the Torah as Moses teaches it in his final addresses. When the Israelites execute the divine tribunal's decision, they pursue righteousness as determined in this case, as well as according to the overall understanding of righteousness as taught in the Torah.

In verse 11b Moses' application of a formula that applies to fidelity to the covenant reinforces this conclusion. Imposing the same rigorous standards of compliance to a specific revelation from God as he does to the Torah in general (5:32; 17:20; 28:14), Moses considers it a deviation "to the right or to the left" to inflict punishment more severely or leniently than the ruling prescribed, or to substitute the prescribed sentence with a different action. Therefore, his instructions here conclude with a stern warning: failure to execute the judgment as prescribed is the height of presumption and defiance against God (v. 12a–b). Refusal to listen to the priest who stands in the service of Yahweh, or to the judge who declares Yahweh's verdict, is as reprehensible as idolatry itself (cf. 17:5–7a) and deserves the death penalty.

The goal (v. 12c). Moses ends this panel as he had the previous one (v. 7b) with a declaration of zeal for the purity of the nation. By executing persons who defy God by noncompliance with his verdict, the evil of rebellion is purged from Israel and righteousness is maintained. Whether rendered by local adjudicators or the central tribunal, every decision advances the agenda of *ṣedeq ṣedeq* ("righteousness, only righteousness"; see 16:20).

Conclusion (17:13)

MOSES CONCLUDES THE UNIT that began in 16:18 by repeating a point made in 13:11[12]. Although concern for righteousness is to drive all adjudicatory decisions, intimately tied to this is his concern to instill fear in the

54. See Morrow, *Scribing the Center,* 191–93.
55. Thus Mayes, *Deuteronomy,* 269.

hearts of the people. Whereas chapter 13 sought to instill fear that prevents a person from following an apostate through the severity of the criminal's punishment, here that goal is served through the severity of the punishment of those who defy God by not executing his judgments.

ISRAEL'S HISTORY WITH ṢEDEQ. Israelite compliance with Moses' instructions in 16:18 – 17:13 was short-lived. Within two generations the people had forgotten Yahweh and his gracious acts of deliverance, providential care, and revelation (Judg. 2:10), resulting in a complete loss of the agenda spelled out here: "righteousness, only righteousness." By the time of Eli (1 Sam. 1 – 4), the spiritual and judicial system was so compromised that not even those who served at the central shrine knew Yahweh or the *mišpāṭ* ("oracle, judgment") of the priests (1 Sam. 2:12 – 13). Before long, kings were sponsoring syncretistic faith and religion (1 Kings 11:1 – 13), and overtly pagan forms had invaded the sanctuary itself (2 Kings 21:1 – 9). The problem envisaged in our text is precisely that for which Manasseh would later be condemned: the carved image of Asherah was planted in the house that Yahweh had chosen for his name (2 Kings 21:7). Along with all sorts of social crimes, this provocation led ultimately to the nation's demise at the hands of Assyrians and Babylonians.

When Yahweh sent prophets to warn of coming judgment because of rebellion against him, corruption in the courts topped the list of crimes. Representing the masses, the eighth-century prophet Micah gave classic expression to the problem:

> Her leaders judge for a bribe,
>> her priests teach for a price,
>> and her prophets tell fortunes for money.
> Yet they lean upon the LORD and say,
>> "Is not the LORD among us?
>> No disaster will come upon us." (Mic. 3:11)

This image of corruption in Judah was reinforced by Isaiah, who pronounced woe on those who acquitted the guilty for a bribe but denied justice to the innocent (Isa. 5:23). The problem of corruption in the courts is a common theme in Psalms and the Wisdom writings. On the one hand, expressed positively, at the level of the individual the psalmist acknowledges that God accepts the worship of the person who does what is righteous (*ṣedeq*) and refuses to accept a bribe against the innocent (Ps. 15:2, 5). At the national level, the sage of Israel declared, "Righteousness [*ṣᵉdāqâ*] exalts a nation, but sin is a disgrace to any people" (Prov. 14:34). On the other hand, "A wicked man accepts a bribe in secret to pervert the course of justice" (Prov. 17:23), and "Extortion turns a wise man into a fool, and a bribe corrupts the heart" (Eccl. 7:7).

However, the eclipse of righteousness was not limited to the administration of justice. In 1 Samuel 2 the sons of Eli illustrate how quickly the corruption had set in, and that it extended to the family of the priest. When Israelites came to worship at the central sanctuary in Shiloh, those "wicked men" (1 Sam. 2:12) claimed the best cuts of the sacrificial meat for themselves. Centuries later Jeremiah associated moral crimes (theft, murder, adultery) with idolatry (offering sacrifices to Baal and walking after other gods they had not known), and with contempt for the place that Yahweh had called by his name (Jer. 7:8 – 11). The history of Israel's pursuit of righteousness is a history of failure.

But as the darkness of the judgment descended, visions of hope for the distant future flashed through the clouds. That hope was embodied not by Levitical priests but by a Davidic Messiah, whose name would be "The LORD Our Righteousness" (Jer. 23:6), and who, endowed with the Spirit of Yahweh, would wear a belt of righteousness around his waist (Isa. 11:1 – 5).

Righteousness in the New Testament. When the New Testament opens, one of the first characters to greet the Messiah was a certain Simeon, whom Luke characterizes as "righteous" (*dikaios*) and "devout" (*eulabēs*), "waiting for the consolation of Israel" and obviously exhibiting the presence of the Holy Spirit (Luke 2:25). Whether or not he was a Levitical priest,[56] when Mary and Joseph brought the child Jesus to the temple according to Jewish law, Simeon recognized the significance of this child with his *Nunc Dimittis*:

> Sovereign Lord, as you have promised,
> > you now dismiss your servant in peace.
> For my eyes have seen your salvation,
> > which you have prepared in the sight of all people,
> a light for revelation to the Gentiles
> > and for glory to your people Israel. (Luke 2:28 – 32)

Although Luke classifies the utterance that followed as a blessing, Simeon forecasts trouble and pain for the child:

> This child is destined to cause the falling and rising of many in Israel, and to be a sign that will be spoken against, so that the thoughts of many hearts will be revealed. And a sword will pierce your own soul too. (Luke 2:34 – 35)

---

56. Cf. S. E. Porter, "Simeon 3," *ABD*, 6:26 – 27.

Moved by the Holy Spirit, that was indeed the divine verdict concerning "the Lord's Christ" (Luke 2:26). According to the divine plan, Jesus would not be executed for his own crimes, but he would die as a substitute for a corrupt and idolatrous humanity.

CONTEMPORARY RIGHTEOUSNESS. THE RELEVANCE of this text for our time is obvious. A nation that prides itself in its Judeo-Christian heritage should be known around the world for its commitment to "righteousness, only righteousness." This commitment should characterize the way we stand for and administer justice in international courts. Whether our decisions are cast in the United Nations Security Council in New York or in the International Court of Justice in The Hague, Netherlands, by the standards of covenant righteousness, decisions must always be cast in the interests of others rather than self-interest.

But our recent history is marred by shameful support of regimes that oppress the poor and run roughshod over the rights of common citizens. This is obvious in the Middle East, where our insatiable thirst for oil rather than justice and righteousness has determined our friendships. The world will recognize us as a righteous nation and will recognize the righteousness of the laws by which we live (Deut. 6:8) when they see our willingness to abandon self-interest for the well-being of others.

This commitment should also characterize the way justice is administered in the courts of this land. Righteousness is not served by a system that expects defense attorneys to convince a jury to acquit the guilty or prosecuting attorneys to condemn the innocent by smooth arguments, evasion of evidence to the contrary, and looking for loopholes in the law. Nor is righteousness served when those with means are able to hire the most skillful legal defense team while the economically or ethnically marginalized are at the mercy of assigned lawyers who would rather be on the other side of the case. Nevertheless, we should not expect much of civil authority in a Constantinian world, where religious confessions and pious platitudes camouflage fundamental moral and social rot. In fact, we should probably be surprised when vestiges of concerns for righteousness surface.

"Righteousness, only righteousness" as the watchword of the redeemed. But in Deuteronomy Moses was not preaching to Egyptians or Canaanites, or even Edomites — with whom Israel shared descent from Abraham, the friend of God. Moses was preaching to the redeemed, to those who claimed to be "sons of God," a holy people, chosen and set apart as Yahweh's special treasure for his praise, honor, and glory (Deut. 26:19).

For this reason, the message of Deuteronomy 16:20–17:13 has particular relevance for the church. "Righteousness, only righteousness" should be the watchword of the redeemed, whether they serve individually as agents of light in a dark world or work together within the community of faith.

This will involve uncompromising personal and corporate commitment to the Lord alone, with no room left for other gods or aberrant forms of religious expression. And it will involve seriously disciplining those who stray from this course or encourage others to do so. But the pursuit of righteousness also demands vigilance in moral ethics, especially in the administration of the community. Even more than the state, leaders in the church must be both wise and righteous, refusing to be corrupted by favors from members or to be tempted to pervert "Your kingdom come" into "My kingdom come." This text reminds us also that the responsibility for the pursuit and administration of righteousness should never be left in the hands of appointed officials. It is everyone's business.

Deuteronomy 17:14–20

W hen you enter the land the LORD your God is
giving you and have taken possession of it and
settled in it, and you say, "Let us set a king over
us like all the nations around us," ¹⁵be sure to appoint over
you the king the LORD your God chooses. He must be from
among your own brothers. Do not place a foreigner over
you, one who is not a brother Israelite. ¹⁶The king, moreover, must not acquire great numbers of horses for himself
or make the people return to Egypt to get more of them,
for the LORD has told you, "You are not to go back that way
again." ¹⁷He must not take many wives, or his heart will be
led astray. He must not accumulate large amounts of silver
and gold.

¹⁸When he takes the throne of his kingdom, he is to write
for himself on a scroll a copy of this law, taken from that of
the priests, who are Levites. ¹⁹It is to be with him, and he is
to read it all the days of his life so that he may learn to revere
the LORD his God and follow carefully all the words of this
law and these decrees ²⁰and not consider himself better than
his brothers and turn from the law to the right or to the left.
Then he and his descendants will reign a long time over his
kingdom in Israel.

Original
Meaning

WHILE THE DOMINANCE OF threefold constructions lends coherence to Deuteronomy
17:14–20,[1] this text divides into two parts: the
anticipation of a king in Israel (vv. 14–15), and
the prescribed conduct of Israel's future king (vv. 16–20). Moses' instructions on kingship begin with a lengthy temporal clause describing future

---

1. (1) Three verbs describing Israel's relationship to the land: they enter, possess, and
occupy it (v. 14; cf. 11:30; 12:29; 26:1); (2) three modifying clauses beginning with ʾᵃšer in
vv. 14–15, with reference to the land (v. 14) and the king (v. 15); (3) a threefold prohibition
of "multiplying" horses, women, precious metals (vv. 16–17); (4) the threefold repetition
of lô ("for himself"), highlighting the danger of using the office of kingship in self-service
(vv. 16–17); (5) three duties of the king with respect to the Torah: to write it for himself
(v. 18), to have it with him (v. 19a), and to read it (v. 19b); (6) three reasons for reading the

circumstances when the Israelites might contemplate a monarchy. The structure of verses 14−15 resembles 12:20, with the key issue being cast in the form of direct speech, followed by the declared desire. Since the Israelites lack the authority to effect the expressed desire without Moses' and Yahweh's permission, the verbs in both connote a request.

While the present text offers no clues concerning what might occasion this request, in the ancient Near East kings normally fulfilled three primary roles: (1) as warrior protecting the nation from outside threats; (2) as judge, guaranteeing justice within; (3) as patron of the cult, ensuring the right ordering of worship.[2] However, in verses 16−20 Moses will explicitly repudiate prevailing models of kingship, which heightens the significance of the request, "Let us set a king over us like all the nations around us." Grammatically "like all the nations that are around [me]" could mean "like all the nations [have]," or more likely, "May I have a king [that I may be] like all the nations around me?"[3] Whereas Moses has repeatedly spoken of the seductive force of Canaanite religious ideas, now he speaks of the seductive pull of Canaanite *politeia*. Remarkably, this text perceives kingship in Israel not as a top-down imposition by a powerful ruler, but as a democratic development, in response to the wishes of the community.

The emphatic opening clause of verse 15 reflects Moses' fundamentally positive disposition toward the monarchical system in principle. However, as in his response to the request in 12:23−25, here Moses narrows the parameters of Israel's kingship. First, the king must be chosen by Yahweh. The notion of divinity choosing a person to serve as his royal representative is widely attested in the ancient Near East, from as early as the eighteenth

---

Torah: "that he may learn" (v. 19), "that ... [he] not consider himself better," and "that ... [he not] turn from the law" (v. 20); (7) the threefold goal of learning: "to revere," "to follow," "to do [lit.]" (v. 19). Several actually exhibit a 3 + 1 pattern, in which the fourth element resembles the other three formally but with respect to function stands outside the triad: (1) three verbs in narrative sequence describing the occupation of the land, followed by a fourth that introduces a direct quotation (v. 14); (2) three *ʾašer* clauses in the narrative of vv. 14−15, supplemented by a fourth embedded in direct speech (v. 14b); (3) three occurrences of *lô* ("for himself") in prohibitive statements (vv. 16−17), followed by a fourth imperative statement (v. 18, "he is to write *for himself* a copy of this law"); (4) three infinitive clauses expressing the [immediate] purposes of reading the Torah for the king himself (vv. 19−20a), followed by a fourth (v. 20b) declaring the long range effect of this action (v. 20b). Some of these triads are recognized by Nelson, *Deuteronomy*, 223.

2. Cf. K. W. Whitelam, "Israelite Kingship: The Royal Ideology and Its Opponents," in *The World of Ancient Israel: Sociological, Anthropological and Political Perspectives* (ed. R. E. Clements; Cambridge: Cambridge Univ. Press, 1991), 130.

3. This understanding is implied in 1 Sam. 8:5, which echoes this text, and is explicitly expressed in 1 Sam. 8:19−20.

century BC to beyond the Old Testament period. Moses is even more emphatic about the second qualification, insisting the king must be an Israelite, "from among your own brothers," and then excluding any outsider.[4]

Verses 16−20 address the manner in which kingship is to be exercised in Israel. Continuing in third person, Moses' purpose is not to provide the king with a manual for leadership but to create an image of responsible leadership in the minds of the people. In contrast to the offices of judge (16:18−20; 17:9), priest (17:9; 18:1−8), and prophet (18:9−22), the office of king is presented as optional, subject to the desire of the people. However, Moses reins in temptations to abuse the office by proscribing greed and ambition (vv. 16−17) and by prescribing an extraordinary spiritual and ethical standard for the king (vv. 18−20).

The proscriptions consist of four statements, but they may be reduced to three prohibitions against excessive accumulation of horses, women, and precious metals. The regulation regarding horses is intended to stifle militaristic impulses (cf. Deut. 20:1; Josh. 17:16−18; Judg. 1:19). The command not to go down to Egypt to procure horses warns against being drawn back to the land that had enslaved them (v. 16).[5] The specific warning is missing in previous narratives,[6] but Moses seems to allude to a warning that has not been preserved in the biblical record. He recalls it here to emphasize that a return to Egypt would in effect annul the people's redemption and cancel their covenant relationship with Yahweh.[7]

The prohibition against multiplying women extends far beyond providing the king with unlimited opportunity for sexual gratification.[8] Since marriages were often arranged to strengthen alliances,[9] the institution of the harem enabled kings to be allied simultaneously with many outside

---

4. See comments on 14:21 and 15:3 (cf. also 23:20[21] and 29:22[21]). On the status of the outsider, see D. I. Block, "Sojourner; Alien; Stranger," *ISBE* (rev. ed.), 4:562.

5. For a later warning of kingship as a symbol of slavery, see 1 Sam. 8:9−18. Anatolia would have been the primary source for horses, on which see D. J. Reimer, "Concerning Return to Egypt: Deuteronomy 17:16 and 28:68 Reconsidered," in *Studies in the Pentateuch* (ed. J. A. Emerton; VTSup 41; Leiden: Brill, 1990), 217−29. It seems the Hyksos rulers of Egypt introduced horses and chariotry as vital elements of Egyptian armed forces. See J. Van Seters, *The Hyksos* (New Haven, CT: Yale Univ. Press, 1966), 183−85.

6. Tigay (*Deuteronomy*, 167) interprets v. 16b as a promise what is usually understood as a command: "For Yahweh has said, 'You will never return that way again.'" If so, the promise is negated in the covenant curses (see 28:68).

7. In the face of the fulfillment of the warning of 28:68 in 722 and 586 BC, to later writers "Egypt" was a cipher for the Assyrians and the Babylonians respectively (cf. Hos. 8:13; 9:3; 11:5).

8. Since "wives" connotes a marital relationship, *nāšîm* here is better rendered generically as "women," the reference being to the harem of an oriental king.

9. Cf. 1 Kings 9:15−16; 16:31.

rulers (cf. 1 Kings 11:1), while also providing decoration for the court to impress visitors.[10] But this text seems unconcerned about these considerations. Instead, Moses the pastor views the harem as a threat to spiritual fidelity to Yahweh: The women will turn the king's heart away. The warning concerns defection into idolatry (cf. 7:3–4), though in light of what follows it may involve defection from the Torah in general and the Supreme Command in particular. The reference to "his heart" suggests such defection is not primarily an external act but a fundamental aspect of one's being (cf. 6:5). Like wine and strong drink, pursuing pleasure and status can inhibit the proper exercise of one's responsibilities.[11]

The proscription on excessive accumulation of silver and gold is shorthand for wealth and opulence. In the ancient Near Eastern political world, this wealth was generally amassed at the expense of the people by taxing the citizens and demanding tribute from subject states.

These prohibitions, then, address three major temptations facing ancient rulers: lust for power, lust for status, and lust for wealth. The text does not prohibit the purchase of horses, or marriage, or the accumulation of some silver and gold. The threefold repetition of "for himself" emphasizes the ban concerning the king's exploitation of his office for personal gain.

Moses' positive instructions for the king are even more remarkable than the preceding prohibitions. (1) The king must copy the Torah for himself "when he sits on his throne over his kingdom" (v. 18a, pers. trans.). The NIV interprets this narrowly as the time of his accession,[12] though the later charge to have the Torah with him all the days suggests a more durative sense. This charge is significant for several reasons. (a) It portrays the king, not as a legislator, but as one who receives laws from a higher authority and is himself subject to them: he writes them "for himself." (b) It assumes royal literacy from the outset of the monarchy.[13] (c) As Sonnet observes, the designation "a copy of this law" "implicitly requires a standard copy, an *editio princeps*, from which the transcript is to be made."[14] (d) The Torah is to be copied on a *sēper*,[15] that is, a "written document," probably a specially

10. Note the emphasis in Dan. 1:3–4 on the qualifications of candidates for Nebuchadnezzar's court: youths without defect, handsome, intelligent in every branch of learning, discreet, wise, and knowledgeable in royal protocol.

11. Cf. the warning of Lemuel's mother in Prov. 31:3–9.

12. Thus Mayes, *Deuteronomy*, 273; Tigay, *Deuteronomy*, 168.

13. Similarly J. F. A. Sawyer, *Sacred Languages and Sacred Texts* (New York: Routledge, 1999), 49–51; A. R. Millard, "Books in the Late Bronze Age in the Levant," in *Past Links: Studies in the Languages and Cultures of the Ancient Near East. Fs. Anson Rainey* (ed. S. Izre'el et al. (Israel Oriental Studies 18; Winona Lake, IN: Eisenbrauns, 1998), 171–81.

14. Sonnet, *The Book within the Book*, 74 (cf. Josh. 8:32).

15. Cf. André Lemaire, "Writing and Writing Materials," *ABD*, 6:1004.

tanned leather scroll of sheep or goatskin.[16] (e) By writing his copy in the presence of the Levitical priests, the king recognizes this as a sacred act (31:9–13). As divinely appointed witnesses and custodians of the document, the Levitical priests would ensure that the king copied the entire document, without addition or omission.[17] By the act of copying the Torah, the king declared his spiritual subordination to the priests and to the Torah, the symbol of the covenant that bound Yahweh and Israel.

(2) The king must wear the Torah. Although it may never be treated merely as a good luck charm, the charge "it is to be with him" suggests that like an amulet, the Torah was to accompany the king constantly, providing a written reminder of his personal vassal status before Yahweh and his primary role as model of covenant righteousness.

(3) The king must read the Torah for himself (vv. 19–20).[18] This charge is the most complex. Moses begins with a simple directive, "He is to read it all the days of his life," reinforcing the previous charge to have the document with him constantly. The importance of reading the Torah is highlighted by four purpose clauses, which echo earlier injunctions to the people. (a) Faithful reading of the Torah is key to a proper disposition toward Yahweh. For the first time in the book, the Torah is portrayed as a medium by which the fear of Yahweh is instilled in the heart/mind.[19]

(b) Faithful reading of the Torah is key to a proper disposition toward other members of the covenant community. Echoing 8:13–14, the idiom, "his heart is lifted up" (pers. trans.), warns against the hubris that afflicted many ancient Near Eastern kings.[20] The king may have been specially chosen by Yahweh and installed by the people,[21] but he must resist the temptation to consider himself their superior.

---

16. On which see ibid., 1003; A. R. Millard, *Reading and Writing in the Time of Jesus* (Biblical Seminar 69; Sheffield: Sheffield Academic, 2000), 25–26; M. Haran, "Book–Scrolls in Israel in Pre-exilic Times," *JJS* 33 (1982): 166–67.

17. Cf. 4:2. The production of duplicate written copies of significant documents was widespread in ancient Mesopotamia. Upon completion of the task, scribes would conventionally add a colophon declaring their fidelity to the original that commonly read, "according to its original, written, checked, and copied." See E. Leichty, "The Colophon," in *Studies Presented to A. Leo Oppenheim* (ed. R. D. Biggs and J. A. Brinkman; Chicago: Chicago Univ. Press, 1964), 150.

18. This is the first occurrence *qārā'* in the sense of "to cry out, read," in Deuteronomy (cf. Ex. 24:7). The verb reflects the ancient practice of reading official documents orally.

19. Such fear is learned by (1) observing Yahweh's victories over the enemies (2:25), (2) hearing the voice of Yahweh from the midst of the fire (4:10), and (3) observing the punishment imposed on those who violate the covenant (17:13; 19:20; 21:21). The consequences of the absence of fear are spelled out in the covenant curses (28:58).

20. See Sonnet, *Book within the Book*, 81.

21. Note the fourfold occurrence of the preposition *ʿal* ("over [me/you]") in vv. 14–15.

(c) Faithful reading of the Torah is key to the king's staying on course in his devotion to Yahweh.[22] The clause "[that he not] turn from the law [command] to the right or to the left" echoes 5:31−32. Again the singular "the command" (*hammiṣwâ*) refers to the Supreme Command (see 6:5); that is, the king must demonstrate total covenant commitment to Yahweh.

(d) Faithful reading of the Torah is key to a secure future. Echoing earlier statements applied to Israel,[23] Moses describes the prospect for the king and his sons in terms of lengthened days over his kingdom. Anticipating a dynastic monarchy, the statement applies to the king the principle enunciated in the Decalogue: people's actions determine their own well-being and the well-being of their households (cf. 5:9).

THE REVOLUTIONARY NATURE OF **Israelite kingship.** By incorporating demands that earlier texts had applied to the people of Israel, this passage reinforces the revolutionary nature of Israelite kingship. (1) Whereas the kings of other nations often gained power by force and at the expense of both rivals and subjects, Israel's kingship will be established in response to a democratic impulse and with the blessing of Yahweh.

(2) Whereas foreigners, either usurpers from the outside or imperial overlords, often governed other states, the Israelites were to be governed by one of their own under the imperial reign of Yahweh.

(3) Whereas kings of other nations regularly used their office to satisfy their own lust for power, status, and wealth, Israelite kings were forbidden from doing so.

(4) Whereas other kings were viewed as administrators of justice, the primary role of Israelite kings was to embody the divinely revealed standard of covenantal justice.

(5) Whereas other kings codified laws to protect their own interests and to regulate the conduct of subjects rather than themselves,[24] Israelite laws were codified by Yahweh, interpreted by his spokesman who had no vested interest in kingship, and then required of the king himself.

---

22. It is equivalent to "walking in his ways" (i.e., "the ways of the LORD"; 8:6; 10:12; 11:22; 19:9; 26:17; 28:9; 30:16; 32:4).

23. References to Israel's lengthening their days occur in 4:26, 40; 5:33; 11:9; 22:7; 30:18; 32:47. References to the days lengthening occur in 5:16; 6:2; 25:15.

24. See esp. the prologue to the Law Code of Hammurabi in Roth, *Law Collections*, 76−81. For extrabiblical evidence for comparable ideals for their kings, see "Advice to a Prince," in W. G. Lambert, *Babylonian Wisdom Literature* (Oxford: Clarendon, 1960), 113−15; the Ugaritic *Kirta* (Parker, *UNP*, 41); and Job 29:7−17 and Prov. 31:1−9, both of which concern non-Israelite rulers.

(6) Whereas kings of other nations were elevated above their country-men with epithets like "son of God"[25] and "image of Bel/Shamash,"[26] in Deuteronomy the former title is reserved for the nation of Israel (14:1; 32:6,18; cf. 1:31), and the latter is absent altogether. Apart from "king," the only epithet Israel's monarch may claim is "brother" of his people.

The paradigm of kingship established here should have secured the place of Israel's kings as the appointed rulers over his people. We do hear occasional echoes of this passage in later texts. Although Joshua was not a king chosen by Yahweh in response to the people's request, as the successor of Moses in Joshua 1:8, Yahweh requires of him what this text demands of the king (note the singular). With Psalm 1 the Psalter opens by characterizing a blessed person as one who delights in the Torah of Yahweh and meditates on it day and night. On the surface, this statement seems to democratize the injunction to read the Torah. However, if the Psalter is indeed a fundamentally royal document, as some have argued,[27] this psalm serves particularly as a guide for the king on how to read the Torah (specifically Deuteronomy).

Israel's political history. This text is important for understanding Israel's political history. Years later, when the elders of Israel appealed to Samuel for a king, the appeal echoed Deuteronomy 17:14: "We want a king over us. Then we will be like all the other nations" (1 Sam. 8:19−20). Samuel's prior "pronouncement concerning the king" seems to have been composed against the backdrop of Deuteronomy 17:16−17. He warned the people that the king they demanded would use his office for selfish ends and run roughshod over their interests. Yahweh answered this request by giving them Saul, who as a Benjamite represented the tribe that had proved by deed and disposition to be like the lowest of the nations (Judg. 19−21; cf. Gen. 19). But Saul's rule was doomed from the beginning. Ultimately he served as a foil for the one Yahweh had in mind from the beginning, the man after Yahweh's heart (1 Sam. 13:14).[28]

None of these texts suggests the biblical authors rejected the monarchy in principle. On the contrary, on three occasions God had expressly prom-

---

25. Later Davidic kings will be presented as "the son of God." See 2 Sam. 7:14; Ps. 2:7; 22:9[10]; 89:27−28[28−29]. On "divine sonship" of kings in the ancient world, see J. Fossum, "Son of God," *DDD*, 788−89.

26. See the characterization of Esarhaddon as "the father of the king, my lord, was the very image of Bel, and the king, my lord, is likewise the image of Bel." See S. Parpola, *Letters from Assyrian Scholars* (SAA 10; Helsinki: Helsinki Univ. Press, 1993), 181 (§228:18−20).

27. B. K. Waltke, *An Old Testament Theology: An Exegetical, Canonical, and Thematic Approach* (Grand Rapids: Zondervan, 2007), 871−84.

28. Cf. D. I. Block, "My Servant David: Ancient Israel's Vision of the Messiah," in *Israel's Messiah in the Bible and the Dead Sea Scrolls* (ed. R. S. Hess and M. D. Carroll R.; Grand Rapids: Baker, 2003), 39.

ised Abraham that "kings" would come from him and Sarah (Gen. 17:6, 16; 35:11), an expectation that Genesis 49:9–12 narrows to the tribe of Judah. The present generation had heard the pagan prophet Balaam speak of the king and his kingdom being exalted (Num. 24:7), and of a star and (royal) scepter rising from Jacob/Israel (Num. 24:17). In David the one chosen by Yahweh had arrived.

The paradigm of kingship established in Deuteronomy 17:14–20 provides the lens used by deuteronomistic historians and prophets to evaluate Israel's kings. This is most evident in the portrayal of Solomon in 1 Kings. Although he is most famous for constructing the temple for Yahweh (David's project), he multiplied horses (1 Kings 4:26–28[5:6–8]; 10:26–29) and wives (11:1–13) and amassed vast riches for the crown (10:23). To be fair, the historian does not explicitly condemn Solomon multiplying wealth or horses, but he denounces him sharply for marrying foreign women (11:1–13), forcefully ruling over his countrymen (5:13–18[27–32]), and breaking the covenant (11:9–13, 33). In the end responsibility for Israel's exile rested on the shoulders of kings who abused the people and led the nation in apostasy (2 Kings 24:3–4).[29]

While a few leaders in Israel's history modeled the ideals of the Torah presented here (Joshua, though not a king, Josh. 1:8–9; Hezekiah, 2 Kings 18:3–7; and Josiah, 22:18–19), the failure of Israel's kings combined with Yahweh's promise to David of eternal title to the throne of Israel gave rise to the messianic hope of a future son of David to embody perfectly the Mosaic paradigm for kingship. This expectation was ultimately fulfilled by Jesus the Messiah, the son of David, whose mission was not to bring an end to the Torah but to fulfill it (Matt. 5:17). As the beloved Son of God who fulfills all righteousness (Matt 3:15), he embodies perfectly the ideals of covenant relationship as represented in the Torah. He is the climax of the royal meta-narrative underlying the entire Old Testament and his kingdom is secure.

PREREQUISITE TO THE KING'S **life and well-being.** The role of the king as model citizen of Israel and a vassal of Yahweh is highlighted not only by applying to the king earlier statements pertaining to Israel, but also by the way exposure to the word of God is presented as a prerequisite to life and well-being. Although no single text contains all the elements, the complete chain of events looks something like this:

29. On Deut. 17:14–20 and the later evaluation of Solomon, see G. N. Knoppers, "Rethinking the Relationship between Deuteronomy and the Deuteronomistic History: The Case of Kings," *CBQ* 63 (2002): 393–415.

Reference	Reading ▶	Hearing ▶	Learning ▶	Fearing ▶	Obeying ▶	Living/ Well-being
4:10		✓	✓	✓		
5:23–29		✓		✓	✓	✓
6:1–3			✓	✓	✓	✓
17:13		✓		✓	✓	
17:19–20	✓	✓	✓	✓	✓	✓
19:20		✓		✓	✓	
31:11–13	✓	✓	✓	✓	✓	

This chart shows that 17:19–20 represents the most complete text, lacking only an explicit reference to hearing. However, since reading involved "crying out" and the king was to "read" the Torah to himself, this element is implied. The link between reading the Torah, fearing Yahweh, and prolonged tenure on the throne (the equivalent to the people's long life in the land) presents a recipe for covenant life in the present. Many centuries later Malachi would acknowledge that the solution for spiritual indifference and the absence of fear is careful attention to the Torah of Moses (Mal. 4:4[3:22]).

Guidelines for a theology of ministry. Beyond this general lesson on the importance of reading the Scriptures in the promotion of fear of God, Deuteronomy 17:14–20 offers church leaders an important resource for developing a theology of ministry — guidelines that run against the grain of many modern definitions of church leadership.[30] (1) The paradigm presented here suggests that the forms of leadership in the church need not necessarily follow a prescribed order. The Lord acceded to the people's desire to have a king. In keeping with new circumstances, new forms of government may need to be designed.

(2) Leaders of God's people must be chosen by God. The way the king would be called remained open, but in Israel's own history this election ultimately led to David. Just as the early church was led by persons recognized to have been called by God,[31] so the church today must seek to be led by faithful persons called by God.

---

30. See further D. I. Block, "The Burden of Leadership: The Mosaic Paradigm of Kingship (Deut. 17:14–20)," in *How I Love Your Torah, O LORD!* 118–39. Cf. idem, "Leadership, Leader, Old Testament," in *New Interpreter's Dictionary of the Bible* (ed. K. D. Sakenfeld; Nashville: Abingdon, 2008), 3:620–26.

31. Paul claims to be "a servant of Christ Jesus, called as an apostle and set apart for the gospel of God" (Rom. 1:1).

(3) Godly leaders exist for the well-being of those they lead and refuse to exploit their positions for personal advantage. The three restrictions placed on royal behavior address three common temptations of leaders: an increasingly insatiable lust for power, status, and wealth.[32] In the Bible responsible headship is never about power or privilege; it is always about securing the well-being of those under one's charge.

(4) Functionally and for the sake of the ministry, godly leaders may be perceived as above their peers, but they must acknowledge their subordination to God and to the people. Like the king in Moses' paradigm, leaders of God's people will read the Word of God for their own nurture and discipline, knowing that God holds them accountable for their personal conduct. Significantly, our text says nothing about administrative gifts or persuasive talent.[33]

(5) Godly leaders embody personally the ideals of covenant relationship to which God's people are committed. This may require modification of John Maxwell's favorite leadership proverb, "He who thinks he leads, but has no followers, is only taking a walk."[34] Actually leaders in the church *must* be taking a walk, walking according to the revealed will of God. In so doing, they model the link between knowing the Word and fearing and obeying the Lord (cf. 31:9–13). This may be what Paul intended with his challenge to Timothy in 1 Timothy 4:13–16.

---

32. The titles of the following publications illustrate present-day awareness of these tendencies: D. A. Stewart, *Money, Power and Sex* (New York: Libra, 1965); N. C. M. Hartsock, *Money, Sex and Power: Toward a Feminist Historical Materialism* (New York: Longman, 1983); P. Turner, *Sex, Money and Power: An Essay on Christian Ethics* (Cambridge, MA: Cowley, 1985); R. J. Foster, *The Challenge of the Disciplined Life: Christian Reflections on Money, Sex and Power* (rev. ed.; San Francisco: Harper & Row, 1989); J. L. Jackley, *Below the Beltway: Money, Sex, Power, and Other Fundamentals of Democracy in the Nation's Capital* (Washington, D.C.: Regnery, 1996); D. Sanders, *Power, Money & Sex: How Success Almost Ruined My Life* (Nashville: Word, 1999); P. Rosenfield, *The Club Rules: Power, Money, Sex and Fear: How It Works in Hollywood* (New York: Warner, 1992); G. C. Rubin, *Power, Money, Fame, Sex: A User's Guide* (New York: Atria, 2001).

33. This understanding of leadership contrasts sharply with that of Carnes Lord, of the Naval War Academy, who asserts that leadership presupposes some element of "such traditionally manly qualities as competitiveness, aggression, or, for that matter, the ability to command.... Leadership that is not prepared to disadvantage anyone is hardly leadership at all" (*The Modern Prince: What Leaders Need to Know Now*, quoted by G. Will, "Ending the 'Feminization' of Politics," *Courier Journal*, January 29, 2004, A7).

34. J. C. Maxwell, *The 21 Irrefutable Laws of Leadership: Follow Them and People Will Follow You* (Nashville: Nelson, 1998), 20.

Deuteronomy 18:1–8

T he priests, who are Levites—indeed the whole tribe of Levi—are to have no allotment or inheritance with Israel. They shall live on the offerings made to the LORD by fire, for that is their inheritance. ²They shall have no inheritance among their brothers; the LORD is their inheritance, as he promised them.

³This is the share due the priests from the people who sacrifice a bull or a sheep: the shoulder, the jowls and the inner parts. ⁴You are to give them the firstfruits of your grain, new wine and oil, and the first wool from the shearing of your sheep, ⁵for the LORD your God has chosen them and their descendants out of all your tribes to stand and minister in the LORD's name always.

⁶If a Levite moves from one of your towns anywhere in Israel where he is living, and comes in all earnestness to the place the LORD will choose, ⁷he may minister in the name of the LORD his God like all his fellow Levites who serve there in the presence of the LORD. ⁸He is to share equally in their benefits, even though he has received money from the sale of family possessions.

MOSES NOW SHIFTS ATTENTION from the king as a paradigm of covenantal righteousness to Israel's treatment of the priests as a measure of the people's fidelity to the standards of righteousness. Structurally 18:1–8 divides into three parts: the basis of the Levites' entitlements (vv. 1–2); the nature of the Levites' entitlements (vv. 3–5); the range of the Levites' entitlements (vv. 6–8). Since the text does not address the Levitical priests directly but speaks about them in the third person, the focus is less on the functions of priests than on the Israelites' disposition toward and treatment of them. In keeping with a call for "righteousness, only righteousness" in 16:20 (see comments), Moses presents the people's response to the Levitical priests as a barometer of their disposition toward Yahweh and his covenant.[1]

---

1. Note also the frequent appeals for charity toward the Levitical priests, along with the fatherless, widows, aliens (14:29; 16:11, 14; 26:12–13), and members of the family (12:12, 18–19).

The Basis of the Levites' Entitlements (18:1 – 2)

THE OPENING STATEMENT CONSISTS of four main clauses, each containing the key word *naḥᵃlâ* ("allotment, grant/property"; NIV "inheritance"; see coments on 1:38). The focus is on a group among the Israelites: "the priests," "Levites," and "the whole tribe of Levi." The first expression refers to those who perform sacrificial rituals and other spiritual ministries at the central sanctuary (10:8; 18:18; 27:9 – 14; 31:9), while the latter two suggest these people trace their origins back to Levi (Gen. 29:34).[2] The expressions "with Israel" (v. 1a) and "among their brothers" (v. 2) reflect the relationship between the Levitical priests and other Israelites. Unlike other tribes, Levi received no territorial allotment when Canaan was divided after the conquest.

The key word *naḥᵃlâ* appears in every line in verses 1 – 2. With the exception of a few passages in Deuteronomy, this word refers to the land of Canaan as Israel's property received from Yahweh.[3] Here Moses anticipates the day when the land is conquered and distributed among the tribes as their grants.[4] However, since the Levites will not receive an allotment, they will be denied a base from which to flourish economically like their fellow Israelites. Although the present comments on the Levites' landless status are based on Numbers 18:20 – 26,[5] Moses speaks of the Levites' compensation as "offerings made to the LORD" (i.e., food gifts),[6] returned to Yahweh as his grant rather than the "tithe."

To compensate for their landless status, Yahweh offers himself as the Levitical priests' grant (v. 2b; cf. Num 18:20). Whereas 4:20 (cf. 32:9) designates Israel as Yahweh's *naḥᵃlâ* ("people of grant"), here Yahweh is the *naḥᵃlâ* of the Levitical priests.[7] In effect, Yahweh invites them to eat from his own table; that which the people present to him, he passes on to them. "As he [Yahweh] promised them" (v. 2) reassures the Levites of their security in him, though the following statement obligates the Israelites to provide for them.

---

2. See Driver, *Deuteronomy*, 213 – 14; J. A. Emerton, "Priests and Levites in Deuteronomy," *VT* 12 (1962): 133 – 34.

3. See 4:21, 38; 10:9; 12:9, 12; 14:27, 29; 15:4; 18:1 – 2; 19:10, 14; 20:16; 21:16, 23; 24:4; 25:19 – 26:1; 29:8[7].

4. For the borders of the national grant, see Num. 34:1 – 12; for the procedures for distributing the tribal grants, see Num. 33:54 and 34:16 – 29. The distribution itself is described in Josh. 13 – 19.

5. According to Num. 26:62, their special status with Yahweh also meant that the Levites were not registered among the troops to engage the Canaanites because no grant was given to them among the people of Israel.

6. So also Milgrom, *Numbers*, 124, on Num. 15:10; idem, *Leviticus 1 – 16*, 161 – 62.

7. After the conquest, the Levites received additional compensation in the form of forty-eight Levitical towns, with their surrounding pasturelands (Josh. 21:1 – 42), in fulfillment (cf. v. 2) of Yahweh's earlier promise in Num. 35:1 – 8.

The Nature of the Levites' Entitlements (18:3–5)

WITH THE ANNOUNCEMENT "NOW this is the share due the priests," this second paragraph concretizes what Moses meant by the food gifts of Yahweh and his grant (v. 1). Yahweh may be the Levitical priests' possession, but he takes care of them by means of the sacrifices that the people bring to him. Moses specifies three types of offerings: meat; the crops of the fields, vineyards, and olive groves; and wool (for clothing and blankets). The gifts brought to the priests must be choice gifts: the shoulder,[8] jowls, and the stomach of the animals; the first of the processed grain, wine, olive oil;[9] and the first fleeces of their flocks. These expressions remind the Israelites of Yahweh's abundant provision and reinforce their duty to treat the priests as generously as Yahweh has treated them.

Whereas verse 2 grounded the Levites' privileges in Yahweh's promise, verse 5 bases them in his election. Here Moses summarizes the Levites' roles as professional worshipers of Yahweh: Yahweh has chosen them "to stand [before Yahweh]"[10] and "[to] minister in the LORD's name always" (cf. v. 7; 10:8). This is official court language, authorizing them to enter the Sovereign's presence to minister to him or to receive a commission from him (cf. Dan. 1:4). The reference to "their descendants" highlights the hereditary nature of the priesthood.

The Range of the Levites' Entitlements (18:6–8)

CONTRARY TO MOST ENGLISH translations,[11] the concern in this paragraph is not to grant Levites from the towns permission to serve in the central sanctuary—this is assumed—but to ensure that all Levites have access to the entitlements.[12] The second person expression "your gates" (NIV "your towns") confirms that this text addresses Israelites, charging them to respect the status and privileges of the Levitical priests.

---

8. On the shoulder of a sacrificial animal as a sacred portion in Israel and the ancient Near East, see Milgrom, *Numbers*, 49.

9. This refers not to the first ripened products or the first harvested, but to the first to be processed (cf. Num. 18:12). See Milgrom, *Leviticus 1–16*, 191.

10. While elsewhere this expression applies to the heavenly host standing at Yahweh's right and left hand (2 Chron. 18:18), or to prophets (Zech 3:1; 2 Chron 29:11), Deuteronomy uses it only of Levitical priests (Deut. 10:8; 18:7).

11. ESV and REB represent notable exceptions. The shift from protasis to apodosis is signaled grammatically in v. 8 by the emphatic object-verb-adverb sentence structure. So also Nelson, *Deuteronomy*, 227.

12. The protasis of this paragraph consists of three conditional sentences (vv. 6–7), which are followed by the apodosis in v. 8. All three conditional statements consist of a main clause followed by a modifying clause.

In verses 6−7 Moses invites all Levites to participate in the prerequisites described in verses 3−5 by presenting a hypothetical scenario involving a Levite who leaves his hometown and comes to the central sanctuary.[13] Moses affirms the impulse of a Levite driven by a personal desire to worship at the place that Yahweh has chosen (cf. 12:15), granting full permission not only to worship at the central sanctuary but also to join fellow Levites in ministering in Yahweh's name. Portraying them as "brothers" serving in the name of Yahweh and standing before him, this text assumes neither conflict nor competition between priests who serve at the central sanctuary and those who serve in outlying locations.

On the surface this invitation to Levites from outlying districts seems to contradict Numbers 18, which distinguishes between Aaron and his sons, who are authorized to perform cultic service within the sanctuary, and the Levites, who may not. However, Moses does not specify the rituals they may perform in the temple. These Levites are no threat to the high priest and his sons, who enjoy hereditary title to inner sanctuary service. Their role may be purely auxiliary, but even then they are performing "priestly" service in the presence of Yahweh at his invitation. Since Deuteronomy encourages worshipers from the towns to bring Levites with them to the central sanctuary, it is reasonable to assume they would serve in the presence of Yahweh by tending to the spiritual needs of those from their towns.

In verse 8 Moses finally gets to the point of this paragraph: equal prerequisites for equal service. The expression "a portion like a portion" (NIV "share equally") creates an effective envelope around this passage (cf. v. 1) and highlights Moses' concern for all Levites. He insists that those who move to the central sanctuary are entitled to the food prerequisites of verses 3−5, just like those who are based there. The last clause of verse 8 is unclear. In general, it seems that when Levites move to the central sanctuary, their dues there are not to be reduced simply because they continue to have income from inherited property back home.[14] In any case, it is doubtful the text envisages the move to the central sanctuary to be permanent.[15]

---

13. As in 12:5, the verb *bô'* ("come"; NIV "moves") orients the hearer/reader to the perspective of the speaker, who here represents the voice of the central sanctuary.

14. On *hā'ābôt* ("the fathers"; NIV "family") meaning "patrimony," see T. E. Ranck, "Patrimony in Deuteronomy 18:8—A Possible Explanation," in *The Answers Lie Below: Essays in Honor of Lawrence Edward Toombs* (ed. H. Thompson; Lanham, MD: Univ. Press of America, 1984), 281−85.

15. Several priests performed duties at one place while residing at another: Abiathar (1 Kings 2:26−27), Jeremiah (Jer. 32:6−25). See further, M. Haran, *Temples and Temple Service in Ancient Israel: An Inquiry into Biblical Cult Phenomena and the Historical Setting of the Priestly School* (Winona Lake, IN: Eisenbrauns, 1985), 119−20.

THE LEVITES IN THEIR **towns**. In Numbers 35:1−8 Yahweh commanded the Israelites to set aside forty-eight cities and surrounding pasture-lands scattered throughout the land for the Levites. Joshua 21:1−42 describes the fulfillment of this command, cataloguing the Levitical cities in each tribal territory. Nowhere does the Old Testament explain the function of these cities or the roles the Levites were to play there. The purpose of these cities seems to have been to ensure that every region had access to pastoral care, which would involve caring for the needy, administering cleansing rituals, presiding over local sacrifices (cf. 1 Sam. 9:12−13; cf. 8:16−17; 9:12−24; 16:1−6) and ceremonies of blessings and cursing (cf. 27:9−14; Josh. 8:33), teaching Torah (31:9−13; 33:8−11), generally keeping alive the traditions of Israel, ensuring covenant fidelity, and representing the central sanctuary in the far-flung regions of the land.

While Levitical cities never appear in Old Testament narratives,[16] the shiftlessness of the Levites in Judges 17−18 and 19−20 suggests the Levites themselves quickly lost their spiritual way after the settlement. No doubt their irresponsibility contributed to the national loss of memory regarding Yahweh and his saving acts (Judg. 2:10).[17]

A BIBLICAL THEOLOGY OF **ministry**. This passage has great significance for developing a biblical theology of ministry. (1) To be called into divine service is the highest calling imaginable. The Levites' claim to Yahweh as their special grant and the guarantor of their well-being was unique among the Israelites. However, Yahweh promised to meet their needs indirectly, through the gifts of his people. In their dependence on God, the Levites modeled the relationship with God that Israel as a nation enjoyed and ministers today enjoy.

(2) Because the Lord himself chooses and summons those who stand before him and serve in his name, divine service is a vocation, not a profession. "To stand before God" means that we listen carefully to his voice and commit ourselves to doing his will, and "to serve in his name" means that we receive our authority from him and that everything we do is driven by

---

16. Hence scholarly skepticism regarding these accounts. See J. R. Spencer, "Levitical Cities," *ABD*, 4:310−11.

17. Ezek. 44:15 complains that the Levitical priests in charge of the central sanctuary defected from Yahweh.

the passion to glorify him. Whereas the Scriptures concerning Israel speak of these as privileges reserved for angels (Luke 1:19), prophets (1 Kings 17:1; Jer. 23:18, 22), and priests (Zech. 3:1; Heb. 10:11–12), the New Testament teaching on the priesthood of all believers (1 Peter 2:9) means that because of the work of Jesus Christ believers collectively have direct access to God and responsibility to represent him to the unbelieving world.

A Schematic Portrayal of the Location and Function of the Levitical Cities

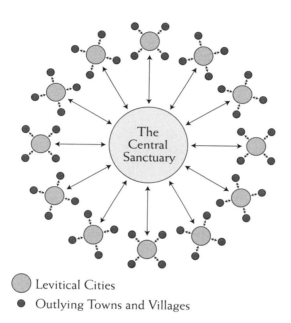

⬤ Levitical Cities

● Outlying Towns and Villages

(3) This passage provides an Old Testament illustration of the truth declared by Paul to Timothy, "The elders who direct the affairs of the church well are worthy of double honor, especially those whose work is preaching and teaching. For the Scripture says, 'Do not muzzle the ox while it is treading out the grain,' and 'The worker deserves his wages'" (1 Tim. 5:17–18). Those called into the Lord's service need to be freed up from the demands of normal gainful employment so that they may attend to the work of the Lord without distraction. In ancient Israel destitute Levites were a disgrace to the nation and a blot on Yahweh's reputation.[18] Similarly today, the manner in which God's people attend to his servants

---

18. Cf. McConville, *Law and Theology in Deuteronomy*, 151.

is a barometer of their spiritual health. A minister in need is a symptom of a people living independently of God. "Righteousness, only righteousness" (see 16:20) demands that God's people care for those whom he has called into his service with generosity and liberality.

Deuteronomy 18:9–22

W hen you enter the land the LORD your God is
giving you, do not learn to imitate the detestable
ways of the nations there. ¹⁰Let no one be found
among you who sacrifices his son or daughter in the fire, who
practices divination or sorcery, interprets omens, engages in
witchcraft, ¹¹or casts spells, or who is a medium or spiritist
or who consults the dead. ¹²Anyone who does these things is
detestable to the LORD, and because of these detestable practices the LORD your God will drive out those nations before
you. ¹³You must be blameless before the LORD your God.

¹⁴The nations you will dispossess listen to those who
practice sorcery or divination. But as for you, the LORD your
God has not permitted you to do so. ¹⁵The LORD your God
will raise up for you a prophet like me from among your own
brothers. You must listen to him. ¹⁶For this is what you asked
of the LORD your God at Horeb on the day of the assembly
when you said, "Let us not hear the voice of the LORD our
God nor see this great fire anymore, or we will die."

¹⁷The LORD said to me: "What they say is good. ¹⁸I will
raise up for them a prophet like you from among their brothers; I will put my words in his mouth, and he will tell them
everything I command him. ¹⁹If anyone does not listen to
my words that the prophet speaks in my name, I myself will
call him to account. ²⁰But a prophet who presumes to speak
in my name anything I have not commanded him to say, or a
prophet who speaks in the name of other gods, must be put
to death."

²¹You may say to yourselves, "How can we know when
a message has not been spoken by the LORD?" ²²If what a
prophet proclaims in the name of the LORD does not take
place or come true, that is a message the LORD has not
spoken. That prophet has spoken presumptuously. Do not be
afraid of him.

UNDOUBTEDLY MANY IN MOSES' audience worried about their future after he was gone. In his first address he reminded them that he would be denied the joy of crossing the Jordan and that Joshua would deliver the land into their hands (1:38; 3:21–22, 28). However, the question remained: What would happen when Joshua was gone as well? Since 16:18 Moses has been answering this question, challenging the people to pursue righteousness, but also reassuring them that they will not be leaderless. He has charged them to appoint judges (16:18), highlighted the role of the priests (17:9–12; 18:1–8), and approved the people's future impulse to set a king over themselves (17:14–20) in order to maintain righteousness. Although Moses served to a greater or lesser degree in all these capacities, none represented his primary role—as conduit for continued divine revelation to the people. To whom should the people turn for a word from God once Moses was gone? In 18:9–22 he answers this question.[1]

Contrary to those who treat 16:18–18:22 as a document on Israelite polity, Deuteronomy 18:9–22 bears scarcely any legal flavor at all. The catalogue of abominable practices in verses 10–11 seeks precision, but the remainder of verses 9–14 consists of theological justification for the taboo on pagan forms of divination (vv. 9, 12) and explicit sermonic exhortation (vv. 13, 14b). Verses 15–22 sound more like a gracious provision of continued access to communication from Yahweh than legal prescription. The passage divides into three parts: the foil for the promise of a prophet like Moses (vv. 9–14); the nature of the promise of a prophet like Moses (vv. 15–20); the challenge to the promise of a prophet like Moses (vv. 21–22). Each part makes its own special contribution to the overall theme of 16:18–18:22: "righteousness, only righteousness" (see comments on 16:20).

The Foil for the Promise of a Prophet Like Moses (18:9–14)

THE THEME OF RIGHTEOUSNESS is particularly evident in this first paragraph, which presents hearer and reader with two contrasting ways: the abominable way of the nations (v. 9b) and the way of perfection with Yahweh (v. 13). The word "abominations" (vv. 9b, 12a, 12b) functions as the key word of this entire paragraph, a conclusion reinforced by the grammatically awkward comment at the end (in v. 14). Two lexically similar but substantively contrasting statements serve as boundaries of this subunit (vv. 9, 14).

---

1. So also Lothar Perlitt, "Mose als Prophet," *Evangelische Theologie* 31 (1971): 596–97. Cf. the repeated occurrence of the verb *šāmaᶜ* ("to listen"; vv. 14, 15, 16, 19).

The first affirms Yahweh's gift of land; the second denies his gift of divinatory revelation.

The opening clause of verse 9 describes the circumstances in which the following instructions will apply. The paragraph displays numerous links with 12:29—31. (1) It opens with a reference to the nations. (2) It sets the stage for the promise of a prophet like Moses by describing a potential problem that the nations will pose. (3) It characterizes the conduct of the nations as "detestable." (4) The cryptic reference to the sacrifice of children abbreviates a fuller and more explicit statement in 12:31. (5) The concluding comment in 18:14 answers to "You must not worship the LORD your God in their way" in 12:31a. It seems that Moses' promise of a prophet in verses 15—18 has intentionally picked up on 12:29—31.

The last clause of verse 9 functions as a theme statement for verses 9—14: "Do not learn to imitate the detestable ways of the nations there." This sets the stage for Moses' description of the way the nations communicate with their gods, or more precisely, manipulate the gods to communicate with them. He prefaces the list of abominable practices with the statement "There shall not be found among you ..." (pers. trans.; cf. 17:2). Verses 10—11 are not exhaustive,[2] but they provide the fullest catalogue of divinatory expressions in the Old Testament.[3] The distinctions between these expressions are not entirely clear, but each makes a specific contribution to the understanding of divination in the ancient Near East.[4]

(1) Passing children through the fire (v. 10; cf. NIV text note). The expression refers to the sacrifice of children and is often associated with the worship of Molech (Lev. 20:2—5).[5] Such offerings were presented as pious fulfillments of vows made to the deity or as expressions of thanksgiving for answered prayers (cf. Judg. 11:34—40).[6] Leviticus 20:2—5 characterizes

---

2. Several forms are missing: dreaming dreams (cf. 13:1—5[2—6]; Gen. 20:3, 6; 37:5, 9; 40:5, 8; 41:11, 15; Judg. 7:13, 15; Dan. 2:1, 3), magic (Gen. 41:8, 24; Ex. 7:11, 22; 8:7, 18, 19[3, 14, 15]; 9:11), and consulting teraphim (2 Kings 23:24; Ezek. 21:21[26]).

3. Compare 2 Kings 17:17; 21:6; 2 Chron. 33:6; Isa. 8:19; Jer. 27:9.

4. On each of these expressions see I. Fischer, *Gotteskünderinnen: Zu einer geschlechterfairen Deutung des Phänomens der Prophetie und der Prophetinnen in der Hebräischen Bibel* (Stuttgart: Kohlhammer, 2000), 43—49.

5. While some argue for an interpretation other than child sacrifice (cf. Tigay, *Deuteronomy*, 465), the links with 12:31 support this interpretation. For full discussion see G. C. Heider, *The Cult of Molech: A Reassessment* (JSOTSup 43; Sheffield: JSOT, 1985); J. Day, *Molech: A God of Human Sacrifice in the Old Testament* (Cambridge: Cambridge Univ. Press, 1989).

6. See L. E. Stager, "The Rite of Child Sacrifice at Carthage," in *New Light on Ancient Carthage* (ed. J. G. Pedley; Ann Arbor: Univ. of Michigan Press, 1980), 1—11. For a popular presentation of the evidence see L. E. Stager and S. R. Wolff, "Child Sacrifice at Carthage— Religious Rite or Population Control," *BAR* 10/1 (1984): 30—51.

child sacrifice as utterly abhorrent. To use this means to manipulate the deity intensifies evil.

(2) Divination (*qᵉsāmîm*). The expression "diviners of divinations" (lit. trans.) involves the most general term for augury.[7] The Old Testament applies the expression to a variety of techniques employed to determine the mind of the gods.[8]

(3) Sorcery (*mᵉᶜônēn*). The meaning of this word is uncertain. While it may be related to "cloud" (*ᶜānān*), we should probably associate it with the root *ᶜnn*, which in the Piel means "to cause to become visible."[9] This suggests some sort of necromantic activity.[10] Elsewhere the expression is associated with witchcraft (Lev. 19:26; Mic. 5:12[11]).[11]

(4) Omens (*mᵉnaḥēš*). This expression probably refers to an interpreter of omens. Although an etymological link with the word *nāḥāš* ("snake") has long been advocated, this seems unlikely in view of the reference to Joseph's "divining" cup in Genesis 44:5, 16.[12]

(5) Witchcraft (*mᵉkaššēp*). Since Exodus 22:18[17] prohibits whatever is meant by this word as a capital crime, it seems to refer to some form of black magic associated with magicians and at least one other class of divinatory expert.[13]

---

7. Cf. Num. 23:23; Josh. 13:22; 1 Sam. 6:2; 28:8; 2 Kings 17:17; Isa. 3:2; 44:25; Jer. 27:9; 29:8; Ezek. 13:9, 23; 21:21–29[26–34]; Mic. 3:6, 7, 11; Zech. 10:2. Cf. F. H. Cryer, *Divination in Ancient Israel and Its Near Eastern Environment: A Socio-Historical Investigation* (JSOTSup 142; Sheffield: JSOT, 1994], 256.

8. Rhabdomancy (Ezek. 21:21[26]), hepatoscopy (Ezek. 21:21[26]), consulting teraphim (2 Kings 23:24; Ezek. 21:21[26]; Zech. 10:2), astrology (Jer. 10:2), hydromancy (Gen. 44:5, 15), and necromancy (1 Sam. 28:3–9). The word "divination" is associated with Ammonites (Jer. 27:3, 9; Ezek. 21:29[34]), Phoenicians, Moabites, and Edomites (Jer. 27:3, 9), Philistines (1 Sam. 6:2), Balaam the Mesopotamian prophet (Num. 22:7; 23:23), as well as Saul and the witch at Endor (1 Sam. 28:8). For a sampling of divination texts from Assyria, see I. Starr, *Queries to the Sungod: Divination and Politics in Sargonid Assyria* (SAA 4; Helsinki: Helsinki Univ. Press, 1990).

9. *HALOT*, 857.

10. Thus also H. L. Bosman, "Redefined Prophecy as Deuteronomic Alternative to Divination in Deut. 18:19–22," *Acts Theologica* 16 (1996): 3.

11. Cf. Judg. 9:37; 2 Kings 21:6; 2 Chron. 33:6; Isa. 2:6; 57:3; Jer. 27:9.

12. Cf. Lev. 19:26; Num. 23:23; 24:1; 2 Kings 17:17; 21:6; 2 Chron. 33:6. The omen literature from ancient Mesopotamia is vast. For sample collections, see E. V. Leichty, *The Omen Series Summa Izbu* (TCS 4; Locust Valley, NY: J. J. Augustin, 1970); R. I. Caplice, *The Akkadian Namburbi Texts: An Introduction* (SANE 1/1; Los Angeles: Undena, 1974). On the meaning of *nāḥāš*, see Cryer (*Divination*, 257–58), who notes that in Jewish tradition this was the *foreign* expression for divination par excellence.

13. Ex. 7:11, "wise men"; Dan. 2:2, "astrologers," and "Chaldaeans." Cf. 2 Kings 9:22; Isa. 47:9,12; Jer. 27:9; Mic. 5:12[11]; Mal. 3:5; 2 Chron. 33:6 (see Cryer, *Divination*, 258).

---

(6) Casting spells (*ḥôbēr ḥāber*). This word appears to be derived from a root "to bind," suggesting one who has the ability to bind someone with a spell.[14]

(7) Mediums (to consult ghosts: *šāʾal ʾôb*). The verb "to ask, consult" is clear, but the etymology of *ʾôb* is not. The term probably refers to the spirit of someone deceased,[15] suggesting the person who asks is a medium able to communicate with the spirit of the dead (cf. 1 Sam. 28:3, 8; Isa. 8:19).

(8) Spiritists (*yiddᵉᶜônî*). The word derives from the root *yādaᶜ* ("to know"). It occurs only in association with *ʾôb* and may represent an alternative expression for one who can communicate with the spirit of a deceased acquaintance.[16]

(9) Calling up the dead (*dôrēš ʾel hammētîm*). "Those who inquire of the dead" clearly speaks of necromancy, consulting the dead. The practice is based on the assumption that the deceased continue to have an influence on the affairs of the living.[17]

The practices in this list are all intended to manipulate deities, supernatural forces, and the spirits of the deceased to act in the worshiper's favor. They are grounded on several fundamental assumptions. (1) There is a link between the natural and supernatural world that makes cooperation between these spheres possible. (2) There is a world of supernatural forces that constantly threaten human beings or that may be harnessed for personal benefit. (3) The wills and operations of supernatural forces may be deciphered in natural phenomena through unsolicited omens (e.g., solar eclipses, birth anomalies) and solicited omens (examining entrails, dropping arrows). (4) By invoking the gods or manipulating other supernatural forces, a person may affect the outcome of events. (5) Since magic is a science, these skills can be taught and learned.[18]

The biblical response to divination, magic, and necromancy presupposes that these practices actually worked.[19] While in certain cases Yahweh

---

14. Cf. Cryer, *Divination*, 259.

15. The word appears elsewhere in Lev. 19:31; 20:6, 27; 1 Sam. 28:3, 9; 2 Kings 21:6; 23:24; 1 Chron. 10:13; 2 Chron. 33:6; Isa. 8:19; 19:3; 29:4.

16. The word appears elsewhere in Lev. 19:31; 20:6, 27; 1 Sam. 28:3,9; 2 Kings 21:6; 23:24; 2 Chron. 33:6; Isa. 8:19; 19:3. Cryer (*Divination*, 261) suggests that RSV's "wizard" is as good as any.

17. This expression occurs elsewhere only in Isa. 8:19, though a similar construction in 12:5 speaks of pilgrimages to the place Yahweh chooses for his name. Cryer (*Divination*, 259) suggests this is synonymous with #7.

18. Thus G. Frantz-Szabó, "Hittite Witchcraft, Magic, and Divination," *CANE*, 3:2007. Hence the warning in v. 9 not to "learn" the abominations of the nations. On divination and magic in the ancient world, see W. Farber, "Witchcraft, Magic and Divination in Ancient Mesopotamia," *CANE* 3:1895 – 910; J.-M. de Tarragon, "Witchcraft, Magic, and Divination in Canaan and Ancient Israel," *CANE*, 3:2071 – 82.

19. Cf. Gen. 44:1 – 5; Ex. 7:11 – 12, 22; 8:7[3]; 1 Sam. 28:8 – 14; Ezek. 21:21 – 22[26 – 27].

overrode fundamentally pagan practices and used them to achieve his own ends, in his eyes divination, magic, and necromancy were as abominable as idolatry itself. The present categorical repudiation of these practices is also grounded on several fundamental convictions. (1) Just as idolatry represents the perverted worship of objects made by human hands (Deut. 4:15–18, 28), so divination, magic, and necromancy represent humanly designed techniques for communicating with the deity that substitute for the gracious communication that Yahweh himself has offered. (2) These divinatory procedures were designed to manipulate deity to fulfill human agendas. This reflects the antithesis of faith and circumvents the means by which Yahweh has promised to speak unambiguously and directly. It also upsets the divine order, which calls on humans to fulfill the divine agenda rather than vice versa. (3) Most significantly, these techniques assume faulty views of the relationship between the natural and supernatural world.

Moses' restates his hostility toward these practices in verses 12–13. Not only are the practices detestable, but "anyone who does these things" is an abomination of Yahweh (v. 12a). Here actor and action are identified. To reinforce the notion, Moses declares that although the Israelites' possession of the land had nothing to do with their own righteousness, the wickedness of the nations living there was a factor in Yahweh's driving them out (cf. 9:4–5).

Verses 13–14 establish the bar of conduct: the nations may listen to fortunetellers and diviners, but Israelites may not. They must be "blameless" (*tāmîm*) in their relationship with Yahweh. This word carries a moral sense expressing the totality of a person's commitment to Yahweh as expressed in the second half of the Shema (6:5; cf. 32:4; Gen. 6:9; 17:1; Job 1:2).[20] This appeal to be blameless reiterates the call for "righteousness, only righteousness," with which this larger section began (see 16:20 and comments).

Verse 14 concludes with an awkward but emphatic note, "But you not thus [i.e., listening to fortunetellers and diviners] did Yahweh your God grant [permission]" (pers. trans.). This may be interpreted as understatement for what Yahweh has prohibited (cf. 17:3), but in light of 4:19, Moses seems to rein in an earlier comment—that Yahweh allotted the astral objects to all the peoples—as authorization for their worship. Moses rejects any appeal to divine revelation to justify pagan forms of communication with Yahweh.

The Nature of the Promise of a Prophet Like Moses (18:15–20)

BECAUSE YAHWEH PROMISES TO provide Israel with prophets, there is no need to resort to divination, magic, and necromancy to determine his

---

20. For a helpful study of *tāmîm* and its ethical significance, see John N. Oswalt, *Called to Be Holy* (Napanee, IN: Evangel, 1999), 46–63.

will.[21] Moses contrasts the multiplicity of techniques the nations use with the singular provision of Yahweh by frontloading the subject in verse 15: "[Instead] a prophet from your midst from among your brothers like me Yahweh your God will raise up for you; to him you must listen" (pers. trans.). Impulses that drive others to abhorrent magical practices[22] will be satisfied in Yahweh's provision of the prophetic institution.

Verse 15 introduces several important features of Israelite prophecy in general and of true prophets in particular. (1) The medium of divine revelation is called a *nābî'* ("one called [by God]"; see also comments on 13:1).

(2) As the designation implies, a true prophet of Yahweh is raised up by Yahweh himself.[23] Here the verb *hēqîm* ("to raise up)" bears a distributive sense, referring not to a single appointment but to a series, from time to time as needed (cf. Judg. 2:18).

(3) True prophets are native Israelites, raised up from "among the brothers" of Israel.

(4) This prophet will be like Moses.[24] While the text does not yet explain what this means, presumably it includes (a) his mediatorial role; (b) access to the presence of Yahweh and membership in his council (Num. 12:7; cf. Jer. 23:16—22); (c) participation in clear, unambiguous, and direct conversation with God (Num. 12:8); and (d) his divine endowment with the spirit of prophecy (cf. Num. 11:25—26). This paradigm of prophecy contrasts starkly to indirect, obscure, and ambiguous divination.

In verses 16—20 Moses takes the Israelites back to Horeb to provide an illustration of the kind of prophecy he has in mind. In his typical narrative style, Moses casts this section in dialogue form. In verse 16b he quotes the people's verbal response to the frightening theophany at Horeb (sixteen words); in verses 17—20 he provides a verbatim report of Yahweh's response (fifty words). The framing narrative illustrates the Mosaic paradigm of prophecy: the people make a request of Yahweh, and Yahweh answers to Moses.

---

21. Cf. Levine, *Numbers*, 200.

22. For further discussion on the relationship between Israelite prophecy and divination, see T. W. Overholt, *Channels of Prophecy: The Social Dynamics of Prophetic Activity* (Minneapolis: Fortress, 1989), 117—47; H. M. Barstad, "No Prophets? Recent Developments in Biblical Prophetic Research and Ancient Near Eastern Prophecy," *JSOT* 57 (1993): 47—49.

23. The verb *hēqîm* ("to raise up" and entrust with a commission) is used elsewhere of divinely appointed saviors (Judg. 3:9, 15), tribal chieftains (Judg. 2:16, 18), a king (1 Kings 14:14), a priest (1 Sam. 2:35), sentries (Jer. 6:17), and shepherds (Jer. 23:4; Ezek. 34:23; Zech. 11:16).

24. On the attributive modifier "like me," highlighting the professional relationship between the one whom Yahweh will raise up and Moses, see A. Schüle, "*Kāmôkā* — der Nächste wie Du: Zur Philologie des Liebesgebotes von Lev. 19,18.34," *Kleine Untersuchungen zur Sprache des Alten Testaments un seiner Umwelt* 2 (2001): 118.

In verse 16, Moses summarizes what he recounted in 4:10—13 and 5:22—26, though the tone and perspective differ. With most translations, the NIV renders the first two statements as cohortatives, but the verbs are indicatives[25] and should be rendered something like: "I cannot continue to hear the voice of Yahweh my God, and as for this great fire, I cannot watch it any more, or I will die."[26] Moses introduced the speech as a request, but his citation omits the petition, noting only the intolerable nature of what the people had witnessed at Horeb.

The opening line in Yahweh's response (v. 17) provides a direct link with the end of 5:28, while 18:18 corresponds roughly to 5:31 and 18:19 to 5:32—33a. Otherwise this speech goes its own way. Since Moses' purpose in chapter 5 was to highlight his role as mediator of revelation in the present, there was no need to cite Yahweh's comments on Moses' significance for the future. As he so often does, oriented to Israel's life in the land, Moses draws out the implications of a past event for their future. In God's mind Moses' prophetic assignment at Horeb both solved a present issue and became paradigmatic for a future succession of prophets. The following discussion follows the threefold structure of Yahweh's speech.

(1) The promise of future prophets like Moses (v. 18a). Except for adjustments in word order and the shift from third to first person, Yahweh's words in verse 18a largely repeat what Moses had said in verse 15 (cf. 5:31a).

(2) The nature of future prophetic activity (v. 18b). This portrayal of prophetic activity is more concrete than in 5:31. Whereas Yahweh had previously told Moses the statutes and laws, in the future he will put his words in prophets' mouths.[27] For Moses this meant passing on the revelation he had received at Sinai, and now the contents of the speeches of Deuteronomy. Whereas 5:31 had characterized Moses' speech as teaching, here prophetic utterance is described as "speaking" all that Yahweh commands him to say.

Moses hereby assures his people that Yahweh will not leave them without authorized teachers when he is gone and they have crossed into the land, nor will they need to go to the nations to learn their ways of communicating with deity (cf. v. 9). Other people consult unreliable mediums, diviners, and magicians, but Yahweh will install his own authorized spokespersons. Others receive only vague and ambiguous messages, but the Israelites will hear the clear and unambiguous word of Yahweh.[28] Moses

---

25. So also Driver, *Deuteronomy*, 228.

26. Similarly Christensen, *Deuteronomy 1:1—21:9*, 401.

27. On the placement of God's words on the mouth of the prophet, see also Ex. 4:15—16; 7:1; Jer. 1:9.

28. Variations of "he will speak all that I command him" occur often in Deuteronomy. Here the clause suggests equivalence in authority between the Torah of Moses and future prophecy.

illustrates his point by speaking in the divine first person. Yahweh had indeed put the words on his mouth.

(3) The *gravitas* of future prophetic activity (vv. 19–20). Moses concludes the citation with Yahweh's appeal to take his prophets' messages seriously. Like the Levitical priests (10:8; 18:5), for the prophet to "speak in my name" (v. 19) is to speak with Yahweh's authority and on his behalf.[29] Yahweh describes the consequence of rejecting his words delivered by the prophet vaguely as "I myself will call him to account." Whoever disobeys the prophet will have to answer to Yahweh, who sent him. To spurn the messenger is to spurn Yahweh.

Yahweh reinforces the *gravitas* of the prophetic ministry with an impassioned word to those who will abuse the office by prophesying falsely. Yahweh identifies two characteristics of false prophets. (a) Presumptuously (see comments on 1:43; 7:13) they may claim to make pronouncements in Yahweh's name when Yahweh has never authorized them to do so. (b) They may speak in the name of other gods (v. 20b). The fate pronounced on such prophets is severe; like those who lead Israelites into the worship of other gods, they must die. While Yahweh does not specify the form of execution, the analogy of chapter 13 and 17:2–7 suggests stoning as the likely means.

The Challenge to the Promise of a Prophet Like Moses (18:21–22).

THE SHIFT TO THE second person of direct address and references to Yahweh in the third person in verse 21 signals a return to the voice of Moses. As elsewhere, Moses introduces a hypothetical interlocutor,[30] who sets the stage for his own comments with a question: How may we recognize a prophetic message that does not come from Yahweh? Whereas Yahweh focused on the marks of a false prophet (v. 20), Moses focuses on the marks of false prophecy. If one can identify a false prophecy, one may identify a false prophet, who should be executed.

On the surface, Moses' answer is not helpful. If utterances that a prophet claims to speak in the name of Yahweh are not fulfilled,[31] the prophecy is false, and the prophet is a charlatan. Since what Yahweh predicts happens

---

29. Cf. Merrill, *Deuteronomy*, 273.

30. The same construction (minus the conjunction), "If you say in your heart/mind" followed by a direct quotation, occurs in 7:17 (cf. 8:17; 9:4). For variations in introductions to interlocutors, see 6:20; 12:20; 13:2[3], 6[7], 13[14]; 17:14.

31. Moses' expressions for nonfulfillment are simple: literally, "The word does not happen and it does not come" (cf. Jer. 28:9). By contrast, a prediction that is fulfilled is referred to as "a word that does not fall" (see Josh. 21:45; 23:14, 15; 1 Kings 8:56; 2 Kings 10:10).

by definition, the pronouncement has not come from him.[32] However, if a prophecy concerns the distant future, the veracity of a statement and the proof of a genuine prophet will be delayed and the prophet may not live to witness his vindication.[33] Moses does not answer this dilemma but concludes this discussion with counsel regarding the proper disposition toward prophets whose words do not come true. This is a sign that such prophets have spoken presumptuously (v. 22), and they should not be feared. The words of false prophets are powerless, and by executing them the people will be standing up for righteousness.

TRUE AND FALSE PROPHECY. This passage is critical for understanding the differences between true and false prophecy, and the significance of the source and authority of the prophecy. The possibilities envisioned by Moses may be represented diagrammatically:

True and False Prophecy in Israel

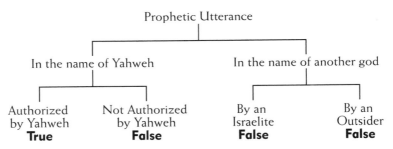

The problem of true versus false prophecy was widely recognized in the ancient Near East. Outside Israel, those seeking a prophetic word often consulted more than one prophetic source to confirm the veracity of an utterance. In Assyria, prophets were considered false if their utterances contradicted the interests of the king or his crown prince.[34] The account

---

32. This distinctive quality of Yahweh's utterances (vis-à-vis lifeless and speechless idols) is reflected in numerous passages in Isaiah: Isa. 41:4, 21–24; 44:24–28; 45:21–25; 46:5–13; 48:3; 55:10; 59:21 (cf. 22:11).

33. See Jer. 29:10; Ezek. 2:5; 33:21–22, 33.

34. For a study of true and false prophecy in Assyria see M. Nissinen, "Falsche Prophetie in neuassyrischer und deuteronomistischer Darstellung," in *Das Deuteronomium und seine Querbeziehungen* (ed. T. Veijola; Schriften der Finnischen Exegetischen Gesellschaft 62; Göttingen: Vandenhoeck & Ruprecht, 1996), 172–95. M. Nissinen, C. L. Seow, and R. K. Ritner have

of Ahab and Micaiah ben Imlah in 1 Kings 22 suggests that occasionally in Israel this criterion was also followed. Ahab had four hundred prophetic lackeys to support his policies (v. 6), but his ally Jehoshaphat requested professional opinion from a prophet of Yahweh to confirm the unanimous utterance of the four hundred (v. 7).[35] Ironically, from the perspective of biblical authors, true prophets tended to oppose the kings, especially when their character and actions were perfidious. A true prophet is one who is true to the divine King, Yahweh himself.

By combining the information provided here with chapter 13, a series of criteria for testing the veracity of a prophet emerge. (1) A true prophet never undermines loyalty to Yahweh or encourages allegiance to any other god (13:1–5[2–6]). (2) A true prophet functions within the Mosaic paradigm, being commissioned by Yahweh and receiving messages from him. Therefore, true prophetic utterances will always be in accordance with and not contrary to the Torah of Moses. (3) True prophecies come to the prophet at God's initiative rather than through professional manipulation of humanly devised means. (4) True prophets speak only in the name of Yahweh. Just as all other claimants to the status of deity are false (cf. 4:28), so all who claim to speak on the authority of another god are deluded and their utterances are lies. (5) The utterances of true prophets are always fulfilled; the nonfulfillment of a prediction confirms the inauthenticity of the predictor.

Based on Exodus 4:1–9, to these we may add a sixth criterion: True prophets may accompany their verbal utterances with authenticating signs. However, since false prophets were able sometimes to do the same (Deut. 13:1–2[2–3]; cf. Ex. 7:10), by itself this criterion is not always reliable. Jeremiah 29:22–23 suggests that the character of the prophet may also serve as a criterion of authenticity.

Later prophets built on Yahweh's comment that he puts his words in prophets' mouths by imagining that prophetic orders were given to prophets just as kings gave orders to their courtiers. Jeremiah denounced false prophets like Zedekiah, who prophesied falsely in Yahweh's name but had never been commissioned by him (Jer. 27:15) and had never stood in his council to receive a message from him (23:16–18). Prophets who typically "tickled the people's ears" with messages of peace are false, in contrast to Jeremiah himself, who found it extremely difficult to convince religious

gathered and published in convenient form first and second millennium BC prophetic texts from Mari, Assyria, Babylonia, Aram (Syria), Ammon, and Egypt in *Prophets and Prophecy in the Ancient Near East* (SBLWAW 12; Atlanta: Society of Biblical Literature, 2003).

35. For analysis of this text and its implications for understanding true and false prophecy see D. I. Block, "What Has Delphi to Do with Samaria? Ambiguity and Delusion in Israelite Prophecy," in *Writing and Ancient Near Eastern Society: Papers in Honour of Alan R. Millard* (ed. P. Bienkowski, C. Mee, and E. Slater; New York/London: T&T Clark, 2005), 189–216.

leaders (priests and prophets) that with his messages of doom, he was actually speaking in the name of Yahweh (Jer. 26:1–19).

Ezekiel encountered the same sort of "auto-inspired" prophets, who presumptuously used all the prophetic formulas. They called people to attention with "Hear the word of the LORD!" (Ezek. 13:2), began their speeches with the citation formula, "This is what the Sovereign LORD says" (13:3), and then stamped their address with the oral signatory formula, "the declaration of the Sovereign LORD" (pers. trans. 13:6, 7).[36] While accounts of the execution of false prophets are rare, the fates of the prophets of Baal (1 Kings 18:19–40; 2 Kings 10:19; cf. Jer. 2:8; 23:13) and Asherah (1 Kings 18:19) demonstrate the seriousness of Yahweh's threats.

Within Deuteronomy, Moses himself functions as the prophet par excellence; his influence in Israel was unmatched (34:10–12). Although scholars debate who "the prophet like Moses" might have been,[37] later texts create the impression that true prophets did indeed function within the Mosaic paradigm. The triad of divine speeches in Judges 2:1–3; 6:7–10; and 10:11–14 are thoroughly Mosaic in tone, vocabulary, and substance; Yahweh did not let one word of Samuel fail, confirming him as prophet in Israel (1 Sam. 3:19–21); David recognized the oracle of Nathan as "this Torah for all humanity" (2 Sam. 7:19, pers. trans.); Yahweh sent Elijah back to Horeb for a fresh revelation of himself and a recommissioning to prophetic service (1 Kings 19:1–21); Yahweh placed his words in Jeremiah's mouth (Jer. 1:9); and Yahweh called on Ezekiel to stand so he could speak with him (Ezek. 1:28–2:1).

Common to these and many more prophetic appearances is the notion that the Mosaic Torah was not the final revelation from God. Mercifully, it seems that every generation was visited by "his servants the prophets."[38] These prophets did not come with radically new messages; their mission was to call the people back to Yahweh and to apply the Torah to new and ever-changing situations.[39] If the people rejected their messages, the prophets pronounced judgment on them, but these pronouncements were rooted in the covenant curses of Leviticus 26 and Deuteronomy 28.

I have suggested above that in this context "a prophet like Moses" refers to a succession of prophets whom Yahweh would raise up, keeping open

---

36. On these prophetic formulae, see Block, *Ezekiel Chapters 1–24*, 32–34.

37. R. Polzin (*Moses and the Deuteronomist: A Literary Study of the Deuteronomic History* [New York: Seabury, 1980], 61) suggests "The 'prophet like Moses' is the narrator of the Deuteronomic History, and through him the Deuteronomist himself."

38. 2 Kings 9:7; 17:13, 23; 21:10; 24:2; Ezra 9:11; Jer. 7:25; 25:4; 26:5; 29:19; 35:15; 44:4; Ezek. 38:17; Dan. 9:6, 10; Amos 3:7; Zech. 1:6.

39. Cf. J. Maier, "Das jüdische Gesetz zwischen Qumran und Septuaginta," in *Im Brennpunkt: Die Septuaginta: Studien zur Entstehung und Bedeutung der Griechischen Bibel* (ed. H.-F. Fabry and U. Offerhaus; BWANT 153; Stuttgart: Kohlhammer, 2001), 161.

the lines of communication with every generation. However, this did not prevent later interpreters from seeing in this "prophet like Moses" an eschatological messianic figure. Although neither this text nor the rest of the Old Testament provides warrant for or evidence of this interpretation, its roots can be traced to the intertestamental period.

Association of Deuteronomy 18:15−18 with an eschatological prophetic Messiah is attested in the apocryphal writings,[40] the Qumran texts,[41] the New Testament,[42] and Samaritan writings.[43] However, this interpretation required a twofold adjustment to the original meaning: the replacement of the distributive meaning of "a prophet like me" with an individual meaning, and the transformation of a text with historical significance into an eschatological statement.[44] This reading does not arise naturally from the text; rather, it imposes on the text a meaning one hopes to find or one needs to have in order to buttress a questionable doctrine.[45] On the one hand,

---

40. 1 Macc. 4:46; 14:41. According to F. Dexinger ("Reflections on the Relationship between Qumran and Samaritan Messianology," in *Qumran Messianism: Studies on the Messianic Expectations in the Dead Sea Scrolls* [eds. J. H. Charlesworth, H. Lichtenberger and G. S. Oegema; Tübingen: Mohr Siebeck, 1998]), the idea of a messianic prophet did not originate with Deuteronomy 18, but this notion quickly found its biblical warrant there.

41. The figure referred to as the "Teacher of Righteousness" in *1QpHab* 8:2−3, or "Interpreter of the Torah" in *4QFlor* [4Q174] 1:11−12. According to *Damascus Covenant* [CD] 6:11a, the one who teaches righteousness will arise at the end of the days. These expressions seem to reflect functions of a "prophet like Moses." On the prophetic Messiah at Qumran, see J. J. Collins, *The Scepter and the Star: The Messiahs in the Dead Sea Scrolls and Other Ancient Literature* (New York; Doubleday, 1995), 112−23.

42. On the perception of Jesus as an eschatological prophet see Matt. 16:14; 20:21; 21:46; Mark 6:15; Luke 7:16; 9:8; John 1:21; 4:19; 6:14; 7:40, 52; 9:17. John 1:19−28 understands John the Baptist this way. Similarly Luke 1:76, where Zechariah refers to him as "the prophet of the Most High," who will prepare the way before the Lord (cf. Matt. 14:5; Mark 11:32; Luke 20:6). In reality Jesus perceived himself as greater than a prophet, whose arrival would be announced by Yahweh's prophetic messenger (Matt. 11:9−10; Luke 7:26−27). For discussion of the perception of Jesus as the eschatological messianic prophet in the New Testament, see D. I. Block, "My Servant David: Ancient Israel's Vision of the Messiah," in *Israel's Messiah in the Bible and the Dead Sea Scrolls* (eds. R. S. Hess and M. D. Carroll R.; Grand Rapids: Baker, 2003), 26−32.

43. In Qumran eschatology the prophetic figure was not a central figure—that role is played by the royal Davidic Messiah. Samaritan tradition reversed the situation; the eschatological vision is dominated by the prophetic figure—there is no royal Messiah. See the full discussion by Dexinger, "Qumran and Samaritan Messianology," 83−99.

44. See ibid., 90−91.

45. Contra S. Dempster ("An 'Extraordinary Fact': Torah and Temple and the Contours of the Hebrew Canon," *TynBul* 48 [1997]: 56, n. 100), it is not "clear that the editor at work here [in Deuteronomy 34] understood the prophecy in 18:18 as a succession culminating in an individual." See further on chapter 34 below.

Jesus is to be identified with Yahweh (incarnate in flesh), who raises up the prophets; on the other, he is the subject of the prophets' proclamation.

GOD SPEAKS TODAY. THIS text offers important lessons for those who would establish a biblical theology of ministry in our own day. Within that theology of ministry we may note the following features. (1) This text reminds us that God speaks to his people graciously in his own time and by his own means. Divination, magic, and efforts to contact the spirits of the netherworld continued into the New Testament era. The disposition of the New Testament toward these practices is precisely that of Moses. The book of Acts recounts several incidents involving magicians, but these characters are viewed as tools of Satan. In each case the power of God triumphed over the powers of darkness.[46]

In his lengthy catalogue of vices in Galatians 5:19–21, Paul lists "witchcraft" (*pharmakeia*) after "idolatry" as a work of the flesh contrary to the Spirit and grounds for exclusion from the kingdom of God. Second Timothy 3:13 speaks of evil men and imposters who deceive (i.e., charlatans), against whose influence the sacred Scriptures are a sure antidote. Elsewhere Paul is keenly aware of the existence of "principalities and powers," which function as minions of Satan. However, through the work of Christ on the cross they have all been defeated (Col. 2:15). Because these powers are hostile to the church, Christians are not to invoke or seek to manipulate them; rather, we must resist them through the power of God (Eph. 6:10–20).[47]

The book of Revelation contains the harshest polemic against divination and magic. With distinct echoes of Deuteronomy (cf. 4:28), Revelation 9:20–21 places "magic arts" in a class with a series of capital crimes. Revelation 21:8 consigns the cowardly, the unbelieving, vile people, murderers, sexually immoral people, "those who practice magic arts," idolaters, and all liars to "the fiery lake of burning sulfur. This is the second death." Based on the disposition of the New Testament, Christians should share Moses' antipathy toward these means of communicating with the supernatural.

(2) In accordance with Yahweh's promise to Israel, the Lord continues to raise up prophetic voices as gifts, ensuring his people of his presence and his desire to communicate with them. Not only does the New Testament

---

46. Acts 8:9–25; 13:4–12; 19:8–20. For brief discussion, see C. E. Arnold, "Magic and Astrology," in *Dictionary of the Later New Testament and Its Developments* (eds. R. P. Martin and P. H. Davids; Downers Grove, IL: InterVarsity Press, 1997), 702–3.

47. For further discussion see C. E. Arnold, "Magic," in *Dictionary of Paul and His Letters* (eds. G. F. Hawthorne and R. P. Martin; Downers Grove, IL: InterVarsity Press, 1993), 582–83.

attest to the ministry of specific prophetic voices,[48] but in two contexts Paul also explicitly acknowledges prophets as divine appointments for the benefit of the church. In his catalogue of offices appointed by God in the church in 1 Corinthians 12:28–29, he lists "prophets" second, between "apostles" and "teachers." Similarly in Ephesians 4:11–14, he lists "prophets" after apostles and before evangelists and pastor teachers.

(3) An authentic prophet of God speaks in God's name, on his behalf, and at his command. Paul serves as a model, regularly opening his letters with affirmations of his apostleship[49] and his status as servant of Jesus Christ.[50] As he declares so emphatically to the Galatian Christians (Gal. 1–2), this means that the word he preaches and teaches is not his own or anyone else's invention, but the message revealed to him by God himself. In fact, the curse he invokes on himself and those (including angels) who would preach any other gospel recalls the death sentence that Yahweh declares on false prophets in Deuteronomy 18:20.

(4) Finally, this passage reminds readers in all ages and contexts to be vigilant in testing the validity of all who preach and teach in God's name. Sounding more like Moses than many realize, 1 John 4:1 warns Christians not to believe every spirit, "but test the spirits to see whether they are from God, because many false prophets have gone out into the world." Similarly, Paul encourages the believers at Thessalonica that even as they welcome prophetic utterances, they must be vigilant in testing all messages, holding fast to what is good and rejecting all that is evil (1 Thess. 5:20–22). In Paul's letter to young Timothy we hear the most explicit warning to reject presumptuous persons who oppose the truth and are corrupted in their minds (2 Tim. 3:1–8).

---

48. Acts 11:27; 13:1; 15:32; 1 Cor. 14:29; Eph. 2:20.

49. Apostles are by definition persons who have received direct revelation from God/Christ and are commissioned by him to proclaim that message to others. Apart from "servant of Christ" this is Paul's favorite official self-designation (Rom. 1:1; 11:13; 1 Cor. 1:1; 9:1–2; 15:9; 2 Cor. 1:1 (cf. 12:12); Gal. 1:1; Eph. 1:1; Col. 1:1; 1 Tim. 1:1; 2:7; 2 Tim. 1:1,11; Titus 1:1 (cf. 1 Pet. 1:1; 2 Pet. 1:1). This is a special issue in the Corinthian correspondence (1 Cor. 4:9; 9:5; 12:28–29; 15:7, 9; 2 Cor. 11:5, 13; 12:11) and Galatians (Gal. 1:17, 19).

50. Rom. 1:1; Gal. 1:10; 1 Tim. 4:6; Titus 1:1; cf. also James 1:1; Jude 1. The expression *doulos Christou* is equivalent to Hebrew *ʿebed yhwh* ("servant of Yahweh"), which was used not only of Moses (Num. 12:7–8; Deut. 34:5; Josh. 1:1, 2, 7, 13, 15; 8:31, 33; 11:12; 12:6; 13:8; 14:7; 18:7; 22:2, 4–5; 2 Kings 18:12; 2 Chron. 1:3; 24:6), but also of the prophets who followed in his train (2 Kings 17:23; 21:10; 24:2; Jer. 25:4; Dan. 9:10; Amos 3:7).

Deuteronomy 19:1–14

❦

Introduction to 19:1–21:9

ALTHOUGH SOME INTERPRET DEUTERONOMY 19:1–21:9 as a commentary on the sanctity of human life as reflected in the fifth command (5:17),[1] the links with the Book of the Covenant make it more likely that Moses is expounding on Exodus 20:22–23:33. While chapter 19 exhibits some links with 16:16–18:22, the attention shifts from authority figures as agents of righteousness to righteousness in everyday life (cf. 16:20). Except for verse 14, Moses here applies fundamental standards of righteousness to a series of issues involving life and death: (1) accidental and intentional manslaughter (19:1–13); (2) legal cases involving capital and lesser crimes (19:15–21); (3) facing death as a warrior in battle (20:1–9); (4) administering the principle of ḥērem (20:10–18); (5) respecting natural life (20:19–20); and (6) dealing with the body of a deceased person discovered in the open field (21:1–9).

When the LORD your God has destroyed the nations whose land he is giving you, and when you have driven them out and settled in their towns and houses, ²then set aside for yourselves three cities centrally located in the land the LORD your God is giving you to possess. ³Build roads to them and divide into three parts the land the LORD your God is giving you as an inheritance, so that anyone who kills a man may flee there.

⁴This is the rule concerning the man who kills another and flees there to save his life—one who kills his neighbor unintentionally, without malice aforethought. ⁵For instance, a man may go into the forest with his neighbor to cut wood, and as he swings his ax to fell a tree, the head may fly off and hit his neighbor and kill him. That man may flee to one of these cities and save his life. ⁶Otherwise, the avenger of blood might pursue him in a rage, overtake him if the distance is too great, and kill him even though he is not deserving of death, since he did it to his neighbor without malice aforethought. ⁷This is why I command you to set aside for yourselves three cities.

---

1. Kaufman, "The Structure of the Deuteronomic Law," 134–37; Georg Braulik, *Die deuteronomischen Gesetze und der Dekalog* (Stuttgart: Katholisches Bibelwerk, 1991), 62–65.

⁸If the LORD your God enlarges your territory, as he promised on oath to your forefathers, and gives you the whole land he promised them, ⁹because you carefully follow all these laws I command you today—to love the LORD your God and to walk always in his ways—then you are to set aside three more cities. ¹⁰Do this so that innocent blood will not be shed in your land, which the LORD your God is giving you as your inheritance, and so that you will not be guilty of bloodshed.

¹¹But if a man hates his neighbor and lies in wait for him, assaults and kills him, and then flees to one of these cities, ¹²the elders of his town shall send for him, bring him back from the city, and hand him over to the avenger of blood to die. ¹³Show him no pity. You must purge from Israel the guilt of shedding innocent blood, so that it may go well with you.

¹⁴Do not move your neighbor's boundary stone set up by your predecessors in the inheritance you receive in the land the LORD your God is giving you to possess.

THE BOUNDARIES OF THE primary literary unit are marked by the opening temporal clause (v. 1)[2] and the change in subject in verse 14. The literary style of 19:1–13 seems more formal and less hortatory than chapters 12–18,[3] but this does not mean Moses has adopted a legislative mode or that this material consists of laws that judges might use in adjudicating specific legal cases.

This becomes apparent when we compare 19:1–13 with Exodus 21:12–14, which apparently underlies it.[4] The legal core of the present text, cast in third person, consists of a formal opening statement (v. 4a), followed by a casuistic presentation of the same two cases of manslaughter (vv. 4b–5, 11), and the required response cast in the second person (vv. 7,

---

2. For similar initial temporal clauses introduced by *kî* ("When"), see 4:25; 6:10, 20; 7:1; 12:20, 29; 17:14; 18:9; 20:1; 21:10; 26:1; 30:1.

3. So also McConville, *Deuteronomy*, 308. Although the text lacks formal imperatives, the principal clauses are dominated by imperfect and *waw* consecutive perfect verbs that have the force of commands.

4. S. M. Paul (*Studies in the Book of the Covenant in the Light of Cuneiform and Biblical Law* [VTSup 18; Leiden: Brill, 1970], 64) observes that these verses contain the only reference to God in the first person in the legal portion of the Book of the Covenant (Ex. 21:2–22:16).

13; like Ex. 21:12 – 14).[5] However, the theological comments around this core give this unit a pronounced sermonic tone, an observation reinforced by other features that are more at home in hortatory addresses than legal ordinances. Verses 5 – 6 sound like a sermon illustration, framed by references to the person's disposition (vv. 4b, 6c). In addition, Moses' portrayal of himself as an authoritative interlocutor in verse 7 and his concluding comment about securing Israel's well-being and purging the blood of the innocent are more paraenetic than legal.

Numbers 35:9 – 34, which provides additional background for our passage, modifies Exodus 21:12 – 14 in keeping with Israel's new circumstances. Once they had claimed all the land, a single place of refuge would be impractical, so Numbers 35:10 – 15 authorizes the selection of six cities of asylum, three on each side of the Jordan. However, the link with the central sanctuary is not lost, since Numbers 35:28 mandates the person seeking asylum to remain in the secure place until the death of the high priest.

The narrative line of the Pentateuch suggests Moses delivered the present instructions shortly after he had received the prescriptions in Numbers 35. While Deuteronomy 4:41 – 42 had reported that Moses set apart three towns east of the Jordan as places of asylum for innocent persons responsible for the death of another,[6] the vocabulary and style of these verses suggest Moses acted in the light of or anticipated his later instructions regarding the asylum towns in Cisjordan (19:8). Except for the geographic phrase (lit.) "beyond the Jordan toward the sunrise," every expression found in 4:41 – 42 recurs in 19:1 – 13. However, within the broader agenda of the second half of the second address announced in 16:20, in Deuteronomy 19:1 – 13 Moses' provision for "towns of refuge/asylum" for those who unwittingly cause another's death is intended to serve the cause of righteousness in the land.

The Provision of Asylum for Innocent Manslaughter (19:1 – 3)

THE OPENING PARAGRAPH SERVES as a thesis statement for the entire unit. Echoing 12:29, verse 1 sets the context by citing three preconditions to when these instructions take effect: Yahweh has cut off the nations (cf. 7:1), the Israelites have dispossesd them, and they occupy their towns and houses. However, whereas in 12:29 Moses only spoke of occupying

---

5. Some suggest vv. 4 – 5 and vv. 11 – 12 represent the original predeuteronomic core, which has been supplemented by a series of deuteronomistic additions. See Mayes, *Deuteronomy*, 284.

6. Bezer in the southern desert plateau for the Reubenites, Ramoth in Gilead for the Gadites, and Golan in Bashan for the Manassites (4:41 – 43; cf. Josh. 20:8).

the Canaanites' land, here he refers to living "in their towns and houses" (cf. 6:10 — 11). Apparently he did not envision the Israelites razing all the Canaanite towns.

Continuing his penchant for triadic expression, verses 2 — 3 prescribe three actions once the Israelites have occupied the land. (1) They must designate three towns in the heartland (NIV "centrally located") to complement the three already set apart east of the Jordan (4:41 — 42) and complete the six called for in Numbers 35:9 — 15. (2) They must establish the routes to the towns of asylum.[7] Since all six asylum towns eventually selected were also Levitical cities, they were invested with a sacral character (cf. Josh 20:7).[8] Even so, it seems "the way/road" and "the land" have been intentionally juxtaposed, suggesting the boundaries of the regions falling under the influence of the respective towns were to be determined by the towns rather than vice versa. The towns were probably selected on the basis of their established significance rather than their centricity.[9] (3) Having identified these three focal points, the Israelites were to divide the entire territory into three regions, for which the towns would function as umbrellas of protection for those fleeing from avengers of blood.

The last sentence of verse 3 declares the purpose of these towns: to serve as refuges for those who inadvertently cause another person's death. Since "to kill" (*rṣḥ*) embraces both intentional and unintentional homicide, those who accidentally caused someone else's death needed protection. This provision recognizes that cases involving unwitting homicide always produce two victims: the person whose life is lost and the one responsible for the act. The provision also recognizes that in the heat of passion the aggrieved family may seek revenge without investigating the circumstances of the tragedy. The asylum would prevent one who is already an emotional victim of his own act from becoming a physical victim of the avengers.[10]

Although ancient treaties included clauses governing the treatment of an overlord's subjects who flee to the town of a vassal, the present

---

7. The NIV's "Build roads to them" assumes the routes are to be prepared and marked in advance so those being pursued by "avengers of blood" may flee freely to their destination. According to ESV, Moses calls for calculating the distances, presumably to ensure the towns were located precisely in the center of the three regions (v. 3b). Cf. P.-E. Dion, "Deuteronomy 19:3: Prepare the Way, or Estimate the Distance?" *Eglise et théologie* 25 (1994): 333 — 41.

8. Some suggest they were temple towns. Moshe Greenberg, "The Biblical Concept of Asylum," *JBL* 78 (1959): 125 — 32; Weinfeld, *DDS*, 236.

9. Contra NIV's "centrally located." This is obvious for Hebron and Shechem, whose special status in Israelite tradition dates back to patriarchal times, and which at this time were recognized as significant Canaanite towns.

10. On the humanitarian aims of this provision, see Greenberg, "The Biblical Concept of Asylum," 125 — 32.

humanitarian concern is missing in those texts.[11] This extraordinary provision[12] shielded unfortunate individuals against further distress.[13]

The Need for the Provision of Asylum
for Innocent Manslaughter (19:4–7, 10)

WHEREAS NUMBERS 35:16–23 focused on the legal rules of evidence,[14] the present text pursues righteousness by providing an illustration of its necessity. Verses 4–7 are a self-contained subunit framed by a formal introduction (v. 4a) and conclusion (v. 7). The introduction illuminates the form and the function of the passage. In keeping with the sermonic nature of this address, verse 4 is best read something like, "Here is an illustration of the killer[15] who flees there [to the town of asylum] that he might live, that is, a person who unintentionally strikes down his neighbor, without having exhibited any prior hostility toward him" (pers. trans.).

Verse 5 presents a concrete situation that might precipitate such a flight. The "killer" goes with his neighbor to the forest to chop wood. As he swings the axe[16] to cut down a tree, the axehead flies off the handle and "finds" his neighbor and kills him. While the verb *māṣā'* means primarily "to find" that for which one is searching, here it refers to a chance encounter,[17] necessitating protection for an innocent person in the form of a refuge to which the individual could flee (v. 5e). Assuming familiarity with the regulations in Numbers 35:24–28, Moses does not need to specify how the people in

---

11. For the nearest equivalent to the present text, see Sefire III:4–6, in J. A. Fitzmyer, "The Treaties of Bar-Ga'yah and Mati'el from Sefire," in *COS*, 2:216. For discussion of Aleppo as a city of refuge, see Jonas C. Greenfield, "Asylum at Aleppo: A Note on Sfire III,4–7," in *Ah, Assyria ...: Studies in Assyrian History and Ancient Near Eastern Historiography Presented to Hayim Tadmor* (eds. M. Cogan and I. Eph'al; Scripta Hierosolymitana 33; Jerusalem, Magnes, 1991), 272–78. Greenfield also discusses temples as asyla in Greek and Latin sources.

12. So also Paul, *Studies in the Book of the Covenant*, 63.

13. Cf. R. Westbrook, *Studies in Biblical and Cuneiform Law* (CahRB 26; Paris: Gabalda, 1988), 79.

14. If the person causes death with an iron, wood, or stone instrument, or his bare hand, he is a murderer and subject to capital punishment.

15. Similarly Nelson, *Deuteronomy*, 237–38.

16. Literally "and his hand is applied to the axe." Cf. the use of pickaxes in the Siloam tunnel inscription in G. I. Davies, *Ancient Hebrew Inscriptions: Corpus and Concordance* (Cambridge: Cambridge Univ. Press, 1991), 4.116 (p. 68).

17. Ex. 21:13, which may be translated idiomatically, "it happened as an act of God," suggests providential involvement in the tragedy. For further discussion, see B. Dinur, "The Religious Character of the Cities of Refuge and the Ceremony of Admission into Them," *ErIsr* 3 [1954]: 135–46 [Hebrew]; viii–ix [English Summary]). For a cuneiform analogue to this act of providence, see CH §249 in Roth, *Law Collections*, 128.

the town of asylum should respond to the fugitive. These regulations call for its citizens to hear the case, adjudicate between the fugitive and the avenger of blood, and respond accordingly to the judgment.[18]

In verse 6 Moses explains why the person would flee: the "avenger of blood" is after him. In the expression "avenger [gôʾēl] of blood" (lit., "the redeemer of blood"),[19] gôʾēl is a technical legal term, denoting a near kinsman responsible for maintaining the integrity of the family and its holdings.[20] Based on an assumption of corporate solidarity, this provision was designed to maintain the wholeness of family relationships even after the person had died.[21] Institutions like this developed in kinship-based societies that lacked a strong central authority.

However, the involvement of the elders as representatives of the community (v. 12) prevented "avengers of blood" from operating independently or being driven by thirst for vengeance. The purpose of the institution was not to foster revenge but to promote righteousness. In cases of murder, righteousness demanded the expiation of the bloodguilt incurred by the death.[22] Moses recognizes that despite the lofty goal of communal righteousness and the expiation of bloodguilt, personal passion could drive avengers of blood (v. 6). In rage they might pursue the "killer," overtake him, and kill him. But since the "killer" in this case has committed no crime and has not previously expressed hatred toward the victim, the sentence of death does not apply. This section concludes with an emphatic reminder to set aside three towns of asylum (v. 7).

---

18. For a helpful discussion of the relationships among the "asylum texts" and the judicial procedures involved in these cases, see Willis, *The Elders of the City*, 118 – 29.

19. References to Israel's redemption from Egypt tend to prefer *pādâ* (7:8; 9:26; 13:5[6]; 15:15; 21:8; 24:18). This word is used to refer to "redeeming" the firstborn (Ex. 13:13 – 15; Num. 18:15 – 17) or offerings (Lev. 27).

20. The Old Testament notes six contexts that called for the intervention of a *gôʾēl*: (1) when hereditary property passes out of the clan (Lev. 25:25 – 30); (2) when a member of the clan has sold himself/herself into slavery because of poverty (25:47 – 55); (3) when the death of a member of the clan calls for compensation and restitution money (Num. 5:8); (4) when a member of the clan is involved in a lawsuit (Job 19:25; Ps. 119:154; Jer. 50:34); (5) when a married relative dies without having fathered a child, by marrying the deceased's widow and providing him with a survivor (Ruth 3:13; cf. Deut. 25:5 – 10); (6) when a member of the clan is murdered by someone outside the clan.

21. See further the studies of the word by Robert L. Hubbard, "The *gôʾēl* in Ancient Israel: The Theology of an Israelite Institution," *BBR* 1 (1991): 3 – 19; idem, "גאל," *NIDOTTE*, 1:789 – 94; Milgrom, *Numbers*, 291 – 92.

22. Cf. 21:1 – 9, where elders deal with unsolved murders. For a concrete case involving an avenger of blood, see 2 Sam. 14:4 – 11, though, as McConville observes (*Deuteronomy*, 311), the text does not identify the avenger either as a member of the victim's family or the city of the person responsible for the death of the victim.

Skipping over verses 8–9, which are parenthetical, verse 10 offers a rationale for the policy: Towns of asylum are needed to prevent innocent blood from being shed in the midst of the land. The expression "innocent blood" refers to the blood of the one responsible for the death of the victim; since the death was accidental, his blood is innocent. Employing the strong "bloodguilt formula," Moses declares that if the community permits the avenger to slay an innocent "killer," they will incur bloodguilt by violating the sanctity of life.

The Expansion of the Provision of Asylum for Innocent Manslaughter (19:8–9)

IN VERSES 8–9 Moses digresses momentarily, contemplating the future when Yahweh expands the Israelites' territory, delivering into their hands all the land he promised on oath to their ancestors. Whereas verses 1–7 had in mind the core Promised Land west of the Jordan, the conditional construction raises the possibility of further expansion (v. 8). Should Israel's territory expand beyond the original tribal allotments, three towns of asylum on each side of the Jordan would be inadequate. Therefore Moses calls for the addition of three more towns of asylum to serve the people living beyond the narrowly defined Promised Land (v. 9b).

However, verse 9 recognizes that just as Israel's prosperity in the land depends on their pursuit of righteousness, so Yahweh's expansion of their territory is contingent on fidelity. Therefore, with a challenge we have often heard before (6:5), Moses appeals for scrupulous devotion to Yahweh demonstrated in action.[23] Yahweh owes nothing to those who do not receive his grace with gratitude and respond to his covenant with obedience.

The Exception to the Provision of Asylum for Manslaughter (19:11–13)

WHEREAS IN THE ANCIENT world protection was generally granted those who sought refuge in temples, Numbers 35 and Deuteronomy 19 insist that no guilty person should be secure in the town of asylum. In proposing a hypothetical scenario that is the opposite of verses 4–10,[24] Moses recognizes the potential for criminals to abuse the institution and reaffirms the demand in Numbers 35 for discrimination between intentional murder and accidental death.

---

23. Cf. 10:12; 11:1, 13; 13:3[4]; 30:6.
24. Num. 35:16–23 dealt with intentional murderer first, followed by the case of the innocent manslayer.

Whereas in verse 4 Moses had characterized the killer and his victim as neighbors on friendly terms, the description of the criminal's actions in verse 11 opens with an announcement of his hostile disposition: "Suppose a man hates his neighbor" (pers. trans.; cf. Ex 21:14a) and plots to kill: He lies in wait, jumps up against his victim, delivers a fatal blow, and then flees to one of the towns of asylum. Omitting any reference to the fugitive's plea for asylum or trial before the congregation (Josh. 20:4, 6), these instructions assume a guilty verdict. Moses demands that the elders of the criminal's community dispatch men to fetch the murderer from the town of asylum and hand him over to the avenger of blood for execution.[25]

Moving from required action to disposition, Moses tries to fortify the community's resolve to deal with the murderer as prescribed by citing the first half of the "no pity formula" (v. 13; cf. 13:8[9]). As a pastor, Moses is realistic; in cases involving relatives, it will be tempting to substitute the sentence of death with economic compensation.[26] However, it is necessary to execute the murderer to purge the nation of the innocent blood of the victim;[27] Israel has been contaminated by the blood of an innocent man. The purgation absolving them of the guilt of the crime can be achieved only by executing the murderer. Until that occurs, culpability for the crime hangs over all the people (v. 10).

Moses concludes these instructions with a reminder that Israel's well-being depends on rigorous defense of innocent blood (v. 13b). Apart from the theological issues involved in purging the blood from Israel, protecting innocent manslayers and executing guilty murderers will serve their own interests. "That it may go well with you" links this passage with others that declare that obedience to the revealed will of Yahweh is "for our good" and credited as "righteousness for us" (6:24—25; cf. 5:33; 10:13).

Righteousness and Greed (19:14)

IF VERSES 1—13 build on the fifth command of the Decalogue, then verse 14 addresses the seventh and tenth commands (5:19, 21b). This verse seems oddly placed, but it is linked to the preceding by its theology of land and vocabulary. The plots of land marked by boundary markers are

---

25. Num. 35:27 suggests that since the murderer is guilty, if the avenger of blood finds him outside the border of the town of asylum and kills him, he does not incur bloodguilt himself.

26. This statement functions as a counterpart to Num. 35:29—34, which prohibits Israelites from avoiding the death penalty by paying a ransom for the life of the murderer.

27. Variations of the purgation formula occur in 13:5[6]; 17:7, 12; 19:13, 19; 21:9, 21; 22:21, 22, 24; 24:7. Except for our text and 21:9, in Deuteronomy the formula always involves purging "the evil" from Israel.

microcosms of the Promised Land as a whole: both represented inviolable "granted" properties. Inserted here, this fragment heightens the significance of respecting others' right to property. Justice outside the town walls—in the fields—is as vital as justice inside the gates. The pursuit of righteousness extends to all of life.

The inviolability of boundary markers is fundamental to a settled agricultural economy, where ownership of land is critical for well-being. The present expression, "set up by your predecessors," assumes a formal procedure allocating parcels of tribal lands to specific clans and families (Num. 26:52–56; 34:13–29; Josh. 14–19). Though evidence is lacking, records of these allotments may have been stored in the central sanctuary. Israelite law viewed Yahweh as the true owner of the land, and the allotments to tribes and families were inviolable.[28] The gravity of these grants is reflected in the covenant curses (27:17) and the custom of kinsmen redeemers (*gôʾēl*) reclaiming land when someone outside the clan possesses it (Lev. 25:23–28).

Bridging Contexts

THE SANCTITY OF LIFE. The foundation for the incommutability of capital punishment as the penalty for homicide is laid in Genesis 9:6: "Whoever sheds the blood of man, by man shall his blood be shed; for in the image of God has God made man." Because human life is sacred, no price is high enough to compensate for its loss. Except for the account of Joshua's assignment of Hebron, Shechem, and Kedesh on the western side of the Jordan and the affirmation of Bezer, Ramoth, and Golan in the Transjordan (Josh. 20:1–9),[29] evidence for cities used as places of asylum in later texts is lacking.

Although it is not specifically mentioned, this distinctively Israelite view of the land may explain why Naboth refused to sell his vineyard to Ahab (1 Kings 21:1–16). However, it also explains why Jezebel, Ahab's wife, had no scruples about confiscating the property. The notion of the inviolability of land holdings, particularly its theological underpinnings, was foreign to this Tyrian princess. In Tyre kings did what they wanted. The notion of asylum remained alive into the monarchy, but rather than being linked to towns of refuge, it was associated with the temple and the horns of the altar. Adonijah's (1 Kings 1:50–53) and Joab's (1 Kings 2:28–29) efforts to save their lives by seeking refuge in the temple proved fruitless.

---

28. Cf. Baker, *Tight Fists or Open Hands*, 99–101.

29. Cf. also Josh. 21:12–13, 21, 27, 32, 38. In addition to Hebron, 1 Chron. 6:57 also names Libnah, Jattir, and Eshtemoa as towns of refuge.

Boundary markers. Echoes of the ordinance involving land markers are heard in two texts in Proverbs.

> Do not move an ancient boundary stone set up by your forefathers. (Prov. 22:28)
> Do not move an ancient boundary stone or encroach on the fields of the fatherless. (23:10)[30]

The latter in particular links this ordinance with Deuteronomy's concern for the poor. In Job 24:1 – 11 the patriarch from Uz cites how "men move boundary stones" as the first in a long series of exploitative crimes that the rich commit against the poor. While the language differs, the seriousness of the problem in later Israelite and Judaean history is reflected in the prophets, who pronounce woe on the greedy "who add house to house and join field to field" (Isa. 5:8), and who seize the fields and houses of the poor, robbing families of their hereditary possession.

 **RESPECT FOR LIFE.** ALTHOUGH Deuteronomy 19:1 – 13 deals with an institution that died long ago, its significance for an enduring theology are profound. While many understand the passage primarily in terms of justice, that justice is merely a subset of a higher and more encompassing value — righteousness. If righteousness is demonstrated first and foremost by unreserved love for God (cf. chap. 13; 16:20 – 17:2), love for God is demonstrated by the way we treat others, especially in our respect for human life.

The Decalogue affirms the right to life as a fundamental human right (Ex. 20:13; Deut. 5:17). This right is not reserved for those with superior intelligence or achievement or for members of one ethnic group; it belongs to all the sons and daughters of Adam via Noah, and by virtue of their status as image-bearers of God (Gen. 9:6). No crime against another human is as heinous as willful homicide, for it involves the intentional elimination of an image of God. Because the demand to execute the perpetrator is rooted in a divine charge to the ancestor of all (Noah), this principle may not be dismissed as an Israelite civil law abrogated in Christ. As Moses declared in Deuteronomy 19:13, personal dispositions, the intimacy of relationships, and sentimentality may not interfere with this righteous demand.

---

30. These proverbs are reminiscent of the beginning of chapter 6 of the Egyptian Instructions of Amenemope: "Do not move the markers on the borders of the fields, nor shift the position of the measuring cord. Do not be greedy for a cubit of land, nor encroach upon the boundaries of a widow" (trans. by Miriam Lichtheim in *COS*, 1:117).

How cheap life has become in our world is reflected in the homicide rates. In the United States in 2008, the Federal Bureau of Investigation reported 14,180 cases of murder and nonnegligent manslaughter, 5.6 per 100,000 population.[31] In our cities the rates are much higher, rising as high as 40 per 100,000 population. The statistics on the relationship between victim and perpetrator are especially troubling. Our text assumes that families will express solidarity and commitment to each other's well-being. However, in our world family loyalties are often sacrificed in precisely this area of behavior. Homicide statistics for the United States in 2008 suggest that 23.3 percent of the murders were committed by family members, and 54.7 percent by other acquaintances (neighbors, friends, boyfriends, etc.).[32] These figures reflect a drastic cheapening of life and the disintegration of the most fundamental relationships. The loss of the idea of covenant, whether it be in relationship to God or in relationship to one another, leads inevitably to a loss of commitment to righteousness.

If this text calls for uncompromising respect for human life, this respect extends also to those who inadvertently take another's life. Whether we interpret these tragedies as chance events or providential acts, accidentally causing another person's death involves no guilt at all.[33] Righteousness and justice demand both that guilty persons be punished and the innocent not be victimized. For this reason, communities committed to righteousness will develop rigorous procedures and institutions designed to establish guilt and innocence, particularly in cases involving manslaughter. Conversely, customs and procedures designed to make the innocent look guilty and the guilty appear innocent are to be condemned as both unrighteous and unjust.

Love. This text reaffirms the importance of love as the underlying disposition toward other human beings. Hatred is an unrighteous disposition of the heart, and rage is her ugly sister. The progeny of these attitudes are hostile and violent acts against others. While we cannot expect neo-Canaanites to govern their lives after the ordinances of God, love for one's fellow human beings, particularly toward members of the household of faith, is the mark of discipleship (John 13:35). Although passions of the unregenerate yield enmity, strife, jealousy, fits of anger, rivalries, dissensions, divisions, "the fruit of the Spirit is love, joy, peace, patience, kind-

---

31. See FBI statistics at www.fbi.gov/ucr/cius2008/offenses/expanded_information/homicide.html (accessed March 2, 2009).

32. See www.fbi.gov/ucr/cius2008/offenses/expanded_information/homicide.html (accessed on March 2, 2009).

33. Though death related to negligence in maintaining a safe environment renders one culpable (cf. 22:8).

ness, goodness, faithfulness, gentleness, self-control; against such things there is no law" (Gal. 5:20–23).

Importance of community. This text illustrates the importance of community. For justice to reign the entire community must be committed to righteousness. This agenda may not be left in the hands of the professionals, who have a propensity to be driven by self-interest rather than the well-being of the community. At the same time, this passage affirms the culpability of the entire community for the crimes of the individual.

The paragon of virtue, Daniel, found himself in exile along with his countrymen; in his prayer in Daniel 9 he recognized that he was a part of the problem—note the preponderance of first person pronouns acknowledging his guilt. In the eyes of God, the guilt of individuals hangs over the community that refuses to deal with the crimes they commit. As a supreme act of grace, Yahweh revealed to ancient Israel a method whereby that guilt could be removed. But as an act of even greater grace, God has revealed to us the means whereby the guilt of humanity can be removed; this is accomplished through the atoning sacrifice of Christ, the ultimate *gôʾēl*, who secures the blessing and life of the righteous and purges them of their sin.

Greed. Finally, in every age God's people need to combat the kind of greed addressed in the ordinance about land markers (v. 14). But the scope of the present ordinance is not restricted to greedy and powerful rulers. The law applies equally to the poor, who out of envy and their own greed may try to seize property held by others. As in the Decalogue, the second person "you" assumes the addressee is the greatest threat to others' security and property. And the "you" here is unqualified. Nothing, not even poverty, justifies the violation of the next person's rights. While this form of greed is rarely expressed in our technological and urbanized context by seizing the neighbor's land, we witness it in the way investors swindle their clients' money, caregivers confiscate the resources of those for whom they are supposed to care, and students claim the ideas of others as their own through the Internet. A community committed to righteousness is characterized by generosity, compassion, and commitment to others' well-being rather than to self-serving avarice and greed.

Deuteronomy 19:15–21

O ne witness is not enough to convict a man accused of any crime or offense he may have committed. A matter must be established by the testimony of two or three witnesses.

¹⁶If a malicious witness takes the stand to accuse a man of a crime, ¹⁷the two men involved in the dispute must stand in the presence of the LORD before the priests and the judges who are in office at the time. ¹⁸The judges must make a thorough investigation, and if the witness proves to be a liar, giving false testimony against his brother, ¹⁹then do to him as he intended to do to his brother. You must purge the evil from among you. ²⁰The rest of the people will hear of this and be afraid, and never again will such an evil thing be done among you. ²¹Show no pity: life for life, eye for eye, tooth for tooth, hand for hand, foot for foot.

THESE GUIDELINES REGARDING WITNESSES in judicial proceedings flesh out the eighth command of the Decalogue (cf. 5:20; cf. 17:6). The text divides into two uneven parts: (1) a call for more than one witness in all cases (v. 15), and (2) instructions on how to deal with malicious witnesses (vv. 16–21). Both are driven by a concern for righteousness in judicial procedures.

Verse 15 is cast as a straightforward appeal for more than one witness in judicial proceedings involving accusations against a person. With three expressions Moses extends the scope of the principle beyond idolatry (17:6), to "any [case involving] crime," "any [case involving] offense," or "any [case involving] offense he may have committed." In all cases, the "testimony" (lit., "mouth") of two or three witnesses is required to establish a case.

The space given to the case of a malicious witness shows that the issue here is not simply justice but righteousness (vv. 16–21). The instructions consist of a clause introducing the problem, followed by the prescribed response. Here the expression *ḥāmās* (NIV, "malicious") refers to judicial violence, verbal action intended to harm another person. In verse 18 this same person is characterized as a "liar." As in 17:6, the problem involves deflecting the legal process from the truth through "false [empty] testimony." The demand for a plurality of witnesses is both reasonable and necessary.[1] It is reasonable because it reduces the chance of mistaken verdicts, especially where verbal testimony is the only means by which to adjudicate a case. It is necessary because without it the judge is left to decide between two opinions — the voice of the accused or the voice of the witness — which raises the specter of prejudice and favoritism.

Verses 17–18 describe the appropriate response to this miscarriage of justice. (1) Accuser and accused must appear before the priests who are serving as judges at that time (cf. 1:17; 17:8–9). Moses speaks explicitly of the litigants standing "in the presence of the LORD,"[2] but then he adds, "before the priests,[3] that is, the judges" (pers. trans.).[4] In keeping with the use of the expression "in the presence of the LORD" elsewhere in the book, we should envision the case being presented at the central sanctuary, where participants would be conscious of Yahweh's supervision of the legal process, heightening the implications of malicious testimony.[5]

(2) The adjudicators are to investigate the case thoroughly (v. 18a). As in 17:4, Moses draws attention to the announcement of the verdict with "and behold" (*binnēh*, not trans. in NIV). The malicious witness has indeed testified falsely against his brother. Identifying the aggrieved party as "his brother" heightens the seriousness of the crime and calls for proportional justice: "as he had plotted[6] against his brother, so you must do to him" (v. 19a, pers. trans.). Repeating the purgation formula (v. 13), in verses 19b–20 Moses presents the rationale for this response: It purges the community of the evil and deters from trumping up charges against their countrymen.

Verse 21 may be interpreted as the conclusion to either this subunit or the entire chapter. As in the case involving the murderer (v. 13a), Moses declares that personal interest and sentimentality are not to jeopardize the administration of justice. He reinforces the need for commitment to

---

1. So also Bovati, *Re-establishing Justice*, 269.

2. On the legal significance of the expression "to stand before [a judge]" see Bovati, *Re-Establishing Justice*, 234–35. On the significance of standing before Yahweh, see Wilson, *Out of the Midst of the Fire*, 176–77.

3. Moses uses the simple expression "the priests" in place of the fuller expression, "the priests, who are Levites" in 17:9.

4. As in 17:9, the conjunction *wᵉ* on *wᵉhaśśōpᵉṭîm* is explicative. Cf. Bovati, *Re-establishing Justice*, 183, n. 33.

5. Cf. 17:8–9. Tigay (*Deuteronomy*, 184) suggests officials are located in the towns throughout the land.

6. The meaning of *zāmam*, "to scheme, plot," is illuminated by Ps. 37:12; the NIV's "as he intended" seems too weak.

proportional justice with a fivefold recitation of equivalencies, generally known as *lex talionis* ("the law of retaliation"). Laws of this type are well attested in ancient Near Eastern documents[7] and the Old Testament (Ex. 21:23 – 25; Lev 24:17 – 21).

For modern readers this principle appears not only to condone but even mandate a "tit for tat," "get even" approach to ethics, and in so doing promotes a culture of escalating violence; but they actually intend the opposite.[8] The laws of *talion* demand that punishment for crimes against another person be proportional to the crimes committed rather than be more severe. Rather than promoting vengeance, the principle of *lex talionis* limited the penalties that adjudicators could impose on offenders.[9] While this approach may explain Exodus 21:23 – 25 and Leviticus 24:17 – 21, the issue in Deuteronomy 19:21 is not punishment for crimes involving bodily injuries, but penalties appropriate for those who maliciously seek to have the court authorize harm against fellows Israelites. Verse 21 fleshes out verse 19. Since false accusations damage personal relations and the very fabric of the community, this principle provides a means of nipping such social cancers in the bud.

RIGHTEOUSNESS IN CASE OF **false accusation.** The Old Testament recounts several cases of malicious testimony coming back to haunt the accuser.[10] According to 1 Kings 21:1 – 16, driven by greed Ahab demanded Naboth's patrimonial property. When Naboth refused to sell it to the king, Queen Jezebel arranged for a mock trial in which two worthless fellows falsely accused Naboth of cursing God and the king, for which the innocent man was executed. When Ahab claimed his land, Elijah declared the divine sentence on the king: "Have you not murdered a man and seized his property? . . . This is what the LORD says: In

---

7. The first law in the Sumerian Laws of Ur–Nammu (2100 BC) states, "If a man commits a homicide, they shall kill that man" (as translated by Roth, *Law Collections*, 17). The Laws of Hammurabi (1750 BC) extend this principle to those who through negligence cause the death of a free man (CH §§229 – 230; Roth, *Law Collections*, 229. Significant discrepancies in punishments reflect the classism of Babylonian society (CH §231).

8. So also, Wright, *Deuteronomy*, 226. For further discussion of the law of *talion*, see Miller, *Ten Commandments*, 244 – 47.

9. So also Thompson, *Deuteronomy*, 218; Labuschagne, *Deuteronomy*, 158.

10. Augustine fancifully interpreted the three witnesses of v. 15 as a veiled reference to the Trinity: "The Trinity, in which is unending stability of truth, was revealed through a mystery. Do you want to have a good case? Have two or three witnesses, the Father and the Son and the Holy Spirit," in *Fathers of the Church: A New Translation* (trans. J. W. Rettig; Washington, D.C.: Catholic Univ. of America, 1993), 88:92.

the place where dogs licked up Naboth's blood, dogs will lick up your blood—yes, yours!'" (21:19). In fulfillment of this oracle, Ahab was killed in battle at Ramoth Gilead, and when the chariot bearing his body returned to Samaria, the dogs did indeed lick up his blood (22:34–38). As for Jezebel, the cursed woman who had trumped up charges against Naboth for cursing God, she would die the most ignominious death, being tossed out the window of her house and having her blood licked up and her flesh eaten by dogs (2 Kings 9:30–37).

Two texts from later times illustrate graphically how some who falsely accused innocent people were punished with the sentence they had wished on the innocent. In Daniel 6 Persian satraps and commissioners fabricated charges of treason against Daniel, for which he was thrown into a pit of lions, as outlined in the policy signed by Darius (6:7[8]). When this "trial by ordeal" proved Daniel innocent, his accusers and their families were tossed into the same pit. The narrator observes that before they landed, the lions had torn them apart (v. 24[25]). Equally dramatic is the case of Haman in the book of Esther. Having trumped up false charges against Mordecai and constructed the gallows in anticipation of his sentence, Haman himself was hanged from those gallows (Est. 7:9–10).

The ethic of *talion*. But what about the ethic of *talion*? Following the lead of the rabbis, who called for compensating all personal injuries (except death) monetarily,[11] many have questioned whether the *lex talionis* was ever intended to be taken literally. Exodus 21:23–25 raises the question of what an eye for an eye and tooth for a tooth may have to do with causing a woman to miscarry.[12] The categorical prohibition of compensation for cases involving intentional homicide in Numbers 35:29–34 suggests this may have been acceptable in nonfatal cases involving bodily injury. But Leviticus 24:17–21 seems unambiguous in its call for equivalent retribution.[13] Recognizing how Yahweh's commands concerning blasphemy are integrated with the laws of *talion* in Leviticus 24:13–23, Milgrom notes perceptively that this statement communicates a profound theological message: Whoever injures a person disfigures the image of God (Gen. 1:27; 9:6b). The law of *talion* assumes that a crime against a person is a crime against God.[14]

---

11. For a discussion of rabbinic understanding of the *talion* texts, see Milgrom, *Leviticus 24–27*, 2136–40. For a reasoned response to rabbinic interpretation, see Levine, Excursus 9, "Retaliation and Compensation in Biblical Criminal Law," in *Leviticus*, 268–70.

12. See the discussion by R. Westbrook, "Lex Talionis and Exodus 21,22–25," *RB* 93 (1986): 52–69.

13. So also Milgrom, *Leviticus 24–27*, 2128–33.

14. Ibid., 2131.

Although not a court case, Samson provides the most obvious illustration of the vengeful and retributive interpretation of the principle. He declared his "Philistine ethic" with "I merely did to them what they did to me" (Judg. 15:11; cf. v. 7), which led to a dramatic escalation of violence, culminating in the death of more than a thousand persons, including Samson's wife and father-in-law. The narrator is aware of the hand of God in these events (14:4), but Samson acts at the level of his senses, without any hint of sensitivity to a greater divine agenda.

Based on Jesus' own words in Matthew 5:38−42, the supposed "tit for tat" ethic of the Old Testament is commonly contrasted with the ethic of the New Testament, which purportedly replaces it with an ethic based on love and forgiveness. Even if the slap on the cheek has no precedent in the Old Testament and involves an insult and only temporary physical discomfort rather than permanent injury, this interpretation misses the point of Jesus' words and misreads the principle of *talion*, which neither condones nor promotes a culture of escalating violence.

GOD IS IN CHARGE. In "The Present Crisis," a poem written in 1844 to inspire leaders of the National Association for the Advancement of Colored People, James Russell Lowell penned these immortal words:

Careless seems the great Avenger; history's pages but record
One death-grapple in the darkness 'twixt old systems and the
    Word;
Truth forever on the scaffold, Wrong forever on the throne, —
Yet that scaffold sways the future, and, behind the dim unknown,
Standeth God within the shadow, keeping watch above his own.[15]

Like this verse, our text calls out to a culture where truth is often sacrificed on the altar of self-interest. The casualties of dishonesty extend far beyond specific targets to the community and the nation. Believers are to be known for their truth-telling, not only in everyday life, but especially in a court of law. For us it should make no difference whether we are speaking under oath (James 5:12). If this is true in cases involving our relationships with outsiders, how much more in our representation of our "brothers and sisters." When called upon to testify in private or public, commitment to

---

15. This poem is readily available on the Internet: e.g., www.bartleby.com/42/805.html (accessed September 21, 2011).

righteousness demands that Christians speak the truth, the whole truth, and nothing but the truth. There is no place for responses that misrepresent or deflect from the discovery of truth,[16] or pleading the Fifth Amendment to protect oneself and hide the truth. Decisive action against those who would hurt others through their lies is needed in order to punish the criminal, deliver the victim, and purge the nation of this cancer.

When Jesus calls New Testament believers to turn the other cheek toward those who abuse them rather than to retaliate with "eye for eye and tooth for tooth" vengeance (Matt. 5:34—42), he does not establish a new ethic. Rather, he reminds his followers that those who bear the name of God live by a distinctive ethic. We do indeed insist that society and the courts uphold the rights of all citizens and protect all from social predators. However, with respect to our own personal relationships, instead of retaliating when our own rights are violated (which may be our legal right), righteous Christians will turn the other cheek and forgive their enemies. They count it a privilege to be persecuted for the sake of righteousness, knowing that this is the mark of a citizen of the kingdom of heaven (Matt. 5:10; 1 Peter 4:12—19).

Indeed, as stated later in the song of Deuteronomy 32 (v. 35) and in Paul's words in Romans 12:19, Yahweh reserves the right to vengeance for himself. Believers' response to abuse is to be characterized by forgiveness, leaving the revenge factor in the hands of God.

16. As in President Clinton's comment when being interrogated for an alleged moral offense, "It depends on what the meaning of the word 'is' is."

Deuteronomy 20:1–20

W hen you go to war against your enemies and see horses and chariots and an army greater than yours, do not be afraid of them, because the LORD your God, who brought you up out of Egypt, will be with you. ²When you are about to go into battle, the priest shall come forward and address the army. ³He shall say: "Hear, O Israel, today you are going into battle against your enemies. Do not be fainthearted or afraid; do not be terrified or give way to panic before them. ⁴For the LORD your God is the one who goes with you to fight for you against your enemies to give you victory."

⁵The officers shall say to the army: "Has anyone built a new house and not dedicated it? Let him go home, or he may die in battle and someone else may dedicate it. ⁶Has anyone planted a vineyard and not begun to enjoy it? Let him go home, or he may die in battle and someone else enjoy it. ⁷Has anyone become pledged to a woman and not married her? Let him go home, or he may die in battle and someone else marry her." ⁸Then the officers shall add, "Is any man afraid or fainthearted? Let him go home so that his brothers will not become disheartened too." ⁹When the officers have finished speaking to the army, they shall appoint commanders over it.

¹⁰When you march up to attack a city, make its people an offer of peace. ¹¹If they accept and open their gates, all the people in it shall be subject to forced labor and shall work for you. ¹²If they refuse to make peace and they engage you in battle, lay siege to that city. ¹³When the LORD your God delivers it into your hand, put to the sword all the men in it. ¹⁴As for the women, the children, the livestock and everything else in the city, you may take these as plunder for yourselves. And you may use the plunder the LORD your God gives you from your enemies. ¹⁵This is how you are to treat all the cities that are at a distance from you and do not belong to the nations nearby.

¹⁶However, in the cities of the nations the LORD your God is giving you as an inheritance, do not leave alive anything

that breathes. [17]Completely destroy them—the Hittites, Amorites, Canaanites, Perizzites, Hivites and Jebusites—as the LORD your God has commanded you. [18]Otherwise, they will teach you to follow all the detestable things they do in worshiping their gods, and you will sin against the LORD your God.

[19]When you lay siege to a city for a long time, fighting against it to capture it, do not destroy its trees by putting an ax to them, because you can eat their fruit. Do not cut them down. Are the trees of the field people, that you should besiege them? [20]However, you may cut down trees that you know are not fruit trees and use them to build siege works until the city at war with you falls.

HAVING DEALT WITH PERSONAL violence in chapter 19, Moses now shifts the focus to corporate violence, the violence of war. The placement of these instructions immediately after the *lex talionis* ("the principle of retaliation") suggests that in warfare even soldiers must recognize the limits of violence, and the state for whom one is fighting must respect this principle when dealing with the enemy. Against the backdrop of Moses' instructions on how to pursue righteousness in the internal affairs of the nation (16:18–19:21), he now instructs the Israelites on pursuing righteousness in external relationships.

Chapter 20, which is devoted entirely to military affairs, divides into three parts: (1) encouraging troops for battle (vv. 1–9); (2) instructions for battle (vv. 10–18); (3) instructions for siege warfare (vv. 19–20). Moses returns to the theme of warfare in three additional texts: 21:10–14; 23:9–14[10–15]; and 24:5.[1] These six texts share several features. All open with a temporal clause introduced by "when" (*kî*). Following the opening clause, all involve a particular aspect of warfare and include a proscription.[2]

---

1. R. Westbrook ("Riddles in Deuteronomic Law," in *Bundesdokument und Gesetz: Studien zum Deuteronomium* [ed. G. Braulik; HBS 4; Freiburg: Herder, 1995], 171) treats 21:1–9 as banditry, a type of warfare.

2. In 20:1–9, fear; in 20:10–15, cruelty to civilian populations of subjugates/conquered cities; in 21:19–20, wanton destruction of nature; in 21:10–14, abuse of captive women taken as wives; in 23:9–14[10–15], casual disposition toward the sanctity of the camp; in 24:5, insensitivity to army recruits. This feature applies also to 20:16–18, which, though lacking the formal introduction, proscribes leaving alive anything that breathes. Cf. A. Rofé, "The Laws of Warfare in the Book of Deuteronomy: Their Origins, Intent and Positivity," *JSOT* 32 (1985): 32.

All address the Israelites as a collective in the second person singular. Five of the six exhibit a remarkably humanitarian tone, expressed toward recruits (20:4–9; 24:5), civilians of subjugated cities (20:10–15; 21:10–14),[3] and even the environment (20:19–20); the sixth (23:9–14[10–15]) secures the presence of Yahweh by prescribing procedures to ensure the sanctity of the camp.

Because of the reference to the principle of "complete destruction" (*ḥērem*) in verses 16–18, this paragraph is often associated with the notion of "holy war" or "Yahweh war" and is distinguished from the rest of the chapter, which concerns "ordinary" warfare.[4] However, the instructions on "ordinary" warfare in this chapter also contain elements associated with *ḥērem*: the involvement of the priest as representative of Yahweh (v. 2); the appeal not to fear (vv. 1, 3); the declaration of Yahweh's presence (vv. 1, 4); the advance announcement of divine victory (v. 4); the acknowledgment of victory as a divine achievement (v. 13); and the recognition of spoil as a gift from Yahweh (v. 14). The primary difference between the *ḥērem* wars against Canaanite towns and other conflicts lies in the way vanquished cities and their populations are to be treated.

Since the three main topics of this chapter are formally introduced with casuistic clauses (vv. 1, 10, 19), some refer to it as a "War Manual."[5] However, the agenda is much more profound, presenting not only a theology of war but also of Israel's place among the nations. Indeed the chapter is dominated by "God statements," which would not normally be included in "laws" or "war manuals" (vv. 1, 4, 13, 16, 17, 18). The key to this chapter is not Israel's relationship to the nations but her relationship to Yahweh, who is always referred to as "the LORD *your God.*" Although some divide the chapter up into primary and secondary elements based on variations in the style and alternations of subject, this approach obscures its thematic coherence and neutralizes its homiletical function. This is not legislation but Torah, pastoral instruction, intended to instill in the Israelites' particular dispositions toward their God and other nations.

Encouraging the Troops for War (20:1–9)

MOSES' INSTRUCTIONS ON WAR begin logically with mustering the troops, for this is where military engagements begin. Although the focus shifts slightly in the midsection, this segment is held together by the framing motif of fear, which dominates verses 1–4 and 8–9.

---

3. A notable exception occurs in 20:16–18, which calls for the annihilation of the populations of Canaanite cities.

4. The expression used by McConville, *Deuteronomy*, 317.

5. Merrill, *Deuteronomy*, 282, 287.

The priest's exhortation (vv. 1–4). Moses begins by describing the context that calls for courage: "When you go to war against your enemies." The clause suggests an offensive rather than defensive military operation.[6] From the reference to Yahweh's presence in their midst (v. 1) and the priest's use of "today" (v. 3), it is obvious Moses has in view primarily the battles against the Canaanite nations (cf. 7:1), whom he had earlier (as here) exhorted his people not to fear (7:18). Not until verse 15 do we learn that he may have more in mind than the wars of conquest of the Promised Land. The collective second person singular suggests that these instructions involve a citizens' army (cf. Num. 1–2; 26) rather than a standing force of professionals, mercenaries, crack troops,[7] or conscripts forced into military service.[8]

For Moses the pastor the primary issue in verses 1–9 is fear. Verses 1–4 address the matter from three perspectives. (1) He acknowledges the cause of fear: the sight of horses and chariots and military forces superior to Israel's own. Although only a minority in the audience had witnessed Yahweh's annihilation of Pharaoh's fleet of horses and chariots at the Red Sea (Ex. 14–15), they were all aware of the threat posed by these movable platforms for launching spears and arrows (cf. Josh. 11:4; 17:16; Judg. 1:19; 4:3).[9] Combined with "people more numerous than you" (NIV, "an army greater than yours"), the description presents a perfect recipe for fear (cf. 7:17).

(2) Moses announces the antidote to fear. As in 7:17, he begins with an appeal, "Do not be afraid of them," followed by a reminder of Yahweh's presence with them. The form of the exhortation involving the durative imperfect calls for courage as a matter of course.[10] The reminder that Yahweh will be with them abbreviates Moses' longer speech in 7:18–21. Arguing from greater to lesser, he reassures Israel that if Yahweh could liberate them by defeating the superior Egyptians, his presence will surely guarantee victory against the Canaanites.

---

6. The idiom *yāṣāʾ lammilḥāmâ* ("to go out for the battle") is a conventional phrase for launching a military campaign. Cf. 2:32; 3:1; 21:10; Judg. 3:10; 20:14, 20, 28; 2 Sam. 21:17; 1 Kings 8:44; 1 Chron. 7:11.

7. Compare David's personal forces (1 Sam. 23:13; 2 Sam. 5:6–10; 15:18; 23:8–39). On the nature of armies in ancient Israel, see P. J. King and L. E. Stager, *Life in Biblical Israel* (Library of Ancient Israel; Louisville: Westminster John Knox, 2001), 239–45; R. de Vaux, *Ancient Israel*, vol. 1, *Social Institutions* (Garden City, NY: McGraw-Hill, 1961), 213–28.

8. Cf. Moses' exhortation to the two and one-half Transjordanian tribes in 3:18–22. This picture is reinforced by the narratives of Joshua and Judges.

9. For images of horse-drawn chariots from ancient Egypt and Assyria see *IBD*, 1:260–62.

10. See also Ex. 14:13. Such expressions are common in threatening situations (cf. Gen 15:1; Judg. 6:23; Joel 2:21, 22) and find exact equivalents in Assyrian oracles of encouragement. See S. Parpola, *Assyrian Prophecies* (SAA 9; Helsinki: Helsinki Univ. Press, 1997), 50.

(3) Moses prescribes a method whereby this fear may be dispelled in the future in specific battle situations. Whereas in the past he had seen the people through crises, in the future that responsibility will rest with the priest.[11] In fact, to ensure that his own voice will be heard whenever the Israelites go out to war, he composes the speech the priests are to deliver to the troops.[12] This speech exhibits the classical features of a military oration (2b–4):[13]

Narrative preamble	When you are about to go into battle, the priest shall come forward and address the army. He shall say:
Call to attention	"Hear, O Israel!
Declaration of the crisis	Today you are going into battle against your enemies.
Appeal for courage	Do not be fainthearted;[14] [do not be] afraid; do not be terrified; [do not] give way to panic before them.
The grounds for encouragement	For the LORD your God is the one who goes with you to fight for you against your enemies to give you victory."

The intensity of the emotional crisis that the sight of formidable enemy forces might create is reflected in the fourfold appeal for courage (cf. 31:6). Verse 4 declares the basis for future courage in the face of powerful enemies (cf. 1:30; 3:22). If verse 1b summarizes 7:18–21, then verse 4 summarizes 7:22–24, where Moses described in greater detail the way Yahweh would deliver the nations of Canaan and their kings into the hands of the Israelites.[15]

---

11. According to Num. 27:21, the priests' duties in the context of warfare included providing oracular guidance by means of the Urim and Thummim. Priests will play a prominent role in the campaign against Jericho (Josh. 6:1–21). For examples of inquiry, see Judg. 1:1–2; 20:23, 27, on which see Block, *Judges, Ruth*, 86–87.

12. For other speeches of Moses prescribed for use in the future, see 6:20 and 26:13.

13. Thus Weinfeld, *DDS*, 45–51. Cf. the orations by David (2 Sam. 10:11–12) and Hezekiah (2 Chron. 32:6–8).

14. This idiom for timidity ("a tender/soft heart") occurs elsewhere in Isa. 7:4; Jer. 51:46. In 2 Kings 22:19 (= 2 Chron. 34:27) it bears the positive sense of a soft heart.

15. On Yahweh as a divine warrior in Deuteronomy see R. D. Nelson, "Divine Warrior Theology in Deuteronomy," in *A God So Near: Essays on Old Testament Theology in Honor of Patrick D. Miller* (eds. B. A. Strawn and N. R. Bowen; Winona Lake, IN: Eisenbrauns, 2003), 241–59. Nelson discusses these verses briefly on pp. 246–47, though his claim that these verses reflect the revival of national aspirations under Josiah is unconvincing.

The officials' speeches (vv. 5–9). In a surprising turn, verse 5 intro-duces a new group of interlocutors, the "officers" (šōṭ'rîm; see comments on 1:16). These seem to have been literate nonmilitary officials, perhaps Levites[16] charged with mustering the troops and keeping records of their names and numbers. This text suggests they were also responsible for screening recruits. Technically verses 5–8 consist of two speeches (vv. 5–7 and v. 8), though the second speech simply carries on the questioning of the first speech. Like verse 3, Moses dictates these speeches so that even after he is gone, recruits will hear his voice as officers try to identify any who should be excused from military service. Moses' penchant for triadic constructions is evident in verses 5–7, which divide into three parts with virtually identical form, as the synopsis of a literal translations shows:[17]

The Speeches of the "Officers" in Deuteronomy 20:5–8

The First Speech			The Second Speech
20:5	20:6	20:7	20:8
Who is the man who has built a new house and has not taken occupancy of it? Let him go back home, or he may die in battle and someone else dedicate it.	Who is the man who has planted a vineyard and not begun to enjoy it? Let him go back home, or he may die in battle and someone else enjoy it.	Who is the man who has been engaged to a woman and not married her? Let him go back home, or he may die in battle and someone else marry her.	Who is the man who is fearful and fainthearted? Let him go back home, or he will cause to melt the heart of his fellows like his own.

The question with which each phase opens reflects a common situation in which a person addresses a crowd. Here the official wants to know if anyone among the troops has just built a house but has not had a chance to occupy it; has planted a vineyard but not yet eaten of its fruit; or has paid the bride price but has not yet consummated the marriage.

Each of these three scenarios demands a brief comment. The mean-ing of ḥānak in the first scenario (v. 5) is uncertain. The NIV's rendering,

16. See 1 Chron. 23:4; 2 Chron. 19:11; 34:13.
17. The speech segments are virtually identical in length, in Hebrew consisting of 17, 16, 16, and 14 words respectively. The modifier "new" in the first column accounts for the difference in the first three.

"dedicate," follows a longstanding tradition. However, the recurrence of this motif in 28:30, where *ḥānak* is substituted with *yāšab bô* ("to live in it") and the absence of any evidence of dedication ceremonies for private homes in the Old Testament suggest the word means simply "to establish residence in."[18] This need not exclude a "housewarming" ceremony of initiation.[19]

The crux of the second scenario involves the expression *ḥillᵉlô* ("begin to enjoy it").[20] According to Leviticus 19:23–25, the fruit of trees could not be eaten for five years. Since this scenario involves grapes rather than fruit trees, the time may have been reduced. A five-year military exemption seems unlikely.

The third scenario involves marriage, the most domestic act of all. In ancient Israel, when parents deemed children to be approaching marriageable age,[21] the father of the groom would contact the parents of the potential spouse and negotiate the terms of marriage, specifically the nature and size of the "marriage present."[22] Agreement by the parents of the bride would signal the engagement, and the bride and groom would be married after a period of betrothal.[23]

While analogues to these military exemptions are attested in extrabiblical literature,[24] nowhere are they expressed as clearly as here. Such

---

18. So also Baker, *Tight Fists or Open Hands*, 104, n. 92.

19. Thus New American Bible. Targum Jonathan reads "affixed the mezuzah [to the doorpost]." For discussions of the term, see S. C. Reif, "Dedicated to חנך," *VT* 22 (1972): 495–501.

20. In the Piel stem the root *ḥll* means "to profane," that is, "to desacralize" something by treating it as nonsacred. NIV's rendering is doubly felicitous, since in the Hiphil stem the same root commonly bears the sense "to begin."

21. Daughters tended to marry at the onset of puberty (about thirteen years of age) and sons a couple of years later.

22. So also G. I. Emmerson, "Women in Ancient Israel," in *The World of Ancient Israel* (ed. R. E. Clements; Cambridge: Cambridge Univ. Press, 1989), 382. The *môhar* was not a purchase price but a deposit delivered to the parents of the bride to promote the stability of the marriage and to strengthen the links between the families of those being married. Cf. Wright, *God's People in God's Land*, 194. According to R. Westbrook (*Old Babylonian Marriage Laws*, AfO Beiheft 23 [Horn: Berger, 1988], 60), the *môhar* was the price paid for the transfer of authority from a girl's father to her husband. See also R. Westbrook and B. Wells, *Everyday Law in Biblical Israel: An Introduction* (Louisville, KY: Westminster John Knox, 2009), 56–61.

23. See further Block, "Marriage and Family in Ancient Israel," 57–58. In 24:5 Moses expands the present policy.

24. For an extrabiblical fourteenth- to thirteenth-century BC analogue, see the Epic of Kirta from Ugarit (*COS*, 1:334). See also Sumerian poems involving Gilgamesh, who apparently excuses all who have a family house or a mother [to care for?], leaving him with fifty single male volunteers. For the translation see A. George, *The Epic of Gilgamesh: A New Translation* (London: Penquin, 2003), 152; cf. also 163.

---

exemptions were governed by the conviction that engagement in warfare rendered persons in transitional states particularly vulnerable. The last sentence of each scenario identifies the problem: the newly married man might be killed in battle, leaving another man to move into his house, to eat the fruit of his vineyard, or to marry the woman who should have been his wife. Policies granting military exemption compassionately affirm family and domestic values[25] and the right to enjoy the blessings of life. These exemptions also represent adaptations of "futility curses," found in ancient Near Eastern treaties and other documents,[26] as well as the covenant curses of Leviticus 26 and Deuteronomy 28:30 – 31, 38 – 40. These futility curses undermine the basic order of the universe, in which a specific cause yields a specific and natural result.

While many treat verses 5 – 7 as independent insertions, these verses also address fears associated with warfare. The fear is not death itself but the consequences of death, both for the individual and for the nation. By exempting these men from military service, Moses provides an answer to both undesirable outcomes.

The officials' second speech (vv. 8 – 9). Speaking of fear, the second speech addresses this issue directly. Although slightly shorter, structurally this speech mimics the three phases of the previous speech. However, the issue in the opening question is not the personal consequences of being killed in battle but the effect of the person's presence among the troops. The expressions describing his disposition, "afraid" and "fainthearted," are borrowed from verse 3. This remarkable statement exempts a would-be warrior from military service out of respect for the psychological effect of his presence on his comrades ("his brothers"). Despite the persistent acknowledgment of Yahweh's hand in Israel's battles, this statement recognizes the human dimension of war. To the fainthearted, the brutality and life-threatening nature of war cause fear. Unlike royal armies manned with conscripted troops, when Israel's citizen army fights Yahweh's wars, the character of individual troops is more important than their numbers.

Verse 9 is transitional, describing the final stage in preparing soldiers for war. After the "officers" have delivered their speeches, and after those with legitimate reasons for exemption and those who are fearful have returned

---

25. For a review of the literature, see W. M. de Bruin, "Die Freistellung vom Militärdienst in Deut. XX 5 – 7: Die Gattung der Wirkungslosigkeitssprüche als Schlüssel zum Verstehen eines alten Brauches," *VT* 49 (1999): 21 – 26.

26. See especially the ninth-century BC bilingual inscription (Akkadian and Aramaic) of Hadad-yith°i in *COS*, 2:154. On ancient Near Eastern and biblical futility curses, see Delbert R. Hillers, *Treaty Curses and the Old Testament Prophets* (Biblica et Orientalia 16; Rome: Pontifical Biblical Institute, 1964), 28 – 29.

home, the officials are to appoint "commanders" to lead the army into battle. Some speculate that the "officers" lacked authority to make such appointments,[27] but given the sacral nature of Israel's warfare, it seems reasonable that these officials might come from the ranks of the Levites.[28] If the king was subordinate to the Levitical priests (17:18), Levitical "officers" could have appointed the captains of the army.

Instructions for the Troops in Battle (20:10−20)

THE OPENING CLAUSE SETS the theme: "When you approach a town to fight against it" (pers. trans.). Like the preceding verses, this text divides into two parts, verses 10−14 and 16−18, with verse 15 functioning as a literary hinge. Moses highlights the differences in military policy between the way Israelites treat distant towns and towns within the Promised Land.

Instructions for distant campaigns (vv. 10−15). While Moses has not indicated that the campaigns envisaged here are anything other than the conquest of Canaan, the contrast between the treatment of targeted cities in verses 10−14 and 7:1−5 raises questions, which Moses will answer in verse 15. The strategies prescribed for military engagement are typical of those followed by Near Eastern kings in military campaigns. Upon approaching a targeted town, the Israelites are to offer it a chance to surrender peacefully.[29] To accept the offer means to accept subject status, though without the horrendous consequences of defeat in battle.

Verses 11−12 present two alternatives open to the targeted town. If "Peace!" is their answer and they open the gates of the city to the Israelites, they are to spare the lives of the entire population of the town (v. 11). However, they may impose corvée labor on them[30] and have them serve as vassals.[31] Alternatively, if they reject peace and "engage you in battle," then the armies of Israel may go on the offensive in subduing the town (v. 12). The sanctioned response involves four stages.

(1) They are to "lay siege" to the town (vv. 12b−13a). In the Old Testament a town is by definition a settlement fortified by walls, towers, and defensive gate structures, precisely the scenario envisaged here. If an invading army could not force its way through the gates or quickly create a breach in the walls, they would lay siege to it, preventing inhabitants from

---

27. Cf. McConville, *Deuteronomy*, 316.

28. Cf. 1 Chron. 23:4; 2 Chron. 19:11; 34:13.

29. On the idiom used in reference to its biblical and ancient Near Eastern context, see D. J. Wiseman, "'Is It Peace?'—Covenant and Diplomacy," *VT* 32 (1982): 311−26, esp. p. 321.

30. For discussion of the "corvée," see G. Klingbeil, "מַס," *NIDOTTE*, 2:992−95; A. Rainey, "Compulsory Labor Gangs in Ancient Israel," *IEJ* 20 (1970): 191−202.

escaping and supplies from being brought in. Depending on the resources inside the city, sieges could last for several years. However, enemy armies would attempt to hasten its fall by trying to penetrate the walls even as the siege was being conducted.[32]

Ezekiel 4:2 provides the most detailed description of siege tactics, listing four typical elements: siege walls, siege ramps, the deployment of troops, and battering rams.[33] Though the citizen armies of Israel would not have had access to the technology or resources of later Assyrian emperors, our text puts no stock in the strategy or technology of the Israelites. The ultimate fall of the city will be credited to Yahweh, who delivers it into their hands (v. 13a).

(2) They are to slaughter all the male inhabitants (v. 13b). Echoing an idiom from 13:15[16] Moses calls for the slaughter of all adult males, who represent the key to resistance and the backbone of the town's economy and administration.

(3) They may plunder the town (v. 14a). With the strong adversative particle *raq* ("only, except"; NIV "as for"), this verse highlights the contrast between the treatment of adult males and the rest of the population. The Israelites may claim the livestock and everything else in the town as booty, and women and children as spoils of war. The instructions regarding women and children are more generous than the treatment they had afforded the Midianites in Numbers 31:15–17. However, the situations are different. The present text envisages campaigns of territorial conquest, whereas in the Midianite battle the Israelites served as agents of divine vengeance (Num. 31:3).

(4) They can make use of the booty (v. 14b). The most common meaning of *ʾākal* is "to eat," but its semantic range is equivalent to English "consume," which may mean "to destroy" (cf. 7:16) or "to use," as in *Consumer Reports*. The latter sense is intended here; the Israelites may use the spoil of battle, receiving it as a gift from Yahweh.

In verse 15 we finally learn why this policy differs so sharply from the policies outlined in chapter 7. These instructions apply to campaigns against "all the cities that are at a distance from you" in contrast to these

---

31. On several occasions in Joshua, Israel substituted annihilation of the population with conscription into forced labor gangs (16:10; 17:13; cf. Judg. 1:28, 30, 33, 35). On use of forced-labor gangs on government projects, see 1 Sam. 8:10–18; 2 Sam. 20:24; 1 Kings 4:6; 5:14. David forced the defeated Ammonites to work for him (2 Sam. 12:31), and Solomon subjected his citizens to periodic corvée labor (1 Kings 5:13–14[27–28]; 9:15, 20–22).

32. On biblical accounts of sieges in their ancient context see K. Lawson Younger Jr., *Ancient Conquest Accounts: A Study in Ancient Near Eastern and Biblical History Writing* (JSOTSup 98; Sheffield: JSOT, 1990).

33. On these tactics see Block, *Ezekiel Chapters 1–24*, 170–73.

towns that "belong to the nations nearby." The latter refers to the land west of the Jordan promised to the fathers, now occupied by the seven Canaanite nations (7:1). The insertion of verses 10–15 suggests that Yahweh's long-range plan for Israel allowed additional conquests. This would probably involve those territories occupied largely by Aramaeans — territory that Yahweh had promised to Abraham (Gen. 15:18–21) and to which Deuteronomy 1:7–8 and 11:24–25 had referred (cf. 19:8–9).

Instructions for campaigns nearby (vv. 16–18). Like verse 14, verse 16 opens with the adversative particle *raq*, which signals a new type of campaign (NIV, "However"). Building on the law of *ḥērem* as prescribed in chapter 7, Moses calls for the total destruction of Canaanite cities and their dedication to Yahweh. As we noted in chapter 7, the verbal expression "to destroy totally" expresses a concept that is as much religious as military. This explains why in 7:1–6 and here the rationale does not address the military threat the enemy poses, but focuses totally on the religious implications of their survival. But what does this paragraph specifically teach about the Israelite approach to the policy of *ḥērem*?

(1) The policy demands the slaughter of the entire human population of the Canaanite towns. Whereas the women and children of distant towns that reject Israel's peaceful overtures are to be spared, in the cities of the land Yahweh is giving to Israel as their grant (*naḥᵃlâ*), nothing "that breathes" is to survive.[34] Towns in the Promised Land proper are to be treated even more severely than the towns east of the Jordan had been (cf. 2:34–35; 3:4–7).

(2) The policy of *ḥērem* is strictly circumscribed. The exception created for distant towns outside the *naḥᵃlâ* demonstrate that this was never intended to be a fundamental part of Israel's military policy (vv. 1–15). This circumscription is reinforced by the explicit naming of the people groups whose towns are targeted both here and in 7:1. The Transjordanian nations to the east (Ammonites, Moabites, Edomites) and the Aramaean city states to the north are excluded.

(3) This policy did not originate with politicians or military leaders but derives from Yahweh himself. The addition of "as the LORD your God has commanded you" at the end of verse 17 drives both hearer and reader to search for antecedent texts.[35] Chapter 7 provides an obvious candidate,[36]

---

34. Josh. 6:21 suggests the Israelites interpreted the phrase "nothing that breathes" (lit., "everything of breath") to mean domesticated livestock (oxen, sheep, donkeys) as well as the entire human population.

35. Cf. Jacob Milgrom, "Profane Slaughter and a Formulaic Key to the Composition of Deuteronomy," *HUCA* 47 (1976): 11–12.

36. Thus Tigay, *Deuteronomy*, 190.

except that those instructions on the ḥērem are cast as speech from Moses' mouth. Here Moses seems to have in mind the treatment of Canaanites prescribed by Yahweh at Sinai (Ex. 23:23 – 33, 34:11 – 16) and reiterated on the plains of Moab (Num. 33:51 – 55). Admittedly the root ḥrm does not appear in the Exodus and Numbers texts, but the antiquity of the notion is demonstrated by the Book of the Covenant (Ex. 22:19[18]) and the Sinaitic laws concerning vows (Lev. 27:28). That Deuteronomy should apply the word ḥrm to the campaigns against the Canaanites in place of gāraš ("to drive out") reflects a crystallization of the agenda in Moses' mind as he approaches the actual invasion of the land.

(4) As noted above, the ḥērem policy was driven by religious rather than genocidal or military considerations: the need to "keep Yahweh's holy people free from syncretism and idolatry."[37] For Israel, implementing ḥērem on a town not only secured its absolute transfer to the divine sphere; it was also intended to secure Israel's survival. At the level of the material, it prevented Israelites from contamination by contact with the "devoted" articles, which would have brought them under the same curse and subject to destruction (7:25 – 26). At the level of the spirit, it cut off the possibility of the Canaanites teaching the Israelites their abominable religious practices (cf. 12:30 – 31; 13:1 – 18[2 – 19]; 18:9).

The earlier texts had explicitly repudiated the worship of Canaanite gods (Ex. 23:24, 33; 34:14 – 15), called for the obliteration of their cultic installations (Ex. 23:24; 34:13; Num. 33:52), prohibited the Israelites from making any covenants with the Canaanites or their gods (Ex. 23:32; 34:15) or intermarrying with the Canaanites (Ex. 34:16), and warned of the seductive attraction of Canaanite religious practices (Ex. 23:33; 34:15). These motifs drive chapter 7 and underlie 20:18.

Moses the pastor is keenly aware of the threat that Canaanite religion poses to the spiritual integrity of God's people. To prepare them for this threat, he reinforces the policy established by Yahweh at Mount Sinai, insisting that the utter elimination of the pagan population is necessary to ensure Israel's fidelity to Yahweh. Presupposing that "law responds to reality *post factum*, only then attempting to govern it,"[38] critical scholars generally insist that these instructions on ḥērem represent a late addition to

---

37. Thus R. Nelson, "*Ḥērem* and the Deuteronomic Social Conscience," in *Deuteronomy and Deuteronomic Literature: Festschrift C.H.W. Brekelmans* (ed. M. Vervenne and J. Lust; BETL 133; Leuven: Leuven Univ. Press/Peeters, 1997), 54.

38. Thus Rofé, "Laws of Warfare in Deuteronomy," 36, who therefore dates the oldest stratum of the Deuteronomic war laws (24:5; 23:10 – 14[11 – 15]; 20:10 – 14,19 – 20) to the middle of the monarchic period, to which a religious zealot and extremist redactor added 20:15 – 18 in the Josianic era.

an earlier core of laws on warfare in Israel.[39] But this reasoning is fallacious. (1) Policies analogous to Israel's ḥērem were widespread in the ancient world and are attested in the second millennium. (2) Laws attempting to prohibit an abuse or undesirable action need not presuppose the abuse is already a problem; they may just as well be preventative, attempting to forestall a potential problem in the future, in which case they argue for the nonexistence of the issue at hand.[40]

Instructions for troops in siege warfare (vv. 19–20). Another temporal clause in verse 19 signals the beginning of the last subsection of this chapter and sets the context for brief instruction on siege warfare. The text envisions difficulty in subduing targeted towns because the inhabitants refuse to engage Israel in battle, forcing them to wear down the town with a protracted siege. It does not specify which towns are in view,[41] but it seems the policies apply to all enemy towns—both near and far, but especially those nearby.[42] Because the Israelites will be taking over the land in the hands of Canaanites, following these instructions becomes even more critical for their own long-range interests.

Remarkably, Moses does not outline a strategy for the Israelites to follow in a protracted siege. Instead, he speaks about preserving the natural environment around the town, charging the people not to destroy the fruit trees by wielding their axes against them. In ancient warfare strategy, the trees of vanquished territories would be cut down for several reasons: (1) as wood for siege structures and fuel for the invaders; (2) as retribution for the enemy's resistance and defiance; (3) as a tactic in psychological warfare, to hasten submission.[43] While the form of the prohibition suggests a compre-

---

39. The dates for the addition of vv. 15–18 vary from the eighth to seventh centuries (M. Weinfeld, "The Ban on the Canaanites in the Biblical Codes and Its Historical Development," in *History and Traditions of Early Israel: Studies Presented to Eduard Nielsen* [ed. A. Lemaire and B. Otzen; VTSup 50; Leiden: Brill, 1993], 142–60), to the time of Josiah (Rofé, "Laws of Warfare in Deuteronomy," 36), to the exile (E. Otto, "Krieg und Religion im Alten Orient und im alten Israel," in *Contimuum und Proprium* [Orientalia biblica und christiana 8; Wiesbaden: Harrassowitz, 1996], 57–58), and the postexilic period (Y. Hoffman, "The Deuteronomistic Concept of the Herem," *ZAW* 111 [1999]: 196–210).

40. So also D. H. Fischer, *Historians' Fallacies: Toward a Logic of Historical Thought* (New York: Harper & Row, 1970), 45.

41. These instructions continue the humanitarian train of thought of vv. 10–14, but that has been interrupted by vv. 15–18. Cf. Nelson, *Deuteronomy*, 247.

42. So also Michael G. Hasel, "The Destruction of Trees in the Moabite Campaign of 2 Kings 3:4–7: A Study in the Laws of Warfare," *AUSS* 40 (2002): 205.

43. See S. Cole, "The Destruction of Orchards in Assyrian Warfare," in *Assyria 1995* (ed. S. Parpola and R. M. Whiting; Proceedings of the 10th Anniversary Symposium of the Neo-Assyrian Text Corpus Project, Helsinki, September 7–11; Helsinki: Helsinki Univ. Press, 1997), 29–40.

hensive policy against cutting down any trees, the motive clause, "because you can eat their fruit," and the specification "fruit trees" in verse 20 focuses on the implications of deforestation for the food supply. In the long term, using the wood of fruit trees to construct siege works[44] is counterproductive to Israel's well-being.

The NIV and most translations render the last clause of verse 19 as a rhetorical question, "Are the trees of the field people, that you should besiege them?" Since trees are immobile, they obviously cannot retreat within the walls for protection, let alone defend themselves against a hostile axe. By this interpretation the statement is devoid of practical considerations and extraordinarily humanitarian and ecological, attempting to inspire sympathy for trees that have neither mind nor heart.[45] While the Hebrew construction is cryptic, it is not cast as a question. It is preferable to interpret the clause more practically and to translate the second half of the verse something like, "You must not cut them down—for humankind [depends on] trees of the field—in order [for the town] to come under the siege before you."[46]

The NKJV interprets the phrase correctly: "for the tree of the field *is* man's *food.*" The expression reflects human subsistence from fruit trees and represents an idiomatic way of saying, "Don't kill the goose that lays the golden eggs," or "Don't bite the hand that feeds you."[47] The trees symbolize life. Since the Israelites will have conquered the fields around the besieged city and eventually will occupy the city, it is contrary to self-interest ruthlessly to cut down the orchards around the city.

HISTORY OF MILITARY EXEMPTIONS. It is difficult to evaluate the degree to which the instructions concerning warfare given here were applied in Israel's conflicts with their enemies. The question of military exemption for reasons of fear surfaces in several narratives.

---

44. These works would include battering rams, ladders, and ramps. On the use of wooden beams and branches in the upper layers of a ramp to improve traction or prevent sinking into the mud of a ramp in later Assyrian siege practices see I. Eph'al, "The Assyrian Siege Ramp at Lachish: Military and Lexical Aspects," *Tel Aviv* 11 (1984): 65.

45. Thus Eph'al, ibid., 23.

46. Similarly N. Wazana, "Are Trees of the Field Human? A Biblical War Law (Deuteronomy 20:19–20) and Neo-Assyrian Propaganda," in *Treasures on Camels' Humps: Historical and Literary Studies from the Ancient Near East Presented to Israel Eph'al* (ed. M. Cogan and D. Kahn; Jerusalem: Magnes, 2008), 279–81.

47. So also ibid., 278–79. However, Wazana mistakenly views this policy as a response to Assyrian military tactics that connected the fate of the enemy with the fate of the trees.

Hushai recognized the demoralizing effect of a fainthearted soldier in the ranks of warriors in his counsel to Absalom in 2 Samuel 17:8 – 10. The element of fear is highlighted even more dramatically in Gideon's reduction of troops in Judges 7:1 – 6. Functioning as one of these officers, Gideon declared, "Anyone who trembles with fear may turn back and leave Mount Gilead" (7:3). When 22,000 troops accepted his release, 10,000 men remained, but these were ultimately reduced to 300. While fear was the occasion for their departure, Judges 7:2 declares in typically Deuteronomic style the true reason for the reduction of fighting men: "in order that Israel may not boast against me that her own strength has saved her" (cf. Deut. 8:17).

History of *ḥērem*. Although the laws of warfare in general and the policy of *ḥērem* in particular as taught here were intended to be determinative for Israel's engagement of the nations, the subsequent narratives suggest the policy of *ḥērem* was inconsistently followed. Joshua seems to have applied the specifications of Deuteronomy 20:16 only to Jericho (Josh. 6:24), Ai (8:26 – 28), and Hazor (11:11 – 13).[48] While the populations of other conquered cities appear to have been annihilated, the cities and their resources were apparently spared for Israelite use, in fulfillment of Deuteronomy 6:10 – 11.

Historiographic references to the policy are rare elsewhere. The expression of *ḥērem* is missing in Joshua 7:22 – 26, but we should interpret the burning of Achan and his household in the light of Deuteronomy 7:25 – 26. Judges 1:17 notes that Judah and Simeon treated Zephath with *ḥērem* warfare and renamed the town Hormah accordingly. While the Amalekites were not included in the Canaanite nations targeted for *ḥērem*, because of their interference with Yahweh's plan for Israel at the time of the exodus, Samuel charged Saul to apply the policy to them (1 Sam. 15). Saul's incomplete compliance contributed ultimately to Yahweh's retraction of kingship from him.

In the latter prophets *ḥērem* functions variously, but especially as a convenient expression for total destruction, often associated with the "day of the LORD."[49] According to Jeremiah 25:9, Yahweh will send Nebuchadnezzar to Palestine as his instrument of *ḥērem* against Judah. In 51:3 the roles are reversed.

---

48. So also V. Philips Long in I. Provan, V. P. Long and T. Longman III, *A Biblical History of Israel* (Louisville: Westminster John Knox, 2003), 140, 154, 173. To this list should be added the Danites' [illegitimate] burning of Laish in Judg. 18:27.

49. For a survey of the use of of *ḥērem* in the latter prophets see M. Fretz, "*Ḥērem* in the Old Testament," in *Essays on War and Peace: Bible and Early Church* (ed. W. M. Swartley; Occasional Papers 9; Elkhart, IN: Institute of Mennonite Studies, 1986), 18 – 20.

While the term *ḥērem* is obviously missing in the New Testament, the concept is not.[50] Based upon LXX's moderate preference for rendering *ḥērem* as *anathema*, which in classical Greek denotes "something dedicated or consecrated to the deity," the motif may be recognized in a series of texts involving curses, though always of individuals.[51] Nowhere, not even in Revelation, is the expression used in a military context, though the image of Babylon going up in smoke in chapter 18 is reminiscent of the burning of Jericho, Ai, and Hazor in Joshua.

INTERPRETING *ḤĒREM* TODAY. No image in the Old Testament is as troublesome, if not offensive, to modern readers as that of Yahweh, the God of Israel, not only tolerating the extermination of the Canaanites, but explicitly prescribing *ḥērem* for all the inhabitants of the land. How can this be reconciled with the New Testament's portrayal of God as a God of love in the person of Jesus Christ and of Yahweh's self-portraiture in the Old Testament as a God of grace and mercy, as expressed, for example, in Exodus 34:6–7?

Deuteronomy 20 itself seems to paint an inconsistent ethical picture. On the one hand, it expresses a remarkably enlightened humanity in: (1) providing military exemption for the fearful and those who have taken important domestic initiatives but have not had a chance to enjoy the fruit of those actions; (2) mandating targeted cities with opportunities for peaceful surrender before attacking; (3) prohibiting Israelites from using the wood of fruit trees to make military hardware. On the other hand, the demand to slaughter all the inhabitants of Canaan—men, women, and children—sounds more like a diabolical plot than a policy prescribed by God as we know him. This policy acknowledges the violence of war, but it also mandates and magnifies it, and portrays Yahweh as an active participant in it. While we justify this policy on textual grounds,[52] how can this genocide be justified morally?

---

50. See Hyung Dae Park, *Finding Herem? A Study of Luke-Acts in the Light of Herem* (LNTS; London: T&T Clark, 2007).

51. Mark 14:71 (Peter employs the verb in committing himself to *ḥērem* if he denies Jesus); Rom. 9:3 (Paul offers to give himself up as *ḥērem* if this would mean the salvation of his own people); 1 Cor. 12:3 (no inspired person says "May Jesus be devoted as *ḥērem*"); 1 Cor. 16:22 ("May those who do not love the Lord be devoted to *ḥērem*"); Gal. 1:8–9 (à la Deut. 13:12–17[13–18], Paul commits anyone who preaches another gospel to *ḥērem*).

52. In Ex. 23:23–33, 34:11–16, and Num. 33:51–55 Yahweh prescribes the action himself. Here we here the voice of his spokesman Moses.

Some have answered the question by allegorizing the notion. The genocidal commands are not meant to be taken at face value but rather were designed to convey some sort of higher truth about Christ. John Cassian, a Scythian monk (from what is modern Bulgaria; ca. AD 360 – 435), suggested that the seven nations whose land God promised to Israel in Deuteronomy 7:1 signify seven virtues necessary to overcome innumerable vices.[53] Some resolve this difficult question by appealing either to the contrasting ethics espoused by the Old and New Testaments, or to progress in revelation.[54] Unless one concedes to some sort of process theology, whereby God's own maturation and progressive enlightenment mirrors that of the human race, neither approach answers the theological question: How can God mandate war and violence in any era? The ethical issues involved in the divine charge to annihilate the Canaanites are complex and cannot be answered quickly. At the risk of being simplistic, those who wrestle with this problem must take into account a series of considerations. In isolation none satisfies completely, but taken together they provide necessary perspective.[55]

1. The policy of *ḥērem* is not a distinctly Old Testament issue. As we noted earlier, similar policies were practiced in the second millennium BC by the Hittites,[56] and in the first millennium by Moabites.[57]
2. The policy of *ḥērem* was divinely prescribed. As the creator of all things and all human beings and as the one who is sovereign over all, God can do anything he wants with anyone and be right in doing so. He was Israel's Commander-in-Chief, and if he commands the Israelites to eliminate the Canaanites, he is perfectly within his rights to do so. He does not need to account to us for his actions or his commands (Jer. 18:6 – 10).
3. The policy of *ḥērem* retains an element of mystery. How could a God of mercy and grace call for the extermination of an entire popula-

---

53. See *Ancient Christian Commentary on Scripture*, Old Testament III, *Exodus, Leviticus, Numbers, Deuteronomy* (ed. J. T. Leinhard; Downers Grove, IL: InterVarsity Press, 2001), 286.

54. According to C. S. Cowles, the Old Testament texts of holy war are "pre-Christ, sub-Christ, and anti-Christ." See "The Case for Radical Discontinuity," in *Show Them No Mercy: Four Views on God and Canaanite Genocide* (Stan Gundry, gen. ed.; Grand Rapids: Zondervan, 2003), 36.

55. For a similar perspective, see Christopher J. H. Wright, *The God I Don't Understand: Reflections on Tough Questions of Faith* (Grand Rapids: Zondervan, 2009), 76 – 108. For fuller discussion of the issues involved, see the essays in *Show Them No Mercy*.

56. See comments on 7:2; see Del Monte, "The Hittite *Ḥērem*," 21 – 45.

57. See K. A. Smelik in *COS*, 2:138. Cf. L. A. S. Monroe, "Israelite, Moabite and Sabaean War-Herem Traditions and the Forging of National Identity: Reconsidering the Sabaean Text RES 3945 in Light of Biblical and Moabite Evidence," *VT* 57 (2007): 318 – 41.

tion? But the ways of God are a mystery. Since we will never completely understand him, we should learn to relax with the questions in our minds. Isaiah 55:8–9 offers some consolation.

4. The policy of *ḥērem* directed at the Canaanites was neither an impulsive nor an arbitrary policy, but the culmination of an ancient plan. While this consideration does not remove the sting of the violence against a targeted race of people, readers of the Pentateuch have anticipated this since Genesis 15:18–21, where Yahweh promised Abraham that after four centuries he would take the land from the peoples of the land and hand it over to Abraham's descendants. Yahweh's fidelity to this promise underlies his call of Moses forty years prior to the delivery of this address (Ex. 3:8; 6:8), and through the defeat of Sihon and Og the Cisjordanian nations were warned of the fate awaiting them. God's elimination of the Canaanites was a necessary step in the history of salvation. For Israel to achieve the goals that he had in mind for them—that they might declare to the world his glory and grace—they needed a clean slate. It is a matter of ethical rather than ethnic cleansing. A holy people requires a holy land.

5. The policy of *ḥērem* was a divinely ordained means of dealing with sin. It was not driven by genocidal or military considerations, but the need to eradicate evil and prevent evil from spreading to the new population. The Canaanites were probably no more degenerate than other peoples of the time and region, but the policy was rooted in the perception of them as particularly wicked (Gen. 15:16). Their practices as a threat to the spiritual and ethical integrity of Israel, the holy people of Yahweh, actually reflect Yahweh's grace toward the other nations, who deserved the same fate.

As Moses had emphatically declared in 9:1–24, this did not mean the Israelites' superior moral state entitled them to the land; rather, it represents Yahweh's strategy for preserving for himself a holy people. But the elimination of the Canaanites was neither the first nor the last time God did/would do this. The difference between the destruction of the Canaanites and all of humanity (except for Noah's family) as described in Genesis 6–9 is one of scale and of agency. God chooses a variety of ways to punish people for wickedness. Sometimes it is through natural disaster, sometimes through plagues or drought or sickness (Lev. 26 and Deut. 28). The difference with the Canaanites is that this time he chose human beings to be the agents of judgment. But he would do so many times in history.

6. The policy of *ḥērem* assumes a paradigmatic role both for Israelites and Canaanites. The latter suffered a fate that ultimately all sinners

will face: the judgment of God. The law of ḥērem is one of many ways in which God executes justice on a sinful people. Later in Deuteronomy, he will catalogue the resources available to him to accomplish this task when Israel herself is the targeted people (32:22−25). Within this list of agents, the sword, which serves metonymically for war, is exceptional because it alone involves the active participation of people in carrying out the plan of God.[58]

While the ḥērem ordinance represents a particular kind of war, in its objectives, the extermination of the Canaanites is of a piece with God's actions against the human population as a whole in the great deluge (Gen. 6−9), his call for the destruction of the Midianites (Num. 31), his destruction of Judah (Ezek. 4−24), and his eschatological defeat of the forces of evil in Revelation. Insofar as the law of ḥērem was directed against a particular target, it depicts in microcosm the fate that awaits all who reject Yahweh as God and Savior. The Scriptures are consistent in their message that evil and rebellion against Yahweh yield death. Apart from the grace of God, this is the fate of all. The difference between Canaanites subject to this law and the ultimate destiny of other sinful inhabitants of the world is that Yahweh used his people Israel as human agents to send them to their fate.

7. The policy of ḥērem applied to a particular people at a particular time. According to Moses, as a fundamental part of Israelite war strategy the law of ḥērem applied only to their conflict with Canaanites. In fact, the scope of this law was strictly circumscribed by restricting it to cities within Israel's Promised Land and listing the targeted peoples by name (7:1; 20:17). Deuteronomy 20 declares unequivocally that this was not to become general policy governing Israel's relationships with the nations. When they engaged in war against other nations, the first goal was to seek peace, and even when offers of peace were refused, to deal humanely with the innocent within the population. Yahweh retained the right to extend the policy to other peoples (e.g., Midianites, Amalekites), but the Israelites were not free to do so on their own. Philistines, Moabites, Ammonites, and Aramaeans were outside the scope of this policy.[59] And, contrary to the way Christians have used these texts, this policy provides no justification for Christian violence against Jews and Muslims in the

58. Cf. H. Eberhard von Waldow, "The Concept of War in the Old Testament," *HBT* 6/2 (1984): 34.

59. This probably accounts for David's repeated queries regarding the will of Yahweh regarding the Philistines in 2 Sam. 5:17−25.

context of the Crusades or European claims to some sort of "manifest destiny" in their slaughter of Native Americans.

8. The policy of *ḥērem* assumed a sense of corporate identity and corporate solidarity that is difficult for modern Westerners to understand. To us each individual is a separate entity, and individual fulfillment is the highest ideal. However, according to the ancient Near Eastern ideal, individuals found their significance and identity in relation to the community. When one person hurts, all hurt; when one prospers, all prosper (1 Cor. 12–14). For this reason, few ancients would have objected when children shared the fate of their parents. This principle applied both to Canaanites and to the Israelites themselves (Ex. 20:3–6; 34:6–7; Deut. 5:8–10).

9. While the policy of *ḥērem* involves a comprehensive call for the extermination, the door was opened for exceptions. It is true that Deuteronomy and other biblical texts consistently portray the Canaanites as enemies of Israel rather than as potential "converts."[60] Nevertheless, the sparing of Rahab and her household demonstrates that Canaanites who acknowledged Yahweh and cast their lot with his people would find grace and deliverance in him. The Canaanites had at least forty years of advance warning (cf. Rahab's confession in Josh. 2:8–11), and any individual who declared faith in Yahweh would be spared. Indeed, so complete was Rahab's incorporation into the community of faith that in the providence of God she became the ancestress of Jesus (Matt. 1:5). If God can save Rahab, he can save anyone.

10. The policy of *ḥērem* plays no favorites. Although seven specific nations were targeted, Moses emphasized that if the Israelites act like Canaanites, abandon Yahweh, and serve other gods, they too will be subject to the same law—men, women, and children (Deut. 7:25–26; 13:12–17[13–18]). The severity of the prescription in 13:15–16[16–17] for Israelite towns that defect exceeds what chapter 7 and 20:16–18 demand of Canaanite towns. Whereas 7:1–5, 25–26 had called for the utter destruction of the people and their cultic installations and artifacts, and 20:16–18 "any [person] that breathes," 13:15–16[16–17] specifies the destruction of the inhabitants of any idolatrous Israelite town and all that was in it, including its livestock. All its booty (cf. 20:14) was to be gathered in the open square and burnt as an offering to Yahweh. With the privilege of bearing the labels "chosen by Yahweh," "people of Yahweh,"

---

60. So also Fretz, "*Ḥērem* in the Old Testament," 15.

"Yahweh's treasure," and "children of Yahweh" comes the weighty responsibility of loving him and representing him well before a watching world. But the Israelites lost sight of their mission, and in 734–22 BC the northern kingdom went the way of the Canaanites, and 586 BC the kingdom of Judah followed.

None of these answers will satisfy everyone, and none of them should be taken in isolation. The challenge for us is that we treasure God's grace in our own lives and pray for him to extend his grace to others. Perhaps when they see what God has done for us, outsiders will, like Rahab, confess faith in our God.

If it was illegitimate for Israelites to extend the scope of the law of *ḥērem* to other nations in Old Testament times, how much less can this be done after the cross and the establishment of the transnational church as God's agents of grace and revelation. Since the "people of God" are no longer defined nationally or ethnically, none of the wars in which contemporary nations engage can be equated with Israel's wars against the Canaanites, and efforts to claim "God is on our side" generally sound presumptuous and arrogant. The church is indeed engaged in warfare; but this conflict is not against flesh and blood, but against principalities and powers arrayed against God and his church. This battle is not fought with physical spears and swords but with all the spiritual resources provided by God (Eph. 6:10–20).

While the New Testament recognizes that the kingdoms of this world will continue to solve their conflicts with violence and war, the troops in the divine army march at the orders of the divine Commander-in-Chief. The Lord calls on his people to return evil directed at them with good, to turn the other cheek to those who abuse them, and like Christ to sacrifice their lives that others may live. In this kingdom of radicals committed to bringing peace rather than war, the next person's right to life always takes precedence over my own.[61] The law of *ḥērem* was never about vengeance in the Old Testament, and Christians must beware of taking vengeance into their own hands. Those who walk by faith trust God to defend his own.

---

61. For eloquent expression of peace as the fundamental policy of Christians, see the many writings of J. H. Yoder, such as *The Politics of Jesus* (2nd ed.; Grand Rapids: Eerdmans, 1994).

Deuteronomy 21:1–9

If a man is found slain, lying in a field in the land the Lord your God is giving you to possess, and it is not known who killed him, ²your elders and judges shall go out and measure the distance from the body to the neighboring towns. ³Then the elders of the town nearest the body shall take a heifer that has never been worked and has never worn a yoke ⁴and lead her down to a valley that has not been plowed or planted and where there is a flowing stream. There in the valley they are to break the heifer's neck. ⁵The priests, the sons of Levi, shall step forward, for the Lord your God has chosen them to minister and to pronounce blessings in the name of the Lord and to decide all cases of dispute and assault. ⁶Then all the elders of the town nearest the body shall wash their hands over the heifer whose neck was broken in the valley, ⁷and they shall declare: "Our hands did not shed this blood, nor did our eyes see it done. ⁸Accept this atonement for your people Israel, whom you have redeemed, O Lord, and do not hold your people guilty of the blood of an innocent man." And the bloodshed will be atoned for. ⁹So you will purge from yourselves the guilt of shedding innocent blood, since you have done what is right in the eyes of the Lord.

Original Meaning

DEUTERONOMY 21 CONSISTS OF five short pieces: verses 1–9, 10–14, 15–17, 18–21, and 22–23. These sections are held together by variations of the land grant formula that frame the chapter (vv. 1, 23); each one opens with a conditional clause ("If, when"), followed by a prescribed response; there is a common concern to separate life and death;[1] and there is an overall chiastic arrangement, with instructions on the rights of the firstborn (vv. 15–17) being the center of gravity.[2] While the word "righteousness" is missing, the entire unit

---

1. C. M. Carmichael, "A Common Element in Five Supposedly Disparate Laws," *VT* 29 (1979): 129–42.
2. A Death and Defilement (vv. 1–9)
     B Basic Family Relationships: Husband and Wife (vv. 10–14)
       C The Rights of the Firstborn (vv. 15–17)
     B´ Basic Family Relationships: Parents and Child (vv. 18–21)
   A´ Death and Defilement (vv. 22–23)

continues the discussion of "righteousness, only righteousness" as announced in 16:20 (see comments), intending to proscribe unrighteous human conduct.

Verses 1–9 exhibit several links with 19:1–13.[3] This text presents a recipe for restoring the deity–nation–land relationship when it has been disturbed through the most serious of human crimes, but it cannot be addressed by dealing with the criminal; his identity is unknown. This is achieved through a ritual designed to atone for the people and to purge from their midst the innocent blood that has been violently shed. The paragraph divides into three parts: (1) The problem (v. 1); (2) The prescription (vv. 2–8b, though broken in v. 6); (3) The result (vv. 8c–9).

The Problem (21:1)

UNLIKE OTHER TEXTS THAT open with "if a man is found," this case does not involve an offender caught in the very act of his misdeed;[4] rather, the pierced body of the victim of a crime is found lying in the open field. While the context suggests the person was murdered, the case is unresolved.[5] The purpose of this unit is not to show how to solve the murder, but how to resolve the spiritual crisis that an unsolved murder creates for the community.

The opening land grant formula illuminates the corporate significance of the crime (v. 1). The goal of the ritual is to restore the symbiotic relationships among Yahweh, Israel, and her land. The reference to land indicates that murder is not merely a crime against a human being but also a crime against Yahweh, for the land is the object of Yahweh's special care (cf. 11:11–12) and the gift he graciously grants to Israel (19:10, 21:23). Murderous acts violate its sanctity.

The Prescription (21:2–8b)

MOSES' INSTRUCTIONS FOR RESOLVING defilement caused by bloodguilt begin with the investigatory procedures (v. 2). He assigns to elders and judges of the region the responsibility for determining who performs the

---

3. The form of the land grant formula found in 21:1 occurs elsewhere only in 19:2 and 19:14; the expression "the blood of an innocent man" (21:8) recalls 19:10 and 13; and 21:9, like 19:1–13, concludes with the purgation formula.

4. Idolater in 17:2; adulterer in 22:22; kidnapper in 24:7. See further, S. Dempster, "The Deuteronomic Formula *kî yimmāṣēʾ* in the Light of Biblical and Ancient Near Eastern Law," *RB* 91 (1984): 188–211.

5. A. Phillips ("Another Look at Murder," *JJS* 28 [1977]: 124–25) observes that the text shows no interest in the victim or his family, or in compensation for the loss of life.

ritual actions. Whereas elders' authority derived from experience and status as heads of families,[6] cases involving more than one community required appointed judges to ensure that the crisis did not degenerate into clan warfare, as towns and villages played the blame game (16:18). Assuming the people in the vicinity of the crime have already been questioned, the officials' task seems simple: measure the distance from the location of the corpse to the towns in the region to determine which is nearest. The purpose of this action is not to establish responsibility for the murder, but to identify the community that should take responsibility for purging Israel of its bloodguilt.

The ritual action of the elders (vv. 3–4, 6–8b). Verse 3 begins abruptly by focusing on the town nearest the victim's body. However, in verse 3b the scope narrows to the elders, who represent the town and ultimately the nation in the expiatory ceremony.[7] Based on the syntax of verses 3b–4 and 6, we may recognize four discrete stages in ritual to be performed.

(1) The elders must select a young heifer that had never been harnessed for work (v. 3b).[8] While the instructions do not explicitly call for an unblemished animal, apparently draft animals were contaminated when humans placed yokes on their necks. Since the ritual involves breaking the animal's neck, an uncontaminated specimen was needed.

(2) The elders remove the heifer to a flowing wadi (v. 4a). Like the heifer, the location of the ritual is described with three qualifications: (a) There must be a wadi flowing with a perpetual stream of water; (b) no service has been performed in it; (c) it has never been planted (with seed). The instructions envisage an Edenic oasis, a virgin river valley where plants grow naturally,[9] rather than a place watered by a stream only in the rainy season.

(3) The elders break the heifer's neck at the wadi (v. 4). Since the action results in the death of the animal, it probably involves a blow to the neck with a large pole or axe. Presumably this method was prescribed to avoid bloodshed, which might explain why a young cow was needed. Seasoned draft animals develop strong neck muscles, making it difficult to break the

---

6. As in the case of the avenger of blood in 19:12.

7. Verse 6 requires the involvement of all the elders of the town, not a representative group.

8. Cattle were used for plowing fields (1 Kings 19:19), treading grain to thresh it (Deut. 25:4), and pulling wagons/carts to transport goods (1 Sam. 6:8–17). Numbers 19:2 also requires that the sacrificial red cow never have worn a yoke.

9. Carmichael ("Five Supposedly Disparate Laws," 131, n. 2) argues the wadi is "eminently cultivable," contra McConville (*Deuteronomy*, 328), who sees the wadi as rocky and unsuitable for cultivation.

neck and perhaps necessitating slitting the jugular—which is to be rigorously avoided in this ritual.[10]

The significance of this aspect of the ritual is unclear.[11] This is obviously not a sacrifice,[12] since it is performed by laypersons far away from any altar. While some interpret this as "a magical procedure for getting rid of sin" (cf. Lev. 16:22),[13] or a substitutionary ritual for the murderer,[14] it seems best to view the ritual as a reenactment of the murder, with the goal of banishing the defilement of the land. An innocent life has been taken in an innocent locale, with rituals performed in such a way that the land does not lose its innocence by absorbing additional blood.

(4) The elders wash their hands over the heifer (v. 6). For the first time the actions in the wadi are linked with the crime. This gesture involves all the elders of the nearest town, reinforcing the conviction that the slaughter of the heifer represents a ritual reenactment of the original murder. While it is unclear why the elders should wash their hands over the heifer, to have the water used to wash their hands dripping onto the animal suggests the ritual was forensic. It provided residents of the town a means whereby they (through their representatives) could declare their innocence before God.[15] This interpretation is supported by the following verbal declaration.

(5) The elders declare their innocence and plead for mercy (vv. 7–8b). The opening, "And they shall answer and say" (pers. trans.), suggests this utterance formally interprets the nonverbal actions.[16] Representatives of the community hereby declare their innocence and plea for absolution from the guilt of murder—they have neither shed this blood[17] nor witnessed the crime.[18] The prescribed speech also calls on the elders to

---

10. On which see G. Brin, "The Firstling of Unclean Animals," *JQR* 68 (1977/78): 12–14.

11. For a survey of scholarly opinions, see Wright, "Deuteronomy 21:1–9," 390–93; Z. Zevit, "The ʿeglâ Ritual of Deuteronomy 21:1–9," *JBL* 95 (1976): 377–90.

12. This form of killing is prescribed elsewhere for animals unsuitable for sacrifice.

13. Von Rad, *Deuteronomy*, 136.

14. Driver, *Deuteronomy*, 141–42.

15. The text does not suggest the murderer is off the hook. Numbers 35:33 explicitly declares that expiation for murder can only be achieved through the execution of the murderer himself. Cf. *m. Sot.* 9:7; *b. Ket.* 37b. Cf. J. Milgrom, "ʿEglah ʿArufah," *EncJud* (2nd ed.), 6:220–21.

16. This is captured by ESV's "They shall testify," but missed by NIV's "declare."

17. As in 19:10 (cf. 27:25) the idiom "to shed blood" is a euphemism for murder, but it also implies that the ground has received the blood of an innocent man and screams for a response from God (cf. Gen. 4:10–11).

18. For a twelfth-century BC analogue from Ugarit concerning a man who was murdered in the city of Arzigana, see J. Nougayrol et al. *Ugaritica 5* (1968) (Paris: Imprimerie Nationale and Librarie Orientaliste Paul Geuthner): 95, 97, ll. 45–50. Cf. the discussion by Westbrook, "Lex Talionis," 64–65.

---

pray that Yahweh will purge his people. The usage of *kappēr* (NIV "accept this atonement"; lit., "Atone!") is exceptional.[19] Whereas in most contexts "atonement" is effected through ritual acts by priests, here Yahweh is the subject of the verb.[20]

Even though the ritual involved only the elders, the prayer has the interests of the nation at heart. The beneficiaries are identified by their relationship to Yahweh, their national name, and the foundation of their relationship to Yahweh: they are Yahweh's people, Israel, the objects of Yahweh's redemptive actions.[21] As in Moses' intercessory prayers (Ex. 33; Num. 14), the elders of the town are to cast themselves and their people on the mercy of Yahweh, but also to challenge him not to annul his redeeming work.

The second part of the petition is more specific, as the elders plead with Yahweh not to hold his people responsible for the innocent blood of the murder victim.[22] Since he places the blood on the people/land, only he can remove the guilt.

These instructions recall Numbers 35:29–34. However, that text focused on expiation for land by means of the blood of the murderer, while this passage provides for purgation when the murderer cannot be identified. The prayer is the key to the passage, expressing confidence that Yahweh will act with mercy when he hears the declaration of innocence, their pleas for atonement, and their reminder of their status with him.

The role of the priests (v. 5). Even though other texts speak of the Levitical priests'[23] sacramental (10:8; 18:5) and judicial (17:8–9) roles, the present statement interrupts the description of a ritual dominated by elders. Apparently, since the people have been unable to identify the criminal and this crime requires the purgation of sin from the land, this is a judicial and sacerdotal issue. But the ritual is conducted before a plurality of priestly officials removed from the central sanctuary and the town courts in a wadi. As in the case of the king who copies the Torah (17:19–20), their presence at this ritual was required to ensure its proper performance and to serve as witnesses. Presumably at the end they will announce the lifting of blood-guilt and the replacement of this curse with the blessing on Yahweh's behalf.

---

19. The verb recurs in 21:8a, 8b; 32:43. Usually the Piel form means "to atone, make atonement," or "to expiate."

20. Cf. 2 Chron. 30:18–19; Pss. 65:3[4]; 78:38; 79:9; Jer. 18:23; Ezek. 16:63.

21. The verb "to redeem, ransom" (*pādâ*) from slavery also occurs in 7:8; 9:26; 13:5[6]; 15:15; 24:18.

22. The idiom "to put innocent blood in the midst of" presents the blood of slain victims as the lens through which Yahweh looks upon the people. The expression occurs only here in the Old Testament (cf. 19:10 and 22:8).

23. The expression, "the priests, the sons of Levi" occurs elsewhere only in 31:9.

The Result (21:8c−9)

MOSES CONCLUDES HIS INSTRUCTIONS with a welcome announcement. If Israel pursues righteousness in relationship to insoluble murder cases this way, the guilt of innocent blood will be purged from their midst (16:20) and they will do what is right in Yahweh's eyes.

THE PRESENT RITUAL RECEIVES a lot of attention in the Talmud,[24] but Old Testament allusions to it are scarce. In 2 Samuel 21:1−14 the perpetrators of the crime are known (Saul and his "blood-stained house," 21:1), but the link between murder and defilement is recognized. David offers to make atonement (*kpr*) that the aggrieved Gibeonites might bless the land grant (*naḥᵃlâ*) of Yahweh (21:3). We may also recognize an allusion, especially to the ritual washing, in Psalm 26:6−7:

> I wash my hands in innocence,
>   and go about your altar, O LORD,
> proclaiming aloud your praise,
>   and telling of all your wonderful deeds.

The psalmist's proclamation probably included his absolution of guilt and declaration of innocence. Ritual handwashing signified a nonverbal declaration of innocence (cf. Matt. 27:24).

THIS SHORT UNIT NOT only reinforces the conviction of the sanctity of human life as espoused in chapter 19, but it also goes beyond that text in recognizing the corporate responsibility of the entire community for the crimes of the individuals. Criminals are indeed responsible for the crimes they commit, but they are not *solely* responsible.[25] When a person violates the righteous standards of God, unless the community responds to the crime, the guilt of the individual rests on the heads of all. We may be calloused to the culture of death in which we live—expressed in four thousand abortions per day in this country, the senseless killing by drug dealers and users, the exploitation of violence in the media—but God is not. It is time to wake up to the curse that

---

24. See L. I. Rabinowitz, "ᶜEglah ᶜArufah," *EncJud* (2nd ed.), 6:221.
25. Cf. Brown, *Deuteronomy*, 204.

hangs over our land, and God's people should lead the way in promoting rituals that will remind us of our sinful condition and the hope of catharsis.

At the same time this text unit offers a fabulous message of grace and hope. Even for cases that are insoluble judicially, Yahweh provides a way of forgiveness for the innocent. These instructions announce to the Israelites a specific response that is guaranteed to be effective, provided their lives are characterized by a commitment to righteousness in all things. However, the hope of sinners is ultimately based not on their own positive efforts, as if these must somehow provide a counterbalance to the evils of the wicked. Rather, as David recognized (Ps. 51:1), the possibility of forgiveness for the individual and the community rests entirely on the compassionate heart of God and his atoning grace — through the sacrifice of Jesus Christ.

Deuteronomy 21:10–23

When you go to war against your enemies and the LORD your God delivers them into your hands and you take captives, ¹¹if you notice among the captives a beautiful woman and are attracted to her, you may take her as your wife. ¹²Bring her into your home and have her shave her head, trim her nails ¹³and put aside the clothes she was wearing when captured. After she has lived in your house and mourned her father and mother for a full month, then you may go to her and be her husband and she shall be your wife. ¹⁴If you are not pleased with her, let her go wherever she wishes. You must not sell her or treat her as a slave, since you have dishonored her.

¹⁵If a man has two wives, and he loves one but not the other, and both bear him sons but the firstborn is the son of the wife he does not love, ¹⁶when he wills his property to his sons, he must not give the rights of the firstborn to the son of the wife he loves in preference to his actual firstborn, the son of the wife he does not love. ¹⁷He must acknowledge the son of his unloved wife as the firstborn by giving him a double share of all he has. That son is the first sign of his father's strength. The right of the firstborn belongs to him.

¹⁸If a man has a stubborn and rebellious son who does not obey his father and mother and will not listen to them when they discipline him, ¹⁹his father and mother shall take hold of him and bring him to the elders at the gate of his town. ²⁰They shall say to the elders, "This son of ours is stubborn and rebellious. He will not obey us. He is a profligate and a drunkard." ²¹Then all the men of his town shall stone him to death. You must purge the evil from among you. All Israel will hear of it and be afraid.

²²If a man guilty of a capital offense is put to death and his body is hung on a tree, ²³you must not leave his body on the tree overnight. Be sure to bury him that same day, because anyone who is hung on a tree is under God's curse. You must not desecrate the land the LORD your God is giving you as an inheritance.

IN DEUTERONOMY 21:10 MOSES' focus shifts from a ritual designed to maintain the purity of the community to family matters. The rest of chapter 21 consists of four fragments devoted to the maintenance of righteousness in marriage and family relationships: (1) the righteous treatment of war brides (vv. 10–14); (2) the righteous treatment of a second-rank wife and her son (vv. 15–17); (3) the righteous treatment of a rebellious son (vv. 18–21); (4) the righteous treatment of a criminal's remains (vv. 22–23).

Righteousness in the Treatment of War Brides (21:10–14)

THE OPENING TEMPORAL CLAUSE and the military theme link this paragraph to the other war texts.[1] It contains an appeal to Israelites to be charitable in their treatment of foreigners who are forced to become a part of the community. It divides into two unequal parts, presenting a primary (vv. 10–13) and a secondary circumstance (v. 14). The primary case calls for charitable treatment of foreign brides when they are first taken; the secondary case, for their charitable treatment in divorce. The principal thrust of the passage is reflected in the concluding motive clause: "since you have dishonored her."[2]

The nature of the degradation (vv. 10–12a). First, Moses attempts to secure the well-being of an enemy woman captured in battle. The description of the warrior's treatment of the war bride sounds calloused,[3] but Moses' disposition is hinted at by the final clause (v. 14). Her degradation occurs in six stages:[4] (1) Yahweh delivers her people into the Israelites' hands (cf. 20:14); (2) the woman is among the captives taken by the Israelites; (3) a warrior notices that she is beautiful; (4) she becomes the object of his affection;[5] (5) he marries her;[6] (6) she is brought back to the home of the warrior. The text does not indicate his marital status. If he is the

---

1. Deut. 20:1–9, 10–15, 16–18, 19–20; 21:10–14; 23:9–14[10–15]; 24:5.

2. On ʿinnâ, meaning to "debase" rather than "rape" or "commit sexual abuse," see E. van Wolde, "Does ʿinnâ Denote Rape? A Semantic Analysis of a Controversial Word," *VT* 52 (2002): 528–44.

3. The warrior's treatment of the woman is summarized with six verbs: (lit.) "you go out," "and you take captives," "and you see," "and you love," "and you take," "and you bring."

4. For discussion and bibliography of the abuse of women in ancient warfare, see Rebekah L. Josberger, "Between Rule and Responsibility: The Role of the ʾAB as Agent of Righteousness in Deuteronomy's Domestic Ideology" (Ph.D. dissertation, The Southern Baptist Theological Seminary, Louisville, 2007), 41–42.

5. The word ḥāšaq was used earlier to describe Yahweh's attachment to Israel (7:7; 10:15).

6. On "to take as a wife" (lāqaḥ lᵊʾiššâ), see *DCH*, 4:573; Block, "Marriage and Family in Ancient Israel," 46–47.

head of the "house" to which he brings her, he probably has at least one additional wife.

Protecting the dignity of the captive woman in marriage (vv. 12b–13). On the surface, for a warrior to marry a captive bride seems innocent. However, Moses realistically recognizes that the system is subject to abuse, as triumphant males exploit and take advantage of female captives. Having none of this, Moses instructs the Israelites how to respect the rights and dignity of wives whom they have captured. (1) The captive bride must be allowed to express her pain at being torn from her people and forced to join an alien community. While having her shave her hair, trim her nails, and remove her native clothing appear to be insulting demands,[7] these actions symbolize her change of status.[8] When her hair and nails grow and she puts on new clothes, she emerges as a new person, with a new identity and new status;[9] she hereby declares nonverbally what Ruth declared verbally to Naomi (Ruth 1:16). The actions also remind her new husband that he is not to treat her as an alien or a slave.

(2) The woman must be permitted to mourn for her father and mother for a month.[10] Whether or not her parents died in the conquest of the town, for this woman they have in effect died, for she has no hope of seeing them again. Moses hereby calls on Israelites to allow others the opportunity to show the same respect for their parents as they are commanded to do (5:16). He also links the consummation of the marriage to the end of the period of mourning; only after she has completed her month of mourning may he have sexual intercourse with her,[11] marry her, and have her formally recognized as his wife. This monthlong quarantine expresses respect for the woman's ties to her family of origin and her own psychological and emotional health, providing a cushion from the shock of being torn from her own family.

---

7. To the rabbis these acts were intended to make her unattractive to the man, so he would rethink his desire to marry this pagan woman. For references see Tigay, *Deuteronomy*, 194, 381–82.

8. Carolyn Pressler, *The View of Women Found in the Deuternomic Family Laws* (Berlin and New York: de Gruyter, 1993), 12.

9. Compare the healed lepers who signify their new status with new clothes (Lev. 14, esp. v. 8), or Gen. 35:2, where the change seems to signify a shift in spiritual allegiance. On the symbolic significance of clothing, see M. E. Vogelzang and W. J. van Bekkum, "Meaning and Symbolism of Clothing in Ancient Near Eastern Texts," in *Scripta Signa Vocis: Studies about Scripts, Scriptures, Scribes and Languages in the Near East Presented to J. H. Hospers by His Pupils, Colleagues and Friends* (ed. H. L. J. Vanstiphout; Groningen: Forsten, 1986), 265–84.

10. On thirty days as the normal period of mourning, see Num. 20:29; Deut. 34:8. For discussion of her mourning, see Calum Carmichael, *The Spirit of Biblical Law* (Athens, GA: Univ. of Georgia Press, 1996), 135.

11. On "to go in to her," as an idiom for sexual intercourse, see Block, "Marriage and Family in Ancient Israel," 46.

Protecting the rights of the captive woman in divorce (v. 14). Recognizing that people's dreams of marriage are not always fulfilled, in verse 14 Moses considers the fate of a captive woman for whom her husband's passion has died.[12] Whatever the cause of this loss of passion, Moses rigorously protects the rights of the foreign wife. If the man decides to divorce his war bride, he may not humiliate her further.[13] On the contrary, by adding "wherever she wishes," he heightens the emphasis on her interests and dignity, freeing her to return home and live with her parents—if they are still alive—or to remarry.[14]

Moses issues two prohibitions for the Israelite husband who would divorce his war bride: By no means may he sell her for silver, nor may he treat her as chattel 'property.[15] He concludes with a rationale for the compassionate treatment of war brides even in divorce. She has already been degraded by being captured and forced to marry the enemy. In other words, the Israelite man may not humiliate (NIV "dishonor") her again by heartlessly treating her as property to be disposed of or exchanged for silver. Through divorce she again loses her status as a member of the Israelite's household.[16]

Righteousness in the Treatment of the Firstborn (21:15−17)

THE PLACEMENT OF THIS provision after verses 10−14 may suggest the captive woman whom the warrior married is still in Moses' mind. The present instructions mention three critical details. (1) A man has two wives, one of whom he favors over the other.[17] (2) Both wives bear a son for their husband. (3) The less favored wife is the first to give birth, presenting the

---

12. Perhaps jealousy of the primary wife or resentment at having mothered the man's "firstborn" (cf. Abraham and Sarah's response to Hagar in Gen. 16 and 21).

13. "Let her go" (Heb. *šillaḥ*) is used elsewhere of releasing slaves (15:12) and divorce (22:19, 29). So also Mal. 2:16, on which see G. P. Hugenberger, *Marriage as a Covenant: Biblical Law and Ethics as Developed from Malachi* (Grand Rapids: Baker, 1998), 72−73.

14. Babylonian marriage documents from the seventh to third centuries speak repeatedly of a released woman being free to "go back to her parental home," or "to her home," or "wherever she wishes." See M. T. Roth, *Babylonian Marriage Agreements: 7th−3rd Centuries B.C.* (AOAT 222; Neukirchen-Vluyn: Neukirchener Verlag, 1989), §§2, 4, 5, 6, 15, 16, 19, 20, 26, 30. For discussion of these texts see D. Instone-Brewer, "Deuteronomy 24:1−4 and the Origin of the Jewish Divorce Certificate," *JJS* 49 (1998): 230−43.

15. *HALOT*, 2:849.

16. So also Josberger, "Between Rule and Responsibility," 68−70.

17. The differences in his disposition are expressed by the antonyms "to love" and "to hate," which punctuate the passage (vv. 15a, 15b, 16b). The latter term need not be interpreted as "hatred, antipathy toward." As in Mal. 1:2−3, it may mean simply "to be indifferent toward, to neglect, or disregard."

---

husband with his "firstborn" (*bᵉkôr*). Because a father could assign this status to a second child, the word should be understood as a designation for rank, of sociological rather than chronological priority. The *bᵉkôr* is the privileged heir, who functions as the *primus inter fratres*, "first among brothers."[18]

If the son of the less-favored wife enjoyed the status of *bᵉkôr*, this could pose a particular problem when the male head of the household divides his property among his heirs (v. 16). Moses does not explicitly outlaw the father's prerogative to choose the primary heir,[19] but he cautions against making this common practice once the Israelites have settled in the land.[20] Responding to this potential situation, verses 16−17a declare that once the father divides the assets, he may not rob the eldest of his rights and status (v. 16) by designating the son of the favored wife as the *bᵉkôr*, but must recognize the natural *bᵉkôr* by giving him a double portion of everything he possesses. The *bᵉkôr's* status as the "the first sign of his [procreative] strength" (v. 17) entitles him to the rights and obligates him to the responsibilities of the firstborn. The double share of the inheritance compensates the *bᵉkôr* for his responsibility to care for the parents in their old age, to provide proper burial upon their decease, and generally to lead the clan after the father is gone. Moses hereby seeks to protect the rights and dignity of the less-favored wife by prohibiting husbands from making children pay for strained relationships between or among parents.

Righteousness in the Treatment of a Rebellious Son (21:18−21)

THE LOCATION OF THIS paragraph may suggest that the incorrigible son represents the son of the favored wife who, being denied *bᵉkôr* status, turns against his parents and wastes his life with rebellion and profligate living.[21] The foundation for these instructions have been laid in the Decalogue (5:16), echoes of which are heard in the twofold reference to both father and mother in verses 18 and 19. The fate of the rebellious son represents the opposite of the blessing that is presented as the reward for honoring one's parents—"that it may go well with you." By having his life cut off, this son experiences the ultimate curse.

---

18. Israel's status as Yahweh's *bᵉkôr* (Ex. 4:22) refers to their place among the nations (cf. Deut. 26:18−19), not their antiquity. On the status of the *bᵉkôr*, see further F. E. Greenspahn, *When Brothers Dwell Together: The Preeminence of Younger Siblings in the Hebrew Bible* (New York/ Oxford: Oxford Univ. Press, 1994), 19, 27, 61−62; Block, "Marriage and Family," 82−85.

19. See Gen. 48:13−20; 49:3−4.

20. Similarly Wright, *Deuteronomy*, 238.

21. Hayim Granot ("Darshanut: The Defiant Son," *JBQ* 26 [1998]: 129−30) suggests the Israelite wife pampered her son to ensure his devotion when forced to share her husband with the new war bride.

The paragraph opens by presenting a hypothetical case of a man with a problematic son who is "stubborn and rebellious" (v. 18), a hendiadys for "stubbornly rebellious" or "utterly incorrigible." The participle suggests the recalcitrance is neither occasional nor isolated, but a pattern by a young man who, while under the roof of his parents, should be assuming his share of the responsibilities within the household. The last clause of verse 18 adds to this image. Despite discipline by his parents, he refuses to listen. While the term "to discipline" (*yissar*) may be used of positive instruction or chastisement for wrongful behavior (22:18; cf. 8:5), here the discipline could have involved any actions ranging from rebuke to flogging.[22]

The description suggests the parents have done all they could to raise their son properly, but he is incorrigible and will not listen to either father or mother. The prescription for this son seems simple. The parents are to seize him, take him to the assembly of the elders in the town where they reside, present their case orally, and leave him with the men of the town, who will stone him to death (vv. 19–21a). Although the procedure appears straightforward, several details deserve comment. (1) The appearance of both father and mother before the elders reflects the status of women in the home.[23] Because contempt for one's mother is as objectionable as rebellion against one's father, her voice also needed to be heard.

(2) The prescribed procedure shows that ultimate authority over life and death rests with the community. Since the body of elders was made up of heads of households, when parents present the case of a rebellious son to them, they appeal to peers to offer their righteous verdict. The effect is to reinforce social structures designed to promote the health of the community. The procedure in the gate is not conceived as a trial in the modern sense. The parents appear before the elders alone; in the proceedings the delinquent son does not defend himself and in so doing present a picture different from that painted by his parents. This does not mean the process was unfairly one-sided. The entire community, including the elders, will have witnessed the son's incorrigibility and the efforts of the parents to correct him. The procedure is driven by a commitment to righteousness within the community when parental efforts fail.

(3) With a formal declaration of his social pathology before the elders, mother and father express their frustrations with an insubordinate son, who

---

22. *Tanakh* follows longstanding rabbinic tradition in translating the term "to flog," in both instances. Cf. Tigay, *Deuteronomy*, 197; J. Fleischman, "Legal Innovation in Deuteronomy XXI 18–20," *VT* 53 (2003): 313. For the ancient disposition toward physical discipline, see Prov. 23:13–14; also 13:24; 29:15.

23. For discussion of the elevated status of wives and mothers in Israel, see Block, "Marriage and Family," 61–69.

has renounced the parental bond. To the vices cited in verse 18 they add that he is "a glutton [NIV 'profligate'] and a drunkard," who wastes the resources of the community (cf. Prov. 23:20–21). The crisis is not caused by naughty children, but by a young man who refuses to grow up and take his rightful place at home and in society.[24] Domestic dysfunction has become a public issue; the son's conduct undermines the social order and communal peace.[25]

(4) Finally, Moses calls on the entire community to administer the punishment—in this case, stoning the incorrigible son to death. Unlike 17:7, which requires witnesses to a crime to initiate the execution, here the parents are not mentioned, presumably out of respect for their affection for their son. Having turned him over to the elders does not mean parental instincts have been stifled.

The instructions conclude with a rationale that highlights the significance of this action for the community. (1) Executing the incorrigible son purges "the evil" from the midst of Israel. Invoking the purgation formula, Moses elevates persistent insubordination to parents to the highest class of crimes that violate fundamental standards of covenant righteousness.[26] (2) Executing the incorrigible son should inspire fear in the hearts and minds of all Israel. This motivation reinforces the links between insubordination to parents and leading fellow Israelites into idolatry (13:11[12]), refusing the judicial decision of the priest or judge (17:11), and false testimony against one's countryman (19:19–20). Reports of this outcome should cause all Israelites to be in awe before their God and fear the fate of those who violate the covenant.

Righteousness in the Treatment of a Criminal's Remains (21:22–23)

OF THE FIVE SUBJECTS dealt with in chapter 21, the disposal of an executed criminal is the shortest—but also the most problematic for modern readers. This topic seems to have been triggered by the reference to the execution of the incorrigible son. The intent of these instructions is to protect the land from the defilement that an exposed body would produce.

Verse 22 assumes three stages in the legal procedure involving a capital crime. (1) It is established that the person is guilty of a crime worthy of death. The opening clause presupposes a careful investigation, leading to

---

24. Fleischman ("Deuteronomy XXI 18–20," 323–27) argues that in refusing to heed his parents' efforts to change his "wayward and defiant" behavior, he denies their authority.

25. For a sociological analysis of the significance of the son's profligate behavior see A. C. Hagedorn, "Guarding the Parent's Honour—Deuteronomy 21.18–21," *JSOT* 88 (2000): 101–21.

26. Cf. 13:5 [6]; 17:7, 12; 19:13, 19; 21:9; 22:21, 22, 24; 24:7.

the conclusion that follows: The suspect has committed a capital crime and must be executed. This class of crimes includes murder, idolatry, and persistent insubordination to parents, but the location of this paragraph suggests Moses may have in mind particularly the incorrigible son. (2) The person has been executed. (3) The person's body is hung on a tree.[27] The verb *tālâ* denotes "to hang up" the corpse of someone already executed. Displaying the body of a criminal by hanging it in a public place[28] served two purposes: to shame the individual even after his death, and to deter others from committing the crime.

Moses prescribes the treatment of the criminal's body that has been hung from a tree from two sides (v. 23a-b). Negatively, the people may not let the corpse hang overnight. Positively, they must bury any criminal on the day of execution. Whereas Israel's neighbors would leave human corpses exposed to be eaten by birds and other scavenging animals,[29] Deuteronomy considers this a most severe curse (28:26). The rationale for burying the body is couched in ambiguous terms: "A person who is hanged is a curse of God" (pers. trans.). The statement raises several questions.

(1) How should we interpret the phrase "a curse of God"? The breadth of support in ancient sources argues for interpreting the phrase as an objective genitive; "the curse of God" refers to something people do to or against God (cf. Lev. 24:15).[30] However, the NIV's "[he] is under God's curse," which assumes a subjective genitive interpretation, is also ancient.[31] Although Paul omits any reference to "God" in Galatians 3:13, this is the interpretation he follows.[32] This approach has dominated Christian interpretation from the beginning.[33]

---

27. Technically, *ʿēṣ* may refer to a tree or a piece of wood. In the latter case, it would mean impaling on a stake, a common practice in ancient Assyria. See M. Greenberg, "Hanging," *IDB*, 1:522; *ANET*, 276, 288, 295, 300.

28. Gen. 40:19, 22; Josh. 8:23, 29; 10:26; 2 Sam 4:12; 21:12. For discussion, see J. A. Fitzmyer, "Crucifixion in Ancient Palestine, Qumran Literature, and the New Testament," *CBQ* 40 (1978): 493–513.

29. Cf. Gen. 40:19; MAL §53.

30. For discussion of the texts supporting this interpretation see Moshe J. Bernstein, "*qllt ʾlhym tlwy* (Deut. 21:23): A Study in Early Jewish Exegesis," *JQR* 74 (1983): 25–37.

31. The LXX reads "for cursed by God is everyone hanged on a tree." The NIV follows LXX in adding "on a tree."

32. This interpretation is reflected also in Targum Neofiti, as well as the Temple Scroll from Qumran. For discussion of these subjective genitive texts see Bernstein, "Early Jewish Exegesis," 24–25.

33. On differences between Jewish and Christian interpretation, see J. M. Lieu, "Reading in Canon and Community: Deuteronomy 21.22–23, A Test Case for Dialogue," in *The Bible in Human Society: Essays in Honour of John Rogerson* (ed. M. Daniel Carroll R. et al.; JSOTSup 200; Sheffield: Sheffield Academic, 1995), 317–34.

---

(2) But this raises a second question: Is the person cursed because his body is hung from a tree, or is he hung from a tree because he is cursed? Since the person who hangs from a tree has suffered "the sentence of death," it appears the person hangs for all to see because he is cursed of God.

This paragraph concludes with a motive clause, expressing concern for the sanctity of the land that Yahweh is giving to Israel. To spare the relatives of the criminal further grief or to prevent the animals from publicly dismembering the body, burying the corpse seems both natural and humane. This command is rooted in the implications of hanging for the land: The exposed corpse defiles the ground on which the people live and from which they draw their sustenance (cf. vv 1−9). The purity of the land demands the body be removed from sight and buried.

ABUSE OF WOMEN. BIBLICAL allusions to these instructions on family and community life are scarce,[34] but illustrations of the abuse of women contemplated here are ubiquitous in the narratives. The behavior of men in these accounts violates the trajectory of Deuteronomy 21. This trajectory, which begins in the Decalogue and continues throughout Moses' second address, seeks to rein in the potential for men to abuse women, including their wives.[35] Scholars have long recognized the attention that Deuteronomy pays to women's rights[36] in its concern for widows (10:17−18, et passim), the involvement of women in worship (12:12, et passim), the manumission of female slaves (15:12), and military exemptions for newly married husbands (20:7). This is the first in a series of texts that focuses on protecting women's dignity within the household.[37] These texts assume that the way men treat women is a barometer of the spiritual climate of the nation.[38]

Although the institution of marriage should have provided security for wives, in ancient Israel not all women were equally secure and equally

---

34. Remarkably the closest illustrations involve Abraham, who sent away his slave wife Hagar (Gen. 21:8−14) and Ezra's commanding the Jews of postexilic Jerusalem to put away their foreign wives (Ezra 10). In both cases God approves the action, presumably as the lesser of two evils.

35. For full discussion see Daniel I. Block, "'You Shall Not Covet Your Neighbor's Wife': A Study in Deuteronomic Domestic Ideology," in *The Gospel According to Moses*, 137−68.

36. Thus Weinfeld, *Deuteronomy 1−11*, 318; idem, *DDS*, 282−92.

37. See also 21:15−21; 22:13−21, 23−29; 24:1−4; 25:5−10. For detailed analysis of these texts, see Josberger, "Between Rule and Responsibility."

38. Though men exhibit a troublesome propensity to twist benign patricentrism into abusive patriarchalism. See Daniel I. Block, "Unspeakable Crimes: The Abuse of Women in the Book of Judges," *SBTJ* 2 (1998): 46−55.

loved. Apart from variations in the characters of their husbands, institutional factors contributing to a woman's insecurity included polygamy, divorce, and widowhood. Polygamy — simultaneous marriage to more than one wife, more precisely polygyny — presented challenges for both husband and wives. Although the Old Testament presents monogamy (one husband, one wife) as the ideal (Gen. 2:24−25), the constitutional texts do not outlaw polygamy for the general population, and narratives report numerous polygamous examples.[39] Multiple wives reflected a man's wealth and status within the community. The only person for whom the practice was expressly forbidden was the king (Deut. 17:17), and that for religious reasons — wives (presumably foreign wives acquired through dynastic marriage) would deflect him from wholehearted devotion to Yahweh.

The stresses created by bigamy and polygyny are evident in several Old Testament narratives. However the tensions do not appear to arise over inheritance or the status of the children in the family, but over the problem of barrenness. In the cases involving Rachel and Hannah, the favored wife was unable to have a child who could be a candidate for the *bᵉkôr*. The words for the favored (*ʾāhab*) and the spurned (*śānēʾ*) wife link our text directly with Jacob's household (Gen. 29:30−31), where the unloved wife was prolific and the loved wife jealous of her sister (30:1). Rachel eventually had two sons, but she did not live long enough to see Joseph assume the role of *bᵉkôr*, nor her younger grandson Ephraim be promised hegemony over the family — ultimately the northern tribes (48:19−20). However, ultimately the status of *bᵉkôr* in relation to the clan is ceded to Judah, the third son of the spurned wife (Gen. 49:8−12).

Hannah's case was similar. Her rival, Peninnah, has sons and daughters (1 Sam. 1:4), but Hannah cannot conceive (1:1−8), causing Peninnah to provoke and irritate her bitterly. While we know nothing of the status of the spurned wife's children, by divinely granted conception and divine call, as prophet and priest Hannah's son Samuel functions as the *bᵉkôr* of the nation. But neither case reflects a struggle between wives over whose son will be the *bᵉkôr*.

Incorrigible children. We cannot tell if Moses' instructions regarding incorrigible children were ever applied in Israel. Eli's sons go their own ways (1 Sam. 2:12−17), refusing to heed the rebuke of their father (2:22−25) and eventually losing their lives for their crimes (2:25, 27−36; 3:10−14; 4:10−18), but the narrator never portrays their crimes as persistent

---

39. Lamech (Gen. 4:23), Abraham (Gen. 16; 25:1−2); Jacob (Gen. 30); Esau (Gen. 26:34; 28:9; 36:1−5); Gideon (Judg. 8:30−31); Elkanah (1 Sam. 1:2); David (1 Sam. 18:17−30; 25:38−43; 2 Sam. 3:2−5); Solomon (1 Kings 3:1; 11:3; Song 6:8); Rehoboam (2 Chron. 11:21). Elkanah was the only commoner mentioned to have had more than one wife.

rebellion against their father; it was directly against Yahweh. Samuel's sons also depart from their father's course (1 Sam. 8:1−3), but this is not cast as rebellion against Samuel. The nearest the narratives come to an event like that envisioned here involves the young lads who mock Elisha as a "baldhead," for which they are mauled and killed by two female bears (2 Kings 2:23−25). However the episode does not involve parents and sons, but a prophet and someone else's children. These are not young adults characterized by stubbornness, rebellion, gluttony, and drunkenness, but naughty small boys mocking a prophetic representative of Yahweh.

Whether or not the penalty Moses prescribed was ever enforced, this text emphasizes the high stock covenantal righteousness places in respect for parents.[40] The refusal to distinguish between respect for father and mother accords with Proverbs 6:20, which places a mother's teaching on par with a father's command. Like later sages in Israel, Moses commends parents for disciplining their children, but he also acknowledges that children make their own choices, and sometimes the courses they choose are opposed to everything they have been taught.[41] In such cases parents are neither culpable for their children's profligate lives, nor are they free to carry out the present policy. That must be left to the community leaders.

Some see this text in the background of Hosea's portrayal of Israel as a rebellious son in Hosea 11.[42] Despite Yahweh's tender care and sustaining love (11:3−4), the son has gone after other gods (v. 2) and persists in turning from him (vv. 5−7). In describing Yahweh's agony over his options, and whether or not to inflict Israel with the ultimate punishment as spelled out in the covenant curses, Hosea offers a rare window into the internal turmoil in Yahweh's mind:

> How can I give you up, Ephraim?
> How can I hand you over, Israel?
> How can I treat you like Admah?
> How can I make you like Zeboiim? (Hos. 11:8a)

In the end his compassion wins out over his fury:

> My heart is changed within me;
> all my compassion is aroused.

---

40. Second Samuel 14−15 recounts Absalom's revolt against his father, David, to which David responds with remarkable magnanimity. Since this is a case of palace intrigue, it differs significantly from the domestic scene envisioned in Deut. 21:18−21.

41. On failed parental discipline, see P. R. Callaway, "Deut. 21:18−21: Proverbial Wisdom and Law," *JBL* 103 (1984): 341−52.

42. See G. A. Yee, "Hosea," in *The Women's Bible Commentary* (exp. ed.; ed. C. A. Newsom and S. H. Ringe; Louisville: Westminster John Knox, 1998), 212−13.

> I will not carry out my fierce anger,
> > nor will I turn and devastate Ephraim.
> For I am God, and not man—
> > the Holy One among you.
> I will not come in wrath. (11:8b–9)

There is no authority to whom Yahweh can appeal, and he surely has the legal right to punish his son. In the end compassion wins out over wrath; restoration is preferred over judgment.

Hanging on a tree overnight. As with the previous instructions, it is difficult to determine the extent to which the Israelites applied the regulations in verses 22–23. According to Joshua 8:29, Joshua obeyed them scrupulously, even with reference to the Canaanite king of Ai. He hung the king on a tree until evening, but at sunset he ordered the removal of the body. His men deposited it at the entrance of the gate of the city and buried it under a heap of stones. Apparently he did the same with the kings of the southern Canaanite alliance (Josh. 10:26–27).

In later times, this passage was interpreted as advocating a form of execution. This is evident especially in the Temple Scroll from Qumran, which elaborates on the present text:

> If a man passes on information against his people or betrays his people to a foreign nation, or does evil against his people, you shall hang him on a tree and he will die. On the evidence of two witnesses or on the evidence of three witnesses he shall be put to death and they shall hang him on the tree. If it happens that a man has committed a capital offence and he escapes amongst the nations and curses his people /and/ the children of Israel, he [*sic*; read "him"] also you shall hang on the tree and he will die. And their corpse shall not spend the night on the tree; instead you shall bury them that day because those hanged on a tree are cursed by God and man; thus you shall not defile the land which I give you for inheritance. (LXIV:7–13)[43]

Clear echoes of our text may be heard in the New Testament, especially in references to the crucifixion of Jesus. In Acts 5:30 and 10:39–40

---

43. As translated by F. Martínez and E. J. C. Tigchelaar, *The Dead Sea Scrolls Study Edition* (Leiden: Brill, 1993), 1287. For discussion of this text see Otto Betz, "The Temple Scroll (*11Qmiqd* 64, 7–13) and the Trial of Jesus," in *Mogilany 1989: Papers on the Dead Sea Scrolls Offered in Memory of Jean Carmignac* (ed. Z. J. Kapera; Krakow: Enigma, 1993), Part I, 101–4. Cf. also the allusion to Deut. 21:22–23 in the Qumran Pesher Nahum (4QpNah [4Q169]) 1.7–8. The report of Alexander Janneus' crucifixion of 800 rebels in 90 BC mentions "one hanged alive from the tree" (*Dead Sea Scrolls Study Edition*, 337; cf. Josephus, *Ant.* 13.14.2).

Peter accuses the Jews of killing Jesus by hanging him on a tree. In Acts 13:28-29 Paul uses similar language; after emphasizing the criminal nature of Jesus' execution ("they found no proper ground for a death sentence," 13:28), he speaks of Jesus' removal from the tree and his burial in a tomb.[44]

MARRIAGE ISSUES AND PRINCIPLES. Deuteronomy 21:10-14 offers our world helpful insights into the biblical view of marriage. (1) Unlike the categorical prohibition of intermarriage with Canaanites in chapter 7, Moses expresses no hesitation in Israelites marrying foreigners. He assumes that, like Ruth, those foreigners will be fully integrated into the community.

(2) This text reminds contemporary readers, especially males, that whether native or alien, women in general and wives in particular must be treated with dignity and respect for their personhood and their identity. The biblical paradigm of marriage and family is clearly patricentric, but this offers God's people no grounds whatsoever for denying women their rights, disregarding their dignity, or treating them as property.

(3) While this passage seems to assume that divorce was not uncommon in ancient Israel, by no means does it endorse this tragedy in a marriage.[45] Whether or not divorce is morally justifiable, like 24:1-4 this text shows it was tolerated in Israel as a legal reality. With Exodus 21:10-11 our text suggests that releasing a slave wife or captive woman whom an Israelite warrior has married is preferable to the man refusing to fulfill his marital duties.

Except for groups that have split off from the Mormon church, the issues dealt with in verses 15-17 seem foreign to the Western world. However, in some parts of the world, particularly in the Muslim world and in sub-Saharan Africa, polygamy is widely practiced. Some social researchers estimate that more than half the men in Kenya are polygamous and one-third of the women are part of a plural marriage.[46] Although the Scriptures do not explicitly ban polygamy, the practical problems the institution raises are well documented. A study of polygamy in Somalia revealed three recurring themes: jealous wives and abusive stepmothers, family honor, and respect for

---

44. See also John 19:31, which adds a new dimension/concern for the sanctity of the Sabbath. For a discussion of these and other New Testament allusions to Deut. 21:22-23 see M. Wilcox, "'Upon the Tree'—Deut. 21:22-23 in the New Testament," *JBL* 96 (1977): 90-94.

45. So also Merrill, *Deuteronomy*, 291. The subject will be discussed in greater detail below on 24:1-4.

46. See http://articles.latimes.com/1999/mar/20/news/mn-19133 (accessed March 8, 2009).

the free will and equality of all.[47] Our text offers perspective on these situations, declaring that the relative status of one's mother in such a context has no bearing on the dignity and humanity of the children. The gospel according to Moses and the gospel according to Jesus call on the redeemed to treat all human beings with the respect due them as image-bearers of God.

The rebellious son passage. Deuteronomy 21:18–21 is a favorite text for modern readers who balk at the authority the Old Testament. Texts like this lead many to reject biblical religion as inhumane and abusive.[48] In Paul's admonitions to children to obey their parents in all things for this is pleasing to the Lord (Eph. 6:1; Col. 3:20), he affirms that the principles governing domestic life in Israel are extended to Christian homes. Paul's observation that this is the only command with a promise (Eph. 6:2) recognizes the link between respect for one's past as embodied in parents and a satisfying future. However, in challenging children to honor their parents with obedience, he recognizes the fine line between appropriate discipline and abusive exasperations (Eph. 6:3; Col. 3:21). In the end all will account to God for the way they have fulfilled their domestic roles.

While some have advocated literal application of this text even for Christians,[49] many simply dismiss this passage as a relic of the old covenant now irrelevant for Christians. If we want to take 2 Timothy 3:16 seriously and recognize that Paul is speaking there of the Old Testament, Christians should try to find a middle way. (1) We recognize that Moses is preaching a farewell address; he is not writing legislation.

(2) As with other constitutional documents of the Pentateuch,[50] the regulations in Deuteronomy were not intended to function as a law code to

---

47. See N. Scruggs, "Somalia," in *International Perspectives on Family Violence and Abuse* (ed. Kathleen Malley-Morrison; New York: Routledge, 2004), 225.

48. See President Barack Obama's reference to Deuteronomy in his address, "Call to Renewal," at the Call to Renewal: A Covenant for a New America conference, June 28, 2006. Available at http://obamaspeeches.com/081-Call_to_Renewal_Keynote_Address. obama-speech.htm (accessed November 1, 2011). Martin Luther interpreted the text allegorically, seeing the son as a teacher in the church, born through the Word, but later corrupted by false teachings. See *Luther's Works*, vol. 9, *Lectures on Deuteronomy* (St. Louis: Concordia, 1960), 215.

49. See *Matthew Henry's Concise Commentary on the Whole Bible* (Nashville: Nelson, 1997), s.v. Deuteronomy 21:18–21: "His own father and mother must complain of him to the elders of the city. Children who forget their duty, must thank themselves, and not blame their parents, if they are regarded with less and less affection. He must be publicly stoned to death by the men of his city. Disobedience to a parent's authority must be very evil, when such a punishment was ordered; nor is it less provoking to God now, though it escapes punishment in this world."

50. The Decalogue (Ex. 20:1–17; Deut. 5:6–21), the "Book of the Covenant" (Ex. 20:22–23:19), the "Instructions on Holiness" (Lev. 17–26).

be administered in the courts. The speeches of Moses provide foundational principles, creating a worldview that begins by recognizing Yahweh's past grace in redeeming Israel from bondage, and then offers guidance in living out those principles. As Moses reiterates so often in the book and as the preamble to the Decalogue emphasizes, Israel is not called primarily to conformity to a code of conduct, but to a relationship with their gracious redeemer.

(3) While we must be cautious about arguing from silence, and while we recognize that the Old Testament narratives do not provide an exhaustive picture of ancient Israelite life, it is striking that the Old Testament provides no hints that these instructions were ever carried out.

(4) Finally, the Jewish interpretive tradition is unanimous in affirming this policy was never applied. Indeed, they engage in remarkable exegetical gymnastics to discount a literal interpretation.[51]

What, then, shall we do with this text? Recognizing it was given to people who claimed to be the community of faith, we do not expect the world to understand or even to want to be governed by biblical principles. But Christians should observe the high stock the Scriptures place on family relations, particularly the responsibility of parents in shaping the faith and lives of their children. Rebellion against parents may be natural, but it is never right. Alexandr Solzhenitsyn rightly insisted that a clear sign of the decadence of a culture is the loss of respect for the older generation.[52] This problem is particularly acute in the modern Western world, where youthfulness rather than maturity is viewed as the ideal, and where, if children are valued, families have become pedocentric. This has produced a narcissistic society, with the individual at the center of the universe, and one's responsibility to the community is diminished.

Texts like this not only place the burden of training children rightly on parents, but they also admit the potential for pain and disappointment, as children make free choices to rebel. The ultimate goal in parenting is to

---

51. (1) The law does not punish except after a warning (e.g., Lev. 19:26), but this text contains no warning (Maimonides, *Mishneh Torah*, "Rebels," Ch. 7); (2) there never has been and never will be a son who fits the definition of a "stubborn and rebellious son" (*t. Sanhedrin* 11:6); (3) the word *bēn* does not apply to a girl or a boy who is not yet *bar mitzwa*; (4) the expression "his father and mother" demands not only that both parents are living, but also that they are without physical defect, even the same height; (5) the parents have to be agreed, and the mother has to be worthy of the father (*m. Sanhedrin*, ch. 8), which means it could never be applied. See the popular commentary by Rabbi Joyce Newmark, "Sparing a Rebellious Son: Ki Tetze *Deuteronomy* 21:10–25:19," *New Jersey Jewish News*, September 11, 2008, available at www.njjewishnews.com/njjn.com/091108/torahSparingTheRebellious-Son.html. See also *b. Sanhedrin* 71a and 72a on Deut. 21:18–21.

52. As cited by Brown, *Deuteronomy*, 210.

promote a healthy community beyond the nuclear family. Indeed, this text raises questions about the validity of the notion of a "nuclear family" itself. It does indeed take a village[53] to raise godly children. In a healthy community, the well-being of every child is everyone's business, and parents with rebellious children should not need to carry the burden alone.

On a tree. Since the manner of execution and the public exposure of the body proposed here have been rejected by virtually all modern peoples, it is difficult to talk about the significance of verses 22−23 for us. Nevertheless, while it concerns a criminal, it may have implications for how we treat the bodies of those who have died. Human beings, no matter how low morally, are still image-bearers of God, and the desecration of the image by mutilation of the body or allowing scavenging creatures to mutilate it is surely a biblical taboo.

However, the most striking significance for Christians is found in the allusion to Deuteronomy 21:22−23 in Galatians 3:13: "Christ redeemed us from the curse of the law by becoming a curse for us, for it is written, 'Cursed is everyone who is hung on a tree.'" In a curious adaptation of this text (substituting "the curse of God" with "the curse of the law," that is, the curse that the law declared on sinners),[54] Paul states the truth concerning ourselves, that we all are sinners deserving the death of the criminal in view in Deuteronomy 21:22−23. This applies also to Jews who try to find salvation by keeping the law rather than by faith, casting themselves on God incarnate in Jesus Christ.

However, Paul also declares the glorious gospel that Christ himself became the curse that we all deserve by virtue of our sinful state. Through his death on the cross, Jesus Christ, the sinless sacrifice, atoned for our sins once and for all, thereby delivering us from the sentence of death that hangs over us all (cf. Rom. 6:23).[55]

---

53. From the title of Hillary Rodham Clinton's book, *It Takes a Village: And Other Lessons Children Teach Us* (New York: Touchstone, 1996). But note the pedocentric implications of the title.

54. "The curse of the law" should not be misinterpreted as if the law itself was the curse any more than "the curse of God" in Deut. 21:23 declares that God himself is a curse.

55. For discussions of this text see Wilcox, "'Upon the Tree,'" 95−99; A. Caneday, "'Redeemed from the Curse of the Law': The Use of Deut. 21:22−23 in Gal. 3:13," *TJ* 10 (1989): 185−209.

Deuteronomy 22:1–12

If you see your brother's ox or sheep straying, do not
ignore it but be sure to take it back to him. ²If the brother
does not live near you or if you do not know who he is,
take it home with you and keep it until he comes looking for
it. Then give it back to him. ³Do the same if you find your
brother's donkey or his cloak or anything he loses. Do not
ignore it.

⁴If you see your brother's donkey or his ox fallen on the
road, do not ignore it. Help him get it to its feet.

⁵A woman must not wear men's clothing, nor a man wear
women's clothing, for the LORD your God detests anyone
who does this.

⁶If you come across a bird's nest beside the road, either
in a tree or on the ground, and the mother is sitting on
the young or on the eggs, do not take the mother with the
young. ⁷You may take the young, but be sure to let the
mother go, so that it may go well with you and you may have
a long life.

⁸When you build a new house, make a parapet around
your roof so that you may not bring the guilt of bloodshed
on your house if someone falls from the roof.

⁹Do not plant two kinds of seed in your vineyard; if you
do, not only the crops you plant but also the fruit of the
vineyard will be defiled.

¹⁰Do not plow with an ox and a donkey yoked together.
¹¹Do not wear clothes of wool and linen woven together.
¹²Make tassels on the four corners of the cloak you wear.

Original Meaning

DEUTERONOMY 22:1–12 contains six fragments.
Although the topics seem disconnected, their
arrangement suggests intentional literary composition, alternating relatively complex instruc-
tions with simple statements. The middle two sections (vv. 6–7, 8) are
cast in casuistic form, while the rest involve second person imperatives.
All six fragments deal with everyday life in the community or household.
Yahweh is named only once (v. 5), but this does not mean the instructions

operate from naturalistic or humanistic foundations. This chapter brings all of life under the rule of "righteousness, only righteousness" (see comments on 16:20).

Righteousness Demonstrated in Care for Domestic Animals (22:1 – 4)

THIS FIRST PARAGRAPH DEALS with two issues: respect for a neighbor's property in general (vv. 2 – 3), framed by statements calling for righteous respect for domestic animals. On first sight verse 1 seems to be interested primarily in restoring property to its owner, but the parallelism of verses 1 and 4[1] suggests these statements should be interpreted together. Both scenarios involve a fellow Israelite's animal in a threatening situation. Verse 1 involves stray sheep or oxen that are vulnerable to wild animals and thieves. Verse 4 involves a pack animal that has fallen down under its load, perhaps the result of slipping or abuse by the owner, who has overloaded it.

At the sight of a stray or fallen animal one might be tempted to ignore it or claim it as one's own property (cf. 5:21). Concerned about the well-being of the animal, Moses addresses the first response. In the face of need, sentimental reflection on the plight of the creatures is insufficient; this is a call for action.[2] The first animal is to be returned to its owner,[3] and the second animal is to be helped back on its feet. Moses prohibits Israelites from ignoring animals that are lost or beasts of burden under stress. Though domestic animals played a vital role in the economy, ownership and control could easily degenerate into abusive treatment.[4]

Verse 2 still concerns the first animal, but the references to a cloak or anything else that is lost in verse 3 generalizes the principle to any personal property and suggests a shift in focus from the creature's interests to that of the owner. A "finders keepers, losers weepers" ethic is to be resisted; whatever one finds is to be returned to its owner. If the owner lives far away

---

1. The first is an adaptation of Ex. 23:4; the second of Ex. 23:5.

2. Tigay (*Deuteronomy*, 199) rightly notes that Deuteronomy commonly anticipates psychological reactions (cf. 15:9, 18), reinforcing our contention that in the book Moses functions primarily as preacher rather than as lawgiver.

3. "Your brother" occurs five times in vv. 1 – 4. Ex. 23:4 calls for this kind of kindness toward one's enemy.

4. The Decalogic requirement to include draft animals in the seventh-day Sabbath rest reflects the same sensitivity to the well-being of domestic animals. On the Deuteronomic disposition toward domestic animals, see D. I. Block, "All Creatures Great and Small: Recovering a Deuteronomic Theology of Animals," in *The Old Testament in the Life of God's People: Essays in Honor of Elmer A. Martens* (ed. J. Isaak; Winona Lake, IN: Eisenbrauns, 2009), 292 – 95, reprinted in *The Gospel According to Moses*, forthcoming.

or if his identity is unknown, the finder must bring the animal home and care for it[5] until the owner comes to claims it, or until the unknown owner identifies himself. This paragraph assumes that the covenant love Israelites have for their neighbors extends to livestock.

Righteousness Demonstrated in
Respect for Sexual Distinctions (22:5)

VERSE 5 CONSISTS OF three clauses; the first two describe the issue and the third lays the foundation for a righteous response. The former represent two sides of the coin expressed in asymmetrical parallelism. Although the NIV assumes synonymity of words here by using the word "clothing" twice, these are two separate words, and the range of meanings for the former (*kᵉlî*) extends beyond "clothing" to vessels and receptacles, utensils, tools and implements, furniture and furnishings, and jewelry.[6] Here it probably refers to any item of decoration normally associated with men. But the second term (*śimlâ*) is more specific, referring to the outer wrapper or mantle.[7]

The prohibition is vague and its meaning uncertain. The characterization of the actions as something that "the LORD your God detests"[8] may suggest an association with idolatry, perhaps a prohibition against cross-dressing and transvestite practices associated with pagan religions. However, the absence of cultic interest in the rest of chapter 22 argues against this view.[9] Similar to verses 9 – 11, this injunction seeks to preserve the order built into creation, specifically the fundamental distinction between male and female. For a person to wear anything associated with the opposite gender confuses one's sexual identity and blurs established boundaries.[10]

---

5. Hebrew lit., "You shall gather it to the midst of your house, and it shall be with you." In multistory houses, the animals occupied the ground floor; otherwise their quarters would be off to one side (cf. 1 Sam. 28:24). On domestic architecture in ancient Israel see King and Stager, *Life in Biblical Israel*, 21 – 35.

6. For these and other meanings and relevant references, see *DCH*, 4:420 – 24.

7. *HALOT*, 1337.

8. This expression occurs elsewhere in 7:25; 12:31; 17:1; 18:12; 23:18[19]; 25:16; 27:15, generally referring to actions or objects that are incompatible with the worship of Yahweh and are abhorrent to him.

9. So also P. J. Harland, "Menswear and Womenswear: A Study of Deuteronomy 22:5," *ExpTim* 110 (1998): 74 – 75.

10. For a study of the problem of cross-dressing in Israel, see N. S. Fox, "Gender Transformation and Transgression: Contextualizing the Prohibition of Cross-Dressing in Deuteronomy 22:5," in *Mishneh Todah: Studies in Deuteronomy and Its Cultural Environment in Honor of Jeffrey H. Tigay* (ed. N. S. Fox, D. A. Glat-Gilad, and M. J. Williams (Winona Lake, IN: Eisenbrauns, 2009), 49 – 71.

Righteousness Demonstrated in
Care for Wild Animals (22:6 – 8)

ALTHOUGH SEVERAL TEXTS CALL for compassion toward domestic animals, this appeal for a tender and sympathetic disposition toward wild birds is unparalleled in the Old Testament.[11] The opening line describes the context to which the following injunctions apply: the chance discovery of a wild bird's nest containing fledglings or eggs, with the mother bird sitting on them. The use of a generic term for bird (cf. 14:11) and the references to nests "beside the road," "in a tree," and "on the ground" cover the full range of possibilities.

While people who discover the nest of a wild bird have several options, Moses offers simple counsel: Israelites may take the eggs/fledglings, but they must spare the mother. Reining in the temptation to cruelty, verse 7 reiterates that if a mother bird is found with its young, the mother is not to be taken. The wisdom of this counsel is obvious: Taking the mother but sparing the young would have meant the death of all, for unhatched eggs and fledgling birds depend on the mother. Israelites are not to kill for killing's sake, nor to exploit natural resources without concern for the survival of the species.[12]

Even so this text appears to ground the instructions in human self-interest. If Israelites will treat birds' nests this way, they will prosper and enjoy long life on the land. The motive clause links this ordinance with other weighty preconditions to longevity (4:40; 5:33; 11:9; cf. 30:18) and highlights its covenantal significance by locating this action in the same class as general statutes Moses has given elsewhere (4:40; 5:29; 6:18; 12:28). The vibrant covenantal relationship involving Yahweh, Israel, and their natural environment represents in microcosm the triangular relationship among God, the earth, and its creatures. The scope of righteous living extends to respect for the life of helpless creatures.[13]

Righteousness Demonstrated in
Care for One's Household (22:8)

HERE MOSES INSTRUCTS ISRAELITES constructing a new house to build a parapet (a low wall or railing) around the roof of the house. This architectural

---

11. For texts calling for sympathy toward domestic animals, see Ex. 34:26; Lev. 22:27 – 28; Deut. 14:21.

12. Cf. Oded Borowski, *Every Living Thing: Daily Use of Animals in Ancient Israel* (Walnut Creek, CA: AltaMira, 1998), 152.

13. See further, Daniel I. Block, "To Serve and to Keep: Toward a Biblical Understanding of Humanity's Responsibility in the Face of the Biodiversity Crisis," in *Keeping God's Earth: The Global Environment in Biblical Perspective* (ed. N. J. Toly and D. I. Block; Downers Grove, IL: InterVarsity Press, 2010), 116 – 42.

feature is necessitated by the design and function of houses in ancient Israel. Houses were often two-storey constructions, with the lower floor housing animals and storing food stuffs, and the upper floor serving as the living quarters. Cooled by the breezes, flat roofs provided a third living space that residents could use for a variety of purposes.[14] Without a barrier around the perimeter, people could step off the roof and fall to their deaths. The final clause of verse 8 holds the head of the household responsible for the life of anyone whose death is the result of negligence.[15]

Righteousness Demonstrated in Farming the Land (22:9—11)

THIS FRAGMENT OF INSTRUCTION exhibits obvious links with Leviticus 19:19, where a similar statement is embedded in a long series of commands describing what being holy just as Yahweh is holy means in everyday life.[16] However, this text only hints at the notion of "holiness," with an odd use of the root *qdš* in verse 9.

The prohibition on seeding a vineyard with other seeds (v. 9). Whereas Leviticus 19:19 prohibits mixing any two kinds of seed in a field, this statement disallows sowing different kinds of plants in a vineyard. The proscription addresses a common practice in ancient and modern times of seeding another crop between the rows of grapevines ("intercropping"), making use of every inch of arable land. However, the motive clause annuls whatever economic benefits the practice might yield, lest the whole crop sown between the vines and the produce of the vineyard be declared sacrosanct (*tiqdaš*)[17] and therefore off limits to the farmer and his family.[18]

---

14. Dry and store grains (Josh. 2:6), sleep (1 Sam. 9:25—26), socialize (Judg. 16:27), relax (2 Sam. 11:2; cf. Dan. 4:29), accommodate guests, or engage in other activity (2 Sam. 16:22; 2 Kings 4:10; Neh. 8:16).

15. Similarly, Ex. 21:33—34 holds anyone who leaves a pit unbarricaded responsible for the loss of animals that might fall into it. For analogous Old Babylonian cases involving responsibility for those "under their roofs" see *CH* §§229—230.

16. On the priority of the Instructions on Holiness, see Michael Fishbane, *Biblical Interpretation in Ancient Israel* (Oxford: Clarendon, 1985), 58—63; J. Milgrom, "Law and Narrative and the Exegesis of Leviticus xix 19," *VT* 46 (1996): 544—48, contra C. M. Carmichael, "Forbidden Mixtures in Deuteronomy xxii 9—11 and Leviticus xix 19," *VT* 45 (1995): 433—48.

17. Cf. *HALOT*, 1073. This is the only occurrence of the Qal form of the verb in Deuteronomy. H.-P. Müller ("קדש," *TLOT*, 3:1105) rightly treats the Qal, which is normally stative, ingressively, "to become holy."

18. NIV "will be defiled" suggests *ṭāmēʾ* ("to be unclean/defiled," cf. 21:23) as the underlying Hebrew expression, when the antonym *qādāš* ("to be holy/sanctified") is used. Hebrew words may be used with opposite meanings (cf. J. Barr, *Comparative Philology and the Text of the Old Testament* [Winona Lake, IN: Eisenbrauns, 2001], 173—77), but here the normal sense is preferred. Many English versions read "forfeited" (ESV, NRSV, NLT, NJPS).

The clause implies consecration of the produce, which means treating it like produce presented at the sanctuary. It seems priests confiscated and set apart for sanctuary use any grain and wine produced in vineyards where another crop was sown.[19]

The prohibition on plowing with two species of animals (v. 10). This prohibition is more concise. Whereas Leviticus 19:19 had referred to domesticated animals generally, here Moses specifies oxen and donkeys; and whereas Leviticus 19:19 had prohibited the *interbreeding* of two kinds of domesticated animals, this proscription forbids yoking oxen and donkeys together. This practice creates a fundamentally incongruous image: the animals' anatomies require different types of harness and a drastically modified yoke to link the two; their unequal strength and stamina could cause the more vigorous to exhaust the weaker. However, to kosher-minded Israelites, these factors were probably less significant than forcing a bond between clean and unclean, which happens when ox and donkey are yoked together.[20]

The prohibition on wearing divergent kinds of fabric (v. 11). Since wool and linen are both agricultural products, this taboo fits logically with the taboo on mixing crops and mixing draft animals. Moses does not justify this taboo, even though it contradicts the prescriptions for the fabric of the tabernacle[21] and the high priest's garments.[22] While forbidden for laypersons, wearing garments of mixed fabrics was reserved for those who served in Yahweh's presence.

In general, it seems that all these prohibitions were intended to guard against boundary violations that defy the order of the universe (Gen. 1).[23] In contrast to the chaotic life of non-Israelites, the life of Yahweh's people is to be characterized by order and clearly defined boundaries. However, the concern goes beyond order in everyday life. These instructions draw clear boundaries between that which is appropriate for deity (mixtures of all sorts) and that which is appropriate for mortals (no mixtures at all).

---

19. See J. Milgrom, "Law and Narrative and the Exegesis of Leviticus xix 19," 546; idem, *Leviticus 1 — 16*, 548 — 49.

20. This probably underlies Paul's injunction in 2 Cor. 6:14 — 15.

21. Ex. 26:1, 31, 36; 27:16; 36:8, 35, 37; 38:18. "Wool" (*ṣemer*) is missing in these texts, but since the ancients had developed technology to dye only wool, the most common textile available, the blue, scarlet, and purple yarns prescribed here were probably spun from wool. Cf. Milgrom, *Leviticus 1 — 16*, 549; P. P. Jensen, *Graded Holiness: A Key to the Priestly Conception of the World* (JSOTSup 106; Sheffield: Sheffield Academic, 1992), 86.

22. Ex. 28:5 — 6, 8, 15; 39:1 — 3, 5; 8. On the Day of Atonement the High Priest wore only linen (Lev. 16:4, 23, 32).

23. Thus C. Houtman, "Another Look at Forbidden Mixtures," *VT* 34 (1984): 226 — 28; cf. M. Douglas, *Purity and Danger: An Analysis of the Concepts of Pollution and Taboo* (London: Routledge and Kegan Paul, 1980), 53.

Certain mixtures were fitting for Yahweh and those who represented him, but not for laypeople who lived before a watching world.

Righteousness Demonstrated in Dress (22:12)

THIS SECTION OF MISCELLANEOUS pastoral instructions ends with an appeal to wear tassels attached to the four corners of one's garment. Moses assumes familiarity with the fuller description in Numbers 15:37 – 41. These tassels had no utilitarian function; they were purely decorative and symbolic. Like words of covenant commitment written on hands and foreheads and on the doorposts of houses and gates (Deut. 6:4 – 9), the tassels reminded the one who wore them and outsiders of Israel's special status as the covenant people of Yahweh.[24]

HISTORY OF THESE LAWS. The narratives of the Old Testament provide few illustrations of lost animals or other property being found and then returned to or held in security for the owners. The circumstances envisioned in verses 1 – 4 are illustrated in 1 Samuel 9, though from the perspective of the person who lost them. When Saul went out looking for his father's donkeys, the family was hoping they would find them in the hands of someone like the person Moses describes. Although Samuel assures Saul that this is in fact the case (1 Sam. 9:20; 10:14 – 20), we do not know who held them or even if Saul brought them back home. Perhaps he had, but the text is more concerned about Saul's finding the kingdom than about finding the animals.

Allusions to the instructions on cross-dressing (v. 5), finding a bird's nest (vv. 6 – 7), parapets on houses (v. 8), and tassels (v. 12) are absent all together. We hear allusions to verses 9 – 10 in the Proverb of the Farmer in Isaiah 28:23 – 29:

> Listen and hear my voice;
>> pay attention and hear what I say.
> When a farmer plows for planting, does he plow continually?
> Does he keep on breaking up and harrowing the soil?

---

24. Cf. M. E. Vogelzang and W. J. van Bekkum ("Meaning and Symbolism of Clothing in Ancient Near Eastern Texts," in *Scripta Signa Vocis: Studies about Scripts, Scriptures, Scribes and Languages in the Near East Presented to J. H. Hospers by His Pupils, Colleagues and Friends* [ed. H. L. J. Vanstiphout; Groningen: E. Forsten, 1986], 277): "The tassels inevitably became the strongest means for reminding Israel of its own characteristic position between the peoples of the world."

When he has leveled the surface,
  does he not sow caraway and scatter cummin?
Does he not plant wheat in its place,
  barley in its plot,
  and spelt in its field?
His God instructs him
  and teaches him the right way.
Caraway is not threshed with a sledge,
  nor is a cartwheel rolled over cummin;
Caraway is beaten out with a rod,
  and cummin with a stick.
Grain must be ground to make bread;
  so one does not go on threshing it forever.
Though he drives the wheels of his threshing cart over it,
  his horses do not grind it.
All this also comes from the LORD Almighty,
  wonderful in counsel and magnificent in wisdom.

Although the text contains technical horticultural vocabulary, some of which is obscure, several theological lessons are obvious. (1) Yahweh, the source of true knowledge is also the source of wisdom for the farmer. (2) The soil is carefully prepared before planting, and the farmer carefully plots his crops, each one assigned its own space. (3) The methods of harvesting are crop specific; different species are in their appointed places and should not be mixed.[25]

CHRISTIANS AND THESE REGULATIONS. Do Christians need to keep these regulations? Many, perhaps most in our churches would say, "No." These instructions are part of ancient Israel's civil and ceremonial laws that have been rendered passé through the work of Christ and have no authority for us. It is true that the kingdom of God has burst the ethnic and ethnocentric boundaries of Yahweh's covenant with Israel, but if we take Matthew 5:17—19 and 2 Timothy 3:16 seriously, perhaps rather than asking whether we need to keep them, we should be asking, "How should we keep these regulations?" Although each segment here represented a specific application of covenantal principles of righteousness within the Israelite context, since the Israel of the Old Testament was to function as a microcosm of humanity at large, underlying all are

---

25. Cf. Borowski, *Agriculture in Iron Age Israel*, 151.

theological principles rooted in the very nature of God and his relation to the world.

As image-bearers of God, charged with the management of the world on his behalf, human beings must tend to animals in distress not only because they belong to our fellow citizens, but for the sake of the animals themselves. The God who pities the livestock of Nineveh (Jon. 4:11) and feeds the birds (Matt. 6:26; Luke 12:24) enjoins his people to be exemplary in the way they treat domestic animals (vv. 1−4) and wild creatures (vv. 6−7).[26] In the Western world we seldom witness the abuse of domestic animals take the form cited here (overloading a donkey), but the well-being of our livestock is jeopardized in more subtle ways—like massive overcrowding in factory farms and the injection of steroids and other chemicals to increase efficiency in the conversion of grain to meat. Moreover, in recent decades we have witnessed the extinction of many species of animals as humans have encroached on animal habitats. Every species was created by God to add its distinctive voice to the glorious cosmic symphony of praise to God. Every species lost is a note of praise lost.[27]

Although the ordinance demanding parapets on houses (v. 8) applies most specifically to Israelites, the responsibilities of householders for the well-being of all who come "under one's roof" was recognized even in extra-biblical law codes.[28] How much more does it apply to Christians, who should seek the welfare of all in their charge. Little imagination is needed to see how this principle should work in our context. In northern climates, it may mean something as simple as keeping ice off the sidewalk so that all who pass by are safe.

The respectful distinction between the sexes reflected in the prohibition on wearing the clothing of the opposite gender and the homosexual conduct often associated with it are reinforced repeatedly in the New Testament. Paul has the sharpest words for these kinds of perversions in Romans 1:24−27. While Christians should never stop loving those for whom cross-dressing is a fetish and those who are confused in their gender identity, the biblical witness coherently and consistently rejects these as tolerable options for God's people.

Few Christians today heed Moses' prohibitions on mixing different varieties of plants in a single plot of land or wearing two different fabrics.

---

26. See further, Richard Bauckham, "Jesus and Animals I: What Did He Teach?" in *Animals on the Agenda: Questions about Animals for Theology and Ethics* (ed. Andrew Linzey and Dorothy Yamamoto; London: SCM, 1998), 33−48; idem, "Jesus and Animals II: What Did He Practise?" 49−60.

27. For detailed discussion of these issues, see Block, "To Serve and to Keep," 116−42.

28. CH §§229−30.

However, underlying these commands is a profoundly theological concern for order. The blurring of boundaries symbolizes chaos. The lives of the redeemed should be characterized by order and resistance to everything that causes disintegration of that order in one's life. Everything about our external conduct and appearance reflects on the name and reputation of our God. To claim the name of Christ (=Yahweh) and to live in a chaotic environment is to misrepresent the one whose name we bear.

Few would see any relevance in Moses' injunction to attach tassels to the corners of the garments. And yet the principle is clear. In a culture increasingly characterized by lewdness and immodesty, the appeal for Christians to adopt distinctive forms of dress gains relevance. Faithful Christians are recognizable by their countercultural values and their sensitivity to the way outsiders read them. While we resist legalism and treating issues of faith as merely or primarily external, verse 12 reminds us that spiritual commitments are not simply matters of the heart. I should indeed "want to be a Christian/more loving/more holy/like Jesus in my heart," but I must declare my commitments publicly, and even more importantly embody the grace of Christ in every aspect of life. Ethical boundaries are determined by our citizenship in heaven, rather than on earth.

Deuteronomy 22:13–30

If a man takes a wife and, after lying with her, dislikes her [14]and slanders her and gives her a bad name, saying, "I married this woman, but when I approached her, I did not find proof of her virginity," [15]then the girl's father and mother shall bring proof that she was a virgin to the town elders at the gate. [16]The girl's father will say to the elders, "I gave my daughter in marriage to this man, but he dislikes her. [17]Now he has slandered her and said, 'I did not find your daughter to be a virgin.' But here is the proof of my daughter's virginity." Then her parents shall display the cloth before the elders of the town, [18]and the elders shall take the man and punish him. [19]They shall fine him a hundred shekels of silver and give them to the girl's father, because this man has given an Israelite virgin a bad name. She shall continue to be his wife; he must not divorce her as long as he lives.

[20]If, however, the charge is true and no proof of the girl's virginity can be found, [21]she shall be brought to the door of her father's house and there the men of her town shall stone her to death. She has done a disgraceful thing in Israel by being promiscuous while still in her father's house. You must purge the evil from among you.

[22]If a man is found sleeping with another man's wife, both the man who slept with her and the woman must die. You must purge the evil from Israel.

[23]If a man happens to meet in a town a virgin pledged to be married and he sleeps with her, [24]you shall take both of them to the gate of that town and stone them to death—the girl because she was in a town and did not scream for help, and the man because he violated another man's wife. You must purge the evil from among you.

[25]But if out in the country a man happens to meet a girl pledged to be married and rapes her, only the man who has done this shall die. [26]Do nothing to the girl; she has committed no sin deserving death. This case is like that of someone who attacks and murders his neighbor, [27]for the man found the girl out in the country, and though the betrothed girl screamed, there was no one to rescue her.

²⁸If a man happens to meet a virgin who is not pledged to be married and rapes her and they are discovered, ²⁹he shall pay the girl's father fifty shekels of silver. He must marry the girl, for he has violated her. He can never divorce her as long as he lives.

³⁰A man is not to marry his father's wife; he must not dishonor his father's bed.

THE REST OF CHAPTER 22, which concerns righteousness in marital and family relations, picks up where 21:10–23 left off. This text divides into two panels, the first instructing how to respond to accusations of sexual infidelity (22:13–21), and the second how to deal with specific sexual misconduct (vv. 22–30).

Righteousness in the Face of Marital Infidelity (22:13–21)

WHILE CRITICAL SCHOLARS TEND to delete the paraenetic features of verses 13–21 as secondary insertions, these are integral to the pastoral tone of the text. In general, this section divides into two uneven parts, presenting a primary case (vv. 13–19), followed by a countercase (vv. 20–21).[1]

The primary case (vv. 13–19). Moses begins by presenting a hypothetical situation in which a man marries a woman (vv. 13–14), but in order to be released from the marriage he trumps up charges against her. Moses casts the case logically as a five-phased process: (1) a man marries a woman (v. 13a); (2) the man consummates the marriage (v. 13b); (3) the man rejects his wife (v. 13c);[2] (4) the man accuses his wife of misconduct (v. 14a); (5) the man publicly shames his wife (v. 14b). The absence of a reason for the rejection in phase 3 suggests an illicit demand for divorce and sets the stage for the presentation of the case to the elders.

The charge in phase 4 may be understood either as "wanton words," that is, unrestrained speech, or "wanton actions," that is, profligate behavior.[3] Since the elders find the woman innocent, the punishment appropriate

---

1. For extrabiblical counterparts to this double case form, see Roth, *Law Collections,* 108–9, 174–75. On the relationship of 22:13–21 to ancient Near Eastern laws, see Willis, *Elders of the City,* 193–206.

2. While *śānēʾ* ("to hate, reject") may be a technical expression for divorce (Judg. 15:2), since Deuteronomy refers to divorce with *šillaḥ* ("to send [from one's house]," 22:19, 29; 24:1, 3), here *śānēʾ* refers to the motivation behind the rejection. So also Pressler, *View of Women,* 23, n. 4. Cf. Hugenberger, *Marriage as a Covenant,* 51–76.

3. Cf. Driver, *Deuteronomy,* 254. NIV translates, he "slanders her and gives her a bad name."

to the crime for which the woman is charged (in this case, death by stoning) should be execution of the man (cf. 19:15—21). However, since he is
"merely" chastised and forced to pay compensation to the woman's father
suggests that the primary issue here is not the veracity of the husband's
charges, but the innocence of his wife. In that case the charge in phase
4 refers to misconduct, which the husband imputes to his wife (cf. v. 17).

The statement in phase 5 reinforces this interpretation. Moses concretizes the slanderous speech in verse 14b by putting self-serving words in his
mouth. Echoing the narrative introduction, the man claims that he took the
woman as his wife, but when he approached her to consummate the marriage, he discovered she was not a virgin.[4] While the man does not give the
evidence for his charge, he had two options, both involving blood. If she
was not menstruating or did not bleed after the first intercourse, he could
conclude either that she was pregnant, or he was not the first man to have
intercourse with her. The parents' words in verse 17 suggests the latter is
the charge. The text does not say why the husband has trumped up this
charge, other than that he wants to get out of a marriage. He thinks he can
achieve his objectives by pressing charges against his wife in court, which
would lead to her execution for adultery (cf. Lev. 20:10).

In verses 15—17 Moses envisions the court proceedings take a surprising
turn. The defendant turns out to be not the woman but the man, who has leveled the charges against her. Therefore, the elders must deal with him before
they deal with the woman. Three features of the judicial procedures are significant. (1) They transpire before elders in the gate of the town where these
people reside, suggesting that adultery is not simply a sinful act between two
consenting adults. In a kinship-based society, healthy marriages are fundamental to the health of the community, linking families that have negotiated
the marital agreement in the first place. Because the divorce sought by this
man and the rumors he has spread have the potential to divide the community, elders representing the extended family units must intervene.

(2) The young woman's parents initiate the proceedings to have their
daughter's sullied reputation cleared. Concern for their own honor may be
a factor,[5] but this case also involves male defense of female honor. The husband's shaming of his wife's honor calls for judicial intervention. Instead of

---

4. The expression *beṭûlîm* ("virginity") derives from *beṭûlâ* (traditionally understood as "virgin") though some now argue that the word means "young girl of marriageable age." See
G. J. Wenham, "*Beṭûlāh*: 'A Girl of Marriageable Age,'" *VT* 22 (1972): 326—48. For a critical
evaluation of Wenham, see Pressler, *View of Women*, 25—26.

5. See A. Phillips, *Deuteronomy* (CBC; Cambridge: Cambridge Univ. Press, 1973), 149;
idem, "Another Look at Adultery," *JSOT* 20 (1981): 6—7; Pressler, *View of Women*, 22—27;
Willis, *Elders of the City*, 224—25.

fulfilling his primary duty of securing the welfare of his wife, he has taken hostile actions against her.

(3) Whereas earlier texts had called for multiple witnesses to establish the truth in a legal case (17:6−7; 19:15), in this case material evidence is presented.[6] The vague reference to "proof of her virginity" in verse 14 is clarified somewhat in verse 17 with "cloth." Although this word normally refers to an outer garment,[7] here it refers either to the garment worn on the night of the wedding or the bed sheet, giving evidence of the breaking of the girl's hymen.[8] The accused woman may have stored the sheet in her "hope chest," as a commemoration of the night of her first intercourse and as concrete evidence of her virginity at the time of her marriage — in case anyone should ever challenge this. This she now produces to her father and mother as proof of her premarital purity.

The speech of the woman's father in verses 16b−17 echoes the man's charges against his wife (vv. 13−14a). However, the father turns the case around and accuses the man of unfaithfulness. He has wrongly rejected his wife and spread false and malicious rumors of her misconduct in the community. After quoting his son-in-law's charge verbatim, he spreads out the bed sheet before the elders, and declares, "Here is the proof of my daughter's virginity."

According to verses 18−19 the evidence of a stained bed sheet trumps the verbal accusations of a treacherous husband. The testimony of the bride's father and the material evidence call for a decisive response against the husband. The elders must take the man and flog him (NIV "punish"), fine him one hundred shekels of silver — to be paid to the father of the young woman as compensation for her sullied reputation[9] — and prohibit him from ever divorcing his wife (v. 19b). While modern readers may find the last prescription troublesome, this requirement aims for a rehabilitative outcome. Because the matter is resolved in a public court of law, the people in the community become guarantors of the man's good behavior.

The fine goes beyond compensating for the injury done to the woman's reputation; it also restores righteousness in Israel. The striking ending of the motive clause in verse 19 assumes that sexual sins are not only personal crimes against another individual; they are also crimes against the entire community.

---

6. Cf. the use of material objects as evidence in Gen. 38:25 (a seal, belt, and staff); Ex. 22:13[12]. (animal remains); Gen. 37:31−33 (a tunic stained with blood); 1 Sam. 26:16 (a spear and jug of water).

7. Deut. 24:10−13 and Ex. 22:26−27[25−26] suggest it was also used for sleeping.

8. To this day in Mediterranean and Arabic lands the sheet used when consummating a marriage is often kept as evidence.

9. Verse 29 suggests the fine was double the fifty shekels paid for a virgin daughter. Cf. Tigay, *Deuteronomy*, 205.

This solution takes seriously the implications for the health of society of the original charges and the extension of the woman's guilt to the covenant community. The court must preserve the good name of all Israelite women, but they must also act to preserve righteousness within the nation as a whole.

The countercase (vv. 20–21). Moses completes the discussion by instructing the court how to proceed if the husband's accusations are confirmed. The description is more concise than the preceding, consisting of summary statements of the opposite result (v. 20), followed by the sentence (v. 21). The former announces simply that the husband is justified in accusing his wife of premarital adultery—proof of virginity is lacking. Failing to produce the stained bed sheet as evidence of innocence, plaintiff and defendant switch roles. The person whose guilt or innocence is at issue is no longer the man who has spread the rumors, but his wife. The punishment for premarital adultery is severe: shameful death by stoning[10] at the entrance to the woman's father's house, because she committed fornication while still at home.[11] This punishment implies the public defaming of the father and his household for having "sold damaged goods" to the husband.[12]

Since marriages in Israel were generally patrilocal, Moses' demand that "the men of her town" rather than the men of the town where she and her husband lived is remarkable. This forces the community that hosted the sinful acts to come to terms with the crime. This conclusion is reinforced by the motive clause and the concluding purgation formula (v. 21). Together, these expressions highlight the heinousness and the communal implications of sexual crimes and declare Moses' main concern—to maintain a holy community of faith before Yahweh. Radical surgery is required to remove those who flaunt contempt for the covenant by promiscuous behavior. Young men and women are to keep themselves pure for their spouse.

Righteousness in the Face of
Sexual Promiscuity (22:22–30 [23:1])

THIS NEXT SET OF instructions seeks to establish righteousness in sexual behavior by presenting three hypothetical adulterous scenarios (vv. 22–29), and an outright apodictic prohibition of sexual relations with one's step-mother (v. 30 [23:1]). The three scenarios exhibit a clear progression, depending on the marital status of the woman: illicit sex with a

---

10. On the place of shame in ancient Israelite law, see V. H. Matthews, "Honor and Shame in Gender-Related Legal Situations in the Hebrew Bible," in *Gender and Law in the Hebrew Bible* (ed. V. H. Matthews et al.; JSOTSup; Sheffield: Sheffield Academic, 1998), 237–42.

11. For extrabiblical support for executing criminals where a crime was committed, see CH §21.

12. Cf. A. Phillips, "Another Look at Adultery," *JSOT* 20 (1981): 10.

married woman (v. 22), illicit sex with a virgin who is betrothed to a man (vv. 23–27), and illicit sex with a virgin not yet betrothed to a man.

Adultery involving a married woman (v. 22). The opening formula, "If a man is found," indicates this case is not about rumors but about adulterers discovered in the very act: A man lies with another man's wife. The opening sentence focuses on the man, but the specified punishment suggests the act was consensual. Moses provides no details on the procedures leading up to the adulterers' execution, nor of the execution itself. However, sandwiched between verses 15–22 and 23–24, the text seems to assume that the person(s) who discovered them in the act would notify the elders of the town and testify against them in a public hearing, whereupon they would be publicly executed by stoning. Since sexual crimes are considered crimes against the fabric of the community and crimes against God, covenantal righteousness demands the purgation of the evil from the midst of Israel, which is achieved by removing the corrupting elements.

Adultery involving a virgin engaged to be married (vv. 23–27). These instructions are more complex, like verses 13–21 (cf. 19:1–13), subdividing into two panels representing a primary case (vv. 23–24) and a countercase (vv. 25–27). The differences in outcome are determined by the location of the offense. Both cases involve a man finding a young woman and engaging in sexual intercourse with her. The woman is referred to by three expressions: "girl [young woman]";[13] "virgin,"[14] and "betrothed girl." The latter two distinguish these cases from the preceding where the adulterous wife was identified as a "wife" (v. 22). Whereas modern Western engagements involve public declarations of intention to marry, betrothal refers to a publicly binding legal act, which explains why in this context the woman was considered "another man's wife" (v. 24).

The primary case (vv. 23–24) concerns an adulterous act committed within the walls of the town, where residents live in close proximity to one another. Since no one heard the woman's cry for help, it is assumed she did not cry out, which suggests the sexual act was consensual. Therefore, both the man and the woman are to be brought to the gate of the town and executed by stoning. While adulterer and adulteress receive the same punishment, the reasons differ. They stone the woman because she did not cry out for help, and the man because he has debased his neighbor's wife[15] and in so doing also violated the honor of his neighbor. However, as in the preceding cases,

---

13. In the previous pericope (22:15, 16, 19, 20, 21) the expression applied to a married woman.

14. On the meaning of this expression see comment on 22:15.

15. The apparently consensual nature of the sexual acts reinforces the notion that in juridical contexts the word does not denote "rape," but serves an evaluative function, best expressed by "debased" (cf. van Wolde, "Does ʿinnâ Denote Rape?" 528–44).

adultery is deemed more than a private act between two consenting adults; it violates the integrity of the nation as a whole. Therefore righteousness demands the death penalty to purge the evil from the midst of the nation.

The countercase (vv. 25–27) highlights the role of the woman as victim. This hypothetical encounter transpires in the open field, where, even if she had cried for help, no one within earshot would have heard her cry. Consequently, she is given the benefit of the doubt, while the man is considered guilty. Having encountered her (v. 27) away from the village in the open country, he seized her and "lay" with her. Comparing the woman's fate to that of the victim of murder (cf. 19:11–13), Moses pronounces the death penalty on the man. However, since the woman is presumed an innocent victim, she shall not die.

Adultery involving a virgin not engaged to be married (vv. 28–29). Of Moses' instructions concerning adultery, this paragraph exhibits the closest links to earlier laws, particularly Exodus 22:16–17[15–16]. Both cases involve a man and a virgin who has not been engaged,[16] though our text casts the actions of the adulterer in a more violent light. Whereas Exodus 22:16[15] considered the man's actions seductive, this text envisions the man seizing the woman and "lying" with her, and the two being caught in the very act. Here the prescribed response focuses entirely on the man. Because he has deflowered and degraded the woman, he must pay the father of the woman fifty shekels. Unlike verse 19, this payment is not considered a fine but the bride price, since upon its payment she becomes his wife in a marriage from which there is to be no divorce as long as they live (cf. v. 19).

Superficially this text seems to go against the general Deuteronomic trajectory of a more humanitarian approach vis-à-vis earlier laws, tightening the ordinance as preserved in Exodus 22:16–17[15–16]. Because the man has degraded the virgin, he must pay the bride price of fifty shekels to her father and take her as his wife, which seems to add insult to injury for the woman. Not only has she been violated, but now she is forced to become his wife. However, if we translate the verb *wᵉnātan* modally, "and he may pay," rather than as an imperative, "he shall pay" (NIV), the tone changes significantly. If her father accepts the bride price and agrees to accept the man as a son-in-law, then the man must fulfill all the marital duties that go with sexual intercourse.[17]

Respecting one's father's sexuality (22:30 [23:1]). This ethical fragment is linked to the preceding by its concern for sexual integrity. However, the apodictic form and the departure from the adulterous cases of the

---

16. In contrast to vv. 23, 25 and 27, which refer to someone who is "pledged to be married." Since this virgin has never been betrothed, her father has not received the bride price due him. See further D. H. Weiss, "A Note on אשר לא ארשׂה," *JBL* 81 (1982): 67–69.

17. For analogues to this text, see the Middle Assyrian Laws §§55–56 (Roth, *Law Collections*, 174–75).

previous paragraphs set it apart.[18] This taboo on sexual intercourse between a man with his father's wife reiterates what Yahweh had prohibited in Leviticus 18:8. The opening clause is cast as a forthright apodictic prohibition on marrying one's father's wife. The case probably does not involve sexual intercourse with one's own mother (cf. Lev. 18:7); rather, it seems to presuppose polygamous family structures (Gen. 35:22; 2 Sam. 16:21—23).[19] Since girls married at a very young age in ancient times,[20] Moses may also be contemplating a scenario in which a man is attracted to his father's former wife, who is free either because of divorce or the husband's death.

The second clause, which the NIV paraphrases as "he must not dishonor his father's bed," gives the rationale for the prohibition. The idiom (lit., "to cover a father's corner") may refer to the garment covering his loins (cf. v. 12), but here it bears sexual overtones. If spreading one's garment over a woman signified covering her nakedness, that is, marrying her (Ruth 3:9; Ezek. 16:8), then to uncover a man's garment signified exposing the person over whom the man had spread his garment. Leviticus 18:8 suggests that to engage in intercourse with one's step-mother desecrates the father's marriage.[21]

SEXUAL PATTERNS IN BIBLICAL **narratives.** While acknowledging the male's initiative in the sexual crimes dealt with here, these instructions reflect a remarkable equality. For women, the outcome of consensual premarital sex was death (vv. 22—24) and of nonconsensual sex, marriage (vv. 28—29). For men it was the same: death or pay the bride price and marry her. While no guilt was incurred by women if they were forced to engage in sexual activity against their will (vv. 22—27), Israel could not tolerate sexually experienced unmarried women.[22] The restrictions on female prostitution[23] and the tenor of narratives involving men with prostitutes suggest the same applied to men.

---

18. The Hebrew Bible links it with the prohibition of various classes of people from the assembly of Yahweh.

19. Wright, *God's People in God's Land*, 208—9; A. Phillips, "Uncovering the Father's Skirt," *VT* 30 (1980): 38—43.

20. According to M. T. Roth ("Age at Marriage and the Household: A Study of Neo-Babylonian and Neo-Assyrian Forms," in *Comparative Studies in Society and History* 29 [1987]: 715—47), brides tended to be in their mid- to late-teens at the time of marriage, while husbands were in their late twenties or early thirties.

21. Cf. W. Dommershausen, "כָּנָף *kānāp*," *TDOT*, 7:231.

22. See further, A. Berlin, "Sex and the Single Girl in Deuteronomy 22," in *Mishneh Todah*, 95—112.

23. Lev. 19:29; 21:7, 14; Deut. 23:17[18].

The narratives of the Old Testament are punctuated with accounts of sexual crimes of all sorts. Perhaps we should not be surprised when Canaanites like Shechem (Gen. 34:2) or Tamar (Gen. 38:14 – 19) behave immorally, but when the covenant people do so against the revealed will of God, their guilt exceeds that of those who do not have the Torah.[24] Although biblical narratives recognize men with remarkable moral fortitude in the face of sexual temptation (Gen. 39:9),[25] they are remarkably frank in their portrayal of the moral failures of Israel's heroes and individuals in their families: the incest of Reuben, the eldest son and natural heir of Jacob (Gen. 35:22); the wanton sexual immorality of Phinehas and Hopni (Eli's sons) with female worshipers (1 Sam. 2:22); David's adulterous affair with his officer's wife (2 Sam. 11:1 – 27); Amnon's rape of his sister (2 Sam. 13:1 – 19). As Israel's/Judah's demise approached, adultery was high on the lists of crimes proving the nation's covenantal infidelity.[26]

But the problem did not end with the Old Testament. Jesus recognized that sexual immorality is not merely an external act; it has its roots in the heart/mind (Matt. 5:27; 15:19; Mark 7:21), and he issued stern warnings against divorce and remarriage because of the adulterous consequences (Matt. 5:32; 19:9; Mark 10:11 – 12; Luke 16:18). Indeed with prophetic fervor he characterized his own generations as evil and adulterous (Matt. 12:39; 16:4; Mark 8:38). The seriousness of sexual immorality not only in society at large but within the early church in particular is reflected in the frequency with which notions of adultery and immorality appear in the New Testament letters[27] and in the book of Revelation.[28]

GENDER ISSUES. THE SEXUAL crimes dealt with in our text are problematic at two levels. Most obviously, they represent violations of the most fundamental of human institutions, the marriage of a man and a woman. To engage in sexual activity outside of marriage is an act of treachery against one's own spouse (Mal. 2:13 – 16) and treachery against the spouse (or prospective spouse, in the case

---

24. Cf. Ezek. 5:5 – 9; 16:48 – 52. Judah recognized that Tamar's righteousness exceeded his own (Gen. 38:26).

25. Note Joseph's response to Potiphar's wife in Gen. 39:9: "How then could I do such a wicked thing and sin against God?"

26. On the problem of adultery in the northern kingdom prior to its demise in the eighth century BC, see Hos. 2:2[4]; 4:2, 13 – 14; on adultery in Judah prior to its demise in the seventh – sixth centuries, see Jer. 3:9; 5:7; 7:9; 23:14; 29:23; Ezek. 16:38; 23:37, 43. Adultery is used metaphorically of Israel's pursuit of other gods in place of her husband, Yahweh.

27. Rom. 13:13; 1 Cor. 5:1, 9 – 11; 6:9, 13, 18; 7:2; 10:8; 2 Cor. 12:21; Gal. 5:19; Eph. 5:3, 5; Col. 3:5; 1 Thess. 4:3; 1 Tim. 1:10; Heb. 13:4; James 4:4; 2 Peter 2:14; Jude 1:7.

28. Rev. 2:14, 20 – 22; 9:21; 14:8; 17:2, 4; 18:3, 9; 19:2; 21:8; 22:15.

of relations with someone not married) of the person with whom one is engaged in this illicit behavior. But God is the witness to all covenants and the guarantor of fidelity,[29] and he holds people accountable for their immorality.

However, the sexual crimes presented here also address issues of gender relations. Many interpret these instructions as irredeemably patriarchal, the primary intention being to defend the rights and honor of men at the expense of women.[30] However, the cultural presuppositions reflected here are millennia removed from modern pervasively egalitarian Western societies. However, our caricatured view of patriarchy, which etymologically means "the rule of the father," is problematic. It evokes images of high-handed and self-serving men whose primary concern was maintaining male honor and male control over the household.

Admittedly, the Hebrew designation of the family unit as a *bêt ʾâb* ("father's house") reflects both the androcentricity of Israelite society in general and the patricentricity of families in particular. Like most ancient Near Eastern cultures Israelite families were patrilineal (official lines of descent were traced through the father's line),[31] patrilocal (married women joined the households of their husbands), and patriarchal (the father governed the household).[32]

**The Patriarchal Family Structure
of Ancient Israelite Narrative**   **The Patricentric Ideal
of Ancient Israel**

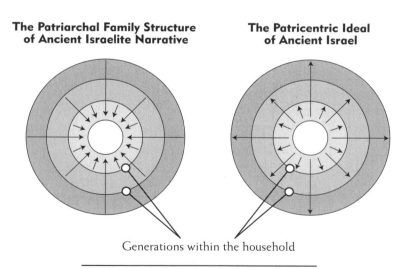

Generations within the household

---

29. Prov. 2:17 refers to marriage as the "covenant of [one's] God."

30. For all the exegetical merit of Carolyn Pressler's work, her contention that these laws only protected the rights of males and reinforced the status of females as their husband's possession is overstated (*View of Women*, 42–43).

31. See the genealogies in Gen. 5; 10; 36; etc.

32. For discussion see R. Patai, *Family, Love and the Bible* (London: Macgibbon & Kee, 1960), 17–18.

But the narratives of the Old Testament expose the problems with patriarchy, inasmuch as responsible rule in the interests of those placed in one's charge may quickly degenerate into self-interested and abusive male behavior.[33] The solution offered by the Old Testament (and the New Testament, for that matter) is not to replace these structures with some sort of egalitarianism that neutralizes gender distinctions and homogenizes roles, but to plead for transformed leadership. In patriarchy the emphasis is on the rule of the head, which often leads to dominance over and exploitation of those within the household for male interests and honor. Sadly, the prediction of Genesis 3:16 has proved to be painfully true: "He will rule over you."

This problem exists at every level of leadership;[34] instead of promoting the health of the community, leaders often undermine it. The patricentrism envisioned in Deuteronomy operates in the reverse direction. There is no denial of traditional family structures—after all, a family is the *bêt ʾāb*—but according to this ideal the emphasis is on the father's responsibility (not power) to care for the household and seek the interests of others above his own.

Although these texts do not gloss over sin committed by females (vv. 20–21, 22, 23–24), their primary concern is to rein in abusive and abominable male behavior: slandering and then seeking to get rid of a wife (vv. 13–19); adultery with a woman betrothed to another man (vv. 23–24); degrading a woman betrothed to another man (vv. 25–27); degrading a virgin (vv. 28–29); and finally abusing one's father and step-mother (v. 30[23:1]). The moral trajectory reflected here characterizes the entire book of Deuteronomy.[35]

A high view of community, family, and human sexuality. The scenarios envisioned in our text may be common, but they are neither normal nor excusable. The covenantal standards signaled by the Decalogue and

---

33. Interpreters rightly characterize as abusive Abraham's passing off his wife Sarah as his sister to save his own skin (Gen. 12:10–20), Lot's offering his two daughters to the thugs of Sodom (Gen. 19:8), Jephthah's sacrificing his daughter (Judg. 11:34–40), the Israelite men's authorizing the remnant of Benjamite warriors to ambush and seize their daughters as they are engaged in celebrative religious dance (Judg. 21:19–24), David's committing adultery with Bathsheba and his murder of her husband (2 Sam. 11:1–27), Amnon's raping his half-sister Tamar (2 Sam. 13:1–19)—to name just a few episodes recounted in Scripture. For keen analysis of some of these troubling texts see P. Trible, *Texts of Terror: Literary Feminist Readings of Biblical Narratives* (OBT; Philadelphia: Fortress, 1984).

34. Hence the instructions for the king in 17:14–20, on which see Block, "The Burden of Leadership," in *How I Love Your Torah, O LORD!* 118–39. For discussion of leadership in the Old Testament see Block, "Leadership, Lead," *NIDB*, 3:620–26.

35. For a preliminary essay on the subject, see Block, "'You Shall Not Covet Your Neighbor's Wife,'" in *The Gospel According to Moses*, 137–68; for a fuller investigation of the matter, see Josberger, "Between Rule and Responsibility."

developed in greater deal in the Deuteronomic Torah call on the "father" (ʾāb) in the "the father's house" (bêt ʾāb) to care for and protect all those under his charge. Because of sheer superior physical power, men exhibit a propensity to exploit and abuse women as if they were nothing more than household property, as disposable as sheep or oxen. Contemporary efforts to determine and reestablish biblical ethical norms must pay attention not only to accounts of the way it was, but also to texts that seek to outline the way it should have been. In this and many other respects, the book of Deuteronomy offers a glorious gospel, setting a trajectory of male-female relations that leads ultimately to Paul's statements in Ephesians 5:25 – 33.

> Husbands, love your wives, just as Christ loved the church and gave himself up for her to make her holy, cleansing her by the washing with water through the word, and to present her to himself as a radiant church, without stain or wrinkle or any other blemish, but holy and blameless. In this same way, husbands ought to love their wives as their own bodies. He who loves his wife loves himself. After all, no one ever hated his own body, but he feeds and cares for it, just as Christ does the church — for we are members of his body. "For this reason a man will leave his father and mother and be united to his wife, and the two will become one flesh." This is a profound mystery — but I am talking about Christ and the church. However, each one of you also must love his wife as he loves himself, and the wife must respect her husband.

Given this perspective on normative patricentrism, a more balanced reading of Deuteronomy 22:13 – 30 [23:1] becomes possible. This chapter reflects a high view of community, family, and human sexuality. It runs against the grain of modern Western approaches, which tend to view human beings atomistically, as independent and self-sufficient, and which view sexual activity as personal matters and sexual sins as purely private.[36] Here Moses teaches modern readers that human sexuality is sacred, that the purity of marriage is to be defended at all cost, and that degeneration in these areas inevitably leads to disintegration of the family as a whole. In a society where the rate of failed marriages is as high among church members as outsiders, Christians in particular need to hear Moses' call for defense of the institution of marriage.

---

36. The communal significance of adultery in Israel contrasts with ancient Mesopotamia, where, according to J. J. Finkelstein ("Sex Offenses in Sumerian Laws," *JAOS* 86 [1966]: 372) adultery "was at bottom a civil invasion of a husband's domain, and it was left to him to take as serious or as lenient a view of the matter as he chose; in practice the inclination was toward the less severe."

Whatever the long-range validity of Moses' (and Yahweh's) demand for executing adulterers — few would approve the punishments for our day — these texts remind us of the heinousness of sexual sins in God's eyes. As long as the standards by which the church responds to these issues are governed by worldly perspectives, so long will her voice on other aspects of justice and morality be rejected as hypocritical and empty. Jesus' disposition on these matters is precisely in line with those of Moses, when he said, "What God has joined together, let man not separate" (Matt. 19:6; Mark 10:9) — which is tantamount to a curse on any who would interfere with another's marriage. And Moses' instructions are no more severe than the warnings of Paul, who declares:

> Do you not know that the wicked will not inherit the kingdom of God? Do not be deceived: Neither the sexually immoral nor idolaters nor adulterers nor male prostitutes nor homosexual offenders nor thieves nor the greedy nor drunkards nor slanderers nor swindlers will inherit the kingdom of God. And that is what some of you were. But you were washed, you were sanctified, you were justified in the name of the Lord Jesus Christ and by the Spirit of our God. (1 Cor. 6:9 – 11)

Contemporary readers are faced with two principal alternatives when faced with texts like Deuteronomy 22:13 – 30: interpret these documents as cultural fossils of a bygone era with no relevance whatsoever for the issues that face readers today, or attempt to understand the permanent values reflected here and find contemporary ways of applying those values. We cast our vote for the latter.

Deuteronomy 23:1–14 [2–15][1]

No one who has been emasculated by crushing or cutting may enter the assembly of the LORD.
²No one born of a forbidden marriage nor any of his descendants may enter the assembly of the LORD, even down to the tenth generation.

³No Ammonite or Moabite or any of his descendants may enter the assembly of the LORD, even down to the tenth generation. ⁴For they did not come to meet you with bread and water on your way when you came out of Egypt, and they hired Balaam son of Beor from Pethor in Aram Naharaim to pronounce a curse on you. ⁵However, the LORD your God would not listen to Balaam but turned the curse into a blessing for you, because the LORD your God loves you. ⁶Do not seek a treaty of friendship with them as long as you live.

⁷Do not abhor an Edomite, for he is your brother. Do not abhor an Egyptian, because you lived as an alien in his country. ⁸The third generation of children born to them may enter the assembly of the LORD.

⁹When you are encamped against your enemies, keep away from everything impure. ¹⁰If one of your men is unclean because of a nocturnal emission, he is to go outside the camp and stay there. ¹¹But as evening approaches he is to wash himself, and at sunset he may return to the camp.

¹²Designate a place outside the camp where you can go to relieve yourself. ¹³As part of your equipment have something to dig with, and when you relieve yourself, dig a hole and cover up your excrement. ¹⁴For the LORD your God moves about in your camp to protect you and to deliver your enemies to you. Your camp must be holy, so that he will not see among you anything indecent and turn away from you.

---

1. Because of differences in the location of the chapter division, the verse numbers in Hebrew are all one higher than the English numbers. For the sake of convenience, the commentary will use only the English numbers.

THE PASTORAL INSTRUCTIONS IN chapter 23 continue the pattern of chapters 21—22, providing counsel on a variety of subjects with a minimal amount of theological or hortatory commentary. While the topics vary considerably, Moses continues his appeal to the Israelites to bring all of life captive to the principle of "righteousness, only righteousness" (see 16:20).

Righteousness in the Assembly of Yahweh (23:1–8)

THE PHRASE TO "ENTER the assembly of the LORD" (*qᵉhal yhwh*) occurs six times, leaving no doubt that guarding the sanctity of the congregation is the primary concern of verses 1–8. The expression "assembly of the LORD" refers to those who have gathered before Yahweh for an audience with him, that is, to hear him speak. Whereas earlier texts had highlighted the inclusive nature of worship (12:7, 12; 16:11, 14), for the first time Moses raises barriers to the assembly. His text divides into two unequal parts, verses 1–6 and verses 7–8. The first part erects walls around "the assembly of the LORD," while the second opens the doors to outsiders.

Defending the sanctity of the assembly of Yahweh (vv. 1–6). Moses erects three barriers to the assembly, each of which is intended to protect the sanctity of the community. The first category of excluded people is emasculated men. The male organs of procreation could have been mutilated either by crushing the testicles[2] or surgically removing them.[3] Whether the cause of deformity was accidental, intentional, or a birth defect, the restriction recalls earlier proscriptions on sacrificing animals with any kind of defect (15:21) or of admitting candidates with any defects to priestly service (Lev. 21:17–23). Moses does not explain why men with deformed genitalia should be excluded. In ancient times prisoners of war, slaves,[4] and men who had committed adultery or engaged in homosexual acts were often castrated,[5] but this prohibition seems has been influenced

---

2. According to Mesopotamian castration procedures, the testicles of boys destined for "eunuchship" would be crushed shortly before they reached puberty. See K. Deller, "The Assyrian Eunuchs and Their Predecessors," in *Priests and Officials in the Ancient Near East* (ed. K. Watanabe; Heidelberg: Universitätsverlag C. Winter, 1999), 305.

3. This second expression refers to one whose penis has been cut off. Cutting off the penis involved more radical surgery than crushing or removing testicles, and seems to have been intended to change a person's gender. See Erra and Ishum, 4.55–56, as translated by S. Dalley, *COS*, 1:113 (p. 413). Some are more cautious about interpreting these as eunuchs. Cf. *CAD*, A/2:341–42 (s.v., *assinnu*) and *CAD*, K:557–9 (s.v., *kurgarrû*).

4. Cf. Herodotus, *Histories* 6.32.

5. MAL §§15, 20.

by pagan religious rites of self-castration, perhaps as an ascetic act of self-torment or in pious imitation of the gods.[6] The reference to males only reflects the exclusively male character of Israel's priestly classes.[7]

Moses' second exclusion identifies the subject by the rare word *mamzēr* (NIV, one "born of a forbidden marriage," v. 2a). While the etymology of the word is uncertain, linked to the preceding this seems to refer to off-spring of prostitutes (cf. vv. 17—18) who lived at pagan cult sites. Moses' earlier warning concerning improper worship (12:30—31) and the linkage of the tenth generation in verse 2b with Ammonites and Moabites in verse 3b reinforce this interpretation. Since Israelites traced both of these peoples to an incestuous act (Gen. 19:37—38), *mamzēr* may refer to one conceived through incestuous intercourse (prohibited in Lev. 18), or more broadly to one born of illicit sexual relationships (Deut. 22:13—29). Such persons were banned from the assembly to the tenth generation, which verse 3 clarifies as "forever."[8] Since children are not responsible for the circumstances of their conception, the ban seems harsh. However, viewed from God's perspective, they are products of abominable unions, and to admit them violates the righteousness that governed Israel as a holy people belonging to Yahweh.[9]

The permanent exclusion of Ammonites and Moabites from "the assembly of the LORD"[10] seems odd (vv. 3—6) in light of the more sympathetic disposition toward Edom in verse 7. Although Moses could have grounded this policy in these peoples' incestuous origins (Gen. 19:30—38), he cites their refusal to greet the Israelites with bread and water when they came up from Egypt and their engagement of Balaam to curse them.[11] Verse 5 is a parenthetical addition, reminding the people of the debt of gratitude they owe to Yahweh for their very existence. Frustrating the Moabites' plan by refusing to use Balaam to curse Israel on Balak's behalf, Yahweh had transformed intended curses into blessings, which become more effusive with each utterance (Num. 23:7—10, 18—24; 24:3—9, 15—19).

---

6. See S. Ribichini, "Eshmun," *DDD*, 307—8. In Assyria, eunuchs could not become priests; as musicians and singers they occasionally participated in religious ceremonies. Thus also Deller, "The Assyrian Eunuchs," 303.

7. Cf. P. Bird, "The Place of Women in the Israelite Cultus," in *Ancient Israelite Religion: Essays in Honor of Frank Moore Cross* (ed. P. D. Miller et al.; Philadelphia: Fortress, 1987), 397—419.

8. Cf. Tigay, *Deuteronomy*, 211.

9. Deut. 7:6; 14:1; 26:19. Cf. Merrill, *Deuteronomy*, 308.

10. Tigay (*Deuteronomy*, 211) suggests "the tenth generation" refers to ten generations after the head of this family entered the land of Israel as a *gēr* ("sojourner").

11. As in Numbers 22:5, Moses introduces the prophet by name (Balaam), patronymic ("son of Beor"), home town ("Pethor"), ethnic affiliation ("Aram"), and geographic region (Naharaim—"of the two rivers," i.e., Euphrates and the Tigris).

The motive clause at the end of verse 5 reminds Israel of the motif that drives the entire book of Deuteronomy: "because the LORD your God loves you." Previously Moses had noted Yahweh's love as the motivating force behind his election and rescue of Israel from Egypt (4:37; 7:8) and his lavish blessing (7:12), but here it underlies Yahweh's protection from hostile military and spiritual forces. Because the Moabites and Ammonites had opposed Yahweh and his agenda regarding the Israelites, the Israelites are never to seek their peace or their welfare. Since "a treaty of friendship" functions as a general expression for well-being in covenantal contexts, this may be a ban on treaties with Ammonites and Moabites.[12]

Opening the doors to the assembly of Yahweh (vv. 7−8). Having closed the door to particular groups in verses 1−6, verse 7 invites the people eventually to open the assembly of Yahweh to outsiders. Moses opens the door with a remarkable statement: "Do not abhor an Edomite/Egyptian." Moses grounds this more tolerant disposition toward the Edomites on Israel's kinship with them (cf. Gen. 25:19−26; cf. Deut. 2:4−7).[13] This conciliatory tone toward Edom (via-à-vis Moabites and Ammonites) may reflect Yahweh's special interest in the direct descendants of Abraham (cf. Gen 27:39−40; 36).

The invitation to Egyptians is even more remarkable, especially in view of the abuse the Israelites had suffered at their hands. However, this disposition is rooted in their role as hosts to Israel: "because you lived as an alien in his country." Here their status as *gēr* ("alien") should be understood favorably (cf. Gen. 26:3). Because the Egyptians hosted them during a precarious phase of their history, they are rewarded by being granted admission to the assembly of Yahweh.[14] Verse 8 qualifies the openness of Israelites toward Edomites and Egyptians. In three generations, presumably once those who were alive at the time of Israel's exodus and desert sojourn have died, their descendants may be welcomed into Yahweh's assembly, provided they, like genuinely pious Israelites, were devoted exclusively to Yahweh (cf. 6:4−5) and lived in keeping with the covenant.

---

12. Similar to the ban on covenants with the Canaanite nations in 7:2. The words occur as parallel elements in the Aramaic Sefire treaty. See W. L. Moran, "Notes on the Treaty Terminology of the Sefire Stelas," *JNES* 22 (1963): 173−76; D. R. Hillers, "A Note on Some Treaty Terminology in the Old Testament," *BASOR* 176 (1964): 46−47.

13. The motif of the brotherly relationship existing between Israel and Edom may be traced throughout the Old Testament, but see especially prophetic condemnation of Edom for stifling natural family affections, and refusing to aid the Israelites in an hour of need (Amos 1:11; Obad. 10−12; cf. also Ps. 137).

14. On this more positive dimension to Israel's Egyptian experience, see M. Cogan, "The Other Egypt: A Welcome Asylum," in *Texts, Temples, and Traditions: A Tribute to Menahem Haran* (ed. M. V. Fox et al.; Winona Lake, IN: Eisenbrauns, 1996), 65−70.

Maintaining Righteousness in the Camp of Israel (23:9 − 14)

THIS IS THE SIXTH of seven war texts in Deuteronomy. Whereas the others tend to highlight humanitarian (20:4−9, 10−15; 21:10−14; 24:5) or environmental issues (20:19−20), this text is concerned with theological and spiritual realities: the integrity of the military camp when Israelites go out to battle. Structurally the paragraph divides readily into three parts.

Theme: a call for purity in the camp (v. 9). Although texts like Exodus 13:18 and 14:19−20 suggest the Israelites as a whole marched out of Egypt as a massive military force, here "camp" refers to the actual fighting force. When they go out on campaigns, they are to guard against anything "impure" (lit., "every evil/bad thing/event"). The expression could refer to a threatening military situation, but in this context the danger is internal and theological; the Israelites are to guard themselves against every spiritual danger.

Exposition: the procedure for maintaining purity in the camp (vv. 10 − 13). Instead of identifying the danger directly, Moses charges the soldiers to guard against it by scrupulously observing purity laws within the camp. While Leviticus 15 identifies bodily discharges as the primary threats to purity,[15] the present concern is the well-being of the army as they anticipate engaging the enemy in the upcoming wars of Yahweh.

Moses begins with instructions regarding seminal emissions (vv. 10−11). When a man out in the field away from his wife becomes unclean through a nocturnal emission of semen, he must leave the camp and remain outside until evening. As evening approaches he shall bathe himself in water, and as the sun is setting he may reenter the camp. This policy would obviously exclude those in this state of impurity from military action. However, concern for holiness superseded concern for military efficiency. Impurity itself is perceived as an active malevolent force whose power can only be checked by ablutions.[16] Even in battle the holy people of Yahweh were to be represented by holy troops.

In verses 12−13 attention shifts to defecation, a daily source of impurity. The Torah has little to say about human excrement,[17] but the present association with nocturnal emissions suggests its impurity derives from its

---

15. On which see Milgrom, *Leviticus 1−16*, 903−1009. In light of more comprehensive texts elsewhere (Lev. 15:1−33; Num. 5:1−4), these instructions regarding defilement in the camp should be viewed as representative.

16. Cf. J. Milgrom, *Leviticus 1−16*, 967−74; idem, "First Day Ablutions in Qumran," in *The Madrid Qumran Congress: Proceedings of the International Congress on the Dead Sea Scrolls, Madrid 1−21 March, 1991* (ed. J. Trebolle Barrera and L. V. Montaner; STDJ 11; Leiden: Brill, 1992), 561−70.

17. But note Ezekiel's horror at defiling food entering his mouth (Ezek. 4:12−15).

source inside the human body rather than the repulsive nature of feces. When the army sets up camp, they (presumably the commanders) are to mark a place outside the camp[18] where the men could relieve themselves. When warriors go out there, they must carry a tool from their kits to dig a hole and bury their feces.[19]

Rationale: the importance of purity in the camp (v. 14). In verse 14 the tone and style change from clinical and hygienic objectivity to theological principle: untended human excretions threaten the very presence of Yahweh. Although some see here a reference to Yahweh accompanying the Israelites into battle,[20] the expression he "moves about in your camp" differs significantly from "he walks with you" in 20:4.[21] The purpose statement, "to protect you and to deliver your enemies to you," reinforces the importance of purity: Yahweh's presence within the camp is the precondition to military victory. These clauses portray him as a divine commander inspecting his troops; if he finds any cause of defilement as he walks about the camp, he will abandon them, forcing them to fight their own battles with their own resources. The expression "anything indecent" expands these instructions to anything that causes contamination: corpses, other bodily excretions, unclean animals, and so on.

ENTERING THE ASSEMBLY OF Yahweh. Allusions to Moses' appeal to guard the assembly of Yahweh (vv. 1 − 8) can be heard in several later texts. When David publicly declares his desire to build the temple, he refers to those gathered in Jerusalem as "the assembly of the LORD" (*qᵉhal yhwh*) and appeals to them to pursue covenant righteousness by obeying the commands of Yahweh their God (1 Chron. 28:8). If 1 Kings 11:1 − 2 has this ordinance in mind, the narrator has lumped Egyptians, Edomites, Sidonians, and Hittites with Moabites and Ammonites and grounded intermarriage with foreigners on their exclusion from the assembly of Yahweh.

Allusions to Deuteronomy 23:1 − 5 are clearer in Nehemiah 13:1 − 3, where the public reading of this very text results in the exclusion of all for-

---

18. As in Num. 2:17, Jer. 6:3, and Ezek. 21:19[24], here it refers to a signpost marking or pointing to the place.

19. The instructions here are remarkably explicit. "When you squat you must dig [a hole] with it; then turn around and cover your excrement" (pers. trans.).

20. Tigay, *Deuteronomy*, 214; Nelson, *Deuteronomy*, 276.

21. Cf. Gen. 3:8, Yahweh Elohim was "walking in the garden"; 2 Sam. 7:6, "I have been moving from place to place with a tent as my dwelling."

eigners from Israel, the expulsion of Tobiah the Ammonite from his temple apartment (vv. 4−9), and apparently the annulment of the Jews' marriages to Ashdodites, Ammonites, and Moabites (vv. 23−26). Lamentations 1:10 identifies Nebuchandezzar's forces with the nations whom Yahweh had forbidden to enter "the assembly belonging to you" (*haqqāhāl lᵉkâ*). Similarly Ezekiel 44:5−9 bans all foreigners from the temple.[22]

However, Isaiah 56:3−8 provides the most striking adaptation of this text. The prophet anticipates a day when "eunuchs" will particpate fully in the worship of Yahweh:

> Let no foreigner who has bound himself to the LORD say,
>   "The LORD will surely exclude me from his people."
> And let not any eunuch complain,
>   "I am only a dry tree."
> For this is what the LORD says:
> "To the eunuchs who keep my Sabbaths,
>   who choose what pleases me
>   and hold fast to my covenant—
> to them I will give within my temple and its walls
>   a memorial and a name
>   better than sons and daughters;
> I will give them an everlasting name
>   that will not be cut off.
> And foreigners who bind themselves to the LORD
>   to serve him,
> to love the name of the LORD,
>   and to worship him,
> all who keep the Sabbath without desecrating it
>   and who hold fast to my covenant—
> these I will bring to my holy mountain
>   and give them joy in my house of prayer.
> Their burnt offerings and sacrifices
>   will be accepted on my altar;
> for my house will be called
>   a house of prayer for all nations."
> The Sovereign LORD declares—
>   he who gathers the exiles of Israel:
> "I will gather still others to them
>   besides those already gathered."

---

22. On later use of Deut. 23:3−8, see Fishbane, *Biblical Interpretation*, 123−29; Tigay, *Deuteronomy*, 477−80.

Although Isaiah characterizes eunuchs as outcasts of Israel, they are obviously committed to righteousness and the life of covenant fidelity as outlined in Deuteronomy. Isaiah envisions an eschatological day when these old barriers will be torn down. Why then should Moses ban eunuchs and Moabites and Ammonites permanently from the assembly of Yahweh? Apparently for him "eunuchs" serves as a cipher for all who oppose wholeness and order in creation and who oppose God's redemptive plan. Isaiah 25:6−7 raises similar questions regarding the categorical and eternal rejection of Moabites and Ammonites. Whereas Isaiah 56:7 predicts a future in which Yahweh's house will be a house of prayer for all peoples, 25:6−7 envisions Yahweh hosting a lavish banquet on his mountain to which all peoples are invited.

Ruth, the Moabite. What about Ruth, a Moabite whose status is reiterated seven times in the short book that goes by her name?[23] Interpreted literally, according to Deuteronomy 23:1−5, David, the king of Israel and principal organizer of temple worship, should have been refused admission to the assembly of Yahweh, as should Jesus the Messiah himself (Matt. 1:1−17). Both were descendants of Perez. Like the eponymous Moab and Ben Ammi, Perez was conceived through an incestuous relationship between Judah and his Canaanite daughter-in-law, Tamar. Perhaps more seriously, being only three generations removed from Ruth, the blood in David's veins was one-eighth Moabite. How could the present ordinance have been violated so flagrantly? And how could Ruth have taken her place alongside Leah and Rachel (Ruth 4:11) and come to be viewed as the supreme paragon of covenantal virtue,[24] even having a canonical book named after her?[25]

It cannot be argued that since the genealogy of David (Ruth 4:18−22) traces the line through males (4:18−22), Ruth's national background is irrelevant. Not only does Deuteronomy 23:2−5 not distinguish descendants on the basis of gender, but the book of Ruth makes a great deal of Ruth's Moabite identity. Perhaps this book illustrates what has been true from the beginning: there have always been two Israels. One Israel is defined by blood and consists of all who are physical descendants of Jacob, while the other is defined by faith and includes all who share the faith of Abra-

---

23. Ruth 1:4, 22; 2:2, 6, 21; 4:5, 10.

24. The expression "woman of nobility" (ʾēšet ḥayil) occurs only in Prov. 31:10−31 and Ruth 3:11.

25. Judging by the dialogue, the center of gravity in the book lies with Boaz, and even Naomi figures more prominently than Ruth. On the book of Ruth as a critical homily on Deuteronomy 23−25, see G. Braulik, "The Book of Ruth as Intra-Biblical Critique of the Deuteronomic Law," *Acta Theologica* 19 (1999): 1−20.

ham and Moses as laid out in Deuteronomy. Those in the former category are also excluded from the assembly of Yahweh because they are spiritual eunuchs. Those in the latter are invited because they live by the commitments expressed in Isaiah 56:3–8 and, like Ruth, have declared, "Your people will be my people and your God my God" (Ruth 1:16–17). Just as Rahab repudiated her spiritual Canaanite identity in Joshua 2:8–13, so Ruth repudiated her Moabite spiritual allegiances and found shelter under the wings of Yahweh (Ruth 2:12).

The spiritualization of the issues involved in verses 9–14 is evident already in the Old Testament, which applies words for human excrement to iniquitous behavior (Prov. 30:12; Isa. 4:4). But Jesus speaks explicitly on these issues in Mark 7:14–23:

> Listen to me, everyone, and understand this. Nothing outside a man can make him "unclean" by going into him. Rather, it is what comes out of a man that makes him "unclean."
>
> ... Don't you see that nothing that enters a man from the outside can make him "unclean"? For it doesn't go into his heart but into his stomach, and then out of his body....
>
> What comes out of a man is what makes him "unclean." For from within, out of men's hearts, come evil thoughts, sexual immorality, theft, murder, adultery, greed, malice, deceit, lewdness, envy, slander, arrogance and folly. All these evils come from inside and make a man "unclean."

A SPIRITUAL BODY. DEUTERONOMY 23:1–8 reminds modern Christian readers that the true Israel is primarily a spiritual body, a community of persons belonging to Yahweh, admitted to his assembly by his gracious invitation, and conditioned on their fidelity to him in life. The psalmists ask, "Who may ascend the hill of the LORD? Who may stand in his holy place?" (Ps. 24:3), and, "Who may dwell in your sanctuary? Who may live on your holy hill?" (Ps. 15:1). The issue here is: "Who is invited to worship in God's presence, and whose worship will God receive favorably?" The answer is clear: "He who has clean hands and a pure heart, who does not lift up his soul to an idol or swear by what is false" (Ps. 24:4), which is concretized in specific behaviors in 15:2–5.

While the call to salvation is unconditional (by grace alone, through faith alone, in Christ alone), the call to worship is conditioned by faith demonstrated in righteous action. Elsewhere Moses speaks of the internal qualification as being circumcised of heart (10:16; 30:6), though in both contexts that disposition is expressed in demonstrated love for God and one's neighbor. Centuries later Paul declared, "A man is not a Jew if he is only one outwardly, nor is circumcision merely outward and physical. No, a man is a Jew if he is one inwardly; and circumcision is circumcision of the heart, by the Spirit, not by the written code. Such a man's praise is not from men, but from God" (Rom. 2:28–29). As a spiritual body, the true Israel recognizes the boundaries that separate this community from the world at large. The assembly of Yahweh welcomes those of genuine faith, but it maintains the highest standards of holiness. Those who stand in opposition to covenantal standards by personal conduct, religious compromise, or indifference and opposition to the work of God are not at home in the church.

God's clean temple. But this passage also reminds us that when outsiders confess and demonstrate faith in Yahweh, the walls of separation based on race or class come down. The portrayal of Edomites and Israelites here provides a paradigm for treating those whom many would dismiss as outsiders by virtue of ethnic background or grudges that derive from relationships in past generations. This text invites readers to bury hatchets, to seek the peace and well-being of those who have no control over what their ancestors have done, and to move on.[26]

Although the New Testament frequently speaks of the agenda of the church in military terms (esp. Eph. 6:10–20), in 1 Corinthians 3:16–17 Paul refers to the church as "God's temple," in which "God's Spirit lives." Therefore, just as the camp of Israel was to be kept pure from defilements (vv. 9–14), so the church must be kept pure and free from sin. Again, the danger does not come from outside; it lurks within.

When I was growing up in a Dutch Mennonite community, we were often told "cleanliness is next to godliness." This dictum may be more biblical than we realize.[27] Within the history of medicine, few events have been as revolutionary as the discovery that many diseases are caused by germs and other microorganisms that flourish in human wastes. Nevertheless, although the practices prescribed here have obvious implications for physical health, this paragraph is not concerned primarily with personal or communal hygiene, but the spiritual well-being of the community. Israel's victory in the battles of Yahweh depended on the ritual purity of the troops and the camp in which they lived. And so it is for us. God's presence among his people requires diligent attention to issues of holiness.

---

26. On the relevance of this text for the Arab-Israeli conflict see Z. W. Falk, "A Peace of Compromise between Israel and the Arabs," in *Pomegranates and Golden Bells: Studies in Biblical, Jewish, and Near Eastern Ritual, Law, and Literature in Honor of Jacob Milgrom* (ed. D. P. Wright et al.; Winona Lake, IN: Eisenbrauns, 1995), 473–78.

27. So also Wright, *Deuteronomy*, 249.

Deuteronomy 23:15–25

I f a slave has taken refuge with you, do not hand him over to his master. [16]Let him live among you wherever he likes and in whatever town he chooses. Do not oppress him.

[17]No Israelite man or woman is to become a shrine prostitute. [18]You must not bring the earnings of a female prostitute or of a male prostitute into the house of the LORD your God to pay any vow, because the LORD your God detests them both.

[19]Do not charge your brother interest, whether on money or food or anything else that may earn interest. [20]You may charge a foreigner interest, but not a brother Israelite, so that the LORD your God may bless you in everything you put your hand to in the land you are entering to possess.

[21]If you make a vow to the LORD your God, do not be slow to pay it, for the LORD your God will certainly demand it of you and you will be guilty of sin. [22]But if you refrain from making a vow, you will not be guilty. [23]Whatever your lips utter you must be sure to do, because you made your vow freely to the LORD your God with your own mouth.

[24]If you enter your neighbor's vineyard, you may eat all the grapes you want, but do not put any in your basket. [25]If you enter your neighbor's grainfield, you may pick kernels with your hands, but you must not put a sickle to his standing grain.

VERSES 15–25 consist of various instructions whose arrangement appears random. However, they exhibit an A B A B A pattern, with the A elements treating horizontal issues (vv. 15–16, 19–20, 24–25), and the B elements dealing with vertical concerns (vv. 17–18, 21–23).[1]

Safeguarding the Rights of a Slave (23:15–16)

THE PERVASIVENESS OF THE problem of runaway slaves is reflected in the frequency with which the issue appears in Mesopotamian[2] and Hittite law

---

1. Cf. Braulik, *Die deuteronomische Gesetze und der Dekalog*, 95–96; Merrill, *Deuteronomy*, 313.
2. See CH §§167–20, as translated by Roth, *Law Collections*, 84–85. Cf. LE §§49–52, ibid., 66–67; LL §12, ibid., 28.

codes[3] and in treaty documents.[4] This instructional fragment casts Israel's vision beyond their own community to the lot of foreign slaves who might seek refuge from their masters within the land of Israel.[5] Moses declares that Israelites are not to send persons who have escaped from their masters back to their (foreign) owners. The prohibited action (lit., "to shut someone in") means to apprehend and imprison the fugitive until the owner arrives, when he would be delivered into the master's hands.[6]

The present provision continues the humanitarian trajectory expressed toward Israelite slaves in chapter 15 and the openness to non-Israelites in the assembly of Yahweh (23:7−8). But the magnanimity of verse 16 is extraordinary.[7] The Israelites must not only let fugitive slaves reside among them, but also allow them to choose a place in any town that seems good to them.[8] Nor may the Israelites exploit and oppress them. The word *hônâ* (from *yānâ*) refers to any kind of mistreatment by which the owner takes advantage of the person's alien status. In effect, foreign slaves who fled to Israel were free to live anywhere without fear.[9] By calling the Israelites to provide safe haven for fugitives, Moses treats the entire land as *terra sancta*.

Safeguarding the Sanctity of the Cult (23:17−18)

THIS FRAGMENT CONSISTS OF three negative commands, followed by a final motive clause. Among these commands, the second is most complex, fea-

---

3. HL §§22−23, as translated by Hoffner, in *Law Collections*, 220.

4. On extradition of slaves, see H. A. Hoffner, "Slavery and Slave Laws in Ancient Hatti and Israel," in *Israel: Ancient Kingdom or Late Invention* (ed. D. I. Block; Nashville: Broadman & Holman, 2008), 145−46, 153−54.

5. Hamilton rightly notes (*Social Justice and Deuteronomy*, 117−21) that together with the release laws in chapter 15, these are the only laws pertaining to slaves in Deuteronomy.

6. This exact practice is reflected in a treaty between the kings of Tunip and Mukiš (as translated by R. S. Hess, *COS*, 2:128 [330]), dating to a century or two before Moses.

7. On the uniqueness of Israel's treatment of runaway slaves, see C. H. Gordon, "The Background of Some Distinctive Values in the Hebrew Bible," in *"Go to the Land I Will Show You": Studies in Honor of Dwight S. Young* (ed. J. E. Coleson and V. H. Matthews; Winona Lake, IN: Eisenbrauns, 1996), 57−59.

8. The form of the statement echoes the refrain of Yahweh's choosing a place to establish his name: "in the place the LORD your God will choose" (cf. 12:5; etc.). This policy contrasts starkly with a clause in the eighth-century BC Sefire Treaty, "You must not give them food or say to them [fugitives from another land], 'Stay quietly in your place'" (*COS*, 2:82 [p. 216]; cf. *ANET*, 660; Tigay, *Deuteronomy*, 215).

9. On the ancient custom of seeking refuge at a sacred shrine, see Ex. 21:12−14. For discussion see Anthony Phillips, *Ancient Israel's Criminal Law: A New Approach to the Decalogue* (New York: Schocken, 1970), 100; J. Milgrom, "Sancta Contagion and Altar/City Asylum," in *Congress Volume: Vienna, 1980* (ed. J. A. Emerton; VTSup 32; Leiden: Brill, 1981), 278−310.

---

turing two critical expressions: "fee of a prostitute," and "hire of a dog" as a coordinate pair. Like most English translations, the NIV interprets the Hebrew phrases here as female and male cult/temple prostitutes respectively, with *zônâ* ("female prostitute") clarifying the former, and *keleb* (lit., "dog") somehow referring to the latter.[10] While some ancient fertility cults included special rites involving worshipers engaging in sexual intercourse with cult functionaries to promote the productivity of their herds and crops and to ensure human fertility,[11] this interpretation is not entirely convincing.[12]

(1) No woman referred to as both *qᵉdēšâ* and a *zônâ* in the Old Testament is associated with cultic activities or a cult center.

(2) In Akkadian texts *qadištu* refers to a woman of special status; she is never portrayed in the role of a prostitute. Since both *qādēš* and *qᵉdēšâ* derive from the root *qdš* ("to be set apart for divine service"), they should not be secularized to mean a prostitute who by virtue of her profession and unmarried status is alienated from the community.[13] The *qᵉdēšô* and *qᵉdēšî* seem to have been young women and men dedicated for service to the gods at the local shrines. Their service may have ranged from menial janitorial service at the shrine to singing and dancing in public events (cf. Judg. 21:19 – 23). As in the ostensibly religious celebrations of Mardi Gras, cultic events often occasioned orgiastic revelry.[14]

---

10. So also *HALOT*, 1075; W. Kornfeld, "קָדֵשׁ," *TDOT*, 12:528; H.-P. Müller, "קָדֵשׁ," *TLOT*, 3:1108–9; J. A. Naudé, "קָדֵשׁ," *NIDOTTE*, 3:886. On cultic prostitution see E. Yamauchi, "Cultic Prostitution: A Case Study in Cultural Diffusion," in *Orient and Occident: Essays Presented to Cyrus H. Gordon on the Occasion of His Sixty-fifth Birthday* (ed. H. A. Hoffner Jr.; AOAT 22; Neukirchen-Vluyn: Neukirchener, 1971), 213–22.

11. See Gen. 38:21–22, cf. v. 15; Deut. 23:18[19]; Hos. 4:14; *CAD*, Q:48–50. This interpretation is widely accepted in the commentaries. See Merrill, *Deuteronomy*, 313; similarly McConville, *Deuteronomy*, 351; Craigie, *Deuteronomy*, 299; Mayes, *Deuteronomy*, 320.

12. For critique, see M. I. Gruber, "Hebrew *qᵉēšâh* and her Canaanite and Akkadian Cognates," *UF* 18 (1986): 133–48; K. van der Toorn, "Female Prostitution in Payment of Vows in ancient Israel," *JBL* 108 (1989): 193–205; idem, "Prostitution (Cultic)," *ABD*, 5:510–13; E. A. Goodfriend, *ABD*, 5:507–9; Tigay, "Excursus 22: The Alleged Practice of Cultic Prostitution in the Ancient Near East," in *Deuteronomy*, 480–81; Nelson, *Deuteronomy*, 280–81.

13. Thus Goodfriend, *ABD*, 5:508, and Gruber, "Hebrew *qᵉdēšâ*,"148. Gruber compares this secular usage of *qdš* with the root *ḥrm* ("to set apart [in Hebrew for destruction])," but in Akkadian it is used of a prostitute, "one set apart."

14. Van der Toorn suggests the ban on transvestism in 22:5 may have been another response to such orgies (*ABD*, 5:510). According to Gen. 28, Judah thought his daughter-in-law was an ordinary prostitute (*zônâ*, v. 15). However, he later referred to her as a *qᵉdēšâ*, presumably to save face, as if sexual activity with a young woman affiliated with a cult shrine was less reprehensible than intercourse with a professional prostitute.

Although the Old Testament describes women in a wide range of religious activities,[15] there is no evidence for female functionaries tied to tabernacle or temple rituals. The consecration of females for cultic service and the involvement of such persons in prostitution here reflects an imitation of foreign cults. If *q^edēšâ* designates a female consecrated for service at a shrine but who also functioned as a prostitute serving male worshipers, then *qādēš* denotes a dedicated male involved in similar service.[16] Apparently they combined official roles with unofficial participation in sexual orgies, either with female worshipers, or more likely gross homosexual acts with male worshipers.

Verse 18 suggests the actions of *q^edēšâ* and *qādēš* had economic significance. The phrase "earnings of a female prostitute" involves a word that always refers to the fee for a prostitute's sexual services.[17] Accordingly, *m^eḥir keleb* (lit., "payment of a dog") refers pejoratively to fees paid for the sexual favors of a *qādēš*.[18] Although other ancient Near Easterners valued dogs for protection and healing and as symbols of loyalty to a master, the Old Testa-

---

15. Presenting gifts for the construction of the tabernacle (Ex. 35:20−29); composing and singing songs of celebration (Ex. 15:1−21; Judg. 5:1−31; 1 Sam. 2:1−10); cultic and processional dance (Ex. 15:20−21; Judg. 21:19−21; Ps. 68:25[26]; Jer. 31:13; cf. women's participation in noncultic celebrative dance: Judg. 11:34; 1 Sam. 18:6−7; 21:11[12]; 29:5); cultic laments (2 Chron. 35:25; Jer. 9:16−17); playing musical instruments in the temple orchestra (1 Chron. 25:5−7) and singing in the temple choir (Ezra 2:65; Neh. 7:67); serving at the entrance to the tent of meeting (Ex. 38:8; 1 Sam. 2:22); participating in cultic meals (1 Sam 1:9); prayer (1 Sam 1:9−18); participating in family worship (Gen. 35:1−7); celebrating the Passover (Ex. 12:43−51); practicing Nazirite asceticism (Num. 6:2; Judg. 13:1−14); making vows (Num. 30:1−15[2−16]). The Old Testament also reports a series of illegitimate female religious activity: false prophecy and magic (Ezek. 13:17−23); necromancy (1 Samuel 28); pagan lamentation in the temple over the death of Tammuz (Ezek. 8:14−15); producing garments and/or decoration of pagan images (2 Kings 23:7); baking cakes and sacrificing to the "Queen of Heaven" (Jer. 7:18; 44:15−19).

16. E. A. Goodfriend ("Could *keleb* in Deuteronomy 23:19 Actually Refer to a Canine?" in *Pomegranates and Golden Bells: Studies in Biblical, Jewish, and Near Eastern Ritual, Law, and Literature in Honor of Jacob Milgrom* (ed. D. P. Wright et al.; Winona Lake, IN: Eisenbrauns, 1995], 386) suggests *qādēš* refers to "a priest of some unorthodox sanctuary, perhaps a high place or *bāmâ* (1 Kings 14:23−24; 22:44, 47)." The root *qdš* is not used of Samuel, but he bore the marks of a legitimate *qādēš*: (1) He was dedicated by Hannah (1:28); (2) he ministered before Yahweh before Eli the priest (2:11; 3:1); (3) he wore the linen ephod (2:18); (4) he grew in stature with Yahweh and humans (2:26); (5) he slept in the temple of Yahweh where the ark of the covenant was (3:3); (6) Yahweh spoke to him directly (3:4−18).

17. Cf. Mic. 1:7 (the identical expression); also Isa. 23:17−18; Ezek. 16:31, 34, 41; Hos. 9:1. See *HALOT*, 1760.

18. Some interpret the expression literally: the full sale price of a dog. Cf. B. Grossfeld, *The Targum Onqelos to Deuteronomy: Translated, with Apparatus, and Notes* (Aramaic Bible 9; Wilmington: Michael Glazier, 1988), 70.

---

ment views them as dangerous and unclean.[19] As scavengers that consume carrion and return to their own vomit (Prov. 26:11), dogs represented the antithesis to holiness.[20] Moses' equation of *q^edēšîm* with "dogs" pejoratively portrays them as engaging in the most disgusting and defiling practices, but also copulating indiscriminately with any available female dog.

The text does not specify the services for which fees are paid. While "fee of a prostitute" is missing in Proverbs 7, this chapter links the payment of vows (v. 14) with brazenly immoral sexual activity. The expression that "the LORD detests them both" places their actions in a category with carved images of pagan deities (7:26; 27:15), pagan service to gods, including child sacrifice (12:30−31), sacrificing blemished animals (17:1), divination, sorcery, magic (18:10−12), transvestism (22:5), and dishonesty in business (25:16). These gifts are rejected as "dirty money."

Safeguarding the Economic Health of the People of Yahweh (23:19−20)

THE REFERENCE TO THE "payment of a dog" in verse 18 may have triggered the shift in attention to another economic issue, the charging of interest on loans. This is the third appeal in the Pentateuch that those with means should be generous to the poor, particularly in the way they handle loans (cf. Ex. 22:25−27 [24−26]; Lev. 25:35−38).[21] Deuteronomy is distinctive in its narrow focus on interest, reflected in the sevenfold occurrence of the root *nšk*. Prohibiting Israelites from charging interest on loans to their countrymen was driven by the sense of community and the desire to inhibit economic stratification, which often resulted in debt-slavery.[22] By addressing would-be lenders rather than borrowers, Moses makes interest-free loans a matter of responsibility for those with means rather than a right of the poor. True righteousness (cf. 16:20) is demonstrated when the rich lend willingly to those in need, without compulsion or desire to profit from someone else's misfortune.

---

19. Ex. 22:31[30]; 2 Kings 9:35−36; Ps. 22:16[17]; Jer. 15:3.

20. See further Goodfriend, "*Keleb* in Deuteronomy," 387−90; J. Crawford, "Caleb the Dog: How a Biblical Good Guy Got a Bad Name," *BRev* 20 (2004): 20−24.

21. For detailed discussion of these texts see E. Neufeld, "The Prohibitions against Loans at Interest in Ancient Hebrew Laws," *HUCA* 26 (1955): 355−57. On the intertextual relationships among these texts see Fishbane, *Biblical Interpretation*, 174−77.

22. Ancient Near Eastern documents occasionally refer to interest-free loans, but the consistent biblical demand is unparalleled. Cf. H. Gamoran, "The Biblical Law against Loans on Interest," *JNES* 30 (1971): 127−34. They often allow exorbitant rates: 20 percent for loans of silver and 33 percent for grain (early second millennium Sumerian laws, LX §§m−n, in Roth, *Law Codes*, 38; eighteenth century BC Laws of Eshnunna, LE §§18a−21, in ibid., 61−62; and Hammurabi, gap §§t−u, in ibid., 97−98).

The Deuteronomic version of the policy exhibits three significant features. (1) The generosity reflected in interest-free loans is to characterize all of life (v. 19). Moses' rhetorical strategy is impressive; by moving from the most overtly economic item, silver, to food, and finally to anything one might need, he opens the eyes to opportunities to assist their countrymen.

(2) The ban on interest for loans does not extend to foreigners (cf. 17:15; 29:22 [21]). Unlike the "alien" who lived among the Israelites, albeit with limited rights, the "foreigner" remained an outsider with no intention of settling down in Israel. The persons envisioned here might have been merchants who bought and sold goods for profit rather than the sheer need for survival. If their business ventures did not succeed, they could always go home.

(3) Finally, this policy seeks to inspire generosity by reminding Israelites that Yahweh's generosity toward them is contingent on their generosity toward each other. The motive clause reflects Yahweh's desire to bless them in the land in every effort to which they put their hands.[23]

Safeguarding Promises (23:21–23)

THE FREQUENCY OF REFERENCES to vows outside the Pentateuch[24] reflects the significance of vows in the ancient world. While neither reiterating nor expanding on earlier instructions (Lev. 27; Num. 30:1–16 [2–17]), this statement highlights three fundamental principles underlying vows. (1) Vows are entirely optional. This is explicitly stated in verse 22 and reinforced in verse 23 with the word "freely."[25]

(2) Once vows are made, they must be kept. Verse 21 warns those who make vows not to delay in making good on the vow, while verse 23 speaks of keeping one's word and acting according to what one has vowed to Yahweh.

(3) Yahweh holds persons accountable for the vows they make. As in 18:19 the expression *dāraš min* means "to require of, to hold one accountable for"—in this case, to punish for what is considered a crime. The emphatic construction, "the LORD your God will certainly demand it of you," reinforces this point. Like failing to keep an oath, failing to fulfill a vow is sin and renders one guilty of theft (cf. Matt. 5:33); technically what has been

---

23. The phrase also occurs in 12:18 and 28:20. Cf. "in all the work of your hands [i.e., that you do]," in 2:7 and 14:29.

24. For studies of this word see C. A. Keller, "נדר," *TLOT*, 719–22; R. Wakely, "נדר," *NIDOTTE*, 3:37–42.

25. For the adverbial use of the word see also Hos. 14:4[5]. Elsewhere the noun refers to voluntary offerings (cf. 12:6, 17; 16:10).

vowed belongs to another person. It is eminently better not to vow at all than to vow and not keep one's promise.

Safeguarding the Trust of Neighbors (vv. 24–25)

THE FINAL INSTRUCTIONAL FRAGMENT is unparalleled in the Pentateuch. Like the preceding, it promotes a community of neighbors who trust one another and look out for one another's welfare. Within an agrarian economy, the right of passers-by to pick grain or fruit from the trees for the journey from the fields they were crossing could create several problems. On the one hand, landowners could be greedy and unreasonable, posting guards at the borders of their land and shooing off passers-by. On the other hand, especially in harvest time, people passing through would be tempted to carry containers and fill them with grapes, or to bring along a sickle (cf. 16:9) with which to cut standing grain and stuff it in their bags.

Moses' instructions as pastoral spokesman for the divine Landlord are simultaneously realistic, generous, and responsible. Except for people whose allotments abutted the boundaries of their town or village, men and women going out to work their fields or to visit friends or relatives in a neighboring village would inevitably need to pass through other people's vineyards, fields of grain, and groves of olives and fruit. Because the land belonged to the nation, landowners must allow casual travelers to pass through their property and let them pick grapes and rub grain out of its heads in their hands for consumption on the journey. However, travelers must respect the rights of the owners of fields and vineyards. This short paragraph makes no reference to God, but it obviously reflects divine values, seeking to base ethics on love and trust.

LATER OLD TESTAMENT ALLUSIONS. The appropriation and application of these diverse instructions in the remainder of the Old Testament are uneven. We will explore allusions to each fragment separately.

The instructions on fugitive slaves (vv. 15–16) do not reflect on the rightness or wrongness of a slave fleeing from his master. Rather, they focus on Israel as a host to such fugitives and remind readers how countercultural Israelite values were to be. Whereas elsewhere masters were allowed and encouraged to rule over slaves with ruthless force, in Israel all human beings, even the slaves who came to them from the outside, were to be treated with dignity and compassion. That Deuteronomy should make such provision for outsiders, but remain silent on the case of fugitive Israelite slaves, is remarkable.

Deuteronomy assumes the institution of slavery, but the Israelite version is to differ radically from their own experience in Egypt and from the American experience. On the one hand, Israelites with economic power over others are to treat their indentured country folk with compassion and generosity (15:1—18), but on the other, the entire land of Israel was to function as a refuge for foreign slaves running away from harsh treatment.[26]

Paul's short epistle to Philemon provides the closest New Testament analogue to the situation reflected here. The apostle writes the letter to Philemon expressly to encourage this Christian slave owner to receive back his fugitive slave, who has in the meantime also become a believer. In this instance Paul's role is analogous to that of the Israelites. Onesimus has not only experienced conversion under his ministry, but he has also sought refuge with him. In resolving the tensions among this triad of believers, Paul does not cite the letter of the law. Moses would have affirmed his appeal to the moral conscience of both slave and master. Recognizing Philemon's rights but against his own personal interests, Paul sends Onesimus back (Philem. 12). However, he sends the letter by the hand of the slave himself, and when Onesimus hands the letter to his master, the minds of all three will meet. As members of the assembly of God, all are equal, but if as members of society distinctions exist, those distinctions are to be tempered by a sense of duty on the part of the subordinate, and by compassion and charity on the part of the superior.

Micah alludes to the fragment in Deuteronomy on the sanctity of the cult (vv. 17—18) in his denunciation of the idolatry of Samaria (Mic. 1:7); as already noted, Proverbs 7 also associates immoral sexual acts with religious devotion. However, this ordinance seems to have been honored more in its inversion than in its direct application. In Ezekiel 16 the exilic prophet paints a particularly graphic picture of Jerusalem taking the resources that Yahweh had graciously lavished on her and using them for idolatrous and harlotrous purposes. In the New Testament, Paul takes the association of idolatry and religious devotion in a different direction when he encourages Christians not to worry about meat that has been offered to idols—since an idol is nothing—unless the act of eating causes someone else to stumble. This sensitivity is remarkably Mosaic.

Echoes of Moses' instructions on charging interest on loans are clearer in the Old Testament. Responding to the question, "Who can be assured of acceptance with Yahweh when they appear before him in worship?" Psalm 15:2—5 presents a list of evidences that one is walking in integrity

---

26. Cf. W. J. Webb, *Slaves, Women & Homosexuals: Exploring the Hermeneutics of Cultural Analysis* (Downers Grove, IL: InterVarsity Press, 2001), 33.

and demonstrating righteousness. The characteristic of a righteous person mentioned in Psalm 12:5[6] echoes Deuteronomy 23:20: "[He] lends his money without usury." Ezekiel's catalogues of the distinctions between a wicked person who is sentenced to death and a righteous person who is sentenced to life refer to this ordinance three times; it is a mark of wickedness to charge interest to a brother and a mark of righteousness not to do so (Ezek. 18:8, 13, 17). In Ezekiel 22:3–12 he climaxes his recitation of abominations and crimes committed by Jerusalem against Yahweh with the charge that she has exploited the poor, expressly noting the charging of usurious interest. While the echo of Leviticus 25:35–38 is clearer, Proverbs 28:8 recognizes the ironic justice when those who increase their wealth through interest and usury end up padding the pockets of those who are gracious to the poor.

The New Testament reiterates both Moses' call for generosity toward the poor and his distinctions between the way the community of faith treats those within and those without. With respect to the latter, Paul enjoins Galatian Christians: "Therefore, as we have opportunity, let us do good to all people, especially to those who belong to the family of believers" (Gal. 6:10). His declaration in Romans 13:9–10 that love does no wrong to a neighbor has caught the spirit of Deuteronomy, as has his encouragement to his readers to please their neighbors for their good (15:2). First Corinthians 5:11 classifies greed with idolatry, sexual immorality and drunkenness.

The most striking application of Moses' instructions on vows (vv. 21–23) involves Jephthah's perverse vow to secure the support of Yahweh in his battle with the Ammonites (Judg. 11:29–40). This vow was not only rash but entirely unnecessary—the Spirit of Yahweh had already come upon him and the troops had rallied behind him. However, half-pagan in disposition and outlook, he followed Canaanite practices in seeking to guarantee divine favor. When the victim of his vow turned out to be his daughter, he lamented that he had opened his mouth to Yahweh and that he could not take back his vow. But abandoning all self-interest, the young girl assured him that keeping his vow was his only recourse.[27]

Even so, that the victim was a human raises questions about what Jephthah should have done.[28] The valorous response would have been to sacrifice his own *šālôm* and leave the vow unfulfilled. To be sure, our text would have considered this sin and subjected him to the curse of Yahweh

---

27. On the connections between Jephthah's vow and our text, see H.-D. Neff, "Jephta und seine Tochter (Jdc. xi 29–40)," *VT* 49 (1999): 206–17.

28. J. C. Exum ("On Judges 11," in *A Feminist Companion to Judges* (Feminist Companion to the Bible 4; ed. A. Brenner; Sheffield: Sheffield Academic Press, 1993, 131) overstates the case in claiming the vow was "irrevocable, irreversible and unalterable."

(which, ironically, is what happened in any case), but it would have spared his daughter and in so doing secured his own future. Jephthah could also have appealed to the loophole that Leviticus 27:1—8 seems to provide and spared her by paying twenty shekels to the priest at the central shrine as compensation for the life of his daughter.[29] While this case is slightly different from that envisioned in Leviticus 27, on the rabbinic principle of *qal wahomer* (lit., "light and heavy") he could have argued that a rule addressing a lesser case would certainly apply in a more serious case involving human life. Finally, Jephthah could have done as he in fact did; fulfill the vow to the letter. The text is silent on whether or not he contemplated a different option.[30]

Judging by the prophetic denunciations of rich landowners abusing the poor in the ways they handle agricultural resources (Amos 8:4; Mic. 2:2), it seems the principles taught in Deuteronomy 23:24—25 were generally disregarded as the end of the nation approached. Remarkably, however, clear echoes of this text are not heard until the time of Christ. The Synoptic Gospels recount Pharisees reporting to Jesus that they have caught his disciples plucking heads of grain and eating the kernels (Matt. 12:1—8; Mark 2:23—28; Luke 6:1—5). Unlike greedy landlords, who might have begrudged the disciples this little bit of food, what troubled the Pharisees was the fact that the "crime" was committed on the Sabbath.

A later uniquely Matthean insertion reflects precisely the spirit of the Mosaic counsel: "But you have neglected the more important matters of the law—justice, mercy and faithfulness. You should have practiced the latter, without neglecting the former" (Matt. 23:23). Formal boundaries of Sabbath behavior had trumped the second half of the Supreme Command, which demonstrated covenant commitment (love) for one's neighbors by permitting them to eat plucked kernels of grain even if it was the Sabbath.

ALIENS IN THE LAND. If we reflect on the contemporary significance of these fragments of pastoral instruction, the answers will be uneven. The first fragment (vv. 15—16) reminds the reader that the community of faith should be a place where those who are oppressed and burdened by exploitative powers may find refuge. While the

---

29. Lev. 27:1—8 regulates cases in which one person vows another, that is, devotes a person to the sanctuary for sacred service, and then for reasons unspecified finds it impossible or impractical to fulfill the vow. On this text, see Milgrom, *Leviticus,* 489; J. E. Hartley, *Leviticus* (WBC; Dallas: Word, 1992), 480—81.

30. For further discussion see Block, *Judges, Ruth,* 375—78.

institution of slavery is officially suppressed around the world, many remain in slavery to abusive landlords, drug lords, pimps, and poverty itself. It is unrealistic to expect secular governments to operate by biblical norms, but the harsh disposition of many evangelicals toward unregistered aliens in this land violates both the spirit and the law of Moses.[31] We must address the illegality of unregistered aliens,[32] not only by insisting on obedience to the laws of the land, but especially by genuine friendship and efforts to help them legalize their presence among us. The Lord is honored and the poor are served when, like Boaz (Ruth 2:12), we ourselves are the wings of God.

Ministry and morality. Moses' call to safeguard the sanctity of the cult reminds us of the dangers of prostitution, not only the prostitution of one's body, but also the prostitution of one's calling. Whether male or female, the call to spiritual ministry demands the most scrupulous attention to one's personal life and the performance of one's professional duties. These are to be fulfilled for the glory of God, not for the pleasure or advantage of the minister. And when ministers cater to worshipers' demands for pleasure without regard to the sanctity of their office or of the community of faith, a serious abomination has been committed. Religious practice and covenantal morality may never be divorced. Resources gathered through illicit means (extortion, theft, immoral business practices, immoral actions) represent "dirty money," repugnant to God.

Charging interest. Deuteronomy's policy concerning interest stands in sharp contrast, not only to ancient Near Eastern law, but also to modern business practices. Recent developments on Wall Street and in the world's financial markets have exposed the greedy underbelly of individualistic capitalism and capitalist individualism.[33] Although Old Testament authors could not have imagined our banking system, where directors amass vast wealth by simply shuffling other people's money, the principles underlying verses 19—20 are especially relevant for the community of the righteous. As the Lord's people, Christians will not exploit others' destitution for personal gain. In the past, certain groups within the Western church have taken

---

31. For an appeal to evangelicals to adopt a more compassionate stance, see Carroll R., *Christians at the Border*.

32. J. K. Hoffmeier (*The Immigration Crisis: Immigrants, Aliens, and the Bible* [Wheaton, IL: Crossway, 2009]) argues for a distinction in our treatment of aliens (Heb. *gērîm*) and illegal aliens (Heb. *bᵉnê nēkār*).

33. The most public representative of the problem is Bernard Madoff, who was sentenced to 150 years in prison for bilking billions of dollars out of clients. See www.cbsnews.com/stories/2009/09/24/60minutes/main5339719.shtml?tag=currentVideoInfo;segmentUtilities (accessed Jan. 15, 1010).

these principles seriously, but hardened commitments to capitalism and free enterprise have a propensity to encourage greed and to blind one to the real needs of others.

Fulfilling vows. Few injunctions that Moses lays on his hearers in Deuteronomy have greater relevance for Christians today than his call to fulfill vows. While the specific subject of verses 21–23 is vows that people make to Yahweh, verse 23a in particular demands much broader application: "Whatever crosses your lips you must keep and do" (pers. trans.). This statement assumes that keeping one's word is a mark of righteousness and a badge of those who belong to the assembly of God. It was to be this way in the Old Testament, and it must be so today. To a culture like ours, which assumes that unless people swear on the Bible or unless they put their commitments in writing people will not keep their word, this text is a fossil from a distant time. Evidently ideals had not changed by New Testament times. In Matthew 5:33–37 Jesus appealed directly to our text to draw the lines of ethical behavior around his own community:

> Again, you have heard that it was said to the people long ago, "Do not break your oath, but keep the oaths you have made to the Lord." But I tell you, Do not swear at all: either by heaven, for it is God's throne; or by the earth, for it is his footstool; or by Jerusalem, for it is the city of the Great King. And do not swear by your head, for you cannot make even one hair white or black. Simply let your "Yes" be "Yes," and your "No," "No"; anything beyond this comes from the evil one.

Few Christians today follow the original Anabaptists in taking these commands literally. But those in this tradition have been closer to the spirit and the letter of Jesus' words than many within the evangelical church. George Gallup observes that differences in ethical behavior between churchgoers and those not religiously active are slight; patterns of lying, cheating, stealing, and "immorality" are virtually indistinguishable.

If the polls conducted by George Barna are valid, in modern America the divorce rate among born-again Christians is actually higher than among unbelievers; and among evangelicals (his surveys distinguish between the groups) it is virtually the same as the general population. Indeed some surveys suggest that divorce rates in some parts of the southern Bible belt are double that of Catholics in the northeast.[34] In Malachi 2:10–16 the prophet calls this moral cancer "breaking faith." Inasmuch as marriage

---

34. For discussion and sources see R. J. Sider, *The Scandal of the Evangelical Conscience* (Grand Rapids: Baker, 2004), 18–20.

ceremonies typically involve vows made in the presence of God, Moses' appeal is especially relevant. We have become a nation of infidels, who do not keep their word.

Generosity. The significance of the final fragment is self-evident. God's people will be compassionate and generous in sharing their resources with others, but they will also be respectful and grateful when they are beneficiaries of that generosity.

Deuteronomy 24:1–5

If a man marries a woman who becomes displeasing to him because he finds something indecent about her, and he writes her a certificate of divorce, gives it to her and sends her from his house, ²and if after she leaves his house she becomes the wife of another man, ³and her second husband dislikes her and writes her a certificate of divorce, gives it to her and sends her from his house, or if he dies, ⁴then her first husband, who divorced her, is not allowed to marry her again after she has been defiled. That would be detestable in the eyes of the LORD. Do not bring sin upon the land the LORD your God is giving you as an inheritance.

⁵If a man has recently married, he must not be sent to war or have any other duty laid on him. For one year he is to be free to stay at home and bring happiness to the wife he has married.

Original Meaning

LIKE CHAPTER 23, DEUTERONOMY 24 deals with a series of topics only loosely related. The concern with the well-being of women within marital relationships in the first five verses illuminates the general concern for righteousness (cf. verse 13; see comments on 16:20) expressed in protecting the interests of the vulnerable.

Righteousness in the Face of Divorce (24:1–4)

FOLLOWING LONGSTANDING RABBINIC TRADITION and the question put to Jesus in Matthew 19:7,[1] some argue that Deuteronomy 24:1b serves not just as a description of divorce procedures but as a ruling on the matter.[2] But several factors raise doubts about this interpretation. (1) Based on ancient Near Eastern divorce laws, it should then have included financial stipulations to the divorce, particularly a statement of the husband's obligations to repay the dowry or the conditions under which he would have been exempt.[3]

---

1. Cf. also Matt. 5:31; 1 Cor. 7:15.

2. Cf. A. Warren, "Did Moses Permit Divorce? Modal *wᵉqāṭal* as Key to New Testament Readings of Deuteronomy 24:1–4," *TynBul* 49 (1998): 39–56; Instone-Brewer, "Deuteronomy 24:1–4 and the Origin of the Jewish Divorce Certificate," 230.

3. Cf. LH §137, 138, 142, 171. On Old Babylonian laws, see Westbrook, *Old Babylonian Marriage Law*, 92; Cf. Neo-Babylonian marriage agreements §§15 and 34 in Roth, *Babylonian Marriage Agreements*, 64–67 and 108–12.

(2) Later use of a prior text is not determinative for the contextual meaning of the earlier text.[4] In fact, Jesus disputed the Pharisees' reading of the text. That Moses *permitted* divorce may simply mean that he left customary procedures in place; he was not making a (new) ruling on this matter.

(3) Although the first husband receives more attention, our text presents the two men in the woman's life as parallel cases (vv. 1b, 3). The repetition of the last three lines in verses 1b and 3 suggests the preceding actions are equivalent, which means that if we interpret the second series conditionally, the first is neither a command nor permission.[5]

(4) The structural parallels between 21:10−14 and this text offer clues on how to interpret this text. Both texts contemplate situations in which a woman is vulnerable to abuse within a marital relationship, and both seek to protect the dignity of a woman who has been rejected by her husband. On this analogy, our text is not intended as a law on divorce but as a prohibition on remarriage,[6] the primary concern being to protect wives from abuse by men, specifically a first husband. Moses does so by reiterating existing procedures for releasing wives from the bonds of marriage and insisting that when a husband divorces his wife, he relinquishes his authority over her. The text follows common diagnostic procedure, reflected in the five headings below.

The problem (v. 1a−c). The opening line suggests the marriage is off to a normal start. However, the grammar[7] signals a complication: the woman did not find grace in the eyes of her husband. While most interpreters try to establish a flaw in the woman that provoked this response, the clause actually exposes a flaw in the man.[8] Verse 1 describes a reciprocally disappointing situation: the woman is disappointed because of what she *does not find* in her husband—grace; the man is disappointed because of something he found in the woman. The text identifies her problem with a vague expression: "something indecent" (NIV).

---

4. McConville (*Deuteronomy*, 358) rightly observes that because New Testament discussions are influenced by contemporary perspectives, they cannot decide the grammar of this text.

5. So also Pressler, *View of Women*, 47.

6. Cf. R. Westbrook, "Prohibition on Restoration of Marriage in Deuteronomy 24:1−4," in *Studies in Bible 1986* (ed. S. Japhet; Scripta Hierosolymitana 31; Jerusalem: Magnes, 1986), 388; Pressler, *View of Women*, 46−47; Hugenberger, *Marriage as a Covenant*, 76−81.

7. Literally, "And it will happen that X does not occur."

8. The noun *ḥēn* speaks of a favorable disposition toward persons in need especially by a person with power. It occurs only here in Deuteronomy.

Opinions on the meaning of this phrase range from "anything at all,"[9] to adultery,[10] to a physical defect.[11] Literally, ʿerwat dābār means "nakedness of a thing." The proximity of this statement to Deut. 23:14[15], the only other place where this phrase occurs, invites the reader to link these two texts. In the earlier passage ʿerwat dābār refers to unburied human excrement, which defiles the Israelite military camp. Obviously defecation is not an immoral act. Since ʿerwâ usually involves the genitals (Ex. 20:26; cf. 28:42), and since this is the woman's problem, the expression is best interpreted as some menstrual irregularity (cf. Mark 5:25–34). The result is a constant state of impurity, curtailing many normal marital activities (cf. Lev. 12:2–8) and rendering her incapable of bearing children. The husband may have learned of her condition after he married her and sought to consummate the marriage. But instead of responding with compassion, he divorced her.

The customary response (v. 1b). Lacking the decency to stand by his wife, the husband initiates divorce procedures. The three-step process summarized in verse 1b was intended not only to free a husband from an undesirable marriage, but also to protect the well-being of his wife. The husband would first write for his wife a certificate of divorce,[12] a document that officially severed the marital bond.[13] Then, the husband would place the certificate in the hands of the woman. The certificate was vital for the woman, especially if the document relinquished the husband's rights to her and her dowry and authorized her to return to her family of origin

---

9. Josephus (*Ant.* 4.8.23) reads "for whatsoever cause." J. J. Collins ("Marriage, Divorce, and Family in Second Temple Judaism," in *Families in Ancient Israel* [ed. L. G. Perdue et al.; Louisville: Westminster John Knox, 1997], 65) suggests the phrase intentionally spreads the net as broadly as possible for "any reason whatsoever."

10. LXX reads "a shameful deed"; *Targums Pseudo-Jonathan and Onqelos*, "transgression." Matt. 5:31–32; 19:7–9 reads *porneia*. This and the previous interpretation are represented by the rabbinic schools of Hillel and Shamai respectively (*m. Giṭṭin* 9:10). However, the present vocabulary and the fact that adultery was punishable by death (22:13–26) seem to exclude a reference to adultery.

11. J. Walton, "The Place of the *hutqaṭṭēl* within the D-Stem Group and Its Implications in Deuteronomy 24:4," *HS* 32 (1991): 14–15; cf. Craigie, *Deuteronomy*, 305.

12. The expression "document of separation/divorce" occurs elsewhere only in Isa. 50:1 and Jer. 3:8.

13. Extrabiblical data suggest the document included (1) a dissolution of marriage formula, "I am not/no longer your husband, and you are not/no longer my wife" (cf. Hos. 2:2[4]; Hugenberger, *Marriage as a Covenant*, 217–25); (2) an explicit declaration of release, authorizing the woman to return home to her father's household or to remarry (cf. Deut. 21:14; D. Instone-Brewer, "Deuteronomy 24:1–4 and the Origin of the Jewish Divorce Certificate," 230–43); (3) a declaration of the return of the dowry (cf. Westbrook, *Old Babylonian Marriage Law*, 79, 92).

or to marry another man. From the man's perspective, the record of the returned dowry would prevent the woman's family from making further claims against him.[14] Finally, the husband would expel the woman from his house.[15]

The complication (vv. 2–3). In describing the results of the divorce proceedings, Moses imagines two developments that could complicate the woman's life. (1) A second husband's disposition toward her may change to rejection. In divorcing her, the second husband follows the same procedures as the first, freeing her to return home to her family or to remarry. (2) Her second husband dies. As in most cultures, the death of a spouse frees a person to remarry. Since widows were economically vulnerable unless a woman was independently wealthy, it would have been in her best interest to remarry, especially if she did not have grown sons.

The proscription (v. 4). Moses declares that if the woman's second husband divorces her or he dies, the original husband may not change his mind and remarry his wife. While scholars have suggested a variety of reasons for denying him the right to remarry her,[16] if ʿerwat dâbâr involves a physical rather than moral problem, the prohibition sought to protect the woman from further abuse from her first husband. The phrase "after she has been defiled" deflects moral accountability away from the woman either to an impersonal physical problem or to someone else.[17]

As in Deuteronomy 21:14, the issue is the degradation of the woman. The man has already degraded her, first by refusing to be gracious to a needy spouse ritually defiled through no fault of her own, and second, by publicizing her personal issue through the divorce proceedings. The preposition "after" suggests the defilement derives not from remarriage to her former husband but from previous events. Even if he regrets having divorced her earlier, she must be protected from further degradation by the man who had forfeited his right to her.

The rationale (v. 4b). Moses justifies prohibiting the remarriage of a woman to her first husband by declaring such an act "detestable" in

---

14. Cf. Instone-Brewer, "Deuteronomy 24:1–4 and the Jewish Certificate of Divorce," 237.

15. Identifying the certificate of divorce as a "document of separation" and the threefold use of the verb "to send away" (vv. 1, 3, 4), suggests *šillaḥ* means "to divorce" (22:19, 29; Mal. 2:16). Cf. Hugenberger, *Marriage as a Covenant*, 72–73.

16. The second marriage had created social tensions; this could be considered incest; greed — the husband would seek to profit from the second marriage. For discussion of the options, see R. Gane, "Old Testament Principles Relating to Divorce and Remarriage," *JATS* 12 (2001): 15–16; Pressler, *View of Women*, 51–59.

17. Davidson (*Flame of Yahweh*, 396–97) rightly notes that the reflexive sense, "she has defiled herself," would have required the Hithpael, as in Lev. 11:24, 43; etc.

Yahweh's sight.[18] Furthermore, remarriage to the first husband would bring sin on the land. The shift to second person reminds the people that they are responsible for maintaining covenantal standards of righteousness (cf. 16:20). If they allow a man to remarry his former wife after she has been married to another, they would bring guilt not only on themselves, but also on the land they have received from Yahweh.

Righteousness in the Face of a Call to Arms (24:5)

THOUGH VERSE 5 SEEMS more at home with earlier war texts, its placement here and its principal concern suggest it belongs to the complex of "family instructions." This text assumes a man has taken a wife but only recently. The concern here is securing the health of any newly established household. A man who has just taken his bride is exempt from military duty (cf. 20:7) and from all outside responsibilities. The awkward clause "have any other duty laid on him" refers to duties that might be imposed on him for the good of the community. He must invest his energies in establishing solid economic and social foundations for his household. Indeed, the exemptions are to apply for one full year.[19]

The verse ends with a remarkable rationale: husbands of new brides are exempt from all communal obligations so they may devote themselves to the happiness of their wives. With keen pastoral insight Moses has painted a picture of marriage that contrasts sharply with that portrayed in verses 1–4. Whereas the two husbands had caused their wife extreme stress, a husband is to pursue righteousness by bringing joy to his wife.

DIVORCE IN SCRIPTURE. SINCE verses 1–4 contain the only explicit instructions on divorce in the Torah, it is important to recognize what this text says and what it does not say. (1) It deals only with the case of divorce initiated by the husband. (2) It demonstrates that in Israel divorce belonged to the realm of internal family law rather than the public courts.[20] (3) It identifies the motivation behind divorce in

---

18. Theoretically, *tô'ēbâ* could be rendered, "for she is detestable," but on the analogy of Lev. 18:22 it refers not to the woman but to the act of remarriage (cf. Pressler, *View of Women*, 49), ranking remarriage with apostasy (7:25; 12:31; etc.), offering blemished offerings (17:1), eating forbidden food (14:3), transvestism (22:5), paying vows with money gained through prostitution (23:18[19]), and heinous sexual sins as in Lev. 18 (cf. vv. 26, 29).

19. The sense "exempt, relieved of responsibility" occurs in Gen. 24:41; Num. 32:22; Josh. 2:20; 1 Kings 15:22.

20. So also Wright, *God's People in God's Land*, 216–17.

only the vaguest of terms: the husband has found ʿerwat dābār in his wife, which probably involves a physical rather than a moral problem. (4) The passage does not seek to regulate divorce per se, but the conduct of the husband after the divorce has occurred. Having humiliated his wife by forcing her to declare herself unclean, he may not reclaim her if she has remarried and then loses her second husband through divorce or death. (5) The legislation seeks to protect the woman by requiring the husband to produce a severance document as legal proof for the dissolution of the marriage. Without this document he could demand her back at any time, and if she would remarry he could accuse her of adultery.[21] (6) While the text provides no moral or theological justification for divorce, it recognizes that divorce was tolerated in ancient Israel as a legal reality. But legal recognition and moral justification are two different issues.

Outside this text, evidence for Israel's disposition toward divorce is sketchy. For humanitarian reasons, Exodus 21:10–11 and Deuteronomy 21:10–14 recognize that releasing a slave-wife or captive woman whom an Israelite warrior had married was preferable to a man refusing to fulfill his marital duties. Presumably as the lesser of two evils, in Genesis 21:8–14 God directed Abraham to send away his slave-wife Hagar. Apart from this episode Old Testament narratives provide few clues on whether or not Israelites adhered to the principles underlying marriage and divorce found here. They report husbands abandoning their wives temporarily (Judg. 14:19–15:8) and wives/concubines abandoning their husbands (Judg. 19), but they do not record a single instance of divorce initiated by a husband or wife until after the exile. According to Ezra 9–10, Ezra ordered the Jews of postexilic Jerusalem to divorce their pagan wives, because these marriages threatened the integrity of the "holy seed."

The postexilic prophet Malachi had such marriages in mind when he condemned his male contemporaries for marrying "the daughters of a foreign god" (i.e., pagans; Mal. 2:11). But then he accused them of "breaking faith" (beḡed) against their wives for divorcing them (2:13–16). While the meaning of "I hate divorce" (v. 16) is clear, the underlying Hebrew is vague and could just as well be rendered "[he who] hates [and] divorces [his wife]."[22] In the combination of śānēʾ ("to hate") and ṣallaḥ ("to send away/divorce"), we hear echoes of Deuteronomy 24:1–4. Moses permitted divorce as a social reality, but he realized the potential for abuse, especially of women, inherent even in customs that had evolved in Israel. Malachi

---

21. So also ibid., 217.

22. For defense of the reading favored here, see Hugenberger, *Marriage as a Covenant*, 66–76.

was more forthright, castigating the men of his time for their treacherous betrayal of their wives and citing the high divorce rate as evidence of the absence of fundamental piety and fear of Yahweh.

The subject of divorce surfaces frequently in the Prophets, but primarily as a metaphor of the rupture in the relationship between Yahweh and Israel. Hosea develops the motif most dramatically. His marriage to Gomer and subsequent loss of her serve as a picture of Yahweh's marriage with Israel. Because of the nation's infidelity and adulteries in going after other gods, Yahweh stifles his compassion and divorces her (2:1−13[3−15]). However, he takes her back, and the marriage flourishes (2:16−25[14−23]). Apart from the sequence of marriage−divorce−remarriage, Hosea's metaphorical picture differs fundamentally from the situation envisaged by Moses in Deuteronomy 24:1−5:

Feature	Literal Marriage, Divorce, and Remarriage in Deuteronomy 24:1−4	Metaphorical Marriage, Divorce, and Remarriage in Hosea 1−3
Disposition of husband to the marriage	Despite having agreed to the marriage, when the time came to consummate it, he changed his mind.	Having promised to the ancestors to enter into covenant relationship with Israel, Yahweh sealed the covenant at Sinai.
Condition of the wife	Physically flawed but morally innocent.	Physically fine but morally flawed.
Disposition of the husband to the wife	Totally lacking in grace.	Lavish in his outpouring of grace before and after the marriage.
Cause of the divorce	The husband's hardness of heart.	The wife's infidelity and adulterous conduct.
Time of the divorce	Before the marriage was consummated.	Centuries after the marriage was sealed.
Sequel to the divorce	Remarriage to another man.	No remarriage; reduced to status of slave on the auction block, but rescued by husband.
Possibility of remarriage	Remarriage to original husband denied.	Remarriage to original husband confirmed.

Yahweh's questions in Jeremiah 3:1 exhibit the clearest echoes of Deuteronomy 24:1−4:

If a man divorces his wife
    and she leaves him and marries another man,

should he return to her again?
Would not the land be completely defiled?
But you have lived as a prostitute with many lovers—
would you return to me?

Remarkably, in the utterances that follow Yahweh invites Israel and Judah back. As in the case of Hosea, the motif of marriage–divorce–remarriage serves as a rhetorical device to wake up the people to their own infidelities. At Sinai Yahweh had bound himself eternally to Israel in a covenant relationship, from which there would be no divorce. Many interpret his abandonment of the land and the exile of the people in 586 BC as evidence of a final divorce—the covenant has been revoked. However, Leviticus 26:44−45 and Deuteronomy 4:29−31 and 30:1−10 declare that the judgment could never be the last word. Even before the people were in the land, Moses anticipated a future rupture of Yahweh's relationship with his people, but he also knew the promised blessings that were fundamental to the marriage contract would be suspended and replaced by divine wrath. But this marriage would not end in divorce. One day estranged husband and wife would be reconciled.

In Matthew 5:31−32 we observe a reflection of early rabbinic interpretation of Deuteronomy 24:1−2. According to the Mishnah the rabbinic schools of Shammai and Hillel offered narrow and broad interpretations respectively of Deuteronomy 24:1−4:

> The school of Shammai say: A man may not divorce his wife unless he has found unchastity in her, for it is written, *Because he hath found in her* indecency *in anything.*
>
> And the school of Hillel say: [He may divorce her] even if she spoiled a dish for him, for it is written, *Because he hath found in her indecency in* anything. R. Akiba says: Even if he found another fairer than she, for it is written, *And it shall be if she find no favour in his eyes....* (Gittin 9:10).[23]

Jesus' interpretation follows the narrower view of Shammai. Indeed, he sets the bar even higher than Deuteronomy 24:1−4, transforming Moses' iteration of a customary provision of a certificate of divorce into a virtual command and restricting legitimate cause for divorce to *porneia* ("marital unfaithfulness"; lit., "sexual immorality"; see also Matt. 19:8−9). Furthermore, he cautions men not to divorce their wives for any other reasons, for in so doing they become responsible for their wives' subsequent adultery, which is what happens when men divorce innocent women and then the latter remarry.

---

23. As translated by H. Danby, *The Mishnah* (London: Oxford, 1933), 321.

Jesus offered this interpretation in the broader context of the Sermon on the Mount, which, like Yahweh's revelation to Israel at Sinai, functions as a covenantal constitutional document governing his relationship with his followers. However, his utterances on divorce and remarriage in Matthew 19:3−9 (//Mark 10:2−12) represent his response to a challenge from the Pharisees. Here he reiterates what he had said earlier, but he also emphasizes that Moses' statements on divorce reflect legally permissible procedures, necessitated by the hardness of human hearts.[24] Moses' instructions were intended to secure the well-being of women in the face of illegitimate divorce. Jesus declares that the provision itself represents a response to a culture that has departed from the divine ideal as reflected in the order of creation. Genesis 1:27 and 2:24 assume that God joins husband and wife together, and that no one may interfere with that union.

The ideals expressed by Paul in 1 Corinthians 7:8−16 are equally high. He virtually excludes legitimate divorce for Christians, declaring that wives should not leave their husbands (v. 10) and husbands should not send their wives away (i.e., divorce them; v. 12). But if a woman abandons her husband, she is not to remarry but to continue to seek reconciliation with him (v. 11). The only context in which a Christian might consider divorce is when one of the parties in the marriage is converted to faith in Christ. Even then the believer may not initiate divorce, for it is hoped that through his/her piety the unbelieving spouse might come to faith (vv. 13−14). But if the unbeliever seeks divorce, the believer may acquiesce, in which case he/she is free to remarry.

MARRIAGE AND DIVORCE FOR **Christians.** According to research into marital patterns in the United States, the divorce rate among professing Christians in some parts of the country is actually higher than among the population as a whole.[25] What can Deuteronomy 24:1−4 teach us that would help us recover a biblical view of marriage and divorce? Here are a few suggestions.

(1) Stable marriages do not just happen; they take effort and must be built on solid foundations. Deuteronomy 24:5 teaches that when people marry, outside responsibilities and distractions should be reduced to a minimum. While a two-week honeymoon offers hope for a good start to the marriage, it is insufficient to prepare for a life of married bliss.

---

24. This comment seems to allude to Moses' comment about the woman finding no grace in the eyes of her husband.

25. See the discussion by Sider, *The Scandal of the Evangelical Conscience,* 18−20.

(2) Because the health of a community depends on the health of marriages, support for newlyweds should be a communal matter. This would mean not only offering communal assistance for getting the marriage off the ground, but also discouraging newlyweds from taking on responsibilities in the church for a specified period—Moses suggests a year.

(3) Because no partners in a marriage are perfect, the health of the marriage requires spouses to be extremely and persistently gracious in responding to the other person's faults. What stressed people need is grace in the eyes of the Lord and in the eyes of their spouses.

(4) Because of the propensity for men to run roughshod over their wives, the church needs to establish specific principles and procedures to ensure that within the context of divorce and remarriage, the welfare of women is protected.

(5) Divorce never happens without violation of the divine ideal and without sin. Divorce arises from hard hearts and represents a final declaration of failure in the most fundamental of human institutions. The culture of divorce in the West offers Christians an extraordinary opportunity to be countercultural. To the extent that in these matters we have behaved like the world, we must repent or face the prospect of God's wrath.[26] To the extent that we model biblical ideals of marriage, we declare to the world the kind of relationship they may enjoy with God through Jesus Christ, the self-sacrificing head and husband of the church.

---

26. For a helpful exegetical and pastoral discussion of these issues, especially as they relate to Matt. 19:3 – 12, see C. L. Blomberg, "Marriage, Divorce, Remarriage, and Celibacy: An Exegesis of Matthew 19:3 – 12," *TrinJ* 11 ns (1990): 161 – 96; A. Köstenberger and D. W. Jones, *God, Marriage, and Family: Rebuilding the Biblical Foundation* (Wheaton, IL: Crossway, 2004), 227 – 58.

Deuteronomy 24:6-22

Do not take a pair of millstones—not even the upper one—as security for a debt, because that would be taking a man's livelihood as security. [7]If a man is caught kidnapping one of his brother Israelites and treats him as a slave or sells him, the kidnapper must die. You must purge the evil from among you.

[8]In cases of leprous diseases be very careful to do exactly as the priests, who are Levites, instruct you. You must follow carefully what I have commanded them. [9]Remember what the LORD your God did to Miriam along the way after you came out of Egypt.

[10]When you make a loan of any kind to your neighbor, do not go into his house to get what he is offering as a pledge. [11]Stay outside and let the man to whom you are making the loan bring the pledge out to you. [12]If the man is poor, do not go to sleep with his pledge in your possession. [13]Return his cloak to him by sunset so that he may sleep in it. Then he will thank you, and it will be regarded as a righteous act in the sight of the LORD your God.

[14]Do not take advantage of a hired man who is poor and needy, whether he is a brother Israelite or an alien living in one of your towns. [15]Pay him his wages each day before sunset, because he is poor and is counting on it. Otherwise he may cry to the LORD against you, and you will be guilty of sin.

[16]Fathers shall not be put to death for their children, nor children put to death for their fathers; each is to die for his own sin.

[17]Do not deprive the alien or the fatherless of justice, or take the cloak of the widow as a pledge. [18]Remember that you were slaves in Egypt and the LORD your God redeemed you from there. That is why I command you to do this.

[19]When you are harvesting in your field and you overlook a sheaf, do not go back to get it. Leave it for the alien, the fatherless and the widow, so that the LORD your God may bless you in all the work of your hands. [20]When you beat the olives from your trees, do not go over the branches a second time. Leave what remains for the alien, the fatherless and the widow. [21]When you harvest the grapes in your vineyard, do

not go over the vines again. Leave what remains for the alien, the fatherless and the widow. [22]Remember that you were slaves in Egypt. That is why I command you to do this.

THE INSTRUCTIONS REGARDING MARRIAGE and family issues in verses 1—5 are followed by a series (14 = 2 x 7) of short paragraphs dealing with a range of issues and only loosely linked thematically. The overarching concern is to develop sensitivity to the plight of the vulnerable in society and instill in persons with means a sense of responsibility for their well-being. This collage of instructions continues the trajectory of compassion found in earlier texts (esp. 15:1—11 and 23:19—20[20—21]), an observation strengthened by reminders of Israel's experience as slaves in Egypt in 24:18 and 22, which echo similar statements in 15:15.

Depriving a Person of Access to Food (24:6)

THIS SINGLE-SENTENCE INSTRUCTIONAL FRAGMENT is cast in impersonal third person form, with an added motive clause. This statement does not prohibit creditors from accepting deposits from debtors, but it prohibits them from demanding as security household items required for subsistence. The handmill, which consists of an upper millstone and a lower stone slab on the ground, provides an apt illustration of the principle.[1] To demand a millstone as a pledge meant depriving a household of the basic instrument for making essential food (bread), which was tantamount to claiming the debtor's life as a pledge.

Depriving a Poor Person of Life Itself (24:7)

THE SECOND FRAGMENT PROHIBITS depriving people of their freedom. Here Moses concretizes and contextualizes the ordinance as given in Exodus 21:16. He identifies the kidnapper as a "brother" of his victim, thereby applying a universal ordinance to members of the covenant community. By highlighting the humiliation of victims, he portrays them as chattel property treated and sold like merchandise (cf. 21:14). By calling for the death penalty to purge the evil from Israel's midst, Moses places this offense in a class with other capital crimes.[2]

---

1. The grinder would kneel on the ground in front of this slab and grind the grain by moving the upper stone back and forth over it. Cf. King and Stager, *Life in Biblical Israel*, 95.

2. Apostasy (13:5[6]), idolatry (17:7), refusing to accept the verdict of a priest (17:12), murder (19:13; 21:9), insubordination to parents (21:21), adultery (22:21, 22, 24), and the noncapital offense of giving a false testimony in court (19:19).

Righteousness in Heeding Authority (24:8–9)

WITHOUT WARNING THE SUBJECT shifts from the righteous response to a personal health issue. On the surface the present concern for skin disease (*ṣāraʿat*) seems to have nothing to do with morality.[3] This note presupposes Leviticus 13–14, which had dealt with the issue in great detail. However, whereas the earlier text involved precise clinical legislation, this is motivational speech, lacking specific information on the nature of the malady or prescriptions for its treatment. Furthermore, whereas the earlier text highlights the role of the priests in the diagnosis and treatment skin diseases, these instructions are addressed to the people, to whom Moses appeals for diligent compliance with the instruction of the Levitical priests. Not doubting his own authority, at the end of verse 8 Moses reinforces his appeal for compliance by linking the voices of Levitical priests with his own and ultimately with God's voice.

Finally, Moses calls for careful attention to the voice of experience, charging the people to remember what happened to Miriam on their journey out of Egypt (Num. 12:10–15). This reminder suggests that the real concern here is not the skin disease but the importance of heeding the instruction of the priests (cf. 17:8–13; 25:2). By this interpretation the "leprous disease" represents Yahweh's punishment for noncompliance with priestly instruction. In any case, this text shows no interest in issues of purity and impurity or why it is inserted among other ethical instructions.

Depriving a Person of Clothing (24:10–13)

THE ILLUSTRATION CHANGES FROM verse 6, but here we find additional instructions on how creditors may lend to the poor. Elaborating on Exodus 22:25–27[24–26], Moses sets the context and presents the case as a general principle. Whereas in the earlier text the loan involved silver and prohibited Israelites from capitalizing on the misfortunes of others, here Moses casts the net more broadly and seeks to limit the psychological damage caused by economic stress. He prohibits creditors from intimidating debtors by entering their houses to demand the pledge. Instead, lenders are to stand outside and wait for borrowers to bring them the pledge. As elsewhere, the goal is a community built on ethical values of trust and compassion.

---

3. For a discussion of *ṣāraʿat*, see J. F. A. Sawyer, "A Note on the Etymology of *ṣāraʿat*," *VT* 26 (1976): 241–45. For recent evidence from Mesopotamian sources suggesting leprosy as a possible interpretation of *ṣārāʿat*, see J. Scurlock and B. R. Andersen, *Diagnoses in Assyrian and Babylonian Medicine: Ancient Sources, Translations, and Modern Medical Analyses* (Urbana: Univ. of Illinois Press, 2005), 70–73.

Verses 12–13 focus on a particular type of borrower, a destitute man, with nothing to offer as collateral but his "outer garment." Since he also uses it as his blanket at night, the creditor must return it to him before sundown. Moses does not say whether the pledge was to be returned for good or if the lender might return every morning to hold the object during the day until the loan is repaid. Whereas Exodus 22:25–27[24–26] encourages compliance by warning creditors that Yahweh defends the debtor, our text offers positive incentives. If the creditor is considerate of the debtor, the latter will bless him.[4] Verse 13 ends with the judicial and divine verdict of innocence/righteousness (ṣᵉdāqâ) on the creditor (cf. 6:25). This response to the poor promotes a healthy relationship between creditor and debtor and pleases Yahweh.

Depriving a Person of Rightful Due (24:14–15)

ALTHOUGH THE REFERENCES TO a poor individual and the appeal to act "before sunset" link this paragraph to the preceding, the attention shifts from a neighbor to a person who contracts his services to an Israelite for wages. Building on Leviticus 19:13, Moses addresses the temptation of employers to exploit their workers, perhaps even seizing pledges by force. The remainder of verse 14 clarifies the status of the potential victim.

The word śākîr ("hired man") refers to a person who is not a member of the household but who is hired for the day to perform specific tasks. Economically he is "poor and needy" (cf. 15:11),[5] sociologically he may be "a brother Israelite or an alien," and geographically, he resides "in your land in your gates" (pers. trans.).

Having challenged his hearers in principle not to take advantage of day laborers, in verse 15 Moses explains what he means: day laborers must be paid at the end of the day in which they perform their services.[6] He concludes with four reasons why they should do so: (1) The hired hand is destitute, having offered his services because he has no independent access to wealth. (2) The man has worked all day in anticipation of payment at the end of the day; he must not be disappointed. (3) Heartless failure to pay will cause the hired man to cry to Yahweh against his employer (cf. 10:18; Ex. 22:27[26]). (4) Failure to pay will render the employer guilty of

---

4. Cf. C. Levin, "The Poor in the Old Testament: Some Observations," *Religion and Theology* 8 (2001): 261. As in other cases involving a lesser person blessing a superior, the verb *brk* may function as a virtual synonym for "praise" (e.g., Ps. 66:8; see also Judg. 5:2, 9).

5. This is a standard pair of words in the Old Testament. Cf. Job 24:14; Ps. 37:14; 40:17[18]; 74:21; 86:1; 109:16, 22.

6. The expression "each day" is shorthand for "the day of his service," which is reinforced with "before sunset."

a crime. The declaration that "it will be [counted] against him as sin" (pers. trans.) is the opposite of the verdict received by creditors who demonstrate righteousness by being gracious to debtors (v. 13; cf. 15:9; 23:20[21]).

Righteousness in Accountability for Crimes: Protecting the Innocent (24:16)

THIS FRAGMENT IS LINKED to the preceding by the word "sin" (*ḥeṭ*). In deny-ing judicial authorities the right to execute children for crimes committed by their fathers,[7] this statement does not contradict the Decalogue.[8] The first command is addressed to fathers, declaring that their actions have implications for all who live within the household (5:9–10). Knowledge that they will be held responsible for the effects their sins have on their families should deter them from actions that violate Yahweh's covenant. Significantly, Old Testament examples of children being punished for crimes committed by parents all involve fundamental violations of the covenant.[9]

Depriving the Poor of Justice (24:17–18)

NOW MOSES RETURNS TO the primary issue of this chapter: demonstrat-ing righteousness toward socially and economically vulnerable persons (cf. 16:20 and comments), specifically promoting the well-being of aliens, the fatherless, and widows. While Exodus 23:6 prohibits perversion of justice in legal proceedings, here Moses applies the principle to the daily treat-ment of the marginalized.

As an illustration he singles out a destitute widow, whose garment a creditor might demand as collateral. In 10:18 he had reassured aliens, the fatherless, and widows that Yahweh is on their side and provides their basic needs. Now he portrays the Israelites with means as extensions of God's gracious hands. Whereas verses 12–13 assume creditors' right to accept a poor man's garment as a deposit for a loan, now Moses prohibits them from demanding the same from a widow.

---

7. Since *yûmat* ("to be put to death") involves judicial execution, here human execution of sentences passed by the courts is in view.

8. In later times that statement was used to argue for the notion of transgenerational accountability as a fundamental principle of Yahweh's covenant with Israel (Jer. 31:29–30; Ezek. 18:2–3). On the significance of the proverb in Ezekiel, see Block, *Ezekiel Chapters 1–24*, 554–90; K. P. Darr, "Proverb Performance and Trans-Generational Retribution in Ezekiel 18," in *Ezekiel's Hierarchical World: Wrestling with a Tiered Reality* (ed. S. L. Cook and C. L. Patton; SBL Symposium Series 31; Atlanta: Society of Biblical Literature, 2004), 199–223.

9. Cf. Deut. 13:15[16]; Josh. 7:24–25; Judg. 21:5–10; 2 Sam 21:1–9. Cf. Tigay, *Deu-teronomy*, 227.

Some suggest Moses' intent is to spare her the indignity of removing mourning garments,[10] but it seems more likely to relate to her gender. Without the protection of a father or husband, a woman appearing in public without her normal clothing could precipitate gossip and charges of immorality.[11] In verse 18 Moses seeks to motivate compassion by reminding all Israelites of their own experience in Egypt.[12] Not only should the memory of their own experience of divine grace stimulate compassion toward all who are disadvantaged, including foreigners, but in so doing they will emulate the character and actions of their God (10:18–19).

Depriving the Poor of Food (24:19–22)

THE THREEFOLD REFERENCE TO aliens, the fatherless, and widows in verses 19–21 and the reference to Israel's slavery in Egypt in verse 22 link this paragraph tightly to the preceding. However, now Moses moves from defensive prohibitions of injustice to offensive guarantees of economic well-being for the vulnerable. He continues his penchant for literary triplets and concludes with a motivational clause that undergirds all three.

Fundamental to Israel's constitution was the notion that Yahweh reserved the right to determine how the land would be used (cf. Lev. 25), part of which included the right of all in the covenant community to a share in its produce.[13] These instructions build on earlier legislation (Lev. 19:9–10; 23:22), where Yahweh had called on landowners to leave the corners of their fields uncut and leave for the poor and the alien whatever they dropped while harvesting the crop. These instructions are even more pastoral, seeking to instill in the covenant community a spirit of generosity that goes far beyond the original legislation. (1) They expand the demographic scope by adding the fatherless and widow to the alien under the rubric of the "poor."

(2) Whereas the earlier laws had spoken only of fields and vineyards, Moses broadens the scope of the principle to include olive groves. This triad of crops is representative, listing the three staples that provided raw materials for bread, olive oil, and wine. But the principle also extends to the fruit of orchards and the produce of vegetable gardens.

(3) Moses expands the benefits to the poor. Since the grain at the edges of fields was often inferior in quality and mixed with weeds, and since grapes

10. Cf. Tigay, *Deuteronomy*, 228.

11. Targum Pseudo-Jonathan adds, "so that evil neighbors shall not arise and bring against her an evil report when you return the pledge to her." As translated by Clarke, *Targum Pseudo-Jonathan: Deuteronomy*, 67.

12. Deut. 5:15; 15:15; 16:12.

13. De Vaux, *Ancient Israel*, 165.

and olives on the ground tended to ripen prematurely or have some defect and quickly spoil, the significance of these provisions was limited. So Moses enjoins landowners and harvesters to leave for the poor whole sheaves of grain already cut and tied but which they had neglected to take home, those grapes still on the vines that harvesters had overlooked, and olives that do not fall to the ground when the branches are beaten to shake them loose. The point is, rather than begrudging fallen and inferior fruit to the poor, the oversights of the harvest and late maturing crops and grapes and olives are to be left intentionally for the benefit of aliens, the fatherless, and widows.

As pastor, Moses seeks to motivate rather than legislate generosity by linking the well-being of the nation to their generosity to the marginalized (v. 19),[14] and, echoing his statement in verse 18, by remembering their own experience as slaves in Egypt. By living the present in the light of Yahweh's grace in the past, their hearts will remain soft toward the poor.

 TREATMENT OF THE POOR in Scripture. Old Testament narrative accounts of persons who lived according to the ethical principles outlined by Moses in these texts are few and far between. Cast in the morally dark period of the judges (Ruth 1:1), Boaz shines as a beacon of light, demonstrating true righteousness in overt act and speech. When Ruth requested permission from Naomi to glean in the field of a man in whose eyes she might find favor (Ruth 2:2), she recognized Israel's current moral problem; as a poor alien and a widow she could not count on anyone allowing her to glean behind the harvesters.

However, having caught the spirit of Torah, Boaz's response went far beyond the letter of the law. (1) He addressed Ruth respectfully and affectionately as "my daughter" (2:8). (2) He invited her to join his own female servants (v. 8). (3) He forbade his male servants from harassing her (vv. 9, 15–16). (4) He invited her to drink from the water jars provided for the members of his own household (v. 9). (5) He blessed her (v. 12). (6) He invited her to his table, encouraging her to dip her bread in his sauce, serving her personally, and giving her food until she was fully satisfied (v. 14). (7) He instructed his workers deliberately to pull grain from their bundles and leave them for her (v. 16). Because of his generosity, Ruth returned to her mother-in-law with as much grain as she could carry. In his overwhelming charity Boaz was not satisfied with merely meeting the demands of the

---

14. In 14:29 and 23:20[21]. the blessing was also tied to acts of compassion toward the marginalized.

earlier laws or even Moses' exposition thereof. With magnanimity and in the spirit of righteousness divinely defined, he recognized himself as the "wings" of Yahweh, under whom the destitute may find shelter (v. 12).

In the Old Testament narratives Boaz has few moral and spiritual peers. On the contrary, Israel's historians understood their history as a history of failure, not only because of their idolatry but also because of their refusal to live according to the covenant standards of righteousness. Second Kings 4:1−7 illustrates the problem. While the use of olive oil as a key motif in the story links this text directly with Deuteronomy 24:20, this short episode does not merely show that Yahweh takes care of the poor—which he does; it also exposes the underlying moral problem of the nation. The substitution of Baal for Yahweh as the object of devotion was accompanied by ethical erosion, demonstrated especially in the treatment of the marginalized. Even if the creditor was within his legal rights to demand her two sons (which is doubtful), his response to the widow's plight obviously violated his moral obligations.

The exploitation of the poor is a prominent motif in the latter prophets. Amos provides classic expression of the problem in the eighth century BC northern kingdom—complete with a reference to Yahweh's past grace:

This is what the LORD says:
"For three sins of Israel,
    even for four, I will not turn back my wrath.
They sell the righteous [*ṣaddîq*] for silver,
    and the needy [*ʾebyôn*] for a pair of sandals.
They trample on the heads of the poor
    as upon the dust of the ground
    and deny justice to the oppressed.
Father and son use the same girl
    and so profane my holy name.
They lie down beside every altar
    on garments taken in pledge.
In the house of their god
    they drink wine taken as fines.
"I destroyed the Amorite before them,
    though he was tall as the cedars
    and strong as the oaks.
I destroyed his fruit above
    and his roots below.
"I brought you up out of Egypt,
    and I led you forty years in the desert
    to give you the land of the Amorites." (Amos 2:6−10)

We find denunciations of the same moral problem and challenges to righteous alternatives in preexilic Judah in Isaiah (Isa. 3:14–15; 10:1–3; 32:7), Jeremiah (Jer. 2:34; 22:16–17), Habakkuk (Hab. 3:14), and Ezekiel (Ezek. 16:49; 18:12; 22:29). Oppression of the poor was a primary precipitant to Yahweh's fury leading to the destruction of Jerusalem, but Zechariah 7:9–12 and Malachi 3:5 attest to the persistence of the problem even in postexilic times.

Despite the legislation in Exodus 22 and the present instructions on taking garments as collateral (vv. 10–12, 17), references to taking garments as collateral in Proverbs 20:16 and Job 22:6, as well as Amos's denunciation of creditors who take the garments of the poor as pledges and then spitefully sleep on them themselves in public places (Amos 2:6–8) suggest this situation was common in Israel's history. An extrabiblical window into economic and social conditions in rural Judah during the time of Josiah is provided by the Mezad Hadshavyahu Ostracon, discovered in 1960 near Yavneh-Yam. The text of this document reads as follows:

> May my lord the governor hear the appeal of his servant. Your servant is a reaper working in Hazar-asam. Your servant finished his harvest and stored it a few days before stopping. After your servant had finished storing the harvest a few days ago, Hoshayahu son of Shobay came and took your servant's garment. After I finished my harvesting a few days ago, he took your servant's garment.
>
> All my companions who were harvesting with me in the heat of the [sun] will testify for me. They will testify that what I have said is true. I am innocent of any [offense.]
>
> [So please return] my garment. If the governor does not consider it his obligation to have [your servant's garment] sent back, [do] it out of pity! You must not remain silent [when your servant is without his garment.][15]

This letter does not explicitly state the garment was taken as collateral for a loan, but the actions of Hoshayahu certainly violate the spirit of the Torah.

Deuteronomy's appeals to compassion toward the poor are based on three considerations: imitation of Yahweh, who demonstrates a special interest in the poor (10:17–19); empathy, remembering their own experience of oppression in Egypt (24:18, 22); and recognition that the future blessing of the nation depended on their compassion toward the poor (v. 19). To these considerations the sage of Israel adds a fourth: acknowl-

---

15. As translated by J. M. Lindenberger, *Ancient Aramaic and Hebrew Letters* (2nd ed.; SBLWAW 14; Atlanta: Society of Biblical Literature, 2003), 110.

edgment that the poor bear God's image, and the way one treats them is a reflection of one's disposition to God:

> He who oppresses the poor shows contempt for their Maker,
>> but whoever is kind to the needy honors God. (Prov. 14:31)

> He who mocks the poor shows contempt for their Maker;
>> whoever gloats over disaster will not go unpunished.
>> (Prov. 17:5)

Explicit echoes of the "social Torah" found in Deuteronomy 24:6 – 22 are scarce in the New Testament. Jesus' declaration that acts of charity for the hungry, the naked, and the imprisoned are actually performed for him (Matt. 25:31 – 46) is rooted in the perspective found in the Proverbs texts. James 2:5 – 6 sounds the most like the prophetic utterances cited above.

> Listen, my dear brothers: Has not God chosen those who are poor in the eyes of the world to be rich in faith and to inherit the kingdom he promised those who love him? But you have insulted the poor man. Is it not the rich who are exploiting you? Are they not the ones who are dragging you into court?

In the references to oppression and mistreatment of the poor in the courts we hear echoes of the voice of Moses.

Reflections of the instructional fragments not concerned overtly with the marginalized in later writings deserve brief comment. As noted above, Deuteronomy 24:7 seems to be concerned only about the abduction of persons for the purpose of selling them into slavery, that is, trafficking human beings. However, its placement immediately after verse 6, whose primary concern is wrongful claims of collateral, invites the reader to interpret this verse within the same social realm.[16] Moses seems to have in mind a scene like that envisioned in Job 24:9:

> The fatherless child is snatched from the breast,
>> the infant of the poor is seized for a debt.

It is possible that the widow in 2 Kings 4:1 – 7 fears the creditor's coming because he is demanding her two sons as collateral for an unpaid debt. Perhaps he hopes to recoup his losses by selling the boys. Moses' prohibition on the seizure of human beings and their sale is reflected in Amos's

---

16. This interpretation is reinforced by the verbal connection with the previous verse. Whereas v. 6 had interpreted taking a person's millstone as security against an unpaid loan metaphorically as taking his very "livelihood" (*nepeš*) as a pledge, v. 7 speaks explicitly of stealing a *nepeš* ("one" in NIV). Similarly Tigay, *Deuteronomy*, 457 – 58.

denunciation of the Philistines and Tyrians for delivering entire populations to Edom, presumably as slaves (Amos 1:6–10).

The instructions concerning skin diseases (vv. 8–9) remind readers in every generation that those whom Yahweh has put into authority are to be respected, their ministry on his behalf to be willingly received. Miriam serves as an illustration to all that God will hold accountable those who reject his will as mediated through his servants.

CONCERN FOR THE POOR and marginalized. As it was in ancient Israel, so today the true barometer of the genuineness of people's faith is not found in creedal utterances, but in their charity toward the poor and the marginalized inside and outside the church. Christian charity toward the poor needs to happen at two levels. (1) Within the spirit of the Torah, individuals within the church should be proactive in caring for the marginalized in their own communities. (2) As communities of faith, churches must respond to the injustices and social cancers that plague the nation and the world. The problem is illustrated by a recent story in the *Chicago Tribune*:

> On a recent afternoon, 15-year-old Marlon Parras stood on a stage in front of 3,000 people and talked about the hardships he and his 13-year-old sister, Emily, have faced since their parents were deported to Guatemala.
>
> He wept as he spoke softly of their parents' decision to leave the children, both American citizens, with relatives and church members so they could continue their education in suburban Atlanta.
>
> "This is not a family," Parras told the crowd that rose to its feet during his emotional testimony. "This is not fair."[17]

While the issue of undocumented aliens is complex, the response of Christians to scenes like this should be different from that of non-Christians. The close identification of many evangelicals with right wing politics and the reputation of hardheartedness toward social concerns they often exhibit are scarcely a credit to the name of Christ. Where is Boaz when so many are looking for "the wings of the Lord"?[18] This issue is not political; it is moral and spiritual.

---

17. *Chicago Tribune*, March 5, 2009.
18. For a helpful discussion of the issues and and proposals for an evangelical response see Carroll R., *Christians at the Border*.

Vicarious punishment. But what of the issue of vicarious punishment (24:16)? Courts should not punish children of criminals more severely than they do those whose families have no history of crime. At the personal level, it is tempting to hold grudges against those who, through no decision of their own, happen to be connected by birth or social organization with those who have committed crimes, but who are long gone. While children are implicated in the effects of their parents' actions, in the administration of justice they may not be held responsible, let alone punished for them.

On the other hand, although this text highlights the importance of individual responsibility for individual crimes, it should not be interpreted in isolation from other texts that highlight communal solidarity and responsibility for the well-being of others. Not only are individuals' personal identities determined by the community in which they live, but their conduct also has a direct bearing on the lives of others, not to mention the bearing of others' actions on them.

Individual and corporate responsibility represent two poles of a continuum, which, if not opposed, often exist in tension.[19] This chapter of Deuteronomy highlights the responsibility of the community to care for individuals, especially those with limited means for taking care of themselves. At the same time, it refuses to allow the members of the community to be dragged into the net of other individuals' misdeeds, especially when this involves actions subject to human judicial decision. The principle of righteousness ($ṣ^edāqâ$) precludes human courts from imposing the sentence for one person's crimes on another person.

---

19. See the helpful study by J. S. Kaminsky, "The Sins of the Fathers: A Theological Investigation of the Biblical Tension between Corporate and Individualized Retribution," *Judaism* 46 (1997): 319–32.

Deuteronomy 25:1–16

W hen men have a dispute, they are to take it to court and the judges will decide the case, acquitting the innocent and condemning the guilty. ²If the guilty man deserves to be beaten, the judge shall make him lie down and have him flogged in his presence with the number of lashes his crime deserves, ³but he must not give him more than forty lashes. If he is flogged more than that, your brother will be degraded in your eyes.

⁴Do not muzzle an ox while it is treading out the grain.

⁵If brothers are living together and one of them dies without a son, his widow must not marry outside the family. Her husband's brother shall take her and marry her and fulfill the duty of a brother-in-law to her. ⁶The first son she bears shall carry on the name of the dead brother so that his name will not be blotted out from Israel.

⁷However, if a man does not want to marry his brother's wife, she shall go to the elders at the town gate and say, "My husband's brother refuses to carry on his brother's name in Israel. He will not fulfill the duty of a brother-in-law to me." ⁸Then the elders of his town shall summon him and talk to him. If he persists in saying, "I do not want to marry her," ⁹his brother's widow shall go up to him in the presence of the elders, take off one of his sandals, spit in his face and say, "This is what is done to the man who will not build up his brother's family line." ¹⁰That man's line shall be known in Israel as The Family of the Unsandaled.

¹¹If two men are fighting and the wife of one of them comes to rescue her husband from his assailant, and she reaches out and seizes him by his private parts, ¹²you shall cut off her hand. Show her no pity.

¹³Do not have two differing weights in your bag—one heavy, one light. ¹⁴Do not have two differing measures in your house—one large, one small. ¹⁵You must have accurate and honest weights and measures, so that you may live long in the land the LORD your God is giving you. ¹⁶For the LORD your God detests anyone who does these things, anyone who deals dishonestly.

DEUTERONOMY 25 CONTINUES THE pattern of chapters 23 and 24, dealing with a series of topics only loosely related, though all in the interest of "righteousness, only righteousness" (16:20, see comments). This chapter breaks down thematically into six parts. The first five offer instructions on protecting the vulnerable whose rights are threatened by Israelites themselves; the last one treats Israel as the vulnerable party, whose very existence has been threatened by outsiders.

Safeguarding Righteousness in the Administration of Justice (25:1–3)

WITH THE FIRST FRAGMENT Moses concludes his instructions on the legal administration of justice in Israel.[1] This paragraph consists of the main case (v. 1), a secondary case (v. 2), and an addendum to prevent excess in the administration of the sentence. The opening statement is vague—a legal case[2] arises between two men, inviting application to any dispute. When a dispute arises that people are unable to settle privately, they may take it to the court for adjudication. The parallel statements in verse 1, "and they shall declare the righteous righteous," and "and they shall declare the wicked wicked" (pers. trans.), express the ideals of true justice. The first declaration signifies acquittal (cf. Ezek 18:9); the second signifies conviction. The subcase in verse 2 is concerned only with cases that call for punishment by flogging. In Deuteronomy this applies only in the case of a man who wrongfully accuses his bride of not being a virgin (22:18).

The specific instructions on the execution of this punishment in verses 2–3 reflect keen concern for justice for both parties. To ensure the executioner does not overstep the bounds of the sentence, the punishment must be administered in the presence of the judge, and the number of lashings must be correlated with the severity of the crime. To protect the dignity of the accused and to prevent excessive public humiliation, Moses sets forty lashes as the absolute maximum sentence. While it is unclear what constitutes excessive public degradation, the identification of the convicted person as "your brother" suggests that even though justice was to be administered by objective standards, floggings were never to be carried out heartlessly. After all, even guilty persons are members of the community.

---

1. Cf. 1:16–17; 10:17–19; 16:18–20; 17:2–13; 19:15–21; 21:1–9, 18–23; 22:13–21; 24:17–18.

2. The expression *rîb* ("lawsuit, legal case") occurs elsewhere in Deuteronomy in 1:12; 17:8; 19:17; 21:5.

Safeguarding Righteousness in the Treatment of Animals (25:4)

ON THE SURFACE THIS apodictic fragment seems unrelated to the preceding. However, since draft animals were often flogged with rods, the command may have been triggered by reference to corporal punishment in verses 2 − 3.[3] The present statement does not address excessive beating of animals, but it displays a "humanitarianism" of a different sort: Oxen used for threshing grain must not be muzzled.[4] The ordinance assumes the ancient practice of threshing grain by having oxen trample the stalks or pull rock-studded sledges over the stalks spread out on the threshing floor. Greedy farmers muzzled their oxen or donkeys to prevent them from eating instead of working, or simply eating that which he hoped to harvest for himself (cf. Prov. 14:4).

This concern for animals accords with the trajectory we have observed repeatedly in Deuteronomy (cf. Prov. 12:10).[5] As in 22:1 − 4 and 6 − 7, Moses' humanitarian concern moves beyond human victims of exploitation to domestic animals. The pursuit of righteousness on the farm will involve care for the creatures in one's charge, just as God himself does (cf. Pss. 104; 147:9).

Safeguarding Righteousness in Relation to Male Sexuality (25:5 − 12)

DEUTERONOMY 25:5 − 12 presents two scenarios with sexual and procreational undertones and involving shameful male (vv. 5 − 10) and female behavior (vv. 11 − 12). However, the paragraphs are linked lexically by the expression "brother/brothers" (cf. also vv. 3 and 5).

Maintaining righteousness in the face of shameful male behavior (vv. 5 − 10). As we have observed in earlier texts, verses 5 − 10 subdivide into a main case (vv. 5 − 6) and a corollary issue (vv. 7 − 10). Both concern the social institution of "levirate marriage." A levirate marriage is a legally sanctioned union between a widow, whose husband has died without having fathered offspring, and the brother of the deceased. Although Deuter-

---

3. Thus Tigay, *Deuteronomy*, 458.

4. On this passage, see J. T. Noonan, Jr., "The Muzzled Ox," *JQR* 70 (1980): 172 − 75; D. Instone-Brewer, "Paul's Literal Interpretation of 'Do Not Muzzle the Ox,'" in *The Trustworthiness of God: Perspectives on the Nature of Scripture* (ed. P. Helm and C. R. Trueman; Grand Rapids: Eerdmans, 2002), 139 − 56; idem, "1 Corinthians 9:9 − 11: A Literal Interpretation of 'Do Not Muzzle the Ox,'" *NTS* 38 (1992): 554 − 65.

5. Note the specification of "ox" and "donkey" and the extension of the right to rest on the Sabbath for "any of your animals" in 5:14; the prohibition of boiling a kid in its mother's milk in 14:21; the charge to restore straying livestock to their owners and to assist animals overburdened with their pack in 22:1 − 4; and the protection of wild birds in 22:6 − 7.

onomy 25:5–10 provides the only formal instruction on the institution in the Old Testament, variations of this type of marriage are widely attested in the ancient world (cf. Gen. 38; Ruth 4).[6]

The levirate institution actually addressed two problems arising from the death of a man without an heir. (1) By marrying the deceased's widow, the *yābām* ("brother-in-law; Lat. *levir*) offered her economic security and physical protection. (2) However, the primary concern here is not the material well-being of the widow, but securing progeny for her deceased husband. Grounded in the conviction that parents lived on in their children[7] and children perpetuate the "name" of their fathers, the levirate addressed the worst curse imaginable—to have one's "seed" cut off and one's name forgotten.[8]

Through the levirate institution the *yābām* could preserve the name of the deceased (Ruth 4:10) and raise up/provide seed for his brother (Gen. 38:8–9). However, this social solution complicated issues of inheritance. Given the links between family and patrimony, in Israel it was critical that property stay within the family (cf. Ruth 4:3, 5, 10). What Moses offers here is not a comprehensive law redressing all these issues, but a pastoral appeal to maintain "the moral integrity and social solidarity"[9] of Israelite families once they have settled in the land. The well-being of the community depends on the preservation of each branch of the family tree and the continued tie of each branch with its patrimonial holdings.

The main case (vv. 5–6) involves two brothers living together. Since one is obviously married, they are not necessarily living under the same roof, though they are part of the same household[10] and responsible for each other's welfare.[11] Tragedy strikes the household when the married brother dies without having fathered a child to continue his branch of the family tree. This left his widow with two options. Either she could return to her own father's household, free to remarry any person she pleased,[12] or she

---

6. Cf. F. Crüsemann, *The Torah: Theology and Social History of Old Testament Law* (trans. A. W. Mahnke; Minneapolis: Fortress, 1996), 254.

7. Cf. J. Pedersen, *Israel: Its Life and Culture* (Atlanta: Scholars, 1991; reprint of 1926 ed.), 1:255–56.

8. Note Jephthah's exclamation of grief in Judg. 11:34–35 at the prospect of his line being cut off.

9. Expressions used by Willis, *Elders of the City*, 304.

10. For a pictorial reconstruction of a joint family compound see King and Stager, *Life in Biblical Israel*, 18.

11. Cf. Z. W. Falk, *Hebrew Law in Biblical Times* (2nd ed.; Provo, UT: Brigham Young Univ. Press/Winona Lake, IN: Eisenbrauns, 2001), 97.

12. Cf. the rights of divorcees as suggested in 21:10–14 and 24:1–4. On these texts see the commentary above.

could remain a part of her husband's household, which obligated a surviving male of the deceased's family to marry her.

Only the latter scenario is envisioned here. Verses 5b–6 describe the righteous response to this situation. Beginning with a prohibition directed at the widow, Moses forbids her from marrying someone "outside the family," for this would not solve the issue of progeny for the deceased. The remainder of verse 5 instructs the deceased's brother how to respond: He must engage in sexual intercourse with his widowed sister-in-law, take her for his wife, and perform the duties of a *yābām*. While the order of these clauses defies custom, the arrangement assumes such a close correlation between marriage and intercourse that these expressions may be interchanged. In no way may this be considered a concession to premarital sex, since the Old Testament never sanctions sexual intercourse or the raising of children outside a permanent marital union.[13]

Verse 6 assumes that the marriage and sexual intercourse achieve their intended goal; the woman conceives and gives birth to a son. While this son is literally her firstborn, as elsewhere the designation *bᵉkôr* refers to his sociological rank, not his chronological priority.[14] Whatever the *bᵉkôr's* role in other circumstances, here he represents the deceased's line; through him both the deceased's name and the integrity of the family patrimony are preserved.

Moses expresses this notion with a strange idiom, translated literally "to rise on the name of the deceased brother,"[15] meaning to establish the deceased's name on his patrimony and prevent his name from being cut off from his kinsfolk (Ruth 4:5; 10). The declared purpose of this marriage was to prevent his name from being "blotted out from Israel." Since family units were sacrosanct, to blot out a man's name meant lopping his branch off the family tree. The institution of levirate marriage provided a legal way to maintain the family line. The son whom the widow bears for the levir will take the name of the deceased as his patronym, and he will then live on through this son and his descendants.

The instructions for the corollary case (vv. 7–10) assume the possibility of exemption for men who prefer not to perform the duties of a levir, though this refusal was not to be taken lightly and involved the stigma

---

13. So also Tigay, *Deuteronomy*, 232.

14. Cf. comments on 21:15.

15. Cf. NIV, "carry on the name of the dead brother." The form of the idiom in Ruth 4:5 and 10 is more natural: "to maintain the name of the dead with his property." A third form of the idiom occurs in Gen. 48:6, to be "reckoned under the names of their brothers." While Num. 27:1–11 allows daughters to inherit property in the absence of sons, this text (v. 5) assumes a male heir.

of shame. The text does not say why a man might not want to marry his brother's widow,[16] but with remarkable latitude Moses authorizes an unwilling levir to opt out of his moral and legal obligations. As in the case of divorce (24:1 – 4), the process prescribed seeks to safeguard the reputation and well-being of the woman who has been struck by two tragedies — the death of her husband and rejection by his brother. Described in considerable detail, the procedure for dealing with an unwilling "brother" allows for a virtuous[17] and assertive[18] response by an aggrieved widow.

(1) Moses authorizes the bereaved widow to present her complaint before the elders at the town gate (v. 7b). As a legally competent plaintiff, he invites her to present her case before the body responsible for applying Israel's family laws.[19] Having lost her husband, who would otherwise defend her interests, she may appeal to the elders to stand up for her. In addition to authorizing women to take their cases to the elders, he also advises the women on how to present their case. Dictating the speech they are to present to the elders, Moses instructs women to declare forthrightly how her brother-in-law has failed his brother by refusing to establish his name in Israel, for he refuses to perform the duties of a *yābām* for her.

(2) Moses charges the elders to summon the *yābām* and speak to him (v. 8a). While not prescribing what they should say, the sequel suggests their goal should be to change his mind, presumably by encouraging him to place the well-being of others above self-interest.

(3) Moses offers the *yābām* the opportunity to speak for himself (v. 8b) and to declare his refusal publicly. His disposition is reflected both in the verb "to persist" and in his declaration, "I do not wish to marry her."

(4) Moses prescribes a ritual of public humiliation of the *yābām*, consisting of several elements. In the sight of the elders the widow is to approach her brother-in-law, pull one of his sandals from his foot, spit in his face, and finally interpret her actions in a public declaration (v. 9). The action represented a symbolic action of shame, but it also symbolized the transfer of the brother-in-law's rights to the deceased's widow and to that portion of the patrimonial estate that her husband would have received when it was

---

16. Cf. Tigay, *Deuteronomy*, 232 – 33. On the vagueness of the *gôʾēl*'s explanation for rejecting the role in Ruth 4:6, see Block, *Judges, Ruth*, 715 – 17.

17. J. R. Ziskind ("The Treatment of Women in Deuteronomy: Moral Absolutism and Practicality — Part I," *JBQ* 27 [1999]: 155 – 56) notes that it would have been perfectly legal for her to accept her brother-in-law's decision not to marry her, take her dowry, and go and marry another man.

18. See V. H. Matthews, "Female Voices: Upholding the Honor of the Household," *BTB* 24 (1994): 9.

19. Cf. 19:12; 21:20; 22:15 – 18. Cf. Nelson, *Deuteronomy*, 299. For full discussion of the role of the elders in this situation, see Willis, *Elders of the City*, 293 – 304.

divided.[20] Since the woman would take the sandal home, it would function like a receipt, providing concrete proof of the present legal proceedings (cf. Ruth 4:7 – 8).[21]

Spitting in the face of the *yābām* is obviously a rude gesture, but with her declaration "This is what is done to the man who will not build up his brother's family line," the widow shows this response is neither impulsive nor idiosyncratic, but accords with established legal procedure. By refusing to be a surrogate father for his deceased brother, the *yābām* is responsible for annihilating the man's name from Israel (cf. v. 6).

These instructions on maintaining righteousness in domestic crises end with a summary of the significance of the ritual (v. 10). The *yābām* who refused to guarantee the memory of his brother may indeed build a house of his own. However, in perpetuity it will be branded as the household of the man who rejected responsibility for the well-being of his own brother, and ultimately the communal good. Interpreted genealogically as "The Family of the Unsandaled," his progeny will bear the stigma of his shameful conduct.

Maintaining righteousness in the face of shameful female behavior (vv. 11 – 12). This short paragraph is linked to the preceding by vocabulary, characters, and motif. However, whereas the previous paragraph concerns shameful behavior by the brother-in-law, this fragment involves shameful behavior by a wife.[22] On the surface, this text recalls Exodus 21:18 – 19 and 22 – 25. However, while in Exodus 21:22 – 25 she was an innocent and passive victim caught in the crossfire of struggling men, here the woman interferes in the fight.

The NIV obscures the likelihood that the men in this scenario are brothers, probably living in the family compound (cf. v. 5). The text offers no cause for the altercation, but in light of the preceding they may have been fighting over inheritance or their respective roles on the estate. The paragraph opens by drawing attention to the men fighting, but the primary interest is in the wife of one of the combatants, who tries to intervene. Her intention is explicitly declared: She wants to rescue her husband from the "hand" of the person who is beating him up. The scene seems strange, since women would hesitate to intervene in such circumstances. However, the primary issue here is not the fact that she would defend her husband, but

---

20. So also Willis, *Elders of the City*, 297.

21. On the relationship of Ruth 4:7 – 8 to this text, see P. A. Kruger, "The Removal of the Sandal in Deuteronomy XXV 9," *VT* 46 (1996): 534 – 59.

22. On Deut. 25:11 – 12 as intentionally shame-inducing rather than talionic or retributive justice, see P. E. Wilson, "Deuteronomy xxv 11 – 12 — One for the Books," *VT* 47 (1997): 220 – 35.

her tactics: She reaches out and grabs his genitals. From the grammar and syntax of the passage as well as the severity of the punishment, this is no innocent gesture; her action is deliberate.

The punishment prescribed seems harsh,[23] and the demand to cut off the woman's hand (v. 12) is shocking and unparalleled in the Old Testament.[24] Since *yād* may be used euphemistically for genitalia,[25] some view this as a form of the *lex talionis*, the woman's hand representing a counterpart to the man's sexual organ.[26] However, the physiological differences between men and women preclude a literal application of the *talion*, and in any case the man has not been injured physically. The reference to the man's genitals as "his appendage of shame"[27] suggests the issue is the woman's shamelessness and immodesty.[28] Whereas verses 5–10 had involved a man who had wrongfully withheld his genitals from a woman, this case involves a man whose genitals have been shamelessly grabbed, perhaps with the intent of injury so he cannot have children.[29] The admonition "show her no pity" highlights the seriousness of the crime and the importance of carrying out the punishment against one who threatens the integrity of the branch of the family tree represented by the man whose genitals were attacked.[30]

Safeguarding Righteousness in Business Transactions (25:13–16)

MOSES CONCLUDES HIS INSTRUCTIONS on righteous living by considering an aspect of life that may be most vulnerable to compromise: everyday economic transactions. These instructions build on Yahweh's own statements in Leviticus 19:35–36. With his twofold reference to *ṣedeq* here in verse 15 (NIV "honest," which occurs 2x in Heb.; lit., "righteous"), Moses creates a striking inclusio with 16:20 (see comments). The significance of

---

23. Cf. CH §§192–195, 219; MAL §A:8–9 (Roth, *Law Collections*, 120–21, 156–57). For discussion of these laws and their relationship to the present text, see Pressler, *The View of Women*, 74–77.

24. Apart from the *lex talionis* (19:21; Ex. 21:23–24), Old Testament laws never call for this kind of mutilation.

25. L. Eslinger, "The Case of an Immodest Lady Wrestler in Deuteronomy 25:11–12," *VT* 31 (1981): 269–81. For a response see P. E. Wilson ("Deuteronomy xxv 11–12," 232–33), who argues that the man was only temporarily disabled.

26. Cf. Phillips, *Ancient Israel's Criminal Law*, 94–95; Craigie, *Deuteronomy*, 316.

27. NIV translates the unusual Hebrew euphemistically as "private parts."

28. Thus Pressler, *The View of Women*, 75, 77.

29. Cf. McConville, *Deuteronomy*, 371.

30. This "no-pity" formula also appears in 13:8[9]; 19:13, 21.

the problem of cheating in business deals throughout the ancient Near East is reflected in the wide range of materials that allude to it.[31]

The present economic fragment divides into three parts, each made up of a pair of statements. The first two pairs consist of perfectly parallel commands cast in apodictic form (vv. 13–14 and 15b, respectively), and the last, of a pair of motive clauses (vv. 15c–16). Verses 13–14 involve the two principal means of measuring commodities. The term *'eben* (lit., "stone") denotes the weights used on balances to weigh goods.[32] This text warns against having two different sets of weights, the lighter one to be used when calculating payment one owes, and the heavier to calculate commodities or money one was owed. The word *kîs* identifies the pouch or bag in which merchants carried their weights. The term *"'êpâ"* (NIV "measures") denotes the size of a vessel used to measure liquid and dry goods.

Verse 15 reiterates Moses' concern for honesty by rephrasing positively his negative commands in verses 13–14. The word *ṣedeq* ("righteous"; NIV "honest") means "in accordance with absolute standards." Together these words create a hendiadys, meaning "perfectly honest" weights and measures. With keen pastoral sense, in verses 15b–16 Moses tries to motivate integrity in business, first by promising long life in the land that Yahweh is giving the Israelites as a reward for honesty, and then by warning that all who commit crimes involving unjust weights and measures are abominable to Yahweh (cf. 18:12; 22:5).

ELSEWHERE IN THE OLD Testament. On this note Moses' pastoral exposition of the statutes, ordinances, and laws revealed by Yahweh through him to Israel at Sinai and later (cf. 12:1) comes to an end. From 12:2–25:16 he has been appealing to his people to demonstrate the wholehearted loyalty to Yahweh he called for in chapters 6–11 in exclusive worship of him (12:2–16:17) and by scrupulous adherence to the terms of the covenant as spelled out previously. In so doing he has sought to apply those terms particularly to the new situation the people will face once they have crossed the Jordan, displaced the Canaanites, and occupied the land. In this chapter Moses has addressed four principal issues,

---

31. See "The Code of Hammurabi" (gap §x in Roth, *Law Collections*, 98); "A Hymn to Shamash" (*COS*, 1:117 lines 107–22, [p. 148], as translated by B. R. Foster); "The Egyptian Book of the Dead" (*ANET*, 34); "The Instruction of Amenemope" (M. Lichtheim in *COS*, 1:47, pp. 119–20).

32. The standard shekel weighed ca. 11.4 grams. Cf. M. A. Powell, "Weights and Measures," *ABD*, 6:906–7.

each of which has implications for the faith and conduct of God's people in our own day.

These issues do not all surface in later writings. Exodus 21:20 refers to a criminal case involving a master beating his servant with a rod, but 1 Kings 12:11 contains the only reference to flogging in Hebrew narratives. Here Rehoboam speaks of disciplining workers with whips and scorpions, that is, barbed whips.[33] Beating was a common means of punishment, but no case of judicial beating as prescribed in verses 1–2 is recorded. In the New Testament, Jesus' beating was but one of the many illegal features of his arrest and trial (Luke 22:63).

The events of Genesis 38 happened long before Moses' present address, but the use of the verb *yibbēm* ("to fulfill the duty of a brother-in-law") in 38:8 suggests this account was written from the perspective of Deuteronomy 25:5–10. A series of events threatened the line of Judah. His firstborn son, Er, died before his wife Tamar bore him a son; Onan refused to serve his brother as a *yābām*; Judah's failure to arrange for his third son Shelah to marry Tamar. Tamar responded by tricking her father-in-law, Judah, to play the role of *yābām*, which led to the birth of twins, Perez and Zerah.[34]

Although the root *ybm* appears only once in the book of Ruth,[35] the book in general and the procedure described in chapter 4 in particular involve the subject of our text. Whereas in Genesis 38 the widow Tamar took the initiative, here the mother of the deceased played that role. While Naomi recognized Boaz as a potential *yābām*, the fact that he was a more distant relative of Mahlon (perhaps uncle or cousin) may explain the use of the word *gō'ēl* ("near relative"; 2:20, et passim) instead of *yābām*. The scene in chapter 4 is the opposite of that envisioned in Deuteronomy 25:7–10. Unlike the unwilling *yābām* in our text, Boaz was eager to preserve the family and patrimony of a kinsman. Whereas the sandal ritual in Deuteronomy is cast as a shaming ritual, here the man who defers to Boaz voluntarily removed his shoe and handed it to Boaz (rather than Ruth)—not as an act of shame, but as legal attestation of a redemptive transaction (cf. Ruth 4:7). In the presence of witnesses, Boaz received the legal right to marry Ruth, and in this way secured the line of Elimelech and Mahlon (4:1–13).

---

33. On which see M. Cogan, *I Kings: A New Translation with Introduction and Commentary* (AB 10; New York: Doubleday, 2000), 349.

34. On levirate marriage in this text, see Willis, *Elders of the City*, 253–62. On the levirate marriage in Judaism, see S. Belkin, "Levirate and Agnate Marriage in Rabbinic and Cognate Literature," *JQR* 60 (1970): 275–329.

35. On which see Block, *Judges, Ruth*, 674–75. The root *ybm* occurs in Ruth only in 1:15, where a feminine noun refers to a sister-in-law.

The temptation to cheat in business deals by reducing or enlarging measuring instruments to one's own advantage (vv. 13−16) afflicts every generation. The book of Proverbs raises the issue three times. In 16:11 the sage declares that no one—not even kings—may tinker with balances and scales because Yahweh owns them and establishes the definitions of "honest" instruments.[36] In 20:10 and 23 the sage picks up the Deuteronomic expression of something that "the LORD detests"; but instead of applying the expression to the person who cheats this way, he applies it to the instruments used to cheat others.

The problem seems to have become especially acute in Israel and Judah as their respective dooms neared. In Amos 8:5 the prophet from Tekoa denounced merchants for shrinking the ephah and inflating the shekel and using false scales. A century and a half later, as part of his description of the new Israelite social and spiritual order, with apodictic authority Ezekiel called on princes not to oppress Yahweh's people with false measuring instruments. Borrowing the language of Deuteronomy he demanded the use of "righteous" (*ṣedeq*) scales, ephahs, and baths (Ezek. 45:10−11). Although the New Testament never refers specifically to cheating with false measurements, Paul's use of expressions like "dishonest gain" (1 Tim. 3:8; Titus 1:7) in his list of disqualifications from leadership positions probably includes cheating.

RIGHTEOUSNESS. MANY REJECT THESE and most of Moses' instructions as having no binding authority for Christians, for they are not explicitly reiterated in the New Testament, and in any case the eschatological new Israel of God has been established.[37] However, this approach rejects the authority of Jesus Christ himself, who declared that he did not come to destroy the "law" (read "Torah"), but to fulfill it (Matt. 5:17), and that the proof of covenant commitment (love) to him (the vine) is keeping his "command," which functions as a collective expression for the revealed will of God (John 14:15, 21; 15:10).

It also neutralizes the force of Paul's declaration in 2 Timothy 3:16 that all Scripture is authoritative and effective for training in "righteousness" (*dikaiosynē*), a thoroughly Deuteronomic notion. Although chapter 25 deals

---

36. See B. K. Waltke, *The Book of Proverbs Chapters 15−31* (NICOT; Grand Rapids: Eerdmans, 2005), 18−19.

37. For discussion of the relevance of Old Testament laws for New Testament Christians, see D. I. Block, "Preaching Old Testament Law to New Testament Christians," in *The Gospel According to Moses*, 104−36; idem, "The Grace of Torah," in *How I Love Your Torah, O LORD!* 17−20.

with specific domestic and economic issues that are culturally conditioned, the underlying theological and ethical principles certainly apply to the faith and conduct of the people of God in our day.

Serving the cause of justice. In verses 1 – 3 Moses reiterates the conviction that the function of legal procedures must always be to establish the truth, which means that when they are followed, the guilty will in fact be convicted and the innocent will be acquitted. Any system (including our own) that acquits those known to be guilty or convicts those known to be innocent cannot be considered a just system. When the guilty are acquitted on a technicality and the innocent are condemned because they do not have access to competent defense counsel, justice has not been served.

At the same time, the punishments appropriate to the crimes must be executed. Those responsible must be cautioned against excess on the one hand, and against dehumanization on the other. Even criminals are members of the community and image-bearers of God, whose dignity must be preserved. While we have been quick to point out the abuses of other countries in the misadministration of justice, the exposure of American treatment of Iraqi prisoners at Abu Ghraib demonstrates that no society is immune to the temptation to abuse its captives.[38]

Animals. In verse 4 Moses calls for the humane treatment of domesticated animals. This charge has greatest relevance for farmers and others who use animals for draft purposes, but the principle underlying this statement extends to all involved in the raising of livestock and poultry. Although for economic reasons farmers cannot cave in to maddening and often naïve demands of some organizations that supposedly defend the rights of animals, the members of the community of faith should be exemplary in their fair and considerate treatment of their stock. Urbanites demand cheap meat, but they are removed from the practical need for farmers to make a living and often do not understand the issues involved in raising livestock. However, when for their own pleasure (as in the case of pets) or out of necessity (seeing-eye dogs), they add God's creatures to their households, righteousness demands a commitment to humane care.

Paul takes the call for an unmuzzled ox in a different direction in 1 Corinthians 9:9 and 1 Timothy 5:18. He appeals to the ordinance to defend the right of those who serve the church to derive their living from the work they do in spreading the gospel. He asks the question, "Is it about oxen that God is concerned?" (1 Cor. 9:9). Assuming a negative answer,

---

38. The abuses have been well documented. See, for example, S. Strasser, ed., *The Abu Ghraib Investigations: The Official Independent Panel and Pentagon Reports on the Shocking Prisoner Abuse in Iraq* (Jackson, TN: Public Affairs, 2004).

some argue that his rhetorical question is possible only if "ox" is inter-preted figuratively of human beings.[39] However, this is unnecessary if one interprets Deuteronomy 25:4 within the context of the entire chapter. Like Paul's own statement, Moses' instructions are addressed to human beings, not to animals. Throughout this chapter his concern has been to develop in his hearers, the people of God, a sensitive and considerate disposition, especially toward the vulnerable. Moses' statement concerning the ox fits this agenda perfectly, extending even to animals the theological principle that in God's economy all workers, human or animal, deserve reward for their labor.[40]

The integrity of the family. In verses 5 – 12 Moses charged his people to be conscientious in defending the integrity of the family. This defense takes place at two levels. (1) It involves each household member looking out for the interests of the others. In this context that meant the establishment of the levirate marriage as an institution to ensure the continued existence of each branch of a family tree. A culture that fails to value children as the continuation of the life of their parents will diminish the dignity and joy of parenthood and soon begin to treat them as independent entities that may be disposed of at will. Christians would do well to recover the notion of the extended family as an organic unity, whose health depends on the well-being of each member. (2) At the same time, we must nurture the sense of privilege that attends with parenthood by affirming and encour-aging maternal and paternal instincts in all who come of age. Meanwhile, verses 11 – 12 caution against behavior within the family that is immodest or threatening to the short- and long-term health of its members.

Business dealings. In verses 13 – 16 Moses has appealed to the com-munity of faith to be exemplary in their business dealings. A more relevant issue in the entire book than the call for integrity in all economic transac-tions can scarcely be imagined. Honest and fair calculation of transactions and scrupulous payment of debts should be the hallmark of those who claim to be God's people. The problem exists not only at the highest levels, as in the outrageous thievery of Bernie Madoff, who bilked trusting inves-tors of billions of dollars, but at the local checkout counter of the grocery store, where we may be tempted to overlook a miscalculation by the clerk

39. Cf. F. W. Grosheide, *Commentary on the First Epistle to the Corinthians* (NICNT; Grand Rapids: Eerdmans, 1953), 205.

40. For a helpful discussion of the hermeneutical issues involved, see W. C. Kaiser Jr., "The Current Crisis in Exegesis and the Apostolic Use of Deuteronomy 25:4 in 1 Corin-thians 9:8 – 10," *JETS* 21 (1978): 3 – 18, esp. 11 – 16. Instone-Brewer ("Paul's Literal Inter-pretation of 'Do Not Muzzle the Ox,'" 139 – 56) argues that Paul follows first-century Jews' assumptions that laws mentioning "ox" apply to any kind of servant, human or animal.

in our favor, and in our offices as we fill out our tax forms. Of course the principle does not apply only to mercantile and financial matters; it also applies to the exchange of ideas (e.g., plagiarism). In a society that seems to become more unethical by the day, Christians should stand out for the fidelity and integrity with which they conduct their business.

Deuteronomy 25:17–19

🔥

R emember what the Amalekites did to you along the
way when you came out of Egypt. ¹⁸When you were
weary and worn out, they met you on your journey
and cut off all who were lagging behind; they had no fear of
God. ¹⁹When the LORD your God gives you rest from all the
enemies around you in the land he is giving you to possess as
an inheritance, you shall blot out the memory of Amalek from
under heaven. Do not forget!

INSERTED AT THE END of fourteen chapters of
appeals to righteousness and covenantal fidelity
demonstrated in total devotion to Yahweh and
compassionate commitment to others, verses
17–19 seem out of place. What has this note to do with the preceding? At
best, the reference to Amalekites links this text to 23:3, which bars Ammonites and Moabites from the assembly of Yahweh for ten generations because
they had hired Balaam to curse them. But now Moses reaches back even
further to the Israelites' pre-Sinai encounter with the Amalekites with a seemingly ruthless charge to blot out every memory of them (cf. Ex. 17:14–16).[1]

Stylistically, verses 17–19 do not exhibit the qualities of "law," which
reminds us again to classify Moses' entire second address as pastoral instruction rather than legislation. Here Moses admonishes the people to take
care of some unfinished business. Two imperatives frame this paragraph
(v. 17a; 19c),[2] which divides into two parts almost equal in length. In the
first Moses charges the Israelites to "remember" the Amalekites' past hostilities (vv. 17–18), and in the second he charges them to "blot out" their
memory from human history (v. 19).

The opening appeal to "remember" Amalek is characteristic of Moses'
rhetorical style.[3] He cites three actions by the Amalekites against Israel

---

1. For Israel's history with this people, see Gen. 36:11–12; Ex. 17:8–16; Num. 13:29;
14:25, 43, 14:45; Judg. 3:13; 6:3, 33; 7:12; 10:12; 12:15; 1 Sam. 14–16; Ps. 83:4–9[5–10].

2. The event in mind is narrated in prose form in Ex. 17:8–16.

3. That they were slaves in Egypt (5:15; 15:15; 16:12; 24:18, 22); Yahweh was their God
(6:12; 8:11, 14, 18, 19); his defeat of the Egyptians (7:18; 16:3); his redemption of Israel
(6:12; 8:14; 15:15; 24:18); his revelation and covenant made at Horeb (4:9–10, 23, 31);
specific actions on their behalf (8:18); his care in the desert (8:2); his punishment of Miriam
(24:9); the people's rebellion (9:7).

that demand response. (1) They opportunistically "cut off" the Israelites along the way when they came out of Egypt. The attack signified unprovoked and malicious intervention in Israel's pilgrimage to Horeb for their appointment with Yahweh. (2) The Amalekites committed barbaric and cowardly atrocities. Fearing to engage the Israelites in a frontal attack, they let the Israelites pass by; then, when they were famished and weary, they attacked powerless stragglers at the rear. These probably involved the weak and the sick, who could not keep up with the main camp and proved easy targets for marauders.[4] (3) The Amalekites did not fear God. Although "to fear God" sometimes bears an ethical sense,[5] the expression should not be limited to the ethical sphere. Moses would never speak of the Amalekites fearing Yahweh, but with this comment he suggests the Amalekite attack involved direct interference in the plan of God.[6]

This interpretation may explain Moses' second charge in verse 19. They are to fulfill this charge when Yahweh has given Israel rest from all their enemies and delivered into their hands the land promised them as their grant.[7] When the Cannanites no longer threaten and they live securely in the land, they must wipe out every vestige of Amalekites. The charge adapts a declaration Moses had heard Yahweh himself issue forty years ago (Ex. 17:12—14). However, he transforms the original divine declaration of purpose into a duty: the people are to "to blot out" the "memory" of the Amalekites.[8]

The paragraph ends with a final appeal to the Israelites: "Do not forget!" But the statement is cryptic: Forget what? Grammatically it could refer to what the Amalekites have done to them and what they will eventually do to the Amalekites—though it conflicts with the command to wipe out the memory of this people. It seems best, therefore, to see this command as answering the "remember" at the beginning of the paragraph, in which case the object of "do not forget" is the preceding command to blot out the Amalekites.[9]

---

4. Cf. Tigay, *Deuteronomy*, 237.

5. That is, as "reverence and obedience toward God's commands coupled with respect for the rights and freedoms of strangers" (e.g., Ex. 1:17, 21).

6. Which may explain why he locates the Amalekite attack "along the way when you came out of Egypt," relating it directly to the exodus, rather than "at Rephidim," as in Ex. 17:8.

7. Cf. Deut. 3:18—22 and 12:9—10.

8. The memory of Yahweh's promise/oath is rendered even more indelible by Moses act of building an altar to commemorate the event and naming it "The LORD is my Banner," in recognition of Yahweh's victory (Ex. 17:15—16).

9. The twenty-second century BC inscription of Utuhegal, king of the Sumerian city-state of Uruk (Erech), provides a striking analogue to Moses' invective against the Amalekites. For the text, see D. Frayne, *Sargonic and Gutian Periods (2334—2113 BC)* (RIME 2; Toronto: Univ. of Toronto Press, 1993), 284—85. For brief discussion, see P. D. Stern, *The Biblical Ḥerem: A Window on Israel's Religious Experience* (BJS 211; Atlanta: Scholars , 1991), 70—72.

THE AMALEKITES IN ISRAEL'S history. The Amalekites resurface at several points in Israel's later history. In the book of Judges they appear with other peoples from the surrounding deserts to oppress and harass Israel.[10] Sometime later, following an initial valiant victory over marauding bands of Amalekites,[11] Samuel informed Saul that Yahweh had not forgotten his earlier declaration of intent to wipe out the Amalekites for what they did to Israel (1 Sam. 15:1–3). Yahweh's expression of intent and his command to Saul to settle the Amalekite question allude to our text:

> I will punish the Amalekites for what they did to Israel when they waylaid them as they came up from Egypt. Now go, attack the Amalekites and totally destroy everything that belongs to them. Do not spare them; put to death men and women, children and infants, cattle and sheep, camels and donkeys. (1 Sam. 15:2–3)

Yahweh through Samuel commissioned Saul as the agent through whom both his promise in Exodus 17:14 and Moses' charge in Deuteronomy 25:19 would be fulfilled. The narrative that follows creates the impression that Saul fulfilled his charge, with the notable exception of sparing King Agag.[12] However, David continued to be involved in conflicts with the Amalekites, apparently winning the decisive victory over them while Saul was being defeated by the Philistines.[13]

Although Saul's campaign is characterized as a mission of *ḥērem*, the narrator makes no attempt to link David's campaign either to Yahweh's promise in Exodus 17:14 or Moses' charge in Deuteronomy 25:19. Remarkably, when the person who claimed to have assisted in the death of Saul identified himself as an Amalekite, David had him killed, not because he was an Amalekite, but because he dared to kill Yahweh's anointed (2 Sam. 1:14–16). Except for later references to spoil that David seized from the Amalekites—along with other nations (2 Sam. 8:12; 1 Chron. 18:11)—the Amalekites appear again only in 1 Chronicles 4:43,[14] which notes that in the days of Hezekiah five hundred Simeonites defeated the remnant of

---

10. Judg. 3:13; 6:3, 33; 7:12; 10:12 (cf. also 12:15). They also appear in Ps. 83:7[8]. in a list of Israel's enemies.

11. 1 Sam. 14:48 echoes Judg. 2:16.

12. This led to Yahweh's final rejection of Saul as king (cf. 1 Sam. 28:18).

13. 1 Sam. 27:8; 30:1–20; 2 Sam. 1:1.

14. On this text see G. Knoppers, *1 Chronicles 1–9: A New Translation with Introduction and Commentary* (AB 12; New York: Doubleday, 2004), 370–71.

Amalekite escapees. Apparently the campaign of elimination called for by Moses in Deuteronomy 25:19 had never been fully carried out.

If Haman the Agagite is to be connected to Agag the Amalekite in the book of Esther,[15] this attests to the persistence of remnants of this people. However, it is unclear whether he was an actual descendant of the Amalekite king Agag, or whether Agagite functions as a pejorative appellative for all who hate the Jews.[16]

TO MANY THIS CALL for the extermination of the Amalekites is as troubling as earlier commands to wipe out the Canaanites. It is small comfort that this text seems to reflect a more enlightened ethic than does the narrative account of Exodus 17:14—16. Whereas the narrative calls for their elimination simply because a people had been attacked, here it is grounded in specific ethical considerations. The Amalekites deserve this fate because they violated fundamental principles of warfare: attacking the Israelites from the rear when they were exhausted and famished, and focusing particularly on those lagging behind. Because of their immoral conduct in war they may be rightly condemned.

However, reducing the present prescription to a moral rather than religious or spiritual issue clouds rather than clarifies the problem. Moses insists on eliminating the Amalekites because they defied God, not only by stifling the fear of divinity that is common to all civilized people, but also by daring to interfere with God at a critical moment in the history of salvation. Yahweh had just rescued the Israelites and was leading them to Sinai, where he would formally confirm them as his covenant people. All this was preparatory to delivering into their hands the land of Canaan so they could flourish there and become his agent of blessing to the whole world. Moses hereby in effect declares, "Woe to any who interfere with the plan of God."

While this text speaks eloquently to the issue of the just pursuit of war, it has little to contribute to contemporary debates about theories of just war. Like his instructions regarding the Canaanite nations listed in 7:1, Moses'

---

15. Esth. 3:1, 10; 8:3, 5; 9:24. Note especially 3:10 and 9:24, which identify him as "Haman the Agagite the son of Hammedatha, the enemy of [all] the Jews."

16. The Targum casts its vote in 3:1 in favor of the former by providing a lengthy genealogy of Haman, tracing his descent from Amalek. Similarly Josephus (*Ant.* 11.6.5, 12). On the history of Jewish interpretation of the Amalekite texts, see L. H. Feldman, *"Remember Amalek!" Vengeance, Zealotry, and Group Destruction in the Bible according to Philo, Pseudo Philo, and Josephus* (Cincinnati: Hebrew Union College Press, 2004); A. Sagi, "The Punishment of Amalek in Jewish Tradition: Coping with the Moral Problem," *HTR* 87 (1994): 323–26.

charge regarding the Amalekites is exceptional. Under no circumstances are these policies to be generalized into national policies of genocide or justification for violent expressions of revenge.

While these observations reflect a realistic interpretation of the present text, there is some virtue in interpreting this text paradigmatically. With roots in the identification of Haman as "the Agagite," Jewish interpretive tradition often perceived the Amalekites as symbols of anti-Semitism.[17] More generally, inasmuch as the Amalekite attack interfered with God's mission of mercy to the world through his chosen people, they represent the forces of evil arrayed against the kingdom of light and salvation, and their doom is also decreed. In the meantime, the people of God do battle with all powers and principalities that are hostile to the kingdom of God. They do so not with military armaments or material resources, but with the armor God has provided and marching forth in the strength he provides (Eph. 6:10–20).

---

17. See Sagi, "The Punishment of Amalek in Jewish Tradition," 323–46; J. Levenson, "Is There a Counterpart in the Hebrew Bible to New Testament Antisemitism," *Journal of Ecumenical Studies* 22 (1985): 242–60.

Deuteronomy 26:1–15

W hen you have entered the land the LORD your God is giving you as an inheritance and have taken possession of it and settled in it, ²take some of the firstfruits of all that you produce from the soil of the land the LORD your God is giving you and put them in a basket. Then go to the place the LORD your God will choose as a dwelling for his Name ³and say to the priest in office at the time, "I declare today to the LORD your God that I have come to the land the LORD swore to our forefathers to give us." ⁴The priest shall take the basket from your hands and set it down in front of the altar of the LORD your God. ⁵Then you shall declare before the LORD your God: "My father was a wandering Aramean, and he went down into Egypt with a few people and lived there and became a great nation, powerful and numerous. ⁶But the Egyptians mistreated us and made us suffer, putting us to hard labor. ⁷Then we cried out to the LORD, the God of our fathers, and the LORD heard our voice and saw our misery, toil and oppression. ⁸So the LORD brought us out of Egypt with a mighty hand and an outstretched arm, with great terror and with miraculous signs and wonders. ⁹He brought us to this place and gave us this land, a land flowing with milk and honey; ¹⁰and now I bring the firstfruits of the soil that you, O LORD, have given me." Place the basket before the LORD your God and bow down before him. ¹¹And you and the Levites and the aliens among you shall rejoice in all the good things the LORD your God has given to you and your household.

¹²When you have finished setting aside a tenth of all your produce in the third year, the year of the tithe, you shall give it to the Levite, the alien, the fatherless and the widow, so that they may eat in your towns and be satisfied. ¹³Then say to the LORD your God: "I have removed from my house the sacred portion and have given it to the Levite, the alien, the fatherless and the widow, according to all you commanded. I have not turned aside from your commands nor have I forgotten any of them. ¹⁴I have not eaten any of the sacred portion while I was in mourning, nor have I removed any of it

while I was unclean, nor have I offered any of it to the dead.
I have obeyed the LORD my God; I have done everything you
commanded me. ¹⁵Look down from heaven, your holy dwelling place, and bless your people Israel and the land you have
given us as you promised on oath to our forefathers, a land
flowing with milk and honey."

MOSES CONCLUDES HIS EXPOSITION on the principles of covenant relationship with an exciting
flourish in chapter 26. This chapter divides into
two unequal parts. Exhibiting numerous links
with 12:2 – 28,[1] 26:1 – 15 contains instructions for liturgical expression of
covenant fidelity in the presence of Yahweh. Verses 16 – 19 function as a
formal conclusion to the second major part of the second address (chaps.
12 – 26). The reference to "decrees and laws" in verses 16 and 17 echo 12:1,
framing chapters 12 – 26 as a grand exposition of the laws and regulations.[2]
By placing instructions on cultic worship at the boundaries, Moses issues a
profound theological message: meaningful and acceptable cultic worship
provides the framework for life. Although prescribed direct speech dominates verses 1 – 15, this segment divides into two parts. Verses 1 – 11 focus
on celebrating Yahweh's faithfulness, and verses 12 – 15 on affirming the
worshiper's fidelity to Yahweh when he worships at the central sanctuary.

Celebrating the Faithfulness of God (26:1 – 11)

THESE VERSES OPEN BY setting the context for the instructions that follow:
after the Israelites have entered the land, taken possession of it, and occupied it.[3] The ritual celebrates the triangular Yahweh – Israel – land covenant
relationship. If Israel will respond to Yahweh's gifts of redemption, cov-

---

1. (1) The rituals occur in the land Yahweh gave to Israel (12:10; cf. 26:1, 3, 9, 15); (2)
they occur at the place that Yahweh would choose to establish his name (12:5, 11, 14, 18,
21, 26; cf. 26:2); (3) they occur "before the LORD your God" (12:7, 12, 18; cf. 26:5, 10, 13);
(4) they involve the entire household and the Levite (12:12, 18; cf. 26:11 – 12); (5) they
include presentation of offerings (12:6, 11; cf. 26:2, 10, 12), (6) joyful celebration (12:7,
12, 18; cf. 26:11), (7) and the blessing of Yahweh (12:7, 15; cf. 26:15); (8) their accept-
ability before Yahweh depends on obedience to all that he has commanded (12:11, 14, 28;
cf. 26:13 – 14).

2. These expressions also frame the first half of the second address. Cf. 5:1 and 11:32. Cf.
N. Lohfink, "Die *ḥuqqîm ûmišpāṭîm* im Buch Deuteronomium und ihre Neubegrenzung durch
Dtn 12,1," *Biblica* 70 (1989): 17 – 18.

3. For this triad of expressions see 11:31 and 12:29, though the opening bears the closest
resemblance to 17:14.

enant, and land with grateful obedience to him, the land will yield its produce in abundance.

Verse 1 sets the stage for a series of ritual actions that extends through verse 11. Excluding the embedded speeches that Moses prescribes for the worshipers, the sequence and structure of this ceremony may be highlighted by listing the actions and the actors in a chiastic manner (the following uses pers. trans.):

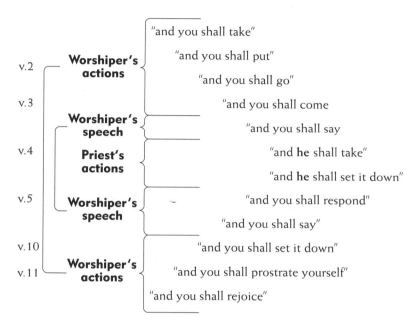

The number of actions (twelve) and the chiastic structure of the text reflect the symmetry of the ritual.[4] Moses' primary intent here is to provide a means by which Israelites may regularly celebrate the goodness Yahweh has lavished first by giving them this good land and then by causing it to yield its produce for their benefit. Responding to the harvest, God's people were to present to Yahweh offerings selected from the first yields of the produce (vv. 2, 10; cf. 18:4).[5]

Neither 18:4 nor the present text specifies when these rituals are to be performed. Since Numbers 28:26a refers to the Festival of Weeks as "the day

4. The chiastic ordering of the material facilitates memorization, on which see D. M. Carr, *Writing on the Tablet of the Heart: Origins of Scripture and Literature* (Oxford: Oxford Univ. Press, 2005), 98–99.

5. On the "firstfruits," see R. O. Rigsby, "First Fruits," *ABD*, 2:796–97; idem, "Firstfruits," *DOTP*, 312–13.

of firstfruits," the offerings envisioned here may have been associated with Pentecost.[6] As in chapter 12, these instructions are addressed to male heads of households (v. 11). While the worshiper's speeches will recognize the corporate benefits of divine grace (vv. 6−10), his personal affirmations employ first person singular verbs (vv. 3, 5, 10). The rituals prescribed in verses 2−11 involve twelve specific verbs, but the actions may be grouped into five phases.

Phase 1: The worshiper's first set of actions (vv. 2−3a). The first phase involves four actions by the worshiper. (1) He is to take some of the first harvestings brought in from his land. Ever mindful of the Israelites' faulty memory (cf. 8:11−18), Moses adds a reminder that the land itself is a gift of Yahweh. (2) The worshiper is to put the offering in a container (NIV "basket"). (3) The worshiper is to go to the place that Yahweh has chosen to establish his name.[7] (4) The worshiper is to "come" to the priest who is in office at the time (cf. 17:9). Since the offering is to be presented before the altar of Yahweh (v. 4), Moses must have in mind the high priest, who receives the gifts on behalf of his colleagues (cf. 18:1−5) and on God's behalf. This may account for the shift from "go" in verse 2 to "come" in verse 3. The worshiper is portrayed as a person who has accepted the invitation to Yahweh's presence offered in chapter 12.

Phase 2: The worshiper's first declaration (v. 3b). The remainder of verse 3 shifts attention from prescribed ritual actions to ritual declaration. With this declaration, the worshiper recognizes the priest "in office at that time" (v. 3a) as both a symbol of divine presence[8] and the official witness to his declaration. His reference to Yahweh as "your [i.e., the priest's] God" does not mean that he is not the farmer's God as well. Rather, it suggests respect before a superior.[9] With this declaration he acknowledges that his firstfruits represent concrete evidence of Yahweh's fidelity to the oath he swore to the ancestors. Whereas outside Israel harvest festivals celebrated the fertility of the land, here the occasion is transformed into a commemoration of Yahweh's fidelity to a greater agenda — the gift of the land itself.

Phase 3: The high priest's actions (v. 4). The priest's response to the worshiper's offering occupies the central position in this sequence of ritual acts. Having heard the farmer's declaration, he receives the gift on Yahweh's behalf.[10] His response turns the tables, acknowledging "the altar of the LORD

---

6. For discussion of the Festival of Weeks, see comments on 16:9−12.

7. On the meaning of this phrase, see comments on 12:5 and 11.

8. The second declaration (vv. 5−10) is made "before the LORD your God."

9. Cf. Deut. 18:7; also Lev. 21:7; 1 Sam. 15:15; 2 Sam. 14:17; 2 Kings 19:4.

10. This is the last of only three references to "the altar" in Deuteronomy (cf. 12:27; 16:21). The paucity of references to any tabernacle or temple appurtenances accords with the overall concern of the book to present a theology of worship rather than to serve as a manual for worship. See also 33:10.

your God" (i.e., the God of the worshiper). The priest's actions declare symbolically that Yahweh has accepted the worshiper's expression of devotion.[11]

Phase 4: The worshiper's second declaration (vv. 5 – 10a). Having observed the priest's actions, the worshiper is to recite a summary history of his people's experience with Yahweh. While Moses introduces the verbal declaration with a formal command, the particle "and now" in verse 10a signals a shift in addressee from the priest to Yahweh, suggesting that the credo (at least vv. 5b–9) is to be recited "before the LORD," not to the priests.[12] Many have recognized that what follows is an early creedal statement (cf. 6:20–25; 11:2–7), cast in celebrative prose, summarizing the Israelites' basic beliefs concerning their origins.[13] Structurally this speech is divided into three parts: (1) an opening statement concerning the social and/or economic status of Israel's ancestor (v. 5b); (2) a survey of Israel's history (vv. 5c–9); and (3) a declaration by the worshiper concerning his present offering (v. 10).

(1) *The status of the ancestor (v. 5b).* The opening statement, "My father was a wandering Aramean," is alliterative and simple, but extremely difficult, with every element up for discussion. First, who is "my father," and in what sense could he be considered an Aramaean? Because elsewhere in Deuteronomy Moses always names the three patriarchs together,[14] earlier statements offer little help in identifying the "father." However, since the narratives of Genesis associate all three patriarchs with Aram (Gen. 11:31; 12:4; 28:1–7; 31:16),[15] "my father" may function as a collective, referring to all three ancestors.[16] In any case, the multiplication of the nation

---

11. The threefold use of the phrase *lipnê yhwh* ("before Yahweh") in vv. 5a and 10b suggests the real presence of Yahweh and the worshiper's awareness of his proximity, which is concretized by "before the altar of the LORD" in verse 4b. See further Wilson, *Out of the Midst of the Fire,"* 187.

12. Cf. v. 3, which has the worshiper making the declaration "to the LORD."

13. G. von Rad ("The Form Critical Problem of the Hexateuch," in *From Genesis to Chronicles: Explorations in Old Testament Theology* [trans. E. Trueman Dicken; ed. K. C. Hanson; Minneapolis: Fortress, 2005], 1–58; idem, *Old Testament Theology* [trans. D. M. G. Stalker; New York: Harper & Row, 1962], 1:121–28) referred to this utterance as "the little historical credo." Biddle (*Deuteronomy*, 382–83) and Nelson (*Deuteronomy*, 308) question his thesis that it is much more ancient than its Deuteronomic literary context.

14. Deut. 1:8; 6:10; 9:27; 29:13[12]; 30:20; 34:4. The final poems mention Jacob alone: 32:9; 33:4, 10, 28.

15. The identification of the site of Jacob and Laban's treaty in Gen. 31:47–49 by Hebrew and Aramaic names, Galeed and Jegar Sahadutha—both of which mean "heap [of stones]," reflects the Aramaean culture of Haran. N. Krause (*"Arami oved avi*: Deuteronomy 26:5," *JBQ* 25/1 [1997]: 31–34) identifies the Aramaean specifically as Abraham.

16. Verse 7 refers to "the LORD, the God of our fathers." Despite Num. 20:14–16, which mentions the descent to Egypt of "our fathers," to conceive of the ancestors of the twelve tribes as Aramaean is difficult. Nevertheless, it is clear from Gen. 34:16 that Cannanites (the people of Shechem) viewed them as aliens.

represents Yahweh's fulfillment of his promise repeated to Abraham, Isaac, and Jacob.[17]

But the modifier "wandering" remains a riddle. Based on the range of meanings of the root of this word, the clause could be translated, "an Aramaean on the point of death."[18] However, since the rest of this credo emphasizes the patriarchs' homelessness rather than their threatened existence, the word may refer to their status as aliens, as reflected explicitly in the verb *gûr* ("to sojourn, live as an alien"), which is used of all three patriarchs.[19] Nonetheless, since both insecurity and wandering are associated with the patriarchs (cf. Gen. 20:11 – 13; Ps. 105:12 – 13), it is difficult to decide whether the term translated "wandering" means "perishing" or "wandering."[20] The ambiguity is probably intentional; when ancient Israelites recited this credo in Hebrew, they perceived the full range of meanings of the word.

(2) *A survey of the history of the ancestor and his descendants (vv. 5c – 9).* The bulk of this credo consists of a summary of the life of the ancestor and the fate and fortunes of his descendants (cf. 4:32 – 40; 6:20 – 25; 11:2 – 7; Num. 20:14 – 16). Moses recalls four stages in Israel's early history.

(a) *Stage 1: Israel's sojourn and growth in Egypt (v. 5c-e).* With three words Moses summarizes the remarkable shift of Israelite fortunes in Egypt (cf. Ex. 1:1 – 7). The ancestor began his sojourn in Egypt as the head of a small clan,[21] but there his household was transformed into a great, strong, and numerous nation.[22] The first clause of verse 5 recalls 10:22, where Moses clarified "a few people" as "seventy persons," and "a great nation, powerful and and numerous"[23] as a population as numerous as the stars of the sky.

---

17. Gen. 15:5; 22:17; 26:4; Ex. 32:13; Deut. 1:10, 22.

18. Thus *DCH*, 1:99. Cf. Gen. 41:50 – 57; 42:1 – 5; 43:1 – 2, 8; 45:7. For various interpretations of the expression, see J. G. Janzen, "The 'Wandering Aramaean' Reconsidered," *VT* 44 (1994): 359 – 75 ["perishing from hunger"]; R. C. Steiner, "The 'Aramean of Deuteronomy 26:5: *Peshat* and *Derash*," in *Tehillah le-Moshe: Biblical and Judaic Studies in Honor of Moshe Greenberg* (ed. M. Cogan, B. L. Eichler, and J. H. Tigay; Winona Lake, IN: Eisenbrauns, 1997), 127 – 38; K. H. Zetterholm, *Portrait of a Villain: Laban the Aramean in Rabbinic Literature* (Interdisciplinary Studies in Ancient Culture and Religion 2; Leuven: Peeters, 2002), 47 — 87, esp. 79 – 87.

19. (1) Abraham: Gen. 12:10; 17:8; 20:1; 21:23, 34; 23:4; 35:27; Ex. 6:4. (2) Isaac: Gen. 26:3; 35:27; 37:1; Ex. 6:4. (3) Jacob: Gen. 28:4; 32:4[5]; 47:9; Ex. 6:4; Ps. 105:12 (= 1 Chron. 16:19), 23.

20. See further, A. R. Millard, "A Wandering Aramean," *JNES* 39 (1980): 153 – 55.

21. Cf. Gen. 12:10, which is echoed in Isa. 52:4.

22. In fulfillment of God's promise to Jacob in Gen. 46:3. The promise has its roots in Gen. 12:2.

23. The triadic expression, "a great, mighty and numerous nation" (pers. trans.) expresses the superlative degree, adapting the emphatic verbal declaration from Ex. 1:7 (cf. Num. 14:12; Deut. 9:14).

(b) *Stage 2: The Egyptian oppression and enslavement (v. 6).* Israel's numerical growth created a crisis for their Egyptian hosts (Ex. 1:8 – 14), who responded by treating the descendants of the ancestor badly and afflicting them with harsh service (cf. Ex. 1:14; 6:9). By switching to the first person plural Moses draws the worshiper and all who hear this confession into the history and fate of the ancestors, particularly the oppression described in Exodus 1.

(c) *Stage 3: Israel's cry to Yahweh and Yahweh's attention (v. 7).* Moses' summary of the Israelites' response to the Egyptian bondage seems more positive than Exodus 2:23 – 25, where the narrator portrayed the cry simply as a cry of distress, which Yahweh happened to hear. This statement suggests the Israelites actually cried out to Yahweh. Yahweh's response to the plight of the wandering Aramaean's descendants is captured with two verbs: Yahweh "heard" their voice, and he "saw" their misery, trouble, and oppression (cf. 4:7 – 8; Ex. 3:7).

(d) *Stage 4: Yahweh's actions on Israel's behalf (vv. 8 – 9).* Echoing Exodus 3:7 – 10 and repeating five of the seven expressions he had used in Deuteronomy 4:34, Moses invites Israelites to celebrate annually Yahweh's past intervention on their behalf.[24] Anticipating the imminent fulfillment of the promise of land to the ancestors and the creedal nature of this passage, Moses describes Yahweh's actions in the past tense (v. 9). If verse 8 had celebrated the magnitude of Yahweh's deliverance by echoing 4:34, this statement celebrates Yahweh's magnanimity in giving the land by echoing earlier descriptions of the land.[25]

This credo exhibits a remarkable historical perspective. In the divine scheme, Egypt played a positive role, functioning as an incubator in which this handful of people could become a nation whose population is now as a numerous as the stars of heaven (Deut. 10:22) and could emerge in the fullness of time (cf. Gen. 15:13 – 16). Viewed positively, the oppression represented the nation's birth pangs, precipitating their separation from their Egyptian hosts (cf. Ps. 105:23 – 38).

(3) *A declaration of the worshiper concerning his offering (v. 10a).* The particle "and now," followed by "look/behold" (not represented in NIV), signals a shift from the past to the worshiper's present ritual performance (v. 10a). Moses hereby calls on the worshiper to speak directly to Yahweh, to declare his gratitude, and to acknowledge Yahweh's gracious provision, symbolized by the container of firstfruits he has brought. Whereas the summary of

---

24. On the meaning of the expressions used in verse 8 to describe Yahweh's victory, see comments on 4:34.

25. First heard in Ex. 3:8, this is the middle of six occurrences of "a land flowing with milk and honey" in Deuteronomy: 6:3; 11:9; 26:9, 15; 27:3; 31:20.

Yahweh's past actions had employed the first person plural, now he speaks as an individual and as the head of a household. With the shift he declares his personal participation in the nation's history, and by giving thanks for the land from which the firstfruits have come, he transforms an annual fertility celebration into a celebration of a historical event: Yahweh's gift of the land to Israel.

Phase 5: The worshiper's actions (vv. 10b–11). The final phase of this ritual (v. 10b) involves actions by the worshiper: He is to set the basket with the firstfruits before Yahweh, and then in a gesture of homage and submission prostrate himself before him. Having done so, he is to invite his entire household, as well as Levites and aliens from his town, to join him in celebrating all the benefactions Yahweh has lavished on them. Like the pilgrimages described in 12:5–12, this is to be a joyful event, presumably involving a meal eaten at the sanctuary in the presence of Yahweh with the entire household, as well as with Levites and aliens whom the worshiper has invited to accompany him to the sanctuary (cf. 12:7, 12, 18; 14:26–27; 16:11, 14).

Affirming Fidelity to the Covenant (26:12–15)

WHILE VERSES 12–15 exhibit many links with the preceding, the focus shifts from Yahweh's faithfulness to Israel to the worshiper's fidelity to Yahweh. Together these two rituals represent the two sides of the coin of covenant relationship: thanksgiving for the privilege (vv. 1–11) and scrupulous fulfillment of the responsibilities (vv. 12–15). This text divides into two parts, describing prerequisites to (v. 12) and the nature of (vv. 13–15) acceptable verbal worship.

(1) *The prerequisite to acceptable confessional worship (v. 12).* Even though verse 12 opens with a reference to the tithe, the primary concern here is the ritual to be performed in the presence of Yahweh when the tithe ordinance has been duly obeyed.[26] Moses' identification of the third year as "the year of the tithe" assumes familiarity with his earlier instructions (14:22–29).[27] However, it is not clear whether this "year of the tithe" was the same year for every household, or was established by communal decision, or whether each household kept its own calendar. The logistical problem of accommodating thousands of worshipers at one time at the central sanctuary at the end of the agricultural year argues for the latter.

---

26. For the tithe in the book, see 12:6, 11, 17; 14:22–27.

27. Echoes of 14:28–29 are clear: (1) the scope: "a tenth of all your produce"; (2) the list of benefactors: Levites, aliens, the fatherless, and widows; (3) the benefit for the poor: "so that they may eat in your towns and be satisfied."

Like the actions and the recitation of the "little historical credo" in verses 1 – 11, the declaration prescribed in verses 13 – 15 is to be recited "in the presence of the LORD your God." Though some have argued that this ritual was to be performed at local sanctuaries (cf. 14:28 – 29), the absence of a reference to a competing place and the literary links between verses 1 – 11 and 12 – 15[28] argue for the central sanctuary as the place where this ritual transpires.[29]

This is not to say the town where the farmer lived was out of the picture. Having contributed his tithe to the marginalized at the gate (v. 12b; cf. 14:28 – 29), every third year the farmer was to go to the central sanctuary for a special ritual performed before Yahweh. Based on his confession in verse 14, it seems that he would have eaten some of it in the meantime, though most would have been given to the poor. The ambiguity seems intentional, to prevent the hearer from simplistically equating this ritual with the actions called for in chapter 14.

Syntactically the temporal clauses carry on to the end of the verse,[30] which suggests that Moses' purpose here is to specify the context of the triennial ritual in verses 13 – 15. The ritual takes place after the act of kindness and is not strictly a part of it. After Israelite farmers have demonstrated covenantal loyalty to Yahweh by taking care of the poor, they are to make a pilgrimage to the central sanctuary and perform the verbal ritual that follows. By linking the triennial tithe to the ritual at the central shrine, Moses reminds his people that care for the marginalized is not merely a noble humanitarian issue; it is expressive of one's covenant relationship with Yahweh.

(2) *The nature of acceptable confessional worship (vv. 13 – 15).* The beginning of the verbal liturgy may be interpreted as a "covenantal code of honor" consisting of nine affirmations, arranged in an A B A pattern; the first and last pairs are cast as affirmations of actions the worshiper has performed, while the middle five consist of negative statements identifying

---

28. The cultic action of verses 12 – 15 exhibits significant links with both verses 1 – 11 and chapter 12: (1) the context (in the land Yahweh has given to Israel: 12:10; cf. 26:1, 3, 9, 15); (2) the divine host ("before the LORD your God": 12:7, 12, 18; cf. 26:5, 10, 13); (3) the nature (presentation of offerings: 12:6, 11; cf. 26:2, 10, 12); (4) the participants (the entire household, Levites, aliens, orphans, and widows: 12:12, 18; cf. 26:1 – 12, 15); (5) the foundation (Yahweh's blessing: 12:7, 15; cf. 26: 15); (7) the human prerequisite to acceptable service (obedience to all that Yahweh has commanded: 12:11, 14, 28; cf. 26:13 – 14); (8) the characterization of offerings as "holy" (12:26; 26:13).

29. For discussion of the options and full defense of this view, see I. Wilson, "Central Sanctuary or Local Settlements? The Location of the Triennial Tithe Declaration (Dtn 26,13 – 15)," *ZAW* 120 (2008): 323 – 40.

30. As in NRSV, NJPSV, ESV; contra NIV.

prohibited behaviors from which he has desisted. The alternation of pairs of specific and general statements reflects the thrust of the Torah of Moses as a whole; far from advocating merely external conformity to set stipulations, he calls for wholehearted grasping of the spirit of covenant relationship, in both its horizontal and vertical dimensions. Although the context of this ritual is the triennial tithe, the declaration never mentions the tithe by name. Instead the opening line refers to this offering as "the sacred [gift]," and the subsequent specific declarations retain this focus with the retrospective pronoun "it."[31] Gifts donated directly to Yahweh are holy, but what farmers donate to take care of the needy in their towns and villages is also holy. After all, they too are images of God (Prov. 14:31; 17:5).

The first declaration involves a strong verb "to remove," used elsewhere in Deuteronomy only of purging evil or bloodguilt from the land.[32] The word reinforces the notion expressed by "to finish" in verse 12a, that the farmer has scrupulously set aside one tenth of all his produce. Echoing verse 12, the second declaration lists the beneficiaries of the worshiper's generosity. The third and fourth declarations perceive the commands as moral territory whose boundaries are defined by God. Here charity toward the poor is seen as representative of compliance with the covenantal stipulations as a whole (cf. 14:28 – 29). With the fourth declaration the worshiper affirms he has taken into account all the commands, though like "you shall give it" in verse 12, the absence of an object on "I have not forgotten [them]" may suggest it is the marginalized rather than the commands that are not forgotten.

With the fifth to the seventh declarations the worshiper's focus shifts from the function and the beneficiaries of the tithe to their proper handling. These statements imply that once a gift had been designated as an offering for the deity, its sanctity must be scrupulously guarded.[33] Moses anticipates three potential sources of defilement, all associated with death. Although many interpret these declarations against the widespread ancient Near Eastern belief that the deceased continued to exert influence

---

31. The tithe is holy because it belongs to Yahweh (Lev. 27:30).

32. "Evil": 13:5[6]; 17:7, 12; 19:19; 21:21; 22:21, 22, 24; 24:7; "bloodguilt": 19:13; 21:9.

33. For Hittite instructions guarding the sanctity of cattle reserved for deity, see *ANET*, 210b-c.

34. Most commentators see here allusions to some such practice (Tigay, *Deuteronomy*, 244; Christensen, *Deuteronomy 21:20 – 34:12*, 642), or to sacrifices to a chthonic deity like Molek (McConville, *Deuteronomy*, 381) or Baal, who bears the epithet "the Dead One" and appears in the Ugaritic myths as a dying and rising god (Craigie, *Deuteronomy*, 323; Merrill, *Deuteronomy*, 336).

on the living after they had died,[34] as in 14:1, reading (lit.) "on account of the dead" is preferred, suggesting the mourning rites defile and disqualify a worshiper from entrance into the presence of Yahweh.[35] These three declarations are less concerned with ensuring the well-being of the poor than with protecting the integrity of the triennial tithe to be presented to Yahweh.

The last two declarations are general in nature. The eighth echoes Exodus 19:5 – 6, suggesting the ritual was to be used as an occasion for personal covenant renewal.[36] With the ninth statement the worshiper acknowledges he is a vassal of Yahweh and declares that he has obeyed Yahweh fully. Locating these instructions at the end of the second address invites readers to interpret this ritual as a token confession of fidelity to the covenant as a whole.

The ritual concludes with a prayer (v. 15), consisting of a five-word request for Yahweh's attention, and a longer and more complex request for his blessing. The verb "to look down" perceives Yahweh as looking out from "your holy dwelling place," that is, from "heaven." By adding "from heaven," the ritual highlights a fundamental mystery of Deuteronomic theology: How can an earthly worshiper be "in the presence of the LORD" (v. 13) and expect Yahweh to hear from heaven? Whereas Israel's neighbors answered the question by erecting statues of the deities in their temples,[37] the present request that Yahweh look down from heaven recalls the use of this verb with God as subject elsewhere (Pss. 14:2; 53:2[3]; 102:19[20]; Lam. 3:50), and accords with the actions he performs "from heaven" (Deut. 4:36) and throughout the Old Testament.[38]

The worshiper's plea for Yahweh to observe *him* from heaven is motivated by a desire for his blessing "on your people Israel." After all, the worshiper is part of the greater entity, Yahweh's covenant nation. He completes the relational triangle by extending the scope of the blessing to the land

---

35. Thus M. Luther, *Luther's Works*, vol. 9, *Lectures on Deuteronomy* (ed. J. Pelikan; Saint Louis: Concordia, 1960), 254; Keil, *Pentateuch*, 3:428. So also more recently B. B. Schmidt, *Israel's Beneficent Dead: Ancestor Cult and Necromancy in Ancient Israelite Religion and Tradition* (Winona Lake, IN: Eisenbrauns, 1996), 190–200.

36. This connection to Ex. 19:5–6 is reinforced by the links with vv. 16–19 below.

37. For a discussion of the way physical objects were transformed into what were perceived to be efficacious images in Assyria, see C. Walker and M. B. Dick, "The Induction of the Cult Image in Ancient Mesopotamia: The Mesopotamian *mîs pî* Ritual," in *Born in Heaven, Made on Earth: The Creation of the Cult Image in the Ancient Near East* (ed. Michael B. Dick; Winona Lake, IN: Eisenbrauns, 1999), 55–122.

38. God hears (2 Chron. 6:21, 23, 25, 30, 33, 35, 39; 7:1, 14; Neh. 9:27–28), speaks (Ex. 20:22; Neh. 9:13), calls (Gen. 21:17; 22:11, 15), thunders [//gives his voice] (2 Sam. 22:14), and his voice falls from heaven (Dan. 4:31).

(cf. v. 9).[39] Although the land is indeed a "good land,"[40] the people are still dependent on Yahweh to bless them and the land (cf. 28:1–14; 33:13–16).

ISRAEL'S HISTORY OF FORGETTING. Despite the creedal nature of this text, specific allusions in later texts are difficult to identify. Indeed, the ritual prescribed here seems to have been "a custom more honour'd in the breach than the observance."[41] This is evident in how quickly the Israelites forgot the favors Yahweh had lavished on them—not only his deliverance of the ancestors from their slavery in Egypt and his gift of the land,[42] but also his blessing the work of their hands in providing crops and flocks and herds. As if ingratitude were not enough, they quickly defected to Baal and the other fertility gods of the Canaanites.

Israelite history is a history of forgetting to give thanks. The people came to take their salvation for granted, their occupation of the land as an unconditional entitlement, and their prosperity as a divine obligation. But Amos reminded his generation that prosperity was not a divine right. On the contrary, because of their rebellion, Yahweh himself caused famines in the land, withholding rain, sending in scorching winds, and calling for insect plagues to devour the crops. Still the people did not return to him (Amos 4:6–9). And 150 years later, even as Nebuchadnezzar's armies attacked the walls of Jerusalem, the people of Judah clung to the promises of their divine patron, having forgotten that with the privilege of covenant relationship come the responsibilities of giving thanks to God for his abundant favors and of showing mercy to others.

When David organized the national religious observances, he appointed Asaph and his brothers (1 Chron. 16:7) and Heman and Jeduthun (16:41) and all kinds of musicians (25:3; cf. 2 Chron. 5:13; 7:6) to lead the congregation in thanksgiving and praise, a pattern followed by other kings as well.[43] This top-down organization of temple worship is inspiring, but our text envisions a spirit of gratitude rising from the ground and from the people. There is no substitute for personal praise of God for mercies that he has lavished on individual households and on the nation as a whole.

---

39. As elsewhere, the reference is primarily to the covenant that Yahweh made with the patriarchs (1:8; 30:20; 34:4), but the oath had been reiterated to the nation that came out of Egypt (Ex. 6:8; 13:11; Num. 14:16; Ezek. 20:6).

40. See 1:35; 3:25; 4:21, 22; 6:18; 8:7, 10; 9:6; 11:17.

41. From William Shakespeare, *Hamlet*, Act 1, Scene 4, lines 7–16.

42. Cf. Judg. 2:2; 6:8–10.

43. Jehoshaphat (2 Chron. 20:21); Hezekiah (30:22; 31:2); Manasseh (33:16).

This principle carries over into the New Testament. In Romans 1:21 Paul declares that the first step in the slide into apostasy is refusal to honor God with thanksgiving. But in 2 Corinthians 9:5 – 15 he lays down the principles of Christian charity:

1. The blessings one receives from God are proportional to one's generosity.
2. True generosity is an individual matter, requiring no legislation.
3. God loves those who give spontaneously and freely.
4. God's blessing is guaranteed for those who are generous.
5. Generosity is not simply a matter of supplying the needs of the poor; God accepts it as an expression of thanksgiving to him.
6. Confession of the gospel of Christ accompanied by acts of obedience to God will cause observers to praise him for the giver's generosity.

In later centuries, if the Israelites remembered the rituals of fellowship and thanksgiving, they tended to view them sacramentally, as though God was obligated to accept their worship irrespective of the condition of their hearts, the nature of their lives, and their disposition toward others. Amos portrays the sanctimonious worship of the people of the northern kingdom with bitter sarcasm:

> "Go to Bethel and sin;
>> go to Gilgal and sin yet more.
> Bring your sacrifices every morning,
>> your tithes every three years.
> Burn leavened bread as a thank offering
>> and brag about your freewill offerings —
> boast about them, you Israelites,
>> for this is what you love to do,"
>>>> declares the Sovereign LORD. (Amos 4:4 – 5)

Isaiah describes Yahweh's attitude toward such empty observances with particular poignancy:

> Hear the word of the LORD,
>> you rulers of Sodom;
> listen to the law [read "Torah"] of our God,
>> you people of Gomorrah!
> "The multitude of your sacrifices —
>> what are they to me?" says the LORD.
> "I have more than enough of burnt offerings,
>> of rams and the fat of fattened animals;

I have no pleasure
in the blood of bulls and lambs and goats.
When you come to appear before me,
who has asked this of you,
this trampling of my courts?
Stop bringing meaningless offerings!
Your incense is detestable to me.
New Moons, Sabbaths and convocations—
I cannot bear your evil assemblies.
Your New Moon festivals and your appointed feasts
my soul hates.
They have become a burden to me;
I am weary of bearing them.
When you spread out your hands in prayer,
I will hide my eyes from you;
even if you offer many prayers,
I will not listen.
Your hands are full of blood;
wash and make yourselves clean.
Take your evil deeds
out of my sight!
Stop doing wrong,
learn to do right!
Seek justice,
encourage the oppressed.
Defend the cause of the fatherless,
plead the case of the widow. (Isa. 1:10–17)

This problem also carries over into the New Testament. Jesus chided the scribes and Pharisees for tithing mint and dill and cumin, but forgetting the weightier matters of Torah, that is, pursuing justice and mercy and faithfulness (Matt. 23:23). Indeed Luke's version contrasts tithing mint and rue and every herb with neglecting justice and the love of God—that is, embodying the love of God in acts of genuine charity toward the poor (Luke 11:42).

ACCEPTABLE WORSHIP. THIS PASSAGE offers Christians today helpful and necessary information on the nature and forms of acceptable worship. (1) True worship is focused on Yahweh. Not surprisingly this text leaves no space for the worship of any other deity. All that the Israelites are and have they owe to him. This is true not only of the daily sustenance they receive from the fruit of the ground, but especially of their status with Yahweh. The Israelites represented the community of the redeemed, who had received the land as a gracious gift from their divine Redeemer.

(2) God's people are a thankful people. This text reminds readers of every age of the importance of specific celebrations devoted to thanksgiving. But true thanksgiving recognizes that God is much more than a fertility deity who provides for his people in the annual cycle of seedtime and harvest. Yahweh's rescue of Israel from the bondage of Egypt was paradigmatic of our redemption from the slavery of sin and our rescue from the kingdom of darkness through the death and resurrection of Jesus Christ. Through the year our Savior has blessed the work of our hands, our minds, and even our technological instruments. It is

> the indispensable duty of all Nations, not only to offer up their supplications to **ALMIGHTY GOD**, the Giver of all good, for his gracious assistance in a time of distress, but also in a solemn and public manner to give him praise for his goodness in general, and especially for great and signal interpositions of his providence in their behalf.[44]

How much more so should this be true of Christians. While we caution against identifying this or any other country as the twenty-first-century heir to Yahweh's favors toward Israel, and we abhor the wars fought against the aboriginal peoples of North America by the first European settlers, we cannot fault the impulse reflected in the "Thanksgiving Proclamation" of 1782, setting aside "a day of solemn **THANKSGIVING to GOD** for all his mercies," and recommending "all ranks, to testify to their gratitude to **GOD** for his goodness, by a cheerful obedience of his laws, and by promoting, each in his station, and by his influence, the practice of true and undefiled religion, which is the great foundation of public prosperity and national happiness." The time has come for God's people to give credit where credit is due, and restore the spiritual dimensions of what has become a secular holiday. Failure to give thanks represents an early stage in the skid to apostasy (cf. Rom. 1:21), and placing one's trust in any other god is the height of ingratitude.[45]

---

44. Excerpted from the "Thanksgiving Proclamation," of the United States Congress in Philadelphia, October 11, 1782, establishing Thursday, November 28 as a day of national thanksgiving. The document is accessible at www.loc.gov/teachers/classroommaterials/presentationsandactivities/presentations/thanksgiving/ (accessed November 28, 2011).
45. See further, R. L. Christensen, "Deuteronomy 26:1–11," *Int* 49 (1995): 59–62.

(3) Through the liturgy prescribed here Moses offers a profoundly holistic approach to issues of faith and life. The contrast between this verbal confession and prevailing patterns in the evangelical church are stark. This text recognizes that devotion to God is demonstrated, not by lip service, but by concrete acts of obedience to the revealed will of God. Had this liturgy been designed today, the prescribed declaration would probably have been "I love you, Lord," or "I worship you, Lord." However, such verbal utterances ring hollow if they do not arise from lips of those who have accepted the path of radical discipleship.

(4) Although fidelity to Yahweh may be demonstrated generally by obedience to all his commands, this triennial tithe provides a true and concrete test of covenantal loyalty. God's people are distinguished by the care they take of those who are marginalized. But their motivation for doing so is not a legalistic sense of duty or obligation, but a recognition that how one operates horizontally, especially how one treats the deprived, is a barometer of the health of the vertical relationships (cf. Prov. 14:31; 17:5).

(5) The concluding confession reminds us of the importance of scrupulous respect for the boundary between the sacred and the profane. Offerings set aside for divine use may not be confiscated for personal consumption, even if the context of the action is ethically and customarily legitimate. Yahweh takes no delight in contaminated or partial gifts.

(6) In concluding these ritual instructions with a petition for divine blessing, Moses recognizes the symbiotic relationship between faith and obedience. True faith is demonstrated by active obedience on the one hand, and by committing ourselves to the favor of God on the other. This liturgy reverses the order expressed by John H. Sammis in the lyrics of the well-known gospel song, "Trust and Obey." God is not to be confused with the genii in Aladdin's lamp, at the service and disposal of any who address him, irrespective of the condition of one's heart or the shape of one's life. Apart from obedience, God's people have no right to expect his blessing.

(7) Finally, this liturgy recognizes a proper balance between the individual and the community. While fidelity to the covenant is demonstrated by the obedience of the individual, fidelity to the covenant also involves a primary concern for the well-being of the community. The liturgist who follows the paradigm established here will quickly move from private and personal confessions of sin and fidelity to prayers for the body.

Deuteronomy 26:16–19

T he LORD your God commands you this day to follow these decrees and laws; carefully observe them with all your heart and with all your soul. [17]You have declared this day that the LORD is your God and that you will walk in his ways, that you will keep his decrees, commands and laws, and that you will obey him. [18]And the LORD has declared this day that you are his people, his treasured possession as he promised, and that you are to keep all his commands. [19]He has declared that he will set you in praise, fame and honor high above all the nations he has made and that you will be a people holy to the LORD your God, as he promised.

THE SIGNIFICANCE OF THIS short paragraph within the flow of Deuteronomy is out of all proportion to its length.[1] These four verses summarize key theological issues of the book and provide a hinge between Moses' lengthy exposition of the specific stipulations and his recitation of the consequences for the nation of their response in chapter 28. Whereas verses 1–15 of this chapter had looked forward to the time when Israel would be well-established in the land, with the opening phrase "this day" in verse 16 Moses refocuses his hearers' attention on the present moment of decision.[2] Although elsewhere the participle construction with "commanding [you]" always has Moses as the subject, for the first time Yahweh issues the commands.[3] Moses hereby reminds his congregation that while he has been speaking, they have actually been hearing the voice of Yahweh their God.

The reference to "these decrees and laws" (haḥuqqîm wᵉhammišpāṭîm) links this verse with earlier combinations of these terms.[4] Together with the

---

1. For detailed study of this text and its function, see S. Guest, "Deuteronomy 26:16–19 as the Central Focus of the Covenantal Framework of Deuteronomy" (Ph.D. diss., The Southern Baptist Theological Seminary, 2009).

2. As with the other 61 occurrences of hayyôm, this expression highlights the "emphatic contemporaneity" that pervades the entire book (thus von Rad, From Genesis to Chronicles, 23).

3. This occurs elsewhere only in Ex. 34:11, where the statement is also contextualized with hayyôm ("today").

4. See comments on 4:1 and 4:45.

verbs "to keep" (*šāmar*) and "to do, practice" (*ʿāśâ*, NIV "carefully observe"), this pair of substantives links this statement stylistically and thematically with 12:1, creating a corresponding bookend at the end of Moses' exposition of specific covenantal issues.

The second part of verse 16 functions as Moses' pastoral exhortation to take seriously the previous statement. The call to "observe" the will of Yahweh with one's whole heart and being represents a practical application of the Shema in 6:4. With this ending Moses reminds his audience that a satisfactory relationship with Yahweh is not expressed merely by creedal confessions or by external conformity to the laws; it requires commitment to doing the will of their covenant Lord.

The repetition of "this day" in verse 17 sets verses 17 – 19 apart from verse 16. Whereas "this day" in verse 16 had formally signaled the conclusion of Moses' exposition of the terms of Yahweh's covenant, by repeating the word in verse 17 he signals the formal incorporation of the Torah that he has proclaimed. Both the syntax and the content of verses 17 – 19 are striking. In keeping with the general tone of the second address, Moses emphasizes that obedience to Yahweh is not to be driven merely by the sense of duty but by keen awareness of the special nature of their relationship. In so doing, he alludes to a formal juridical procedure that he has apparently supervised in the context of his delivery of this address, by which Yahweh and the Israelites who stand before him have formalized their covenant relationship.

Although the lexical and rhetorical links with chapters 5 – 11 observed in Deuteronomy 26:16 are even more pronounced in verses 17 – 19,[5] these verses also look forward, particularly to 28:1, whose links with this text are tight. Deuteronomy 26:17 – 19 divides into two parts, each introduced by a clause involving the Hiphil form of the verb "to speak" and displaying remarkable parallelism.[6] The Hiphil form is best interpreted in a quasi-

---

5. (1) To "walk in his ways" (v. 17; cf. 8:6; 10:12; 11:22; also 28:9; 30:16); (2) the three-fold designation of the covenant stipulations, "his decrees, commands and laws" (v. 17; cf. 5:31; 6:1; 7:11; 8:11; 11:1; also 30:16); (3) "listen to/obey his voice" (v. 17; cf. 9:23; also 28:1; 30:2, 8, 20); (4) to become "his treasured possession" (v. 18; cf. 7:6; also 14:2); (5) "a people holy to the LORD your God" (v. 19; cf. 7:6; also 14:2, 21; 28:9).

6. These represent the only occurrences of the Hiphil form of *ʾāmar* ("to say") in the entire Old Testament. NIV's rendering obscures the exceptional construction and miscon-strues these statements by attributing the respective statements to the wrong persons. It also contradicts the structure of covenant relationship, which is grounded in Yahweh's free and gracious election of Israel, who must demonstrate acceptance of this status through faithful obedience. So also C. Levin, "Über den 'Color Hierenianus' des Deuteronomiums," in *Das Deuteronomium und seine Querbeziehungen* (Schriften der Finnischen Exegetischen Gesellschaft 32; Göttingen: Vandenhoeck & Ruprecht, 1996), 120.

juridical sense; the parties to an agreement hear the other party declare their commitment to the terms of the relationship hereby established. Normally it would be out of place for a human vassal to force the divine Suzerain into saying anything;[7] therefore the causative Hiphil should probably be interpreted more softly, something like "You have accepted/acknowledged Yahweh's declaration that he will be your God," and "Yahweh has accepted/acknowledged your declaration that you will be his treasured people."[8] The term "covenant" is missing from this paragraph, but the declarations that follow show they involve the formalization of a covenant relationship.

These verses obviously involve two declarations, the first by Yahweh (v. 17) and the second by the people (vv. 18–19). The two parts exhibit remarkable grammatical parallelism in that both involve four elements expressed with infinitives construct. While the parallelism is clear, it is not so clear who says what or how it was said. As the presiding officer in the covenant ratification rituals, through indirect speech Moses summarizes the privileges each party accepts and the obligations to which they commit themselves, and in so doing creates some syntactical ambiguities. The respective speeches may be identified as follows:

Moses' voice: Today, you have had Yahweh declare:
God's voice: *"I will be your God,*
And you shall walk in my ways,
And you shall keep my ordinances, and my commands, and my laws,
And you shall listen to my voice."
Moses' voice: Today, Yahweh has had you declare:
The people's voice: *"We will be your treasured people —*
just as you promised us —
And we will keep all your commands;
And you shall set us high above all the nations you have made
for praise, fame, and honor;
And we will be a holy people belonging to Yahweh our God —
just as you promised" (pers. trans.)[9]

Each speech consists of a declaration of the status within the relationship that the respective speakers accept for themselves, and a commitment to the

7. Thus Lohfink, *Great Themes from the Old Testament*, 393 n. 47.
8. Cf. NRSV and NJB. For discussion of the present form see T. C. Vriezen, "Das hiphʿil von ʾāmar in Deut. 26,17.18," *Jaarbericht van het Vooraziatische-Egyptisch Geselschap Ex oriente lux* 17 (1964): 207–10.
9. Cf. Guest, 117–26.

obligations to which they recognize the others to have committed themselves. Yahweh accepts the status of being Israel's God, in fulfillment of the oft-repeated promise embodied in the covenant formula,[10] and Israel accepts the status of being Yahweh's treasured people and a holy people belonging to him. Additionally, the Israelites commit themselves to keeping all Yahweh's commands, in fulfillment of Yahweh's charge in verse 17b. The obligations to which each party recognizes the other to have committed himself are expressed with active verbs. Yahweh calls on Israel to walk in his ways, to keep all his commands, and to listen to his voice, while Israel recognizes Yahweh's commitment to set them high above all the nations he has made, for praise, fame, and honor.

The mutuality of this declaration and the evocation of reciprocal commitments is remarkable,[11] though not without precedent in the making of treaties/covenants in the ancient world.[12] Our text seems to presuppose an oral version of the procedure delineated in these treaties, according to which Israel heard Yahweh declare his commitment to them through the mediation of Moses, and Yahweh heard the people declare their commitment to him.

With these declarations, the present generation standing before Moses is (re)constituted as the privileged "people of the LORD" (cf. 27:9; 29:13[12]). However, despite the remarkable bilaterality and mutuality of the affirmations, this is no parity treaty: (1) Israel's relationship to Yahweh has its roots in his ancient promises; (2) while Israel's obligations involve scrupulous obedience to Yahweh's revealed will, Yahweh does not reciprocate and commit himself to doing Israel's will; (3) although Yahweh is Israel's God, Israel is his possession, analogous to the treasure of kings, and his holy possession; (4) although Yahweh will set Israel high above the nations, Israel has no authority or power to set Yahweh above the gods; (5) although Israel will be elevated high above the nations, this is not for her glory but for the glory of Yahweh.

---

10. "I will be your God and you shall be my people." On the formula see Seock-Tae Sohn, "'I Will Be Your God and You Will Be My People': The Origin and Background of the Covenant Formula," in *Ki Baruch Hu': Ancient Near Eastern, Biblical, and Judaic Studies in Honor of Baruch A. Levine* (ed. by R. Chazan, William W. Hallo, and Lawrence H. Schiffman; Winona Lake, IN: Eisenbrauns, 1999), 364; Hugenberger, *Marriage as a Covenant*; P. Kalluveettil, *Declaration and Covenant: A Comprehensive Review of Covenant Formulae from the Old Testament and the Ancient Near East* (AnBib 88; Rome: Biblical Institute, 1982); K. Baltzer, *The Covenant Formulary* (Oxford: Blackwell, 1971).

11. Cf. M. A. Friedman, "Israel's Response in Hosea 2:17b: 'You Are My Husband,'" *JBL* 99 (1980): 202.

12. The former is illustrated most dramatically by the treaty between Rameses II of Egypt and the Hittite king Hattusili III in the thirteenth century BC. The treaty has been preserved in two versions, but they are cast so that the Egyptian version records the commitments of the Hittite king and the Hittite version contains the commitments of the Egyptian king. These are conveniently juxtaposed in *ANET*, 199–203.

This concluding statement deserves further comment. By declaring that Yahweh will set Israel high above the nations that he has made, Moses casts his gaze far beyond the Cis- and Transjordanian regions to the world as a whole. This notion is reiterated in 28:1–14 in an economic and political sense as well as in 32:8–9 in an administrative sense (cf. 15:6). In short, Israel will be the head over all and the tail to no one (v. 13). While 26:19 does not describe how Israel will be elevated above the nations, it summarizes the effects: "in praise, fame and honor." The NIV rendering suggests that the goal is Israel's praise, fame and glory (cf. Zeph. 3:19–20).[13] However, given the flow of the book as a whole and later echoes of this text, it is best to ascribe the glory to God.[14] Neither in Deuteronomy nor anywhere else is Israel's standing among the nations ever to be a source of national pride (cf. 7:7; 8:17–18; 9:4–24).[15]

Furthermore, 10:21 declares that Israel is to recognize Yahweh as their praise, because of all that *he has done for them* (cf. 28:9–10). In effect, Israel is to reflect the glory and grace of the God whose name they bear, which will lead the nations to fear them because of that name (cf. 28:1–14).[16] This interpretation of the "praise, fame and honor" expressed by the nations is reinforced by Israel's acceptance of her status as a treasured and holy people belonging to Yahweh. By adding "as he promised" after both phrases in verses 18 and 19, Moses alludes to the benefactions delineated in Exodus 19:5–6. Like Aaron, Israel is to fulfill a priestly role, declaring to the nations the glory of her God and drawing the nations to him.

THE MISSIOLOGICAL AGENDA. WITH this final declaration of Israel's special status in the divine plan of salvation history, Moses concludes his exposition on the stipulations of the covenant (12:1–26:19). All that remains in this address is to specify the consequences for Israel of her response to the challenge and privilege of covenant relationship with Yahweh (28:1–29:1[28:69]).

Like the ancient Israelites, modern readers of Deuteronomy may be tempted to view God's election of Israel and his revelation of his will to them as ends in themselves. A superficial reading of the Sinai narratives (Ex. 19–Num. 9) might support this interpretation. Apart from the Egyptians,

---

13. NRSV preserves the ambiguity: "for him to set you high above all nations that he has made, in praise and in fame and in honor" (cf. NASV, NJB).

14. Thus NEB and REB: "to bring *him* praise and fame and glory."

15. So also Wright, *Deuteronomy*, 272–73.

16. Cf. 4:6–8; Jer. 13:11; 33:9.

from whose clutches Yahweh delivered the Israelites, and the Canaanites, whose land Yahweh is about to hand over to them, references to the outside world are rare. Twice Yahweh declares that he separated Israel from the peoples (Lev. 20:24, 26); occasionally the nations witness Yahweh's actions on Israel's behalf (Ex. 34:10; Lev. 26:45; Num. 14:15); and Balaam foresaw Israel's victory over the nations (Num. 24:8). However, the tables are reversed in the covenant curses, which warn of the nations invading Israel and the people perishing among the nations (Lev. 26:33, 38).

Although Israel's missionary function receives scant emphasis in the Sinai narratives, this does not mean it is absent. On the contrary, Israel's redemption and constitution as the people of Yahweh are set within the context of his missiological agenda. If Israel would keep Yahweh's covenant and listen to his voice, they would be his treasured possession, his kingdom of priests, and his holy nation (Ex. 19:5–6). By adding "the whole earth is mine" in 19:5, Yahweh declares his universal goal. He has called Israel to himself and revealed his will to them that the world might learn of the benefits of his glory and grace.

As Abraham's descendants, Israel is called to fulfill the mission God announced to him in the first recorded encounter: "All peoples on earth will be blessed through you" (Gen. 12:3). When Yahweh called Abraham to a covenant relationship with himself, when he incorporated the Israelites into this covenant and fleshed out the nature of this covenant at Sinai, and when this covenant was renewed on the plains of Moab, the nations were in view. Through obedience to Yahweh's will the Israelites would declare publicly how righteous are his statutes (4:6–8) and how gracious is their God.

In Deuteronomy the pattern for missions is fundamentally centripetal.[17] While the world watched, Yahweh delivered Israel from her Egyptian bondage, entered into a covenant relationship with her, put Canaan into her hands, and blessed her. As his covenant partner, Israel played a paradigmatic role; what Yahweh had done for them he sought to do for all. However, like Rahab and Ruth, those who seek him must come to Israel. The Pentateuch lacks a missionary mandate like the Great Commission in Matthew 28:18–20, commanding the Israelites to go to the nations and to proclaim the gospel of divine grace. Instead, God placed Israel at the center of the nations (cf. Ezek. 5:5) so that when outsiders saw what Yahweh had done for them, they would praise Yahweh and join Israel in covenant relationship with him.

The partial fulfillment of this mission in the heyday of the monarchy under David and Solomon is reflected in the doxology of the Queen of Sheba in 1 Kings 10:9: "Praise be to the LORD your God, who has delighted in you and placed you on the throne of Israel. Because of the LORD's eternal

---

17. Though Jonah's mission to Nineveh demonstrates that it was not exclusively so.

love for Israel, he has made you king, to maintain justice and righteousness." Sadly, however, the history of Israel and her mission as a "light for the nations" (Isa. 42:6) was a history of failure. Instead of bringing praise to the name of Yahweh, they brought shame to his name with their moral failure and finally their exile (Ezek. 36:17–21).

With the coming of Christ and the establishment of a covenant community that transcends national and ethnic boundaries, God's missionary strategy shifts from an essentially centripetal paradigm to a fundamentally centrifugal pattern. Jesus announces the shift in strategy from "come see what God has done for his people" to "Go tell the world what God has done for you" (cf. Matt. 28:18–20). This new paradigm is illustrated dramatically in the book of Acts with the successive outpourings of the Holy Spirit on Jews in Jerusalem (Acts 2), Samaritans (Acts 8), Gentile God-fearers in the land (Acts 10), and the Ephesians as representatives of Gentiles on foreign soil (Acts 19). Indeed Paul, whose relationship to the gospel of Christ, the Redeemer from sin, is analogous to that of Moses' relationship to the gospel of Yahweh, the Redeemer from bondage, was expressly called to proclaim this gospel to the Gentiles (Rom. 11:13; 15:15–16).

However, to conclude that a centrifugal approach has totally displaced the centripetal strategy is simplistic. In 1 Peter 2:9–12 Peter's understanding of Christians' missionary role is similar to that of Israel's. Though addressed to believers scattered among the Gentiles, there is no hint they had traveled to Gentile lands in a conscious missionary effort. Rather, like ancient Israel among the nations, these Christians resided in pagan communities. Through their own experience of God's grace and by their godly conduct, they were to proclaim the excellencies of the one who had called them out of darkness into his marvelous light. Jesus also assumed this paradigm when he characterized believers as salt and light (Matt. 5:13–16). Indeed the Scriptures close with a glorious vision of people from every tribe and nation redeemed and gathered around the Lamb to worship him (Rev. 5:9; 7:9). This is the supreme example of centripetal missiological strategy.

MISSION FOR CHRISTIANS. WITH these comments on the missiological significance of Deuteronomy 26:16–19 we have touched on the significance of this passage for Christians today.[18] This short text provides a summary statement of the privileges and

---

18. For a discussion of this passage with particular focus on its missionary implications see D. I. Block, "The Privilege of Calling: The Mosaic Paradigm for Missions (Deut. 26:16–19)," *How I Love Your Torah, O LORD!* 140–61.

obligations of covenant relationship. In Christ we observe the supreme demonstration of God's commitment to us. In Christ we hear God say, "I will be your God and you will be my people," a refrain whose echoes are heard in 2 Corinthians 6:16 and Revelation 21:3. Through his saving work we have become his treasured possession and his holy people. This is our privilege as the new covenant people.

However, with every privilege come responsibilities. If Yahweh required his people Israel to respond to his grace with wholehearted obedience, the same is true for us. In healthy covenant relationships the parties to the covenant commit themselves to acting in the interests of the other person. The same is true of our covenant relationship with God. As Yahweh incarnate, Jesus said, "If you love me [i.e., are covenantally committed to me], you will keep my commands" (pers. trans. of John 14:15; cf. 14:21; 15:10). The charge involves more than simply doing everything Jesus tells the disciples from now on. Rather, "my commands" (*entolas*)[19] is shorthand for the divine will revealed in the context of his covenant with Israel. The God who spoke at Sinai is none other than the Lord Jesus Christ, and the fruit he calls us to bear is the fruit of righteous conduct, joyful obedience to his will, as revealed in the Torah.

If Yahweh was glorified through the righteous and faithful conduct of his people Israel, the same is true of the new Israel of God. Indeed, Jesus reminds his disciples that his Father is glorified in this—that the disciples prove to be his disciples by bearing much fruit. As we do so, the glory and grace of the heavenly Father will radiate forth from us, drawing people to him like a great magnet. May believers everywhere be faithful in proclaiming his grace, and may many heed his call to go to the ends of the earth, so that everyone may know that Yahweh, incarnate in Jesus Christ, is God and Lord of all—for his praise, fame, and glory.

---

19. The word *entolas*, which echoes Deut. 26:18 (for Heb. *miṣwôt*), occurs forty times in Deuteronomy LXX: 4:2, 40; 5:29, 31; 6:1–2, 17, 25; 7:9, 11; 8:1–2, 6, 11; 10:13; 11:8, 13, 22, 27, 28; 13:4, 18[5, 19]; 15:5; 16:12; 17:19, 20; 19:9; 26:13, 18; 27:1, 10; 28:1, 13, 15, 45; 30:8, 10, 11, 16.

Deuteronomy 27:1–26

Moses and the elders of Israel commanded the people: "Keep all these commands that I give you today. ²When you have crossed the Jordan into the land the LORD your God is giving you, set up some large stones and coat them with plaster. ³Write on them all the words of this law when you have crossed over to enter the land the LORD your God is giving you, a land flowing with milk and honey, just as the LORD, the God of your fathers, promised you. ⁴And when you have crossed the Jordan, set up these stones on Mount Ebal, as I command you today, and coat them with plaster. ⁵Build there an altar to the LORD your God, an altar of stones. Do not use any iron tool upon them. ⁶Build the altar of the LORD your God with fieldstones and offer burnt offerings on it to the LORD your God. ⁷Sacrifice fellowship offerings there, eating them and rejoicing in the presence of the LORD your God. ⁸And you shall write very clearly all the words of this law on these stones you have set up."

⁹Then Moses and the priests, who are Levites, said to all Israel, "Be silent, O Israel, and listen! You have now become the people of the LORD your God. ¹⁰Obey the LORD your God and follow his commands and decrees that I give you today."

¹¹On the same day Moses commanded the people:

¹²When you have crossed the Jordan, these tribes shall stand on Mount Gerizim to bless the people: Simeon, Levi, Judah, Issachar, Joseph and Benjamin. ¹³And these tribes shall stand on Mount Ebal to pronounce curses: Reuben, Gad, Asher, Zebulun, Dan and Naphtali.

¹⁴The Levites shall recite to all the people of Israel in a loud voice:

¹⁵"Cursed is the man who carves an image or casts an idol—a thing detestable to the LORD, the work of the craftsman's hands—and sets it up in secret."

Then all the people shall say,

"Amen!"

¹⁶"Cursed is the man who dishonors his father or his mother."

Then all the people shall say,

"Amen!"

17"Cursed is the man who moves his neighbor's boundary stone."

Then all the people shall say,

"Amen!"

18"Cursed is the man who leads the blind astray on the road."

Then all the people shall say,

"Amen!"

19"Cursed is the man who withholds justice from the alien, the fatherless or the widow."

Then all the people shall say,

"Amen!"

20"Cursed is the man who sleeps with his father's wife, for he dishonors his father's bed."

Then all the people shall say,

"Amen!"

21"Cursed is the man who has sexual relations with any animal."

Then all the people shall say,

"Amen!"

22"Cursed is the man who sleeps with his sister, the daughter of his father or the daughter of his mother."

Then all the people shall say,

"Amen!"

23"Cursed is the man who sleeps with his mother-in-law."

Then all the people shall say,

"Amen!"

24"Cursed is the man who kills his neighbor secretly."

Then all the people shall say,

"Amen!"

25"Cursed is the man who accepts a bribe to kill an innocent person."

Then all the people shall say,

"Amen!"

26"Cursed is the man who does not uphold the words of this law by carrying them out."

Then all the people shall say,

"Amen!"

EVEN TO CASUAL READERS chapter 27 seems intrusive.[1] It interrupts the otherwise smooth flow from Deuteronomy 26:16−19 to 28:1−14— which are linked by common vocabulary and motifs—and introduces a distinctive genre and content. The present chapter consists of three distinct speeches, each with its own narrative introduction and speaker(s) (vv. 1, 9, 11); it seems ill-connected with the preceding or what follows and might have made more sense after 31:29. While any explanation for the present arrangement is speculative, perhaps 11:26−32 provides the best clue for the insertion of this chapter between 26:16−19 and 28:1. There Moses had called for a blessing and curse ritual on Mounts Gerizim and Ebal respectively. Indeed, the large block of material preserved in 26:16−28:68 exhibits a reverse resumptive expository relationship to 11:26−32.[2] The correspondence in structures may be illustrated as follows:

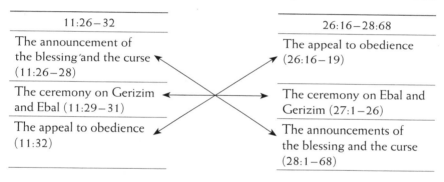

11:26−32	26:16−28:68
The announcement of the blessing and the curse (11:26−28)	The appeal to obedience (26:16−19)
The ceremony on Gerizim and Ebal (11:29−31)	The ceremony on Ebal and Gerizim (27:1−26)
The appeal to obedience (11:32)	The announcements of the blessing and the curse (28:1−68)

Critical scholars tend to interpret chapter 27 as a combination of separate Gilgal and Shechem traditions,[3] though some recognize a unified text and argue that this chapter follows the model of a royal land grant ceremony described on Babylonian boundary stone inscriptions.[4] While the latter impulse is sound, recent advances in understanding these stones call for a refinement of the thesis.[5] Like ancient *naru* inscriptions, this chapter

---

1. Cf. Block, "Recovering the Voice of Moses," in *The Gospel According to Moses*, 29.

2. Similarly McConville, *Deuteronomy*, 387.

3. Cf. O. Eissfeldt, "Gilgal or Shechem," in *Proclamation and Presence* (ed. J. I. Durham and J. R. Porter; Richmond: John Knox, 1970), 90−101. For a brief recent representation of this approach see Biddle, *Deuteronomy*, 395.

4. A. E. Hill, "The Ebal Ceremony as Hebrew Land Grant," *JETS* 31 (1988): 399−406.

5. K. E. Slanski (*The Babylonian Entitlement narûs* [kudurrus]: *A Study in their Form and Function* [ASOR Books 9; Boston: American Schools of Oriental Research, 2003]) has established that such inscriptions were not limited to geographic boundaries but extended to other entitlements.

involves: (1) references to the erection of inscribed stones (vv. 2−4, 8); (2) the construction of an altar to the deity (vv. 5−7); (3) a listing of witnesses (vv. 12−13); (4) the speech of representatives of the divine owner (v. 14); and (5) a series of curses invoked upon those who would violate the inscription (vv. 15−26). These features make good sense in their ancient Near Eastern context and contribute to a theology far greater than the sum of the parts of the chapter.[6]

As noted above, Deuteronomy 27 comprises three parts of unequal length and arranged in an ABA pattern; the two larger parts (vv. 1−8; vv. 11−26) sandwich a short hortatory challenge (vv. 9−10). Although the rituals of the two outside parts diverge widely, the accounts are linked in several ways. (1) For the first time in Deuteronomy both speeches open with the verb "to command, charge." (2) In contrast to covenant renewal rituals alluded to elsewhere in the book (11:26−28; 26:16−19; 29:2[1]−30:20; 31:24−30), both involve future rituals to be performed in the Promised Land (vv. 2, 4, and 12). (3) Both rituals are to take place on Mount Ebal (vv. 4, 13), though the latter also adds the name of Mount Gerizim, located next to Ebal.

Completing the Covenantal Triangle: Yahweh—Israel—Land (27:1−8)

FOR THE FIRST TIME the narrator has Moses formally charge the people with an obligation and refers to accomplices in the speech act, that is, "the elders." Structurally the speech divides into three parts: (1) a brief opening appeal to scrupulous adherence to the present prescriptions (v. 1b); (2) a summary of the instructions regarding the prescribed ritual (vv. 2−3); (3) a more detailed description of the prescribed ritual (vv. 4−8).

The opening appeal (v. 1) establishes the context in which the following prescriptions are to be applied, linking the moment formally with the series of events reflected in the book of Deuteronomy as a whole. The vocabulary is familiar, resembling many appeals found elsewhere in the book.[7] "All these commands" to which Moses refers are not the prescribed rituals that follow, but the "the entire covenantal charge" embodied in "this Torah, this body of instruction" (vv. 3, 8, 26),[8] that is, the speeches of Deuteronomy. The final word of verse 1 ("today") reminds the reader of the

---

6. For a theological interpretation of the chapter as a whole, see by P. A. Barker, "The Theology of Deuteronomy 27," *TynBul* 49 (1998): 277−303.

7. See 6:25; 8:1; 11:8, 22; 15:5; 19:9.

8. See also Tigay, *Deuteronomy*, 247−48. For references to "this Torah" elsewhere, see 1:5; 4:8; 17:18, 19; 28:58, 61; 29:29[28]; 31:9, 11, 12, 24; 32:46.

distance between the time of this address, that is, the day of decision and commitment, and the time to implement the following rituals.

The remainder of the address concerns a special one-time ritual that the Israelites are to perform when they reach their destination. The instructions divide into two parts, verses 2–3 and 4–8 respectively. Although these segments exhibit distinctive emphases, the repetition of key phrases and expressions reflects a deliberately constructed and coherent whole. The beginning of each segment is signaled by "and it shall be" (*wᵉhāyâ*), followed by a declaration that the ceremony is to be performed after the Israelites have crossed the Jordan. Thereafter the skeletons of both panels are represented by the following triad of commands (pers. trans.):

> You shall set up [large] stones,
> And you shall plaster them with plaster,
> And you shall write on them all the words of this Torah.

The first panel emphasizes the context of the ritual; the second highlights the ritual itself, twice adding a fourth element to the commands: "And you shall build an altar to Yahweh your God" (pers. trans.).

Panel A (vv. 2–3). Setting the chronological context, Moses announces that the rituals to follow are to be performed "on the day" (NIV "when") the Israelites cross the Jordan into the land that Yahweh has promised them. He highlights the significance of the moment by twice declaring that Israel is crossing over "into the land the LORD your God is giving you," by describing the land as a desirable land "flowing with milk and honey,"[9] and by ending the panel with "just as the LORD, the God of your fathers, promised you" (cf. Gen. 17:8). These rituals celebrate Yahweh's grace, and the inscribed stones serve as permanent reminders of his faithfulness. The instructions for the ritual in verses 2b–3a are clear and reduced to the barest details. The challenge for the reader is establishing the significance of these actions.

Erecting stone monuments. The use of the verb "to set up, erect" suggests that the stones in question are vertical pillars.[10] Finding an analogue in later Greek traditions of colonization, some scholars propose the pillars served as monuments to the conclusion of a journey.[11] Others argue that Ebal is the "place" that Yahweh would choose for his name to dwell, and that the stone monument here is a victory stela on which is inscribed Yahweh's

---

9. Cf. Deut. 6:3; 11:9; 26:9, 15; 27:3; 31:20.

10. Israelites erected pillars as memorials to conquests (1 Sam. 7:12; 1 Chron. 18:3), and other political achievements (2 Sam. 18:18), to treaties (Gen. 31:45), and as religious symbols of devotion (Gen. 28:18, 22; 35:14; Josh. 24:26, 27).

11. M. Weinfeld, "The Pattern of the Israelite Settlement in Canaan," in *Congress Volume Jerusalem 1986* (ed. J. A. Emerton; VTSup40; Leiden: Brill, 1988), 280.

name.[12] However, the plural in verses 2–3 seems to call for the erection of more than one pillar. While the text does not specify their exact number, the number of tribes involved in the liturgical imprecations may suggest twelve (vv. 12–13), in which case this part of the ritual would echo the original covenant ratification ceremony celebrated at Sinai (Ex. 24:4).[13]

Plastering the stones. The command to plaster the stones involves the verb *śîd*, derived from a noun that denotes "lime." The plaster probably involved a white alkaline compound consisting of water and calcium oxide—derived from limestone readily available in the vicinity of Ebal and Gerizim—and readily applied to surfaces. As the moisture evaporates, the plaster hardens, leaving a smooth coating over the object.[14] While the scribes would probably etch the text of the Torah on the stone pillars with a sharp object, they could also write it with ink or paint. In either case, exposed to the elements the text would quickly wear away, and all that would be left as a memorial to this event were the pillars themselves. Though these could have been reused as a rallying point, these instructions call for a one-time ritual use involving the text of the Torah Moses has been promulgating.

Writing the Torah on the stones. The expression "all the words of this Torah" suggests the scribes were to include all of Moses' present addresses on the pillars (cf. 4:2; 17:18). The logistical problems involved in transcribing "all the words of this Torah" are less than they seem at first sight. The three speeches of Moses in Deuteronomy are considerably longer than Hammurabi's law code, which takes up less than three-fourths of the surface area of the seven-foot stela of Hammurabi.[15] While the entire text

---

12. See Richter, *The Deuteronomistic History and the Name Theology*, 139–42; idem, "The Place of the Name in Deuteronomy," *VT* 57 (2007): 343–44. This interpretation is unlikely because: (1) the chapter makes no reference to the "name" or to the chosen place; (2) although the conquest of Jericho was a significant achievement and could perhaps be viewed as a deposit of certain future victories, the victory over the Canaanites had in fact not yet been accomplished; (3) the cultic prescriptions involving the "place" in Deuteronomy 12 differ markedly from those prescribed here; (4) perhaps most significant, whereas the former called for regular and repeated observances at the "place," this chapter calls for a one-time event.

13. Cf. Josh. 4:5.

14. During the Iron Age plaster was commonly used to waterproof cisterns, and occasionally wealthier people would plaster the walls and floors of their houses. See further L. G. Herr, "Plaster," *ISBE* (rev. ed.), 3:883. For a late ninth century BC example of text written on plaster, see the Deir ʿAlla inscription (*COS* 2.27).

15. Whereas the Law Code was written in syllabic cuneiform script in contrast to Deuteronomy's consonantal alphabetic script, a precise comparison of the originals is difficult. L. W. King's English translation (*The Code of Hammurabi* [Whitefish, MT: Kessinger, 2004; reprint of 1910 edition]) of the Code has slightly more than 11,000 words, which compares with ca. 14,500 for NIV's translation of Moses' second address. In Hebrew the word count for Moses' three speeches is ca. 12,000 words.

---

of Moses' speeches could easily have been transcribed on two six-foot stelae, if we assume twelve pillars, each pillar would have contained about 1,000 words.

Panel B (vv. 4 – 8). The framework of the second panel (vv. 4, 8) repeats the essential information presented in the first, though in abbreviated form. However, now Moses specifies the site as "on Mount Ebal."[16] This location is logical on several counts. (1) If one plots a straight line between the northernmost and southernmost borders of the land, Mounts Ebal and Gerizim appear precisely at the midpoint.[17] (2) Mount Ebal is one of the highest mountains in the region; from its peak one could see most of the Promised Land. (3) Located near Shechem, the region of Ebal and Gerizim was extremely important in Israel's history and tradition (Gen. 12:6 – 7; 33:18 – 20). This ceremony invites the nation to acknowledge God's faithfulness in finally fulfilling his promise to the ancestors.

Verses 5 – 7 instruct the people on the rituals to be performed on Mount Ebal. They begin with a charge to build an altar, specifying natural stones (cf. vv. 2 – 4) rather than stones chiseled to shape with an iron tool. While this altar is distinguished from the altar used in worship at the tabernacle or temple, the proscription recalls Exodus 20:25. Apparently, just as animals to be sacrificed were to be "without defect" (Lev. 1:3) and without "any serious flaw" (Deut. 15:21), so the stones of this altar were to be whole and complete. To improve on them with human effort and man-made tools was to defile them.[18]

In verses 6b – 7 Moses calls for whole burnt offerings (^cōlōt) and peace/fellowship offerings ($š^elāmîm$) to be sacrificed to Yahweh on the altar, and for celebration by feasting in his presence. The former are mentioned in chapter 12 (vv. 6, 11, 27), but verse 7 contains the only reference to the latter in the book. Deriving from the root $šlm$ ("to be whole"), these sacrifices

---

16. The Samaritan Pentateuch and one LXX manuscript (Papyrus Giessen 19) read Mount Gerizim. For discussion, see E. Tov, *Textual Criticism of the Hebrew Bible* (Minneapolis: Fortress, 1992), 94 – 95.

17. That is, at the midpoint of a straight line drawn between Dan and Beersheba, which soon functioned as a stereotypical definition of the extremities of the land of Israel (Judg. 20:1; 1 Sam. 3:20; 2 Sam. 3:10; 17:11; 24:2, 15; 1 Kings 4:25; 1 Chron. 21:2; 2 Chron. 30:5; Amos 8:14). Judg. 9:37 refers to Gerizim as "the center of the land," though LXX renders the phrase "navel of the earth."

18. So also S. M. Olyan, "Why an Altar of Unfinished Stones? Some Thoughts on Ex 20,25 and Dtn 27,5–6," *ZAW* 108 (1996): 161–71. Although its function is disputed, at Ebal archaeologists have discovered a large structure made of uncut stones and filled with soil dated in the early Iron Age, when the Israelites were settling in the land. See A. Zertal, "Ebal, Mount," *ABD*, 2:255–58; idem, "An Early Iron Age Cultic Site on Mount Ebal," *TA* 13 – 14 (1986–1987): 105–65; idem, "Has Joshua's Altar Been Found on Mount Ebal?" *BAR* 11 (1985): 26–44.

celebrated the health of the relationship between deity and subject,[19] which explains why the *šᵉlāmîm* may be eaten with joy in Yahweh's presence. Although the phrase "in the presence of the LORD your God" is usually associated with the central sanctuary, these instructions assume the real presence of Yahweh at this altar as well. The altar is Yahweh's table; from it he receives the "whole burnt offering" and around it the people consume the "peace/fellowship offerings."

The combination of whole burnt offerings and peace offerings links this event not only with the altar law in Exodus 20:24 – 26, but even more significantly with Exodus 24:1 – 11. As in our text, there the sacrifices offered at Sinai are associated with twelve pillars representing the tribes of Israel (v. 4) and eating in the presence of Yahweh (v. 11), which provides one more clue to the significance of this ritual. Like the procedure at Sinai, this ceremony is covenantal. Whereas the Sinai event had sealed the bipartite relationship between people and deity, the third party (the land) was missing. The purpose of this ritual was to integrate the land in this complex of relationships and to secure Israel's title to that which Yahweh promised long ago. By eating the covenant meal in the presence of Yahweh *in the land he has given them*, the Israelites celebrate the completion of the triangle.

God
Yahweh

People   **Land**
Israel   Canaan

The panel closes with a charge to copy the Torah carefully on the stone pillars (v. 8). At least this is how NIV and most translations understand the Hebrew expression used here. However, recent discussions suggest this phrase speaks more to the purpose of the inscription than the nature of the script. From the perspective of speech-act theory, whereas Moses' oral proclamation of the Torah had the effect of legally binding this generation of Israelites to the covenant their parents had signed on to at Sinai and Abraham had signed on to by accepting circumcision as the mark of the

---

19. On *šᵉlāmîm*, see R. E. Averbeck, "שׁלם," *NIDOTTE*, 4:130 – 43; Milgrom, *Leviticus 1 – 8*, 217 – 25; G. A. Anderson, "Sacrifices and Sacrificial Offerings: Old Testament," *ABD*, 5:878 – 79. B. Levine (*In the Presence of the Lord* [Leiden: Brill, 1974], 3 – 54) interprets this as "an efficacious gift of greeting," offered "in the presence of the Lord."

covenant (Gen. 17), so inscribing the Torah on these pillars bound the land legally to this covenant.[20] Performed as soon as the Israelites entered the land, the ceremonies signaled the beginning of the full functioning of the tripartite covenant relationship.

The Charge of Moses and the Levites (27:9–10)

SANDWICHED BETWEEN TWO LARGER sections involving future rituals to be performed at Ebal we find a hortatory fragment that brings the audience back to the present. This citation, which involves the Levitical priests, seems to be excerpted from a longer speech, perhaps given in the context of 31:24–29. Moses recognizes that if it has been difficult to keep his people on track in their covenant relationship with Yahweh while he was with them, there will be little to restrain them after his death (v. 27). The present speech would have fit well in this context.

While 27:6–7 anticipates celebration before Yahweh, the opening appeal, "Be silent, O Israel, and listen!" and the declaration of the significance of the ceremonies in which they have just participated signal the solemnity of the present moment: They have become a people belonging to Yahweh (26:16–19).[21] The "today" of verse 9 (NIV "now") points to the specific moment of covenant renewal on the Plains of Moab. In fulfillment of Yahweh's promise in Genesis 17:7, at Sinai the Israelites had been integrated into his covenant with Abraham and become the people of Yahweh. But that generation was gone, necessitating the confirmation of the covenant under the supervision of Moses on the Plains of Moab. Through Moses' promulgation of the Torah (1:5) and formal covenant renewal ceremonies (26:16–19; cf. 29:10–13[9–12]), this generation had confirmed themselves as the privileged people of Yahweh.[22]

As in 26:16–19, this declaration is followed by an appeal to fidelity to the covenant Lord. Moses cautions the people not to assume that formal rituals of devotion are all that Yahweh demands. Covenantal fidelity is demonstrated through listening to Yahweh's voice (v. 10a) and scrupulously observing the commands expounded upon orally by Moses, transcribed on the pillars of stone, and eventually preserved in written Torah (31:9–13). His instructions are not to be treated merely as museum pieces or literary artifacts, but as guides to life.

---

20. See the note on 1:5 above, p.55, The text makes no reference to reading the Torah before the people.

21. This is the only occurrence of the Niphal plus *lamedh* to express entrance into a state. Previously Deuteronomy always used the Qal form of the expression, *hāyâ lᵉᶜām* ("to become [his] people"). Cf. 4:20; 7:6; 14:2; 26:18.

22. The covenant made with Abraham and with Israel at Sinai (and confirmed in Moab) is one and the same. See Hwang, "The Rhetoric of Remembrance," 269–355.

Appealing for Covenantal Fidelity in
the Promised Land (27:11 – 26)

IN VERSES 11 – 26 Moses' attention returns to the future ceremony to be performed at Mounts Gerizim and Ebal (v. 12a). Whereas verses 1 – 8 involved only nonverbal actions,[23] the liturgy prescribed here is entirely verbal. The text divides stylistically and substantively into two parts. In verses 11 – 13 the Levites participate as a group alongside the rest of the tribes; in verses 14 – 26 they are at the center of the action pronouncing the curses. The first part anticipates the proclamation of blessings and curses, while the second reports only the latter. It seems these two segments represent two phases of a complex ritual involving the recitation of both blessings and curses as part of a covenant renewal ceremony (some version of chap. 28?). Apparently the utterance of the curses in verses 14 – 26 has a different function altogether. There is no need to assume an antiphonal recitation of the blessings and curses or to envision the tribes reciting anything at all — other than "Amen" after each imprecation. Verses 12 – 23 suggest the respective groups are to stand while the blessings and curses are recited, probably by someone else.

The prescribed arrangements for the blessings and the curses (vv. 11 – 13). Unlike the preceding speeches, verse 11 suggests Moses gave the following instructions by himself. Verses 12 – 13 are cast in symmetrical form, describing the purpose, location, and arrangement of the tribes for the liturgy on the respective mountains. On the surface, the first purpose clause ("to bless," *lamed* + infinitive construct) suggests the tribes serve as speakers, but the grammar of the second is less clear. The circumlocution involving the preposition ʿal ("concerning"), followed by the definite noun "the curse," may intentionally avoid having the tribes actually cursing the people.[24] If the meaning of the *lamed* in the first is adjusted to the preposition ʿal in the second, functioning as a *lamed* of reference, neither expression involves verbal participation by the tribes. Apparently when the blessings and curses were proclaimed, the tribes on the respective mountains would rise.[25] Moses provides no rationale for this arrangement.[26]

The list of tribal names in verses 12 – 13 is archaic, based on realities prior to the isolation of Levi as the priestly tribe and the division of Joseph

---

23. There is no reference to reading the Torah that is transcribed onto the pillars.

24. Thus Tigay, *Deuteronomy*, 253.

25. In either case, the grammatical construction deviates markedly from 11:29, where Moses spoke of "placing the blessing on Mount Gerizim and the curse on Mount Ebal."

26. For the possibilities, see Mayes, *Deuteronomy*, 217 – 18; Barker, "The Theology of Deuteronomy 27," 288.

into Ephraim and Manasseh.[27] The tribal sequence reflects both geography and genealogy. Except for Issachar, the tribes stationed on the northern slope of Gerizim were allocated land to the south of the site of this ritual. Except for Dan, the tribes stationed on the southern slope of Ebal were allocated land either to the north or across the Jordan. The tribes stationed on Gerizim included those descended from Rachel (Joseph and Benjamin), plus the two Leah tribes destined to dominate Israel's religious and political life (Levi and Judah).[28] To these were added two more Leah tribes, Simeon (closely associated with Judah in the distribution of land) and Issachar, whose territory abutted that of Manasseh (Joseph). The remaining Leah tribes (Reuben and Zebulun) were left to be grouped with the descendants of Jacob's concubines, Bilhah (Dan, Napthali) and Zilpah (Gad, Asher).

Deuteronomy 27:11 – 13 does not specify which blessings and curses were to be recited. The absence of blessings in verses 15 – 26 renders unlikely the view that it involved these curses. This interpretation is reinforced by the shift in vocabulary, from *haqqᵉlālâ* ("the curse," v. 13) to *ʾārûr* ("cursed be," vv. 15 – 26). If the latter curses are identified with the curse of verse 13, Moses should either have used the root *ʾrr* in verse 13 or the root *qll* in verses 15 – 26. Instead, verse 12 speaks of "blessing" (*bērēk*) and verse 13 of cursing (*qᵉlālâ*), the same roots found in 11:29. Therefore, it seems best to associate the blessings and curses in verses 11 – 13 with chapter 28.

The present ritual was to be a defining moment in Israel's history[29] as the people celebrated the completion of the covenantal triangle. The ritual prescribed in verses 11 – 13 functions as a verbal equivalent to the sprinkling of the blood on the people in Exodus 24:8, binding the Israelites once more to the covenant made at Sinai and renewed on the Plains of Moab under the supervision of Moses. However, this time Mounts Ebal and Gerizim are present not only as witnesses to the blessings and curses, but as the repository to the Torah itself (the inscribed pillars of uncut stones taken from the region), and the land of Canaan (now Israel) is also engaged as a vital partner in the covenantal relationship.

The imprecatory ritual (vv. 14 – 26). This is a self-contained subunit, with its own formal introduction (v. 14), followed by twelve imprecations

---

27. The order differs but the entries accord with the names of Jacob's sons in Genesis 49 and the names of the tribes in Deuteronomy 33. Cf. the Song of Deborah and Barak in Judges 5, which omits Levi and splits Joseph into Ephraim and Machir, the latter representing Manasseh. See Block, *Judges, Ruth*, 232.

28. There is no real contradiction here between Levi as a tribe that stands with the rest of the tribes and the references to the Levites in vv. 9 and 14. In Deuteronomy the latter expression refers to the Levites as priestly functionaries (cf. 10:9; 14:29; 31:9, 25 – 26). Cf. McConville, *Deuteronomy*, 391.

29. Cf. J. M. Cohen, "When Did We Become a Nation?" *JBQ* 31 (2003): 260 – 62.

(vv. 15 – 26). The significance if this imprecatory liturgy may be suggested by rituals reflected in ancient Mesopotamian *narû* inscriptions. These inscriptions divide into two principal parts. The operative parts specify the terms of the entitlement and present legal and historical circumstances that legitimize the acquisition. The imprecative segments seek "to ensure the inviolability of the entitlement and the ability of the recipient to hold the entitlement permanently, that is, to pass it down at his death to his heirs for all time."[30]

While the parallels to the present ritual are obvious, *narû* inscriptions exhibit significant differences with our text. (1) The transcription of the Torah on plastered stones rather than chiseling the text in durable rock suggests the permanence of the entitlement does not depend on the existence of this document but is guaranteed by the copy in the custody of the Levitical priests. (2) Whereas the imprecations on *narû* stones sought to ensure the inviolability of the entitlement by invoking divine curses on those who violated the entitlement, the Torah written by Moses and copied on these pillars sought to secure the fidelity of the beneficiaries to the divine Superior, who had graciously granted them title to the land. (3) Whereas the second division of *narû* inscriptions sought to motivate fidelity only through imprecations, the corresponding part of the Torah begins with a lavish description of blessings that attend the entitlement (28:1 – 14).

The movement from verses 12 – 13 to 14 suggests the ritual of verses 15 – 26 is intended as a response to the blessings and curses recited — presumably by leading Levites as liturgical leaders. The size of the assembly and the role of the mountains as witnesses require the Levites to declare the curses "in a loud voice." By receiving the declarations, these mountains are incorporated in the deity – nation – and covenantal triangle and become witnesses to the oath under which the Israelites place themselves. In so doing, they recognize that should the people prove unfaithful, Moses is not the one who curses them; they have invoked the curse on themselves.

Verses 15 – 26 consist of twelve imprecations, which has led scholars to refer to this text as the *Dodecalogue* ("the twelve words"). The quota of twelve imprecations probably derives from the preceding listing of twelve tribes, binding all twelve tribes to them and facilitating memorization and recitation. The imprecations are stereotypical in form, beginning with a verbal anathema, followed by a reference to the person cursed.[31] The first and last anathemas (vv. 15, 26) are syntactically more complex than the

---

30. Slanski, *The Babylonian Entitlement* narûs (kudurrus), 288.

31. For curses elsewhere in the Old Testament, see Gen. 3:14; 4:11; 9:25; 27:29; 49:7; Num. 24:9; 28:16 – 19; Josh. 6:26; Jdg 5:23; 21:18; 1 Sam. 14:24, 28; Jer 11:3; 17:5; 20:14, 15; 48:10. For discussion see R. P. Gordon, "Curse, Malediction," *NIDOTTE*, 4:491 – 93.

rest, identifying the criminal action by means of relative clauses rather than a participle to identify the crime. This syntactical frame warns against breaking the Supreme Command through idolatry (v. 15) and violating the covenant as laid out in the Torah (v, 26).

The imprecations exhibit a modified chiastic structure:

1 Idolatry (secret)	A	Violation of the supreme Command
2 Dishonoring parents	B	Violation of fundamental domestic order
3 Moving a neighbor's landmark	C	Violation of a neighbor's rights
4 Misleading the blind		
5 Perverting the rights of the alien, fatherless, and widow	D	Violation of the rights of the economically marginalized
6 Having intercourse with one's [step]mother		
7 Having intercourse with an animal	E	Violation of domestic sexual boundaries
8 Having intercourse with one's sibling		
9 Having intercourse with one's mother-in-law		
10 Striking down a neighbor (secret)	C'	Violation of a neighbor's rights
11 Accepting a bribe is crime against life	B'	Violation of fundamental social order
12 General disregard of the Torah	A'	Violation of the covenant in principle

Imprecations for violating sexual taboos represent the center of gravity (##6–9). While the catalog omits several capital crimes, the crimes listed represent the kinds of offenses that need to be purged from Israel. The defiling effects of human sin intensify the seriousness of the crimes listed here, for they jeopardize the land's performance in the triadic covenantal relationship.

This imprecatory ritual implies that covenantal righteousness could not be enforced merely through the courts. Casting the taboos as imprecations places violators under divine sanction. The verb ʾārûr ("Cursed is") commits perpetrators into the hands of God, who supervises the moral order and will ultimately establish righteousness through the punishment of evildoers.[32] In this ritual the people bind themselves to these consequences by answering each of the Levites' proclamations in unison, "Amen." Since this word functions as a solemn formula by which the hearers accept the

---

32. See the excellent discussion by E. Gerstenberger, "' ... (He/They) Shall Be Put to Death': Life-Preserving Divine Threats in Old Testament Law," *Ex Aud* 11 (1995): 43–61, esp. 48–49 on Deut. 27:15–26.

declared curse, the present ritual functions as a verbal equivalent to the ritual in Exodus 24:8. Each imprecation deserves brief comment.

#1 *Private household idolatry (v. 15).* The curses open with an imprecation on anyone who constructs idolatrous images and secretly sets them up in his house (cf. 4:28; Judg. 17:3, 4).[33] Unlike the golden calf, which served as a public national symbol (9:12, 16), this curse has in mind small household idols that could be clandestinely manufactured and set up within a house. As in 7:25 and 12:31, Moses characterizes such a practice as "detestable" (*tôʿēbâ*) to Yahweh, an expression used elsewhere of various socio-religious crimes (cf. 17:1; 18:12; 22:5; 23:18[19]; 25:16).

#2 *Disrespectful treatment of parents (v. 16).* The mistreatment of father and mother is expressed by an unusual word that conveys the opposite of "to honor" (5:16). This category of behavior obviously includes the blatant rebellion dealt with in 21:18–21, but the scope is much broader, referring to any verbal or physical action by which children demean parents.

#3 *Moving a landmark (v. 17).* The wording of this imprecation derives from 19:14. In Israel moving a boundary stone was viewed not only as a violation of others' right to their own property, but also as a crime against Yahweh, the ultimate owner of the land (Lev. 25:23), who had through casting the lot personally allotted the land to the respective clans and families.

#4 *Misleading the blind (v. 18).* This is the first of two curses addressed to those who take advantage of others' misfortune. While the curse addresses a particular kind of handicap (blindness), the underlying principle extends to persons with other physical deficiencies, as reflected in Leviticus 19:14 and extrabiblical texts.[34]

#5 *Subverting the rights of the marginalized (v. 19).* Like the curse on those who move boundaries (v. 17), the wording derives from earlier instruction in 24:17.[35] Common to aliens, the fatherless, and widows in a patricentric world like Israel's is the absence of an adult male to defend their rights and secure their well-being. Through their compassionate administration of justice and care for the poor, the Israelites are to emulate their God (10:18).

The next four anathemas concern sexual crimes. Those listed here may have been selected because they involve crimes committed within the household and could be easily covered up. Though adultery is not men-

---

33. See comments on 4:16, 23, 25; 5:8.

34. Compare the ca. twelfth-century BC Egyptian Instruction of Amenemope: "Do not laugh at a blind man, nor tease a dwarf, nor cause hardship for the lame." Translation by M. Lichtheim, COS, 1:47 (p. 121). Earlier Amenemope had written, "Beware of robbing a wretch, of attacking a cripple."

35. Cf. also 16:19; Ex. 23:2, 6; Lam. 3:35; cf. also Prov. 18:5.

tioned, it involves a rendezvous with a woman from outside the family, which would naturally arouse suspicion.

#6 *Incest with one's father's wife (v. 20).* Whereas 22:30[23:1] forbids marrying one's father's former wife, this curse condemns males who engage in sexual intercourse with their stepmother (cf. Lev. 18:7–8).[36] Like the fourth command of the Decalogue, which also seeks to preserve parental honor, in this context this is the only curse grounded with a motive clause. "For he would uncover the skirt of his father" (pers. trans.) is a euphemism for violating the sanctity of the marriage, though this act would also violate the taboo expressed in the second curse (v. 16).

#7. *Intercourse with an animal (v. 21).* Engaging in sexual relations with animals seems to have been a relatively common practice in the ancient world.[37] This curse extends the taboo in Israel to all animals. Whereas Leviticus 18:23 condemns such acts, whether committed by a man or woman, as defiling and perverse, other texts expressly declare them capital crimes (Ex. 22:19[18]; Lev. 20:15–16). Apparently bestiality was deemed such a heinous offense because it blurs the boundaries between the creaturely world and humankind created as image-bearers of God (Gen. 1:26–28). The roots of this disposition go back to Eden, where God created woman because none of the animals was an appropriate counterpart for the man (Gen. 2:18–25).

#8 *Incest with one's sister (v. 22).* This taboo concerns sexual intercourse between siblings, specifically condemning such relations with one's half-sister (lit., "daughter of his father") or one's full sister ("daughter of his mother"). This practice was common in royal circles of ancient Egypt,[38] and apparently in Phoenicia.[39]

#9 *Sexual intercourse with one's mother-in-law (v. 23).* The curse on a man who has sexual intercourse with his mother-in-law accords with Leviticus 20:14,

---

36. The situation could arise if a father remarries after the death of one's mother, or if he remarries after his divorce from one's mother, or if he is in a bigamous or polygamous situation. Whereas the prohibition on sexual relations with one's mother in Lev. 18:7–8 guards the relationship between mother and son, this taboo speaks only of the father's honor.

37. For discussion of Hittite laws condemning those who engage in sexual relations with animals, see H. A. Hoffner, "Incest, Sodomy and Bestiality in the Ancient Near East," in *Orient and Occident: Essays Presented to Cyrus H. Gordon on the Occasion of his Sixty-fifth Birthday* (ed. H. A. Hoffner Jr.; Neukirchen-Vluyn: Neukirchener Verlag, 1973), 81–90.

38. See J. Èerny, "Consanguineous Marriages in Pharaonic Egypt," *JEA* 40 (1964): 23–39; for later times, see W. Scheidel, "Brother Sister Marriage in Roman Egypt," *Journal of Biosocial Science* 3 (1997): 361–71.

39. The sarcophagus inscription of ʾEshmunʿazar II of Sidon (fifth century BC) suggests this king's father (Tabnit) and mother (ʾUmmiashtart) had a common father, Eshmunazzar I. See *COS*, 2:57.

---

which condemns this act as "wicked" and calls for capital punishment in the form of burning.

#10 *Striking one's neighbor in secret (v. 24).* It is unclear whether this curse involves simply striking one's neighbor in secret or intentionally killing a person by striking him. The formulation may be intentionally vague to cover any physical violence that threatens the well-being of the community.

#11 *Accepting a bribe to condemn an innocent person (v. 25).* This curse addresses a legal situation, like that envisaged in 16:19. However, here the case involves either paying a bribe to a witness in court to ensure testimony supporting fallacious charges against an innocent person that lead ultimately to his death, or paying a bribe to a judge so he condemns an innocent person to death—in which case this curse strengthens the ordinance in Exodus 23:6—7.

#12 *Failure to uphold the terms of this Torah (v. 26).* The imprecations conclude with a general curse on all who will not uphold "the words of this law." As in verses 3 and 8, "the words of this law" refer minimally to the instructions in Moses' second address, but they may include the first and third addresses as well. The appeal to establish the words of the Torah "by carrying them out" reminds the Israelites that the Torah was given not as an external badge of identity or an artifact to be analyzed and dissected, but as a document to govern conduct. Whereas in 8:18 "to confirm a covenant" had declared Yahweh's fidelity to his covenant commitments, this imprecation calls for Israelite fidelity to him and invests Moses' words with permanent canonical authority.

OLD TESTAMENT ALLUSIONS. OLD Testament allusions to the ceremonies prescribed here are rare. The names of the mountains Ebal and Gerizim occur outside Deuteronomy (cf. 11:29) only in Joshua 8:30—35, though Gerizim appears alone in Judges 9:7.[40] The former reports that after the conquest of Jericho and Ai, Joshua led the Israelites in a ritual "just as Moses the servant of Yahweh had commanded the people, and just as it is written in the book of the Torah of Moses" (pers. trans.). As described, this event involved (1) constructing an altar of uncut stones; (2) presenting whole burnt and peace/fellowship offerings on it; (3) transcribing the Torah of Moses that he had written on stones in the pres-

---

40. We may hear an allusion to Moses' appeal to the Levites to answer loudly in Micah's invocation of the mountains as witnesses to the case that Yahweh has against his people (Mic. 6:1—2).

ence of the people;[41] (4) dividing the population into two halves to stand in front of Mounts Gerizim and Ebal, respectively, for the blessing of the people; and (5) reading the blessings and the curses just as they are recorded in the Torah of Moses. The text concludes by noting that Joshua read the Mosaic Torah in its entirety before all the people, including women, small children, and aliens living among them.

Although Deuteronomy 27:1—8 is silent about the ark or the Levitical priests who carried it, Joshua 8:33 makes these the focal point. Presumably the ark was stationed between the two groups of tribes, in the valley between Ebal and Gerizim—in full view of the participants in the ceremony. Since the ark represented the ruling presence of Yahweh, with this addition the narrator presents Yahweh as a witness to and a participant in the rites performed here. Remarkably, whereas Deuteronomy 27:14—26 calls for a recitation of imprecations at the end of the ceremony, Joshua 8:33 ends by noting Joshua's scrupulous adherence to Moses' prescriptions (vv. 31, 33, 35; cf. 1:8). This was indeed a historic milestone: for the first time, deity, nation, and land were all together. Echoes of Deuteronomy 27 in the covenant renewal ceremony at Shechem recounted in Joshua 24, particularly Joshua's commentary on the stone that he erects (v. 27), reinforce this interpretation.

The only other reference to either of these mountains occurs in Judges 9:7, which describes Jotham standing on Mount Gerizim overlooking Shechem and proclaiming his antimonarchic fable concerning Abimelech. In postbiblical times Gerizim took on special significance especially in the Samaritan tradition. This was the site of their temple—as opposed to Jerusalem, which explains why the Samaritan Pentateuch, the only Scriptures the Samaritan sect recognized, consistently identified Gerizim as the only legitimate center of Yahweh worship.[42]

This tradition is recognized in 2 Maccabees 6:2, and Josephus (*Ant* 11.8.2, 7), but it surfaces in the New Testament in John 4:20—22. Although

---

41. The text does not mention pillars; it seems to assume the stones are the stones of which the altar is built. Cf. C. Begg, "The Cisjordanian Altar(s) and their Associated Rites According to Josephus," *BZ* 41 (1997): 195.

42. Not only does the Samaritan read "Gerizim" in place of "Ebal" in 27:4—5, but all allusions to Jerusalem in the Pentateuch are changed to Gerizim (e.g., Abraham sacrifices Isaac on Mount Moreh near Shechem, instead of Moriah in Gen. 22:2). Assuming the first command to be an introduction to the Decalogue, the Samaritans add a tenth command highlighting the sanctity of Mount Gerizim. Since the Samaritans viewed Shechem to have been chosen as the place of worship during the time of the patriarchs (Gen. 12:6; 33:18—20), in Deuteronomy the "the place the LORD will choose," is changed to "the place the LORD has chosen." On these ideological adaptations, see Tov, *Textual Criticism*, 94—95; B. K. Waltke, "Samaritan Pentateuch," *ABD*, 5:938.

not identified by name, Jesus' conversation with the Samaritan woman reflects the distinctive Samaritan tradition. In response to her comment that "our fathers worshiped on this mountain, but you Jews claim that the place where we must worship is in Jerusalem," Jesus replied not only that the time is coming when neither "this mountain" nor Jerusalem will matter, but also that the Samaritans worship the Father in ignorance. Although the Samaritans were misled, this account testifies to the long-range significance of Moses' instructions in Deuteronomy 27.[43]

Allusions to the imprecations recited at the end of the liturgy of Deuteronomy 27 are scarce. "They have treated father and mother with contempt" in Ezekiel 22:7 may echo Deuteronomy 27:16, and "In you men accept bribes to shed blood" in Ezekiel 22:12 may echo Deuteronomy 27:25. These texts and the rest of the Old Testament suggest these curses were honored more in the breach than in the observance. Illustrations of violations abound in the narratives.

- Micah erected an idolatrous image in his house (Judg. 17:3 – 4), which was later confiscated and used by the Danites (18:14 – 31); Solomon and many kings after him sponsored idolatrous state cults (1 Kings 11:1 – 10; cf. Manasseh in 2 Kings 21:1 – 9).
- David's son Absalom dishonored him by grasping for his throne (2 Sam. 15).
- Ahab seized the vineyard of Naboth located next to the palace (1 Kings 21).
- The widow and sons of a son of the prophets were exploited by a creditor (2 Kings 4:1 – 7).
- Reuben had intercourse with his stepmother Bilhah (Gen. 35:22; cf. 49:4); symbolic of his claim to the throne of David, Absalom publicly had intercourse with his father's concubines (2 Sam. 16:21 – 23), and Solomon seems to have interpreted Adonijah's request to marry Abishag, David's companion, as some such crime (1 Kings 2:13 – 25).
- Though he is not explicitly criticized for it, Abraham married his half-sister (Gen. 20:12). Amnon raped his sister Tamar (2 Sam. 13).
- David had his trusted warrior Uriah killed (2 Sam. 11).
- The historian summarizes the history of Israel as a history of violating the Torah and all the laws of God (2 Kings 17:34 – 35). A notable exception was Josiah, whose declared goal was "to establish

---

43. For a report on recent excavations of Gerizim, including evidence for a temple in Nehemiah's time, see Y. Magen, "Bells, Pendants, Snakes & Stones: A Samaritan Temple to the Lord on Mt. Gerizim," *BAR* 36/6 (November/December 2010): 26 – 35, 70.

the words of the Torah written in the scroll found in the temple" (2 Kings 23:24, pers. trans.).[44]

THE AMAZING GRACE OF God. Although the chapter ends on a serious note, contemporary readers do well to recognize in the rituals performed on Mounts Gerizim and Ebal the amazing grace of God. (1) God always keeps his Word. The prescribed ceremonies proclaim Yahweh's faithfulness to his covenant promises to the ancestors (vv. 2–3) and to the nation that came out of Egypt forty years earlier. When the Israelites perform these rituals, they will finally be at home in the land that Yahweh has given them, celebrating the covenantal union that exists among deity (Yahweh), people (Israel), and land (Canaan).

(2) With the Israelites, we need to rejoice that God has revealed his will. The Torah the Israelites are to inscribe on the stone pillars in the heart of their new homeland symbolized for them their covenant relationship with God. We do a disservice to Moses and to the Torah that he proclaims in this book if we equate this word with "law," for the Torah is much more than law — just as the Decalogue is much more than commands. In expounding the law Moses continually reminds the people that they are the products of this grace, and their obedience is to arise both from a recognition of past grace and in anticipation of grace still to come.

(3) If the inscription of the Torah on the stone pillars symbolizes Yahweh's gracious revelation of his will, then the altar symbolizes his gracious presence among them and his desire to have the Israelites before him. Whereas in 12:1–15 Yahweh had invited his people to his presence without reference to the altar, here the altar functions as the table on which the peace offerings are presented and at which the people eat and rejoice in the presence of Yahweh (vv. 6–7).[45] By eating the peace/fellowship sacrifices in the presence of the divine host, the Israelites celebrated the covenant bond that Yahweh had graciously established with them.[46]

These rituals signify Israel's security and hope in Yahweh. Of course, the peace they celebrate is made possible only through the work of Jesus Christ, whose sacrificial work underlies all these rituals. And the peace

44. Note the correspondence between "he shall establish the words of this Torah" in Deut. 27:26 and "he established the words of the Torah written on the document" in 2 Kings 23:24 (both pers. trans.).

45. Barker recognizes that the altar and the sacrifices lie at the heart of the Mount Ebal rituals ("The Theology of Deuteronomy 27," 295).

46. Cf. R. E. Averbeck, "Offerings and Sacrifices," *NIDOTTE*, 4:1001.

they will celebrate at Gerizim and Ebal expresses in microcosm the peace we enjoy and the heavenly inheritance we will one day claim in the very presence of God. We who were once far away have been brought near through the blood of Christ, for he himself is our peace, having destroyed the barrier between Israel and us, and created in himself one new person out of two (Eph. 4:12−15).

(4) Interrupting the ritual prescriptions, we hear Moses and the Levites reminding the Israelites that they become the people of Yahweh by grace alone (vv. 9−10). While the significance of this for Israel has been spelled out in 7:6; 14:1−2; and 26:16−19, we rejoice because as the new Israel of God, we too have become his sons, the objects of his gracious election, his special treasure, a holy people belonging to him (1 Peter 2:9−10). The awareness of our status as the Lord's covenant people should inspire us to scrupulous but joyful obedience to his revealed will.

(5) Moses' charge to the tribes—all twelve of them—to participate in the ceremony of blessing and cursing reminds them and modern readers of a notion that will be developed more fully in 30:15−20. Even as they enter the land, the people are to know that two ways are open to them: the way of blessing and the way of the curse. By referring to both, he anticipates chapter 28. Furthermore, by involving all the tribes, Moses reminds them that they all have equal access to the benefits of the land they have entered as well as to the delights it offers. This understanding of the people of God is remarkably egalitarian.

(6) The concluding imprecatory ceremony functions as a gracious reminder of the consequences of disobedience. The fact that Moses concludes his instructions concerning the rituals to be performed on Mounts Ebal and Gerizim with a series of curses—as stern as these are—culminating in a comprehensive warning against any violation of the covenant as represented in the Torah, accords with earlier expressions of pessimism concerning the nation's present and future spiritual condition (cf. 5:29; 9:7−24; 12:8).

Nevertheless, to interpret this ritual as a declaration that Israel is already under the curse of the law is to misunderstand the function of curses in covenantal contexts. They never serve as sentences for guilt already incurred but as gracious warnings against future infidelity. Their purpose is positive—to motivate obedience. If God's goodness does not stimulate his people to faith and righteous conduct, perhaps warnings like this will. Accordingly, these curses are not so much a prediction of Israel's certain

---

47. For discussion, see L. L. Norris, "The Function of New Testament Warning Passages: A Speech Act Theory Approach" (PhD diss., Wheaton College, Wheaton, IL, 2011).

doom as a reminder that through disobedience his people store up for themselves the wrath of God (cf. Rom. 2:4–5; Gal. 6:8). Even these warnings are grace, like Jesus' words in John 15:1–15, and as Paul will declare in Romans 11:17–24 and Colossians 1:21–23, for they serve the pastoral purpose of keeping the people of God spiritually on track.[47]

With this chapter we learn the full story of Israel's paradigmatic experience of grace. When Yahweh rescued this people from Egypt and established his covenant with them at Sinai, he inaugurated the eschatology announced to Abraham centuries ago in Genesis 15:13–16 and 17:3–8. Through these events those who had been slaves in Egypt were redeemed and at Sinai adopted as children of God (cf. Deut. 14:1–2). But the full realization of the promise still awaited them. Through the ceremonies in this chapter, the Israelites were invited to celebrate the eschatology realized when they crossed the Jordan. Now deity, people, and land were finally together. Inaugurated eschatology had given way to realized eschatology.

The Israelite experience is paradigmatic of our own. Through the sacrifice of Jesus Christ on the cross, we have been rescued from the bondage of sin and declared to be children of God. But the benefits of this redemption and adoption are not yet fully realized. We live in eager anticipation of the receipt of the grant/inheritance reserved for us (Rom. 8:9–17; Eph. 1:3–14). That will be an even greater and more glorious day of celebration.

Deuteronomy 28:1–29:1[28:69]

If you fully obey the LORD your God and carefully follow all his commands I give you today, the LORD your God will set you high above all the nations on earth. ²All these blessings will come upon you and accompany you if you obey the LORD your God:

³You will be blessed in the city and blessed in the country.

⁴The fruit of your womb will be blessed, and the crops of your land and the young of your livestock—the calves of your herds and the lambs of your flocks.

⁵Your basket and your kneading trough will be blessed.

⁶You will be blessed when you come in and blessed when you go out.

⁷The LORD will grant that the enemies who rise up against you will be defeated before you. They will come at you from one direction but flee from you in seven.

⁸The LORD will send a blessing on your barns and on everything you put your hand to. The LORD your God will bless you in the land he is giving you.

⁹The LORD will establish you as his holy people, as he promised you on oath, if you keep the commands of the LORD your God and walk in his ways. ¹⁰Then all the peoples on earth will see that you are called by the name of the LORD, and they will fear you. ¹¹The LORD will grant you abundant prosperity—in the fruit of your womb, the young of your livestock and the crops of your ground—in the land he swore to your forefathers to give you.

¹²The LORD will open the heavens, the storehouse of his bounty, to send rain on your land in season and to bless all the work of your hands. You will lend to many nations but will borrow from none. ¹³The LORD will make you the head, not the tail. If you pay attention to the commands of the LORD your God that I give you this day and carefully follow them, you will always be at the top, never at the bottom. ¹⁴Do not turn aside from any of the commands I give you today, to the right or to the left, following other gods and serving them.

¹⁵However, if you do not obey the LORD your God and do not carefully follow all his commands and decrees I am giving you today, all these curses will come upon you and overtake you:

¹⁶You will be cursed in the city and cursed in the country. ¹⁷Your basket and your kneading trough will be cursed. ¹⁸The fruit of your womb will be cursed, and the crops of your land, and the calves of your herds and the lambs of your flocks. ¹⁹You will be cursed when you come in and cursed when you go out.

²⁰The Lord will send on you curses, confusion and rebuke in everything you put your hand to, until you are destroyed and come to sudden ruin because of the evil you have done in forsaking him. ²¹The Lord will plague you with diseases until he has destroyed you from the land you are entering to possess. ²²The Lord will strike you with wasting disease, with fever and inflammation, with scorching heat and drought, with blight and mildew, which will plague you until you perish. ²³The sky over your head will be bronze, the ground beneath you iron. ²⁴The Lord will turn the rain of your country into dust and powder; it will come down from the skies until you are destroyed.

²⁵The Lord will cause you to be defeated before your enemies. You will come at them from one direction but flee from them in seven, and you will become a thing of horror to all the kingdoms on earth. ²⁶Your carcasses will be food for all the birds of the air and the beasts of the earth, and there will be no one to frighten them away. ²⁷The Lord will afflict you with the boils of Egypt and with tumors, festering sores and the itch, from which you cannot be cured. ²⁸The Lord will afflict you with madness, blindness and confusion of mind. ²⁹At midday you will grope about like a blind man in the dark. You will be unsuccessful in everything you do; day after day you will be oppressed and robbed, with no one to rescue you.

³⁰You will be pledged to be married to a woman, but another will take her and ravish her. You will build a house, but you will not live in it. You will plant a vineyard, but you will not even begin to enjoy its fruit. ³¹Your ox will be slaughtered before your eyes, but you will eat none of it. Your donkey will be forcibly taken from you and will not be returned. Your sheep will be given to your enemies, and no one will rescue them. ³²Your sons and daughters will be given to another nation, and you will wear out your eyes watching for them day after day, powerless to lift a hand. ³³A people that you do not know will eat what your land and labor produce, and you will have nothing but cruel oppression all your days. ³⁴The sights

you see will drive you mad. [35]The LORD will afflict your knees and legs with painful boils that cannot be cured, spreading from the soles of your feet to the top of your head.

[36]The LORD will drive you and the king you set over you to a nation unknown to you or your fathers. There you will worship other gods, gods of wood and stone. [37]You will become a thing of horror and an object of scorn and ridicule to all the nations where the LORD will drive you.

[38]You will sow much seed in the field but you will harvest little, because locusts will devour it. [39]You will plant vineyards and cultivate them but you will not drink the wine or gather the grapes, because worms will eat them. [40]You will have olive trees throughout your country but you will not use the oil, because the olives will drop off. [41]You will have sons and daughters but you will not keep them, because they will go into captivity. [42]Swarms of locusts will take over all your trees and the crops of your land.

[43]The alien who lives among you will rise above you higher and higher, but you will sink lower and lower. [44]He will lend to you, but you will not lend to him. He will be the head, but you will be the tail.

[45]All these curses will come upon you. They will pursue you and overtake you until you are destroyed, because you did not obey the LORD your God and observe the commands and decrees he gave you. [46]They will be a sign and a wonder to you and your descendants forever. [47]Because you did not serve the LORD your God joyfully and gladly in the time of prosperity, [48]therefore in hunger and thirst, in nakedness and dire poverty, you will serve the enemies the LORD sends against you. He will put an iron yoke on your neck until he has destroyed you.

[49]The LORD will bring a nation against you from far away, from the ends of the earth, like an eagle swooping down, a nation whose language you will not understand, [50]a fierce-looking nation without respect for the old or pity for the young. [51]They will devour the young of your livestock and the crops of your land until you are destroyed. They will leave you no grain, new wine or oil, nor any calves of your herds or lambs of your flocks until you are ruined. [52]They will lay siege to all the cities throughout your land until the high fortified walls in which you trust fall down. They will besiege all the cities throughout the land the LORD your God is giving you.

⁵³Because of the suffering that your enemy will inflict
on you during the siege, you will eat the fruit of the womb,
the flesh of the sons and daughters the LORD your God has
given you. ⁵⁴Even the most gentle and sensitive man among
you will have no compassion on his own brother or the wife
he loves or his surviving children, ⁵⁵and he will not give to
one of them any of the flesh of his children that he is eating.
It will be all he has left because of the suffering your enemy
will inflict on you during the siege of all your cities. ⁵⁶The
most gentle and sensitive woman among you — so sensitive
and gentle that she would not venture to touch the ground
with the sole of her foot — will begrudge the husband she
loves and her own son or daughter ⁵⁷the afterbirth from her
womb and the children she bears. For she intends to eat them
secretly during the siege and in the distress that your enemy
will inflict on you in your cities.

⁵⁸If you do not carefully follow all the words of this law,
which are written in this book, and do not revere this glorious and awesome name — the LORD your God — ⁵⁹the LORD
will send fearful plagues on you and your descendants, harsh
and prolonged disasters, and severe and lingering illnesses.
⁶⁰He will bring upon you all the diseases of Egypt that you
dreaded, and they will cling to you. ⁶¹The LORD will also
bring on you every kind of sickness and disaster not recorded
in this Book of the Law, until you are destroyed. ⁶²You who
were as numerous as the stars in the sky will be left but few in
number, because you did not obey the LORD your God. ⁶³Just
as it pleased the LORD to make you prosper and increase in
number, so it will please him to ruin and destroy you. You will
be uprooted from the land you are entering to possess.

⁶⁴Then the LORD will scatter you among all nations, from
one end of the earth to the other. There you will worship
other gods — gods of wood and stone, which neither you
nor your fathers have known. ⁶⁵Among those nations you
will find no repose, no resting place for the sole of your
foot. There the LORD will give you an anxious mind, eyes
weary with longing, and a despairing heart. ⁶⁶You will live
in constant suspense, filled with dread both night and day,
never sure of your life. ⁶⁷In the morning you will say, "If only
it were evening!" and in the evening, "If only it were morning!" — because of the terror that will fill your hearts and
the sights that your eyes will see. ⁶⁸The LORD will send you

back in ships to Egypt on a journey I said you should never make again. There you will offer yourselves for sale to your enemies as male and female slaves, but no one will buy you. 29:1These are the terms of the covenant the LORD commanded Moses to make with the Israelites in Moab, in addition to the covenant he had made with them at Horeb.

CHAPTER 28 BRINGS MOSES' second address to a close. Several features suggest that in the oral delivery chapter 28 followed immediately after chapter 26: (1) Deuteronomy 28:1−2, 9−11 and 26:16−19 exhibit a series of thematic and lexical and stylistic links;[1] (2) following ancient treaty form, these blessings and curses appear naturally after the Israelites have confirmed their status as Yahweh's covenant people (26:16−19); (3) Deuteronomy 29:1[28:69] expressly declares that these utterances were delivered in the context of a covenantal renewal ceremony;[2] (4) concluding the address on covenant relationship with blessings and curses brings it into line with the conclusion to the covenant revelation at Sinai (Lev. 26). If the structure of chapters 12−26 and 28 resembles that of the so-called "Holiness Code" of Leviticus 17−26, the correspondence between the concluding colophons is particularly striking:

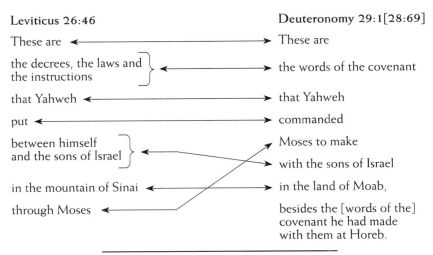

Leviticus 26:46	Deuteronomy 29:1[28:69]
These are	These are
the decrees, the laws and the instructions	the words of the covenant
that Yahweh	that Yahweh
put	commanded
between himself and the sons of Israel	Moses to make
	with the sons of Israel
in the mountain of Sinai	in the land of Moab,
through Moses	besides the [words of the] covenant he had made with them at Horeb.

1. Appeals for scrupulous obedience to all Yahweh's commands and to "walk in his ways"; the promise that Yahweh will set Israel high above the nations; references to Israel as a holy people belonging to Yahweh.

2. The ending of this unit is disputed. English translations follow the Vulgate in seeing 29:1[28:69] as the introduction to chap. 29, which accords with the location of analogous titular

The structure of Deuteronomy 12 − 26 generally and the curses in 28 particularly seems to be patterned after the "Holiness Code." The most significant deviation in the latter involves the omission of the hopeful declaration that Israel's history will not end in exile (Lev. 26:40 − 45). But this lack is more apparent than real, for this hope had been announced at the end of the first address (4:30 − 31) and will be developed in detail in Deuteronomy 30:1 − 10.

However, the links between Deuteronomy 28 and Leviticus 26 extend beyond structural features to the blessings and curses themselves. Many motifs in Deuteronomy 28 derive from Leviticus 26 (e.g., Lev. 26:30 − 31; Deut. 28:36b − 37, 64; cf. 4:27 − 28). Sometimes vocabulary is borrowed from Leviticus, but it is often modified.[3] Scholars also recognize the links between Deuteronomy's version of the covenant curses and imprecations found in extrabiblical treaty documents.[4] Indeed, most disasters anticipated for Israel (vv. 20 − 68) appear outside the Bible.[5] These imprecations seem to derive from "the broad pool of traditional curse topics and formulae that had long existed and grown up through many centuries, of which we now see only glimpses."[6]

Deuteronomy 28 divides structurally into two uneven panels, consisting respectively of blessings awaiting the Israelites if they are faithful to their covenant Lord (vv. 1 − 14), and curses if they persist in rebellion against

---

declarations in Deuteronomy (1:1; 4:44, 45; 12:1; 33:1), and the use of "covenant" as the key word in chapter 29 (vv. 9, 12, 14, 21, 25[8, 11, 13, 20, 24]). While Deut. 29:1[28:69] is obviously transitional, the Hebrew versification, which includes this verse in chapter 28, is well-founded. See H. F. van Rooy, "Deuteronomy 28, 69 — Superscript or Subscript," *JNWSL* 14 (1988): 215 − 22.

3. E.g., the portrayal of drought as hardening the heavens and the pulverizing the earth (Lev. 26:19; Deut. 28:23 − 24).

4. See D. R. Hillers, *Treaty-Curses and the Old Testament Prophets* (BibOr 16; Rome: Pontifical Biblical Institute, 1964). Hillers discusses Leviticus 26 and Deuteronomy 28 on pp. 30 − 42. Also see Deut. 28:15, 45 − 47, 58; cf. Sefire 1A:14 and 24 (*COS*, 2:213 − 14); the Vassal Treaties of Esarhaddon (hereafter VTE) §§410, 513 (*ANET*, 538 − 39); Deut. 28:58, 61; cf. Sefire 1B:23, 28, 33 (*COS*, 2:214 − 15); Deut. 28:62 − 63; cf. Sefire 1B: 23, 38, (*COS*, 2:215).

5. Based on links between this chapter and the Vassal Treaties of Esarhaddon in particular, many critical scholars assume that Deuteronomy 28 was inspired by neo-Assyrian vassal treaty form. However, the differences in these documents are more striking than the similarities and links with second millennium BC treaties and are at least as strong as with first millennium texts. For discussion, see M. Zehnder, "Building on Stone? Deuteronomy and Esarhaddon's Loyalty Oaths (Part 1): Some Preliminary Observations," *BBR* 19.3 (2009): 341 − 74; "Building on Stone? Deuteronomy and Esarhaddon's Loyalty Oaths (Part 2): Some Additional Observations" *BBR* 19.4 (2009): 511 − 35.

6. K. A. Kitchen, *On the Reliability of the Old Testament* (Grand Rapids: Eerdmans, 2003), 294.

him (vv. 15–68). The space devoted to the curses reflects the chapter's paraenetic purpose. Like the imprecations in 27:15–26, these curses seek to motivate fidelity and deter Israelites from violating the terms of the covenant.[7] Moses' aim is pastoral: to impress on the minds of his audience the seriousness of disobedience. By assenting to the specified consequences in the ratification ritual, for good or ill, the Israelites seal their own fate.[8]

Assuming that 26:16–19 originally stood at the head of this chapter, the conclusion to Moses' second address originally exhibits the following structure:

Introduction: The Privilege and Responsibilities of Covenant Relationship (26:16–19)	
The blessings (28:1–14)	The curses (28:15–68)
The precondition to blessing (28:1–2)	The precondition to curse (28:15)
Formulaic declarations of blessing (28:3–6)	Formulaic declarations of curse (28:16–19)
Detailed exposition of blessing (28:7–14)	Detailed exposition of curse (28:20–68)
Colophonic Conclusion (29:1[Heb. 28:69])	

The Way of Blessing and Summary of the Way of the Curse (28:1–19)

ALTHOUGH VERSES 15–19 formally introduce the long imprecatory section, since they mirror the introduction to the blessing section (vv. 1–6), a comparative commentary may be helpful. Each part consists of a formal introduction, followed by a series of blessings/curses that represent the consequences of the choices the people make.

The preconditions to blessing and curse (28:1–2; 28:15). While the NIV obscures these features, the opening lines of the two panels exhibit remarkable parallelism. As in extrabiblical texts,[9] whether or not people listen to their suzerain's voice tests their fidelity as vassals (vv. 1, 15; cf. Ex. 19:5). The addition of "today" in both brings Moses' hearers back to the present and reminds readers that chapter 27 has been a textual digression. While the words for "blessings" and "curses" are the same as those encoun-

---

7. Similarly D. J. McCarthy, *Treaty and Covenant: A Study in Form in the Ancient Oriental Documents and in the Old Testament* (AnBib 21; Rome: Pontifical Biblical Institute, 1963), 176.

8. This interpretation is reinforced in 29:12–13[11–12], 20–21[18–20], 24–28[23–27].

9. For discussion, see Kalluveettil, *Declaration and Covenant*, 153–59.

tered in 11:26–29 and 27:12–13, here and throughout the chapter the concepts are portrayed as animate beings that come upon their targets. The opening to the first panel promises Israel that if they will walk in the ways of Yahweh, he will set them high above the nations of the earth (cf. 26:19; 7:14). Verse 13 expands on the motif of Israel's exaltation in the context of the blessings, but verses 43–44 develop its antithesis, Israel's subjugation through the curses.

The formulaic declarations of blessing and curse (28:3–6; 28:16–19). With a few minor exceptions, the formulaic declarations of blessing and curse continue the mirror-image rhetorical strategy. The text includes six declarations each of blessing and cursing, yielding a total of twelve and matching the division of the tribes in 27:11–13. The outer benedictions/maledictions involved standardized pairs of opposites—"town" and "country"; "your coming in" and "your going out"—which function as merisms for "wherever you are" and "wherever you go," respectively. The middle pair in each case is more complex. Whereas the outside pairs involve the Israelites' own general well-being, these pairs pronounce the benediction/malediction upon the fruits of human effort (vv. 4, 17–18).

These formulaic blessings and curses define Israel's well-being in agricultural terms and are grounded on the underlying premise that the land belongs to Yahweh; he determines whether it fulfills its role within the covenantal triangle involving deity, people, and land.[10] While Israel's neighbors looked to fertility gods for their economic security, these opening statements declare that Israel's well-being depends on their fidelity to Yahweh.

The way of blessing (28:7–14). Although verses 7–13 expound on verses 3–6, this paragraph exhibits independent stylistic and structural integrity. The skeleton consists of seven principal clauses. Except for the third (v. 8b), in Hebrew each statement highlights Yahweh's role by beginning with a verb and explicitly identifying Yahweh as the subject. As a whole the unit summarizes the rewards for covenant obedience, though verses 9 and 13b–14 remind the hearers that these benefactions are not unconditional entitlements (cf. vv. 1–2). Within this relationship Israel will never be able to claim credit for the blessings they enjoy, but they will be held fully liable if the blessings do not materialize. Appearing in the center of roughly chiastically arranged benefactions (vv. 9–10), Moses highlights Israel's special relationship with Yahweh, envisioning a glorious future in which the covenantal triangle is fully operative and *shalom* pervades. The

---

10. Cf. E. W. Davies, "Land: Its Rights and Privileges," in *The World of Ancient Israel: Sociological, Anthropological and Political Perspectives* (ed. R. E. Clements; Cambridge: Cambridge Univ. Press, 1989), 349–69.

benefactions are best treated in logical order rather than serially as they appear in the text.

Echoing 15:4, in verse 8b Moses issues a general promise that Yahweh will bless the nation in the land. Presenting the ideal of the trilateral relationship in its most elementary form, this statement could have served as a heading to this entire list of blessings. In verses 8a and 11 − 12a Moses promises fertility and material prosperity as certain rewards for faithfulness. The proof of Yahweh's blessing on all human effort (cf. v. 20)[11] will be evident in Israel's barns (v. 8a). Fleshing out this general promise of material well-being in verses 11 − 12a, Moses adds an effusive promise — "the LORD will grant you abundant prosperity" — and then specifies the dimensions of that prosperity: large families, large herds, and abundant crops (v. 11). As in verse 4, this triad reflects the three areas of primary concern in fertility religions.

However, since this prosperity will happen on the land that Yahweh had sworn to the patriarchs, the blessing is linked to the ancient promises. Moses concretizes the image of prosperity in verse 12a by portraying Yahweh as the owner of a heavenly "storehouse,"[12] who opens the chute and lets the rains gush out on the land. This statement is inspired by Leviticus 26:4, but the image is also reminiscent of Ugaritic myths that refer to Baal's releasing the rains over the earth.[13] Moses hereby declares polemically that the productivity of the land is determined by Yahweh, not Baal. In addition to extraordinary fertility within the land, in verses 7 and 12b − 13 Moses promises Israel hegemony over the nations. Speaking metaphorically, he declares that Yahweh will make them "the head" of all and "the tail" of none (v. 13a). This hegemony will involve total military (v. 7)[14] and economic (vv. 12b − 13a; cf. 15:6) superiority over the nations.

As noted above, verses 9 − 10 represent the theological heart of this paragraph and the climax of all the blessings in verses 1 − 14. Echoing 26:18 − 19, Moses articulates Yahweh's ideal for his people and their privileges as his covenant partner (cf. Ex. 19:5 − 6). Whereas 26:19 had spoken of Yahweh setting Israel high above all the nations, here Moses envisions him establishing Israel as his holy people. That this involves the fulfillment of an earlier commitment is highlighted by the verb "to establish" and the

---

11. "Everything you put your hand to" in v. 8a is equivalent to "all the work of your hands" in v. 12. Cf. 12:18; 15:10; 23:20[21]; 28:8, 20.

12. On the heavens as a storehouse filled with Yahweh's resources, see Job 37:1 − 13; 38:22; Ps. 104:13; Ezek. 34:25 − 30.

13. For the text in transliteration and translation see *UNP*, 132 − 37.

14. They will attack Israel as a united force coming on one road, but flee in seven. As in 7:1 "seven ways" speaks of totality; the survivors will seek every possible escape route.

addition of "as he promised you on oath." The notion of Israel as Yahweh's holy people is familiar from 7:6; 14:2, 21. However, in keeping with Exodus 19:5−6, the fulfillment of Yahweh's covenantal promises will be contingent on their living according to his revealed will, here referred to as "keeping" his commands and "walking in his ways." These are shorthand expressions for all that Yahweh requires of Israel (cf. 10:12−13).

When Yahweh establishes Israel as his holy people, then all the nations of the earth will see that Israel is branded with his name. Translated literally ("that the name of Yahweh is read/called upon you"), this expression derives from the practice of inscribing or branding one's name on property.[15] When the nations read Yahweh's name on Israel, they will recognize both that he owns them[16] and that their well-being is a reflection of their divine Suzerain.[17] They will transfer the awe that is rightly expressed before God to the people who bear his awesome name. This comment correlates with Moses' declaration in 26:19 that the nations' recognition of Israel will ultimately result in the praise, renown, and glory of Yahweh.

By characterizing the nations' response as "fear," Moses links this statement with Genesis 9:2, and in so doing hints at Israel's role in the biblical metanarrative of redemption. As his "holy people," Israel was chosen to bear the name of their divine Redeemer and of the Creator of all nations (26:19). They represent humanity in microcosm, exercising authority on Yahweh's behalf and evoking the response of awe from those over whom they exercise dominion.

The Way of the Curse (28:20−68)

IN VERSE 20 WE arrive at the longest literary unit in Deuteronomy. Whereas the imprecations of 27:15−26 and 28:15−19 are formulaic in nature, the curses in verses 20−68 are cast in impassioned rhetorical style and expound in exhaustive detail the reversal of the blessings specified in verses 7−13. When heard orally, these curses create terror in the mind of the hearer.

Several features of the text contribute to their shuddering effect. (1) As in verses 7−13 Yahweh is the subject of all the significant verbs. (2) Moses emphasizes Yahweh's intentions with a series of expressions involving the preposition "until": until Israel is destroyed/he destroys her (vv. 20, 24, 45,

15. On the practice of branding slaves with the name of their owners in Mesopotamia, see M. A. Dandamaev, *Slavery in Babylonia from Nabopolassar to Alexander the Great (626−331 BC)* (rev. ed.; DeKalb, IL: Northern Illinois Univ. Press, 1984), 78, 229−34. See also our discussion of the second command of the Decalogue (5:11) above.

16. See also 2 Chron. 7:14, and esp. Isa. 63:19.

17. For further discussion, see D. I. Block, "Bearing the Name of the LORD with Honor," in *How I Love Your Torah, O LORD!* 61−72.

51, 61; vv. 48, 63), Israel perishes (vv. 20, 22), her defenses crumble (v. 52), and he has made an end of Israel (v. 21). These hyperbolic expressions declare Yahweh's goal: to destroy the covenantal triangle and in effect "wipe out" the nation itself. (3) Moses highlights Israel's hopelessness by punctuating the litany of disasters with declarations of the absence of any relief.[18] (4) By means of a seemingly endless catalogue of secondary agents of doom, Moses warns that Yahweh will marshal every conceivable agent of destruction against his people. (5) At critical junctures Moses inserts reminders of the causes of these disasters. Although Yahweh is directly involved in Israel's demise, the Israelites will be destroyed because they have been unfaithful to him (vv. 20, 45, 47, 62).

On first sight, the catalogue of curses seems erratic and disjointed. The opening declaration (v. 20) may be interpreted as a heading for the entire section, summarizing the key issues in the imprecations: (1) the source of Israel's doom; (2) the agents of doom; (3) the scope of doom; (4) the goal of doom; and (5) the reason for Israel's doom. Thereafter the location of conditional and motive clauses offers the best clues to the structure of these curses.

A new conditional clause in verse 58 divides the text into two unequal parts: verses 20–57 and verses 58–68. Within the first part verses 45–48 are transitional, offering a theological interpretation of Israel's eventual doom. Within this segment verses 45–46 summarize verses 20–44 and verses 47–48 introduce verses 49–57. These structural signals point to three recognizable literary panels — three volleys of woe intended to motivate Israel to fidelity and love for their Redeemer.

(1) **The way of doom: the first volley (28:20–46).** Verses 20 and 45–46 frame the first volley of woes, announcing the issues involved. While linked in substance, the styles of these bookends differ. Whereas verse 20 has Yahweh dispatching the agents of Israel's doom, verse 45 compares the curses to an animal pursuing and overtaking its prey. Whereas in verse 20 Yahweh commissions a triad of agents of doom against Israel, verse 45 replaces these with a triad of verbs. Whereas verse 20 identifies the targets of doom as the work of the Israelites' hands, verse 45 identifies the Israelites themselves as the targets. Whereas verse 20 declares that Yahweh's actions against Israel are precipitated by the people's evil deeds and their abandonment of Yahweh, verse 45 specifies the offenses as refusing to obey Yahweh, not keeping his commands and decrees.

---

18. There will be no one to frighten away the scavenging beast and birds, who come to devour the corpses of Israel's slain (v. 26); there will be no one to save (vv. 29, 31); there will be nothing their hand can do (v. 32); and there will be no one to buy their freedom (v. 68).

The reference to the long-range effects of Yahweh's actions against Israel in verse 46 represents the most striking difference between these borders: They will be a "sign" and "wonder" forever.[19] The text does not specify what Yahweh's actions against Israel will prove, but it appears the lessons will include Yahweh's marshaling the forces of heaven and earth to punish those who resist him and to achieve his purposes in accordance with his word. Between these borders Moses threatens a litany of disasters, illustrating the curse, panic, and frustration referred to in verse 20. Although he moves from one topic to another, the passage divides into three paragraphs, successively increasing in length and intensity, like three blasts of the watchman's trumpet (vv. 20–26; vv. 27–34; vv. 35–45). The core of each paragraph involves three broad categories of calamities cited in Leviticus 26:25–26: sword, pestilence, and famine.

The first alarm (vv. 21–26). The first alarm involves three agents of disaster: the plague (vv. 21–22a), crop failure (vv. 22b–24), and military defeat (vv. 25–26). While outside Israel the word *deber* (NIV "diseases") identified the demon of pestilence,[20] here allusions to malevolent spirits are thoroughly demythologized. The expression refers to epidemics like the bubonic plague that often afflict animal and human populations ravaged by famine and battle. Yahweh will cause this plague to cling to its victim like fleas attached to skin and bite them.[21]

In verse 22 Moses becomes more specific, listing seven afflictions with which Yahweh will strike his people. The catalogue of seven afflictions expresses Yahweh's sovereignty over all agents of death and destruction. The first four entries elaborate on *deber* in verse 21 and specify diseases at Yahweh's disposal: wasting disease,[22] fever,[23] inflammation,[24] and scorching heat.[25] The fifth refers to the sword (*ḥereb*), which functions as shorthand for Israel's defeat by enemy armies (cf. vv. 25–26),[26] and the last two refer to crop diseases.

---

19. In 13:12[13]. these expressions identify supernatural actions performed by prophets to prove their authenticity.

20. See G. del Ollmo Lete, "Deber," *DDD*, 231–32.

21. On the bubonic plague in ancient Mesopotamia, see J. Scurlock and B. R. Andersen, *Diagnoses in Assyrian and Babylonian Medicine* (Urbana: Univ. of Illinois Press, 2005), 73–74. In Mesopotamia, the plague was occasionally described as a demon of pestilence "eating" his victims, as if he were an insect with a particular thirst for human blood (ibid, 472).

22. Cf. also Lev. 26:16. This probably refers to tuberculosis. Cf. *HALOT*, 1463.

23. Cf also Lev. 26:16. This probably refers to some sort of inflammation, perhaps fever. Cf. *HALOT*, 1067; Tigay, *Deuteronomy*, 262.

24. This may be another term for "fever." Cf. *HALOT*, 223.

25. This probably refers to a feverish heat. Cf. *HALOT*, 352, 357.

26. Contra NIV, which renders this as "drought."

The next two verses (vv. 23 – 24) spell out the crop afflictions. Like the four expressions for human illnesses, the meanings of the terms for crop diseases are uncertain. "Blight" apparently refers to premature drying of grain growing in the fields, perhaps because of the desiccating effect of scorching east wind. "Mildew" seems to involve pathological yellowing of grain, attributable to plant disease, inadequate nutrients in the soil, or drought. These verses echo Leviticus 26:19, which also portrays the heavens as a sheet of metal preventing moisture above the firmament from watering the earth, and the ground as hardened and resisting cultivation. Verse 24 envisions precipitants from the heavens. However, this is not rain but powdery dust that falls on the people, like dust storms whipped up by the hot desert winds (sirocco) common in the Middle East.

The reference to the sword (*ḥereb*) in verse 22 anticipates the threats of verses 25 – 26. Reversing the blessing of verse 7, Yahweh threatens to hand Israel over to her enemies to be struck down and forced to flee. Instead of being "high above all the nations on earth" (v. 1; cf. 26:19), they will present the kingdoms of the earth with an image of terror (cf. 2 Chron. 29:8). Verse 26 concretizes the horror of defeat in battle. The corpses of the slain are left out in the open field as carrion for scavenging birds and mammals — perhaps the greatest indignity of all. In the ancient world bodies were often discarded in the open and left to be eaten by wild animals,[27] especially the bodies of those who had broken contracts and treaty oaths.[28]

The second alarm (vv. 27 – 34). The second alarm also presents three categories of disaster: pestilence, famine, sword. As in verses 21 – 22a, the curses in verses 27 – 29a, 34 threaten the personal health of the Israelites. A pair of identical clauses highlights Yahweh's role in Israel's future disaster (vv. 27a, 28a, cf. v. 35a), to be followed by a list of agents he will engage. The seven listed here correspond to the seven listed after the same principal clause in verse 22, though now the first four involve incurable skin ailments, while the last three are psychosomatic and psychological in nature.[29] As in verse 22, the meanings of some of these expressions are uncertain. "Boils" refers to some sort of skin disease, perhaps an ulcer or a boil (NIV; cf. Ex. 9:8 – 12).[30] "Tumors" involves some kind of swelling, and "festering sores" point to infectious skin lesions; "the itch" occurs only here. Verse 28 adds

---

27. See Hillers' discussion of this curse, *Treaty-Curses*, 68 – 69.

28. As translated by Parpola and Watanabe, *Neo-Assyrian Treaties and Loyalty Oaths*, 46. See also F. C. Fensham, "The Curse of the Dry Bones in Ezekiel 37:1 – 14 Changed to a Blessing of Resurrection," *JNWSL* 13 (1987): 60. Cf. Jer. 7:33; 34:17 – 20; Ezek. 37:1 – 2.

29. So also Tigay, *Deuteronomy*, 263.

30. Like the earlier words for "fever" and "inflammation" (v. 22), the word used here derives from a root meaning "to be warm."

three more diseases (cf. Zech. 12:4): "madness,[31] blindness [cf. 1 Sam. 21:14–15(15–16)] and confusion of mind." This may refer to the bewilderment that attends the kinds of disasters described in this chapter.[32]

Verse 29 illustrates how these mental disorders manifest themselves. Disoriented, in broad daylight people will grope their way around like a blind man in his perpetual darkness (cf. v. 34). Generally speaking, verses 29c and 33b establish the context of this segment: "day after day you will be oppressed and robbed." This declaration, coupled with the expressions of hopelessness in vv. 29, 31, and 32, suggests the effects of an overwhelming military defeat.

Compounding the crisis, verse 29b announces the theme of utter futility, which is then developed by means of a series of futility curses[33] involving grievous domestic and economic abuses. (1) *The futility of betrothal* (v. 30a). A man will be betrothed to a woman, but another man will ravish her (cf. 21:10–14).[34] (2) *The futility of home construction* (v. 30b). The reference to Israelites building houses but not dwelling in them reverses the fate the present generation is about to impose on the Canaanites (6:10–11). (3) *The futility of agricultural efforts* (v. 30c). The threat of planting vineyards but not enjoying the fruit of the vine also reverses the image of 6:10–11. (4) *The futility of owning livestock* (v. 31). Referring to the three most important domestic animals—oxen, donkeys, sheep—this curse warns of their confiscation by invaders. (5) *The futility of having children* (v. 32). The Israelites' children will be seized and delivered over to merchants to be sold in the international slave trade. Parents will look on helplessly and spend the rest of their lives "crying their eyes out" for them.[35] (6) *The futility of all human effort* (v. 33). Verse 33 summarizes the tragedy of the preceding. The Israelites will not eat the fruit of their own ground or consume any products of their toil.

The third alarm (vv. 35–44). Like the first alarm, this paragraph subdivides into three parts, dealing successively with illnesses (v. 35), military defeat (vv. 36–37), and famine (vv. 38–42). It ends with a warning of the internal social effects of Israel's calamities (vv. 43–44).

---

31. Tigay (*Deuteronomy*, 264) interprets this as "stupefaction, psychological disorientation."

32. For discussion of mental disorders in ancient Mesopotamia see Scurlock and Andersen, *Diagnoses*, 367–85.

33. For extrabiblical analogues to these "futility curses," see the Tell Fekheriye bilingual inscription (*COS*, 2:34[p. 154]). For discussion of these "futility curses," see T. G. Crawford, *Blessing and Curse in Syro-Palestinian Inscriptions of the Iron Age* (American University Studies 7/120; New York: Peter Lang, 1992), 170–73.

34. The rare word used here involves raping women in the context of battle and conquest (Isa. 13:16; Zech. 14:2).

35. Thus Tigay, *Deuteronomy*, 265.

Picking up the motif mentioned in verse 27, verse 35 returns to "the boils of Egypt," though now Moses adds that they will affect the knees and legs particularly, rendering movement difficult. Not only will this plague be incurable; the boils will cover the entire body from the soles of their feet to the crowns of their heads.

Whereas the first alarm spoke explicitly of Yahweh causing Israel's defeat at the hands of enemy armies (vv. 24−25), and the second dealt with oppression of Israel's citizens that will attend such a defeat (vv. 29b−34), the third predicts Israel's exile from the land (vv. 36−37). (1) Reiterating notions expressed earlier in 4:27−28, Moses speaks of Yahweh's direct involvement in driving his people into exile (28:36). Borrowing vocabulary from 17:14−15, he inserts a surprising but sarcastic reference to Israel's king.[36]

(2) Moses speaks again of Israel's exile among the nations, characterized ominously as "unknown to you or your fathers" (cf. 13:6[7]), an expression intended to strike fear in the hearts of the Israelites. In a final blow to the tripartite covenantal relationship celebrated in chapter 27, they will be exiled to an alien land.

(3) Moses declares that there, among the nations, the Israelites "will worship other gods, gods of wood and stone" (v. 36; cf. 4:28). Their privileged status as vassals of Yahweh will be exchanged for vassaldom to lifeless idols. Whereas non-Israelites perceived idols as living objects indwelt by the spirit of the deity they represented, to Moses idols were concrete objects at best and "detestable images" (29:17[16]) at worst.

Verse 37 summarizes the effects of these calamities on Israel's standing among the nations. Expanding on 4:27−28 and and 28:25, this statement inverts verse 10 and especially 26:19. Moses replaces three expressions of privilege in the latter with three expressions of shame: "horror," "object of scorn," and "ridicule." The first word expresses the nations' shock at Israel's fate.[37] The second suggests that the name "Israel" will become proverbial for disaster; they will become a classic illustration of misfortune and rejection by a deity. Deriving from a root meaning "to repeat," the third word suggests that Israel will become the object of ridiculing conversations.

In verses 38−42 Moses resumes his threat of famine as judgment, but his tactics change. Now the lack of food will not be caused by drought and plant diseases but insects—though he interrupts this series of "futility curses" by warning of the deportation of the children (v. 41). This threat

---

36. Without reference to his divine election. Cf. Samuel's comment in 1 Sam. 12:13.

37. Cf. 29:22−24[21−23]. This expression is common in Jeremiah's oracles of judgment: Jer. 2:15; 4:7; etc. See also 2 Kings 22:19; 2 Chron. 29:8; 30:7; Ps. 73:19; Isa. 5:9; 13:9; Hos. 5:9; Joel 1:7; Mic. 6:16; Zeph. 2:15; Zech. 7:14.

might have been included more logically after verse 36, but its present location places "the fruit of the womb" alongside "the fruit of the ground." The catalogue of futility curses involves the entire range of ancient Palestinian agricultural activity: fields of grain (v. 38), vineyards (v. 39), olive groves (v. 40), and fruit trees (v. 41). The crop failures are caused by little creatures that Yahweh will send to devour and despoil the crops before they can be harvested. "Locusts" (v. 38) are grass-eating insects that fly in vast swarms and devour everything in sight.[38] "Worms" (v. 39) refers to fruit grubs that attack the grapes.[39] The meaning of "swarms of locusts" (v. 42) is uncertain, but it probably refers to a species of beetle that kills vegetation by attacking leaves or stems.[40]

Verses 43–44 reverse the blessing in verses 12–13 (cf. 23:20[21]) and invert the Israelites' situation during the plagues of Egypt (Ex. 8:23–24[19–20]; 9:4, 6): Aliens will come and live among the Israelites. "The alien" could refer to foreign nations, but this is better interpreted as a divinely imposed reversal whereby Israelites in the land are targeted for judgment while sojourners and guest workers are spared (cf. Lev. 25:47).

In verses 45–46 Moses provides a summary conclusion to the litany of disasters (identified as "all these curses") described in verses 20–44. These threats describe Israel's certain future if they abandon Yahweh and serve other gods (v. 29).

(2) The way of doom: the second volley (28:47–57). As severe as the preceding covenant curses are, now the effects become horrific. This volley is concerned with only one issue: the utter degradation of Israel through siege by a foreign enemy. The panel divides into three parts: the underlying causes of the disaster (vv. 47–48), the tactics of Yahweh's agent in the disaster (vv. 49–52), and the horrific consequences of the disaster (vv. 53–57). The climactic build-up is reflected in the increasing lengths of each segment.

The underlying causes of Israel's demise (vv. 47–48). In summarizing the reasons for Israel's demise these verses offer a study in contrasts: because Israel "did not serve the LORD your God," they "will serve the enemies the LORD sends"; famine, thirst, and nakedness will replace joy and exuberance; total deprivation will replace abundance. These images identify the ultimate and the immediate causes of Israel's fall.

Moses begins by declaring that ultimately Israel herself will be responsible for the threatened disasters (v. 47). The adverbial expressions "joyfully"

---

38. See T. Hiebert, "Joel, Book of," *ABD*, 3:876; Borowski, *Every Living Thing*, 159–60.
39. *HALOT*, 1702.
40. See M. Lubetski, "Beetlemania of Bygone Times," *JSOT* 91 (2000): 3–26.

and "gladly" highlight the disposition Yahweh's generous provision should evoke. "In the time of prosperity" is shorthand for "on account of all that the LORD has done for you." Recalling 6:10–12, this threat warns the people not to forget Yahweh, especially when they are enjoying the good things the land produces for them.[41] Because the Israelites refuse to serve their Benefactor, Yahweh will provide alternative masters (v. 49). He "will bring" enemies to attack and pillage Israel, leaving them hungry, thirsty, and naked (v. 48). In place of the gracious yoke of the covenant, Yahweh himself will impose a yoke of iron on the necks of Israel until he has destroyed them (v. 48).[42] This yoke they will not be able to break.

The character and tactics of Yahweh's agent (vv. 49 – 52). Inverting the promises of 26:19 and 28:1, 13, Moses frames this paragraph with declarations of Yahweh's involvement in Israel's demise (vv. 49, 52). However, between these frames his focus shifts from Yahweh, who will be immediately responsible for Israel's demise, to the terrifying nature and tactics of his agent. Verses 49–50 characterize Yahweh's agent of doom with five bold brushstrokes, each of which intensifies the terror of Israel's demise. (1) The enemy will come "from the ends of the earth." What is near is familiar; what is distant is mysterious and fearful. (2) The enemy will be fast. Like an eagle swooping down on his prey, he will attack his targets suddenly and without warning. (3) The enemy will speak an unintelligible language. This rules out negotiations and contributes to horror.[43] (4) The enemy will be "fierce-looking" (lit., "strong of face"), which expresses both the terror of a victim and the resolve of the attacker. (5) The enemy will be heartless, showing no respect for the aged or mercy toward the young.[44]

The ruthless disposition of Yahweh's agent is matched by his ruthless actions (vv. 51–52). (1) He will consume the Israelites' livestock and crops from the ground. Borrowing expressions from 7:13, Moses presents these actions as the ironic reversal of the blessings. (2) He will besiege the Israelites throughout the land. Condemning the Israelites "trusting" in their high walls and defensive gate structures (cf. 3:5), in verse 52 Moses predicts that all the fortifications in the land that Yahweh had granted to Israel will come crashing down before the invader. The deity–nation–land covenantal triangle will collapse like the walls of Israel's cities.

---

41. Deut. 32:13–15 offers a poetic description of the problem of ingratitude.

42. Cf. "an iron yoke" in Jer. 28:14. Ancient Near Easterners often spoke of a vassal's relationship to his overlord as bearing his yoke (cf. Jer. 2:20; 5:5; cf. 27:8, 11, 12; 30:8–9).

43. Later prophets apply the idiom to the Assyrians (Isa. 33:19) and the Babylonians (Jer. 5:15).

44. Cf. the characterization of the Assyrians in Isa. 13:18, and the Babylonians in Lam. 4:16 and 5:12–13.

The horrific consequences of Yahweh's actions against Israel (vv. 53−57). Borrowing images from Leviticus 26:27−29, this paragraph opens with a general thesis statement, which is followed by two frightful scenes of cannibalism. While the opening declaration highlights the occasion of the crisis—in siege and in distress—this paragraph offers commentary on the "fruit of your womb" in verse 18. When the "fruit of your land" and the "fruit of your herds" are exhausted, people will resort to eating the "fruit of your womb."[45] The last clause highlights the horrific social effect of Israel's sins and the theological dimension of the tragedy: The people devour their own offspring whom they had received as gracious gifts from Yahweh.[46]

Moses develops this theme in two parallel panels, illustrating how men and women respectively respond to the crisis precipitated by the siege (vv. 54−55, 56−57). Both panels begin by highlighting the cultural refinement of the people who are reduced to eating their own children. While fathers are described as "most gentle and sensitive" (v. 54), Moses concretizes mothers' delicacy by describing those who consume their children as being unable to bear the thought of letting the soles of their feet touch the ground (v. 56). These characterizations reflect the dehumanization that results from the actions of Yahweh's agent.

Both panels also depict men and women turning against members of their own families. The image of the woman who becomes hostile even toward her afterbirth is shocking (vv. 56−57a). Verses 55 and 57b paint two pictures of unspeakable horror. The first image is tragic: Exhibiting no compassion toward his brothers and remaining children, the father refuses to share with them the flesh of his children. The second is grotesque: The mother secretly eats her children, and like an animal she also devours the afterbirth.[47]

(3) **The way of doom: the third volley (28:58−68).** Following a summary of the basis of all the curses in this chapter (v. 58), the final volley of doom presents four threats: (1) disease (vv. 59−63b), (2) exile away from the land (vv. 63c−64), (3) restlessness (vv. 65−67), and (4) return to Egypt (v. 68). Although each section ends with the effect of the disaster on the people, the paragraph is framed by ominous references to Egypt.

---

45. All three phrases have been encountered in the literal Hebrew in the summary blessings of verse 4 and the curse of verse 18.

46. The motif of cannibalism in times of crisis and famine is common in ancient Near Eastern documents. See *ANET*, 298c; *ARAB*, 2:794. For treaty curses threatening cannibalism, Parpola and Watanabe, *Neo-Assyrian Treaties and Loyalty Oaths*, 11 (cf. *ANET*, 533), 46 (cf. *ANET*, 538), and 52 (cf. *ANET*, 539).

47. See 2 Kings 6:28−29; Lam. 4:10. Also see Isa. 9:19−21[18−20]; 49:26; Jer. 19:9; Ezek. 5:9−10; Zech. 11:9.

Moses opens this section with a reminder to his immediate audience that the horrific fate described in this chapter is inevitable if they do not live scrupulously according to "all the words of this Torah that are written in this document" (pers. trans. of v. 58),[48] and if they "do not revere this glorious and awesome name—the LORD your God." The construction in verse 58 (lit., "keep by doing . . . and by fearing") reminds the Israelites that covenantal fidelity involves both obedience to the will of the covenant Lord and due concern for his honor. This is the only reference to fearing the "glorious and awesome name" of God in Deuteronomy.[49]

Part of the function of the original theophany at Sinai had been to instill in the people awe before Yahweh to deter them from sin and to inspire fidelity.[50] Moses' present instruction in the Torah (6:2) and future readings are to serve the same purpose (17:19; 31:12−13). The remainder of this paragraph highlights the consequences of failure to honor the name of Yahweh. Echoing the language and building on ideas expressed in 4:26−29, Moses threatens the Israelites with a complete reversal of their salvation history by means of plagues and diseases (vv. 59−63b), dispersion (vv. 63c−67), and enslavement (v. 68).

Moses highlights the intensity of the plagues with which Yahweh will strike Israel by: (1) describing the afflictions with a rare verb (*hiplāʾ*), meaning "to perform an exceptional act" (NIV "fearful"); (2) modifying the afflictions with intense adjectives (v. 59); (3) threatening to bring back against Israel every dreaded disease of Egypt (v. 60a);[51] (4) speaking of persistence, adding, "They will cling to you" (v. 60b); (5) broadening the scope of the plague to include disasters not specified in the written record of this Torah (v. 61; cf. 29:20−21[19−20]); (6) declaring Yahweh's determination to destroy[52] Israel (v. 61b); (7) and announcing the result to be a direct reversal of the promises to the ancestors of innumerable progeny (v. 62).

The construction of verse 63 signals a new and shocking dimension in this litany of horror: the termination of the nation−land association by dispersing the population among the nations (vv. 63−67). Moses begins by speaking shockingly of a change in Yahweh's disposition toward his people.

---

48. The statement suggests that Moses either delivered his addresses from written drafts or he intended to transcribe them as soon as they had been delivered. Cf. 17:18; 31:9.

49. See elsewhere Isa. 59:19; Mic. 6:9; Mal. 4:2 (cf. the antonym, "to despise the name," in 1:6); Pss. 61:5[6]; 86:11; 102:16[17]; Neh. 1:11; also Rev. 11:18.

50. Cf. 4:10; 5:29; and Ex. 20:20.

51. Echoing 7:15, the statement reverses Yahweh's earlier rescue from the diseases of Egypt.

52. Elsewhere this verb applies to the inhabitants of the land, whom the Israelites will dispossess: 7:2−24; 9:3; 12:30; 31:3−4; 33:27.

Where previously Yahweh had delighted in causing Israel to flourish, now he will delight in their destruction. The notion is troubling to modern readers, but read within the ancient conceptual environment, it contrasts sharply with the notions of Israel's neighbors. Where others attributed such calamities to demonic forces and hostile deities, Yahwism refuses to take the easy way out. These statements reflect the other side of Yahweh's passion: When his people trample underfoot his grace, his passions will be ignited against them.

The purpose of his hostile actions against his own people goes beyond severing Israel's tie with her land (v. 63c) to a rupturing of the people's ties with their deity (v. 64). The characterization of Israel's new objects of worship as gods that "neither you nor your fathers have known" highlights the contrast between Yahweh, who has graciously revealed himself to his people by word and deed (cf. 4:6 – 15, 32 – 40), and the gods of the nations, who never speak or act (cf. Jer. 10:5).

Verses 65 – 66 describe the Israelites' physical and emotional state in exile: Yahweh himself will rob them of all joy and meaning in life, and the distress over their demise will haunt them wherever they go. Moses highlights Yahweh's involvement in their restlessness by portraying their "anxious mind,"[53] "eyes weary with longing," and "a despondent heart"[54] as antigifts. In verses 66 – 67 he concretizes their despair by introducing hypothetical interlocutors, whose lips express their emotional state. The picture of Israel's restlessness recalls the "dread" of Egypt and other nations in the face of Yahweh's judgment (Ex. 15:16; Num. 22:3), and the dread of the Canaanites in the face of the Israelites' arrival (Deut. 2:25; 11:25).

Moses' warning of Israel's doom concludes in verse 68 with an unequivocal image of the reversal of Israel's history. Whereas in 17:16 Moses had warned the people never to return to Egypt, now he announces that as a climactic act of divine judgment for persistent apostasy Yahweh will take them back there himself, and there they will be put up for auction as slaves. However, that they should be transported there in ships is puzzling.[55] Moses may have added the reference to ships intentionally to add to the Israelites' trauma; for a landed people the prospect of a journey by sea could have been frightening. Alternatively, these ships may represent

---

53. The characterization of the heart/mind (*lēb*) as "anxious, agitated" contrasts with the kinds of hearts Yahweh gives elsewhere: a heart to know Yahweh (29:4[3]; Jer. 24:7); a listening/understanding heart (1 Kings 3:9); a single heart to fear Yahweh (Jer. 32:39); a new heart (Ezek. 11:19; 36:26); a heart of flesh, i.e., a responsive heart (Ezek 36:26); a single heart to do the king's will (2 Chron. 30:12).

54. This expression speaks of utter emotional and physical exhaustion.

55. On the international slave trade, see Joel 3:6[4:6]; Amos 1:9.

some nation's (Egypt's or Tyre's?) economic and mercantile power. Even so, Yahweh will commandeer those symbols of pride and independence and use these vessels to send his people off into slavery.

This curse is rendered even more puzzling by Moses' reference to his previous assertion that Israel will never see Egypt again. Apparently alluding to a promise not recorded in the Pentateuch, Moses hereby reinforces the notion that Yahweh's punitive actions signify his suspension of the benefits that have been Israel's as his redeemed and covenant people. Back in Egypt they will try to sell themselves to their enemies to serve as male and female slaves, but even as slaves they will be deemed worthless. Perhaps the Egyptians will reject them because they recognize the Israelites as victims of some horrific curse (cf. 29:22–28[21–27]), and they fear that contact with them could bring on them the same awful fate.

Colophonic Conclusion (29:1 [28:69])

ASSUMING THE PHRASE "THE terms of the covenant" in 29:1[28:69] and 29:8[7] refers to the stipulations expounded in Moses' second address, this narrative comment brings the report of that address to a conclusion. The characterization of the covenant as "that which Yahweh commanded Moses to make [lit., 'cut'] with the descendants of Israel" (pers. trans.) highlights Moses' role as authorized interpreter of its stipulations and the one who presides over the covenant renewal ceremonies reflected in Deuteronomy. If Moses "cuts" this covenant with the descendants of Israel, he does so on Yahweh's behalf (cf. 31:16).

Although many interpret this statement as distinguishing between the covenant made on the Plains of Moab and one Yahweh previously made with Israel at Sinai, this distinction is unwarranted. Since Moses opened his second address by reciting the Decalogue (5:6–21), the essence of covenant relationship obviously remains the same, as do both Yahweh's and Israel's roles within that relationship. What is happening on the Plains of Moab is not the establishment of a new covenant, but the renewal of the original covenant first made with Abraham and then established with Israel at Sinai. Since the people standing before Moses were not involved in the proceedings at Horeb forty years earlier, these procedures are necessary to bind this generation to the covenant ratified at Horeb (5:2–3) and to ensure that they enter the Promised Land as the covenant people of Yahweh.

The preceding address has provided the people with a theological and ethical trajectory by which the basic covenantal principles should be applied once they enter that land. Accordingly, the expression "in addition to the covenant he had made with them at Horeb" (29:1[28:69]) refers to the ceremonies involved in the renewal and ratification of the covenant with the present generation.[56] When Moses "cuts this covenant," he supervises new ceremonies whereby the new generation commits itself to the old covenant. This means that as a result of his exposition, the people have a fuller understanding of the original event and the stipulations revealed at Horeb, but also that they commit themselves to Moses' interpretation in this address of the words associated with that covenant (the Decalogue, Book of the Covenant, Instructions on Holiness, etc.). In short, the covenant referred to in 29:1[28:69] should not be viewed as a new covenant but as a supplement to the one made at Sinai, which itself represented the fulfillment and elaboration of Yahweh's covenant with Abraham (Gen. 17:7−8).

A DARK VIEW OF the God of the Old Testament? Modern readers often recoil before the horrific scenes envisioned here—and especially before the images of this bloodthirsty God who "delights" in perpetrating these violent acts (28:63), especially if we read verses 15−68 without first reading verses 1−14 or in isolation from all that has preceded in Moses' second address. How can this view of God be justified or reconciled with the view of God presented in the New Testament? Perhaps Marcion was right; perhaps the god of the Old Testament was a different divinity than the God of the New Testament, embodied in Jesus Christ.[57]

However, recent advances in speech-act theory have heightened our appreciation for the rhetorical and homiletical significance of these blessings and curses for Moses' original audience and for later generations who would hear them read in settings of communal worship (Deut. 31:9−13).[58] The question we need to ask is: What did Moses intend to do with his words in this chapter? The words on the page represent Moses' *locutions;*

---

56. We should not interpret the expression, "in addition to the covenant" to mean "in contrast to," "in contradiction to," or "in opposition to." The phrase is elliptical and should be interpreted "in addition to [the terms of] the covenant he made with them at Horeb," thus matching "the terms of the covenant" at the beginning of the verse. For defense of the unity of the covenant made at Sinai and confirmed by this generation in Moab, see P. A. Barker, *The Triumph of Grace in Deuteronomy: Faithless Israel, Faithful Yahweh in Deuteronomy* (Paternoster Biblical Monographs; Carlisle, UK; Waynesboro, GA: Paternoster: 2004), 112−16.

57. Marcion was a first-century AD heretic.

58. On the place of speech-act theory in biblical interpretation, see K. J. Vanhoozer, *Is There a Meaning in This Text? The Bible, the Reader, and the Morality of Literary Knowledge* (Grand Rapids: Zondervan, 1998), 201−80.

what he intended to accomplish with the words is called his *illocution*; and how the audience interpreted his words and responded to them is referred to as the *perlocution*. In these blessings and curses we observe Moses' illocutionary pastoral agenda reaching its climax. At the end of his lengthy address on the privileges and responsibility of covenant relationship with Yahweh, this is in effect an altar call, a call to fear the honored and awesome name of Yahweh and to demonstrate that fear in grateful submission to his lordship and obedience to his will (v. 58; cf. 11:26–28; 30:11–20). Moses is a pastor, who sets before the people the way of life and the way of death. Both the lavish promises of blessing as a reward for obedience and the horrific warnings of doom as consequences of rebellion were intended to get the hearers' attention, to arouse fear, and to warn the people what it would be like to fall into the hands of an angry God.[59]

History of the covenant. The history of Israel is a history of the rejection of Moses' message. Earlier we emphasized that in Deuteronomy 28 Moses builds on the covenant blessings and curses as revealed by Yahweh himself in Leviticus 26. Given the lengthy lists of curses in ancient Near Eastern treaty documents, we should not be surprised to learn that these blessings and curses represent fundamental elements of the covenant that Yahweh made with Israel.[60] This means that when the northern kingdom of Israel experienced the horrors predicted here in 722 BC at the hands of the Assyrians, and their Judaean counterparts experienced them in 586 BC at the hands of the Babylonians, this represented not the termination of Yahweh's covenant with his people, but the fulfillment of its fine print.

Tragically, the nearer those doomsdays came, the more the people, particularly the Judaeans, clung to Yahweh as their divine Protector. Their security was based on four divine commitments: (1) Yahweh's irrevocable gift of the land of Canaan to Abraham and his descendants; (2) Yahweh's irrevocable covenant marriage with his people at Sinai; (3) Yahweh's irrevocable grant of the throne over Israel to David and his descendants; (4) Yahweh's irrevocable choice of Jerusalem as his dwelling place.[61] However, the

---

59. Cf. D. B. Sandy, *Plowshares & Pruning Hooks: Rethinking the Language of Biblical Prophecy and Apocalyptic* (Downers Grove, IL: InterVarsity Press, 2002), 89.

60. Note the colophonic conclusion to the stipulations of the covenant ratified at Sinai in Lev. 26:46: "These are the decrees, the laws and the instructions [NIV 'regulations'] that the LORD established on Mount Sinai between himself and the Israelites through Moses." Significantly this statement occurs immediately after a reference to the covenant with the ancestors whom Yahweh brought out of Egypt, including the covenant formula, and after the list of blessings and curses.

61. For fuller discussion, see Block, *Ezekiel Chapters 1–24*, 7–9, 16.

people forgot that with the benefactions associated with these divine commitments came the responsibility of serving Yahweh as the agent of grace and revelation to the world, which meant living according to the ways of Yahweh as revealed in his covenant. They also forgot that the blessings and curses of Leviticus 26 and Deuteronomy 28 were built into the covenant itself—which explains why the warnings of doom in prophets like Jeremiah and Ezekiel depended so heavily on the covenant curses.

By the late seventh century BC, idolatry, contempt for Yahweh, and rejection of his will were so deeply entrenched that Yahweh could no longer tolerate the evil of their ways. Indeed, he would have been untrue to his covenant commitments if he had turned a blind eye to persistent infidelity and had not imposed the curses spelled out here. In the words of Ezekiel (speaking for Yahweh), "I am Yahweh, I have spoken, and I will do [what I have said]" (pers. trans.).[62] These declarations refer less to Ezekiel's own prophetic utterances than to Yahweh's original covenantal commitments, which included his threats of doom.

While echoes of and allusions to specific elements of the blessings and curses may be heard throughout the Old Testament, their significance is graphically illustrated in 2 Kings 22, which records the discovery of the Torah document in the temple and Josiah's response to the discovery. When Shaphan the scribe read the Torah document to him, the king tore his clothes. Fearful that Yahweh would pour his fury out on his people according to all that is written in the Torah because of their history of refusing to live according to its teachings (v. 13), Josiah demanded that his officials immediately inquire of Yahweh concerning the words of the document. In an oracular pronouncement, the prophet Huldah declared the divine resolve to bring "disaster" on the land and its inhabitants, that is, "everything written in the book" (v. 16). Through her Yahweh announced that because they had abandoned him in favor of other gods, the time for the outpouring of his wrath had come (v. 17). While Josiah himself would be spared the horrors of Judah's end, the day of the nation's desolation[63] and curse[64] had been set. Nothing Josiah could do would stave off Yahweh's fury.

And when it happened, Judah's doom transpired precisely as and in fulfillment of the curses of the Torah. While the deluded people accused Yahweh of reneging on his commitments, with remarkable perception in his prayer Daniel recognized the reality:

---

62. See Ezek. 12:25; 17:24; 22:14; 36:36; 37:14.
63. The phrase *hāyâ lᵉsammâ* in 2 Kings 22:19 is borrowed from Deut. 28:37.
64. The singular *qᵉlālâ* alludes to the plural "the curses" in Deut. 28:15, 45.

We have not obeyed the LORD our God or kept the laws he gave us through his servants the prophets. All Israel has transgressed your law and turned away, refusing to obey you.

Therefore the curses and sworn judgments written in the Law of Moses, the servant of God, have been poured out on us, because we have sinned against you. You have fulfilled the words spoken against us and against our rulers by bringing upon us great disaster. Under the whole heaven nothing has ever been done like what has been done to Jerusalem. Just as it is written in the Law of Moses, all this disaster has come upon us, yet we have not sought the favor of the LORD our God by turning from our sins and giving attention to your truth. The LORD did not hesitate to bring the disaster upon us, for the LORD our God is righteous in everything he does; yet we have not obeyed him. (Dan. 9:9–14)

Perhaps what is most remarkable is the amazing patience and grace of Yahweh. He would have been totally within his covenantal rights to have imposed these curses on Israel much earlier and in many circumstances: in the premonarchic period of the judges, during the reign of Solomon (1 Kings 11–12), and repeatedly thereafter as king after king—both northern and Judean—led the people down the path of apostasy and idolatry. But Yahweh waited. To be sure, he imposed the curses one or two at a time (Amos 4:6–13), hoping this would wake up his people and cause them to return to him. He was indeed patient (Ex. 34:6–7).

Finally, after centuries of putting up with their perfidy, Yahweh had had enough. When the northern kingdom fell to the Assyrians in 734–722 BC and the southern kingdom—along with the Davidic monarchy—fell to the Babylonians in 586 BC, the people experienced the horrors precisely as predicted in these covenant curses.[65] However, neither the fall of Israel or the fall of Judah meant that Yahweh had cancelled or broken off his covenant. On the contrary, these events confirmed that the covenant was still in force. The blessings were suspended and replaced with the curse, exactly as spelled out in the covenant document (Lev. 26) and as proclaimed by Moses (Deut. 28).

Contemporary Significance

SINCE THE NEW TESTAMENT declares explicitly that in Christ we are redeemed from the curse of the law (Gal. 3:13), it is easy for Christians to dismiss Deuteronomy 28 (and Lev. 26) as a fossil from a bygone age—interesting for its antiquarian value to some, but ulti-

---

65. See D. Stuart, *Hosea–Jonah* (WBC 31; Waco, TX: Word, 1987), xxxi–xlii.

mately irrelevant. However, we need always to be asking, what is there of permanent value for us in texts like this? To this question we offer several answers.

Imprecatory strategy. Moses' imprecatory rhetorical strategy in this chapter is not unique to the book of Deuteronomy or the Old Testament; it is also picked up in the New Testament. In keeping with Moses' opening appeal to heed the voice of Yahweh as the test of fidelity to the covenant Lord (Deut. 28:1–2) and reiterated throughout the litany of curses,[66] Jesus declared to his disciples, "If you love me [i.e., are covenantally committed to me], keep my commands" (John 14:15, 21, pers. trans.). Indeed, in the sequence of the call to obedience to Christ in John 14 and the parable of the vine and the vinedresser in John 15, we observe a New Testament equivalent to the blessings and curses of Deuteronomy 28. Specifically, Jesus seeks to motivate fidelity by promising that those branches that bear fruit—which in the context means keeping his commands—will abide in his love and experience full joy (vv. 10–12), but those branches that do not bear fruit will be lopped off and tossed into the fire (v. 6). The former obviously answers to the blessings of Deuteronomy 28:1–14, while the latter answers to the curses (28:15–68).

This rhetorical strategy also occurs in New Testament letters. For example, Paul writes:

> Once you were alienated from God and were enemies in your minds because of your evil behavior. But now he has reconciled you by Christ's physical body through death to present you holy in his sight, without blemish and free from accusation—if you continue in your faith, established and firm, not moved from the hope held out in the gospel. (Col. 1:21–23)

Like Moses, Paul is addressing people who claim to be God's people. Yet he needs to warn them that unless they continue in their faith, their presentation before Christ as holy and innocent is jeopardized. Writing to Gentile Christians in Rome, Paul is even more specific:

> If some of the branches have been broken off, and you, though a wild olive shoot, have been grafted in among the others and now share in the nourishing sap from the olive root, do not boast over those branches. If you do, consider this: You do not support the root, but the root supports you. You will say then, "Branches were broken off so that I could be grafted in." Granted. But they were broken off because of unbelief, and you stand by faith. Do not be arrogant, but

---

66. Deut. 28:9, 13–15, 20, 45, 47, 58, 62.

be afraid. For if God did not spare the natural branches, he will not spare you either.

Consider therefore the kindness and sternness of God: sternness to those who fell, but kindness to you, provided that you continue in his kindness. Otherwise, you also will be cut off. And if they do not persist in unbelief, they will be grafted in, for God is able to graft them in again. After all, if you were cut out of an olive tree that is wild by nature, and contrary to nature were grafted into a cultivated olive tree, how much more readily will these, the natural branches, be grafted into their own olive tree! (Rom. 11:17–24)

In Hebrews 10:28–31 the author of this book compares the fate of the Israelites with the potential fate of his audience:

Anyone who rejected the law of Moses died without mercy on the testimony of two or three witnesses. How much more severely do you think a man deserves to be punished who has trampled the Son of God under foot, who has treated as an unholy thing the blood of the covenant that sanctified him, and who has insulted the Spirit of grace? For we know him who said, "It is mine to avenge; I will repay," and again, "The Lord will judge his people." It is a dreadful thing to fall into the hands of the living God.

Guarding against presumption. The warnings in such texts are intended to guard against presumption. Like the Israelites of the Old Testament, Christians may be tempted to presume upon the grace of God and take their standing with him for granted. However, these warnings aim to elicit both hope and fear; in so doing they provide an antidote to apostasy and rebellion.[67]

As a corollary, this passage reminds readers in every generation that prosperity and freedom may never be regarded as fundamental and unconditional rights. The call to relationship with God in Christ to bear his name is a glorious privilege (Deut. 28:8–10; cf. 1 Pet. 4:12–19), to which we must respond with faith demonstrated through obedience to the revealed will of God. Fidelity to him may provoke the ire of others, but it will win the Lord's praise. However, failure to live according to the will of the Suzerain may win the praise of others, but it will provoke the ire of God.

Yahweh remains sovereign. This text reminds contemporary readers that although Yahweh always keeps his word, he retains full sovereignty

67. For fuller discussion of these and other texts like this, see L. L. Norris, "The Function of New Testament Warning Passages: A Speech Act Theory Approach" (PhD dissertation, Wheaton College, Wheaton, IL, 2011).

over all affairs of the universe. He sets up nations, and he brings them down. He does so by employing natural means of drought, disease, and calamities of every sort, and by using human agents. In contrast to the peoples of the ancient Near East, calamities are not the result of demonic forces. The covenant Lord has the right and power to inflict them even on his own people, should they abandon him. This text reminds believers in every age that there is no eternal security for those who live in sin. All confessions to the contrary, in the end the true test of faith is found in the life of the believer.

Representing God to the world. Far from preaching a gospel of health and wealth, as we find in many contemporary preachers,[68] Deuteronomy 28 reminds readers in every age that by redeeming his people, God calls them to the glorious privilege of representing him to the world and demonstrating by their lives the transforming power of Christ. That privilege is highlighted by verses 1 and 9 – 10, which summarize God's vision for his people, whether Old Testament Israel or the church today. His goal is to set us high above all the nations of the earth — though not for our sakes, but for the sake of him whose name we bear.

We have been called out of the world to be his holy people and are called by the name of the Lord (v. 10; lit., "the name of Yahweh is read on us"). If the name of the Lord is read on us, that must mean it has been stamped on us. Either we have been branded by his name (cf. comments on 5:11), or like Israel's high priest (Ex. 28:35), we wear a medal on our foreheads inscribed, "Holy to the LORD." This brand reflects the mission to which we have been called: declaring to the world in life and testimony what God in his grace can do for sinners.

However, as Yahweh himself declared in Exodus 19:4 – 6 and Moses reiterated in Deuteronomy 26:16 – 19, the fulfillment of that mission depends on the fidelity of his people — listening to his voice and keeping his covenant. Israel was not called for Israel's sake, but for the sake of God's mission of redemption for the world. And so it is with us. According to Ephesians, the Lord chooses sinners and adopts them as his children; he stamps them with his name and calls them to be holy and blameless (Eph. 1:3 – 5); he sets them high above the nations (1:11 – 14) and lavishes on them the riches of his grace and every spiritual blessing. All these divine actions were intended so that those who were the first to hope in Christ

---

68. See especially Joel Osteen, *Your Best Life Now: 7 Steps to Living at Your Full Potential* (Nashville: Faith Words, 2004). For a critique, see David van Biema and Jeff Chu, "Does God Want You to Be Rich?" *Time* (Sunday, September 10, 2006). For a helpful response to this kind of gospel, see W. C. Kaiser, "The Old Testament Case for Material Blessings and the Contemporary Believer," *TJ* 9 (1988): 151 – 69.

should live to the praise of his glory (1:6). Called to "praise, fame and honor" (Deut. 26:19), may we never forget the hope of our calling and the riches of the glory of his inheritance in the saints. And may we never forget that "we are God's workmanship, created in Christ Jesus to do good works, which God prepared in advance for us to do" (Eph. 2:10), which means living a life worthy of the calling that we have received (4:1).

Indeed, the remainder of Ephesians (chaps. 4–6) functions as the equivalent to Deuteronomy 12–26. Given this high calling, the severity of the consequences of rejecting the responsibilities that come with that calling becomes understandable. In the words of Jesus, every branch that does not bear fruit (works of righteousness) is cut off, withers, and is thrown into the fire and burned (John 15:2, 6). This is a solemn warning to believers in every age.

Deuteronomy 29:2–28[1–27][1]

✹

Introduction to Deuteronomy 29:2[1]–30:20

WITHIN THE OVERALL FLOW of Deuteronomy, chapters 29–30 represent Moses' third and final sermon before he dies (34:1–12). The sermon divides into shorter subparts, but it is held together by a series of literary features: (1) an emphasis on the immediate rhetorical context ("today, this day");[2] (2) the vocabulary of the curse (and blessing);[3] (3) references to "the covenant written in the document of the Torah" (pers. trans. of 29:21); (4) references to the "heart/mind" as the seat of the problem and focus of the solution;[4] (5) echoes of chapter 4 that resound throughout these two chapters (see below); (6) extensive links to the remainder of the first address (chaps. 1–3) and the lengthy second address;[5] (7) the adaptation of ancient Near Eastern treaty vocabulary and form, which spans the chapters;[6] and (8) the motif of knowledge and ignorance.[7]

Despite these unifying features, scholars have found a variety of bases for dissecting the material into primary and secondary strata.[8] However, abrupt transitions and changes in style may derive from the rhetorical nature and sermonic intention of these chapters, if not the original oral situation. Here Moses' final pastoral addresses reach their climax, as he urges his people to accept God's will as revealed at Sinai and expounded in

---

1. Because of differences in the location of the chapter division, the verse numbers in Hebrew are all one lower than the English numbers. For the sake of convenience, the commentary will use only the English numbers.

2. See 29:4, 10, 12, 13, 15a, 15b, 18, 28; 30:2, 8, 11, 15, 16, 18a, 18b, 19.

3. See *haqqᵉlālâ*, "curse" (29:27; 30:1, 19); *hāʾālâ/ʾālôt*, "covenant imprecation/imprecations, curse/curses" (29:12, 14, 19, 20, 21; 30:7), and specifically *ʾālôt habbᵉrît*, "the imprecations of the covenant" (29:21).

4. Deut. 29:4, 18, 19; 30:1, 2, 6, 10, 14, 17.

5. For a discussion of these links see Timothy A. Lenchak, *Choose Life! A Rhetorical-Critical Investigation of Deuteronomy 28,69–30:20* (Rome: Pontifical Biblical Institute, 1993), 114–18.

6. The following elements have been identified: the historical prologue (29:2b–9); the declaration of commitment (29:10–15); the stipulations (29:16–20a); the appeal to witnesses (30:19a); the blessings and the curses (30:15–18, 19b–20). This is a modified version of the scheme proposed by A. Rofé, "The Covenant in the Land of Moab (Deuteronomy 28:69–30:20," in *Das Deuteronomium: Entstehung, Gestalt und Botschaft* (ed. N. Lohfink; BETL 68; Louvain: Louvain Univ. Press, 1985), 310–20; reprinted in *A Song of Power and the Power of Song* (ed. D. L. Christensen; Winona Lake, IN: Eisenbrauns, 1993), 269–80.

7. Deut. 29:4, 24, 29; 30:11–14.

8. For surveys of recent approaches, see Barker, *Triumph of Grace*, 108–10; Lenchak, *Choose Life!* 32–36.

"this book of the Torah," and to choose life rather than death by ordering their lives according to the will of God.

We may only speculate about the circumstances in which this final address was delivered. References to the blessings and curses assume the audience was familiar with the contents of chapter 28 and suggest the ceremonies taking place "today/this day" (29:10 − 13) are to be distinguished from those alluded to in 26:16 − 19. But we do not know how much time separated this address from the Israelites' earlier acceptance of the covenant (chaps. 12 − 26, 28). Apparently, having transcribed his first and second addresses, Moses reconvened the assembly (29:2) to issue a final appeal for covenantal fidelity and to supervise a final ritual by which the people bind themselves once more to the covenant. Perhaps he perceives this as the first phase of a ceremony the Israelites will conclude at Shechem as prescribed in chapter 27.

Based on content and temporal signals, the speech consists of five parts arranged in an ABABA pattern, with the "A" sections being addressed to Moses' immediate audience and the "B" sections relating to the future. The flow of the former (29:2 − 13, 29; 30:11 − 20) is relatively smooth, suggesting these represent the main body of the original oration, and that the latter (29:14 − 28; 30:1 − 10), which concern the future, represent digressions from the main plot. In its present form, Moses' final address may be interpreted as a four-act drama involving Yahweh and his covenant people. The first two and the last acts subdivide into two scenes each, while the climactic third act consists of a single scene. This plot may be portrayed as on page 673.

Moses summoned all the Israelites and said to them: Your eyes have seen all that the LORD did in Egypt to Pharaoh, to all his officials and to all his land. ³With your own eyes you saw those great trials, those miraculous signs and great wonders. ⁴But to this day the LORD has not given you a mind that understands or eyes that see or ears that hear. ⁵During the forty years that I led you through the desert, your clothes did not wear out, nor did the sandals on your feet. ⁶You ate no bread and drank no wine or other fermented drink. I did this so that you might know that I am the LORD your God.

⁷When you reached this place, Sihon king of Heshbon and Og king of Bashan came out to fight against us, but we defeated them. ⁸We took their land and gave it as an inheritance to the Reubenites, the Gadites and the half-tribe of Manasseh.

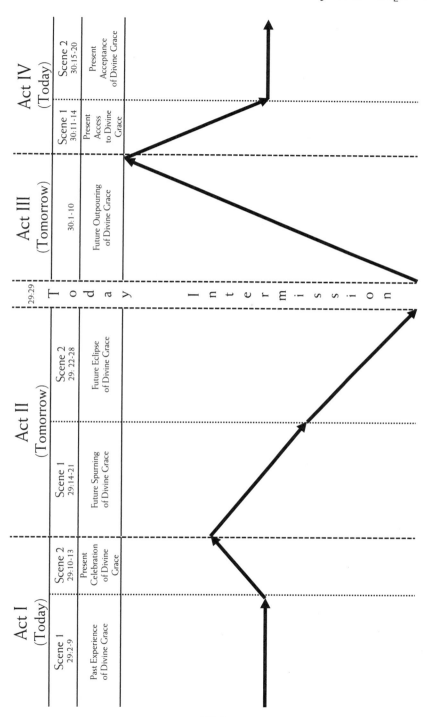

⁹Carefully follow the terms of this covenant, so that you may prosper in everything you do. ¹⁰All of you are standing today in the presence of the LORD your God—your leaders and chief men, your elders and officials, and all the other men of Israel, ¹¹together with your children and your wives, and the aliens living in your camps who chop your wood and carry your water. ¹²You are standing here in order to enter into a covenant with the LORD your God, a covenant the LORD is making with you this day and sealing with an oath, ¹³to confirm you this day as his people, that he may be your God as he promised you and as he swore to your fathers, Abraham, Isaac and Jacob. ¹⁴I am making this covenant, with its oath, not only with you ¹⁵who are standing here with us today in the presence of the LORD our God but also with those who are not here today.

¹⁶You yourselves know how we lived in Egypt and how we passed through the countries on the way here. ¹⁷You saw among them their detestable images and idols of wood and stone, of silver and gold. ¹⁸Make sure there is no man or woman, clan or tribe among you today whose heart turns away from the LORD our God to go and worship the gods of those nations; make sure there is no root among you that produces such bitter poison.

¹⁹When such a person hears the words of this oath, he invokes a blessing on himself and therefore thinks, "I will be safe, even though I persist in going my own way." This will bring disaster on the watered land as well as the dry. ²⁰The LORD will never be willing to forgive him; his wrath and zeal will burn against that man. All the curses written in this book will fall upon him, and the LORD will blot out his name from under heaven. ²¹The LORD will single him out from all the tribes of Israel for disaster, according to all the curses of the covenant written in this Book of the Law.

²²Your children who follow you in later generations and foreigners who come from distant lands will see the calamities that have fallen on the land and the diseases with which the LORD has afflicted it. ²³The whole land will be a burning waste of salt and sulfur—nothing planted, nothing sprouting, no vegetation growing on it. It will be like the destruction of Sodom and Gomorrah, Admah and Zeboiim, which the LORD overthrew in fierce anger. ²⁴All the nations will ask:

"Why has the LORD done this to this land? Why this fierce, burning anger?"

²⁵And the answer will be: "It is because this people abandoned the covenant of the LORD, the God of their fathers, the covenant he made with them when he brought them out of Egypt. ²⁶They went off and worshiped other gods and bowed down to them, gods they did not know, gods he had not given them. ²⁷Therefore the LORD's anger burned against this land, so that he brought on it all the curses written in this book. ²⁸In furious anger and in great wrath the LORD uprooted them from their land and thrust them into another land, as it is now."

AS SUGGESTED BY THE diagram, chapter 29 involves two acts, the first involving the celebration of the grace of covenant (vv. 2–13), and the second involving the spurning of that grace (vv. 14–28).

Act I: Celebrating the Grace of Covenant Today (29:2–13)

THE NARRATIVE INTRODUCTION (V. 2) signals the beginning of a formal speech in a formal context.[9] Moses situates his final address in the present (vv. 4, 10, 12), but he begins by calling on the people to recall Yahweh's past grace (vv. 2–9) and to commit themselves to the one who has been so gracious to them (vv. 10–13).

Remembering Yahweh's past grace today (vv. 2–9). The opening paragraph consists of a collage of words, phrases, and clauses found elsewhere in Deuteronomy. The significant new elements involve references to the deprivations (v. 4; i.e., no heart to know, eyes to see, ears to hear; v. 6, not consuming bread and wine), and the purpose clause in verse 9, which employs the expression "to prosper" (which occurs only here in Deuteronomy). This section reviews Israel's experiences with Yahweh leading to the present moment (vv. 2c–8), followed by a brief call for response (v. 9). The historical summary focuses on Yahweh's redemptive actions and providential care on Israel's behalf (vv. 2b–6), as well as Israel's response to the Transjordanian kings (vv. 6–7). Each of these subdivides further into a remembrance of Yahweh's actions (vv. 2b–3, 5), followed by a statement of deprivation (vv. 4, 6).

---

9. As in Ex. 12:21; 36:2; Lev. 10:4; Deut. 5:1; 31:7

Since most in the assembly were born during the forty years in the desert and did not witness the nation's rescue from Egypt, Moses draws all of them into Yahweh's past actions by speaking as if they were eyewitnesses to those events.[10] Through their renewal of the covenant that Yahweh made with Israel at Sinai, the present generation may identify with their predecessors, who saw the amazing signs and wonders that Yahweh performed in Egypt.

Verse 4 is difficult, but retaining the word order of the Hebrew may help: "But the LORD has not given you a mind that understands or eyes that see or ears that hear, until this day."[11] Following the reference to the understanding "mind," "eyes" and "ears" denote mental capacities of perception and understanding.[12] Whereas the exodus generation as a whole did not grasp the revelatory, redemptive, and covenantal significance of Yahweh's actions (9:1–24; cf. 1:19–46), this generation knows; through Moses' final pastoral addresses Yahweh has given Israel a heart to know, eyes to see, and ears to hear.[13] The covenant renewal ceremony that follows and Moses' statements in 30:11–14 assume this knowledge.

In Moses' recollection of Yahweh's actions during the desert wanderings, he speaks in first person with Yahweh's voice. While this recollection is comparable to 8:2–4, the focus changes slightly here. (1) Whereas Moses had previously observed that throughout their travels the Israelites' feet had never been sore, now Yahweh declares that their sandals did not wear out. (2) Whereas Moses had previously highlighted the deprivation of food and the provision of manna as a test, now he declares that the test served a revelatory purpose as well. Like the great acts of the exodus (4:32–40) it proved that he is Yahweh, their God. Instead of bread, wine, and other alcoholic beverages (staple products of agricultural effort), Yahweh had sustained them with manna and water.[14] Apparently the desert deprivations were to accomplish in the exodus generation what Yahweh's miraculous saving actions had failed to achieve.

The second part of this historical review focuses on the present generation's response to Sihon of Heshbon and Og of Bashan. Whereas the refusal to enter Canaan from Kadesh Barnea (1:1–40) had proved the previous

---

10. Cf. 3:21; 4:3, 9; 5:24; 10:21; 11:7.

11. So also Tigay, *Deuteronomy*, 275. In effect, the previous generation had become like idols of wood and stone that Moses characterized in 4:28 as neither seeing nor hearing nor eating nor smelling. Cf. Pss. 115:4–8; 135:15–18.

12. The triad of "mind," "eyes," and "ears" occurs elsewhere in Isa. 6:10; 32:3–4; Jer. 5:21; Ezek. 40:4. This concept underlies Paul's idiom in Eph. 1:18, "having the eyes of your hearts enlightened that you may know."

13. This interprets "until this day" broadly as the present context of Moses' final addresses, not simply the day of this phase of the covenant renewal ceremony. Cf. comments on 1:5.

14. And quail: Ex. 16:13; Num. 11:31–32; Ps. 105:40.

generation's faithlessness, this generation's attacks on the Amorite kings demonstrated their trust in Yahweh. The allocation of the Transjordanian land to the Reubenites, Gadites, and the half-tribe of Manasseh concretized and testified to that faith.

Within the chapter as a whole, verse 9 is a hinge. Here Moses challenges his audience to continue to prove their faith in Yahweh, keeping the words of this covenant by doing them. The covenant ceremonies Moses is about to supervise involve a reaffirmation of the commitments made earlier by the exodus generation and by the people gathered here in the presence of Moses (26:16–19). The clause "so that you may prosper in everything you do" highlights the future importance of maintaining the commitment the Israelites had shown in their victory over the Amorite kings. The dimensions of this prosperity are summarized in the blessings of 28:1–14.

Claiming Yahweh's grace today (vv. 10–13). Although most scholars extend the paragraph through verse 15, the syntax requires the division reflected here. Verses 10–13 comprise one complex sentence, whose core is represented by a principal clause followed by two purpose clauses, both of which subdivide into two parts:

You are presenting yourselves this day before Yahweh your God

    (1) that you may enter into (a) the covenant of Yahweh your God

                    (b) and his sanctions

   (2) and that (a) he may confirm you as his people

            (b) and he may be your God. (pers. trans.)

The remainder is commentary, with the syntactical construction, choice of vocabulary, and threefold reference to "today" combining to portray a formal ceremonial event.

The nature of the event. The opening clause sets the agenda. The Niphal form of *nāṣab* ("present oneself") means "to take one's stand" and captures with one word what Moses had expressed with two in 4:10. The phrase "before Yahweh your God" reinforces this interpretation, linking what is about to transpire with the covenantal ritual of the exodus generation at Sinai/Horeb.

The participants in the event. In the remainder of verses 10–11 Moses lists the participants in the covenantal proceedings. Beginning with a comprehensive expression "all of you," he provides the longest catalogue of participants in a formal religious event in the entire Old Testament. The eight entries seem to be arranged from greatest to least, but they divide into two groups on the basis of content (the first four involve titular and administrative designations) and syntax (the last member of each set of four begins with the conjunction). Three of the administrative designations have been encountered earlier in the book.[15] Although elsewhere in the book, the fourth designation (*šibṭêkem*) always means "your tribes" (1:15; 5:23; 12:5; 31:28), this does not suit the present context. Since the word *šebeṭ* derives from a root meaning "rod, staff," it seems best to interpret the word as "tribal staff-holder"—hence a tribal official.[16]

The second quartette of participants includes common people: men, children, wives, aliens. Moses highlights the inclusive nature of the event by expanding on the last entry. The reference to outsiders as those "who chop your wood and carry your water" involves a stereotypical pair, which is shorthand for aliens engaged in all kinds of menial labor.[17]

The purpose of the event. This assembly had two purposes. (1) Through these rituals the people "enter into the covenant of Yahweh your God and his oath" (v. 12, pers. trans.). The idiom used here, "to pass over [*ʿābar*] into a covenant,"[18] may derive from a ritual in which the parties to a covenant cut an animal in two and then bind themselves to its terms by passing between the parts.[19] Consistent with the biblical testimony elsewhere, Moses refers to this covenant as Yahweh's covenant, not Israel's, and the oath as "his oath."

Although the idiom "to cut [*krt*] a covenant" (NIV "make") often involves a new covenant,[20] this interpretation does not suit the present case.[21] The word "oath" derives from *ʾlh*, a root meaning "to swear, to curse, to take an oath" (cf. Ezek. 16:59; 17:19). The pair of expressions, "the covenant of Yahweh and his oath," is a hendiadys, "his sworn covenant"—that is, a treaty that concludes with a curse. In the ritual of covenant making, the oath involved a conditional imprecation, calling for the curses if the party taking the oath fails to keep the terms of the treaty.

---

15. For "your heads/leaders," see 1:15; 5:23; for "your chief men," see 5:23; 19:12; 21:2–4, 6, 19–20; 22:15–18; 25:7–9; 27:1; 29:10; 31:9, 28; 32:7; for "your elders," see 1:15; 16:18; 31:28.

16. For discussion of the issues and other possibilities, see Lenchak, *Choose Life!* 94–95.

17. Cf. Josh. 9:21–27, where the Israelites assigned these tasks to Gibeonites after their deception was exposed.

18. The expression occurs only here in the Old Testament, substituting for the more common "to enter into [*bôʾ*] a covenant" (see 2 Chron. 15:12; Jer. 34:10; Ezek. 16:8). For a discussion of these and other formulaic expressions for entering into a covenant relationship see M. Weinfeld, "*bᵉrît*," *TDOT*, 2:255–56.

19. Cf. Gen. 15:9–10, 17; Jer. 34:18. On the ceremony in the ancient Near East, see Weinfeld, *TDOT*, 2:262–63.

20. See Dumbrell, *Covenant and Creation*, 15–26.

21. Nor is it always the case elsewhere. Ezekiel seems to use this expression interchangeably with "to establish a covenant" (cf. Ezek. 16:60; 34:25).

(2) Through these rituals Yahweh confirms Israel as his people and himself as their God. Moses' adaptation of the covenant formula in verse 13 recalls not only commitments expressed in 26:17–18, but also the event at Sinai by which Yahweh had bound himself to the exodus generation (Ex. 29:45; Lev. 26:11–12). Moses declares expressly that the present ritual represents a fulfillment of earlier promises to this people.[22] With this statement Moses seems to recall Yahweh's address to him in Exodus 6:2–8, but he also casts his gaze far beyond Yahweh's promises to the exodus generation, to his oath to the ancestors (Gen 17:7).[23] The covenant that he promised to "establish" with Abraham and his descendants is the covenant he established with Abraham's descendants at Sinai (Ex. 19–24), and he now confirms on the Plains of Moab with the generation about to move in and take the Promised Land.[24] Although the people had already engaged in some sort of covenant renewal ritual on the Plains of Moab (26:16–19), Moses seems to have deemed it necessary to supervise a ratification ritual one more time.

Act II: Despising the Grace of Covenant Tomorrow (29:14–28)

IN VERSES 14–21, Moses addresses the consequences of despising the grace that Yahweh offered to Israel in receiving them as his covenant people. Moses sets the stage with an opening declaration of intent (vv. 14–15) and a recollective digression (vv. 16–17). The remainder of the chapter deals successively with an individual as a representative of the Israelite community who betrays the covenant and the covenant Lord (vv. 18–21), and with the effects of Israel's collective rebellion on the territorial apex of the covenantal triangle (vv. 22–28). Structurally and conceptually verses 14–21 build on 4:25–28. Both texts anticipate future apostasy and subdivide into similar parts: (1) the context of the apostasy (4:25a; 29:14–15); (2) the nature of the apostasy (4:25b; 29:16–18); (3) the geographic consequences of the apostasy (4:26–28; 29:19–21).

Setting the stage (vv. 14–17). Moses begins by extending his vision beyond the present ritual to Israel's future performance. However, he

---

22. The formula "as he promised you" occurs frequently in Deuteronomy: 1:11, 21; 6:19; 9:3; 10:9; 11:25; 12:20; 15:6; 18:2; 26:18, 19; 27:3; 31:3. In Deuteronomy this clause always speaks of an earlier "promise," found in sources on which Deuteronomy draws. See J. Milgrom, "Profane Slaughter and a Formulaic Key to the Composition of Deuteronomy," *HUCA* 47 (1976): 3–4.

23. Cf. 1:8; 6:10; 9:5; 30:20; 34:4.

24. For discussion of the relationship between these texts and these covenants, see J. Hwang, *The Rhetoric of Remembrance: An Exegetical and Theological Investigation into the 'Fathers' in Deuteronomy* (Winona Lake, IN: Eisenbrauns, forthcoming).

immediately interrupts himself with a parenthetical reminder of Israel's past experience with idolatry (vv. 16−17), to be followed by the completion of the thought in verses 18−21 with two negative purpose clauses.

The construction of verses 14−15 is emphatic, both by a second reference to "this covenant with its oath" (referring to the privileges and warnings built into the covenant) and by its word order. In verse 15 Moses reiterates that all who presently stand before Yahweh are indeed bound to the privileges and responsibilities that attend covenantal relationship with Yahweh, but then he complicates matters by including "those who are not here today." Although technically this could refer to absentees or non-Israelites, verses 10−11 exclude the former, and verse 13 excludes the latter, identifying the parties to this covenant as those whom Yahweh had claimed as his people. Moses does not clarify the enigma until the beginning of the next subsection (v. 22). Despite the vagueness of this statement, the commitments made here by Israel and Yahweh were binding for future generations.

As if his mind is running ahead of him, in verses 16−17 Moses digresses with reflections on the Israelites' life in Egypt and their crossing through the territory of other nations on their journey to the present location. However, the journey itself is not his concern. Rather, it is the shocking sight of the idolatry of the nations through whose lands they passed. Moses may have had in mind the Moabites in particular (cf. 4:3; also Num. 25:1−3), but the reference to Egypt suggests that Israel's encounter with idolatry began there. Although Yahweh's signs and wonders represented attacks on the gods of Egypt (Deut. 4:32−40; cf. Ex. 12:12; 18:11), the Exodus narratives are silent on Israelite idolatry before the golden calf incident at Sinai.[25]

Moses' epithets for idols reflect his disposition toward idolatry. The word *šiqqûṣîm* (NIV "detestable images") derives from a root meaning "abhorrent, disgusting." Moses borrows the second expression (*gillûlîm*, NIV "idols") from Leviticus 26:30.[26] Meaning "round things" and having reference primarily to sheep feces, the epithet itself is a caustic comment on idolatry.[27] Although these designations for idols emphasize their worthlessness and repugnancy, Moses' list of the materials from which idols were

25. But see Josh. 24:14. The present statement may underlie Ezekiel's perception of the Israelites' idolatrous past (Ezek. 20:5−9, on which see Block, *Ezekiel Chapters 1−24*, 624−30, especially 628−29). This conclusion is reinforced by the prophet's favorite designation for idols. See further below.

26. Thirty-nine of the word's forty-eight occurrences in the Old Testament are found in Ezekiel. For a full discussion of the word see D. Bodi, "Les *gillûlîm* chez Ézéchiel et dans l'Ancien Testament et les différentes pratiques cultuelles associées à ce terme," *RB* 100 (1995): 481−510.

27. Bodi, ibid., captures the intended sense with "shitgods." On the meaning of *gillûlîm*, see Block, *Ezekiel Chapters 1−24*, 227−28.

made (v. 17) seems to treat them as valuable objects. However, according to 4:28, these are pathetic lifeless creations of human hands.

The personal consequences of infidelity (vv. 18−21). Having digressed momentarily, Moses returns to the issue that preoccupies him. He fears that despite having bound themselves to the covenant, for some individuals the temptation of idolatry may prove too strong. Adopting a tone and style reminiscent of chapter 13, Moses warns the present and future generations that, unlike the gods of the nations, Yahweh will brook no rivals (29:18). His warning consists of two clauses. (1) He warns against tolerating an individual in their midst who should turn away from Yahweh to serve other gods. With the idiom "whose heart turns" (cf. 30:17),[28] Moses returns to one of the key words in this speech (*lēb*, "heart/mind"),[29] a term that identifies the seat of thought as well as of the will, emotion, and passion. Whereas verse 4 suggested that Yahweh had not given the previous generation a heart to know, here the heart knows what it wants to do: to abandon Yahweh and submit to other gods.

Continuing his propensity in this address to group subjects in fours, Moses identifies four potential apostates: a man, a woman, a clan, a tribe. Because verses 19−21 focus on the apostasy and arrogant response of an individual, some argue that this paragraph concerns primarily individual infidelity.[30] However, the quartette of subjects in verse 18 suggests a corporate interest as well. Furthermore, the sequel (vv. 22−28) portrays the effects of corporate and national rebellion. While interest in the individual is obvious, this person is singled out as a representative of the nation. The actions he performs, the disposition he expresses, and the fate he experiences represent the actions, disposition, and fate of the apostate nation as a whole.

(2) Moses warns against the poisonous nature of idolatry. Rendered literally, the last clause in verse 18 reads literally: "Lest there be among you a root bearing the fruit of poison and wormwood." Since roots do not actually bear fruit, the word used here probably represents "stock" from which branches grow (cf. 2 Kings 19:30; Job 14:17).[31] Here poison and wormwood function metaphorically for the unsavory and lethal effects of idolatry. If the idolatry itself will not kill, then the curse will—as described in verses 19−21.[32]

---

28. Deut. 17:17 speaks of apostasy as the heart/mind "turning aside," presumably from following the way of Yahweh (so also Jer. 17:5; Ezek. 6:9; Ps. 101:4).

29. Cf. 29:4, 18, 19; 30:2, 6 [3x], 10, 14, 17.

30. Cf. McConville, *Deuteronomy*, 416−17, 420.

31. On the fruits specified here, see I. Jacob and W. Jacob, "Flora," *ABD*, 2:816; M. G. Reddish, "Wormwood," *ABD*, 6:973.

32. These two words are combined to express the threat of divine punishment in Jer. 9:15[14] and 23:15, and to describe the fulfillment of the threat in Lam 3:15, 19.

Verse 19 introduces the idolater himself, summarizing his anticipated response to hearing "the words of this oath." Once again Moses concretizes the scenario by casting the apostate's reaction in the form of direct but internal speech ("in his heart/mind"; NIV "thinks"). Rendered literally, "And he will bless himself" here probably means something like, "And he will congratulate himself."[33] Lacking the heart/mind spoken of in verse 4, this man pays no heed to the sanctions to which he and all Israelites have bound themselves and imagines himself secure.

The opening line of the idolater's utterance is clear (v. 19b), reflecting the smugness of a man who imagines that the blessings listed in 28:1–14 are guaranteed for him unconditionally. However, what follows is extremely obscure. NIV's "even though" interprets the introductory particle *kî* concessively, though a conditional ("if") or causal ("because"), or even an emphatic "indeed," are also possible. The answer depends on the meaning of the remainder of the clause.[34] Although the idiom used here is usually rendered "stubbornness of heart," since few would congratulate themselves for being stubborn, we should probably interpret it more positively: "I will be resolute." But about what? Based on its usage elsewhere, the relatively rare verb *sâpâ* means something like "to eliminate, to sweep away." Apparently "watered and dry" functions as a merism, in which case this statement speaks of sweeping everything away.

But to what does this refer?[35] Interpreted within the broader context, the idolater's comment in verse 19b represents his response to a reminder of "the words of this oath." If "oath" refers to sanctions accompanying the covenant, then Moses seems to have in mind all of chapter 28, with *hârâwâ* ("the watered environment") referring to the blessings (28:1–14) and *haṣṣᵉmēʾâ* ("the parched environment") referring to the curses (28:15–68). More specifically, in context it seems to refer to the written document the person reads before the idolater.[36] To reconstruct the scene, an Israelite who has previously bound himself on oath to Yahweh's covenant reneges on his commitment and pursues an idolatrous course. Upon discovering this, someone warns him of the error and danger of his way by reading to him from the written copy of the Torah the curses associated with the cov-

---

33. So also McConville, *Deuteronomy*, 413.

34. NIV's periphrastic rendering, "even though I persist in going my own way," glosses over the problems.

35. NIV's "This will bring disaster on the watered land as well as the dry," is meaningless in the context, and like most English translations mistakenly removes this clause from the idolater's speech. For further discussion of the issues see McConville, *Deuteronomy*, 412; Nielsen, *Deuteronomy*, 336; Tigay, *Deuteronomy*, 280.

36. Note the references to the written record of the oath/curse in vv. 20 and 21.

enant. But the idolater responds defiantly, claiming all will be well for him. Seizing the document from the person who read the curses, he destroys the whole thing — both the blessings and the curses — thinking he can get away with it.

In verses 20 – 21 Moses predicts Yahweh's reaction, with the opening line serving as a theme statement. Though Moses might have declared Yahweh as unwilling to spare that man, he speaks of refusing forgiveness. Nothing will change Yahweh's disposition: not the idolater's own pleas for indulgence,[37] nor the mediatory atonement ritual of a priest,[38] nor the intervention of a responsible family member,[39] nor the intercession of a godly mediator.[40] By his idolatry and highhanded response to the warnings, the idolater has sealed his own fate.

Moses describes the actual fate of the idolater in the remainder of verses 20 – 21. (1) Employing an obvious anthropomorphism, he declares that Yahweh's anger and passion will "smoke" against that man.[41] (2) Every sanction recorded in this document will settle down on the idolater. (3) Yahweh will wipe out the idolater's name from under the heavens. With this idiom Moses asserts that Israelites who turn to idols will be subject to the same fate he had earlier prescribed for Canaanites (7:24) and Amalekites (25:19).[42] (4) Yahweh will single out the idolater from all the tribes of Israel as a particular target of disaster. Whereas Yahweh had earlier separated Israel from the Egyptians to spare them from calamity, now he will do the opposite. Here Moses declares that an idolatrous man may not find security in the group. Whatever the fate or fortune of the rest of the tribes, this person's doom is sealed; he will be struck with all the sanctions of the covenant recorded in the Torah document.

The geographic consequences of collective infidelity (vv. 22 – 28). The segment begun in verse 14 reaches its climax as Moses moves from the personal consequences of infidelity to the horrific collective consequences. Meanwhile his focus shifts from the people who have rebelled

---

37. According to 2 Chron. 7:14, when Yahweh's people humble themselves, and pray, and seek his face, and turn from their wicked ways, he will forgive. Cf. Naaman's request for forgiveness in 2 Kings 5:18.

38. Cf. the rituals that result in forgiveness in Lev. 4:20, 26, 31, 35; 5:10, 13, 16, 18; 6:7[5:26]; 19:22; Num. 15:25 – 28.

39. Cf. Num. 30:5, 8, 12[6, 9, 13].

40. Num. 14:20; note also Daniel's intercession on behalf of his people in Dan. 9:19. For discussion of the verb used here, see J. P. J. Olivier, *NIDOTTE*, 3:259 – 64.

41. On the image of an angry person's nose smoking see also Ps. 74:1 (see also comments on 4:24).

42. This was also the fate that Yahweh had threatened for the entire nation for worshiping the calf at Horeb (9:14).

against Yahweh to the land he had given to them. With this shift comes a change in style and genre. Ninety of these 117 words are cast as direct speech,[43] involving three different voices: (1) of descendants of the present generation of Israelites and foreign visitors to the land of Israel, who set the stage (vv. 22 – 23); (2) of all the nations, who raise the theological question posed by what the first voice describes (v. 23); (3) of a hypothetical respondent, who offers a theological explanation for the sight (vv. 25 – 28).

The first speech (vv. 22 – 23). Verse 22 is taken up with identifying the speakers in the first address. Moses begins with a general designation, "the later generations," which in context and in the light of the links with 4:25 – 31 suggests a distant future.[44] He qualifies the phrase with two types of people who will observe the devastation of the land: "your children who follow you" and "foreigners who come from distant lands." The singular form (lit., "foreigner") answers to the singular idolater in verses 18 – 20 and functions as a representative of visitors from distant lands. According to verse 23 the speech is precipitated by the sight that greets these observers: "the calamities that have fallen on the land," and "the diseases with which the LORD has afflicted it." These expressions are shorthand for all the curses in 28:20 – 68, though they bear closest links with 28:59. Remarkably Moses ascribes to the land afflictions normally experienced by humans.

The speech itself begins tersely with three nouns, "sulphur, salt, burning,"[45] followed by a triad of negative expressions of the visible effects. (1) The first word denotes a yellow crystalline substance found in regions of volcanic activity that ignites readily in air, giving off suffocating fumes.[46] While this chemical may be used either as a fungicide or for reducing alkalinity in the soil, excessive amounts sterilize the soil.

(2) The substance represented by the word "salt" is used both as a seasoning (Job 6:6) and as a sterilizing agent. However, Judges 9:45 and several extrabiblical references to spreading salt on conquered territory suggest this gesture also served to render the land infertile and to invoke a horrendous curse on the land.[47]

(3) The third word derives from a root meaning "to burn" (*śrp*) and is expressly associated with fire in Numbers 16:37. Here the expression refers

---

43. NIV obscures the oral character of v. 21 by beginning the direct speech in v. 24.

44. Contra those who specify the next generation: ESV, NRSV, McConville, *Deuteronomy*, 412.

45. The NIV switches these around.

46. Elsewhere this term is often associated with fire (Gen. 19:24; Ps. 11:6; Isa. 30:33; Ezek. 38:22); cf. pitch in Isa. 34:9.

47. On salt as symbol of barrenness and desolation, see Ps. 107:34; Jer. 17:6; Zeph. 2:9. Cf. S. Gevirtz, "Jericho and Shechem: A Religio-Literary Aspect of City Destruction," *VT* 13 (1963): 52 – 62. See also comments on 7:2 – 5.

to the sight of a landscape that has been torched, presumably by fire and sulfur from heaven.

The triad of expressions following these three words describes the devastating effects of the sulfur, salt, and fire on the landscape: "nothing planted, nothing sprouting, no vegetation growing on it." The sight reminds observers of the utter devastation of Sodom, Gomorrah, Admah, and Zeboiim.[48] Indeed the noun *maḥpēkâ* ("destruction") appears to have become part of the stock vocabulary used in recounting that event.[49]

The second speech (v. 24). The introduction of new speakers highlights the irony of the situation. Whereas Yahweh's design was that the nations should witness Israel's privileged status (26:19; cf. 28:1), here "all the nations" witness her demise. However, technically the nations' questions are not about the people of Israel; they concern their land: "Why has Yahweh treated this land like this? Why this extreme outburst of his fury?" (pers. trans.). These are the questions any ancient Near Easterner would have asked;[50] the sight of such devastation would naturally be interpreted as evidence of divine fury.

The third speech (vv. 25 – 28). Moses does not identify the speakers behind the third speech. Since they speak of Israelites in third person, they must be outsiders, though they seem well aware of Israel's special relationship with Yahweh and the covenant he had made with them. The speech itself divides into two virtually equal parts, the first (vv. 25 – 26) dealing with human causation behind Israel's fate, and the second (vv. 26 – 27) with Yahweh's response.

(1) Israel's treachery is the ultimate cause of their fate (vv. 25 – 26). Here the speakers realize that Israel's destruction is the result of rebellion against their divine Lord. They recognize four dimensions of Israel's treachery. (a) They have abandoned the covenant of Yahweh, the God of their ancestors.[51] One's first impulse is to interpret this as the covenant made with the patriarchs, by which Yahweh swore to give the land of Canaan to them and their descendants as an eternal possession.[52] However, echoing Leviticus 26:45, Moses

---

48. Although Genesis 18 – 19 speaks only of the destruction of Sodom and Gomorrah, the addition of Admah and Zeboiim, mentioned in Gen. 10:19 and 14:2, 8, is picked up by Hosea in Hos. 11:8.

49. The word is always associated with Sodom and Gomorrah: Isa. 1:7; 13:19; Jer. 49:18; 50:40; Amos 4:11.

50. For a similar response to Ashurbanipal's devastation of Arabia for rebelling against him, see *ANET*, 299 – 300.

51. This is one of only five instances where Israel's infidelity is referred to as "abandoning the covenant." Cf. 1 Kings 19:10, 14; Jer. 22:9; Dan. 11:30.

52. Cf. Deut. 1:8; 6:10; 9:5, 27; 30:20; 34:4.

specifies the time when this covenant was made: "when he brought them out of the land of Egypt." This clause points unequivocally to the covenant he made with Israel at Horeb (cf. 29:1 [28:69]). (b) The Israelites have gone after other gods. The prohibition against worship of other deities is fundamental to Yahweh's covenant with Israel, as expressed in the preamble to the Decalogue and the Supreme Command (5:6−10) and in the Shema (6:4−5). (c) They submitted to other gods. As elsewhere in the book, to "serve [Heb. ʿābad; NIV 'worship'] other gods" involves accepting the status of vassal before the deity. (d) They prostrated themselves before strange gods. Moses refers to them as "gods they did not know, gods he had not given them," in contrast to Yahweh, who had called Israel to an intimate covenant relationship with himself and had claimed Israel as his special allotment (32:9).

(2) Yahweh's fury is the immediate cause of Israel's fate (vv. 27−28). In the observers' description of Yahweh's response to Israel's treachery, the attention returns to the land. Intensifying the picture of divine fury begun in verses 20 and 24, the hypothetical interlocutor heaps up a series of expressions unparalleled in the Old Testament: Yahweh fumes at the nose (v. 27)[53] and acts in rage (v. 28), fury, and great wrath (v. 28). The observers' speech concludes by summarizing how Yahweh had expressed his anger. They acknowledge that Yahweh has imposed on the land "all the curses written in this book" (v. 27), uprooted[54] the population from the land, and tossed them away to a different land (v. 28).[55]

This speech is filled with irony. Like those who had come out of Egypt (cf. v. 4), the future generation of Israelites envisioned here seems clueless about spiritual realities, apparently having forgotten Yahweh their God,[56] his covenant (4:23; cf. 29:25), and the event at which they formally became the people of Yahweh (cf. 4:9−14). Furthermore, they abandoned the one who had revealed himself so dramatically in their rescue from Egypt and at Sinai in favor of other gods that they did not know (v. 26; cf. 11:28; 13:2[3], 13[14]). By contrast, the anonymous speaker is keenly aware of the special covenant relationship that existed between Yahweh and Israel: of Israel's origins in

---

53. Cf. 6:15; 7:4; 11:17; 31:17. This idiom derives from the natural phenomenon of hot breath issuing from the nose of an infuriated creature. Cf. v. 20, which speaks of the "nose" of Yahweh "burning" with rage.

54. The verb "to uproot" occurs only here in Deuteronomy, but is a favorite for the destructive judgmental actions of Yahweh in Jeremiah: Jer. 1:10; 12:14−15, 17; 18:7; 24:6; 31:28; 42:10; 45:4; cf. also 1 Kings 14:15.

55. The verb "to throw" occurs only here in Deuteronomy, but is also used elsewhere of Yahweh casting his people out of his presence: 2 Kings 13:23; 24:20 = Jer. 52:3; Jer. 7:15; 2 Chron. 7:20, cf. 1 Kings 9:7.

56. Cf. 6:12; 8:11, 14, 19.

Egypt and Yahweh's gracious acts of redemption, of Yahweh's passion for his people, of his personal involvement in their demise, and of the written Torah and every curse written in it. The concluding note, "as it is now," does not refer to the immediate rhetorical situation, but reflects the context and perspective of the interlocutor. "Now" is the day of Israel's judgment.

ISRAEL'S SUBSEQUENT HISTORY. MOST of the themes addressed in this chapter have been heard before. Perhaps more than anything, here Moses reinforces the notion that a covenant relationship with Yahweh is an incredible privilege. Of all the nations on earth Yahweh picked Israel for a special role. Since Israel owed her very existence to her gracious divine Suzerain, Yahweh's demand for complete and undivided devotion was reasonable. In the first half of his final address Moses reminds his people of the awful consequences of abandoning the covenant. Even in this reminder we see the grace of God, for he takes no pleasure in the death of the wicked but in their life (Ezek. 33:11).

But Moses' vision of the nation's future proves true. According to Judges 2:10 − 11, the spiritual recidivism anticipated here set in within decades of this speech. Seven times the narrator declares that the descendants of Israel did evil in the eyes of Yahweh,[57] and twice that they did right in their own eyes (17:6; 21:25). In Judges 17 − 18 the family of Micah illustrates the role of individuals in the apostasy. While the idea to craft an idol originated with Micah's mother (17:3 − 4), the narrator attributes responsibility for the cult shrine and its administration to Micah (17:5, 9 − 13; 18:14 − 26). Rather than denouncing this evil, the shiftless Levite became a priest in this apostate establishment (17:7 − 13). And when the Danites came along and confiscated the idols and the artifacts related to the cult, the sins of an individual became the sins of a tribe and a clan (18:19). Not until the very end (18:30) does the narrator let the reader in on the horrific secret: the apostate priest was Moses' own grandson Jonathan!

The books of Kings describe how the sins of individuals in Judges become the sins of the nation, as one king after another led them down the infuriating path of idolatry. Finally, in 722 BC the curses envisioned in this text fell on the northern kingdom, and in 586 BC Jerusalem and Judah fell, leaving the nations to puzzle over the role of Yahweh in the fate of his people. Their perplexity is expressed with the question, "Where is their

---

57. Judg. 2:11; 3:7, 12; 4:1; 6:1; 10:6; 13:1. In three of these he specifies the evil as viola-tion of the Supreme Command: they abandoned Yahweh, served other gods, and provoked divine anger (2:11 − 12; 3:7 − 8; 10:6 − 7).

God?"[58] In an oracle to Solomon after the dedication of the temple, Yahweh warns the king and all his successors not to forget Moses' final address:

> As for you, if you walk before me in integrity of heart and uprightness, as David your father did, and do all I command and observe my decrees and laws, I will establish your royal throne over Israel forever, as I promised David your father when I said, "You shall never fail to have a man on the throne of Israel."
>
> But if you or your sons turn away from me and do not observe the commands and decrees I have given you and go off to serve other gods and worship them, then I will cut off Israel from the land I have given them and will reject this temple I have consecrated for my Name. Israel will then become a byword and an object of ridicule among all peoples. And though this temple is now imposing, all who pass by will be appalled and will scoff and say, "Why has the LORD done such a thing to this land and to this temple?" People will answer, "Because they have forsaken the LORD their God, who brought their fathers out of Egypt, and have embraced other gods, worshiping and serving them — that is why the LORD brought all this disaster on them." (1 Kings 9:4 − 9)

Centuries later, as the doom of Judah approached, the prophet Jeremiah warned his people with echoes of this text:

> For this is what the LORD says about the palace of the king of Judah:
>
> "Though you are like Gilead to me,
>   like the summit of Lebanon,
> I will surely make you like a desert,
>   like towns not inhabited.
> I will send destroyers against you,
>   each man with his weapons,
> and they will cut up your fine cedar beams
>   and throw them into the fire.
>
> "People from many nations will pass by this city and will ask one another, 'Why has the LORD done such a thing to this great city?' And the answer will be: 'Because they have forsaken the covenant of the LORD their God and have worshiped and served other gods.'" (Jer. 22:6 − 9).[59]

---

58. Pss. 42:10[11]; 79:10; 115:2; Joel 2:17.
59. See also Jer. 5:19; 16:10 − 13.

In a bizarre caricature of Deuteronomy 29:4, Isaiah 6:9−10 appropriated Moses' declaration that in the past Yahweh had not given to Israel a mind to know, eyes to see, or ears to hear, to the hardened dispositions of his own time. Isaiah's prophetic ministry would have the opposite effect on his audience; their hearts will be rendered even more insensitive, their eyes more blind, and their ears more deaf, which reflects Yahweh's determination to carry out "all the curses written in this book of the Torah," in fulfillment of 29:18−28.[60] In Ezekiel 12:2 the exiled prophet applies Deuteronomy 29:4 to Judah's immediate situation, presenting the unseeing eyes and unhearing ears as evidence of the nation's rebellion against Yahweh.

More than a millennium later, in Romans 11:8 Paul picked up on Deuteronomy 29:4 and applied it to his own generation of Jews. His opening comment, "as it is written," suggests that he was consciously quoting Moses. The correspondence between his citation and the LXX Greek rendering of the Hebrew is evident when translations of the two texts are juxtaposed:

Deuteronomy 29:4	Romans 11:8
	As it is written,
But Yahweh has not given you	"God gave them
a heart to understand	a spirit of stupor,
or eyes to see	eyes so that they could not see
or ears to hear,	and ears so that they could not hear,
to this day,	to this very day."

But Paul's application of Moses' final address to the Jews of his day does not end with a comparison between their hardened condition and the anticipated rebellion of Israel in Deuteronomy 29:18−28. On the contrary, anticipating chapter 30, Paul bases his hope for the Jews as ethnic Israel on Moses' word that judgment cannot be the last word. As Talstra observes,

> Paul, the Jew, may, like the prophet Elijah, have felt alone, but that feeling is not allowed to dominate. The situation is comparable to that in 1 Kings 19: the relationship between God and Israel

---

60. G. K. Beale (*We Become What We Worship: A Biblical Theology of Idolatry* [Downers Grove, IL: InterVarsity Press, 2008], 71−76) argues that in having unseeing eyes and unhearing ears the exodus generation of Israelites became like the idols they worshiped.

has not ended. The teaching of Jesus and his disciples by no means implies an end to the covenant of God and Israel, but fits into it.[61]

INDIVIDUAL RESPONSIBILITY WITHIN THE cove-nantal relationship. What are Christians today to make of this chapter and its horrific images of divine fury and earthly devastation? We may summarize several significant lessons that every generation of believers needs to hear. For one thing, this chapter highlights the motif of individual responsibility within the covenantal relationship. It is not only nations or communities as groups that relate to God—positively or negatively. Individuals who trample underfoot his grace render themselves the particular targets of divine wrath (vv. 20−21) and may not seek cover under the national umbrella as they pursue their rebellious ways. If humanly designed weapons can single out precise targets in a larger space, Yahweh's aim is even deadlier.

The tragic missiological consequences of infidelity. This chapter also highlights for readers of the book the tragic missiological consequences of infidelity. Yahweh did not establish his covenant with Israel in a corner, nor did he intend for her to be insular in her enjoyment of his blessing. He chose Israel in the first place that she might be a kingdom of priests, a holy people among the nations, intervening on their behalf before him and serving as his agents of revelation and blessing. Moses' second address ended with repeated references to Yahweh's design for his people: to raise them high above the nations for his praise, fame, and honor (26:19; 28:9−10). This chapter emphasizes that if the prosperity of Israel redounds to the glory of God among the nations, the opposite is also true when they observe the horrendous consequences of infidelity.

Outsiders. Finally, verses 22−28 in particular remind us that sometimes outsiders are more sensitive to divine truth than those who claim to be God's people. Despite the Israelites' experience of deliverance from Egypt, their acceptance of covenant relationship, and their reception of the rev-

---

61. E. Talstra, "Texts and Their Readers: On Reading the Old Testament in the Context of Theology," in *The Rediscovery of the Hebrew Bible* (ed. J. W. Dyk et al.; ACEBT Supplement 1; Maastricht: Shaker, 1999), 109. We might recognize another indirect allusion to Deuteronomy 29 in Rom. 11: 3−5, where Paul quotes Elijah's complaint in 1 Kings 19:10 that the people have destroyed Yahweh's altars and killed his prophets, lamenting that he only is left. What he leaves off is Elijah's opening charge against his own people: they have abandoned Yahweh's covenant, which obviously derives from Deut. 29:25. As noted above, the idiom occurs only in Deut. 29:25; 1 Kings 19:10, 14; Jer. 22:9; and Dan. 11:30.

elation in the form of statutes and ordinances at Sinai and beyond, Moses' generation took these privileges for granted and failed to grasp the significance of all that their eyes had seen and their ears had heard.

Things were not markedly different in Paul's day. In Romans 9:4–5 Paul speaks of his kinsmen after the flesh possessing the privileges of adoption as sons, the glory (glorious revelation?), the covenants, the Torah, the divinely revealed and effective system of cultic rituals, the promises, and the traditions, but they do not grasp the significance of the climactic revelation of God in Jesus Christ. He is the fulfillment of all the promises and the goal of all revelation (Rom. 10:4). Whoever calls on his name will be saved (10:13). As outsiders, those who were previously mere observers of all that God has done for and to his chosen people have, by faith in Christ, been grafted into the olive tree (Rom. 11:17–24). This is not a cause for pride, but for humbly rejoicing in God's grace toward us.

In the meantime, with Paul our heart's desire and prayer to God for his chosen people is that their minds will know, their eyes will see, and their ears will hear the glorious gospel of salvation in Jesus Christ—who is over all, God blessed forever. Amen (Rom. 9:5).

Deuteronomy 29:29[28]–30:10

The secret things belong to the LORD our God, but the things revealed belong to us and to our children forever, that we may follow all the words of this law. ³⁰:¹When all these blessings and curses I have set before you come upon you and you take them to heart wherever the LORD your God disperses you among the nations, ²and when you and your children return to the LORD your God and obey him with all your heart and with all your soul according to everything I command you today, ³then the LORD your God will restore your fortunes and have compassion on you and gather you again from all the nations where he scattered you. ⁴Even if you have been banished to the most distant land under the heavens, from there the LORD your God will gather you and bring you back. ⁵He will bring you to the land that belonged to your fathers, and you will take possession of it. He will make you more prosperous and numerous than your fathers. ⁶The LORD your God will circumcise your hearts and the hearts of your descendants, so that you may love him with all your heart and with all your soul, and live. ⁷The LORD your God will put all these curses on your enemies who hate and persecute you. ⁸You will again obey the LORD and follow all his commands I am giving you today. ⁹Then the LORD your God will make you most prosperous in all the work of your hands and in the fruit of your womb, the young of your livestock and the crops of your land. The LORD will again delight in you and make you prosperous, just as he delighted in your fathers, ¹⁰if you obey the LORD your God and keep his commands and decrees that are written in this Book of the Law and turn to the LORD your God with all your heart and with all your soul.

Original Meaning

THE TRANSITION FROM THE horrors and darkness of divine fury in chapter 29 to the brilliant sunshine of divine grace in chapter 30 would be abrupt if it were not cushioned by 29:29. As a transitional statement, it makes more sense to treat it as an introduction to chapter 30 than the conclusion to chapter 29, for it opens the door to the contemplation of a new future for Israel.

Today: Wondering about Covenant Grace (29:29)

BRINGING HIS HEARERS BACK to the present, Moses contrasts "secret things" belonging to Yahweh with "things revealed" belonging to the audience and to their descendants in perpetuity. The meaning of the latter is clarified by the last clause—the Torah that Moses has been expounding for the past twenty-five chapters.[1] Whereas the previous generation lacked the disposition to receive the revelation (v. 4), Moses' present audience has been given a clear understanding of the will of Yahweh and the nature of covenant relationship.

Commentators have interpreted the "secret things" reserved by/for Yahweh variously as hidden sins,[2] the oral Torah,[3] wisdom,[4] or the mystery of divine providence.[5] The last suggestion offers the most promise. Similar to 4:28—31, this statement serves as a transition from judgment to restoration in the distant future. However, in contrast to 4:28—31, which attributes the shift to Yahweh's compassionate character and his irrevocable commitment to his covenant with the ancestors, the change in divine disposition becomes more pressing in this text. How could the gracious Redeemer who had been abandoned in favor of other gods even contemplate ultimate renewal of the covenant? This is the mystery of divine providence.[6]

Whatever the significance of the "secret things," Moses' insertion of this statement provides a psychological buffer between the darkness of chapter 29 and the brilliance of chapter 30. Like the intermission between acts in a theatrical performance, this esoteric reflection on wisdom prepares for the change in tone and direction. Without this literary pause, the shift from 29:28[27] to 30:1 would be intolerably abrupt.

---

1. This conclusion will be reinforced in the following chapter, particularly 30:11—14 and 30:15—20. Cf. Barker, *Triumph of Grace*, 139—40.

2. Like those cited in 27:15 and 24. See Rofé, "Covenant in the Land of Moab," 313. Cf. also Ps. 19:12[13].

3. Thus the rabbis, on which see A. Shemesh and C. Weman, "Hidden Things and Their Revelation," *RevQ* 18 (1998): 409—27. At Qumran v. 29 was read as a *pesher* on their history; the hidden things were reserved for God during the First Temple Period (when Israelites broke the revealed commands), but they were revealed in the Second Temple Period to the members of the Community. See CD 3:9—20; 5:20—6:11.

4. Some note the link with Job 28:21, which speaks of wisdom as hidden and inaccessible to human beings. Cf. G. Braulik, *Deuteronomium II 16,18—34,12* (Neue Echter Bible 28; Würzburg: Echter Verlag, 1992), 216.

5. After observing that the secret things are undefined, Barker comments, "Whatever they are, they are not necessary for man to know. God has revealed all that is needed for obedience" (*Triumph of Grace*, 140).

6. If the "today" segments (29:2—13[1—12]; 29:29; 30:11—20) represent the core of this address, then the hidden things contrast not only to "all the words of this Torah" but also to "the command" in 30:11 and "the word" in 30:14.

Act III: Trusting in the Grace of Covenant Tomorrow (30:1–10)

UNLIKE LEVITICUS 26:40–45, the blessings and curses in Deuteronomy 28 do not anticipate renewal after the judgment. However, this lack is more than made up for by 30:1–10. Indeed, with this arrangement Moses has heightened the significance of the renewal spoken of in Leviticus 26,[7] and the links between Deuteronomy 30:1–10 and chapter 28 suggest this entire address should be read in the light of the covenant curses presented there.[8]

When the curtain rises after 29:29, the tone has changed completely, though the mysteries of divine providence remain and leave the reader asking a host of questions. After the flagrant spurning of his grace described in chapter 29, how could Yahweh receive his people again? What is the relationship between Israel's return to Yahweh and Yahweh's return to them? Does Yahweh return to Israel because she has made the first move in returning to him, or is the process reversed?[9] While the issues involved in the debate are important, theological agendas from outside should not interfere with a natural reading of the text.

Deuteronomy 30 represents the climax of the gospel according to Moses as he has proclaimed it in this book. Employing the second person of direct address, Moses brings his present audience into these future events. Much of the theological freight of this section is carried by key words. The most important of these is the root *šûb* ("to return, turn back"), which occurs seven times, with some variation in meaning.[10] Since four of the seven involve Israel as the subject (vv. 1, 2, 8, 10) and three involve Yahweh (vv. 3a, 3b, 9), Israel's future restoration obviously requires a change in the disposition

---

7. J. Krasovec ("The Distinctive Hebrew Testimony to Renewal Based on Forgiveness," *Zeitschrift für altorientalische und biblische Rechtsgeschichte* 5 [1999]: 226) interprets 30:1–10 as a counterpart to Lev. 26:40–45.

8. Krasovec (ibid., 230) suggests they came from the same author.

9. For representation of the first view see Driver, *Deuteronomy*, 328; Craigie, *Deuteronomy*, 363; Tigay, *Deuteronomy*, 283–84; Biddle, *Deuteronomy*, 444. For representation of the second view, see Wright, *Deuteronomy*, 289–90; and esp. Barker, *Triumph of Grace*, 144–45; K. Turner, *The Death of Deaths in the Death of Israel: Deuteronomy's Theology of Exile* (Eugene, OR: Wipf and Stock, 2010), 173–79, though he adopts a more moderate stance in "When Does God Circumcise the Heart in Israel's Restoration from Exile? Deuteronomy 30:1–10 and Its Implications for the Christian Doctrine of Salvation," a paper presented to the Evangelical Theological Society, Washington, D.C., 2006.

10. A. Rofé ("The Covenant in the Land of Moab [Deuteronomy 28:69–30:20]: Historico-Literary, Comparative and Form-Critical Considerations," in *Das Deuteronomium: Entstehung, Gestalt und Botschaft* (ed. N. Lohfink; BETL 68; Leuven: Leuven Univ. Press, 1985), 311) describes this passage as "a majestic fugue" on the theme of *šûb*. For a full study of the word, see W. L. Holladay, *The Root שוב in the Old Testament (with Particular References to Its Usage in Covenantal Contexts)* (Leiden: Brill, 1958).

of both parties. These along with other repeated elements function as glue holding this literary unit together. The subthemes interwoven throughout this passage exhibit an exquisite chiastic arrangement (pers. trans.):[11]

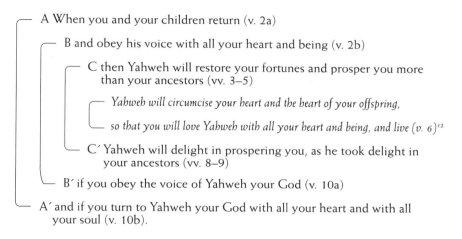

A When you and your children return (v. 2a)

    B and obey his voice with all your heart and being (v. 2b)

        C then Yahweh will restore your fortunes and prosper you more than your ancestors (vv. 3–5)

            Yahweh will circumcise your heart and the heart of your offspring,

            so that you will love Yahweh with all your heart and being, and live (v. 6)[12]

        C′ Yahweh will delight in prospering you, as he took delight in your ancestors (vv. 8–9)

    B′ if you obey the voice of Yahweh your God (v. 10a)

A′ and if you turn to Yahweh your God with all your heart and with all your soul (v. 10b).

This is a gloriously holistic text, announcing the full restoration of the triadic covenantal relationship. Based on syntactical and conceptual markers, the text breaks down into the following segments: (1) the restoration of the bilateral relationship between Yahweh and Israel (vv. 1–3); (2) the divine restoration of the trilateral covenant relationship (vv. 4–7); (3) the human proof of the restoration (v. 8); (4) the environmental proof of the restoration (vv. 9–10).

The Restoration of the Bilateral Relationship between Yahweh and Israel (vv. 1–3)

THE OPENING "WHEN" CLAUSE identifies the context in which the restoration of the bilateral relationship will transpire. The verse begins with "When all these *haddᵉbârîm*." While many translate *haddᵉbârîm* simply as "things" (and the NIV omits translating it), in Deuteronomy and the Pentateuch as a whole the expression always means "all these words."[13] Moses clarifies the phrase with "the blessing and the curse" (pers. trans.), which points back to chapter 28. The modifying clause, "[which] I have set before you,"

---

11. Cf. Wright, *Deuteronomy*, 289.

12. Verse 7 is omitted because it deals with what Yahweh will do to the nations rather than Israel, though these actions ultimately are for Israel's benefit.

13. Gen. 20:8; 29:13; Ex. 19:7; 20:1; 24:8; Num. 16:31; Deut. 4:30; 12:28; 30:1; 32:45.

reinforces this interpretation. Moses has been doing things with words—trying to inspire fidelity with promises as rewards for obedience and with warnings as the consequences of disobedience. When his predictions have been fulfilled, the events foreseen in verses 1b–3 will occur (cf. 4:30).

Moses begins his description of Israel's restoration by summarizing the changes in the relationship between the people and Yahweh. (1) Concerning the people (vv. 1b–2), the Israelites will experience a change in disposition. Among all the nations where Yahweh their God has banished them, they will come to their senses. In the clause rendered by the NIV as "you take them to heart," the verb *bēšîb* ("to turn x back") actually lacks an object. If we assume "all these words" (v. 1b) to be the object, then in exile the Israelites will reverse their hardened disposition (cf. 29:19[18]) and in effect recast as a confession what Moses had presented as a third person interpretation in 29:25–28[24–27].

(2) The Israelites will then experience a change in orientation: they "will return to the LORD your God," a verbatim quotation from 4:30. This signifies a reversal of past patterns of behavior characterized as "abandoning" Yahweh (28:20) or his covenant (29:25[24]), and turning aside from his way (9:12) or from him to serve other gods (11:16), to name a few.

(3) The Israelites will experience a change in receptiveness: they will finally listen to the voice of Yahweh (NIV "obey"; cf. 4:30).[14] The coordinate expression "with all your heart and with all your being" (NIV "soul"; vv. 2, 6, 10) picks up a refrain heard often in the book[15] and highlights the completeness of the people's "repentance."

Additional echoes of 4:29–31 occur in verse 3 as Moses shifts his attention to Yahweh's new disposition and actions. (1) Yahweh's intentions concerning Israel will change; he will restore their fortunes.[16] Here the reversal involves lifting the judgment and restoring the relationship between the people of Israel and their land. (2) Yahweh's disposition toward Israel will change; he will show compassion to them (cf. 4:31). As in 13:17[18], the change seems contingent on Israel's listening to his voice and doing what is right in his sight. (3) Yahweh's orientation regarding Israel will change; he will "turn around." The verb here expresses Yahweh's fundamental reori-

---

14. This clause serves as a refrain in the book: 4:30; 8:20; 9:23; 13:4, 18 [5, 19]; 15:5; 21:18, 20; 26:14, 17; 27:10; 28:1–2, 15, 45, 62; 30:2, 8, 10, 20.

15. Deut. 4:29; 6:5; 10:12–13; 11:13–15; 13:3[4]; 26:16.

16. This is the first of twenty-five occurrences of this idiom in the Old Testament, and its only occurrence in Deuteronomy. In Job 42:10 the expression involved restoration of the beleaguered man's original good fortune. For discussions of the idiom, see J. M. Bracke, "*šûb šᵉbût*: A Reappraisal," *ZAW* 97 (1985): 233–44; J. A. Thompson and E. A. Martens, "שׁוּב," *NIDOTTE*, 4:58–59.

entation. Instead of turning from Israel and operating as their enemy, he will turn toward them and act on their behalf. (4) Yahweh's treatment of Israel will change. Whereas previously he had scattered them among the nations, now he will gather them (cf. 4:27; 28:64). While we hear nothing yet of the restoration of the people to the land, this divine action represents a necessary first step in reversing their uprooting (29:28[27]).

The Restoration of the Trilateral Relationships Involving Yahweh, Israel, and the Land (30:4−7)

THE SYNTAX OF VERSE 4 signals a shift in flow, though the repetition of the verb "to gather" suggests that verses 4−5 expand on the last clause in verse 3 and highlight the comprehensiveness of the restoration. Moses begins this subunit by addressing the nation−land relationship of the triangle (vv. 4−5). His solution involves five elements, expressed with five verbs. The language is generally familiar, though a few details call for further comment. The second verb, "to take" (NIV "bring back") is cryptic. The link with 4:20—the only other occurrence with Yahweh as the subject and Israel as the object—suggests the verb signifies a concrete affirmation of election; Yahweh will claim Israel as his own possession once more. The third verb, "to bring" (v. 5), suggests Yahweh is bringing them home and to himself (cf. comments on 12:5). Furthermore, the addition of "and you will take possession of [the land]," implies permanence. Yahweh's original delight, expressed concretely in the blessings of 28:1−14, will return. The picture will be complete when Yahweh fulfills his ancient promise to Abraham to multiply his descendants once more (6:3; 13:17[18]).[17] In fact, Yahweh will cause the population to exceed that of their ancestors before the exile.[18] Finally, the national ideals announced in the covenant with Abraham and confirmed when the Israelites were incorporated in this covenant at Horeb will be realized.

In verse 6 Moses addresses the heart of the problem: Israel's ruptured relationship with Yahweh. In so doing he reintroduces a notion presented in 10:16, where he had called on the Israelites to "circumcise" their hearts. The metaphor refers to removing all psychological, moral, and spiritual barriers to true devotion to Yahweh, resulting in undivided love and obedience. While a positive disposition toward God is a prerequisite to restoration, Moses acknowledges that permanent and total covenant commitment can be achieved neither by appealing to the people to get themselves right

---

17. Cf. Gen. 16:10; 17:2, 20; 22:17; 26:4, 24; 28:3; 35:11; 48:4.

18. For references to Israel prospering in the land and multiplication of the population, see also 6:3; 7:13; 30:16.

with Yahweh nor by mere returning to the land. On the contrary, national infidelity not only seems inevitable; it poses an ever-present danger for this generation.[19] However, Moses has also declared that however certain Israel's failure may be, so certain is the conviction that alienation from Yahweh and exile cannot be the last word (cf. 4:28–31).

Verse 6 brings us close to unraveling the mysteries of divine providence and grace (cf. 29:29[28]). Moses declares that Yahweh will secure permanent and total devotion through circumcising the hearts of those whom he brings back from the exile and of their descendants. He expresses the goal of this surgery with a simple infinitive phrase: "to love the LORD your God." As elsewhere, "love" denotes commitment demonstrated in actions that serve the interests and pleasure of one's covenant partner. This could not be achieved by legislation; it required a radical new act, the surgical removal of the symbols of the old affections. With this act, the goal of life and the ideal expressed by the Shema (6:4–5) will be realized.[20]

With this heart surgery the covenantal triangle will be totally restored. Before Moses completes the picture by dealing with implications of this renewal for the land (v. 9), he takes a quick glance at the nations around (v. 7). Concomitant with Israel's spiritual restoration, Yahweh will repair their standing among the nations, imposing the sanctions that his own people had experienced in 29:22–28[21–27] on those who served as his agents of punishment. Part of the mystery of divine providence is that Yahweh exercises full freedom over all nations. Like Gog and Magog in Ezekiel 38–39, Yahweh may call them in to carry out his mission, but as haters of his people they are his enemies, and their wickedness must be addressed.

The Human Proof of Restoration (30:8)

THE OPENING "AS FOR you, you will turn ..." (pers. trans.) in verse 8 signals a shift of focus from the divine actions in verses 4–7 back to the human response. Repeating notions expressed in verse 2, verse 8 describes what will be demanded of Israel in the future and actually predicts the fulfillment of those demands. Yahweh's people will exhibit a new orientation, a new receptiveness, and a new obedience in compliance with Moses' teaching. Moses' optimism regarding Israel as a nation presupposes a divine act of heart circumcision. He expresses no confidence in the human will to maintain the course.

---

19. See 5:29; 9:6, 13, 24; 13:2[3]; 31:16–18, 27–29.

20. Since elsewhere Moses suggests this goal will be achieved through reading/hearing the Torah (17:19–20; 31:11–13), circumcising the heart is equivalent to implanting the Torah in peoples' hearts.

The Environmental Proof of the Restoration (30:9–10)

EXPANDING ON VERSE 5, Moses draws his hearers' attention back to Yahweh, who causes the land to fulfill its role in the tripartite covenant relationship. In describing the environmental evidences of this new order, he highlights Israel's special relationship with Yahweh by what these two will do for each other. He announces the effect of Yahweh's beneficent actions in the opening clause: He will cause the Israelites to prosper in all they do. Echoing the blessing in 28:11, Moses develops three dimensions of this prosperity: in their own progeny, in the progeny of their livestock, and in the productivity of the ground. Yahweh's lavish blessing of Israel arises from a new orientation and disposition toward his people.

Reiterating his earlier promise, Yahweh declares that he will "turn toward Israel"[21] with renewed delight over them (cf. 28:63). Since the patriarchs never actually enjoyed the benefits of the full triangular covenantal relationship, "your fathers" refers to the present generation, who will receive the land and ultimately be viewed as the ancestors of the exiled generations (cf. 4:25; 29:22[21]). Accordingly, although Moses seems to view Israel's future apostasy as inevitable, he anticipates this will be preceded by a period of fidelity and prosperity. The promise of 7:12–16; 8:11–13; and 11:13–15 is not merely a utopian dream for the eschatological future (cf. 32:13–14); it will happen to this generation and/or their descendants.

In verse 10 Moses brings this section to a close with one more reminder that although the triangular covenantal relationships will be fully restored, his people should not view these promises as unconditional predictions, irrespective of their disposition. (1) The Israelites must pay full attention to the voice of Yahweh, which means ordering their conduct according to his commands and decrees as written in "this book of the Torah."[22] This written document represents not only a written transcript of Moses' pastoral addresses but also congealed divine oral communication. Since Yahweh's voice is expressly identified with a written text, in the Torah of Moses Israelites of all generations have access to the divine voice.

(2) Israel must return to Yahweh her God with all her heart/mind and her entire being. Whereas verse 3 had called on Israel to return to Yahweh and listen to his voice with all their heart/mind and being, here Moses reverses the order, saying they must listen to his voice and return to Yahweh with their entire heart and being.

---

21. As in vv. 3c and 8, the NIV obscures the reference to reorientation by treating *yâsûb*, "he will return," as an adverb, "again."

22. The expression "in this book of the Torah" is identical to the form in 29:21[20], but different from 28:61, "written in the book of this Torah." Note that "book" (*sēper*) is not book in a technical sense but a written document—in all likelihood, a vellum or parchment scroll.

The Hebrew particle *kî* occurs three times in verses 9–10 and poses a critical issue in interpreting this paragraph. Should we interpret this expression causally ("because"), or conditionally ("if"), or temporally ("when")? Theoretically any of these is possible.[23] However, since *kî* clauses following a main clause normally bear a causal sense,[24] these three clauses declare both the grounds and the certainty of Israel's newfound prosperity: Yahweh will bless Israel because he will delight in her (v. 9b), because they will listen to his voice (v. 10a), and because they will return to him.[25] Moses' earlier appeal to "circumcise your hearts" and his repetitious calls for love, fear, obedience, and service of Yahweh (esp. 10:12–16) rest on this possibility. It seems the missing element in Israel's history would not be the ability to keep the will of Yahweh, but the will to do so, an issue taken up more fully in following paragraphs.

In Deuteronomy 30:1–10 Moses reiterates and expounds on his vision of Israel's future as summarized in 4:30–31 and envisioned in Leviticus 26:40–45. Perhaps herein lies the answer to the divine mystery in 29:29[28]. Why would Yahweh turn again to Israel in such a lavish outpouring of covenantal love? Because in the end his mercy wins out over his fury, and his commitment to his people is eternal. The judgment will not and cannot be the last word.

MOSES, JEREMIAH, AND PAUL. In this portrait of Israel's inevitable restoration Moses has planted numerous seeds that will sprout and grow in later texts.[26] Jeremiah paints his picture of Israel's restoration climaxing in the establishment of a new covenant (Jer. 31:27–37) with this passage in the background. In the prophet's declara-

---

23. The NIV disregards the first occurrence, treating the last clause of v. 9 as an independent clause; in v. 10 *kî* is translated twice as "if."

24. Thus A. Aejmelaeus, "Function and Interpretation of *kî* in Biblical Hebrew," *JBL* 105 (1986): 202–7.

25. Cf. ibid., 202–8. Contra McConville, *Deuteronomy*, 428; syntactically, the temporal interpretation seems least likely and depends too much on theological assumptions regarding Israel's incapacity to turn to Yahweh prior to his circumcision of their heart in 10:16.

26. My interpretation obviously assumes the chronological priority of Deuteronomy over Jeremiah. See G. Vanoni, "Anspielungen und Zitate innerhalb der hebräischen Bibel: Am Beispiel von Dtn 4,29; Deut 30,3 und Jer 29,13–14," in *Jeremia und die deuteronomische Bewegung* (ed. W. Gross; BBB 98; Weinheim: Beltz Athenäum, 1995), 383–95. Contrariwise, M. Z. Brettler argues that Deuteronomy 30:1–10 is based on Jeremiah. See "Predestination in Deuteronomy 30.1–10," in *Those Elusive Deuteronomists: The Phenomenon of Pan-Deuteronomists* (ed. L. S. Schearing and S. L. McKenzie; JSOTSup 268; Sheffield: Sheffield Academic, 1999), 171–88.

tion of his thesis in Jeremiah 30:3 we hear clear lexical and conceptual echoes of Deuteronomy 30:1–10. Although Jeremiah does not refer to the circumcision of the heart, his understanding of the divine inscription of the Torah on the hearts of the people and his vision for all Israel participating in the new order fall within the same theological field.

Like Moses, Jeremiah is fully aware that there are two Israels. On the one hand, there is the Israel that claims status before God and before the nations by virtue of descent from Abraham, their identification with the exodus from Egypt through the annual celebration of the Passover, and their possession of the Torah; this is Paul's "Israel after the flesh."[27] On the other hand, there is true spiritual Israel, for whom the Shema (Deut. 6:4–5) is the watchword. Like Josiah centuries later, they turn to Yahweh with all their inner beings, their persons, and their resources (2 Kings 23:25); like Caleb and Rahab and Ruth (who were Gentiles by blood), they have a different Spirit and follow Yahweh fully (cf. Num. 14:24; Deut. 1:36; Josh. 14:8); and like David, they trust Yahweh fully (2 Sam. 22:2–51). Historically, times when the boundaries of these two Israel's coalesced were rare. The contrast between the two may be portrayed graphically as follows:

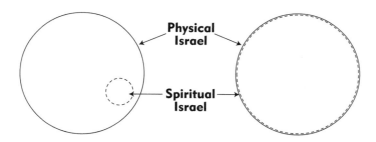

But the image envisioned here is different. As pictured on the right, Moses looks forward to a time when the boundaries of physical and spiritual Israel will be coterminous. All Israel will be circumcised of heart; all will love Yahweh; all will listen to his voice and live according to the Torah of Moses; and all will participate in Yahweh's favor.

This is the ideal that Jeremiah has in mind. Taking a page out of Moses' notebook, he castigates his people for being uncircumcised of heart (4:4; 6:10; 9:25–26), but in Jeremiah 31:31–34 he looks beyond the judgment to the day when "all Israel" will (1) have the Torah inscribed on their hearts, (2) be related to Yahweh by covenant, (3) know him, and (4) will have experienced the forgiveness of their sins. None of these four features is

---

27. Rom. 4:1; 9:3, 5; Gal. 4:23, 29.

absolutely new; from the beginning there has been a remnant who enjoyed these gifts of grace. The only new feature of the "new covenant" is its scope. Speaking with Yahweh's voice the prophet looks forward to a day when all Israel will embrace him (cf. v. 22) and the boundaries of spiritual Israel will match the boundaries of physical Israel.

Affirmed from both sides, the bond of commitment will be indissoluble. In the new covenant there is no freedom from the law, nor is there any adjustment in God's standards of righteousness. Jeremiah envisions a future[28] when the original Torah of Yahweh will be internalized in the hearts of all Israel and all Israel will be freed to walk in the ways of Yahweh. The so-called "new covenant" is not actually new; it means the fulfillment and realization of the ideals represented in God's covenant with Abraham, which were transferred to the entire nation at Sinai and renewed with this generation on the Plains of Moab.[29]

The return of the Jews from Babylon in 538 BC demonstrated that Yahweh had not forgotten his people or his word through Moses. Weaned of idolatry, the returnees rebuilt Jerusalem as the spiritually renewed covenant people of Yahweh. However, neither Moses nor later biblical interpreters would have envisioned this as the complete fulfillment of Deuteronomy 30:1 – 10, for this event was a renewal only "in small measure" (cf. Ezek 11:16). The pillars on which their hope was based were only partially reconstructed:

1. They occupied only a small portion of the land originally promised to the ancestors.
2. Although ca. 50,000 returned (Ezra 2:64 – 65), these were primarily Judahites and Levites and represented only a small portion of Israelites scattered throughout the ancient Near East.
3. Zerubbabel, a descendant of David, was back, but the kingship was not restored; he was merely a governor of a province under the control of Persia (Hag. 1:12 – 15; 2:23).
4. The temple was rebuilt, but it was a pathetic version of the glorious original; in any case, the glory of Yahweh apparently never returned (cf. Hag. 2:1 – 9).

---

28. The expression "the days are coming" recurs in vv. 27, 31, 38.

29. In context, Jer. 31:27 – 40 is entirely parochial; only Israel is in view here. Ezekiel does not speak of heart circumcision, but replaces this image with the metaphor of heart transplant language. Echoing Moses' ambivalence in Deuteronomy, in one moment he calls on the Israelites to get themselves a new heart and a new spirit (Ezek. 18:31; cf. Deut. 10:16), and in the next speaks of Yahweh transplanting the people's spirit and heart (11:19; 36:24 – 34; cf. Deut. 30:6). Like Moses, Ezekiel sees the proof of spiritual renewal as obedience to God's will.

This picture obviously does not match the ideal set by Moses, but it was a deposit of Yahweh's continued commitment to his people.

Deuteronomy 30:1–10 also provides the roots of Pauline thought. In response to Judaizers, who argued that Gentiles needed to be circumcised physically to have access to Yahweh's covenant, Paul argued that the covenant people of God are not identified by physical circumcision but by internal circumcision of the heart by the Spirit. Punning on the name Judah ("praise"), he declared that true Israel (Jews) receive their praise from God and not from humans (Rom. 2:25–29). Refracted through Jeremiah's vision of the future, Paul looked forward to the fulfillment of the Mosaic ideal when "all Israel will be saved" (Rom. 11:26).

This prospect of hope for a renewal of the relationship between Yahweh and his estranged subjects contrasts sharply with realities assumed in ancient Near Eastern suzerainty treaties. While these political documents present the relationship between suzerain and vassal with familial language like "father" and "son," respectively, human suzerains tended to be concerned primarily to protect their own interests; treaty curses are never followed by expressions of hope for renewal of the relationship after the curses have been inflicted by the gods. Moreover, whereas political suzerains invoked the deities as third parties to reward or punish traitors in the subjunctive mood, Yahweh declares the consequences of obedience and disobedience in the declarative mood and poses as guarantor of both the sanctions and ultimate restoration in the first person.[30]

Although Yahweh performs the legislative, executive, and judicial functions, he also exercises complete freedom to renew the relationship after the curses have been imposed. His original election of the ancestors was driven by broader missiological concerns, but in his relationship with Israel he always operated in his people's interests. Yahweh's power and status were never jeopardized by their rebellion; driven by his compassionate heart and his irrevocable commitment to his people (4:30–31), he was free to declare the judgment ended and to offer them a new start. Deuteronomy 30:1–10 offers powerful testimony to Yahweh's eternal commitment to his people.[31]

THE PRESENT STATE OF **Israel.** Deuteronomy 30:1–10 bears profound significance for Christians today at three levels. First, it offers guidance for a Christian perspective on the present state of Israel. On the one hand, the existence of a homeland for the Jewish

---

30. Cf. Krasovec, "Distinctive Hebrew Testimony," 234.
31. Cf. Ex. 31:16–17; Lev. 24:8; 26:40–45; Judg. 2:1; Ps. 111:2–9; Isa. 24:4–5; 54:4–10.

people in the land of Israel cannot be dismissed merely as an accident of history. After two thousand years in the diaspora, the descendants of Abraham from all over the world have recreated a state in the land promised to his descendants. This is evidence of a most remarkable providence.

Even so, we recognize that the present state of Israel is not the fulfillment of Moses' vision or of the vision of the prophets who succeeded him. The preconditions established for the renewal of the covenantal triangle have not been fulfilled. While some Jews scrupulously follow ritual and kosher laws of Judaism, Israel today is essentially a secular state; furthermore, their treatment of Palestinians and other aliens in their midst exhibits little evidence of a national movement characterized by a circumcised heart and the moral vision summarized in Deuteronomy 10:12–22. Apart from the faith and the fear of God demonstrated in actions that seek the well-being of the next person ahead of one's own, there is no divine right to the land.

We pray for the peace of Jerusalem, but we also pray for the peace of the region. Israel's calling is to serve as a microcosm of a world that longs for shalom; this involves fidelity to God and the concomitant blessing of God. Applying Joel 2:32[3:5] directly to Christ, Paul declared that true devotion to Yahweh is demonstrated by faith in Jesus Christ, for "everyone who calls on the name of the Lord will be saved" (Rom. 10:13).[32]

God and the covenant relationship. As Paul emphasizes in Romans 2, Deuteronomy 30:1–10 provides a paradigm for the way God establishes a covenant relationship with those who earnestly seek him. On the one hand, a positive relationship with God calls for a change in our disposition as we come to our senses and recognize the rebellion of our ways; a change in orientation as we move away from the path of evil and rebellion; and a willingness to hear the voice of God, calling us to faith and establishing the course on which we must go (Acts 3:19; 8:22).[33] The message of Scripture

---

32. On which see D. I. Block, "Who Do Commentators Say 'the Lord' Is? The Scandalous Rock of Romans 10:13," in *On the Writing of New Testament Commentaries: Festschrift for Grant Osborne on the Occasion of His 70th Birthday* (ed. S. Porter and E. Schnabel (Leiden: Brill, 2012), forthcoming.

33. M. Boda notes rightly that Deuteronomy has little to say about forgiveness and atonement as solutions for violation of the covenant. The emphasis is on divine compassion and restoration as a response to human repentance. See chapter 7, "Deuteronomy," in *A Severe Mercy: Sin and Its Remedy in the Old Testament* (Siphrut 1; Winona Lake, IN: Eisenbrauns, 2009), 97–114. While theologians often argue that repentance itself is the result of a prior divine work, this text will not allow a reductionistic explanation of the process of salvation. Here the sequence is penitence, which involves deep reflection on and acknowledgement of sin, followed by turning around and wholehearted obedience. Only the latter is presented as the result of the divine work of God in circumcising human hearts.

is consistent: The human preconditions for relationship with God include faith and repentance, which Paul speaks of as putting off the old corrupt self and putting on the new self (Col. 3:9−10).

On the other hand, this spiritual renewal is effected by a gracious divine act. When God withdraws his hand of judgment from us who deserve it— for all fall short of God's glorious standard (Rom. 3:23)—when his disposition and orientation changes from wrath to compassion, and when he circumcises human hearts by a gracious and undeserved act of transformation, a relationship with him is established. All whose hearts are circumcised will love him wholeheartedly and will demonstrate that love in joyful obedience to his will.

The new covenant. From the perspective of this side of the cross, the conceptual links between this text and the new covenant forces us to ask about the role of Christ, who makes this new covenant relationship possible. When Jesus instituted the Lord's Supper, of the fruit of the vine, he said, "This cup is the new covenant in my blood, which is poured out for you" (Luke 22:20). Through the work of Christ we are brought near to God to enjoy covenant relationship with him; through Christ we come to know the Father; through the sacrifice of Christ our sins are forgiven; and through Christ and his Spirit our minds are renewed and his Torah is inscribed on our hearts. The work of Christ, whose mission was established before the foundation of the world (1 Peter 1:18−21), provides the basis for all God's covenants. Through Christ's work the holiness of God is satisfied and his wrath toward us is lifted and replaced with mercy.

Deuteronomy 30:11–20

Now what I am commanding you today is not too difficult for you or beyond your reach. ¹²It is not up in heaven, so that you have to ask, "Who will ascend into heaven to get it and proclaim it to us so we may obey it?" ¹³Nor is it beyond the sea, so that you have to ask, "Who will cross the sea to get it and proclaim it to us so we may obey it?" ¹⁴No, the word is very near you; it is in your mouth and in your heart so you may obey it.

¹⁵See, I set before you today life and prosperity, death and destruction. ¹⁶For I command you today to love the LORD your God, to walk in his ways, and to keep his commands, decrees and laws; then you will live and increase, and the LORD your God will bless you in the land you are entering to possess.

¹⁷But if your heart turns away and you are not obedient, and if you are drawn away to bow down to other gods and worship them, ¹⁸I declare to you this day that you will certainly be destroyed. You will not live long in the land you are crossing the Jordan to enter and possess.

¹⁹This day I call heaven and earth as witnesses against you that I have set before you life and death, blessings and curses. Now choose life, so that you and your children may live ²⁰and that you may love the LORD your God, listen to his voice, and hold fast to him. For the LORD is your life, and he will give you many years in the land he swore to give to your fathers, Abraham, Isaac and Jacob.

Original Meaning

IN THESE VERSES MOSES brings his audience back to the present with a final appeal. His pastoral concern is clear as he reminds the Israelites of the reasonableness of the covenantal demands (vv. 11–14) and challenges them to choose the right course (vv. 15–20).

The Accessibility of the Revelation of God (30:11–14)

IN VERSES 11–14 Moses reiterates that the demands of covenant relationship are not unknowable, unreasonable, incomprehensible, or impossible.

On the contrary, they are accessible and doable. Seldom in the book has the argumentation been so tight. Beginning with a thesis statement expressed negatively (v. 11), Moses presents two supporting arguments virtually identical in style and structure, and then concludes with a positive answer to the opening thesis.

The paragraph opens with the particle *kî* (NIV "Now"), marking the peak or climax of the third address.[1] In 29:14[13] Moses had thrust his audience forward to the distant future, warning them not to slide into apostasy (29:14—28[13—27]), but ultimately offering hope that in the end Yahweh's compassion will win over his anger (30:1—10). If we read the main body of this covenant renewal oration (29:2—13, 29[1—12, 28]; 30:11—20) as a continuous narrative, the particle *kî* links this paragraph directly to 29:29[28], suggesting that verses 11—14 expand on "all the words of this law [Torah]" that have been revealed to the Israelites.[2] In the opening declaration, "this command" (*hammiṣwâ*, untrans. in NIV) refers to all the covenantal demands.[3] While some suggest this word serves as a virtual synonym for *hattôrâ*, "the Torah, instruction,"[4] the singular form may also refer to the Supreme Command—under which all others are subsumed—expressed in the first command of the Decalogue and the second part of the Shema (6:5; cf. 10:12—21).

In 30:12—13 Moses inserts the voices of two hypothetical interlocutors, through whom he makes two important disclaimers about the command. (1) The command is not "too difficult" (*niplē^ʾt*) for the Israelites' comprehension or performance (v. 11). This word may refer either to something beyond one's understanding[5] or beyond one's power to perform.[6] Here Moses probably intends the word to be understood in the broadest sense. The command is not so baffling that only a magician can grasp it, nor is it so difficult that it demands superhuman strength. For Yahweh to have

---

1. On the use of *kî* to mark a prominent juncture, see C. M. Follingstad, *Deictic Viewpoint in Biblical Hebrew Text: A Syntagmatic and Paradigmatic Analysis of the Particle כִּי* (Dallas: SIL, 2001), 52.

2. So also E. Aurelius, "Heilsgegenwart im Wort: Dtn 30,11—14," in *Liebe und Gebot. Studien zum Deuteronomium* (ed. L. Perlitt Festschrift, R. G. Kratz and H. Spieckermann; (FRLANT 190; Göttingen: Vandenhoeck & Ruprecht, 2000), 15.

3. Cf. Deut. 6:25; 11:22; 15:5; 19:9. Deut. 30:11 lit. translates: "this command that I am commanding you today"; it echoes 15:5 verbatim.

4. Tigay, *Deuteronomy*, 74, 286.

5. In Ex. 34:10 a cognate noun refers to Yahweh's marvelous deeds on behalf of his people. In Deut. 17:8 the Niphal verb involves an insoluble legal case. Prov. 30:18 associates this word with incomprehensibility.

6. See 2 Sam. 13:2; Zech. 8:6. It is used with reference to Yahweh in Gen. 18:14; Jer. 32:17, 27.

imposed on his people a standard of conduct that was impossible to achieve would not have been a gracious act, but the ultimate in tyranny.

(2) The command is not out of reach. Moses makes this point with two illustrations cast in virtually identical form. Imagining a person embarking on a long journey to retrieve the command and then returning with it and teaching it to the people, Moses juxtaposes heaven and sea as a merism to express "any conceivable destination."[7] Several extrabiblical texts provide analogues to Moses' comment.[8] Although Moses was probably unaware of this cosmic journey tradition, his comment appears to answer the questions raised by the righteous sufferer in *Ludlul Bēl Nēmeqi*: "Who knows the will of the gods in heaven? Who understands the plans of the underworld gods? Where have mortals learnt the way of a god?"[9]

In contrast to the inaccessibility of the minds of the gods, the revelation of God, that is, "the word," is right here and need not be retrieved from a distant place. The switch from "this command" in verse 11 to "the word" in verse 14 appears stylistic, but the choice invites association with "the words," which collectively designate Moses' instructions (cf. 1:1). Moses' equation of "this command" and "the word" provides further insight into the significance of his final addresses. In contrast to the secret things that Yahweh has reserved for himself (29:29[28]), through Moses' speeches Yahweh's revelation is brought near to the present generation, and the people are given a mind to know, eyes to see, and ears to hear (cf. 29:4[3]).

The expression "near" suggests a link with 4:7–8, which speaks of Yahweh's nearness to Israel. What is true of Yahweh is also true of "this command." Verse 14 indicates the revelation is extremely near, in their mouths and in their minds/hearts; by recitation they commit it to memory.[10] Through the concluding purpose clause in this verse, Moses declares that

---

7. This pair of expressions serves as a shorthand version of opposites listed elsewhere in the Old Testament (Job 11:8–9; Ps. 139:8–9; cf. Job 28). In Amarna Letter 264 a Canaanite king describes his loyalty to Pharaoh: "Should we go up into the sky, or should we go down into the netherworld, our head is in your hand" (transl. by Moran, *Amarna Letters*, 313).

8. For example, see "Etana," in Foster, *Before the Muses*, 533–54; Tablets IX–XI in the Epic of Gilgamesh. For translation of the latter see A. George, trans., *The Epic of Gilgamesh: The Babylonian Epic Poem and Other Texts in Akkadian and Sumerian* (London: Penguin, 2000), 70–100; also *ANET*, 88–97.

9. *Ludlul Bēl Nēmeqi* 1.36–38, as translated by Lambert, *Babylonian Wisdom Literature*, 41. See also the question raised in "The Dialogue of Pessimism": "Who is so tall as to ascend to the heavens? Who is so broad as to compass the underworld?" (ibid., 148–49, ll. 83–84). On the relationship of these texts to Deut. 30:11–12, see F. E. Greenspahn, "A Mesopotamian Proverb and Its Biblical Reverberations," *JAOS* 114 (1994): 35.

10. Deut. 30:11 and 14 adapt 6:6: "These commandments that I give you today are to be upon your hearts."

---

his instruction is to guide the Israelites' conduct. The statement assumes that both the Supreme Command and the detailed body of instructions that flow from it are, in fact, doable. In calling for wholehearted obedience, Yahweh does not demand what is unknowable, impossible, or unreasonable. If Israel fails—and they will (31:16–18)—it will not be because the people *cannot* keep the law because the bar is impossibly high, but that they *will not* keep it. While every generation will produce individuals who are righteous and loyal to Yahweh (i.e., true Israelites), here the concern is spiritual recidivism of the nation as a whole. Their success depends on the fidelity of the group.

The Two Ways (vv. 15–20)

MOSES CONCLUDES HIS THIRD address with an urgent appeal to choose wisely between the two options he has been presenting all along (cf. 11:26–28). The structure of the present paragraph may be highlighted graphically as follows (pers. trans. below):

	See, I set before you today	
The Choice	life and prosperity	death and disaster.

The Conditions	which I am commanding
	    you today
	by loving Yahweh your
	    God
	by walking in his ways,
	and to keep his commands
	decrees
	and laws;
		But if your heart
		    turns away
		and you do not obey
		and you are seduced
		and you prostrate yourself
		    before other gods
		and serve them

	I declare to you this day	

The Consequences	then you will live
	    and increase,
	and Yahweh your God
	    will bless you
	in the land
	you are entering
	to possess it.
		that you will certainly
		    be destroyed.
		Your days shall not
		    be lengthened
		on the soil
		you are crossing the Jordan
		    to enter
		to possess it.

In view of the language,[11] many consider this unit a distillation of "Deuteronomic theology," according to which obedience results in blessing

---

11. For the demands, cf. 10:12; 11:1, 22; for the promises/threats, cf. 4:1; 7:13; 8:1.

and disobedience results in the curse.[12] Adopting a style imitated in later wisdom writings,[13] Moses the teacher/preacher presents two options and outlines the consequences of each. If they demonstrate love for Yahweh by walking in his ways and obeying all his commands, they will enjoy life and prosperity; but if they turn away from Yahweh and his way, they "will certainly be destroyed" (v. 18). Here "the life" and "the good" (lit. trans.; note the article in the Heb.) represent functional equivalents to "the blessing" (11:26; 28:1−14), while "the death and the destruction" (again, note the article) represent the curse (11:26; 28:15−68).

Verse 16 begins awkwardly in Hebrew with a subordinate clause that elsewhere refers to something that Moses has previously commanded.[14] In 11:27, "if you obey the commands of the LORD your God" precedes this clause, which suggests that here in 30:16, either Moses assumes the people would have filled in the blank, or the omission represents a scribal lapse.[15] Accordingly, the following infinitives should be interpreted modally: Israel obeys the commands of Yahweh that Moses is commanding them "by loving" Yahweh their God, "by walking" in his ways, and "by keeping" his commands, decrees, and laws (cf. 10:12). The consequences of infidelity involve the opposites of the benefactions Moses had promised as reward for fidelity: instead of life, death; instead of good, disaster.[16]

Naturally, the kinds of behavior that bring on death and disaster involve a change in disposition away from Yahweh, demonstrated in disobedience and worship of other gods (vv. 17−18). Whereas obedience yields life, multiplication, and blessing in the land the Israelites are entering, disobedience yields certain destruction, death, and shortened life spans in the land they are entering. By inserting "I declare to you this day" (v. 18) between the conditions and the consequences of disobedience, Moses adds solemnity to the warning.

Moses concludes his final address with an impassioned appeal to choose rightly (v. 19). Repeating a statement from the paraenetic ending to the

---

12. Cf. the discussion by W. Brueggemann, "The Shrill Voice of the Wounded Party," *HBT* 21 (1999): 1−25.

13. The sage contrasts life and death as a motivational theme in Prov. 11:19; 14:27; 18:21. See also G. H. Wilson, "'The Words of the Wise': The Intent and Significance of Qohelet 12:9−14," *JBL* 103 (1984): 186−87. In association with Deut. 11:26−28 and 30:15−18, Wilson cites Prov. 3:33−35; 4:10−19; 8:32−36.

14. In this chapter alone, see vv. 1a, 1b, 2, 3, 5, 7, 8, 11, 16b, 18.

15. Perhaps an error by homoioarcton, the scribe's eye having skipped from the first *ʾᵃšer* to the second, resulting in the loss of the intervening material. ESV and NRSV follow LXX, which includes the missing clause. So also McConville, *Deuteronomy*, 423; Nelson, *Deuteronomy*, 345, 346. NIV's reading is possible, though unlikely.

16. On *tôb* ("good") and *raʿ* ("evil") as polar opposites see C. Westermann, *Genesis 1−11: A Continental Commentary* (Minneapolis: Fortress, 1994), 328−33.

first address (4:26), he calls on the heavens and the earth to testify against Israel that he has presented these options to them. The Hebrew of the second half of verse 19 is emphatic: "The life and the death I have put before you; the blessing and the curse" (pers. trans.). The references to life and death reiterate the opening of this paragraph (v. 15), and the references to the blessing and the curse are borrowed from 11:26–27.

The final call to "choose life" at the end of verse 19 represents both the high point of Moses' final address and the climax of his preaching on the plains of Moab. This clause governs the rest of verses 19 and 20, being followed immediately by a purpose clause and then by three modal infinitives. To choose life means to demonstrate covenant commitment ("love") to Yahweh in actions that serve his interests, to "listen" to the voice of Yahweh, and to "hold fast" to him alone.[17]

But the choice is binary: life or death. The three infinitives with which verse 20 opens assume that proper choices involve the entire person and that Israel holds the keys to life in their own hands. Here Moses understands "life" in both quantitative and qualitative terms. "Life" means a long life in which the effects of sin and premature death are staved off. But it also means dwelling in the land that Yahweh had promised on oath to give to their ancestors. With this last reference to the ancestors Moses has come full circle, ending where he began—with the people on the verge of the Promised Land and with Yahweh's sworn promises ringing in his ears. Yahweh always keeps his word; the question here is, will the people keep theirs?

MOSES' PREACHING CONTINUES. ALTHOUGH Moses' farewell addresses to his congregation have ended, his voice is not silenced. The sound of his preaching rings through the centuries, not only through the sermons preserved in the book of Deuteronomy, but also in the compositions of historians, prophets, sages, and psalmists, who remind us that those who claim to be God's people always stand at the moment of decision: Will we love God? Will we listen to his voice? Will we hold fast to him alone?

Joshua picked up Moses' plea in his own farewell address with the challenge: "Choose for yourselves this day whom you will serve, whether the gods your forefathers served beyond the River, or the gods of the Amorites, in whose land you are living." And then he presented himself as a model,

---

17. On *dābaq* ("to hold fast, cling to"), see comments on 4:4; 10:20; 11:22; 13:4[5]. Deut. 11:22 contains a similar triad of requirements, though "to walk in all his ways" substitutes for listening to his voice between the other two.

"As for me and my household, we will serve the LORD" (Josh. 24:15). Sadly, the history of Israel is a history of wrong choices. To be sure, there were individuals who chose life. The history of the nation is framed by two such persons. For his loyalty, at the beginning Caleb gained the honorific title "my servant," and enjoyed the delights of dwelling in the land, because he possessed a different spirit and followed Yahweh fully (Num. 14:24).[18] At the end, Josiah received the supreme commendation: "Before him there was no king like him, who turned to Yahweh with his whole inner being, his whole person, and all his resources, according to the entire Torah of Moses" (2 Kings 23:25, pers. trans.). But in the swirl of Judah's final decades, even his life was cut short by a "random" Egyptian arrow.

The author of Hebrews summarizes well the exodus generation's rejection of the glorious grace of Yahweh demonstrated in election, redemption, covenant, and providential care: "For we also have had the gospel preached to us, just as they did; but the message they heard was of no value to them, because those who heard did not combine it with faith" (Heb. 4:2; cf. Num. 32:11–12). The same was true of their grandchildren. According to Judges, within a generation after crossing the Jordan, the Israelites repeatedly made wrong choices, bringing on themselves the covenant curses. They chose death rather than life, and only by Yahweh's grace did the nation emerge at the end of second millennium BC more or less intact—physically at least. But spiritually they all did what was right in their own eyes (Judg. 17:6; 21:25).

After the establishment of the Davidic monarchy, within a generation Israel's kings led the way in wrong choices, greasing the nation's downward slide to destruction. Israel's choice of death was so fixed that Isaiah could rhetorically twist the notion of Israel's covenant relationship with Yahweh into their own "covenant with death" (Isa. 28:15, 18). Overcome by the power of their flesh (cf. Rom. 8:3), the Israelites refused to link the good news represented by Yahweh's offer of life with faith (e.g., Num. 14:11). Instead of circumcising their hearts and submitting to the divine circumcision, they hardened their hearts, refused to listen to Yahweh's voice, and broke the covenant (cf. Heb. 8:9 [Jer. 31:32]). This led to Yahweh's suspension of his promised blessing and the imposition of the covenant curses.

Paul and Deuteronomy 30. However, Moses and the prophets, particularly Jeremiah (Jer. 31:1–40) and Ezekiel (Ezek. 34; 36:13–38; 37:1–28), and Paul in the New Testament (Romans 9–11), insisted that Israel's story would not end with the exile. Through God's gracious work in fulfillment of his covenant commitments, the nation would rise again and fulfill the ideals Moses declared in his farewell addresses. However, when Paul spoke

---

18. With Joshua, Caleb remained true to Yahweh (Num. 14:24; Deut. 1:36; Josh. 14:8–9, 14), in contrast to the rest of the generation that came out of Egypt (Num. 32:11–12).

of Christ being brought down from heaven and brought up from the abyss, he took the present text in a surprising direction. The following synopsis of literal translations shows that his argument was based loosely on the Septuagintal reading of Deuteronomy 30:11–14:

Deuteronomy 30:11–14 (LXX)	Romans 10:6b–8
For this command that I am commanding you today is not excessive or far away;	
It is not in heaven *above*, saying	*Do not say in your heart,*
'Who will go up to heaven for us	'Who will go up to heaven
and get it to us	*that is, to bring Christ down?'*
so hearing it we may do [it]?'	
	or
Nor is it beyond the sea, saying,	
'Who will cross over	'Who will *go down to the Abyss*
beyond the sea for us	*that is, to bring Christ up from the dead?'*
and bring it to us	
	But what does it say,
so hearing it we may do [it].'	
The word is very near	'Near you is the word,
in your mouth and in your heart	in your mouth and in your heart.'
and in your hand to do it.	
	That is, the word of faith that we proclaim.

New Testament scholars have gone to great lengths to rationalize Paul's christological adaptation of this text.[19] However, we must remember that Paul functions primarily as a rhetorician rather than as a scholar engaged in grammatical-historical exegesis as we practice it. His intent was not to unlock the mysteries of Moses' statement in Deuteronomy 30:11–14, but to exalt Christ by highlighting him as the climax of the covenant[20] for all who believe (Rom. 10:4), and to expose Jewish abuse of the law by divorcing it from faith and claiming access to relationship with God on the basis of superior righteousness (cf. Rom. 9:30–32).[21] Paul began his argument by appealing to Yahweh's own promise in Leviticus 18:5, that those who

---

19. See esp. T. Schreiner, *Romans* (BECNT; Grand Rapids: Baker, 1998), 550–63; D. J. Moo, *The Epistle to the Romans* (NICNT; Grand Rapids: Eerdmans, 1996), 644–60.

20. "The end of the law" (Rom. 10:4). Our expression is borrowed from N. T. Wright, *The Climax of the Covenant: Christ and the Law in Pauline Theology* (Minneapolis: Fortress, 1993), 241.

21. An implication of Paul's citation of Deut. 9:4 (LXX), in the original context of which Moses destroys the notion that Israel's entitlement to the land of Canaan rested on superior righteousness. Cf. Schreiner, *Romans*, 558; Moo, *Romans*, 650–51.

faithfully keep the ordinances and laws will live by them. This is in perfect harmony with the spirit of the entire book of Deuteronomy[22] and accords with the disposition of psalmists, who delight in keeping Torah and find in obedience to Torah the way of life.[23]

Remarkably, Deuteronomy lacks the Hebrew equivalent of Paul's *pistis* ("faith"). However, the absence of the word does not mean the absence of the concept. The offer of life as a reward for obedience in Deuteronomy assumes obedience to be expression of faith, an outworking of exclusive devotion to and fear of Yahweh.[24] We should not confuse the ideals of the Torah as laid out in Deuteronomy generally and 30:11 − 14 in particular with Israel's historical response to the same. Paul cannot hereby be correcting a flaw in the Torah, for that would contradict its perfections by virtue of its divine origin. Romans 10:5 and 6 − 9 do not represent opposing notions, as if in its original context the law offered a "works righteousness," in contrast to the "righteousness by faith" for which Paul appeals. Rather, Paul hereby corrects a contemporary misinterpretation and misuse of the law. His Jewish detractors treat obedience to the law as the ticket into the kingdom of God, when that ticket is to be understood as a gracious gift to be received only by faith. Paul and Moses agree that divine soteriological favor is not won through obedience to the law; rather, willing obedience to the law is proof that one has accepted by faith the grace that God has offered (cf. Deut. 6:20 − 25).

We should also be cautious when wrestling with the relationship between Paul's use of excerpts from Deuteronomy 30:12 − 14 and their function in the original context. No doubt Paul understood the intent of Moses' words in their original context. In fact, he brilliantly recognizes the analogous relationship between the "command/word" in Deuteronomy 30:11, 14, and Christ. For the Israelites of Moses' day to learn the will of Yahweh required no effort at all, for Yahweh had freely and graciously revealed his will. Indeed, to have commissioned agents to go and fetch a word from God either from heaven or from some far-off land would have been an act of unbelief and a repudiation of the grace already received.

Paul applies the same principle to Christ. There is no need to go up to heaven or down to the netherworld to retrieve Christ. In the incarnation Christ came down from heaven, and in the resurrection he came up from the abyss. Whereas in the original context faith was demonstrated by accepting the Torah and submitting to Yahweh, in the wake of the resur-

---

22. Deut. 4:1; 6:20 − 25; 8:1, 3; 30:6, 16.

23. Pss. 19:7 − 14 [8 − 15]; 119: 16, 24, 25, 35, 40, 47, 48, 62, 70, 77, 92, 93, 97, 113, 119, 127, 140, 143, 156, 159, 163, 167, 175.

24. Deut. 4:10; 5:29; 6:2, 4 − 5, 13, 24; 10:12, 20; 13:4[5]; 17:19; 31:12 − 13.

rection, faith is demonstrated in accepting Christ and in submitting to him. Jesus is more than the embodiment of the law; because he is Yahweh incarnate, he, rather than the law, is now "the focus of God's revelatory word."[25]

But how can Paul link the "command"/"word" in Deuteronomy 30:11–14 with Christ? Is this some sort of midrashic exegesis or an ancient rhetorical method? Although we cannot be sure Moses was making the link here, the use of the adjective *qârôb* to describe the "nearness" of the word in verse 14 recalls Moses' statement in 4:7 that Yahweh, Israel's God, is "near" (*qᵉrôbîm*) to his people. Indeed within the reception history of Moses' final address, Yahweh and the Torah are intimately associated—so intimate that in Psalm 119 human actions and dispositions we would expect to be directed toward Yahweh are directed instead toward the word/command, as if God is identified with the word. In many instances expressions for "law"/"word"/"Torah" can be substituted with the divine name Yahweh.[26]

Given these associations of the "word" with Yahweh, Paul's substitution of Jesus Christ for the "command"/"word" in Deuteronomy 30:11, 14 begins to make sense. In the context of Romans 10 Paul's goal is to prove not only that Jesus Christ is analogous to the Torah declared by Moses, but also that Jesus is to be identified with Yahweh, to whom the Israelites were to be committed without reservation and on whose behalf Moses spoke. This is suggested in Romans 10:8b by Paul's association of "the word of faith that we are proclaiming" with the confession "Jesus is Lord" in 10:9.

But what is the meaning of the confession, "Jesus is Lord" (*kyrion Iēsoun*)? On first impulse it is tempting to interpret this as a confession of Jesus' lordship, perhaps in response to Caesarian demands to accept the Roman emperor as lord. However, the word *kyrios* ("lord") in the New Testament was used as an epithet, reflecting both Hebrew *ᵓᵃdôn* ("Lord") and the divine name *yhwh* ("Yahweh"). By the latter interpretation, the confession signifies "Jesus is Yahweh,"[27] which differs from verse 12, where the characterization of Jesus as "Lord of all" obviously speaks to his sovereignty rather than his identity.[28]

---

25. Thus Moo, *Romans*, 653.

26. Cf. Aurelius, "Heilsgegenwart im Wort," 23–24. The following involve citations in which expressions for the "word"/"command"/"Torah" could be replaced by the divine name Yahweh: Pss. 119:19 (cf. 27:9; 69:17[18]; 102:3[4]; 143:7), 20, 31 (cf. 63:9[10]; Deut. 10:20), 41, 42 (cf. 56:4[5]); 46 (cf. Isa. 61:6); 47 (cf. Deut. 6:5; Pss. 26:8; 31:23[24]; 97:10; 116:1; 145:20), 48 (cf. Pss. 28:2; 63:4[5]); 114 (cf. vv. 43, 74; 147; cf. 31:24[25]; 33:18, 22; 69:3[4]; 71:5; 147:11; 130:7; 131:3).

27. The ambiguity has its roots in LXX, which regularly renders both the tetragrammaton (*yhwh*) and *ᵓᵃdôn* as *kyrios*.

28. Cf. C. E. B. Cranfield, *Romans: A Shorter Commentary* (Grand Rapids: Eerdmans, 1985), 258–60.

This interpretation of *kyrion Iēsoun* is reinforced by several additional features. (1) Leviticus 18:5, which Romans 10:5 quotes, is framed by the divine self-introduction formula: "I am Yahweh, your God; and you shall keep my ordinances and laws, by the doing of which you shall live; I am Yahweh" (pers. trans.).[29] (2) Just as the signs and wonders of Egypt fulfilled Yahweh's self-revelatory goals, so God's raising of Jesus from the dead proved his identity with Yahweh (Rom. 10:7). (3) Paul's punctuation of Romans 10:1 – 13 with soteriological language (vv. 1, 9, 13) suggests he was looking back beyond Moses' address in Deuteronomy 29 – 30 to the exodus. (4) Finally by applying Joel 2:32[3:5] to Christ (v. 13), Paul identifies Jesus with Yahweh. Accordingly, the confession *kyrion Iēsoun* ("Jesus is Yahweh") resembles a similar confession in Philippians 2:9 – 11: *kyrios Iēsous Christos* ("Jesus Christ is Yahweh").[30]

Paul's identification of Christ with Yahweh is not intended primarily to contrast the law as a way of works righteousness and the righteousness that comes by faith, but to up the ante for his Jewish audience. Whereas Moses challenged the Israelites to demonstrate faith by choosing life and submitting to the Torah, Paul declares that in view of the death and resurrection of Christ, those who would be saved must put their faith in Jesus Christ, who is Yahweh come in the flesh. As the "the end of the law," Jesus is both the perfect embodiment of Torah righteousness and the embodiment of Yahweh himself, the source of the Torah. Thus the incarnation goes far beyond the revelation involved in the Torah. Whereas Moses could only mediate divine grace by teaching Torah, in Jesus grace and truth are embodied (John 1:17).[31]

In recognizing this link between the "command"/"word" in Deuteronomy 30:11, 14, we may have solved the riddle of Paul's citation of this verse in Romans 10:6 – 8, but we may also have stumbled upon the riddle represented by the prologue of John's gospel. What is said of Christ, the divine Word, in John 1:1 – 18 could be said of the revealed word in Deuteronomy. Moreover, what is said of John the Baptizer is true of Moses: "He himself was not the light; he came only as a witness to the light" (John 1:8). The juxtaposing of rejection and belief in John 1:11 – 12 is analogous to Moses' challenge in Deuteronomy 30:15 – 20 to choose life. John 1:14

---

29. That "live" here means "remain alive" or even "enjoy life" rather than "conduct one's life" is confirmed by the conclusion to this chapter (Lev. 18:29 – 30), which warns the Israelites not to practice evil, lest they be cut off.

30. For further discussion, see Block, "Who Do Commentators Say 'the Lord' Is"? forthcoming.

31. The contrast here is not between law and grace, but between mediated grace and embodied grace (cf. John 1:16).

finally explains the link between the presence of Yahweh in Deuteronomy 4:7 – 8 and the presence of the "word" in 30:11, 14. The grace represented by the Torah mediated by Moses is now embodied in Christ. Through Christ, God has revealed the "hidden things" of Deuteronomy 29:29[28]. If this interpretation is correct, then 29:29[28] and 30:11 – 14 provide the first hint in the book of the glorious events with which the New Testament opens. In light of the incarnation, the crucifixion, and the resurrection, we see in Christ the grace of God embodied. Therefore, whoever will call upon the name of Yahweh — that is, Christ — will be saved.

 GOD'S SELF-REVELATION. THE SIGNIFICANCE of a text like this for the church today is no mystery. As heirs of God's revelation to Israel and as those who understand the climactic revelation in Christ, we celebrate the grace expressed in the name Immanuel. God is near, and his will is clearly revealed. In our post-Christian spiritual environment, the quest for the mind of God takes many forms: Eastern religions, meditation, fascination with the cultic practices of aboriginal populations, and hunger after "words of knowledge." This text reminds us that God has taken the initiative in revealing himself; no human quests to the far corners of the globe or into the deep recesses of the soul are needed.

A further dimension to the good news of this passage is that what God has revealed of himself — in the Word and in Christ — is clear, and the response that he calls forth from us is doable. God does not demand of his people that they jump over nine-story buildings; he asks the reasonable and calls for the doable. That he should have revealed himself to us is marvelous, but that which he asks of us is plain: to demonstrate love for God in Christ through joyful obedience and grateful service.

Choose life! While Israel failed collectively, God's response to individuals who choose life offers inspiration to all. Although we must caution against an unhealthy individualism, the facts remain that God takes no pleasure in the death of anyone (Ezek. 18:32), and that the course of life is open to all. Ezekiel 18 emphasizes that there are no victims; people's standing before God and their ultimate destiny — life or death — is in their own hands. Such is the gospel according to Moses, and such is the gospel according to Jesus, who invites us to "enter through the narrow gate. For wide is the gate and broad is the road that leads to destruction, and many enter through it" (Matt. 7:13). This is not only a warning against choosing the wrong path that leads to death and destruction, but also an invitation to choose the path of life. Thanks be to God!

Deuteronomy 31:1–30

🔥

Introduction to Deuteronomy 31–34

THE OPENING LINE OF chapter 31 signals a transition from hortatory proclamation in chapters 29–30 to narrative. This narrative carries through to the
end of the book, completing the story summarized proleptically in Genesis
15:13–21. While completing the metanarrative of the Pentateuch, these
chapters also connect with Deuteronomy 1–3, bringing to an end the personal story of Moses.[1] Like many narratives of significant persons in the
Old Testament, the biography of Moses ends with a death narrative.[2] The
account of Moses' demise is more complex than that of any other character
in the Old Testament, but it incorporates most of the elements found in the
ideal form of biblical death narratives.[3]

This death story itself divides into two parts. The first describes Moses'
actions to ensure Israel's future well-being (31:1–32:47). The second concerns the account of his death and burial (32:48–34:12). Lengthy poems
represent the center of gravity in both segments (32:1–43; 33:2–29).

Then Moses went out and spoke these words to all
Israel: [2]"I am now a hundred and twenty years old
and I am no longer able to lead you. The LORD has
said to me, 'You shall not cross the Jordan.' [3]The LORD your
God himself will cross over ahead of you. He will destroy
these nations before you, and you will take possession of
their land. Joshua also will cross over ahead of you, as the
LORD said. [4]And the LORD will do to them what he did to
Sihon and Og, the kings of the Amorites, whom he destroyed

---

1. Some interpret chapters 1–3 and 31–34 as the outer frames of the book (D. L. Christensen, "Form and Structure in Deuteronomy 1–11," in *Das Deuteronomium* (ed. N. Lohfink;
BETL 68; Leuven: Leuven Univ. Press, 1985), 138; Merrill, *Deuteronomy*, 396), while others
treat chap. 31 as a continuation of chap. 3 (J. D. Levenson, "Who Inserted the Book of the
Torah?" *HTR* 68 [1976]: 209). But these interpretations gloss over basic differences between
chaps. 1–3, which consist of continuous speech by Moses, and chap. 31, which is narrative
with embedded speeches.

2. The text is framed by Moses' announcement of his imminent death (31:2) and the
narrator's eulogy in 34:10–12.

3. For a study of this death narrative, see B. H. Cribb, *Speaking on the Brink of Sheol: Form and
Message of Old Testament Death Stories* (Gorgias Dissertations: Biblical Studies 43; Piscataway,
NJ: Gorgias, 2009), 180–220.

along with their land. ⁵The LORD will deliver them to you, and you must do to them all that I have commanded you. ⁶Be strong and courageous. Do not be afraid or terrified because of them, for the LORD your God goes with you; he will never leave you nor forsake you."

⁷Then Moses summoned Joshua and said to him in the presence of all Israel, "Be strong and courageous, for you must go with this people into the land that the LORD swore to their forefathers to give them, and you must divide it among them as their inheritance. ⁸The LORD himself goes before you and will be with you; he will never leave you nor forsake you. Do not be afraid; do not be discouraged."

⁹So Moses wrote down this law and gave it to the priests, the sons of Levi, who carried the ark of the covenant of the LORD, and to all the elders of Israel. ¹⁰Then Moses commanded them: "At the end of every seven years, in the year for canceling debts, during the Feast of Tabernacles, ¹¹when all Israel comes to appear before the LORD your God at the place he will choose, you shall read this law before them in their hearing. ¹²Assemble the people—men, women and children, and the aliens living in your towns—so they can listen and learn to fear the LORD your God and follow carefully all the words of this law. ¹³Their children, who do not know this law, must hear it and learn to fear the LORD your God as long as you live in the land you are crossing the Jordan to possess."

¹⁴The LORD said to Moses, "Now the day of your death is near. Call Joshua and present yourselves at the Tent of Meeting, where I will commission him." So Moses and Joshua came and presented themselves at the Tent of Meeting.

¹⁵Then the LORD appeared at the Tent in a pillar of cloud, and the cloud stood over the entrance to the Tent. ¹⁶And the LORD said to Moses: "You are going to rest with your fathers, and these people will soon prostitute themselves to the foreign gods of the land they are entering. They will forsake me and break the covenant I made with them. ¹⁷On that day I will become angry with them and forsake them; I will hide my face from them, and they will be destroyed. Many disasters and difficulties will come upon them, and on that day they will ask, 'Have not these disasters come upon us because our God is not with us?' ¹⁸And I will certainly hide my face on

that day because of all their wickedness in turning to other gods.

[19]"Now write down for yourselves this song and teach it to the Israelites and have them sing it, so that it may be a witness for me against them. [20]When I have brought them into the land flowing with milk and honey, the land I promised on oath to their forefathers, and when they eat their fill and thrive, they will turn to other gods and worship them, rejecting me and breaking my covenant. [21]And when many disasters and difficulties come upon them, this song will testify against them, because it will not be forgotten by their descendants. I know what they are disposed to do, even before I bring them into the land I promised them on oath." [22]So Moses wrote down this song that day and taught it to the Israelites.

[23]The LORD gave this command to Joshua son of Nun: "Be strong and courageous, for you will bring the Israelites into the land I promised them on oath, and I myself will be with you."

[24]After Moses finished writing in a book the words of this law from beginning to end, [25]he gave this command to the Levites who carried the ark of the covenant of the LORD: [26]"Take this Book of the Law and place it beside the ark of the covenant of the LORD your God. There it will remain as a witness against you. [27]For I know how rebellious and stiff-necked you are. If you have been rebellious against the LORD while I am still alive and with you, how much more will you rebel after I die! [28]Assemble before me all the elders of your tribes and all your officials, so that I can speak these words in their hearing and call heaven and earth to testify against them. [29]For I know that after my death you are sure to become utterly corrupt and to turn from the way I have commanded you. In days to come, disaster will fall upon you because you will do evil in the sight of the LORD and provoke him to anger by what your hands have made."

[30]And Moses recited the words of this song from beginning to end in the hearing of the whole assembly of Israel.

CHAPTER 31 CONSISTS PRIMARILY of alternating long and short speeches. The three short addresses involve the installation of Joshua, while the longer addresses concern the transcription of the Torah.[4] The pattern of topics is somewhat convoluted:

A. The Appointment of Joshua as Moses' Successor (31:1–8)
   B. The Torah (31:9–13)
A. The Appointment of Joshua as Moses' Successor (31:14–15)
      C. The National Anthem (31:16–22)
A. The Appointment of Joshua (31:23)
   B. The Torah (31:24–27)
      C. The National Anthem (31:28–32:44)
   B. The Torah (32:45–47)

This material may originally have consisted of three separate speeches. If so, by breaking them up and intertwining them, the editor suggests all three were integral to Moses' concern to ensure Israel's future fidelity and realization of Yahweh's promises. In essence, chapters 31–32 function as "a textual witness or memorial," a perpetual reminder of the covenant renewed on the Plains of Moab, of Yahweh's enduring commitment to them, and of the response required of them. Its memorial status is reinforced by the root ʿd ("witness"), which occurs repeatedly (31:2, 19, 21, 26, 27, 28; 32:46).[5] Remarkably, Moses has no interest in erecting memorials to himself; the only legacy that concerns him is a people who never forget Yahweh's covenant with Israel.

The Installation of Joshua as Moses' Successor: Part I (31:1–8)

THESE EIGHT VERSES CONSIST of two speeches united by subject and by genre. Both are classified as "encouragement speeches"—a designation suggested by the repeated charge (vv. 6, 7), and reinforced by negative imperatives (vv. 6, 8), as well as by reminders of Yahweh's covenant faithfulness. The

---

4. On the structure and composition of this chapter, see Tigay, *Deuteronomy*, 502–7; E. Talstra, "Deuteronomy 31: Confusion or Conclusion? The Story of Moses' Three-fold Succession," in *Deuteronomy and Deuteronomic Literature: Festschrift C. H. W. Brekelmans* (ed. by M. Vervenne and J. Lust; Leuven: Leuven Univ. Press, 1997), 87–110; A. Rofé, "The Composition of Deuteronomy 31 in the Light of a Conjecture about Inversion in the Order of Columns in the Biblical Text," *Shnaton* 3 (1979): 59–76.

5. Cf. B. Britt, *Rewriting Moses: The Narrative Eclipse of the Text* (JSOTSup 402; Gender, Culture Theory 14; London: T&T Clark 2004), 140. The noun ʿēd can apply either to persons (17:6–7; 19:15–16) or to concrete objects (Josh. 24:27–28; Isa. 30:8) as witnesses.

first speech (vv. 2 − 6), referring to Joshua in the third person, is addressed to the people. The second is addressed to Joshua (v. 7b).

Moses' challenge for the people (31:1 − 6). The narrative opens awkwardly, but verse 1 shifts attention from the nature of covenantal relationship to steps taken to "put the house in order."[6] Though some classify this as a "war oration,"[7] like the preceding addresses, this speech has a profoundly pastoral tone. It divides into three parts: (1) Moses' announcement of his impending demise (v. 2); (2) Moses' promise of Yahweh's continued presence (vv. 3 − 5); (3) Moses' appeal for courage and confidence (v. 6). The middle section is the center of gravity.

Whereas other death stories tend to begin with the narrator's announcement of the character's old age and impending death, here Moses announces his own demise (v. 2). But he does so indirectly, simply announcing his old age and his inability to "lead"[8] the people any longer. Moses' 120 years were perfectly proportioned: his early years in Egypt, forty years (Acts 7:23, 30); his years as sojourner in Midian, forty years (Ex. 7:7); as leader of Israel, forty years (Deut. 1:3). Moses' quotation of the words of Yahweh betray deep disappointment if not bitterness.[9] He gives neither the reason for this refusal nor the circumstances in which it had been declared.

After reminding the people of his imminent demise, Moses directs their attention to Yahweh's continued presence (vv. 3 − 5). His promise of future divine favor consists of seven clauses by which he makes three points. (1) The people will not embark on the campaign of conquest leaderless; they will be led by Yahweh and his designated agent (v. 3a, d). While the first statement recalls 9:3, its echo in verse 3d highlights Joshua's role as the representative of Yahweh (cf. Josh. 5:13 − 15). "As the LORD has said" at

---

6. The opening verb, "and he went," anticipates the series of movements by Moses in this chapter. While the NIV reflects the reading of the MT, because this construction, which involves the verb *hālak* ("to go"), followed by a verb of speech without further comment on where Moses might have gone, is unprecedented, many read, "When Moses finished speaking these words," with LXX and a Qumran fragment (1QDeut[b] [1Q5], in *DJD* 1 [1955], pl. X, fig. 13 and p. 59), and in conformity with the convention reflected in Gen. 17:22 and Deut. 32:45. Thus Mayes, *Deuteronomy*, 372 − 73; Tigay, *Deuteronomy*, 289, 400; Nelson, *Deuteronomy*, 353. However, the more difficult reading and less conventional MT is preferred over the LXX and the Qumran readings. So also F. Nwachukwu, "The Textual Differences between the MT and the LXX of Deuteronomy 31: A Response to Leo Laberge," in *Bundesdokument und Gesetz: Studien zum Deuterononmium* (ed. G. Braulik; HBS 4; Freiburg: Herder, 1995), 88 − 90.

7. Nelson, *Deuteronomy*, 358.

8. NIV's "to lead you" is a periphrastic rendering of the merismic phrase, "to go out and come in," which in Num. 27:17 refers expressly to the exercise of military leadership (cf. also Deut. 28:6).

9. Toward the people: 1:37 − 38; 4:21; toward Yahweh: 3:24 − 27.

the end of verse 3 alludes to 3:28, where Yahweh had said Joshua would go before the people and secure possession of the land.

(2) Yahweh will deal with the Canaanite nations himself. Moses promises that Yahweh will destroy them (v. 3b), and then he reminds Israel of recent victories over the Amorite kings as concrete illustrations of Yahweh's anticipated actions against the Canaanites (vv. 4−5a). He strengthens the promise by adding that Yahweh will indeed deliver them into the hands of the Israelites.

(3) Moses charges the Israelites to engage the enemy and claim the victory that Yahweh wins. Whereas in verse 3c he does so with one word, in verse 5 he commands the Israelites to deal with the Canaanites according to his earlier charges (cf. chaps. 7, 20).

Moses concludes this brief speech with an impassioned appeal to his people to take courage and put full confidence in Yahweh (v. 6). He expresses the former with two pairs of admonishments. The first pair is cast positively, "Be strong and courageous" (cf. vv. 7, 23),[10] and the second is cast negatively, "Do not be afraid or terrified" (cf. 20:3). The object of fear is identified vaguely as "them," that is, the nations referred to in verse 3. Moses then declares the grounds for courage: Yahweh is marching with them as the divine Warrior.

Echoing reassurances heard earlier in 20:1 and 4, he declares that Yahweh will not fail the Israelites or abandon them (cf. v. 8; 1 Chron. 28:20). The first expression involves the metaphor of slackening or relaxing (the hands) (cf. 4:31). The second ("forsake, abandon") occurs here for the first time with Yahweh as the subject.[11] Intimating that the Israelites had come to rely on Moses' personal presence for their security, this speech reminds them that their future success does not depend on human leaders but on God's presence, who will not relax as their divine patron or abandon them altogether.

Moses' challenge for Joshua (31:7−8). In verse 7a Moses' attention shifts from the people to Joshua (cf. vv. 14, 23).[12] Unlike Yahweh's speech to Joshua in verse 23 (cf. v. 14), here Moses has two audiences: Joshua and all Israel. Whereas Yahweh had spoken to Moses at Sinai in the hearing of the people that they "might believe in [Moses] forever" (Ex. 19:9, pers. trans.), now Moses publicly passes the mantle to his trusted lieutenant (cf. Num. 27:18−19), so they will see Joshua as the divinely chosen successor.

---

10. The pair of expressions occurs in the plural elsewhere in Josh. 10:25 and 2 Chron. 32:7, and in the singular in Josh. 1:6, 7, 9, 18; 1 Chron. 22:13; 28:20.

11. Cf. also v. 17. The Heb. verb ʿāzab ("abandon, forsake") is used of Israel abandoning Yahweh in v. 16 and 28:20 or his covenant in 29:25[24].

12. This short speech builds on comments made in the first address in 1:38; 3:21−22, 28. For the narrative account of the event, see Num. 27:15−23.

The hortatory framework, "Be strong and courageous" (v. 7, echoing v. 6), and "Do not be afraid; do not be discouraged" (v. 8), sets the tone of this speech. Between these appeals Moses describes Joshua's task and assures him of Yahweh's aid.[13] His summary commission focuses on two phases of the events that await him and the Israelites: Joshua will bring this people into the land Yahweh had sworn to give to the ancestors,[14] and Joshua will distribute among the Israelites the land Yahweh had reserved for them as their special grant.

Unless the hortatory verb "to be strong" implies a military context,[15] neither here nor in the earlier charges (1:38; 3:28) does Moses refer explicitly to Joshua's role as military leader. Verse 8 offers Joshua the grounds for courage: Yahweh goes before him and guarantees his presence. "He will never leave you nor forsake you" repeats verbatim the conclusion to Moses' speech for the people in verse 6.

The Deposition of the Torah (31:9–13)

THIS PARAGRAPH INTERRUPTS THE flow of thought, separating Moses' commissioning speech for Joshua from Yahweh's direct address to him (vv. 14–15, 23). The paragraph is carefully constructed, consisting of a narrative introduction (vv. 9–10a) and an address to the Levitical priests and all the elders of Israel (vv. 10b–13). While the editor's intent is evident in the verbal echoes of 10:1–9,[16] the focus of attention here is the Torah that Moses had been proclaiming since the beginning of the book (vv. 9, 11, 12).

The narrative preamble (v. 9) highlights three specific actions by Moses in relation to the Torah. (1) Moses wrote down this Torah. Although Deuteronomy presents Moses primarily as a self-conscious oral communicator of the Torah,[17] for the first time he appears as a scribe. The contents of this "written" document are specified as "all the words of this Torah that

---

13. For a form-critical study of narratives involving the commission of a person for an office or task, see D. J. McCarthy, "An Installation Genre?" *JBL* 90 (1971): 31–41.

14. The formula occurs elsewhere in 1:8; 6:18; 8:1; 9:5; 11:9, 21; 26:3; 28:11; 30:20.

15. This verb tends to be used in texts involving the installation of a military leader, but is often replaced by verbs like "to make, do" in contexts involving civil or religious duties. See McCarthy, "Installation Genre?" 34–35.

16. See C. T. Begg, "The Tables (Deut. X) and the Lawbook (Deut. 31)," *VT* 33 (1983): 97–98.

17. The expression "this Torah" (*hattôrâ hazzō[>]t*) occurs repeatedly elsewhere: 1:5 (written by the narrator's pen); 4:8; 17:18, 19; 27:3, 8, 26; 28:58, 61; 29:29[28]. (from the lips of Moses). For additional references to written documents, see 4:13; 5:22; 10:4; 17:18; 27:3, 8. On the possibility of a document referring to itself as a written document, see J. Chinitz, "The Word *Torah* in the Torah," *JBQ* 33 (2005): 243–45.

are written in this document" (cf. 28:58), "his commands and his statutes that are written in this document of the Torah" (30:10), "the curses [of the covenant] written in this document" (29:20, 21, 27[19, 20, 26]; all pers. trans.).[18]

(2) Moses hands the Torah to the Levitical priests and to all the elders of Israel. Whereas Yahweh had previously entrusted the Decalogue to Moses (5:22; 10:4), now Moses entrusts the written copy of his exposition of the covenant to community leaders for safekeeping. Moses' action strengthens the link between the Torah document he produced and the original covenant document produced by Yahweh,[19] and he seeks to ensure that no one will tamper with this sacred text (cf. 4:2; 12:32).

But the narrator also notes the involvement of all the elders of Israel. While priests represented Yahweh to the people and the people to Yahweh, these civil authorities represent the people in covenant relationship with each other. The involvement of priestly and civil authorities anticipates the bifurcation of roles after Moses' death.[20] Moses' handling of the Torah accords with the ancient Near Eastern practice of preparing written copies of covenants for use in ratification and renewal ceremonies.[21] But the precedent goes back to Sinai. Just as Yahweh had prepared written documents for the vassal after orally declaring the basic terms of the covenant, so Moses follows up his oral exposition of the covenant and the renewal ceremonies with a written copy of the agreement.

(3) Moses charges the Levitical priests and elders to read the Torah regularly before the people. This charge, which takes up the bulk of this paragraph, consists of three principal declarations: read this Torah (v. 11); assemble the people (v. 12); let their children hear and learn to fear Yahweh (v. 13). The links between this speech and Moses' account of what

---

18. The characterization of Moses as the author of "this Torah" contrasts with the Decalogue itself, whose author was Yahweh (10:4). See further, R. Venema, "YHWH or Moses? A Question of Authorship: Exodus 34:28–Deuteronomy 10:4; 31:9, 24," in *YHWH—Kyrios—Antitheism or the Power of the Word: Festschrift für Rochus Zuurmond anlässlich seiner Emeritierung am 26. Januar 1996* (ed. K. A. Deurloo and J. Diebner; DBAT Beiheft 14; Amsterdam/Heidelberg: DBAT, 1996), 69–76. NIV's rendering of *sēper* as "book" is misleading. Books as we know them (codices consisting of sheets that could be written on both sides and bound on one edge) were not used until shortly before Christ. Presumably Moses used a leather scroll of lambskin or parchment. Cf. M. Haran, "Scribal Workmanship in Biblical Times," *Tarbiz* 50 (1980–1981): 71–72; Alan R. Millard, "Writing," *DOTP*, 904–11.

19. See further discussion below on vv. 24–26.

20. This had also been anticipated in chapter 27:1–8. Together these leaders of the people will continue Moses' role. Similarly Sonnet, *Book within the Book,* 139–40, after Braulik, *Deuteronomium II,* 223; N. Lohfink, "Die ältesten Israels und der Bund zum Zusammenhang von Dtn 5,23; 26:17–19; 27,1, 9f und 31,9," *BN* 67 (1993): 26–42.

21. Cf. Weinfeld, *DDS,* 63–64. See comments on 10:1–9.

happened at Sinai in 4:10 are striking. Apparently future readings of the Torah will provide succeeding generations with regular opportunities for renewal and actualization of their covenant relationship with him.[22]

Verses 10b−11 set the context for the reading of the Torah by providing four vital details: (a) at the end of the seventh year,[23] (b) at the time appointed for cancelling debts and releasing indentured Israelite servants (cf. 15:1−18), (c) on the festival of Sukkoth,[24] (d) when all Israel is gathered at the central sanctuary to seek the face of Yahweh their God. Linking the reading with the canceling of debts will remind all Israelites of their common status as benefactors of Yahweh's gracious redemption.

The festival of Sukkoth commemorated the Israelites' dwelling in portable booths when they came out of Egypt (Lev. 23:43) and Yahweh's gracious provision in the desert.[25] The alternative name, Festival of Ingathering (Ex. 23:16; 34:22), highlights its location after the harvest had been processed and stored. The celebrative nature of this festival made it a most attractive event and ensured that the Torah would be read publicly at a time when the largest number of pilgrims were at the central sanctuary. The reference to gathering at the central sanctuary to see the face of God highlights the direct and personal nature of the encounter with him at the sanctuary.[26] Moses' command to read "this Torah" assumes that by hearing the text of the Torah, the people will have an encounter with Yahweh as direct as had the Israelites on Mount Horeb (4:10).

Echoing Yahweh's order at the original Horeb event (4:10), in verse 12 Moses charges the Levitical priests and elders to assemble the people that they might participate in this covenant renewal ritual. He highlights the comprehensiveness of the gathering by listing four specific classes of people: men, women, children, aliens.[27] While legal requirements obligated only males to appear before Yahweh at the three great festivals (16:16), the spirit of the law called for heads of households to bring with them their entire community to hear the Torah. Moses expresses the purpose of the

22. Cf. McConville, *Deuteronomy*, 439.

23. According to Lev. 23:34−44, Sukkoth was to be celebrated in the middle of the seventh month on Tishri 15−21. The association of the end of the seventh year with the festival of Sukkoth suggests Moses had in mind the informal agricultural calendar rather than the official liturgical calendar.

24. In Jewish tradition the eighth day of this festival ends with the celebration *Simḥat Torah*, "The Joy of Torah." This service focuses on the Torah as God's gracious gift to his people.

25. Tigay, *Deuteronomy*, 291.

26. Ex. 24:10 is even more direct when the narrator notes that the Israelites "saw the God of Israel" at Sinai.

27. This list is shorthand for the fuller listing in 16:14.

reading with a series of verbs (cf. 17:19–20): reading yields hearing, which yields learning, which yields fearing, which yields obedience, which yields life.

In verse 13 Moses expresses concern for future generations. Responding to human propensity to forget one's commitments (cf. 29:14–15), reading the Torah every seventh year ensures that no child will be left behind or reach adulthood without having heard the Torah at least twice.[28]

The Installation of Joshua as Moses' Successor: Part II (31:14–15, 23)

THE TEXT TAKES A surprising turn at verse 14, resuming the subject of Joshua's installation. But now we near the voice of Yahweh speaking directly to Moses, inviting him and Joshua for a private audience with him in the Tent of Meeting. The formality of the occasion is reflected in (1) the opening "See" (NIV "Now"); (2) Yahweh's charge to Moses to summon Joshua for an audience with him; (3) the use of the formal verb "to present oneself"; (4) Yahweh's announcement of the purpose of this audience: to commission him; (5) the location of the audience: in the Tent of Meeting.

In the Exodus and Sinai narratives the designation "Tent of Appointments" applies to two different portable structures:[29] the cultic tabernacle sanctuary located at the center of the Israelite camp, and the tent pitched outside the camp to which God came for special appointments (Ex. 33:7–11; Num. 12:4–5). The latter is involved here. When Moses and Joshua present themselves inside the Tent of Meeting, Yahweh appears in a pillar of cloud, which stands at the doorway of the Tent. Like the tabernacle housing the ark, the Tent of Meeting symbolized the desire of the holy and transcendent deity to dwell among and communicate with mortal human beings.

Verses 14–15 lead the reader to expect a speech from Yahweh for Moses and Joshua. While verses 16–21 deal with Moses' succession, remarkably

---

28. On the septennial ritual as an educational commemoration of the covenant made at Sinai and renewed on the Plains of Moab rather than as a repeated covenant renewal ceremony, see Craigie, *Deuteronomy*, 371; W. L. Holladay, "A Proposal for Reflections in the Book of Jeremiah of the Seven-Year Recitation of the Law in Deuteronomy (Deut. 31:10–13)," in *Das Deuteronomium* (ed. N. Lohfink; BETL 68; Louvain: Louvain Univ. Press, 1985), 326–28.

29. Cf. M. Haran, "The ʾōhel mōʿēd in Pentateuchal Sources," *JSS* 5 (1960): 50–65. For a critique of the view that the Tent of Meeting and the tabernacle represent different notions of divine presence, see I. Wilson, "Merely a Container? The Ark in Deuteronomy," in *Temple and Worship in Biblical Israel* (ed. J. Day; London: T&T Clark, 2007), 212–49. For discussion of the relationship between these two Tents of Meeting, see M. Haran, *Temples and Temple Service in Ancient Israel: An Inquiry into Biblical Cult Phenomena and the Historical Setting of the Priestly School* (Winona Lake, IN: Eisenbrauns, 1985), 264–69.

after his death he is to be replaced with a Song. Joshua is not a part of the picture until verse 23, which contains Yahweh's commissioning speech for him as Moses' successor. Verse 23 opens awkwardly in Hebrew without an explicitly subject: "And he charged," which NIV correctly fills in as "the LORD."[30] It seems this fragment was originally attached to verse 15 and was separated from its context by the insertion of Yahweh's speech to Moses in vv. 17–21. Except for the change from third person to first person, in verse 23 Yahweh summarizes Moses' installation speech in verses 7–8, exhorting Joshua to be strong and brave; declaring his role—he will lead the Israelites into the Promised Land; stating the significance of Joshua's action—this represents the fulfillment of Yahweh's promise; and promising Yahweh's presence. The narrator does not explain why he has included two installation addresses, though it seems that Yahweh's private commissioning may have been for Joshua's personal benefit, reassuring him that he is the divinely appointed successor to Moses.

The Preamble to Israel's National Anthem (31:16–22)

ON FIRST SIGHT VERSES 16–22 seem unrelated to the induction of Joshua. Here Yahweh introduces the Song (preserved in chap. 32) with a speech predicting Israel's future apostasy (vv. 16–18) and describing his answer to the crisis this will create (vv. 19–21).

The problem: Israel's apparently inevitable apostasy (vv. 16–18). Beginning abruptly by announcing Moses' imminent death, Yahweh describes the consequences of this event as a chain of actions and responses. He softens the directness of the opening announcement slightly by speaking euphemistically of Moses' demise as "lying with the ancestors."[31] Obviously Moses' death has great significance not only for himself, but especially for the people. Yahweh describes the Israelites' anticipated response to Moses' departure with four verbs: (1) They will "rise" (untrans. in NIV) in rebellion against Yahweh; (2) they will "prostitute themselves" to foreign gods of the land they are entering (cf. Ex. 34:15–16);[32] (3) they will "forsake" Yahweh (cf. 29:25[24]); and (4) they will "break the covenant."

It is fitting that Yahweh should speak of Israel's infidelity as "prostitution," since his relationship with Israel is portrayed in marital terms, and

---

30. While the nearest antecedent of the pronoun "he" is Moses in v. 22, it is clear from the first person verbs that Yahweh is the speaker.

31. NIV reads "rest with the fathers." The idiom derives from the common practice of burying the deceased in family tombs, but it also reflects a common Israelite view that in death people are gathered to Sheol, where they join their kin reclining on beds (cf. 32:50).

32. Cf. Judg 2:17; 8:27, 33; 1 Chron. 5:25; cf. also Lev. 17:7; 20:5; Ezek. 20:30.

his jealousy/passion is kindled whenever his people flirt with other gods.[33] Furthermore, the gods competing for the people's allegiance are lusty fertility gods, who will seduce the Israelites with promises of prosperity and security. The reference to the covenant the people will break (cf. v. 20) as "my covenant," and the comment "[that] I made [lit., 'cut'] with him," highlight the monergistic nature of the covenant. Yahweh chose the covenant partner; he set the terms and graciously revealed them to his people; he graciously announced the consequences of fidelity/infidelity.

The three expressions Yahweh uses to describe his response to Israel's apostasy reflect the intensity of his rage (v. 17a). While Moses had spoken earlier of Yahweh's anger and his abandonment of his people,[34] the idiom "to hide the face"[35] occurs here for the first time. The expression signifies the withdrawal of favor.[36] In ancient courtly contexts, for a king to turn his face from a subject signaled disaster,[37] though the idiom was often applied to gods as well.[38]

As in extrabiblical texts, when a deity hid his face the effects were devastating (v. 17b). Yahweh speaks of the resultant "disasters" and "difficulties" as carnivorous beasts that seek and devour prey. To the disasters the people will respond with a curious rhetorical question: "Have not these disasters come upon us because our God is not with us?" The question itself represents the answer to a prior query. Remarkably, in 29:24−25[23−24] the heathen nations' answer to a related question was more accurate than the Israelites' own explanation: The people's demise is indeed the result of divine wrath, but the ultimate cause is their abandoning of the covenant that Yahweh made with them. The Israelites' explanation here may be theologically correct, but the tone is wrong. They accuse Yahweh of failure to keep his covenant promises, when ultimate responsibility lies in their own

---

33. See esp. Hos. 4:12−14. For a study of the metaphor see P. Bird, "'To Play the Harlot': An Inquiry into an Old Testament Metaphor," *Gender and Difference in Ancient Israel* (ed. P. L. Day; Minneapolis: Fortress, 1989), 75−94.

34. This threat reverses the promise of 31:6, 8; cf. also 29:27[26].

35. For a summary of the dimensions of the hidden face of God and references, see *HALOT*, 771−72.

36. See the positive counterpart to the expression in the Aaronic blessing (Num. 6:25−26). For related Akkadian idioms, see A. L. Oppenheim, "Idiomatic Akkadian," *JAOS* 61 (1941): 256−57; S. E. Balentine, *The Hiding of the Face of God in the Old Testament* (New York: Oxford, 1983), 22−28.

37. Cf. "I shall turn (and) die if the crown prince my lord turns away his face from me," in L. Waterman, *Royal Correspondence of the Assyrian Empire*, Part II: *Translation and Transliteration* (Ann Arbor: Univ. of Michigan Press, 1930−36), 114−15.

38. See "A Prayer of Lamentation to Ishtar," in *ANET*, 385, and the complaint of the afflicted in *Ludlul bēl nēmeqi* ("The Babylonian Job"), in Lambert, *Babylonian Wisdom Literature*, 38, line 4. Except for Job 13:14; 34:29, the idiom describes Yahweh's reaction to covenant betrayal.

perfidy (v. 18; cf. Ezek. 8:12; 9:9). This final statement involves an effective wordplay on the root *pnh* ("to face"). When Yahweh hides his "face," he refuses his attention; when the Israelites "face" other gods (cf. v. 20), they look to them for their security.[39]

The Solution: A Song (31:19–21)

AS IN 4:1 AND 10:12, *we*ʿ*attâ* (NIV "Now") in verse 19 signals a transition from the first to the second half of Yahweh's speech, introducing the logical sequel to the preceding. In light of the previous speech, we might have expected Yahweh formally to pass Moses' mantle to Joshua. Remarkably, instead of appointing a pastoral successor to hold the nation together spiritually and to keep it on its covenantal course, he commissions a song. Indeed verses 19–21 suggest that Yahweh's primary reason for calling Moses and Joshua to the Tent of Meeting was to communicate to them this Song, which would serve as a sort of national anthem for the people.

The Hebrew word *šîr* may refer to a song to be sung or a poem to be recited,[40] and it defines the genre of the composition. Delivering this Song involves two actions: transcribing it as written text and presenting it orally to the people (v. 19). By charging Moses to teach it to the Israelites, Yahweh requires him to do with the Song what he had done with the Torah in his preceding addresses (4:14; 5:31; 6:1). This suggests that teaching involves not only recitation, but also interpretation and hortatory appeals.[41]

Verse 19b suggests the Song was to serve a legal function. Indeed the scene envisioned fits the genre of a *rîb* ("legal dispute"). Whereas earlier legal contexts had witnesses to a crime testifying, Yahweh intends for this Song itself to function as the witness. It will testify for Yahweh by declaring his fidelity in the face of the people's apparently inevitable infidelity (cf. v. 21); it will remind Israel that when they experience the covenant curses, this will be Yahweh's just and predicted response for having trampled underfoot his grace. This knowledge will be important in the future, especially when outsiders deduce from Israel's disasters that their divine patron has either been unable or unwilling to defend his people against foreign powers and their gods.[42] As we will see, the Song combats such erroneous responses.

---

39. Cf. also Job 36:21; Hos. 3:1; also Ps. 40:4[5].

40. On the difference between "poem" and "song," see D. Lipton, *Longing for Egypt and Other Unexpected Biblical Tales* [Hebrew Bible Monographs 15; Sheffield: Phoenix, 2008), 189–90. On the singing or oral recitation of written poetry in Mesopotamia, see J. Tigay, *The Evolution of the Gilgamesh Epic* (Philadelphia: Univ. of Pennsylvania Press, 1982), 107, n. 2.

41. The idiom used here, "to put it on their lips," means teaching it thoroughly so the people have memorized it and can recite.

42. Cf. Jer. 30:17; 33:24; Ezek. 36:20–21;

Contra the NIV, rather than describing the temporal context in which the Song will fulfill its function, verse 20 establishes the grounds for its testimonial role.[43] Apparently assuming that Israel's apostasy and judgment are inevitable, in the face of these events the Song will remind them of the divine favor they have spurned and will declare that for their deeds they have experienced the calamities precisely as predicted. In the end Yahweh will be vindicated and Israel's rebellion against their beneficent Suzerain will be exposed.

Verse 20 summarizes *vaticinium ante eventum* (prediction before the event), future historical developments that necessitate the Song. Just as Israel's past began and ended with Yahweh's gracious actions,[44] so their future depends on Yahweh's gracious acts. Fulfilling his sworn promise to the ancestors,[45] Yahweh will deliver into their hands the land, which will yield its produce and enable them to eat, be satisfied, and grow fat. Although we have heard of the danger this would pose before (6:11; 8:10, 12; 11:15), for the first time we read of them being fat (NIV "thrive"). The expression speaks of a satiety that causes the beneficiaries of Yahweh's largesse to forget the source of their abundance and to attribute their well-being to the fertility gods of Canaan (cf. 6:10 – 15; 8:11 – 14; 11:8 – 17; 32:13 – 14).

The remainder of verse 20 describes Israel's response to Yahweh's lavish generosity: They will turn to other gods, serve them as vassals, spurn Yahweh, and break his covenant. Juxtaposed with verse 16, to "turn to other gods" and to "serve them" (NIV "worship") in verse 18 substitute for to "rise" and to "prostitute themselves to the foreign gods." Correspondingly, to "spurn me" (NIV "reject") and "break my covenant" substitute for to "forsake me" and to "break the covenant I made with them" in verse 16. The reference to spurning Yahweh is new in the book and prepares the reader for Yahweh's reciprocal response in 32:19.

The opening expression in verse 21 signals a new movement in this litany of Israelite apostasy. "Many disasters and difficulties" represent new participants in Israel's future and serve as a shorthand expression for all the covenant curses outlined in 28:15 – 68. However, as subjects of the verb, these otherwise inanimate entities appear as active agents that attack

---

43. If *kî* introduces a temporal clause ("when"), then the protasis should extend through v. 21 (thus NJPS). The sequence of verbs in v. 20 opens with an imperfect, followed by seven *waw* consecutive perfects, which regularly expresses a series of real events rather than hypothetical future events construed as past events. The decision to end the protasis at "when they eat their fill and thrive" and to begin the apodosis with "they will turn" is arbitrary.

44. Deut. 4:32 – 40; 6:20 – 25; etc.

45. Deut. 1:8, 35; 6:10, 18, 23; 7:13; 8:1; 9:5; 10:11; 11:9, 21; 19:8; 26:3, 15; 28:11; 30:20; 31:7, 20.

("come upon") Israel like a wild animal attacks its prey.[46] In this desperate context the words of the Song will testify to the fidelity and grace of Yahweh and the ingratitude and rebellion of his people. The inserted clause, "because it will not be forgotten from the mouth of his seed" (pers. trans.), reinforces the anthemic nature of the Song that follows; it is intended to be sung in perpetuity. As Israel's national anthem,[47] it will remind the people of their origins in the gracious acts of Yahweh and warn them against trampling underfoot his generosity. But it also offers hope. Like the ending to Moses' third address, it declares that after judgment, Yahweh will vindicate his reputation and his people.

The concluding clauses of verse 21 reiterate the need for the Song. Yahweh's pessimism concerning Israel's spiritual condition has surfaced elsewhere in Deuteronomy (5:28—29; 9:24; 12:8; 31:27), but this is the most explicit declaration of the apparent inevitability of Israel's failure to keep the covenant. Of course, the problem is not with the covenant; the faults lie entirely with the people. Yahweh's awareness of the people's intent to rebel "today," even before he has given them the land he swore to give them, confirms that the apostasy described in verse 20 involves a certain future reality.

After recounting Yahweh's speech, the narrator reports that Moses did as Yahweh had instructed him (v. 22). He wrote down the words of the Song "that day" and taught these words to the descendants of Israel. By repeating the verbs "to write" and "to teach" (cf. v. 19), the narrator highlights Moses' scrupulosity in carrying out the divine orders.

Moses' Concluding Speech (31:24—29)

BASED ON THE SUBJECT matter, this short paragraph divides into three parts: (1) a preamble to Moses' speech (vv. 24—25); (2) final instructions regarding the Torah (vv. 26—27); (3) instructions regarding Israel's national anthem (vv. 28—30). Although the latter two may represent separate utterances associated with earlier elements of this chapter, by combining them the narrator suggests the depositions of the Torah and the Song reflect a common concern.

(1) By noting that Moses' charge to the Levites is issued after he has finished writing the words of the Torah, the narrator links what follows to verses 9—13. Assuming that this statement refers to Moses' transcription of his addresses, the written Torah represents a remarkable literary

---

46. The verb echoes 4:30.

47. On which see Daniel I. Block, "The Power of Song: Reflection on Ancient Israel's National Anthem (Deuteronomy 32)," in *How I Love Your Torah, O LORD!* 162—88.

achievement, though not unprecedented in terms of length.[48] While verse 25 reiterates what we have known from verses 9 – 10, it is more focused on identifying the addressees — the Levites, particularly those charged with carrying the ark of the covenant of Yahweh — though verse 27 suggests Moses will also address the people in general.

(2) Moses' instructions for the Levites divides into three parts: (a) commands on what to do with the Torah (v. 26a, 26b); (b) a statement of the Torah's function (v. 26c); (c) a declaration of his awareness of Israel's propensity to rebel (v. 27). By handing the written copy of the Torah to the Levites, Moses designates them as custodians of the document, and by having them place it beside the ark, he acknowledges Yahweh as its source and divine Guarantor (cf. 10:1 – 2).

Once produced, the Torah scroll was probably put in a clay jar or wooden box for safekeeping.[49] Ancient practices illumine the command to place the written copy of the Torah document beside the ark. When two people or groups made a treaty, each party took a written copy home and deposited it in the sanctuary, in recognition of the deity's role as guarantor of the covenant and for periodic retrieval to use in covenant renewal rituals. The present act means Moses' pastoral instructions are as binding as the Decalogue itself, though by placing the Torah scroll beside rather than inside the ark Moses ensures its accessibility. While verses 9 – 13 require the Levites to read the Torah every seven years at the Festival of Sukkoth, it was probably also used in other worship events, not to mention the requirement of kings to copy it for themselves (17:18 – 20).

Like the Song mentioned in verses 19 – 21, the written copy of the Torah will serve as a witness against the Israelites. Although he is addressing the Levites primarily, the expression "against you" (v. 26) suggests they functioned as representatives of Israel. Like the Song, the Torah recounts the remarkable grace of Yahweh in establishing Israel as his covenant partner, warns the Israelites of the consequences of rebellion, and holds out for the nation a positive future beyond the judgment (4:19 – 31; 30:1 – 20).[50]

48. Considered together, the speeches of Moses compare in length with the Mesopotamian Gilgamesh epic. For discussion of this issue, see A. R. Millard, "Books in the Late Bronze Age in the Levant," in *Past Links: Studies in the Languages and Cultures of the Ancient Near East* (ed. S. Izre'el et al.; Israel Oriental Studies 18; Winona Lake, In: Eisenbrauns, 1998), 171 – 81.

49. Cf. Jer. 32:14. On the storage of treasured documents in boxes in Egypt, see *ANET*, 495a; M. Lichtheim, *Ancient Egyptian Literature*, vol. 3, *The Late Period* (Berkeley: Univ. of California Press, 1980), 129 – 31; for a reference to tablet containers in ancient Mesopotamia, see the Gilgamesh Epic, tablet 1, 22 – 25. Cf. Tigay, *Gilgamesh Epic*, 263, note on 1:22.

50. On the Song as an expression of the heart of Deuteronomy, see A. Lee, "The Narrative Function of the Song of Moses in the Contents of Deuteronomy and Genesis-Kings" (Ph.D diss., University of Gloucestershire, 2010).

Furthermore, similar to the Decalogue (Ex. 24), the written copy of the Torah beside the ark testifies to the covenant renewal proceedings by which the present generation had bound themselves to Yahweh.

As Yahweh had done in relationship to the Song (v. 21), in verse 27 Moses grounds the actions regarding the Torah in his awareness of the people's spiritual condition. However, whereas Yahweh described the shallowness of Israel's devotion in the vaguest of terms, here Moses is more specific: The people are "rebellious" and "stiff-necked."[51] Indeed, Moses accuses the people of persistent rebellion against Yahweh and expresses the knowledge that once he is gone, they will show their true colors. Moses' reference to his death clarifies his statement in verse 2 and Yahweh's euphemistic announcement in verse 16.

(3) Moses' instructions concerning the Song in verses 28–29 consist of a command to the Levites to act (v. 28a), the purpose of that action (v. 28b–c), and a rationale for it (v. 29). Moses begins by commanding the Levites to assemble the "elders" and "officials" of Israel for an audience with him (cf. vv. 12, 30).[52] Whereas in verse 12 we learned of the purpose of the assembly from the perspective of the audience, here Moses declares the purpose from his perspective—that he may speak in their hearing and summon the heavens and the earth to testify against the people. In accord with common legal proceedings, this brings the number of witnesses to three: the heavens and the earth (v. 28), the Song (v. 19), and the Torah (v. 26).[53]

Verse 29 reinforces verse 27, showing that Moses shares Yahweh's pessimistic view of the spiritual state of the people (cf. v. 21). Like Yahweh (v. 16), he knows that as soon as he is gone, the people will become "utterly corrupt" and "turn from the way" they were taught. Moses describes the effects of their apparently inevitable rebellion with one simple statement: "Disaster"[54] will strike them in the end.[55] Although some interpret the phrase "in days to come" eschatologically,[56] as in 4:30 it means no more

---

51. On the meaning of these expressions, see comments on 9:6–7.

52. On šōṭᵉrîm, see comments on 1:15.

53. On the nature and purpose of appealing to heaven and earth as witnesses see comments on 4:26 and 30:19.

54. The article on "disaster" suggests a specific outcome, doubtless as the application of the curses of chapter 28.

55. Cf. the fuller statements in chapter 28 and 29:20–28[19–27].

56. For an eschatological interpretation of the phrase, see especially J. H. Sailhamer, *The Pentateuch as Narrative: A Biblical–Theological Commentary* (Grand Rapids: Zondervan, 1992), 36–37, 475; idem, *The Meaning of the Pentateuch: Revelation, Composition and Interpretation* (Downers Grove, IL: InterVarsity Press, 2009), 36, 332–33, 343.

than "in the distant future."[57] Moses ends on an extremely pessimistic note: The Israelites will do evil in the eyes of Yahweh, provoking his fury. As elsewhere (4:25; 9:18; 17:2), "the evil" points primarily to the violation of the Supreme Command, that is, the first principle of covenant relationship. "To provoke him" reduces to a single word the divine passion described earlier in verses 17−18 and in 29:23−28[22−27].

The narrator has the last word in this chapter, reporting that Moses recited all the words of this song in the hearing of the whole assembly. As in verse 24, the addition of "from beginning to end" highlights his scrupulosity in fulfilling his charge as pastor to the people.

THE WRITINGS OF MOSES. Although chapter 31 is a complex literary piece, it offers remarkable insight into ancient Israel's view of the nature and importance of their written Scriptures, particularly the Torah.[58] (1) The Deuteronomic Torah in its entirety was divinely inspired, authoritative, canonical, and sacred. Announced by the narrator in the introduction (1:3) and reiterated throughout, Moses has been instructing the people just as Yahweh had commanded him. Having presented his profoundly theological interpretation of Yahweh's revelation in the great events of the exodus from Egypt, covenant-making at Sinai, provision and guidance in the desert, victory over the Amorite kings, and the imminent conquest of the Promised Land, on the one hand, and the specific revelation associated with the covenant at Sinai, on the other hand, Moses has transcribed his speeches, handed them to the priests for safekeeping next to the ark of the covenant, and then charged them to read them to all the people regularly when they gather for worship.

More than any other text in the Old Testament, chapter 31 binds Moses to a written document more tightly than any of the prophets who follow in his train. Critical scholars generally dismiss this chapter as fictional and view Deuteronomy as a pseudepigraph created centuries later to lend authority to Josiah's reforms,[59] but herein we find the roots of the Jewish and Christian tradition that Moses wrote the Pentateuch. This chapter provides the basis for a variety of expressions found in Old Testament:

---

57. The same applies to Gen. 49:1, where the expression is not a *terminus technicus* for the eschaton, but a reference to a distant future event. Cf. V. P. Hamilton, *The Book of Genesis Chapters 18−50* (NICOT; Grand Rapids: Eerdmans, 1995), 646.

58. Cf. the discussion in Tigay, *Deuteronomy*, 498.

59. See Fishbane, *Biblical Interpretation in Ancient Israel*, 436; Sonnet, *The Book within the Book*, 259−67.

"the book of the Law of Moses,"[60] "the book of Moses" (2 Chron. 25:4; 35:12; Neh. 13:1), "the Law of Moses,"[61] "the book of the Law of the LORD that had been given through Moses" (2 Chron. 34:14), and "the words of Yahweh by the hand of Moses" (2 Chron. 35:6, pers. trans.). This tradition carries over into the New Testament in references to "the Law of Moses,"[62] "the book of Moses" (Mark 12:26), "Moses" as a substitute for "the Law,"[63] "what [Moses] wrote" (John 5:47), vague references to laws that Moses commanded,[64] "the customs Moses handed down to us" (Acts 6:14), statements like "Moses wrote" (Luke 20:28; cf. Deut. 25:5), and "Moses says" (Rom. 10:19). In the Gospels Jesus himself frequently refers to Moses as a recognized authority in Jewish tradition and as an authority behind his own teachings.

While it is probably an exaggeration to insist that Moses' own hand put together the entire Pentateuch as we have it, or even the book of Deuteronomy, the speeches in this book represent the Torah of Moses par excellence. Although readers of the Old Testament often assume that expressions translated as "the law of the LORD" refer to the Pentateuch as a whole, the default view should rather be that "the Torah of Yahweh" and "the Torah of Moses" refer particularly to the book of Deuteronomy. This book is the heart of the Torah that the priests were to teach and model,[65] in which psalmists delighted,[66] to which the prophets appealed,[67] by which faithful kings ruled,[68] and by which righteous citizens lived (Ps. 1).

This was the book—long neglected—that Josiah's officials found in the temple and which provided the theological impetus for his wide-ranging reforms (2 Kings 22–23); this was the book that Ezra read to the community of returned exiles on the occasion of the Festival of Booths (Neh. 8). And as the light of Old Testament prophecy was going out, this was the book to which Malachi called his people to return (Mal. 4:4). The book of Deuteronomy provides the theological base for virtually the entire Old

---

60. Josh. 8:31, 32; 23:6; 2 Kings 14:6; Neh. 8:1.

61. 1 Kings 2:3; 2 Kings 23:25; 2 Chron. 23:18; 30:16; Ezra 3:2; 7:6; Dan. 9:11, 13; Mal. 4:4[3:22].

62. Luke 2:22; 24:44; John 7:23; Acts 13:39; 15:5 (cf. "the manner of Moses" in v. 1); 28:23; 1 Cor. 9:9; Heb. 10:28.

63. Luke 16:29, 31; 24:27; John 5:45, 46; Acts 6:11; 21:21; 26:22; 2 Cor. 3:15.

64. Matt 8:4; 19:7, 8; 22:24; Mark 1:44; 7:10; 10:3, 4; Luke 5:14; John 8:5; Acts 6:14.

65. Deut. 33:10; 2 Chron. 15:3; 19:8; Mal. 2:6, 9; cf. Jer. 18:18; Ezek. 7:26; Ezra 7:10.

66. Pss. 1:2; 19:7–14[8–15]; 119; etc. On the Torah in Deuteronomy as the primary referent behind psalmists' references to the Torah, see P. Miller, "Deuteronomy and the Psalms: Evoking a Biblical Conversation," *JBL* 118 (1999): 3–18.

67. Isa. 1:10; 5:24; 8:20; 30:9; 51:7.

68. 1 Kings 2:2–4; 2 Kings 14:6; 22:11; 23:25.

(and New) Testament and is the paradigm for much of its literary style. Luke 16:19−31 and John 5:19−47 illustrate the enormous stature of Moses in the tradition of Judaism at the turn of the ages. In the Torah the Jews heard Moses' prophetic voice, and in the Torah they read what he wrote.

Even though Deuteronomy 31 underlies the tradition of Moses as the man behind the Torah, the picture it paints of him is remarkably modest, standing in sharpest contrast to ancient rulers associated with law. In the law code of Hammurabi, the eighteenth-century BC Babylonian king claims to have been chosen by the gods "to make justice prevail in the land, to abolish the wicked and the evil, to prevent the strong from oppressing the weak,"[69] and commissioned by Marduk "to provide just ways for the people of the land (in order to attain) appropriate behavior."[70] Even so, his egotistical self-portrait in the prologue is the opposite of the Mosaic portrait painted here and in the rest of the book. Characterized by the narrator elsewhere as the humblest man on earth (Num. 12:3), Moses erected no monuments in his own honor, and he never referred to the Torah as "my Torah," or "the Torah of Moses." It is simply "this document of the Torah," whose authority rests entirely on Yahweh who charged him to speak these words.

Inclusive. Deuteronomy 31 also emphasizes that the covenant principles spelled out in the Torah apply to all. In the picture of worship painted by 31:9−13 we recognize a remarkably democratic and egalitarian tone. The image of women and aliens at worship here and throughout the Old Testament presents a sharp contrast to the misogynistic attitudes that developed in the intertestamental period. Like 12:12, this text invites entire households—parents, sons and daughters, male and female servants, resident Levites—to appear before Yahweh to hear the Torah. Unlike the temple that Herod built to appease the Jews, which had separate courts for the women and for Gentiles,[71] none of the Old Testament designs of structures for worship (tabernacle, Davidic temple, Ezekiel's temple) excluded women or even segregated them from men. And nowhere in the Old Testament do we hear misogynistic venom like that spewed by Ben Sirach,[72] or recited in prayer every day by many orthodox Jews around the world:

---

69. LH i.1−6, as translated by Roth, *COS*, 2:131, p. 336.

70. LH v.14−25, ibid, p. 337.

71. For discussion and diagrams of Herod's temple, see L. Ritmeyer, *The Quest: Revealing the Temple Mount in Jerusalem* (Jerusalem: Carta, 2006), 348−55; also *EncJud* (2nd ed., 2007), 19:612.

72. See Sir 25:13−26:12. For a brief discussion of this issue in Ben Sirach, see J. J. Collins, "Marriage, Divorce, and Family in Second Temple Judaism," in *Families in Ancient Israel* (ed. L. G. Perdue et al.; Louisville: Westminster John Knox, 997), 143−45; for fuller treatment see W. C. Trenchard, *Ben Sira's View of Women: A Literary Analysis* (BJS 38; Chico, CA: Scholars, 1982).

Blessed are You Hashem, our God, King of the world, for not
making me a Gentile,
Blessed are You Hashem, our God, King of the world, for not
making me a woman.
Blessed are You Hashem, our God, King of the world, for not
making me a boor.[73]

The privilege of covenant relationship is open to all who identify with
Yahweh by faith; all may delight in the knowledge that they are Yahweh's
children, his special treasure, his sanctified people. While the Torah provides concrete testimony to Israel's privileged standing before Yahweh, it
also holds the entire community accountable to its demands. To be sure,
Deuteronomy 17:14—20 singles out the king as under its authority, but
by reading the Torah every seven years before all the people, the Levites
were to call every member to *ṣedeq ṣedeq* ("righteousness, only righteousness,"
16:20)—that is, devotion to Yahweh demonstrated in the pursuit of his
glory and the well-being of one's neighbor.

The reading of the Torah. The lack of Old Testament evidence for carrying out the instructions given here has led some to interpret chapter 31 as "a
purely utopian provision."[74] However, analogous testimonial function of prior
texts has been identified in ancient Hittite treaty documents.[75] In the face
of an outbreak of plagues, the fourteenth-century Hittite king Mursilis was
directed by an oracle to two tablets on which were recorded the oaths that
the Hittites had made to the gods. From these tablets Mursilis learned that the
plagues had been caused by the Hittites' violation of these oaths, which led
him to plead for mercy from the gods.[76] Josiah reacted similarly when, in the
course of refurbishing the temple, his workers discovered the Torah document
there (2 Kings 22—23). He accepted its testimonial function and earnestly
sought for divine grace, for which the narrator characterized him as one who
sought Yahweh with all his heart/mind, his being, and his resources.[77] But
the narrator made no attempt to link the reading of the Torah with Sukkoth.

---

73. *Tosefta Berakhot* 6:16. For discussion of its origin and meaning, see J. Tabory, "The
Benedictions of Self-Identity and the Changing Status of Women and of Orthodoxy," in
Kenishta: Studies of the Synagogue World (ed. J. Tabory; Bar-Ilan: Bar-Ilan Univ. Press, 2001),
107–38.

74. Nelson, *Deuteronomy*, 359, though some have argued that during the late monarchy
the Torah was actually recited every seven years. See Holladay, "A Proposal for Reflections
in the Book of Jeremiah," 326–28.

75. See Tigay, *Deuteronomy*, 297.

76. See "Mursili's 'Second' Plague Prayer to the Storm-God of Hatti (CTH 378.II)," in
I. Singer, *Hittite Prayers* (SBLWAW 11; Atlanta: Society of Biblical Literature, 2002), 57–61;
cf. *ANET*, 394–96.

77. The Hebrew expression represents a verbatim quotation of Deut. 6:5.

The issues are different, however, in Nehemiah 8, which reports Ezra's reading the Torah to the returnees from exile. The narrator emphasizes that this gathering involved all the people — men, women, children — and explicitly associates it with Sukkoth (vv. 14 – 18).[78] While it is unclear whether the reading occurred as a part of the festival or the reading of the Torah precipitated the observance, the link is explicitly recognized. Whereas the Old Testament never prescribes the reading of the Decalogue, the Book of the Covenant, or the Instructions on Holiness in cultic observances, from the beginning Moses envisioned the written Torah would play a significant role in Israel's worship.

In Joshua 1 we hear the clearest echoes of this chapter, which is not surprising, since the events described there appear to have happened within weeks, if not days of the speeches delivered here. This chapter is remarkable for its picking up on both the charges to Joshua (Josh. 1:6 – 7, 9; cf. Deut. 31:7 – 8, 23) and the importance of the written Torah (Josh. 1:7 – 8; cf. Deut. 31:9 – 13, 26 – 27). Admittedly the latter involved only Joshua rather than the assembly of all the people, as if the new leader assumes the role of a king (cf. Deut. 17:14 – 20). Yahweh's appeal for fidelity to the Torah as the prerequisite to success in the military campaigns that lay ahead perceived Joshua as the embodiment of the nation.

The great commission given by Jesus to his apostles in Matthew 28:18 – 20 provides a striking New Testament equivalent to this chapter:

> All authority in heaven and on earth has been given to me. Therefore go and make disciples of all nations, baptizing them in the name of the Father and of the Son and of the Holy Spirit, and teaching them to obey everything I have commanded you. And surely I am with you always, to the very end of the age.

We hear echoes of Deuteronomy 31 in the reference to "heaven and earth," the appeal to teach God's people everything Jesus has commanded them, and the promise of his presence.

---

78. Although the date of the event is not recorded, the assembly of the postexilic community under the leadership of Ezra for the express purpose of reading the Torah bears the marks of an effort to fulfill Moses' present charge. This understanding is reinforced by the people cutting palm branches and living in booths for seven days. Some argue that this occasion actually coincided with the year and dates of release. See J. Blenkinsopp, *Ezra – Nehemiah: A Commentary* (OTL; Philadelphia: Westminster, 1988), 293; F. C. Fensham, *The Books of Ezra and Nehemiah* (NICOT; Grand Rapids: Eerdmans, 1982), 221.

FORMULA FOR SUCCESS. THE significance of this chapter for the contemporary church is profound. The formula for success in the kingdom of God remains the same. As was the case with the divine and Mosaic commissioning of Joshua, on the one hand, and the great commissioning of the apostles by Jesus, on the other, Yahweh always provides the leadership needed to fulfill his calling. While every generation of leaders must hand the baton to successors, thankfully, neither new leaders nor the people in their charge are left to their own resources. The keys to the fulfillment of God's mission remain acceptance of the commission received from him and trust in his promised presence.

Times of transition represent tests of faith: Will we and our leaders put our confidence in God, or will we turn to false gods, on the one hand, or to despair, on the other? The history of Israel demonstrates that despite every privilege and every needed provision, those who claim to be God's people have the propensity to be distracted by other objects of devotion, to falter in their faith, and to lose sight of their mission as the agents of divine blessing. But the Israelites did not have a monopoly on infidelity. The course of church history is littered with leaders and entire groups of people abandoning the Lord, paying no heed to his will as revealed in the Torah and the rest of the Scriptures, and succumbing to the gods of this world. These remain ever-present dangers.

Reading and hearing God's Word. This passage highlights the importance of reading and hearing the Word of God in worship. If the call to formal communal worship is fundamentally an invitation to appear before the divine King for an audience with him (cf. 31:11), surely what he has to say to his people is more important than what they have to say to him. The psalmist wrote, "Today if you hear his voice, do not harden your hearts as they did at Meribah, as you did that day at Massah" (Ps. 95:7—8). Since in hearing the Scriptures read we are hearing the voice of God, evangelicals in particular must rediscover that through reading the written Word of God, worshipers hear the voice of God.

Despite what creedal statements testify, the relative absence of the Scriptures is one of the marks of contemporary evangelical worship. At best the Scriptures are read piecemeal and impatiently that we might get on with the sermon—as if the preacher stands in the place of Moses and his interpretation is as authoritative as the very words that proceed from the mouth of God. At worst, we do not open the Scriptures at all. In our drive to be contemporary and relevant, sometimes advertently and often inadvertently we dismiss the reading of the Scriptures as a fossil whose vitality and usefulness has died long ago. In the process we displace the life-giving and life-declaring voice of God with the foolish and seductive babbling of mortals, and the possibility of true worship is foreclosed. With Moses, Malachi 4:4[3:22] assumes that when people hear the Word of God, they will learn to fear God. And when they fear God, they will commit themselves to unconditional and total obedience to his will. The mark of a true encounter with God and true worship is the transformed life.

The hardness of the human heart. This chapter testifies to the hardness of the human heart. Despite the freshness of the memory of Yahweh's redeeming acts, the covenant renewal ceremony on the Plains of Moab, and Yahweh's imminent deliverance of the land into the people's hands, both Yahweh and Moses recognize the inevitable — the people will abandon him and the covenant in favor of the lusty gods of the land. In advance he provides the people with two witnesses to his own faithfulness to his promises — the Torah and the Song. When the people have apostasized and have experience the threatened disasters written in the Torah, the written copies of the Torah and the Song of Yahweh (chap. 32) will declare his fidelity and their own infidelity. A fuller treatment of the implications of the role of this song awaits an examination of the Song itself, but this chapter testifies to the power of a song. Modern readers may be amazed that when the restraining influence of Moses is removed, God replaces him, not with a second Moses figure, but with a song. People are what they sing.

Deuteronomy 32:1–47

🔥

¹Listen, O heavens, and I will speak;
    hear, O earth, the words of my mouth.
²Let my teaching fall like rain
    and my words descend like dew,
like showers on new grass,
    like abundant rain on tender plants.

3I will proclaim the name of the Lord.
    Oh, praise the greatness of our God!
⁴He is the Rock, his works are perfect,
    and all his ways are just.
A faithful God who does no wrong,
    upright and just is he.

⁵They have acted corruptly toward him;
    to their shame they are no longer his children,
    but a warped and crooked generation.
⁶Is this the way you repay the LORD,
    O foolish and unwise people?
Is he not your Father, your Creator,
    who made you and formed you?

⁷Remember the days of old;
    consider the generations long past.
Ask your father and he will tell you,
    your elders, and they will explain to you.
⁸When the Most High gave the nations their inheritance,
    when he divided all mankind,
he set up boundaries for the peoples
    according to the number of the sons of Israel.
⁹For the LORD's portion is his people,
    Jacob his allotted inheritance.

¹⁰In a desert land he found him,
    in a barren and howling waste.
He shielded him and cared for him;
    he guarded him as the apple of his eye,
¹¹like an eagle that stirs up its nest
    and hovers over its young,

that spreads its wings to catch them
    and carries them on its pinions.
¹²The LORD alone led him;
    no foreign god was with him.

¹³He made him ride on the heights of the land
    and fed him with the fruit of the fields.
He nourished him with honey from the rock,
    and with oil from the flinty crag,
¹⁴with curds and milk from herd and flock
    and with fattened lambs and goats,
with choice rams of Bashan
    and the finest kernels of wheat.
You drank the foaming blood of the grape.

¹⁵Jeshurun grew fat and kicked;
    filled with food, he became heavy and sleek.
He abandoned the God who made him
    and rejected the Rock his Savior.
¹⁶They made him jealous with their foreign gods
    and angered him with their detestable idols.
¹⁷They sacrificed to demons, which are not God—
    gods they had not known,
    gods that recently appeared,
    gods your fathers did not fear.
¹⁸You deserted the Rock, who fathered you;
    you forgot the God who gave you birth.

¹⁹The LORD saw this and rejected them
    because he was angered by his sons and daughters.
²⁰"I will hide my face from them," he said,
    "and see what their end will be;
for they are a perverse generation,
    children who are unfaithful.
²¹They made me jealous by what is no god
    and angered me with their worthless idols.
I will make them envious by those who are not a people;
    I will make them angry by a nation that has no
        understanding.
²²For a fire has been kindled by my wrath,
    one that burns to the realm of death below.
It will devour the earth and its harvests

and set afire the foundations of the mountains.

²³"I will heap calamities upon them
and spend my arrows against them.
²⁴I will send wasting famine against them,
consuming pestilence and deadly plague;
I will send against them the fangs of wild beasts,
the venom of vipers that glide in the dust.
²⁵In the street the sword will make them childless;
in their homes terror will reign.
Young men and young women will perish,
infants and gray-haired men.
²⁶I said I would scatter them
and blot out their memory from mankind,
²⁷but I dreaded the taunt of the enemy,
lest the adversary misunderstand
and say, 'Our hand has triumphed;
the LORD has not done all this.'"

²⁸They are a nation without sense,
there is no discernment in them.
²⁹If only they were wise and would understand this
and discern what their end will be!
³⁰How could one man chase a thousand,
or two put ten thousand to flight,
unless their Rock had sold them,
unless the LORD had given them up?
³¹For their rock is not like our Rock,
as even our enemies concede.
³²Their vine comes from the vine of Sodom
and from the fields of Gomorrah.
Their grapes are filled with poison,
and their clusters with bitterness.
³³Their wine is the venom of serpents,
the deadly poison of cobras.

³⁴"Have I not kept this in reserve
and sealed it in my vaults?
³⁵It is mine to avenge; I will repay.
In due time their foot will slip;
their day of disaster is near
and their doom rushes upon them."

³⁶The LORD will judge his people
> and have compassion on his servants
when he sees their strength is gone
> and no one is left, slave or free.
³⁷He will say: "Now where are their gods,
> the rock they took refuge in,
³⁸the gods who ate the fat of their sacrifices
> and drank the wine of their drink offerings?
Let them rise up to help you!
> Let them give you shelter!

³⁹"See now that I myself am He!
> There is no god besides me.
I put to death and I bring to life,
> I have wounded and I will heal,
> and no one can deliver out of my hand.
⁴⁰I lift my hand to heaven and declare:
> As surely as I live forever,
⁴¹when I sharpen my flashing sword
> and my hand grasps it in judgment,
I will take vengeance on my adversaries
> and repay those who hate me.
⁴²I will make my arrows drunk with blood,
> while my sword devours flesh:
the blood of the slain and the captives,
> the heads of the enemy leaders."

⁴³Rejoice, O nations, with his people,
> for he will avenge the blood of his servants;
he will take vengeance on his enemies
> and make atonement for his land and people.

⁴⁴Moses came with Joshua son of Nun and spoke all the words of this song in the hearing of the people. ⁴⁵When Moses finished reciting all these words to all Israel, ⁴⁶he said to them, "Take to heart all the words I have solemnly declared to you this day, so that you may command your children to obey carefully all the words of this law. ⁴⁷They are not just idle words for you—they are your life. By them you will live long in the land you are crossing the Jordan to possess."

ALTHOUGH THE NIV LABELS this chapter as "The Song of Moses," it should really be called "The Song of Yahweh,"[1] because Yahweh inspired it and dictated it to Joshua and Moses in the Tent of Meeting (31:14–21). Whereas in Moses' preaching we hear the voice of God refracted through the orations of a man, this song was composed by God and then performed by Moses precisely as he had heard it (31:30; 32:44).[2] Even more directly than Moses' sermons, this is "the word of God."

Efforts to establish the structure of the Song must take into account the emphasis it places on speech. Although Yahweh dictated the words (31:19) and Moses relayed them all to the people (31:30), fourteen verbs and nouns of speech point to utterances that have been embedded in the Song (cf. vv. 20–26, 34–38). The result is a complex song, involving no fewer than four degrees of direct discourse.[3] Based on these demarcations of the speeches and syntactical signals,[4] we may divide the Song into sections and stanzas as follows:

A. The Exordium: A Call to Acknowledge the Perfections of Yahweh (vv. 1–4)
B. The Recollection: A Call to Acknowledge the Imperfections of Yahweh's People (vv. 5–18)
   Stanza I: The Thesis Statement (vv. 5–6)
   Stanza II: A Call to Remember Yahweh's Grace (vv. 7–14)
   Stanza III: Trampling Underfoot the Grace of Yahweh (vv. 15–18)
C. The Confession: A Call to Recognize the Justice of Yahweh (vv. 19–35)

---

1. "The song of Moses the servant of God, and the song of the Lamb" in Revelation 15:3 are often associated with this text, but the epithet may just as well refer to Exodus 15, which explicitly celebrates Yahweh's deliverance of the Israelites from their tyrannical Egyptian overlords, which is paradigmatic of the salvation provided by the Lamb.

2. On the song as composed and commissioned by God, see further, T. Giles and W. J. Doan, *Twice-Used Songs: Performance Criticism of the Songs of Ancient Israel* (Peabody, MA: Hendrickson, 2009), 108–9.

3. Cf. J. P. Fokkelman, *Major Poems of the Hebrew Bible, at the Interface of Prosody and Structural Analysis*, vol. 1, *Ex. 15, Deut. 32, and Job 3* (Studia Semitica Neerlandica; Assen: Van Gorcum, 1998), 58–62.

4. Contra prevailing perceptions, the particle *kî* functions fundamentally as a discourse marker, which may function causally ("because," v. 20), or temporally ("when," v. 36c), though neither is certain. For full discussion, see Follingstad, *Deictic Viewpoint in Biblical Hebrew Text*.

Stanza I: Yahweh's Justice in Dealing with His Own People
(vv. 19–25)
Stanza II: Yahweh's Justice in Dealing with Israel's Enemies
(vv. 26–35)
D. The Gospel: A Call to Treasure the Compassion of Yahweh
(vv. 36–42)
E. The Coda: A Call to Celebrate the Deliverance of Yahweh (v. 43)

Based on the opening call for witnesses and the argumentation of the Song, the text has often been interpreted as a *rîb*, a prophetic lawsuit.[5] However, this interpretation overlooks the significance of expansions that have nothing to do with lawsuits (vv. 2, 30–43) and elements that are associated more with wisdom literature than with legal proceedings.[6] The legal features are actually quite muted, taking second place to liturgical features,[7] which are reinforced by the narrative context of the poem (31:19–22).[8] Whatever technical term we ascribe to the poem, its didactic function is clear. In addition to proclaiming the greatness of Yahweh, the Song provides a constant reminder to the Israelites of their origins (rooted in Yahweh's grace) and their demise (rooted in their perfidious response to grace), which demonstrates Yahweh's justice in punishing them and points to the resolution of the broken relationship through Yahweh's future acts of grace.[9]

While some ascribe the Song to late prophetic circles,[10] recent studies have argued for an earlier date. It may be one of the earliest literary pieces

---

5. See H. B. Huffmon, "The Covenant Lawsuit in the Prophets," *JBL* 78 (1959): 285; cf. G. E. Wright, "The Lawsuit of God: A Form-Critical Study of Deuteronomy 32," in *Israel's Prophetic Heritage* (ed. B. W. Anderson et al.; New York: Harper: 1962), 26–67; J. M. Wiebe, "The Form, Setting and Meaning of the Song of Moses," *Studia Biblica et Theologica* 17 (1989): 119–63.

6. See esp. J. R. Boston, "The Wisdom Influence upon the Song of Moses," *JBL* 87 (1968): 198–202.

7. These features include (1) the designation as a song rather than a legal case; (2) frequent alternation of persons moving back and forth among first, second, and third persons; (3) alternation of speakers; (4) series of commands (vv. 3, 7, 39, 43) and interrogatives (vv. 6, 30, 34, 37–38); (5) concluding call to praise (v. 43).

8. Cf. M. Thiessen, "The Form and Function of the Song of Moses (Deuteronomy 32:1–43)," *JBL* 123 (2004): 407–24; M. Leuchter, "Why Is the Song of Moses in the Book of Deuteronomy?" *VT* 57 (2007): 314.

9. Similarly J. R. Boston, "The Song of Moses: Deuteronomy 32:1–43" (PhD diss.; Ann Arbor, MI: University Microfilms, 1966), 191, 149–52, 187–91.

10. Mayes, *Deuteronomy*, 381. For further discussion see R. Bergey, "The Song of Moses (Deuteronomy 32.1–43) and Isaianic Prophecies: A Case of Early Intertextuality?" *JSOT* 28/1 (2003): 34–36; also S. A. Nigosian, "The Song of Moses (DT 32): A Structural Analysis," *ETL* 72 (1996): 5–7.

in the Old Testament.[11] As is the case with many psalms, this song provides few hints of a historical context that might have precipitated it.[12] Since it includes both archaic and late lexical and syntactical features,[13] the Song itself and the surrounding narrative provide the best clues to its origins.

As suggested earlier, this song serves as a sort of national anthem, intended to function as a "witness" in perpetuity (31:21) by reminding the people that they owed their existence to Yahweh and warning against abandoning him in favor of other gods. Moses had personally performed these functions for the past forty years, but once he is gone, the Song must take over and keep the people on spiritual course. This anthemic function accounts for the absence of specific historical references: to be perpetually relevant required removing time-bound details. As an anthem, this song would have been recited, sung, or performed when the people assembled for worship. At which liturgical events this happened we may only speculate. However, the association of this song with the reading of the Torah at Sukkoth (Festival of Booths) in chapter 31 may provide a clue. How it might have been used in worship is unclear. However, observing specified and implied shifts in speaker, we may imagine an antiphonal liturgy something like this:[14]

Verses	Content	Speaker
1—3	Introduction	Leader of the service
4	Creedal affirmation	Congregation
Pause		
5—6	Summary declaration of the indictment	Leader of the service
7	Call to remember Yahweh's grace	Leader of the Service
8—14f	Recitation of Yahweh's grace	Man or men in the assembly
14g—18	Declaration of the indictment of the people	Leader of the service
Pause		
19—20a	Declaration of Yahweh's sentence	Leader of the service

11. For full discussion of the history of scholarship on Deuteronomy 32, see P. Sanders, *The Provenance of Deuteronomy 32* (OtSt 37; Leiden: Brill, 1996), 1—98.

12. So also Fokkelman, *Major Poems*, 142—43.

13. See S. Nigosian, "Linguistic Patterns of Deuteronomy 32," *Bib* 78 (1997): 206—24.

14. This is an adaptation of Thiessen's reconstruction. For fuller discussion, see D. I. Block, "The Power of Song," 173—79

20b–27c	Recitation of Yahweh's judgment speech	Priest or cultic prophet
27d–e	Declaration by the nations	Appointed man in the assembly
28–29	Description of the nations	Priest or cultic prophet
30	Question asked of the nations	Leader of the service
31	Declaration of the Israelites	Congregation
32–35	Recitation of Yahweh's description of Israel's enemies	Priest or cultic prophet
Pause		
36–37a	Declaration of Yahweh's commitment to his people	Priest or cultic prophet
37b–38	Recitation of Israel's challenge to the nations	Congregation
39–42	Recitation of Yahweh's judgment speech against the nations	Priest or cultic prophet
43	Concluding summons to praise	Congregation

In essence, songs like this were written "to reconstruct the past in such a way as to assist in forming a *concrete social identity* among the reading and listening audience with the goal of creating a commitment or *obligation* to a specific ideal, value or belief."[15] This is certainly true of Deuteronomy 32. This song rehearses in lyric form the essence of Moses' preaching, appealing to every generation to acknowledge Yahweh's work of grace on their behalf, to reject all other spiritual allegiances, to recognize the consequences of infidelity, and to rejoice in the hope that ultimately Yahweh's commitment to them is immutable.

The Exordium: A Call to Acknowledge the Perfections of Yahweh (32:1–4)

THE OPENING TO THE Song offers four critical elements involved in the rhetorical situation envisaged: (1) the audience (v. 1); (2) the means (v. 2); (3) the rhetor's goal (v. 3); (4) the subject (v. 4). As elsewhere in the book, the "heavens" and the "earth" represent the entire cosmos. In light of earlier appeals (4:26; 30:19; 31:28), verse 1 looks like a call for witnesses in a legal case. However, the exordium suggests that this song does not envision a legal situation; this is a song of praise to Yahweh from the lips of a human that the world needs to hear.

---

15. Giles and Doan, *Twice-Used Songs*, 22 (italics theirs).

Verse 2 describes the means by which the singer will praise Yahweh — "my teaching" and "my words" — but he focuses on the refreshing effect of his words. With artful parallelism he compares his words to "rain," "dew," "showers," and "abundant rain." Linked to verse 1, the words for moisture are arranged in an ABBA order, with the first and last expressions suggesting rains that fall from the heavens, and the middle two referring to moisture that appears spontaneously from the earth (Gen. 1:11 – 12; 2:5). This verse suggests that the words of praise for Yahweh (cf. v. 3) will precipitate new productivity and fertility in the cosmos.

The focus particle *kî* (omitted in NIV) at the beginning of verse 3 signals a shift in attention from the words of the Song to the singer's intent: to glorify Yahweh. Exodus 34:5 – 6 illustrates the meaning of "I will proclaim the name." In the second line the singer appeals to the audience to join him in ascribing greatness to Israel's God. The Song does this by reciting his attributes (v. 4), his gracious deeds on behalf of his people (vv. 5 – 14), his righteous anger in response to their rebellion (vv. 15 – 25), his justice in dealing with Israel's enemies (vv. 26 – 35), and ultimately his compassionate atonement for his own people (vv. 36 – 43). The reference to Yahweh by name and the epithet "our God" express the perspective of faithful Israelites in every generation.

Although verse 4 does not contain a new verb of speech, this seems to represent an embedded utterance, fulfilling the singer's promise to proclaim the name of Yahweh (v. 3). Like the Shema (6:4 – 5), this is a confessional statement, announcing the theme of Israel's national anthem. The mantra is carefully constructed, declaring the theme with a single word and then providing commentary in the form of a series of nominal clauses. The first line introduces a key motif in this song. The word "rock" appears twice in its natural sense (vv. 13a, 13b), five times as an epithet of Yahweh (vv. 4, 15, 18, 30, 31b), and twice in reference to foreign gods (vv. 31, 37). By contrasting Yahweh and the "rock" in which the nations put their trust (vv. 31, 37), the word connotes strength, stability, and permanence;[16] Israel finds her security in Yahweh alone.[17]

Five nominal sentences citing six characteristics of the Rock follow this opening exclamation. (1) The activity of the Rock is "perfect," which suggests that all Yahweh's actions are flawless — in contrast to other gods ("rocks") who are declared to be nothing (vv. 31, 37).[18] (2) All the ways of

---

16. Cf. C. J. Labuschagne, *The Incomparability of Yahweh in the Old Testament* (Pretoria Oriental Series 5; Leiden: Brill, 1966), 70–71, 115–16.

17. Cf. 1 Sam. 2:2; 2 Sam. 22:32. In 2 Sam. 23:3 David's calls Yahweh the "Rock of Israel" (cf. Isa. 30:29).

18. Isa. 41:24 characterizes other gods as "less than nothing" and their work as utterly worthless.

the Rock are "just"; that is, everything he does serves the cause of justice. (3) The Rock is "the faithful God [El]." This cryptic phrase summarizes 7:9–10, offering a lyrical exposition of the earlier statement. It celebrates the two sides to Yahweh's faithfulness, first in his calling and providing for Israel (vv. 8–14), and then in his judgment of those "who hate" him (vv. 15–43). (4) The Rock "does no wrong."[19] (5) The Rock is righteous (NIV "upright"; *ṣaddîq*) and upright (NIV "just"; *yāšār*). The former expression refers to living and acting according to principles established by covenant (cf. 16:20),[20] while the latter derives from a root meaning "to be straight" (cf. 6:18; 12:25; 13:19[20]; 21:9).

The Recollection: A Call to Acknowledge the Imperfections of Yahweh's People (32:5–18)

THIS SECTION OF THE poem consists of three stanzas: verses 5–6, 7–14, 15–18. With its remarkable description of God's grace toward Israel, the middle stanza is obviously the center of gravity, being sandwiched between two pointed descriptions of Israel's faithless response.

Stanza I: The thesis statement (vv. 5–6). The first stanza begins ambiguously. Although the initial clause lacks an antecedent specifying the subject as well as an explanation of how the corruption occurred, the context suggests it must be Israel, and the use of the verb elsewhere for future apostasy (4:16, 25; 31:29) indicates the corruption involves violation of the Supreme Command through idolatry.

A series of cryptic clauses describe this corrupt people. (1) They are Yahweh's "non-children." The expression suspends if not reverses Yahweh's formal adoption of Israel as his children at Sinai (14:1).[21] (2) They are a blemished (NIV "shame[ful]") lot. Using a word normally applied to defective sacrificial animals, the singer contrasts the corruption of Israel with the perfection of Yahweh's work (v. 4) and negates their status as "a people holy to the LORD."[22] (3) They are "a warped and crooked generation." Elsewhere the former expression is contrasted with integrity (Prov. 19:1; 28:6), loyalty, and perfection (2 Sam. 22:26–27); the second word occurs only here. Proverbs 8:8 uses derivatives of these two words to represent the opposite of "righteousness."

---

19. Cf. 25:16; Ezek. 18:8, 24, 26; 33:13–18; Jer. 2:5.

20. In 4:8, the expression applies to the terms of the covenant itself; in 16:19 and 25:1 it refers to the faithful human party to the covenant.

21. Cf. the name of Hosea's son, "Not-My-People" (Hos. 1:9). The expression "children given to corruption" in Isa. 1:4 echoes the present text.

22. Cf. 7:6; 14:1; 26:19; 28:9.

The rhetorical questions of verse 6 confirm that verse 5 has contrasted the perfections of Yahweh (v. 4) with Israel's deep-seated imperfections, particularly its use of the verb *gāmal* (NIV "repay"). The rhetorical question in the first line calls for a negative answer, but the characterization of the Israelites in the second line as "foolish" and "unwise" suggests they have answered it positively. In Psalm 74:18 "foolish people" refers to those who stupidly revile the name of Yahweh.[23] Together these words negate Israel's status as recognized by the nations in 4:6.

The second half of verse 6 uses another rhetorical question to hint at the nature of their corruption: Yahweh is their Father (1:31; 8:5), but they have treated him shamefully. Here Yahweh's fatherhood relates primarily to his being the source of Israel's existence, which is expressed with a triad of verbs. "Your Creator" is used of acquisition,[24] but the term may relate either to childbirth (Gen. 4:1) or to creation (Ps. 139:13; cf. Prov. 8:22). The second verb, "who made you," involves the most common Hebrew word for "to make," but in several contexts it relates to God's creation of humanity in general (Prov. 14:31; Isa. 17:7; Jer. 27:5) and to Israel in particular (Pss. 95:6; 100:3; Hos. 8:14). The third ("formed") means fundamentally to fix or establish, but the present creative nuance is reflected also in Psalm 119:73. Together, these rhetorical questions highlight the folly of Israel's response to Yahweh's work on her behalf.

Stanza II: A call to remember Yahweh's grace (vv. 7–14). These verses recite the divine actions establishing Israel and elevating her high above the nations. This exposition opens with an appeal to remember Israel's past. If the hearers themselves cannot remember, they may consult their fathers and elders, the guardians and repositories of history in preliterate societies. The invitation recalls 4:32, though here the *terminus a quo* is implied in the expressions "days of old" and "generations long past." The rest of this stanza summarizes the response of the fathers/elders to the request, highlighting four significant stages of the nation's history.

(1) *Yahweh's election of Israel and her special relationship with him (vv. 8–9).* With elegant parallelism the elders recall the establishment of Israel's special relationship to Yahweh. Identified in the opening line as "Most High,"[25] verse 8 suggests Yahweh's primary action involved establishing international boundaries (cf. Gen 10:5, 32). As noted on 1:38, the expression "to give as a grant" (NIV "give ... their inheritance") is a feudal expression referring to the apportionment of property by the lord to his subjects.

---

23. Cf. Job 2:10; Pss. 14:1; 39:9[10]; 53:1[2]; 74:22.
24. *HALOT*, 1111–13.
25. Elyon suggests a supreme deity. See Elnes and Miller, "Elyon," *DDD*, 295.

But what was apportioned, and who were the beneficiaries of the distribution? The NIV assumes the distribution involved territory granted to the nations,[26] but on contextual and syntactical grounds, "nations" should be understood as the object of the verb. (a) Verse 9 presents Jacob/Israel as the personal "grant" of Yahweh.[27] (b) The first two cola of verse 8 specify the context for the main event — when Elyon fixed[28] the boundaries of the peoples. Although the beneficiaries of the apportionment are not explicitly identified, the last line of verse 8 provides a clue, especially if we prefer the reading of a Qumran fragment (4QDeut[j]) and the Septuagint ("according to the sons of God") over the Hebrew Masoretic text.[29] These semidivine heavenly beings serve as Yahweh's agents of providence on earth. Accordingly, Yahweh divided the "sons of man" into "nations," and then apportioned them to the "sons of God," to be their patrons and protectors on his behalf.

Verse 9 highlights Israel's special status within this cosmic administrative structure. Whereas Yahweh apportioned the nations to the "sons of God," he claimed Jacob as his own "portion" and his "allotted possession" (NIV "inheritance"). "Possession" (*naḥᵃlâ*) usually refers to the land that Yahweh allots to Israel,[30] but in 4:20 Moses spoke of Yahweh claiming his people themselves as his "possession." Whereas the lore of other ancient peoples involving the origins of relationships between gods and their respective territories[31] focused on the deities' territorial holdings, like the rest of the Old Testament, this text emphasizes the relationship between Yahweh and his people.

(2) *Yahweh's rescue of Israel from a threatening situation and his care for her in the desert (vv. 10–11).* In this strophe the allusion shifts from the exodus (v. 9) to Israel's

---

26. On the nations and their relationships to lands, see also Isa. 10:13; Amos 9:7; Acts 17:26.

27. "Jacob" is the birth name of the ancestor of "Israel," who derived their national name from the name that God gave him (Gen. 32:28[29]); Jacob is never used in the Old Testament as a territorial designation.

28. Cf. Ps. 74:17 and Prov. 15:25. On the verb, see Sanders, *Provenance of Deuteronomy 32*, 155 and 297–315.

29. The NIV follows MT, but see the text note. For defense "sons of God" rather than "sons of Israel," see Block, *The Gods of the Nations*, 25–32; M. Heiser, "Monotheism, Polytheism, Monolatry, or Henotheism? Toward an Assessment of Divine Plurality in the Hebrew Bible," *BBR* 18/1 (2008): 17–18.

30. Deut. 4:21, 38; 10:9; 15:4; 18:2; 19:10; 20:16; 21:23; 24:4; 25:19; 26:1.

31. For a discussion of these traditions see Block, *Gods of the Nations*, 21–25. For contemporary African traditions of the relationship between the high god and the lesser gods of the tribes, see L. Ugwuanya Nwosu, "The Nations and the Sons of God in Deuteronomy 32: Perspectives on Evangelical Strategies in Non-monotheistic Cultures," *Bible Bhashyam* 22 (1996): 29–32.

experience in the desert of Sinai. The bland expression in the first line ("in a desert land") is colorized with "in a barren and howling waste" in the second. The word translated "howling" assumes a connection with a verb that denotes the howling of jackals and other desert creatures (cf. Mic. 1:8). This verse does not specify why the desert threatened Israel (cf. 8:15), but the vocabulary suggests a slow death of thirst or the sudden attack of hungry desert creatures.

However, apparently just in time Yahweh came by and "found" Israel (v. 10a; cf. Hos. 9:9 – 10; 13:4 – 6; Ezek. 16:1 – 8). The second half of verse 10 highlights Yahweh's response to this vulnerable people. Like an army circling a village of defenseless women and children to keep the enemy at bay, he surrounded them and protected them. The simile in the last line of this verse intensifies the image of Yahweh's protection; he guarded them as his precious treasure. This interpretation of the literal expression "the apple of his eye" has a long history.[32] Whatever its derivation, this became a fixed expression for "to treat with love and care" (cf. 8:15 – 16).[33]

Verse 11 introduces another image of divine care, referring to four actions an eagle might take to secure the well-being of its young. It "hovers" over them, spreads its wings, takes hold of the eaglet, and carries it away with its pinions flapping.[34] The image involves an adult bird picking up the eaglet with its beak and soaring away. The inspiration for the statement may come from Exodus 19:4. The strophe ends with a summary declaration that if the Israelites ever made it through the desert, it was entirely to Yahweh's credit (v. 12). The first colon expresses the notion positively: Yahweh "alone led" Israel;[35] the last clause expresses it negatively — "no foreign god" accompanied Israel (cf. 31:16).

(3) *Yahweh's endowment of Israel with all good things (vv. 13 – 14).* The last strophe envisions Yahweh's leading Israel through the Promised Land in triumphant procession. The first line portrays Israel's arrival as an army of chariots riding over the "heights of the land." The high places could either refer to the

---

32. For discussion of the English idiom, see M. B. Ogle, "The Apple of the Eye," *Transactions of the American Philosophical Society* 73 (1942): 181–91.

33. Sanders, *Provenance of Deuteronomy 32*, 163.

34. The word *ʾebrâ* ("pinion") occurs elsewhere in Job 39:13; Ps. 68:13[14]; 91:4; Job 39:13. The common understanding of an adult eagle picking up its young, placing it on its pinions, and giving it a ride is fanciful and unnatural. While some claim to have witnessed such a sight (G. R. Driver, "Once Again: Birds in the Bible," *PEQ* 90 [1958]: 56–57), others dispute it (H. G. L. Peels, "On the Wings of the Eagle (Dtn 32,11) — An Old Misunderstanding," *ZAW* 106 [1994]: 300–303). This interpretation recalls the legendary Mesopotamian picture of Etana flying to heaven on the back of an eagle (*COS*, 1:131 [p. 457]).

35. This alludes to the pillar of cloud by day and fire by night. Cf. Ex. 13:17, 21; 15:13; Neh. 9:12, 19; Pss. 77:20[21]; 78:14, 53. In Pss. 23:3; 77:20[21]; 78:52–53 the verb for "led" (*nhh*) speaks of the tender care of a shepherd.

highlands of Canaan (1:7, 19–20, 41, 43, 44; 3:25) or serve as a cipher for religious installations in Canaan. The references to feasting on the resources of the land in the following lines point to the former interpretation.

The rest of verses 13–14, then, highlights the agricultural benefits that the land yields for Israel.[36] (1) Yahweh provides food spontaneously from the rock. "Nourishing him with honey from the rock and oil from the flinty crag" is a metaphor for such prosperity that both desirable products (honey) and economic staples (olive oil) ooze from the land.[37]

(2) Yahweh provides food through livestock. This includes milk products[38] and the flesh of animals: young rams fattened for slaughter,[39] mature rams, male goats, and choice cattle (lit., "sons of Bashan," an idiomatic expression for fattened bovines).[40] Fat was considered especially nutritious and often represented the productivity of the land (Pss. 81:17; 147:14).

(3) Yahweh provides food through the soil. Just as fat around kidneys was the most desirable product of rams (Lev. 3:3–4; Isa. 34:6), so "fat of the kidneys of wheat" (pers. trans.) refers to the highest quality wheat or flour.[41] The phrase "blood of grapes" refers either to common red or specialty wine. The stanza ends with a surprising verbal clause: "You drank foaming [wine]." Here wine in the fermentation stage highlights the Israelites' joy in the produce provided by the land that Yahweh had given them.

Stanza III: Trampling underfoot the grace of Yahweh (vv. 15–18). The concern of this stanza is Israel's violation of the Supreme Command. The subject is presented from two sides: Israel's abandonment of Yahweh (vv. 15, 18) and their pursuit of other gods (vv. 16–17). The opening line highlights the material benefits of Yahweh's grace. The reference to Israel as "Jeshurun" (cf. 33:5, 26; Isa. 44:2), Yahweh's affectionate epithet for his people, heightens the tragedy.[42] The description of Jeshurun that follows suggests the name is used ironically. The "straight one" on whom Yahweh

---

36. The text alludes to earlier statements in 6:11; 7:13; 8:7–10; and 11:15.

37. The image of sucking honey and oil from the rock portrays the rock as a wet nurse on Yahweh's behalf. On Yahweh satisfying Israel with honey from the rock, see also Ps. 81:16[17]. The word for "honey" may refer to the juice of grapes or figs. Cf. McConville, *Deuteronomy*, 455.

38. On processed milk products like butter, curds, and yogurt, see Borowski, *Every Living Thing*, 54–56.

39. *HALOT*, 496; Borowski, *Every Living Thing*, 20, 83.

40. Contra NIV's "choice rams." Bashan was renowned for its fine cattle: Ezek. 39:18; Micah 7:14; Ps. 22:12[13].

41. Hence NIV's "finest kernels of wheat." Cf. fat of wheat in Ps. 81:16[17]; the fat of oil and new wine (Num. 18:12).

42. For a study of the name and its meaning see M. J. Mulder, *TDOT*, 6:472–77. The name is related to the Hebrew word *yâšar*, which means "straight."

had lavished his affection (vv. 7–14) has acted perversely through abominable acts of devotion to other gods (vv. 16–17).

The image of perversion pervades the entire stanza. The tone is set by the rare denominative verb "to be, become fat," which appears in two different forms at the beginning of each of the first two cola of verse 15. In isolation the present metaphor could be interpreted positively (vv. 13–14), but as a heading for this stanza it represents the opposite, "fat of mind," i.e., stupid (cf. Isa. 6:10; Jer. 5:28). Since all five verbs in the first two cola apply most naturally to farm animals, the Song paints a picture of a prize calf whose senses have been dulled by the glut of food and whose corpulence is highlighted in the second line: the calf grew fat and became stout and plump.

The rich food and prosperity (vv. 13–14) have obviously had an effect on the consumer's disposition. In verse 15a Israel kicks like an animal, a colorful image of revolt against its provider. With elegant parallelism, in verse 15b the poet laments Israel's abandonment of her divine Creator and Savior. The choice of *nāṭaš* rather than *ʿāzab* for "abandon" is striking. While usually used of Yahweh giving up on his people,[43] here *nāṭaš* speaks of the people abandoning him (cf. Jer. 15:6). The second verb (*nābal*) (Piel) means to treat with contempt, as if the object is a fool (cf. v. 6). Instead of honoring Yahweh their father and generous divine benefactor, they despise him.

The target of their contempt is clear: "God," and "the Rock" of salvation (v. 15). The reference to the Rock that saves is striking. Although rocks are normally associated with defense,[44] by going on the offensive, this Rock created a people for himself by choosing them, providing for them in the desert, and granting them prosperity in his land (vv. 8–14), as well as by destroying the enemies who threatened and held them captive.[45]

Verses 16–17 shift the focus from Israel's foolish response to Yahweh to their ridiculous response to other gods. We may treat these verses together by noting first the objects of Israel's perverse devotion and then the effects this has on Israel's true divine Benefactor. The Song employs seven expressions for false gods. (1) They are "strangers" (NIV "foreign"), illicit and prohibited objects of worship. (2) They are "abominations" (NIV "detestable"). (3) They are *šēdîm*. The rendering of this word as "demons" derives from LXX and the Vulgate's *daemonibus*.[46] While demons were viewed as

---

43. Judg. 6:13; 1 Sam. 12:22; 1 Kings 8:57; 2 Kings 21:14; Isa. 2:6; Jer. 7:29; 23:33, 39; Pss. 27:9; 94:14.

44. 2 Sam. 22:3; Pss. 18:2[3]; 62:2, 6–7[3, 7–8]; Isa. 17:10.

45. Similarly 2 Sam. 22:47; Ps. 18:46[47]. In Ps. 89:26[27]. David uses this word of Yahweh, who has adopted him as his son and granted him eternal kingship.

46. While this word is common for demons in postbiblical Jewish Aramaic, it occurs elsewhere in the Old Testament only in Ps. 106:37, where it serves as a correlative of "effigies, idols."

agents of disorder and death in the world outside Israel, the Hebrew Bible provides little information on them.[47] Though *šēdîm* is commonly treated as a loanword from an Akkadian word meaning protective spirits,[48] in light of the references to the *šdyn* in the Deir ʿAlla texts from the ninth to eighth century BC,[49] it seems best to interpret this as a designation for beings viewed to be actual divinities.[50]

(4) The Israelite objects of devotion are nongods. The phrase "not God" rejects any effort to equate the *šēdîm* with true divinity. (5) They are "unknown gods." The expression recalls earlier statements[51] and highlights the contrast with Yahweh, who had revealed himself by name to the Israelites. (6) They are novelties ("gods that appeared recently"), in contrast to Yahweh/Elyon, "the ancient God" (33:27), who has been operating in Israel's interest since the day the nations were distributed among the sons of God (v. 8).[52] (7) They are gods the ancestors "did not fear."

Verse 18 returns to the notions with which the strophe had opened (v. 15): Israel has forgotten Yahweh. This notion is expressed by curiously conflating paternal and maternal elements. While masculine in form, the verbs describing Yahweh's actions involve a female role. Whereas the first may be applied either to mothers[53] or to fathers,[54] the second ("who gave you birth") obviously involves a maternal experience.[55] By portraying Israel as the child of Yahweh, who exhibits both fatherly (v. 6) and motherly (v. 18) qualities, the Song highlights Israel's dependence on Yahweh for her very existence.[56] In forgetting Yahweh, they have truly trampled underfoot his grace.

---

47. K. van der Toorn, "The Theology of Demons in Mesopotamia and Israel: Popular Belief and Scholarly Speculation," in *Die Dämonen: Die Dämonologie der israelitisch-jüdischen und frühchristlichen Literatur im Kontext ihrer Umwelt* (eds A. Lange et al.; Tübingen: Mohr Siebeck, 2003), 61–83.

48. The word may also refer to malevolent spirits. See *CAD*, 17/2:256–59.

49. See J. A. Hackett, *The Balaam Text from Deir ʿAlla* (HSM 31; Chico, CA: Scholar, 1980), 85–89.

50. See H. Niehr, *TDOT*, 14:418–24; M. Weippert, *TLOT*, 3:1304–10, esp. 1307.

51. See 11:28; 13:2, 6, 13[3, 7, 14]; 28:64; 29:26[25].

52. Cf. Judg. 5:8, "they choose new gods" (thus NIV; cf. Tigay, *Deuteronomy*, 306); but see Block, *Judges, Ruth*, 226–27 ("God chose new [leaders]").

53. Gen. 3:16; Job 14:1; 15:14; 25:4 (women); Jer. 14:5 (doe); 17:11 (female partridge).

54. Gen. 4:18; 10:8; 1 Chron. 1:10; Prov. 17:21; 23:22; Dan. 11:6.

55. Isa. 51:2; Job 39:1. LXX resists the portrayal of God as a woman who bears children, rendering it with a participle that means "the one who fed you." Thus also Sanders, *Provenance of Deuteronomy 32*, 186.

56. So also Tigay, *Deuteronomy*, 307. Tigay notes that in ancient Syrian and Hittite inscriptions, kings were described as both father and mother of their subjects. See the eighth-century BC Phoenician inscription of Azatiwada, *COS*, 2:31 (p. 149), and the ninth-century BC inscription of Kilamuwa, *COS*, 2:30 (p. 148).

The Confession: A Call to Recognize
the Justice of Yahweh (32:19–35)

IN VERSE 19 THE Song turns to Yahweh's reaction to Israel's rebellion. The poet's central thesis is that Yahweh's punishment of his people is just, but so is his response to those who take advantage of them for their own sakes. This section opens with a narrative introduction (v. 19), but the remainder is cast entirely in the form of a divine speech in the first person.

Stanza I: Yahweh's justice in dealing with his own people (vv. 19–25). In this first stanza, Yahweh declares his resolve to withdraw his presence from his people (vv. 20–21) and send in his agents of death (vv. 22–25). The singer begins by announcing the theme. The change in divine disposition is expressed with two verbs: "the LORD saw" and "rejected." The first highlights the contrast between Yahweh and the non-gods to whom the Israelites had turned (4:28); the second is ambiguous because it lacks an object. However, the meaning of the verb is clarified in verses 20–25: Yahweh's sons and daughters, who have provoked him.

Yahweh's disposition toward his people (vv. 20–21). This poetic strophe opens with a declaration of Yahweh's resolve: "Let me hide [my face]" and "Let me see" (pers. trans.). The first statement recalls Yahweh's prediction in the narrative preamble to the Song (31:16b–18). The second line is not an expression of openness, as if Yahweh has no awareness or control over Israel's destiny. The emphasis on his control in the following verses suggests this statement should be interpreted as ironic, if not even stronger, "Let me see to [i.e., determine] their end."[57]

Verses 20c–21b summarize the basis for Yahweh's rejection of his people, presenting first the external (v. 20c–d) and then the internal grounds (v. 21a–b). Externally, Israel's punishment is justified because they are "perverse"[58] and totally lacking in fidelity. Internally, Yahweh's rejection of Israel is fueled by his fury. With their exchange of the only true God in favor of non-gods and "futilities" (NIV "worthless idols"), they have ignited his passion and stoked his anger (Deut. 5:9). The expressions for other gods are intentionally pejorative.[59] Similar to Moses' descriptions of these gods elsewhere in the book (4:28; 29:17[16]), Yahweh dismisses them as unresponsive to devotion. He denies their objective existence (cf. v. 17), describing them as *ḥᵃbālîm* ("vapor, soap bubbles"), evanescent and lacking substance.[60]

---

57. On *ʾaḥᵃrît* meaning "outcome," see also below on v. 29.

58. This form occurs elsewhere only in Proverbs, where it speaks of a person who turns truth upside down (Prov. 2:12, 14; 6:14; 8:13; 10:31, 32; 16:28, 30; 23:33).

59. Cf. Block, "Other Religions in Old Testament Theology," 61–62.

60. On *hebel* ("absurdity, futility") as a designation of idols, see also 2 Kings 17:15; Ps. 31:6[7]; Jer. 2:5; 10:8, 15; 14:22; 16:19; 51:18; Jonah 2:8[9]. This word occurs frequently in Ecclesiastes.

In verse 21c–d Yahweh declares his intention in rejecting Israel. Applying the principle of *talion*, he will treat them as they have treated him. They
have ignited his passion by substituting him for a "non-god"; he will ignite
theirs by substituting them with a "non-people."[61] They have provoked
his ire with "futilities"; he will provoke their ire with a "nation that has no
understanding." Yahweh will exchange his "smart" people for an "idiotic"
nation. In effect, barbarians have replaced a civilized people as the object
of Yahweh's affections.

Yahweh's actions against his people (vv. 22 – 25). The focus particle *kî* at the
beginning of verse 22 ("For") signals a shift to the actions that Yahweh
threatens against Israel. The expression of divine fury begins cosmically
(v. 22) and then zeroes in on the Israelites themselves (vv. 23 – 25). Verse
22 opens with a simple announcement that a flame has been ignited in
Yahweh's nostrils.[62] But the fire does not remain there; it spreads to the
lowest recesses of Sheol (NIV "death") and will devour the entire earth and
its produce, and it will set ablaze the very "foundations of the mountains."
The scope of Yahweh's anger has reached cosmic proportions.[63]

However, in verses 23 – 25 Yahweh's fury against the cosmos gives way
to a particular target, identified vaguely with the third person plural pronoun ("them"), and then specified in verse 25 as young men and young
women, nursing children, and grey haired men. But who are they? Even
though Yahweh's people have not been referred to since verse 15, all who
hear the Song will know the target is Israel, which renders the following
description all the more frightening.

Verse 23 serves as a thesis statement, highlighting Yahweh's role and
identifying the genre of calamities that follow. Verse 23a classifies the
gathering storm as "evils," a general expression for "calamities" (NIV). The
second colon casts the theme in metaphorical form,[64] employing "arrows"
as shorthand for all the ammunition at Yahweh's disposal. Many of these
weapons are associated with ancient conceptions of the demonic world.
The boundaries of several blur, but each deserves brief comment.

Starvation. The word "wasting famine" occurs only here in the Old
Testament. That this parade of deadly divine weapons should be headed by
"famine" reflects the role of starvation in ancient warfare. If *rāʿab* is intended

---

61. Hosea's naming his son "Not-My-People" (Hos. 1:9) apparently alludes to this text,
but he exploits the phrase in a new way.

62. This interpretation is reinforced by Jer. 15:14 and 17:4, which employ the same noun
and verb and speak of a fire kindled in Yahweh's nose.

63. "Foundations of the mountains" occurs elsewhere only in 2 Sam. 22:8 (= Ps. 18:7[8]).

64. Deut. 32:42; Num. 24:8; 2 Sam. 22:15 = Ps. 18:14[15]; Pss. 7:14; 38:2[3]; 64:78. ;
91:5–6; 120:4; 144:6; Job 6:4; Lam. 3:12–13; Ezek. 5:16–17; Hab. 3:11; Zech. 9:14.

as a proper name,[65] then the previous word should probably be revocalized as *mᵉzî*, yielding the sense, "My sucker, Raᶜab," to match the preceding "my arrows" and to go with the following "my warrior, Resheph."[66]

Epidemic. Although NIV's "consuming pestilence" assumes the first word is a passive form of a verb meaning "to eat," it is preferable to derive the word from *lāḥam* ("to fight")[67] and to treat the second word as a proper name: Resheph. Resheph, whose symbol was the arrow,[68] often appears in extrabiblical texts as the demon of epidemics and death.[69]

Pestilence. The NIV's "deadly plague" is difficult. *Qeteb* is probably a proper noun. Though some connect it with the sirocco wind or the heat of midday,[70] most understand this as the name of the demon of pestilence.[71] In view of recent evidence, the word for "deadly" should be understood as "poisonous,"[72] yielding "Qeteb, my poisonous one."

While these agents appear in the covenant curses (28:20–22, 48) and the names originate in pagan demonology,[73] in orthodox Yahwism the entities involved have all been thoroughly demythologized. Yahweh is in complete control of all forces of death, including those that other peoples identify with malevolent spirits from the netherworld. However, Yahweh also has other more natural weapons at his disposal.

Vicious animals. The verb "to send" is regularly used for Yahweh's dispatching of messengers and prophets as well as agents of death and destruction (cf. 7:20). Here the agents are fearful animals, with "the fangs of the wild beasts."[74]

---

65. Some treat this as "The Hungry One," an epithet for Death/Mot not only here but also in Jer. 18:21; Ps. 33:19; Job 18:12. See N. J. Tromp, *Primitive Conceptions of Death and the Netherworld in the Old Testament* (BibOr 21; Rome, 1969), 107–10; N. Wyatt, "Qeteb," *DDD*, 673.

66. Thus J. C. De Moor, "'O Death, Where Is Thy Sting?'" in *Ascribe to the Lord: Biblical and Other Studies in Memory of P. C. Craigie* (ed. L. Eslinger and G. Taylor; JSOTSup 67; Sheffield: JSOT, 1988), 105.

67. In Qal, Pss. 35:1; 56:1, 2[2, 3]; in Niphal, Deut. 1:30, 41, 42; 3:22; 20:4; etc.

68. On this figure, see J. Day, "New Light on the Mythological Background of the Allusion to Resheph in Habakkuk III 5," *VT* 29 (1979): 259–74. The figure has recently surfaced on a stela from Tell el-Borg in Egypt. See J. K. Hoffmeier and K. A. Kitchen, Reshep and Astarte in North Sinai: A Recently Discovered Stela from Tell el–Borg, *Egypt and the Levant* 17 (2007): 127–36.

69. See P. Xella, "Resheph," *DDD*, 700–703.

70. See Sanders, *Provenance of Deuteronomy 32*, 196.

71. On this deity see N. Wyatt, "Qeteb," *DDD*, 673–74.

72. See D. Pardee, "'Venom' in Job 20:14," *ZAW* 91 (1979): 401–16. See C. Cohen, "Poison," *EncJud* (2nd ed.), 16:283–84.

73. Cf. van der Toorn, "Theology of Demons," 63–65.

74. Cf. also Joel 1:6; Job 4:10; 41:14[6].

Venom of vipers. Verse 24d moves from the teeth of the animals to the deadly venom (lit., "heat"; cf. v. 33) of snakes, identified as those creatures that "glide in the dust."[75]

Sword. Whether we interpret as a common noun, "sword," or as a proper noun, *Ḥereb*, the word functions as shorthand for the slaughter of warfare. The effect of the sword is expressed by the verb "to bereave of children," which other texts attribute to wild animals.[76]

Terror. While NIV and most translations interpret this noun as a common noun, *ʾEmah* may also be a proper noun, a personification of the terror that causes those who have taken refuge inside their homes to collapse.[77] The place of refuge refers to the inner rooms of a house, the ancient equivalent of a fallout shelter. The terror that Yahweh had threatened as a weapon against Israel's enemies (Ex. 23:26−28; cf. 15:15−16) will be turned against his own people.

The final two cola of verse 25 summarize the scope of the disaster with two pairs of expressions. The first involves a conventional pair referring to males and females in their youthful prime.[78] The second pair, "[nursing] infants"[79] and "gray-haired men," functions as a merism, emphasizing that none will survive the attack of Yahweh's agents of wrath. While the language used to identify the divine agents differs significantly from the covenant curses in Deuteronomy 28, it is clear the Song envisions the same situation.

Stanza II: Yahweh's justice in dealing with Israel's enemies (vv. 26−35). The verb "I said" signals the start of an embedded speech in which the audience overhears Yahweh contemplating the implications of his actions against Israel.[80] In the end we learn why he did not utterly reject his people, despite their horrendous ingratitude and rebellion. The strophe begins with a past conversation that Yahweh had with himself. He admits that he had intended to "scatter them" and to "blot out their memory." This second line is shocking. While it involves different vocabulary, Yahweh would do to them what they were to do to the Canaanites (7:24).

---

75. The meaning of the expression is illustrated by Mic. 7:17. Cf. also Gen. 3:14.

76. Lev. 26:22; Ezek 5:17; 14:15. Jer. 15:7 and Hos. 9:12 speak of Yahweh robbing people of their children directly.

77. Perhaps as a correlative of "terror of the night" in Ps. 91:5 (associated with Deber and Qeteb, v. 6), and "the terrors of God" arrayed against Job in Job 6:4. On Terror as a demonic entity see M. Malul, "Terror of the Night," *DDD*, 851−54.

78. For this pair of expressions, see 2 Chron. 36:17; Pss. 78:63; 148:12; Isa. 23:4; 62:5; Jer. 51:22; Lam. 1:15, 18; 2:21; Ezek. 9:6; Amos 8:13; Zech. 9:17.

79. Cf. Song 8:1; Joel 2:16.

80. Cf. the helpful theological analysis offered by von Rad, *Deuteronomy*, 198−99.

Verse 27 explains why Yahweh backed off from this plan: He feared provocation (NIV "taunt") from the adversaries of God's people. Apparently Yahweh was troubled by the possibility that the enemies would draw false conclusions regarding their role in Israel's demise. The Song declares the enemies' response through direct speech by an interlocutor. The first clause reflects the gesture of a victor raising his hand in triumph.[81] The second represents the opposite side of the coin. Despite all the first person verbs in verses 19–25, they will say that it was not Yahweh who destroyed Israel. Yahweh would not tolerate this besmirching of his reputation (9:28; cf. Ex. 32:12; Num. 14:13–16). The enemies' declaration produces a change in the divine Sovereign's disposition, as the object of his ire shifts to those he had sent as agents of his people's punishment. Ultimately, Yahweh spares Israel to salvage his reputation.[82]

The focus particle *kî* functions as structural marker in verses 28, 31, 32, and 35c. In verse 28 (untrans. in NIV) it signals the beginning of a report from Yahweh's point of view,[83] as Yahweh renders his verdict on the arrogant enemies. They may have been chosen as instruments of divine judgment, but this decision was not based on their inherent qualifications or moral superiority (cf. 9:4–7). To the contrary, verses 28–29 highlight the enemy's stupidity — of which their arrogant claim of verse 27 is primary proof. While some understand the subject of verses 28–30 to be Israel,[84] the natural antecedents for the third person pronouns throughout verses 28–35 are the "enemy" and the "adversary" of verse 27. The portrayal of Israel's enemies resembles the portrayal in wisdom literature of fools who refuse to acknowledge Yahweh.[85] Verse 29 presents evidence of the enemy's ignorance by posing a hypothetical and unreal condition. Were the nations wise, they would get it, that is, grasp their end (cf. v. 20). Since verses 36–42 promise a positive end for Israel,[86] the present statement concerns the enemy's destiny (cf. Ps. 73:16–19).

Without warning in verse 30 someone asks a rhetorical question. But who is the inquirer? Since the third person pronouns in the third and fourth lines rule out an Israelite, this must be an outsider who watches the tables turn.[87] These lines answer the query of the first two. Whereas

---

81. Cf. Ex. 14:8 (the Israelites march out of Egypt "with hands held high"); Mic. 5:9[8]. (Israel's hand over the enemy); Ps. 89:13[14]. (Yahweh's hand over all).

82. See further D. A. Glatt-Gilad, "Yahweh's Honor at Stake: A Divine Conundrum," *JSOT* 98 (2002): 69–71.

83. So also Peter Gentry, in private communication.

84. Craigie, *Deuteronomy*, 386; Merrill, *Deuteronomy*, 421.

85. See Job 12:12; 32:11; Prov. 2:11; 3:13; 10:23; 14:29; 15:21; 17:27; 19:8; 20:5; etc.

86. Cf. also Deut. 8:16 and Job 42:12.

87. Cf. the answer provided by the unnamed speaker in Deut. 29:25–27[24–26]. In the cultic performance, someone in the congregation may have shouted out this question. Sanders (*Provenance of Deuteronomy* 32, 212–13) suggests that in vv. 30–31 we hear the poet's voice.

the nations think they have won the victory by their own military efforts (v. 27c–d), the speaker asserts that the Israelites' survival is due entirely to the work of God.[88] The God who had contemplated letting his people be destroyed (v. 26) has turned around and stood up for them.

The focus particle *kî* ("For") and the shift to first person plural in verse 31 signal a new speaker, who recognizes the uniqueness of Yahweh among the gods of the nations (cf. vv. 15–18, 21). The statement assumes the catalog of Yahweh's distinctive characteristics referred to in the Song, as well as the nature of the gods of the nations. But the meaning of the last line of verse 31 is unclear. NIV's "concede" interprets the last word (*pᵉlîlîm*) in the light of Exodus 1:22 and Job 31:11, where it seems to refer to arbiters in judicial cases. This interpretation suggests that in the end the enemies will acknowledge that Yahweh is incomparable. However, it seems preferable to associate *pᵉlîlîm* with the Akkadian verb "to guard"[89] and to see the phrase used here as "our enemies' guardians," the counterpart to "our Rock" in v. 31a.[90]

The opening *kî* in verse 32 (untrans. in NIV) signals another shift in perspective, returning to the voice of Yahweh, which will carry through to the end of verse 35. While the image of Sodom and Gomorrah as places renowned for agricultural productivity is ancient (Gen. 13:10), by linking Israel's enemies with these cities Yahweh recognizes their great potential: Their vine derives from the same stock as that grown in Sodom, and their tendrils derive from the stock of Gomorrah. But how different is the promise from the fulfillment! Instead of finding *Vitis vinifera* yielding grapes for wine,[91] those who picked the fruit discovered these were wild plants that produced lethal and bitter fruit (cf. 2 Kings 4:38–40).

The rest of verses 32 and 33 suggests the grapes are poisonous and their clusters deadly—as deadly as the venom of serpents and as cruel as the

---

88. The comment, "Unless their Rock had sold them, unless the LORD had given them up," involves two forms of the divine committal formula, used in military contexts to declare that a deity had given one of the parties in battle into the hands of the other. On the formula, which appears five times in Judges (2:14; 3:8; 4:2, 9; 10:7), see Block, *Judges, Ruth*, 147–48.

89. Thus Tigay, *Deuteronomy*, 310–11. For discussion see E. A. Speiser, "The Stem PLL in Hebrew," *JBL* 82 (1963): 103–6; idem, "PALIL and Congeners: A Sampling of Apotropaic Symbols," *Assyriological Studies* 16 (1965): 389.

90. Though this requires either a reversal of the order of words in a genitive relation (for other examples of this anomaly, see Tigay, *Deuteronomy*, 404, n. 135), or emending the text so that it reads: "See, their rock is not like our Rock, nor [are] the guardians of our enemies [like our Guardian]."

91. Cf. Judg. 9:13. Note also "the blood of grapes" that the Israelites drank in v. 14, above.

poison of cobras.[92] With the references to Sodom and Gomorrah, Yahweh subtly hinted at the enemies' destiny (v. 29) and provided a clue to the riddle that follows in verses 34 – 35. The strophe opens with a rhetorical question. "Have I not kept this in reserve with me and sealed it in my vaults [i.e., treasuries]?" But what has been stored up? It seems best to treat "their wine" in verse 33 as the antecedent of "it." Yahweh has kept under lock and key the poisonous wine from Sodom and Gomorrah, reserved for the day when he will serve it to Israel's enemies.[93]

According to verse 35, because Yahweh controls the nations' fate, their judgment is certain. The opening phrase, "It is mine to avenge," affirms the notion of the previous verse. Yahweh has stored the poisonous wine in his treasuries until the time is right to wreak vengeance on those who refuse to acknowledge his role in their defeat of Israel. Although the Masoretes pointed the following word as a Piel verb ("to make restitution, restore balance") as a correlative of "vengeance," it obviously functions as a noun, a second object in Yahweh's possession, if not in his storehouse. Yahweh operates according to principle, giving the wicked what they deserve and balancing crime and punishment. Indeed, the poison is reserved for the time when their feet fail. Given the reference to wine in verse 33, the phrase "their feet will slip" evokes images of an intoxicated man struggling to walk. However, more to the point of the present text, faltering feet is a metaphor for experiencing calamity.[94]

The second half of verse 35 clarifies the "time" of the divine vengeance. The expressions for the calamity awaiting the nations are striking. The first, "disaster," occurs elsewhere in the Old Testament,[95] but its meaning is clarified by Ezekiel 35:5, which pairs "the time of doom" with "the time of their final punishment." The second expression, "doom," involves a hapax form.[96] Here the plural form refers to "impending disasters"; poisonous wine now stored in Yahweh's storehouse is about to be served.

The Gospel: A Call to Treasure the Compassion of Yahweh (32:36 – 42)

AGAIN THE FOCUS PARTICLE *kî* in verse 36 (untrans. in NIV) signals a new movement in this song. This stanza opens with the voice of the poet, but

---

92. This is probably the Egyptian cobra, the most dangerous snake in the region. On the varieties of snakes referred to in the Old Testament see J. Feliks, "Snakes," *EncJud* (2nd ed.), 18:695 – 96.

93. Isa. 51:17, 22; Jer. 25:15 – 29; 51:7; Ezek. 33:31 – 34; Rev. 14:10; 16:19.

94. In the Psalms especially, a person whose foot does not "slip" is secure. Cf. Pss. 38:16[17]; 66:9; 121:3.

95. 2 Sam. 22:19 = Ps. 18:18[19]; Job 21:30; Prov. 27:10; Jer. 18:17; 46:21; Ob. 13.

96. Though see related forms in *šāpaṭ* (10:3; Job 3:8; 15:24).

in verse 37 Yahweh quickly resumes his speech. Verse 36 announces the theme with two chiastically structured lines. The first verb (*dîn*) involves a legal expression meaning "to judge," but in cases involving the oppressed or needy, it means "to champion the cause of."[97] The second involves a Hithpael of the root *nḥm* (NIV "have compassion"; cf. Ps. 135:14; Num. 23:19).[98] While Yahweh and Moses deem Israel's future infidelity and judgment to be inevitable (Deut. 31:16–18, 20–21), already in 4:31 Moses had declared the present assertion of divine empathy to be rooted in Yahweh's character as a compassionate God. This stanza celebrates the extraordinary fact that Yahweh will intervene on Israel's behalf against those who tried to destroy them.

The second half of verse 36 sets the context of his change in disposition. The expression "their strength is gone" (lit., "their hand evaporates") contrasts Israel's powerlessness with the boast of the enemies (v. 27c). But the Song adds a remarkable little detail: Yahweh sees! In contrast to the foreign gods (4:28) and reversing the hiding of his face earlier (v. 20), Yahweh notices that the Israelites are at the end of their resources. The last line expands on the enemies' loss of power: Their leaders have disappeared. Reinforcing the first half of the verse, the scarcity of leaders motivates Yahweh to intervene.

In verses 37–38 Yahweh's voice returns and carries on through verse 42. He begins by taunting the Israelites for having put their confidence in other gods. The rhetorical question (v. 37a) alludes to verses 15–18, ironically and sarcastically using the generic singular "rock." The gods the people have chosen are mere pebbles, in contrast to Yahweh, the omnipotent and perfectly just Rock (v. 4). In verse 38 the mockery turns to idols themselves. Recognizing the importance of keeping gods satisfied, Yahweh challenges the gods they have chosen to come to their aid by asking where the gods are who accepted their devotees' sacrifices and libations. The triad of action verbs reinforces the sarcasm: "Let them rise, assist you, and be your hiding place" (pers. trans.). These expressions all play on the reference to the gods as "rock" in verse 37.

Those who heard this song will have recognized in the introduction to verse 39 the climax. The unparalleled heaping up of attention-grabbing expressions, "See! Now! Note! I! I am he!" (pers. trans.), which focuses hearers' attention on Yahweh, who declares self-assuredly, "There is no God beside me." Whether we interpret ʿimmād as "with me" or "besides me,"

---

97. So NJPS. Of God: Gen. 30:6; Ps. 54:1[3]; of human officials: Prov. 31:9; Jer. 5:28; 21:12; 22:16.

98. The Niphal is used often to express God's sorrow or his change in disposition toward an object. E. g., Gen. 6:6–7; Ex. 32:12, 14; 1 Sam. 15:11, 29, 35; Jon. 3:9–10; 4:2.

Yahweh alone controls the events of history. He is sui generis; no one shares status or rank with him.[99] The remainder of verse 39 and indeed verses 40–42 elaborate on Yahweh's exclusive control over the fates and fortunes of human beings, beginning with two merismic statements that highlight his supreme authority over life and death. If Israel has suffered, this has indeed been the work of Yahweh, but the switch to an imperfect verb turns this statement into a promise: Yahweh will certainly heal his people. The last line of verse 39 emphasizes that when he acts on Israel's behalf, no outside power—neither divine nor human—can stop him.[100]

The final strophe (vv. 40–42) seals Israel's future. With a dramatic non-verbal gesture and an emphatic verbal declaration, Yahweh assures Israel that he will deal with their enemies once and for all. While some interpret the idiom "to lift the hand" as a metaphor for Yahweh's active involvement in defense of Israel,[101] the added prepositional phrase "to heaven" and the following oath formula suggest a legal gesture of raising the hand in association with swearing an oath.[102] By adding "forever," Yahweh guarantees the defeat of the enemy with a certainty equal to that of his oath to Abraham in Genesis 22:16.

Verses 41 and 42 reinforce the substance of the divinely sworn affidavit, beginning with a reference to the context: when Yahweh, the divine warrior, prepares his weapons for battle. The first line speaks literally of sharpening "the lightning of my sword."[103] But Yahweh's weapons of war are also weapons of judgment. If the first half of verse 41 sets the stage, the second half announces the action. Alluding back to verse 35, Yahweh declares that

---

99. The use of "I [alone] am he" in Isaiah confirms this: Isa. 41:4; 43:9–13, 25; 46:3–4; 48:12; 51:12; 52:6.

100. Cf. 1 Sam. 2:6–7; 2 Kings 5:7; Hos. 6:1–2; Ezek. 17:24; Job 5:18.

101. See J. Lust, "For I Lift My Hand to Heaven and Swear: Deut. 32:40," in *Studies in Deuteronomy in Honour of C. J. Labuschagne* (ed. F. G. Martínez; VTSup 53; Leiden: Brill, 1994), 155–64.

102. Cf. also Å. Viberg, *Symbols of Law: A Contextual Analysis of Legal Symbolic Acts in the Old Testament* (CBOTS 34; Stockholm: Almqvist and Wiksell, 1992), 19–32; Nigosian, "Song of Moses," 20. This idiom occurs elsewhere with Yahweh as subject in Ex. 6:8; Num. 14:30; Ps. 106:26; Neh. 9:15; Ezek. 20:5, 6, 15, 23, 28, 42; 36:7. The gesture is also attested in the eighth-century BC Aramaic inscription of Panamuwa from Zenjirli in Turkey (*COS*, 2.36, p. 157). On the grammar of the oath formula see M. R. Lehmann, "Biblical Oaths," *ZAW* 81 (1969): 74–92.

103. Alluding to the image of the polished blade flashing in the sunlight (cf. Nah. 3:2–3; Ezek. 21:14–16[19–21]). The lightning may also refer to bolts Yahweh uses like a sword to slaughter (cf. 2 Sam. 22:14–16; Hab 3:11), in which case this statement involves a pointed polemic against Baal. See further, J. Day, "Echoes of Baal's Seven Thunders and Lightnings in Psalm XXIX and Habakkuk III 9 and the Identity of the Seraphim in Isaiah VI," *VT* 29 (1979): 143–51. Baal is also linked with lightning in ancient iconographic representations. See *ANEP*, 168, §290.

he will repay his enemies. The sword he had placed in the hands of Israel's enemies (v. 25) he will now wield against them to restore ethical balance.

In verse 42 the picture turns grotesque. Yahweh portrays his sword and arrows as carnivorous beasts that cannot get enough of human blood and human flesh.[104] The last two cola of this verse specify the fare with which these weapons gorge themselves. While the first line obviously refers to the blood of those slain by the sword and those who have been captured, the meaning of the second line is uncertain. The NIV follows an ancient interpretive tradition rendering *parʿôt* as "leaders," while others suggest a reference to the hairy heads of the enemy, perhaps alluding to the unkempt and disheveled appearance of captives.[105] The lexical issues are far from settled, but the general significance of this strophe is clear: Yahweh will rise on behalf of his people and punish their enemies for their arrogance and brutality to Israel.

The Coda: A Call to Celebrate Yahweh's Deliverance (32:43)

ISRAEL'S NATIONAL ANTHEM ENDS on a festive note, appealing to the nations to join in the celebration of Yahweh's gracious acts on behalf of Israel. Unfortunately, the interpretation of this final strophe is frustrated by the most serious textual problems in the chapter, if not in the book. Following MT the NIV presents a shorter ending consisting of four cola. The strophe makes sense, but it raises questions whether the verse is complete as it stands. The LXX, Targum Neofiti, and fragments from Qumran reinforce suspicions regarding the MT. While scholars disagree in their assessment of this evidence,[106] we find the arguments for the eight-line reading of LXX to be persuasive and will base our commentary on this reading:[107]

---

104. While the notion of arrows drinking occurs only here, the image of a sword devouring its victims is common in the Old Testament (2 Sam. 2:26; 11:25; Isa. 1:20; 34:5−6; Jer. 46:10; etc.), and elsewhere (*ANET*, 540, ll. 635−36).

105. For further discussion see T. Kronholm, *TDOT*, 12:98−101.

106. Some argue for retaining MT: Fokkelman, *Major Poems of the Hebrew Bible*, 130; some for a reading as short as MT, but differing significantly: A. Rofé, "The End of the Song of Moses (Deuteronomy 32:43)," in *Liebe und Gebot: Studien zum Deuteronomium, L. Perlitt Festschrift* (eds. R. G. Kratz and H. Spieckermann; Göttingen: Vandenhoeck & Ruprecht, 2000), 164−72; most favor the six-cola reading reflected in 4QDeutq: Nelson, *Deuteronomy*, 379−80; van der Kooij, "The Ending of the Song of Moses," 93−100; a few support the eight-cola reading of LXX.

107. See further, Block, "The Power of Song," 185−88. So also Jason S. DeRouchie, in personal communication. Note that in Romans 15:10, Paul quotes the third line of Deuteronomy 32:43 LXX verbatim as Scripture: "Rejoice, O Gentiles with his people." Similarly R. H. Bell, "Deuteronomy 32 and the Origin of the Jealousy Motif in Romans 9−11," in *Provoked to Jealousy: The Origin and Purpose of the Jealousy Motif in Romans 9−11* (WUNT 2/63; Tübingen: Mohr Siebeck, 1994), 259. Apparently Paul deemed the LXX version of Deuteronomy 32:43 to be authoritative Scripture.

Rejoice, O heavens with him,
>and bow down to him, all sons of God.
Rejoice, O nations, with his people.
>And let all the messengers of God strengthen themselves.
[See,] the blood of his sons he will avenge,
>and he will avenge and take vengeance on his enemies.
He will pay back those who hate him,
>and atone for the land of his people.

The switch from first person forms in verse 42 to third person in verse 43 signals a shift in speaker from Yahweh (vv. 37−42) to the poet. The object of praise is not named, but Yahweh is referred to at least twelve times, eight explicitly by means of pronominal suffixes on nouns, and four implicitly in third person singular verbs, to which we should add the phrases "sons of *God*" and "messengers of *God*." These features keep the attention focused squarely on Yahweh. The way the coda refers to Israel reinforces this interpretation. Considering the complete collapse of the relationship between deity and nation in verses 15−25, the fact that the nation should be referred to as "his children"[108] and "his people" alone is cause for celebration, for it declares that the promise of verse 36a−b has been fulfilled.

The opening lines identify the addressees as "heavens" and "all sons of God." This correlation expressions suggests *šāmayim* ("heavens") abbreviates "all the host of heaven" (4:19; 17:3) and refers to "celestial beings,"[109] who are called on to shout in celebration and to prostrate themselves before Yahweh in submission and homage. Here the "sons of God" are residents of the heavens (cf. v. 8; 4:19). Their role as agents of divine providence among the peoples is reinforced in line 4, which identifies them as "messengers of God." However, they may not compete with Yahweh for the affections of his people. The Song invites these heavenly beings to celebrate with Israel, acknowledging Yahweh's role in punishing his (and Israel's) enemies and in renewing his relationship with his people. Line 3 invites the nations to join Yahweh's people in the celebration.

In the last four lines the hearers turn their sights from the heavenly scene to the earthly. The lines are arranged chiastically, with the outside cola focusing on Yahweh's actions on Israel's behalf and the inside lines dealing with their enemies. This arrangement highlights the echo of verse 41c−d and its function as a shorthand expression for Yahweh's fuller decla-

---

108. MT reads "his servants."

109. On this interpretation also for Ps. 89:5[6] and Job 15:15, see Sanders, *Provenance of Deuteronomy 32*, 250.

ration of his defeat of his adversaries in verses 39–42. The second bicolon presents the other side of the coin. If Yahweh defeats his enemies, he does so in the interests of his people by avenging the blood of his sons and making atonement for his land and his people.[110] The need for atonement for land is created by human blood violently shed (Num. 35:30–34) and unburied corpses (Deut. 21:23) that defile the land—the effects of the slaughter of the Israelites (v. 43c; cf. 25).

Viewed as a whole, verse 43 presents the hosts of heaven and the nations with three reasons to celebrate and pay homage to Yahweh: (1) Yahweh has restored his relationship with Israel; (2) Yahweh has taken vengeance on Israel's (and his own) enemies; (3) Yahweh has made atonement for the land. In so doing he has reversed the earlier dissolution of the tripartite relationship involving deity–nation–people precipitated by Israel's idolatry. This is cause for celebration not only by the Israelite beneficiaries of the divine action—as in this song—but also by the hosts of heaven and the nations, indeed the entire universe.

The Epilogue to Israel's National Anthem (32:44–47)

HAVING QUOTED ISRAEL'S ANTHEM, the narrator draws the reader back to the context in which the Song was delivered. The second half of verse 44 recapitulates 31:30, and verse 45 reiterates the last phrase of 31:30, "until it was finished." But Moses is not content with merely reciting the poem. As Israel's pastor he adds an exhortation in verse 46 for all the assembled people, charging them to take everything he has said with all seriousness. The NIV's "solemnly declare" (or "testify") reiterates 31:20–21 and indicates that the Song serves as "a witness" against the people. Echoing the sequel to the Shema in 6:6–9, Moses emphasizes how seriously they must take his instruction. From the inside out they are to commit themselves to all the words with which he has admonished them, and they are to pass on all his teachings to their children, charging them to keep all the words of this Torah by doing them.

In verse 47 Moses reiterates the importance for Israel's future of heeding his instruction. Stated negatively, they are not to treat his teaching as frivolous or trivial; stated positively, Moses' words are the keys to Israel's life; their existence in the land they are about to enter depends on their commitment to these words (cf. 6:24–25; 30:20; 31:12–13). In identifying his words with the revelation of God, Moses provides his people with the key to their future.

---

110. The verb *kippēr* ("to atone for, to cleanse") occurs elsewhere in Deuteronomy only in 21:8.

ECHOES OF THE SONG in the Old Testament. Having worked our way through the Song, we may now look back first and see how it fits into the overall program and message of Deuteronomy. Although many argue that the Song is textually erratic,[111] its conceptual framework is clearly at home in the theology of the book.[112] Of the nine characteristic Deuteronomic themes identified by Weinfeld,[113] six are clearly represented in this song:[114] (1) the struggle against idolatry (vv. 8–9, 15–18, 21, 37); (2) Israel's election, exodus, and covenant (vv. 9–11, 15, 18); (3) the monotheistic creed (vv. 4, 12, 39); (4) observance of the Torah and loyalty to the covenant (vv. 13–15); (5) inheritance of the land (vv. 13–15); (6) retribution and material motivation (vv. 19–20, 22–27, 41–43).

Some attribute the differences in language and the addition of new tenets in the Torah of Deuteronomy to the temporal distance of several centuries between the Song and the rest of the book,[115] but these may just as well be attributed to the genre and functions of the texts. Whereas the Torah is cast as a series of addresses to be read privately by the king (17:18–20) and publicly at least every seven years (31:9–13), this song is by definition a poem, composed to be sung or recited in liturgical contexts and/or sung as the national anthem wherever the people live. The embedding of the Song in Moses' sermons is deliberate, reminding the reader in memorable lyric form of the gospel that he has been promulgating. Far from functioning as a loosely connected appendix, this song rings in our ears as a glorious summary of Moses' preaching.

Whereas echoes of the Decalogue, the basic covenantal document, are rare in the Old Testament, echoes of the Song embedded in Deuteronomy 32 are ubiquitous. The psalmists speak of the futility of idols with particular poignancy and sarcasm. While the vocabulary is slightly different, Psalm

---

111. See the discussion on pages 746–49..

112. For full defense of this view, see now A. Lee, "The Narrative Function of the Song of Moses in the Contents of Deuteronomy and Genesis-Kings" (D.Phil. diss.; University of Gloucestershire, 2010).

113. Weinfeld, *DDS*, 1.

114. See the discussion by S. Schweitzer, "Deuteronomy 32 and 33 as Proto-Deuteronomic Texts," *Proceedings EGL & MWBS* 22 (2002): 82–89. The only missing elements are the centralization of the cult, fulfillment of prophecy, and the election of the Davidic dynasty. Contra J. Pakkala ("The Date of the Oldest Edition of Deuteronomy," *ZAW* 3 [2009]: 388–401), the absence of these features suggests a date of composition prior to the establishment of the monarchy rather than in the Persian period.

115. Schweitzer, "Deuteronomy 32 and 33," 86.

115:1−8 offers commentary on this text, beginning by ascribing glory to the name of Yahweh (115:1a),[116] celebrating his attributes of covenant loyalty (*ḥesed*) (v. 1b),[117] bringing in the nations who say, "Where is their God?" (v. 2), declaring his absolute freedom and sovereignty (v. 3),[118] and then describing the absurdity of idols:

> But their idols are silver and gold,
>> made by the hands of men.
> They have mouths, but cannot speak,
>> eyes, but they cannot see;
> they have ears, but cannot hear,
>> noses, but they cannot smell;
> they have hands, but cannot feel,
>> feet, but they cannot walk;
>> nor can they utter a sound with their throats.
> Those who make them will be like them,
>> and so will all who trust in them. (vv. 4−8)

Borrowing is equally evident in Psalm 135, which begins by calling for praise to the name of Yahweh (v. 1−3; cf. Deut. 32:3−4), declaring Yahweh's election of Jacob for himself and Israel's status as his treasured possession (v. 4), stating his greatness and absolute freedom and sovereignty (v. 5), employing elements from his treasuries (v. 7; cf. Deut. 32:34), quoting verbatim Deuteronomy 32:36, "For the LORD will vindicate his people and have compassion on his servants" (v. 14), and repeating the mockery of idols found in Psalm 115 (quoted above).

The celebration of Israel's special status, the spoof of idolatry, and the declaration of Israel's ultimate restoration in Isaiah 44 is laced with echoes of this song: (1) Jacob's election and formation from the womb (44:1−2; cf. Deut. 32:8−9, 18); (2) the affectionate epithet, Jeshurun (44:2; cf. Deut. 32:15); (3) the declaration that there is no god besides Yahweh (44:8; cf. Deut. 32:39); (4) the lithic epithet, "the Rock" (44:8; cf. Deut. 32:4, 15, 31); (5) the mockery of idols, which turn out to be lies in people's hands (44:9−20; cf. Deut. 32:15−17, 21, 37); (6) the announcement of Israel's restoration (44:21−27), specifically confirming the word of his servant (44:26), which alludes to the promissory ending of the Song (Deut. 32:36, 43); and (7) the appeal to the cosmos, including the heavens, to join in the celebration of Israel's restoration (44:23; cf. Deut. 32:43a).

---

116. Cf. Deut. 32:3, where the poet proclaims the name of Yahweh and ascribes greatness to him.

117. Cf. Deut. 32:4, where the poet ascribes faithfulness and righteousness to him.

118. "Our God is in heaven; he does whatever pleases him" summarizes Deut. 32:38−42.

The influence of the Song is evident in the prophets, particularly Isaiah,[119] Jeremiah,[120] and Ezekiel.[121] This is most striking in Ezekiel 16, which adapts and transforms the Song's portrayal of the rise, demise, and ultimate restoration of Israel into a powerful oracle of grace, judgment, and hope. Although Ezekiel's primary concern in this chapter is Israel's spiritual harlotry, by borrowing themes and vocabulary from Deuteronomy 32 and imitating the plot structure of the Song, he has confirmed its role as a "witness" for Yahweh and against Israel and transformed it into a powerful rhetorical device.[122] If Israel goes into exile—and she does—it is because Yahweh has fulfilled his covenant threats (28:15–68) and made good on the warning embedded in Israel's national anthem.

Post–Old Testament testimony. While prophets marshaled the Song's words of judgment to warn the people of the consequences of their rebellion and to encourage reform[123] in the nation's darkest hours, to the faithful this song will have inspired great hope. Second Maccabees 7 preserves a striking illustration of the latter. In the face of torture for refusing to transgress the Torah of the ancestors, people encouraged each other with the words of Deuteronomy 32:36: "The Lord God is watching over us and in truth has compassion on us, as Moses declared in his song that bore witness against the people to their faces, when he said, 'And he will have compassion on his servants'" (v. 6; cf. v. 36).[124] As noted earlier, we may only speculate on how the Song might have been used liturgically in early Israelite worship. Josephus offers interesting insight into an early Jewish tradition:

> He [Moses] recited to them a poem in hexameter verse, which he has moreover bequeathed in a book preserved in the temple, containing a prediction of future events, in accordance with which all

---

119. See Bergey, "The Song of Moses (Deuteronomy 32.1–43) and Isaianic Prophecies," 33–54; also Nigosian, "The Song of Moses (DT 32)," 5–7.

120. See W. Holladay, "Jeremiah and Moses: Further Observations," *JBL* 85 (1966): 17–27.

121. For an examination of the influence of the Song on the portrayal of the nations in Ezekiel see B. Gosse, "Deutéronome 32,1–43 et les redaction des livre d'Ezéchiel et d'Isaïe," *ZAW* 107 (1995): 110–17.

122. For a detailed discussion of the links, see J. Gile, "Ezekiel 16 and the Song of Moses: A Prophetic Transformation," *JBL* 130 (2011): 87–108.

123. J. R. Lundbom argues that Josiah based his reforms strictly on Huldah's interpretation of the Song. See "Lawbook of the Josianic Reform," *CBQ* 38 (1976): 293–302. However, whether it was the Torah (chaps. 4–28) or the Song, these documents complement each other.

124. Cf. A. van der Kooij, "The Use of the Greek Bible in II Maccabees," *JNWSL* 25 (1999): 131.

has come and is coming to pass, the seer having in no whit strayed from the truth. All these books he consigned to the priests, together with the ark, in which he had deposited the Ten Words written on two tablets, and the tabernacle. (*Ant.* 4.8.44)

According to rabbinic tradition, Levites would read portions of the Song in the temple on the Sabbath over a six-week cycle, while worshipers presented their additional offerings; when they came to the end, they would repeat the cycle.[125] Since a separate scroll apparently containing only Deuteronomy 32 has surfaced in Qumran (4QDeutq),[126] it seems this text was used separately either as part of a liturgy or for instructional purposes. That the Song's influence carries over into the New Testament is evident from Paul's quotation of Deuteronomy 32:43 (LXX) in Romans 15:10 and his development of the motif of "jealousy" in Romans 9—11.[127]

While Israel's poets and prophets obviously did not forget the national anthem, if the people ever sang it or participated in liturgical performances involving the Song, this must have quickly become a mere ritual, because it did not keep the Israelites on course with Yahweh. Despite Yahweh's and Moses' efforts to keep the Song ringing in their ears and recited on their lips, it did not take long for them to trample underfoot his grace and to abandon their Rock in favor of the worthless "pebbles" of the nations.

THE POWER OF MUSIC. What is the enduring theological significance of the Song? The question may be addressed at several levels. At the literary level, this chapter testifies to the power of music not only to express lofty theological ideas, but also to shape people's lives. In a sense we are what we sing or what we play. If we would understand another culture, the first step is not to read essays about it by dispassionate observers, but to listen to the music, to feel the rhythm of its songs, to hear the story of its poetry.

This is no less true of the church than of the cultures of the people who make up the church. Luther said, "If any would not sing and talk of what Christ has wrought for us, he shows thereby that he does not really believe." However, Luther misunderstood Old Testament worship completely when he added, "and that he belongs not into the New Testament,

---

125. For references, see Tigay, *Deuteronomy*, 546, n. 35.

126. See P. Skehan, "A Fragment of the 'Song of Moses' (Deut 32) from Qumran," *BASOR* 136 (1954): 12—15.

127. See further, Bell, *Provoked to Jealousy*, 259.

which is an era of joy, but into the Old, which produces not the spirit of joy, but of unhappiness and discontent."[128] In keeping with the spirit of worship in chapters 12, 14, and 26, this song was given to Israel to testify to them not only of the God with whom they were related by covenant, but also of themselves and their own proclivity to unbelief and to going their own way. Whereas to this point in their history Moses had kept them on course spiritually and theologically, when they would be dispersed to their tribal allotments, no central leader could perform this function anymore.

But if a leader cannot accompany all the people to all their scattered territories, a song can. God's people should be characterized not only by enthusiastic song, but also by a song that goes beyond slogans and sound bites and empty repetitions, such as characterize the music of the world (Matt. 6:7). The song of God's people must declare God's just sovereignty over the universe, rehearse the history of God's grace to his people, offer frank assessments of our own condition, warn us against the folly of forgetfulness and idolatry, and give us hope for the future. Deuteronomy 32 was that kind of gift to Israel.

Theology. At the theological level, the Song is unparalleled within the book of Deuteronomy, if not the entire Old Testament, for its concentrated but extraordinarily lofty theology. That theology is presented in several ways.

1. Through names and epithets of Yahweh: He is Yahweh (v. 3, etc.), our God (v. 3), the Rock (vv. 4, 15, 18, 30, 31), El (v. 4), Father (v. 6), Elyon (v. 8), and the One and Only (v. 39).
2. Through recitation of his attributes: He is great (v. 3), faithful (v. 4), lacking any fault (v. 4), righteous (v. 4), upright (v. 4), impassioned (vv. 16, 21), provoked (v. 20), angry (v. 22), and compassionate (v. 36).
3. Through rehearsal of his cosmic actions: He divides the population of the earth into peoples, places them in the charge of his heavenly agents, allocates the lands to the nations (v. 8), and uses the forces of nature in acts of judgment (vv. 31–42). When he acts against the nations, he does so in defense of his own honor and out of compassion for his people.
4. Through rehearsal of his actions on behalf of his people: He created them and established them (v. 6), he fathered them (18), out of all the nations he chose them for a special relationship with himself (v. 9), he rescued them in the desert (v. 10), he cared for them

---

128. In his preface to the *Velentin Babst Gesangbuch* (1545), as cited in W. E. Buzsin, "Luther on Music," *Musical Quarterly* 32 (1946): 83.

(vv. 10–11), he lavishly provided for them (vv. 12–14), he is their Savior (v. 15), he punishes them (vv. 20–25), he rescues them from the enemy (vv. 26–42), and he makes atonement for his land and his people (v. 43).

These are all worthy reasons to praise the Lord!

Assessment of the human condition. The Song presents a frank assessment of the human condition, especially our propensity to trample underfoot God's grace by refusing to give thanks, and if we recognize our dependence on higher powers, to bow down to idols that are pathetic figments of the human imagination. John Calvin taught us centuries ago that human nature is "a perpetual factory of idols."[129]

But what are idols? Are they limited to three-dimensional images erected in sanctuaries for worship? In our world, where television shows like *American Idol* annually present new objects of adulation to millions of viewers, the word has come to be associated primarily with musicians and other entertainers who have won the adulation and dervish devotion of their fans. While our text does not define the word "idolatry," it declares that idolatry (1) is evidence of a corrupt, warped, and twisted culture (v. 5); (2) infects us when we forget our origins in the undeserved and gracious acts of God (vv. 6–15, 18); (3) is an irrational and foolish response to our environment (vv. 16–18, 21); (4) is incompatible with true faith and inevitably provokes the wrath of God (vv. 19–22); and (5) is treachery of the highest order, replacing confidence in and loyalty to the Rock, the only God who exists and who alone exercises sovereign control over the universe (vv. 39–41) for pathetic pebbles, which have no power at all, and whose spiritual significance is an illusion.

Modern Westerners do not tend to bow down to physical images, but idols are not limited to physical representations of deities. An idol is anything that robs God of our devotion and in which we trust, to which we look for significance, meaning, and security. The idols of our day include money, pleasure, beauty, science, human reason, and power.[130] Job's description of idolatry is not only brilliant, but also modern:

---

129. John Calvin, *Institutes of the Christian Religion* (ed. J. T. McNeill; trans. F. L. Battles; LCC 20; London: SCM, 1960), 1:108. This entire chapter (11) is devoted to a repudiation of images of the divine, responding particularly to images in Roman Catholic worship.

130. For a powerful critique of contemporary idolatry, see Timothy Keller, *Counterfeit Gods: The Empty Promises of Money, Sex, and Power, and the Only Hope that Matters* (New York: Dutton, 2009). See also his address, "The Grand Demythologizer: The Gospel and Idolatry," at www.thegospelcoalition.org/resources/video/The-Grand-Demythologizer-The-Gospel-and-Idolatry. See also the classic treatment by the seventeenth-century Puritan David Clarkson, "Soul Idolatry Excludes Men out of Heaven," in *The Works of David Clarkson* (Carlisle, PA: Banner of Truth Trust, 1988 [reprint of 1864 edition]), 2:299–333.

. If I have put my trust in gold
    or said to pure gold, "You are my security,"
if I have rejoiced over my great wealth,
    the fortune my hands had gained,
if I have regarded the sun in its radiance
    or the moon moving in splendor,
so that my heart was secretly enticed
    and my hand offered them a kiss of homage,
then these also would be sins to be judged,
    for I would have been unfaithful to God on high. (Job
    31:24—28)

In our day, when tolerance of alternative beliefs is touted as the highest virtue, the message of this song is as offensive as the Supreme Command, the first "word" of the Decalogue. The exclusiveness of Yahwism in the ancient Israelite context is matched only by the exclusivist message of the New Testament. In orthodox Yahwism Yahweh brooks no rivals; similarly, the gospel declares that salvation is found only in Christ (John 14:6; Acts 4:12).

Glorious hope. Finally, for individuals who flounder and for a church that has lost its way, this passage offers glorious hope. Yes, rebellion and ingratitude must be punished, but we may find hope in God's covenant commitment and his great compassion, which in Christ triumphs over his wrath. For the church and for humanity, the judgment will not be the last word; we look forward to the day when the entire universe will be transformed into a symphony of praise to God. Through the work of Christ, God has rendered vengeance on all the forces of evil and made atonement for his people (cf. v. 43).

Deuteronomy 32:48–52

On that same day the LORD told Moses, ⁴⁹"Go up into the Abarim Range to Mount Nebo in Moab, across from Jericho, and view Canaan, the land I am giving the Israelites as their own possession. ⁵⁰There on the mountain that you have climbed you will die and be gathered to your people, just as your brother Aaron died on Mount Hor and was gathered to his people. ⁵¹This is because both of you broke faith with me in the presence of the Israelites at the waters of Meribah Kadesh in the Desert of Zin and because you did not uphold my holiness among the Israelites. ⁵²Therefore, you will see the land only from a distance; you will not enter the land I am giving to the people of Israel."

FOLLOWING A NARRATIVE INTRODUCTION, this paragraph is cast entirely as divine speech. The opening phrase, "on that same day," ties the Song with Moses' preparations for his demise, which he had anticipated in his first address (3:23–28) and more recently in 31:2. Yahweh himself had announced Moses' death in 31:14–15, but to this point he has focused on its implications for the people. Given Moses' role in the divine agenda, it is fitting that the last words we hear from Yahweh's mouth in Moses' lifetime are directed to his agent.

By modern Western standards, this speech is strange. The tone of the first part seems matter-of-fact, if not calloused. Instead of expressing gratitude for the work Moses has done for Yahweh's people during the past forty years, Yahweh's tone is accusatory, reminding him of his infidelity at Meribah Kadesh and reiterating that he will not enter the land. The negative nature of this speech becomes even more apparent when it is compared with Numbers 27:12–14, which the narrator seems to have adapted here. This address is twice as long as the earlier version, and the additions here affect the tone dramatically. The skeleton of the speech is represented by the quartette of commands: "go up," "view," "die," "be gathered" (vv. 49–51). It concludes with a climactic indicative statement (v. 52), which must have been the most painful of all.

(1) The first of Yahweh's commands is to climb Mount Nebo (v. 49a). The mountain is identified here by two names (cf. "Mount Pisgah" in 3:27).

The article and the plural form ("Abarim") suggest the name refers not to a single point but to the range of mountains east of the Dead Sea between the Arnon Gorge and Wadi Hesban. Mount Nebo (modern Jebel en-Nebu) itself rises 2,739 feet above sea level, providing an excellent location from which to view the whole land. In 34:1 the note that Moses ascends from the Plains of Moab to Mount Nebo, to the top of "[the] Pisgah," across from Jericho, clarifies the relationship between Nebo and Pisgah. As noted on 3:27, since *pisgâ* always occurs with the article, this is likely a common noun, meaning something like "the ridge," perhaps the ridge of which Nebo is the peak.

(2) Yahweh invites Moses to view the Promised Land (v. 49b). Technically, the verb "view" is an imperative, though here it also functions as an invitation to Moses to receive his consolation prize, namely, to see the Promised Land (cf. 3:27). This is obviously small consolation, for while it would concretize for him the completion of his mission, it would also concretize his loss, as he gazes on what might have been. This is the only reference to "the land of Canaan" in the book (i.e., "Canaan" used as a geographic name). Whereas elsewhere in the land grant formula, Moses had always spoken of national territories as their "grant of land" (or "inheritance") or their "possession" (*yᵉrušśâ*), referring to it as a "holding" (*ᵃḥuzzâ*; NIV "possession") links this passage with Leviticus 25:45 and Numbers 32:5, 22, 29.

(3) Yahweh instructs Moses to die on the mountain (v. 50a). This extraordinary command is matched elsewhere only by Job's wife's order for her husband (Job 2:9). Moses' forty-year investment in Yahweh's mission did not exempt him from the fate that inevitably strikes all. He too must submit to the one and only God, who kills and gives life (v. 39).[1]

(4) Yahweh commands Moses to be gathered to his people (v. 50b). The passive form "be gathered to your people" is odd.[2] But the idiom derives from the practice of burying bodies of the deceased in family tombs, together with the remains of those predeceased. Obviously Moses will not be buried in a family tomb, but as was the case with his brother Aaron (cf. Num. 27:13), in death his spirit will join the spirits of kinsfolk in Sheol.

---

1. Cf. Dennis T. Olsen, *Deuteronomy and the Death of Moses* (Minneapolis: Fortress, 1994), 150.

2. With the exception of 2 Kings 22:20 (= 2 Chron. 34:28) this euphemism for death occurs only in the Niphal. The idiom occurs only here in Deuteronomy, but it is common in earlier narratives: with "people": Gen. 25:8, 17; 35:29; 49:29, 33; Num. 20:24; 27:13; 31:2; with "fathers": Judg. 2:10; without prepositional phrase: Num. 20:26; Isa. 57:1.

In verse 51 Yahweh reiterates why Moses may not enter the Promised Land (cf. Num. 20:12; 27:14).[3] While our text does not describe Moses' act of rebellion at Meribah Kadesh, Yahweh interprets it as breaking faith and a failure to recognize his sanctity. The verb for "break faith" (*mâ'al*) in the Old Testament usually refers to Israelite infidelity to Yahweh.[4] In striking the rock Moses had misrepresented Yahweh publicly, violated his own representative role, and failed to respect Yahweh's unique and sacred status. To Yahweh, striking the rock reflected a cavalier disposition toward him, as though Moses could adapt Yahweh's commands as he wanted. Moreover, in relating directly to the rock rather than the Rock, he had committed an idolatrous act.

Yahweh's present indictment highlights the communal implications of Moses' actions; he had publicly failed to uphold Yahweh's holiness. As leader of the people and representative of Yahweh, he had struck the rock when Yahweh had commanded him to speak to it. While his act may have been a gesture of frustration, to God it involved publicly usurping what is otherwise a divine agenda. Remarkably, it worked—water issued from the rock. Moses may have looked like a magician—but it cost him his life and his mission.

The twofold reference in verse 51 to Moses' committing his offense "in the midst of the descendants of Israel" (pers. trans.) reinforces its magnitude in Yahweh's eyes. Specifying that Moses' failure occurred at "Meribah Kadesh in the Desert of Zin"[5] links the act geographically with the people's rebellion (1:19−46; Num. 20:3, 13). While modern interpreters take offense at the harshness of Yahweh's treatment of Moses, the punishment was fair and fitting.[6] If the people were sentenced to die in the desert because they had rebelled against (Deut. 1:26) and refused to trust Yahweh (1:32; Num. 14:11, 23), this should also apply to their leader.

Verse 52 summarizes Yahweh's earlier response to Moses' demand to be permitted to enter the land (3:27). Yahweh's tone is stern. Moses may indeed "see" the land visually, but he may not "experience" it.[7] He is barred entry to

---

3. For discussion of these texts, especially the reason for the exclusion of Moses, see W. Lee, "The Exclusion of Moses from the Promised Land: A Conceptual Approach," in *The Changing Face of Form Criticism for the Twenty-first Century* (ed. M. A. Sweeney and E. Ben Zvi; Grand Rapids: Eerdmans, 2003), 217−39.

4. Numbers 5:6 describes wronging another person in any way as being "unfaithful to the LORD."

5. The Desert of Zin is the region around Kadesh Barnea, forming the southern frontier of the Promised Land.

6. So also Milgrom, *Numbers*, 166.

7. On the verb *râ'â* meaning "to experience," see Esth. 9:26; Lam. 2:16.

the land promised to the ancestors and identified as the goal of this adventure in Yahweh's first encounter with him (Ex. 3:8). The sting of the final clause must have been particularly acute; those who stood before Moses throughout his farewell addresses will enter, but he must remain behind.

TWO SIDES OF MOSES. Who would have thought that Israel's faithlessness in refusing to enter the land would have such dire consequences for Moses? In the end, the man who had twice rejected the status of patriarch and eponymous ancestor and through his intercession secured Israel's survival—at Sinai (Ex. 32:10–14) and Kadesh Barnea (Num. 14:11–24)—was denied the pleasure of seeing Yahweh's grand mission completed. In his first address Moses had blamed the people repeatedly for his own exclusion from the Promised Land (1:37; 3:23–29; 4:15–24). Their lack of confidence in Yahweh (1:32) had led to rebellion (1:26, 43) and had dragged him down with them. However, Yahweh would have none of this blame game. Responsibility for Moses' exclusion from the land rested squarely on his own shoulders.

The contradictions in attribution of blame for Moses not being able to enter the land between Numbers 20:12–13 and Deuteronomy 32:48–52 on the one hand, and Moses' first address in Deuteronomy on the other, are more apparent than real. The first two involve narratives that recount the event from Yahweh's point of view, whereas Moses' earlier statements reflected his own negative disposition toward his people. Both are true. Given the sequence of events as outlined in Numbers, the people could be blamed for Moses' failure to enter the land. Had they trusted Yahweh and moved in from Kadesh Barnea, this event at Meribah Kadesh would never have happened and Moses would not have provoked Yahweh's ire. Indeed, Moses would have enjoyed thirty-eight years of life in the Promised Land.

Later psalmists associated Meribah primarily with the people's rebellion, particularly their refusal to listen to the voice of Yahweh (Pss. 81:7[8]; 95:8; 106:32), but pay little attention to Moses' fate. Psalm 106:32–33 recognizes both sides, though it refers to Moses' sin and to his end only in the vaguest of terms:

By the waters of Meribah they angered the LORD,
    and trouble came to Moses because of them;
for they rebelled against the Spirit of God,
    and rash words came from Moses' lips.

Apart from this reference, neither the Old nor the New Testament ever alludes to Moses' rebellion. Rather, the image of this "servant of the LORD" becomes increasingly idealized. By itself Deuteronomy 32:48–52 paints a rather tarnished picture of Moses, but in the arrangement of the book we observe the narrator's efforts to protect the image of this man. Had chapter 34, which portrays Moses in glowing colors, been placed immediately after this episode—the book would have closed with a conflicted portrait of the man. On the one hand, he was a failure as a leader, who showed contempt for the holiness of Yahweh and proved unable to complete the mission on which he had embarked forty years earlier. On the other hand, he departs as a 120-year-old man whose vigor had not diminished (34:7) and whose image would tower over all the prophets who succeed him (34:9–12). He knew Yahweh and performed signs and wonders "in the sight of all Israel" (34:12) more intimately than any prophet in history.[8]

By inserting the benedictions of chapter 33 in an otherwise coherent narrative, the narrator has ensured that readers close the book with a positive image of the man in their minds. Insofar as Moses is refused entry into the Promised Land, he shares the fate of his people. However, as we will see in 34:6, his ultimate demise is quite different. He does not die in the desert with the generation who refuses to enter the land. He dies alone on Mount Nebo, but in his burial he is honored more than any human in history: he is "gathered to the fathers" by Yahweh himself.

THE BURDEN AND DANGERS of ministry. In this paragraph we observe that the privilege of leadership over God's people comes with a heavy burden. From those who have been given much, much is required (Luke 12:48). Those who are called to lead must lead according to the will of the one who has called them. In this respect, Moses failed at Meribah Kadesh by disregarding the voice of God and giving vent to his own frustration. Concerning his failure, Aaron Wildavsky comments eloquently:

> At Meribah Moses substitutes force for faith. In his hand the rod reduces a divinely ordered act to a trickster's shenanigans. But the import runs deeper. If Moses' strongest leadership quality has been his ability to identify with the people, then the lack of faith at Meribah is a double one. Moses not only distances himself from God by doubting the adequacy of his work but also distances himself from the people by assuming power that was God's. Tired of the incessant

---

8. The statement counterbalances the earlier comment that he failed to treat Yahweh as holy "among the Israelites" (32:51).

murmurings, Moses taunts the people just before he strikes the rock: "Hear now, ye rebels; must we fetch you water from this rock?" (Num 20:10).

Instead of exhorting a stiffnecked people to greater faith, Moses condescends to their plea with an arrogant jeer. His words imply acceptance of the people's evil (separating himself from it) rather than hope of overcoming it. "Ye rebels" assumes very much what Aaron had presumed in trying to rationalize fashioning the Golden Calf. At that point, Aaron had lamely pleaded for Moses' sympathy: "thou knowest thy people, that they are set on mischief" (Exod. 32:22). Like Aaron's defense then, Moses' "Hear now, ye rebels" now becomes its own accusation. Similarly Moses taunts the people with rebelliousness, yet is himself rebelling when he smites the rock without authority — the authority God alone can provide. Perhaps, after all, Moses does have more authority than he, or any man, can handle.[9]

Wildavsky adds that in usurping divine authority, Moses has become guilty of the worst form of idolatry — self-worship.

The language the Scriptures associate with Moses' actions with respect to the rock is telling: not trusting in Yahweh (Num. 20:12), treachery or breaking faith (Deut. 32:51), speaking rash words (Ps. 106:33), but particularly a refusal to defend the holiness of Yahweh before the people (Num. 20:12; Deut. 32:51). When the people accused Moses of engaging in a diabolical plot to destroy them in the desert (Num. 20:3−5), in his self-absorption and his absorption with his own staff (vv. 8−9), he shirked his pastoral duty. Instead of defending the sanctity of Yahweh and demonstrating the power of the divine word (cf. v. 8), he taunted the people (v. 10) and presumptuously flaunted his own power by striking the rock.

In so doing Moses illustrates the dangers of pastoral ministry. Instead of being concerned about the reputation of God and the health of his people, we are often tempted to respond to criticism with idolatrous acts of independence. This always shames the name of the Lord and jeopardizes the success of our efforts within the mission of God. Within the history of that mission those who are called to carry the burden often prove the biggest hindrances. However, we can take heart knowing that ultimately no one is indispensable; God's cosmic mission will be fulfilled by a Leader who is flawless: Jesus Christ, the perfectly righteous one.

---

9. Aaron Wildavsky, *Moses as Political Leader* (Jerusalem: Shalem, 2005), 176.

Deuteronomy 33:1-29

🔥

This is the blessing that Moses the man of God pronounced on the Israelites before his death. ²He said:

"The LORD came from Sinai
    and dawned over them from Seir;
he shone forth from Mount Paran.
He came with myriads of holy ones
    from the south, from his mountain slopes.
³Surely it is you who love the people;
    all the holy ones are in your hand.
At your feet they all bow down,
    and from you receive instruction,
⁴the law that Moses gave us,
    the possession of the assembly of Jacob.
⁵He was king over Jeshurun
    when the leaders of the people assembled,
    along with the tribes of Israel.
⁶"Let Reuben live and not die,
    nor his men be few."

⁷And this he said about Judah:

"Hear, O LORD, the cry of Judah;
    bring him to his people.
With his own hands he defends his cause.
    Oh, be his help against his foes!"

⁸About Levi he said:

"Your Thummim and Urim belong
    to the man you favored.
You tested him at Massah;
    you contended with him at the waters of Meribah.
⁹He said of his father and mother,
    'I have no regard for them.'
He did not recognize his brothers
    or acknowledge his own children,
but he watched over your word
    and guarded your covenant.
¹⁰He teaches your precepts to Jacob
    and your law to Israel.

He offers incense before you
     and whole burnt offerings on your altar.
[11]Bless all his skills, O LORD,
     and be pleased with the work of his hands.
Smite the loins of those who rise up against him;
     strike his foes till they rise no more."

[12]About Benjamin he said:

"Let the beloved of the LORD rest secure in him,
     for he shields him all day long,
     and the one the LORD loves rests between his shoulders."

[13]About Joseph he said:

"May the LORD bless his land
     with the precious dew from heaven above
     and with the deep waters that lie below;
[14]with the best the sun brings forth
     and the finest the moon can yield;
[15]with the choicest gifts of the ancient mountains
     and the fruitfulness of the everlasting hills;
[16]with the best gifts of the earth and its fullness
     and the favor of him who dwelt in the burning bush.
Let all these rest on the head of Joseph,
     on the brow of the prince among his brothers.
[17]In majesty he is like a firstborn bull;
     his horns are the horns of a wild ox.
With them he will gore the nations,
     even those at the ends of the earth.
Such are the ten thousands of Ephraim;
     such are the thousands of Manasseh."

[18]About Zebulun he said:

"Rejoice, Zebulun, in your going out,
     and you, Issachar, in your tents.
[19]They will summon peoples to the mountain
     and there offer sacrifices of righteousness;
they will feast on the abundance of the seas,
     on the treasures hidden in the sand."

[20]About Gad he said:

"Blessed is he who enlarges Gad's domain!
     Gad lives there like a lion,

tearing at arm or head.
²¹He chose the best land for himself;
the leader's portion was kept for him.
When the heads of the people assembled,
he carried out the LORD's righteous will,
and his judgments concerning Israel."

²²About Dan he said:

"Dan is a lion's cub,
springing out of Bashan."

²³About Naphtali he said:

"Naphtali is abounding with the favor of the LORD
and is full of his blessing;
he will inherit southward to the lake."

²⁴About Asher he said:

"Most blessed of sons is Asher;
let him be favored by his brothers,
and let him bathe his feet in oil.
²⁵The bolts of your gates will be iron and bronze,
and your strength will equal your days.

²⁶"There is no one like the God of Jeshurun,
who rides on the heavens to help you
and on the clouds in his majesty.
²⁷The eternal God is your refuge,
and underneath are the everlasting arms.
He will drive out your enemy before you,
saying, 'Destroy him!'
²⁸So Israel will live in safety alone;
Jacob's spring is secure
in a land of grain and new wine,
where the heavens drop dew.
²⁹Blessed are you, O Israel!
Who is like you,
a people saved by the LORD?
He is your shield and helper
and your glorious sword.
Your enemies will cower before you,
and you will trample down their high places."

MOSES' DEATH LOOMS OVER the congregation of Israel and the book of Deuteronomy. Having delivered his final pastoral addresses, installed Joshua as successor, taught the people the Song, and received Yahweh's command to climb Mount Nebo, all that remains in the extended liturgical event reflected by Deuteronomy is the blessing of the congregation.

As noted in the previous unit, chapter 34 flows smoothly after 32:52, which suggests that the benedictions in chapter 33 were delivered earlier and inserted here to buffer Yahweh's negative evaluation of Moses in 32:48–52 from the narrator's own eulogy in 34:1–12. Despite the bitterness toward the people and God expressed in Moses' first address, and Yahweh's predictions of Israel's spiritual recidivism as soon as Moses will pass from the scene (31:16–21), Israel's pastor is able to look beyond his personal disappointments and the fickleness of the people to their future in the Promised Land.

Although Deuteronomy 33 is cast in elegant ancient Hebrew poetry, this composition differs markedly from chapter 32. (1) Whereas the surrounding prose treats the Song as integral to the narrative, the benediction is only loosely related to the context by a chronological note fixing the occasion of the utterance (33:1). (2) Whereas the Song functioned as a "witness" (31:19, 21) *for* Yahweh and *against* Israel, the prose preamble identifies this poem generically as a "blessing," which functions *for* Israel.[1] (3) Whereas the Song has a cohesive story line, Deuteronomy 33 consists of a series of benedictory fragments strung together like a string of pearls. (4) Whereas the Song was concerned with Israel as a whole, here the focus is on individual tribes. (5) Although the theology of the opening exordium (vv. 2–5) and concluding coda (vv. 26–29) compare with the exordium and coda of the Song, the intervening blessings focus on Yahweh's role in guaranteeing the well-being of individual tribes.

Despite these differences, this chapter resembles the Song in exhibiting a mixture of archaic grammatical and syntactical features and features characteristic of later Hebrew. This makes it difficult to date the blessings based on the language,[2] and we are driven back to the poem itself to determine

---

1. B. Kelly prefers a more neutral label, "tribal sayings," because some of these "blessings" do not bless: "Quantitative Analysis of the Tribal Sayings in Deuteronomy 33 and Its Significance for the Poem's Overall Structure," in *Milk and Honey: Essays on Ancient Israel and the Bible in Appreciation of the Judaic Studies Program at the University of California, San Diego* (ed. S. Malena and D. Miano; Winona Lake, IN: Eisenbrauns, 2007), 54.

2. The following represent the major variations in dating: (1) eleventh century BC: F. M. Cross and D. N. Freedman, "The Blessing of Moses," *JBL* 67 (1948): 192; C. J. Labuschagne,

the most likely context for its composition. The portrait of corporate Israel as an assembly of tribes idealistically united under the kingship of Yahweh in the land (vv. 26–29) and the romantic portrayal of individual tribes point to an early premonarchic date. If this chapter consists of fragments of originally separate pronouncements, their present arrangement based on geographical location may suggest a post-settlement context, when the Danites were established in the north. While deuteronomistic language is subdued, the text incorporates no fewer than seven of the nine tenets identified by scholars as deuteronomistic.[3] As with chapter 32, the chapter's linguistic character suggests it was composed early, but it has undergone some linguistic and grammatical updating.

Deuteronomy 33 exhibits several marks of intentional and artful design. (1) The tribal benedictions are framed by hymnic pieces virtually identical in size (33:1–5, 26–29). (2) Within the collection of blessings, Levi and Joseph represent the tribal center of gravity, receiving as much attention as all the rest combined. This interest not only anticipates the future religious and political significance of these tribes, but also reflects their significance within Israel in the recent past (cf. Gen. 45–50; Ex. 32:25–29; Num. 25:7–13).[4] At the same time, given the tribe of Judah's later significance of the Davidic monarchy and its separate existence as a nation, the relatively little attention that Judah receives is striking.

The poetic blessing of Jacob in Genesis 49 provides the closest analogue to Deuteronomy 33. Although these two texts display several formal and thematic similarities, they also exhibit significant differences. Whereas the blessings of Genesis 49 are addressed to Jacob's immediate sons, these blessings are addressed to the tribes of Israel. Whereas Genesis 49 tends to cast the blessings as predictions of the future, here they are cast largely in the jussive as wishes for the future. Whereas Genesis 49 lists the tribes more or less according to the birth order and rank of Jacob's sons, here the order

---

"The Tribes in the Blessing of Moses," in *Language and Meaning: Studies in Hebrew Language and Biblical Exegesis: Papers Read at the Joint British-Dutch Old Testament Conference Held at London, 1973* (ed. J. Barr et al.; OtSt 19; Leiden: Brill, 1974), 101. (2) Ninth to eighth century BC: von Rad, *Deuteronomy*, 208; Nelson, *Deuteronomy*, 387; R. J. Tournay, "Le psaume et les benedictions de Moïse," *RevB* 103 (1996); 196–212 (time of Jeroboam II). (3) Sixth century BC or later: S. Beyerle, *Der Mosesegen im Deuteronomium* (BZAW 250; Berlin/New York: de Gruyter, 1997), 275–85.

3. S. Schweitzer "Deuteronomy 32 and 33 as Proto-Deuteronomic Texts," *Proceedings EGL & MWBS* 22 (2002): 87.

4. According to Kelly ("Quantitative Analysis," 60–61) the tribal sayings minus v. 21 (a "divider") consist of 70 cola averaging seven syllables each in length, symbolic of all Israel gathered before Moses. This fits with Freedman's observation that the exordium and coda (minus the peroration, v. 29b) each consist of fourteen lines.

seems to be affected by geography. Perhaps because Simeon's allotment was within the territory of Judah, Moses has no blessing for this tribe.[5]

Introduction and Exordium (33:1–5)

THE NARRATIVE PREAMBLE (V. 1) reminds readers that what follows is part of Moses' preparations for his death. In contrast to leaders of the peoples around Israel, Moses is not concerned about his personal legacy.[6] As Israel's pastor and virtual father of this large household, he takes great pains to ensure the well-being of those who survive him.[7] Explicitly classified a "blessing" (*bᵉrâkâ*), these utterances involve pronouncements of goodwill and invocations of divine favor on the tribes. Typically the favors invoked in such blessings revolve around fertility, status, peace, and security.[8]

Remarkably the narrator introduces Moses in relation to God rather than the people; he was "the man of God."[9] Although the phrase refers primarily to a person's official standing with Yahweh, it is ambiguous and may also describe his character: Moses was a "godly man." Placed immediately after Yahweh's characterization of Moses as one who had broken faith with him and had not treated him as holy (32:51), the epithet reflects the narrator's admiration for the man.

The exordium proper takes up verses 2–5, portraying Yahweh in glorious theophanic form, coming from the mountains in the desert, presumably to deliver his people and to be acknowledged as king over all the tribes of Israel. Verse 2 describes in cryptic form the divine warrior's appearance to Israel. In this and other poems celebrating Yahweh's military actions,[10] he

---

5. Simeon was involved (with his brother Levi) in the treacherous affair involving Dinah and the Shechemites (Gen. 34:25), and the idolatry and immorality at Baal Peor (Num. 25:6–15). After the opening chapter of Judges, the tribe of Simeon is named only twice in the narratives of the Old Testament (2 Chron. 15:9; 34:6).

6. On the place of the blessings in Old Testament death narratives, see Cribb, *Speaking on the Brink of Sheol.*

7. The perception of Moses as patriarch in the tradition of Abraham, Isaac, and Jacob dates back to the golden calf incident at Sinai, when Yahweh offered to destroy the nation and start his program over with Moses as the head and presumptive eponymous ancestor of his people (Ex. 32:10). Although Moses rejected this offer, Yahweh later declared that he had made his covenant *with Moses* and Israel (34:27–28), and he publicly demonstrated Moses' special role by having his own glory radiate from Moses whenever he came from an appointment with him (34:29–35).

8. See the emphases in the blessings of Deut. 28:1–14.

9. Cf. Josh. 14:6; Ezra 3:2; Ps. 90:1. This epithet was also used of David (Neh. 12:24, 36), and in later texts often functions as a title for prophets (see 1 Sam. 9:7–10; 1 Kings 12:22; 13:4–31 [14x]; 17:18; 20:28; 2 Kings 1:9–13 [5x]; 4:7–40 [10x]). Targum Neofiti reads "prophet of Yahweh" (Deut. 33:1).

10. See Ex. 15:1–18; Judg. 5:2–5; Ps. 68:7–10[8–11]; Hab. 3:2–15.

fights on Israel's behalf, rescuing them from enemies who hold them in bondage (Egypt) and who interfere in their march toward destiny (Amalekites, Moabites, Amorites, etc.). Accompanied by his heavenly host, nothing can stop him.

Moses identifies the place from which Yahweh comes by three names: Sinai,[11] Seir,[12] and Mount Paran.[13] To Moses and his people these names refer to the mountainous region to the south, where they had experienced the glory of Yahweh thirty-eight years ago. But here Yahweh's appearance is a military moment.[14] His movements are described with three verbs: he "came" from Sinai, he "dawned" on Israel from Seir, and he "shone forth" from Mount Paran. While the second verb normally applies to the rising of the sun, it may also apply to dawning light more generally.[15] The verb "to shine forth" is relatively rare, being used elsewhere primarily of Yahweh's glory radiating from him.[16]

The last two lines of verse 2 are difficult in Hebrew, but we should interpret what is actually a singular ("holy one") as a collective designation for the "holy ones" (cf. NIV), which occurs in verse 3. These "holy ones" are the angelic host who serve Yahweh in his heavenly court and accompany the divine warrior as a royal entourage.[17] The word *ʾšdt* in the last line is problematic. Although MT vocalizes it as two words (*ʾēš* and *dât*, "fire" and "law") and its marginal note instructs readers to pronounce it as two,[18] the

---

11. This is the only occurrence of the name Sinai in the book, which has always referred to the mountain of revelation as Horeb (1:2, 6, 19; 4:10, 15; 5:2; 9:8; 18:16; 29:1[28:69]). Based on this text and Judg. 5:4−5 some argue for locating Sinai in Arabia. See R. S. Hendel, "Where Is Mount Sinai?" *BRev* 16 (2000): 8.

12. This is the region south of the Dead Sea (1:44; 2:1, 4−5, 8, 12, 22, 29), though the Israelites also applied this name to the eastern Negev (cf. 1:2, 44; Num. 20:16). On Seir, see E. A. Knauf, "Seir," *ABD*, 5:1072−74.

13. The location of Mount Paran is uncertain, but the name probably refers to a peak or highland region in the desert of Paran, mentioned in 1:1.

14. On the portrayal of Yahweh as the divine warrior in this text, see P. D. Miller Jr., "Two Critical Notes on Psalm 68 and Deuteronomy 33," *HTR* 56 (1964): 241−43.

15. Isa. 60:2 echoes the present metaphorical use of the expression for a glorious theophanic appearance of Yahweh

16. Pss. 50:2; 80:1[2]; 94:1; Job 3:4.

17. Ps. 68:5−8[6−9] offers commentary on this verse.

18. The marginal note in the Aleppo Codex is even more explicit: "written as one word and read as two words." Thus R. C. Steiner, "דָּת and עָיִן: Two Verbs Masquerading as Nouns in Moses' Blessing (Deuteronomy 33:2, 28)," *JBL* 115 (1996): 693. Some read a single word, which suggests that MT is a corruption of "at his [Yahweh's] right hand, Asherah." See M. Weinfeld, "Feminine Features in the Imagery of God in Israel: The Sacred Marriage and the Sacred Tree," *VT* 46 (1996): 527−28; C. McCarthy, "Moving from the Margins: Issues of Text and Context in Deuteronomy," in *Congress Volume Basel 2001* (ed. A. Lemaire; VTSup 92; Leiden: Brill, 2002), 126−34.

Septuagint not only renders it as one but translates it incomprehensibly as "angels."[19] This reading reflects a late tradition that angels mediated the law Sinai.[20] It seems best to treat *dāt* as a contracted feminine form of the verb *dāʾâ* ("to fly"), used of the flight of an eagle,[21] which creates the image of Yahweh arriving in brilliant splendor, accompanied by a myriad of holy ones, and sending out fire from his right.[22]

Verse 3 highlights Yahweh's special relationship to Israel, with the first line focusing on his love for the people and the second on their status. Whereas the singular "holy one" (v. 2) served as a collective expression for Yahweh's heavenly entourage, here the plural "holy ones" refers to his earthly attendants. This characterization of the Israelites reflects their position as "a people holy to the LORD,"[23] which means they are secure in his protective care, but also under his authority, following "at [his] feet" and receiving "instruction" from him.

Taken together verses 2 – 3 paint a picture of Yahweh's universal authority, balancing his superiority over the heavenly hosts with his sovereignty over Israel. Moses emphasizes Israel's role in Yahweh's earthly agenda. What the angels are to his cosmic administration, the Israelites are to the earthly. This idealized picture of Yahweh's holy ones investing their energies in the divine agenda provides significant background for interpreting the blessings.

The third person reference to Moses and the reference to the giving of the Torah in verse 4 catch the reader by surprise. If this represents the people's response to the theophany and their privileged status,[24] it expresses remarkable respect for the man and his mediatory role; as mediator of divine revelation, he is one of Yahweh's attendants. The word *tôrâ* (NIV "law") may allude to Moses' addresses,[25] and the verb "he gave [NIV 'commanded']" to Moses' verbal activity in the addresses.[26] However, linked to the previous verse, this Torah may be identified with his commands that have now become the special "possession" of the Israelites (cf. 4:8). Referring to the benefactors as "the assembly of Jacob" links this text even more closely with Genesis 49, where Jacob summons his sons to assemble.

---

19. On which see A. F. L. Beeston, "Angels in Deuteronomy 33²," *JTS* n.s. 2 (1951): 30–31.

20. See Josephus *Ant.* 15.5.3; Acts 7:53; Gal. 3:19; Heb. 2:2.

21. Thus Steiner, "Two Verbs," 695–96. Cf. Deut. 28:49; Jer. 48:40; 49:22.

22. NIV's "from the south, from his mountain slopes," is unlikely.

23. Cf. Deut. 7:6; 14:2, 21; 26:19. Note also Lev. 11:44, 45; 19:2; 20:7, 26; Num. 15:40; but esp. Num. 16:3.

24. Craigie, *Deuteronomy*, 393.

25. Deut. 17:18; 28:58, 61; 29:21[20]; 30:10; 31:24, 26.

26. Deut. 1:16, 18; 3:18, 21; 12:21; 24:8; 27:1; 31:5. Tigay (*Deuteronomy*, 321) doubts this *torah* refers to Deuteronomy.

The exordium closes by celebrating Yahweh's kingship in Israel. Moses' preceding proclamation of the Torah was the climactic episode in a series of events by which Yahweh's royal authority over Israel was affirmed. Verse 5 suggests the gathering of the tribes on the plains of Moab was a royal event, the climactic moment in the march of a divine warrior from Sinai/Paran to the land that he and his hosts are about to conquer. Identifying Israel as "Jeshurun,"[27] Yahweh's special name for his people, reinforces the expression "you who love the people" in verse 3. This verse paints a colorful verbal picture of the exalted and triumphant King of Israel. In the face of his own imminent death, Moses hereby declares publicly that although he will be departing, the Israelites remain the objects of Yahweh's affection, and they may cross the Jordan confidently, knowing that their divine King will lead the way into the enemy territory.

The Blessings of Reuben and Judah (33:6 – 7)

THE COLLECTION OF BENEDICTIONS opens unannounced with the blessing of Reuben. Reuben's reputation is mixed in the narratives of Genesis (cf. Gen. 35:22; 37:18 – 29; 49:3 – 4), but Moses' blessing is in effect a prayer for Reuben, implicitly appealing to Yahweh to spare him in the face of an apparently precarious future. While the troop records in Numbers 2 and 26 point to a relatively robust population, Moses envisions a reduction, perhaps because they will settle outside the actual Promised Land (Deut. 3:12 – 17).[28]

In contrast to Jacob's clear vision of Judah (Gen. 49:8 – 12), Moses' blessing is extremely modest. It consists of four lines, beginning with a plea to Yahweh to hear the Judahites' prayers — apparently when they head into battle — and to provide protection so they may return safely from their campaigns. Whether we read line three concessively ("Though his hands contend for him") or jussively ("Let his hands contend for him"), the blessing concludes with a plea for Yahweh to aid Judah against their adversaries. The tribe's fate and fortune are in the hands of Yahweh, the nation's divine Warrior.

The Blessing of Levi (33:8 – 11)

THE LENGTH OF THE Levites' blessing reflects Moses' relationship to this tribe (Ex. 6:16 – 27) and their spiritual role among the people. While verse

---

27. See comments on 32:15.

28. See Josh. 13:15 – 23 for the tribal boundaries. Reuben's precarious geographic position is reflected in the ninth-century BC inscription of Mesha, which lists Nebo, Medeba, and Baal-Meon, all Reubenite cites, among his conquests from Israel (*COS*, 2:23 [pp. 137 – 38]). In addition, the Song of Deborah and Barak criticizes Reuben for refusing to participate in the wars against the Canaanites (Judg. 5:15 – 16), though they had apparently actively engaged their own enemies (1 Chron. 5:18 – 22).

11 hints at a military role for this tribe, the emphasis is on their spiritual ministry among the people. This blessing envisions four responsibilities for the Levites, all of them custodial: of the Thummim and Urim (v. 8), the covenant (v. 9), divine revelation (v. 10a—b), and the sacrificial liturgy (v. 10c—d).

The verb seems to have dropped out of the opening line of verse 8, which should probably be reconstructed as follows: "Give to Levi your Thummim, and your Urim to the godly man."[29] Thummim and Urim[30] identify the two small stones carried by the high priest in a pouch in his pectoral (Ex. 28:30; Lev. 8:8). The Old Testament does not give a clear picture of their nature or the manner in which they were to be manipulated. They seem to have been small stones or sticks cast like lots for binary decisions (cf. Num. 27:21; Ezra 2:63; Neh. 7:65).

Our text suggests the Levites were awarded custody of the Urim and Thummim because of the fidelity they demonstrated at Massah and Meribah. The term *ḥāsîd* ("godly, loyal one"; NIV "the man you favored") identifies one who exhibits the loyalty and commitment that Yahweh himself demonstrates toward Israel by his keeping his covenant (7:9, 12). The names Massah ("place of testing") and Meribah ("place of contention") involve plays on words associated with two contexts in which Yahweh provided water for the people in the desert. The accounts of these events in Exodus 17:1—7 and Numbers 20:1—13 do not mention the involvement of the Levites, which suggests this image conflates elements of the events at these places of testing with Israel's rebellion in the worship of the golden calf at Sinai (Ex. 32:25—29) and the immorality of Baal Peor (Num. 25:1—13). In both instances the Levites stood up to defend Yahweh. If the event in view is that reported in Numbers 20, then the place that proved Moses' own undoing (cf. 32:50—52) was the place of the Levites' elevation in stature with God.

In verse 9 Moses' commendation of the Levites for sacrificing loyalty to family in defense of Yahweh's word and covenant seems to have in mind the golden calf incident at Sinai (cf. Ex. 32:26—29; Num. 25:11—12). By their actions they kept the word of Yahweh and guarded his covenant, but also lived up to Moses' charge in Deuteronomy 13 to execute anyone who would lead the people away from Yahweh.

---

29. Cf. *BHQ*, 158*—59*. The scribe's eye seems to have skipped from one reference to Levi to the other.

30. Everywhere else the order is Urim and Thummim. See Ex. 28:30; Lev. 8:8; Num. 27:21; 1 Sam. 14:41 (following the versions); Ezra 2:63; Neh. 7:65. For a detailed study of the Urim and Thummim, see Cornelis Van Dam, *The Urim and Thummim: A Means of Revelation in Ancient Israel* (Winona Lake, IN: Eisenbrauns, 1997); also M. Greenberg, "Urim and Thummim," *EncJud* (2nd ed.), 20:422—23.

Verse 10a-b highlights the charge to the Levites' to teach Yahweh's precepts and his Torah. These two expressions represent the divine revelation given at Sinai (cf. Ex. 21:1) and Moses' exposition of that revelation (cf. Deut. 31:9–13). While the role of Levites as readers and teachers of Torah does not figure prominently in the biblical narratives,[31] we hear accusations of failure in this regard in the prophets.[32] Apparently one of the functions of the Levitical cities was to provide bases from which the Levites could teach Torah in every corner of the country.

The last two lines of verse 10 highlight the Levites' liturgical role. The references to "incense" and "whole burnt offerings" are shorthand for the entire tabernacle ritual system prescribed in Exodus and Leviticus. The reference to "incense in your nostrils" alludes to the practice of waving incense before a deity's image to evoke a smile of approval.

Reaching a climax in verse 11, the blessing of Levi involves two spheres of existence. (1) Moses invokes Yahweh's blessing on the Levites' substance. While the word rendered "skills" in the NIV is capable of a wide range of meanings,[33] in this context "resources" captures the required sense. Because the Levites lacked their own territorial allotment, they were especially dependent on Yahweh. Verse 11b moves from what Yahweh does for the Levites to what they do for him. The plea for Yahweh to be pleased with the work of the Levites' hands shows that not even professional clergy may presume acceptance before him.

(2) Moses invokes Yahweh's protection of the Levites. Although Exodus 32:25–29 and Numbers 25:6–7 portray Levites wielding weapons of war in defense of Yahweh's honor, as a rule they were probably unarmed. For their well-being they depended on the favor of the people and the protection of God. The present request for Yahweh to "smite the loins" of adversaries is idiomatic. This blessing assumes that to oppose the Levites is to oppose God.

The Blessings of Benjamin and Joseph (33:12–17)

AFTER BLESSING THREE LEAH tribes the benediction turns to the tribes descended from Rachel: Benjamin and Joseph. The blessing for Benjamin is fragmentary and textually problematic. The redundant *ʿlyw* (NIV "in him")

---

31. But note their prominence in Nehemiah 8, a postexilic text.

32. Ezek. 22:26; Mal. 2:1–9. On the relationship between the latter and the blessing of Levi, see R. Fuller, "The Blessing of Levi in Dtn 33, Mal 2, and Qumran," in *Konsequente Traditionsgeschichte: Festschrift für Klaus Baltzer zum 65. Geburtstag* (ed. R. Bartelmus et al.; OBO 126; Göttingen: Vandenhoeck & Ruprecht, 1993), 37–40.

33. Cf. R. Wakely, *NIDOTTE*, 2:116–26.

seems to be a scribal error for the divine name "Elyon,"[34] suggesting an original something like the following:

> The beloved of Yahweh dwells securely,
>> Elyon shields him all day,
>> and between his shoulders he dwells. (pers. trans.)

In any case, the blessing opens with an affectionate epithet. Here Benjamin is not merely the beloved son of his father (cf. Gen. 44:20), but the "beloved" of Yahweh (cf. 2 Sam. 12:25). The blessing proper focuses on Benjamin's security under Yahweh's protective care: "May he dwell securely, may Elyon protect him constantly; may Israel dwell between Yahweh's shoulders." The last statement evokes the image of a parent holding a child in protective embrace.[35] Such a positive image of Benjamin would have been unthinkable after the events described in Judges 19–21, reinforcing the view that this entire benediction antedates the monarchy.

In the blessing of Joseph we reach a second center of gravity. Past and present history offer sufficient warrant for the amount of attention given to Joseph and the tribe's status reflected here: (1) the benediction exhibits conceptual and lexical links with Genesis 49:22–26; (2) Joseph was the tribe of Joshua; (3) the narratives of Joseph dominate the last fifteen chapters of Genesis. The fact this blessing is identical in length to that of Levi (52 words) may reflect the nature of Israel's leadership under Josephite and Levite tribes after Moses' death (Joshua was an Ephraimite).

Whereas previous blessings focused on the security of particular tribes, this blessing opens with an effusive prayer for blessing of the land. This may have been inspired by the names of the eponymous ancestors: "Joseph" means "May he increase/add," (cf. Gen. 30:24) and Ephraim means "to be fruitful" (cf. Gen. 41:52). But the tone is set by the key word *meged* ("choicest [fruit]"), which occurs five times in verses 13–16. From the same semantic field, verse 15a adds *rōʾš* ("head") in the sense of "foremost things." Although the opening line of this litany recognizes Yahweh as the source of all good things, the picture involves the covenantal triangle, with deity, people, and land all fulfilling their functions within this relationship.

The blessing marshals the entire cosmos in Joseph's interest: the heavens, which yield their dew; the "deep waters" that lie below (cf. 8:7); the

---

34. LXX reads *theos* ("God") and 4QDeut[h] reads "God," in both cases. Nelson, *Deuteronomy*, 384–85.

35. Some interpret Yahweh as the subject who rests between Benjamin's shoulders, which represent the hills of the territory of Benjamin that flank the sanctuary, perhaps of Bethel. See J. D. Heck, "The Missing Sanctuary of Deut 33:12," *JBL* 103 (1984): 523–29. See further G. R. Stone, "Sheltering under Divine Wings," *Buried History* 30 (1994): 58–66.

"sun," which all ancients recognized as essential for the land to yield its produce; the "moon"; "the ancient mountains; the everlasting hills";[36] and "the earth and its fullness"—a comprehensive expression for living things, vegetation, and animals, which the earth yields in abundance. The list concludes with a declaration that prosperity is dependent on the good will of Yahweh, identified here by the unusual epithet, (lit.) "the one who inhabits the bush." The NIV's "who dwelt in the burning bush" fills out the allusion to the bush that would not burn up in Exodus 3:2—4.[37]

In verses 16—17 we hear several allusions to the portrayal of Joseph in Genesis. Verse 16 begins with a prayer that all these agricultural favors will rest like a diadem on the "head" of Joseph.[38] The verse ends by characterizing Joseph as "prince among his brothers," a phrase also borrowed from Genesis. While Genesis 45:8 describes Joseph's status in Egypt, the present text identifies him as prince of his brothers (cf. 1 Chron. 5:1—2).

Verse 17 elaborates on Joseph's status as firstborn with impressive bovine imagery.[39] Joseph is a majestic specimen, with magnificent horns like a wild ox.[40] The targets of Joseph's rampage are the "nations" to "the ends of the earth." The blessing concludes by clarifying the meaning of "his horns" (v. 17b). They are the "myriads" (NIV "ten thousands") of Ephraim and the "thousands" of Manasseh. As Jacob does in Genesis 48:15—20, Moses gives pride of place to Ephraim by naming him first and ascribing to him "myriads" of troops.[41]

The Blessings of Zebulun, Issachar, and Gad (33:18—21)

IN VERSES 18—25 Moses addresses the six northern tribes in five short fragments. As with Ephraim and Manasseh, in verse 18 he honors Zebulun by departing from the birth order and naming the younger tribe first. The blessing of Zebulun and Issachar opens with a call to "rejoice," followed by

36. Hills and mountains metonymically represent olive groves and vineyards cultivated on hilltops.

37. Hence Targum Neofiti's expansion, "Who made the Glory of his Shekinah dwell in the thorn bush." Tigay (*Deuteronomy*, 328) understands the expression as an intentional pun on the name Manasseh.

38. The word "head" here is *qodqôd* (also occurs in 28:35). The word is borrowed from Gen. 49:26.

39. For a discussion of "firstborn" (*bᵉkôr*), see 21:15; *HALOT*, 131; *DCH*, 1.170.

40. Hebrew *rᵉʾēm* refers to the European and Middle Eastern branch of bovines known as aurochs, now extinct. Cf. Borowski, *Every Living Thing*, 190—91. Job 39:9—10 characterizes them as wild and impossible to domesticate. In Balaam's oracles, God himself is a "wild ox," whose horns protect Israel as he brings them out of Egypt (Num. 23:22; 24:8).

41. Against convention, Moses refers to the "ten thousands" first (cf. Deut. 32:30; Judg. 20:10; 1 Sam. 18:7; Mic. 6:7).

an enigmatic reference to Zebulun "going out" and Issachar "in your tents." While the former may allude to Zebulun's trading or fishing ventures, in contrast to Issachar's nomadic dwellings, we should treat these two lines as a merism, equivalent to "when you go out and when you come in."[42] Zebulun and Issachar are to rejoice wherever they are.

Moses holds off the reason for the celebration until the end (v. 19b–c), where he speaks of these tribes harvesting the products of the sea and the seashore. The harvest would include primary marine resources like fish and shells (used for making jewelry, lamps, and dyes), as well as products of maritime trade: timber, precious metals, pottery, and agricultural products from abroad.[43] He describes the mercantile enterprise strangely as "sucking" (NIV "feast on") abundance from the seas and the hidden treasures of the sand. Like Genesis 49:13, this blessing envisions Zebulun and Issachar along the coast in Phoenician territory rather than inland as described in Joshua 19:10–23.

In the middle Moses refers enigmatically to calling peoples to the mountains to offer righteous sacrifices. This reference is uncertain. As in verse 3, "peoples" refers to kinsfolk, as opposed to outsiders (cf. v. 17). Presumably the "righteous sacrifices" involve celebrations called for by the verb "rejoice" at the beginning, but on which "mountain" is unclear.[44] This is probably a generic expression for the location of the festivals, overlooking the sea and the seashore.

Strictly speaking the blessing involving Gad (vv. 20–21) actually pronounces the benediction on the one who enlarges Gad, that is, Yahweh himself, in which case "blessed is" means in effect "praise be" to God. The enlargement of Gad represents a fulfillment of the name, which means "good fortune," and probably has more to do with increasing the population than expanding the territory. Though the vocabulary differs, the image of Gad as a lion borrows from Jacob's blessing of Judah in Genesis 49:9. The two verbs reflect the two activities for which these large felines are known: sleeping and devouring prey.

Verse 21 anticipates Gad's future commitments and challenges. The first two cola allude to Gad's request to be granted a portion of the land of the Amorites east of the Jordan River (Num. 32:1–2). Joshua 22 shows that

---

42. Num. 27:17, 21; Deut. 28:6, 19; 31:2; 1 Kings 3:7; 2 Chron. 1:10.

43. The trade potential is illustrated dramatically by the recovery of a fourteenth-century BC merchant sailing vessel off the coast of Uluburun in Southern Turkey. For a popular illustrated study, see G. F. Bass, "Oldest Known Shipwreck Reveals Splendors of the Bronze Age," *National Geographic* 172/6 (1987): 692–733.

44. See S. Ahituv, "Zebulun and the Sea," in *Studies in Historical Geography and Biblical Historiography: Presented to Zecharia Kallai* (ed. G. Galil and M. Weinfeld; VTSup 81; Leiden: Brill, 2000), 5.

this decision would present serious challenges in the future, especially their relationship to the other tribes and their access to the spiritual heritage. But like Lot in Genesis 13:8–11, the Gadites "saw" this land and chose what they deemed best for themselves. Moses acceded to their request and reserved for them favorable territory, characterized as "the leader's portion."

The last three lines praise the Gadites for their spiritual commitments. When the heads of the people assembled, they fulfilled the ideals of the covenant by executing the righteousness of Yahweh and living according to his "judgments." Many translations render the phrase *ṣidqat yhwh* as "the justice of the LORD" (NIV "the LORD's righteous will"); this term does include the notion of social justice, but it should be interpreted more broadly as "righteousness" as laid down in the Sinai revelation and the Mosaic Torah (cf. 16:20). To be sure, righteousness involves justice, but it refers to conduct according to all his righteous "decrees" and "laws" (Deut. 4:8) and "walking in all the ways of the LORD," which include religious, ceremonial, civil, social, and personal prescriptions as well.

The Blessings of Dan, Naphtali, and Asher (33:22–25)

MOSES' BLESSING OF DAN is the shortest of all (v. 22). Although uttered by Moses, the placement of this fragment among the northern tribes suggests these blessings were gathered and arranged after the Danite's migration to Laish (Judg. 18). However, there is additional logic in locating Dan after Gad. Like Gad (v. 20), Dan is compared to a lion cub leaping from Bashan (cf. Gen. 49:9).

The blessing of Naphtali (v. 23) sounds like a collage of expressions that have been heard earlier, but they are now combined in the first two lines to present an image of superlative well-being and satisfaction with the favor and the blessing of Yahweh (cf. Prov. 10:22). The last line charges Naphtali to take possession of the west and the southland. The NIV's "southward to the lake" understands the first word in its normal sense. However, in this context involving directions, the word translated "lake" probably means "west."[45]

In the blessing of Asher Moses prays for both fertility and security. The first two lines request for Asher's supremacy among the tribes in the blessing and favor with God. The material dimension of that favor is expressed by a curious idiom, "let him bathe his feet in oil." The expression imagines the olive trees of Galilee so productive that streams of oil run down the hills.[46]

---

45. So also Gen. 12:8; 13:14; Ex. 10:19; 27:12; Josh. 8:9; Ezek. 41:12; 42:19; Zech. 14:4.

46. J. R. Porter ("The Interpretation of Deuteronomy xxxiii 24–5," *VT* 44 [1994]: 268–69) argues that this is a ritual act endowing the troops with vigor and fleetness of foot for military duty.

Verse 25 pleads for Naphtali's security, expressed in terms of bronze and iron gate-bolts. The expression for "bolts of your gates" reflects the fact that in ancient Palestine defensive gate structures were complex installations, consisting of double doors made of thick boards, barred by a heavy horizontal beam slid through slots in the doorposts. The reference to iron and bronze adds to the image of prosperity and security. Any town that could make its bolts of solid iron or copper was prosperous indeed.[47] The blessing concludes with a proverb: "As your days, so your security" (pers. trans.) The meaning of the expression is somewhat difficult to ascertain, but the impulse reflected in early versions to render the word as "strength" is sound.[48]

The Coda (33:26–29)

THE CODA PICKS UP where the exordium had left off, praising Yahweh for his lavish support for Israel (vv. 26–27) and congratulating Israel for having a God like Yahweh (vv. 28–29). This stanza divides into three artfully composed parts, with the first (vv. 26–27) and last (v. 29) being identical in length by word count (19 words) framing the shorter center (v. 28). The outer parts both begin with a vocative address and highlight Yahweh's rescue of Israel from her enemies, while the center focuses on Israel enjoying the security he has provided.

The opening line of verse 26 declares the incomparability of God. Here Moses uses the term "El," which may either be a generic expression for deity or claim for him the title of the high God in Canaanite mythology. The following line, which speaks of Yahweh riding through the heavens/skies in "majesty"[49] to come to the aid of his people, points in the latter direction (cf. Ps. 104:3). This imagery recalls Canaanite myths of the storm god Baal, one of whose stock epithets was "rider of the clouds."[50] By claiming these epithets for Yahweh, Moses declares his jurisdiction over all the spheres that Canaanites had distributed among the gods.

The first two lines of verse 27 declare in a nutshell the Israelites' basis of security. (1) They know their God is eternal. With the epithet "eternal God," Moses claims for Yahweh the status of El, whose titles included "king, father of years."[51] Inoculating his people against the virus of Canaan-

---

47. Bronze and iron gate-bolts are mentioned in 1 Kings 4:13; Ps. 107:16; Isa. 45:2.

48. See Porter, "The Interpretation of Deuteronomy XXXIII 24–25," 269–70.

49. Used of Yahweh elsewhere only in Ps. 68:34[35]; cf. Ps. 93:1; Isa. 26:10.

50. *CTA* 1.2:IV.8, 28. For discussion of this link to Canaanite mythology, see J. Day, *Yahweh and the Gods and Goddesses of Canaan* (JSOTSup 265; Sheffield: Sheffield Academic, 2000), 91–98.

51. Baal Cycle, KTU 1.6:I.36 (*UNP*, 153).

ite fertility religion, Moses declares that Yahweh, not the otiose and aging Canaanite El, is the key to Israel's well-being.

(2) The Israelites are secure because Yahweh is their defender. Defensively he provides a safe dwelling place[52] and sustains them with his strong, "everlasting arms." Taken together, Moses created the image of a strong father who provides a safe and secure home for his family and who holds them in a protective embrace.

(3) But Yahweh's actions on Israel's behalf are also offensive; he goes before Israel, defeating the enemy and sending out his agents with the charge "Destroy him!" It is difficult to know whether the charge is issued to Israel or to his nonhuman agents (32:23 – 24, 40 – 41). This is indeed a picture of total security. Yahweh rides *above* Israel, he upholds his people from *below*, and he marches on *ahead* of them.

Verse 28 functions as a fulcrum between two hymnic celebrations of privilege, describing a domestic scene of perfect bliss. While the meaning of the first of the opening parallel lines is clear, the second is enigmatic, until we recognize the precision of the parallelism. As is normally the case, the first line employs common vocabulary: the verb "to live" and the modifier "in safety" (cf. v. 12). But the second has long been a riddle. The NIV follows longstanding tradition in attaching "alone" to the preceding line and interpreting ʿên as "fountain, spring." But this is difficult grammatically and conceptually. If "alone, secluded" is attached to the following line and ʿên treated as a verb "to reside," synonymous with "live" (šākan),[53] the parallelism is complete: "So Israel lived in safety, Jacob lived alone" (cf. ESV), and the image of security is reinforced.

The last two lines of verse 28 highlight Israel's prosperity, while subtly continuing the polemic against pagan religious notions. Israel is at home in a land that yields grain and high quality wine. As in 7:13 – 14, these words also serve a polemical function, being cognate to the names of the gods Dagan and Tirshu/Tirash, respectively. As staple agricultural products, grain and wine function as a merism referring to full prosperity.

Moses concludes his blessing of the tribes on a celebrative note, congratulating the Israelites for the privilege that is theirs of being the people of Yahweh. Whereas the coda had begun by declaring the incomparability of Israel's God, it ends by declaring the incomparability of God's people. They are the beneficiaries of his rescue and protection. The first statement is vague enough to include other experiences of rescue, but it alludes

52. See 26:15. The word is used of a lair for lions in Job 38:40; Ps. 104:22; Song 4:8; Amos 3:4; Nah. 2:13.

53. For defense of this interpretation, see Steiner, "Two Verbs Masquerading as Nouns," 696 – 98.

primarily to Israel's deliverance from the Egyptians (cf. 4:32–40). The second statement identifies Yahweh metaphorically as Israel's Shield of help and her Sword of triumph. Whereas "shield" is a common metaphor for Yahweh in the Old Testament,[54] this is the only reference to him as "sword." Whereas in verse 26 the word had spoken of Yahweh's "preeminence," here it applies to his people: Yahweh is the defender of Israel's majesty.

The last two lines testify dramatically to the kind of preeminence Moses had spoken of earlier in 26:19 and 28:1, 10–14. The meaning of the rare word translated as "cower" in the NIV is determined by the context. With the last line, Moses presents the image of subjugated persons cringing prostrate before their victor and the victor placing his foot on their backs,[55] a practice attested in both literary word and the iconography from the ancient Near East.[56]

MOSES' FAREWELL ADDRESS. IN the ancient world nation states typically derived their name from the people's perceived ancestor, and the people's sense of cohesion was based on a sense of ethnic cohesion based on a sense of common descent from that ancestor (e.g., Moabites, Edomites, Israelites). Although Moses was obviously the first and founding leader of Israel as a nation, despite Yahweh's offer to make of him a great nation (Ex. 32:10), Moses made no effort to change Israel's story or to secure allegiance to himself. And in contrast to the leaders of other nations, he made no effort to secure his personal legacy by erecting memorials to himself.[57] Instead in his final days he poured out his energies in "setting his house in order" and securing the well-being of the people he had led for forty years. These efforts involved primarily words: words of

---

54. Gen. 15:1; 2 Sam. 22:3, 31, 36 (= Ps. 18:2, 30, 35[3, 31, 36]); Pss. 3:3[4]; 28:7; 33:20; 59:11[12]; 84:11[12]; 115:9–11; 144:2; Prov. 2:7; 30:5.

55. In Josh. 10:24 the victor places his foot on the neck of the vanquished (cf. also 1 Kings 5:3[17] and Ps. 110:1, the latter of which speaks of the enemies as the Davidic king's footstool.

56. See O. Keel, *The Symbolism of the Biblical World* (New York: Seabury, 1978), 253–56; *ANEP* §249; F. J. Yurco, "3,200-Year-Old Picture of Israelites Found in Egypt," *BAR* 16/5 (September–October, 1990): 30.

57. For a summary discussion of the memorial projects of Rameses II, see K. A. Kitchen, "Ramesses II," in *The Oxford Encyclopedia of Ancient Egypt* (ed. D. G. Redford; Oxford: Oxford Univ. Press, 2001), 3:117; idem, *Pharaoh Triumphant: The Life and Times of Ramesses II* (Warminster, England: Aries & Phillips, 1982), 174–82. For the Neo-Assyrian period see the reliefs of Sennacherib from Nineveh and of Ashurbanipal II from Nimrud (Calah) in the British Museum.

exhortation to fidelity to Israel's gracious Redeemer and Lord (his three addresses), words of encouragement to the people and Joshua for the challenges they will soon face (31:1–8), words of song that serve as a national anthem (32:1–43), and words of blessing (33:1–26).

Moses' blessing of the tribes follows the ancient pattern of heads of households gathering their clans around them for a final blessing before their demise. In the New Testament Jesus picked up the practice when, immediately prior to his own death, he called his disciples around him for final conversations and to bless them (John 13–16). Once Judas had left, Jesus began his lengthy address to the disciples who remained. Remarkably, although he repeatedly drew attention to his Father in heaven, he presented himself as the focus of the disciples' trust and security: They trust in God; they must trust in him (14:1). He bequeathed to them his peace (14:27; 16:33), promising them that in him they would find all the resources needed to cope with a hostile world: (1) the hope of a future with him (14:3); (2) resources for any circumstance (14:13–14); (3) divine presence and aid in the person of the Holy Spirit (14:16, 26; 15:26; 16:7); (4) his and the Father's love (15:1–15; 16:25–27; cf. Deut. 33:3); (5) reminders of their divine election (15:15–19); (6) their ultimate triumph (16:33). All these notions are thoroughly Deuteronomic, and they also address universal concerns. Jesus, Yahweh incarnate, is indeed "the way and the truth and the life" (14:6).

Theological notions in the Blessing of Moses. The Blessing of Moses, especially the hymnic frame, reinforces many theological notions introduced earlier in Deuteronomy. First and foremost, Israel is uniquely privileged to have Yahweh as their God. He is the divine Warrior who comes from Sinai/Paran, arrayed in splendor and accompanied by his heavenly hosts. When he steps down on earth, to his forces he adds his earthly entourage, the nation of Israel, claiming them as his "holy ones" and committing himself to being their divine patron. This eternal God has appeared again in person in the latter days as the incarnate Son of God. Although the "Hymn to Christ" in Philippians 2:6–11 speaks of Christ's emptying himself, taking on the form of a servant, and dying on a cross, other texts remind us that in his incarnation he shed none of his glory. After decades of reflection on the significance of Jesus' life John wrote: "The Word became flesh and made his dwelling among us. We have seen his glory, the glory of the One and Only, who came from the Father, full of grace and truth" (John 1:14). And the author of Hebrews declares:

> The Son is the radiance of God's glory and the exact representation of his being, sustaining all things by his powerful hand. After he provided purification for sins, he sat down at the right hand of the

Majesty in heaven. So he became as much superior to the angels as the name he has inherited is superior to theirs. (Heb. 1:3−4)

Like the Song of Yahweh in chapter 32, the Blessing of Moses proclaims a theology that underlies all of Scripture. In contrast to pagan gods, images of which may be physically present and visible but who are impotent inventions of depraved imaginations, the imageless Yahweh reveals himself in glorious splendor and through verbal communication as sovereign Lord and King over all the powers of heaven and earth and as the divine Warrior who vanquishes all who oppose him. He is the one who has chosen for himself a people whom he sanctifies and declares his holy ones, whom he loves and addresses by the affectionate name, Jeshurun. If the Israelites will accept his grace and his lordship, their security and well-being are guaranteed.

Unfortunately, the history of the nation is a history of frustration and failure. Because Israel refused to trust Yahweh their God and spurned his protective grace, the reality of their history differed radically from the hope and the promise declared here. In the end, the divine Warrior who first appeared to deliver them and to bring them to the Promised Land became their enemy. The privileges of salvation, protection, well-being, and divine presence may not be taken for granted.

DEPENDENCE ON GOD FOR all things. This text, particularly the blessings of the individual tribes, present considerable challenges for modern readers. What am I to do with the promise to Naphtali or Moses' word for Dan? I am not a Danite; I do not live in the part of the world where the Danites lived; the issues I face day by day are quite different from the issues faced by the Reubenites or Asherites or Josephites.

Still, in surveying all these blessings, one hears a common theme expressed in a dozen variations. In the face of opposition from those who oppose God and his kingdom and represent the kingdom of darkness, God's people are fully dependent on their divine patron for their well-being. They may rest in the strong arms of Yahweh, who rides above them (v. 26), who upholds them from below (v. 27), and who drives out the enemy before them. Our God does indeed supply all our needs according to his riches in glory in Christ Jesus (Phil. 4:19). The people of Israel were probably not surprised to hear Moses warn them of the hostile world they face, but the coda declares that they will not face it alone. God's people are secure in him.

A transformation of Moses' promises. Even as we find our security in Christ and recognize that God assumes responsibility for our well-being, we are cautioned against the abuse of texts like this by claiming them as unconditional promises of material prosperity. When the New Testament church was established, the covenant community became an international community, which meant that God's reputation and the advance of the gospel were no longer tied to one state or one people; this text's promises of material well-being have been transformed. A transnational and global Christianity may not claim these promises of dipping feet in oil and other idioms of agricultural prosperity as literal and unconditional foundations for the health and wealth gospel peddled by so many today and exported around the world, particularly in places of desperate poverty.

One of America's most popular preachers declares that by his death Jesus Christ frees us from our bad habits and addictions, fear and worry, discouragement and depression, poverty and lack, and low self-esteem,[58] as if these freedoms are unconditional entitlements. But they never have been, not even for the ancient Israelites. True well-being and security are found in Jesus Christ, through whose death and resurrection a personal relationship with God is secured. This does not mean that we are immune from disaster, but that when disaster strikes, our well-being is ensured. The gospel calls us to take up the cross and to suffer for the cause of Christ. Making material prosperity and physical health our passion is idolatry, a modern version of Canaanite fertility religion.

Nevertheless, in Christ we do find glorious reassurance that God is as interested in the genuine well-being of his people as we are. Just as he fulfilled his Word in delivering the Promised Land into the Israelites' hands, so he fulfills his Word in granting us every spiritual blessing in heavenly places in Christ (Eph 1:3). The life of faith is indeed lived out in the everyday struggles of life. God does not promise to solve every problem, but he does promise to be there in those struggles.

Ecclesiology for the people of God. Above we addressed the picture of God that Moses paints with these blessings. But what about the people of God? For those with eyes to see, this benediction, particularly the framework, offers a profound ecclesiology, highlighting the privileges that come with membership in the assembly of God's people. Like the faithful in ancient Israel, we are the recipients of the divine revelation (v. 2), the objects of his love, identified by a special name (vv. 3, 5), his holy ones held by his hand (v. 3), the people to whom God has revealed his will (vv. 3–4; cf. 4:7–8), citizens of his kingdom (v. 5), the secure beneficiaries of his

---

58. Hear Joel Osteen at www.youtube.com/watch?v=di9–PebV634&NR=1.

defense (vv. 26–27), and his lavish provision (v. 28), but, most fundamentally, the undeserving recipients of his salvation.

As in the Lord's Prayer, issues relating to physical well-being are framed by and subordinated to the sheer privilege of calling God our Father, King, Savior, and Defender. To bear the name of Christ and to hear him address us as his beloved are reasons enough to celebrate and keep our focus on him. Through Christ we claim the adoption as sons, the glory, the covenants, the revelation of God's will, the service of worship, and the promises. May God be blessed forever! (Rom. 9:4–6).

Deuteronomy 34:1–12

T hen Moses climbed Mount Nebo from the plains of Moab to the top of Pisgah, across from Jericho. There the LORD showed him the whole land—from Gilead to Dan, ²all of Naphtali, the territory of Ephraim and Manasseh, all the land of Judah as far as the western sea, ³the Negev and the whole region from the Valley of Jericho, the City of Palms, as far as Zoar. ⁴Then the LORD said to him, "This is the land I promised on oath to Abraham, Isaac and Jacob when I said, 'I will give it to your descendants.' I have let you see it with your eyes, but you will not cross over into it."

⁵And Moses the servant of the LORD died there in Moab, as the LORD had said. ⁶He buried him in Moab, in the valley opposite Beth Peor, but to this day no one knows where his grave is. ⁷Moses was a hundred and twenty years old when he died, yet his eyes were not weak nor his strength gone. ⁸The Israelites grieved for Moses in the plains of Moab thirty days, until the time of weeping and mourning was over.

⁹Now Joshua son of Nun was filled with the spirit of wisdom because Moses had laid his hands on him. So the Israelites listened to him and did what the LORD had commanded Moses.

¹⁰Since then, no prophet has risen in Israel like Moses, whom the LORD knew face to face, ¹¹who did all those miraculous signs and wonders the LORD sent him to do in Egypt— to Pharaoh and to all his officials and to his whole land. ¹²For no one has ever shown the mighty power or performed the awesome deeds that Moses did in the sight of all Israel.

FOR THIRTY-THREE CHAPTERS READERS have been listening in on a sacred event, as Israel's pastor has been preparing his congregation for life in the Promised Land. The gospel according to Moses has been rich in grace: the gift of salvation, free and undeserved; the gift of covenant, personal and intimate; the gift of revelation, profound and unparalleled; the gift of providence, patient and loving; and the gift of a home, over the Jordan about to be delivered into their hands. They have heard Moses expound on these themes with eloquence (1:6–30:20), sing them with passion (32:1–43), and apply them with enthusiasm (33:1–29). In chapter 34 that voice is silenced. The only voices we hear are the voice of Yahweh (34:4) and the voice of the narrator, whose reflections on the man exhibit obvious admiration and awe.

We have heard the voice of the narrator before (1:1–5; 4:41–5:1a; 29:1[28:69]), but now for the first time he holds our attention. The events described conclude the death narrative formally begun in chapter 31.[1] By this point in the drama, Moses has done all he could do to set his house in order. He has commissioned a successor (31:1–8, 23), provided a written transcript of his farewell pastoral sermons and arranged for the regular reading of this Torah in the future (31:9–13, 24–29), taught the people a national anthem (31:14–22, 30; 32:47), and pronounced his benediction on the tribes (33:1–29). All that remains is the report of his death and the people's response to his passing. This is the function of chapter 34.[2]

The Report of Moses' Death (34:1–6)

FOR A MAN WHO played such an important role in the history of Israel, the account of Moses' death is remarkably modest, standing in sharpest contrast to elaborate texts, images, inscriptions, and monuments that significant persons outside Israel produced to commemorate their lives. Nowhere in the narratives of the Pentateuch or in his speeches on the Plains of Moab does he express the least interest in memorializing his name. Although Moses recognizes that his teaching is divinely authorized, he never calls it "my Torah," or "the Torah of Moses." It is simply (lit.) "this Torah," or "this document of the Torah,"[3] which he taught the people "as the LORD commanded" him.[4] Later writers refer to Deuteronomy as "the *tôrâ* of Moses,"[5] but Moses does not create the Torah as a memorial to himself; it is entirely a memorial to Yahweh's grace.

---

1. Implicitly by Moses himself (31:2); explicitly by Yahweh (31:14, 16); explicitly by Moses (31:29); explicitly by Yahweh (32:50). Olsen demonstrates convincingly (*Deuteronomy and the Death of Moses*) that we must read the entire book of Deuteronomy from the perspective of Moses' death.

2. For full discussions of the nature and function of Deuteronomy 34 as the conclusion to the Pentateuch, see C. Frevel, "Ein vielsagender Abschied: Exegetische Blicke auf den Tod des Mose in Dtn 34,1–12," *BZ* 435 (2001): 209–34. F. G. López ("Deut 34, DTR History and the Pentateuch," in *Studies in Deuteronomy in Honour of C. J. Labuschagne on the Occasion of His 65th Birthday* (ed. F. G. Martínez, et al.; VTSup 53; Leiden: Brill, 1994], 47–61) recognizes that Deuteronomy 34 could be read either as *"one single narrative"* or at three successive levels, as most critical scholars do. Our commentary will follow the former approach.

3. Deut. 17:18–19; 27:3, 8, 26; 28:58, 61; 29:21, 29[20, 28]; 30:10; 31:9, 11, 12, 24, 26; 32:46.

4. Deut. 1:3; 4:5; 6:24–25; 10:5; cf. 34:9;

5. Josh. 8:31–32; 23:6; 1 Kings 2:3; 2 Kings 14:6; 23:25; 2 Chron. 23:18; 30:16; Ezra 3:2; 7:6; Neh. 8:1; Dan. 9:11, 13; Mal. 4:4[3:22]; Luke 2:22; 24:44; John 7:23; Acts 13:39; Acts 15:5; 28:23; 1 Cor. 9:9; Heb. 10:28.

As the final death report, Deuteronomy 34 recounts Moses' ascent up Mount Nebo, his observation of the land (vv. 1 − 4), and his death and burial (vv. 5 − 6). The opening sentence and structural and lexical links between this text and 32:49 − 52 suggest this chapter continues that narrative (cf. 34:5), which was interrupted by the inserted poem blessing the tribes (33:1 − 29). The benediction may have fit more naturally after 32:47, suggesting the editor of the book intentionally created a buffer between Yahweh's negative assessment of Moses (32:48 − 52) and his own much more positive eulogy. The present location of the blessing also creates the impression that as Moses climbed Mount Nebo, he turned around, saw the Israelites below him, and pronounced these blessings.

This is the first occurrence of the phrase "plains of Moab" in Deuteronomy.[6] The word translated "plains" generally denotes "wasteland," which suggests the people were camped in the desert north of this mountain range (cf. Num. 21:20). As noted on 3:27 and 32:49, Pisgah probably designates the mountain ridge of which Nebo is the peak, providing an excellent view of the land across the Jordan. The concluding phrase, "across from Jericho," highlights both the geographical and historical contexts: Moses is on the very edge of the Promised Land, within sight of the major city of the region and the first target of the Israelites' campaign of conquest. Although chapter 34 opens with a report of Moses' ascent, the bulk of the paragraph focuses on Yahweh's actions (vv. 1b, 4, 6). Verses 1b − 3 describe the sequel to Yahweh's order to Moses in 3:27 and 32:49. But the emphasis shifts from Moses seeing the land to Yahweh showing it to him.

The narrator highlights the scope of the survey more emphatically than in 3:27 in three ways. (1) He opens with "the LORD showed him the whole land" (v. 1). Since the extremities named below would probably have been beyond the range of the naked eye, Yahweh may have granted Moses extraordinary vision.

(2) The narrator specifies the regions surveyed. Moving in a counterclockwise direction, Moses looks straight north to Gilead (representing the eastern Transjordanian territories), to Napthali (representing the northern region between the Sea of Galilee and the Mediterranean), Ephraim and Manasseh (representing the Israelite heartland across the Jordan), Judah (the region between the Dead Sea and the Mediterranean), the Negev (the southern region as far as the Sinai peninsula), and coming full circle to the southern part of the Ghor, the rift valley dominated by the city of Jericho, "the City of Palms."

---

6. The expression recurs in v. 8. See also Num. 22:1; 26:3, 63; 31:12; 33:48 − 50; 35:1; 36:13; Josh. 13:32.

(3) The narrator mentions the extremities of Moses' gaze: from Gilead a hundred miles north as far as Dan, at the foot of Mount Hermon, sixty miles west as far as the western sea, and fifty miles south as far south as Zoar (cf. Gen. 19:22).[7] Like Deuteronomy 33:22, the naming of Dan presupposes the migration of the Danites (Judg. 18), suggesting the book of Deuteronomy received its final form a century or more after Moses' death. At the same time, the toponymic definition of the extremities as from Dan to Zoar may suggest that the account antedates the later period when "from Dan to Beersheba" became the stereotypical expression for the extreme northern and southern boundaries (e.g., 1 Sam. 3:20). While this emphasis on geography matches the focus of 1:1−5, the perspective has shifted from retrospection to prospection, anticipating Israel's crossing the Jordan and occupation of the land.

In verse 4, Yahweh addresses Moses, declaring to him that this is indeed the land he had promised on oath to the ancestors. He summarizes the content of the oath in another embedded speech: "to your seed I will give it" (cf. 1:8; 11:9; pers. trans.).[8] For Israel this declaration brings the book to an end on a hopeful note, but for Moses it was extremely painful. Without rehearsing the cause as he had in 32:50−52, Yahweh reminds him once more that he will not cross over there. Moses may only gaze at the prize with his eyes. With this statement, the forty-year conversation that Yahweh had initiated with his trusted servant in Midian (Ex. 3:6−10) ends. Moses will not experience the realization of the promise, but he will leave the stage knowing that Yahweh has been faithful both to the ancestors and to him.

The announcement of Moses' death in verse 5 is brief and to the point. But even his death confirms Yahweh's fidelity, for his demise transpires "as the LORD said." This expression often refers to a command issued by Yahweh (e.g, Ex. 17:1; Num. 33:2, 38), which suggests that even in his death Moses proves a faithful servant (cf. 32:50). But the statement may also refer to Yahweh's fulfillment of his own earlier prediction of Moses' death (31:14).

In verse 5 the narrator identifies Moses by the honorific title "the servant of the LORD" for the first time.[9] The notion of human beings func-

---

7. Modern es-Safi on Wadi Zered, several miles south of the Dead Sea. See M. C. Astour, "Zoar," *ABD*, 6:1107.

8. Introducing the oath with "when I said" (lit., "saying") signals a quotation of Gen. 12:7. So also López, "Deut 34, DTR History and the Pentateuch," 55. Cf. Gen. 15:18; 24:7; 26:4; 48:4; Ex. 32:13; 33:1.

9. The epithet had been used earlier in Ex. 14:31 and Num. 12:8, and resurfaces repeatedly in Joshua (1:1−2, 7; etc.) and dozens of times thereafter. For the honorific nature of the title, see *HALOT*, 775.

tioning as servants of deities was widespread in the ancient Near East and is reflected in theophoric names that employ the root ʿebed in Hebrew (e.g., Obadiah, "one who serves Yahweh").[10] Although the word "servant" may denote menial status, phrases like "servant of the king" for court officials demonstrate that in contexts like this, it bears honorific significance (2 Kings 25:8).[11]

From a hagiographic perspective, the notice of Moses' burial in verse 6 is striking on two accounts. (1) Whereas in the ancient world members of the family normally disposed of the body of the deceased, the narrator notes that Moses was buried by Yahweh himself. (2) Although the narrator specifies that he was buried in a valley in the land of Moab opposite Beth Peor (cf. 3:29; 4:3, 46), he adds that at the time of writing, the location was unknown. This comment intensifies the tragedy of Moses' death. He died not having achieved the goal that obsessed him and was buried on foreign soil. Moses had reached his heavenly destination without having reached his earthly home. God had been with Moses throughout his life, but Moses was alone with God in his death.

The Response to Moses' Death (34:7 – 8)

IN VERSE 7 THE focus returns to Moses. In keeping with other biblical death narratives,[12] the first statement reports Moses' age at the time of his death: 120 years (cf. 31:2). But the narrator adds an interesting detail about Moses' remarkable physical condition: when he died, he had 20/20 vision[13] and his vigor had not waned. What the narrator meant by "nor his strength gone" is unclear. Most translations understand this expression to mean something like "life force, virility," but some argue that it refers to his skin, which had not lost its moisture and become wrinkled.[14] In

---

10. For Mari, see H. B. Huffmon, *Amorite Personal Names in the Mari Texts: A Structural and Lexical Study* (Baltimore: John Hopkins Univ. Press, 1965), 118–19, 189; the Amarna Letters, R. S. Hess, *Amarna Personal Names* [Winona Lake, IN: Eisenbrauns, 1996], 7–13, 244); Phoenician texts, F. L. Benz, *Personal Names in the Phoenician and Punic Inscriptions* (Studia Pohl 8; Rome: Pontifical Biblical Institute, 1972), 371; Ugarit, F. Gröndahl, *Die Personnenamender Texte aus Ugarit* (Studia Pohl 1; Rome: Pontifical Biblical Institute, 1967), 80, 105; Aramaic, M. Maraqten, *Die semitischen Personennamen in den alt- und reischsaramäischen Inschriften aus Vorderasien* (Hildesheim: Olms Verlag, 1988), 94, 192.

11. This interpretation is reinforced by archaeologists' discovery of dozens of seals from ancient Palestine referring to the bearer of the seal as "servant of the king" or servant of a specific king, as in the famous seal of "Shama servant of Jeroboam." Slaves did not have seals.

12. See Cribb, *Speaking from the Brink of Sheol*, 218–23.

13. The same verb regarding "weak" eyes is used of Isaac's eyes in Gen. 27:1; cf. also Job 17:7 and Zech. 11:17.

14. E.g., Tigay, *Deuteronomy*, 338.

---

either case, the years in the desert affected Moses quite differently from his fellow Israelites, who all died prematurely (8:4). Moses died neither of old age nor disease, but simply because within the divine plan his time was up. As the Israelites had done for Aaron (Num. 20:29), they mourned Moses' passing for thirty days (v. 8), apparently the conventional length of mourning in ancient Israel.[15]

Epitaph: The Narrator's Commentary on Moses (34:9 – 12)

ALTHOUGH NEITHER THE NARRATIVES of Exodus through Numbers nor Moses' first speech in Deuteronomy mask the flaws in the man's temperament and character, the narrator's extreme admiration for Moses is evident in the conclusion to this book. The grammatical construction of the first sentence of verse 9 shifts the attention from Moses to Joshua son of Nun, but in so doing it still honors Moses. Because Moses had laid his hands on Joshua,[16] the latter was filled with the spirit of wisdom and the people listened to him as Yahweh had commanded through Moses.

The expression "spirit of wisdom" occurs elsewhere in the Old Testament in Exodus 28:3 and Isaiah 11:1 – 2. In both, it represents a special divine endowment for the fulfillment of a divinely ordained role. Through Moses' ritual gesture Joshua was authorized and empowered to administer the nation justly and to embody the righteousness of the Torah (cf. 17:14 – 20).[17] This "spirit of wisdom" is distinct from the "spirit" attributed to Joshua in Numbers 27:18. (1) Whereas in the earlier passage *rûaḥ* refers to the proper disposition toward Yahweh that Joshua exhibited prior to his ordination, here the narrator declares that Joshua was divinely endowed with the spirit of wisdom *because* Moses ordained him.

(2) Whereas the earlier passage has Moses taking hold of Joshua and laying his hand on him, this text lacks any reference to Moses' "taking" him and replaces the singular "hand" with the plural "hands." Rituals involving both hands result in the transference of something from one object to another (cf. Lev. 16:21).[18] While not explicitly declared, the present

---

15. Cf. the seventy-day mourning of Jacob by the Egyptians in Gen. 50:3. In Deut. 21:13 Moses required Israelite soldiers to grant foreign wives taken in battle a month to grieve, presumably for the loss of their parents.

16. See the full discussion by K. Mattingly, "Joshua's Reception of the Laying on of Hands, Part 2: Deuteronomy 34:7[sic, read 9] and Conclusion," *AUSS* 39 (2002): 89 – 103.

17. For full discussion of the wisdom motif in Deuteronomy, see G. Braulik, "'Weisheit' im Buch Deuteronomium," in *Weisheitausserhalb der kanonischen Weisheitsschriften* (ed. B. Janowski; Veröffentlichungen der Wissenschaftlichen Gesellschaft für Theologie 10; Gütersloh: Chr. Kaiser, 1996), 39 – 69.

18. So also Braulik, "'Weisheit' im Buch Deuteronomium," 64.

statement assumes that Moses possessed the same spirit of wisdom, and that when he laid his hands on Joshua, that divine spirit passed from him to Joshua. Recognizing the significance of this liturgical act and undoubtedly the evidence of the spirit in Joshua, the people responded to him with loyalty and obedience.

The narrator concludes his biography of Moses with an unrestrained eulogy. At the time of writing, Israel had seen no prophet comparable in stature and power with Moses. The reference to Moses as "prophet" recalls 18:15. Moses performed many administrative, judicial, and even priestly functions, but he is never identified as a judge, ruler, priest, or lawgiver.[19] In Moses' own mind and in the narrator's mind he was the paradigmatic prophet. With his use of the verb "to rise," the narrator links his eulogy with Moses' own prediction in 18:15, that Yahweh would raise up an authoritative prophet like him from among the people.

The reference to Moses' incomparability as prophet implies that some time had elapsed between the death of Moses and the writing of this epitaph and that Israel had been served by a series of prophetic successors to Moses by this time. The narrator explains in considerable detail why he deemed Moses to be exceptional. (1) No other prophet was as intimate with Yahweh as Moses was: Yahweh knew him "face to face." The idiom speaks of an intimate and direct relationship — without need for an intermediary (cf. Ex. 33:11; Num. 12:6 – 8).

(2) No other prophet performed the kinds of actions that Moses did on Yahweh's behalf (v. 11). In fact, Yahweh sent him to perform "signs and wonders" in the land of Egypt before Pharaoh, all his servants, and his entire land, and to demonstrate his "mighty power" in the sight of the Israelites. Previously in Deuteronomy Moses always attributed these portentous acts to Yahweh himself (4:34; 6:22; 7:19; 11:3; 26:8; 29:3[2]). Apparently to the narrator these signs and wonders both served the divine revelatory agenda and authenticated Moses as the indisputable prophet of Yahweh.[20] With this statement the narrator has not only eulogized Moses; he has also reinforced his words in 4:2; 12:32[13:1], as well as the narrator's own comments in 31:24, 30. He thus validates the speeches of Moses and their final committal to writing in the book of Deuteronomy.[21]

---

19. Num. 27:17 perceives Moses' role primarily as that of a pastor. For fuller discussion, see D. I. Block, "Will the Real Moses Please Rise," in *The Gospel According to Moses*, 68 – 103.

20. Thus Tigay, *Deuteronomy*, 340.

21. In this respect the ending to Deuteronomy resembles the ending to the law code of Hammurabi, on which see J. Tigay, "The Significance of the End of Deuteronomy (Deut 30:10 – 12)," in *Temples, Texts, and Traditions: A Tribute to Menahem Haran* (ed. M. Fox; Winona Lake, IN: Eisenbrauns, 1995), 137 – 43.

Bridging Contexts

MOSES AS THE PROPHET? While David is arguably the most important human figure in the Old Testament,[22] the image of Moses towers over the history of Israel from beginning to end, extending even to the New Testament. Despite his flaws and his personal failure to reach the Promised Land, Moses was the prophet par excellence. In his life, his actions, and his person, he embodied self-sacrificing service for Yahweh and for his people. Later authors would eulogize him as "the servant of the LORD,"[23] the "man of God,"[24] and "his chosen one" (Ps. 106:23). The New Testament association of Moses with the prophets[25] follows a longstanding tradition. In fact, according to Hosea 12:13[14], it was as "a prophet" that Yahweh engaged Moses to lead Israel out of Egypt and to guard them.

While many readers find the portrayal of Moses in the narratives that began in Exodus 1 and end in Deuteronomy 34 and in the speeches of Deuteronomy to be larger than life,[26] in both Old and New Testaments temptations to idolize him are resisted. Peter comes close, responding to Jesus' transfiguration on the mountain between Moses and Elijah with a proposal to build three tabernacles, one for each of these figures. Apparently he thought that by associating Jesus with these two prophets of Israel, he would elevate him. But the gospel narratives quickly deflect the attention away from Moses and Elijah (who disappear) to Jesus, God's beloved Son and his Chosen One, who remains alone on the mountain.[27]

Some see in the references to the prophet whom Yahweh will raise up in Deuteronomy 18:15 and especially the narrator's observation that no prophet like Moses has yet appeared in Israel in 34:10 hints that the prophetic spirit had ceased in Israel and been replaced by Scripture, and

---

22. The name David appears 1023 times, which is more than Moses (762) and Abram/Abraham (61/175=236) combined. The discrepancy in frequency is especially striking when texts excluding the narratives of their lives are considered. The name Moses appears fewer than 120 times in Joshua to Malachi; David's name appears 424 times. In the poetic books Moses name appears 8 times (including the superscription to Psalm 90); David's 88 (including superscriptions). In the prophets Moses' name appears 7 times; David's 36 times.

23. Josh. 1:1, 2, 7, 13, 15; 8:31, 33; 9:24; 11:12, 15; 12:6; 13:8; 14:7; 18:7; 22:2, 4, 5; 1 Kings 8:53, 56; 2 Kings 18:12; 21:8; 1 Chron. 6:49[34]; 2 Chron. 1:3; 24:6, 9; Neh. 1:7, 8; 9:14; 10:29[30]; Ps. 105:26; Dan. 9:11; Mal. 4:4[3:22]; Heb. 3:5; Rev. 15:3.

24. Josh. 14:6; 1 Chron. 23:14; 2 Chron. 30:16; Ezra 3:2; Ps. 90:1.

25. Luke 16:29, 31; 24:27, 44; John 1:45; Acts 26:22; 28:23.

26. See G. W. Coates, "Legendary Motifs in the Moses Death Reports," *CBQ* 39 (1977): 34–44.

27. Matt 17:1–8; Mark 9:2–8; Luke 9:28–36.

the stage has been set for an eschatological prophet.[28] The Qumran community developed two different dispositions toward Moses as an eschatological figure. In some circles the prophet "like Moses" (18:15–19) was expected to accompany the Messiahs of Aaron and Israel.[29] Others perceived the Teacher of Righteousness as a prophet after the model of Moses, that is, the authoritative leader and lawgiver of a new Israel still wandering in the desert in these last days.[30]

The New Testament provides ample evidence that many in Palestine at the time of Christ were awaiting an eschatological prophetic messiah. However, the role of eschatological prophet was fulfilled by John the Baptist, not Jesus.[31] In Acts 3:12–26 Peter seems to have interpreted the prophet like Moses of Deuteronomy 18:15 in a collective sense, referring to the prophets whose predictions were fulfilled in Jesus the Messiah (v. 20), the servant raised up by God (v. 26).

Acts 7:20–44 provides a clear picture of the view of Moses in early Christianity. In Stephen's lengthy survey of Moses' role in the history of Israel, he refers to him as the one who had said to the Israelites, "God will send you a prophet like me from your own people" (v. 37). As is the case with Acts 3:22, New Testament scholars generally see in "a prophet like me" a reference to Christ.[32] But this interpretation detracts from the overall thrust of the speech, whose purpose is to trace the history of Israel's spiritual obstinacy. Stephen does indeed devote a major portion of his speech to Moses, specifically reviewing his call to the ministry of deliverance (vv. 20–34), followed by a summary statement of the people's rejection of him despite his lofty standing with God and his status in the community (vv. 35–38), and ending with a prolonged indictment (vv. 39–43). The citation of Deuteronomy 18:15 occurs within Acts 7:35–38, where the emphasis is clearly on Moses, the one sent by God to rule and deliver Israel

---

28. Cf. J. Sailhamer, *Introduction to Old Testament Theology: A Canonical Approach* (Grand Rapids: Zondervan, 1995), 245–49; S. Dempster, "An 'Extraordinary Fact': Torah and Temple and the Contours of the Hebrew Canon," *TynB* 48 (1997): 53–56.

29. Testimonia 4Q175; 1QS ix:11.

30. See 1QpHab 2:1–2; 7:4–5. For further discussion see D. K. Falk, "Moses," in *Encyclopedia of the Dead Sea Scrolls* (ed. L. H. Schiffman and J. C. VanderKam; Oxford: Oxford Univ. Press, 2000), 1:577. Compare the portrayal of Moses as the ideal king if not divinized Jewish hero in Philo and rabbinic literature. See J. van Seters, "Moses," in *The Biblical World* (ed. J. Barton; Routledge, 2002), 205; S. Pearce, "King Moses: Notes on Philo's Portrait of Moses as an Ideal Leader in the Life of Moses," *Mélanges de l'Université Saint-Joseph* 57 (2004): 37–74.

31. See John 1:19–28; also Matt. 14:5; Mark 11:32; Luke 1:76.

32. See, e.g., Ben Witherington III, *The Acts of the Apostles: A Social-Rhetorical Commentary* (Grand Rapids: Eerdmans, 1998), 271; John B. Polhill, *Acts* (NAC 26; Nashville: Broadman, 1992), 199–200.

(v. 35), the one who performed signs and wonders before them for forty years (v. 36), the paradigmatic prophet (v. 37), the one who received the oracles from God, and who passed them on to the people. We detract from Stephen's focus if we isolate the quotation in v. 37 and impose on it a messianic significance. Here Stephen's attention is not on "a prophet like me," let alone the Messiah,[33] but on "me," that is, Moses, who predicts that he is not the last prophet God will raise up. At best this passage allows for an analogical link between Moses and Jesus; the rejection of Jesus fits Israel's longstanding pattern of rebellion against God, as supremely illustrated by their response to Moses, his agent of deliverance and revelation.[34]

Some scholars find in 34:10 evidence for a fundamental messianic hope pervading the entire Pentateuch and the anticipation of a messianic prophet still to come who will supersede Moses.[35] However, this interpretation depends on a predisposition to look for messianic notions everywhere and is without foundation in the text itself. It is preferable to read the statement simply as an observation that at the time of the final composition of the book of Deuteronomy, and perhaps the Pentateuch as a whole, no prophet had arisen in Israel who could match the status, power, and influence of Moses.

Yahweh's faithfulness. Apart from celebrating Moses' life, this closing chapter celebrates Yahweh's faithfulness. The Promised Land is literally in sight. Promises that were heard for the first time in Genesis 12:3 and that punctuated the patriarchal and exodus narratives are about to be fulfilled. All that remains is for Moses to die and his trusted lieutenant to take over. Led by Joshua, the Israelites will quickly take the land, but the real challenge will come thereafter. Will the voice of Israel's greatest prophet continue to ring in the people's ears, and will the people remain true to Yahweh after Moses and his successor are gone? The opening chapters of Judges show how short-lived Israel's fidelity to the instruction of their beloved pastor would be. Indeed, the identification of Jonathan, the son of Gershom, the son of Moses, as the priest of the aberrant cult at Dan in Judges 18:30 suggests that the recidivism infected Moses' own family within two generations.

But even as the closing chapter celebrates the life of Moses, it throws his death into starkest relief. We have been waiting for this moment since 31:1,

---

33. Ernst Haenchen (*The Acts of the Apostles: A Commentary* [Philadelphia: Westminster, 1971], 282) is correct in observing that "the speaker does not come to the theme of Jesus until verse 52."

34. Cf. Jesus' parable of vine-growers who killed the servants and finally the son of the landowner: Matt. 20:33–46; Mark 12:1–12; Luke 20:9–18.

35. John Sailhamer, "The Messiah and the Hebrew Bible," *JETS* 44 (2001): 5–23, esp. p. 23.

making this the longest and most complex death narrative in the Old Testament. And in truth, the shadow of Moses' imminent death has hung over the entire book. After all, the speeches we have heard in chapters 1−30 are the addresses of the head of this vast household preparing his people for his departure. By preserving these speeches, the narrator reminds his readers that the book as a whole is not about Moses; it is about the people's relationship to Yahweh. Human leaders come and go; the question will be: Will God's people be true to the eternal God? Will they allow Yahweh to lead them, not only in campaigns of conquest under Joshua, but also in paths of righteousness wherever they settle and live. The journey is not over until they are home spiritually as well as physically. The narratives in Joshua through Kings report how badly Israel fared.

The account of the death and burial of Moses on the mountain forces the reader to ask, "Now what?" The answer lies in the recognition that in the end, Israel's fate is not in the hands of Moses. He is not the one who actually brought them out of Egypt and sustained them through the desert wanderings, and he will not complete the mission by delivering the Promised Land into their hands. The rest of the Scriptures are commentary not only on how Israel responded, but also on the fidelity of Yahweh, who will complete the present mission without Moses[36] and who will patiently work with his people. Moses has merely been his mouthpiece, the interpreter of his great and gracious revelatory acts, whose aim was always to point his people to Yahweh their Redeemer.

Ultimately the New Testament gospel becomes the supreme fulfillment of the events begun here. As Moses had introduced the people to Yahweh, in all his grace and glory, so John the Baptist will introduce us to Jesus, Yahweh incarnate, through whose awesome signs and wonders his divine glory is revealed and we are delivered, not from the bondage of Egypt but from the bondage of sin. Through God's gracious call we are adopted as God's sons and daughters; and through his sustaining power we receive the eternal grant of life—to the praise of his glory (Eph. 1:1−14)!

Presumably the absence of any tradition about Moses' grave in the Old Testament reflects a deliberate aversion to the potential apotheosis of Moses, which might have developed from the veneration of his grave as a sacred place.[37] But this lack of information did not prevent the Israelites, especially the Jews in the intertestamental and rabbinic periods, from speculating about Moses' departure from the earth. According to Josephus (*Ant*

---

36. N. Lohfink rightly notes that when Moses died, Yahweh's mission for his people was only one-half complete. See "Moses Tod, die Tora und die alttestamentliche Sonntagslesung," *Theologie und Philosophie* 71 (1996): 481−94.

37. Thus M. Greenberg and S. D. Sperling, "Moses," *EncJud* (2nd ed.), 14:530.

4.8.48), Moses recorded his own death in anticipation of stories being told that he entered heaven alive because of his surpassing righteousness. The epistle of Jude (v. 9) alludes to a story involving a dispute between Michael the archangel and the devil over the body of Moses. This tale apparently was included in the lost ending of a first-century BC document known as the *Testament of Moses*.[38] In Jewish tradition the rabbis would debate whether Moses even died or was transported directly to heaven.[39]

Laying on of hands. When Moses laid his hands on Joshua, he performed a ritual by which divine authority and power is transferred from one person to another. This ritual resurfaces in the New Testament. Jesus often laid his hands on the sick and healed them,[40] and the apostles carried on this tradition (Acts 28:8). But the gesture was a special part of the ordination ritual, by which people were recognized as called of God and sent out with the authority of those who laid their hands on them — and ultimately the authority of God.[41] In Acts 13:2 − 4 the Holy Spirit is portrayed as the sending agent. Generally it was perceived that by this gesture the Holy Spirit himself passed through the hands to the ordinand (Acts 8:19).[42] In John 20:21 − 23 Jesus performs the gesture somewhat differently — presumably because he is God himself. Instead of laying his hands on his disciples, Jesus breathes on them, declaring, "Receive the Holy Spirit." In this way he authorizes them to declare the forgiveness of sins.

MOSES NOT PARADIGMATIC. IF Moses was the paradigmatic prophet of all Scripture, both Old and New Testaments, we need to consider whether he may serve as a paradigm for ministers of the gospel today. We recognize at the outset that Moses was an imperfect vessel, resistant to God's call, on occasion hotheaded and reckless in his performance of his duties, and frustrated with his people. However, by God's grace and through his pursuit of righteousness, this dishonorable vessel became "an instrument for noble purposes, made holy, useful to the

---

38. For the text see R. H. Charles, *The Apocrypha and Pseudepigrapha of the Old Testament* (Oxford: Clarendon, 1913), 2:105 − 7. See further R. Bauckham, *Jude, 2 Peter* (WBC 50; Waco, TX: Word, 1983), 47 − 48, 65 − 76.

39. For bibliography and discussion see A. J. Heschel, *Heavenly Torah: As Refracted through the Generations* (ed. and trans. G. Tucker; New York: Continuum, 2007), 353 − 54.

40. Mark 5:23; 6:5; 8:23, 25; Luke 4:40; 13:13.

41. Acts 6:6 (deacons); 13:2 − 4 (Paul and Barnabas); 1 Tim. 4:14 (Timothy).

42. This gesture of ordination is distinct from the gesture by which new converts received the Holy Spirit, as confirmation of their inclusion within the new covenant community (Acts 8:17, Samaritans; 19:6, Ephesians).

Master and prepared to do any good work" (2 Tim. 2:21). We recognize also that he was called to a unique mission within the context of God's program of salvation for the world. Once Egypt's role as incubator in which Jacob's seventy descendants could grow into an innumerable host had been fulfilled (Deut. 10:22; 26:5–10), in the fullness of time (Gen. 15:13–16) and in response to the cries of the Israelites (Ex. 2:23–25), God called this man to be the agent through whom his deliverance, protection, and revelation would be accomplished.

Contrary to the comment of the Israelites at Sinai (Ex. 32:1), Moses was not the deliverer, for Yahweh was the one who brought Israel out of Egypt.[43] Moses was merely the (privileged and burdened) human agent through whom Yahweh would perform this saving work (Ex. 3–4; Hos. 12:13[14]). The New Testament recognizes Moses as a key figure in this climactic moment of grace: "From the fullness of his grace we have all received one blessing superceding another; for the Torah was given through Moses, while grace and truth happened in Jesus Christ" (John 1:16–17, pers. trans.). Because of Moses' unique place in God's salvation history, several aspects of his ministry are not intended necessarily to be paradigmatic. The narrator recognizes that for the signs and wonders and awesome acts of power that Moses performed, he was without equal, and later Scriptures offer no hint that prophets viewed this aspect of his ministry as a bar they would aspire to reach or even view as normative.[44]

The same seems true in the New Testament. The incarnation, death, and resurrection of Christ, as well as the birth of the church, were accompanied by revelatory signs and wonders, authenticating Jesus as Yahweh come in the flesh and announcing the dawn of the new age. But neither the New Testament correspondence in general nor the Pastoral Letters in particular suggest these were to become enduring and normative evidences of the work of the Spirit of God. Like Pastor Moses, the authors of the letters call for submission to Christ demonstrated in renewed minds and transformed lives. These are the true evidences of the work of God.

Moses as paradigmatic. However, in other respects the pastoral ministry of Moses is paradigmatic. All who are called to divine service should surely emulate his passion for the agenda to which God has called them, his determination to preach only in accordance with the revealed will of

---

43. Note how Yahweh consistently introduces himself: "I am the LORD your God, who brought you out of of Egypt, out of the land of slavery" (e.g., Deut. 5:6).

44. The nearest exception is Elisha, whose ministry is characterized by miracles. Although his signs and wonders also served a revelatory purpose—to prove that Yahweh, not Baal, is God in Israel—in magnitude and significance they did not match Moses' miracles, and no miracles were as public as Moses' acts of power.

God, his plea for gratitude for the grace of God in salvation and providential care, his call for wholehearted and full-bodied obedience to God's will as the proper response to divine grace, his realistic view of his congregation, his vision of the church in God's program of salvation for the world (Deut. 26:19), his refusal to erect monuments in his own honor, and his confidence in God to do his work by his means. The flavor of ministry that arises from these commitments differs greatly from the self-serving, egotistical, and pandering paradigm of ministry that drives so much of the evangelical world.

Moses was a shepherd after the order of Christ as described in 1 Peter 5:1–6, and after the order of Yahweh as celebrated in Psalm 23 — perhaps the finest pastoral text in Scripture. Like Yahweh — incarnate in the good Shepherd, Jesus Christ — Moses provided his people what they really needed: nourishment and rest. He guided them in paths of righteousness; he walked with them through valleys of deepest darkness; and he invited them to come and celebrate in the presence of the Lord. May the Lord raise up for his work in our day pastors in the order of Christ our Shepherd. May his servants find inspiration for their ministry in Moses, the humblest man on earth (Num. 12:3), and may they find nourishment in the life-giving Torah he left as a monument to the honor and praise of God.

Scripture Index

Scripture Index

Scripture Index

Scripture Index

Scripture Index

Scripture Index

Scripture Index

Index of Ancient Literature Outside the Biblical Tradition

Ancient Jewish Sources

Selected Subject Index

Selected Subject Index

Selected Subject Index

Selected Subject Index

Author Index

Author Index

Author Index